# Lecture Notes in Computer Science 4261

*Commenced Publication in 1973*
Founding and Former Series Editors:
Gerhard Goos, Juris Hartmanis, and Jan van Leeuwen

## Editorial Board

Yueting Zhuang   Shiqiang Yang
Yong Rui   Qinming He (Eds.)

# Advances in Multimedia Information Processing – PCM 2006

7th Pacific Rim Conference on Multimedia
Hangzhou, China, November 2-4, 2006
Proceedings

 Springer

Volume Editors

Yueting Zhuang
Qinming He
Zhejiang University, College of Computer Science
Hangzhou, 310027, P.R. China
E-mail: {yzhuang, hqm@zju.edu.cn

Shiqiang Yang
Tsinghua University, Department of Computer Science and Technology
Beijing 100084, China
E-mail: yangshq@tsinghua.edu.cn

Yong Rui
Microsoft China R&D Group, China
E-mail: yongrui@microsoft.com

Library of Congress Control Number: 2006935258

CR Subject Classification (1998): H.5.1, H.3, H.5, C.2, H.4, I.3, K.6, I.7, I.4

LNCS Sublibrary: SL 3 – Information Systems and Application, incl. Internet/Web
and HCI

ISSN        0302-9743
ISBN-10     3-540-48766-2 Springer Berlin Heidelberg New York
ISBN-13     978-3-540-48766-1 Springer Berlin Heidelberg New York

Springer is a part of Springer Science+Business Media

springer.com

© Springer-Verlag Berlin Heidelberg 2006
Printed in Germany

Typesetting: Camera-ready by author, data conversion by Scientific Publishing Services, Chennai, India
Printed on acid-free paper      SPIN: 11922162      06/3142      5 4 3 2 1 0

# Preface

Welcome to the proceedings of the 7th Pacific-Rim Conference on Multimedia (PCM 2006) held at Zhejiang University, Hangzhou, China, November 2-4, 2006. Following the success of the previous conferences, PCM 2000 in Sydney, PCM 2001 in Beijing, PCM 2002 in Hsinchu, PCM 2003 in Singapore, PCM 2004 in Tokyo, and PCM 2005 in Jeju, PCM 2006 again brought together researchers, developers, practitioners, and educators in the field of multimedia from around the world. Both theoretical breakthroughs and practical systems were presented at the conference. There were sessions from multimedia retrieval to multimedia coding to multimedia security, covering a wide spectrum of multimedia research.

PCM 2006 featured a comprehensive program including keynote talks, regular paper presentations, and special sessions. We received 755 submissions and the number was the largest among all the PCMs. From such a large number of submissions, we accepted only 116 oral presentations. We kindly acknowledge the great support provided by the Program Committee members in the reviewing of submissions, as well as the additional reviewers who generously spent many hours. The many useful comments provided by the reviewing process are very useful to authors' current and future research.

This conference would not have been successful without the help of so many people. We greatly appreciate the support from our Organizing Committee Chairs Fei Wu, Nicu Sebe, Hao Yin, Daniel Gatica-Perez, Lifeng Sun, Alejandro Jaimes, Li Zhao, Jiangqin Wu, Shijian Luo, Jianguang Weng, Honglun Hou, Xilin Chen, Qing Li, Hari Sundaram, Rainer Lienhart, Kiyoharu Aizawa, Yo-Sung Ho, Mark Liao, Qibin Sun, Liu Jian, Yao Cheng, Zhang Xiafen, Zhang hong, Zhou xin and advisory chairs, Sun-Yuan Kung, Thomas S. Huang, and Hongjiang Zhang. Special thanks go to Fei Wu, the organization Vice Chair, who spent countless hours in preparing the conference. Last but not least, we would like to thank the sponsorship of National Natural Science Foundation of China, Insigma Technology Co.,Ltd, Microsoft Research, and Y.C. Tang Disciplinary Development Fund (Zhejiang University).

August 2006

Yunhe Pan
Yueting Zhuang
Shiqiang Yang
Yong Rui
Qinming He

# Organization

PCM 2006 was organized by the College of Computer Science and Technology, Zhejiang University.

## Organization Members

**Conference Chair**
Yunhe Pan                     Zhejiang University, China

**Program Co-chairs**
Yueting Zhuang                Zhejiang University,China
Shiqiang Yang                 Tsinghua University, China
Yong Rui                      Microsoft Research, USA

**Organizing Chair**
Qinming He                    Zhejiang University, China

**Organizing Vice-Chair**
Fei Wu                        Zhejiang University, China

**Tutorial Co-chairs**
Nicu Sebe                     University of Amsterdam, Netherlands

**Special Sessions Co-chairs**
Daniel Gatica-Perez           IDIAP/EPFL, Switzerland
Lifeng Sun                    Tsinghua University, China

**Poster/Exhibition Co-chairs**
Alejandro Jaimes              FXPAL, Japan
Li Zhao                       Tsinghua University, China

**Financial Chair**
Shijian Luo                   Zhejiang University, China

**Registration Chair**
Jianguang Weng                Zhejiang University, China

**Web Chair**
Honglun Hou                   Zhejiang University, China

**Publicity and Liaison Chairs**

| | |
|---|---|
| Xilin Chen | Institute of Computing Technology, CAS, China |
| Qing Li | City University of Hong Kong, China |
| Hari Sundaram | Arizona State University, USA |
| Rainer Lienhart | University of Augsburg, Germany |
| Kiyoharu Aizawa | University of Tokyo, Japan |
| Yo-Sung Ho Gwangju | Institute of Science and Technology, Korea |
| Mark Liao | Academia Sinica, Taiwan, China |
| Qibin Sun | I2R, Singapore |

**Advisory Committee**

| | |
|---|---|
| Sun-Yuan Kung | Princeton University, USA |
| Thomas S. Huang | University of Illinois at Urbana Champaign, USA |
| Hongjiang Zhang | Microsoft Research Asia, China |

## Program Committee

Aggelos Katsaggelos (Northwestern University, USA)
Ajay Divakaran (Mitsubishi Labs, USA)
Alejandro Jaimes (FX Pal Japan, Fuji Xerox, USA)
Alan Hanjalic (Delft University of Technology, Netherlands)
Anthony T. S. Ho (University of Surrey, UK)
Asanobu Kitamoto (National Institute of Informatics, Japan)
Bernard Merialdo (Eurocom, France)
Bo Shen (HP Labs, USA)
Chabane Djeraba (LIFL, France)
Changsheng Xu (Agency for Science, Technology and Research, Singapore)
Chong-Wah Ngo (City University of Hong Kong, Hong Kong)
Chi-Man Pun (University of Macau, Macau)
Dongge Li (Motorola Labs, USA)
Dongming Lu (Zhejiang University, China)
Feng Jing (Microsoft, China)
Goh Wooi Boon (Nanyang Technological University, Singapore)
Gopal Pingali (IBM Research, USA)
Hae Kwang Kim (Sejong University, Korea)
Hae Yong Kim (University of São Paulo, Brazil)
Heather Yu (Panasonic, USA)
Hitoshi Kiya (Tokyo Metropolitan University, Japan)
Huamin Feng (Beijing Electronic Science and Technology Institute, China)
Hyeran Byun (Yonsei University, Korea)
Hyoung Joong Kim(Kwangwoon University, Korea)
Ichiro Ide (Nagoya University, Japan)
Irene H. Y. Gu (Chalmers, Sweden)
Jenq-Nenq Hwang (University of Washington, USA)
Jeong A. Lee (Chosun University, Korea)

Yihong Gong (NEC Laboratories America, USA)
Yi Wu (Intel, USA)
You Jip Won (Hanyang University, Korea)
Youngjun Yoo (TI, USA)
Young Shik Moon (Hanyang University, Korea)
Yuanchun Shi (Tsinghua University, China)
Yung-Chang Chen (Tsing Hua University, Taiwan, China)
Yuntao Qian (Zhejiang University, China)
Zhengxing Sun (Nanjing University, China)
Zhigeng Pan (Zhejiang University, China)
Zhi-hua Zhou (Nanjing University, China)

## Additional Reviewer List

Aimin Pan (Microsoft Research Asia, China)
Alin Alecu (Vrije Universiteit Brussel, Belgium)
Arnaud Dupuis (IRISA - INRIA, France)
Bart Jansen (Vrije Universiteit Brussel, Belgium)
Bin Li (Nanyang Technological University, Singapore)
Caroline Fontaine (IRISA - CNRS, France)
Chiyomi Miyajima (Nagoya University, Japan)
Christel Chamaret (IRISA - INRIA, France)
Dan Costin (Vrije Universiteit Brussel, Belgium)
Daoqiang Zhang (Nanjing University, China)
Duc Tran (University of Dayton, USA)
Emilie Dumont (Institut Eurecom, France)
Fabio Verdicchio (Vrije Universiteit Brussel, Belgium)
Fenn-Huei Sheu (Taiwan Ocean University, Taiwan, China)
Georgios Patsis (Vrije Universiteit Brussel, Belgium)
Guillaume Gravier (IRISA - CNRS, France)
Helene Richy (IRISA - Universite de Rennes 1, France)
Huiyang Zhou (University of Central Florida, USA)
Jan Lievens (Vrije Universiteit Brussel, Belgium)
Jean-Luc Dugelay (Institut Eurecom, France)
Jie Tang (Nanjing University, China)
Jing Tian (Nanyang Technological University, Singapore)
Jinhua Guo (University of Michigan-Dearborn, USA)
Joakim Jiten (Institut Eurecom, France)
Jong-il Park (Hanyang University, Korea)
Julien Bourgeois (Universite de France-Comte, France)
Kazuya Kodama (National Institute of Informatics, Japan)
KeijiYanai (University of Electro-Communications, Japan)
Kenny Wang (Wayne State University, USA)
Khanh Vu (University of Central Florida, USA)
Lei Chen (HKUST, China)

Luce Morin (IRISA - Universite de Rennes 1, France)
Mei Han (NEC Labs, USA)
Mikio Ikeda (Yokkaichi University, Japan)
Min Feng (Microsoft Research Asia, China
Motohiko Isaka (Kwansei Gakuin University, Japan)
Nilesh Patel (University of Michigan-Dearborn, USA)
Olivier Crave (IRISA - INRIA, France)
Remi Trichet (Institut Eurecom, France)
Rudi Deklerck (Vrije Universiteit Brussel, Belgium)
Shengyang Dai (Northwestern University, USA)
Steven Tondeur (Vrije Universiteit Brussel, Belgium)
Tai Mei (Microsoft Research Asia, China
Takanori Nishino (Nagoya University, Japan)
Teddy Furon (IRISA - INRIA, France)
Tim Bruylants (Vrije Universiteit Brussel, Belgium)
Tim Dams (Vrije Universiteit Brussel - Hogeschool Antwerpen, Belgium)
Tom Clerckx (Vrije Universiteit Brussel, Belgium)
Tomokazu Takahashi (JSPS/Nagoya University, Japan)
Venkatesh Babu (Norwegian University of Science and Technology, Norway)
Werner Verhelst (Vrije Universiteit Brussel, Belgium)
Whoi-Yul Yura Kim (Hanyang University, Korea)
Xavier Naturel (IRISA - INRIA, France)
Xiao Wu (City University of Hong Kong, Hong Kong)
Xiaoyan Sun (Microsoft Research Asia, China)
Yan Lu (Microsoft Research Asia, China)
Yan Zhang (Nanjing University, China)
Ying Cai (Iowa State University, USA)
Yuan Yuan (Aston University, UK)
Yves Mathieu (Ecole Nationale Superieure des Telecommunications, France)

## Sponsoring Institutions

National Natural Science Foundation of China
Insigma Technology Co.,Ltd
Microsoft Reasearch
Y.C. Tang Disciplinary Development Fund (Zhejiang University, China)

# Table of Contents

# Expressive Speech Recognition and Synthesis as Enabling Technologies for Affective Robot-Child Communication

Selma Yilmazyildiz, Wesley Mattheyses, Yorgos Patsis, and Werner Verhelst

Vrije Universiteit Brussel, dept. ETRO-DSSP
Pleinlaan 2, B-1050 Brussels, Belgium
{Selma.Yilmazyildiz, wmatthey}@vub.ac.be
{gpatsis, wverhels}@etro.vub.ac.be

**Abstract.** This paper presents our recent and current work on expressive speech synthesis and recognition as enabling technologies for affective robot-child interaction. We show that current expression recognition systems could be used to discriminate between several archetypical emotions, but also that the old adage "there's no data like more data" is more than ever valid in this field. A new speech synthesizer was developed that is capable of high quality concatenative synthesis. This system will be used in the robot to synthesize expressive nonsense speech by using prosody transplantation and a recorded database with expressive speech examples. With these enabling components lining up, we are getting ready to start experiments towards hopefully effective child-machine communication of affect and emotion.

## 1 Introduction

In Belgium alone some 300.000 children need to be hospitalized for long periods of time or suffer from chronic diseases [1]. Different projects exist which aim at using Information and Communication Technologies (ICT) like Internet and WebCams to allow these children to stay in contact with their parents, to virtually attend lectures at their school, etc. [1], [2]

Together with the Anty foundation and the Robotics and Multibody Mechanics research group at our university, we participate in a project that aims at designing a furry friendly robot called Anty [3], [4]. Anty will provide access to ICT means like a PC and WiMAX in a child-friendly form and will act as a friendly companion for the young hospitalized child. It is our task to design the vocal communication system for Anty. Since it will be a long time before a real speech dialog with a machine will become possible through speech understanding techniques, we choose to develop an affective communication system that can recognize expressive meaning in the child's voice, such as the child's intent or emotional state, and that can reply using synthesized affective nonsense speech.

The paper is organized as follows: in section 2 we describe our current emotion recognition system, in section 3 we describe our expressive synthesis system and in section 4 we conclude with a discussion.

Y. Zhuang et al. (Eds.): PCM 2006, LNCS 4261, pp. 1–8, 2006.

## 2  Automatic Classification of Emotions in Speech

It is well known that speech contains acoustic features that vary with the speaker's affective state. The effects of emotion in speech tend to alter pitch, timing, voice quality and articulation of the speech signal [5]. The goal of an emotional speech recognizer is to classify statistical measures of these acoustic features into classes that represent different affective states.

In our own work, we mainly used a segment based approach (SBA) for emotion classification. As illustrated in Fig. 1, statistical measures of acoustic features are calculated for the whole utterance as well as for each of its voiced segments. We used 12 statistical measures of pitch, intensity and spectral shape variation.

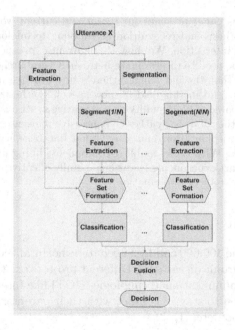

**Fig. 1.** Main components of the segment based approach for emotion classification

Four different emotional databases (Kismet, BabyEars, Berlin and Danish) have been used and ten-fold cross validation has been mostly applied as the testing paradigm. Fig. 2 shows the results that we obtained with our SBA approach and with our own implementation of the AIBO emotion recognition system [6]. It can be noted that these results compare favourably to those that have been previously reported in the literature for these databases ([5], [7], [8], [9]).

In [10], we also reported some detailed cross database experiments. In these experiments the databases Kismet and BabyEars were paired and the emotional

| | Kismet | | BabyEars | | Berlin | | Danish | |
|---|---|---|---|---|---|---|---|---|
| MLA | AIBO | SBA | AIBO | SBA | AIBO | SBA | AIBO | SBA |
| SVM | 83.7 | 83.2 | 65.8 | 67.9 | 75.5 | 65.5 | 63.5 | 56.8 |
| KNN | 82.2 | 86.6 | 61.5 | 68.7 | 67.7 | 59.0 | 49.7 | 55.6 |
| ADA-C4.5 | 84.63 | 81 | 61.5 | 63.4 | 74.6 | 46.0 | 64.1 | 59.7 |

**Fig. 2.** Percentage recognition accuracy for emotion classification on four different databases with two different systems and three different machine learning algorithms

classes that did not occur in both databases were dropped. The remaining common emotions were Approval, Attention and Prohibition. In a first set of experiments, training was performed on one of the databases and testing on the other. This off-corpus testing on the two corpora showed virtually no improvement over baseline classification (i.e., always classifying the test samples as belonging to the most frequent class in the test database). On the other hand, when the two corpora are merged into a single large corpus, classification accuracy is only slightly reduced compared to the scores obtained on the individual databases.

In other words, we found evidence suggesting that emotional corpora of the same emotion classes recorded under different conditions can be used to construct a single classifier capable of distinguishing the emotions in the merged corpora. The classifier learned using the merged corpora is more robust than a classifier learned on a single corpus because it can deal with emotions in speech that is recorded in more than one setting and from more speakers.

The emotional databases that are available contain only a small number of speakers and emotions and with the feature sets that are usually employed in the field, there is little generalization accross databases, resulting in database dependent classifiers. Furtunately, we also found that we can make the systems more robust by using much larger training databases. Moreover, adding robustness to the feature set that is used to represent the emotion in the utterance could compensate for the lack of vast amounts of training data. It would therefore be interesting to investigate the use of acoustic features that mimic the process of perception of emotions by humans.

# 3  Synthesis of Affective Nonsense Speech

## 3.1  System Design

We designed a system for producing affective speech that uses a database with natural expressive speech samples from a professional speaker and a database with naturally spoken neutral speech samples from the same speaker. Details of the construction of these databases are given in section 3.2.

In order to produce a nonsense utterance with a given desired emotion, the synthesizer randomly selects an expressive speech sample of the proper type from the first database and uses this as a prosodic template. Next, a nonsense carrier phrase is constructed that has the same syllabic structure as the selected prosodic template. As explained in detail in section 3.3, this is done by concatenating segments from the database with neutral speech samples. Except that inter-segment compatibility aspects are taken into account, the segments to be concatenated are selected ad random.

Finally, the same pitch and timing structure as found in the prosodic template is copied on the nonsense carrier phrase, a process that is known as prosodic transplantation [11], [12] and that effectively provides the synthetic output with a same intonational pattern as the natural example. The prosodic modification technique used in this prosody transplantation is summarized in section 3.4.

Besides working in accordance with the concept of prosodic transplantation, we believe that the strength of our synthesizer mainly resides in its high quality and low complexity that was achieved by using an overlap-add technique for both the segment concatenation and the prosodic modification, in accordance with the source filter interpretation of pitch synchronized overlap-add (PSOLA) [13], as introduced in [14]. As will be explained, according to this interpretation, the synthesizer can make use of the series of pitch markers to fulfill the concatenation. More details about the synthesizer can also be found in [15].

## 3.2   Speech Database

In order to produce expressive speech as close as possible to natural emotional speech, the quality of the prosodic templates was an important parameter. The speaker should be able to keep a same voice quality while recording the neutral text and he should be able to express the desired emotions convincingly. Our databases were constructed from the speech samples of a professional speaker.

Four primary human emotions (anger, joy, sadness and fear) were included. First, samples of expressive and neutral utterances were recorded in an anechoic chamber. Next, the utterances to use in the databases were selected through an evaluation process using four criteria: color of the voice, the emotion perceived in the utterance, closeness to the intended emotion, and the quality of the portraying (faked/real). Each utterance was rated by four researchers who are familiar with speech processing and one amateur musician. Finally, 14 utterances were selected for inclusion in the database.

An interactive segmentation tool was developed based on the MEL-cepstral distances between the hanning windowed frames on the left and the right of each sample point. Large MEL-scale cepstral distances are an indication of a phone transition, small distances indicate stationary speech parts. The tool we developed plots these distances and, given the desired number of segments, the user can specify the appropriate cut-points. These are stored in a meta-data file that can be used for constructing the nonsense carrier utterances by concatenating randomly selected speech segments from the database. Fig. 3 illustrates this segmentation process.

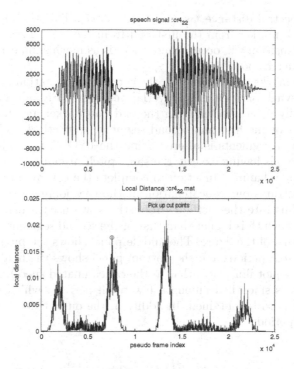

**Fig. 3.** MEL-cepstral distance based manual segmentation. The upper panel shows the speech utterance 'not ring'. The bottom panel shows the MEL-scale cepstral distances.

## 3.3 Segment Concatenation

The synthesizer has to concatenate the selected segments in an appropriate way in order to construct a fluently sounding speech signal. While concatenating speech segments, one has to cope with two problems. First, the concatenation technique must smooth the transition between the two signals in time, otherwise these transitions will appear to abrupt and the concatenated speech would not sound fluent, but chopped. Further, while joining voiced speech signals, the introduction of irregular pitch periods at the transition point has to be avoided, since these would cause audible concatenation artifacts.

As mentioned before, we opted to use PSOLA to perform the prosody transplantation. PSOLA needs to identify the exact location of every individual pitch period in the voiced speech segments using so-called pitch markers. The quality of the output signal greatly depends on the correctness of these markers and we designed an efficient and robust algorithm to accomplish this pitch marking [16].

Obviously, by choosing pitch markers as the segments cut-points, we can assure that the periodicity of the speech signal will not be disrupted by the concatenation procedure. In order to further enhance the concatenation quality, we designed an optimization method that selects the best cut-markers according to a MEL-scale spectral distance, as suggested in [17]. This technique selects for each join a pitch marker from the first and from the second segment in such a way that the transition will occur where there is as much similarity between the two speech signals as possible.

Once the cut marks are determined, the actual concatenation problem is tackled by a pitch-synchronous window/overlap technique. First, a number of pitch periods (typically 5) is selected from the end cut-marker and from the beginning cut-marker of the first and second segment, respectively. Then, the pitch of these two short segments is altered using the PSOLA technique, which will result in two signals having exactly the same pitch. Finally, the two signals are cross-faded using a hanning-function to complete the concatenation.

Figure 4 illustrates our concatenation method by joining two voiced speech segments. To illustrate the method's robustness, we used a first segment that has a pitch value which is higher than that of the second segment, as one can see in the upper panel of the figure. The middle panel shows the pitch-alignment of the extracted pitch periods and the bottom panel shows the final concatenated speech. This last plot illustrates that in the concatenated speech signal the segment transition is smoothed among a few pitch periods, which is necessary if a fluent output is to be obtained. In addition, the output does not suffer from irregular pitch periods.

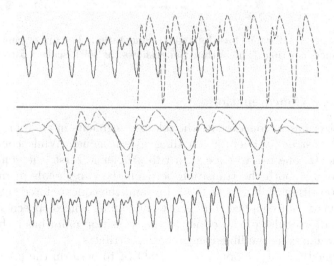

**Fig. 4.** Pitch-synchronous concatenation. The upper panel illustrates the segments to be concatenated, the middle panel illustrates the pitch-synchronized waveshapes, and the lower panel illustrates the result after cross-fading.

The proposed concatenation technique delivers results of the same auditive quality as some more complex concatenation methods found in the literature. The technique has been systematically judged against a spectral interpolation approach and it was concluded that the computationally more complex interpolation could not outperform the proposed overlap-add method.

## 3.4 Adding Prosody

At this point we need to apply the correct prosody to the concatenated nonsense speech signal by using the PSOLA technique for altering the timing and the pitch of the speech. The pitch markers of the nonsense speech can be simply computed from the pitch markers of the concatenated segments. These will then be used as analysis-pitch markers for the PSOLA technique.

At the same time, each sample point that indicates a phoneme transition in the synthesizer's databases is memorized in the meta-data. By using these transition points the synthesizer calculates the inherent length of each phoneme present in the concatenated signal and in the prosodic template. Using these two sets of values, the amount of time-stretching that is necessary to provide the output speech with the correct timing properties is computed. Subsequently, the PSOLA algorithm will synthesize the output signal by using a time varying time-stretch value going from phoneme to phoneme. The synthesis-pitch markers used by the PSOLA operation determine the pitch of the final output [14]. Obviously, it suffices to calculate these pitch markers based on the pitch-parameters of the prosodic template to ensure that the imposed intonation curve is correctly assigned to the final speech signal.

## 4 Concluding Discussion

We presented our recent and current work on expressive speech synthesis and recognition as enabling technologies for affective robot-child interaction.

We showed that our current expression recognition system obtains competitive results and could be used to discriminate between several archetypical emotions. However, we also showed that in this field the old adage "there's no data like more data" is more than ever valid and in order to avoid having to record hughe databases with expressive child speech, we plan to open a parallel track to investigate robust features for emotion recognition as well as psychoacoustically motivated dimensions of expressive speech.

We also designed a lightweight speech synthesis system that was successfully used as a replacement for the back-end of the NeXTeNS open source text-to-speech synthesis system for Dutch, thereby turning it into a Flemish speaking text-to-speech application [15]. We are using the same acoustic synthesis modules to construct a system for synthesizing expressive nonsense speech that copies the intonation from a database with expressive speech examples onto a neutral synthetic carrier phrase. In our future work we plan to investigate whether and how aspects of voice quality should be incorporated in the system.

With these enabling components lined up, we are getting ready to enter a new and very exciting research phase where we can start experiments towards hopefully effective child-machine communication of affect and emotion.

## Acknowledgements

Parts of the research reported on in this paper were supported by the IWOIB project Link II - Voice Modification of the Brussels region, by the IWT projects SPACE (sbo/040102) and SMS4PA-II (O&O/040803), by the IBBT projects VIN and A4MC3, and by the research fund of the Vrije Universiteit Brussel.

## References

1. Simon et Odil: Website for hospitalized children. http://www.simonodil.com/
2. IBBT research project ASCIT: Again at my School by fostering Communication through Interactive Technologies for long term sick children. https://projects.ibbt.be/ascit/
3. Anty project website: http://anty.vub.ac.be/
4. Anty foundation website: http://www.anty.org/
5. Breazeal, C., Aryananda, L.: Recognition of Affective Communicative Intent in Robot-Directed Speech. In: Autonomous Robots, vol. 12, (2002) pp. 83–104
6. Oudeyer, P.: The production and recognition of emotions in speech: features and algorithms. International Journal of Human-Computer Studies, Vol. 59 (2003) 157–183
7. Slaney, M., McRoberts, G. A Recognition System for Affective Vocalization. Speech Communication, 39 (2003) 367–384
8. Ververidis, D., Kotropolos, C.: Automatic speech classification to five emotional states based on gender information. Proceedings of Eusipco-2004 (2004) 341–344
9. Hammal, Z., Bozkurt, B., Couvreur, L., Unay, D., Caplier, A., Dutoit, T.: Passive versus active: vocal classification system. Proceedings of Eusipco-2005 (2005)
10. Shami, M., Verhelst, W.: Automatic Classification of Emotions in Speech Using Multi-Corpora Approaches. In: Proc. of the second annual IEEE BENELUX/DSP Valley Signal Processing Symposium SPS-DARTS (2006)
11. Verhelst, W., Borger, M.: Intra-Speaker Transplantation of Speech Characteristics. An Application of Waveform Vocoding Techniques and DTW. Proceedings of Eurospeech'91, Genova (1991) 1319–1322
12. Van Coile, B., Van Tichelen, L., Vorstermans, A., Staessen, M.: Protran: A Prosody Transplantation Tool for Text-To-Speech Applications. Proceedings of the International Conference on Spoken Language Processing ICSLP94, Yokohama (1994) 423–426
13. Moulines, E., Charpentier, F.: Pitch-Synchronous Waveform Processing Techniques for Text-to-Speech Synthesis Using Diphones. Speech Communication, volume 9 (1990) 453-467
14. Verhelst, W.: On the Quality of Speech Produced by Impulse Driven Linear Systems. Proceedings of the International Conference on Acoustics, Speech and Signal Processing - ICASSP-91 (1991) 501–504
15. Mattheyses, W.: Vlaamstalige tekst-naar-spraak systemen met PSOLA (Flemish text-to-speech systems with PSOLA, in Dutch). Master thesis, Vrije Universiteit Brussel (2006)
16. Mattheyses, W., Verhelst, W., Verhoeve, P.: Robust Pitch Marking for Prosodic Modification of Speech Using TD-PSOLA. Proceedings of the IEEE Benelux/DSP Valley Signal Processing Symposium, SPS-DARTS (2006) 43–46
17. Conkie, A., Isard, I.: Optimal coupling of diphones. Proceedings of the 2nd ESCA/IEEE Workshop on Speech Synthesis - SSW2 (1994)

# Embodied Conversational Agents:
# Computing and Rendering Realistic Gaze Patterns

Gérard Bailly, Frédéric Elisei, Stephan Raidt, Alix Casari, and Antoine Picot

Institut de la Communication Parlée, 46 av. Félix Viallet, 38031 Grenoble - France
{gerard.bailly, frederic.elisei, stephan.raidt, alix.casari,
antoine.picot}@icp.inpg.fr

**Abstract.** We describe here our efforts for modeling multimodal signals exchanged by interlocutors when interacting face-to-face. This data is then used to control embodied conversational agents able to engage into a realistic face-to-face interaction with human partners. This paper focuses on the generation and rendering of realistic gaze patterns. The problems encountered and solutions proposed claim for a stronger coupling between research fields such as audiovisual signal processing, linguistics and psychosocial sciences for the sake of efficient and realistic human-computer interaction.

**Keywords:** Embodied conversational agents, talking faces, audiovisual speech synthesis, face-to-face interaction.

## 1 Introduction

Building Embodied Conversational Agents (ECA) able to engage a convincing face-to-face conversation with a human partner is certainly one of the most challenging Turing test one can imagine (Cassell, Sullivan et al. 2000). The challenge is far more complex than the experimental conditions of the Loebner Prize[1] where dialog is conducted via textual information: the ECA should not only convince the human partner that the linguistic and paralinguistic contents of the generated answers to human inquiries have been built by a human intelligence, but also generate the proper multimodal signals that should fool human perception. We are however very close to being able to conduct such experiments. Automatic learning techniques that model perception/action loops at various levels of human-human interaction are surely key technologies for building convincing conversational agents. George, the talkative bot that won the Loebner Prize 2005, learned its conversation skills from the interactions it had with visitors to the Jabberwacky website, and through chats with its creator, Mr Carpenter. Similarly the first Turing test involving a non interactive virtual speaker (Geiger, Ezzat et al. 2003) has demonstrated that image-based facial animation techniques are able to generate and render convincing face and head movements.

Combining a pertinent dialog management with convincing videorealistic animation is still not sufficient to reach a real sense of presence (Riva, Davide et al.

---

[1] The Loebner Prize for artificial intelligence awards each year the computer program that delivers the most human-like responses to questions given by a panel of judges over a computer terminal.

Y. Zhuang et al. (Eds.): PCM 2006, LNCS 4261, pp. 9–18, 2006.

2003). The sense of "being there" requires the featuring of basic components of situated face-to-face communication such as mixed initiative, back channeling, turn taking management, etc. The interaction requires a detailed scene analysis and a control loop that knows about the rules of social interaction: the analysis and comprehension of an embodied interaction is deeply grounded in our senses and actuators and we do have strong expectations on how dialogic information is encoded into multimodal signals.

Appropriate interaction loops have thus to be implemented. They have to synchronize at least two different perception/action loops. On the one hand there are low-frequency dialogic loops. They require analysis, comprehension and synthesis of dialog acts with time scales of the order of a few utterances. On the other hand there are interaction loops of higher frequency. These include the prompt reactions to exogenous stimuli such as sudden events arising in the environments or eye saccades of the interlocutor. The YTTM model (Thórisson 2002) of turn-taking possesses three layered feedback loops (reactive, process control and content). Content and reactive loops correspond to the two loops previously sketched. The intermediate process control loop is responsible for the willful control of the social interaction (starts and stops, breaks, back-channeling, etc). In all interaction models, information- and signal-driven interactions should then be coupled to guarantee efficiency, believability, trustfulness and user-friendliness of the information retrieval.

We describe here part of our efforts for designing virtual ECAs that are sensitive to the environment (virtual and real) in which they interact with human partners. We focus here on the control of eye gaze. We describe the multiple scientific and technological challenges we face, the solutions that have been proposed in the literature and the ones we have implemented and tested.

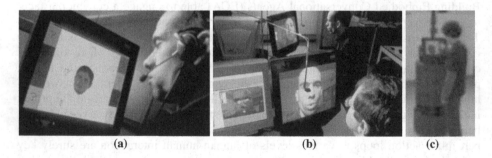

(a)                              (b)                              (c)

**Fig. 1.** Face-to-face interaction: (a) gaming with an ECA; (b) studying human gaze patterns; (c) our ECA mounted on the Rackham mobile robot at the Space city in Toulouse – France (Clodic, Fleury et al. 2006). Copyright CNRS for (a) and (b).

## 2  Gaze and Mutual Gaze Patterns

The sampling process with which the eye explores the field of sight consists of fixations, smooth pursuits and saccades. Saccades are the rapid eye movements (approx. 25-40ms duration) with which the high-resolution central field (the fovea) is pointed to the area of interest. Fixations (and slow eye movements) of relatively long duration (300ms) enable the visual system to analyze that area (e.g. identify objects or humans). They are characterized by microsaccades that compensate for retinal adaptation. Functionally these two components correspond to two complementary visual streams, a 'where'- and a 'what'-stream (Grossberg 2003). The 'what'-stream is responsible for object recognition, the 'where'-stream localises where these objects and events are. The 'what'-stream is assumed to be allocentric, i.e. object centered, whereas the 'where'-stream is egocentric, i.e. observer centered. An additional mechanism, called smooth pursuit, locks slowly moving interest points in the fovea.

Scrutinizing a scene (either a static picture or a video) is more complicated than just moving from one salient feature of the scene to the next. Perceptual salience is not the only determinant of interest. The cognitive demand of the scrutinizing task has a striking impact on the human audiovisual analysis of scenes and their interpretation. Yarbus (1967) showed notably that eye gaze patterns are influenced by the instructions given to the observer during the examination of pictures. Similarly Vatikiotis-Bateson et al (1998) showed that eye gaze patterns of perceivers during audiovisual speech perception are influenced both by environmental conditions (audio signal-to-noise ratio) and by the recognition task (identification of phonetic segments vs. the sentence's modality). Attention is also essential: Simons and Chabris (1999) suggest that attention is essential to consciously perceive any aspect of a scene. Major changes to scenes may be ignored ('change blindness') and objects may even not be perceived ('attentional blindness') if they are not in our focus of attention.

Finally, eye gaze is an essential component of face-to-face interaction. Eyes constitute a very special stimulus in a visual scene. Gaze and eye-contact are important cues for the development of social activity and speech acquisition (Carpenter and Tomasello 2000): theories of mind[2] (Scassellati 2001) rely on the ability of computing eye direction of others. In conversation, gaze is involved in the regulation of turn taking, accentuation and organization of discourse (Argyle and Cook 1976; Kendon 1967). We are also very sensitive to the gaze of others when directed towards objects of interest within our field of view or even outside (Pourtois, Sander et al. 2004). In the Posner cueing paradigm (1980), observers' performance in detecting a target is typically quicker in trials in which the target is present at the location indicated by a former visual cue than in trials in which the target appears at the uncued location. The outstanding prominence of the human face in this respect was shown by Langton et al. (1999; 2000). Driver et al. (1999) have shown that a concomitant eye gaze also speeds reaction time.

The data presented so far show that gaze control is a complex cognitive activity that not only depends on the environment – that of course includes other humans – but also on our own cognitive demands.

# 3  Computational Models for the Observation of Natural Scenes

Most robots incorporate a computational model for observing their environment. Mobile robots use the results for planning displacements and avoid obstacles. Anthropoid robots embed cameras at eyes location and the movements that are

---

[2] The ability to understand that others have beliefs, desires and intentions that are different from one's own (Baron-Cohen, Leslie et al. 1985; Premack and Woodruff 1978).

necessary for controlling their field of view informs indirectly human partners on their focus of interest. Most sociable anthropoid robots control gaze for communication needs: robots constructed by the Humanoid Robotics Group at the MIT Artificial Intelligence Laboratory have been designed to mimic the sensory and motor capabilities of the human system. The robots should be able to detect stimuli that humans find relevant, should be able to respond to stimuli in a human-like manner. The first computational theory of mind built by Scassellati (Scassellati 2001) was already incorporating a complex control of eye gaze et neck movements for pointing and signalling shared visual attention. Robita developed at Waseda University (Matsusaka, Tojo et al. 2003) points to objects and regulates turn taking in group conversation by gaze direction.

**Fig. 2.** Models for observing natural scenes. Left: eye saccades of the ECA developed by Itty et al (Itti, Dhavale et al. 2003) are sequenced by points of interest computed from a video input. Right: Sun (Sun 2003) uses a multiscale segmentation to scrutinize an image by successive zoom-ins and -outs.

Most gaze control strategies for ECA are more elementary. When no contextual audiovisual stimuli are available (e.g. for web-based ECA), the basic strategy consists in globally reproducing blinks and gaze paths learnt by statistical models from human data (Lee, Badler et al. 2002). Attempts to regulate an ECA gaze from video input are quite recent: Itti et al (2003) propose a visual attention system that drives the eye gaze of an ECA from natural visual scenes. This system consists in computing three maps: (a) a saliency map, a bottom-up path that computes a global saliency for each pixel of the current image that combines color, orientation and flow cues; (b) a pertinence map, a top-down path that modulates the saliency map according to cognitive demands (e.g. follow white objects… that may cause attention blindness to events connected to darker areas of the scene), and (c) an attention map that is responsible with the observation strategy that switches between the successive points of interest. The attention map also handles temporary Inhibition Of Return (IOR) so that all points of interest in a scene have a chance to be in focus. Although mostly tested on still images, the object-based attention framework proposed by Sun (2003) is based on a multi-scale segmentation of the image that computes a hierarchy of the points of interest as function of salience, granularity and size of the objects.

We recently implemented a eye gaze control system that builds on Itti et al proposal but replaces the pertinence and attention maps with a detector/tracker of regions of interest as well as with a temporary inhibition of return that rules the content of an attention stack (Xu and Chun 2006) that memorizes position and appearance of previous regions of interest. The object detector is responsible for detecting known objects (such as faces) that triggers further predetermined scrutation (such as focus on mouth and eyes for speaking faces) and for building statistical models of the shape and appearance of unknown objects (based yet on color histogram). If necessary, the detector uses the built characteristics to perform a smooth pursuit using a Kalman filter (see figure 3). Once the object of interest does not move and fixation has been long enough for recognizing/building a model of the object, the object is pushed in the attention stack and the system seeks for the next salient object. While none is found, the system pops back the objects stored in the attention stack. The stack is also used for storing temporally the characteristics of an object that has not been entirely processed when a more salient object bumps in the scene: the exogenous stimulus is urgently processed and the system goes back to its normal sequential exploration.

Two natural videos have been used for testing (see figure 3): the first scene features a subject waiving colored objects in front of him while the second one features several person passing behind a subject facing the camera. Gaze patterns computed by our system have been compared to human ones recorded using a non invasive Tobii® eyetracker: main differences occur when innate objects have a stronger intrinsic salience than faces in the scene (see figure 4). Subjects are in fact more sensitive to faces than clothing since human faces are of most importance for understanding natural scenes. When interacting with people, events occurring in the immediate environment have also an impact on gaze and gaze interpretation. For instance, Pourtois et al (2004) have shown that facial expressions of your interlocutor is interpreted very differently depending on whether his gaze are directed to you or not.

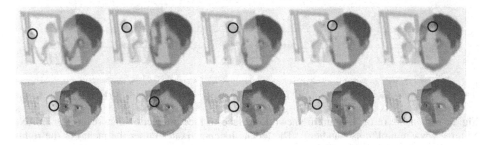

**Fig. 3.** An ECA exploring a visual scene. The ECA scrutinizes a real scene displayed on a transparent screen. Key frames are displayed. A black circle materializes the point of interest for each image. Top: a subject waves a blue book in front of the ECA and the module responsible for smooth pursuit controls the gaze. Bottom: a person passes behind the interlocutor and a saccade is performed to track this new object of interest.

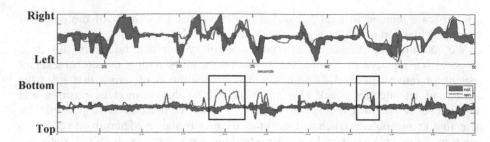

**Fig. 4.** Comparing gaze trajectories (top: horizontal displacement; bottom vertical displacement) generated by our eye gaze control system with those recorded from subjects observing
the same scene (the colored gauge is obtained by computing the variance between 5 subjects).
Major differences (enlightened) are observed in vertical displacement where the control system
is sometimes attracted by saturated colors of clothes of people passing in the background
rather than their faces.

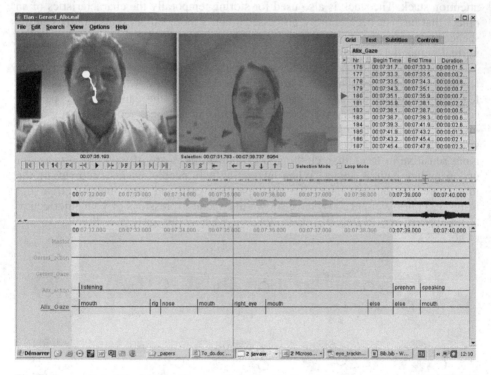

**Fig. 5.** Screenshot of the labeling framework for face-to-face interaction data (using the ELAN
editor® www.mpi.nl/tools/elan.html). The female listener fixates either the mouth or the right
eye of the male speaker when he is uttering a SUS utterance (see text).

## 4   Gaze Patterns in Face-to-Face Interaction

When interacting, people mostly gaze at the other's face and gesturing. While speech
is clearly audiovisual (Stork and Hennecke 1996), facial expressions and gaze also

inform us about the physical, emotional and mental state of the interlocutor. Together with gesturing, they participate in signaling discourse structure, ruling turn taking and maintaining mutual interest. Context-aware ECA should be reactive to gaze patterns of their interlocutors and implement these complex interaction rules (Thórisson 2002).

Most data on eye movement of perceivers during audiovisual speech perception have been gathered using non interactive audiovisual recordings (Vatikiotis-Bateson, Eigsti et al. 1998). Several experiments have however shown that live gaze patterns are significantly different from screening (Gullberg and Holmqvist 2001): social rules have in fact a strong impact on communication when interacting face-to-face.

We conducted preliminary experiments for determining the natural gaze interplays between interlocutors according to their social status, their roles in the conversation and the dialog task. We illustrate below the complex gaze patterns already observed in a simple task such as repeating the other's utterance. The experimental setting involves two cameras coupled with two eye trackers (see figure 1b) that monitor the gaze patterns of the interlocutors when interacting through two screens. We checked that this setting enables an acceptable spatial cognition so that each interlocutor correctly perceives what part of his face the other is looking at. The task just consisted in a speech game where Semantically Unpredictable Sentences (see Benoît, Grice et al. 1996, for description of SUS) uttered by one speaker in noisy environment have to be repeated with no error by his interlocutor. The speaker has of course to correct the repeated utterance as long as the repetition is incorrect. Mutual attention is thus essential to the success of interaction. Preliminary results (see Table 1) confirm for example that prephonatory (preparing to speak) activity is characterized by a gaze away from the face of the interlocutor. Eyes and mouth are all scrutinized when first listening to SUS whereas gaze during verification is focused on the mouth: gaze patterns are of course highly depending on cognitive demands (Yarbus 1967).

**Table 1.** Gaze data from speaker X when interacting with speaker Y. A turn consists in trying to repeat a SUS uttered by the partner with no error. Percentage of time spent on mouth and eyes regions is given for various actions and roles of the interlocutors.

|            |               | Regions of the face of Y gazed by X | | | |
|------------|---------------|-------|----------|-----------|-------|
| SUS giver  | Actions of X  | Mouth | Left eye | Right eye | Other |
| X          | Prephonatory  | 48,1  | 0        | 6,9       | 45,0  |
|            | Speaking      | 91,6  | 0        | 5,1       | 3,3   |
|            | Listening     | 82,0  | 0        | 6,7       | 11,3  |
| Y          | Listening     | 64,0  | 14,6     | 17,8      | 3,6   |
|            | Speaking      | 48,4  | 29,2     | 19,2      | 3,2   |
|            | Prephonatory  | 18,7  | 10,2     | 37,6      | 33,5  |

# 5   Comments

A control model for eyes direction should not only rely on a context-aware multimodal scene analysis and a basic comprehension of the user's intentions and social rules but also rely on a faithful scene synthesis. Gaze patterns should be rendered so that human partners perceive the intended multimodal deixis and mutual attention. In a preceding paper (Raidt, Bailly et al. 2006), we have shown that our ECA is able to efficiently attract users' attention towards its focus of interest. We currently investigate the impact of the eye gaze rendering on performance. Eyelids deformations as well as head movements participate to the elaboration of gaze direction: adequate prediction of these deformations according to gaze direction reinforces perception of spatial cognition.

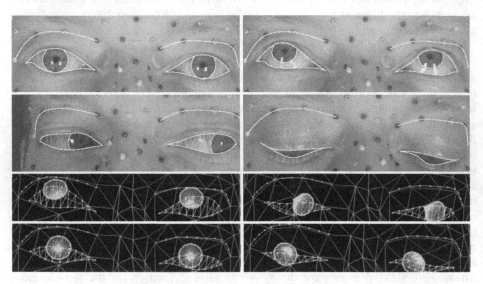

**Fig. 6.** A 3D statistical shape model that reproduces geometric deformations of the eyelids of one subject depending on gaze direction

# 6 Conclusions

This paper sketches a research framework for giving ECA the gift of situated human interaction. The landscape on eye gaze research is of course incomplete and gaze is one part of the facial actions that humans involve in face-to-face conversation. Gestural scores should be properly orchestrated so that complementary and redundant information is delivered at the right tempo to the interlocutor. Human behavior is so complex and subtle that computational models should be grounded on quantitative data (please refer for example to Bailly, Elisei et al. 2006, for a study of facial movements involved in conversation). Interaction rules should be completed with interaction loops that take into account the necessary coupling between signals extracted by a detailed multimodal scene analysis and the comprehension of the discourse and speaker's desires and beliefs that the artificial intelligence is able to built. Part of the success and realism of the interaction is surely in the intelligent use the artificial intelligence can make of the symptoms of the comprehension of the interaction the human partners who are present in the scene offer for free.

# Acknowledgments

The authors want to thank Jan Cornelis, Hichem Sahli and Werner Verhelst for their kind invitation. The technical support from Alain Arnal and Christophe Savariaux was essential. This work is financed by the GIS PEGASUS, the ELESA research federation and the Presence project of the Cluster Rhones-Alpes InfoLog.

# References

1. Argyle, M. and M. Cook (1976). Gaze and mutual gaze. London, Cambridge University Press.
2. Bailly, G., F. Elisei, P. Badin and C. Savariaux (2006). Degrees of freedom of facial movements in face-to-face conversational speech. International Workshop on Multimodal Corpora, Genoa - Italy: 33-36.
3. Baron-Cohen, S., A. Leslie and U. Frith (1985). "Does the autistic child have a "theory of mind"?" Cognition 21: 37-46.
4. Benoît, C., M. Grice and V. Hazan (1996). "The SUS test: A method for the assessment of text-to-speech synthesis intelligibility using Semantically Unpredictable Sentences." Speech Communication 18: 381-392.
5. Carpenter, M. and M. Tomasello (2000). Joint attention, cultural learning and language acquisition: Implications for children with autism. Communicative and language intervention series. Autism spectrum disorders: A transactional perspective. A. M. Wetherby and B. M. Prizant. Baltimore, Paul H. Brooks Publishing. 9: 30–54.
6. Cassell, J., J. Sullivan, S. Prevost and E. Churchill (2000). Embodied Conversational Agents. Cambridge, MIT Press.
7. Clodic, A., S. Fleury, R. Alami, R. Chatila, G. Bailly, L. Brèthes, M. Cottret, P. Danès, x. Dollat, F. Elisei, I. Ferrané and M. Herrb (2006). Rackham: an interactive robot-guide. IEEE International Workshop on Robots and Human Interactive Communications, Hatfield, UK
8. Driver, J., G. Davis, P. Riccardelli, P. Kidd, E. Maxwell and S. Baron-Cohen (1999). "Shared attention and the social brain : gaze perception triggers automatic visuospatial orienting in adults." Visual Cognition 6 (5): 509-540.
9. Geiger, G., T. Ezzat and T. Poggio (2003). Perceptual evaluation of video-realistic speech. CBCL Paper #224/AI Memo #2003-003, Cambridge, MA, Massachusetts Institute of Technology.
10. Grossberg, S. (2003). "How does the cerebral cortex work? development, learning, attention, and 3d vision by laminar circuits of visual cortex." Behavioral and Cognitive Neuroscience Reviews 2: 47-76.
11. Gullberg, M. and K. Holmqvist (2001). Visual attention towards gestures in face-to-face interaction vs. on screen. International Gesture Workshop, London, UK: 206-214.
12. Itti, L., N. Dhavale and F. Pighin (2003). Realistic avatar eye and head animation using a neurobiological model of visual attention. SPIE 48th Annual International Symposium on Optical Science and Technology, San Diego, CA: 64-78.
13. Kendon, A. (1967). "Some functions of gaze-direction in social interaction." Acta Psychologica 26: 22-63.
14. Langton, S. and V. Bruce (1999). "Reflexive visual orienting in response to the social attention of others." Visual Cognition 6 (5): 541-567.
15. Langton, S., J. Watt and V. Bruce (2000). "Do the eyes have it ? Cues to the direction of social attention." Trends in Cognitive Sciences 4 (2): 50-59.

16. Lee, S. P., J. B. Badler and N. Badler (2002). "Eyes alive." ACM Transaction on Graphics **21** (3): 637-644.
17. Matsusaka, Y., T. Tojo and T. Kobayashi (2003). "Conversation Robot Participating in Group Conversation." IEICE Transaction of Information and System **E86-D** (1): 26-36.
18. Posner, M. I. (1980). "Orienting of attention." Quarterly Journal of Experimental Psychology **32**: 3-25.
19. Pourtois, G., D. Sander, M. Andres, D. Grandjean, L. Reveret, E. Olivier and P. Vuilleumier (2004). "Dissociable roles of the human somatosensory and superior temporal cortices for processing social face signals." European Journal of Neuroscience **20**: 3507-3515.
20. Premack, D. and G. Woodruff (1978). "Does the chimpanzee have a theory of mind?" Behavioral and brain sciences **1**: 515-526.
21. Raidt, S., G. Bailly and F. Elisei (2006). Does a virtual talking face generate proper multimodal cues to draw user's attention towards interest points? Language Ressources and Evaluation Conference (LREC), Genova - Italy: 2544-2549.
22. Riva, G., F. Davide and W. A. IJsselsteijn (2003). Being there: concepts, effects and measurements of user presence in synthetic environments. Amsterdam, IOS Press.
23. Scassellati, B. (2001). Foundations for a theory of mind for a humanoid robot. Department of Computer Science and Electrical Engineering. Boston - MA, MIT: 174 p.
24. Simons, D. J. and C. F. Chabris (1999). "Gorillas in our midst: sustained inattentional blindness for dynamic events." Perception **28**: 1059-1074.
25. Stork, D. G. and M. E. Hennecke (1996). Speechreading by Humans and Machines. Berlin, Germany, Springer.
26. Sun, Y. (2003). Hierarchical object-based visual attention for machine vision. PhD Thesis. Institute of Perception, Action and Behaviour. School of Informatics. Edinburgh, University of Edinburgh: 169 p.
27. Thórisson, K. (2002). Natural turn-taking needs no manual: computational theory and model from perception to action. Multimodality in language and speech systems. B. Granström, D. House and I. Karlsson. Dordrecht, The Netherlands, Kluwer Academic: 173–207.
28. Vatikiotis-Bateson, E., I.-M. Eigsti, S. Yano and K. G. Munhall (1998). "Eye movement of perceivers during audiovisual speech perception." Perception & Psychophysics **60**: 926-940.
29. Xu, Y. and M. M. Chun (2006). "Dissociable neural mechanisms supporting visual short-term memory for objects." Nature **440**: 91-95.
30. Yarbus, A. L. (1967). Eye movements during perception of complex objects. Eye Movements and Vision'. L. A. Riggs. New York, Plenum Press. **VII**: 171-196.

# DBN Based Models for Audio-Visual Speech Analysis and Recognition

Ilse Ravyse[1], Dongmei Jiang[3], Xiaoyue Jiang[3], Guoyun Lv[3], Yunshu Hou[3],
Hichem Sahli[1,2], and Rongchun Zhao[3]

[1] Joint Research Group on Audio Visual Signal Processing (AVSP)
[1] Vrije Universiteit Brussel, Department ETRO,
Pleinlaan 2, 1050 Brussel
{icravyse, hsahli}@etro.vub.ac.be
[2] IMEC, Kapeldreef 75, 3001 Leuven
[3] Northwestern Polytechnical University, School of Computer Science,
127 Youyi Xilu, Xi'an 710072, P.R. China
{jiangdm, rczhao}@nwpu.edu.cn
http://etro.vub.ac.be

**Abstract.** We present an audio-visual automatic speech recognition system, which significantly improves speech recognition performance over a wide range of acoustic noise levels, as well as under clean audio conditions. The system consists of three components: (i) a visual module, (ii) an acoustic module, and (iii) a Dynamic Bayesian Network-based recognition module. The vision module, locates and tracks the speaker head, and mouth movements and extracts relevant speech features represented by contour information and 3D deformations of lip movements. The acoustic module extracts noise-robust features, i.e. the Mel Filterbank Cepstrum Coefficients (MFCCs). Finally we propose two models based on Dynamic Bayesian Networks (DBN) to either consider the single audio and video streams or to integrate the features from the audio and visual streams. We also compare the proposed DBN based system with classical Hidden Markov Model. The novelty of the developed framework is the persistence of the audiovisual speech signal characteristics from the extraction step, through the learning step. Experiments on continuous audiovisual speech show that the segmentation boundaries of phones in the audio stream and visemes in the video stream are close to manual segmentation boundaries.

## 1 Introduction

Automatic speech recognition (ASR) is of great importance in human-machine interfaces, but despite extensive effort over decades, acoustic-based recognition systems remain too inaccurate for the vast majority of conceivable applications, especially those in noisy environments, e.g. crowded envirenment. While incremental advances may be expected along the current ASR paradigm, e.g. using acoustic multi-stream Dynamic Bayesian Networks (DBN) [1, 2, 3], novel approaches in particular those utilizing visual information as well are being studied. Such multi-modal Audio-Visual ASR systems have already been shown to

Y. Zhuang et al. (Eds.): PCM 2006, LNCS 4261, pp. 19–30, 2006.

have superior recognition accuracy, especially in noisy conditions [4,5,6]. The use of visual features in audio-visual speech recognition is motivated by the speech formation mechanism and the natural speech ability of humans to reduce audio ambiguities using visual cues. Moreover, the visual information provides complementary cues that cannot be corrupted by the acoustic noise of the environment. However, problems such as the selection of the optimal set of visual features, and the optimal models for audio-visual integration remain challenging research topics. In this paper, we provide improvements to the existing methods for visual feature estimation and we propose speech recognition models based on Dynamic Bayesian Networks (DBN) which are extension of the model proposed in [7].

The proposed framework for audio-visual analysis is as follows. Visemes are recognized in the bimodal speech by means of their characteristic features in both the audio and visual streams. The novelty in our framework is the integration method of both signal properties in a learning scheme. The learning scheme of visemes distinguishes itself from the existing audio-only word recognizers because it is able to segment the timing of the visual features. We have currently constructed a single DBN model to recognize phoneme segments from the audio stream, and a similar single DBN model to recognize viseme segments from the corresponding image stream. Considering the study of the correlation and asynchrony of audio and video, these models can be seen as the foundation for a multi-stream DBN model that recognizes the audio-visual units from the audio-visual speech.

We intend to apply the framework in automatic lip-sync using animation of virtual faces [8] to improve the robustness of audio speech in noisy environments.

The paper is organized as follows. Section 2.1 discusses the visual features extraction, starting from the detection and tracking of the speaker's head in the image sequence, followed by the detailed extraction of mouth motion, and section 2.2 lists the audio features. The usage of the extracted features in audiovisual speech recognition is explained in section 3, along with experimental results. Concluding remarks and future plans are outlined in section 4.

## 2     Audio-Visual Features Extraction

### 2.1     Visual Feature Extraction

Robust location of the speaker's face and the facial features, specifically the mouth region, and the extraction of a discriminant set of visual observation vectors are key elements in an audio-video speech recognition system. The cascade algorithm for visual feature extraction used in our system consists of the following steps: face detection and tracking, mouth region detection and lip contour extraction for 2D and 3D feature estimation. In the following we describe in details each of these steps.

**Head Detection and Tracking.** The first step of the analysis is the detection and tracking of the speaker's face in the video stream. For this purpose we use a previously developed head detection and tracking method [9]. The head detection consists of a two-step process: (a) face candidates selection, carried out here by clustering the pixel values in the $YC_rC_b$ color space and producing labeled skin-colored regions $\{R_i\}_{i=1}^N$ and their best fit ellipse $E_i = (x_i, y_i, a_i, b_i, \theta)$ being the center coordinates, the major and minor axes length, and the orientation respectively, and (b) the face verification that selects the best face candidate. In the verification step a global face cue measure $M_i$, combining gray-tone cues and ellipse shape cues $Q_j$, $j = 1, \ldots, 4$, is estimated for each face candidate region $R_i$. Combining shape and facial feature cues ensures an adequate detection of the face. The face candidate that has the maximal measure $M_i$ localizes the head region in the image.

The tracking of the detected head in the subsequent image frames is performed via a kernel-based method wherein a joint spatial-color probability density characterizes the head region [9].

Figure 1 illustrates the tracking method. Samples are taken from the initial ellipse region in the first image, called *model target*, to evaluate the model target joint spatial-color kernel-based probability density function (p.f.d.). A hypothesis is made that the true target will be represented as a transformation of this model target by using a motion and illumination change model. The hypothesized target is in fact the modeled new look in the current image frame of the initially detected object. A *hypothesized target* is therefore represented by the *hypothesized p.d.f.* which is the transformed model p.d.f. To verify this hypothesis, samples of the next image are taken within the transformed model target boundary to create the *candidate target* and the joint spatial-color distribution of these samples is compared to the *hypothesized p.d.f.* using a distance-measure. A new set of transformation parameters is selected by minimizing the distance-measure. The parameter estimation or tracking algorithm lets the target's region converge to the true object's region via changes in the parameter set.

This kernel-based approach proved to be robust to the 3-dimensional motion of the face(see Figure 2). Moreover, incorporating an illumination model into the tracking equations enables us to cope with potentially distracting illumination changes.

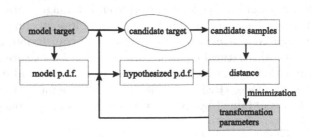

**Fig. 1.** Tracking algorithm

**2D Lip Contour Extraction.** The contour of the lips is obtained through the Bayesian Tangent Shape Model (BTSM) [10]. Figure 2 shows several successful results of the lip contour extraction.

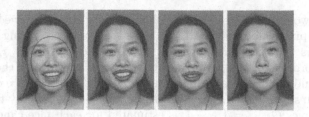

**Fig. 2.** Face detection/tracking and lip contour extraction

The lip contour is used to estimate a visual feature vector consisting of the mouth opening measures shown in Figure 3. In total, 42 mouth features have been identified based on the automatically labeled landmark feature points: 5 vertical distances between the outer contour feature points; 1 horizontal distance between the outer lip corners; 4 angles; 3 vertical distances between the inner contour feature points; 1 horizontal distance between the inner lip corners; and the first order and second order regression coefficient (delta and acceleration in the image frames at 25 fps) of the previous measures.

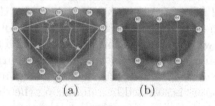

(a)          (b)

**Fig. 3.** Vertical and horizontal opening distances and angle features of the mouth: (a) outer contour features; (b) inner contour features

**3D Lip Motion Extraction.** All facial expressions are produced by the 3D deformation of the skin, the face shape (due to articulation), as well as the rigid head movements. Estimating 3D deformation from 2D image sequences is an ill-posed problem which we solved in [11] by imposing physical constraints on the face motion: the rigid motion consists of a rotation and translation relative to the projection axes, and the natural deformations of the facial features are induced by distributed muscle forces which are modeled in a mechanical displacement-based finite element model (FEM). In this model, 3D deformation, also called scene flow $\mathbf{W}$ [12], is obtained by solving the following energy function

$$\widehat{\mathbf{W}} = \arg\min_{\mathbf{W}} \left[ \left( \sum_{k=1}^{m} \| \mathbf{u}_k - \widetilde{\mathbf{u}}(\mathbf{W}_k) \|^2 \right) + \psi \right] \tag{1}$$

where $\mathbf{u}$ is the estimated optical flow and $\widetilde{\mathbf{u}}(\mathbf{W})$ the parameterized optical flow constructed as the projection of $\mathbf{W}$, the sum is taken over all the vertices of the wire-frame face model, and $\psi$ are regularization terms expressing the smoothly varying muscles forces that lie tangential to the face surface.

Equation 1 is solved using the quasi-Newton trust region method where in each iteration the displacements are obtained from solving the mechanical FEM with the updated forces input.

This approach for 3D motion motion extraction has the advantage that the muscle topology does not need to be fixed as in the mass-spring models [13], and that the face motions are not restricted to geometrical transformations as in [14]. The output of the deformation estimation around the mouth is not only the displacement of the feature points, but also the direction and magnitude of the forces needed for the articulation. 3D deformation (motion) estimation results are shown in Figure 4, and Figure 5 illustrates the estimated forces at automatically labeled landmarks.

$$(a) \qquad\qquad\qquad (b)$$

**Fig. 4.** 3D Lip motion extraction: (a) mouth initialization on first frame; (b) mouth motion estimation at fourth frame

**Fig. 5.** Total estimated forces (at 3 landmarks) allowing the 3D deformation of the lip from the first frame to the fourth frame of Figure 4

## 2.2   Audio Features

The acoustic features are computed with a frame rate of 100frames/s. Each speech frame is converted to 39 acoustic parameters: 12 MFCCs (Mel Filterbank Cepstrum Coefficients [15]), 12 $\Delta$MFCCs, 12 $\Delta\Delta$MFCCs, energy, $\Delta$ energy, $\Delta\Delta$ energy;

# 3   Audiovisual Recognition

## 3.1   DBN Model for Speech Segmentation

In recent years, single stream DBN and multi-stream DBN are applied to continuous speech recognition, and improvements have been achieved in the recognition rates of words, as well as in the robustness to background noise [1, 7].

In our framework, we design two single-stream DBN based learning schemes: the first segments audio speech into phone sequence, and the second segments visual speech to viseme sequence. In the following the audio-based DBN model is described, for the video the same model is used. The training data consists of the audio and video features extracted from labeled (word and phone/viseme) sentences.

The DBN models in Figure 6 represents the unflattened and hierarchical structures for a speech recognition system. It consists of an initialization with a *Prologue* part, a *Chunk* part that is repeated every time frame (t), and a closure of a sentence with an *Epliogue* part. Every horizontal row of nodes in Figure 6 depicts a separate temporal layer of random variables. The arcs between the nodes are either deterministic (straight lines) or random (dotted lines) relationships between the random variables, expressed as conditional probability distributions (CPD). The specific placement of the arcs is done according to the Bigram language model [7].

In the training model, the random variables *Word Counter* $(WC)$ and *Skip Silence* $(SS)$, denote the position of the current word or silence in the sentence, respectively. The other random variables in Figure 6 are: (i) the number of *words* in a sentence (W); (ii) the occurrence of a *transition to another word* $(WT)$, with $WT = 1$ denoting the start of a new word, and $WT = 0$ denoting the continuation of the current word; (iii) the number of *phone position* in the word $(PP)$; (iv) the occurrence of a *transition to another phone* $(PT)$, defined similarly as $WT$; and (v) the *phone identification* $(P)$, e.g. 'f' is the first phone and 'vl' is the first viseme in the word 'four'.

In our model, as opposed to the state-of-the-art word level speech recognition systems [1,3], we have changed the often used *Whole Word State* nodes into the phone/viseme nodes $(P)$ with a word-phone(or viseme) dictionary.

We Now define the CPDs, for each level of nodes of Figure 6. First, the acoustic feature $o_t$ is a random function of the phone in the conditional probability function $p(o_t|P_t)$, which is calculated by a Gaussian Mixture Model(GMM) as in a typical Hidden Markov Model (HMM) system. Next, the phone variable $P_t$ is fully deterministic of its parents $PP_t$ and $W_t$. This means that given the current word and phone position, the phone is known with certainty:

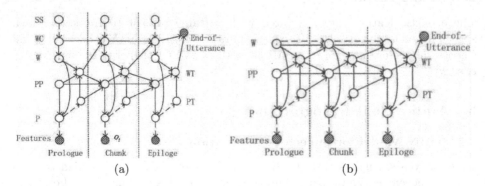

(a)                                              (b)

**Fig. 6.** DBN models: (a) training, (b) recognition

$$p(P_t = i | PP_t = k, W_t = w) =$$
$$\begin{cases} 1 \text{ if } i \text{ is the } k^{th} \text{ phone in word } w \\ 0 \text{ otherwise} \end{cases} \tag{2}$$

The phone transition variable $PT_t$ is a binary indicator that specifies when the model should advance to the next phone. $p(PT_t | P_t)$ takes its cue from the phone variable $P_t$ meaning that each phone may have its own duration distribution. For each phone, there is a nonzero probability of either staying at a phone or moving to the next phone. But only when $p(PT_t | P_t)$ is 1, $PT_t$ is assigned as 1 which means a phone transition is occurring.

Another important hidden variable is the phone position ($PP$), which denotes the position of the current phone in a word:

$$PP_t = \begin{cases} PP_{t-1} & \text{if } PT_{t-1} = 0 \\ 1 + PP_{t-1} & \text{if } PT_{t-1} = 1 \text{ and } WT_{t-1} = 0 \\ 0 & \text{if } WT_{t-1} = 1 \end{cases} \tag{3}$$

Furthermore, the other deterministic transition is the word transition ($WT$). Here a word transition ($WT_t = 1$) occurs only if there is a phone transition ($PT_t = 1$) from the last phone position ($PP_t = k$) of a word ($W_{t-1} = w$):

$$WT_t = \begin{cases} 1 \text{ if } PT_t = 1 \text{ and } lastphone(k, w) \\ 0 \text{ if } PT_t = 1 \text{ and } \sim lastphone(k, w) \\ 0 \text{ if } PT_t = 0 \end{cases} \tag{4}$$

where $lastphone(k,w)$ is a binary indicator that specifies if the phone reaches the last position $k$ of a word $w$ (known from the word-to-phone dictionary).

$$lastphone(k, w) = \begin{cases} 1 \text{ if } PP_t = k \text{ and } W_{t-1} = w \\ 0 \ otherwise \end{cases} \tag{5}$$

Finally, the word variable ($W$) uses the switching parent functionality, where the existence (or implementation) of an arc can depend on the value of some other variable(s) in the network, referred to as the switching parent(s). In this case, the switching parent is the word transition variable. When the word transition is zero ($WT_{t-1} = 0$), it causes the word variable $W_t$ to copy its previous value, i.e., $W_t = W_{t-1}$ with probability one. When a word transition occurs ($WT_{t-1} = 1$), however, it switches to the word-to-word arc and uses the bigram language model probability $p(W_t | W_{t-1})$. So these DBN models switch implementations of a CPD from a deterministic function to a random bigram language model, i.e. *bigram* which means the probability of one word transiting to another word whose value comes from the statistics of the training script sentences.

$$p(W_t = i | W_{t-1} = j, WT_t = k) = \begin{cases} 1 & \text{if} & \text{i=j} & \text{and} & \text{k=0} \\ \text{bigram} & \text{if} & \text{k=1} \\ 0 & \text{otherwise} \end{cases} \tag{6}$$

In the training DBN model, the Word Counter ($WC$) node is incremented according to the following CPD:

$$p(WC_t = i|WC_{t-1} = j, WT_{t-1} = k, SS = l) =$$

$$\begin{cases} 1 \text{ if } i{=}j \text{ and } k{=}0 \\ 1 \text{ if } i{=}j \text{ and } bound(w,j) = 1, k = 1 \\ 1 \text{ if } i{=}j{+}1 \text{ and } bound(w,j) = 0, l = 0, k = 1 \\ 1 \text{ if } i{=}j{+}2 \text{ and } bound(w,j) = 0, l = 1, k = 1, realword(w) = 1 \\ 1 \text{ if } i{=}j{+}1 \text{ and } bound(w,j) = 0, l = 1, k = 1, realword(w) = 0 \\ 0 \text{ } otherwise \end{cases} \quad (7)$$

where $bound(w,j)$ is a binary indicator specifying if the position $j$ of the current word $w$ exceeds the boundary of the training sentence, if so, $bound(w,j) = 1$. $realword(w) = 1$ means the coming word $w$ after silence is a word with real meaning.

The estimation/training of the above defined CPDs in the DBN is implemented with the generalized EM algorithm with the graphical model toolkit GMTK [1]. In the recognition process the inference algorithm [1] find the best path through the nodes of the DBN structure to represent the audio or visual speech in the best way by a time series of words as well as phones/visemes.

Using the same notation, the proposed multi-stream DBN model is illustrated in Figure 7. Its advantage is that it not only considers the asynchrony between the audio and the visual stream by assigning the phone position ($PP$) and the viseme position ($VP$) independently, but also takes into account their tight correlation by incorporating the conditions from both streams into the word transition ($WT$), through the arcs from $PP$ and $PT$ to $WT$, as well as the arcs from $VP$ and $VT$ to $WT$.

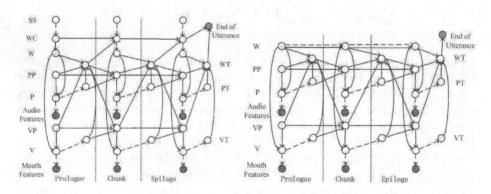

**Fig. 7.** Multi-stream DBN model

## 3.2  Experiments

We recorded our own audiovisual database with the scripts of the Aurura 3.0 audio database containing connected digits. 100 recorded sentences are selected to be used as training data, and another 50 sentences as testing data. In the phone DBN recognition experiments, we first extract a word-to-phone dictionary from the standard TIMITDIC dictionary [16] for the ten digits, as well as silence and short pause 'sp'. Actually, only 22 phones are used due to the small size of the vocabulary. In the viseme DBN recognition experiments, we first map the word-to-phone dictionary to a word-to-viseme dictionary using a mapping table we previously proposed in [8].

**Recognition Results.** For the single audio stream DBN, Table 1, summarizes the word recognition rates (WRR) using only acoustic features with white noise at different SNRs. Compared to trained triphone HMMs (implemented using HTK), one can notice that with the proposed DBN model we obtain equivalent results in case of 'clean' signal and better results with strong noise.

**Table 1.** Word Recognition Rate v.s. SNR

|     | clean | 40db | 30db | 20db | 15db | 10db | 0db |
|-----|-------|------|------|------|------|------|------|
| HMM | 99.06 | 99.06 | 99.06 | 94.34 | 81.13 | 58.49 | 30.19 |
| DBN | 99.06 | 99.06 | 98.11 | 87.74 | 84.91 | 69.81 | 35.85 |

For the single video stream DBN, the word recognition rates has been of 67.26 percent for all SNR levels. This is normal as the visual data is not affected by acoustic noise.

**Segmentation Results.** To illustrate the segmentation results we used a simple audio-video stream corresponding to the sentence "two nine". Table 2 shows the phones segmentation results from the audio stream, while Table 3 shows the visemes segmentation from visual stream.

**Table 2.** Phone Segmentation Results

| Phoneme | sil | t | uw | sp | n | ay | n | sil |
|---------|-----|---|-----|-----|---|-----|---|-----|
| HMM(ms) | - | 0-510 | 510-820 | 820-820 | 820-950 | 950-1230 | 1230-1460 | 1460-1620 |
| DBN(ms) | 0-420 | 430-540 | 550-820 | 830-840 | 850-970 | 980-1200 | 1210-1340 | 1350-1610 |

**Table 3.** Viseme Segmentation Results

| Viseme | vn | vd | vp | vj | vm | vg | vp | vc | vp | vb | vm | vj |
|--------|-----|-----|-----|-----|-----|------|------|------|------|------|------|------|
| DBN(image frame) | 0-4 | 5-5 | 6-6 | 7-8 | 9-9 | 10-16 | 17-17 | 18-29 | 30-30 | 31-31 | 32-36 | 37-38 |

The segmentation results together with the temporal changes of audio and visual features are illustrated in Figure 8, using the following mapping between visemes and phones: viseme 'vm' corresponds to the mouth shape of the phone 't', 'vg' to phone 'uw', 'vp' to phone 'n', 'vc' to phone 'ay', and 'vj' means silence (sil in Table 2). Some mouth images (frames) of the visemes are also shown.

From the phone and viseme segmentation results, one can notice that the viseme boundaries are normally 20 ms to 30 ms earlier than their corresponding phones. Similar results, from subjective evaluations, have been reported in [17]. From Figure 8, we also see that even when we can't hear any voice (silence), we can observe some mouth movements in the images. This explains why there are some visemes recognized in the silence fragments of the audio stream, as shown in Table 3.

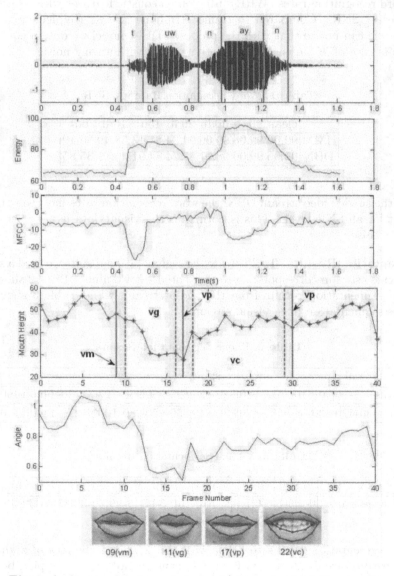

**Fig. 8.** Audio visual features and phone/viseme segmentation results

# 4  Discussion

We have described a framework to recognize audiovisual speech. In the learning scheme with DBN models we use the visual features to segment visemes and the audio features to segment phones. Word recognition results from audio show that DBN model is more robust to very noisy background than HMM. The visual speech recognition is robust against noise, namely word recognition rate keeps about 67.26 percent in all noise levels.

This improvement of the intelligibility of the speech in noisy environments, together with the accurately extracted time boundaries of phones and visemes, can be used to synthesize speech and mouth shapes in a talking virtual face.

The integration framework of the audio and visual modalities is extendible to other scenarios than visual speech. In particular, we plan to address the emotion recognition in the audiovisual video.

## Acknowledgement

This research has been conducted within the *Audio Visual Speech Recognition and Synthesis: Bimodal Approach* project funded in the framework of the Bilateral Scientific and Technological Collaboration between Flanders, Belgium (BILO4/CN/02A) and the Ministry of Science and Technology (MOST), China ([2004]487).

## References

1. Bilmes, J., Zweig, G.: The graphical modelds toolkit:an open source software system for speech and time-series processing. In: Proceedings of the IEEE Internation Conf. on Acoustic Speech and Signal Processing(ICASSP). Volume 4. (2002) 3916–3919
2. Jeff Bilmes, G.Z., et al: Discriminatively structured dynamic graphical models for speech recognition. Technical report, JHU 2001 Summer Workshop (2001)
3. Y.Zhang, Q. Diao, S.W.C., J.Bilmes: Dbn based multi-stream models for speech. In: Proceedings of the IEEE Internation Conf. on Acoustic Speech and Signal Processing(ICASSP). (2003)
4. G.Gravier, G.Potamianos, C.: Asynchrony modeling for audio visual speech recognition. In: Proceedings of Human Language Technology Conference. (2002)
5. G.N.Gawdy, A.Subramanya, C.J.: Dbn based multi-stream models for audio visual speech recognition. In: Proceedings of the IEEE Internation Conf. on Acoustic Speech and Signal Processing(ICASSP). (2004)
6. Xin Lei, Gang Ji, T.N.J.B., Ostendorf, M.: Dbn-based multi-stream mandarin toneme recogntion. In: Proceedings of the IEEE Internation Conf. on Acoustic Speech and Signal Processing(ICASSP). (2005)
7. Bilmes, J., Bartels, C.: Graphical model architecture for speech recognition. In: IEEE signal processing magazine. Volume 89. (2005)
8. Lei, X., Dongmei, J., Ravyse, I., Verhelst, W., Sahli, H., Slavova, V., Rongchun, Z.: Context dependent viseme models for voice driven animation. In: 4th EURASIP Conference focused on Video/Image Processing and Multimedia Communications, EC-VIP-MC 2003, Zagreb, Croatia, July 2-4, 2003. Volume 2. (2003) 649–654

9. Ravyse, I., Enescu, V., Sahli, H.: Kernel-based head tracker for videophony. In: The IEEE International Conference on Image Processing 2005 (ICIP2005), Genoa, Italy, 11-14/09/2005. Volume 3. (2005) 1068–1071

10. Zhou, Y., Gu, L., Zhang, H.J.: Bayesian tangent shape model: Estimating shape and pose parameters via bayesian inference. In: Proceedings of the 2003 IEEE Conference on Computer Vision and Pattern Recognition(CVPR2003). Volume 1. (2003) 109–118

11. Ravyse, I.:    Facial  Analysis  and  Synthesis.    PhD thesis, Vrije Universiteit Brussel, Dept. Electronics and Informatics, Belgium (2006) online: www.etro.vub.ac.be/Personal/icravyse/RavysePhDThesis.pdf.

12. Vedula, S., Baker, S., Rander, P., Collins, R., Kanade, T.: Three-dimensional scene flow. IEEE Transactions on Pattern Analysis and Machine Intelligence **27** (2005) 137–154

13. Lee, Y., Terzopoulos, D., , Waters, K.: Constructing physicsbased facial models of individuals. In: Proceedings of the Graphics Interface '93 Conference, Toronto, ON, Canada. (1993) 1–8

14. Eisert, P.: Very Low Bit-Rate Video Coding Using 3-D Models. PhD thesis, Universitat Erlangen, Shaker Verlag, Aachen, Germany (2000) ISBN 3-8265-8308-6.

15. Steven B.Davis, P.M.: Comparison of parametric representation for monosyllable word recognition in continuously spoken sentences. IEEE Transactions on Acoustics, Speech, and Signal Processing **28** (1980) 357–366

16. : (http://www.ldc.upenn.edu/doc/timit/timitdic.txt)

17. J.Beskow, I.Karlson, J.G.: Synface-a talking head telephone for the hearing-impaired. In et al, K., ed.: Computers Helping People with Special Needs. (2004) 1178–1186

# An Extensive Method to Detect the Image Digital Watermarking Based on the Known Template

Yang Feng, Senlin Luo, and Limin Pan

Dept. of Electronics Engineering, Beijing Institute of Technology,
Beijing, China, 100081
bitluosenlin@sina.com

**Abstract.** There are many types of digital watermarking algorithms, but each type corresponds with a certain detecting method to detect the watermark. However, the embedding method is usually unknown, so that it is not possible to know whether the hidden information exists or not. An extensive digital watermarking detecting method based on the known template is proposed in this paper. This method extracts some feature parameters form the spatial, DCT and DWT domains of the image and template, and then use some detecting strategies on those parameters to detect the watermark. The experiment result shows that the correct detecting rate is more than 97%. Obviously, the extensive digital watermarking detection method can be realized, and the method is valuable in theory and practice.

**Keywords:** digital watermarking; extensive detection; correlative detection.

## 1 Introduction

With the fast growing of network and media techniques, there has been growing interest in developing effective techniques to discourage the unauthorized duplication of digital data like audio, image and video. In traditional method, cryptology is often used to protect them, but when the cryptograph has been decoded, copying and republishing of the digital data would be out of control. The appearance of digital watermarking can change this status, digital watermarking is a new technique which protects the copyright in the circumstance of the open network, it also can attest the source and integrality of digital data[1][2][3]. Authors of digital media embed some information into their works by using an unappreciable method, and those information can not be found unless via a corresponsive detector.

Developing of digital watermarking techniques is in a high speed, there have been many types of digital watermarking methods. But each type is independent from each other, so the detection of each one should correspond with the method of embedding.

Generally, Methods of Images digital watermarking can be divided into two types, methods in spatial domain and methods in transform domain. And methods of transform domain can be divided into DCT domain methods and DWT domain (wavelet domain) methods. Cox. I. J, professor of Imperial College London, has proposed a frame of two steps watermarking detection[2][4], as Fig 1. The array of the

Y. Zhuang et al. (Eds.): PCM 2006, LNCS 4261, pp. 31–40, 2006.

watermarking image (the image which will be detected) in symbol spatial is extracted by the watermark extractor. And then, the watermarking information (hidden information) can be detected from the array by a simple detector. This simple detector could be a linear correlate detector, unitary correlate detector or correlate coefficient detector.

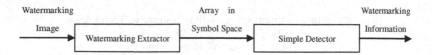

**Fig. 1.** Frame of the two steps watermarking detection

However, the method of embedding is usually unknown in the process of watermarking detection. There are more than one hundred methods of digital watermarking embedding, and because of the time consuming and the uncertainty detecting result, it is nearly impossible to use every corresponsive method to detect the watermarking information. In that way, does any extensive watermarking detection methods exist? By the analyzing of the digital watermarking embedding and detecting algorithms, an extensive images watermarking detection method is proposed in this paper, this method extract the feature parameters form the spatial, DCT and DWT domain (array in symbol space) of the image. These parameters would be taken for the inputs of a watermarking detector, and the result of the watermarking detector is the detecting value to judge the hidden information exists or not. The experimental result shows that the method of extensive digital watermarking detection can be realized, and it is very effective.

## 2 Method of Extensive Image Digital Watermarking Detection

### 2.1 Theoretic Analyze

Usually, two techniques are proposed for watermarking embedding[1 2 3 5]

$$v_i' = v_i + \alpha w_i \tag{1}$$

$$v_i' = v_i(1 + \alpha w_i) \tag{2}$$

In above equations, $v_i$ is the feature parameter of the original image, and $v_i'$ is the feature parameter of the watermarking image in spatial, DCT and DWT domains (the image which has been embedded some watermarking information); $w_i$ is the feature parameter of the template; $\alpha$ is the embedding intensity. Equation (1) is the additive embedding method, and equation (2) is the multiplicative embedding method. Each of them could increase the correlation between the image and the template. Thus, the calculation of the correlation between the image and the template can be used for watermarking detection. The formula of unitary correlation is as follows [6]:

$$z_{nc}(V, W_r) = \sum_{i=0}^{n} \overline{V}[i]\overline{W}_r[i], \quad \overline{V}[i] = \frac{V[i]}{|V|}, \quad \overline{W}_r[i] = \frac{W_r[i]}{|W_r|} \tag{3}$$

In the equation (3), $z_{nc}$ is the unitary correlate value between $v$ and $w_r$. The unitary correlate value between two arrays means the cosine of their angle. That is:

$$\frac{V \cdot W_r}{|V||W_r|} > \tau_{nc} \Leftrightarrow \theta < \tau_\theta, \quad \tau_\theta = \cos^{-1}(\tau_{nc}) \tag{4}$$

From the equation (4), the unitary correlate value $z_{nc}$ between feature parameters of the image and the template can be gotten, and then compared with the threshold $\tau_{nc}$ ($\tau_{nc}$ is an experimental value), if $z_{nc} < \tau_{nc}$, the watermarking information should not exist, or else it exists.

From above analyzing, a group of results could be obtained by comparing the unitary correlate values, and then integrating the comparing results to get the final detecting result.

## 2.2 The Framework of the Extensive Detection Method

As the Fig 2, is procedure of extensive images digital watermarking detection, the method has three steps: classifying images and templates; extracting and combining feature parameters of them; using some detecting strategies on those parameters to detect the watermark, and integrating the results.

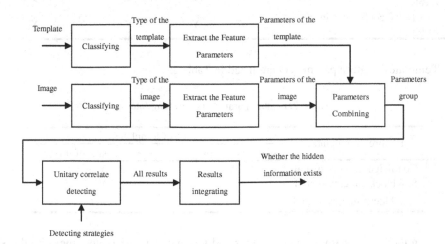

**Fig. 2.** Procedure of extensive images digital watermarking detection based on the known template

Images should be divided into two types: gray images and color images, and each type should be divided into three sub-types: non-compressed, compressed by JPEG and compressed by JPEG 2000. Templates should be divided into two types: smaller than image in size and in the same size of the image. After then, different feature parameters of images and templates can by extracted. The feature parameters of the images are listed in Table 1, the sign of "Y" means that the feature parameter in the head of the column could be extracted from the images of the type in the head of the row.

**Table 1.** Feature parameters and watermarking images

| Feature parameters of templates | Types of the images | | | | | |
| | Gray images | | | Color images | | |
| | Non-pressed | Pressed by JPEG | Pressed by JPEG 2000 | Non-pressed | Pressed by JPEG | Pressed by JPEG 2000 |
|---|---|---|---|---|---|---|
| Coefficient in gray spatial | Y | — | — | — | — | — |
| Coefficient in RGB spatial | — | — | — | Y | — | — |
| DCT coefficient in gray spatial | Y | Y | — | — | — | — |
| 8×8 DCT coefficient in gray spatial | Y | Y | — | — | — | — |
| DCT coefficient in YCbCr spatial | — | — | — | Y | Y | — |
| 8×8 DCT coefficient in YCbCr spatial | — | — | — | Y | Y | — |
| DWT coefficient in M levels | Y | Y | Y | Y | Y | Y |
| 8×8 DWT coefficient in M levels | Y | Y | Y | Y | Y | Y |

Templates' feature parameters are listed in Table 2:

**Table 2.** Feature parameters and templates

| Feature of templates | Types of templates | |
| | Smaller than images | At the same size of images |
|---|---|---|
| Coefficient in gray spatial | Y | Y |
| 8×8 blocks in gray spatial | — | Y |
| m×n blocks in gray spatial | Y | — |

When the feature parameters of images and templates are extracted, they should be combined together, the parameters of image should be combined with parameters of template. Table 3 shows feature parameters of the image and its corresponsive parameters of the template.

**Table 3.** Feature parameters of watermarking images and templates

| Feature parameters of images | Feature parameters of templates | | |
| --- | --- | --- | --- |
| | Coefficient in gray spatial | 8×8 blocks in gray spatial | m×n blocks in gray spatial |
| Coefficient in gray spatial | Y | — | — |
| Coefficient in RGB spatial | Y | — | — |
| DCT coefficient in gray spatial | Y | — | — |
| 8×8 DCT coefficient in gray spatial | — | Y | Y |
| DCT coefficient in YCbCr spatial | Y | — | — |
| 8×8 DCT coefficient in YCbCr spatial | — | Y | Y |
| DWT coefficient in M levels | Y | — | — |
| 8×8 DWT coefficient in M levels | — | — | Y |

Some detecting strategies should be use to calculate the unitary correlate values of the groups in table 3. Detection values $z_1, z_2, ... z_n$ from these strategies should be compared with their corresponsive thresholds $\tau_1, \tau_2, ... \tau_n$, and then the final detecting result is obtained by fusing the comparing results.

## 2.3  Detecting Strategies

There are 10 groups of parameters in the Table 3, they correspond with 6 different detecting strategies, and these strategies are showed in Table 4.

**Table 4.** Detecting strategies

| Detecting strategies | parameters (image parameters + template parameters) |
| --- | --- |
| Strategy 1 | Coefficient in gray spatial + Coefficient in gray spatial ; |
| Strategy 2 | Coefficient in RGB spatial + Coefficient in gray spatial ; |
| Strategy 3 | DCT coefficient in gray spatial + Coefficient in gray spatial ; |
| | DCT coefficient in YCbCr spatial + Coefficient in gray spatial ; |
| Strategy 4 | 8×8 DCT coefficient in gray spatial + 8×8 blocks in gray spatial; |
| | 8×8 DCT coefficient in YCbCr spatial + 8×8 blocks in gray spatial; |
| | 8×8 DCT coefficient in gray spatial + m×n blocks in gray spatial; |
| | 8×8 DCT coefficient in YCbCr spatial + m×n blocks in gray spatial; |
| Strategy 5 | DWT coefficient in M levels + Coefficient in gray spatial ; |
| Strategy 6 | 8×8 DWT coefficient in M levels + m×n blocks in gray spatial. |

Suppose that $V$ denotes the feature parameter of the image; $W_r$ denotes the feature parameter of the template.

**Strategy 1:** In strategy 1, unitary correlate values between $V$ and $W_r$ should be calculated by scanning. The front data of $V$ is used to calculate with $W_r$, and then, $V$ is shifted, calculated with $W_r$, ... From the whole process, a group of detecting values $z_{11}, z_{12}, ..., z_{1N}$ should be produced; the mean of them is the final detecting value of this strategy. The formula is as follows:

$$z_1 = \frac{1}{N} \sum_i^N z_{1i} \tag{5}$$

The whole process is simulated in Matlab platform as follows:

```
len_v = length (v);
len_w = length (w);
% detected on scanning.
for offset = 0 : 1 : ( len_v - len_w )
    vw = v ((offset + 1) : (offset + len_w ) );
    % calculates the unitary correlate value
    %between vw and w.
    z( offset + 1 ) = UniCorrelate( vw, w );
end
% calculate the mean of all detecting values
z1 = mean( z );
```

**Strategy 2:** In this strategy, $V$ has two-dimension matrix with three sub-vectors (RGB). Unitary correlate values between $V$ and $W_r$ should be calculated by scanning in these three sub-arrays, and there would produce three groups of detecting values: $z_{21}^{(R)}, z_{22}^{(R)}, ..., z_{2N}^{(R)}, \quad z_{21}^{(G)}, z_{22}^{(G)}, ..., z_{2N}^{(G)}, \quad z_{21}^{(B)}, z_{22}^{(B)}, ..., z_{2N}^{(B)}$, the mean of them is the final detecting value of strategy 2, that is:

$$z_2 = \max\{z^{(R)}, z^{(G)}, z^{(B)}\}$$

$$z^{(R)} = \frac{1}{N} \sum_i^N z_{2i}^{(R)}, \quad z^{(G)} = \frac{1}{N} \sum_i^N z_{2i}^{(G)}, \quad z^{(B)} = \frac{1}{N} \sum_i^N z_{2i}^{(B)} \tag{6}$$

**Strategy 3:** $V$ is transformed into $V'$ with Zigzag. $V'$ is an array in frequency domain. Elements of $V'$ are frequency parameters of the image. They are from low frequency to high frequency. The Unitary correlate value between $V'$ and $W_r$ is the detecting value of strategy 3. The formula is as follows:

$$z_3 = \frac{1}{N} \sum_i^N z_{3i} \tag{7}$$

**Strategy 4:** $V(i)$ is transformed into $V'(i)$ with Zigzag ($i$ means the number of the block, and $i$ from 1 to N). Elements of $V'(i)$ are frequency parameters of the image block $i$. They are from low frequency to high frequency. Calculate the unitary correlate value between $V'(i)$ and $W(i)$, and get a group of detecting value $z_{41}(i), z_{42}(i),..., z_{4m}(i)$, the mean of them is the detecting value of strategy 4. The formula is as follows:

$$z_4 = \frac{1}{mN}\sum_{i=0}^{N}\sum_{j=0}^{m} z_{4j}(i) \tag{8}$$

N denotes the amount of the blocks.

**Strategy 5:** In this strategy, $V$ has four sub-vectors, $V^{(ca)}, V^{(ch)}, V^{(cv)}, V^{(cd)}$. The unitary correlate values between $W_r$ and each sub-vector of $V$ should be calculated by scanning. There are four groups of detecting values: $z_{51}^{(ca)}, z_{52}^{(ca)},..., z_{5N}^{(ca)}$ , $z_{51}^{(ch)}, z_{52}^{(ch)},..., z_{5N}^{(ch)}$ , $z_{51}^{(cv)}, z_{52}^{(cv)},..., z_{5N}^{(cv)}$ , $z_{51}^{(cd)}, z_{52}^{(cd)},..., z_{5N}^{(cd)}$ . The formula is as follows:

$$z_5 = \max\{z^{(ca)}, z^{(ch)}, z^{(cv)}, z^{(cd)}\}$$

$$z^{(ca)} = \frac{1}{N}\sum_{i=0}^{N} z_{5i}^{(ca)} \quad z^{(ch)} = \frac{1}{N}\sum_{i=0}^{N} z_{5i}^{(ch)}$$

$$z^{(cv)} = \frac{1}{N}\sum_{i=0}^{N} z_{5i}^{(cv)} \quad z^{(cd)} = \frac{1}{N}\sum_{i=0}^{N} z_{5i}^{(cd)} \tag{9}$$

**Strategy 6:** Calculate the unitary correlate values between $W(i)$ and each sub-vector of $V(i)$ by scanning ($i$ means the number of the block, $i$ from 1 to N). There would be 4×N groups of detecting values: $z^{(ca)}(1), z^{(ch)}(1), z^{(cv)}(1), z^{(cd)}(1)$ , $z^{(ca)}(2), z^{(ch)}(2), z^{(cv)}(2), z^{(cd)}(2)$ , ... , $z^{(ca)}(N), z^{(ch)}(N), z^{(cv)}(N), z^{(cd)}(N)$ , N denotes the account of the blocks. The formula of final detecting value is as follows:

$$z_6 = \frac{1}{N}\sum_{i=0}^{N} z(i) \tag{10}$$

$$z(i) = \max\{z_i^{(ca)}, z_i^{(ch)}, z_i^{(cv)}, z_i^{(cd)}\}$$

## 3   Experiments and Results

In the experiments, 720 images which are 256×256 pixel in size are used, all the images were produced from 120 standard images by 6 different methods of digital watermarking embedding [2 6 7 8 9 10]. Methods of embedding are listed in Table 5. All standard images and templates are from Standard Image Database of Signal & Image Processing Institute, Electrical Engineering Department, School of Engineering, and University of Southern California (USC).

**Table 5.** Watermarking images in the experiment

| No. | Count | Method of Embedding |
|---|---|---|
| 1 | 120 | Direct embed the information, which is modulated by template into gray-scale of gray-images. |
| 2 | 120 | Direct embed the information, which is modulated by template into color-scale of color-images. |
| 3 | 120 | Direct embed the information, which is modulated by template into DCT domain of images |
| 4 | 120 | Embed the information, which is modulated by template into 8×8 DCT domain of images. |
| 5 | 120 | Direct embed the information, which is modulated by template into DWT domain of images. |
| 6 | 120 | Embed the information, which is modulated by template into 8×8 DWT domain of images. |

All produced images and their original images were used by the method of extensive images digital watermarking detection, in total, there were 120 results of original images and 720 results of watermarking images. The Probability distribution of the detecting values is showed in Fig 3. X-axis denotes the detecting values, Y-axis denotes the probability of detecting values, real line denotes the probability distribution of watermarking images' detecting values, broken line denotes the probability distribution of original images' detecting values.

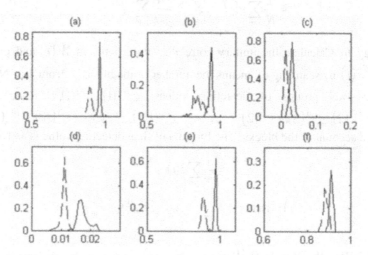

**Fig. 3.** Probability distribution of detecting values (a) Strategy 1, (b) Strategy 2, (c) Strategy 3, (d) Strategy 4, (e) Strategy 5, (f) Strategy 6

Fig 3 shows that means of original images detecting values are smaller than that of watermarking images. Thus, watermarking images can be distinguished from original images by choosing appropriate thresholds. In this experiment, thresholds of 6 strategies are listed in Table 6:

**Table 6.** Thresholds of detecting values

| Detecting strategies | Thresholds | Detecting rate (%) | Error rate (%) |
|---|---|---|---|
| Strategy 1 | 0.917 | 100.00 | 0 |
| Strategy 2 | 0.902 | 98.33 | 2.50 |
| Strategy 3 | 0.014 | 100.00 | 2.56 |
| Strategy 4 | 0.013 | 100.00 | 0.85 |
| Strategy 5 | 0.910 | 100.00 | 0 |
| Strategy 6 | 0.902 | 84.62 | 4.27 |
| Mean | — | 97.16 | 1.70 |

Table 6 shows that the correct rate of the detecting method proposed in this paper is 97.16%, and the error detecting rate is 1.70%. Obviously, the extensive watermarking detection method has achieved very good capability.

If lower thresholds were used, the correct detecting rate could reach a higher level, but the error detecting rate would be higher too. Oppositely, if higher thresholds were used, the error detecting rate could be lower, but the correct detecting rate would be lower too.

## 4 Conclusions

A new method of digital watermarking detection for images is proposed by this paper, this method is extensive in some extent. It's based on the known templates, the images and templates' feature parameters in spatial, DCT and DWT domains should be extracted, and than combined these parameters to obtain the detecting values by using the unitary correlative detection method; these detecting values show the correlation between images and their templates in different domains and different positions, so images can be divided into watermarking images or non-watermarking images by the comparing between these detecting values and thresholds.

The method in this paper suits the detection for some methods of digital watermarking based on templates which need templates to modulate the hidden information for embedding. For these embedding methods, the method of detection in this paper can detect whether hidden information exists in an image, without knowing the method of embedding. And the correct detecting rate can achieve a high level (about 97.16%) and the error rate is in a low level (about 1.70%). This paper proves that extensive detection of digital watermarking can be realized in some extent (for example, based on known templates). This extensive detecting method is very important and useful in application of information hidden and information security. The method of extensive digital watermarking detection based on unknown templates will be the next study.

## References

1. Frank Hartung. Multimedia Watermarking Techniques [D]. Proceedings of the IEEE. 1999, 7(87), 1079~1107.
2. Cox I.J, Miller L.M, Bloom J.A. Digital Watermarking [M]. Beijing: Electronic Industries Press, 2003.

3. WANG Baoyou, WANG Junjie, HU Yunfa.A Review of Copyright Protection by Digital Watermarking Techniques [J]. Computer Application and Software. 2004, 1(21): 30~87. (in Chinese)

4. Cox I J, Kilian J, Leighton T, et al. Secure spread spectrum watermarking for multimedia [J]. IEEE Trans. on Image Processing, 1997,6 (12):1673-1687.

5. ZHANG Jun, WANG Nengchao, SHI Baochang. Public Watermarking for Digital Images [J]. Journal of Computer-Aided Design & Computer Graphics. 2002, 4(14): 365~368. (in Chinese)

6. SUN Shenghe, LU Zheming, NIU Xiamu. Digital Watermarking Techniques and Applications [M]. Beijing: Science Press, 2004. (in Chinese)

7. HU Ming, PING Xijian, DING Yihong. A Blind Information Hiding Algorithm Based on DCT Domain of Image [J]. Computer Engineering and Applications. 2003,5:89~104. (in Chinese)

8. LIU Jinghong, YAO Wei. A Watermarking Algorithm with Hight Definition [J] . Computer Engineering and Applications. 2004, 30: 76~115. (in Chinese)

9. MA Miao, TIAN Hongpeng, ZHANG Huiqun. A Wavelet Energy Based Algorithm of Visible Watermark [J]. Journal of Xian University Sicence and Technology. 2002, 22(2):199~215. (in Chinese)

10. ZHANG Xiaofeng, DUAN Huilong. Image Watermarking Based on Wavelet Transform [J]. Computer Engineering and Applications. 2004, 11: 64~204. (in Chinese)

# Fast Mode Decision Algorithm in H.263+/H.264 Intra Transcoder

Min Li[1] and Guiming He[2]

[1] Computer School of Wuhan University, Wuhan, 430072 Hubei, China
[2] Electrical School of Wuhan University, Wuhan, 430072 Hubei, China
[1] reaphope@163.com , [2] gmhe@whu.edu.cn

**Abstract.** In this paper, we proposed a fast mode decision algorithm in transform-domain for H.263+ to H.264 intra transcoder. In the transcoder, the residual signals carried by H.263+ bitstreams are threshold controlled to decide whether we should reuse the prediction direction provided by H.263+ or re-estimate the prediction direction. Then the DCT coefficients in H.263+ bitstreams are converted to H.264 transform coefficients entirely in the transform-domain. Finally, by using the new prediction mode and direction, the H.264 transform residual coefficients are coded to generate the H.264 bitstream. The simulation results show the performance of the proposed algorithm is close to that of a cascaded pixel-domain transcoder (CPDT) while transcoding computation complexity is significantly lower.

**Keywords:** transform-domain, pixel-domain, CPDT, transcoding.

## 1 Introduction

H.263+, or H.263 version 2, is backward compatible with H.263. The objective of H.263+ is to broaden the range of applications and to improve compression efficiency. H.263+ offers many improvements over H.263[1]. Nowadays, H.263+ has been widely used in a number of applications from videoconferencing to distance learning. And in some areas such as UTMS mobiles, H.263+ is compulsory.

H.264/AVC [2] is the latest international video coding standard jointly developed by the ITU-T Video Coding Experts Group and the ISO/IEC Moving Picture Experts Group. Compared to other video coding standard, it achieves higher coding efficiency by employing techniques such as variable block-size motion estimation and mode decision, intra prediction, and multiple reference frames. Due to its superior compression efficiency, it is expected to replace other video-coding standards in a wide range of applications. However, considering the fact that H.26x and MPEG-x have been successfully used in many applications, the complete migrations to H.264 will take several years. So, there is a need to convert video in H.26x format or MPEG-x format to video of H.264 format. This would enable more efficient network transmission and storage.

In this paper, we will discuss some problems about H.263+ to H.264 transcoding which belongs to inhomogeneous transcoding. Many approaches [3]~[5] exist to improve transcoding of inter macroblock, usually, they reuse the motion vectors and

Y. Zhuang et al. (Eds.): PCM 2006, LNCS 4261, pp. 41–47, 2006.

apply vector refining and re-quantization on inter macroblocks in order to reduce the bitrate. Compared to inter macroblock transcoding, intra macroblocks are less considered. In [6],a novel intra-frame prediction algorithm has been introduced to reduce the computation complexity in MPEG-2/H.264 transcoders, since MPEG-2 is quite different from H.263+ in many aspects, so it is not suitable for H.263+ to H.264 transcoding. In[7],a fast transcoding algorithm of intra-frames between H.263 and H.264 is proposed, but the transcoding architecture is based on pixel-domain. Although it reduce the computation complexity about 30% compared to fully search, it has to perform inversing transform and transforming which will cost a lot of time. As we all known, transform domain techniques may be simpler since they eliminate the need of inverse transform and transform. In [8],Yeping Su presents an efficient way to transcode intra-frame from MPEG-2 to H.264 in transform-domain ,but in his proposed transcoding architecture, they use DCT coefficient and reference marcoblocks in pixel-domain to decide the prediction mode and residual signal, this is apparently unreasonable. Here we proposed a fast mode decision algorithm in transform-domain for intra-frame in the H.263+ to H.264 transcoder. The simulation results show the performance of our proposed algorithm is close to that of a cascaded pixel-domain transcoder(CPDT) while transcoding complexity is significantly lower.

The rest of the paper is organized as follows: section 2 discusses the issues to be addressed for intra transcoding operations. In section 3,we introduce a fast intra-frame prediction algorithm suitable for the transcoding of H.263+ to H.264.In section 4,we carry out a performance evaluation of the proposed algorithm in terms of its computation complexity、 bit rate and PSNR results. Finally, section 5 concludes the paper.

## 2  Issues and Approaches

In the context of H.263+ to H.264 intra transcoding, there are two main issues to be addressed, the first one is converting H.263+ DCT coefficient to H.264 transform coefficient, which will be referred to as HT; the second one is the reuse and re-estimation problem of H.263+ intra prediction mode.

H.264 standard uses an integer transform based on $4 \times 4$ block, and H.263+ standards use a Discrete Cosine Transform (DCT) based on $8 \times 8$ block. In order to realize transcoding in transform-domain, we have to convert the input 8x8 DCT coefficients to 4x4 H.264 transform coefficients at first, hereinafter referred as DTH-transform.

The conventional method is convert DCT coefficient into pixel-domain by inverting DCT transform, then convert the pixel-domain coefficient to DCT coefficient by 4x4 DCT integer transform. See figure 1.

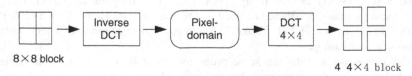

Fig. 1. Conventional method

In order to speed-up this process, we can use the transform domain DCT-to-HT conversion method introduced in [9]:

$$F_1'=A \times F_1 \times A^T. \tag{1}$$

$F_1'$ denotes four 4×4 block of H.264 transform coefficient, $F_1$ denotes an 8×8 block of DCT coefficients, A is the kernel matrix and it is defined as follows:

$$A= \begin{bmatrix}
1.4142 & 1.2815 & 0 & -0.45 & 0 & 0.3007 & 0 & -0.2549 \\
0 & 0.9236 & 2.2304 & 1.7799 & 0 & -0.8638 & -0.1585 & 0.4824 \\
0 & -0.1056 & 0 & 0.7259 & 1.4142 & 1.0864 & 0 & -0.5308 \\
0 & 0.1169 & 0.1585 & -0.0922 & 0 & 1.0379 & 2.2304 & 1.975 \\
1.4142 & -1.2815 & 0 & 0.45 & 0 & -0.3007 & 0 & 0.2549 \\
0 & 0.9236 & -2.2304 & 1.7799 & 0 & -0.8638 & 0.1585 & 0.4824 \\
0 & 0.1056 & 0 & -0.7259 & 1.4142 & -1.0864 & 0 & 0.5308 \\
0 & 0.1169 & -0.1585 & -0.0922 & 0 & 1.0379 & -2.2304 & 1.975
\end{bmatrix}$$

This process transforms the 8×8 DCT coefficients $F_1$ into four 4×4 H.264 transform coefficients $F_1'$ by using the kernel matrix A. Since matrix A contains many zero-valued elements, this process is significantly less complexity and can save about 30% of operations compared with the procedure depicted in Figure 3.

In H.263+, there is one intra-prediction mode and it is defined within frequency domain. This intra-prediction mode consists of three different prediction options: DC only, vertical DC and AC, horizontal DC and AC. This direction is used for all 4 luminance and both chrominance blocks equivalently.

In contrast to H.263, where the predicted signal consists of DCT coefficients, the prediction process in H.264 is defined within the pixel domain. H.264 has three different prediction mode: Intra4 ,Intra16 and Intra8. The first two modes are for luminance blocks, and the third mode is for chrominance blocks. For Intra4 mode, there exist 9 prediction directions while for Intra16 and Intra8, there are only 4 prediction directions.

Although there are remarkable differences for the intra-prediction process between H.263+ and H.264, the reusing information is possible. Since there are some similarities between the basic patterns of the directions which are defined for both standards, and these patterns are vertical, horizontal stripes and DC prediction, thus the coded direction can be used as estimation for re-encoding the bit stream.

## 3 Transform Intra-frame in Transform-Domain

The architecture of our proposed transform-domain intra transcoder is depicted in Fig. 2.The incoming H.263+ bit stream is variable length decoded and inverse quantized at first. Then the prediction mode, direction and the residual sum of the intra macroblock is given to "PRED" stage for threshold controlling, then the 8×8 DCT coefficients are transformed to 4×4 DCT coefficient by DTH-transform. More exactly, the prediction direction is reused if the residual sum of current intra macroblock is smaller than threshold T (dash line shows), otherwise, if the residual sum of current intra macroblock is bigger than threshold T, the prediction direction should be re-estimated in transform-domain. (solid line shows).After the prediction mode and direction have been decided, we can get the prediction value and the residual signal in transform-domain, after re-quantization, on one hand, the prediction mode and residual signal are entropy encoded and send out, on the other hand, they are inverse quantized and stored in the "Reference Macroblock" as reference value. Our approach simplifies the intra-frame prediction by reusing the intra-prediction mode and DCT coefficients available from H.263+. The exact algorithm works as follows:

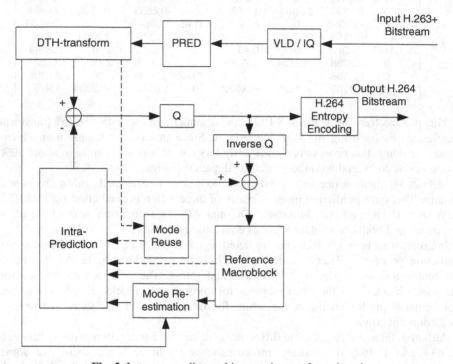

**Fig. 2.** Intra transcoding architecture in transform-domain

Step1. Calculate the error residual sum $R_i$ for each 8 x 8 block $i$;

Step2. For all 4 luminance block in a macroblock, if all $R_i < T_i$, ( $i \in \{ 1 \ldots 4 \}$ ) and the direction of four blocks are all the same, use Intra16 mode,and the new direction is the same as those of H.263+; if all $R_i < T_i$ ( $i \in \{ 1 \ldots 4 \}$ ),but the direction of four blocks are different, select Intra4 mode but reuse the direction of every block directly.

Step3. For all 4 luminance block in a macroblock, if $R_i > T_i$ ( $i \in \{ 1 \ldots 4 \}$ ), select Intra4 mode and re-estimate the direction for the ith block. The re-estimating process is as follows: performing DTH- transform and convert the 8×8 DCT coefficient into 4×4 coefficient at first, then re-estimate directions in transform-domain, after Rate Distortion Optimized (RDO) in transform-domain [6], we can get the most suitable prediction direction. Using the new mode and the corresponding direction, the error residual is calculated and transformed, after entropy coding, it is written into the H.264 output bit stream.

Step4. For chrominance blocks, if $R_5$ > T or $R_6$ > T, re-estimate chrominance prediction direction, otherwise, reuse directions of H.263+.

Step5. For all chrominance and luminance blocks, if the direction is not available in H.264 because of missing reference pixels, re-estimation is used. The re-estimation process is the same as step3.

Large experiments show the main impact on performance loss is due to wrong mode selection, which strongly depends on the threshold T. To improve the algorithm's performance, we introduce the relationship between QP and T, namely, $T=K \cdot QP^{3/2}+C$.

## 4  Simulation Results

In order to evaluate our proposed algorithm, we have implemented the proposed transcoder based on H.264 reference software JM9.0 [10]. Throughout our experiments, we have used various video sequences with the same frame rate (30 frames/s) and format (CIF). Every frame of each sequence is encoded as Intra-frame in order to obtain results for intra-frame prediction only.

Two transcoders are evaluated: Cascaded Pixel Domain Transcoder (CPDT) and Transform-domain Transcoder with Fast intra mode decision (TTF). The computational complexity is measured using the runtime of the entire transcoder. The Rate-Distortion performance is also measured between the output H.264 video and the corresponding raw video.

Table 1 shows the complexity reductions of TTF over CPDT.The computation saving of TTF over CPDT is around 50%. The reason behind this fact is that in both intra16 and intra4 mode, the use of the prediction direction 0,1 and 2 are more than 50% of the times. Furthermore, we can see the computation reduction Silent sequence got is 44.6%, among all sequences, it is the lowest one. For compared to other sequences, there are more motions in Silent sequence, thus it need to re-estimate more macroblocks' prediction directions and the re-estimation process will cost a lot of time. On the contrary, Costguard and Stefan get higher computation reduction, they are 55.6% and 53.2% respectively, compared to other three sequences, they have reused more macroblocks' prediction directions and re-estimated less macroblocks' prediction directions. At the same time, we can see when use our proposed algorithm, the lower the QP values, the higher the computation complexity, since selecting small QP, the T also will be small and more macroblocks should be re-estimated.

Fig3 and Fig4 show the PSNR and bitrate for both transcoders. From them we can see, compared to CPDT, the PSNRs are only slightly decreased while the bitrate is slightly increased by using our proposed algorithm. When QP is 30,the PSNR decreased 0.45dB,when QP is 45,the PSNR decreased 0.8dB. Depending on the output bitrate, we measured an increment between 5% at high data rates and 9% at low data rates.

From the experimental results, we can see when QP increased, the computation complexity is decreased while the PSNR is increased. Since for high QP the threshold T is higher, more macroblock will be re-estimated, thus the computation process will be more complexity and the prediction direction will be more accurate.

## 5 Conclusion

We proposed a transform-domain H.263+ to H.264 intra video transcoder. The transform-domain architecture is equivalent to the conventional pixel-domain implementation in terms of functionality, but it has significantly lower complexity. We achieved the complexity reduction by taking advantage of direct DCT-to-DCT coefficient conversion and transform-domain mode decision. We also presented a fast intra mode decision algorithm utilizing transform-domain features that can further reduce its computational complexity. Simulation results show that we can achieve significant computational reduction without sacrificing video quality.

**Table 1.** Comparison of computation complexity for CPDT transcoder and TTF transcoder

|  |  | News | Costguard | Foreman | Stefan | Silent |
|---|---|---|---|---|---|---|
| CPDT(ms) | QP=30 | 75139 | 48891 | 70351 | 64019 | 69434 |
|  | QP=45 | 68411 | 42632 | 62485 | 59675 | 63325 |
| TTF(ms) | QP=30 | 39212 | 21085 | 34096 | 34281 | 40211 |
|  | QP=45 | 35209 | 18972 | 29225 | 29983 | 35108 |
| Computation | QP=30 | 47.9% | 56.9% | 51.5% | 46.5% | 42.1% |
| Reduction | QP=45 | 48.5% | 55.6% | 53.2% | 49.8% | 44.6% |

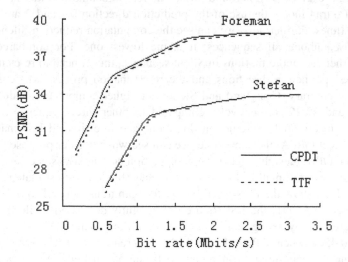

**Fig. 3.** RD-Results for transcoding intra macroblocks from H.263+ to H.264(QP=30)

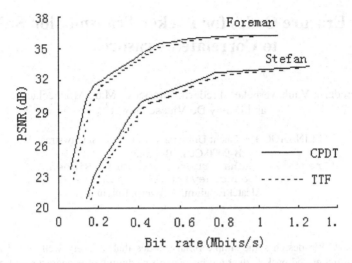

**Fig. 4.** RD-Results for transcoding intra macroblocks from H.263+ to H.264(QP=45)

## References

1. Draft ITU-T Recommendation and Final Draft International Standard of Joint Video Specification (ITU-T Rec. H.264 I ISO/ IEC 14496-10 AVC)(2003)
2. ITU Telecom. Standardization Sector of ITU. : Video coding for low bitrate communication. *Draft ITU-T Recommendation H.263 Version 2*(1997).
3. Tan Yap-Peng,Sun Haiwei.:Fast motion re-estimation for arbitrary downsizing video transcoding using H.264/AVC standard. *IEEE Transactions on Consumer Electronics,* vol.50, no.3 (2004) 887-894
4. Chia-Wen Lin, Yuh-Reuy Lee. : Fast algorithms for DCT-domain video transcoding. *International Conference on Image Processing* (2001) 421-424
5. Zhi Zhou,Shijun Sun,Shawmin Lei,ect. : Motion Information and Coding Mode Reuse for MPEG-2 to H.264 Transcoding. *IEEE International Symposium on Circuits and Systems* (2005) 1230-1233
6. Gerardo Fernaindez-Escribano, Pedro Cuenca, Luis Orozco-Barbosa,ect.:Computational Complexity Reduction of Intra-frame prediction in MPEG-2/H.264 Video Transcoders. *IEEE International Conference on Multimedia and Expo* (2005) 707 – 710.
7. Jens Bialkowski,Andre Kaup,Klaus Illgner. : Fast Transcoding of Intra Frames Between H.263 and H.264.*2004 International Conference on Image Processing* (2004) 2785~2788
8. Yeping Su, Jun Xin, Anthony Vetro,ect. : Efficient MPEG-2 to H.264/AVC Intra Transcoding in Transform-domain. *IEEE International Symposium on Circuits and Systems*.vol.2 (2005) 2785~2788
9. Jun Xin,Anthony Vetro ,Huifang Sun. :Converting DCT Coefficients to H.264/AVC Transform Coefficients", Pacific-Rim Conference on Multimedia (2004)
10. JVT Reference Software official version JM9.0. http://iphome.hhi.de/suehring/tml/ download/old_jm/jm90.zip

# Binary Erasure Codes for Packet Transmission Subject to Correlated Erasures

Frederik Vanhaverbeke[1], Frederik Simoens[1], Marc Moeneclaey[1],
and Danny De Vleeschauwer[2]

[1] TELIN/DIGCOM, Ghent University, Sint-Pietersnieuwstraat 41,
B-9000 Gent, Belgium
{Frederik..Vanhaverbeke, Frederik.Simoens,
Marc.Moeneclaey}@telin.ugent.be
[2] Alcatel Belgium, Antwerp, Belgium

**Abstract.** We design some simple binary codes that are very well suited to reconstruct erased packets over a transmission medium that is characterized by correlation between subsequent erasures. We demonstrate the effectiveness of these codes for the transmission of video packets for HDTV over a DSL connection.

**Keywords:** Triple play, IPTV, video over DSL, Forward Error Correction.

## 1 Introduction

When information is packetized and sent over a transmission medium, it is common practice to provide protection on the physical layer against transmission errors (e.g., by using a Forward Error Correcting (FEC) code [1]). But even with this protection, the occasional erasure of packets cannot be avoided. Indeed, the data link layer will typically detect whether or not a packet is hit by residual transmission errors by verifying the Cyclic Redundancy Check (CRC) sum of the packet; when the checksum is wrong at some point during the transmission, the packet is eliminated before even reaching the receiver. Hence, in order to recover these eliminated packets, it is desirable to have additional protection of the packets on the transport layer.

A straightforward way to protect the transmitted packets is to use an erasure code [1-3]. This involves collecting K consecutive information packets, computing N-K parity packets, and transmitting the total set of N packets. When a limited number of these N packets get lost, the K information packets can still be reconstructed from the remaining packets. Although codes come in many kinds and have been investigated very extensively in recent decades (e.g. [4]), only a small subset of them are viable candidates for many applications. Indeed, the use of erasure codes comes at a price in terms of transmission overhead and latency, which both ought to be kept as low as possible (e.g. for video transmission). As a consequence, one should try to limit at the same time K (which determines the latency) and the ratio (N-K)/K (which determines the overhead).

Y. Zhuang et al. (Eds.): PCM 2006, LNCS 4261, pp. 48–55, 2006.

As far as erasure coding is concerned, it should be kept in mind that the FEC coding on the physical layer and the nature of the transmission channel can have as an effect that the destruction of several *subsequent* packets is more likely than the random destruction of packets. As a consequence, there is some special interest in codes that are attuned to the specific problem of erasure bursts. This urges us to focus our attention in this paper on codes that are especially capable to deal with bursts of erasures. Other aspects to keep in mind are the processing delay and the hardware complexity associated with erasure decoding, which should remain as low as possible. In this respect, binary codes [1] deserve our special attention, because their decoding complexity is smaller than that for Reed-Solomon (RS) codes [5].

In this article, we systematically design erasure codes that meet the stringent requirements set out above. So, we restrict our attention to systematic binary codes because of the inherent low decoding complexity. We also limit ourselves to codes with low overhead and a low number of information packets K (i.e. low latency) that are able to restore bursts of (subsequent) erasures rather than random erasures over the codeword. In section 2, we briefly describe the concept of erasure coding on the transport layer, and develop some codes for erasure bursts consisting of two or three consecutive erasures. In section 3, we illustrate the efficacy of these codes in the special application of video transmission for High Definition TeleVision (HDTV) [6] over a DSL connection [7]. Finally, section 4 summarizes our findings.

## 2  Erasure Codes for Packet Protection

In order to apply erasure coding to a stream of information packets, we collect a set of K successive information packets (say $\mathbf{B}_1$, $\mathbf{B}_2$, ..., $\mathbf{B}_K$) of size $\Gamma$ (bits), and we use these packets to construct (N-K) parity (FEC) packets (say $\mathbf{P}_1$, $\mathbf{P}_2$, ..., $\mathbf{P}_{N-K}$) of the same size that are transmitted along with these information packets (see figure 1). The set of the $k$th bits of these N packets make up a codeword $\mathbf{c}^{(k)}$ of a common binary (N,K) code with generator matrix $\mathbf{G}$ and parity matrix $\mathbf{\Omega}$:[1]:

$$\mathbf{c}^{(k)} = \left( \underbrace{B_{1,k}, B_{2,k}, ..., B_{K,k}}_{\mathbf{b}^{(k)}}, P_{1,k}, ..., P_{N-K,k} \right) = \mathbf{b}^{(k)}.\underbrace{[\mathbf{I}_K \ \ \mathbf{\Omega}]}_{\mathbf{G}} \tag{1}$$

where $B_{s,k}$ and $P_{t,k}$ are the $k$th bit (k = 0, ..., $\Gamma$-1) of packet $\mathbf{B}_s$ and $\mathbf{P}_t$ respectively, and $\mathbf{I}_K$ is the identity matrix of order K. For our convenience, we will refer to $\mathbf{C} = (\mathbf{B}_1, \mathbf{B}_2, ..., \mathbf{B}_K, \mathbf{P}_1, ..., \mathbf{P}_{N-K})$ as a 'Packet CodeWord (PCW)'.

Assume that some of the packets of a transmitted PCW $\mathbf{C}$ are erased during transmission. In that case, all constituent codewords $\mathbf{c}^{(k)}$ (k = 0, ..., $\Gamma$-1) will exhibit erasures at the very positions corresponding to those erased packets. In order to restore the erased packets, one can try to solve for the erased bits in each codeword $\mathbf{c}^{(k)}$ by means of the set of equations

$$\tilde{\mathbf{c}}^{(k)}.\begin{bmatrix} \mathbf{\Omega} \\ \mathbf{I}_{N-K} \end{bmatrix} = \tilde{\mathbf{c}}^{(k)}.\mathbf{H}^T = 0 \tag{2}$$

where $\mathbf{H} = [\boldsymbol{\Omega}^T \; \mathbf{I}_{N-K}]$ is the check matrix. In (2), $\tilde{\mathbf{c}}^{(k)}$ is the word that is composed of the correctly received code bits of $\mathbf{c}^{(k)}$ and code bits that are unknown since they have been erased during transmission. Once the erased codebits have been recovered through (2) for all codewords $\mathbf{c}^{(k)}$ ($k = 0, \ldots, \Gamma\text{-}1$), we immediately can reconstruct the erased packets.

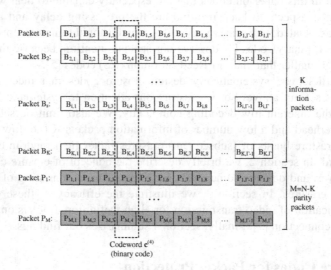

Codeword $\mathbf{c}^{(4)}$
(binary code)

**Fig. 1.** Relation between information packets and constituent codewords

Unfortunately, solving (2) for the erased codebits will be possible only when the columns of $\mathbf{H}$ corresponding to these codebits are independent. Although it is possible to recover a single erasure by means of a single parity check code [1], the reconstruction of more than one erasure will be less straightforward. In fact, it can be shown [1] that the maximum number of erased packets $e_{max}$ that can be resolved independent of their position by a binary $(N,K)$ code has to meet the following two inequalities:

$$\sum_{i=0}^{\lfloor e_{max}/2 \rfloor} \binom{N}{i} \leq 2^{N-K} \;\; ; \;\; e_{max} \leq N - K \tag{3}$$

For $e_{max} = 2$ and 3, (3) reduces to:

$$e_{max} = 2,3 \quad \rightarrow \quad N \leq 2^{N-K} - 1 \; ; \; N - K \geq e_{max} \tag{4}$$

In table 1, we illustrate the minimum required overhead and the corresponding codeword length $N_{min\text{-}overhead}$ for a binary code with $e_{max} = 2$ or 3 as a function of the number of parity packets $(N-K)$. From this table, we see that binary codes with the ability to recover *every* double or triple erasure cannot have at the same time a low latency (low N) and a low overhead.

**Table 1.** Required overhead and $N_{min\text{-}overhead}$ for binary codes that can recover all double or triple erasures (note: for triple erasures only N-K $\geq$ 3 applies)

| N-K | (N-K)/N | $N_{min\text{-}overhead}$ |
|:---:|:---:|:---:|
| 2 | $\geq 66\%$ | 3 |
| 3 | $\geq 43\%$ | 7 |
| 4 | $\geq 27\%$ | 15 |
| 5 | $\geq 16\%$ | 31 |
| 6 | $\geq 10\%$ | 63 |
| 7 | $\geq 6\%$ | 127 |

However, in many applications it is not a must to be able to recover all double or triple erasures. In fact, a substantial quality improvement can oftentimes be achieved by the use of codes that allow for the reconstruction of the most frequently observed double or triple erasures. In this paper, we will focus on a system where subsequent packet erasures are correlated as represented in the transition diagram of figure 2, that is determined entirely by the conditional probabilities $p_1$ = Pr[packet i+1 is erased | packet i is not erased] and $p_2$ = Pr[packet i+1 is erased | packet i is erased]. Depending on the value of $p_2$, the probability of a burst of two (three) subsequent erasures may be substantially higher than the probability of all other double or triple erasures. By consequence, the packet error rate may be dominated by these bursts of multiple erasures, and a substantial system improvement could be achieved by application of binary codes that allow for the correction of all these potential bursts of erasures (but not all other multiple erasures). In the following two sections, we turn our attention to binary codes with low latency and low overhead that are able to recover all bursts of respectively two and three erasures. In section 3, we will illustrate the effectiveness of these special codes for the special case of HDTV transmission over a DSL line.

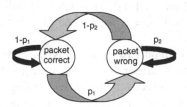

**Fig. 2.** State diagram that describes correlation between successive erasures

## 2.1  Binary Codes with Two Parity Bits for Correlated Erasures

For a binary code with two parity bits, the check matrix $\mathbf{H}$ is given by $\mathbf{H} = [\mathbf{\Omega}^T \mid \mathbf{I}_2]$, where the columns of $\mathbf{\Omega}^T$ can take three possible values: $[0\ 1]^T$, $[1\ 0]^T$ and $[1\ 1]^T$. From (2), we can tell immediately that we will not be able to recover *any* triple erasure, since no three columns of **H** can be linearly independent. On the other hand, two erasures can be resolved if and only if the corresponding columns of **H** are independent, i.e. the columns have to be different. By selecting for **H** a matrix where no two subsequent columns are equal, all erasure bursts of length two can be resolved. Such a matrix **H** can easily be designed for any N. For instance, a matrix that satisfies these requirements for N = 3n, is given by

$$\mathbf{H'} = \underbrace{\left[\mathbf{Z} \quad \mathbf{Z} \quad ... \quad \mathbf{Z}\right]}_{n \ times} \quad with \quad \mathbf{Z} = \begin{bmatrix} 1 & 1 & 0 \\ 1 & 0 & 1 \end{bmatrix} \tag{5}$$

For N = 3n-k (k = 1, 2), one can simply omit the first k columns of **H'** to obtain a valid check matrix. Codes with check matrix (5) will allow for the recovery of *all* double subsequent erasures. Although these codes do not have the potential to recover all other double erasures, they will allow for the recovery of many other double (non-subsequent) erasures as well, as long as the columns of the corresponding erased bits are different.

## 2.2 Binary Codes with Three Parity Bits for Correlated Erasures

The check matrix **H** for a binary code with three parity bits is given by $\mathbf{H} = [\mathbf{\Omega}^T \mid \mathbf{I_3}]$, where the columns of $\mathbf{\Omega}^T$ can take 7 possible values: $[0\ 0\ 1]^T$, $[0\ 1\ 0]^T$, $[0\ 1\ 1]^T$, $[1\ 0\ 0]^T$, $[1\ 0\ 1]^T$, $[1\ 1\ 0]^T$ and $[1\ 1\ 1]^T$. In analogy to what was discussed in the previous section, this code cannot recover any quadruple erasure, although it can recover all subsequent double erasures by making sure that no two subsequent columns of **H** are equal. When N = 7n, a possible realization of **H** that meets this requirement is

$$\mathbf{H''} = \underbrace{\left[\mathbf{Z'} \quad \mathbf{Z'} \quad ... \quad \mathbf{Z'}\right]}_{n \ times} \quad with \quad \mathbf{Z'} = \left[\mathbf{Z''} \begin{array}{ccc} 1 & 0 & 0 \\ 0 & 1 & 0 \\ 0 & 0 & 1 \end{array}\right] \tag{6}$$

where the columns of **Z''** are $[0\ 1\ 1]^T$, $[1\ 0\ 1]^T$, $[1\ 1\ 0]^T$ and $[1\ 1\ 1]^T$, placed in a random order. When N = 7n-k (k = 1, ..., 6), one can omit the first k columns of **H''** to obtain a valid matrix **H**.

As opposed to the case with only two parity bits, the code with three parity bits can be designed to resolve triple erasures. All we have to do is make sure that for the triple erasures we want to recover, the corresponding three columns of **H''** are linearly independent, i.e. no two columns of the three are equal and the modulo-2 sum of the three columns is different from zero. Focusing now on codes with check matrices of type **H''**, in order to be able to recover all busts of three subsequent erasures, we have to search for a matrix **Z'** that meets the following requirements:

1. All three subsequent columns of **Z'** are linearly independent
2. The first two columns and the last column of **Z'** are linearly independent
3. The first column and the last two columns of **Z'** are linearly independent

In figure 3, we search by means of a tree diagram for a matrix $(\mathbf{Z'})^T$ that meets these requirements. The search is started from the rows 5-7 of $(\mathbf{Z'})^T$, which make up $\mathbf{I_3}$. In order to find the possibilities for row 4, we write out all possible rows that are different from the rows 5-7 and independent of the rows 5 and 6. The possibilities for row 3 are the rows that are different from the rows 4-7 (for the relevant branches) and independent of the rows 4 and 5. The same procedure is repeated up to row 1. Four branches seem to come to a dead end, while four other matrices are not valid (crossed on figure 3), since the resulting $\mathbf{Z'}$ does not meet the above mentioned condition 2 or 3. So, the tree search has led to the following two possibilities for $\mathbf{Z'}$:

$$\mathbf{Z_1'} = \begin{bmatrix} 1 & 0 & 1 & 1 & 1 & 0 & 0 \\ 1 & 1 & 1 & 0 & 0 & 1 & 0 \\ 0 & 1 & 1 & 1 & 0 & 0 & 1 \end{bmatrix} \qquad \mathbf{Z_2'} = \begin{bmatrix} 1 & 1 & 1 & 0 & 1 & 0 & 0 \\ 0 & 1 & 1 & 1 & 0 & 1 & 0 \\ 1 & 1 & 0 & 1 & 0 & 0 & 1 \end{bmatrix} \qquad (7)$$

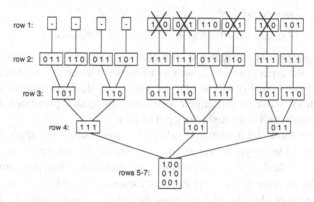

**Fig. 3.** Tree search for binary codes that can resolve all erasure bursts of length three

## 3   Case in Point: HDTV over DSL Line

To illustrate the effectiveness of the codes presented in the previous section in a practical system, we will examine the performance of these codes in the case of packet transmission for HDTV over a DSL connection operating at 20 Mb/s. For this application, the latency (caused by the FEC code) should not exceed about 100 ms in order to keep the zapping delay low, while the overhead has to be restricted to about 5% in order not to hamper the transmission on the connection [8]. In addition, even when the video data is interleaved to counter the impulsive noise, there will remain some residual correlation between successive erasures (as modeled in figure 2) due to the coding on the physical layer.

When we protect the video packet by means of an erasure code, the presence of one or more irrecoverable erased *video* packets in the PCW typically results in a visible distortion of the video image. With $P_{EC}$ the probability that at least one video packet of a PCW can not be recovered after erasure decoding, the mean time between visible distortions $T_{MTBVD}$ is given by[1]

$$T_{MTBVD} = \frac{K.\Gamma}{R_{vid}.P_{EC}} \qquad (2)$$

where $\Gamma$ is the size of the video packet (consisting of 7 MPEG-TS packets [9] of 188 bytes each, i.e., about 11e3 bits), $R_{vid}$ is the net video bitrate (taken as 8 Mbit/s [8]) and $K\Gamma/R_{vid}$ equals the duration of a PCW. For HDTV, one aims at achieving $T_{MTBVD}$ ≥ 12h, corresponding to no more than 1 Visible Distortion in Twelve hours (VDT). Hence, one needs to select a code that has low enough a $P_{EC}$ to reach this goal.

Unfortunately, the latitude in selecting the FEC codes for this application is very much restricted by the aforementioned requirements of low latency and low overhead. In fact, apart from the requirement of low (de)coding complexity, the requirements on the code can be summarized as:

$$\begin{cases} latency \leq 100ms & \Leftrightarrow & K \leq 72 \\ overhead \leq 5\% & \Leftrightarrow & (N-K)/K \leq 5\% \\ T_{MTBVD} \geq 12h & \Leftrightarrow & P_{EC} \geq K\Gamma/(R_{vid}.12h) \end{cases} \qquad (3)$$

The first two requirements imply that the number of parity packets of the code can not be higher than 3. Referring to table 1, we can immediately see that no binary code that meets the requirements of (3) will be able to resolve all double erasures. However, as there is correlation between subsequent erasures, the codes presented in section 2 might be able to provide for a satisfactory performance.

In figure 4, we show the achievable value of $T_{MTBVD}$ when we apply the codes of section 2 over a wide range of values $p_2$ (see figure 2), where $p_1$ is fixed at the realistic value $p_1 = 4e-5$. As a comparison, we also added the performance of the Single Parity Check code (SPC) and Reed-Solomon codes with two or three parity packets. One can show that the highest possible value of $p_2$ amounts to 0.14, namely when all video packets are transmitted back-to-back. In reality, the probability that two packets are back-to-back will be given by some value q, and it can be shown that for realistic traffic profiles the value of q does not exceed about 0.1 (i.e. $p_2 < 0.014$). As a consequence, the binary code with three parity bits derived in section 2.2, always achieves the goal of less than 1 VDT in any realistic scenario ($p_2 < 0.014$). As a matter of fact, this binary code achieves a performance of about 0.2 VDT for all practical values of $p_2$. The code of section 2.1 with just two parity packets appears to show a satisfactory performance (i.e. about or somewhat less than 1 VDT) for $p_2 \approx$ 0.014, but is certainly up to the task of packet protection for values of $p_2$ lower than 0.014. This performance is to be compared with the performance of the more complex RS codes that have about the same acceptable upper limits on $p_2$ in order to achieve less than 1 VDT. Hence, the very simple binary codes of section 2 allow for an equally efficient protection of the video packets as the more complex RS codes.

---

[1] We assume that the transmission of the parity packets has no material impact on the transmission time of a packet codeword, e.g. by transmitting the parity packets in an uninterrupted batch after the video packets. As a result, the transmission time of a packet codeword is determined exclusively by the number of video packets K.

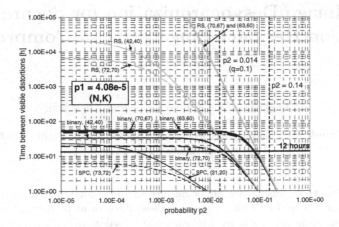

**Fig. 4.** Comparison of the various codes with correlated erasures

## 4  Conclusions

In this paper, we designed some very simple binary codes that are especially suited to protect packets on the transport layer over a system where subsequent packet erasures are correlated. We demonstrated the efficiency of these codes in the special case of HDTV over a DSL line, and we found that these codes allow for a video quality that is almost as good as the quality achievable through the more complex RS codes.

## References

1. G.C. Clark and J.B. Cain. *Error-correction coding for digital communications*. Plenum Press, 1981.
2. W.C. Huffman and V. Pless, *Fundamentals of Error-Correcting Codes*, Cambridge University Press, 2003.
3. R.H. Morelos-Zaragoza, *The Art of Error Correcting Coding*, Wiley, West-Sussex, 2002.
4. C. Berrou and A. Glavieux, "Near Optimum Error Correctin Coding and Decoding," *IEEE Transactions on Communications*, vol. 44, pp. 1261-1271, October 1996.
5. S.B. Wicker and V. K. Bhargava, *Reed-Solomon codes and their Applications*, IEEE Press, 1994.
6. "Parameter values for the HDTV+ standards for production and international programme exchange," *ITU-R recommendation BT. 709-5*, 2002.
7. "Overview of digital subscriber line (DSL) Recommendations," *ITU-T Recommendations G.995.1*, February 2001.
8. M. Watson, "Proposal for evaluation process for forward error correction codes for DVB-IPI," *DVB IP document TM-IPI2084*, September 2005.
9. D. Hoffman, V. Goyal, M. Civanlar, G. Fernando, "RTP Payload Format for MPEG1/MPEG2 Video," *IETF RFC2250*, January 1998.

# Image Desynchronization for Secure Collusion-Resilient Fingerprint in Compression Domain

Zhongxuan Liu, Shiguo Lian, and Zhen Ren

France Telecom R & D Beijing, 2 Science Institute South Rd, Beijing, 100080, China
zhongxuan.liu@orange-ft.com

**Abstract.** Collusion is a major menace to image fingerprint. Recently, an idea is introduced for collusion-resilient fingerprint by desynchronizing images in raw data. In this paper, we consider compression domain image desynchronization method and its system security. First, appropriate desynchronization forms for compression domain are presented; secondly, the system security is discussed and a secure scheme is proposed; thirdly, for evaluating the visual degradation of space desynchronization, we propose a metric called Synchronized Degradation Metric (SDM). Performance analysis including the experiments indicate the effectiveness of the proposed scheme and the metric.

## 1 Introduction

Now there are increasing availability of copying devices for digital media data, which makes restraining illegal redistribution of multimedia objects an important issue. One promising solution is to embed imperceptible information into media to indicate the ownership or the user of the media. Fingerprint is to embed the user's information into the media by watermarking technique. In this case every user will receive visually the same while in fact different copies. When the media is illegally redistributed, the information in the media will be used to identify the illegal users.

A most serious menace for fingerprint is the collusion attack. This attack combines several copies of a media and derives a copy hard to identify the information of the attackers. This kind of attack is classified into two categories [1]: linear collusion (average and cut-and-paste collusion) and nonlinear collusion (minimum, maximum and median collusion). To this problem, some solutions have been proposed. Orthogonal fingerprinting [2] makes each fingerprint orthogonal to another and keeps the colluded copy still detectable. The disadvantages of this method include the high cost on fingerprinting detection and the limitation in customer population [1]. The other method is coded fingerprinting which carefully designs the fingerprinting in codeword that can detect the colluders partially or completely. The Boneh-Shaw scheme [3][4] and the combinatorial design based code [1] belong to this method which suffers the LCCA attack [5].

Recently, a new method called desynchronization based fingerprint [6][7] for collusion-resilient fingerprint (DCRF) was proposed. This method aims to make

Y. Zhuang et al. (Eds.): PCM 2006, LNCS 4261, pp. 56–63, 2006.

collusion impractical: by desynchronizing the carrier, the colluded copy has serious quality degradation and no commercial value. Virtues of DCRF are: firstly, it avoids the difficulty of tracing traitors through colluded copies. Although the methods such as orthogonal and coded fingerprint have the ability to implement the difficult task of tracing traitors, when more users, more colluders and combined attacks including the all kinds of collusion attacks are considered, finishing the task is too difficult [1][5]. secondly, because collusion does not need to be considered for fingerprint coding, much shorter code is needed which makes the media support more users or degrade less.

In most cases, image should be transmitted in compression format. For Celik's scheme [7], to finish the desynchronization, the image needs to be decompressed firstly, processed and finally compressed. In our paper, a new scheme for directly desynchronizing image in compression domain is proposed. In this case the processing does not need the decompression and compression. Additionally, a metric for evaluating both the desynchronization and collusion is given.

In this paper, a DCRF scheme in compression domain is proposed. In Section 2, suitable DCRF forms for compression domain image are shown. The performance of the proposed scheme based on the DCRF forms are analyzed in Section 3. In Section 4, a metric for space desynchronization and collusion degradation is given followed by conclusions and future work in Section 5.

## 2    Suitable DCRF Forms for Compression Domain Image

There have been quite a few papers discussing compression domain processing [8]. For images, since the compression process of JPEG is composed of block DCT, Zig-zag scanning, quantization, RLE (run length encoding) and entropy coding, the compression domain processing is classified into several types: the processing after DCT, after scanning, et al (here JPEG standard is considered because it is well used for image compression). Operators in compression domain are also given, such as point operators with some predetermined values or another image, filtering, resizing, rotation and others [8]. Condensation is introduced to sparse the coefficient matrix [9]. Compared with space domain processing, compression domain processing is computing efficient because of two reasons: one is that most of the coefficients will be zero which saves memory; the other is that the computing of IDCT and DCT is saved which reduces the time cost [8]. In the following content, the suitable DCRF operators for compression domain image will be discussed.

There're many kinds of desynchronization operators proposed for attacking image watermarking such as RST, random warping et al. While for compression domain processing, several conditions should be satisfied for saving time cost and memory consuming:

1. Local random operations such as random warping should not be used because doing so in compression domain is difficult. The same random operation is applied to a line of the image is more reasonable;

2. The operators dealing with complex locating and inter-block computing should not be used. For images, it is better for the operator to utilize only blocks neighboring to each other in scanning order;
3. The operators should not impact the visual quality of the image apparently.

Because of the above constraints, the most fitful desynchronization forms are translation and shearing especially those operations along the horizontal direction. For horizontal translation and shearing, only several MCUs (Minimum Coded Units) of DCT coefficients need to be saved. For vertical translation and shearing, several rows of MCUs need to be saved. The parameters used for desynchronization include horizontal and vertical translation/shearing, and the rotations computed by horizontally and vertically shearing [8].

We revise the algorithm in [8] for DCT domain translation and shearing with image size unchanged (because compression domain resizing is complex and transmitted image copies should be with the same size):

For the first block of a row or a column:

$$B = \sum_i L_i AR_i^1 (i = 1, ..., N).$$

For the other blocks of a row or a column:

$$B = \sum_i L_i(\tilde{A} * R_i^2 + A * R_i^3).$$

Here $A$ is the current block and $\tilde{A}$ is the former block.

$$R_i^1 = [P_1(i-1) \quad P_2(N-i+1)]$$

$$R_i^2 = [P_3(i-1) \quad P_4(N-i+1)]$$

$$R_i^3 = [P_4(i-1) \quad P_2(N-i+1)]$$

where $P_1(i)$ is the $N$ by $i$ zero matrix except with the first row elements being 1, $P_2(i)$ is the $N$ by $i$ zero matrix except with the upper $i$ by $i$ matrix being the identity matrix, $P_3(i)$ is the $N$ by $i$ zero matrix except with the lower $i$ by $i$ matrix being the identity matrix and $P_4(i)$ is the $N$ by $i$ zero matrix.

Because DCT can be described as follows:

$$T(A) = CAC^t,$$

then

$$T^{-1}(T(L_iAR_i)) = T^{-1}(CL_iAR_iC^t)$$

$$= T^{-1}(CL_iC^tCAC^tCR_iC^t) = T^{-1}(T(L_i)T(A)T(R_i)). \tag{1}$$

By this method, $T(L_i)$ and $T(R_i)$ can be computed off-line.

# 3   The Proposed Scheme Based on DCRF Forms

## 3.1   The Proposed Scheme

In our method, oblivious watermarking is used: The $i^{th}$ fingerprinted signal is formed as

$$S_i = \phi_i(S) + F_i$$

where $\phi_i(\cdot)$ is the desynchronizing function, $F_i$ is the $i^{th}$ embedded fingerprint. Compared with non-oblivious watermarking [7], oblivious watermarking can avoid the problem of transmitting original copy and the hardness of resynchronization especially when the received copies have been influenced by compression and noise. The integral system illustrated in Fig. 1 is explained as follows:

1. A key is used to generate space desynchronization pattern parameters;
2. The picture is partially decompressed to get DCT coefficients;
3. The coefficients are space desynchronized according to the parameters;
4. Fingerprint is embedded into the sequence before (or after) run length and entropy coding.

In this scheme, the extraction process utilizes the blind watermarking extraction techniques [10]. By this scheme, the desynchronization in detection end or the resynchronization in detection end are both avoided, which improve the detection efficiency and security.

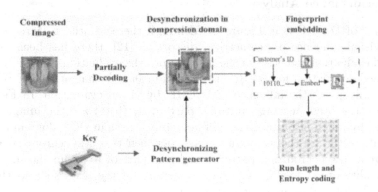

**Fig. 1.** Our proposed DCRF

## 3.2   The Methods to Improve the System Security

The attacks to the strategy in Figure 1 include four aspects:

1. The desynchronized copy may suffer malicious attacks such as redesynchronization and recompression. Robust blind watermarking embedding and extraction technique [10] is better for coping with this attack;

2. With or without some post processing, the copy after collusion may have no apparent artifacts. For coping with this attack, the discretizing step of the parameters for desynchronizing should be large enough while not influencing visual quality apparently [6];
3. The desynchronized copies may be registered to a certain copy [7]. For dealing with this attack [7], larger range of the parameters for desynchronizing should be used which can increase the seeking range of registration;
4. When the desynchronizing pattern database is published (for example, as part of standard) or known by attackers, the desynchronizing patterns of the copies may be guessed. For this attack, large space for the desynchronizing parameters is needed (determining the key space). While in [6] (see Table 1 of [6]), there're only 256 kinds of composition considered which will limit the security. Here, we propose a secure DCT domain DCRF named as "divided DCT domain DCRF" (DDDCRF, $D^3CRF$): divide the image into parts and apply different desynchronization patterns for different parts. For maintaining visual quality: the moving distance in neighbor parts should not be larger than one or two pixels. By the method, the original $O(1)$ parameter space is enlarged to be $O(N)$ ($N$ is the pixel number). For example, assume 8 levels are permitted for the translation of a line, and neighbor lines are translated with different levels and the difference is no more than one. For a $512 * 512$ image, only considering horizontal translation, the translation parameter space is $8^{512/8} = 8^{64}$ which is much larger than 256 in [6].

### 3.3   Performance Analysis

The result of $D^3CRF$ is in Figure 2. Although there's initial research of evaluating visual influence of geometrical distortion [12], there has been no wide accepted evaluation metrics. On the other hand, the evaluation using PSNR and normalized correlation for $D^3CRF$ is very the same to that of DCRF [7], then here we only judge the influence of $D^3CRF$ by visual evaluation. In Figure 2, (a)(d) are the original image and one part of it, (b)(e) are the image desynchronized by different patterns for different block rows in DCT domain and one part of it, (c)(f) are the averaging image between two desynchronized images by different desynchronizing patterns and one part of it. From the figure, the visual quality of colluded copy is bad especially for the texts such as the "US Air Force" and the textures such as the mountains.

The comparison between the features of Celik's method [7] and $D^3CRF$ is in Table 1.

## 4   Synchronized Degradation Metric (SDM)

Although geometric distortion is a very hot topic for watermarking research, the methods of evaluating geometric distortion are very few. Most of geometric distortion evaluation is by subjective method [11]. There has been also research for objective evaluation for geometric distortion [12], but from our knowing there's

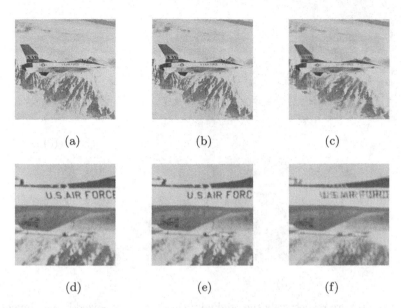

(a)                    (b)                    (c)

(d)                    (e)                    (f)

**Fig. 2.** Illustration for D³CRF: (a)(d) Original Airplane image and one part of it; (b)(e) The Airplane image after using D³CRF and one part of it; (c)(f) Collusion result of two images after using divided D³CRF and one part of it

**Table 1.** Comparison of D³CRF and method of Celik

| Method | D³CRF | Celik's method |
|---|---|---|
| Security | High | Middle |
| Efficiency | High / middle | Middle |
| Robustness | Middle | Middle |
| Compression compliant | With | Without |

no research for evaluating space desynchronized images' collusion distortion. Here, we propose a metric called SDM for evaluating both space desynchronized and colluded copies:

$$SDM(P_{Desyn}) = \alpha \cdot PSNR(Ima_{Resyn}) + \beta \cdot log10(\text{Max}(P_{min}, P_{Resyn}) * P_{ini}).$$

where $PSNR(\cdot)$ is operator for computing $PSNR$ of image, $Ima_{Resyn}$ is resynchronized image, $P_{Resyn}$ is the value for this resynchronization, and $\alpha, \beta, P_{min}, P_{ini}$ are parameters. In our experiments, we only consider horizontal translation for analysis convenience, $\alpha = 1, \beta = -5, P_{min} = 0.1, P_{ini} = 20$. In Fig.3, (a)~(e) are respectively the original image, desynchronized image, image with noise, image with both desynchronization and noise, colluded image of different desynchronized images. From Fig.3, the visual effect of (b) is visually much better than (c)~(e), while $PSNR$ of (b) is worse than or similar to (c) (see (a) of Fig.4), then $PSNR$ is not appropriate for evaluating visual degradation of

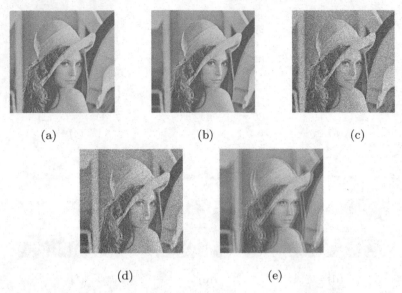

(a)                    (b)                    (c)

(d)                    (e)

**Fig. 3.** (a)∼ (e) are respectively the original image, desynchronized image, image with noise, image with both desynchronization and noise, colluded image of different desynchronized images

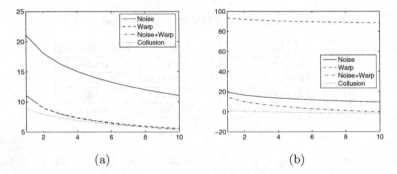

(a)                              (b)

**Fig. 4.** (a)$PSNR$ of noised, warped, noised and warped, colluded images with different warped parameters or different variance Gaussian noise; (b)$SDM$ of different noised, warped, noised and warped, colluded images

desynchronization and collusion. Compared with $PSNR$, SDM of (b) in Fig.3 is better than (c)∼(e) in Fig.3 (see (b) of Fig.4). Then, SDM is more uniform to human's perception.

## 5   Conclusion and Future Work

In this paper, a secure D³CRF scheme is proposed. Virtues of D³CRF include: firstly, it does not need to solve the difficult problems of extracting the user ID from colluded medias and punishing the attendees; secondly, security is enhanced by introducing blind fingerprint extraction and enlarging desynchronization parameter space; thirdly, the method processes JPEG compressed image directly and does not need to decompress and compress the image. In the future, $D^3CRF$ system in compression domain will be studied for video processing. Compared with the mature technique of high efficient JPEG compression and decompression, high efficiency compression domain operation for desynchronization should be devised.

# References

1. Wu, M., Trappe, W., Wang, Z.J., and Liu, R.: Collusion-resistant fingerprinting for multimedia. IEEE Signal Processing Magazine, **21(2)**, (2004), 15-27.
2. Wang, Z.J., Wu, M., Zhao, H.V., Trappe, W, and Liu K.J.R.: Anti-collusion forensics of multimedia fingerprinting using orthogonal modulation. IEEE Trans. Image Processing. **14(6)**, (2005), 804-821.
3. Boneh, D., and Shaw, J.: Collusion-secure fingerprinting for digital data. IEEE Trans. Inform. Theory, **44(5)**, (1998), 1897-1905.
4. Schaathun, H.G.: The Boneh-Shaw fingerprinting scheme is better than we thought. IEEE Trans. Information Forensics and Security, **1(2)**, (2006), 248-255.
5. Wu, Y.D.: Linear combination collusion attack and its application on an anti-collusion fingerprinting. IEEE ICASSP 2005, **II.** 13-16, Philadelphia, USA.
6. Mao, Y.N., and Mihcak, K.: Collusion-resistantintentional de-synchronization for digital video fingerprinting. IEEE ICIP 2005, vol. **1**, 237-240 .
7. Celik, M.U., Sharma, G., and Tekalp, A.M.: Collusion-resilient fingerprinting by random pre-warping. IEEE Signal Processing Letters, **11(10)**, (2004), 831-835.
8. Chang, S.F.: Compressed-domain techniques for image/video indexing and manipulation. IEEE ICIP 1995, Vol. **1**, 23-26.
9. Smith, B.C., and Rowe, L.A.: Fast software processing of motion JPEG video. ACM Multimedia 1994, 77-88.
10. Lee, J.S., Tsai, C.T., and Ko, C.H.: Image watermarking through attack simulation. Optical Engineering, **45(2)**, (2006), 027001/1-11.
11. Setyawan, I., and Lagendijk, R.L.: Perceptual quality impact of geometric distortion in images. 25-th Symposium on Information Theory in the Benelux, June 2-4, 2004, 217-224.
12. Setyawan I., and Lagendijk, R.L.: Human perception of geometric distortions in images. SPIE Security, Steganography, and Watermarking of Multimedia Contents 2004, 256-267.

# A Format-Compliant Encryption Framework for JPEG2000 Image Code-Streams in Broadcasting Applications*

Jinyong Fang and Jun Sun

Institute of Image Communication and Information Processing, Shanghai Jiaotong University, Shanghai 200030, China
jyfang@sjtu.edu.cn, sunjun@cdtv.org.cn

**Abstract.** The increased popularity of multimedia applications such as JPEG2000 places a great demand on efficient data storage and transmission techniques. Unfortunately, traditional encryption techniques have some limits for JPEG2000 images, which are considered only to be common data. In this paper, an efficient secure encryption scheme for JPEG2000 code-streams in broadcasting applications is proposed. The scheme does not introduce superfluous JPEG2000 markers in the protected code-stream and achieves full information protection for data confidentiality. It also deals with the stream data in sequence and is computationally efficient and memory saving.

**Keywords:** JPEG2000, Format-Compliant encryption, JPSEC, Broadcasting application.

## 1 Introduction

In the latest still image compression standard JPEG2000, the syntax requires that any two consecutive bytes in the encrypted packet body should be less than 0xFF90 [1]. A JPEG2000 code-stream is composed of markers and data packets. The markers with values restricted to the interval [0xFF90, 0xFFFF] are used to delimit various logical units of the code-stream, facilitate random access, and maintain synchronization in the event of error-prone transmission. The packets carry the content bit-streams whose codewords (any two contiguous bytes) are not in the interval [0xFF90, 0xFFFF]. Since the output of a good cipher appears "random", straightforward application of a cipher to encrypt code-stream packets is bound to produce encrypted packets, which include superfluous markers. Such markers will cause potentially serious decoding problems (such as loss of code-stream synchronization and erroneous or faulty image transcoding). To overcome the superfluous markers problem, the encryption method must be JPEG2000 code-stream syntax compliant. Such a compliant encryption method does not introduce superfluous markers in the encrypted packets and maintains all the desirable properties of the original code-streams.

* This work is supported by Ningbo Industrial Scientific and Technological project (2005-B100003) and Natural science foundation of Ningbo, China. (2005A620002).

Y. Zhuang et al. (Eds.): PCM 2006, LNCS 4261, pp. 64–71, 2006.

Conan[2] described a technique which selectively encrypt JPEG2000 code-streams in order to generate compliant encrypt JPEG2000. In that scheme, if any byte, says $X$, has a value less then 0xF0, the four LSBs (Least Significant Bits) of $X$ are encrypted with a block cipher. Clearly, the security of this scheme is weak. Wu and Ma[3] proposed two packet-level encryption schemes based on stream ciphers and block ciphers respectively. They showed that the two schemes protected most of the code-stream data. However, they are not able to regain synchronization when some transmission error occurs. These algorithms are adopted by on-going JPSEC, which is the part 8 of JPEG2000 and is concerned with all the security aspects of JPEG2000 image codestreams. Later Wu and Deng[4] gave a code-block level compliant scheme. They claimed that this scheme could provide full protection of code-streams. However, this algorithm needs iterative operations to achieve practicable key stream and has a probability of never generating conditional-satisfied encrypted code-stream. Even if it can generate compliant out streams in some cases, its iterative method is computationally inefficient.

In this paper we propose a new scheme to encrypt and decrypt the code-stream in sequence and provide full protection of the information.

## 2  Brief Description for JPEG2000 Packet Structure

The structure of a JPEG2000 packet is depicted in Fig.1. A packet consists of a packet header followed by a packet body. To note, the Standard ensures that none of the code-stream's delimiting marker codes (these all lie in the range 0xFF90 through 0xFFFF) can appear in the packet-stream except marker segment SOP (start of packet) and marker EPH (end of packet header).

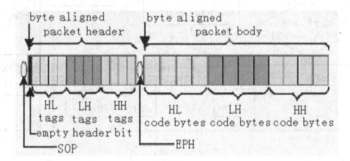

**Fig. 1.** JPEG2000 packet structure

## 3  Compliant Code-Stream Encryption Scheme Description

To hold the JPEG2000 structure, the proposed scheme is to encrypt the packet body data. The marker codes (ranging from 0xFF90 to 0xFFFF) will be kept their original values and will not appear in the packet body. Let $M$ express a part of packet body, and $M = m_1 \| m_2 \| \ldots \| m_n$, where $\|$ denotes concatenation and each $m_i$ depicts one byte in $M$. In the same way, we denote ciphertext as $C = c_1 \| c_2 \| \ldots \| c_n$, where $c_i$ depicts one byte.

## 3.1 Encryption Algorithm

Generate the key stream as a byte sequence. Discard those bytes with value of 0x0、0x70、0xE0. This constraint is to ensure the byte with value of 0xFF will change its value while encrypting. Denote the result key stream as $S = s_1 \| s_2 \| \ldots \| s_n$, where $s_i$ denotes one byte. Use $c_{mid}$ to mark whether the previous byte is once encrypted to 0xFF.

The encryption algorithm is illustrated in Fig.2.

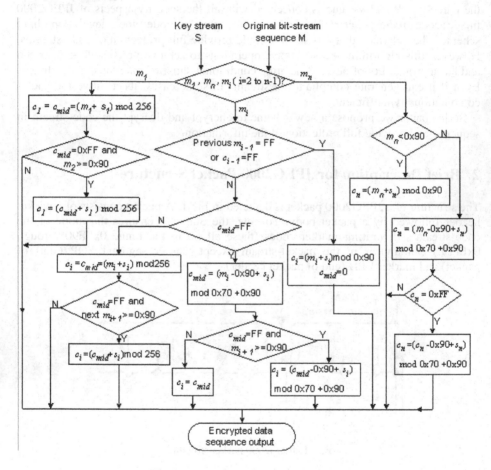

**Fig. 2.** Diagram of compliant encryption

① For the first byte $m_1$, if $c_{mid}$ equals 0xFF in the first encryption and $m_2 \geq 0x90$, $c_{mid}$ should be encrypted for a second time and $m_2$ will be encrypted to $c_2 \geq 0x90$ in the next step. Otherwise, no special processing needs to be done and $c_1 = c_{mid}$. It is worth noting that If $c_{mid} = 0xFF$ and $m_2 < 0x90$, $m_2$ will be encrypted to $c_2 \leq 0x90$ in the next step. In this way, we can infer whether a byte 0xFF needs to be decrypted for a second time in consideration of the next cipher-byte while decrypting.

② For $m_i$ ($i=2$ to $n-1$), seven kinds of cases may occur, in which Fig.3 depicts six special cases.

The first case is $m_{i-1}$ =0xFF and the second is $c_{i-1}$ =0xFF. These cases indicate that $m_i$ is less than 0x90. Therefore, keep the encrypted byte $c_i$ less than 0x90 too. Thus $c_i$ can indicate the previous byte need to be decrypted only once. These cases are also depicted in Fig. 3 (a) and (b).

If the first two cases are not true and $c_{mid}$ = 0xFF, which indicates current $m_i$ >= 0x90, it shows that the previous byte was encrypted to 0xFF ever and was encrypted twice. So $m_i$ should be encrypted into a value no less than 0x90. In this way, we can conclude whether the previous byte needs to be processed twice while decrypting. Then if the new $c_{mid}$ =0xFF and the next byte $m_{i+1}$ >=0x90, $m_i$ needs to be encrypted for a second time, which is the third case. It is also depicted in Fig. 3 (f). Otherwise, if the new $c_{mid}$ ≠0xFF or $m_{i+1}$ <0x90, the fourth case and the fifth case occur. Then let $c_i$ = $c_{mid}$. They are also depicted in Fig. 3 (d) and (e) respectively.

If the above cases are not true, the last two cases occur. In these two cases, the previous $m_{i-1}$ ≠0xFF and $c_{i-1}$ ≠0xFF and $c_{mid}$ ≠0xFF. So the encryption of current $m_i$ is independent of the previous byte $m_{i-1}$ and can be processed the same as the first packet byte $m_1$. Fig.3(c) also depicts the case in which $m_i$ is encrypted twice.

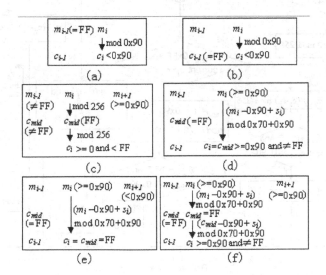

**Fig. 3.** Special cases in encryption process

③ The last packet byte $m_n$ is processed to ensure that $c_n$ is of the same range as $m_n$. In other words, it may either belong to interval [0,0x8F] or belong to interval [0x90, 0xFF]. Because the JPEG2000 compressed code-stream does not allow 0xFF as the ending byte for each Code-block Contribution to Packet (CCP), our scheme selects CCP as the processing unit because the end byte of CCP is non-0xFF. If the last byte is encrypted to $c_n$ =0xFF, $c_n$ is encrypted for a second time by $s_n$. Thus the last byte is ensured to never be 0xFF.

## 3.2 Decryption Algorithm

In the decryption process, we also deal with the encrypted JPEG2000 code-streams in sequence. Generate the same key stream $S$ as that in the encryption algorithm firstly. Then decrypt each cipher byte according to the case it belongs to. This process is just an inverse to the encryption. We use $m_{mid}$ to mark whether the previous cipher byte is decrypted to 0xFF just like $c_{mid}$ in encryption algorithm. Fig.4 depicts the decryption algorithm.

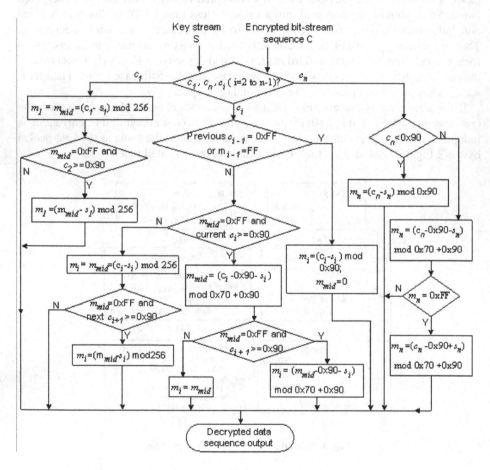

**Fig. 4.** Diagram of compliant decryption

①For the first byte $c_1$, let $m_{mid}$ =(c1 – s1) mod 256. If $m_{mid}$ =0xFF and $c_2$ >=0x90, it shows a second time of decryption needs to be done, otherwise, $m_1$ =$m_{mid}$.

②For $i$=2 to n-1,

a) If $c_{i-1}$ =0xFF or $m_{i-1}$ = 0xFF, it shows that the correspondent mi is less than 0x90. So $m_i$ =( $c_i$ – $s_i$) mod 0x90, $m_{mid}$ =0x0.

b) Otherwise, if $m_{mid}$ =0xFF and $c_i$ >= 0x90, which indicates $m_i$ is also >=0x90, let $m_{mid} = (c_i - 0x90 - s_i)$ mod 0x70+0x90. Then if the new $m_{mid}$ =0xFF and $c_{i+1}$ >= 0x90, it indicates $m_i$ was encrypted twice and a second decryption is needed, or else let $m_i$ equal to $m_{mid}$.

c) If the previous cases are not true, the current byte is independent of the previous byte. So the decryption process is the same as the first byte.

③ For the last byte $c_n$, we first judge which range it belongs to, then it is decrypted according to the correspondent formula. When the recovered $m_n$ is 0xFF, it needs to be decrypted for a second time.

## 4  Security Analysis

In our scheme, $s_i$ in the key-stream will never be 0□0x70 or 0xE0. For byte 0, the ciphertext will never be 0,0x70, 0xE0; for byte 1, the ciphertext will never be 1, 0x71, 0xE1,.... Therefore, if our scheme is used in non-broadcasting applications, in which there may be many different key streams for a same original content, based on the observation of the ciphertext pattern, the attacker may guess the original byte. In other words, if the attacker get protected code-streams generated from the same original codestream for $k$ times, he can guess byte 0 if there is no 0, 0x70 and 0xE0 in the same position of the protected streams. For one cipherbyte, $k$ should be 0x6F at least. Let $n$ denote the number of possible ciphertext value. In our scheme $n$=0x6F and $k$>=$n$.

Let $Aj$ ={one byte with value of $j$ does not occur when attacker gets ciphertext for $k$ times}, Then

$$p(A_j) = \frac{(n-1)^k}{n^k} = (1-\frac{1}{n})^k \qquad j = 1,2,...,n. \qquad (1)$$

Similarly, $A_i \cap A_j$ ={Value $i$ and value $j$ do not occur when attacker gets cipherbyte for $k$ times}. It is easy to check

$$p(A_i \cap A_j) = \frac{(n-2)^k}{n^k} = (1-\frac{2}{n})^k \qquad i,j = 1,2,...,n, i \neq j. \qquad (2)$$

......

$$p(A_{i_1} \cap A_{i_2} \cap,...,\cap A_{i_{n-1}}) = (1-\frac{n-1}{n})^k \qquad i_1,i_2,...,i_{n-1} \in \{1,2,...,n\}. \qquad (3)$$

So the probability that $n$ possible bytes do not occur is

$$p(A_1 \cap A_2 \cap,...,\cap A_{n-1} \cap A_n) = (1-\frac{n}{n})^k = 0. \qquad (4)$$

Let
$$S_1 = \sum_{j=1}^{n} p(A_j) = n\frac{(n-1)^k}{n^k} = C_n^1(1-\frac{1}{n})^k, \tag{5}$$

$$S_2 = \sum_{i<j}^{n} p(A_i \cap A_j) = C_n^2(1-\frac{2}{n})^k, \tag{6}$$

......

$$S_{n-1} = \sum_{i_1<i_2<...<i_{n-1}} p(A_{i_1} \cap A_{i_2} \cap ... \cap A_{i_{n-1}}) = C_n^{n-1}(1-\frac{n-1}{n})^k. \tag{7}$$

$$S_n = 0. \tag{8}$$

Now we assume $A$={at least one possible cipherbyte for an original byte does not occur when the attacker gets ciphertext for $k$ times}.

Then we have $p(A) = p(\bigcup_{j=1}^{n} A_j) = S_1 - S_2 + S_3 - ... + (-1)^n S_{n-1}.$ $\qquad$ (9)

Let $B$={each possible cipherbyte for an original byte has occurred when the attacker gets ciphertext for $k$ times}, Therefore

$$p(B) = 1 - p(A) = 1 - S_1 + S_2 + ... + (-1)^{n-1} S_{n-1}$$
$$= 1 - C_n^1(1-\frac{1}{n})^k + C_n^2(1-\frac{2}{n})^k - ... + (-1)^{n-1} C_n^{n-1}(1-\frac{n-1}{n})^k. \tag{10}$$

Obviously, $p(B)$ in Eq.(10) is the probability of guessing the individual byte. We set $k$=500, which means the attacker get ciphertext for the same original byte for 500 times. In this case, the probability of information recovered is 0.2893. For a group of bytes, we assume that each byte in the code-stream is independent, so the probability of guessing them is $\{p(B)\}^m$, where $m$ denotes the length of the group of bytes. For example, If $m$=100 and $k$ is also 500, the probability of guessing them is 1.3664e-54, which means it is difficult to recover an image code-stream because of its large sizes and the scheme is safe. As $k$ is getting larger and larger, the probability increases rapidly. Therefore this vulnerability limits the applications of our scheme. It cannot be used in the condition that the attacker can get large different copies of the same information. So the broadcasting mode is appropriate, in which only one key stream is used for the same original bit-stream. Thus the attackers can't recover the original information with cipher-only attack.

## 5   Experimental Results

Fig. 5a and Fig. 5b show the origin and encrypted Lena image respectively. The encrypted view of the image is totally incomprehensible.

**Fig. 5.** Experiment result. a) Origin image b) encrypted image.

# 6 Conclusion

In this paper, a method of compliant encryption for JPEG2000 code-streams in broadcasting applications is proposed. The scheme provides full protection for image information. Because the encryption and decryption of the code-streams are in sequence, much less memory is needed. Also in this scheme there are at most two iterations in encryption and decryption of each byte. Therefore it is computationally efficient and is easy to be implemented into FPGA based coding and decoding architectures. So our scheme is especially practicable for large images. Furthermore, the fully compliant encrypted code-streams maintain all the nice characteristics of original JPEG2000 code-streams, such as error resilience and scalability.

# References

1. 'Information Technology – JPEG2000 image coding system', ISO/IEC International Standard 154441, ITU Recommendation T.800, 2000
2. Conan Vania, Sadourny Yulen and Thomann Stève: 'Symmetric Block Cipher Based Protection: Contribution to JPSEC,' ISO/IEC JTC 1/SC 29/WG1 N2771, Oct.2003
3. Wu H.J. and Ma D.: 'Efficient and Secure Encryption Schemes for JPEG2000,' ICASSP 2004, pp. V869-872
4. Wu Y.D., and Robert Deng: 'Compliant Encryption of JPEG2000 Codestreams,' IEEE ICIP, Oct. 2004, Singapore, ISBN 0-7803-8555-1

# Euclidean Distance Transform of Digital Images in Arbitrary Dimensions

Dong Xu[1,2] and Hua Li[1]

[1] Key Laboratory of Intelligent Information Processing, Institute of Computing Technology,
Chinese Academy of Sciences
Beijing P.O. Box 2704, 100080, P.R. China
[2] Graduate University of Chinese Academy of Sciences
{xudong, lihua}@ict.ac.cn

**Abstract.** A new algorithm for Euclidean distance transform is proposed in this paper. It propagates from the boundary to the inner of object layer by layer, like the inverse propagation of water wave. It can be applied in every dimensional space and has linear time complexity. Euclidean distance transformations of digital images in 2-D and 3-D are conducted in the experiments. Voronoi diagram and Delaunay triangulation can also be produced by this method.

## 1 Introduction

Distance transform (DT) is the transformation that converts a digital binary image to another gray scale image in which the value of each pixel in the object is the minimum distance from the background to that pixel by a predefined distance function. Three distance functions are often used in practice, which are City-block distance, Chessboard distance and Euclidean distance. In this paper, we mainly concentrate on the Euclidean distance transform (EDT).

The signed Euclidean distance transform which represented the displacement of a pixel from the nearest background point, was defined in [1], and exploited in applications like curve smoothing, detecting dominant points in digital curves, finding convex hulls etc. Mitchell et al used a gray scale mathematical morphology approach for Euclidean distance transform [2], [3]. Morphological erosion is an operation which selects the minimum value from the combination of an image and the predefined weighted structure element within a window, so it is appropriate for EDT. And they applied decomposition properties of mathematical morphology for parallel computing. Shih et al achieved correct and efficient EDT by size-invariant four-scan algorithm in [4] and two-scan based algorithm in [5]. Vincent [6] encoded the objects boundaries as chains and propagated these structures in the image using rewriting rules. This method could achieve exact results and was very efficient. Other variations of fast and exact EDT methods were given in [7] and [8].

Several linear time algorithms were proposed recently, many of which were based on the pre-computed Voronoi diagrams [9], [10] and [11]. The emphasis of some articles is on exploiting a general method in arbitrary dimensions like [11] and [12].

Y. Zhuang et al. (Eds.): PCM 2006, LNCS 4261, pp. 72–79, 2006.
© Springer-Verlag Berlin Heidelberg 2006

Some literature developed methods for parallel computing or hardware implementation of Euclidean distance transform. Zhang et al implemented Euclidean distance transform in real time with stack filters using only binary logic gates [13].

The results of distance transforms may be very useful in skeleton extraction [14], [15], [16], shortest path planning [17], shape description [18]. Leymarie et al [18] proposed a novel method for shape description of planar objects. They combined EDT with an active contour model to minimize an energy function and extract a Euclidean skeleton. EDT was applied in the application of medical image processing such as automated path finding in virtual endoscopy and analysis of 3D pathological sample images in [19].

In this paper, we propose an algorithm to deal with Euclidean distance transform which has the properties as follows:

I   The algorithm has a uniform framework and can be applied in arbitrary dimensions.
II  The algorithm has the linear computational complexity of O(m), where m is the number of pixels in the object.
III The algorithm can be applied in dynamic images whose boundary doesn't need to be close and its pixels can increase dynamically.
IV  Voronoi diagram and Delaunay triangulation can be two byproducts of this algorithm.

The remainder of the paper is organized as follows. In section 2, we elaborate on the principle of the proposed algorithm. Analysis and discussion are presented in section 3. Some results of Euclidean distance transformation in 2-D and 3D are illustrated in section 4. We conclude the paper and open perspectives for future work in the end.

## 2   Boundary Propagation Algorithm

### 2.1   Basic Terms

In this part, we define some basic symbols which may be used throughout the paper and without the limitation of dimensions. Suppose I is an binary image in n-dimensional space, in which O is the set of pixels in the object, and $B = \overline{O}$ is the set of pixels on the background. $X = (x_1, x_2, ..., x_n) \in Z^n$ is a pixel in image I and m=|O| is the total number of pixels in the object. The value of the pixel X is defined as follows:

$$f(X) = \begin{cases} 1 & if\ X \in O \\ 0 & if\ X \in B \end{cases} \tag{1}$$

The neighborhood N(X) of pixel X in n-dimensional space is given as below. It can be found that when n=2, the neighborhood is 8-connected neighborhood and when n=3, it becomes 26-connected neighborhood. There are at most $3^n - 1$ adjacent pixels of a pixel in n-dimensional image when the pixel is not on the boundary of the image.

$$N(X) = \{Y \mid Y = (y_1, y_2, ..., y_n) \in I, \mid y_i - x_i \mid \leq 1, 1 \leq i \leq n, Y \neq X \} \tag{2}$$

Next, we give the definition of the set of boundary pixels S. It belongs to the background and is the outlier or the neighboring shell of the object.

$$S = \{Y \mid Y \in B, \exists X \in O : Y \in N(X)\} \tag{3}$$

The goal of Euclidean distance transform of a pixel X in the object is to find the minimal Euclidean distance from background pixels to X, that is also equivalent to find the pixel in S which minimizes the distance between the pixel X and the background. Function g represents the Euclidean distance transform from binary image I to gray scale image $I'$, and d means Euclidean distance.

$$g(X) = d(X, B) = d(X, S) = \min\{d(X, Y), Y \in S\} \tag{4}$$

At last, to a pixel X in the object, we define the nearest pixel in background as NP(X). Generally, there is may be more than one pixel which has the smallest Euclidean distance. In this situation, we select one of them randomly.

$$NP(X) = \arg\min_{Y}\{d(X, Y), Y \in S\} \tag{5}$$

For the sake of the requirement of the algorithm, NP(X) also has definition when $X \in S$. S was also called zero-distance set in [1] since the Euclidean distance of pixels in S equal to zero from this definition.

$$NP(X) = X \quad if \ X \in S \tag{6}$$

## 2.2 Propagation Algorithm

The propagation algorithm comes from the inverse analysis of the results from signed Euclidean distance transform [1] and Voronoi diagram [10]. For every pixel X in the object after the signed Euclidean distance transform, NP(X) can be computed from the displacement. Hence, the field in the object can be divided into at most |S| parts according to all the nearest boundary pixels NP(X), $X \in O$. This kind of division makes up of a Voronoi diagram in n-dimensional space.

The algorithm propagates from the boundary pixels to the object pixels layer by layer, like the inverse propagation of water wave. It is very similar to the algorithm presented in [6] by Vincent, which was suitable for the exact EDT of closed boundary. Here, we use a data structure—queue Q to record one layer of pixels and iterate it until the queue is empty. For each pixel X in the object, we save its information of the nearest boundary pixels NP(X), minimal Euclidean distance dmin(X) etc. There are mainly two operations—insert and delete to the queue. Clear procedure of this algorithm is given by the following pseudocode.

*// Initialization*
*Q=S;*
*For (each X in O)*

```
{
    dmin(X)=+∞;
    NP(X)=NULL;
}
// Iteration
while (Q!=empty)
{
    get the first element Y in Q;
    for(each Z in N(Y))
        if (Z ∈O && NP(Z)!=NP(Y) && dmin(Z)>d(Z,NP(Y)))
        {
            NP(Z)=NP(Y);
            dmin(Z)=d(Z,NP(Y));
            insert Z to the end of Q;
        }
    delete Y;
}
```

In the *initialization* part, we set S as the initial queue, and let Euclidean distance of each pixel X be a very large integer. In the *iteration* part, to a pixel Y in the queue, we propagate it to its nearest neighborhood $N(Y)$. If a pixel Z in the neighborhood hasn't been handled or the current minimal distance $dmin(Z)$ is larger than the distance between Z and $NP(Y)$, then the nearest pixel in background $NP(Z)$ inherits from Y by $NP(Z)=NP(Y)$.

# 3  Algorithm Analysis and Discussions

## 3.1  Computational Complexity

The efficiency of the algorithm is comparable with that in [6], we give the upper bound of the computational complexity for further analysis here. The *iteration* part occupies most of the computation time in this algorithm. We don't discuss the implementation of square root, addition and multiplication operations here, which has been well solved in former literature. Instead, we concern with the number of insert operation, which is proportional to the computation time. Suppose $m=|O|$ is the number of pixels in the object. Each pixel is inserted to the queue at least once, but the upper bound can not be determined because of the complicated shapes of the object. On average, the times of insert operation of a pixel X is less than the number of its direct neighborhood $N(X)$. This is because the nearest boundary pixel $NP(X)$ can be propagated from any direction of its neighborhood.

Based on the above analysis, the computational complexity of the algorithm is $O((3^n-1)m)$ in n-dimensional space. In 2-D and 3-D, the linear time complexity are $O(8m)$ and $O(26m)$ respectively, which can also be approved by summing up the number of insert operation in experiments. Since $NP(Z)!=NP(Y)$ and $dmin(Z)>d(Z,NP(Y))$ are the conditions for insert operation in the pseudocode, the pixel Z doesn't need to be put into the queue anymore if it has found the correct $NP(Z)$.

## 3.2  Accuracy Discussion

Vincent pointed out many algorithms suffered from inaccurate problem of the transformed results and illustrated it in two sketches. He solved this problem and achieved exact Euclidean distance transform by decomposing the boundary of the object into several convex chains. However, his algorithm had a limitation that the object must have a close boundary.

To this boundary propagation algorithm, the only imprecise distance comes from the isolated pixel in the object. Isolated pixel X means that NP(X) is different from any of the NP(Y), Y∈N(X). The Euclidean distance of this kind of isolated pixel can not be correctly computed, but it appears rarely in practice. It should be pointed out that in some applications of distance transformation like skeleton extraction, a consistent distribution of the object pixels is preferred according to the nearest boundary pixels. In other words, our algorithm could have some advantages in these applications.

## 4  Experimental Results

### 4.1  Dynamic Insert Operation

Some of the literature for EDT is based on a scanning flow, such as [4] and [5]. After the scanning, the EDT results of the whole image are got. If the boundary pixels increase dynamically with time, the boundary propagation algorithm is more dominant because it only acts on the partial area surrounding the newly added pixels. Hence, this algorithm is compatible to others' and can be used afterwards in dynamic images. The left of Fig. 1 shows a Euclidean distance map with 7 boundary points (zero-distance set), which are denoted as red points. We randomly add another three boundary points in the image. The new Euclidean distance map is given in the right of Fig. 1. As we can see, the algorithm becomes faster when the number of boundary points increases. This is because there are fewer pixels whose Euclidean distances need to be modified as the new boundary pixel added in.

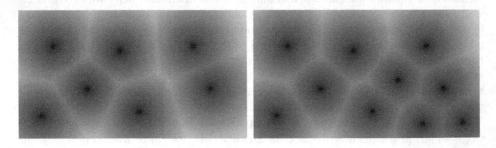

**Fig. 1.** Left: Euclidean distance map of 7 boundary points. Right: Euclidean distance map of the left image with three new boundary points added in.

## 4.2  Byproducts of the Algorithm

Paper [10] and [11] constructed the Voronoi diagram firstly and then built Euclidean distance based on it. In this algorithm, we produce Euclidean distance directly and avoid Voronoi diagram, but it can be an accessory of the algorithm. In the Euclidean distance map, if a pixel has the same minimal distance to two or more boundary pixels, then it is in the edge of Voronoi diagram. Blue lines in the left of Fig. 2. constitute the Voronoi diagram after we have generated the Euclidean distance map. If two boundary pixels share one edge in the Voronoi diagram, then there exists an edge between them in the corresponding delaunay triangulation, which is desribled by green lines in the right of Fig. 2.

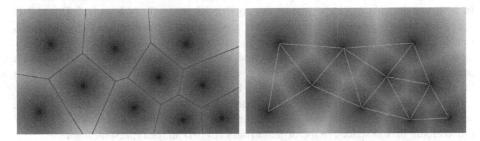

**Fig. 2.** Left: Voronoi diagram from Euclidean distance map. Right: Delaunay triangulation from Euclidean distance map.

## 4.3  EDT Examples in 2-D and 3-D

Here, we give two examples of Euclidean distance map of real image or object with close boundary in 2-D and 3-D.

Butterfly is a commonly used image for Euclidean distance transformation and skeleton extraction in 2-D. The left of Fig. 3 shows the distance transform result of

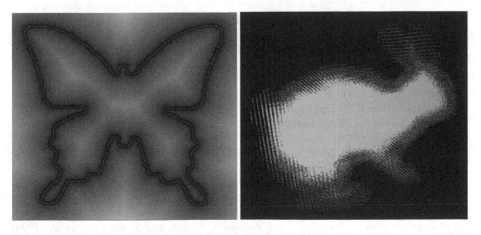

**Fig. 3.** Left: Euclidean distance map of the butterfly. Right: Euclidean distance map of the bunny model.

our algorithm. The close boundary is denoted by red pixels. In 3-D space, since it is hard to show the values of Euclidean distances, we regard them as the sizes of the voxels when rendering. In the following example—the right of Fig. 3, we first get the voxels of the bunny model by a voxelization method. Boundary propagation algorithm is carried out to this 3-D digital image afterwards. It can be seen that the voxels near the boundary are rendered by small points and voxels far from the boundary are of big size.

# 5  Conclusions and Future Work

In this paper, we introduce a novel method to compute Euclidean distance transform in arbitrary dimensions. Experiments are conducted successfully both in 2-D and 3-D space for visualization of the results. This propagation algorithm has the advantages that it can be used in dynamic images in arbitrary dimensional space and has linear complexity. By experiments, we also find that the algorithm is very efficient. It achieves real-time to compute EDT when new boundary pixel is added to Fig. 1. It takes only few seconds to compute EDT in Fig. 3.

In the future, the distance transformation results can be applied in various fields, such as skeleton extraction and shape description. Connectivity and simplification of the skeleton in 3-D space are the urgent affairs for 3-D shape representation.

# Acknowledgments

This work is supported by National Key Basic Research Plan (Grant No. 2004CB318006) and National Natural Science Foundation of China (Grant No. 60533090).

# References

[1] Ye Q. Z.: The Signed Euclidean Distance Transform and Its Applications. Proc. ninth Int. Conf. Pattern Recognition. (1988) 495-499
[2] Huang C. T., Mitchell O. R.: A Euclidean Distance Transform Using Grayscale Morphology Decomposition. IEEE Trans. Pattern Analysis and Machine Intelligence. 16 (1994) 443-448
[3] Shih F. Y., Mitchell O. R.: A Mathematical Morphology Approach to Euclidean Distance Transformation. IEEE Trans. Image Processing. 1 (1992) 197-204
[4] Shih F. Y., Liu J. J.: Size-invariant Four-scan Euclidean Distance Transformation. Pattern Recognition. 31 (1998) 1761-1766
[5] Shih F. Y., Wu Y. T.: The Efficient Algorithms for Achieving Euclidean Distance Transformation. IEEE Trans. Image Processing. 13 (2004) 1078-1091
[6] Vincent L.: Exact Euclidean Distance Function by Chain Propagations. IEEE Proc. Computer Vision and Pattern Recognition. (1991) 520-525
[7] Cuisenaire O. , Macq B.: Fast and Exact Signed Euclidean Distance Transformation with Linear Complexity. Proc. Int. Conf. Acoustics, Speech, and Signal Processing. (1990) 3293-3296

[8]  Schouten T., Broek E. V. D.: Fast Exact Euclidean Distance (FEED) Transformation. Int. Conf. Pattern Recognition. (2004) 594-597

[9]  Breu H., Gil J., Kirkpatrick D., Werman M.: "Linear Time Euclidean Distance Transform Algorithms", IEEE Trans. Pattern Analysis and Machine Intelligence. 17 (1995) 529-533

[10] Guan W. G., Ma S. D.: A List-Processing Approach to Compute Voronoi Diagrams and the Euclidean Distance Transform. IEEE Trans. Pattern Analysis and Machine Intelligence. 20 (1998) 757-761

[11] Maurer C. R. Jr., Qi R. S., Raghavan V.: A Linear Time Algorithm for Computing Exact Euclidean Distance Transforms of Binary Images in Arbitrary Dimensions. IEEE Trans. Pattern Analysis and Machine Intelligence. 25 (2003) 265-270

[12] Ragnemalm I.: The Euclidean Distance Transform in Arbitrary Dmensions. Int. Conf. Image Processing and its Applications. (1992) 290-293

[13] Zhang S., Karim M. A.: Euclidean Distance Transform by Stack Filters. IEEE Signal Processing Letters. 6 (1999) 253-256

[14] Capson D. W., Fung A. C.: Connected Skeletons from 3D Distance Transforms. Southwest Symposium on Image Analysis and Interpretation. (1998) 174-179

[15] Golland P., Grimson W. E. L.: Fixed Topology Skeletons. IEEE Proc. Computer Vision and Pattern Recognition. (2000) 10-17

[16] Choi W. P., Lam K. M., Siu W. C.: Extraction of the Euclidean Skeleton Based on a Connectivity Criterion. Pattern Recognition. 36 (2003) 721-729

[17] Shih F. Y., Wu Y. -T.: "Three-dimensional Euclidean Distance Transformation and its Application to Shortest Path Planning", Pattern Recognition. 37 (2004) 79-92

[18] Leymarie F., Levine M. D.: Simulating the Grassfire Transform Using an Active Contour Model. IEEE Trans. Pattern Analysis and Machine Intelligence. 14 (1992) 56-75

[19] Toriwaki J., Mori K.: Distance Transformation and Skeletonization of 3D Pictures and Their Applications to Medical Images. Digital and Image Geometry: Advanced Lectures. (2001) 412-429

# JPEG2000 Steganography Possibly Secure Against Histogram-Based Attack

Hideki Noda[1], Yohsuke Tsukamizu[2], and Michiharu Niimi[1]

[1] Kyushu Institute of Technology, Dept. of Systems Innovation and Informatics,
680-4 Kawazu, Iizuka, 820-8502 Japan
{noda, niimi}@mip.ces.kyutech.ac.jp
[2] Kyushu Institute of Technology,
Dept. of Electrical, Electronic and Computer Engineering,
1-1 Sensui-cho, Tobata-ku, Kitakyushu, 804-8550 Japan
tukamizu@know.comp.kyutech.ac.jp

**Abstract.** This paper presents two steganographic methods for JPEG2000 still images which preserve histograms of discrete wavelet transform (DWT) coefficients. The first one is a histogram quasi-preserving method using quantization index modulation (QIM) with a dead zone in DWT domain. The second one is a histogram preserving method based on histogram matching using two quantizers with a dead zone. Comparing with a conventional JPEG2000 steganography, the two methods show better histogram preservation. The proposed methods are promising candidates for secure JPEG2000 steganography against histogram-based attack.

## 1 Introduction

Steganography is the practice of hiding or camouflaging secret data in an innocent looking dummy container. This container may be a digital still image, audio file, or video file. Once the data has been embedded, it may be transferred across insecure lines or posted in public places. Therefore, the dummy container should seem innocent under most examinations. On the other hand, steganalysis is the task of attacking steganographic systems. Considering the aim of steganography, it might be sufficient if an attacker can detect the presence of hidden data in a container.

In steganography using digital images, data embedding into compressed images should be primarily considered since images are usually compressed before being transmitted. The JPEG compression using the discrete cosine transform (DCT) is now the most common compression standard for still images, and therefore a number of steganographic methods have already been proposed for JPEG images [1]-[6]. Several steganalysis methods for JPEG steganography have also been proposed to detect whether messages are embedded or not in a JPEG image [2],[7]. Such steganalysis methods usually exploit some changes on the histogram of quantized DCT coefficients caused by embedding.

JPEG2000 using the discrete wavelet transform (DWT) is an incoming image coding standard which has rich desirable features and is believed to be used

Y. Zhuang et al. (Eds.): PCM 2006, LNCS 4261, pp. 80–87, 2006.

widely. Therefore steganographic methods for JPEG2000 images might be commonly used in the near future but only a few methods have been proposed before now [8],[9]. As far as we know, steganalysis for JPEG2000 steganography has not been studied yet.

This paper presents two steganographic methods for JPEG2000 still images which can preserve histograms of quantized DWT coefficients. The histogram preservation should be a necessary requirement for secure JPEG2000 steganography since steganalysis for JPEG2000 steganography is likely to exploit histogram changes by embedding. The first method is a histogram quasi-preserving method which uses quantization index modulation (QIM) [10] in DWT domain with a device not to change the after-embedding histogram excessively. The second one is a histogram preserving method which uses a histogram matching technique using two quantizers, where the representatives of each quantizer are given in advance and the intervals for each representative are set so as to preserve the histogram of cover image. Here we call the first method QIM-JPEG2000 steganography and the second one histogram matching JPEG2000 (HM-JPEG2000) steganography.

## 2    Histogram Preserving and Quasi-preserving JPEG2000 Steganography

Two JPEG2000 steganographic methods using two quantizers in DWT domain are here presented. In principle these two methods follow our previous methods in DCT domain for JPEG images [6]. However, unlike JPEG compression, there is a problem in JPEG2000 compression that a true quantization step size for a DWT coefficient is not known at the quantization step of DWT coefficients. Since the problem is resolved later in Section 3, at the moment we assume that the true quantization step size is known at the quantization step.

### 2.1    Histogram Quasi-preserving QIM-JPEG2000 Steganography

Consider applying QIM [10] using two different quantizers to embed binary data at the quantization step of DWT coefficients. Each bit (zero or one) of binary data is embedded in such a way that one of two quantizers is used for quantization of a DWT coefficient, which corresponds to embed zero, and the other quantizer is used to embed one.

Assuming that the probabilities of zero and one are same in binary data to be embedded, consider how histograms of quantized DWT coefficients change after embedding. This assumption is quite natural since any compressed data has such property. From now on, we assume that DWT coefficients belonging to a codeblock[1] are divided by its quantization step size in advance and then two codebooks, $C^0$ and $C^1$, for two quantizers can be defined as $C^0 = \{0, \pm(2j + 0.5); j \in \{1, 2, \ldots\}\}$ and $C^1 = \{\pm(2j + 1.5); j \in \{0, 1, 2, \ldots\}\}$ for all frequency

---

[1] The codeblock is a unit processing block in JPEG2000 coding, as described in Section 3. The quantization step size can be different from codeblock to codeblock.

subbands. Let $h_i$ and $h_{-i}$, $i \in \{1, 2, \ldots\}$ denote the number of DWT coefficients whose values $w$ are in the interval $i \leq w < i+1$ and $-i-1 < w \leq -i$, respectively, and $h_0$ in the interval $-1 < w < 1$. These settings reflect the feature of JPEG2000 that the absolute values of DWT coefficients are bit-plane-encoded to integers and decoded by adding 0.5 to the encoded absolute value except for 0, i.e., for example, $w = -3.8$ is encoded as -3 and decoded as -3.5. Let $h_i^-$ and $h_i^+$ denote the number of DWT coefficients in the lower and higher half interval of $h_i$, respectively, and therefore $h_i^- + h_i^+ = h_i$. After embedding by QIM, the histogram $h_i$ is changed to $h_i'$ as

$$h_i' = \frac{1}{2}h_i + \frac{1}{2}(h_{i-1}^+ + h_{i+1}^-). \tag{1}$$

The change in (1) can be understood as follows. For example, if $i$ is a positive even number, and $C^0$ is used for embedding zero, half of DWT coefficients in the interval $i \leq w < i+1$ are used for embedding zero and their quantized coefficients are unchanged after embedding. However the other half, $(h_i^- + h_i^+)/2$ coefficients are used for embedding one, resulting in that $h_i^-/2$ coefficients are quantized to $i-1$ and $h_i^+/2$ coefficients to $i+1$. Alternatively, $h_{i-1}^+/2$ coefficients from the bin $i-1$ and $h_{i+1}^-/2$ coefficients from the bin $i+1$ are quantized to $i$ for embedding zero. With similar consideration, it is easily understood that the change shown in (1) holds true for any number $i$.

Eq. (1) indicates that if $h_i = h_{i-1}^+ + h_{i+1}^-$, then the number in the bin $i$ does not change. In particular for $i = 0, \pm 1$, however, much difference between $h_i$ and $h_{i-1}^+ + h_{i+1}^-$ causes the significant change on $h_i'$ after embedding. That is, since $h_0$ is usually larger than $h_1$ and $h_{-1}$, the most significant changes are decrease of $h_0$ and increase of $h_1$ and $h_{-1}$. Therefore a straightforward application of QIM in the DWT domain cannot be allowed for secure steganography against histogram-based attacks.

Now let us try to preserve $h_0$, $h_1$ and $h_{-1}$ after embedding. We introduce a dead zone for DWT coefficients $w$, $t_d^- < w < t_d^+$ ($-1 < t_d^- < 0 < t_d^+ < 1$) where DWT coefficients are not used for embedding. The number of positive DWT coefficients $N_d^+$ and that of negative coefficients $N_d^-$ in the dead zone are described as $N_d^+ = N(0 < w < t_d^+)$ and $N_d^- = N(t_d^- < w < 0)$, respectively. $t_d^+$ and $t_d^-$ are determined by optimum $N_d^+$ and $N_d^-$ values which minimize the histogram changes for the bins 0 and $\pm 1$.

By introducing the aforementioned dead zone, part of $h_0^+$ and $h_0^-$, i.e., $h_0^+ - N_d^+$ and $h_0^- - N_d^-$ are used for embedding, and therefore $h_0'$, $h_1'$ and $h_{-1}'$ become as follows.

$$h_0' = N_d^+ + N_d^- + \frac{1}{2}\{(h_0^+ - N_d^+) + (h_0^- - N_d^-)\} + \frac{1}{2}(h_{-1}^+ + h_1^-)$$

$$h_1' = \frac{1}{2}(h_1^- + h_1^+) + \frac{1}{2}\{(h_0^+ - N_d^+) + h_2^-\}$$

$$h_{-1}' = \frac{1}{2}(h_{-1}^- + h_{-1}^+) + \frac{1}{2}\{h_{-2}^+ + (h_0^- - N_d^-)\}$$

The optimum values for $N_d^+$ and $N_d^-$ can be derived by minimizing the sum of squared histogram changes over bin indices 0 and $\pm 1$, $\sum_{i=-1}^{1}(h_i - h_i')^2$. Note that in the proposed QIM-JPEG2000 steganography, quantized coefficients 0s cannot be treated as zeroes embedded in them, because they cannot be discriminated from 0s in the dead zone. Regarding this problem and its solution, see [6].

## 2.2   Histogram Preserving HM-JPEG2000 Steganography

Consider histogram matching at quantization step of DWT coefficients, assuming that the probabilities of zero and one are same in binary data to be embedded. Histogram matching is here considered separately for positive coefficient part and negative one, since there sometimes exists asymmetry between both parts. In the following, the matching for positive part is only described (negative part can be treated in the same way).

Two quantizers, $Q^0(w)$ and $Q^1(w)$ are prepared: the former used to embed zero and the latter to embed one.

$$Q^0(w) = \begin{cases} 0, & t_0^0 < w < t_1^0, \\ 2j + 0.5, & t_j^0 < w < t_{j+1}^0, \ j \in \{1, 2, \ldots\}, \end{cases} \tag{2}$$

$$Q^1(w) = 2j + 1.5, \ t_j^1 < w < t_{j+1}^1, \ j \in \{0, 1, 2, \ldots\}, \tag{3}$$

where $w$ is a positive DWT coefficient and $t_0^0 = t_0^1 = 0$. The decision threshold values $t_j^0, j \in \{1, 2, \ldots\}$ for $Q^0(w)$ are set so that they satisfy

$$\frac{1}{2}N(t_j^0 < w < t_{j+1}^0) = \begin{cases} h_0^+ & \text{for } j = 0 \\ h_{2j} & \text{for } j \in \{1, 2, \ldots\}, \end{cases} \tag{4}$$

where $N(t_j^0 < w < t_{j+1}^0)$ depicts the number of coefficients in the interval $t_j^0 < w < t_{j+1}^0$. Note that $1/2$ in (4) means that half of relevant coefficients are used for embedding zero and its number is adjusted to $h_0^+$ or $h_{2j}$ of cover image to preserve the histogram of cover image. The decision threshold values $t_j^1, j \in \{1, 2, \ldots\}$ for $Q^1(w)$ are similarly set as they satisfy

$$\frac{1}{2}N(t_j^1 < w < t_{j+1}^1) = h_{2j+1}, \ j \in \{0, 1, 2, \ldots\}. \tag{5}$$

From Eqs. (4) and (5), it is found that histogram preservation can be realized if $h_0^+ + \sum_{j=1}^{\infty} h_{2j} = \sum_{j=0}^{\infty} h_{2j+1} = N(0 < w < \infty)/2$ . The condition $h_0^+ + \sum_{j=1}^{\infty} h_{2j} = \sum_{j=0}^{\infty} h_{2j+1}$, i.e., $\sharp even = \sharp odd$ does not hold true in general. The relation $\sharp even > \sharp odd$ usually holds true, and in high frequency (low level) subbands, $\sharp even \gg \sharp odd$ because $h_0^+$ is much larger than others.

Consider how to match after-embedding histogram with before-embedding one under the relation of $\sharp even > \sharp odd$. We introduce a dead zone, $0 < w < t_d$ ($t_d < 1$) in which DWT coefficients are not used for embedding. $t_d$ is determined as it fulfills

$$N_d = N(0 < w < t_d) = \sharp even - \sharp odd. \tag{6}$$

Eq. (6) means that $\sharp odd$ is equal to $\sharp even$ with least $N_d$ coefficients removed. Then using $t_d$ and $N_d$, the decision threshold values $t_j^0, t_j^1, j \in \{1, 2, \ldots\}$ for $Q^0(w)$ and $Q^1(w)$ are set so that they satisfy

$$\frac{1}{2}N(t_d < w < t_1^0) = h_0^+ - N_d \tag{7}$$

$$\frac{1}{2}N(t_j^0 < w < t_{j+1}^0) = h_{2j}, \ j \in \{1, 2, \ldots\}, \tag{8}$$

$$\frac{1}{2}N(t_d < w < t_1^1) = h_1 \tag{9}$$

$$\frac{1}{2}N(t_j^1 < w < t_{j+1}^1) = h_{2j+1}, \ j \in \{1, 2, \ldots\}, \tag{10}$$

respectively. Eqs. (7) to (10) indicate that $\sharp odd$ and $\sharp even - N_d$ are equal to $N(t_d < w < \infty)/2$ and then histogram matching becomes possible.

## 3   Implementation of the Proposed JPEG2000 Steganography

JPEG2000 encoder consists of several fundamental components: pre-processing, DWT, quantization, arithmetic coding (tier-1 coding), and bit-stream organization (tier-2 coding) [11] (see the left part of Fig. 1). Pre-processing includes inter-component transformation for multi-component images, typically color images. After the DWT is applied to each component, wavelet coefficients are quantized uniformly with dead zone. The quantized wavelet coefficients are then bit-plane encoded by arithmetic coding. In JPEG2000, each subband of the wavelet transformed image is encoded independently of the other subbands. Furthermore, each subband is partitioned into small blocks called codeblocks, and each codeblock is independently encoded. The compressed data from the codeblocks are organized into units called packets and layers in tier-2 coding, where the bit-stream of each codeblock is truncated in an optimal way to minimize distortion subject to the constraint on bit rate. This rate-distortion optimization determines the optimal number of bit-planes for each codeblock under the given bit rate. That is, the true quantization step sizes for DWT coefficients are determined at the final stage of compression.

Considering the aforementioned feature of JPEG2000, data embedding by the proposed JPEG2000 steganography is decided to be performed after the arithmetic decoding in decoding process, where the optimal bit-plane structure and the true quantization step sizes for a given bit rate are available. The procedure for data embedding and extraction in the proposed JPEG2000 steganography is shown in Fig. 1. The proposed JPEG2000 steganography was implemented using JJ2000 Java software of JPEG2000 compression [12].

The entire process to embed data follows the solid line arrows shown in Fig. 1. An image is encoded into JPEG2000 bit-stream, whose size can be met almost exactly to a target bit rate. The JPEG2000 bit-stream is then decoded, but decoding is halted after the arithmetic decoding. At this point, given raw DWT coefficients and the true quantization step sizes, data embedding can be carried out using two quantizers. The quantized DWT coefficients modified by embedding are then subjected to JPEG2000 encoding again, which produces secret-data-embedded JPEG2000 bit-stream.

The data extraction procedure follows the dashed arrows in the middle part of Fig. 1. JPEG2000 decoding of the secret-data-embedded bit-stream starts from bit-stream unorganization and is halted after the arithmetic decoding. At this point, extraction of secret data is carried out using the quantized DWT coefficients.

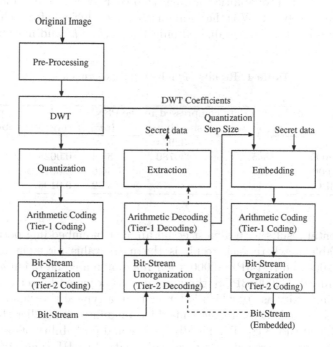

**Fig. 1.** A flowchart of data embedding and extraction in the proposed JPEG2000 steganography

## 4  Experiments

The proposed QIM-JPEG2000 and HM-JPEG2000 were evaluated comparing with JPEG2000-BPCS steganography [8], which is the first JPEG2000 stegano-graphic method proposed by us. JPEG2000-BPCS embeds data into complex blocks in the least significant bit-planes of quantized DWT coefficients. The complexity of each block can be measured and it is used to determine whether the block is complex enough to embed data. These three methods were tested using eight standard images: Lena, Barbara, Mandrill, Airplane, Boat, Goldhill, Peppers, and Zelda. These images are 512 × 512 pixels in size, 8 bit per pixel (bpp) gray images, and were compressed with 1 bpp as the before-embedding target bit rate.

The histogram change can be measured by Kullback-Leibler divergence, which is defined as

$$D_{KL} = \sum_i P_i \log \frac{P_i}{P_i'}$$
$$= \sum_i \frac{h_i}{N} \log \frac{h_i}{h_i'}, \tag{11}$$

where $P_i$ and $P_i'$ are probabilities of quantized coefficient $i$ before and after embedding, respectively, and $N$ is the total number of coefficients for each frequency subband. Here Eq. (11) was evaluated only for nonzero $h_i$ and nonzero $h_i'$.

**Table 1.** Results of embedding experiments

| method | embedded data size (bytes) | compressed image size (bytes) | PSNR (dB) | KL divergence | prob. of embedding (%) |
|---|---|---|---|---|---|
| (no embedding) | - | 32974 | 38.0 | - | 1.4 |
| QIM-JPEG2000 | 3855 | 39780 | 35.4 | 0.0028 | 0.8 |
| HM-JPEG2000 | 3781 | 39919 | 34.6 | 0.0012 | 1.2 |
| JPEG2000-BPCS | 3711 | 39315 | 35.2 | 0.0106 | 26.8 |

Experimental results with almost equal amount of embedding performed are shown in Table 1, where each result is the mean value for eight images. For QIM-JPEG2000 and HM-JPEG2000, their maximum amount of embedding was performed. In JPEG2000-BPCS, the amount was adjusted by setting a threshold of the complexity as 10, which is larger than a typical threshold value 8 for $4 \times 4$ block size, and therefore the embedded amount was smaller than that in usual JPEG2000-BPCS [8]. The KL divergence and probability of embedding in the table are those averaged over three subbands (LH, HL, and HH subband) of third-level in five-level wavelet transform used. The third-level subbands are here selected considering the balance between the total number of DWT coefficients and the number of non-zero DWT coefficients in a subband. That is, in a higher level subband, the total number of coefficients is smaller and therefore its histogram is less reliable, and in a lower level subband, the number of non-zero coefficients is smaller. The KL divergence value for JPEG2000-BPCS is much larger than those for QIM-JPEG2000 and HM-JPEG2000. Smaller KL divergence values represent better histogram preservation. Regarding histogram preservation, HM-JPEG2000 is the best as is expected, but in terms of quality (PSNR value) of stego image, it is the worst. The probability of embedding [2] is a measure related with the chi-square attack to steganography based on the least significant bit (LSB) flipping, i.e., the probability of chi-square statistic under the condition that the LSB flipping is applied. It could be concluded that the chi-square attack cannot work for the proposed methods but it may possibly detect the embedding by JPEG2000-BPCS.

## 5  Conclusions

Two JPEG2000 steganographic methods, QIM-JPEG2000 and HM-JPEG2000 have been presented. QIM-JPEG2000 is a histogram quasi-preserving method using QIM with a dead zone and HM-JPEG2000 is a histogram preserving method based on histogram matching using two quantizers with a dead zone. Comparing with JPEG2000-BPCS steganography, the two methods show better histogram preservation. It is also shown that the chi-square attack cannot work for the proposed methods. The proposed methods are promising candidates for secure JPEG2000 steganography against histogram-based steganalysis.

## References

1. Upham D.: (1997) http://ftp.funet.fi/pub/crypt/cypherpunks/steganography/jsteg/
2. Westfeld A.: F5 - A steganographic algorithm: high capacity despite better steganalysis. Lecture Notes in Computer Science, Vol.2137 (2001) 289-302
3. Provos N.: Defending against statistical steganalysis. 10th USENIX Security Symposium (2001)
4. Eggers J.J., Bauml R., Girod B.: A communications approach to image steganography. Proceedings of SPIE, Vol.4675 (2002) 26-37
5. Sallee F.: Model-based steganography. Lecture Notes in Computer Science, Vol.2939 (2004) 154-167
6. Noda H., Niimi M., Kawaguchi E.: High performance JPEG steganography using quantization index modulation in DCT domain. Pattern Recognition Letters **27** (2006) 455-461
7. Fridrich J., Goljan M., Hogea D.: New methodology for breaking steganographic techniques for JPEGs. Proceedings of SPIE, Vol.5020 (2003) 143-155
8. Noda H., Spaulding J., Shirazi M.N., Kawaguchi E.: Application of bit-plane decomposition steganography to JPEG2000 encoded images. IEEE Signal Processing Letters **9**(12) (2002) 410-413
9. Su P.C., Kuo C.C.J.: Steganography in JPEG2000 compressed images. IEEE Trans. on Consumer Electronics **49**(4) (2003) 824-832
10. Chen B., Wornell G.W.: Quantization index modulation: A class of provably good methods for digital watermarking and information embedding. IEEE Trans. on Information Theory **47**(4) (2001) 1423-1443
11. Rabbani M., Joshi R.: An overview of JPEG 2000 still image compression standard. Signal Processing: Image Communication **17** (2002) 3-48
12. JJ2000 website. http://jj2000.epfl.ch/index.html

# Perceptual Depth Estimation from a Single 2D Image Based on Visual Perception Theory

Li Bing, Xu De, Feng Songhe, Wu Aimin, and Yang Xu

Institute of Computer Science, Beijing Jiaotong University, Beijing, China, 100044
binggege@people.com.cn, xd@computer.njtu.edu.cn,
Songhe_Feng@163.com, wuaimin@sohu.com, yangxubj@126.com

**Abstract.** The depth of image is conventionally defined as the distance between the corresponding scene point of the image and the pinhole of the camera, which is not harmony with the depth perception of human vision. In this paper we define a new perceptual depth of image which is perceived by human vision. The traditional computation models of image depth are all based on the physical imaging model, which ignore the human depth perception. This paper presents a novel computation model based on the visual perception theory. In this approach, we can get the relative perceptual depth from a single 2-D image. Experimental results show that our model is effective and corresponds to the human perception.

## 1 Introduction

The depth information of a scene is very important in computer vision. It is a useful clue, for instance, for the purpose of object recognition and scene interpretation. The traditional definition of the depth of a visible surface is the distance from the surface to the camera. i.e., it is the distance between the surface to the thin convex lens[1]. This definition is not harmony with the human depth perception, thus we redefine a perceptual depth conception based on the visual perception in this paper.

So far, various methods for depth estimation have been proposed. The method of stereopsis [2] is most popular of them. In this method, the same scene is imaged by two different cameras at two different positions. And then we can get the depth from the binocular disparity. In addition to this method, researchers have used the camera focus for depth recovery, which is called depth-from-focus (DFF) method [1, 3, 4, 5]. This method is based on the defocus and blurring in the image to determine its depth. Besides these, A. Torralba and A. Oliva proposed another depth estimation algorithm called depth estimation from image structure [6], which is based on the whole scene structure that does not rely on specific objects. In these methods, some just use a single 2-D image to estimate the depth [1, 6, 7]. Depth estimation from a single image is simple and more usually used in many situations. In our method, we also only use a single image.

All these depth estimation methods are only derivate from physical image model, which neglect the depth perception of human beings. The depth of image is just the depth which human perceive from the image. In this paper, a depth estimation model

Y. Zhuang et al. (Eds.): PCM 2006, LNCS 4261, pp. 88–95, 2006.

based on visual perception theory is proposed. Both the physical imaging process and the human depth perception are considered in our model.

This paper is organized as follows. In Section 2, some principles about depth perception in visual perception theory is described. Then we propose the definition of perceptual depth and computable model of depth estimation based on visual perception theory in section 3. The experimental results using this model are presented in Section 4. Section 5 concludes this paper.

## 2 Some Depth Perception Theories

In this paper, we mainly use two theories in the visual psychology. One is depth perception theory and the other is the size constancy theory. The two theories are discovered by psychologists long before. We will discuss these theories in the follow sections.

### 2.1 Depth Perception

Human beings always perceive the depth correctly and quickly. How do human beings get the depth from the images on their retinas? According to scientific researches, visual psychologists have concluded five main clues for the depth perception: binocular disparity, convergence, motion parallax, accommodation, and pictorial cues. [8]

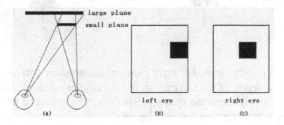

**Fig. 1.** Example of binocular disparity: because the two planes have different distances from the observer, the images on retinas are different. (A) is the image on the left retina; (B) is the image on the right retina.

Fig. 1 shows an example of the binocular disparity. The vision system can estimate the depth according to the disparity of the two images. If the images in two eyes are same, it means that the large plane and the small plane are on a same plane. The convergence, motion parallax and accommodation factors are illustrated as Fig. 2.

The four factors above are so important for depth perception, but they all have less, even no, use when observer looks at a single 2-D image. Depths still can be perceived by human in certain conditions. In this situation, the pictorial cues play a key role. What are pictorial cues? Pictorial cues include perspective, shade, and occlusion and so on. Generally, all the depth cues like these in the image are called pictorial cues [8]. If there is no pictorial cue; human beings can perceive nothing about depth from a single 2-D image. So pictorial cues are necessary for depth estimation from a single image. Different pictorial cue gives us different depth perception. Consequently, our depth estimation method just uses the real ground cue in the image. Fig.3 shows an example about different pictorial cues.

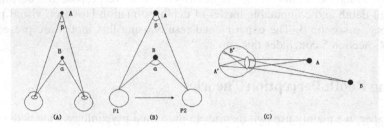

**Fig. 2.** Three factors of depth perception: (A) shows convergence factor. The two eyes converge at a certain point: angle α is larger than angle β because of the different depths. (B) describes the factor of motion parallax. Point A is farther than point from the observer. When the observer moves from P1 to P2, the change angles of the two points are α and β, α is obviously larger than β. Accommodation factor is shown in picture (C).When the observer stares at A, point B, which is father than point A, is blurry in human eyes.

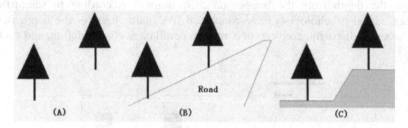

**Fig. 3.** Example about pictorial cues: Different pictorial cue gives us different depth perception. We have no idea about depths of the two trees in (A) because of no cue of image. The two trees have different depths in (B) due to the road's perspective. The depths of the two trees we perceived in (C) are same, but they have different heights.

## 2.2 Perceptual Size Constancy

Our perception of objects is far more constant or stable than our retinal images. Retinal images change with the movement of the eyes, the head and our position, together with changing light. If we relied only on retinal images for visual perception we would always be conscious of people growing physically bigger when they came closer, objects changing their shapes whenever we moved, and colors changing with every shift in lighting conditions. Counteracting the chaos of constant change in retinal images, the visual properties of objects tend to remain constant in consciousness. This phenomenon is called perceptual constancy in visual psychology theory. Psychologists classified the perceptual constancy into four categories: color constancy, brightness constancy, size constancy and shape constancy [9, 10].

The size constancy is playing a key role in human vision in recognizing objects. Psychologists have discovered computation theory of size constancy [8]. They have got an expression to compute the perceptual size as:

$$S = k \times A \times D \tag{1}$$

where S is the object's perceptual size, A is the angle of view, D is the perceptual depth of object, k is the zoom coefficient of human eyes or camera, it keep invariable in a certain imaging process. The angle of view A can be represented by the size of object in the image.

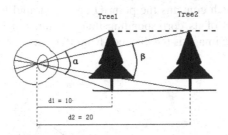

**Fig. 4.** Example of computation of size constancy: The images of two trees in human retina have different heights. Tree 1's image is higher than tree 2's in the retina, but the heights which human perceive are same.

Fig. 4 shows an example of the computation theory of the size constancy. The view angles of the two trees are $\alpha$ and $\beta$. The view angle can be represented by the size of object in the image. We define the sizes of the trees in the image as $S_1$ and $S_2$. In addition, according to the pinhole imaging model, the size of the object in image is in inverse proportion to the distance between the object and the observer. From equation (1), we can compute the perceptual size of the two trees, we define the perceptual size of the two trees are PS$_1$ and PS$_2$, the relationship between $PS_1$ and $PS_2$ is as follow

$$\frac{PS1}{PS2} = \frac{k \times \alpha \times d_1}{k \times \beta \times d_2} = \frac{\alpha}{\beta} \times \frac{d_1}{d_2} = 1 \tag{2}$$

From the computation of the size constancy, we find the perceptual size of tree1 is equal to the perceptual size of tree2. Although they have different size images on human retina, the sizes human perceive are same.

## 3 Perceptual Depth Estimation

In this section, we mainly discuss the depth estimation method. But above all, we define a novel image depth called perceptual depth (PD) based on the visual perception theory.

### 3.1 Definition of Perceptual Depth

The traditional definition of image depth is not harmony with human depth perception. According to visual cognition theory and our common sense, human vision perceives the distance from the foot of object to human foot (foot-to-foot), rather than from other parts of the object to human eye, as the depth of this object, because the ground supporting feet of objects is the most important reference surface for depth perception of human vision [11]. In fig.5, the scene points P' and Q' have the same depths, because they have a same foot. All the points on a same straight line on the ground, which is parallel to the image plane, will be perceived as the same depth, just like line $L_1$ and $L_2$ in the Fig. 5. Consequently, we define the distance from the scene point to the plane, which contains the point O and is parallel to the Image Plane, as Perceptual Depth (PD) of its corresponding image point. For instance, in Fig.5, the PD of the point p in the image is the distance from P' to E.

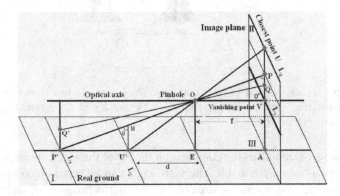

**Fig. 5.** The pinhole imaging model with real ground: O is the pinhole, f is the focus distance. Image plane is vertical with the real ground plane.

## 3.2 Perceptual Depth Estimation

We will use the geometrical optics knowledge and the visual perception theory to estimate the perceptual depth. Fig.5 shows the pinhole imaging model with real ground. P' and U', which images are P and U relatively, are on the ground. In the image, U' is the nearest point to the pinhole. The distance between U' and E is d. The horizon (vanishing line) between the real ground and the real sky surely projects along the optical axis onto the image plane, and form the image line $L_3$, which must be parallel to the real ground plane, as shown in Fig.5. O' must be the center point in the image.

According to physical imaging process, line $P'U'$ and $U'M$ have a same image in the image plane, that is $PU$. We denote length of line $PU$ as $h$. According to the equation (1), the perceptual size of $U'M$, which is noted as $PS_1$, can be obtained as:

$$PS_1 = k \times |PU| \times |U'E| = k \times h \times d \tag{3}$$

And then we denote the perceptual size of $P'U'$ as $PS_2$, according to the geometrical relation, we can compute $PS_2$ as follow:

$$PS_2 = PS_1 \times \tan \theta \tag{4}$$

where $\theta$ is $\angle P'MU'$, which is equal to $\angle OPO'$. And tan $\angle OPO'$ can be computed as follow according to geometry:

$$\tan\theta = \tan\angle OPO' = \frac{OO'}{|PO'|} = \frac{f}{|PO'|} \qquad (5)$$

where $f$ is the focus distance. Because O' is the center of the image and $|PU|=h$, suppose the height of image is $H$, so $|PO'|=H/2 - h$. And in equation (3), if $k=1/f$, $PS_1$ is just the real size of $U'M$. Consequently, let $k=1/f,$, we can get $PS_2$ form (3), (4) and (5) as follow:

$$PS_2 = k \times h \times d \times \frac{f}{|PO'|} = \frac{1}{f} \times h \times d \times \frac{f}{H/2 - h} = \frac{h}{H/2 - h} \times d \qquad (6)$$

Suppose the Y-coordinate of point $P$ in the image is $P_y$, and pixel is used as the unit of $H$, h and $P_y$. Then h can be expressed as $(H - P_y)$. The perceptual depth of P' in Fig. 5 is denoted as PD, which can be described as follow:

$$PD = PS_2 + |U'E| = \frac{h}{H/2 - h} \times d + d = \frac{H/2}{H/2 - h} \times d = \frac{H}{2P_y - H} \times d \quad (H/2 < P_y < H) \qquad (7)$$

From equation (7), image height H and Y-coordinate of $P$ can be easily obtained from an image. If knowing the depth of closest point $U'$ that is d in the equation or any point's distance in the ground, we can compute the perceptual depth of any point in the real ground. And the depths of objects can be obtained through its referenced foot on the ground. If d is not known, the relative depth of each point can be computed by equation (7) using d as the unit. So given a single 2-D image, we can obtain the depths easily form equation (7).

## 4  Experimental Results

We use our method to estimate the *PD* in the follow 2 images and measure the real data to check our method. The detail experiment data is shown in the table 1.

(A)                                                          (B)

**Fig. 6.** Estimate the PD of trees in the two images: The number of tree becomes bigger from nearness to farness in the two images. The nearest right tree in (A) is 1st, the farthest tree is 7th. The nearest right tree in (B) is 1st, the farthest one is 8th.

**Table 1.** The height and width of the two images are 2048 and 1480 relatively. CPD is the distance of the closest point, RPD is the relative perceptural depth; PD is perceptual depth, which is computed by our method; RD is real depth that is obtained by measurement; RE is relative error and ARE is average of relative error.

| Image | Object | CPD (m) | $P_y$ (pixle) | RPD | PD (m) | RD | RE | ARE |
|-------|--------|---------|---------------|-----|--------|-----|------|-----|
| Fig.7 (A) | 1$^{st}$ tree | 2.9 | 1070 | 2.242 | 6.503 | 7 | 7.1% | 14.95% |
| | 2$^{nd}$ tree | 2.9 | 935 | 3.795 | 11.005 | 11.9 | 7.52% | |
| | 3$^{rd}$ tree | 2.9 | 872 | 5.606 | 16.258 | 16.9 | 3.80% | |
| | 4$^{th}$ tree | 2.9 | 832 | 8.044 | 23.326 | 21.9 | 6.51% | |
| | 5$^{th}$ tree | 2.9 | 811 | 10.423 | 30.225 | 26.8 | 12.78% | |
| | 6$^{th}$ tree | 2.9 | 793 | 13.962 | 40.491 | 31.7 | 27.73% | |
| | 7$^{th}$ tree | 2.9 | 782 | 17.619 | 51.095 | 36.7 | 39.22% | |
| Fig.7 (B) | 1$^{st}$ tree | 3.9 | 1130 | 1.897 | 7.398 | 7.4 | 0.00% | 3.51% |
| | 2$^{nd}$ tree | 3.9 | 953 | 3.474 | 13.549 | 13.6 | 3.72% | |
| | 3$^{rd}$ tree | 3.9 | 884 | 5.139 | 20.042 | 20.0 | 2.08% | |
| | 4$^{th}$ tree | 3.9 | 849 | 6.789 | 26.477 | 26.0 | 1.83% | |
| | 5$^{th}$ tree | 3.9 | 810 | 10.571 | 41.229 | 40.3 | 2.30% | |
| | 6$^{th}$ tree | 3.9 | 799 | 12.542 | 48.915 | 46.3 | 5.65% | |
| | 7$^{th}$ tree | 3.9 | 790 | 14.800 | 57.720 | 54.3 | 6.30% | |
| | 8$^{th}$ tree | 3.9 | 785 | 16.444 | 64.133 | 60.4 | 6.18% | |

From the table 1, comparison of the real value with the perceptual depth is shown in Fig. 7. We can safely draw a conclusion that the farther is the object from the observer, the larger is the relative error. This conclusion is also consistent with human visual perception. In fact, if the object is far enough, human beings also can't perceive the depth accurately.

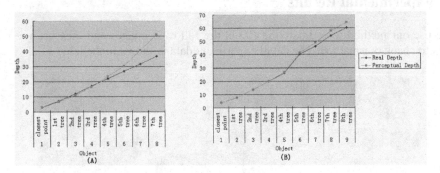

**Fig. 7.** The change curves of the two experiments: (A) is the curve of Fig.6(A); (B) is the change curve of Fig.6(B)

The two charts in Fig.7 show that relative error in image (A) is larger than image (B). The reason is that optical axis of the camera is not completely horizontal in image (A). From our many experiments, we find the perceptual depth we estimate is relative accurate in the condition that the angle made by optical axis of camera and horizon is between -30 degrees and 30 degrees. That means in this range, our method can be used effectively. The greatest strongpoint of our method is that only one image and no priori information is needed. The computation in our method is also simple and the parameters are easily to obtain.

## 5 Conclusion

Image depth is a very important clue in computer vision. In this paper, deriving from human visual perception, we give a new definition of image depth (PD). The visual perception theory is continuously used to obtain the computation of the perceptual depth. This depth estimation method is simple, quick, general and effective, which has an extensive use. From beginning to end, both the physical model and human perception are considered. We tentatively introduce the depth perception into the computer vision and get an effective depth estimation method. It is maybe a novel effective way to solve some problems in CV with visual perception theory.

## References

1. Lai Shang-Hong, Fu Chang-Wu, Chang Shyang: A Generalized Depth Estimation Algorithm With a Single Image. IEEE Trans. on Pattern Analysis and Machine Intelligence (1992) 405 – 411.
2. Songde Ma, Zhengyou Zhang: Computer vision. Science Press, China (1998) 52-93.
3. P. Grossmann: Depth from Focus. Patt. Recogn. Lett. (1987) Vol. 5, 63-69
4. A. N. Rajagopalan, S. Chuandhuri, Uma Mudenagudi: Depth Estimation and Image Restoration Using Defocused Stereo Pairs. IEEE Trans. On Pattern Analysis and Machine Intelligence (2004) 1521-1525.
5. P. Favaro, S. Soatto: A Geometric Approach to Shape from Defocus. IEEE Trans. on Pattern Analysis and Machine Intelligence (2005) 406 - 417 .
6. A. Torralba, A. Oliva: Depth Estimation from Image Structure. IEEE Trans. on Pattern Analysis and Machine Intelligence(2002) 1226-1238.
7. D. Jelinek, C. J. Taylor: Reconstruction of Linearly parameterized Models from Single Images with a Camera of Unknown Focal Length. IEEE Trans. On Pattern Analysis and Machine Intelligence (2002) 1226-1238
8. I. Rock: Perception. Scientific American Books, Inc. (1984).
9. Qigang Gao: A Computation Model for Understanding Three-Dimensional View Space. IEEE conf. on ICSMC(1996) 941-946.
10. Qigang Gao, Andrew K. C. Wong, Shang-Hua Wang: Estimating Face-pose Consistency Based on Synthetic View Space. IEEE Trans. on system, man, cybernetics(1998) 1191-1199.
11. J.J. Gibson: The Ecological Approach to Visual Perception. Boston, Houghton Mifflin (1979) 156-164.

# A System for Generating Personalized Virtual News

Jian-Jun Xu, Jun Wen, Dan-Wen Chen, Yu-Xiang Xie, and Ling-Da Wu

Center for Multimedia Technology, National University of Defense Technology, Changsha,
410073, China
{jianjunxu, junwen, dwchen, yxxie, wld}@nudt.edu.cn

**Abstract.** To improve the degree of immersion for strategic situation representation in strategic war gaming, the concept of virtual news and automatic generation model are presented in this paper. Via analyzing characteristic of news video, the design and generation algorithm for virtual news narrative template are given, which borrow the idea of Natural Language Process and combine the specialties of news video. And the narrative template revise algorithm is also proposed based on time constraints. Virtual News is automatically generated driven by virtual news narrative template, which retrieving relative news segments in multimedia database and selecting appropriate representation method based on the model- EEDU (Extended Entity-Description-Utility). This approach can generate virtual news according to text description about strategic situation provided by users, and furthermore provide personalized service for decision-makers. Finally, experiment results are used to indicate the validity of our system.

## 1 Introduction

News is new information about some subjects which the public has interest in. It has the characteristic of specialties, novelty, and interests and so on [1]. But virtual news is not real news edited by TV stations and generated to represent strategic situation according to the strategic war gaming simulation course of some round. Its goal is to show the cause and effect of news event streams happened during some periods of simulation for decision maker. It is organized based on the collected and processed news information materials.

PERSEUS project [8] creates personalized multimedia news portals, which provides relevant information, selected from newswire sites on the Internet and augmented by video clips automatically extracted from TV broadcasts. A personalized video story generation approach [2] based on the user's interests is presented, but these systems above does not consider the narration in news and virtual news representation style. A framework [4] for home movie making is presented and implemented, where there are essentially three phases to make film. (1) Storyboarding: Entails the selection of a narrative template, a decision as to the intent of the production, and the resulting automatic generation of a storyboard. (2) Directing: Footage is actually captured, according to the generated storyboard of phase 1. (3)Editing: The captured footage is assembled into the final film according to the storyboard. The approach in [4] provides a workflow for film making but it is not appropriate for our work. Because

Y. Zhuang et al. (Eds.): PCM 2006, LNCS 4261, pp. 96–105, 2006.

the time for decision making between rounds in strategic simulation is restricted, it's impossible to take a long time to go to the locale to capture and create relative materials for our purposes. Therefore the collected, existed and processed news video, picture, audio must be utilized fully in our system.

Considering the characteristic of strategic simulation virtual news has following specialty: (1) Fast generation. Because of the continuity and pressure of strategic simulation process, virtual news must be generated quickly so that decision makers can understand the changing situation in time. (2) Time constraints. The length of generated virtual news is about 15 minutes and cannot be too long to affect the process of strategic simulation. Automatic generation of virtual news is driven by the strategic situation description text documents like news report provided by users and the length of these documents is different. These documents introduce the content of some event in detail and the audio track of virtual news video is created by speech systemization engine based on documents. If all the content of one document is read by anchor, the synthesized speech will be too long for the final generated virtual news video. So the important task of our system is to process the text documents based on time constraints of strategic simulation.

The following parts of this paper are organized as follows: Section2 gives our system an overview. Section 3 introduces the automatic generation of virtual news narrative template and implementation algorithm. And the method for virtual news template revision based on time constraints is presented. In section 4, we discuss the multimedia materials retrieval model—EEDU and representation style for virtual news. In the section 5 the experiment result is given. At last, in section 6, we draw conclusion for our system and give some ideas to improve the system in the future.

## 2   System Architecture of Virtual News Generation

An overview of the implemented system architecture can be seen in Fig.1. Generally speaking, the system includes the main 3 phases: automatic generation of virtual news narrative template, multimedia materials retrieval and virtual news video generation (as shown in grey block). The specific block diagram of our system is as follows:

(1) User provides a set of news description documents like internet news report about some event;
(2) Analyze text document sequentially and generate news heading, anchor commentary, time and so on for each news document;
(3) Generate virtual news narrative template using processed text document with news heading, announcement commentary, time etc;
(4) Revise the narrative template based on time constraints until satisfy condition of time restriction. The computing of time lies on the length of the synthesized speech of anchor commentary in template.
(5) Search appropriate media materials driven by narrative template based on model EEDU and select appropriate representation style for virtual news;
(6) Synthesize media materials and generate virtual news video for decision-makers.

The approach for representing situation via virtual news is like telling stories to decision makers and show the effect and cause of an event clearly, which will be great help for decision makers.

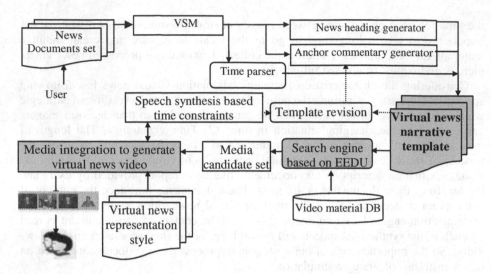

**Fig. 1.** The block diagram of generating virtual news automatically

## 3  Automatic Generation of Virtual News Narrative Template

### 3.1  Establishment of Virtual News Narrative Template

Considering the criterion of news report video like CCTV news, we establish the following virtual news narrative template to represent the virtual news for satisfying the needs of user:

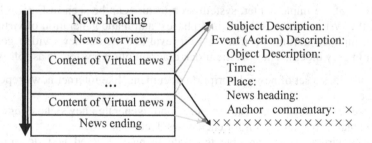

**Fig. 2.** Fig2 (a) shows the virtual news narrative template, and Fig2 (b) the specific content format for the k$^{th}$ virtual news

News heading →news overview →content representation of the first news →…→content representation of the *n*th news→ news ending (Fig.2(a)). From Fig.2 (a) it shows that there many virtual news in a template. And each virtual news has its own description format including subject description, object description, time, place, event, action, anchor commentary about news (Fig.2 (b)). The description format of each virtual news content embodies many essential elements of news report, such as Who, When, Where, What, How and so on. Virtual news narrative template is the base for generating virtual news, which not only provides standard format, but also is the key part for retrieving relative media materials.

## 3.2 Automatic Generation of Virtual News Narrative Template

The goal of this phase is to generate the virtual news narrative template from a set of documents about a subject provided by user. The elements of each virtual news in narrative template can be extracted by information extraction technology combing with technology of natural language process (NLP). The tasks of creating virtual news narrative template include automatic generation of time, place, anchor commentary and news heading from documents etc.

(1) Time extraction
Time is one of the most important elements in news report, which represents the time that an event happens. The standard time format in this paper is defined as follows: time= yyyy-MM-dd-hh-mm-ss. There are three kinds of time: (1) Absolute time. It is easy to convert this kind of time into the standard format, such as "2008□ 9□ 1□" in Chinese can be converted into the following standard time format: 2008-09-01-00-00-00; (2) Relative time. Relative time can be obtained by extracting or setting some time reference point in document; (3) Fuzzy time. Because it is fuzzy there is no way transforming this kind of time into standard time format. For example, "few day ago". This kind of time will be processed manually.

Because time of strategic simulation is often virtual and not relative to real time, attributes of documents such as the latest modified time and creation time cannot be used for time extract. We achieve time by the time mark tagged during the words segmentation in a document. And each round of strategic simulation has its own virtual time interval. Assume that the interval of the $J$th round is $\left[time_b^J, time_e^J\right]$, if the extracted time is not in the interval, time will be designated manually. The case of place extraction is like time.

(2) Anchor commentary extraction
Anchor commentary in narrative template is important element for introducing news content in detail, which will be read by anchors. Anchor commentary extraction is implemented like news abstraction generation. Our approach uses conventional vector space model to represent documents. Each document is represented by a vector of weighted terms. Document, paragraphs, and sentences in paragraph are represents term vector with the same length. And the similarity between document and paragraph, paragraph and sentence are computed by cosine distance. The relative concept definition of algorithm for anchor commentary extraction and detailed algorithm description are defined as allows:

**Definiton 1.** Let $T$ denote a document, and let $V(T) = (W_1, W_2, \cdots, W_K)$ denote term's weight vector for document $T$, $W_i$ represents the $i$ th term's weight. For weight of term in body of document $T$, we use traditional "ltc" version of the $tf \cdot idf$ scheme [3].

**Definiton 2.** Let $P_i$ denote a paragraph in document $T$. $V(P_i) = (W_{i1}, W_{i2}, \cdots, W_{ik})$ denote term's weight vector in $P_i$, where $W_{ij}$ represents the $j$ th term's weight in the $i$ th paragraph.

**Definiton 3.** Let $S_{ij}$ denote the $j$ th sentence in the $i$ th paragraph in document $T$ , $V(S_{ij}) = (W_{ij1}, W_{ij2}, \cdots, W_{ijk})$ denote term's weight vector in $S_{ij}$ , where $W_{ijm}$ represents the weight of the $m$ th term.

**Definiton 4.** The similarity between paragraph $P_i$ and document $T$ is define

as: $S(P_i,T) = \dfrac{V(P_i) \bullet V(T)}{|V(P_i)| \bullet |V(T)|}$ ,where $V(P_i) \bullet V(T) = \sum\limits_{j=1}^{k} W_{ij} \times W_j$ , $W_{ij} \in V(P_i)$ , $W_j \in V(T)$ ,

$|V(P_u)| = \left( W_{i1}^2 + W_{i2}^2 + \cdots + W_{ik}^2 \right)^{\frac{1}{2}}$ , $|V(T)| = \left( W_1^2 + W_2^2 + \cdots + W_k^2 \right)^{\frac{1}{2}}$ .

**Definiton 5.** The similarity between sentence $S_{ij}$ and paragraph $P_i$ is defined as:

$S(S_{ij},P_i) = \dfrac{V(S_{ij}) \bullet V(P_i)}{|V(S_{ij}) \bullet V(P_i)|}$ , where $W_{ijm} \in V(S_{ij})$, $W_{im} \in V(P_i)$.

**Algorithm 1.** The extraction algorithm of anchor commentary is described in detail as follows:

   Step1: Construct term vector $V(T)$ for a given input document $T$;
   Step2: Extract all paragraphs for a document and construct term vector $V(P_i)$ for each paragraph;
   Step3: Compute similarity between each paragraph and document by formula $S(P_i,T)$;
   Step4: If $S(P_i,T) > \theta$(predefined threshold, 0.65)☐$P_i$ is considered as a subject paragraph. First and last paragraph are processed as subject paragraph no matter what the similarity is more than threshold;
   Step5: Construct term vector $V(S_{ij})$ for each sentence in subject paragraph;
   Step6: Computing the similarity $S(S_{ij},P_i)$ between each sentence $S_{ij}$ in subject paragraph $i$ and paragraph $i$;
   Step7: Sentences of subject paragraph are ordered by descend based on $S(S_{ij}, Pi)$. The sentences with higher similarity $S(S_{ij},P_i)$ is selected as subject sentence. In this paper the sentence selection ratio is 0.3, which will be adjusted based on time constraints discussed in next section;
   Step8: All sentences labeled as subject sentence in document are organized as a rough commentary according to the sentence's sequence in original document.

   After all subject sentences are extracted, we use sentence parser approach [5] to extract syntactical structures to fill the narrative template.

### 3.3   Virtual News Template Revision Based on Time Constraints

To satisfy the requirements of the characteristic of time constraints between the rounds of strategic simulation, the revision method based on time reduction for each virtual news is adopted in this paper. It mainly reduces the length of anchor commentary because the anchor speech is created by speech synthesize engine and the synthesized speech's time must fulfill the time constraints. Suppose the total time of virtual news is $L$ minutes, there is $N$ news, denoted as $VN = \{VN_1, \cdots, VN_N\}$. Assume that the synthesized time is $L_k$ corresponding to the $k^{th}$ virtual news's anchor commentary. To satisfy the condition $\sum_{i=1}^{N} L_i \leq L$, time reduction method must be adopted to revise the virtual news narrative template. There are two kinds of tactics for time reduction: average tactics and importance tactics. Our system uses the average tactics as default and allows user to select appropriate time reduction tactics.

(1)Average tactics
Average tactics means that all virtual news in template is of the same importance. So the time assigned for introducing the news content is identical. First scan the virtual news sequentially. Then compute the time of synthesized speech for anchor commentary. If time is more than average time, we use algorithm1 to generate anchor commentary again and reduce the number of selected subject sentences until satisfy the time constraints.

(2) Importance tactics
All news is ordered by its importance and urgency. The more important and urgent virtual news is, the more possibility of keeping original length of anchor commentary. We use the principle of top $n$, which computing the maximum value of $i$ satisfying the condition $\sum_{i=1}^{n} L_i \succ L$.

## 4   Generation of Virtual News Based on Narrative Template

Narrative template is the most important part in automatic generation of virtual news. It describes the whole virtual news along timeline and introduces the content for each virtual news in detail. And it is also the base of the following process, such as the retrieval of media materials relative to news.

### 4.1  Multimedia Materials Retrieval Based on EEDU Model

We propose a multimedia retrieval model – EEDU by extending the EDU model, which is the abbreviation of Extended Entity-Description-Utility (Ref Fig.3). Some concepts used in EEDU will be introduced next.

(1) **Entity Space.** Entity space includes many kinds of entities from videos, images, audios or graphics. The so-called entity is the existence in multimedia. It can be notional, or physical. Take video for example, from top to bottom, we regard all video files, stories, scenes, shots and frames as entities. Entities at different levels form the structure of videos, and each entity has its attributes and predications. Entity is, in fact, a subset of videos, images, audios and graphics□which can be temporal or spatial. Supposing a video segment containing N shots, then the $k^{th}$ shot can be described in this way: $Shot_k = \{f_s \in P(f) \mid start(k) \leq f_s \leq end(k)\}, k \in [1, N]$,Where $f_s$ is a frame, $P(f)$ is the set of all frames, $start(k)$ and $end(k)$ is the start and the end frame number of shot $k$ respectively.

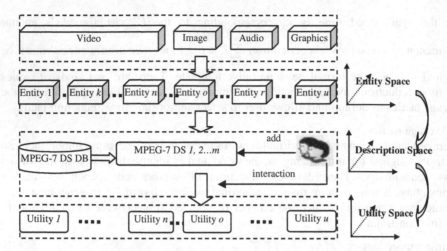

**Fig. 3.** Search Engine based on EEDU (Extended Entity-Description-Utility)

**(2) Description Space.** Description is the abstract and general explanation of an entity. Different from the original information, description is the processed and extracted information, which can be more understandable. Description space is the set of descriptions. Here we use the description schema (DS) in MPEG-7 to describe the content of an entity. For example, SemanticTime DS, SemanticPlace DS, Event DS, Object DS, Face DS etc at the conceptual layer are used.

Different levels of entities have different descriptions. The description of an entity is formed from several descriptors. For example, entity $E_k$ can be described as follows: $D_{E_k} = \{d_{k1}, d_{k2}, d_{k3}, ...\}$, Where $d_{k1}$, $d_{k2}$, $d_{k3}$, ... are descriptors of the entity. Users can add descriptors to the entity.

**(3) Utility Space.** Utility is the contribution of an entity. In other words, it explains how much work the entity does in representing some concept. We use descriptions of each entity to evaluate the utility. And by the utility function, we can get a series of utilities. Based on these utilities, we can finally select entity with highest utility.

Generating utility from descriptions, which can be shown as follows:
$U = \varphi(D)$, where $U = (u_1, u_2, ..., u_n)^T$ and $\varphi$ means the utility function. Supposing it is the simple weight sum function, then $u_k = \sum_{j=1}^{m} w_j \cdot \overline{d_{ij}}$, where $\sum_{j=1}^{m} w_j = 1$, and $\overline{d_{ij}}$ is the normalization utility of the $j^{th}$ description of entity $i$. For different kinds of media and users with different interests, the weight of each descriptor is not invariable. We calculate the initial weight according to user's custom and experience. When user interacts with our system, the weight will be adjusted.

### 4.2 Multimedia Materials Retrieval Based on EEDU Model

After the relative media materials with highest similarity to narrative template are retrieved by EEDU model, appropriate representation style for virtual news must be

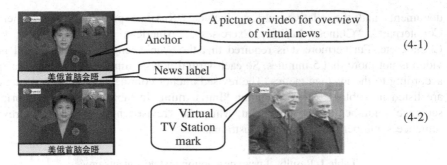

**Fig. 4.** two representation styles for virtual news

selected to make the generated virtual news video like real news video. There are two styles for representation adopted in our system as follows (Fig.4):

(1) Anchor shot+ little window (a picture or video for overview of virtual news) (Fig. 4-1): In this kind of representation style only anchor shot appears and anchor introduces all the news content by speech.
(2) Anchor shot+ little window□and then introduce the detailed news content by speech and video, picture, or graphics (Fig.4-2).

The description of the representation style for virtual news is based on XML, which adopts the method of DES timeline [6]. The description includes the information about the time and space of the materials in generated virtual news video.

The synthesized time of news's anchor commentary is determined during the process of section 3. Then the technology of DES (DirectShow Editing Service) [6] is used to synthesize many multimedia materials searched by EEDU. It considers the representation style and the following rules:

(1) Process of station mark and closed caption. During the collection of media materials the method for TV station mark and caption detection [7] is used and then detected areas are processed with mosaic.
(2) Consistency of anchor materials. To keep continuity of news video program, the anchor appeared in materials must be only one and cannot change during the program. If the anchors in multimedia materials often change, the reality of generated news program will be reduced.

## 5 Experiment Results

Our experiment is carried out in Pentium 4 2.0 Ghz CPU, 512 RAM and Windows 2000 professional system. To test the effectiveness of the proposed method, experiments are carried out on the news materials collected from the CCTV news and Phoenix news. The news materials are processed into shots, scenes, and stories etc and annotated with semantics, which is the base of our system. To generate the personalized virtual news, user provides situation description text like news report after some periods of strategic simulation ends. In our experiments, user submitted 10 documents and the relative subjects include "Russia's president hosts American Counterpart", "Chinese Military Exercises", "American Defense Minister visits China", etc. Furthermore it is required that the whole length of final virtual news video is not more that 5 minutes. So each virtual news's time is less than 30 seconds according to the average tactics. The revised anchor commentary of each documents are listed in Table 1. The 3$^{rd}$ column "Initial num" in table1 refers to the original sentence's number of one document, while the "revised num" denotes the revised sentence's number based on time constraints.

**Table 1.** Results of news description text documents process

| Virtual news ID | Subjects | Initial num | Revised num | Revised time | Time |
|---|---|---|---|---|---|
| VN1 | Russia's president hosts American Counterpart | 19 | 17 | 00:25″ | 2009-10-1 |
| VN2 | Foreign minister's station | 17 | 15 | 00:22″ | 2009-10-2 |
| VN3 | American Defense Minister visits China | 19 | 18 | 00:24″ | 2009-10-2 |
| VN4 | Chinese Military Exercises | 25 | 21 | 00:30″ | 2009-10-3 |
| ⋮ | ⋮ | ⋮ | ⋮ | ⋮ | ⋮ |

Fig.5 (a) shows the user interface of anchor commentary extraction. The final generated virtual news video program along timeline is shown in Fig.5 (b).

From the above experiment results we can draw the conclusion that the text process algorithm can satisfy the time constraints during the generation of virtual news. And the generated personalized virtual news video introduces the news clearly like telling stories to users and augments the immersion of strategic simulation. But the shortcoming of the virtual news is that the lipping of anchor is not matching with the synthesized speech, which is also the emphasis of our future work.

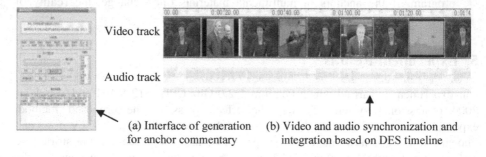

Video track

Audio track

(a) Interface of generation          (b) Video and audio synchronization and
    for anchor commentary                integration based on DES timeline

**Fig. 5.** Relative interface of our system for generating virtual news automatically

# 6  Conclusions

This paper introduces our system for generating virtual news automatically and discusses the relative approach, which has the following three phases: (1) Virtual news narrative template is generated by information extraction combing natural language process automatically and revised based on time constraints. (2)The relative media materials are retrieved based on model EEDU. (3) Virtual news video is generated by DES considering the representation style. The proposed approach in this paper augments the degree of automation for virtual news's generation, which can improve the immersion of strategic simulation and help decision makers to understand the current situation for further decision making.

# References

1. D Randall. The Universal Journalist, Second Edition[M]. London: Photo Press, 2000.
2. Zhang Xian-hai, WU Ling-da, XIE Yu-xiang. Research of automatic generation and representation for personalized video story based on classification. Application Research of Computers, 2000, vol.7, pp18~20.(in Chinese).
3. Salton, G., Buchley, C.: Term-weighting approach in automatic text retrieval. Information Processing & Management (1988) 24(5): 513-523.
4. Brett Adams and Svetha Venkatesh. Taming the roving camera: A framework for creating professional home movies through narrative and kinesthetic elements[R]. International conference on Multimedia Modeling 2004, Poster, Brisbane, QLD, Australia, January, 2004.
5. XU Yan-yong, ZHOU Xian-zhong, JING Xiang-he etc. Chinese Sentence Parsing Based on Maximum Entropy Model. ACTA ELECTRONICA SINICA,Vol.31, No.11, 2003: 1608-1612.(in Chinese)
6. DirectX SDK. http:// msdn.microsoft.com/windows/DirectX/default.aspx.
7. Xie Yuxiang. Research on News Video Mining Technology Supporting Intelligence Analysis [D]. Ph D, National University of Defense Technology, 2004. 4.
8. PERSEUS: Personalized Multimedia News Portal Victor O. Kulesh, Valery A. Petrushin, Ishwar K. Sethi IASTED International Conference on Artificial Intelligence Applications (AIA 2001), 4-7 September 2001, Marbella, Spain.

# Image Fingerprinting Scheme for Print-and-Capture Model

Won-gyum Kim, Seon Hwa Lee, and Yong-seok Seo

Digital Contents Research Division, Electronics and Telecommunication Research
Institute (ETRI),
161 Gajeong-dong, Yuseong-gu, Daejon, Korea
{wgkim, seonhwa, yongseok}@etri.re.kr
http://www.etri.re.kr

**Abstract.** This paper addresses an image fingerprinting scheme for the print-to-capture model performed by a photo printer and digital camera. When capturing an image by a digital camera, various kinds of distortions such as noise, geometrical distortions, and lens distortions are applied slightly and simultaneously. In this paper, we consider several steps to extract fingerprints from the distorted image in print-and capture scenario. To embed ID into an image as a fingerprint, multi-bits embedding is applied. We embed 64 bits ID information as a fingerprint into spatial domain of color images. In order to restore a captured image from distortions a noise reduction filter is performed and a rectilinear tiling pattern is used as a template. To make the template a multi-bits fingerprint is embedded repeatedly like a tiling pattern into the spatial domain of the image. We show that the extracting is successful from the image captured by a digital camera through the experiment.

## 1 Introduction

Digital fingerprinting is a technique for enforcing digital rights policies whereby unique labels are inserted into content prior to distribution. Developing specification of fingerprinting (watermarking) schemes depends on the application which means their usage scenario. In general the design of fingerprinting (watermarking) schemes focuses on specific attacks: compression, additive noise, blurring, sharpening, collusion and geometrical distortions. It is so difficult to handle against those kinds of attacks together that the fingerprinting schemes are quite different according to applications.

Recently, as a kind of illegal distribution behavior, the method by a digital photo printer and a digital camera are used widely. For example, high-quality still images like nude and advertisement images serviced with fee through mobile and Internet are printed by a high-performance digital photo printer and used in magazine (or poster, advertisement stuff, interior, etc.) illegally. Digital fingerprinting can be a good alternative solution for this problem. The content owner (or seller) can extract fingerprinting information from the image and trace a re-distributor back.

Some fingerprinting techniques based on watermarking have been proposed [1][3][4][9] for embedding information in multimedia signals. But, these techniques are not enough to present the variety of customer information as a fingerprint. To

Y. Zhuang et al. (Eds.): PCM 2006, LNCS 4261, pp. 106 – 113, 2006.

identify lots of customers' multi-bits embedding scheme is required. Additionally, in a captured image by digital camera there exist many distortions slightly. So a new fingerprinting scheme which considers these kinds of distortions is also required.

Generally high-quality still images for advertisement (or poster) have high-price rate. By this reason, high-quality still images are copied illegally very well and used widely for the purpose of advertisement in magazine or interior poster, etc. In this case it is not easy to trace the first illegal re-distributor unless a customer ID is embedded into the image as a fingerprint. The motivation of this paper is to trace the customer who re-distributes illegally at first using a customer ID from the printed images. In this paper, to obtain a still image from off-line(magazine or poster) we use a high-performance digital camera. The reasons we choose a digital camera as an image acquisition device are that a digital camera is one of convenient mobile devices and is spread well in public.

The most difficult thing to extract fingerprint from the captured image is to restore the image from distortions due to D/A-A/D conversion. In this case we can predict these kinds of distortions from the fingerprinted and captured image.

- Geometrical Distortion
  - RST distortion: According to the angle of the camera geometrical distortions such as RST(rotation, scaling, and translation) are occurred slightly.
  - Cropping: After capturing the image the boundary portion of the image could be cropped.
  - Perspective: Due to the distance between a camera and a picture perspective distortion could be occurred. This distortion also produces trapezoid geometric distortion.
  - Lens distortion: If a distorted lens is used then the curvature of the lens is changed. It makes the image concave or convex.
- Illumination Distortion: This distortion includes the refraction caused by shining a bright light or sunburst into the camera. Distortions are light and sunburst distortions.
- Quality Degradation: Due to the skill of a photographer and performance of the digital camera the quality of the original image could be degraded. This distortion such as blurring is occurred when the camera is out of focus.

In this paper, we propose a new fingerprinting scheme which embeds 64 bits customer ID into the spatial domain of a color image and print out using a photo printer and extract this ID from the image captured by a digital camera. Additionally we do not consider collusion attacks because we conclude that it is not easy to collude together in the proposed scenario. In this In Section 2, we show how to embed and extract fingerprinting information. Experimental results and conclusion are shown in Section 3 and 4.

## 2  Proposed Fingerprinting Scheme

### 2.1  Embedding

In the fingerprinting system accommodation of multi-bits is necessary because the amount of fingerprinting data to be embedded is not small and customer information is also complex. In this paper, we construct a 64-bits fingerprinting code and embed into the spatial domain of the image repeatedly. Assume that we are given a 64-bits message which can be separated as 8 symbols whose length is 8 bits.

In the proposed scheme we assume that each symbol can has only Alphabet capital and small letters and numeric numbers from 0 to 9, $S=\{s_1, s_2, s_3,...,s_N\} \in \{a,...,z,A,...,Z,0,...,9\}$. Then, we generate random sequences for every symbol from a secret key which can be represented in $r_i \in \{-1, +1\}$. Therefore, the total number of possible sequence, $r_i$ is $(26 \times 2+10)*8 = 496$. We assume that all 496 random sequences are orthogonal each other. The length of the random sequence depends on the size of unit block in this scheme. In order to produce fingerprint signal, $F$, the only eight random sequences corresponding to eight fingerprint symbols are selected and merged together. Finally the sign of the merged sequence is taken as follows:

$$F = sign \left( \sum_{i=1}^{8} r_i(s_i) \right)$$

Next, we describe how to embed the fingerprint signal into an image adaptively. HVS(Human Visual System) is a weighted function to make the image robust to various kinds of attacks and to improve imperceptibility. In the proposed scheme we design a simple HVS function for the spatial domain of the image. The basic idea of our HVS is that fingerprint is embedded strongly into the less recognizable regions of the image. To do this, we separate the image into three regions; flat, strong edge, texture region. A criterion of area is as follows:

$$x(i, j)=\begin{cases} Flat & if \ Std(i, j) \le 2 \\ Strong \ edge & if \ Edge(i, j) > T \\ Texture & if \ StD(i, j) > 2 \end{cases} \quad where \quad T = Aver_{Edge}(I)+2*StD_{Edge}(I)$$

$Aver(i,j)$, $Std(i,j)$, and $Edge(i,j)$ are local average, standard deviation and edge detection value on $x(i,j)$ respectively. For edge detection Prewitt operator is used. $Aver_{Edge}(I)$ and $StD_{Edge}(I)$ are average and standard deviation of edge detection values, $Edge(i,j)$. HVS function is as follows:

$$\lambda(i, j) = \begin{cases} \alpha & Flat, Strong \ edge \ area \\ StD(i, j) * WF(Avg(i, j)) & Otherwise \end{cases}$$
$$where, \quad WF(i) = (2 - \tanh(i/25))/3, \quad i = [0...255]$$

$\alpha$ is minimum embedding strength and set to 2. $WF(*)$ is a weighted function for dark and bright area. So, fingerprint is embedded strongly by this function because these areas are less sensitive than normal area.

To extract fingerprint correctly from the image captured by a digital camera, it is important to restore the image from geometrical distortions. In the proposed system a rectilinear tiling pattern is used to do this. To construct the latticed template random sequence, R, described the previous section is embedded repeatedly as shape of unit block. Embedded unit blocks are used as a template to restore the captured image. In this paper, the size of unit block is 128x128. For instance if the image size is 512x512, then unit block is embedded 16 times repeatedly around the center point of the image. In extracting step minimum 9 points from the center of the image are extracted and we can construct a latticed template using these points. If the image size is

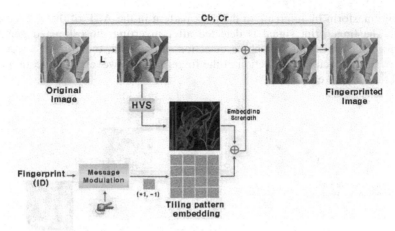

**Fig. 1.** Overall embedding process; Embedding domain is luminance channel of the spatial of the image. The fingerprint is a customer ID consisting 8 ASCII characters and numerical number from 0 to 9. The size of unit block is 128x128. In the case of Lena image, fingerprint signal is embedding 16 times repeatedly. Minimum size of the image for resistance against geometrical distortions is 512x512.

not multiple of 128, the unit blocks are embedded into the available area of the image from the center point. The overall embedding steps are described in Fig. 1.

## 2.2 Extracting

In this paper, a general correlation detector is used to extract a fingerprint. But, pre-processing is needed before extraction because much noise and various kinds of distortions are performed in the captured image. Extracting process proposed in this paper consists of 2 steps; image restoration including resizing and noise reduction, and fingerprint detection. Fig. 2 shows the overall extracting process for print-to-capture model. For blind extracting original estimation step is needed. In original estimation the noise signal including fingerprinting signal is filtered using an adaptive wiener filter.

As we described in Section 1, there is too much noise in the captured image depending on a digital camera and photographing condition. In the proposed system, to reduce false alarm probability, resizing and pre-filtering for noise reduction are applied before extracting. When taking a photo by a digital camera, the size of image is too big because the resolution of a digital camera is high in general. So, we cut out the real image from the captured image and resize appropriately and an adaptive wiener filter is applied to remove the noise.

After removing the noise, the image restoration by reverse information is needed to extract a fingerprint from the geometrically distorted image. Geometric attacks are thought of as one of the most dangerous attacks in the digital watermarking and fingerprinting area. Auto-correlation function (ACF)-based watermarking is known to have great potential for combating geometric attacks [2][5]. It handles geometric attacks by embedding a periodic pattern. Due to the periodicity, periodic peaks are found in the ACF of the fingerprint. The fingerprint detector estimates the applied geometric transform by referring to the peak pattern in the ACF of the extracted fingerprint. The fingerprint signal is detected after inverting the estimated geometric transform. Because of this two-phase detection mechanism, the correct detection of the AC peaks is crucial for detection of the fingerprint. However, the detection of the AC peaks is still not easy.

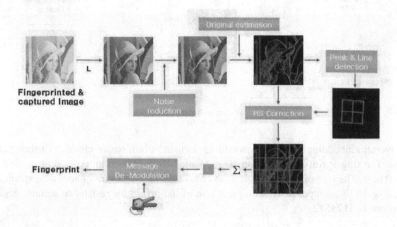

**Fig. 2.** Overall extracting process; Extracting is completed by the order of luminance channel selection, noise reduction, original estimation, RS correction, accumulation, and message de-modulation. In this process translation correction is not needed because the location of maximum correlation peak is not important in message de-modulation step. Translation error just changes the location of maximum correlation peak.

In the proposed system reverse information is calculated from the latticed template pattern which is detected by auto-correlation function (ACF). We can detect 16 peaks at least because a unit block consisting of random sequences is embedded repeatedly in the embedding process, but it is 9 peaks in the center of the image that are only needed to detect the latticed template. In this paper, using the latticed template consisting of 9 peaks is proposed to calculate reverse information of the distorted image. In the proposed system we apply auto-correlation function to the wiener-filter coefficients because the fingerprint is noise-like pseudorandom sequence. We use the average of 3x3 local variance of the whole image as an estimated noise variance in the wiener filter.

In practice, as many candidate peaks are detected after performing auto-correlation function, we choose 9 peaks which construct a lattice template as following steps.

Step 1: Choose a maximum peak value in local window. The size of local window used in this proposed system is from 16x16 to 64x64.

Step 2: Choose 3 peaks on a line satisfying next 2 conditions among remaining candidate peaks after Step 1.

    A.    $|distA - distB| \leq \tau$ and $|distC| \leq \tau$

    B.    $|Angle| \leq \nu$ and $|Angle| \leq 90 - \nu$

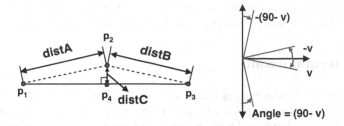

Where, |*distA*| and |*Angle*| are the distance between two peaks and difference of the gradient between two lines. The threshold τ(pixels) and v(degree) are decided experimentally according to the performance of the system. Through the proposed steps we can get 6 lines consisting of 3 peaks from the captured image that is shown in Fig.3.

Image restoration for rotation and scaling is performed by the template consisting of 6 lines. As we also know the original template pattern, we can calculate reverse angle and scaling factor without difficulty. Other geometrical distortions like projection can be corrected by reforming the detected template to a perfect square. As the worst case when detecting only 1 line we can estimate reverse angle and scaling factor from the line. The advantage of the latticed template proposed in this paper is that correcting process for non-linear distortions is simpler than other template patterns proposed before[2][5].

(a) All possible lines        (b) Template        (c) Restored image

**Fig. 3.** After detecting peaks from ACF, all possible lines consisting 3 candidate peaks are selected like image (a). Lines are filtered by angle and distance conditions from all possible lines and construct a lattice-like template showed in (b). From the template reverse angle and scaling rates are calculated and restore image like (c).

To extract fingerprinting symbols is performed by correlation detector used in general watermarking scheme. At first, we generate 496 random sequences representing symbols from a secret key used in the embedding process. Next, the fingerprinting signal is estimated by performing the wiener filter on the restored image. The noise variance of the wiener filter is the average of the local variances of the whole image. The estimate signal is divided into 128x128 unit blocks and summed together.

Fingerprinting symbols are calculated by performing cross-correlation function between the summed block(the estimated fingerprint) and 496(62*8 symbols) random sequences(the reference fingerprint) each. For each symbol the random sequence which has max correlation value is chosen as a fingerprint symbol. In the proposed method translation correction is not needed because the only random sequence which has max correlation value is chosen without any consideration of the location of the peak.

## 3   Experimental Results

Test is performed on color images whose size is from 1283x770 to 1425x870 and the printed image size is around A4 size. A HP Photosmart 7960 photo printer which supports 600 dpi resolution and high-quality photo paper are used to print out images. The digital camera used when capturing images is FUJI FinePix S2 Pro, which supports 5 mega pixels image size.

We first embed a fingerprint ID into images and hang them on the wall or board in various parts of the laboratory and get a captured image using a digital camera and a tripod. Finally we cut and resize the captured image and apply a wiener filter to remove noise, and then we try to extract a fingerprint ID using the proposed scheme. When taking a captured image we control focus range to choose appropriate scaling factor of the image. Available scaling range covered by the proposed scheme is from 90% to 110%.

**Table 1.** Detection results for test images

| Mode | Test images | Success | Detection rate(%) |
|------|-------------|---------|-------------------|
| TIFF | 30 | 27 | 90.0 |
| JPEG | 30 | 26 | 86.7 |

Table 1 shows the detection results. We try to extract fingerprint IDs from 30 images and succeed in extracting IDs completely in 27 images in TIFF mode of the digital camera.  PSNR of the test images after fingerprinting is 38 dB on average. Detection rate is almost same in two modes because the digital camera uses high-performance JPEG quality to compress a picture. Fig. 4 shows the example of the test images.

**Fig. 4.** The test and success images; the images hanging on board in the first row are the captured images digital camera in JPEG mode. The images in the second row are re-edited images. Unnecessary background like board is removed roughly using image editing software. We succeed extracting fingerprints from all 4 images using the proposed scheme.

# 4 Conclusion

In this paper, we propose an image fingerprinting scheme for print-to-capture scenario performed by a photo printer and a digital camera. To embed ID into an image as a fingerprint multi-bits embedding is applied. 64-bits ID information is embedded as a fingerprint into spatial domain of color images. This embedding method doesn't need to correct translation error. In order to restore a captured image from distortions a noise reduction filter is performed and a rectilinear tiling pattern is used as a template. To make the template a multi-bits fingerprint is embedded repeatedly like a tiling pattern into the spatial domain of the image. In extracting process to detect template noise reduction filter is performed first and correlation peaks are calculated by ACF function. Finally lattice-like template is derived from candidate peaks using angle and distance conditions and image is restored. In experiment we embed fingerprints into 30 high-quality images and hang them on broad. We also show that the extracting is successful from the image captured by a digital camera through the experiment.

# References

1. M. Wu, W. Trappe, Z. J. Wang, and K. J. R. Liu, "Collusion-Resistant Fingerprinting for Multimedia," *IEEE Signal Processing Magazine*, pp.15-27, 2004.
2. S. Pereira, and T. Pun, "Robust Template Matching for Affine Resistant Image Watermarks," *IEEE Transaction on Image Processing*, vol. 9, No. 6, pp.1123-1129, 2000.
3. D. Boneh, J. Shaw, "Collusion-Secure Fingerprinting for Digital Data," *IEEE Transaction on Information Theory*, vol. 44, no. 5, pp. 1897-1905, Sep. 1998.
4. J. Dittmann, "Combining digital watermarks and collusion secure fingerprints for customer copy monitoring," *Proc. IEE Seminar Sec. Image & Image Authentication*, pp.128-132, Mar. 2000.
5. M. Kutter, "Watermarking resisting to translation, rotation, and scaling." *Proc. Multimedia systems and applications*, SPIE 3528, 423-431, 1998.
6. J. S. Lim, "Digital image enhancement and noise filtering by use of local statistics," *IEEE Trans. Pattern Anal. Machine Intell.*, Vol. PAMI-2 No.2, pp.165-168, Mar. 1980
7. L. Yu, X. Niu, and S. Sun, "Print-and-scan model and watermarking countermeasure," *Image and Vision Computing*, pp.1-8, 2005
8. Z.J.Wang, M. Wu, H. Zhao, W. Trappe, and K.J.R. Liu, "Resistance of Orthogonal Gaussian Fingerprint to Collusion Attacks," *in Proc. of IEEE Int. Conf. on Acoustics, Speech, and Signal Processing(ICASSP'03)*, pp.724-727, Hong Kong, Apr. 2003
9. D. Kirovski, H.S. Malvar, and Y. Yacobi. "Multimedia Content Screening using a Dual Watermarking and Fingerprinting System,"*ACM Multimedia*, 2002

# 16×16 Integer Cosine Transform for HD Video Coding

Jie Dong and King N. Ngan

Dept. of Electronic Engineering, The Chinese University of Hong Kong
Hong Kong SAR
{jdong, knngan}@ee.cuhk.edu.hk

**Abstract.** High-Definition (HD) videos often contain rich details as well as large homogeneous regions. To exploit such a property, Variable Block-size Transforms (VBT) should be in place so that transform block size can adapt to local activities. In this paper, we propose a 16×16 Integer Cosine Transform (ICT) for HD video coding, which is simple and efficient. This 16×16 ICT is integrated into the AVS Zengqiang Profile and used adaptively as an alternative to the 8×8 ICT. Experimental results show that 16×16 transform can be a very efficient coding tool especially for HD video coding.

**Keywords:** HD video coding, ICT, AVS.

## 1 Introduction

High-Definition (HD) videos often contain rich details as well as large homogeneous regions. In other words, spatial correlation varies greatly throughout an HD video sequence. To exploit such a property, Variable Block-size Transforms (VBT) should be employed, such that smoother regions can be transformed using larger transforms for better energy compaction and better visual quality, and for more detailed areas, smaller transforms can avoid the ringing artifacts and reduce complexity.

The existing video coding systems with VBT use 8×8 as the largest transform block size. However, our study shows that 16×16 transforms are very efficient in coding large homogeneous regions in HD videos, thus improving the overall performance. In this paper, a 16×16 transform is proposed to the Audio Video Coding Standard (AVS) Zengqiang Profile [1] which is the developing profile of the national standard of China aiming at HD video coding. Since there is an 8×8 ICT already existing in the AVS Zengqiang Profile, the 2 transforms are used adaptively according to the local activities of frames. The proposed 16×16 transform is designed as a type of Integer Cosine Transform (ICT), which was first introduced by W. K. Cham in 1989 [2] and has been further developed in recent years. ICT can be implemented using integer arithmetic without mismatch between encoder and decoder and if well-designed, can provide almost the same compression efficiency as Discrete Cosine Transform (DCT).

The contribution of this paper mainly lies in 2 parts. Firstly, a 16×16 ICT is designed, which avoids mismatch between encoder and decoder and has very close decorrelation capability to that of the DCT. Furthermore, to minimize the increasing computational complexity caused by the additional larger transform, we design the 16×16 ICT suitable for simple 16-bit integer arithmetic implementation and compatible

Y. Zhuang et al. (Eds.): PCM 2006, LNCS 4261, pp. 114–121, 2006.

with the 8×8 one. Secondly, to integrate the proposed 16×16 ICT into the AVS Zengqiang Profile, the related problems of transform size selection, 16×16 intra prediction, and 16×16 block entropy coding have been solved.

The remainder of the paper is organized as follows. A brief review of ICT is given in Section 2. Section 3 describes the proposed 16×16 ICT. Section 4 introduces in detail how the related problems are solved when the 16×16 ICT is integrated into the AVS Zengqiang Profile. Section 5 reports the experimental results, followed by the conclusion in Section 6.

## 2  Review of ICT

ICT originates from the DCT in order to simplify the computation of DCT and it enables bit-exact implementations. Its transform matrix is generated from the DCT matrix with the principle of dyadic symmetry [2] and contains only integers. Since the transform matrix is not normalized, a normalization process, known as scaling, is required after transformation. The process of transformation and scaling can be expressed by (1) and (2), respectively,

$$F_{n \times n} = T_n \times f_{n \times n} \times T_n^T \tag{1}$$

$$S_{n \times n} = F_{n \times n} // R_{n \times n} \tag{2}$$

where $f_{n \times n}$ is the input data, $T_n$ is the n×n transform matrix, $S_{n \times n}$ is the transformed data and symbol // indicates that each element of the left matrix is divided by the element at the same position of the right one. The elements in matrix $R_{n \times n}$ are all integers and can be derived from the norms of basis vectors of $T_n$. Interested readers may refer to [2] for details.

The divisions in (2) are usually approximated by integer multiplication and shifting as shown in (3),

$$S_{n \times n} = F_{n \times n} \otimes P_{n \times n} >> N \tag{3}$$

where symbol $\otimes$ indicates that each element of the left matrix is multiplied by the element at the same position of the right one and $>>N$ means right shifting $N$ bits. $R_{n \times n}$ from (2) and $P_{n \times n}$ from (3) satisfy (4) and $P_{n \times n}$ is defined as the scaling matrix.

$$P_{n \times n}(i, j) \times R_{n \times n}(i, j) = 2^N \tag{4}$$

Similarly, for the inverse ICT, the whole process including inverse scaling and inverse transformation can be represented in (5) as

$$f_{n \times n} = \left( T_n^T \times (S_{n \times n} \otimes P_{n \times n}) \times T_n \right) >> N \tag{5}$$

## 3  The Proposed 16×16 ICT

### 3.1  16-Bit Integer Implementation

As shown in (6), the transform matrix $T_{16}$ is very simple. All coefficients have only 7 different magnitudes and can be represented by 5-bit integers. Due to the small magnitudes of the coefficients, the transform matrix is suitable for 16-bit integer arithmetic implementation.

$$T_{16} = \begin{bmatrix} 8 & 8 & 8 & 8 & 8 & 8 & 8 & 8 & 8 & 8 & 8 & 8 & 8 & 8 & 8 & 8 \\ 11 & 11 & 11 & 9 & 8 & 6 & 4 & 1 & -1 & -4 & -6 & -8 & -9 & -11 & -11 & -11 \\ 10 & 9 & 6 & 2 & -2 & -6 & -9 & -10 & -10 & -9 & -6 & -2 & 2 & 6 & 9 & 10 \\ 8 & 6 & 4 & 1 & -11 & -11 & -11 & -9 & 9 & 11 & 11 & 11 & -1 & -4 & -6 & -8 \\ 10 & 4 & -4 & -10 & -10 & -4 & 4 & 10 & 10 & 4 & -4 & -10 & -10 & -4 & 4 & 10 \\ 11 & 9 & -11 & -11 & -4 & -1 & 8 & 6 & -6 & -8 & 1 & 4 & 11 & 11 & -9 & -11 \\ 9 & -2 & -10 & -6 & 6 & 10 & 2 & -9 & -9 & 2 & 10 & 6 & -6 & -10 & -2 & 9 \\ 1 & 4 & -6 & -8 & 9 & 11 & -11 & -11 & 11 & 11 & -11 & -9 & 8 & 6 & -4 & -1 \\ 8 & -8 & -8 & 8 & 8 & -8 & -8 & 8 & 8 & -8 & -8 & 8 & 8 & -8 & -8 & 8 \\ 4 & -1 & -8 & 6 & 11 & -9 & -11 & 11 & -11 & 11 & 9 & -11 & -6 & 8 & 1 & -4 \\ 6 & -10 & 2 & 9 & -9 & -2 & 10 & -6 & -6 & 10 & -2 & -9 & 9 & 2 & -10 & 6 \\ 11 & -11 & -9 & 11 & -6 & 8 & 1 & -4 & 4 & -1 & -8 & 6 & -11 & 9 & 11 & -11 \\ 4 & -10 & 10 & -4 & -4 & 10 & -10 & 4 & 4 & -10 & 10 & -4 & -4 & 10 & -10 & 4 \\ 9 & -11 & 11 & -11 & -1 & 4 & -6 & 8 & -8 & 6 & -4 & 1 & 11 & -11 & 11 & -9 \\ 2 & -6 & 9 & -10 & 10 & -9 & 6 & -2 & -2 & 6 & -9 & 10 & -10 & 9 & -6 & 2 \\ 6 & -8 & 1 & -4 & 11 & -11 & 9 & -11 & 11 & -9 & 11 & -11 & 4 & -1 & 8 & -6 \end{bmatrix} \tag{6}$$

The 8×8 ICT in the AVS Zengqiang Profile is a type of Pre-scaled Integer Transform (PIT) [3], which means that the scaling of the inverse ICT is moved to the encoder side and combined with that of the forward ICT as one single process. With PIT, there is no scaling and thus no scaling matrix stored for decoding, whilst the computational complexity and memory requirement on the encoder side remain unchanged. Due to these advantages of PIT and to be compatible with the 8×8 ICT, the proposed 16×16 ICT is also designed as a PIT.

The whole process of ICT, including transformation and scaling, can be implemented by (7) and (8), respectively.

$$F_{16 \times 16} = \left( T_{16} \times f_{16 \times 16} \times T_{16}^T + 2^6 \right) >> 7 \tag{7}$$

$$S_{16 \times 16} = \left( F_{16 \times 16} \otimes P_{16 \times 16} + 2^{15} \right) >> 16 \tag{8}$$

Right shifting 7 bits in (7) and 16 bits in (8) guarantee that the intermediate results for multiplication or addition are all smaller than 16 bits. And the factors, $2^6$ and $2^{15}$ in (7) and (8) are for rounding.

For inverse ICT, since the PIT is employed, the inverse scaling step is saved and the implementation of (5) is simplified as below:

$$b_{16 \times 16} = \left( S_{16 \times 16} \times T_{16} + 2^2 \right) >> 3 \tag{9}$$

$$f_{16 \times 16} = \left( T_{16}^T \times b_{16 \times 16} + 2^6 \right) >> 7 \tag{10}$$

Right shifting 3 bits for horizontal transform in (9) and 7 bits for vertical transform in (10) ensure that any intermediate result in the inverse ICT process is smaller than 16 bits.

## 3.2   The Performance of the 16×16 ICT

Besides the simple structure, the proposed ICT also shows good energy compaction capability especially in those homogeneous regions in HD videos. This is because the first 3 basis vectors of the transform matrix which represent relatively low frequency components resemble those of the DCT, including the same dyadic symmetries. Suppose that the input data are so highly correlated which can be approximated by a 1-D first-order stationary Markov source with correlation coefficient ρ tending to 1. Table 1 shows the transform efficiency of Karhunen-Loeve Transform (KLT), DCT and the proposed ICT, respectively, with different ρ, where the transform efficiency η can be calculated by (11). As evident in Table 1, the efficiency of the proposed ICT is very close to that of the DCT, especially when the input data is very highly correlated, e.g., ρ= 0.95.

$$\eta = \frac{\sum_{i=1}^{15}\left|S_{16\times16}(i,i)\right|}{\sum_{i=0}^{15}\sum_{j=0}^{15}\left|S_{16\times16}(i,j)\right|} \tag{11}$$

**Table 1.** The transform efficiency of different transforms

| ρ | KLT | DCT | Proposed ICT |
|------|------|------|--------------|
| 0.95 | 1.00 | 0.88 | 0.86 |
| 0.90 | 1.00 | 0.83 | 0.79 |
| 0.85 | 1.00 | 0.80 | 0.75 |

Another merit of the transform matrix is that the norms of basis vectors are very close to each other. This property is very important when PIT is employed, because with PIT, the inverse scaling is moved to the encoder side, which can be viewed as applying a frequency weighting matrix to the transformed signals. In order not to alter the energy distribution of the signals in the transform domain significantly, the coefficients in the scaling matrix should be closed to each other, which can be guaranteed by making the norms of basis vectors in the transform matrix very close to each other.

### 3.3  The Compatibility with the 8×8 ICT in the AVS Zengqiang Profile

It is nature that the 16×16 DCT is compatible with the 8×8 one. However, it is not always true for ICT. To ensure that the proposed 16×16 ICT can be compatible with the 8×8 one used in the AVS Zengqiang Profile, we extended the 8 basis vectors in the 8×8 transform matrix by the fifteenth even dyadic symmetry to form the even rows in (6). For the odd rows in (6), we slightly modified the dyadic symmetries in the 16×16 DCT matrix in order to ensure orthogonality whilst keeping the magnitudes of the coefficients small enough. It has been proved in 3.2 that the degradation of decorrelation capability caused by alteration of dyadic symmetry is negligible.

#### 3.3.1  Compatible Transformation

To show how the 8×8 transformation in the AVS Zengqiang Profile is involved in the proposed 16×16 one, two modules, defined as $T_{8u}$ and $T_{8d}$ in (12), can be extracted from (6) and $T_{8u}$ is exactly the same as the 8×8 transform matrix. Figure 1 shows how these two modules work for the 16×16 forward transformation when implemented by butterfly structure. Instead of using butterfly structure, these two modules in Figure 1 can also be implemented directly using matrix multiplication.

$$
T_{8u} = \begin{bmatrix}
8 & 8 & 8 & 8 & 8 & 8 & 8 & 8 \\
10 & 9 & 6 & 2 & -2 & -6 & -9 & -10 \\
10 & 4 & -4 & -10 & -10 & -4 & 4 & 10 \\
9 & -2 & -10 & -6 & 6 & 10 & 2 & -9 \\
8 & -8 & -8 & 8 & 8 & -8 & -8 & 8 \\
6 & -10 & 2 & 9 & -9 & -2 & 10 & -6 \\
4 & -10 & 10 & -4 & -4 & 10 & -10 & 4 \\
2 & -6 & 9 & -10 & 10 & -9 & 6 & -2
\end{bmatrix}
\quad
T_{8d} = \begin{bmatrix}
11 & 11 & 11 & 9 & 8 & 6 & 4 & 1 \\
8 & 6 & 4 & 1 & -11 & -11 & -11 & -9 \\
11 & 9 & -11 & -11 & -4 & -1 & 8 & 6 \\
1 & 4 & -6 & -8 & 9 & 11 & -11 & -11 \\
4 & -1 & -8 & 6 & 11 & -9 & -11 & 11 \\
11 & -11 & -9 & 11 & -6 & 8 & 1 & -4 \\
9 & -11 & 11 & -11 & -1 & 4 & -6 & 8 \\
6 & -8 & 1 & -4 & 11 & -11 & 9 & -11
\end{bmatrix}
\tag{12}
$$

Since the 8×8 transform matrix, $T_{8u}$, is involved in the 16×16 one, not only can an independent module set up specially for the 8×8 transformation be saved, but also the output date from the 8×8 transformation can be reused by the 16×16 one.

The compatibility of the forward transformations has been described in detail, and it is very similar for the case of inverse ones.

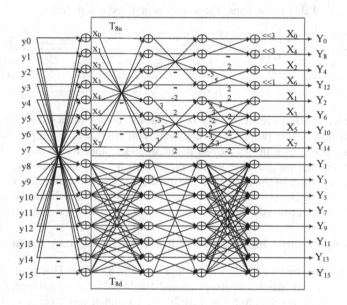

**Fig. 1.** The 16×16 forward transform butterfly structure

### 3.3.2  Compatible Scaling Matrix

As mentioned in Section 2, the process of scaling is for normalization and thus the scaling matrix can be derived by the norms of basis vectors in the corresponding transform matrix [2]. Because the even rows in (6) are obtained by extending the 8 basis vectors in the 8×8 transform matrix using the fifteenth even dyadic symmetry, the relationship between their scaling matrices, $P_{8\times8}$ and $P_{16\times16}$ can be shown in (13). Interested readers may refer to [4] for how the relationship is obtained.

$$
P_{8\times8}(i, j) = P_{16\times16}(2i, 2j) \times 4
\tag{13}
$$

(13) shows that $P_{16\times16}$ (2*i*, 2*j*) is one quarter of $P_{8\times8}$ (*i*, *j*) and this difference can be easily ironed out by shifting, which means that $P_{16\times16}$ (2*i*, 2*j*) can be used as $P_{8\times8}$ (*i*, *j*), if *N*, the bits of right shifting in (3), for the 8×8 scaling is 2 bits less than that for the 16×16 scaling. Therefore, the compatibility of scaling matrix is achieved and the memory specially for storing an 8×8 scaling matrix can be saved.

# 4  Integration of the 16×16 ICT into the AVS Zengqiang Profile

## 4.1  Transform Size Selection

Luminance components in a Macroblock (MB) can be transformed by one 16×16 transform, or alternatively by four 8×8 transforms. The selection of the optimum transform size is performed using a criterion of rate-distortion (R-D) cost that can be calculated by (14) with a proper Lagrange multiplierλ[5]. In (14), the SSD(MB) means the summation of square difference between the original and reconstructed MB and bits(MB) is the total bits used to code the MB. The two block-size transforms are tried one by one and their R-D costs are calculated respectively. The one with the lower cost is selected.

$$\text{cost} = \text{SSD(MB)} + \lambda\text{bits(MB)} \qquad (14)$$

With this selection criterion, the best R-D performance can be achieved, but a 1-bit binary signal should be transmitted in every MB header to indicate which transform is used.

## 4.2  16×16 Intra Prediction

The largest block size for intra prediction in the current AVS Zengqiang Profile is 8×8, and to apply the 16×16 ICT to intra-coded MB, the 16×16 intra prediction must be in place. Five prediction directions are used, including DC, horizontal, vertical, down-right and down-left, all of which are very similar to those for 8×8. However, intra prediction with large block size is more likely to introduce visible artifacts, since more pixels are predicted from the same source [6]. So, instead of using the reference pixels directly, a 3-tap low-pass filter [1 2 1]/4 is applied to the reference pixels before they are used, as shown in Figure 2. As for the DC mode, the predicted value is the average of all the available top and left neighboring pixels.

## 4.3  16×16 Block Entropy Coding

In the AVS Zengqiang Profile, the 8×8 residual blocks are coded by Context-based Adaptive Binary Arithmetic Coding (CABAC) [1]. Its arithmetic coding engine can code sources with various statistics by using different probability models. Therefore, instead of designing new codebooks, an additional set of probability models specially for the 16×16 residual blocks is designed that can be updated adaptively according to the changes of the source statistics. The arithmetic coding engine remains unchanged.

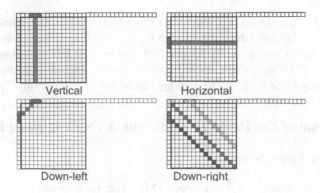

**Fig. 2.** 16×16 intra prediction modes

## 5 Experimental Results

The proposed 16×16 ICT is integrated into the RM62b platform which is the latest version of the reference software of the AVS Zengqiang Profile. For every MB, it is used adaptively as an alternative to the 8×8 ICT. Extensive experiments have been done and the test conditions are listed in Table 2. Both the forward and inverse ICT are implemented with 16-bit simple integer arithmetic as described in Section 3.

The performance improvement of coding different HD sequences is shown in Table 3, which can be represented by PSNR gain for equal bit rate in the second column or by saved bit rate in terms of the same PSNR in the third column, using the proposed method in [7]. It is obvious that the coding efficiency is significantly improved

**Table 2.** Test conditions

| Sequence Structure | IBBPBBP…. |
|---|---|
| Intra Period | 0.5 second |
| FME | ON |
| Deblocking Filter | ON |
| R-D Optimization | ON |
| QP | Fixed(22, 28, 34, 40) |
| Rate Control | OFF |
| Interlace Handling | PAFF |
| Reference Frame | 2 |
| Search Range | ±32 |
| Frame Rate | 60 FPS (Progressive) |
| | 30 FPS (Interlace) |
| Resolution | 1280x720 (Progressive), |
| | 1920x1088 (Interlace) |

since none of them is smaller than 0.1 dB. Whilst the average gain is almost 0.2 dB, for the best case of Kayak, the gain is up to 0.39 dB. From the fourth column of Table 3 which gives the percentage of MBs coded by the 16×16 ICT, we can safely conclude that the 16×16 ICT is very useful in HD video coding because more than half of the MBs are coded by it. The only case where the 16×16 ICT usage is less than 50% is the Fireworks which is full of low-correlated details.

**Table 3.** Experimental results

| Test sequence | PSNR gain (dB) | Bit rate saved (%) | MB using 16×16 (%) |
|---------------|----------------|--------------------|--------------------|
| City | 0.123 | -4.39 | 72.02 |
| Crew | 0.219 | -9.81 | 73.07 |
| Fireworks | 0.162 | -2.19 | 45.69 |
| Flamingo | 0.120 | -2.26 | 50.05 |
| Kayak | 0.389 | -5.75 | 66.41 |
| Riverbed | 0.235 | -4.77 | 80.88 |
| ShuttleStart | 0.163 | -6.87 | 75.34 |
| Optis | 0.136 | -5.21 | 70.58 |
| **Average** | **0.193** | **-5.16** | **66.76** |

## 6 Conclusion

In this paper, we propose a 16×16 ICT, specially designed for HD video coding, which is efficient and simple to implement. This 16×16 ICT is integrated into the AVS Zengqiang Profile and used adaptively as an alternative to the 8×8 ICT. The experimental results show that with the 16×16 ICT, the coding efficiency is greatly improved with the average gain around 0.2 dB. Hence, it can be concluded that the 16×16 ICT is a useful coding tool for HD video coding.

## References

1. AVS Video Group, "Information technology – Advanced coding of audio and video – Part 2: Video (AVS-X WD 3.0)", AVS Doc. AVS-N1242, Dec. 2005.
2. Cham, W.K., "Development of integer cosine transforms by the principle of dyadic symmetry", Proc. IEE, I, 136,(4), pp. 276-282, 1989.
3. Ci-Xun Zhang, Jian Lou, Lu Yu, Jie Dong, W. K. Cham "The Technique of Pre-Scaled Integer Transform in Hybrid Video Coding", IEEE ISCAS, 2005. Vol. 1, pp. 316-319, May 2005.
4. Jie Dong, Jian Lou, Ci-Xun Zhang and Lu Yu, "A new approach to compatible adaptive block-size transforms", Visual Communication and Image Processing, 2005, Vol. 5960, pp. 38-47, July 2005.
5. T. Wiegand and B. Girod, "Lagrangian multiplier selection in hybrid video coder control", in Proc. ICIP 2001, Thessaloniki, Greece, Oct. 2001.
6. Mathias Wien, "Variable Block-Size Transforms for H.264/AVC", IEEE Trans. Circuits Syst. Video Technol., vol. 13, pp. 560–576, July 2003.
7. G. Bjontegaard, "Calculation of average PSNR differences between RD-curves", ITU-T SG16 Doc. VCEG-M33, 2001.

# Heegard-Berger Video Coding Using LMMSE Estimator

Xiaopeng Fan, Oscar Au, Yan Chen, and Jiantao Zhou

Department of ECE, Hong Kong University of Science and Technology,
Kowloon, HK SAR, China
{eexp, eeau, eecyan, eejtzhou}@ust.hk

**Abstract.** In this paper a novel distributed video coding scheme was proposed based on Heegard-Berger coding theorem, rather than Wyner-Ziv theorem. The main advantage of HB coding is that the decoder can still decode and output a coarse reconstruction, even if side information degrade or absent. And if side information present or upgrade at decoder, a better reconstruction can be achieved. This robust feature can solve the problem lies in Wyner-Ziv video coding that the encoder can hardly decide the bit rate because rate-distortion was affected by the side information known only at the decoder. This feature also leaded to our HB video coding scheme with 2 decoding level of which we first reconstruct a coarse reconstruction frame without side information, and do motion search in previous reconstructed frame to find side information, then reconstruct a fine reconstruction frame through HB decoding again, with side information available.

**Keywords:** Distributed video coding, Heegard-Berger coding, Side information, LMMSE.

## 1 Introduction

### 1.1 Distributed Source Coding

The basis of distributed source coding is a surprising conclusion proved by Slepian and Wolf in 1970s, that for lossless coding of 2 correlated sources, there's no rate gap between separate encoding and joint encoding, as long as decode jointly [1]. Wyner and Ziv extend this to lossy coding and build up a rate distortion formula for coding with side information at decoder side only [2]. They also proved that in quadratic Gaussian case, coding efficiency loss is zero even if side information is not available at encoder [3]. For many other sources, the gaps are also proved to be bounded [4].

Generally, distributed source coding [10] was based on Wyner-Ziv theorem and in practical borrows a lot from channel coding [14][15]. The key idea is consider a virtual channel between the source and the side information. Encoder uses a systematic error correcting code, for example using Turbo [11] or LDPC [12][13], to generate parity bits of the source and send them to decoder and discard the systematic bits. Decoder regards side information as noisy version of systematic bits and corrects them back to original source bits, with the help of parity bits received from encoder.

Y. Zhuang et al. (Eds.): PCM 2006, LNCS 4261, pp. 122–130, 2006.

## 1.2  Problem in Wyner-Ziv Video Coding

WZ coding scheme can achieve good compression, but in practical for none-stationary source such as video, it is very hard to decide bit rate at encoder. This is because after quantization, the minimum bit rate, i.e. the conditional entropy, depends on side information which may be better or worse than expected in encoder. Degraded side information can cause decoding failure while upgraded side information means redundancy in bit stream. Actually it was proved in [4] that when side information may degrade at decoder, redundant bitrate need to be paid.

One solution is to introduce a feedback channel [17]. Encoder encode parity bits in recursive way[18] and send them to decoder little by little, and decoder will send back a symbol to encoder when decoding succeed. Obviously this feedback channel solution is restricted to online decoding application only. Actually the introducing of this feedback make the encoder not strictly distributed. And more important it increases the delay latency by the sum of decoding delay and feedback delay.

Another solution is to let encoder estimate the correlation between source and prediction [16]. But this estimation scheme cannot be used in a strict distributed video coding application in which encoder can not access the side information at all, such as camera array. Even if for other applications, rate redundancy and decoding failure problem still exist, because the estimation can not be perfect and sophisticated to keep the low complexity advantage of distributed video coding.

Actually these two solutions are common in that they fix the distortion and try to find optimal rate for uncertain side information, which were hard and even impossible for some cases.

## 1.3  Proposed Heegard-Berger Video Coding

In this paper, we canceled the feedback channel by fixing the rate so that the distortion may depend on the quality of side information. WZ coding was substituted by Heegard-Berger coding [5][6]. One important feature of HB coding is that the codeword can always be decoded even if without side information. And if the side information is available at decoder, a fine version of the coded image can be reconstructed. This feature lead to our HB video coding scheme with 2 level decoding in which we first reconstruct a coarse version frame and use it to find prediction and then reconstruct a fine version frame with the prediction available.

Since there was very few research in finding HB code till now, in this paper an implementation was given, by cascading traditional lossy coder and a post processing linear minimum mean square error (LMMSE) estimator. This implementation, although not very complicated, was actually optimal in some cases.

Remain parts of this paper was organized as following: In section 2, HB theorem was introduced through quadratic Gaussian case. In section 3, the proposed HB video coding system was described. Then in section 4, simulation details and results were given with a performance comparison with those state-of-art Wyner-Ziv video coding.

# 2  Heegard-Berger Coding

The main difference between HB coder and WZ coder is that HB coder can decode either with or without side information. Figure 1 is the diagram of HB coder. Encoder encodes X into bitstream. At decoder side, if Y is not available, a coarse version reconstruction $\hat{X}_1$ can be decoded. If Y is available, a fine reconstruction $\hat{X}_0$ can be obtained. For example in quadratic Gaussian case Y=X+N, it was proved that for all $D_1 \leq \sigma_X^2$ :

$$R_{HB}(D) = 1/2\log^+[\sigma_X^2 \sigma_N^2 /(D_0(D_1 + \sigma_N^2))]$$

where $\log^+(x) = \max(\log(x), 0)$ and $D_1$, $D_0$ denote respectively the distortion of $\hat{X}_1$ and $\hat{X}_0$ from X.

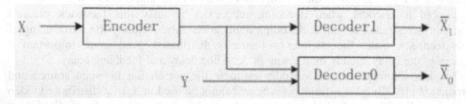

**Fig. 1.** Heegard-Berger Coding System

Generally $R_{HB}(D_1,D_0) \geq R_{WZ}(D_0)$, which is the cost to achieve the flexibility to reconstruct a coarse version without side information available. But there are also some cases that $R_{HB}(D_1,D_0) = R_{WZ}(D_0)$. Actually we will show later that in our usage model, HB coder can outperform WZC because it benefit from a better side information Y. A detail explanation was given in next section.

## 3 Proposed Heegard-Berger Video Coding

### 3.1 Whole Framework

HB frame are used as interframe instead of P frame. For a HB frame, without doing motion estimation and intra prediction, each frame X is coded by a frame-HB encoder and send to decoder. At decoder side, first a coarse version reconstruct image $\hat{X}_1$ was decoded by HB decoder 1, then if the decoder is not powerful, it may stop and the complexity is just similar to traditional I frame decoder. But if the decoder device is powerful enough, it may treat the coarse version reconstruction $\hat{X}_1$ as X, and do motion search in last reconstruction frame and find a prediction Y for current frame. Then HB decoder 0 was used to reconstruct a fine version image $\hat{X}_0$.

Since motion compensation at decoder can only partially remove temple redundancy, in our implementation, DCT was also used to exploit spatial redundancy.

But unfortunately, there is no practical HB coding scheme till now. However we will show in next section that, in quadratic Gaussian case, actually we can implement one kind of HB coder by cascading traditional lossy coder and a post processing linear minimum mean square error (LMMSE) estimator. The assumption of quadratic Gaussian case was reasonable, because after DCT transform, distribution of coefficients can be considered as Gaussian roughly. In section 3.2 we compared and

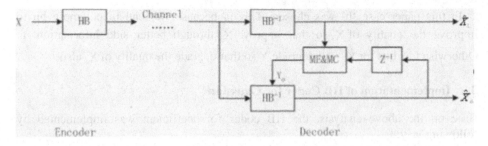

**Fig. 2.** Proposed Video Codec ($Z^{-1}$ is 1 frame delay)

selected from 3 class of HB coder. And in section 3.3, the implementation of our HB coder was introduced.

### 3.2 Selection of HB Coder for Gaussian

We assume the distribution of DCT coefficient is Gaussian and Y=X+N, and X, Y, N denote source, side information and noise respectively, i.e. X is the DCT coefficient we want to compress, Y is the coefficient from motion compensated block, N is the residue between X and Y.

Similar to MDC coding 8, we classify HB coding into 3 classes:

a) No excess rate case: $R_{HB}(D_1,D_0) = R_{WZ}(D_0)$. Where $R_{WZ}(D_0)$ denote the rate of Wyner-Ziv coder to achieve distortion $D_0$.
b) No excess marginal rate case: $R_{HB}(D_1,D_0) = R_X(D_1)$. This means that we put all bit rate to improve the quality of $\hat{X}_1$ and the quality gain from $\hat{X}_1$ to $\hat{X}_0$ is totally comes from the side information Y.
c) General case: Situations between case 'a' and case 'b' are general cases in which distortion $D_1$ and $D_0$ are balanced.

Among the three cases, for fixed bit rate, class 'a' has the lowest distortion (best performance) when side information is available but highest distortion when side information not available. Class 'b' is just the opposite of class 'a'. And class 'c' is between class 'a' and 'b'.

Class 'a' i.e. WZ coder was widely used currently in distributed video coding. But it's not suitable for our usage model, because we expect $\hat{X}_1$ to be in good quality so that we can find better Y after motion estimation. Actually we proved in theorem 1 in appendix that in this case $D_1 \geq \sigma_X^2$, i.e. SNR of $\hat{X}_1$ is not more than 0dB.

Class 'c' can be implemented by a successive refinement scheme [7], i.e. first encode X to get $\hat{X}_1$ at decoder side, and then encode X to get $\hat{X}_0$ at decoder side given Y at decoder and $\hat{X}_1$ at both encoder and decoder.

Class 'b' can be implemented by cascading a lossy coder and a LMMSE estimation module at decoder: $\hat{X}_0 = E(X|\hat{X}_1, Y)$. We proved in theorem 2 in appendix that this scheme is optimal for quadratic Gaussian case.

In this paper case 'b' was chosen. This is because we tend to put more bit to improve the quality of $\hat{X}_1$ so that improve $\hat{X}_0$ through better side information Y. Otherwise few bits for $\hat{X}_1$ will degrade Y so that degrade the quality of $\hat{X}_0$ also.

### 3.3  Implementation of HB Coder for Gaussian

Base on the above analysis, the HB coder for coefficient was implemented by following way:

At encoder side, a general lossy coder consists of quantization and entropy coding was used to encode each coefficient X, and $\hat{X}_1$ was the expected reconstruction of X at decoder side. Simultaneously, $D_1 = E[(\hat{X}_1 - X)^2]$ in SNR format for every 11 macroblock (1 slice) was also encoded and transmitted to decoder.

At decoder side, first bitstream was decoded to get $\hat{X}_1$, then after motion search and side information Y available, a LMMSE estimator was used to get $\hat{X}_0$, the best estimation of X given $\hat{X}_1$ and Y, by:

$$\hat{X}_0 = aY + b\hat{X}_1,$$

Where a and b are estimation weights and $a = D_1 /(D_1 + \sigma_N^2)$, $b = \sigma_N^2 /(D_1 + \sigma_N^2)$

But because $\sigma_N^2 = E[(X - Y)^2]$ is not available for both encoder and decoder, we use $\sigma_\Delta^2 = E[(\hat{X}_1 - Y)^2]$ instead, which was obtained from motion estimation module at decoder.

## 4  Experimental Result

We implemented the HB video codec proposed in section 3 and assessed its performance for QCIF video sequences. The test condition was same as in [19]. Every 8th frame is a key frame and the remaining frames are HB frames. The 1st 100 odd frames of Salesman, Foreman, Mobile and Paris QCIF sequences at 15 fps were tested.

Key frame was encoded to I frame, with a fixed quantization parameter, using a standard H263+ codec. For encoding a HB frame, 8 x 8 DCT was followed by quantization and entropy coding, similar as in H263+. $D_1$ for every slice consists of 11 macroblocks was coded (in SNR format, i.e $10\log_{10}(D_1)$) by DPCM with 3 bits uniform quantizer with QP step size 1.0dB and coded by FLC, which means that the difference of $D_1$ (in SNR format) from neighbor slice was quantized and clipped into the range -4.0dB~+4.0dB, and quantized with maximum distortion 0.5dB, or say 1.12 times. $D_1$ was simply coded by FLC rather than VLC because the bit rate was already very insignificant (0.42kb/s[1]) compared with bit rate for coefficients.

---

[1] In our simulation, only $D_1$ for luminance component was transmitted and also, at decoder side, only estimation weights a and b of luminance component was calculated. Cb and Cr component just copy those weights from luminance.

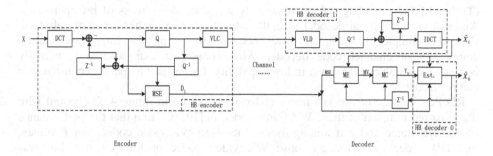

**Fig. 3.** An implementation of proposed video codec ($Z^{-1}$ is 1 frame delay and Est. is LMMSE estimator)

In [19], to achieve higher RD performance, at encoder side last frame was used as prediction of current frame in a 'zero motion' way, i.e. only the residual frame was coded. Our HB video codec also benefit from this scheme. Different from [19], in our codec the subtraction was done in transform domain so that there's no need to do IDCT at encoder side. The encoder stored the reconstruct coefficients for last frame and used them as prediction for coefficients of current frame.

Obviously the encoding system is similar to H263 intraframe encoder except first the quantization noise variance $D_1$ was coded, and second residue coefficient rather than coefficient itself was coded. Figure 3 illustrate the diagram of the HB coding system. It's obvious that the encode complexity is only slightly more than intraframe encoder (by a dequantization module, and a MSE module), and less than zero motion P-frame encoder because we needn't do IDCT.

At decoder side, first a coarse reconstruction $\hat{X}_1$ was decoded and then an 8x8 integer pixel motion estimation was performed in last reconstruct frame $\hat{X}_0^*$, treating $\hat{X}_1$ as current frame. After get motion compensated frame Y, the best guess of X given $\hat{X}_1$ and Y was calculated by $\hat{X}_0 = aY + b\hat{X}_1$.

And the calculation was done for each 8x8 block in spatial domain rather than DCT transform domain to save computation complexity. This did not affect the result because $a$ and $b$ are fixed for whole block and DCT transform is linear transform.

Because the motion vector obtained base on $\hat{X}_1$ may not be optimal especially when $D_1 = E[(\hat{X}_1 - X)^2]$ is high, a motion field filter was adopted to refine the motion vectors obtained from motion estimation. In detail, when calculating SSE, not only pixels in current block but also those in neighbor blocks were considered. New SSE of current block (i,j) is the weighted average of current block and its four neighbour blocks:

$$SSE'_{i,j}(x, y) = \lambda * SSE_{i,j}(x, y) + (1 - \lambda) * Avg(SSE_{m,n}(x, y))$$
$$(m,n) \in NeighbourBlock(i, j)$$

Where $\lambda$ is the weight of current block and in our test we set $\lambda = 0.75$.

Compared with distributed video coding schemes in [16]~[19] based on WZ coder, the proposed scheme has less complexity in both encoder and decoder side. This is because the implementation of WZ coder require binarilization and channel code

(Turbo, LDPC) encoding, which is actually not low due to mass of bit operations. And as to complexity at decoder side, the advantage of our scheme is more obvious. First the complexity is much lower because we avoid the huge computation complexity of channel code decoder. More important, our scheme is actually complexity scalable and even if in low capability devices still a coarse reconstruction can be decoded.

RD Performance of our HB frame codec was showed in figure 4. Compared with the most recent result of those WZ frame codec in [19], we find that the performance of this HB frame codec is among those state-of-art WZ video codec. For Foreman, this HB codec outperformed those WZ video codec at low bit rate but was outperformed by some of them at high bit rate. For Salesman, this HB codec outperform those WZ video codec more than 1dB at all bit rate, and approach H263+ interframe codec.

It's not surprising that our HB video can outperform WZ video coder in some cases. This is because we benefit from more accurate motion compensation, by putting more bits in $\hat{X}_1$, the coarse reconstruction frame, than those WZ coder put in hash.

Regarding to the distortion gap between $\hat{X}_0$ and $\hat{X}_1$, if Y is not available, i.e. no motion estimation was done at decoder side, the loss (difference of $D_1$ and $D_0$ in PSNR) is up to 0.6dB for low bit rate and down to 0.2dB for high bit rate for Foreman and Mobile, and near to 0 dB for Salesman and Paris. This indicated that for low motion video sequences, since residual coefficient coding is already good enough, motion estimation at decoder side can not contribute more.

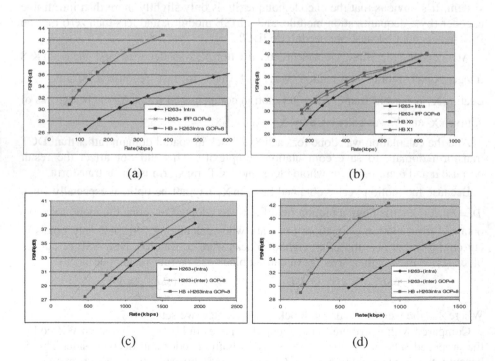

(a)  (b)

(c)  (d)

**Fig. 4.** RD comparison on QCIF sequences (a) Saleman (b) Foreman (c) Mobile (d) Paris

# 5  Conclusion and Furture Work

In this paper Heegard-Berger theorem was proposed to be used in distributed video coding. A HB coder for Gaussian source was implemented, by cascading traditional lossy coder and a post processing LMMSE module. Experiment results show that this video codec achieve similar performance of those distributed video codec based on Wyner-Ziv theorem, with less complexity at both encoder and decoder, and no feedback channel, and computational scalability at decoder, i.e. an acceptable reconstruction can still be decoded even if the computational capability of decoder is as low as encoder.

Since the LMMSE estimation scheme in this paper is relatively an initial implementation of HB coder, it can be expected that the proposed HB video coding scheme with a two level decoder would perform better if more sophisticated HB coder was adopted. So for future works, a class 'c' HB codec can be investigated to take place the class 'b' HB codec in this paper to further improve RD performance.

# References

1. J. D. Slepian and J. K. Wolf, "Noiseless coding of correlated information sources," IEEE Trans. Inf. Theory, vol. IT-19, pp. 471–480, Jul. 1973.
2. A. D. Wyner and J. Ziv, "The rate-distortion function for source coding with side information at the decoder," IEEE Trans. Inf. Theory, vol. IT-22, no. 1, pp. 1–10, Jan. 1976.
3. A. D. Wyner, "The rate-distortion function for source coding with side information at the decoder—II: general sources," Inf. Control, vol. 38, no. 1, pp. 60–80, Jul. 1978.
4. R. Zamir, "The Rate Loss in the Wyner-Ziv Problem," IEEE Trans. Inf. Theory, vol. it-42, no. 6, Nov. 1996.
5. C. Heegard and T. Berger, "Rate distortion when side information may be absent," IEEE Trans. Inform. Theory, vol. IT-31, pp. 727-734, Nov. 1985.
6. A. Kaspi, "Rate-distortion when side-information may be present at the decoder," IEEE Trans. Information Theory, vol. 40, pp. 2031–2034, Nov. 1994.
7. Y. Steinberg and N. Merhav, "On successive refinement for the Wyner-Ziv problem," IEEE Trans. Information Theory, vol. 50, pp. 1636–1654, Aug. 2004.
8. A. A. El Gamal and T. M. Cover, "Achievable rates for multiple descriptions," IEEE Trans. Inform. Theory, vol. IT-28, pp. 851 -857, Nov. 1982.
9. M. Fleming and M. Effros, "Rate-distortion with mixed types of side information," in Proc. IEEE Symposium Information Theory, p. 144, Jun.-Jul 2003.
10. S. S. Pradhan and K. Ramchandran, "Distributed source coding using syndromes (DISCUS): design and construction," in Proc. IEEE Data Compression Conf., 1999, pp. 158–167.
11. J. García-Frías, "Compression of correlated binary sources using turbo codes," IEEE Commun. Lett., vol. 5, no. 10, pp. 417–419, Oct. 2001.
12. , "Compression of binary sources with side information at the decoder using LDPC codes," IEEE Commun. Lett., vol. 6, no. 10, pp. 440–442, Oct. 2002.
13. D. Schonberg, S. S. Pradhan, and K. Ramchandran, "LDPC codes can approach the Slepian–Wolf bound for general binary sources," presented at the Allerton Conf. Communication, Control, and Computing, Champaign, IL, 2002.

14. T. P. Coleman, A. H. Lee, M. Medard, and M. Effros, "On some new approaches to practical Slepian–Wolf compression inspired by channel coding," in Proc. IEEE Data Compression Conf., 2004, pp. 282–291.
15. V. Stankovic, A. D. Liveris, Z. Xiong, and C. N. Georghiades, "Design of Slepian–Wolf codes by channel code partitioning," in Proc. IEEE Data Compression Conf., 2004, pp. 302–311.
16. Puri, R., Ramchandran, K, "PRISM: A 'reversed' multimedia coding paradigm," In: Proc. IEEE International Conference on Image Processing, Barcelona, Spain (2003)
17. Aaron, A., Girod, B, "Wyner-Ziv video coding with low encoder complexity," In: Proc. IEEE International Conference on Image Processing, San Francisco, CA (2004)
18. Varodayan, D., Aaron, A., Girod, B, "Rate-adaptive distributed source coding using Low-Density Parity Check codes," In: Proc. Asilomar Conference on Signals and Systems, Pacific Grove, CA (2005)
19. Aaron, A., Varodayan, D., Girod, B, "Wyner-Ziv Residual Coding of Video," In: Proc. Picture Coding Symposium, Beijing, China (2006)

## Appendix: Proof of Theorems

**Theorem 1:** For quadratic Gaussian case, if $R_{HB}(D_0,D_1)=R_{WZ}(D_0)$, then $D_1 \geq \sigma_X^2$

Proof: The proof is straight forward because RD function for HBC and WZC can be written as:

$$R_{HB}(D) = \frac{1}{2}\log^+ \frac{\sigma_X^2 \sigma_N^2}{D_0(\min(D_1,\sigma_X^2)+\sigma_N^2)}, \text{ and } R_{WZ}(D_0) = \frac{1}{2}\log^+ \frac{\sigma_X{}^2 \sigma_N{}^2}{(\sigma_X{}^2+\sigma_N{}^2)D_0}$$

comparing the two equations immediately yield: $\min(D_1,\sigma_X^2) = \sigma_X^2$, i.e. $D_1 \geq \sigma_X^2$

**Theorem 2:** For quadratic Gaussian case, if $R_{HB}(D_0,D_1)=R_X(D_1)$, then $D_0 = \dfrac{D_1\sigma_N^2}{D_1+\sigma_N^2}$

Proof: Similar with in proof of theorem 1, we have:

$$R_{HB}(D) = 1/2\log^+[\sigma_X^2 \sigma_N^2 /(D_0(D_1+\sigma_N^2))] = R_X(D_1) = 1/2\log^+(\sigma_X^2 / D_1),$$

$$\text{so that } D_0 = \frac{D_1\sigma_N^2}{D_1+\sigma_N^2}.$$

which is just the LMMSE estimation noise of $\hat{X}_0 = E(X|\hat{X}_1, Y)$

# Real-Time BSD-Driven Adaptation Along the Temporal Axis of H.264/AVC Bitstreams

Wesley De Neve, Davy De Schrijver, Davy Van Deursen,
Peter Lambert, and Rik Van de Walle

Ghent University - IBBT
Department of Electronics and Information Systems - Multimedia Lab
Gaston Crommenlaan 8 bus 201, B-9050 Ledeberg-Ghent, Belgium
{wesley.deneve, davy.deschrijver, davy.vandeursen,
peter.lambert, rik.vandewalle}@ugent.be
http://multimedialab.elis.ugent.be

**Abstract.** MPEG-21 BSDL offers a solution for exposing the structure of a binary media resource as an XML description, and for the generation of a tailored media resource using a transformed XML description. The main contribution of this paper is the introduction of a real-time work flow for the XML-driven adaptation of H.264/AVC bitstreams in the temporal domain. This real-time approach, which is in line with the vision of MPEG-21 BSDL, is made possible by two key technologies: BFlavor (BSDL + XFlavor) for the efficient generation of XML descriptions and Streaming Transformations for XML (STX) for the efficient transformation of these descriptions. Our work flow is validated in several applications, all using H.264/AVC bitstreams: the exploitation and emulation of temporal scalability, as well as the creation of video skims using key frame selection. Special attention is paid to the deployment of hierarchical B pictures and to the use of placeholder slices for synchronization purposes. Extensive performance data are also provided.

**Keywords:** BSDL, H.264/AVC, STX, temporal scalability, video skims.

## 1 Introduction

Video adaptation is an active area of interest for the research and standardization community [1]. The major purpose of a framework for video adaptation is to customize video resources such that the resulting bitstreams meet the constraints of a certain usage environment. This makes it possible to optimize the Quality of Experience (QoE) of the end-user. Several adaptation strategies can be identified, either operating at a semantic level (e.g., removal of violent scenes), at a structural level (e.g., picture dropping), or at a signal-processing level (e.g., coefficient dropping). In this paper, we introduce a real-time work flow for the structural adaptation of H.264/AVC bitstreams along their temporal axis, based on describing their high-level syntax in XML. Our approach enables applications such as the exploitation and emulation of temporal scalability in streaming scenarios, as well as the creation of video highlights in off-line use cases.

Y. Zhuang et al. (Eds.): PCM 2006, LNCS 4261, pp. 131–140, 2006.

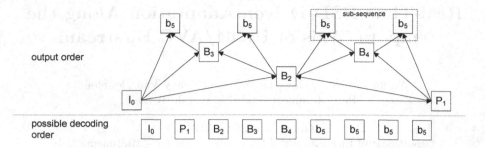

**Fig. 1.** The IbBbBbBbP coding pattern containing four sub-sequence layers

This paper is organized as follows. Section 2 introduces the two main enabling technologies, while Sect. 3 discusses several methods for the XML-driven extraction of bitstreams of multiple frame rates from a single coded H.264/AVC bitstream. Finally, Sect. 4 concludes this manuscript.

## 2   Enabling Technologies

### 2.1   Temporal Scalability in H.264/AVC

In video coding formats prior to H.264/AVC, temporal scalability is typically realized by the disposal of bidirectionally predicted pictures (B pictures). However, H.264/AVC only defines I, P, and B slices, and not I, P, and B pictures. Second, a coded picture can comprise a mixture of different types of slices. Finally, B slices can be used as a reference for the reconstruction of other slices [2].

Therefore, the recommended technique for achieving temporal scalability in H.264/AVC is to rely on the concept of sub-sequences [3] [4]. A sub-sequence represents a number of inter-dependent pictures that can be disposed without affecting the decoding of the remaining bitstream. In practice, these units of content adaptation are typically created by relying on a hierarchical coding pattern. This is a coding structure in which the use of reordering between picture decoding order and picture output order takes the form of building up a coarse-to-fine structuring of temporal dependencies. Nowadays, it is common to implement such a coding pattern using B slice coded pictures [5] (further referred to as hierarchical B pictures). However, hierarchical I slice or P slice coded pictures can be used as well (if coding efficiency is less important than encoding and decoding complexity), or a mix of the different slice and picture types.

An example coding pattern, offering four temporal levels, is shown in Fig. 1. A capital letter denotes a reference picture; a small letter a non-reference picture. Each picture is tagged with the value of frame_num. This syntax element acts as a counter that is incremented *after* the decoding of a reference picture, a functionality useful for the purpose of error concealment and content adaptation. Note that a hierarchical coding pattern is typically a good structure in terms of coding efficiency, but not in terms of end-to-end delay.

## 2.2    BSD-Driven Content Adaptation

**MPEG-21 BSDL.** The MPEG-21 Digital Item Adaptation (MPEG-21 DIA) standard addresses issues resulting from the desire to access multimedia content anywhere, anytime, and with any device. This concept is better known as Universal Multimedia Access (UMA). The MPEG-21 Bitstream Syntax Description Language (MPEG-21 BSDL) is a description tool that is part of MPEG-21 DIA. The language in question is a modification of W3C XML Schema to describe the (high-level) structure of a particular media format (file format, coding format) [6]. This results in a document called a Bitstream Syntax Schema (BS Schema). It contains the necessary information for exposing the structure of a binary media resource as an XML-based text document, called Bitstream Syntax Description (BSD), and for the creation of a tailored media resource using a transformed BSD. This media resource is then suited for playback in a particular usage environment, for instance constrained in terms of processing power.

In a BSDL-based content adaptation framework, the generation of a BSD is done by a format-neutral software module called BintoBSD Parser, while the adapted bitstream is constructed by a format-agnostic engine called BSDtoBin Parser. How to transform a BSD is not in the scope of MPEG-21 BSDL. In this paper, Streaming Transformations for XML (STX) are used for the transformation of BSDs (see further). The functioning of BintoBSD and BSDtoBin is guided by a BS Schema for a particular media format. As such, the BintoBSD and BSDtoBin Parsers constitute the pillars of a generic software framework for media format-unaware content adaptation, and of which the operation is entirely steered by XML-based technologies (e.g., XML, XML Schema, STX).

Finally, the main advantages of BSD-driven adaptation of binary media resources can be summarized as follows:

- the complexity of the content adaptation step is shifted from the compressed domain to the XML domain, allowing the reuse of standard XML tools (e.g., editors, transformation engines) and an integration with other XML-oriented metadata specifications (e.g., the MPEG-7 standard);
- the high-level nature of the BSDs allows to think about a media resource on how it is organized in terms of headers, packets, and layers of data;
- a *format-agnostic* content adaptation engine can be implemented (i.e., a combination of a BSD adaptation engine and BSDL's BSDtoBin Parser).

**BFlavor.** The first version of the MPEG-21 BSDL specification is characterized by a number of performance issues with respect to the automatic generation of BSDs. Indeed, a format-agnostic BintoBSD Parser has to store the entire BSD in the system memory in order to support the at-run time evaluation of an arbitrary set of XPath 1.0 expressions. These XPath expressions are used to get access to XML-structured information that is already retrieved from a media resource, needed by a BintoBSD Parser for its decision-making while progressively parsing a bitstream. This behavior of BintoBSD results in an increasing memory usage

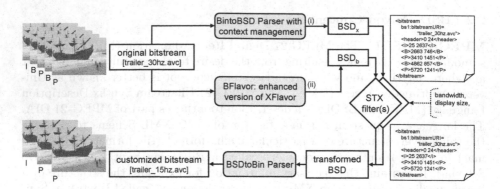

**Fig. 2.** BSD-driven media content adaptation, using BFlavor, STX, and BSDL

and a decreasing processing speed during the generation of an XML description for the high-level structure of a media resource.

Two different solutions were developed by the authors of this paper to address the performance issues of BSDL's BintoBSD process:

1. the first approach adds a number of new attributes to BSDL, allowing a BintoBSD Parser to keep the in-memory tree representation of a BSD minimal while still guaranteeing a correct output for the BintoBSD process [7];
2. the second solution consists of the development of a new description tool for translating the structure of a binary media resource into an XML description, called BFlavor (BSDL + XFlavor) [8] [9].

BFlavor is the result of a modification of XFlavor to efficiently support BSDL features. It allows to describe the structure of a media resource in an object-oriented manner, after which it is possible to automatically create a BS Schema, as well as a code base for a format-specific parser. This automatically generated parser is subsequently able to generate BSDs that are compliant with the automatically generated BS Schema. As such, this implies that the resulting BSDs can be further processed by the upstream tools in a BSDL-based adaptation chain, such as a format-neutral BSDtoBin Parser.

Fig. 2 provides a high-level overview of our XML-based content adaptation chain. It illustrates the two different approaches for creating BSDL-compliant BSDs: (1) by relying on an optimized BintoBSD Parser, using our extensions to BSDL; (2) using a BFlavor-based parser. The transformation of the BSDs is done by relying on STX while the adapted bitstreams are constructed using BSDL's BSDtoBin Parser.

## 3   Bitstream Extraction in H.264/AVC

In this section, a few experiments are discussed that were set up to evaluate the expressive power and performance of the XML-driven content adaptation chain

**Table 1.** Bitstream characteristics for The New World movie trailer

| ID | coding pattern | frame rate (Hz) | resolution | #slices/ picture | #NALUs[a] | duration (s) | $size_o$ (MB) |
|---|---|---|---|---|---|---|---|
| $TNW_1$ | IbBbBbBbP | 23.98 | 848x352 | 5 | 17808 | 148 | 42.9 |
| $TNW_2$ | IbBbBbBbP | 23.98 | 1280x544 | 5 | 17808 | 148 | 78.7 |
| $TNW_3$ | IbBbBbBbP | 23.98 | 1904x800 | 5 | 17808 | 148 | 126.0 |

[a] NALU stands for Network Abstraction Layer Unit; $size_o$ stands for original file size.

**Table 2.** BSD generation using an optimized BintoBSD Parser and BFlavor

| ID | $BintoBSD_m$ Parser | | | | BFlavor | | | |
|---|---|---|---|---|---|---|---|---|
| | throughput (NALU/s) | $MC^a$ (MB) | BSD (MB) | $BSD_c$ (KB) | throughput (NALU/s) | MC (MB) | BSD (MB) | $BSD_c$ (KB) |
| $TNW_1$ | 124 | 1.7 | 44.3 | 326 | 1164 | 0.7 | 28.9 | 308 |
| $TNW_2$ | 110 | 1.7 | 44.2 | 335 | 777 | 0.7 | 29.0 | 317 |
| $TNW_3$ | 97 | 1.7 | 44.3 | 332 | 533 | 0.7 | 29.0 | 314 |

[a] MC stands for peak heap Memory Consumption; $BSD_c$ for compressed BSD size.

as proposed in Fig. 2. The focus is hereby put on the real-time adaptation of H.264/AVC bitstreams along the temporal axis. The media resources involved are three different versions of the same movie trailer, called The New World[1]. The performance analysis was done by breaking up the XML-driven content adaptation chain in its three fundamental building blocks: BSD generation, BSD transformation, and bitstream construction. Real-time means that every building block, typically running in a pipelined fashion on different processing nodes, is able to achieve a throughput that is at least as fast as the playback speed of the original media resource.

The most important properties of the bitstreams used, encoded with the H.264/AVC reference software (JM 10.2), are shown in Table 1. The coding pattern employed is visualized by Fig. 1. The results were obtained on a PC with an Intel Pentium IV 2.61 GHz CPU and 512 MB of memory. All time measurements were done 11 times, after which an average was taken of the last 10 runs in order to take into account the startup latency. BSDs were compressed using WinRAR 3.0's default text compression algorithm. The anatomy of the H.264/AVC bitstreams was described up to and including the syntax elements of the slice headers, once in MPEG-21 BSDL and once in BFlavor.

### 3.1 BSD Generation

Table 2 summarizes the results obtained during the generation of BSDs for the bitstreams involved. The BFlavor-based parser outperforms our optimized BintoBSD Parser on all metrics applied: the parser is faster than real-time for all bitstreams used (i.e., its throughput is always higher than the playback speed of 23.98 x 5 NALUs/s or 120 NALU/s) and is characterized by a very low memory footprint. The BFlavor-driven parser also produces textual BSDs that are much

---

[1] Online available at: http://www.apple.com/trailers/.

**Table 3.** BSD transformation using STX and tailored bitstream construction using BSDL's format-neutral BSDtoBin Parser

| ID | operation | BSD transformation | | | | bitstream reconstruction | | |
|---|---|---|---|---|---|---|---|---|
| | | throughput (NALUs/s) | MC (MB) | BSD (MB) | $BSD_c$ (KB) | throughput (NALUs/s) | MC (MB) | $size_a$ (MB) |
| $TNW_1$ | remove $EL^a$ 3 | 835 | 1.2 | 21.5 | 159.0 | 406.2 | 2.0 | 98.4 |
| $TNW_2$ | remove EL 2 + 3 | 980 | 1.2 | 11.0 | 81.0 | 361.2 | 2.3 | 65.2 |
| $TNW_3$ | remove EL 1 + 2 + 3 | 1098 | 1.3 | 5.8 | 41.0 | 264.3 | 2.2 | 38.6 |
| $TNW_1$ | replace EL 3 | 537 | 1.7 | 36.9 | 194.0 | 515.2 | 2.1 | 98.5 |
| $TNW_2$ | replace EL 2 + 3 | 445 | 1.7 | 33.5 | 121.0 | 554.7 | 2.3 | 65.3 |
| $TNW_3$ | replace EL 1 + 2 + 3 | 447 | 1.3 | 33.1 | 84.6 | 537.2 | 2.2 | 38.8 |

[a] EL stands for enhancement layer.

smaller than those created by the BintoBSD Parser. This is due to the design of our manually created BS Schema (used by the BintoBSD and BSDtoBin Parser): it is less optimized than BFlavor's automatically generated BS Schema (only used by a BSDtoBin Parser) for the purpose of readability.

## 3.2 BSD Tranformation and Bitstream Reconstruction

The transformation of the BSDs was done using Streaming Transformations for XML (STX)[2]. This transformation language is intended as a high-speed, low memory consumption alternative to XSLT as it does not require the construction of an in-memory tree. As such, STX is suitable for the transformation of large XML documents with a repetitive structure, which are typical characteristics for BSDs describing the high-level structure of compressed video bitstreams. Indeed, several publications have shown that XSLT, as well as a hybrid combination of STX/XSLT, are unusable in the context of XML-driven video adaptation, due to a respective high memory consumption and high implementation overhead [10].

A number of STX stylesheets were implemented in the context of this research, dependent on the targeted use case. In what follows, the semantics and performance of the different transformation steps are outlined in more detail.

**Exploiting Temporal Scalability by Dropping Slices.** A first STX stylesheet was written to drop the different temporal enhancement layers as visualized in Fig. 1. The decision-making process was implemented by checking the values of the following syntax elements: `nal_ref_idc`, `slice_type`, and `frame_num`. The value of `gaps_in_frame_num_value_allowed_flag` in the Sequence Parameter Set (SPS) was modified to one, signaling to a decoder that reference pictures were intentionally dropped. As shown in the upper half of Table 3, the implementation of the removal operations, at the level of a BSD, can be done very efficiently in terms of processing time and memory consumption needed. The STX engine used was the Joost STX processor (version 2005-05-21).

**Emulation of Temporal Scalability Using Placeholder Slices.** In the context of digital video coding, it is important to separate the concept of what

---

[2] Online available at `http://stx.sourceforge.net/`.

is encoded in the bitstream, which is essentially a compact set of instructions to tell a decoder how to decode the video data, from the concept of what is the decision-making process of an encoder. The latter process is not described in a video coding standard, since it is not relevant to achieving interoperability. Consequently, an encoder has a large amount of freedom about how to decide what to tell a decoder to do. This freedom can also be exploited by a content adaptation engine to offer a solution for resynchronization issues that may occur after the adaptation of an elementary bitstream in the temporal domain.

The traditional view of temporal scalability is to remove certain coded pictures from a bitstream while still obtaining a decodable remaining sequence of pictures. This approach is typically applied when using BSD-driven bitstream thinning. However, a major drawback of this method is that it fails when, for instance, the remaining pictures are to be resynchronized with an audio stream.

Elementary bitstreams usually do not convey (absolute) timing information as this responsibility is typically assigned to the systems layer (e.g., file formats, network protocols), and not to the coding layer. Consequently, after having dropped certain pictures in a bitstream, it is often impossible to synchronize the remaining pictures with a corresponding audio stream without an external knowledge, an observation that is especially true when varying coding patterns are in use. Therefore, we propose to exploit temporal scalability in elementary video bitstreams by replacing coded pictures with placeholder pictures, a technique that operates at the same level as BSDL, i.e. at the coding layer [10].

A placeholder or dummy picture is defined as a picture that is identical to a particular reference picture, or that is constructed by relying on a well-defined interpolation process between different reference pictures. Therefore, only a limited amount of information needs to be transmitted to signal placeholder pictures to a decoder. Placeholder pictures are used to fill up the gaps that are created in a bitstream due to the disposal of certain pictures, a technique that is further referred to as the emulation of temporal scalability. This approach makes it straightforward to maintain synchronization with other media streams in a particular container format, especially when a varying coding structure is in use because the total number of pictures remains the same after the adaptation step. As such, from the bitstream's point of view, emulating temporal scalability can be considered a substitution operation, and not a removal operation.

Several STX stylesheets were developed to translate the B slices in the temporal enhancement layers of the H.264/AVC bitstreams to skipped B slices and skipped P slices (see Fig. 3).

- A picture consisting of skipped B slices tells an H.264/AVC decoder to reconstruct the picture by doing an interpolation between the previous picture and the next picture in output order[3].
- A picture consisting of skipped P slices instructs a decoder to output the last picture in the decoded picture buffer[4].

---

[3] The interpolated picture is computed based on the relative temporal positions of the list 0 and list 1 (decoded) reference pictures.

[4] This is, the first (decoded) reference picture in list 0.

```
<stx:group name="BtoskippedP">
  <stx:template match="jvt:coded_slice_of_a_non_IDR_picture" public="no">
    <stx:element name="coded_slice_of_a_skipped_non_IDR_picture" namespace="h264_avc">
      <stx:process-children group="BtoskippedP"/>
    </stx:element>
  </stx:template>
  <stx:template match="jvt:slice_layer_without_partitioning_rbsp" public="no">
    <stx:element name="skipped_slice_layer_without_partitioning_rbsp" namespace="h264_avc">
      <stx:process-children group="BtoskippedP"/>
    </stx:element>
  </stx:template>
  <stx:template match="jvt:slice_type" public="no">
    <stx:element name="slice_type" namespace="h264_avc">0</stx:element>
  </stx:template>
  <stx:template match="jvt:slice_qp_delta" public="no">
    <stx:element name="slice_qp_delta" namespace="h264_avc">0</stx:element>
  </stx:template>
  <stx:template match="jvt:if_slice_type_eq_B" public="no"/>
  <stx:template match="jvt:slice_data" public="no">
    <stx:element name="skipped_slice_data" namespace="h264_avc">
      <stx:element name="mb_skip_run" namespace="h264_avc">234</stx:element>
      <stx:element name="rbsp_trailing_bits" namespace="h264_avc">
        <stx:element name="rbsp_stop_one_bit" namespace="h264_avc">1</stx:element>
        <stx:element name="rbsp_alignment_zero_bit" namespace="h264_avc">0</stx:element>
      </stx:element>
    </stx:element>
  </stx:template>
</stx:group>
```

**Fig. 3.** Extract of the STX stylesheet for translating B slices to skipped P slices in the XML domain. Similar logic is used for translating I and P slices to skipped P slices.

Skipped B slices were used as a substitute for the B slices in the third enhancement layer when only this layer is to be removed; the use of skipped P slices would lead to a wrong output order (i.e., $I_0B_4B_3B_4B_2B_4B_4B_4P_1$), due to the fact that $B_4$ is the last picture in the decoded picture buffer. Skipped P slices were used as a substitute for all B slices when at least two enhancement layers are replaced; a correct output order can be obtained then (e.g., $I_0B_2B_2B_2B_2B_2B_2B_2P_1$ when dropping two enhancement layers).

Performance results are provided in the lower half of Table 3. It is clear that the translation operations, which are entirely expressed in the XML domain, can be executed in real time. The same observation is true for the behaviour of BSDL's BSDtoBin Parser [11]. The overhead of the skipped slices in the resulting bitstreams can be ignored, as one can notice in the column with label $size_a$.

**Video Skims by Key Frame Selection.** Finally, our XML-driven content adaptation approach was also used for the production of video skims. These compact abstractions of long video sequences are typically created by filtering out relevant pictures, e.g. key pictures that are located near the beginning of a shot. Therefore, a STX stylesheet was implemented that takes as input the shot detection information as produced by the IBM MPEG-7 Annotation Tool[5] , and that subsequently identifies and marks the I slice coded pictures located near the start of a shot. More precisely, the information about the different shots is embedded by the STX stylesheet as additional attributes in a BSD (see Fig. 4). The resulting BSD is then provided as input to a next STX stylesheet; it filters out the relevant I slice coded pictures and translates all remaining I and B slices to skipped P slices to maintain synchronization with the original audio stream.

---

[5] Online available at: http://www.alphaworks.ibm.com/tech/videoannex.

```
<bitstream xmlns="h264_avc" xmlns:jvt="h264_avc" bitstreamURI="the_new_world_h480p_IbBbBbBb.h264">
  <byte_stream>
    <byte_stream_nal_unit pic_cnt="0" shot="false">
      <!-- Sequence Parameter Set -->
    </byte_stream_nal_unit>
    <byte_stream_nal_unit pic_cnt="0" shot="false">
      <!-- Picture Parameter Set -->
    </byte_stream_nal_unit>
    <byte_stream_nal_unit pic_cnt="1" shot="true">
      <!-- First coded slice of I_0 (an IDR picture) -->
    </byte_stream_nal_unit>
    <byte_stream_nal_unit pic_cnt="2" shot="false">
      <!-- First coded slice of I_1 (a non-IDR picture) -->
    </byte_stream_nal_unit>
    <byte_stream_nal_unit pic_cnt="3" shot="false">
      <!-- First coded slice of B_2 (a non-IDR picture) -->
    </byte_stream_nal_unit>
    <!-- Remaining byte stream NALUs in decoding order -->
  </byte_stream>
</bitstream>
```

**Fig. 4.** Embedding shot information as additional attributes in a BSD

Note that the IbBbBbBb coding pattern was used instead of IbBbBbBbP, offering random access at regular picture intervals as every picture in the base layer is encoded as an I slice coded picture. The summary of the video bitstream also results in a significant reduction of its file size: from 44.7 MB to 4.40 MB when $TNW_1$ is used with the IbBbBbBb pattern. This technique may be of particular interest for the repurposing of content for constrained usage environments.

## 4 Conclusions

This paper introduced a real-time work flow for the description-driven adaptation of H.264/AVC bitstreams along their temporal axis. The key technologies used were BFlavor for the generation of BSDs, STX for the transformation of BSDs, and BSDL's format-neutral BSDtoBin Parser for the construction of tailored bitstreams. Our approach was validated in several use cases: the exploitation of temporal scalability by dropping certain slices; the emulation of temporal scalability by relying on skipped slices; and the creation of video skims. The use of video skims, new in the context of BSD-based video adaptation, is made possible by enriching a BSD with additional metadata to steer the BSD adaptation process. As an example, an overall pipelined throughput of at least 447 NALUs/s was achieved when emulating temporal scalability in a high-definition H.264/AVC bitstream by substituting all slices in the enhancement layers by skipped P slices, together with a combined memory use of less than 5 MB.

A remaining bottleneck in this content adaptation system is the size of the textual BSDs. Further research will also concentrate on shifting the focus of BSD-driven content adaptation from a structural level to a semantic level.

**Acknowledgments.** The research activities that have been described in this paper were funded by Ghent University, the Interdisciplinary Institute for Broadband Technology (IBBT), the Institute for the Promotion of Innovation by

Science and Technology in Flanders (IWT), the Fund for Scientific Research-Flanders (FWO-Flanders), the Belgian Federal Science Policy Office (BFSPO), and the European Union.

# References

1. Chang, S.-F., Vetro, A.: Video Adaptation: Concepts, Technology, and Open Issues. Proc. the IEEE 93 (1) (2005) 145-158
2. Sullivan, G.J., Wiegand, T.: Video Compression - From Concepts to the H.264/AVC Standard. Proc. the IEEE 93 (1) (2005) 18-31
3. Tian, D., Hannuksela, M., Gabbouj, M.: Sub-sequence Video Coding for Improved Temporal Scalability. Proceedings 2005 IEEE International Symposium on Circuits and Systems (ISCAS 2005), pages 6074-6077, Kobe, Japan, May 2005
4. De Neve, W., Van Deursen, D., De Schrijver, D., De Wolf, K., Van de Walle, R.: Using Bitstream Structure Descriptions for the Exploitation of Multi-layered Temporal Scalability in H.264/AVC's Base Specification. Lecture Notes in Computer Science, Volume 3767, pages 641-652, Oct 2005
5. Schwarz, H., Marpe, D., Wiegand, T.: Analysis of Hierarchical B Pictures and MCTF. Proceedings 2006 International Conference on Multimedia & Expo (ICME 2006), Toronto, Canada, July 2006
6. Panis, G., Hutter, A., Heuer, J., Hellwagner, H., Kosch, H., Timmerer, T., Devillers, S., Amielh, M.: Bitstream Syntax Description: A Tool for Multimedia Resource Adaptation within MPEG-21. Signal Processing: Image Communication 18 (2003) 721-747
7. De Schrijver, D., De Neve, W., De Wolf, K., Van de Walle, R.: Generating MPEG-21 BSDL Descriptions Using Context-Related Attributes. Proceedings of the 7th IEEE International Symposium on Multimedia (ISM 2005), pages 79-86, USA, December 2005
8. Van Deursen, D., De Neve, W., De Schrijver, D., Van de Walle, R.: BFlavor: an Optimized XML-based Framework for Multimedia Content Customization. Proceedings of the 25th Picture Coding Symposium (PCS 2006), 6 pp on CD-ROM, Beijing, China, April 2006
9. De Neve, W., Van Deursen, D., De Schrijver, D., De Wolf, K., Lerouge, S., Van de Walle, R.: BFlavor: a harmonized approach to media resource adaptation, inspired by MPEG-21 BSDL and XFlavor. Accepted for publication in EURASIP Signal Processing: Image Communication, Elsevier.
10. De Neve, W., De Schrijver, D., Van de Walle, D., Lambert, P., Van de Walle, R.: Description-Based Substitution Methods for Emulating Temporal Scalability in State-of-the-Art Video Coding Formats. Proceedings of the 7th International Workshop on Image Analysis for Multimedia Interactive Services (WIAMIS 2006), pages 83-86, Incheon, Korea, 2006
11. Devillers, S., Timmerer, C., Heuer, J., Hellwagner, H.: Bitstream Syntax Description-Based Adaptation in Streaming and Constrained Environments. IEEE Trans. Multimedia 7 (3) (2005) 463-470

# Optimal Image Watermark Decoding

Wenming Lu, Wanqing Li, Rei Safavi-Naini, and Philip Ogunbona

University of Wollongong, NSW 2522, Australia
{wl86, wanqing, rei, philipo}@uow.edu.au

**Abstract.** Not much has been done in utilizing the available information at the decoder to optimize the decoding performance of watermarking systems. This paper focuses on analyzing different decoding methods, namely, Minimum Distance, Maximum Likelihood and Maximum *a-posteriori* decoding given varying information at the decoder in the blind detection context. Specifically, we propose to employ Markov random fields to model the prior information given the embedded message is a structured logo. The application of these decoding methods in Quantization Index Modulation systems shows that the decoding performance can be improved by Maximum Likelihood decoding that exploits the property of the attack and Maximum *a-posteriori* decoding that utilizes the modeled prior information in addition to the property of the attack.

## 1 Introduction

An image watermarking system is subject to three conflicting requirements: invisibility, robustness and capacity. Invisibility requires that the original and the watermarked images look perceptually identical; robustness implies that a useful version of the embedded message can be recovered after attacks; given the fixed invisibility and robustness, it is desirable to embed as much information as possible.

Figure 1 is a block diagram depicting the processes involved in a typical watermarking system: embedding, attacking channel and detection. The embedder takes an image, $\mathbf{x}$, as input into which the message $m_e$ of length $l_{m_e}$, is to be embedded. The message, $m_e \in \{0,1\}^{l_{m_e}}$, is either in its original binary form or error correction coded to aid subsequent decoding. Note that before the message is embedded into the image, it may undergo some pre-processing, such as dividing the image into blocks, transforming the image into another convenient domain and extracting coefficients or feature vectors as the embedding signals, $\mathbf{x}^w(\mathrm{x}_1^w, \mathrm{x}_2^w, \cdots, \mathrm{x}_n^w)$, $n=l_{m_e}$. The encoder then maps $t$-th bit, $t = 1, 2, \cdots, n$, of $m_e$ to a watermark signal that is inserted into $\mathrm{x}_t^w$ to produce the watermarked signal $\mathrm{s}_t^w$. The mapping is usually subject to a secret key, $k$, that determines the security of the watermarking system. All watermarked signals $\mathbf{s}^w(\mathrm{s}_1^w, \mathrm{s}_2^w, \cdots, \mathrm{s}_n^w)$, are appropriately processed and assembled to produce the watermarked image $\mathbf{s}$ in the pixel domain.

The watermarked image, $\mathbf{s}$, goes through the attack channel, $C$, which may include common signal processing, incidental modifications or even intentional attacks, before being received at the detector as $\mathbf{y}$, a distorted version of $\mathbf{s}$. Inside the detector, some pre-processing similar to that employed at the embedder is

Y. Zhuang et al. (Eds.): PCM 2006, LNCS 4261, pp. 141–149, 2006.

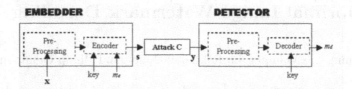

**Fig. 1.** A typical watermarking system

applied to produce possibly distorted watermarked signals, $\mathbf{y}^w$ ($y_1^w, y_2^w, \cdots, y_n^w$), $n=l_{m_e}$. For each watermark signal, $y_t^w$, a detection value, $d_t$, is calculated based on the watermark signal generated using the same key, $k$. We denote as $d$-$map$, $\mathbf{d}$, all calculated detection values, $d_1, d_2, \cdots, d_n$. The decoding problem can be formulated as the estimation of the message $m_d$ based on the $d$-$map$, $\mathbf{d}$.

Most of existing literature has focused on optimizing the embedding process. Efforts in this direction include the class of host-signal interference non-rejecting systems, e.g., the Spread Spectrum (SS) system [1]; the class of host-signal rejecting systems, e.g. Quantization Index Modulation (QIM) [3]; and encoder with the side information [2]. Various strategy to seek the best domain and the most appropriate embedding signals for achieving robustness against a set of possible attacks [5, 4, 6] have been studied in the past.

## 1.1   Contribution of the Paper

In this paper we focus on the detector and develop strategy to utilize any information available at the decoder. Knowledge of the model of the attack can be used to implement noise (distortion) removal or reduction, in the received image $\mathbf{y}$ [1]. Most decoders to date have relied on the $d$-$map$ calculated on the distorted image, $\mathbf{y}$, and estimated the embedded message based on analysis of $\mathbf{y}$. We refer to this simple decoding method as Minimum Distance (MD) decoding.

For any watermarking system, the detection values, $\mathbf{d} \in d$-$map$, are random variables that possess some probability distribution. The impact of an attack can be reflected in the change of the distribution. In other words, the distribution of detection values can be considered as a characterization of the attack that the watermarked image has gone through and a maximum likelihood (ML) decoder can utilize such information to improve the decoding. In [7], an ML decoder was proposed for QIM systems. However there was no conscious exploitation of the property of the attack to which the image was subjected. Attacks may change the distribution of the detection values in different ways and without the appropriate estimation of the property of the attack, ML does not necessarily improve the decoding performance.

The distributions of the bits in the binary representation of the embedded message vary with different messages and can be exploited if appropriately modeled. Specifically for structured logos, the neighborhood dependency can be modeled by Markov random field, MRF, to estimate prior information about such message. Maximum *a-posteriori*, MAP, decoding is then adopted to exploit prior information and the property of the attack to enhance the decoding performance. We analyze these three decoding methods under the assumption of availability of different information at the decoder. Through experimentation we provide examples of applying the decoding methods in a QIM system and compare performances. Results show that proper estimation of the attack's property and modeling of the prior information can certainly be used by ML or MAP decoders to boost the decoding performance.

# 2  Optimal Image Watermark Decoding

## 2.1  Minimum Distance (MD) Decoding

The MD decoder only has access to the *d-map*, $\mathbf{d}$, calculated from $\mathbf{y}$. For each watermarked unit $y_t^w$, we define $\delta_t^0$ and $\delta_t^1$ as the distances between $y_t^w$ and the nearest bit 0 and 1 centroid, respectively. For any watermarking system $W$, there exists a function $F_W(.)$ that maps the detection value to the pair $(\delta_t^0, \delta_t^1)$, i.e., $(\delta_t^0, \delta_t^1) = F_W(d_t)$. Generally, for a message, $m$, we define the aggregated distances to nearest bit 1 and 0 centroid as, $\mathbf{d}_{\{\mathbf{y},m\}} = \sqrt{\sum_t^n \left(\delta_t^{b_t}\right)^2}$, with $b_t$ as the $t$-th bit of message $m$. The MD decoding strategy is to find a message $\hat{m}$ that minimizes $\mathbf{d}_{\{\mathbf{y},m\}}$. In other words the estimated message $\hat{m}$, is,

$$\hat{m} = \arg\min_m \mathbf{d}_{\{\mathbf{y},m\}} \tag{1}$$

Note that $\mathbf{d}_{\{\mathbf{y},m\}}$ is minimized if each $\delta_t^{b_t}$ is minimized and the decoding can be carried on each embedding unit independently,

$$b_t = \begin{cases} 1 \text{ if } \delta_t^0 > \delta_t^1 \\ 0 \text{ if } \delta_t^0 \le \delta_t^1 \end{cases} \tag{2}$$

where $b_t$ represents the bit decoded on $y_t^w$, and $m_d = \{b_1, b_2, \cdots, b_n\}$.

## 2.2  Maximum Likelihood (ML) Decoding

For a given attack, $C$, let $p_C(\mathbf{d}|m)$ be the probability of the *d-map*, $\mathbf{d}$, conditioned on the embedded message, $m$. The decoding strategy is to choose the message $\hat{m}$ that maximizes the conditional probability, i.e.,

$$\hat{m} = \arg\max_m p(\mathbf{d}|m) \tag{3}$$

The number of possible messages is considerably large and in most cases the calculation of $p_C(\mathbf{d}|m)$ cannot be done in reasonable time. Therefore, it is often assumed that the noise added to each unit $s_t^w$ is independent. If we assume that the data model, $p(d_t|b_t)$, represents the conditional probability of the detection value $d_t$ conditioned on embedding bit $b_t$ in a unit after the attack $C$,

$$p(\mathbf{d}|m) = \prod_{t=0}^{n=l_m} p(d_t|b_t) \tag{4}$$

$p(\mathbf{d}|m)$ can then be maximized when each bit $b_t$ is individually optimized.

In contrast with MD decoding, ML exploits both the data model of the attack and the *d-map*. Rather than employ pre-decoding noise reduction processing, ML decoding estimates the data model, i.e., the modification of the distribution of the detection values, and utilizes it to enhance the decoding.

## 2.3   Maximum *a-posteriori* (MAP) Decoding

When the message is a binary bit map, such as a logo with some spatial structure, incorporation of the structural information into the decoding may further improve the robustness. We propose to model the prior structural information using Markov random field (MRF) [9, 8]. MAP decoding can employ such modeled prior information to further improve the decoding.

Let $D = \{D_t : 1 \leq t \leq N\}$ be a random field defined on a lattice $L$, where $N = w \times h = l_{m_e}$ is the number of bits and $t = j + w \times i$ is the index of the bit at $(i, j)$. We consider a *d-map*, $\mathbf{d}$, the vector of the detection values, that is calculated from $\mathbf{y}$ as a realization of the $D = \{D_t : t \in L\}$, $\mathbf{d}^* = \{d_t : t \in L\}$. We also consider the embedded logo $m_e$ as a true but unknown labeling of the *d-map* and assume that the labeling is a realization of a random field $M = \{M_t : t \in L\}$, $m^* = \{b_t : t \in L\}$, where $b_t \in \{0, 1\}$. Then the problem of decoding the embedded logo can be formulated as an estimation of the labels, $\hat{m}$, that maximizes the *a- posteriori* probability [8] given the observed *d-map*. The $\hat{m}$ then becomes the estimated message $m_d$. Using Bayes rule

$$p(M = m | D = \mathbf{d}) \propto p(D = \mathbf{d} | M = m) p(M = m) \tag{5}$$

Assuming $M$ is an MRF defined in a neighborhood system, $\eta$, and $\{D_t, t = 1, 2, \cdots, N\}$ is conditionally independent and each $D_t$ has the same conditional pdf, $f(d_t | b_t)$, dependent only on $b_t$ , then Eq.( 5) becomes

$$p(M = m | D = \mathbf{d}) \propto \prod_{t \in L} f(d_t | b_t) p(b_t | b_{\partial t}) \tag{6}$$

where $p(d_t | b_t)$ is known as the data model that captures the property of the attack and $p(b_t | b_{\partial t}) = \frac{e^{-u(b_t | b_{\partial t})}}{Z_t}$ is the prior pdf, known as the prior model, of $b_t$ given its neighbors, $b_{\partial t}$, defined in a neighborhood system $\eta_t$ [8]. $Z_t$ is a partition function and $u(\cdot)$ is usually referred to as an energy function. With the given models, the MAP estimation of the embedded message is

$$\hat{m} = \arg\max_{m \in \Omega} \prod_{t \in L} f(d_t | b_t) p(b_t | b_{\partial t}) \tag{7}$$

It is not computationally feasible to find an optimum solution of Eq.( 7). However, there are three well-known algorithms for local optimum solutions: Simulated Annealing (SA) [9], Maximizer of Posterior Marginal (MPM) [8] and Iterated Conditional Modes (ICM) [10]. We adopted ICM due to its simplicity and reasonable performance. ICM is a deterministic algorithm and iteratively updates the current decoding $\hat{b}_t$ at pixel $t$ on the basis of the observation *d-map* and the decoding of its neighbors. The locality property of MRF has led to the updating rule for the ICM algorithm

$$\hat{b}_t = \arg\max_{b_t} f(d_t|b_t)p(b_t|b_{\partial t}) \tag{8}$$

The prior model, or especially the energy function $u(\cdot)$, can be empirically defined over cliques in a second-order neighborhood system [9] as

$$u(b_t|b_{\partial t}) = -(\gamma + \beta \sum_{s \in \partial t} \delta(b_t - b_s)) \tag{9}$$

where $\gamma$ enforces the utilization of the probability of the embedded bits and $\beta$ is a parameter to encourage (big value) or discourage (small value) the spatial coherency of the decoded bits and $\delta(\cdot)$ is a delta function. When embedded messages are random or unknown to the decoder, $p(M = m)$ is equiprobable for all possible messages, MAP decoding then degrades to ML decoding.

## 3   Application to QIM

In QIM, each detection value $d_t$ contains $d^0$ and $d^1$ that represent the distances between $y_t^w$ and the nearest bit 0 and 1 centroid, respectively. $F_{QIM}$ then yields,

$$\begin{cases} \delta_t^0 = d_t^0 \\ \delta_t^1 = d_t^1 \end{cases} \tag{10}$$

With ML and MAP, the data models against certain attacks must be either theoretically or empirically derived. For the modeled prior information, the parameters such as the bit probabilities of the message and the influences from different directions should be estimated either in advance or adaptively adjusted during the decoding for MAP decoders.

### 3.1   Experimental Results

The results of application of the three decoding methods only on QIM are reported for the sake of brevity. Images are divided into $4 \times 4$ blocks; QIM is applied on averages of blocks [6]. The quantization step $\Delta$ is set to 10, so that the PSNR between the original and watermarked images is around 38.8. We test a total of 80, $512 \times 512$ gray-scale images that contains reasonably large number of 1.3 million $4 \times 4$ blocks. Those images are also carefully selected to cover a wide range of texture, contrast, edge strength and directions. Random messages and ten logos with varying geometric shapes, numbers and characters are chosen as the message and repeatedly embedded into the images. ICM is adopted to implement the MAP decoding. In ICM, for logos, $\beta = 1$, thus assuming same influences from all directions; and $\alpha = 0$, so that no bit probability is employed. ICM converges in less than 6 iterations in most cases; for random messages, ICM runs for one iteration and $\beta = 0$ and $\alpha$ is set to match the bit probability for messages.

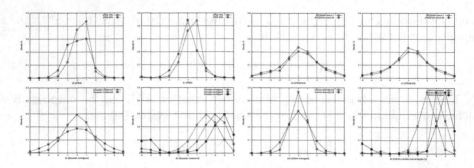

**Fig. 2.** (*Top*): from *left* to *right*, $d^0$, $d^1$ distributions after JPEG and $d^0$, $d^1$ after JPEG2000; (*Bottom*): some data models of Gaussian and uniform attacks

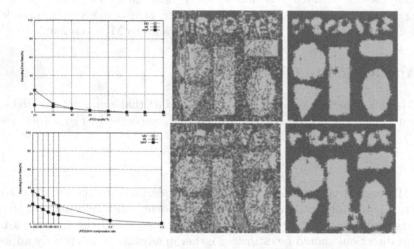

**Fig. 3.** (*Top*) MD, ML and MAP against JPEG(*left*); JPEG 20% attack:(*middle*)MD and ML decoded logo, DER=21.7%; (*right*)MAP(ICM 6 iterations), DER=5.9%; (*Bottom*) MD, ML and MAP against JPEG2000; JPEG2000 rate=0.05 attack: (*middle*)MD and ML decoded logo, DER=28.8%; (*right*)MAP(ICM 6 iterations), DER=9.6%

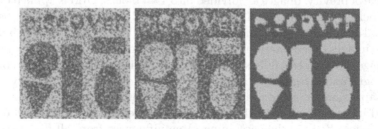

**Fig. 4.** Decoded logo against uniform[-2,8] attack:MD(*left*) DER=75.5%;ML(*middle*) DER=23.5%;MAP(*right*)(ICM 3 iterations), DER=6%

The Gaussian noise $N(\mu, \sigma)$, the uniform noise$[\eta_1, \eta_2]$, JPEG and JPEG2000, are used to attack watermarked images. Fig.2 (*Top*) shows the distribution of $d^0$ and $d^1$ after JPEG and JPEG2000 compression at two different levels for applying QIM on local averages. Our goal is to compare the performances of decoding methods and therefore we do not discuss the estimation of data models in detail. We may approximate the pdf as a Laplacian distribution with different means and variances, $p(d = d_t) = \frac{1}{2\sigma}e^{\frac{-|d_t-\mu|}{2\sigma}}$. In experiments, we set $\mu$=0 and $\sigma$=5, half of $\Delta$, for simplicity. Fig.2 (*Bottom*) from left to right shows the distributions of $d^0$ after Gaussian attacks $N(\mu=0,\sigma=5)$, $N(\mu=0,\sigma=8)$; $N(\mu=2,\sigma=5)$, $N(\mu=3,\sigma=5)$ and $N(\mu=4,\sigma=5)$; the data models of uniform attacks [-5,5] and[-8,8]; [-3,7]($\mu$=2), [-2,8]($\mu$=3) and [-1,9]($\mu$=4). The distributions of $d^1$ is similar to those of $d^0$. Clearly, the distributions of $d^0$ and $d^1$ are quite different in the face of different attacks or even same attacks but with different parameters.

Fig.3 and 5 shows the plotted curves of Decoding Error Rate (DER) for MD, ML and MAP against the chosen attacks. For JPEG, JPEG2000 and white noise attack, ML and MD are equivalent. However, ML outperforms MD against non-white Gaussian and uniform noise at higher level of attack strength. And for all high levels of attack, MAP continue to outperform ML on decoding logos. Some of MD, ML and MAP decoded logos from the host image *lena* against JPEG 20%, JPEG2000 rate of 0.05 compression and a uniform attack are also shown in Fig.3 and 4 for visually justifying the results. In Fig.5 (*right*), ML can also correct the error bits against non-white noise on decoding random messages, but MAP shows very limited edge over ML in this case. The results clearly show that the appropriate utilization in the property of the attack and the modeled prior information by ML or MAP decoder effectively improves the decoding performance.

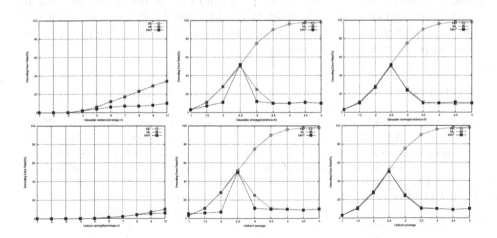

**Fig. 5.** (*Top*) MD, ML and MAP against Gaussian: (*left*) on logos, $\mu$=0, $\sigma$ 1-10; (*middel*) on logos , (*right*) on random messages $\mu$ 1-5, $\sigma$ =5; (*Bottom*) MD, ML and MAP against uniform: (*left*) on logos $\mu$=0, $\eta_1$ -1 to -5 and $\eta_2$ 1-5; (*middel*) on logos, (*right*) on random messages $\mu$ from 1-5, $\eta_1$ -4 to -1 and $\eta_2$ 6-9

## 4   Discussion and Conclusion

### 4.1   Discussion

It has to be pointed out that the proposed MD, ML and MAP decoding can be applied to other systems by appropriate derivation of $(\delta^0, \delta^1)$ from $d_t$, *i.e.*, deriving the function $F(.)$ for a particular system. For instance, in the case of SS the correlation coefficient, $d_{cc}$, can be the detection value. The possible detection lies in the interval [-1,1]. Note that the signals that share the same direction with $w$ results in $d_{cc}$ of 1 and those share similar sign with $-w$ produces $d_{cc}$ of -1. $w$ and $-w$ can be equivalently treated as a set of the bit 1 and 0 centroid in SS and $F_{SS}$ can then be defined as

$$\begin{cases} \delta_t^0 = d_{cc,t} - (-1) \\ \delta_t^1 = 1 - d_{cc,t} \end{cases} \tag{11}$$

Other watermarking systems could similarly derive the definition of the $(\delta^0, \delta^1)$ and then apply the appropriate decoding method.

### 4.2   Conclusion

Existing literature focused on improving the performance of watermarking systems at the embedder by choosing the appropriate domain and embedding signal, or encoding with the side information. We focus on analyzing three different decoding methods given varying information at the decoder. ML decoding is adopted for exploiting the property of the attack to which the image is subjected. We also propose to model the prior information about the structured message by random fields and apply MAP decoding to exploit such information. Experimental results show that depending on the available information the decoding performance can be improved.

## References

[1] I.J.Cox, M.Miller and J.Bloom, Digital watermarking, Morgan Kaufmann, 2002.
[2] I.J. Cox, M.L. Miller and A. McKellips, Watermarking as communications with side information, Proceedings of the IEEE, 1999, Vol.87, No.7, pp1127-1141.
[3] B. Chen, Design and analysis of digital watermarking, information embedding, and data hiding systems, MIT, 2000, PhD. Dissertation, Cambridge, MA.
[4] V.Licks, R.Jordan and P.Gonzlez, An exact expression for the bit error probability in angle qim watermarking under simultaneous amplitude scaling and AWGN attacks, ICASSP, 2005.
[5] A. Piper, R.Safavi-Naini and A.Mertins, Resolution and quality scalable spread spectrum image watermarking, Proc. ACM Multi.& Sec. Workshop, 2005, New York.
[6] W. Lu, W. Li, R. Safavi-Naini and P. Ogunbona, A new QIM-based image watermarking method and system, 2005 Asia-Pacific Workshop on Visual Information Processing, Hong Kong, 2005, pp160-164.

[7] L. Gang, A. N. Akansu and M. Ramkumar, Periodic signaling scheme in oblivious data hiding, Proc. ASILOMAR (34th), 2000, pp1851-1855.

[8] R.C. Dubes and A.K. Jain, Random field models in image analysis, Journal of Applied Statistics, 1989, Vol.16, No.2, pp131-163.

[9] S. Geman and D. Geman, Stochastic relaxation, Gibbs distributions, and the Bayesian restoration of images, IEEE Trans. on Pattern Analysis and Machine Intelligence, 1984, PAMI-6, No.6, pp721-741.

[10] J. Besag, On the Statistical Analysis of Dirty Pictures, J. R. Statist. Soc. B, vol.48, No.3, pp259-302, 1986.

# Diagonal Discrete Cosine Transforms for Image Coding

Jingjing Fu and Bing Zeng

Department of Electrical and Electronic Engineering
The Hong Kong University of Science and Technology
Clearwater Bay, Kowloon, Hong Kong
{jjfu, eezeng}@ust.hk

**Abstract.** A new block-based DCT framework has been developed recently in[1] in which the first transform may choose to follow a direction other than the vertical or horizontal one – the default direction in the conventional DCT. In this paper, we focus on two diagonal directions because they are visually more important than other directions in an image block (except the vertical and horizontal ones). Specifically, we re-formulate the framework of two diagonal DCTs and use them in combination with the conventional DCT. We will discuss issues such as the directional mode selection and the cross-check of directional modes. Some experimental results are provided to demonstrate the effectiveness of our proposed diagonal DCT's in image coding applications.

## 1 Introduction

Over the past three decades, a lot of image compression methods have been developed, such as predictive coding, transform-based coding, vector quantization, and sub-band/wavelet coding. Among various image coding techniques, the block-based transform approach has become particularly successful, thanks to its simplicity, excellent energy compaction in the transform domain, super compromise between bit-rate and quantization errors, etc.

With almost no exception, each transform-based scheme chooses the 2-D discrete cosine transform (DCT) that is applied on individual image blocks of a square size $N \times N$. Practically, this conventional DCT is always implemented separately through two 1-D DCT's, one along the vertical direction and another along the horizontal direction; and it does not make any difference by doing the vertical direction first or the horizontal direction first.

Both vertical and horizontal directions are important according to the human visual system (HVS). In the meantime, a lot of blocks in an image do contain vertical and/or horizontal edge(s). Thus, the conventional DCT seems to be the best choice for image blocks in which vertical and/or horizontal edges are dominating. On the other hand, however, there also exist other directions in an image block that are perhaps as equally important as the vertical and horizontal ones, e.g., two diagonal directions. For instance, let us consider two image blocks as shown in Fig. 1 where two constant regions are separated along one diagonal direction. Then, it is easy to understand that the conventional DCT may not be the most appropriate choice, as some unnecessary non-zero AC coefficients will be generated.

Y. Zhuang et al. (Eds.): PCM 2006, LNCS 4261, pp. 150–158, 2006.
© Springer-Verlag Berlin Heidelberg 2006

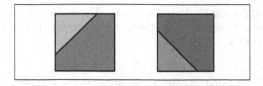

**Fig. 1.** Two image blocks that contain diagonal edges

In order to avoid this defect, we have recently developed a block-based directional DCT framework in [1]. In this framework, the first transform may choose to follow a direction from a total number of seven modes, namely, vertical/horizontal (Mode 0), diagonal down-left (Mode 3), diagonal down-right (Mode 4), vertical-right (Mode 5), horizontal-down (Mode 6), vertical-left (Mode 7), and horizontal-up (Mode 8). In principle, these are the same as the intra prediction modes defined in H.264 [3] where the vertical mode and horizontal mode have been merged into a single one as both are the same as the conventional DCT.

In this paper, we focus on two diagonal directions (i.e., Modes 3 and 4), because they are visually more important than Modes 5-8. In the next section, we will re-formulate the framework for these two diagonal DCT's. Two practical issues will be discussed in Section 3, i.e., the directional mode selection and the cross-check of directional mode. Some simulation results are shown in Section 4 to illustrate the effectiveness of our diagonal DCT's. Finally, Section 5 presents some conclusions.

## 2 Diagonal Discrete Cosine Transforms

For simplicity, all results presented in this section are based on image blocks of size $4 \times 4$ : $a = [a_{u,v}]_{4\times4}$ ; whereas the extension to the $N \times N$ block size is straightforward.

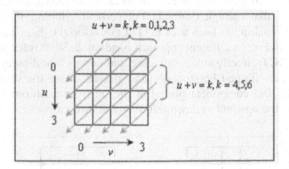

**Fig. 2.** A $4 \times 4$ image block in which the first DCT is performed along the diagonal down-left direction

Let us consider the diagonal down-left mode (Mode 3) first. As shown in Fig. 2, the first DCT will be performed along the diagonal down-left direction, i.e., for each diagonal line with $u + v = k$ , $k = 0, \cdots, 6$ . Totally, there are 7 diagonal DCT's in the first step, whose lengths are $[N_k] = [1,2,3,4,3,2,1]$. The resulting coefficients after each DCT are placed back along the corresponding diagonal line and expressed into a group of diagonal vectors

$$A_k = [A_{0,k}, A_{1,k}, \cdots, A_{N_k-1,k}]^T, \qquad k = 0,1,\cdots,6 \qquad (1)$$

Notice that each diagonal vector $A_k$ is of a different length $N_k$, with the DC component placed at bottom-left position, followed by the first AC component and so on, along the bottom-left to up-right diagonal direction, see left part of Fig. 3 for the details.

Next, four L-shaped DCT's are applied, see the middle part of Fig. 3, where the coefficients along each L-shaped line are $[A_{u,v}]_{v=u:6-u}$ for $u = 0,\cdots,3$. The coefficients after the second-step DCT's are denoted as $[\hat{A}_{u,v}]_{v=0:6-2u}$ for $u = 0,\cdots,3$ and placed back along the corresponding L-shaped line, see the right part of Fig. 3.

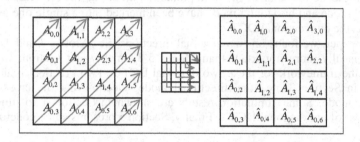

**Fig. 3.** Left: arrangement of coefficients after the first DCT. Middle: four L-shaped DCT's in the second step. Right: arrangement of coefficient after the second DCT.

Clearly, all coefficients produced after two transforms fit into the 4×4 block exactly. Therefore, any available zigzag scanning can be used directly to convert the 2-D coefficient block to a 1-D sequence so as to facilitate the runlength-based VLC.

It can be derived that a simple (horizontal or vertical) flipping of Mode 3 will yield Mode 4. This relationship has been used in [1] to develop the diagonal DCT for Mode 4. In this paper, however, a different approach is adopted. With reference to Fig. 4, we perform the first DCT directly along each diagonal down-right direction. All resulting coefficients are then flipped horizontally and placed along the diagonal down-left direction, with the DC component placed at the up-right position, followed by AC components along the up-right to down-left diagonal direction.

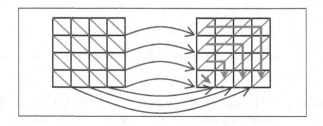

**Fig. 4.** Diagonal down-right DCT (Mode 4)

After making this new arrangement, we need to use a different DCT in the second step, which is now an anti L-shaped one. As will be described in the next section, this arrangement consequently facilitates a cross-check so as to automatically distinguish Mode 3 and Mode 4 without sending any overhead bits for representing the mode information. Also, a cross-check between Mode 0 and Mode 3/4 will be discussed in the next section.

As both diagonal DCT's formulated above are of a different length in different diagonal line, they cannot be applied directly on image blocks, because they would suffer from the so-called *mean weighting defect* [2]. To understand this in detail, let us consider the simple example of a spatially uniform image block, i.e., all pixels in the block have the same gray value. After the diagonal DCT in the first step, all AC coefficients are zero, but the resulting DC coefficients will become different for different diagonal lines. Consequently, the L-shaped (or anti L-shaped) DCT's in the second step will unavoidably generate some unnecessary non-zero AC coefficients – which is rather absurd.

One way to solve this problem is to modify the weighting factor used in the DCT matrix. However, the DCT matrix after such modification will become to be a non-unitary one, whereas the transform coding theory suggests that the use of a non-unitary transform is highly disadvantageous for coding efficiency, because it would suffer from the so-called *noise weighting defect* [2] - some statistics of quantization errors, e.g., spatial distribution of error variances or the frequency characteristics of the error signal, will be weighted in an uncontrollable manner.

To solve this dilemma problem, Kauff and Schuur proposed a novel method that consists of two steps: (1) DC separation and (2) ΔDC correction, in their work on SA-DCT [2]. This method can be readily applied in our case, with a brief description as follows.

In the DC separation step, the mean value $m$ of an image block is calculated and it will be quantized to $\overline{m}$. Then, $m$ is subtracted from the initial image block, and, subsequently, the diagonal DCT and L-shaped (or anti L-shaped) DCT are applied in the first and second steps, respectively, on the resulting zero-mean image block.

In the ΔDC correction step, the DC component produced above will be set to zero and thus will not be transmitted; while all AC components will be quantized. Next, the L-shaped or anti L-shaped IDCT is applied. Then, a ΔDC term is computed and the ΔDC correction will be done before the diagonal IDCT. Finally the quantized mean value $\overline{m}$ will be added back to the reconstructed image block.

It has been demonstrated in [2] that the ΔDC method is consistently better than modifying the weighting factor by 1-2 dB, and such conclusion has been confirmed in our experimental results. Therefore, the ΔDC method is always adopted in our diagonal DCT-based image coding.

# 3   Diagonal DCT-Based Image Coding

There are a number of other issues that need to be solved before the developed diagonal DCT framework can be applied in image coding.

*A. Selection of best DCT mode*
It is easy to understand that two diagonal DCT's formulated above have to be used together with the conventional DCT - thus resulting in three DCT modes: Mode 0

(conventional DCT), Mode 3 (diagonal down-left DCT), and Mode 4 (diagonal down-right DCT). Clearly, how to effectively select the most suitable mode for each image block is an important issue. However, we choose to leave it as one of our future works; instead, a brute-force method is adopted here: we run quantization and VLC for three modes and select the best according to a productive rate-distortion criterion – the product of the MSE and bit-count in each image block.

*B. Cross-check of DCT modes*
It seems that two (overhead) bits are needed to represent the selected DCT mode for each image block. In practice, however, we can reduce this number significantly, as explained in the following.

First of all, overhead bits of each image block are introduced in two stages. At the first stage, one overhead bit is used to distinguish the conventional mode (Mode 0) and the diagonal mode (Mode 3 or 4). Another overhead bit is needed at the second stage only when the diagonal mode is called at the first stage so as to distinguish Mode 3 and Mode 4. We observed from our simulation results that usually more than half of image blocks will choose Mode 0 according to the productive R-D criterion described above, consequently, the average number of bits per block for representing the mode information can be reduced to be below 1.5.

To further reduce the number of overhead bits per block, we propose to carry out a two-stage cross-check, with some details described below. Suppose that an image block $B$ is coded in a mode that is unknown. After the inverse VLC, inverse zigzag scanning, and de-quantization, we obtain the DCT coefficients of $B$ and then apply the IDCT according to Mode 0, Mode 3 and Mode 4, respectively, with the reconstructed blocks denoted as $B_0$, $B_3$, and $B_4$.

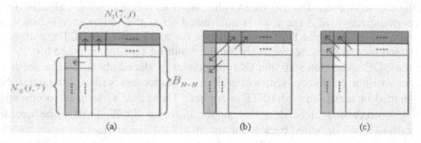

**Fig. 5.** Neighbor difference pattern of three modes (a) Mode 0 (b) Mode 3 (c) Mode 4

Next, we compute the neighbor difference of $B_0$, $B_3$ and $B_4$ using Eq. (2) according to the information of the image blocks which have been reconstructed.

$$Diff_0 = \sum_{i=0}^{N-2} \left| B_0(i,0) - N_0(i,7) \right| + \sum_{j=0}^{N-1} \left| B_0(0,j) - N_1(7,j) \right|$$

$$Diff_3 = \sum_{i=0}^{N-2} \left| B_3(i,0) - N_0(i+1,7) \right| + \sum_{j=0}^{N-1} \left| B_3(0,j) - N_1(7,j+1) \right| \quad (2)$$

$$Diff_4 = \sum_{i=0}^{N-2} \left| B_4(i,0) - N_0(i-1,7) \right| + \sum_{j=0}^{N-1} \left| B_4(0,j) - N_1(7,j-1) \right|$$

The results will be processed in two stages ( $Diff$ is the minimum value of $Diff_0$ , $Diff_3$ , $Diff_4$ ):

*Stage 1*: Mode 0 is called if $Diff = Diff_0$ ; Mode 3/4 is called otherwise.

*Stage 2*: Mode 3 is called if $Diff = Diff_3$ ; Mode 4 is called otherwise.

In the first stage, we attempt to distinguish Mode 0 from Mode 3/4 where neighbor difference method is used. Let's use $P_1$ to denote the correct cross-check rate (i.e., Mode 0 is correctly detected as Mode 0 or Mode 3/4 is correctly detected as Mode 3/4); whereas $1 - P_1$ will be the wrong cross-check rate (i.e., Mode 0 is incorrectly detected as Mode 3/4 or Mode 3/4 is incorrectly detected as Mode 0). Suppose that such a cross-check is done at the encoder side. Clearly, one bit per block is needed to tell whether the cross-check is correct or not, and this bit needs to be sent as overhead. Based on $P_1$ , these overhead bits within an entire image can be further coded in an arithmetic coding so that the average number of overhead bits per block $E_1$ can be approximated as

$$E_1 = -P_1 \log_2 P_1 - (1 - P_1) \log_2 (1 - P_1) \tag{3}$$

which represents the entropy of a two-symbol memoryless source with probability distribution $[P_1 \quad 1 - P_1]$ and is always smaller than 1.

The same principle is applied in the second stage to distinguish Mode 3 and Mode4, after a diagonal mode is called in the first stage. $P_2$ is used to denote the correct cross-check rate (i.e., Mode 3 is correctly detected as Mode 3 or Mode 4 is correctly detected as Mode 4); whereas $1 - P_2$ will be the wrong cross-check rate (i.e., Mode3 is incorrectly detected as Mode4 or Mode4 is incorrectly detected as Mode3). Thus, the average number of overhead bits per block $E_2$ in this stage is approximately

$$E_2 = -P_2 \log_2 P_2 - (1 - P_2) \log_2 (1 - P_2). \tag{4}$$

Finally, the average number of overall overhead bits per block is

$$E = E_1 + E_2 \cdot P \tag{5}$$

where $P$ represents the percentage of image blocks that have chosen Mode 3 or 4 according to the productive R-D criterion described earlier.

Clearly, $E$ would be very small if the cross-check is highly accurate in both stages, i.e., $P_1 \gg 1 - P_1$ and $P_2 \gg 1 - P_2$ . In this paper, we only tested a gradient-based scheme where the horizontal and vertical gradients are computed in Mode 0, while two diagonal gradients (down-left and down-right) are computed in Modes 3 and 4, respectively, referring to Eq. (2). Our results show that the correct cross-check rate is about 75~95% at both stages and the average number of overhead bits per block has been reduced to the range 0.45~1.2 for all test data and quantization parameters.

It is worth to point out that all overhead bits can be ignored completely if our diagonal DCT's are used in combination with the intra prediction modes defined in H.264 [3] for the coding of all intra blocks – which is indeed one of our future works. On the other hand, our another future work is to attempt to apply such diagonal

DCT's in motion-compensated frames in video coding. In this scenario, (significantly) reducing the number of overhead bits becomes quite crucial.

## 4   Experimental Results

In this section, we provide some experimental results to illustrate our diagonal DCT framework. To this end, we select the first frames of four video sequences: "Akiyo", "Foreman", "Stefan", and "Mobile" (of the CIF format). We fix the block size at $8 \times 8$ for all test data and implement the H.263 quantization/VLC in which the QP value is selected in the range [3, 31] with incremental step being set at 2.

Some simulation results are shown in Fig. 6, where only image blocks that have chosen Mode 3 or 4 in our diagonal DCT framework are included. It is clear that a significant gain has been achieved for the frames of "Akiyo" and "Foreman": ranging from over 1 dB in the high bit-rate end to 3-4 dB in the low bit-rate end. The gain is also quite noticeable (0.5~2.0 dB) for the frames of "Stefan" and "Mobile".

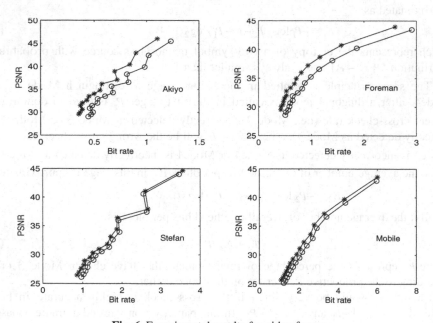

**Fig. 6.** Experimental results for video frames

Figure 7 shows the distribution of modes in each test data when QP=20, in which Mode 0, Mode 3, and Mode 4 are represented as black (with gray value = 5), a gray-color (with gray value = 128), and white (with gray value = 250), respectively. While the distribution seems rather random in general, we do observe some patterns (in white-color) at the up-right corner of "Foreman". It is easy to justify that these patterns are the desired ones as the texture of "Foreman" at this corner is highly oriented along the diagonal down-right direction (Mode 4).

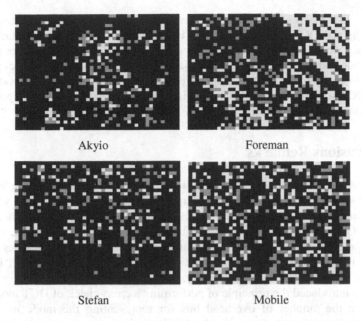

**Fig. 7.** Distribution of various DCT modes for four video frames (QP = 20)

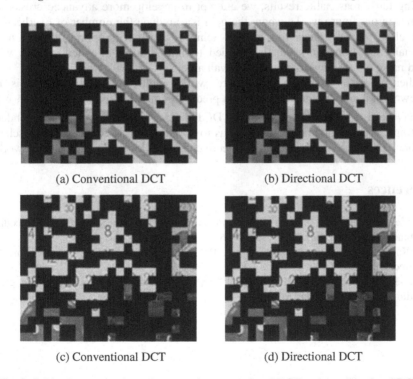

(a) Conventional DCT                      (b) Directional DCT

(c) Conventional DCT                      (d) Directional DCT

**Fig. 8.** Subjective comparisons between the conventional DCT and our directional DCT

Finally, Fig. 8 gives some subjective comparisons between the conventional DCT and our diagonal DCT for the frames of "Foreman" and "Mobile". All black blocks indicate that Mode 0 has been chosen in our diagonal DCT so that the conventional DCT and our diagonal DCT produce the same result. The purpose of blacking these blocks is to highlight all blocks that have chosen a diagonal coding mode in our diagonal DCT scheme. It is clear that the visual quality achieved in our diagonal DCT has been improved significantly.

## 5  Conclusions Remarks

In this paper, we formulated a new framework for two diagonal DCT's in which the first transform can choose to follow a diagonal direction, instead of the vertical or horizontal one - the default direction in the conventional DCT. To complement the diagonal DCT in the first step, the second transform is arranged to be an L-shaped or anti L-shaped one. By selecting the best suited one from three DCT modes for each individual image block, we demonstrated that a remarkable coding gain has been achieved in the rate-distortion performance.

We also introduced the principle of performing a cross-check of DCT modes so as to minimize the number of overhead bits for representing the mode information. While a simple gradient-based cross-check scheme has been adopted in this paper – yielding fairly reasonable results, we attempt to develop more advanced cross-check schemes in our future works where the goal is to reduce the number of overhead bits to be close to zero. Once this goal is achieved - we feel optimistic with it, our diagonal DCT framework can be applied to inter frames in video coding, which would make our framework much more valuable.

Other research issues in our future works include: implementing this new framework in combination with the intra prediction modes developed in H.264 where we may need to develop integer-based DCT's for a non-$2^M$ length; independently selecting the DCT mode effectively so as to avoid the brute-force selection scheme; and theoretical analysis to justify the effectiveness of our diagonal DCT framework.

## References

1. B. Zeng, "Directional discrete cosine transforms – a new framework for image coding," submitted to *IEEE Trans. CSVT*, Jan. 2006.
2. P. Kauff and K. Schuur, "Shape-adaptive DCT with block-based DC separation and ΔDC correction," *IEEE Trans. CSVT*, vol. 8, pp. 237-242, June 1998.
3. ITU-T Rec. H.264 | ISO/IEC 14496-10 (AVC), "Advanced video coding for generic audiovisual services", March 2005.

# Synthesizing Variational Direction and Scale Texture on Planar Region

Yan-Wen Guo[1,2,*], Xiao-Dong Xu[1], Xi Chen[1], Jin Wang[1], and Qun-Sheng Peng[1]

[1] State Key Lab of CAD and CG, Zhejiang University, Hangzhou 310027, China
[2] State Key Lab for Novel Software Technology, Nanjing University, Nanjing 210093, China
{ywguo, xuxiaodong, xchen, jwang, peng}@cad.zju.edu.cn

**Abstract.** Traditional 2D texture synthesis methods mainly focus on seamlessly generating a big size texture, with coherent texture direction and homogeneous texture scale, from an input sample. This paper presents a method of synthesizing texture with variational direction and scale on arbitrary planar region. The user first decomposes the interest region into a set of triangles, on which a vector field is subsequently specified for controlling the direction and scale of the synthesized texture. The variational texture direction and scale are achieved by mapping a suitable texture patch found in the sample via matching a check-mask, which is rotated and zoomed according to the vector field in advance. To account for the texture discontinuity induced by not well matching or different texture directions/scales between adjacent triangles, a feature based boundary optimization technique is further developed. Experimental results show the satisfactory synthesis results.

**Keywords:** Computer graphics, texture synthesis, texture direction and scale, feature matching.

## 1 Introduction

Texture synthesis means generating a big size texture from an input texture sample, such that the big size texture appears similar pattern with the sample locally while presents some stochastic attribute globally. As its wide applications in game/film producing, virtual reality, etc., texture synthesis has been widely studied by the researchers of computer vision/graphics for many years [1-11].

Earlier methods emphasize on analyzing the stochastic property of the texture [1-6], and apply obtained texture model to supervise the synthesis process. Recently, some methods deem the synthesis process as a Markov process and texture the given region based on neighbors' matching [7-11]. That is, to synthesize texture on a certain region, a rectangular patch is recursively textured to fill in this region, and the current patch to be textured is only related with its neighbors' texture. Although nearly seamless synthesis results can be obtained with

---

[*] Corresponding author.

Y. Zhuang et al. (Eds.): PCM 2006, LNCS 4261, pp. 159–166, 2006.

above methods, most of them can only generate texture with identical texture direction and homogeneous texture scale on a rectangular region. It is difficult for them to conveniently synthesize texture with variational texture direction or scale. However, this class of texture is much useful and universal in our life, such as the tiles of winding road, the pattern of fabric, tree's skin, etc.

In this paper, we present a method of synthesizing texture with variational direction and scale. The method still regards the synthesis process as a Markov process, while applies triangle as the synthesis unit. So we can generate texture on arbitrary 2D region. The variational direction is achieved by rotating the current triangle to be textured and a check-mask, with the angle composed of a given referenced vector and the specified vector adhering to the current triangle, when searching for the suitable texture patch in the sample. Meanwhile, variational scale is generated by zooming in or out the current triangle and its check-mask according to the proportion between the module of the referenced vector and that of the specified vector. To relax texture discontinuity between adjacent triangles, we further introduce a feature matching and warping based boundary optimization technique, which in fact results in resolving the "assignment problem" in linear programming with high efficiency. It is convenient to extend this method to directly synthesize variational texture on surface.

The rest of this paper is organized as follows. Section 2 introduces some related work. We provide the method of synthesizing variational texture detailedly in section 3, and present the feature based matching and warping technique in section 4. Some experimental results are given in section 5. The last section summarizes our work and highlights the future work.

## 2   Related Work

Earlier methods concentrated on analyzing the texture models and can be classified by the models they applied, such as reaction-diffusion [1], and random field models [2-3], etc. Some also used hybrid models that include a periodic component and a stochastic component [4].

Recently, neighborhood based methods have attracted much attention and achieved significant progress [7-11]. The most important stage of these methods is to search for a suitable texture pixel/patch in the input sample, which is most matched with its neighbors' existent texture. Among these methods, applying pixel as the synthesis unit and texturing a pixel in each step can achieve fine results, but the efficiency is low. Although applying patch as the unit can enhance the performance, texture discontinuity between adjacent patches is a key issue that should be addressed carefully.

To resolve this problem, some methods perform a fusion operation in the common region of the current patch and the existing one, whereas the methods in [8][10] optimize the patch merging stage and find a best texture segmentation by dynamic programming or graph cut technique. With the help of feature map, Wu et al. developed a novel algorithm to perform feature matching and alignment by measuring structural similarity [11], and got remarkable synthesis results.

# 3    Synthesizing Variational Texture

Our method of texture synthesis adopts triangle as the synthesis unit. As any 2D region with close boundaries can be triangulated by the standard Delaunay algorithm, we can synthesize texture on arbitrary planar region.

In the following, we mainly describe the method of synthesizing texture on the triangulated region, and how to generate the effect of variational direction and scale. First of all, the creation of vector field will be addressed.

## 3.1    Creation of Vector Field

After triangulating the interest region, we need designate the vector field on this region for controlling the synthesized texture's direction and scale. The user first specifies the vectors of a few seed-triangles, then the inverse distance weighted interpolation method is used to generate the vectors on the rest of the triangles. Besides the vector field, a referenced vector should also be given by the user, which indicates the standard texture direction/scale in sample.

## 3.2    Texture Synthesis on Triangles

Our method is still neighborhood based. However, it is not feasible to texture the triangulated region with scan line order as most previous methods have done. Instead, we use a priority based traversal method to texture each triangle. The priority of a triangle is defined as the number of its neighbors that have been synthesized. Initially, all the triangles included in the region are pushed into a priority queue with zero priorities. After this, the triangle with the highest priority will be iteratively removed from the queue and be textured, and the priority queue is refreshed simultaneously.

It it obvious that, for the first time, since the triangle removed from the queue has zero priority, this triangle is filled with an arbitrary texture patch selected from the sample. Additionally, the priority of each triangle in fact predicates the constraints to this triangle. That is, the higher priority, the more constraints its check-mask includes. Synthesizing the triangle with the highest priority in each step can actually facilitate searching for the matched texture patch, and reduce efficiently the discontinuity between adjacent triangles.

In the following subsections, we exploit some details of the algorithm.

## 3.3    Extraction of Check-Mask

Classical neighborhood based methods, like [5, 7], utilize the overlapped region between the current unit and its adjacent synthesized ones as the template to search for the best matched texture patch in the sample, which works well for most kinds of textures.

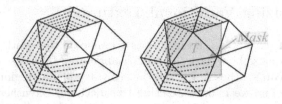

**Fig. 1.** Check-mask. The left: the current triangle $T$ and its synthesize adjacent neighbors (filled with blue dashed. The right: the check-mask, which is a square surrounding the $T$.

However, in our method, we can not easily define a regular template as most previous methods have done, for the unknown and irregular shape of the synthesized triangles. Instead, we define here a check-mask, which is in fact a square surrounding the current triangle as shown in Fig. 1. Assume that the triangles filled with the blue dashed have been textured (the left figure). Then their corresponding region lying in the blue square (the right figure) will take effect during the searching process, while the rest area in the mask is useless.

The size of the check-mask is selected in proportion to the size of the bounding box of the current triangle. In fact, the smaller the mask is, the faster the searching speed is; or else the lower the speed is. Nevertheless, if the mask is too small, the continuity or structure of the synthesized texture can not be well preserved. So it is a balance to felicitously select its size. We empirically value the mask 1.2 multiple of the bounding box in our experiments, and restrict its width within 20 pixels as well to ensure the synthesis speed. Experimental results show that this mechanism for choosing the mask works well in most cases.

### 3.4    Transformation of Check-Mask

To generate the effect of variational texture direction and scale, we need transform the check-mask in the light of the specified vector of the current triangle $T$. The transformation here in fact can be factorized into a rotation part answering for the variational direction, and a zoom one accounting for the different scale. The check-mask is rotated in term of the angle between the referenced vector specified and the vector of $T$, and zoomed in or out according to the proportion between the module of the referenced vector and that of $T$'s vector.

Once we have transformed the check-mask, we can search for the suitable texture patch for $T$ in the sample. The searching process is performed by traversing all possible positions of the mask in scan-line order in the sample, and computing the color difference between the color of the mask and that of its corresponding position in the sample. The position with the minimal color difference indicates the texture patch best matched, which are therewith mapped to the position of $T$ in the interest region.

# 4   A Feature Based Boundary Optimization Technique

For most neighborhood based methods, a key issue existent is the texture discontinuity at the boundary of the adjacent synthesis units. This problem is much more serious in our method incurred by different texture directions and scales between adjacent units. To resolve this problem, we introduce here a feature matching and warping based post processing technique to optimize the boundary.

In fact, for textures with salient features, especially highly structured textures, discontinuity is frequently caused by mismatching of features at the edges of triangles. So if we can rematch the features near the common edge and align them with minor deformation, the synthesis effect will be notably enhanced.

## 4.1   Feature Matching

Suppose $T_P$ is the current triangle textured, and $T_Q$ is one of its neighbors synthesized. We first detect the feature points, for example the image gradient exceeding a given threshold, on the common edge of $T_P$ and $T_Q$. Assume that they are: $S_P = \{p_1, p_2, ..., p_n\}$ for $T_P$ and $S_Q = \{q_1, q_2, ..., q_m\}$ for $T_Q$ respectively (see Fig. 2). Our idea is to find a best match between the points of $S_P$ and those in $S_Q$, relying on which, we align the textures near the common edge via minor deformation.

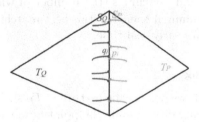

**Fig. 2.** Rematch of features. The blue/green curves represent the features detected for $T_Q/T_P$ near the common edge, on which the blue/green nodes are the feature points to be matched and aligned.

We first define the matching energy about two points $p_i$, $q_j$ as:

$$f_{i,j} = \omega_1 f_d(p_i, q_j) + \omega_2 f_c(p_i, q_j) + \omega_3 f_g(p_i, q_j). \tag{1}$$

Where $f_d$ is the normalized Euler distance between two points punishing the large distortion and ensuring small texture deformation. $f_c$, $f_g$ denote the normalized color and gradient differences respectively. $\omega_1$, $\omega_2$ and $\omega_3$ are the weights balancing the actions of $f_d$, $f_c$ and $f_g$, which are valued with $0.4, 0.3, 0.3$ in our experiments.

Then the total energy for matching the points between $S_P$ and $S_Q$ is specified as:

$$F(P,Q) = \sum_{k=1}^{min(n,m)} f_{ik,jk}, \quad (1 \leq i_k \leq n, 1 \leq j_k \leq m). \tag{2}$$

For a valid matching of (2), the following terms are required. (a) Any two points in $S_P$ should be matched with dissimilar points in $S_Q$. For two points in $S_Q$, the term is the same. (b) The points in one set should be orderly matched with the points in the other set. That is, cross matching is forbidden, since that will cause texture jumping.

According to above conditions, note that, since the points number of $S_P$ may be not equal to $S_Q$, some redundant points are automatically abandoned after the matching process. The points in $S_P$ or $S_Q$ with the less number will be fully matched.

The objective function for the best matching is thus:

$$\arg \min_{\{ik,jk,(k=1,\ldots,min(n,m),1\leq ik\leq n,1\leq jk\leq m)\}} F(P,Q).$$

In fact, solving such a function can be easily converted into solving a "assignment problem" in linear programming, by adding some virtual points in the set with less points. The detailed solution can be found in [12]. However, as the number of feature points lying on the common edge is usually not large, we only need to enumerate all valid matchings (the number of which totals $C_{max(n,m)}^{min(n,m)}$), then the one with the minimal energy is the best matching. In most cases, the solution can be found in nearly real-time.

### 4.2   Texture Warping

With the matched result, we deform the texture of $T_P$ slightly along the common edge. Without losing generality, assume the point number of $S_P$ is less than $S_Q$. Thus any point included in $S_P$ is matched with a point in $S_Q$.

**Fig. 3.** Comparision between the results with (the left) and without (the right) our algorithm

We first add some virtual points along an edge parallel to the common edge, which have the same number with the points in $S_P$ and preserve consistently relative positions on this edge with the points of $S_P$ on the common edge. The region of $T_P$ near the common edge is then uniformly triangulated with these points. Finally, the texture in each triangle is mapped to its new triangle resulting from the feature matching process. Fig. 3 compares the synthesis results generated with and without the algorithm.

## 5 Experimental Results

We have performed our experiments on an Intel Pentium IV 1.6GHz PC with 512MB main memory under the Windows XP operating system. Figs. 4, 5 demonstrate our experimental results.

Fig. 4 (a) & (b) give two synthesis results with direction field in vortex shape. The rectangle region consists of 96 triangles, and synthesis timing is 25 seconds. Fig. 4 (c) & (d) demonstrates two results. The synthesized textures become larger progressively from the top-right angle to the bottom-left of the square. We divide the rectangle region into 128 triangles, and fulfill the synthesis using 32 seconds. Fig. 4 (e) show the corresponding direction field for Fig. 4 (c) & (d).

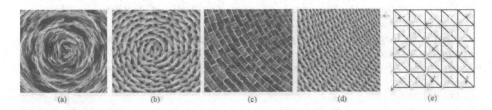

**Fig. 4.** Synthesis results. The direction field is similar to that shown in Fig. 1. Resolution is (256*256).

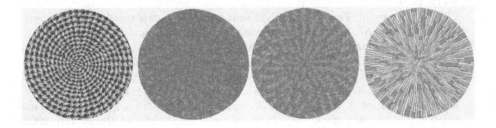

**Fig. 5.** Synthesis results. The diameter of each synthesized texture is 256 pixels.

Fig. 5 shows the results of synthesizing circular texture, whose scale around the center is smaller than that near the border. The circle is divided into 400 triangles, and it takes 96 seconds to synthesize one result.

# 6    Conclusions and Future Work

We have presented a method for synthesizing 2D texture with variational direction and scale, which was not dealt with by previous methods. By searching in the sample a check-mask transformed automatically according to the specified vector, the synthesized texture varies progressively satisfying the user's will. Furthermore, a feature based matching and warping post processing technique is developed, to treat with texture discontinuity between adjacent units. In the future we intend to extend our method to directly synthesize variational texture on 3D surface.

## Acknowledgement

This paper is supported by National 973 program (No. 2002CB312101), NSFC grant (No.60403038) and CUHK Direct Research Grant(No.2050349).

## References

1. Witkin A, Kass M. Reaction-diffusion textures. In *Porc. SIGGRAPH91*, LasVegas, July 1991, pp.299-308.
2. Fournier A, Fussel D, Carpenter L. Computer rendering of stochastic models. *Communications of the ACM*, 1982, 25(6): 371-384.
3. Bennis C, Gagalowicz A. 2-D macroscopic texture synthesis. *Computer Graphics Forum*, 1989, 8(4): 291-300.
4. Francos, J. M., Meiri, A. Z., Porat, B. A Unified TextureModel Based on a 2DWold-Like Decomposition. *IEEE Transactions on Signal Processing*, 1993, 41: 2665C 2678.
5. Heeger D J, Bergen J R. Pyramid-based texture analysis/synthesis. In *Proc. SIGGRAPH95*, Los Angeles, August 1995, pp.229-238.
6. Portilla J, Simoncelli E P. A parametric texture model based on joint statistics of complex wavelet coefficients. *International Journal of Computer Vision*, 2000, 40(1): 49-70.
7. Wei L Y, Levoy M, Fast Texture Synthesis using Tree-structured Vector Quantization, In *Proc. SIGGRAPH00*, San Antonio, July 2000, pp.479-488.
8. Efros A A, Freeman W T. Image quilting for texture synthesis and transfer. In *Proc. SIGGRAPH01*, Los Angeles, August 2001, pp.341-346.
9. Liang L, Liu C, Xu Y Q, Guo B N, Shum H-Y. Real-time texture synthesis by patch-based sampling. *ACM Trans. Graphics*, 2001, 20(3): 127-150.
10. Kwatra V, Schodl A, Essa I, Turg G, Bobick A. Graphcut textures: image and video synthesis using graph cuts. In *Proc. SIGGRAPH03*, San Diego, July 2003, pp.277-286.
11. Wu Q, Yu Y Zh. Feature matching and deformation for texture synthesis. In *Proc. SIGGRAPH04*, Los Angeles, August 2004. pp.364-367.
12. Hillier F. S, Lieberman G. J. Introduction To Operations Research(7th edition). Prentice Hall, 2002.

# Fast Content-Based Image Retrieval Based on Equal-Average K-Nearest-Neighbor Search Schemes

Zhe-Ming Lu[1,2], Hans Burkhardt[2], and Sebastian Boehmer[2]

[1] Visual Information Analysis and Processing Research Center, Harbin Institute of Technology
Shenzhen Graduate School, Room 417, Building No.4, HIT Campus Shenzhen University
Town, Xili, Shenzhen 518055 P.R. China
zhemingl@yahoo.com
[2] Institute for Computer Science, University of Freiburg, Georges-Koehler-Allee 052,
room 01-030, 79110 Freiburg i.Br., Germany
Hans.burkhardt@informatik.uni-freiburg.de

**Abstract.** The four most important issues in content-based image retrieval (CBIR) are how to extract features from an image, how to represent these features, how to search the images similar to the query image based on these features as fast as we can and how to perform relevance feedback. This paper mainly concerns the third problem. The traditional features such as color, shape and texture are extracted offline from all images in the database to compose a feature database, each element being a feature vector. The "linear scaling to unit variance" normalization method is used to equalize each dimension of the feature vector. A fast search method named equal-average K nearest neighbor search (EKNNS) is then used to find the first K nearest neighbors of the query feature vector as soon as possible based on the squared Euclidean distortion measure. Experimental results show that the proposed retrieval method can largely speed up the retrieval process, especially for large database and high feature vector dimension.

**Keywords:** Image Retrieval, Content-based Image Retrieval, Fast .K-Nearest Neighbor Search.

## 1 Introduction

The amount of digital visual information over the Internet has grown exponentially in recent three decades, which brings the research upsurge in visual information retrieval (VIR). The ultimate goal of VIR is to retrieve desired images or video clips among massive amounts of visual data in a fast, efficient, semantically meaningful, friendly, and location-independent manner. Over the past three decades, there have been basically three ways of retrieving previously stored multimedia data, i.e., free browsing, text-based retrieval [1] and content-based retrieval [2]. Free browsing is only acceptable for the occasional user and cannot be extended to users who frequently need to retrieve specific multimedia information for professional applications. It is a tedious, inefficient, and time-consuming process and it becomes completely impractical for large databases. Text-based retrieval has two big problems associated with the

Y. Zhuang et al. (Eds.): PCM 2006, LNCS 4261, pp. 167–174, 2006.
© Springer-Verlag Berlin Heidelberg 2006

cataloguing phase: 1) the considerable amount of time and effort needed to manually annotate each individual image or clip; and 2) the imprecision associated with the subjective human perception of the contents being annotated. In a content-based visual information retrieval (CBVIR) system, instead of being manually annotated by keywords, images are indexed by their own visual content, such as color [3], texture [4], object's shape and movement [5], which are more essential and closer to the human perceptual system than the keywords used in text-based image retrieval systems.

The four most important issues in content-based image retrieval (CBIR) are how to extract features from an image, how to represent these features, how to search the images similar to the query image based on these features as fast as we can and how to perform relevance feedback. This paper concerns the third problem. The main idea of this paper is to introduce the fast search algorithm [6] formerly used in K-nearest-neighbor (KNN) classification to CBIR systems. This fast search algorithm is derived from the equal-average nearest neighbor search algorithm [7], which is used in fast codeword search for a vector quantization (VQ) [8] based encoding system. In fact, a lot of newly-developed fast codeword search algorithms [9,10] can be also introduced in KNN classification and CBIR. Considering the extra storage requirements and offline computation burden, we select the simplest one, i.e., the equal-average K-nearest-neighbor search algorithm [6]. Another purpose of the proposed scheme is to introduce the vector quantization technique in CBIR systems. In fact, VQ codebook design techniques have been used to classify the images in the database before retrieval [11, 12]. However, they don't take into account the problem how to speed up the process of the similarity comparison, which is the main concern in this paper.

## 2 Feature Database Construction

In this section, we introduce how to construct a feature database offline. This process includes three sub-processes, i.e., feature extraction, feature vector normalization and feature vector sorting. In this paper, we select four kinds of features, i.e., color, texture, shape and global translation-rotation-invariant features. All of these features are based on the HSV color space. The dimension of all selected features is 200, including 192-dimensional color features based on three color components, 3-dimensional texture features based on V component, 4-dimensional shape features [13] based on the V component and a 1-dimensional global invariant feature [14] based on the V component. Each feature vector is computed and normalized offline.

When the Euclidean distance is used to measure similarity between images in content-based image retrieval, it implicitly assigns more weight to features with large variances than those with small variances. In order to reduce this effect, we should normalize each dimension and thus make each dimension have the same range. In this paper, we use the "linear scaling to unit variance" method [15]. Assume the feature vector $\mathbf{y}_i = (y_{i,1}, y_{i,2}, y_{i,3}, ..., y_{i,D})$ has been extracted from the image $\mathbf{M}_i$, $i = 0,1,..., I-1$, where $D$ is the dimension of each feature vector and $I$ is the number of images in the database. To normalize each component into the same range [-1, 1], we use the following equation:

$$\hat{y}_{i,j} = \begin{cases} \dfrac{y_{i,j} - m_j}{3 \cdot \sigma_j} & \left| \dfrac{y_{i,j} - m_j}{3 \cdot \sigma_j} \right| \le 1 \\[2mm] -1 & \dfrac{y_{i,j} - m_j}{3 \cdot \sigma_j} < -1 \\[2mm] 1 & \dfrac{y_{i,j} - m_j}{3 \cdot \sigma_j} > 1 \end{cases} \quad (i = 0,1,\ldots,I-1, \ j = 1,2,\ldots,D) \tag{1}$$

where $\hat{y}_{i,j}$ is the normalized feature vector component, and

$$m_j = \frac{1}{I} \sum_{i=0}^{I-1} y_{i,j}$$

$$\sigma_j = \sqrt{\frac{1}{I-1} \sum_{i=0}^{I-1} (y_{i,j} - m_j)^2} \tag{2}$$

After normalization, we use the following weighted Euclidean squared distance to denote the difference between two normalized feature vectors.

$$\overline{d}(\hat{x}, \hat{y}) = \sum_{l=1}^{4} \left[ w_l \cdot \frac{1}{D_l} d(\hat{x}_l, \hat{y}_l) \right] = \sum_{l=1}^{4} \left[ \frac{w_l}{D_l} \sum_{i=1}^{D_l} (\hat{x}_{l,i} - \hat{y}_{l,i})^2 \right]$$

$$= \sum_{l=1}^{4} \left[ \sum_{i=1}^{D_l} \left( \sqrt{\frac{w_l}{D_l}} \cdot \hat{x}_{l,i} - \sqrt{\frac{w_l}{D_l}} \cdot \hat{y}_{l,i} \right)^2 \right] = \sum_{l=1}^{4} \left[ \sum_{i=1}^{D_l} (\tilde{x}_{l,i} - \tilde{y}_{l,i})^2 \right] = d(\tilde{x}, \tilde{y}) \tag{3}$$

where $\hat{x}$ and $\hat{y}$ are two normalized feature vectors of $x$ and $y$ respectively, $\hat{x}_l$ and $\hat{y}_l$ are the $l$-th sub-vectors, $D_l$ is the dimension for the $l$-th sub-vector, and $\hat{x}_{l,i}$ and $\hat{y}_{l,i}$ are the components of the vector $\hat{x}_l$ and $\hat{y}_l$ respectively. Because our fast algorithm is based on squared Euclidean distance measure, we convert the distance form from $\overline{d}(\hat{x}, \hat{y})$ into $d(\tilde{x}, \tilde{y})$, where $\tilde{x}$ and $\tilde{y}$ are called weighted normalized feature vectors, $\tilde{x}_{l,i} = \hat{x}_{l,i} \cdot \sqrt{w_l / D_l}$ and $\tilde{y}_{l,i} = \hat{y}_{l,i} \cdot \sqrt{w_l / D_l}$ are the components of sub-vectors $\tilde{x}_l$ and $\tilde{y}_l$ respectively. In our test systems, $D_1=192$, $D_2=3$, $D_3=4$, $D_4=1$ and thus $D=200$ and we use $w_1=w_2=w_3=w_4=0.25$.

In order to perform a fast search more efficiently, we should sort the feature vectors in the ascending order of the mean value calculated from each weighted normalized feature vector, i.e.,

$$\forall 0 \le i \le j \le I-1, \ \tilde{m}_i \le \tilde{m}_j \tag{4}$$

Where

$$\tilde{m}_i = \frac{1}{D} \sum_{k=1}^{D} \tilde{y}_{i,k} \qquad \tilde{m}_j = \frac{1}{D} \sum_{k=1}^{D} \tilde{y}_{j,k} \tag{5}$$

Note that we should also save the mean values of weighted normalized vectors in the feature database file. We can view this value as the first dimension of the weighted normalized vector, namely the sorted weighted normalized vector can be denoted as follows.

$$\hat{y}_i = \{\tilde{y}_{i,0}, \tilde{y}_i\} = (\tilde{y}_{i,0}, \tilde{y}_{i,1},..., \tilde{y}_{i,D}) = (\tilde{m}_i, \tilde{y}_{i,1},..., \tilde{y}_{i,D}) \quad (i = 0,1,...,I-1) \qquad (6)$$

Where $\hat{y}_i$ is the $i$-th sorted weighted normalized $D+1$ dimensional feature vector in the feature database.

## 3 Proposed Fast Image Retrieval Method

In this section, we give a new fast search method. Assume the total number of images in the database is $I$, the user wants to get the first $M$ ( $M \leq I$ ) most similar images to the query image, but the system interface can only display R images in each page. Thus the required number of pages for displaying is $P=[(M-1)/R]+1$. Here, [ ] denotes the operation to get the integer part. In most cases, $P > 1$ but $P$ is small and the users want to get the first P pages of most similar images (i.e. the first $K = P \cdot R$ most similar images) at the same time before displaying. In the conventional query-by-example CBIR system, the similarity comparison is performed between the input feature vector and each feature vector in the database, which is referred to as a full search (FS) scheme, where we should search the whole database to get the first $P$ pages of most similar images. Different from that, in this paper, we propose a fast retrieval algorithm to obtain the first $K = P \cdot R$ most similar images as soon as possible. First we give Theorem 1, which is the foundation of EKNNS, as follows.

**Theorem 1:** Define $A_D(\tilde{x}, \tilde{y}_p) = \sqrt{d(\tilde{x}, \tilde{y}_p)/D}$, where $\tilde{x}$ is a weighted normalized $D$-dimensional query feature vector and $\tilde{y}_p$ is the $p$-th weighted normalized $D$-dimensional feature vector from database ($0 \leq p \leq I-1$). Assume that the current minimum distortion is $d_{\min} = d(\tilde{x}, \tilde{y}_p)$, and the mean values of $\tilde{x}$ and $\tilde{y}_i$ ( $i = 0,1,...,I-1$ ) are $\tilde{m}_x$ and $\tilde{m}_i$, respectively. If $|\tilde{m}_i - \tilde{m}_x| \geq A_D(\tilde{x}, \tilde{y}_p)$, then $d(\tilde{x}, \tilde{y}_i) \geq d(\tilde{x}, \tilde{y}_p)$.

The proof of this theorem can be referred to [7]. Based on this theorem, we know that if $\tilde{m}_i < \tilde{m}_x - A_D(\tilde{x}, \tilde{y}_p)$ or $\tilde{m}_i > \tilde{m}_x + A_D(\tilde{x}, \tilde{y}_p)$, then the distortion of vector $\tilde{y}_i$ must be larger than $\tilde{y}_p$. Thus, if we have sorted the feature vectors in the ascending order of their means, we can search the nearest vector by modifying $A_D(\tilde{x}, \tilde{y}_p)$ iteratively. Developed from this conclusion, the main idea of EKNNS is: If we have gotten $K$ vectors and the vector from them with the largest distortion is $\tilde{y}_{index\_max}$, we can ensure that there are at least $K$ vectors that have less distortion than those with mean values out of the interval [ $\tilde{m}_x - A_D(\tilde{x}, \tilde{y}_{index\_max})$ , $\tilde{m}_x + A_D(\tilde{x}, \tilde{y}_{index\_max})$ ].

By searching the candidates near the initial best match vector $\tilde{y}_p$ in an up-and-down manner and updating the $K$ vectors iteratively, we can reduce the searching range. The algorithm can be illustrated as follows:

Step 1: If the query image is outside of the image database, then we need to calculate the query image's weighted normalized feature vector $\tilde{x}$ and its mean value $\tilde{m}_x$. In the mean-value-sorted feature database, get the initial index $p$ of the vector with the minimum mean distance from the query vector's mean value by the following bisecting method.

Step 1.0: Set $i = 0, j = I - 1$. If $\tilde{m}_x \geq \tilde{m}_j$, then set $p = j$ and go to Step 2; If $\tilde{m}_x \leq \tilde{m}_i$, then set $p = i$ and go to Step 2.

Step 1.1: Set $p = (i + j)/2$. If $\tilde{m}_x \leq \tilde{m}_p$, then $j = p$; Otherwise $i = p$.

Step 1.2: If $j - i > 1$, go to Step 1.1.

Step 1.3: If $\left| \tilde{m}_x - \tilde{m}_j \right| \geq \left| \tilde{m}_x - \tilde{m}_i \right|$, then $p = i$; Otherwise $p = j$.

Step2: Define two flags, $flag1 = false$ and $flag2 = false$, which denote whether the search process can be terminated or not in the up and down search directions respectively. Set $low = p - K/2$, $high = p + K/2 - 1$. If $low < 0$, then $low = 0$, $high = K - 1$ and $flag1 = true$. If $high > I - 1$, then $high = I - 1$, $low = I - K$ and $flag2 = true$. Calculate and sort the distances $d(\tilde{x}, \tilde{y}_{low}), d(\tilde{x}, \tilde{y}_{low+1}), ..., d(\tilde{x}, \tilde{y}_{high})$ in the ascending order based on bubble sort method. Save the corresponding distances in the array $d_{min}[i]$ and their indices in the array $index[i]$, $i = 0,1,..., K - 1$.

Step 3: Search the $K$ best-match vectors to the query vector. Note that we don't require searching the vectors with the indices from $low$ to $high$.

Step 3.0: Set $j = \min\{p - low + 1, high - p + 1\}$. If $low = 0$, then $j = high - p + 1$. If $high = I - 1$, then $j = p - low + 1$. Set $\tilde{m}_{min} = \tilde{m}_x - A_D(\tilde{x}, \tilde{y}_{index[K-1]})$ and $\tilde{m}_{max} = \tilde{m}_x + A_D(\tilde{x}, \tilde{y}_{index[K-1]})$.

Step 3.1: If $flag1 = true$ and also $flag2 = true$, then the algorithm can be terminated with the final $K$ indices of the most similar vectors, $index[i]$, $i = 0,1,..., K - 1$.

Step 3.2: If $flag1 = true$, go to Step 3.3. If $p - j < 0$ or $\tilde{m}_{p-j} < \tilde{m}_{min}$, then $flag1 = true$, go to Step 3.3. Otherwise, we use partial distance search (PDS) method [16] to compute $d(\tilde{x}, \tilde{y}_{p-j})$, if $d(\tilde{x}, \tilde{y}_{p-j}) < d(\tilde{x}, \tilde{y}_{index[K-1]})$, then insert $d(\tilde{x}, \tilde{y}_{p-j})$ into $d_{min}[i]$ and index $p - j$ into $index[i]$ in the ascending order of distances, and also update the lower and upper limits of means, $\tilde{m}_{min} = \tilde{m}_x - A_D(\tilde{x}, \tilde{y}_{index[K-1]})$ and $\tilde{m}_{max} = \tilde{m}_x + A_D(\tilde{x}, \tilde{y}_{index[K-1]})$.

Step 3.3: If $flag2 = true$, go to Step 3.4. If $p + j \geq I$ or $\tilde{m}_{p+j} > \tilde{m}_{max}$, then $flag2 = true$, go to Step 3.4. Otherwise, we use the partial distance search (PDS) method to compute $d(\tilde{x}, \tilde{y}_{p+j})$, if $d(\tilde{x}, \tilde{y}_{p+j}) < d(\tilde{x}, \tilde{y}_{index[K-1]})$, then insert $d(\tilde{x}, \tilde{y}_{p+j})$ into array $d_{\min}[i]$ and index $p + j$ into array $index[i]$ in the ascending order of distances, and also update the lower and upper limits of means, $\tilde{m}_{\min} = \tilde{m}_x - A_D(\tilde{x}, \tilde{y}_{index[K-1]})$ and $\tilde{m}_{\max} = \tilde{m}_x + A_D(\tilde{x}, \tilde{y}_{index[K-1]})$.

Step 3.4: Set $j = j + 1$, go to Step 3.1.

## 4   Experimental Results

To demonstrate the effectiveness of the proposed methods, we use two databases in the experiments. The first one is a database with 1000 images of size $384 \times 256$ or $256 \times 384$, which are classified into ten classes (i.e., People, Beach, Building, Bus, Dinosaur, Elephant, Flower, Horse, Mountain and Food), each class including 100 images. This database is used to test the performances of recall vs. time and precision vs. time. The other is a database with 20000 images of various sizes (without classification), which is only used to test the time performance. In our experiments, we use a Pentium IV computer with 2.80GHz CPU to test the performance. First we compute the feature vectors offline for all images in the database, and also normalize, weight and sort them offline. Each weighted normalized feature vector is a 200-dimensional vector, which includes 192-dimensional color features, 3-dimensional texture features, 4-dimensional shape features and 1-dimensional invariant feature as described in Section 2. We do following two experiments.

The first experiment is based on the classified 1000 images. We randomly select 2 images from each class, and thus totally 20 images, as the test query images. For each test query image, we perform the full search method and our proposed EKNNS method respectively with $P$=1, 2, 3, 4, 5, 6, i.e., the six cases where the users want to obtain $K$=16, 32, 48, 64, 80, 96 returned images. Then we can obtain corresponding required time, recall and precision performances for these 6 cases respectively. For each case, we average the time, recall and precision over the 20 test query images. After averaging, we can compare EKNNS with FS search method by the performance of recall, precision and time as shown in Table 1. Note that, for the full search method, no matter how many images are returned for users, it has to perform the whole search over all images in the database, so the required time in each case is the same for the full search method. For our EKNNS algorithm, because $P$ only varies from 1 to 6, and is not so large, so the required time is also nearly the same for various returned pages.

The second experiment is based on unclassified 20000 images. This experiment is only to show the time performance of the full search method and EKNNS for different numbers of pages, i.e., $P$ varies from 1 to 10, the ten cases are $K$=16, 32,..., 160. We randomly select 40 images from the database to be the test query images. For each test image, we obtain the required time for each case and each method. After averaging the required time for each case and each method over the 40 test query images, we obtain the curve as shown in Fig. 1.

From the experimental results, we can see that the proposed EKNNS algorithm only needs 18% time of the full search method while guaranteeing the same recall and precision in the case of $K=16$, $D=200$ and $I=1000$. And when $K$ varies from 16 to 160, $D=200$ and $I=20000$, the proposed EKNNS only needs 2%-3% of the required full search time. For $K \ll I$, the EKNNS algorithm needs nearly the same time for various returned pages, which means the EKNNS is affected less by the number of returned images.

**Table 1.** Comparisons of FS and EKNNS algorithms with 1000 classified images (D=200)

| Returned Pages | $P=1$<br>$K=16$ | $P=2$<br>$K=32$ | $P=3$<br>$K=48$ | $P=4$<br>$K=64$ | $P=5$<br>$K=80$ | $P=6$<br>$K=96$ |
|---|---|---|---|---|---|---|
| Average Precision | 70.31% | 59.06% | 53.44% | 49.06% | 45.5% | 41.56% |
| Average Recall | 11.25% | 18.9% | 25.65% | 31.4% | 36.4% | 39.9% |
| FS CPU Time | 16ms | 16ms | 16ms | 16ms | 16ms | 16ms |
| EKNNS CPU Time | 3ms | 3ms | 3ms | 3ms | 3.1ms | 3.2ms |

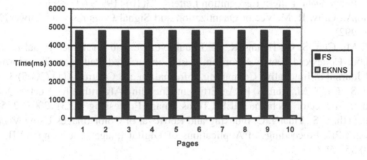

**Fig. 1.** Experimental results based on 20000 unclassified images

## 5 Conclusions

In this paper, two novel fast schemes named EKNNS and IEKNNS for CBIR are presented. These methods are suitable for the CBIR systems with multiple displaying pages, large databases and high-dimensional feature vectors. These methods exploit the mean values of the feature vectors to speed up the search process while guaranteeing the same performances of recall and precision. Experimental results demonstrate the efficiency of the proposed methods.

## Acknowledgments

This work was supported by the Alexander von Humboldt Foundation Fellowship (Germany) grant, ID: CHN 1115969 STP and the Program for New Century Excellent Talents in University of China under grant NCET-04-0329.

# References

1. Chang, N. S., Fu, K. S. Fu. Query-by-Pictorial-Example. IEEE Transactions on Software Engineering. 6(6) (1980) 519-524
2. Long, F. H., Zhang, H. J., Feng, D. D. Fundamentals of Content-based Image Retrieval, in: D. D. Feng, W. C. Siu, H. J. Zhang (Ed.),Multimedia Information Retrieval & Management-Technological Fundamentals and Applications, Springer-Verlag, New York(2003)1-26
3. Yamada, A., Kasutani, E., Ohta, M., Ochiai, H., Matoba, H. Visual Program Navigation System Based on Spatial Distribution of Color. Proc. IEEE International Conference on Consumer Electronics, (2000) 280-281
4. Kuan, J. P. K., Joyce, D. W., Lewis, P. H. Texture Content Based Retrieval Using Text Descriptions. SPIE Proc. of Storage and Retrieval for Image and Video Databases VII, vol. 3656, (1999) 75-85
5. Lee, K., Street, W. N. Incremental Feature Weight Learning and Its Application to a Shape Based Query System. Pattern Recognition Letters 23(7) (2002) 865-874
6. Pan, J. S., Qiao, Y. L., Sun, S. H. A Fast K Nearest Neighbors Classification Algorithm. IEICE Transactions on Fundamentals. E87-A(4) (2004) 961-963
7. Guan, L., Kamel, M. Equal-average Hyperplane Partitioning Method for Vector Quantization of Image Data. Pattern Recognition Letters. 13(10) (1992) 693-699
8. Gersho,A., Gray, R. M. Vector Quantization and Signal Compression. Kluwer, Norwood, MA, (1992)
9. Lu, Z. M., Chu, S. C., Huang, K. C.. Equal-average Equal-variance Equal-norm Nearest Neighbor Codeword Search Algorithm Based on Ordered Hadamard Transform. International Journal of Innovative Computing, Information and Control. 1(1) (2005) 35-41
10. Pan, J. S., Lu, Z. M., Sun, S. H. An Efficient Encoding Algorithm for Vector Quantization Based on Subvector Technique. IEEE Trans. Image Processing. 12(3) (2003) 265-270
11. Panchanathan, S., Huang, C. Indexing and Retrieval of Color Images Using Vector Quantization. SPIE Proceedings of Applications of Digital Image Processing XXII, vol. 3808 (1999) 558-568
12. Uchiyama, T., Takekawa, N., Kaneko, H., Yamaguchi, M., Ohyama, N. Multispectral Image Retrieval Using Vector Quantization. Proc. IEEE International Conference on Image Processing, vol. 1, (2001) 30-33
13. Belkasim, S. O., Shridhar, M., Ahmadi, M. Pattern Recognition with Moment Invariants: a Comparative Study. Pattern Recognition. 24(12) (1991) 1117-1138
14. Siggelkow, S., Burkhardt, H. Fast Invariant Feature Extraction for Image Retrieval, in: R. C. Veltkamp, H. Burkhardt, H. P. Kriegel (Ed.), State-of-the-Art in Content-Based Image and Video Retrieval, Kluwer Academic, Boston (2001) 43-68
15. Iqbal, Q., Aggarwal, J. K. Combining Structure, Color and Texture for Image Retrieval: a Performance Evaluation. International Conference on Pattern Recognition (ICPR), vol. 2, (2002) 438-443
16. Bei, C. D., Gray, R. M.. An Improvement of the Minimum Distortion Encoding Algorithm for Vector Quantization. IEEE Transactions on Communications. 33(10) (1985) 1132-1133

# Characterizing User Behavior to Improve Quality of Streaming Service over P2P Networks

Yun Tang[1], Lifeng Sun[2], Jianguang Luo[1], and Yuzhuo Zhong[2]

[1] Department of Computer Science and Technology,
Tsinghua University, Beijing 100084, P.R. China
{tangyun98, luojg03}@mails.tsinghua.edu.cn
[2] {sunlf, zyz-dcs}@mail.tsinghua.edu.cn

**Abstract.** The universal recognition that it is critical to improve the performance of existing systems and protocols with the understanding to practical service experiences motivates us to discuss this issue in the context of peer-to-peer (P2P) streaming. With the benefit of both practical traces from traditional client-server (C/S) service systems and logs from P2P live broadcasting system, in this paper we first characterize end user behaviors in terms of online duration and reveal the statistically positive correlation between elapsed online duration and expected remaining online time. Then we explore the feasibility to improve the quality of streaming service over P2P networks by proposing Low Disruption Tree Construction (LDTC) algorithm to take the online duration information into account when peers self-organize into the service overlay. The experiment results show that LDTC could achieve higher stability of video date delivery tree and in turn improve the quality of streaming service.

## 1   Introduction

The increasing growth of Internet and digital content industry introduces a new area of interaction between huge volume of information and end users. Particularly, streaming media contents, especially in the form of video, to a large population of end users remains interesting and challenging. At the system design stand, a rich body of literature discussed application layer multicast or overlay multicast approaches [1,2,3,4] in past years to tackle with the scalability problem without the need of network infrastructure support. Recently, the peer-to-peer (P2P) technique emerged as the most prospective means in this arena since it effectively explored the cooperative paradigm among numerous end users. Each peer, also interchangeably called node or user, plays the role of both client and server at the same time and hence the system capacity is amplified. Besides the popular P2P file sharing and VoIP applications on the Internet, BitTorrent [5] and Skype [6] for instance, many P2P live video streaming systems were also designed and deployed to broadcast TV programs [7,9]. Our experiences have demonstrated that it could scale to reliably support a great number of users [8].

At the measurement study side, the prolific areas of research attempted to offer insightful understandings towards existing systems or protocols and essentially

Y. Zhuang et al. (Eds.): PCM 2006, LNCS 4261, pp. 175–184, 2006.
© Springer-Verlag Berlin Heidelberg 2006

came in two flavors. The first category of previous work commonly examined server workload, user characteristics and streaming performance of traditional client-server (C/S) or CDN-based live video streaming service [10,11], while the other category [12,13,14] analyzed P2P traffic, system capacity and message protocols of P2P file sharing and VoIP applications mentioned above. Although it is generally believed that it is critical to look at how the real systems work before the further betterments could be carried out, little research has been done in the context of P2P live streaming possibly due to practical difficulties.

Accordingly, the introductory summary frames out that there is both a need and an opportunity to investigate corresponding issues and further enable new classes of next generation P2P networks. As the first step, we aim to explore the feasibility of the interplay between practical properties and system design in this paper and our study goes beyond exiting work in following two aspects.

*1) Characterizing user behavior in C/S and P2P live streaming service.* We make statistical analysis to both more than **10 million** service traces from traditional C/S system in CCTV[1] and service logs from a practical P2P system with concurrent online users more than **200,000** for live broadcasting Spring Festival Evening show in Jan. 2006 over global Internet. We characterize end user behavior in terms of online duration and reveal the statistically positive correlation between elapsed online duration and expected remaining online time.

*2) Improving service quality with the aid of user characteristics.* We propose the Low Disruption Tree Construction (LDTC) algorithm to exploit the above practical-oriented feature. LDTC takes the online duration information into account when peers organize the service overlay. The experiment results show that LDTC could achieve higher stability of video date delivery tree and in turn improve the quality of streaming service. To the best of our knowledge, this is the first work to integrate practical observations into the design philosophy of P2P live video streaming.

The balance of this paper is organized as follows. Sec.2 presents the statistic analysis to service traces and reveals inherent characteristics of user behavior. Then we propose Low Disruption Tree Construction algorithm in details and present the experiment results in Sec.3. Sec.4 discusses some future work and ends this paper.

## 2    Statistical Analysis to User Behaviors

A characteristic in P2P network is that the peers change their behaviors and join or leave the service group continuously and independently, resulting in high dynamic in overlay topology and peer membership. In particular, the frequent turnover of upstream peers substantially poses great challenge on comfortable playback quality at end users in streaming applications. From this viewpoint, the stability of peer community is intuitively one of most vital factors for global system performance and thus we select the online duration of rational users as the first metric to model user behavior in the following two subsections.

---

[1] CCTV: China Central Television Station, http://www.cctv.com.

## 2.1 Online Duration Analysis in C/S Architecture

It should be stressed that since *end users have little knowledge and concerns on whether the service is provided via C/S or P2P technique*, it is important and feasible to analyze user behaviors in C/S approaches which might be analogous to those in P2P networks. We hence retrieved more than 10 million traces between Oct. 2004 and Jan. 2005 from central streaming servers at CCTV global websites. Tab.1 lists the basic information of those service traces, including the effective traces and average online duration at each channel(CCTV-News, CCTV-4 and CCTV-9).

**Table 1.** Information of service traces

| Channel | Effective traces | Average online | Synthesized parameters |
|---|---|---|---|
| 1.CCTV-News | 8,314,245 | 772 seconds | $(\mu, \sigma) = (4.421, 1.672)$ |
| 2.CCTV-4 | 2,349,934 | 542 seconds | $(\mu, \sigma) = (4.037, 1.464)$ |
| 3.CCTV-9 | 676,807 | 704 seconds | $(\mu, \sigma) = (4.161, 1.438)$ |
| In total | 11,340,986 | 720 seconds | NULL |

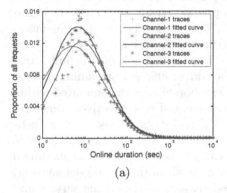 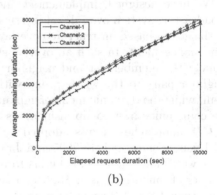

(a)  (b)

**Fig. 1.** Analysis to online duration of practical service traces: (a)Distribution of online duration and fitted curves; (b)Relation between elapsed online duration and expected remaining online time

To reveal the intrinsic characteristics within the online duration, we depict the percentage and cumulative percentage of various online duration distributions, as show in Fig.1(a). Clearly, although the populations (that is, effective traces) vary in different channels, all the three statistical results substantially follow the lognormal distribution. The last column in Tab.1 further provides the synthesized parameters for lognormal distribution in Fig.1(a). The distinctness of each $(\mu, \sigma)$ pair indicates the differences between each channel, potentially comprising contents, popularity and so on.

Only the lognormal distribution characteristic, however, is far from enough. In P2P networks, each peer is typically served by others and thus the stable peer-pair cooperation is of significance in P2P live streaming service. If we denote $p(t)$ as the online duration probability density, then the expected remaining online time of peers with elapsed online duration $T$ could be statstically calculated as:

$$E(t - T|t \geq T) = \frac{\int_T^\infty (t-T)p(t)dt}{\int_T^\infty p(t)dt} \tag{1}$$

Fig.1(b) further depicts the statistical relation between elapsed online duration and expected remaining online time. Observe that users who have enjoyed the service for a longer time would be statistically willing to spend more time. The main reason of this positive correlation may reside in the "*popularity-driven*" access pattern and synchronous nature of live video programs.

## 2.2   Online Duration Analysis in P2P Network

As discussed, it could be boldly conjectured that there would be the approximate positive correlation in P2P live streaming systems. Therefore we attempt to capture the online duration characteristic in P2P service community in this subsection.

We have designed, implemented and deployed a practical P2P live video broadcasting system over global Internet in previous study [8]. Our work builds on the gossip-based unstructured overlay [15,16] to perform distributed membership management. In such an overlay structure, each peer maintains two lists, namely the member list and neighbor list. The video packets transmit along neighbor pairs to the whole group with the aid of efficient streaming mechanism, while the dynamic membership and neighborship are disseminated within the community in a gossip fashion. As a scalable and cost-effective alternative to C/S approaches, it was adopted by CCTV to live broadcast Spring Festival Evening show at Feb. 2005 and Jan. 2006. In the first deployment in 2005, there were more than 500,000 users from about 66 countries with the maximum number of concurrent users 15,239 on Feb. 8th, 2005. In the second deployment, more than 1,800,000 users from about 70 countries subscribed the service and the maximum concurrent users reached its peak about 200,000 on Jan. 28th, 2006, as shown in Fig.2(a).

We then examine the logs to reveal online duration evolution of peers. Fig.2(b) shows the cumulative distribution of the online session duration. Observe that nearly 50% peers spent less than 200 seconds in the community, which indicated that many peers would not stay for a long time, while there were also roughly 20% users who would like to keep active for more than 30 minutes. Besides, we depict the relation between elapsed online duration and expected remaining online duration in Fig.2(c). It is obvious that peers who had stayed longer also would be expected to spend more time, as similar to that in C/S architecture.

Towards this end, the practical traces and logs from C/S and P2P systems offer in-depth statistical characteristic of user online duration. While the result of "*the older, the longer*" in both approaches seems quite intuitive, it essentially reflects the stability of service group, which could be deemed important for efficient system design and comfortable service quality in P2P networks.

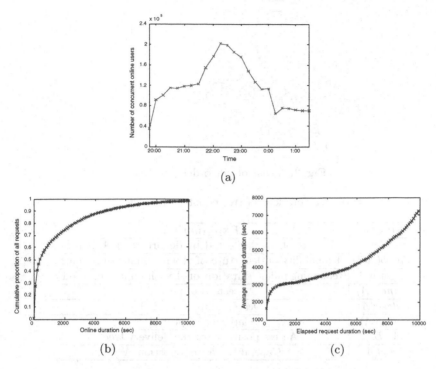

**Fig. 2.** Analysis to online duration of practical service logs: (a)Practical system evolution at Jan. 28th, 2006; (b)CDF of online duration; (c)Relation between elapsed online duration and expected remaining online time

## 3   LDTC: Low Disruption Tree Construction Algorithm

In this section, we mainly present one feasible algorithm to improve quality of streaming service by constructing video data delivery tree with the information of users' online duration. At the heart of this algorithm is to employ those peers with longer online duration as the bone of the tree, as well as to diminish the descendants' amount of those who are just active for a short while, resulting in low disruption of packets transmission and in turn high streaming quality.

Before proceeding, let us consider Fig.3 as a representative example. We assume video packets transmit along the simplified tree paths in the right rectangle instead of practical gossip-based overlay mesh for ease of presentation. Apparently the departures of peers $B$ and $D$ have more negative impacts on the stability of video transmission than those of the leaf peers $C$ and $E$ (in simplified model). Note that here we only discuss natural turnover rather than the unexpected failure of peers or links. Then we start the design of proposed LDTC with formal notations in Tab.2.

According to the statistical study in Sec.2, there is a positive correlation between elapsed online duration $t$ and expected remaining online duration $remn(t)$. And a larger $remn(A, t)$ implies lower possibility for a peer to leave, that is, lower

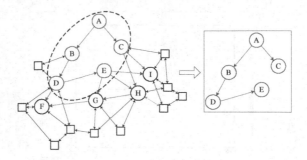

**Fig. 3.** A case of video delivery tree

**Table 2.** Notations of tree construction algorithm

| Notation | Explanation |
|----------|-------------|
| $affc(A)$ | Number of peers affected by departure of $A$, $A \in P$ |
| $prob(A,t)$ | Probability of departure of $A$ with online duration $t$ |
| $remn(A)$ | Remaining online duration of $A$ with online duration $t$ |
| $ance(A)$ | Ancestors of peer $A$ |
| $desc(A)$ | Descendants of peer $A$ |
| $cap(A)$ | Capacity of peer $A$ |
| $A', B', ...$ | Access positions of the delivery tree |
| $cap(A')$ | Capacity of access postion $A'$ |

$prob(A,t)$. As $t$ increases, $E(prob(A,t))$ decreases. Then we could calculate the expectation of disruptions (in terms of affected peers) as:

$$E(affc(P)) = E(\sum_{\forall A \in P} prob(A) \cdot affc(A)) = \sum_{\forall A \in P} (E(prob(A)) \cdot |desc(A)|) \quad (2)$$

The aim of providing stable transmission is hence translated into constructing a delivery tree with lower $E(affc(P))$. Besides, for peer $A$, it is also possible to affect the packets forwarding if $A$'s upstream ancestors leave, that is,

$$E(affc(P)) = E(\sum_{\forall A \in P} \sum_{\forall N \in ance(A)} prob(N)) = \sum_{\forall A \in P} \sum_{\forall N \in ance(A)} (E(prob(N)) \quad (3)$$

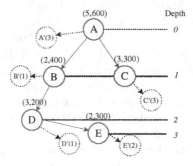

**Fig. 4.** Tree construction with candidate access positions

We now proceed to propose the low disruption tree construction (LDTC) algorithm. As extension to Fig.3, Fig.4 schematically depicts the candidate access positions $\zeta$ for a new participant $F$, where $\zeta = \{A', B', C', D', E'\}$. The 2-tuple, $(5, 600)$ for example, is assumed to present the service capacity (in terms of descendants) and elapsed online duration. The details of LDTC are summarized as following steps.

---

**LDTC tree construction algorithm steps:**

1. Calculate the average depth of the delivery tree. In Fig.4, the average depth is $l = (0 + 1 + 1 + 2 + 3)/5 = 1.4$;

2. Rank the candidate access positions in $\zeta$ whose depths are not more than $\lceil l \rceil$ in ascending sort as $\zeta_1$. If there is no candidate position whose depth is more than $\lceil l \rceil$, then $\zeta_1$ will be composed by those with minimum depths. In Fig.4, $\zeta_1 = \{\{A'\}, \{B', C'\}\}$;

3. Rank in descending sort the candidate positions in $\zeta_1$ according to the ancestors online duration to obtain $\zeta_2$;

4. For the new participant $F$, calculate the number $m$ of peers whose service capacity are more than that of $F$ and the number $n$ of total peers in delivery tree after $F$'s join. In Fig.4, if $cap(F) = 2$, then $m = 3, n = 6$;

5. Calculate the ratio $r$ as $r = (m + 1)/n$, number of available capacity at each depth $C = \{c_1, c_2, \ldots\}$ and potential position as $p = \lceil r \cdot \sum_i c_i \rceil$. In Fig.4, $r = 0.67$, $cap(A') = 3$, $cap(B') = 3$, $cap(C') = 1$, $C = \{c_1 = 3, c_2 = 4\}$, $p = \lceil 0.67 \times 7 \rceil = 5$;

6. Select the access position in $\zeta_2$ according to $C$ and $p$ in previous step. In Fig.4, since $p = 5 > c_1 = 3$, $F$ has to subscribe at depth 2 and thus select $B'$ to join the delivery tree;

7. If there are more than one peer in $\zeta_2$ with same conditions, then randomly select one as the access position for $F$.

---

To testify the proposed LDTC algorithm, we conduct simulation experiments and compare it with other tree construction algorithms. Tab.3 lists the basic experiment setup and note that here we just adopt a median $(\mu, \sigma)$ to simulate the online duration distribution of peers. The experiments compare the following five tree construction algorithms:

(1)**Random:** randomly select access positions in the tree;

(2)**Min-depth:** Select the access position with minimum depth in the tree;

(3)**Max-online:** Select the access position with maximum online duration;

(4)**Proposed:** Proposed LDTC algorithm;

(5)**Contrastive:** Randomly sort in step 3 in proposed LDTC algorithm.

Fig.5 depicts the average depths and accumulative disruptions in Random, Min-depth, Max-online and Proposed algorithms. All the results are averaged by 10-round experiments. Observe that the average depth in Proposed algorithm is even smaller than that in Min-depth because we intentionally deploy peers with larger capacity to get closer to the source root while Min-depth actually achieves the local optimal minimum depth. Proposed algorithm also exhibit the best performance in terms of tree disruption as compared to other algorithms

**Table 3.** Simulation experiment setup

| Parameter | Value or range |
|---|---|
| Simulation time | 100000 seconds |
| Capacity of root peer | 10 |
| User arrival pattern | $\lambda = 1$ (Poisson process) |
| Online duration | $(\mu, \sigma) = (4.4, 1.6)$ (Lognormal distribution) |
| Peer capacity | $\mu = 2$ (Exponential distribution) |

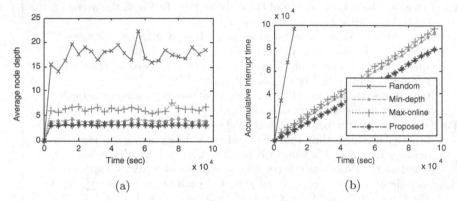

(a)    (b)

**Fig. 5.** Simulation results of random, min-depth, max-online and proposed algorithms

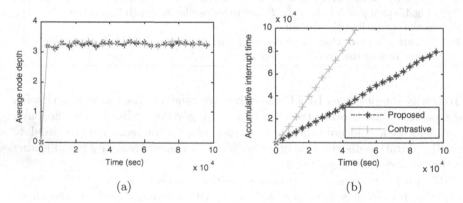

(a)    (b)

**Fig. 6.** Comparisons between proposed algorithm and contrastive algorithm

in Fig.5(b). Fig.6 compares the Proposed and Contrastive algorithm in terms of average depth and accumulative disruptions. Since they differ from each other only with respect to the sort method of candidate positions, the average depth should be the same, as shown in Fig.6(a). The distinctness in Fig.6(b) indicates that the online duration essentially provides higher stability when constructing the tree and confirms the effectiveness of LDTC. Although LDTC seems quite simple, we claim that in this paper we mainly explore the feasibility to improve quality of streaming service with the benefit of practical properties and how to retrieve users' private information, e.g. service capacity and online duration, will be investigated in future work.

## 4    Conclusion and Future Work

In this paper, we mainly investigate the issue of leveraging practical service experiences to guide the design of P2P live streaming system and in turn improve the quality of streaming service. Our contributions come in two-fold. Firstly, we make statistical analysis to service traces from the C/S system and P2P system and then reveal statistically positive correlation between elapsed online duration and expected remaining online time. Secondly, we are motivated to propose Low Disruption Tree Construction algorithm with the benefit of the practical characteristic. It takes the online duration of peers into account when constructing video data delivery tree and hence offers higher stability for streaming service.

Future research could proceed along several arenas. One is to evaluate the overheads of LDTC and retrieve peers information in a distributed manner. It is also interesting to characterize user behavior profile in a more comprehensive manner for further improvements.

## Acknowledgement

The authors gracefully thank the anonymous reviewers for their comments. This work is supported by the National Natural Science Foundation of China under Grant No.60432030 and No.60503063.

## References

1. Yang-hua Chu, Sanjay G. Rao, Hui Zhang: A Case for End System Multicast. In Proc. of 2000 ACM SIGMETRICS (2000) 1-12.
2. Suman Banerjee, Bobby Bhattacharjee, Christopher Kommareddy: Scalable Application Layer Multicast. In Proc. of 2002 ACM SIGCOMM (2002) 205-217.
3. Miguel Castro, Peter Druschel, et al: SplitStream: High-Bandwidth Multicast in Cooperative Environments. In Proc. of 2003 ACM SOSP (2003) 298-313.
4. Miguel Castro, Peter Druschel, Anne-Marie Kermarrec, Antony Rowstron: SCRIBE: A Large-Scale and Decentralized Application-Level Multicast Infrastructure. IEEE Journal on Selected Areas in Communications, vol. 20, no. 8, (2002) 100-110.
5. B. Cohen. BitTorrent. http://www.bitconjuer.com/BitTorrent/.
6. Skype, http://www.skype.com.
7. Xinyan Zhang, Jiangchuan Liu, Bo Li, Yum, Y.-S.P.: CoolStreaming/DONet: A Data-Driven Overlay Network for Efficient Live Media Streaming. In Proc. of 2005 IEEE INFOCOM (2005) 2102-2111.
8. Meng Zhang, Li Zhao, Yun Tang, Jianguang Luo, Shiqiang Yang: Large-Scale Live Media Streaming over Peer-to-Peer Networks through Global Internet. In Proc. of 2005 P2MMS ACM MULTIMEDIA (2005) 21-28.

9. PPLive site: http://www.pplive.com.
10. Eveline Veloso, Virglio Almeida, Wagner Meira, Azer Bestavros, Shudong Jin: A Hierarchical Characterization of a Live Streaming Media Workload. In Proc. of 2002 ACM SIGCOMM IMC (2002) 117-130.
11. Kunwadee Sripanidkulchai, Bruce Maggs, Hui Zhang: An Analysis of Live Streaming Workloads on the Internet. In Proc. of 2004 ACM SIGCOMM IMC (2004) 41-54.
12. Saikat Guha, Neil Daswani, Ravi Jain: An Experimental Study of the Skype Peer to Peer VoIP System. The 5th International Workshop on Peer-to-Peer Systems (2006), available at http://iptps06.cs.ucsb.edu/.
13. Stefan Saroiu, P. Krishna Gummadi, Steven D. Gribble: A Measurement Study of Peer-to-Peer File Sharing Systems. In Proc. of 2002 SPIE MMCN (2002) 156-170.
14. Dongyu Qiu, R. Srikant: Modeling and Performance Analysis of BitTorrent-Like Peer-to-Peer Networks. In Proc. of 2004 ACM SIGCOMM (2004) 367-378.
15. Suman Banerjee, Seungjoon Lee, Bobby Bhattacharjee, Aravind Srinivasan: Resilient Multicast Using Overlays. In Proc. of 2003 ACM SIGMETRICS (2003) 102-113.
16. Vivek Vishnumurthy, Paul Francis: On Heterogeneous Overlay Construction and Random Node Selection in Unstructured P2P Networks. In Proc. of 2006 IEEE INFOCOM (2006), To Appear.

# Interacting Activity Recognition Using Hierarchical Durational-State Dynamic Bayesian Network

Youtian Du, Feng Chen, Wenli Xu, and Weidong Zhang

Department of Automation, Tsinghua University, Beijing, 100084, China
dyt02@mails.tsinghua.edu.cn,
{chenfeng, xuwl}@mail.tsinghua.edu.cn,
zwd03@mails.tsinghua.edu.cn

**Abstract.** Activity recognition is one of the most challenging problems in the high-level computer vision field. In this paper, we present a novel approach to interacting activity recognition based on dynamic Bayesian network (DBN). In this approach the features representing the human activities are divided into two classes: global features and local features, which are on two different spatial scales. To model and recognize human interacting activities, we propose a hierarchical durational-state DBN model (HDS-DBN). HDS-DBN combines the global features with local ones organically and reveals structure of interacting activities well. The effectiveness of this approach is demonstrated by experiments.

**Keywords:** interacting activity recognition, dynamic Bayesian network, global feature, local feature.

## 1 Introduction

Activity recognition is one of the most important open areas in the high-level computer vision, in which many theories of other fields are involved such as pattern recognition and artificial intelligence. It is a complex and challenging task due to the ambiguity caused by human body articulation, mutual occlusion, environment, etc.

Over the last decade there has been growing interest in the activity recognition [1,2]. However, few efforts were put into understanding human activities that have substantial extent in time or involve interactions between people [1,3].

### 1.1 Related Work

In the field of activity recognition, probabilistic graph models, especially temporal sequential models such as hidden Markov models (HMMs), are adopted and have become the most popular approaches.

The conventional HMM is inadequate to model complex activities because it cannot characterize the hierarchic and shared structure embedded in the activities. To recognize interactions between two objects, Brand et al.[4] proposed

Y. Zhuang et al. (Eds.): PCM 2006, LNCS 4261, pp. 185–192, 2006.

a coupled hidden markov model(CHMM), which can model two correlative dynamic processes. Based on CHMM, Oliver et al.[3] described a Bayesian computer vision system for modeling and recognizing human interactions, and features were extracted based on trajectories. Experimental results indicated that coupled hidden Markov model (CHMM) was superior to HMM in interacting activity recognition. Park and Aggarwal[5] estimated the body part poses and overall body poses with low level and high level of Bayesian network respectively, and recognized two-person interactions with DBN. To interpret group activities, Gong and Xiang [6] proposed a dynamically multi-linked hidden markov model with the structure determined by Bayesian Information Criterion (BIC). Liu and Chua [7] decomposed the observation of HMMs in multi-agent activity recognition, which can solve the case that agent number is variable.

## 1.2  Our Approach

In this paper, a new approach is proposed to the recognition of human interacting activities involving two persons. First, features of the motion are divided into two classes: global features and local features, which represent activities on the different spatial scales. Second, a hierarchical durational-state DBN model structure (HDS-DBN) is presented to model and recognize interacting activities, combining the two classes of features organically.

The advantages of the approach are: (1) these two classes of features represent interacting activities more accurately and completely; (2) HDS-DBN reveals interacting activity structures well; (3) HDS-DBN overcomes the defect of exponential distribution of duration in conventional HMM and some of its extensions.

## 2  Global Feature and Local Feature

Features play a crucial role in activity recognition. A large amount of work toward interacting activity recognition has only extracted features based on object trajectories to represent activities, but obviously such features are not exact especially to represent sophisticated activities. To overcome this defect, more complex features should be extracted [4]. In this paper, features are extracted on two different spatial scales, which are named global features and local features respectively. Global features generally consider each object as a point, and describe the motion trajectory on a large spatial scale and the relations between objects or between object and scene. Local features represent the motion details such as bow, which cannot be described exactly by global features. Fig.1 shows the architecture of feature extraction.

Global features measure the position, velocity of each object, and from these data a global feature vector is constructed which consists of:

(1) $v_i$, the magnitude of velocity of each person, which can be obtained by $v_i = \sqrt{v_{xi}^2 + v_{yi}^2}$, where $v_{xi}$ and $v_{yi}$ are velocities of person $i$ ($i = 1, 2$) in the $x$ and $y$ direction respectively,

(2) $d$, the distance between two persons,

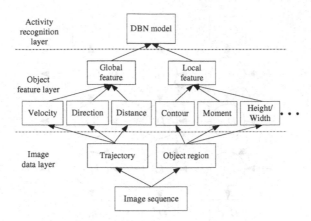

**Fig. 1.** Feature extraction graph. The left part of the graph shows the global feature extraction, and the right shows the local feature extraction.

(3) $s$, the angle between motion directions of the two persons. Note that the value of $s$ is zero when one or both persons are stationary.

Different from global features, local features describe the human motion details, and they are more various and complicated to select. In the current work the local feature vector is composed of the aspect ratio $\gamma_i$ of the bounding box surrounding human region, and the angle of inclination of human body which is denoted by $\alpha_i$. The first element is discriminative between stand and squat, and the second one is an easy and reasonable selection to roughly distinguish between walk and run because the pose of body is different between these two movements.

## 3   Modeling and Recognizing Interaction Activities

### 3.1   Model Framework

In this paper, a hierarchical durational-state dynamic Bayesian network (HDS-DBN) is proposed to model interacting activities. There are three kinds of states in HDS-DBN: global activity state, duration state and local activity state. Global activity state is associated with the activity on a large spatial scale or relations between people or between people and scene, and it produces global features. Duration state indicates how long the corresponding global activity state will last from current time, that is, the remaining duration of the global activity state. Local state embodies the motion details or posture of each person and it produces local features. Hence, the model including such three kinds of states above can model an interacting activity completely. Fig.2 shows the HDS-DBN structure, where $G_t$ and $L_t$ denote the global activity state and the local one at time $t$ respectively. $D_t$ is the duration state and means the remaining duration of state $G_t$ at time $t$. $O_t^1$ and $O_t^2$ are the global features and local ones at time $t$ respectively.

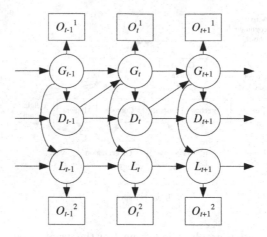

**Fig. 2.** HDS-DBN model structure

To a common activity, the global activity state holds the dominant role, while the local one shows the details of the activity. So in the HDS-DBN model, we only consider the effect from the global activity state to the local one. With this model, the two classes of features are combined organically. Generally, activities last a long duration. To overcome the defect of exponential distribution of duration in conventional HMM, a duration state $D_t$ is added in HDS-DBN model with uniform distribution for modeling the global activity state $G_t$. Actually the local activity state $L_t$ also lasts a duration, but in this paper we don't consider it for the reduction of model complexity. Actually, the duration state of global activity state also benefits the local one.

The parameter set $\Theta$ of HDS-DBN $\lambda$ contains the prior probabilities $P(G_1)$ and $P(L_1)$, the observation probabilities $P(O_t^1|G_t)$ and $P(O_t^2|L_t)$, the transition probabilities $P(G_t|G_{t-1}, D_{t-1})$, $P(L_t|L_{t-1}, G_t)$, and $P(D_t|D_{t-1}, G_t)$. These parameters are expressed as follows:

$$P(G_t = j|G_{t-1} = i, D_{t-1} = d) = \begin{cases} \delta(i-j) & if\, d > 0 \\ A^1(i,j) & if\, d = 0 \end{cases}, \tag{1}$$

$$P(L_t = j|L_{t-1} = i, G_t = k) = A^2(i,j,k), \tag{2}$$

$$P(D_t = d'|D_{t-1} = d, G_t = i) = \begin{cases} p_i(d') & if\, d = 0 \\ \delta(d' - d + 1) & if\, d \neq 0 \end{cases}, \tag{3}$$

$$P(O_t^1|G_t = i) = \sum_{k=1}^{M_g} \omega_k N(O_t^1, \mu_{ik}, \Sigma_{ik}), \tag{4}$$

$$P(O_t^2|L_t = i) = \sum_{k=1}^{M_l} \eta_k N(O_t^2, \mu_{ik}, \Sigma_{ik}). \tag{5}$$

Where $A^1$ and $A^2$ are transition matrixes, $\delta(\cdot)$ is the Dirac function, $p_i(\cdot)$ is a uniform distribution function, $N(x, \mu_{ik}, \Sigma_{ik})$ is a Gaussian distribution function with mean vector $\mu_{ik}$ and covariance matrix $\Sigma_{ik}$, and $M_g$ and $M_l$ are the numbers of elements in GMM for the two observation distributions respectively.

## 3.2   Parameter Estimation and Inference

We assume that a total of $m$ global activity states have been visited in the sequence and we denote these states as $G^1, G^2, \cdots, G^m$ with durations associated with each state of $d_1, d_2, \cdots, d_m$. The joint probability of observation $O = ((O_1^1, O_1^2), (O_2^1, O_2^2), \cdots, (O_T^1, O_T^2))^1$ and activity state $S = (G, D, L)$ for HDS-DBN model $\lambda$ is given by

$$P(O, S|\lambda) = P(G^1)P(L_1)p_{G^1}(d_1) \prod_{t=1}^{d_1} a^2_{G^1 L_{t-1} L_t} P(O_t^1|G^1)P(O_t^2|L_t)$$

$$\cdot \prod_{r=2}^{m} [a^1_{G^{r-1} G^r} p_{G^r}(d_r) \prod_{t=d_1+\ldots d_{r-1}+1}^{d_1+\ldots d_r} a^2_{G^r L_{t-1} L_t} P(O_t^1|G^r)P(O_t^2|L_t)], \qquad (6)$$

where $a^1_{G^{r-1} G^r}$ and $a^2_{G^r L_{t-1} L_t}$ are the elements of $A^1$ and $A^2$ respectively.

In the learning process, the parameters $\Theta$ of the HDS-DBN $\lambda$ model are estimated to model the corresponding predefined interacting activities. Given a sequence of training data of the form $O_{1:T}$, the maximum likelihood parameters $\hat{\Theta}$ are estimated according to the following equation:

$$\hat{\Theta} = \arg\max_{\Theta} P(O_{1:T}|\Theta). \qquad (7)$$

For the space limitation of the paper, the estimation results are not given here.

Activity recognition is the inference process given HDS-DBN model structure and estimated parameters. Given a set of HDS-DBN mode $\lambda = \{\lambda_1, \lambda_2, \cdots, \lambda_C\}$, where $C$ is the number of models, we select $c$ as the class label of the test activity with observations $O_{1:T}$, where

$$c = \arg\max_i P(\lambda_i|O_{1:T}). \qquad (8)$$

## 3.3   HDS-DBN Model Structure Analysis

A criterion of a good model is to describe the given observation data better. Here we adopt Schwarz's Bayesian Information Criterion (BIC)[8] to measure the goodness of HDS-DBN model against that of another in describing a given dataset. For a model parameterized by a $K$-dimensional vector, the BIC is defined as:

$$BIC = -2\log L(\lambda) + K \log N,$$

where $\lambda$ is the model, and $N$ is the size of the dataset.

---

[1] Sometimes we denote $(O_t^1, O_t^2)$ with $O_t$ for simplicity.

In the interaction recognition, we have several HDS-DBN models $\{\lambda_1, \lambda_2, \ldots, \lambda_C\}$, which correspond different classes of interactions respectively. The parameter dimension of each model probably is different due to the different state number selected in the model. Hence the Schwarz's BIC cannot be adopted directly in our work, and it is modified in our work as follows:

$$BIC = \sum_{c=1}^{C} (\sum_{i=1}^{M_c} -2\log P(d_i^c | \lambda_c) + k_c \log N_c) , \qquad (9)$$

where $d_i^c$ is the $i$th data in the $c$th class, $k_c$ is the parameter dimension of model $\lambda_c$, $M_c$ is the number of sample of each class, and $N_c$ is the size of each class of data, $c = 1, 2, \cdots C$. The modified BIC can measure goodness a set of models which have the same structure, and each model corresponds a class of data. In the subsection 4.2, the comparison between HDS-DBN and HMM is shown based on the modified BIC.

## 4   Experimental Results

Experiments were conducted on recognizing interacting activities between two persons in the scenes of parking lot and footway. The video data is captured by digital camera with the frame size $352 \times 288$.

We consider five different interacting activities:

(1) Inter1: Two people walk on the same path in the same direction with relatively constant distance.
(2) Inter2: Two people walk on the same path in the opposite direction.
(3) Inter3: Two people run on the same path in the opposite direction.
(4) Inter4: Two people walk in the opposite direction on the same path. They chat with each other when meeting, and then go on separately.
(5) Inter5: Two people approach and meet, one puts an object on the ground and goes away, and the other takes this object and goes away.

For each activity, we have about 30 samples, and each sample has about 300 frames. The dataset is halved, with one half used for learning and the other half for testing. Some key frames of Inter5 are shown in figure4. We employ sliding window with window length 10 frames and step length 5 frames when extracting features.

### 4.1   Recognition Results

According to the complexity of the various activities, HDS-DBN includes three to five global activity states and three local activity states. Three to five elements of GMM are used to model the distribution of observations generated by each global activity state or local one. Table 1 shows the results of the interacting activity recognition, in which the diagonal components mean the amount of activities recognized correctly.

**Fig. 3.** Key frames in Inter5 (we only show the interesting regions of original images )

**Table 1.** Recognition results

|        | Inter1 | Inter2 | Inter3 | Inter4 | Inter5 |
|--------|--------|--------|--------|--------|--------|
| Inter1 | 15     | 0      | 0      | 0      | 0      |
| Inter2 | 0      | 12     | 1      | 0      | 0      |
| Inter3 | 0      | 1      | 18     | 0      | 0      |
| Inter4 | 0      | 0      | 0      | 15     | 0      |
| Inter5 | 0      | 0      | 0      | 0      | 11     |

To testify the performance of HDS-DBN, we recognize the same activities using HMMs with three to six states. Table 2 illustrates the accuracy of interacting activities recognition with HMMs and with HDS-DBN. The second column of table 2 means observation data of HMM are global features, and the third column means observation data include both global features and local features. The last column means observation data of HDS-DBN are not only a kind of feature, but both global features and local features, which is decided by its structure. Our approach is superior to HMMs for recognizing the interacting activities, more significantly, identifying complex activities such as Inter5.

## 4.2  Model Structure Analysis Results

We have calculated the BIC of both HDS-DBN models and HMMs given the same 86 sequences, which include total testing data and partial training data. To HDS-DBN models, the Log-likelihood value, with constant 10 as the base, is -5 951.4, the parameter dimension $k_c(c = 1, 2, 3, 4, 5)$ of model $\lambda_c$ corresponding to each interacting activity is 312,312,312,435,590, and the size of each class of activity data is 285, 315, 281, 545, 404 respectively, where each size is equal to the sum of length of each sample in the corresponding class. Hence the *BIC*

**Table 2.** Comparison between HMMs and HDS-DBN(%)

|        | HMM(1) | HMM(2) | HDS-DBN |
|--------|--------|--------|---------|
| Inter1 | 100    | 100    | 100     |
| Inter2 | 84.62  | 92.31  | 92.31   |
| Inter3 | 84.21  | 84.21  | 94.74   |
| Inter4 | 93.33  | 100    | 100     |
| Inter5 | 63.64  | 81.82  | 100     |

value of HDS-DBN is 16 940. To HMMs, the Log-likelihood value is -9 343.3, the parameter dimension $k_c$ of model $\lambda_c$ corresponding to each interacting activity is 736,736,736,1 150,1 150$^2$. The *BIC* value of HMMs is 30 279 given the same data. Hence we know the structure of HDS-DBN is better than that of HMMs.

## 5    Conclusions

This paper presents a novel approach to the recognition of human interacting activities. In the work, we divide features into global features and local features, and propose a new DBN model structure named HDS-DBN to model interacting activities completely. HDS-DBN combines the two classes of features together organically and reveals the structure of interacting activities well.In addition, it overcomes the defect of exponential distribution of duration in conventional HMM. Experimental results demonstrate that HDS-DBN model has the reasonable structure and can recognize interacting activities with high correct rates.

## References

1. Aggarwal, J.K., Park, S.: Human Motion: Modeling and Recognition of Actions and Interactions. In Proc. 3DPVT (2004) 640–647
2. Wang, L., Hu, W., Tan, T.: Recent developments in human motion analysis. Pattern Recognition 36 (2003) 585-601
3. Oliver, N.M., Rosario, B., Pentland, A.P.: A Bayesian computer vision system for modeling human interactions. IEEE Trans. PAMI 22 (2000) 831–843
4. Brand, M., Oliver, N., Pentland, A.: Coupled hidden Markov models for complex action recognition. In Proc. CVPR (1997) 994-999
5. Park, S., Aggarwal, J.K.: A hierarchical Bayesian network for event recognition of human actions and interactions. Multimedia Systems 10 (2004) 164-179
6. Gong, S., Xiang, T.: Recognition of group activities using dynamic probabilistic networks. In Proc. ICCV. (2003) 742–749
7. Liu, X., Chua, C.: Multi-agent activity recognition using observation decomposed hidden markov models. Image and vision computing 24 (2006) 166-175
8. Schwarz, G.: Estimating the dimension of a model. The Annals of Statistics 6 (1978) 461-464

---

[2] Such high parameter dimension of HMMs and HDS-DBN is mainly caused by covariances of the Gaussian observation distribution as equations (4) and (5).

# Improving the Image Retrieval Results Via Topic Coverage Graph

Kai Song[1], Yonghong Tian[1], and Tiejun Huang[2]

[1] Institute of Computing Technology,
Chinese Academy of Science, Beijing, 100080, China
[2] School of Electronics Engineering and Computer Science, Peking University
{ksong, yhtian, tjhuang}@jdl.ac.cn

**Abstract.** In the area of image retrieval, search engines are tender to retrieve images that are most relevant to the users' queries. Nevertheless, in most cases, queries cannot be represented just by several query words. Therefore, it is necessary to provide relevant retrieval results with broad topic-coverage to meet the users' ambiguous needs. In this paper, a re-ranking method based on topic coverage analysis is proposed to perform the refinement of retrieval results. A graph called Topic Coverage Graph (TCG) is constructed to model the degree of mutual topic coverage among images. Then, Topic Richness Score (TRS), which is calculated based on TCG, is used to measure the importance of each image in improving the topic coverage of image retrieval results. Experimental results on over 20,000 images demonstrate that our proposed approach is effective in improving the topic coverage of retrieval results without loss of relevance.

**Keywords:** Image retrieval, re-rank, topic coverage.

## 1 Introduction

In recent years, the area of image retrieval has drawn extensive attention from researchers around the world [1]. In semantic-based image retrieval, lots of methods are introduced to overcome the so-called semantic gap between low-level visual features and high-level semantic features of image. In [2,3], strategies of relevance feedback are used to learn the users' requirement and therefore retrieve more query-related images. Multi-modal analysis [4,5,6,7,8] is another method that discovers the semantics of images by exploiting the synergy of texts, audio, video information. In previous works, most of the image search engines tend to provide users a list of retrieval results with respect to the relevance score of each image to the query. This scheme is effective when users' needs are clear and they care much about the precision and recall in the results. Nevertheless, in most cases, users cannot describe their requests only by several query words accurately. Therefore their actual requirements are ambiguous. For example, the top retrieval results often fall into a specific subtopics of the queries and users cannot find the images they want from the retrieval results with limited topic coverage.

Y. Zhuang et al. (Eds.): PCM 2006, LNCS 4261, pp. 193–200, 2006.

Therefore, it is necessary to provide relevant retrieval results with broad topic-coverage to meet the users' ambiguous and various needs. As reported in [9], most people said they preferred the retrieval results with broad and interesting topics. Previous works on diversifying document retrieval results has showed great promise in web search engines [10]. In the literature of image retrieval, several approaches have been proposed to achieve such target. Goh *et al* [11] exploit a SVM-based active learning algorithm, which incorporates diversity [12] for image retrieval. A two-scale image retrieval scheme using meta-information feedback is another attempt [13]. The early methods mainly focus on low-level visual feature similarities, either by clustering and picking up the top results in each cluster or calculating the angle of two visual feature vectors. This paradigm is based on the hypothesis that topic-related images tend to be closely associated together in visual feature space. Nevertheless, most topic-related images are scattered in visual space and can hardly clustered together. Take the images of cars with different colors for instance, they are scattered in different visual clusters. Furthermore, images in the same cluster may contain different topics. The cluster of the color blue may contain sky, sea, or the uniform of Italian soccer team. Therefore, only choosing the top images in each cluster will result in enormous loss in topic coverage.

All the investigations motivate us to propose a semantic-based re-ranking method to enrich the topic coverage of image retrieval results. In this paper, images are modeled as a graph called Topic Coverage Graph (TCG), whose edges indicate the degree of mutual topic coverage among images. Then, Topic Richness Score (TRS), which is calculated based on the graph, is used to measure the importance of each image in improving the topic coverage of image retrieval results. Images with high scores are more likely to enrich topic coverage of retrieval results and should be ranked in top place in the results. A re-ranking algorithm is applied according to the topic richness score in the end of our proposed method. Five researchers are invited to evaluate the re-ranked results both in topic coverage and relevance. The experimental results demonstrate that our proposed approach is effective in diversifying the topic coverage of image retrieval results and the re-ranking method outperforms the clustering method in improving the topic coverage of retrieval results significantly without the loss of relevance.

The rest of the paper is organized as follows. We introduce the proposed method in detail in section 2. In section 3, experiments and evaluations are reported. We conclude our work in section 4.

## 2   The Re-ranking Method

The framework of our proposed re-ranking method is illustrated in Figure 1. For a given image retrieval set generated by a certain image search engine, a Topic Coverage Graph (TCG) is constructed to model the degree of mutual topic coverage among images. Based on the graph, we calculate Topic Richness Score (TRS), which is introduced to measure the importance of each image in improving the topic coverage of image retrieval results. In the process of re-ranking, images with highest TRS are chosen to be presented in the top retrieval results in each iteration to diversify the retrieval results.

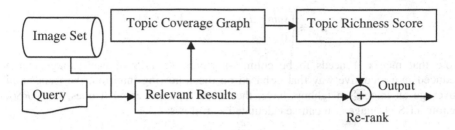

**Fig. 1.** Framework of the proposed re-ranking method

## 2.1 Topic Coverage Graph Construction

Let image set $I=\{i_1, i_2, ..., i_n\}$ denote the retrieval results generated by a certain image search engine. We assume that all the images in $I$ are annotated by several words. Since annotation is not the main concern in this paper, we investigate the state of art of annotation and topic discovery in [7,8,14]. The method in [8] requires no parameter tuning, no clustering, no user-determined constant and has been proved to be effective in automatic image annotation. Therefore, we adopt it as our annotation strategy and assume it is effective and accurate. Let $W_k(1 \leq k \leq n)$ denote the annotation set of image $i_k(1 \leq k \leq n)$. Each different word in annotations is considered as a different topic. The similarity between an image pair $i_j$ and $i_k$ is defined as:

$$sim(i_j, i_k) = \begin{cases} \dfrac{|W_k \cap W_j|}{|W_k|} & k \neq j \\ 0 & k = j \end{cases} \tag{1}$$

Where $|\cdot|$ denotes the set cardinality. Intuitively, $sim(i_j, i_k)$ reflects the degree of mutual topic coverage in an image pair. $sim(i_j, i_k)=1$ represents that image $i_j$ covers all the topics in $i_k$, and $sim(i_j, i_k)=0$ represents image $i_j$ and $i_k$ contain totally different topics. Note that the similarity defined here is asymmetric, which reflects the asymmetry of mutual topic coverage in an image pair.

If images are considered as nodes, they can be modeled as a directed-weighed graph. Each edge in the graph is assigned a weight $sim(i_j, i_k)$, which indicates the similarities between the corresponding images. Since the graph is constructed based on the value of $sim(i_j, i_k)$, which represents the degree of mutual topic coverage among images, we call the graph Topic Coverage Graph (TCG). A group of heavily linked nodes in the graph represents images with high topic-overlapping, while images connected by week link cover various topics.

## 2.2 Topic Richness Score Calculation

We use Topic Richness Score (TRS) to measure the importance of each image in improving topic coverage of retrieval results. TCG is used to perform the calculation. Let $A$ denote the adjacency matrix of TCG. Each entry of $A$ corresponds to the weight of an edge in the graph. The formal definition is given as follows:

$$a_{jk} = \begin{cases} sim(i_j, i_k) & k \neq j \\ 0 & k = j \end{cases} \tag{2}$$

Note that matrix $A$ needs to be column-normalized. TRS of each image can be deduced in a recursive way that is based on the following intuition: the richer topic coverage an image's neighbors have, the richer topic coverage it does. Let $TRS(i_k)$ denote TRS of image $i_k$, it can be calculated as follows:

$$TRS(i_k) = \sum_{j=1, j \neq i}^{n} a_{kj} TRS(i_j) \tag{3}$$

$a_{kj}$ is used as the weight of TRS computation because it quantitatively characterizes the degree of mutual topic coverage between an image pair. Let $\vec{\omega} = [TRS(i_1), TRS(i_2), \cdots, TRS(i_n)]_{n \times 1}$, (3) can be written in a matrix form:

$$\vec{\omega} = M\vec{\omega} \tag{4}$$

Since topic-overlapping does not exist in every image pair, it is possible that the matrix $A$ has all-zero rows. This will cause failure in eigenvector computation. Similar to the random jumping factor in PageRank, a dumping factor $c$ is introduced to overcome the problem:

$$\vec{\omega} = cM\vec{\omega} + \frac{1-c}{n}\vec{e} \tag{5}$$

Where $\vec{e}$ is a column vector with all its $n$ elements equaling to 1. $c$ is set to 0.85 in our method. By solving equation (5), we obtain TRS of every image in $I$.

The process of TRS calculation can be explained as a random walk model [15, 16]. Given a topic, our goal is to find the image, which has the greatest probability to diversify topic coverage of retrieval results. The random walker chooses the edge in two rules: (1) with the probability $c$, the walker reaches another node in current group, which is composed of heavily-linked nodes; (2) with the probability of $(1-c)$, the walker jumps out of current group and reaches another group. $\vec{\omega}$, the solution of equation (5), represents the stationary probability of each image in diversifying the retrieval results.

## 2.3   The Re-ranking Method

Generally, given a retrieval result in terms of the relevance to the query, images with high TRS are chosen to be presented in the top retrieval results so that the image set of top results are various in topics. Note that topics that are contained in the chosen images become less important in enriching topic coverage in further steps. Based on the intuition, our re-ranking strategy is to decrease the scores of the images whose topic-related images have already been chosen in the top results. The steps of the methods are described as follows:

*Step 0. Initialize set $R = \Phi$, which denotes the retrieval set after re-ranking, set $I = \{i_1, i_2, \cdots, i_n\}$, which denotes the retrieval results generated by a certain search engine,*

*Step 1.  Sort all the elements in set I by their TRS in descending order.*
*Step 2.  Put the image $i_k$ with the highest TRS from set I to set R. For j≠k, re-calculate*
*          TRS in the following way: TRS($i_j$)= TRS($i_j$)- $a_{jk}$ · TRS($i_k$)*
*Step 3.  Re-sort the images in set I by the updated TRS in descending order.*
*Step 4.  Go to Step 2 until top N retrieval results are chosen.*

In Step 2, we impose a penalty algorithm to the images, which are topic-related to image $i_k$. The more an image is topic-related to image $i_k$, the more penalties it obtains.

## 3  Experiments

Our experiments are based on 718 annotated words and over 20,000 illustrations extracted from digital books in China-American Digital Academic Library (CADAL) project. For the illustration dataset, our specific consideration lies in that illustration is a typical collection covers repetitive topics because of the cross-topics in digital books. Therefore, our proposed approach is more likely to show the improvements in diversifying the retrieval results compared with other methods.

In our experiments, we choose 20 queries and the top 50 retrieval results of each query are passed to our approach and k-means algorithm separately to re-rank top 20 results that often draw most attentions of users. For k-means algorithm, we set $k$=20 and pick up the top 1 result of each cluster to generate the top 20 results. We compare the re-ranked retrieval results generated by our method with those by the clustering technique (e.g. k-means).

In order to evaluate the effectiveness of the proposed approach, five researchers in the area of image retrieval are invited to evaluate topic coverage of the re-ranked results. They are asked to count the number of topics in the re-ranked results (both by our method and k-means) of each query. Since the criteria of topic classifying vary from user to user, results are evaluated in the form of relative changes, which is defined as follows:

$$\Delta = \frac{1}{N}\sum_{i=1}^{N}(T_i^{TRS} - T_i^{k-means}) \tag{7}$$

Where $N$ is the number of users and $N$=5 in our experiments. $T_i^{TRS}$ denotes the number of topics in the results re-ranked by our method given by user $i$ and $T_i^{k-means}$ denotes the number of topics in the results re-ranked by k-means given by user $i$. Table 1 shows the relative changes in top 20 retrieval results of each query.

From Table 1, we can tell that our proposed re-ranking method based on TRS improves the topic coverage in top 20 retrieval results significantly compared with k-means algorithm. For the query *forest*, we present the top 10 retrieval result to illustrate the improvement in topic coverage.

In figure 3, most images in the results re-ranked by k-means are related to forest landscape. In figure 3, more subtopics related to forest are covered in the retrieval results, including forest insects, forest product laboratory, forest animals, the Rocky

**Table 1.** Relative changes in top 20 results of 20 queries

| No. | Relative Changes | No. | Relative Changes |
|-----|------------------|-----|------------------|
| 1   | +5.2             | 11  | +4.2             |
| 2   | +4.8             | 12  | +4.0             |
| 3   | +4.2             | 13  | +4.8             |
| 4   | +3.0             | 14  | +2.8             |
| 5   | +3.8             | 15  | +4.8             |
| 6   | +4.4             | 16  | +4.2             |
| 7   | +3.2             | 17  | +5.0             |
| 8   | +5.4             | 18  | +3.8             |
| 9   | +4.8             | 19  | +3.6             |
| 10  | +4.6             | 20  | +4.2             |

**Fig. 2.** Top 10 retrieval results after re-ranking by k-means

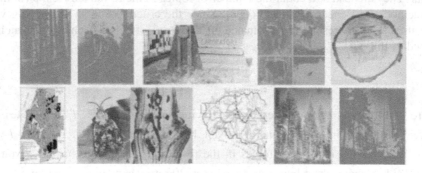

**Fig. 3.** Top 10 retrieval results after re-ranking by TRS

Mountain district of the forest service, forest resources of the Douglas-Fir Region. Retrieval results showed in Figure 2 and Figure 3 demonstrate that our proposed method achieves more topic coverage improvement in retrieval results.

Although the proposed method achieves significant improvements in topic coverage of the top retrieval results, we cannot simply obtain the improvement at the cost of losing relevance in the results. Therefore, the five researchers are also asked to give the relevance score of each image in top20 results before and after re-ranking (2-relevant, 1-hard to tell, 0-irrelevant). The average relevance score (ARS) of an image set $I$ is calculated as follows:

$$ARS(I) = \frac{1}{MN} \sum_{k=1}^{N} \sum_{j=1}^{M} RS_k(i_j) \tag{8}$$

$M$ denotes the number of images in set $I$ ($M=20$ in our method). $RS_k(i_j)$ denotes the relevance score of image $i_j$ given by user $k$.

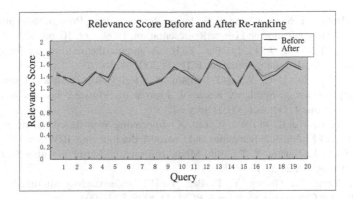

**Fig. 4.** Relevance score before and after re-ranking

Figure 4 illustrates the average relevance score of each query before and after re-ranking. From Figure 4, we can tell that our proposed approach almost has no influence on the relevance of retrieval results.

## 4 Conclusions and Future Work

In the area of image retrieval, relevance is used to evaluate the quality of retrieval results. However, it seems that such criterion does not necessarily ensure the satisfaction from users due to their ambiguous requirements. In this paper, a re-ranking method is proposed to provide images with more query-related subtopics in top retrieval results. In our method, we use topic coverage graph to model the degree of mutual topic coverage among images. Based on the graph, topic richness score is calculated to measure the importance of each image in improving topic coverage of retrieval results. Finally, a new ranking method is introduced to re-rank the retrieval results to enrich topic variety of top image retrieval results. Experimental results demonstrate that our proposed approach is effective in improving the topic coverage of retrieval results without loss of relevance. Post-retrieval processing is an important and rewarding technique in enhancing the quality of image retrieval results and therefore deserves more attention in the area of image retrieval. Our future work includes applying our method to other areas of information retrieval (e.g. text, video retrieval) and scaling our method to larger dataset.

## Acknowledgement

The project in our paper is supported by China-American Digital Academic Library (CADAL) project (No. CADAL2004002) and the Hi-Tech Research and Development Program (863) of China (No. 2003AA119010). We also acknowledge the efforts of the five evaluators.

## References

1. Rui, Y., Huang, T. S. and Chang, S. F.: Image Retrieval: Past, Present, and Future. Journal of Visual Communication and Image Representation, 1999, Vol. 10, pp.1-23
2. Zhuang, Y. T., Yang, J., Li, Q., Pan, Y. H.: A graphic-theoretic model for incremental relevance feedback in image retrieval. ICIP (1) 2002: 413-416
3. Kim, D. H., Chung, C. W. and Barnard, K.: Relevance Feedback Using Adaptive Clustering for Image Similarity Retrieval. Journal of Software Systems and Software, Volume 78, Issue 1, October 2005, Pages 9-23.
4. Zhuang, Y. T., Wu, C. M., Wu, F., Liu, X.: Improving Web-Based Learning: Automatic Annotation of Multimedia Semantics and Cross-Media Indexing. ICWL 2004: 255-262
5. Li, Q., Yang, J., Zhuang, Y. T.: Multi-Modal Information Retrieval with a Semantic View Mechanism. AINA 2005: 133-138.
6. Wu, F., Yang, Y., Zhuang, Y. T., Pan, Y. H.: Understanding Multimedia Document Semantics for Cross-Media Retrieval. PCM (1) 2005: 993-1004.
7. Duygulu, P., Barnard, K., Freitas, N., and Forsyth, D. A.: Object recognition as machine translation: Learning a lexicon for a fixed image vocabulary. In 7th ECCV conference, volume 4, pp. 97–112, 2002.
8. Pan, J. Y., Yang, H. J., Faloutsos, C., and Duygulu, P.: Automatic Multimedia Cross-modal Correlation Discovery. In Proceedings of the 10th ACM SIGKDD Conference, pp. 653-658, Aug 2004.
9. Carbonell, J. and Goldstein, J.: The use of MMR, diversity-based reranking for reordering documents and producing summaries. In Proceedings of the 21$^{st}$ ACM SIGIR 1998, 335-336.
10. Zhang, B. Y., Li, H., Liu, Y., Ji, L., Xi, W. S., Fan, W. G., Chen, Z., Ma, W. Y.: Improving web search results using affinity graph". In Proceedings of the 28th annual international ACM SIGIR, pp. 504-511, 2005.
11. Goh, K. S., Chang, E. Y., Lai, W. C.: Multimodal concept-dependent active learning for image retrieval. In Proceedings of the 12th annual ACM international conference on Multimedia, pp. 564-571, 2004.
12. Brinker, K. :Incorporating diversity in active learning with support vector machines. In Proceedings of the 20th International Conf. on Machine Learning, pp. 59--66, 2003.
13. Li, J. Two-scale image retrieval with significant meta-information feedback.. In Proceedings of the 13th ACM international conference on Multimedia, pp. 499-502, 2005.
14. Zhou, X. S. and Huang, T. S.: Unifying keywords and visual contents in image retrieval. *IEEE MultiMedia*, 9(2):23--33, 2002.
15. Brin, S. and Page, L.: The anatomy of a large-scale hyper-textual web search engine. In Proceedings of the Seventh International World Wide Web Conference, 1998.
16. Haveliwala, T. H.: Topic-sensitive PageRank. In WWW2002, May 7-11 2002.

# Relevance Feedback for Sketch Retrieval
# Based on Linear Programming Classification

Bin Li, Zhengxing Sun[*], Shuang Liang, Yaoye Zhang, and Bo Yuan

State Key Lab for Novel Software Technology, Nanjing University, P.R. China, 210093
szx@nju.edu.cn

**Abstract.** Relevance feedback plays as an important role in sketch retrieval as it does in existing content-based retrieval. This paper presents a method of relevance feedback for sketch retrieval by means of Linear Programming (LP) classification. A LP classifier is designed to do online training and feature selection simultaneously. Combined with feature selection, it can select a set of user-sensitive features and perform classification well facing a small number of training samples. Experiments prove the proposed method both effective and efficient for relevance feedback in sketch retrieval.

**Keywords:** Relevance Feedback, Sketch Retrieval, Linear Programming (LP).

## 1 Introduction

Due to the fluent and lightweight nature of freehand drawing, sketch-based graphical communications has attracted a lot of attention [1][2]. While more and more sketchy shapes would be created and collected in database as a new data type in multimedia database [3], sketch retrieval has come into being [4][5] to retrieve useful information from the sketches for users with a sketch-based query. However, similar to the needs of existing content retrieval, such as text information retrieval and visual information retrieval, benefiting from advances in sketch retrieval cannot be expected before the availability of relevance feedback.

The goal of relevance feedback in content retrieval is to learn user's preference and bridge the semantic gap between low-level features and high-level concepts [6]. Usually, relevance feedback puts user in the loop through asking the user to give feedbacks regarding the relevance of the current outputs of the system. The user marks those results as either relevant or non-relevant and then feeds back to the system. Based on this feedback, the system presents another set of better results. The system learns user's preference through this iterative process, and improves the retrieval performance.

Early works on relevance feedback mainly employ query vector modification and weighting adjustment. Owning to the lack of optimality consideration, researchers begin to look at this problem from a systematic point by formulating it into a learning problem. Many popular machine learning techniques were employed to relevance feedback, such as Decision Tree [7], Nearest-Neighbor classifiers [8], Bayesian

---

[*] Corresponding author.

Y. Zhuang et al. (Eds.): PCM 2006, LNCS 4261, pp. 201–210, 2006.

classifiers [9] and Support Vector Machines [10], etc. Among those, SVM-based techniques are the most attractive techniques to solve the relevance feedback problem. Based on the original two-class SVM, one-class SVM [11] and biased SVM [12] were proposed against the imbalance between the positive and negative samples. However, it is often difficult to collect enough training data for classifier through the users' annotation in the relevance feedback process. Learning in the small sample case is a tough problem in relevance feedback, because classifiers' performance will largely drop when facing insufficient training samples. Furthermore, most of the existing approaches treat all features of content equally, and the user-sensitive features set by means of feature selection [13]. In fact, the benefits of feature selection are not only to find the user-sensitive features set, but also to reduce the computation complexity.

In this paper, our key idea for the relevance feedback of sketch retrieval is to constrain the candidate samples according to the classification results learned from users' feedback and to find the user-sensitive features using feature selection. We bring accordingly the technique of Linear Programming (LP) classification into the process of relevance feedback. A LP classifier is designed to do training and feature selection simultaneously. Combined with feature selection, it can select a set of the user-sensitive features and perform classification well with a small number of samples. In terms of LP classifier, our proposed process of sketch retrieval can be described as follow. After submitting initial query to sketch retrieval engine, user first annotates the candidate results returned by the engine as relevant or non-relevant ones. The LP classifier is trained online by the users' annotated samples, and the user-sensitive features are selected according to their contribution to classification of the candidates. The trained LP classifier is then used to classify the candidates into the positives and the negatives. The similarity between the positives and the original query are updated with the combination of their similarities in both the user-sensitive feature space and the original feature spaces. Finally, the candidates are re-ranked according to their updated similarities as the output of relevance feedback.

The rest of paper is organized as following. The principle of the Linear Programming (LP) classifier with feature selection is introduced in section 2. In section 3, the similarity calculation of relevance feedback is discussed in detail. Finally, some experiments and conclusions are given.

## 2  Linear Programming Classifier with Feature Selection

In the early 1960s, the Linear Programming (LP) technique [14] was used to solve the pattern separation problem. Later, a robust LP technique [15] was proposed to deal with linear inseparability, which always generates a linear surface as an optimal separator for two linearly inseparable sets. In order to cope with the feature selection problem, the new LP classifier has been proposed for combining the feature selection with the classifier training process [16].

Here is our notation for describing LP classifier in detail. For a vector x in the n-dimensional space $\mathbb{R}^n$, $x_+$ denotes the vector in $\mathbb{R}^n$ with components $(x_+)_i = \max\{x_i, 0\}$, a vector of ones in a space of arbitrary dimension will be denoted by e. The 1-norm of x, $\sum_{i=1}^{n} x_i$ , will be denoted by $\|x\|_1$ . The vector $|x|_*$ has components, which are equal to 1 if the corresponding components of $\omega$ are nonzero and 0 if the corresponding components of $\omega$ are zero. For a real matrix $M \in \mathbb{R}^{m \times n}$ , $M^T$ denotes the transpose matrix.

Generally speaking, a binary classification problem can be formalized as a task to estimate a function $f : \mathbb{R}^n \rightarrow \{-1,+1\}$ based on independent identically distributed data:

$$(x_1, y_1), \cdots, (x_l, y_l) \in X \times Y, \ X = \mathbb{R}^n, Y = \{-1,+1\} \tag{1}$$

where, the training instances are vectors in n-dimensional space, $l$ is the number of training instances. Accordingly, given two sets of samples, $A$ and $B$ in $\mathbb{R}^n$ , the task of LP classifier is to find the linear function $f(x) = \omega^T x - \gamma$ , which stratifies: $f(x) > 0$ if $x \in A$ and $f(x) \leq 0$ if $x \in B$ .

Obviously, the function determines a strict separating plane $\omega^T x = \gamma$ with the n-dimensional normal $\omega \in \mathbb{R}^n$ and the real number $\gamma$ that separates sample set $A$ from $B$ .

Practically, the LP classifier has to deal with the linear inseparable case because of overlap between the positive and negative points. A robust LP formulation [14] is proposed which generates a plane that minimizes an average sum of misclassified points belonging to two disjoint point sets. The LP classifier is based on the following error-minimizing optimization problem:

$$\min_{\omega,\gamma} \frac{1}{m} \|(-A\omega + e\gamma + e)_+\|_1 + \frac{1}{k} \|(B\omega - e\gamma + e)_+\|_1 \tag{2}$$

Where, $A \in \mathbb{R}^{m \times n}$ represents the m points of the set $A$ , $B \in \mathbb{R}^{k \times n}$ represents the k points of the set $B$ .

The error-minimizing problem in equation (2) is equivalent to a robust linear programming problem, which solves the classification problem through minimizing the average sum of misclassification errors of the points, as follow:

$$\min_{\omega,\gamma,y,z} (\frac{e^T y}{m} + \frac{e^T z}{k}), \ s.t. \begin{cases} -A\omega + e\gamma + e \leq y \\ -A\omega + e\gamma + e \leq y \\ y \geq 0, z \geq 0 \end{cases} \tag{3}$$

Feature selection is imposed by suppressing as many components of the normal vector $\omega$ to the separating plane which gives an acceptable discrimination between point sets $A$ and $B$ . It is achieved by introducing an extra term with parameter $\lambda \in [0,1)$ into the objective function while weighting the original objective function by parameter $(1-\lambda)$ [16]. The objective function is reformulated as equation (4).

$$\min_{\omega,\gamma,y,z} (1-\lambda)(\frac{e^T y}{m} + \frac{e^T z}{k}) + \lambda e^T |\omega|_*, \quad s.t. \begin{cases} -A\omega + e\gamma + e \leq y \\ -A\omega + e\gamma + e \leq y \\ y \geq 0, z \geq 0 \end{cases} \tag{4}$$

Note that $e^T |\omega|_*$ is simply a count of the nonzero elements in the normal vector $\omega$, and this is the key point to combining feature selection with classifier training. Equation (4) balances the error in separating the sets $A$ and $B$, $(\frac{e^T y}{m} + \frac{e^T z}{k})$, and the number of nonzero elements of $\omega$, $e^T |\omega|_*$. Furthermore, all the features corresponding to zero elements of $\omega$ are removed, so the features are selected after LP optimization.

Guo and Dyer [17] developed a method called feature selection via linear programming (FSLP) to deal with the extra term in the objective function of equation (4). A simple term $e^T s$ with only one weighting parameter $\mu$ is introduced to replace the extra term. LP formulation with feature selection is produced as following:

$$\min_{\omega,\gamma,y,z} (\frac{e^T y}{m} + \frac{e^T z}{k}) + \mu e^T s, \quad s.t. \begin{cases} -A\omega + e\gamma + e \leq y \\ -A\omega + e\gamma + e \leq y \\ s \leq \omega \leq s \\ y \geq 0, z \geq 0 \end{cases} \tag{5}$$

where, $\mu$ is the balance parameter and $s$ is the component-wise absolute value of $\omega$.

Based on the decision function determined by the normal vector $\omega$ and the real number $\gamma$, we can know the instances inside the boundary will be predicted as positive, otherwise, as negative. Simultaneously, feature selection has been selected via the LP classifier training.

## 3   Similarity Measure Constrained by the LP Classifier

In our method, Generalized Ellipsoid Distance is introduced to model the distance between two samples as equation (6):

$$ED(x,q) = (x-q)^T W(x-q) \tag{6}$$

Here, $W$ is a real symmetric full matrix that gives a generalized ellipsoid distance function. Actually, the solution to the optimal distance matrix $W$ can be formulated as a minimization problem and the author in [18] shown how to find the solution. The smaller the value of Ellipsoid distance, or in other words, the closer the two feature vectors are, the more similar the two corresponding samples look like, and vice versa. We introduce a threshold to normalize the similarity, so the similarity between samples can be calculated from the Ellipsoid distances as follows:

$$SIM(x,q) = \begin{cases} 0 & if \ ED(x,q) \geq threshold \\ 1 - \dfrac{ED(x,q)}{threshold} & otherwise \end{cases} \tag{7}$$

Given a query, the LP classifier is trained online and features are selected based on user's feedback. The trained LP classifier is then used to classify the candidates into the positives and the negatives. At the ranking phase, the positive and negative samples are treated differently. The similarity between the positives and the original query are updated with the combination of their similarities in both the user-sensitive feature space and the original feature spaces. On the contrary, the negatives are ranked based on their similarity to the query sample using the original features.

Accordingly, we can formulate the overall similarity measure as follows:

$$S(x,q) = \begin{cases} \alpha \times SIM(x,q) + \beta \times SIM(x_s,q_s) & if \ D(x,\Theta) \geq 0 \\ SIM(x,q) \times MinSim & otherwise \end{cases} \tag{8}$$

Where, the parameters $\alpha$ and $\beta$ represent the importance of the original features and the selected features, $x_s$ stands for the sample's selected features generated by the LP classifier, and $D(x,\Theta)$ is the distance of $x$ to the classifier boundary characterized by a parameter set $\Theta$. The distance $D(x,\Theta)$ is calculated by equation (9):

$$D(x,\Theta) = \omega^T x - \gamma \tag{9}$$

where $\omega, \gamma$ are determined by the LP classifier. $MinSim$ is the minimal similarity among the positive samples. $SIM(x,q) \times MinSim$ can be viewed as a kind of normalization of the negative samples' similarity so that the negative samples' similarity will be less than the positive ones'.

## 4   Experiments and Evaluation

Our proposed relevance feedback algorithm is evaluated with sketch retrieval using a sketchy symbol database. For the data collection, we chose 30 kinds of mechanical engineering symbols and 25 electric symbols, which resulted in a database of 55 classes of sketchy symbols, as shown in **Fig. 1**. For each of the 55 classes, ten persons are asked to draw 20 sketchy symbols respectively. So there are a total of 1100 sketchy symbols in the database. We employ spatial relations graph spectrum as the retrieval features to represent the content of sketchy symbol, which has been proved the availability of content representation for sketchy symbol retrieval in our previous

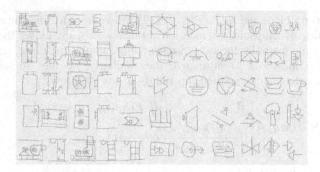

Fig. 1. Illustration of All 55 classes of sketchy symbols

work [6]. Our experiment environment is a PC with Pentium 4 2.4G CPU, 512MB memory, running on Windows XP and Visual C++ 6.0.

There are two goals in our evaluation. First, we want to find out whether the LP classifier is robust enough for relevance feedback. The true positive rate (TP) and the true negative rate (TN) are employed to evaluate the classifier's accuracy. The true positive rate is the proportion of positive cases that were correctly identified. The true negative rate is defined as the proportion of negatives cases that were classified correctly. Second, we want to see if the retrieval performance can be improved based on the scheme proposed above. Recall and precision are used to evaluate the retrieval performance. Recall is the ratio of the number of relevant images returned to the total number of relevant images. Precision is the ratio of the number of relevant images returned to the total number of images returned.

In order to evaluate the LP classifier's recognition accuracy, we randomly select $m$ categories of sketchy symbols, which contain 1 positive class and $m-1$ negative classes. For the positive class, $n$ instances are picked as training data and 10 instances are picked as test data. For each negative class, 1 instance is picked as training data and 10 instances are picked as test data. The true positive rate and the true negative rate are recorded and the whole process is repeated for 10 times to produce average value as the final result. To simulate the sample distribution in relevance feedback, we used $m=2, 5, 10, 15$ and $n=1, 2, 3, 4, 5, 6$ in experiment. The experimental results are shown in **Fig. 2**, where **Fig. 2**(a) illustrates the true positive rate curve varied with the number of training samples and **Fig. 2**(b) illustrates the true negative rate curve varied with the number of training samples.

As shown in **Fig. 2**(a), with the increase of the categories $m$ of sketchy symbols, the true positive rate goes down because more categories mean that the ratio of positive training samples to negative samples becomes less. However, when $m$ equals to 15, the true positive rate reaches about 90% with 6 positive training samples, though it is practically impossible that there are 15 categories of sketchy symbols in the retrieval candidates. It means that even when the category number of the candidates returned to users reaches 15, the LP classifier is still available for relevance feedback. In **Fig. 2**(b), the true negative rate is a little lower than the true positive rate in the experiment but the misclassified negative samples in relevance feedback can be corrected later through the similarity calculating. That is to say, from

**Fig. 2**, we can see that about 5 positive instances are sufficient for both the true positive rate and the true negative rate, which means that the LP classifier performs well when facing small training samples. In conclusion, the LP classifier is robust enough in the small training sample case and it will be also proved in the next experiment on relevance feedback performance.

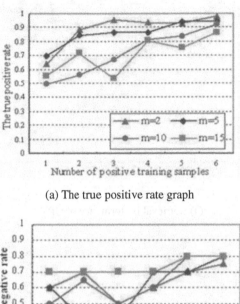

(a) The true positive rate graph

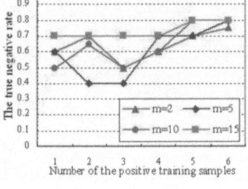

(b) The true negative rate graph

**Fig. 2.** Recognition accuracy of the LP classifier

In the second experiment, we evaluate the retrieval performance of our method on the sketchy symbols database, comparing with the relevance feedback algorithm using query point movement (QPM). A category is first picked from the database randomly, and this category is assumed to be the user's query target. The system then improves retrieval results by relevance feedbacks. In each of iterations of the relevance feedback process, 40 images are picked from the database and labeled as either relevant or non-relevant based on the ground truth of the database. The precision and recall are then recorded, and the whole process is repeated for 10 times to produce the average precision and recall as the final result. The experimental results are shown in

Fig. 3, where Fig. 3(a) illustrate the Precision-Recall curve of the relevance feedback using QPM and Fig. 3(b) illustrate the Precision-Recall curve of the relevance feedback using our designed LP classifier.

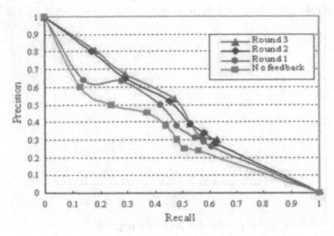

(a) Retrieval performance of QPV

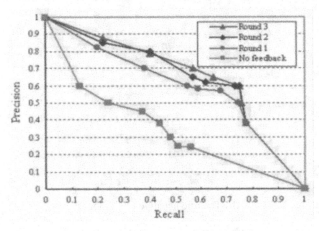

(b) Retrieval performance of LP classifier

Fig. 3. Retrieval performance for relevance feedback

From Fig. 3, we can see that the Precision-Recall curve of our proposed method goes up faster than the QPV method's, especially in the first round. When the precision is 0.5, after the first round feedback, the recall of the LP classifier based method improves to 0.75 compared to QPV method's 0.42. After 3 times feedback round, the Precision-Recall curve of our proposed method is significantly improved contrast with QPV method's one. It means that the LP classifier based relevance feedback can improve the retrieval performance better than the method using QPM, meanwhile, it also proves that the LP classifier can find the user-sensitive features effectively in terms of feature selection.

The time cost used in the retrieval process is also a much-concerned factor for evaluation the relevance feedback method's performance. In our experiment, the average response time is 9.3 milliseconds, which is fast enough for real-time interaction.

## 5 Conclusion

Training and feature selection of classifier with small set of samples is one of the key problems in relevance feedback. In this paper, we employ the linear programming techniques for solving this problem in sketch retrieval. We take into consideration the users' perceptual difference in relevance feedback and design a LP classifier to do online training and feature selection simultaneously, where the LP classifier is trained online by the users' annotated samples, and the user-sensitive features are selected according to their contribution to classification of the candidates. It can be suited for the need of small training samples in relevance feedback. The experimental results prove that relevance feedback based on LP classifier is effective and promising for improving the retrieval performance in sketch retrieval.

However, much more factors affect the performance of relevance feedback algorithm and it is probably safe to say that no simple scheme is likely to capture users' retrieval intentions for sketches. More researches are needed to develop better feature representation of sketch content and to improve the LP classifier's generalization capability.

## Acknowledgments

This paper is supported by the grants from "the National Natural Science Foundation of China" [Project No. 69903006 and 60373065], and "the Program for New Century Excellent Talents in University of China" [Project No. NCET-04-04605].

## References

1. Zhengxing Sun, Wenyin Liu, Binbin Peng, Bin Zhang and Jianyong Sun, User adaptation for online sketchy shape recognition, Lecture Notes in Computer Science, Vol. 3088, 2004, pp. 303-314.
2. Zhengxing Sun and Jing Liu, Informal user interfaces for graphical computing, Lecture Notes in Computer Science, Vol. 3784, 2005, pp. 675-682.
3. Walid G. Aref, Daniel Barbará, Daniel P. Lopresti, Ink as a First-Class Datatype in Multimedia Databases, Multimedia Databases, Springer-Verlag, 1995, pp.113-163.
4. Daniel P. Lopresti, Ink as Multimedia Data, In: Proceedings of the Fourth Intl. Conference on Information, Systems, Analysis and Synthesis, Orlando FL, 1998. 122-128.
5. Shuang Liang, Zhengxing Sun and Bin Li, Sketch Retrieval Based on Spatial Relations, Proceedings of International Conference on Computer Graphics, Imaging and Visualization (cgiv05), Beijing, China, July, 2005, pp 24-29.

6. T.S. Huang and X.S. Zhou, Image retrieval with relevance feedback: From heuristic weight adjustment to optimal learning methods, in International Conference in Image Processing (ICIP'01), Thessaloniki, Greece, October 2001.

7. MacArthus S.D, Brodley C.E, Shyu C, Relevance feedback decision trees in content-based image retrieval, in Proceedings of IEEE Workshop on Content-Based Access to Image and Video Libraries, South Carolina, 2000.

8. P. Wu and B, S. Manjunath, Adaptive nearest neighbour search for relevance feedback in large image database. In ACM Multimedia conference, 2001.

9. I. J. Cox, M. L. Miller, T. P. Minka, T.V. Papathomas, and P.N. Yianilos, The Bayesian image retrieval system, PicHunter: Theory, implementation and psychophysical experiments, IEEE Transactions on Image Processing, vol. 9, no. 1, pp. 20–37, 2000.

10. P. Hong, Q. Tian, and T. S. Huang, Incorporate support vector machines to content-based image retrieval with relevant feedback, in Proceedings of IEEE International Conference on Image Processing, Vancouver, BC, Canada, 2000.

11. Chen Y, Zhou X.S, Huang T.S, One-class SVM for learning in image retrieval, in Proceedings of International Conference on Image Processing, Greece, 2001.

12. Chu-Hong Hoi, Chi-Hang Chan, Kaizhu Huang, Michael R Lyu and Irwin King, Biased Support Vector Machine for Relevance Feedback in Image Retrieval, in Proceedings of International Joint Conference on Neural Networks, Budapest, Hungary, 2004.

13. A. Jain and D. Zongker, Feature selection: Evaluation, application, and small sample performance, IEEE Transactions on Pattern Analysis and Machine Intelligence, 1997.

14. O. L. Mangasarian, Linear and nonlinear separation of patterns by linear programming, Operations Research, vol. 9, pp. 444-452, 1965.

15. K. P. Bennett and O. L. Mangasarian, Robust linear programming discrimination of tow linearly inseparable sets, Optimization Method and Software, vol. 1, pp. 23-34, 1992.

16. P. S. Bradley and O. L. Mangasarian, Feature selection via concave minimization and support vector machines, in proceeding of. 5th International Conference on Machine Learning, 82-90, 1998.

17. G. Guo and C. R. Dyer, Learning from examples in the small sample case: Face expression Recognition, IEEE Transactions on Systems Man. and Cybernetics, vol. 35, no.3, pp. 477-488, 2005.

18. Y. Ishikawa, R. Subramanya, and C. Faloutsos, MindReader : Querying databases through multiple examples, in Proceedings of 24th International Conference on Very Large Data Bases(VLDB'98), pp. 218-227, 1998.

# Hierarchical Motion-Compensated Frame Interpolation Based on the Pyramid Structure

Gun-Ill Lee and Rae-Hong Park

Department of Electronic Engineeging, Sogang University
C. P. O. Box 1142, Seoul 100-611, Korea
gilee201@nate.com, rhpark@sogang.ac.kr

**Abstract.** This paper presents a hierarchical motion-compensated frame interpolation (HMCFI) algorithm based on the pyramid structure for high-quality video reconstruction. Conversion between images having different frame rates produces motion jitter and blurring near moving object boundaries. To reduce degradation in video quality, the proposed algorithm performs motion estimation (ME) and motion-compensated frame interpolation (MCFI) at each level of the Gaussian/Laplacian image pyramids. In experiments, the frame rate of the progressive video sequence is up-converted by a factor of two and the performance of the proposed HMCFI algorithm is compared with that of conventional frame interpolation methods.

**Keywords:** Gaussian/Laplacian image pyramids, hierarchical motion-compensated frame interpolation, motion estimation, pyramid structure.

## 1 Introduction

Video compression techniques basically improve the encoding performance by exploiting the temporal redundancy between subsequent frames as well as the spatial redundancy existing within a frame. Most of video coding standards utilize motion estimation (ME) and motion compensation (MC) to remove the temporal redundancy, thus accurate ME is required for efficient video compression [1][2]. In low bit rate transmission systems such as video telephone and video conferencing, the number of transmission bits must be reduced as much as possible to meet real-time requirements and bandwidth constraints [3]-[4]. For this goal, the number of transmitted frames is reduced by frame subsampling at the encoder, and then skipped frames are reconstructed by temporal frame interpolation at the decoder.

Conventional frame repetition, temporal linear interpolation, and spatio-temporal filtering have been used for frame interpolation for their simplicity of implementation. However, they give jerky motions and blurring at object boundaries since they utilize intensity information only. Recently, motion-compensated frame interpolation (MCFI) techniques have been used to reduce the visual artifacts [5]-[7]. They make use of the detected motion vectors (MVs), in which accurate ME is important for faithful reconstruction of interpolated frames. In MCFI, the motion information of

Y. Zhuang et al. (Eds.): PCM 2006, LNCS 4261, pp. 211–220, 2006.

transmitted frames is used for reconstruction of interpolated frames. For high-quality video, accurate ME is needed to obtain true MV fields. Several methods such as three-dimensional (3-D) recursive search BMA and hierarchical BMA (HBMA) have been proposed to estimate true MV fields [8]. An MCFI that considers occlusion (covered/uncovered regions) uses skipping fields or frames at the encoder and reconstructs the missing frames using MCFI at the decoder [9]. In moving picture experts group (MPEG)-2 [10], bidirectional ME is used to interpolate a B-frame between two (I or P) reference frames. One of three prediction modes (forward, backward, and bidirectional) is selected depending on the mean square difference (MSD) using two MVs (forward and backward MVs). Then the current macroblock (MB) is interpolated according to the selected MB prediction mode using the previous and/or current frames, in which the estimated MV field is transmitted.

In the proposed algorithm, we decompose each of the current and previous frames into a number of Gaussian/Laplacian images. The input frames are decomposed into lowpass and highpass components and, at each level, ME and frame interpolation are performed. The interpolated frame at current level is expanded and used for ME at next level. We perform ME and MCFI hierarchically from top level (coarsest resolution) to bottom level (original resolution), obtaining final interpolated frames at bottom level.

The rest of the paper is organized as follows. The proposed HMCFI algorithm is presented in Section 2. Experimental results and discussions are shown in Section 3. Finally, conclusions are given in Section 4.

## 2  Proposed HMCFI Algorithm

The proposed HMCFI algorithm is based on the Gaussian/Laplacian image pyramid structures [11]. The image pyramid approach represents an image as a set of images having different resolutions/scales and processes independently at each resolution level. The image pyramid technique supports various scalabilities according to image resolution, image size, frequency band, and amount of data. It is a coarse-to-fine technique that supports a progressive transmission. Examples of its applications include ME, still image/video coding, noise reduction, edge detection, and image matching.

The hierarchical image pyramid structure is composed of Gaussian and Laplacian pyramids. The Gaussian pyramid is a set of lower resolution images acquired by lowpass filtering and then decimation. The Laplacian pyramid is defined by the difference image between two Gaussian images at adjacent levels. It contains high frequency components such as edges in an image.

We can construct Gaussian and Laplacian pyramids of the previous frame. Using the decomposed Gaussian/Laplacian images of the previous frame and the current frame, we perform both ME and frame interpolation at each level, which is different from the HBMA-based frame interpolation technique that uses the MV obtained from hierarchical ME [8] for final frame interpolation. The proposed HMCFI algorithm employs different ME and interpolation procedures depending on the type of the pyramid level: top, intermediate, and bottom levels, which are explained in the following.

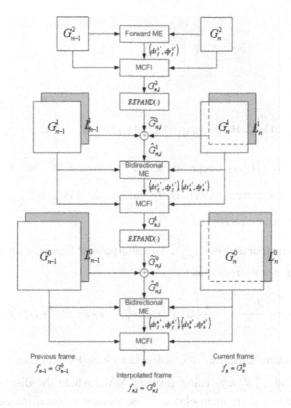

**Fig. 1.** Block diagram of the proposed HMCFI algorithm ($L$=3)

## 2.1  Top Level Processing

Fig. 1 shows the block diagram of the proposed HMCFI algorithm with the number of levels $L$ equal to three, in which frame interpolation results at upper level are delivered to lower level. At each level, different types of ME and MCFI are performed. The different block size is applied to ME at each level since the resolution of each level is different. Let $M \times N$ denote the size of a block for block matching.

**Forward ME.** To obtain the MVs, forward ME is performed using a BMA. The block size at top level is $M/4 \times N/4$ for block matching and the search range is $\pm R$.

To obtain more accurate MVs, half-pixel accuracy spiral search is applied [8]. The mean absolute difference (MAD), as a matching function or a distortion measure can be written as

$$MAD\left(dx_f^{L-1}, dy_f^{L-1}\right) = \frac{16}{MN} \sum_{x=1}^{M/4} \sum_{y=1}^{N/4} \left| G_n^{L-1}(x, y) - G_{n-1}^{L-1}\left(x + dx_f^{L-1}, y + dy_f^{L-1}\right)\right|, \tag{1}$$

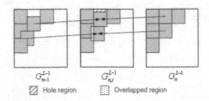

$G_{n-1}^{L-1}$          $G_{n,i}^{L-1}$          $G_{n}^{L-1}$

▨ Hole region          ▥ Overlapped region

**Fig. 2.** Holes and overlapped regions at top level

where $G_n^{L-1}(x,y)$ ( $G_{n-1}^{L-1}(x,y)$ ) represents the luminance of the $(L-1)$th Gaussian image at $(x,y)$ of the current (previous) frame and the MV $\left(dx_f^{L-1^*}, dy_f^{L-1^*}\right)$ denotes the displacement that minimizes (1).

**Bidirectional reconstruction of $G_{n,i}^{L-1}$.** The interpolated Gaussian image $G_{n,i}^{L-1}$ using bidirectional MC is reconstructed as

$$G_{n,i}^{L-1}\left(x+\frac{dx_f^{L-1^*}}{2}, y+\frac{dy_f^{L-1^*}}{2}\right) = \frac{1}{2}\left\{G_{n-1}^{L-1}\left(x+dx_f^{L-1^*}, y+dy_f^{L-1^*}\right) + G_n^{L-1}(x,y)\right\}. \tag{2}$$

Interpolated Gaussian frames are reconstructed block by block of size $M/4 \times N/4$ from $G_{n-1}^{L-1}(x,y)$ and $G_n^{L-1}(x,y)$ using forward MVs, where the displacement in the interpolated frame is linearly interpolated. If the location of the displacement is not on the integer grid, the intensity value on the fractional grid is bilinearly interpolated using intensity values of neighboring pixels on the integer grid.

**Hole and overlapped region processing.** Hole and overlapped regions are generated in the interpolated frame since the grid of the motion compensated block is not matched to that of the interpolated frame. To overcome this defect, we apply the hole and overlapped region processing. Fig. 2 shows holes and overlapped regions generated in the interpolated frame $G_{n,i}^{L-1}$. They are detected by pixelwise flags that are incremented by one when the pixel in the interpolated frame $G_{n,i}^{L-1}(x,y)$ is covered by the block specified by the displacement in MC. The total number of occurrences covered by the motion-compensated block in the interpolated frame is stored. Hole regions (overlapped regions) consist of pixels with the flag value equal to zero (larger than one).

To process hole regions, we use causal spatio-temporal filtering as error concealment. We consider the intensity $G_{n,i}^{L-1}(x,y)$ at hole pixel along with three neighboring intensities ($G_{n,i}^{L-1}(x-1,y)$ , $G_{n,i}^{L-1}(x,y-1)$ , and $G_{n,i}^{L-1}(x+1,y-1)$) in the interpolated frame. We also consider the intensities $G_{n-1}^{L-1}(x,y)$ and $G_n^{L-1}(x,y)$ at pixels in the previous and current frames, respectively, and compute a sum of the absolute differences (SAD) as a matching function. The SADs can be written as

$$SAD_{n,prev} = \left| G_{n-1}^{L-1}(x,y) - G_{n,i}^{L-1}(x-1,y) \right| + \left| G_{n-1}^{L-1}(x,y) - G_{n,i}^{L-1}(x,y-1) \right| + \left| G_{n-1}^{L-1}(x,y) - G_{n,i}^{L-1}(x+1,y-1) \right|$$

$$SAD_{n,cur} = \left| G_n^{L-1}(x,y) - G_{n,i}^{L-1}(x-1,y) \right| + \left| G_n^{L-1}(x,y) - G_{n,i}^{L-1}(x,y-1) \right| + \left| G_n^{L-1}(x,y) - G_{n,i}^{L-1}(x+1,y-1) \right| \tag{3}$$

where the subscript prev (cur) denotes the previous (current) frame.

Two SAD values ($SAD_{n,prev}$ and $SAD_{n,cur}$) computed by (3) are compared and the intensity value $G_{n-1}^{L-1}(x,y)$ or $G_n^{L-1}(x,y)$ yielding a smaller SAD value replaces the intensity value at that (hole) point. The smaller the SAD value, the more the intensity value at hole pixel similar to neighboring intensity values.

Overlapped regions are detected by the regions having the flag value greater than one. We compare block MADs of several candidate blocks that cover the pixel $(x,y)$ in the interpolated frame, select the block yielding the smallest block MAD, and reconstruct the pixel in the overlapped region using that block.

## 2.2 Intermediate Level Processing

**Construction of $G_{n,i}^{L-2}$.** The interpolated frame at top level ($l = L-1$) is delivered to the next intermediate level ($l = L-2$) for ME. The interpolated frame at top level must be expanded to have the same resolution as the image at next intermediate level. The expanded image $\tilde{G}_{n,i}^{L-2}$ is a blurred image, from which it is difficult to estimate accurate MVs. So we add to $\tilde{G}_{n,i}^{L-2}$ the high frequency (detailed) information that is obtained from Laplacian pyramid images $L_{n-1}^{L-2}$ and $L_n^{L-2}$ using MC. Finally, the Gaussian image $\hat{G}_{n,i}^{L-2}$ for bidirectional ME can be written as

$$\hat{G}_{n,i}^{L-2}(x,y) = EXPAND\left(G_{n,i}^{L-1}(x,y)\right) + \frac{1}{2}\left\{ L_{n-1}^{L-2}\left(x + dx_f^{L-1^*}, y + dy_f^{L-1^*}\right) + L_n^{L-2}\left(x - dx_f^{L-1^*}, y - dy_f^{L-1^*}\right) \right\}. \tag{4}$$

Note that the grid is generated in the interpolated frame.

**Bidirectional ME.** The bidirectional ME used in MPEG-2 [10] is performed at intermediate level by using the interpolated frame in (4) as the reference frame. Note that no holes and overlapped regions exist in the reference frame at intermediate level, in which the interpolated frame corresponds to the reference frame on which the block grid is generated.

Forward ME and backward ME are performed to detect forward and backward MVs $\left(dx_f^{L-2^*}, dy_f^{L-2^*}\right)$ and $\left(dx_b^{L-2^*}, dy_b^{L-2^*}\right)$, respectively, using $\hat{G}_{n,i}^{L-2}$ and the Gaussian images $G_{n-1}^{L-2}$ and $G_n^{L-2}$ of the previous and current frames at current level. The block size for ME is $M/2 \times N/2$ and the search range is $\pm 2R$.

**Prediction mode selection.** Using the forward and backward MVs, the prediction mode at current MB is selected depending on the MSDs:

Forward prediction : $MSD_f \leq MSD_b, MSD_f \leq MSD_{bi}$

Backward prediction : $MSD_b \leq MSD_{bi}$ (5)

Bidirectional prediction : otherwise,

where $MSD_f$ ($MSD_b$) represents a forward (backward) MSD using the forward (backward) MV and $MSD_{bi}$ denotes the bidirectional MSD using both forward and backward MVs.

**Frame interpolation at level $(L-2)$.** According to the prediction mode of the current MB, the different MCFI scheme is applied. If the prediction mode of the current MB is forward (backward), then the MB value of the Gaussian image of the previous (current) frame is used. If the prediction mode is bidirectional, then the average MB value of the Gaussian images of the previous and current frames is used.

**Construction of $G_{n,i}^l$ ($1 \leq l < L-2$).** The interpolated frame $G_{n,i}^l$ at intermediate level ($1 \leq l < L-2$) is delivered to next level for bidirectional ME. To have the same resolution as the pyramid images $G_{n-1}^l$ and $G_n^l$ at next level, the interpolated frame $G_{n,i}^{l+1}$ at upper level must be expanded. The expanded Gaussian image $\tilde{G}_{n,i}^l, 1 \leq l < L-2$, is obtained by an $EXPAND(\cdot)$ operator. Similarly, we add to $\tilde{G}_{n,i}^l$ the Laplacian images compensated using $L_{n-1}^l$ and $L_n^l$. As in MCFI, we can obtain $\hat{G}_{n,i}^l, 1 \leq l < L-2$, using the prediction mode information and the Laplacian images:

$$\hat{G}_{n,i}^l(x,y) = EXPAND\left(G_{n,i}^{l+1}(x,y)\right)$$

$$+ \begin{cases} L_{n-1}^l\left(x + 2 \times dx_f^{l*}, y + 2 \times dy_f^{l*}\right) & \text{for forward prediction} \\ L_n^l\left(x - 2 \times dx_b^{l*}, y - 2 \times dy_b^{l*}\right) & \text{for backward prediction} \\ \frac{1}{2}\left\{ L_{n-1}^l\left(x + 2 \times dx_f^{l*}, y + 2 \times dy_f^{l*}\right) + L_n^l\left(x - 2 \times dx_b^{l*}, y - 2 \times dy_b^{l*}\right) \right\} & \text{otherwise.} \end{cases}$$
(6)

**Bidirectional ME using $G_{n,i}^l$ ($1 \leq l < L-2$) with the small search range.** The MB prediction mode and estimated MVs are delivered to next level. At next level, bidirectional ME is performed with a small search range. The MVs delivered to next level are defined by

$$\begin{cases} dx^{l*} = 2 \times dx^{l+1*} + \Delta dx^{l*} \\ dy^{l*} = 2 \times dy^{l+1*} + \Delta dy^{l*}, \quad 1 \leq l < L-2 \end{cases}$$
(7)

where $\left(dx^{l+1*}, dy^{l+1*}\right)$ denotes the MV at intermediate level $(l+1)$, whereas $\left(\Delta dx^{l*}, \Delta dy^{l*}\right)$ signifies the incremental MV refined at intermediate level $l$.

**Frame interpolation at level** $l$ $(1 \leq l < L-2)$. Using the delivered MB prediction mode information and estimated MVs, frame interpolation is performed. The final interpolated frame is delivered to bottom level for MV refinement. Note that frame interpolation is done using forward and backward MVs depending on the prediction mode.

## 2.3 Bottom Level Processing

**Bidirectional ME.** Using $\hat{G}_{n,i}^0$ and the Gaussian pyramid images $G_{n-1}^0$ and $G_n^0$ at bottom level, bidirectional ME is performed for MV refinement. The block size for block matching is $M \times N$ with a small search range of $\pm(R-3)$. The MVs at bottom level are defined by

$$\begin{cases} dx^{0^*} = 2 \times dx^{1^*} + \Delta dx^{0^*} \\ dy^{0^*} = 2 \times dy^{1^*} + \Delta dy^{0^*}, \end{cases} \tag{8}$$

where $\left(dx^{1^*}, dy^{1^*}\right)$ denotes the MV at level 1 and $\left(\Delta dx^{0^*}, \Delta dy^{0^*}\right)$ signifies the incremental MV refined at bottom level $(l=0)$.

**Frame interpolation.** Using the MB prediction mode information delivered from intermediate level and estimated MVs, frame interpolation is performed at bottom level. Similar to MCFI performed at intermediate levels, different MCFI is applied according to the prediction mode of the current MB.

# 3 Experimental Results and Discussions

We present experimental results with two test common intermediate format (CIF) video sequences (352×288, 30 frames): *Akiyo* and *News*. The *Akiyo* sequence is used to evaluate how the frame interpolation algorithm performs on sequences with small motions whereas the *News* sequence is used to test the performance of the frame interpolation algorithm for sequences containing large and complicated motions (e.g., the dancer in the background). In experiments, we assume that two frames $f_n$ and $f_{n+2}$ are given and the missing frame $f_{n+1}$ is reconstructed by frame interpolation, in which the frame rate is up-converted by a factor of two. In conventional MCFI algorithms such as the HBMA based method [8], the four-region segmentation based method (FRS) [9], and the prediction mode decision based method (PMD) in MPEG-2 [10], the missing frames are estimated using the MV information of the skipped frames. Note that the proposed HMCFI algorithm does not use the MV information.

The first experiments are performed with frames 49-80 of the *Akiyo* sequence. Note that half-pixel accuracy spiral search for ME is applied to all methods considered. The HBMA algorithm uses three-level Gaussian/Laplacian pyramids. At each level, the different block size is employed ( 4×4, 8×8, and 16×16 from top to bottom levels), and the different search range is used ( [−5,5], [−3,3], and [−2,2]

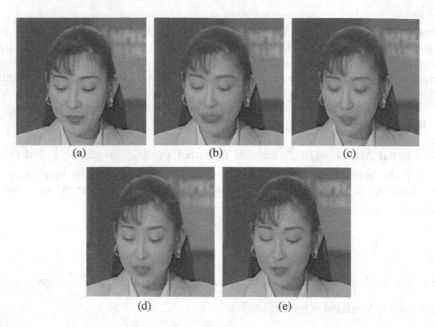

**Fig. 3.** Simulation results (*Akiyo* sequence). (a) Original (missing) 65th frame, (b) frame interpolated by HBMA, (c) frame interpolated by FRS, (d) frame interpolated by PMD, (e) frame interpolated by the proposed HMCFI algorithm.

from top to bottom levels). The FRS and PMD algorithms use 16×16 blocks with the search range equal to [−10,10]. The proposed HMCFI algorithm also uses three-level Gaussian/Laplacian pyramids as in the HBMA algorithm. The block size is varied (4×4, 8×8, and 16×16 from top to bottom levels) and the different search range is used ([−5,5], [−10,10], and [−2,2] from top to bottom levels).

Fig. 3 shows experimental results of the *Akiyo* sequence. Fig. 3(a) illustrates the 65th (missing) frame reconstructed using the 64th and 66th frames. Figs. 3(b) and 3(c) show the frames interpolated by the HBMA and the FRS, respectively, which are severely distorted near eyes and mouth. On the contrary, the frames interpolated by the PMD and the proposed HMCFI algorithm shown in Figs. 3(d) and 3(e), respectively, are well reconstructed.

The second experiments are performed with frames 49-80 of the *News* sequence. The same parameter values are used for both *Akiyo* and *News* sequences. Fig. 4 shows experimental results of the *News* sequence. Fig. 4(a) illustrates the 66th (missing) frame reconstructed using the 65th and 67th frames. Figs. 4(b) and 4(c) show the frames interpolated by the HBMA and the FRS, respectively. Similar to the *Akiyo* sequence cases, Figs. 4(b) and 4(c) give blocky effects, which are totally unacceptable. Fig. 4(d) shows the frame interpolated by the PMD, in which an afterimage (artifact) exists. Fig. 4(e) shows the frame interpolated by the proposed HMCFI algorithm that does not yield an afterimage, showing high visual quality.

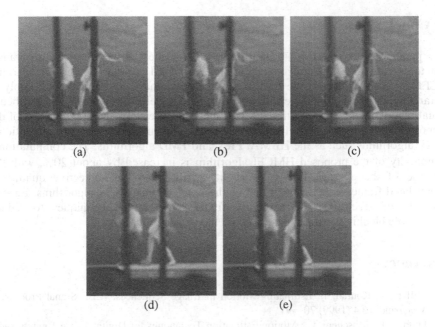

**Fig. 4.** Simulation results (*News* sequence). (a) Original (missing) 66th frame, (b) frame interpolated by HBMA, (c) frame interpolated by FRS, (d) frame interpolated by PMD, (e) frame interpolated by the proposed HMCFI algorithm.

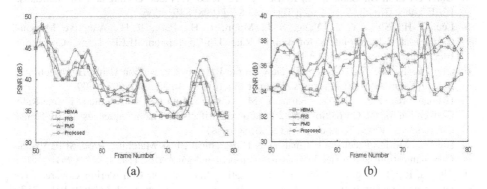

**Fig. 5.** PSNR comparison of four methods as a function of the frame index. (a) *Akiyo* sequence, (b) *News* sequence.

Figs. 5(a) and 5(b) show the PSNR of four different methods as a function of the frame index for the *Akiyo* and *News* sequences, respectively. In both test sequences, the proposed HMCFI algorithm gives a higher PSNR than the conventional MCFI algorithms. Even though the HBMA requires a low computation load for ME, it yields a lower PSNR than other MCFI algorithms. Since the PSNR is not always a reliable measure for image quality evaluation, it is desirable to compare the subjective visual quality. As shown in Figs. 3 and 4, the proposed HMCFI algorithm gives the best visual quality as well as the PSNR.

# 4  Conclusions

This paper presents an HMCFI algorithm based on the Gaussian/Laplacian pyramid structures for frame rate up-conversion. The proposed algorithm performs ME and MCFI at each level of the Gaussian/Laplacian image pyramids. We apply a hierarchical approach to frame interpolation, which yields a higher PSNR and better visual quality than the conventional MCFI methods. We show the effectiveness of the proposed HMCFI algorithm for video sequences compared with the conventional MCFI algorithms such as the HBMA, FRS, and PMD algorithms. The computational complexity of the proposed HMCFI algorithm is increased by about 20%, with the increase of the average PSNR by about 1.2dB. Also the subjective quality of interpolated frames is better than that of the conventional MCFI algorithms. Further research will focus on the pixelwise frame interpolation techniques to reduce undesirable blocking artifacts generated by blockwise processing.

# References

1. Stiller, C., Konrad, J.: Estimating Motion in Image Sequences. IEEE Signal Processing Magazine, 16 4 (1999) 70 − 91.
2. Dufaux, F., Moscheni, F.,: Motion Estimation Techniques for Digital TV: A Review and a New Contribution. Proc. IEEE, 83 (1995) 858 − 876.
3. Reed, E.C., Dufaux, F.: Constrained Bit-Rate Control for Very Low Bit-Rate Streaming-Video Applications. IEEE Trans. Circuits Syst. Video Technol., 11 7 (2001) 882 − 889.
4. Cote, G., Erol, B., Gallant, M., Kossentini, F.: H.263+: Video Coding at Low Bit Rates. IEEE Trans. Circuits Syst. Video Technol., 8 7 (1998) 849 − 866.
5. Lee, S.-H., Shin, Y.-C., Yang, S.-J., Moon, H.-H., Park, R.-H.: Adaptive Motion-Compensated Interpolation for Frame Rate Up-Conversion. IEEE Trans. Consumer Electronics, 48 3 (2002) 444 − 450.
6. Choi, B.-T., Lee, S.-H., Ko, S.-J.: New Frame Rate Up-Conversion Using Bi-Directional Motion Estimation. IEEE Trans. Consumer Electronics, 46 3 (2000) 603 − 609.
7. Hilman, K., Park, H.-W., Kim, Y.-M.: Using Motion Compensated Frame-Rate Conversion for the Correction of 3:2 Pulldown Artifacts in Video Sequences. IEEE Trans. Circuits Syst. Video Technol., 10 6 (2000) 869 − 877.
8. Bierling, M.: Displacement Estimation by Hierarchical Block Matching. Proc. SPIE Visual Communications and Image Processing, Cambridge, MA, 1001 2 (1988) 942 − 951.
9. Thoma, R., Bierling, M.: Motion Compensating Interpolation Considering Covered and Uncovered Background. Signal Processing: Image Communications, 1 2 (1989) 191 − 212.
10. ISO/IEC JTC1/SC29/WG11 MPEG93/N457, MPEG-2 Test Model Version 5, Mar. 1993.
11. Burt, P.J., Adelson, E.H.: The Laplacian Pyramid as a Compact Image Code. IEEE Trans. Communications, 31 4 (1983) 532 − 540.

# Varying Microphone Patterns for Meeting Speech Segmentation Using Spatial Audio Cues

Eva Cheng*, Ian Burnett, and Christian Ritz

Whisper Labs, School of Electrical, Computer and Telecommunications Engineering
University of Wollongong, Wollongong NSW Australia 2522
Ph.: +61 (0)2 4221 3785; Fax: +61 (0)2 4221 3236
{ecc04, ianb, critz}@uow.edu.au

**Abstract.** Meetings, common to many business environments, generally involve stationary participants. Thus, participant location information can be used to segment meeting speech recordings into each speaker's 'turn'. The authors' previous work proposed the use of spatial audio cues to represent the speaker locations. This paper studies the validity of using spatial audio cues for meeting speech segmentation by investigating the effect of varying microphone pattern on the spatial cues. Experiments conducted on recordings of a real acoustic environment indicate that the relationship between speaker location and spatial audio cues strongly depends on the microphone pattern.

**Keywords:** spatial audio cues, meeting audio analysis, microphone arrays.

## 1 Introduction

Meetings recordings are currently difficult to access offline as users potentially have to search through hours of audio/video data to find segments of interest. Efficient 'browsing' of meeting recordings is thus of great interest to many business environments. Research groups currently focus on meeting analysis to facilitate effective meeting browsing [1]. Browsing requires the meeting to be segmented and annotated with semantically meaningful information such as speaker identification, speaker location, speech summary, transcript or level of participant interaction e.g. monologue, group discussion or presentation.

Many of the annotations can be derived from the meeting audio recordings alone. A fundamental way to segment meeting audio is by each speaker's period of participation, or 'turn'. For such segmentation, Lathoud et al. represented speaker location information as Time Delay Estimations (TDE) derived from omnidirectional recordings, using Generalized Cross Correlation (GCC) based techniques such as GCC-PHAT and SRP-PHAT [2].

The authors' previous work extended the concept of using speaker location information for meeting speech segmentation by representing speaker location information with spatial audio cues [3]. The cues are derived from the spatial cues in Spatial Audio Coding (SAC) [4, 5]. When applied to meeting speech segmentation,

---

* Partially supported by the CSIRO ICT Centre, Australia.

Y. Zhuang et al. (Eds.): PCM 2006, LNCS 4261, pp. 221–228, 2006.

previous work found that the spatial cues detected multiple concurrent speakers, whereas GCC-based approaches tended to only detect the strongest speaker in a given speech frame [3].

This paper further investigates the validity of using spatial audio cues for meeting speech segmentation. Simulated meetings recorded with different microphone patterns are analyzed to explore the how microphone pattern affects the relationship between the spatial cues and speaker location. SAC techniques have not been previously investigated with microphone array recordings. Rather, research has focused on resynthesising spatialised recordings e.g. 5.1 surround [6].

In the remainder of this paper, Section 2 outlines the spatial cues extraction from the recorded speech. Section 3 describes the meeting recording setup, while Section 4 presents the results obtained from these recordings. Section 5 concludes the paper.

# 2   Spatial Audio Coding

SAC aims to compactly represent multichannel audio for storage and transmission over mediums such as the Internet. In the encoder, spatial cues are extracted from the $C$-channel input audio (where $C > 1$) and the audio is downmixed into $D$ channels (where $D < C$). The $D$-channel downmix and associated 'side information' (spatial cues) are sent to the decoder for resynthesis into $C$-channels which aim to recreate the original perceptual 'spatial image' for the user.

This paper explores the use of spatial audio cues for the purposes of meeting speech segmentation by speaker turn. The spatial audio cues, derived from SAC, represent the *perceptual* speaker location information contained in the speech recordings. Psychoacoustic studies have shown that humans localize sound sources with two main cues: Interaural Level Difference (ILD) and Interaural Time Difference (ITD) [7]. These psychoacoustic concepts are adopted by SAC approaches to derive level and time or phase-based spatial cues from multichannel audio. This paper employs spatial cues originally introduced by the following SAC schemes: Binaural Cue Coding (BCC) [4] and Parametric Stereo Coding (PSC) [5].

## 2.1   Spatial Audio Coding Cues

BCC and PSC encoders accept $C$-channel input, where $C = 2$ for PSC. Each time-domain channel, $c$, is split into $M$ frames using 50% overlapped windows. The frequency-domain spectrum, $X_{c,m}[k]$, is obtained by an $N$-point Discrete Fourier Transform (DFT) for each channel, $c$, and frame, $m$ [7][8]. The human hearing system uses non-uniform frequency subbands known as 'critical bands' [7]. Thus, $X_{c,m}[k]$ is decomposed into non-overlapping subbands of bandwidths that match these critical bands. The DFT coefficients in each subband are denoted by $k \in \{A_{b-1}, A_{b-1} + 1, \ldots, A_b - 1\}$, where $A_b$ are the subband boundaries and $A_0 = 0$.

BCC calculates the following spatial cues between each input channel $c$ ($2 \leq c \leq C$) and a reference channel (taken to be channel one i.e. $C = 1$), for each frame, $m$, and each subband, $b$ [4]:

- Inter-Channel Level Difference (ICLD)

$$ICLD_p[b] = 10\log_{10}\left(\frac{P_2[b]}{P_1[b]}\right); P_c[b] = \sum_{k=A_{b-1}}^{A_b-1}|X_c[k]|^2 , \tag{1}$$

- Inter-Channel Time Difference (ICTD), which estimates the average phase delay for subbands below 1.5kHz. Subbands above 1.5kHz estimate the group delay.

The PSC encoder extracts the following spatial cues between the two input channels for each frame, $m$, and each subband, $b$ [5]:

- Inter-channel Intensity Difference (IID)

$$IID[b] = 10\log_{10}\left(\frac{\sum_{k=A_{b-1}}^{A_b-1}X_1[k]X_1^*[k]}{\sum_{k=A_{b-1}}^{A_b-1}X_2[k]X_2^*[k]}\right), \tag{2}$$

- Inter-channel Phase Difference (IPD), limited to the range $-\pi \le IPD[b] \le \pi$ ,

$$IPD[b] = \angle\left(\sum_{k=A_{b-1}}^{A_b-1}X_1[k]X_2^*[k]\right). \tag{3}$$

The human auditory system is less sensitive to interaural phase differences at frequencies greater than approximately 2kHz [7]. Thus, BCC splits the ICTD calculation at 1.5kHz and PSC only estimates the IPD cue for subbands below 2kHz.

Previous research showed that the ICTD from BCC did not exhibit a strong nor consistent relationship with speaker location [3]. Thus, this paper implements a combined BCC and PSC encoder where only the ICLD (which is effectively the same calculation as the IID) and IPD cues are estimated.

## 3 Meeting Recordings

To simulate a real meeting environment, recordings were made in an immersive spatial audio playback system. Fig. 1 illustrates the recording setup. The Configurable Hemisphere Environment for Spatialised Sound (CHESS) [8] was used to simulate a meeting with five participants equally spaced (i.e. 72° apart) in a circle approximately 3m in diameter. Each participant was represented by a loudspeaker which played clean speech sourced from one person.

Clean speech was obtained from the Australian National Database of Spoken Languages (ANDOSL). Five native Australian speakers, two female and three male, were chosen as the meeting 'participants'. The ANDOSL speech files were upsampled to 44.1kHz from 20kHz, and normalized with silence removed. Previous work showed that silence segments produced ambiguous spatial cues, since no speaker location information exists in such segments [3].

To simulate a meeting, each of the five loudspeakers was played in turn (from Spkr1 to Spkr5 in Fig. 1). Each participant's turn ranged from 1-1.5 minutes in duration. This resulted in a 6.5 minute long 'meeting' of non-overlapped speech.

To record the speech, two AKG C414 B-XL II multi-pattern microphones were placed in the centre of the 'meeting environment', spaced 20cm apart. All experiments utilized the two microphones in the Mic 1 and Mic 2 positions, as shown in Fig. 1. Microphones recorded the speech which was then sampled at 44.1kHz and stored at 24 bits/sample.

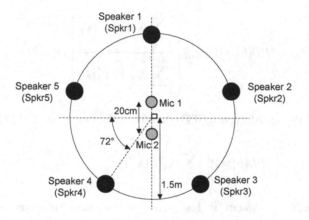

**Fig. 1.** Recording setup

# 4  Results

The simulated 'meetings' were recorded in CHESS [8] using the two microphones configured as a pair of omnidirectional, cardioid, hypercardioid, or figure-8 pattern microphones. For each of the four microphone patterns under study, spatial cues were estimated from the pair of recordings using the combined BCC/PSC spatial audio encoder. At a sampling rate of 44.1kHz, this resulted in a decomposition of 21 subbands and a DFT of length 2048 was used.

Fig. 2 plots the ICLD and IPD spatial cues as a function of time. The mean of each speaker's 'turn' is shown as the solid line. The mean was calculated based upon the ground truth segmentation from the original speech. The shown ICLD is taken from the subband centered at 2.5kHz, which is a frequency region that exhibits strong speech activity. In contrast, the displayed IPD is taken from the subband centered at 382Hz, since pitch information dominates at low frequencies. Fig. 2 shows that the spatial cues vary significantly depending on the microphone pattern used.

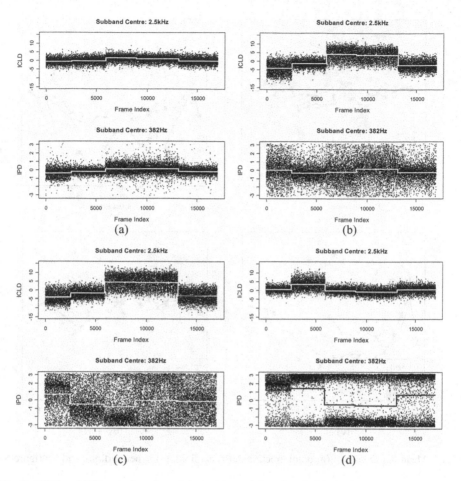

**Fig. 2.** ICLD and IPD as a function of time: (a) omnidirectional, (b) cardioid, (c) hypercardioid, and (d) figure-8 microphones

## 4.1 ICLD

Fig. 3 illustrates the mean and the 95% confidence interval (CI) of the ICLD cue in each subband for each speaker. The mean was calculated across all the frames from each speaker's 'turn' for each subband.

The cardioid (Fig. 3b) and hypercardioid (Fig. 3c) patterns clearly show three groups of ICLD trends across the subbands. Ideally, the five different speakers should exhibit five distinct ICLD trends. However, this is not possible with one microphone pair: in that case, sound localization is limited to sources that are not equidistant between the two microphones. Thus, the three trends seen in Figs. 3b and 3c correspond to Speaker 1, and the equidistant pairs of Speakers 2 and 5, and Speakers 3 and 4 (see Fig. 2). In contrast, the omnidirectional (Fig. 3a) and figure-8 (Fig. 3d) recordings cannot clearly distinguish between the five spatially separated speakers based on the ICLD cue.

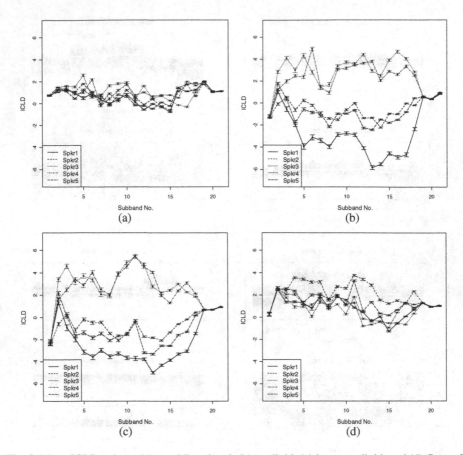

**Fig. 3.** Mean ICLD values: (a) omnidirectional, (b) cardioid, (c) hypercardioid, and (d) figure-8

The authors' previous work showed that the ICLD represented spatial information, independent of the speaker characteristics [3]. These findings are confirmed by the cardioid and hypercardioid results in Figs. 3b and 3c. These microphone patterns are better suited to the level-based spatial cue because the single lobe directionality limits the influence of background noise that can corrupt ICLD estimation.

In Fig. 3, the ICLD cue does not show inter-speaker trends for very low or very high frequencies. For the first (centered at 27Hz) and last three subbands (centered at 12kHz, 15kHz, 19kHz), all five speakers exhibit similar means for all microphone patterns. At high frequencies, although the recordings were sampled at 44.1kHz, the original speech was sampled at 20kHz and hence no frequency information exists above 10kHz. In the low frequency subband, however, there is little speech activity in this frequency region and thus minimal spatial information exists.

In Fig. 3, the mean ICLD value per speaker varies across the subbands. This is due to the prominence of speech activity around certain frequency regions. In addition, the ICLD calculation already combines the contribution from a range of DFT frequency bins (see Equation 1).

## 4.2  IPD

Fig. 4 illustrates the mean and 95% CI of the IPD cue in each subband for each speaker's 'turn'. The opposite trends to Fig. 3 are shown in Fig. 4. In Fig. 4, the IPD cue from the cardioid (Fig. 4b) and hypercardioid (Fig. 4c) pattern recordings do not show significant differences between the five speakers. Similarly to the ICLD cue, Speakers 2 and 5, and Speakers 3 and 4 should exhibit similar IPD cues due to the microphone placement. The pattern that best shows this trend is the omnidirectional microphone (Fig. 4a). For the figure-8 recordings (Fig. 4d), the cues from Speakers 3 and 4 match more clearly than those from Speakers 2 and 5.

The superior performance of the omnidirectional microphones for IPD cue estimation is consistent with previous work, which found that omnidirectional patterns are best suited to TDE [2]. The TDE calculation, like the IPD cue (see Equation 3), involves cross-correlation estimation. Such calculations require spatially distributed microphones that record the same signal but vary according to degradation from the acoustic environment. The omnidirectional pattern fits this requirement, while the directional patterns record signals that vary depending on the source

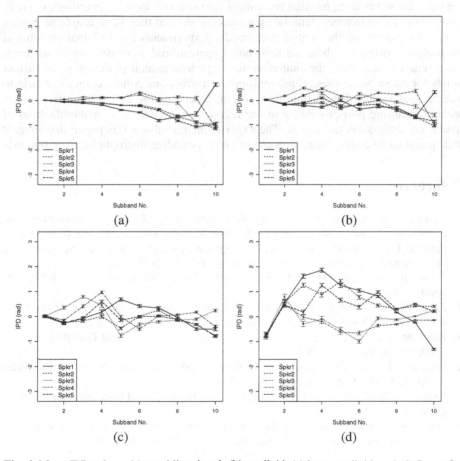

**Fig. 4.** Mean IPD values: (a) omnidirectional, (b) cardioid, (c) hypercardioid, and (d) figure-8

direction relative to the main pickup lobe/s. Thus, the figure-8 pattern performs better than the cardioid and hypercardioid patterns for the IPD cue in Fig. 4. By having two main pickup lobes, figure-8 patterns can capture signals which do not differ as much between spatially distributed microphones compared to single main lobe patterns.

Similarly to the ICLD cue, the means of the IPD vary across the subbands. In addition, the means of the IPD from the different speakers converge to similar values in the first subband (centered at 27Hz). The lack of spatial information in the first subband is because of little pitch or speech activity in these frequency regions. Due to the psychoacoustically motivated subband decomposition, low frequency subbands also contain fewer DFT bins. Hence, frequency bins that do not contain information are more likely to corrupt the spatial cue estimation in these smaller subbands.

## 5  Conclusion

Experiments in this paper have shown that spatial audio cues, derived from spatial audio coding, do strongly correspond to changing speaker location. Thus, spatial cues are valid for segmenting meeting recordings into speaker 'turns'. Recordings made in a real acoustic environment simulating a meeting showed that the microphone pattern significantly affected the spatial cue trends. Experiments showed that directional microphone patterns such as cardioid and hypercardioid were best suited to level-based cues. In contrast, the omnidirectional pattern exhibited the most consistent trends for phase-based cues. Thus, appropriate microphone pattern choice can help to reduce spatial cue degradation from room reverberation and background noise, without requiring post-processing of the recordings, spatial cues, or modification of spatial cue estimation techniques. The experimental results in this paper also suggest that spatial audio coding techniques are suitable for coding microphone array signals.

## References

1. Tucker, S. and Whittaker S.: Accessing Multimodal Meeting Data: Systems, Problems and Possibilities. Lecture Notes in Computer Science, Springer-Verlag, vol. 3361, (2005) 1-11.
2. Lathoud, G., McCowan, I., and Moore, D.: Segmenting Multiple Concurrent Speakers using Microphone Arrays. Proc. Eurospeech '03, Geneva (2003) 2889-2892.
3. Cheng, E. et al.: Using Spatial Cues for Meeting Speech Segmentation. Proc. ICME '05, Amsterdam, (2005).
4. Faller, C. and Baumgarte, F.: Binaural Cue Coding – Part II: Schemes and Applications. IEEE Trans. On Speech and Audio Processing, vol. 11, no. 6, (2003) 520-531.
5. Breebaart, J. et al.: High Quality Parametric Spatial Audio Coding at Low Bitrates. AES 116th Convention, Berlin, (2004).
6. Breebaart, J. et al.: MPEG Spatial Audio Coding/MPEG Surround: Overview and Current Status. AES 119th Convention, New York, (2005).
7. Blauert, J.: Spatial Hearing: The Psychophysics of Human Sound Localization, MIT Press, Cambridge, (1997).
8. Schiemer, G. et al.: Configurable Hemisphere Environment for Spatialised Sound. Proc. Australian Computer Music Conference (ACMC '04), Wellington, (2004).

# Region-Based Sub-pixel Motion Estimation from Noisy, Blurred, and Down-Sampled Sequences

Osama A. Omer and Toshihisa Tanaka

Department of Electrical and Electronic Engineering, Tokyo University of Agriculture and Technology, 2-24-16, Nakacho, Koganei-shi, Tokyo 184-8588, Japan
osama@sip.tuat.ac.jp, tanakat@cc.tuat.ac.jp

**Abstract.** Motion estimation is one of the most important steps in super-resolution algorithms for a video sequence, which require estimating motion from a noisy, blurred, and down-sampled sequence; therefore the motion estimation has to be robust. In this paper, we propose a robust sub-pixel motion estimation algorithm based on region matching. Non-rectangular regions are first extracted by using a so-called watershed transform. For each region, the best matching region in a previous frame is found to get the integer-pixel motion vector. Then in order to refine the accuracy of the estimated motion vector, we search the eight sub-pixels around the estimated motion vector for a sub-pixel motion vector. Performance of our proposed algorithm is compared with the well known full search with both integer-pixel and sup-pixel accuracy. Also it is compared with the integer-pixel region matching algorithm for several noisy video sequences with various noise variances. The results show that our proposed algorithm is the most suitable for noisy, blurred, and down-sampled sequences among these conventional algorithms.

**Keywords:** Sub-pixel motion estimation, watershed transform, region matching, super-resolution.

## 1 Introduction

Sub-pixel motion estimation techniques are widely used in video coding. Motion estimation with sub-pixel accuracy in hybrid video coding schemes possesses higher coding efficiency than that with integer-pixel accuracy [1, 2]. However, it requires more computation for additional processes such as interpolation and search with sub-pixels. Block matching algorithms are frequently used in the standard video coding schemes. However, block matching algorithms suffer from the blocking artifacts. Also the residual will be large due to the fault assumption of constant motion vector within each block. As the residual increases, the bit rate increases. The goal of motion estimation for super resolution (SR) is to find the exact motion of each pixel. However, it is quite difficult to find correct motions of all pixels. Existing algorithms of motion estimation search for approximation to the real motion of each pixel to improve estimation accuracy. Therefore, motion estimation with sub-pixel accuracy is a necessary step

Y. Zhuang et al. (Eds.): PCM 2006, LNCS 4261, pp. 229–236, 2006.

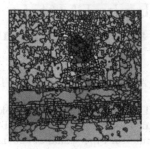

**Fig. 1.** The segmented arbitrary shaped regions

in SR techniques for a video sequence [3, 4, 5]. Moreover, the sub-pixel information required for SR reconstruction must be estimated from noisy, blurred, and down-sampled observed data. A requirement for an algorithm working well under these conditions increasingly arises. Many algorithms have been proposed to estimate motion with sub-pixel accuracy [1, 2]; however a few of them treats with low resolution sequences [2]. Motivated by an application to SR for video, in this paper, we propose an algorithm for motion estimation based on arbitrary shaped region matching with sub-pixel accuracy. The proposed algorithm uses the model introduced in [1] to estimate the motion-compensated prediction errors of the neighbors of the integer-pixel motion vector. Our contribution consists of three points; the first is to use watershed transform based on rain-falling simulation [6, 7] to segment each current frame into arbitrary shaped regions which are further used for region matching instead of block matching. The second is to search for the best motion vector in three steps like three step search (TSS) algorithm [8] which needs less computation time than full search (FS) algorithm. The third is that to use different models to find sub-pixel motion vectors depending on the best matching position with integer-pixel accuracy. The simulation results of the proposed algorithm are compared with that of the well known FS algorithm, the region based algorithm with integer-pixel accuracy, and the full search with sub-pixel accuracy for both noise-free and noisy, blurred and down-sampled sequences. The organization of this paper is as follows. In Section 2, we introduce the proposed algorithm, which is divided into two sub-sections. In Section 3, the simulation results are presented. Finally the conclusion of the paper is presented in Section 4.

## 2  Robust Sub-pixel Motion Estimation

### 2.1  Integer-Pixel Motion Vector

The first step in the proposed algorithm is to use the watershed transform based on the rain-falling simulation [6] to segment the current frame into arbitrary shaped regions as shown in fig.1. This step will create a number of lakes grouping all the pixels that lie within a certain threshold. This can reduce the influence of

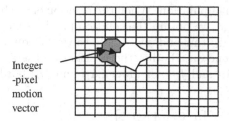

**Fig. 2.** The arbitrary shaped region matching

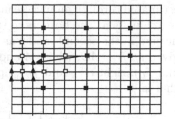

**Fig. 3.** TSS algorithm

Integer
-pixel
motion
vector

noise and reduce the oversegmentation problem. These regions are shifted right, left, up, and down in order to search for the best matching region in three steps in the same way as TSS algorithm [8]. The best matching position gives the integer-pixel motion vector, as illustrated in Figs. 2 and 3.

## 2.2 Sub-pixel Accuracy Step

In this step the accuracy of the motion vector is modified by searching for the best matching position within the eight sub-pixels around the estimated integer-pixel motion vector in the previous step. The following models have been proposed in [1] to predict the errors of motion compensation.

$$f_1(x,y) = c_1x^2y^2 + c_2x^2y + c_3x^2 + c_4xy^2 + c_5xy + c_6x + c_7y^2 + c_8y + c_9, \quad (1)$$
$$f_2(x,y) = c_1x^2 + c_2xy + c_3y^2 + c_4x + c_5y + c_6, \quad (2)$$
$$f_3(x,y) = c_1xy + c_2x + c_3y + c_4, \quad (3)$$

where $f_i(x,y)$ denotes the error at the $(x,y)$-pixel, and $(0,0)$ is the best matching position obtained in the previous steps. The coefficients here can be determined by the errors at 3×3 integer-pixel positions around the motion vector, while for the corner positions, the errors at 2×2 integer positions are calculated, and for the boundary positions, the errors at either 2×3 or 3×2 positions are utilized depending on the boundary. Specifically, the equation given as

$$
\begin{bmatrix}
f(-1,-1) \\
f(0,-1) \\
f(1,-1) \\
f(-1,0) \\
f(0,0) \\
f(1,0) \\
f(-1,1) \\
f(0,-1) \\
f(1,1)
\end{bmatrix}
=
\begin{bmatrix}
1 & -1 & 1 & -1 & 1 & -1 & 1 & -1 & 1 \\
0 & 0 & 0 & 0 & 0 & 0 & 1 & -1 & 1 \\
1 & -1 & 1 & 1 & -1 & 1 & 1 & -1 & 1 \\
0 & 0 & 1 & 0 & 0 & -1 & 0 & 0 & 1 \\
0 & 0 & 0 & 0 & 0 & 0 & 0 & 0 & 1 \\
0 & 0 & 1 & 0 & 0 & 1 & 0 & 0 & 1 \\
1 & 1 & 1 & -1 & -1 & -1 & 1 & 1 & 1 \\
0 & 0 & 0 & 0 & 0 & 0 & 1 & 1 & 1 \\
1 & 1 & 1 & 1 & 1 & 1 & 1 & 1 & 1
\end{bmatrix}
\begin{bmatrix}
c_1 \\
c_2 \\
c_3 \\
c_4 \\
c_5 \\
c_6 \\
c_7 \\
c_8 \\
c_9
\end{bmatrix}
\quad (4)
$$

represents the estimation model for coefficient $c_1, c_2, \ldots, c_9$ in the normal case where the position of the motion vector is neither at the corner nor at the border. Then the error at sub-pixel positions can be computed easily by the coefficients estimated through an inverse matrix manipulation. When the position of the best matching is at the borders of the image, we obtain the solution for the six coefficients in the second model as in (2). To this end, we should solve the equation given as $f = AC$, where $A$ and $f$ depend on whether the position is at left ($A_L$ and $f_L$), right ($A_R$ and $f_R$), upper ($A_U$ and $f_U$), or lower ($A_D$ and $f_D$) border, that is,

$$A_L = \begin{bmatrix} 1 & 1 & -1 & 1 & -1 & 1 \\ 0 & 0 & 0 & 1 & -1 & 1 \\ 1 & 0 & -1 & 0 & 0 & 1 \\ 0 & 0 & 0 & 0 & 0 & 1 \\ 1 & -1 & -1 & 1 & 1 & 1 \\ 0 & 0 & 0 & 1 & 1 & 1 \end{bmatrix}, A_R = \begin{bmatrix} 0 & 0 & 0 & 1 & -1 & 1 \\ 1 & -1 & 1 & 1 & -1 & 1 \\ 0 & 0 & 0 & 0 & 0 & 1 \\ 1 & 0 & 1 & 0 & 0 & 1 \\ 0 & 0 & 0 & 1 & 1 & 1 \\ 1 & 1 & 1 & 1 & 1 & 1 \end{bmatrix},$$

$$f_L = [f(-1,-1), f(0,-1), f(-1,0), f(0,0), f(-1,1), f(0,1)]^T,$$
$$f_R = [f(0,-1), f(1,-1), f(0,0), f(1,0), f(0,1), f(1,1)]^T,$$

$$A_U = \begin{bmatrix} 1 & 1 & -1 & 1 & -1 & 1 \\ 0 & 0 & 0 & 1 & -1 & 1 \\ 1 & -1 & 1 & 1 & -1 & 1 \\ 1 & 0 & -1 & 0 & 0 & 1 \\ 0 & 0 & 0 & 0 & 0 & 1 \\ 1 & 0 & 1 & 0 & 0 & 1 \end{bmatrix}, A_D = \begin{bmatrix} 1 & 0 & -1 & 0 & 0 & 1 \\ 0 & 0 & 0 & 0 & 0 & 1 \\ 1 & 0 & 1 & 0 & 0 & 1 \\ 1 & -1 & -1 & 1 & 1 & 1 \\ 0 & 0 & 0 & 1 & 1 & 1 \\ 1 & 1 & 1 & 1 & 1 & 1 \end{bmatrix},$$

$$f_U = [f(-1,-1), f(0,-1), f(1,-1), f(-1,0), f(0,1), f(1,0)]^T,$$
$$f_D = [f(-1,0), f(0,0), f(1,0), f(-1,1), f(0,1), f(1,1)]^T.$$
$$c = [c_1, c_2, c_3, c_4, c_5, c_6]^T,$$

When the position of the best matching is at the corner, we should solve one of four equations which can be used to get the solution for the four coefficients of the third model as in (3), by using matrices shown below:

$$A_{LU} = \begin{bmatrix} 1 & -1 & -1 & 1 \\ 0 & 0 & -1 & 1 \\ 0 & -1 & 0 & 1 \\ 0 & 0 & 0 & 1 \end{bmatrix}, A_{LD} = \begin{bmatrix} 0 & -1 & 0 & 1 \\ 0 & 0 & 0 & 1 \\ -1 & -1 & 1 & 1 \\ 0 & 0 & 1 & 1 \end{bmatrix},$$

$$A_{RU} = \begin{bmatrix} 0 & 0 & -1 & 1 \\ -1 & 1 & -1 & 1 \\ 0 & 0 & 0 & 1 \\ 0 & 1 & 0 & 1 \end{bmatrix}, A_{RD} = \begin{bmatrix} 0 & 0 & 0 & 1 \\ 0 & 1 & 0 & 1 \\ 0 & 0 & 1 & 1 \\ 1 & 1 & 1 & 1 \end{bmatrix},$$

$$f_{LU} = [f(-1,-1), f(0,-1), f(-1,0), f(0,0)]^T,$$
$$f_{LD} = [f(-1,0), f(0,0), f(-1,1), f(0,-1)]^T,$$
$$f_{RU} = [f(0,-1), f(1,-1), f(0,0), f(1,0)]^T,$$
$$f_{RD} = [f(0,0), f(1,0), f(0,1), f(1,1)]^T,$$
$$c = [c_1, c_2, c_3, c_4]^T$$

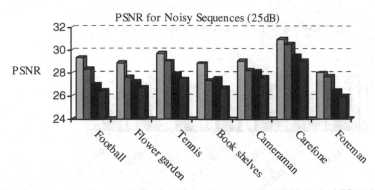

**Fig. 4.** PSNR Quality measure for blurred, noisy, and down-sampled sequences (25dB)

In summary, the proposed algorithm alternates among the three models depending on the position of the integer motion vector.

## 3   Simulation Results

The proposed algorithm is tested by different image sequences including fast motion and slow motion with white Gaussian noise with different SNR to confirm the effectiveness and robustness. We examined the well known test video sequences such as *football*, *tennis* and *carefone* sequences and slow motion sequences such as *flower garden*, and *foreman* sequences. We also tested video sequences with a synthetic motion created by shifting a still image with sub-pixel accuracy such as *cameraman* and *book shelves* images. All these sequences are blurred, degraded by additive noise with different signal-to-noise ratio (SNR), and down-sampled to simulate conditions similar to super-resolution case. The algorithm is compared with the well known block matching full search with sub-pixel accuracy proposed by Jung et el. [1], and also compared with the full search algorithm with integer-pixel accuracy. Moreover, it is compared with the region matching with integer-pixel accuracy algorithm. The simulation results show that the proposed algorithm give better quality than all the other three algorithms for noisy sequences. Figure 4 shows the results for noisy sequences with additive white Gaussian noise (25dB). Also, Figure 5 shows the results for noisy sequences with additive white Gaussian noise (20dB). In both cases, the size of the blocks for the block-based FS algorithm was 8×8. Figures 6 and 7show the results of different SNR for *football*, and *flower garden* sequences respectively. In these figures, we can observe the effect of noises with several noise levels. It is interesting that the proposed method is more robust for the images with higher noise levels. This implies that the proposed algorithm is more appropriate to the application to super-resolution. Figure 8 shows comparison between the compensated frames resulting from different algorithms with 25dB Gaussian noise.

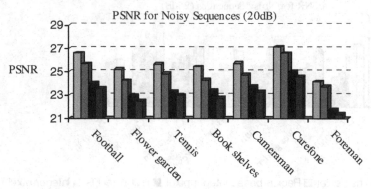

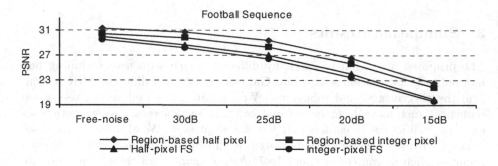

**Fig. 5.** PSNR Quality measure for blurred, down-sampled and noisy sequences (20dB)

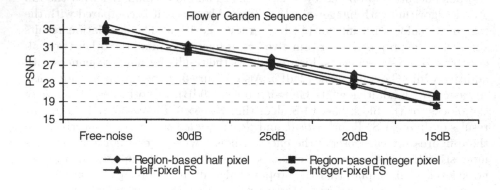

**Fig. 6.** PSNR quality measure with different noise for football sequence

**Fig. 7.** PSNR quality measure with different noise for flower garden sequence

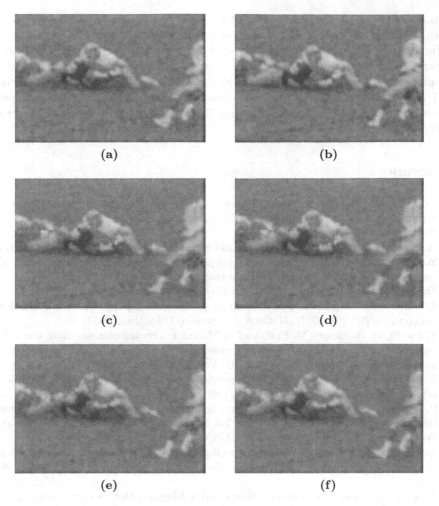

**Fig. 8.** Comparison of conventional methods with the proposed algorithm. The $1^{st}$ frame, which is noisy, blurred and down-sampled, is the reference for the $2^{nd}$ frame: (a) $1^{st}$ (reference) frame (25dB), (b) $2^{nd}$ frame to be estimated (25dB), (c) compensated frame using integer-pixel FS algorithm, (d) compensated frame using half-pixel FS algorithm, (e) compensated frame using region-based integer-pixel algorithm, and (f) compensated frame using the proposed algorithm.

We observe the blocking effect in Fig. 8 (c) and (d), however, our region-based algorithm doesn't generate blocking artifacts.

## 4   Conclusion

We have proposed a novel motion estimation algorithm for blurred, noisy and down-sampled sequences with sub-pixel accuracy. The proposed algorithm consists of two main steps, the first is the integer pixel motion estimation which based on TSS for each arbitrary shaped region, and the second is the accuracy refinement by searching for the best matching within the sub-pixel positions around the detected integer-pixel motion vector. The proposed algorithm gave promising results for low resolution sequences with slow/fast motion for blurred and noisy video sequences. An application the proposed algorithm to super-resolution for video sequence is on-going. This extension will be reported in the near future.

# References

1. Jung W. Suh, and Jechang Jeong, Fast sub-pixel motion estimation techniques having lower computational complexity, IEEE Trans. on Consumer Electronics, Vol. 50, No. 3, August 2004.
2. Sean Borman, Robert L. Stevenson, Block-matching sub-pixel motion estimation from noisy, under-sampled frames: an empirical performance evaluation, SPIE Visual Communications and Image Processing, 1999.
3. Zhongding Jiang, Tien-Tsin Wong and Hujun Bao, Practical super-resolution from dynamic video sequences, in Proceedings of IEEE Computer Vision and Pattern Recognition (CVPR 2003), Madison, Wisconsin, USA, June 2003.
4. S. Farsiu, D. Robinson, M. Elad, and P. Milanfar, Dynamic demosaicing and color super-sesolution of video sequences, Proceedings of the SPIE conference on image reconstruction from incomplete data III, Vol. 5562, October 2004.
5. C. Bishop, A. Blake. B. Marthi Super-resolution enhancement of video,Artificial Intelligence and Statistics (AISTATS), 2003.
6. P. De Smet and D. De Vleschauwer Performance and scalability of highly optimized rainfalling watershed algorithm, Proc. Int. Conf. on Imaging Science, Systems and Technology, CISST98, Las Vegas, NV, USA, July 1998, pp. 266- 273 .
7. Vincent, L., and Soille, P. Watersheds in digital spaces: an efficient algorithm based on immersion simulations, IEEE Trans. Patt. Anal. Mach. Intell. 13, 6 (1991), 583-598.
8. T. Koga, K. Linuma, A. Hirano, Y Iijima and T Ishiguro, Motion compensated Interframe coding for video conferencing, in Proc. Nat. Telecomm. Conf., New Orleans, LA, pp. G5.3.1-5.3.5., Nov. 29-Dec.3, 1981.

# Differential Operation Based Palmprint Authentication for Multimedia Security

Xiangqian Wu[1], Kuanquan Wang[1], and David Zhang[2]

[1] School of Computer Science and Technology,
Harbin Institute of Technology (HIT), Harbin 150001, China
{xqwu, wangkq}@hit.edu.cn
http://biometrics.hit.edu.cn
[2] Biometric Research Centre, Department of Computing,
Hong Kong Polytechnic University, Kowloon, Hong Kong
csdzhang@comp.polyu.edu.hk

**Abstract.** This paper presents a novel approach of palmprint authentication for multimedia security by using the differential operation. In this approach, a differential operation is first conducted to the palmprint image in horizontal direction. And then the palmprint is encoded according to the sign of the value of each pixel of the differential image. This code is called DiffCode of the palmprint. The size of DiffCode is 128 bytes, which is the smallest one among the existing palmprint features and suitable for multimedia security. The similarity of two DiffCode is measured using their Hamming distance. This approach is tested on the public PolyU Palmprint Database and the EER is 0.6%, which is comparable with the existing palmprint recognition methods.

**Keywords:** Multimedia security; biometrics; palmprint authenrication; differential operation.

## 1 Introduction

In the computerized society, most multimedia are in digital formats, which are easy to be modified and reproduced. Biometric based personal recognition is one of the effective methods to prohibit the multimedia signals from illegal reproduction and modification [1, 2]. Within biometrics, the most widely used biometric feature is the fingerprint [3, 4, 5, 6] and the most reliable feature is the iris [3, 7]. However, it is very difficult to extract small unique features (known as minutiae) from unclear fingerprints [5, 6] and the iris input devices are expensive. Other biometric features, such as the face and the voice, are as yet not sufficiently accurate. The palmprint is a relatively new biometric feature. Compared with other currently available features, palmprint has several advantages [8]. Palmprints contain more information than fingerprints, so they are more distinctive. Palmprint capture devices are much cheaper than iris devices. Palmprints contain additional distinctive features such as principal lines and wrinkles, which can be extracted from low-resolution images. By combining all features of palms, such as palm geometry, ridge and valley features, and principal lines and wrinkles, it is possible to build a highly accurate biometrics system.

Y. Zhuang et al. (Eds.): PCM 2006, LNCS 4261, pp. 237–244, 2006.

Many algorithms have been developed for palmprint recognition in the last several years. Han [9] used Sobel and morphological operations to extract line-like features from palmprints. Similarly, for verification, Kumar [10] used other directional masks to extract line-like features. Wu [11] used Fisher's linear discriminant to extract the algebraic feature (called Fisherpalms). The performance of these methods are heavily affected by the illuminance. Zhang [12, 13] used 2-D Gabor filters to extract the texture features (called PalmCode) from low-resolution palmprint images and employed these features to implement a highly accurate online palmprint recognition system. In this paper, we encoded a palmprint using the differential operation. This code is called DiffCode. In the matching stage, the Hamming distance is used to measure the similarity of the DiffCodes.

When palmprints are captured, the position, direction and amount of stretching of a palm may vary so that even palmprints from the same palm may have a little rotation and translation. Furthermore, palms differ in size. Hence palmprint images should be orientated and normalized before feature extraction and matching. The palmprints used in this paper are from the Polyu Palmprint Database [14]. The samples in this database are captured by a CCD based palmprint capture device [12]. In this device, there are some pegs between fingers to limit the palm's stretching, translation and rotation. These pegs separate the fingers, forming holes between the forefinger and the middle finger, and between the ring finger and the little finger. In this paper, we use the preprocessing technique described in [12] to align the palmprints. In this technique, the tangent of these two holes are computed and used to align the palmprint. The central part of the image, which is $128 \times 128$, is then cropped to represent the whole palmprint. Such preprocessing greatly reduces the translation and rotation of the palmprints captured from the same palms. Figure 1 shows a palmprint and its cropped image.

The rest of this paper is organized as follows. Section 2 discusses diffCode extraction. Section 3 presents the similarity measurement of palmprints. Section 4 contains some experimental results. And in Section 5, we provide some conclusions.

## 2   DiffCode Extraction

Let $I$ denote a palmprint image and $G_\sigma$ denote a 2D Gaussian filter with the variance $\sigma$. The palmprint is first filtered by $G_\sigma$ as below:

$$I_f = I * G_\theta \tag{1}$$

where $*$ is the convolution operator.

Then the difference of $I_f$ in the horizontal direction is computed as following:

$$D = I_f * b \tag{2}$$

$$b = [-1, 1] \tag{3}$$

where $*$ is the convolution operator.

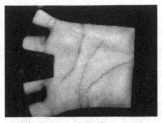 

(a) Original Palmprint (b) Cropped Image

**Fig. 1.** An example of the palmprint and its cropped image

Finally, the palmprint is encoded according to the sign of each pixel of $D$:

$$C(i,j) = \begin{cases} 1, & \text{if } D(i,j) > 0; \\ 0, & \text{otherwise.} \end{cases} \tag{4}$$

$C$ is called DiffCode of the palmprint $I$. The size of the preprocessed palmprint is $128 \times 128$. Extra experiments shows that the image with $32 \times 32$ is enough for the DiffCode extraction and matching. Therefore, before compute the DiffCode, we resize the image from $128 \times 128$ to $32 \times 32$. Hence the size of the DiffCode is $32 \times 32$. Figure 2 shows some examples of DiffCode. From this figure, the DiffCode preserves the structure information of the lines on a palm.

## 3 Similarity Measurement of DiffCode

Because all DiffCodes have the same length, we can use Hamming distance to define their similarity. Let $C_1, C_2$ be two DiffCodes, their Hamming distance ($H(C_1, C_2)$) is defined as the number of the places where the corresponding values of $C_1$ and $C_2$ are different. That is,

$$H(C_1, C_2) = \sum_{i=1}^{32} \sum_{j=1}^{32} C_1(i,j) \otimes C_2(i,j) \tag{5}$$

where $\otimes$ is the logical **XOR** operation.

The matching score of two DiffCodes $C_1$ and $C_2$ is then defined as below:

$$S(C_1, C_2) = 1 - \frac{H(C_1, C_2)}{32 \times 32} \tag{6}$$

Actually, $S(C_1, C_2)$ is the percentage of the places where $C_1$ and $C_2$ have the same values.

Obviously, $S(C_1, C_2)$ is between 0 and 1 and the larger the matching score, the greater the similarity between $C_1$ and $C_2$. The matching score of a perfect match is 1. Figure 3 shows the matching results of Figure 2. In this figure, the

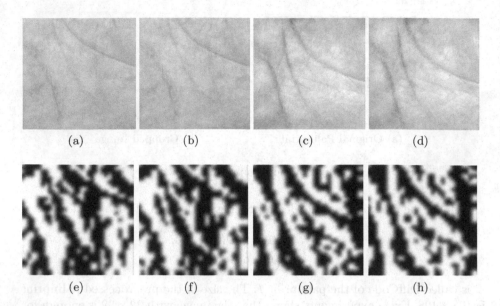

**Fig. 2.** Some examples of DiffCodes. (a) and (b) are two palmprint samples from a palm; (c) and (d) are two palmprint samples from another palm; (e)-(h) are the DiffCodes of (a)-(d), respectively.

white points of the images represent that the value of the corresponding places in $C_1$ and $C_2$ are same. Their matching scores are listed in Table 1. According to this table, the matching scores of the DiffCodes from the same palms are much larger than that of the ones from different palms.

**Table 1.** Matching Scores of the DiffCodes in Figure 2

| No. of DiffCodes | Figure 2(e) | Figure 2(f) | Figure 2(g) | Figure 2(h) |
|---|---|---|---|---|
| Figure 2(e) | 1 | 0.8623 | 0.5811 | 0.5489 |
| Figure 2(f) | - | 1 | 0.5867 | 0.5633 |
| Figure 2(g) | - | - | 1 | 0.8418 |
| Figure 2(h) | - | - | - | 1 |

## 4    Experimental Results

We employed the PolyU Palmprint Database [14] to test our approach. This database contains 600 grayscale images captured from 100 different palms by a CCD-based device. Six samples from each of these palms were collected in two sessions, where three samples were captured in the first session and the other three in the second session. The average interval between the first and the second collection was two months. Some typical samples in this database are shown in

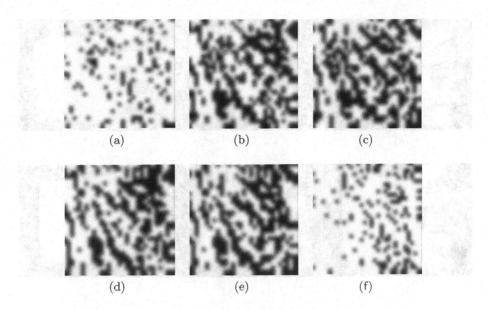

(a)                    (b)                    (c)

(d)                    (e)                    (f)

**Fig. 3.** Matching Results of Figure 2. (a)-(f) are the matching results of Figure 2(e) and 2(f), Figure 2(e) and 2(g), Figure 2(e) and 2(h), Figure 2(f) and 2(g), Figure 2(f) and 2(h), Figure 2(g) and 2(h), respectively.

Figure 4, in which the last two samples were captured from the same palm at different sessions. According to this figure, the lighting condition in different sessions is very different. In our experiments, the variance of the 2D gaussian filter $\sigma$ is chosen as 0.5.

In order to investigate the performance of the proposed approach, each sample in the database is matched against the other samples. The matching between palmprints which were captured from the same palm is defined as a genuine matching. Otherwise, the matching is defined as an impostor matching. A total of 179, 700 (600 × 599/2) matchings have been performed, in which 1500 matchings are genuine matchings. Figure 5 shows the genuine and impostor matching scores distribution. There are two distinct peaks in the distributions of the matching scores. One peak (located around 0.82) corresponds to genuine matching scores while the other peak (located around 0.55) corresponds to impostor matching scores. The Receiver Operating Characteristic (ROC) curve, which plots the pairs (FAR, FRR) with different thresholds, is shown in Figure 6. For comparisons, the FusionCode method [13], which is an improvement of the PalmCode algorithm [12], is also implemented on this database. In the FusionCode method, each sample is also matched with the others. The ROC curve of the FusionCode method is also plotted in Figure 6 and the corresponding equal error rates (EERs) are listed in Table 2. According to the figure, the whole curve of the DiffCode approach is below that of the FusionCode method, which means that the performance of the proposed approach is better than that

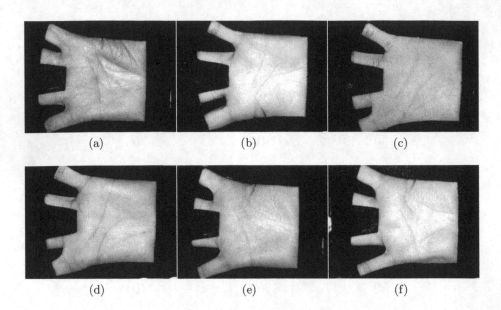

(a)                    (b)                    (c)

(d)                    (e)                    (f)

**Fig. 4.** Some typical samples in the Polyu Palmprint Database

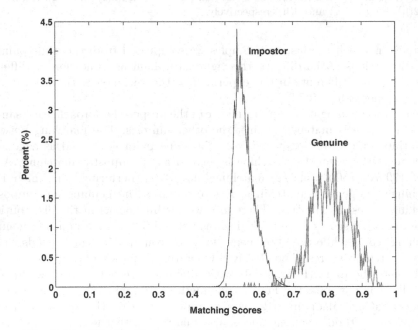

**Fig. 5.** The Distributions of Genuine and Impostor Matching Scores

of the FusionCode method. From Table 2, the EER of the DiffCode approach is
0.13% smaller than that of FusionCode. Furthermore, the size of a DiffCode is
$(32 \times 32) \div 8 = 128$ bytes, which is 1/3 of the size of the FusionCode.

**Table 2.** Comparisons of Different Palmprint Recognition Methods

| Method | DiffCode | FusionCode |
|---|---|---|
| EER (%) | 0.64 | 0.77 |
| Feature Size (bytes) | 128 | 384 |

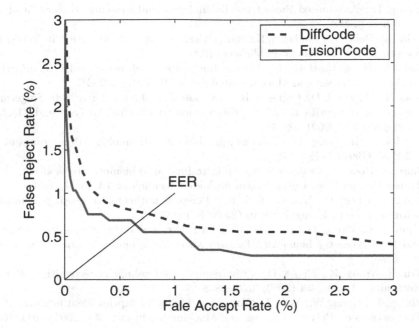

**Fig. 6.** The ROC Curve of the Proposed Approach and FusionCode Method

## 5    Conclusion and Future Work

A novel approach to palmprint authentication is presented in this paper. The palmprint DiffCode is extracted using differential operation. The similarity of the DiffCode is defined using their Hamming distance. The size of the diffCode is only 128 bytes, which is the smallest palmprint feature, and therefore very suitable for the multimedia security. The experimental results clearly shows the high accuracy of this approach.

In future, we will integrate the diffCode into the multimedia systems.

## Acknowledgements

This work is supported by the National Natural Science Foundation of China (No. 60441005), the Key-Project of the 11th-Five-Year Plan of Educational Science of Hei Longjiang Province, China (No. HZG160) and the Development Program for Outstanding Young Teachers in Harbin Institute of Technology.

# References

1. Golshani, F.: Computational Biometrics, Multimedia Analysis, and Security. IEEE MultiMedia **10** (2003) c2,1
2. Jain, A., Bolle, R., Pankanti, S.: Techniques for Securing Multimedia Content in Consumer Electronic Appliances using Biometric Signatures. IEEE Transactions on Consumer Electronics **51** (2005) 545–551
3. Zhang, D.: Automated Biometrics–Technologies and Systems. Kluwer Academic Publishers (2000)
4. Jain, A., Bolle, R., Pankanti, S.: Biometrics: Personal Identification in Networked Society. Kluwer Academic Publishers (1999)
5. Jain, A., Hong, L., Bolle, R.: On-line fingerprint verification. IEEE Transactions on Pattern Analysis and Machine Intelligence **19** (1997) 302–313
6. Maio, D., Maltoni, D., Cappelli, R., Wayman, J.L., Jain, A.: Fvc2000: Fingerprint verification competition. IEEE Transactions on Pattern Analysis and Machine Intelligence **24** (2002) 402–412
7. Wildes, R.: Iris recognition: an emerging biometric technology. Proceedings of the IEEE **85** (1997) 1348–1363
8. Jain, A., Ross, A., Prabhakar, S.: An introduction to biometric recognition. IEEE Transaction on Circuit and System for Video Technology **14** (2004) 4–20
9. Han, C., Chen, H., Lin, C., Fan, K.: Personal authentication using palm-print features. Pattern Recognition **36** (2003) 371–381
10. Kumar, A., Wong, D., Shen, H., Jain, A.: Personal verification using palmprint and hand geometry biometric. Lecture Notes in Computer Science **2688** (2003) 668–678
11. Wu, X., Wang, K., Zhang, D.: Fisherpalms based palmprint recognition. Pattern Recognition Letters **24** (2003) 2829–2838
12. Zhang, D., Kong, W., You, J., Wong, M.: Online palmprint identification. IEEE Transactions on Pattern Analysis and Machine Intelligence **25** (2003) 1041–1050
13. Kong, A.W., Zhang, D.: Feature-level fusion for effective palmprint authentication. Internatrional Conference on Biometric Authentication, LNCS **3072** (2004) 761–767
14. Polyu palmprint palmprint database. http://www.comp.polyu.edu.hk/biometrics/

# A Broadcast Model for Web Image Annotation

Jia Li[1], Ting Liu[1], Weiqiang Wang[1,2], and Wen Gao[1]

[1] Institute of Computing Technology, CAS, Beijing 100080, China
[2] Graduate University of Chinese Academy of Sciences (GUCAS)
{jli, tliu, wqwang, wgao}@jdl.ac.cn

**Abstract.** Automatic annotation of Web image has great potential in improving the performance of web image retrieval. This paper presents a Broadcast Model (BM) for Web image annotation. In this model, pages are divided into blocks and the annotation of image is realized through the interaction of information from blocks and relevant web pages. Broadcast means each block will receive information (just like signals) from relevant web pages and modify its feature vector according to this information. Compared with most existing image annotation systems, the proposed algorithm utilizes the associated information not only from the page where images locate, but also from other related pages. Based on generated annotations, a retrieval application is implemented to evaluate the proposed annotation algorithm. The preliminary experimental result shows that this model is effective for the annotation of web image and will reduce the number of the result images and the time cost in the retrieval.

**Keywords:** Web image annotation; retrieval; Broadcast Model.

## 1 Introduction

Content-based web image retrieval [4] is quite popular now. Images on the Internet usually can be annotated through the cues from other information. Some existing algorithms [2,7] first divide a web page into blocks through a certain page segmentation algorithm, such as [1,5,6] to make each block contain a single topic. Then the image in the block is annotated through the cues from ALT (alternate text), texts and links in that block. But these algorithms ignore the content of the block while measuring its importance. Sometimes appropriate words for annotating an image can't be found within the page where the image locates.

To overcome these disadvantages, we present a Broadcast Model (BM). In this model information used to annotate an image can locate at anywhere in a website, and the importance of each block is calculated with respect to their content.

In the remaining parts, Section 2 gives a clustering method for page segmentation. Section 3 describes the proposed BM and presents an iterative implementation for BM. Section 4 gives experimental results. Section 5 concludes the paper.

Y. Zhuang et al. (Eds.): PCM 2006, LNCS 4261, pp. 245–251, 2006.

## 2  Page Segmentation

In our algorithm, a web page is first divided into blocks through the following clustering procedure:

**Step 1:** Extract all the basic elements in a web page, such as images, links or texts, which can be identified by different tags <img>, <a> <#text> respectively. The size and position for each basic element is directly recorded.

**Step 2:** Images with a large enough area and a proper width-height-ratio are considered to be valid.

**Step 3:** Cluster basic elements into rectangle blocks based on the following rules.

1)  Each element is considered as a block. A block $B_i$ contained by another block $B_j$ will be combined into it.

2)  For two blocks that don't both contain valid images, they will clustered to a new block if the new rectangle block does not intersect with other existing blocks.

**Step 4:** for each block $B_k$, evaluate its importance $I(B_k)$ by formula (1):

$$I(B_k) = WA(B_k) / \sum_{j=1}^{N} WA(B_j), \tag{1}$$

$$WA(B_j) = W^{valid} \times S_j^{valid} + W^{invalid} \times S_j^{Invalid} + W^{link} \times S_j^{link} + W^{text} \times S_j^{text}, \tag{2}$$

Where $S_j^{valid}$, $S_j^{invalid}$, $S_j^{link}$, $S_j^{text}$ denotes the total area of valid images, invalid images, links, and texts in block $B_j$, and $W^{valid}$, $W^{invalid}$, $W^{link}$, $W^{text}$ denote the weights of the corresponding basic elements. Generally we have $W^{valid} > W^{text} \geq W^{link} > W^{invalid}$. Fig.1 gives an example of page segmentation result.

 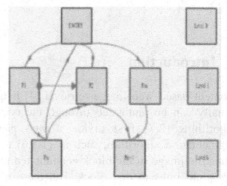

**Fig. 1.** An example of page segmentation          **Fig. 2.** A structure graph of a website

## 3  Broadcast Model (BM)

"Broadcast" here means an interaction between blocks and web pages. In this section, we first give an overview of the proposed broadcast model in subsection 3.1, and then present an iterative implementation of BM.

## 3.1 Overview

For pages in a website, they are organized together through hyperlinks. We use $s \xrightarrow{1} T$ to denote a hyperlink from an object $s$ to another object $T$. Objects here can be a page or a block. Correspondingly, $B_i \xrightarrow{N} P_{jN}$ denotes a path from a block $B_i$ to a page $P_{jN}$ through $N$ leaps. The structure of a website is illustrated in Fig. 2. The entry in Fig.2 denotes the first page of the website and levels are extracted from the address of pages. Generally a page $P_m$ in low level tends to be more general in content than $P_n$ in high level. In the model, the content in a block $B_i$ is only related with information in the pages in higher levels. The information correlation reduces as the distance between $B_i$ and the pages increases. Normalized Gaussian function will be used to model this correlation as in formula (3):

$$E(x) = \frac{G(x)}{G(0)} \quad G(x) = \frac{1}{\sqrt{2\pi}} \exp[-\frac{x^2}{2}] \quad x = 0,1,2,3\ldots\ldots \tag{3}$$

$E(N)$ shows the information correlation between a block and a page N steps away from it. When $x \geq 3, E(x) < 0.011$. So only information in pages one or two steps away from a block are used when annotating an image in the block in our model.

For an object (a page or a block), we use a feature vector $F = [<W_1, D_1>,...,<W_i, D_i>,...,<W_N, D_N>]$ to characterize its content. Here $<W_i, D_i>$ $i = 1,2,...N$ denote a keyword and its descriptive factors (DF), which show the importance of a keyword for describing the content of the object. We use $D_j' = D_j / \sum_{i=1}^{N} D_i$ to normalize a feature vector and let $D_1 \geq D_2 ..... \geq D_N$. In our model, the max length of the feature vector for a page is longer than that for a block, since we usually need more words to characterize the content of a page than a block. For valid images in a block, we use keywords and their importance in the feature vector for the block to annotate them. An iterative process is developed to evaluate the values of feature vectors for different blocks or pages.

## 3.2 An Iterative Algorithm to Implement BM

The proposed algorithm to implement BM assumes that most information useful for annotating an image locates in nearby pages or ALT/surrounding texts/links in the block the image belongs to.

### 3.2.1 Initialization

After pages are divided into blocks and the importance of each block are calculated, we start up the annotation of images through the following initialization procedure.

**Step 1:** For each block, add keywords and their occurrences from surrounding texts, links and ALT (if any) into the feature vector of that block with different weights, since their importance in the annotation are different. The information in a link usually summarizes a topic about the page it links to. So keywords and their frequencies associated with the link are also added to the feature vector of the page it links to.

**Step 2:** For the feature vector of each block, the first $N_b$ keywords $w_i$ with largest weighted frequencies $f_i$ ( $i = 1, 2, ..., N_b$ ) are reserved. The descriptive factor for $w_i$ is calculated by $D_i = f_i / \sum_{n=1}^{k} f_n$ , where k is the length of the feature vector, $k \leq N_b$ .

**Step 3:** For each page, keywords from outside links and all the blocks in the page are sorted into a list according to their frequencies which are further weighted by the importance of the block it belongs to before sorting. The first $N_p$ keywords and keywords from outside links are used to represent the content of the page. Then normalize the feature vector of each page.

### 3.2.2  Annotating Valid Images

In the iterative procedure, the feature vector of each block is updated to make it better summarize the topic in the block, i.e., determine the suitable keywords and their proper DF values for the description of the topic. The details of the iteration algorithm are summarized as follows:

Step 1:   Set the current iteration times Time=0, and the total iteration times T.

Step 2: Process all the blocks and pages:

For each page $P_i$ :

(a) For each block $B_j$ in page $P_i$ which contains valid images, let $S = [<W_1, D_1>, ..., <W_i, D_i>, ..., <W_N, D_N>]$ denote its feature vector.

1)   Calculate two thresholds $T_H = \sum_{i=1}^{N} D_i / N$ and $T_L = \beta T_H$ , $\beta \in (0,1)$ . Based on these two thresholds, the feature vector $S$ is divided into three parts. Let $D_1 \geq ... \geq D_{N1} \geq T_H \geq D_{N1+1}... \geq D_{N2} \geq T_L \geq D_{N2+1}... \geq D_N$ and a metrics $\Omega$ is defined in formula (4) to measure how well $S$ is for the description of the topic.

$$\Omega = (\sum_{i=1}^{N1} D_i + \frac{1}{2} \sum_{i=N1+1}^{N2} D_i) / (\sum_{i=N2+1}^{N} D_i + \frac{1}{2} \sum_{i=N1+1}^{N2} D_i), \quad (4)$$

Then Normalize $S$ and calculate the $\Omega$ value based on it.

2)   Calculate the feature vector $S_{out}$ representing information from other pages useful for annotation. It is obtained through weighting all the feature vectors of the pages one or two steps away from $B_j$ with $E(0)$ and $E(1)$ respectively. Only the first $N_p$ keywords in $S_{out}$ with largest weighted DF value are reserved. Then $S_{out}$ is normalized.

3)   Modify feature vector $S$ using $S_{out}$ through the following three steps:

**Enhance:** For each keyword $W_k$ whose DF value $D_k$ is less than $T_H$ , if $W_k$ also appears in $S_{out}$ with DF value $D_k^{'}$ , $D_k$ in $S$ is replaced with $D_k + D_k^{'}$ when this change can increase the $\Omega$ value of a new $S$ . Since the words with DF values greater than $T_H$ are considered to be already proper for annotation, we don't enhance them in the same way.

**Reduce:** Normalize $S$ and omit words whose DF values are less than $T_L$ .

**Disturb:** Calculate the new $\Omega$ value based on $S$ . If the number of keywords in $S$ is low or the change of $\Omega$ values after the current iteration is lower than a predefined threshold, the keyword (with the smallest DF value in $S_{out}$ ), which doesn't appear in $S$ , is added into $S$ . That means we add disturbance into $S$ from gentle to great in order to reach a global optimization and try not to induce the over-unsteadiness of $S$ . Then $S$ is normalized again.

(b) Modify the feature vector for the page $P_i$ based on the change of feature vectors of all the blocks in it.

Step 3: If Time < T then makes Time=Time+1 and go to step 2. Otherwise end the iterative procedure and take the feature vector in each block as the annotation of images in them.

The goal of the iterative procedure is to make the value of $\Omega$ for the feature vector of each block containing valid images as high as possible, and at the same time to keep a proper number of keywords in the feature vector. After the iteration, the feature vectors of blocks will contain a proper number of words and proper DF values to denote the topic in the block. Then they will be considered to be more effective as the annotation of the image in this block.

# 4   Experiments

In our experiment 15890 pages are crawled from http://www.nationalgeographic.com, and the number of images is 20189. In the experiment, the area of valid images is required to exceed 6000 pixels and width-height-ratio for valid images is between 0.2 and 5. $W^{valid} = 20, W^{link} = 1, W^{invalid} = 1$ and $W^{text}$ is set with respect to text properties, such as font, font size and background. In the iterative procedure, we set $N_B = 10, N_p = 10$ , $\beta = 0.5$ . A text-based image retrieval platform is used to evaluate the effectiveness of generated annotation for images. In the retrieval system, a user can query images with several words that form a query vector $Q$ with equal DF values initially. An image will gain a score increase by $D_X \times D_Y$ if a keyword $W_i$ in $Q$ is one of its annotation keywords, where $D_X$ and $D_Y$ are their DF values in the annotation of the image and the query vector $Q$ respectively. After that the images with positive scores are shown to the user.

200 valid images are randomly selected and described with three keywords by a user at most. These images are retrieved and the results are used to evaluate the annotation. We will evaluate our model through three aspects: rank of the expected

images in the result, average time cost in the retrieval process and average number of images generated in the retrieval. A better annotation will cause small ranks, little average time cost and small average number of results generated in the retrieval. To make a comparison we also check these three aspects in the result without using the BM. The percentages of results whose rank in the retrieval result are smaller than specific values are shown in Fig. 3.

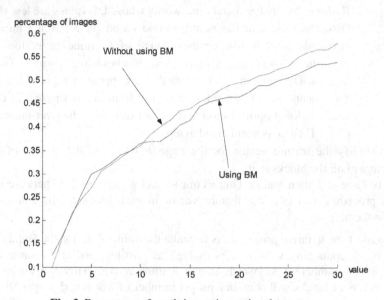

**Fig. 3.** Percentage of result image in user's tolerance range

Further analysis reveals that the percentage of images with ranks less than 30 are almost the same whether using BM or not. But when using BM, the average time used in the retrieval is about 10% less than the average time cost in the retrieval without using BM. And the average number of result images whose score is positive in the retrieval is also 17% less than the average result number without using BM. That is because the length of feature vectors used for the annotation of images is shorter and only eminent words are left. The experiment shows that when using BM, the time cost in the retrieval and the average number of result images have a certain reduction while ranks of the expected images change a little.

## 5  Conclusions

In this paper we present a method to evaluate the importance of a block after the page segmentation procedure. Based on the segmentation algorithm we propose a broadcast model algorithm to choose valid annotation for images on the Internet from associated information. In this model the source of the keywords for annotating an image is not limited to a web page where the image locates. In the future we will extend our work to a larger set of web pages and low-level features will be used for the annotation of images.

# References

[1] Deng Cai, Shipeng Yu, Ji-Rong Wen, Wei-Ying Ma. VIPS: a vision-based page segmentation algorithm. Microsoft Technical Report, MSR-TR-2003-79, 2003

[2] Deng Cai, Xiaofei He, Wei-Ying Ma, Ji-Rong Wen and Hong-Jiang Zhang, Organizing WWW Images Based on the Analysis of Page Layout and Web Link Structure,2004 IEEE International Conference on Multimedia and Expo., Taipei, Jun. 2004.

[3] Huamin Feng, Rui Shi, and Tat-Seng. Chua. A bootstrapping framework for annotating and retrieving WWW images. ACM International Conference Multimedia 2004, pages 960-967, 2004.

[4] M. L. Kherfi, D. Ziou and A.Bernadi, Image Retrieval from the World Wide Web: Issues, Techniques and Systems. ACM Computing Surveys, vol 36, no. 1, March 2004.

[5] S. Chakrabarti. Integrating the document object model with hyperlinks for enhanced topic distillation and information extraction. In Proc. of the 10th International Conference on World Wide Web, pages 211--220, 2001.

[6] Shian-Hua Lin, Jan-Ming Ho. Discovering Informative Content Blocks from Web Documents. In Proc. of the SIGKDD'02 Conf., pages 588--593, 2002

[7] S. P .Li, S. Huang, G. R.Xue, Y. Yu," Block-based language modeling approach towards web search " In Proc. of the seventh Asia-Pacific Web Conference (APWeb2005), March 29 - April 1, 2005, Shanghai, China.

# An Approach to the Compression of Residual Data with GPCA in Video Coding

Lei Yao, Jian Liu, and Jiangqin Wu

College of Computer Science, Zhejiang University,
Hangzhou, 310027, China
leiyzju@yahoo.com.cn, {ken3300, wujq}@zju.edu.cn

**Abstract.** Generalized Principle Component Analysis (GPCA) is a global solution to identify a mixture of linear models for signals. This method has been proved to be efficient in compressing natural images. In this paper we try to introduce GPCA into video coding. We focus on encoding residual frames with GPCA in place of classical DCT, and also propose to use it in MCTF based scalable video coding. Experiments show that GPCA really gets better PSNR with the same amount of data components as DCT, and this method is promising in our scalable video coding scheme.

**Keywords:** Generalized Principle Component Analysis (GPCA), Discrete Cosine Transform (DCT), Scalable Video Coding (SVC), prediction error, residual frame.

## 1 Introduction

Ever since the 1980s, block-based predictive/transform coding (also called hybrid coding) has dominated the video compression technologies. The motion compensated prediction and DCT strategies (MC/DCT) have been widely used in all the MPEG and ITU-T video coding standards. The recent H.264/AVC video coding technology [1], which also inherited the MC/DCT method, has achieved unprecedented compression gain. Nevertheless, further improving the efficiency of video coding becomes a more challenging job nowadays.

Much effort has been made to find new ways of video coding with computer vision and image processing technologies. Segmentation-based coding tries to segment an image into regions with similar textures, by coding the shapes of the segments and modeling the textures, a higher coding efficiency can be achieved [2, 3]. Object-based coding tries to understand the semantic content of the video. This will probably be the key to the optimal solution of video coding problem. A lot of work has been done on using PCA in modeling objects, especially human faces in video scenes [4, 5]. However, these ideas have not developed into very mature technologies and are often confines to limited conditions.

René Vidal, Yi Ma et al. [6, 7, 8] proposed an algebraic geometric approach to the problem of estimating a mixture of linear subspaces from sample data points, the so called Generalized Principle Component Analysis (GPCA) approach. This approach has found various applications in 2D and 3D motion segmentation, image segmentation and

Y. Zhuang et al. (Eds.): PCM 2006, LNCS 4261, pp. 252 – 261, 2006.

compression, and video segmentation. Especially in image compression, GPCA with a multi-scale scheme shows exciting results that are better than the state-of-the-art wavelet based image representation [7]. This inspired us that such an efficient representation of still images will also be very useful in representing video data, and a similar multi-scale scheme has been used in some scalable video coding frameworks [10]. In fact, GPCA can find a hybrid linear model for any given image, and segment the pixels in an image into several groups with each group in a particular linear subspace. That means the pixels in the same group usually has the homogenous textures or belongs to the same object. In this way, we can segment an image without using complex computer vision technologies, and at the same time encode each segment with some bases and coefficients.

This paper proposes to use GPCA method instead of DCT to encode the prediction error of motion compensation. Since motion compensated prediction has been proved to be a very good technology to remove data correlation in temporal and spatial directions, we still employ it in our coding framework. For the prediction errors, we use GPCA to replace DCT. We experimented with GPCA coding on single prediction residual images, as well as a group of residual images tiled together, and found that GPCA can achieve a better peak signal to noise ratio (PSNR) with less components than DCT. Further more, we also found that by keeping different ratio of components, we can implement a scalable coding scheme which seems very promising.

Section 2 presents an introduction to the use of GPCA in our coding framework. Section 3 presents the scalable video coding scheme using GPCA. Experimental results are shown in Section 4. Conclusion and future work are presented at last.

## 2 Representing Prediction Error Image with GPCA

The major video coding standards have similar functional blocks, as shown in Figure 1. Motion compensated prediction is used to reduce temporal redundancy, transform is used to reduce spatial redundancy, quantization is used for bit-rate control, and entropy coding is used to reduce statistical redundancy. In this paper, we deal with the spatial redundancy, where we use GPCA method instead of the typical DCT transform.

**Disadvantages of DCT**
DCT stemmed from Fourier transform. It converts the image into the frequency domain and represents it by a superposition of basis functions. These basic functions are fixed by the transform, and thus may not be suitable for every image. Moreover, Fourier series have a Gibbs phenomenon which implies that DCT is not a good tool to represent discontinuities in an imagery signal.

**Disadvantages of Standard PCA**
Principle Component Analysis (PCA) is a technique to identify patterns in data and compress the data by reducing the number of dimensions without much loss of the information. It tries to convert the imagery data into the optimal subspace with reduced number of dimensions and represent it with a superposition of the subspace bases. In contrast to DCT, PCA transforms the image into a subspace which is adaptive to the

specific image. However, PCA is efficient only when the image data conforms to a single distribution model. On the contrary, residual frames and images usually contain several heterogeneous regions which cannot fit well in a single model. As a result, this method of data compression is not suitable to be employed directly in video coding. Given a set of vectors generated from the original residual data, we need first to segment the vectors into groups before applying PCA to compress the data. The hybrid linear model presented in [7, 8] suits the problem addressed here as well.

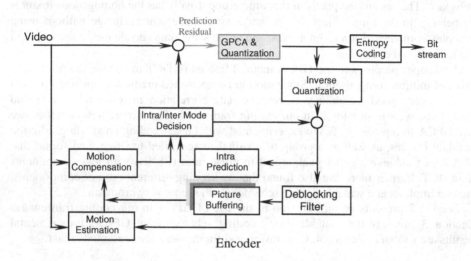

**Fig. 1.** The block diagram of H.264 algorithm, where integer DCT transform is replaced by GPCA, as shown by the colored block

**Hybrid Linear Models and GPCA**

In this paper we use hybrid linear models (which can be identified by GPCA) to represent residual frames. We first treat each residual frame as separate pictures. Then we encode a group of residual frames using the hybrid linear model.

GPCA algorithm deals with a set of samples from an ambient space. So we first convert a residual frame into vectors that reside in a space $\mathbb{R}^D$. Given a residual frame $f$ with width $W$ and height $H$. Inspired by the approach presented in [9], we first divide the frame into $l \times m$ equal sized blocks. Every $l \times m$ block is then stacked into a vector $v$. In this way, the vector $v$ resides in a $D$ dimensional space, with $D = \sum_{i=1}^{Num} c_i$, where $c_i$ is the number of samples for a color component in a $l \times m$ block, and $Num$ is the number of color components. For our YUV420 format frame image, $c = 6$, with 4 samples for Luma value and 2 samples each for Cb and Cr value. In this way, a residual frame $f$ is represented by a set of vectors $\{x_i \in \mathbb{R}^D\}_{i=1}^N$, $N = W \times H / (l \times m)$.

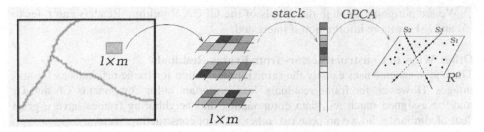

**Fig. 2.** Converting a residual frame into a set of vectors. The frame is divided into equal-sized $1 \times m$ blocks. Different color components of each block is stacked into a vector, which is fed into the GPCA algorithm to identify a hybrid linear model.

The vector set $\left\{ x_i \in \mathbb{R}^D \right\}_{i=1}^N$ is then subtracted by the mean vector $\bar{x} = \frac{1}{N} \sum_1^N x_i$, resulting in a vector set which has a zero mean. The set $\Delta X = \{ x_i - \bar{x}, i = 1, \cdots, N \}$ can be represented by its SVD decomposition $\Delta X = USV^T$, and the first $d$ columns of $U$ become the projection base $P \in R^{d \times D}$. The reduced dimension $d$ and the PCA coefficients $C$ are computed as follows.

$$S = diagonal(\alpha_1, \alpha_2, \cdots, \alpha_D)$$

$$d = \min_{k=1,\cdots,D-1} (\sum_{i=k+1}^{D} \alpha_i^2 < \varepsilon)$$

$$C = S(1:d, 1:d)V^T(1:d,:)$$

Using GPCA algorithm, $C$ is further segmented into $n$ groups, $G = \{ g_i \in R^{d \times n_i}, i = 1, \cdots, n \}$, where $n_i$ is the number of vectors that belong to group $i$. Each group $g_i$ is then represented by a set of bases $b_i \in R^{sd_i \times d}$, where $sd_i$ is the dimension of the subspace that $g_i$ belongs to, and coefficients $C_i = R^{sd_i \times n_i}$ similar to that in the first step. So far we can convert a frame to a set of coefficients:

$$Frame = P + \{C_i + b_i + meanVector_i\} + meanVector$$

And the total number of coefficients is

$$Count = d \times D + \sum_{i=1}^{n} (sd_i \times (n_i + d) + d) + D$$

Once a hybrid linear model is identified for a given frame residual image, the residual image can be coded by several sets of bases and coefficients (one set of bases and one set of coefficients for each subspace). Unimportant components, i.e., small coefficients, can be discarded to reduce bit rate.

We are not going through the details of the GPCA algorithm. Readers can refer to [6] and [8] for more information if interested.

**Other Ways to Construct Vectors from Frame Residuals**

The above scheme uses exactly the same representation for frame residuals as for still images. However, for frame residuals, less important color components Cb and Cr may be assigned much less data components, and neighboring frames have a great deal of similarity. So we propose two other ways of constructing vectors.

To cope with the disparity between the Luma and Cb/Cr color components, we process different components separately. We extend the window size from $2 \times 2$ to $2 \times 4$ and the vector space becomes $R^{D \times N}$, where $D = 8$ for a window size of $2 \times 4$, and $N = W \times H / 8$ is the number of vectors for Luma component. The vector sets of a frame and the final PCA representation is as follows:

$$\left\{ y\_vectors \in R^{D \times N}, u\_vectors \in R^{D \times N/4}, v\_vectors \in R^{D \times N/4} \right\}$$

$$Frame = \left\{ \begin{matrix} P_c + \{C_{ci} + b_{ci} + meanVector_{ci}, i = 1, \cdots, n\} + meanVector_c, \\ c = y, u, v \end{matrix} \right\}$$

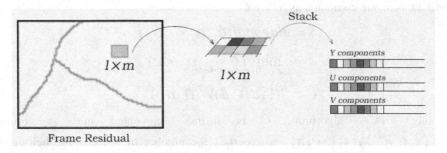

**Fig. 3.** Constructing vectors by treating Y, U and V color components separately. That is, stacking different color components into 3 separate vectors.

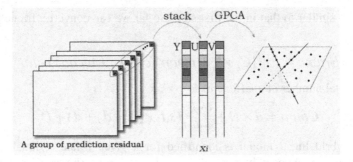

**Fig. 4.** Construct vectors from a group of residual frames, i.e., stack the pixel at the same position in a group of residual frames in to one vector. Again, the three different color components are processed separately.

To exploit the correlations among neighboring frames, we line up all the pixels at the same position in a group of frames (namely, a GOP). Assume that the size of the frame group is $l$, then the size of the vector will be $l$. Again, the three color components are processed separately. Concerning the information loss and computational complexity of high-dimensional matrix, the GPCA algorithm performs more efficiently when the ambient space has a relatively lower dimension. But as the dimension of the vector space increases, PCA can be used to reduce the dimension of the data before applying GPCA. Thus the size of the vector should be chosen carefully. We chose to use $2 \times 2, 2 \times 4$ blocks and GOP size of 15 in our experiments.

## 3 Scalable Video Coding (SVC) Scheme with GPCA

With the development of motion compensated temporal filtering (MCTF), scalable video coding has made remarkable progress in recent years. Aside from spatial and temporal scalability, the open-loop structure of temporal sub-band coding makes it convenient to incorporate SNR scalability [9, 10]. We found that the GPCA residual frame representation presented above is also a potential technology to facilitate SNR scalable coding. We simply use GPCA to encode the high-pass and low-pass pictures after the temporal sub-band filtering, as shown in Figure 5.

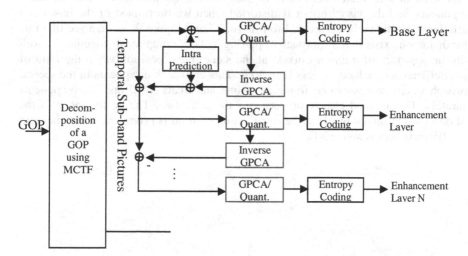

**Fig. 5.** SNR scalable coding scheme with GPCA

Our scheme of scalability is implemented by adaptively changing the dimension of the subspaces. In the hybrid linear model of the residual frames, sample vectors are segmented into groups. Different groups may reside in subspaces with different dimensions. But we set a same dimension bound for each group. If the bound is $B$, the number of dimensions for all groups should not be higher than $B$. Groups with dimension less than or equal to $B$ are unchanged, and groups with higher dimension are cut to be $B$-dimensional subspaces. The information loss is the part represented by the discarded bases. The number of dropped coefficients is then:

$$\sum_{i=1}^{n}\left((Dim_{g_i} - B)\times(vecCount_{g_i} + vecDim_{g_i})\right),$$

where $Dim_{g_i}$ is the dimension of the subspace $g_i$, $vecCount_{g_i}$ is the number of vectors in group i, $vecDim_{g_i}$ is the dimension of the vector.

## 4   Implementation and Experimental Results

In our experiment, the input is the residual of each frame, which is generated by subtracting the predicted frame from the original picture. Before applying GPCA on the data, PCA is used to reduce the dimension of the data. Ultimately, the input of the GPCA algorithm is the PCA coefficients rather than the original residual data, and the PCA projection bases are stored for future restructure of the frames.

We conduct a comparison of our method with DCT on the reference software of H.264/AVC scalable extension, JSVM2.0. The DCT transform block is of size 4x4. Assume the number of coefficients is $C$ and the proportion of kept coefficients is *ratio*, we set the $(1-ratio)\times C$ least important elements to zero.

We found in the experiment that the approach of putting the three color components in one vector suffers from the information loss in Cb and Cr color components, and the visual effect is distorted when we drop most of the bases and coefficients, as shown in Figure 6. From Figure 7 and Figure 9, we can see that this color distortion exists in the approach of putting Y, U, V components together, as well as in the approach of lining up pixels at the same frame position when the ratio of kept coefficients is reduced to less than 30%. This drawback disappears in the second approach which processes one frame at a time and treats Y, U and V components separately. This method clearly outperforms the other two. The performance of the method of lining up the pixels at the same frame position is promising when the ratio of coefficients kept is above 30%.

(a)                                                    (b)

**Fig. 6.** (a) the approach of putting Y, U, V components together with 16.41% data components kept. (b) the approach of processing one frame at a time and treats Y, U and V components separately with 12.46% data components kept.

By reducing the dimension of the subspace, we also implement the scalable coding scheme mentioned in Section 3. Since the importance of the eigenvectors of the SVD decomposition is in decreasing order, the latter part of the base vectors is trivial compared to the first several ones. Thus the information loss of dropping those unimportant components is not critical.

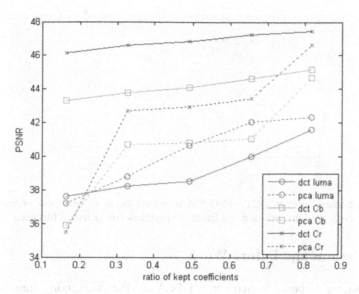

**Fig. 7.** Comparison between DCT and GPCA in which the input vectors are constructed by putting Y, U, V components of a 2x2 block together. Conducted on **foreman** sequence.

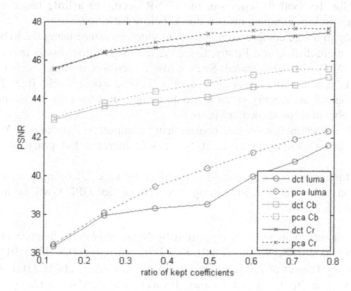

**Fig. 8.** Comparison between DCT and GPCA. Input vectors are constructed from 2x4 blocks, and the Y, U and V color components are processed separately. Conducted on **foreman**.

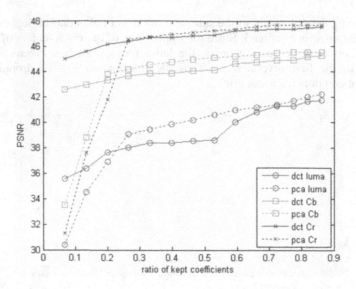

**Fig. 9.** Comparison between DCT and GPCA in which the input vectors are constructed by lining up pixels at the same position of a frame. Experiment conducted on **foreman**.

## 5   Conclusions and Future Work

In this paper, we proposed to incorporate GPCA into the video coding framework. We tested the approach on several video sequences, like foreman, football, vectra and news. Generally, the performance of our method is better than the DCT approach except that for the football sequence, the PSNR decreases a little faster than DCT when the ratio of kept components is reduced below 40%.

Comparing to image compression, encoding video sequence using the hybrid linear model faces more difficulties. Firstly, the $2 \times 2$ block partition results in a 6-element vector for a YUV420 video frame. Such a low dimension is not enough for GPCA dimension reduction, while larger block size will cause worse block effect. Secondly, U/V color channel are usually given less data components than the Y channel, which leads to the phenomenon shown in Figure 6.

So far all the segmentation and restructuring computation is done in MATLAB. Optimizing the algorithm to make it faster will increase the practicality of our method.

In the future, more research can be done on using GPCA for object based motion compensation and scalable video coding. We believe that GPCA will be a powerful tool in video compression.

**Acknowledgments.** This work is supported by National Natural Science Foundation of China (No.60525108, No.60533090), 973 Program (No.2002CB312101), Science and Technology Project of Zhejiang Province (2005C13032, 2005C11001-05), and China-US Million Book Digital Library Project (www.cadal.zju.edu.cn ). Special thanks go to Prof. Yueting Zhuang and Dr. Fei Wu at College of Computer Science, Zhejiang University for their valuable advice.

# References

1. "Text of Final Committee Draft of Joint Video Specification" (ITU-T Rec. H.264 | ISO/IEC 14496-10 AVC), ISO/IEC JTC1/SC29/WG11, MPEG02/N4920, July 2002, Klagenfurt, AT, USA.
2. L. Torres and M. Kunt, Video Coding: "The Second Generation Approach. Englewood Cliffs", NJ: Kluwer, 1996.
3. P. Salembier, L. Torres, F. Meyer, and C. Gu, "Region-based video coding using mathematical morphology," Proc. IEEE, vol. 83, no. 6, pp. 843–857, Jun. 1995.
4. Asaad Hakeem, Khurram Shafique, and Mubarak Shah, "An Objectbased Video Coding Framework for Video Sequences Obtained From Static Cameras", ACM Multimedia '05 Singapore.
5. A. Smolic, T. Sikora, and J.-R. Ohm, "Long-term global motion estimation and its application for sprite coding, content description, and segmentation," IEEE Trans. Circuits Syst. Video Technol., vol. 9, no. 8, pp. 1227–1242, Dec. 1999.
6. Ren'e Vidal, Yi Ma, Shankar Sastry, "Generalized Principal Component Analysis (GPCA)", Proceedings of the 2003 IEEE Computer Society Conference on Computer Vision and Pattern Recognition (CVPR'03) 1063-6919/03, 2003 IEEE.
7. Wei Hong, John Wright, Kun Huang, Yi Ma: "A Multi-Scale Hybrid Linear Model for Lossy Image Representation". ICCV 2005: 764-771
8. Kun Huang, Allen Y. Yang, Yi Ma: "Sparse representation of images with hybrid linear models". ICIP 2004: 1281-1284
9. Heiko Schwarz, Detlev Marpe, and Thomas Wiegand, "SNR-SCALABLE EXTENSION OF H.264/AVC", Proc. IEEE International Conference on Image Processing (ICIP 2004)
10. Heiko Schwarz, Detlev Marpe, and Thomas Wiegand, "MCTF AND SCALABILITY EXTENSION OF H.264/AVC", Proc. of PCS, San Francisco, CA, USA, Dec. 2004.

# A Robust Approach for Object Recognition

Yuanning Li[1], Weiqiang Wang[2], and Wen Gao[1]

[1] Institute of Computing Technology, Chinese Academy of Sciences, Beijing, China, 100080
[2] Graduate School, Chinese Academy of Sciences, Beijing, China, 100039
{ynli, wqwang, wgao}@jdl.ac.cn

**Abstract.** In this paper, we present a robust and unsupervised approach for recognition of object categories, RTSI-pLSA, which overcomes the weakness of TSI-pLSA in recognizing rotated objects in images. Our approach uses radial template to describe spatial information (position, scale and orientation) of an object. A bottom up heuristical and unsupervised scheme is also proposed to estimate spatial parameters of object. Experimental results show the RTSI-pLSA can effectively recognize object categories, especially in recognizing rotated, translated, or scaled objects in images. It lowers the error rate by about 10%, compared with TSI-pLSA. Thus, it is a more robust approach for unsupervised object recognition.

**Keywords:** Object recognition, pLSA.

## 1 Introduction

Recognition of Object categories within images is a challenging issue in computer vision and multimedia analysis. It refers to detecting the existence of an instance of an object category in a given image. Many methods of representation of objects [1] or object categories [2][3][6] have been presented. The bag-of-words model [7] becomes very popular. Each visual word in the model corresponds to a descriptor of the appearance of a local region. The representation method based on local appearance shows robustness to occlusions, geometric deformation or illumination variance.

Recently some researchers have made efforts to apply the successful techniques of unsupervised topic discovery in document classification to address some vision issues. Sivic et.al. [4] has applied Probabilistic Latent Semantic Analysis(pLSA) to tackling object recognition. Li and Perona [5] have applied Latent Dirichlet Allocation(LDA) to scene analysis. These approaches are based on the bag of words model [7].A weakness of them is that they disregard information about the spatial layout of local features, having severely limited descriptive ability.

Modeling spatial layout of local features is a challenge in object recognition. The key is to find correspondence between the model and parts of object within images. Many papers use different schemes to tackle this problem, while very few methods keep robust when objects in images are deformed by translation, rotation and scaling. Felzenszwalb and Huttenlocher [8] present a parts-and-structure model where the dependence in spatial relations between parts is tree-structured. This model is used to find people in images. Berg and Malik [9] propose a scheme based on deformable

Y. Zhuang et al. (Eds.): PCM 2006, LNCS 4261, pp. 262–269, 2006.
© Springer-Verlag Berlin Heidelberg 2006

shape matching where the correspondence between the model and features in the image is posed as an integer quadratic programming problem. Fergus [10] integrates location information into pLSA model and achieves translation and scale invariance. In fact, robustness to rotation is also a significant and practical demand in object recognition. Inspired by the works [4] and [10], we present an approach to classifying objects that can be rotated, translated or scaling from a set of unlabelled images.

In this paper, we first introduce Probabilistic Latent Semantic Analysis (pLSA) to visual domain. Then we utilize radial template to describe spatial states of objects (position, scale and orientation) in images. We extend pLSA through incorporating spatial information to classify objects. A bottom up heuristic and unsupervised scheme for estimating object spatial information within images is also proposed to cope with rotation, translation and scale. To compare with the existing object recognition approaches, we test the leant model on standard dataset and obtain a competitive performance in rotation, translation and scale.

## 2   Rotation, Translation and Scale Invariant pLSA (RTSI-pLSA)

We proposed an extension to pLSA model to incorporate spatial information among visual words, so that it can model objects in images with rotation, translation and scale invariance.

### 2.1   Applying Probabilistic Latent Semantic Analysis (pLSA) to Visual Domain

Probabilistic Latent Semantic Analysis (pLSA) is an unsupervised method in text document analysis [11]. It is used to discover topics for a document using the bag-of-words document representation. For the issue of object recognition in images, we can regard *images* as *documents, object categories* as *topics,* and *visual word* (descriptors of local regions) as *words* to apply pLSA, just as shown in Table1. So an image containing several object instances corresponds to a mixture of topics.

**Table 1.** Different concepts within pLSA as applied to the text and visual domains

|     | Text domain | Image domain |
| --- | --- | --- |
| $d$ | Document | Image |
| $z$ | Topic | Object category |
| $w$ | Word | Visual word |

To simplify the representation of visual word, all descriptors from training images are vector quantized, forming a fixed visual codebook. Suppose we have a collection of images $D=[d_1,...,d_N]$ with visual words from the visual codebook $W=[w_1,..,w_V]$ . A $V{\times}N$ matrix $C$ can be constructed and its element $C(i,j)$ denotes the occurrences of $w_i(i=1,...,V)$ in image $d_j(j=1,...,N)$. The joint probability $P(w, d)$ can be rewritten as

$$P(w,d) = \sum_z P(w \mid z)P(z \mid d)P(d) \qquad (1)$$

where $P(w|z)$ denotes occurrence of a visual word in a topic, $P(z|d)$ denotes the probability of a image associated with a topic. The probability distributions $P(w|z)$ and $P(z|d)$ in the model are learnt using EM which maximizes the likelihood of the model over data. An image $d$ is classified by running EM with $P(w|z)$ fixed, estimating $P(z|d)$. A detailed explanation of the model can be found in [4] [11][12].

## 2.2  Model Spatial Information of Object with a Modified Radial Template

Radial template in [14] is used to detect rotated faces, as shown in Figure1(a). We propose a modified radiate template to model objects. Appearances of an object in images vary with its position $(a, b)$, scale$(s)$, and orientation $(o)$. As illustrated in Figure1 (b), we use the modified radial template to describe objects. The center$(c)$ of the template that covers the object specifies the position $(a, b)$ of the centroid of object. Diameter of the template indicates the scale of the object. The polar axis indicates template's orientation which is consistent with the orientation $(o)$ of object. For simplicity, we quantize all possible orientations into 8 directions. Location $(x)$ in the image is quantized in $X(X = 10)$ bins: one in the template center, eight in different orientations around the center and one in the large background region $X_{bg}$. As a result, each visual word in the image falls in one of these bins. The estimation of the parameters $(a, b, s, o)$ for an object is discussed in subsection 2.4.

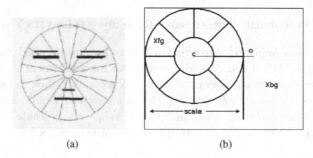

(a)                              (b)

**Fig. 1.** (a) Original definition of Radial Template in [14]. (b) Modified Radial Template for object recognition.

## 2.3  Incorporate Spatial Information to pLSA

To incorporate spatial information into pLSA, we introduce a second latent variable $p$ which represents the spatial parameters of an object in an image. The difference from the scheme in [10] is that the latent variable $p$ has an additional orientation$(o)$ parameter, besides position$(a, b)$ and scale$(s)$.

As illustrated in Figure1 (b), the location of a visual word $w$ is quantized into a bin in the radial template, and we use $x$ to denote the index of the bin. Then we model $w$ and $x$ jointly. $P(w|z)$ in pLSA becomes $P(w,x|p,z)$. The graphical model is shown in Figure2. To simplify our method, we only model $P(w,x|z)$ as Equation (2), and it can be represented by an array with the size $(V \times X) \times Z$. $P(w,x|z)$ captures the co-occurrence of a visual word and its location within a topic.

$$P(w,x\mid z)=\sum_{p}P(w,x,p\mid z)=\sum_{p}P(w,x\mid p,z)P(p\mid z)=\sum_{p}P(w,x\mid p,z)P(p) \qquad (2)$$

$P(p)$ in Equation (2) is a multinomial density over possible $p$. The joint probability model in Equation (1) becomes Equation (3).

$$P(d,w,x)=\sum_{z}P(w,x\mid z)P(z\mid d)P(d) \qquad (3)$$

The similar update procedure as pLSA can be applied to the new model(see Appendix). We calculate the initial values of $P(w,x\mid z)$ by moving the radial template over the candidate $p$ based on Equation (2) and aggregating results in learning stage.

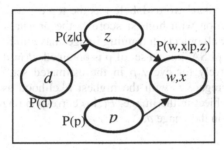

**Fig. 2.** Graphical model for RTSI-pLSA

### 2.4 Estimate Spatial Parameters of an Object

Since the parameters of an object may take values in a large range, it is time-consuming to marginalize exhaustively over scales, locations, and orientations in an image. So we develop a bottom up heuristic and unsupervised algorithm to identify a small set of $p$ for each topic, which makes the computation much efficient in learning and recognition stage. The algorithm of estimating the spatial parameters of objects is summarized as follows:

(1) Apply the standard pLSA to a training set to classify all visual words in an image into different topics. The visual words labeled by a topic $z$ in the image should satisfy:  $P(w\mid z)>P(w\mid z_i)$; $z_i \neq z$. In recognition stage, the average density of the visual words on the radial template, $\overline{P(w\mid z)}=\dfrac{\sum\limits_{x\in X_{fg}}P(w,x\mid z)}{X_{fg}}$ , is used to weight each visual word for a specific topic.

(2) Estimate the scale($s$) and position($a$, $b$) parameters of an object.

For all the visual words labeled as the same topic, we use a set of mixtures of Gaussians with K components, (K =1, 2 in our experiments) to fit the distribution of the locations of these visual words. The mean of each component is considered as a possible position for the centroid of an object, while its axis-aligned variance is used to estimate the scale of the object. Since more than one object in the same category may exist in an image, the mixtures of Gaussians with different numbers of components are tried. We use flat density for $P(p)$, since we have no prior knowledge to show a specific parameter $p$ has priority to others.

(3) Estimate the orientation($o$) parameter of an object.

In recognition, we quantize all possible orientations in 8 directions to simplify the search of rotation space. Then the system votes for each direction to identify the orientation of an object. Given a topic $z$, the score of the orientation in the direction $o(o= k\times 45^o$, k = 0...7) is calculated by equation (4).

$$score(p(o)) = \sum_{i=1}^{N} P(w_i, x_i \mid z, p(o))$$ (4)

$N$ is the number of all the visual words labeled as the topic $z$. $x_i$ is the bin index in a radial template. The direction with highest score is the orientation of an object. In learning stage, we suppose all objects in training images have no rotation ($o$=0).

In recognition of RTSI-pLSA, once a set of p is obtained, $P(w,x|z)$ is kept fixed and $P(z|d)$ is computed iteratively for every $p$ in the estimated set. When the iterative procedure converges, we regard $p^*$ with the highest likelihood as the most possible spatial parameters of the object in the image. $P(z|d)$ corresponding to $p^*$ indicates the object categories depicted in the image $d$.

## 3 Experiments

To evaluate our method, we compare the performance of pLSA [4], TSI-pLSA [10], and our RTSI-pLSA on the Caltech data. Four categories in the Caltech data are used in our experiments. They are airplanes(1075 images), motorbikes(827 images), face(435 images), and background (901 images). Two detectors, saliency operator [13] and DoG [1], are used to locate interesting regions in our system. Each interesting region is characterized by a 72 dimensional SIFT descriptor (3×3 spatial grids were used). To make our approach robust to rotation, we have all patches' orientation normalized before histograming. No further normalization was carried out. In each experiment, 100 images are randomly chosen from each category as the training set, and the remaining images are used for test. We use K-means algorithm to quantize the extracted SIFT descriptors from the training images to obtain a codebook of visual words. The evaluation results are obtained through averaging multiple experiment results.

We first compare the performance of the three approaches under different sizes of codebooks. The related experiment results are shown in Figure3(a) and Table.2. For each approach, we notice the error rate varies slightly when the codebook sizes are larger than 800. Under the same codebook, TSI-pLSA and RTSI-pLSA show a significant improvement over pLSA. So incorporation of spatial information is effective to lower the error rate of object classification. The experimental results also show that TSI-pLSA and RTSI-pLSA have almost the same error rate. Since objects in each category of the Caltech set have different sizes and positions, we think TSI-pLSA and RTSI-pLSA have comparable performance in dealing with the two kinds of transformations, i.e. translation and scaling.

Since the orientation of objects in the Caltech set does not show apparent variance, we construct a new test dataset through rotating the images a random angle around their centers, before performance comparison of the three models in dealing with rotation. The corresponding classification error rates are shown in Figure 3 (b) and listed in Table3. pLSA does not consider any spatial information, we can see that rotation affects little on pLSA. Although TSI-pLSA models objects through taking position and scale into account, the experimental results show that it has the highest error rate. The proposed RTSI-pLSA decrease about 10% in error rate and shows significant improvement in handling rotation cases, compared with TSI-pLSA.

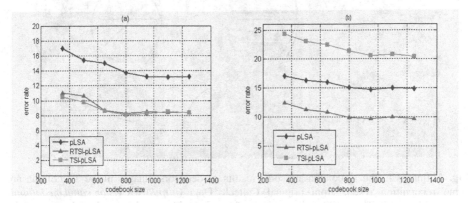

**Fig. 3.** (a) Average error rate of pLSA, TSI-pLSA and RTSI-pLSA under different codebook size (b) Average error rate of rotated Caltech data with different codebook size

**Table 2.** Error rate of different classes (Codebook size K = 800)

| Categories | pLSA | TSI-pLSA | RTSI-pLSA |
|------------|------|----------|-----------|
| Airplane | 13.8 | 5.8 | 8.9 |
| Face | 12.9 | 11.5 | 6.2 |
| Motorbike | 14.0 | 7.5 | 8.6 |
| Average | 13.7 | 8.1 | 8.3 |

**Table 3.** Error rate of different classes (Codebook size K = 800)

| Categories | pLSA | TSI-pLSA | RTSI-pLSA |
|------------|------|----------|-----------|
| Airplane | 17.1 | 21.5 | 12.1 |
| Face | 14.0 | 19.3 | 6.4 |
| Motorbike | 13.6 | 23.5 | 11.3 |
| Average | 15.1 | 21.4 | 9.9 |

From the experimental results on the Caltech dataset, some tentative conclusion can be drawn. Modeling local patches' appearance and spatial information jointly is helpful for object recognition. The proposed RTSI-pLSA can still classify rotated, translated or scaled objects in images effectively, even if training data does not contain the related examples, and TSI-pLSA has a weak performance in such situation, compared with RTSI-pLSA.

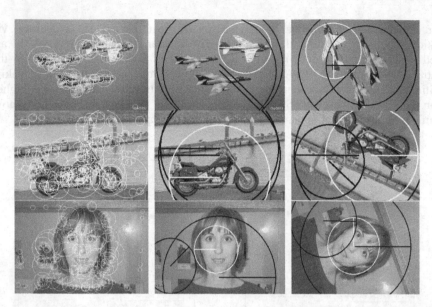

**Fig. 4.** Images in the 1st column are some results of detectors. Images in the 2nd column are some recognition results from original Caltech Data (*http://www.vision.caltech.edu/html-files/archive.html*). The most possible object is bounded with the white circle. Diameter of the circle indicates the scale of the object and the line starting from the center of the circle specifies the orientation of object. Images in the 3rd column are recognition results from random rotated Caltech data.

## 4 Conclusion

We propose an unsupervised approach for recognizing object categories within images, RTSI-pLSA that learns visual object categories by modeling appearance of local patches and their spatial information jointly. We also propose a bottom up heuristic scheme to estimate parameters of spatial information of objects. The experimental results show the proposed RTSI-pLSA can effectively recognize object categories within images. The RTSI-pLSA has an impressive advantage in recognizing rotated, translated or scaled object, even when training data have no related examples. In such situation, it can lower the error rate by 10% or so compared with TSI-pLSA. Thus, RTSI-pLSA is a more robust approach for object recognition.

## References

1. D.Lowe: Object recognition from local scale-invariant feature. In Proc. International Conference on Computer Vision (ICCV 1999)
2. R.Fergus, P. Perona and A. Zisserman: Object class recognition by unsupervised scale-invariant learning. In Proc. the IEEE Conference on Computer Vision and Pattern Recognition (2000).
3. Li Fei-Fei, Rob Fergus, Pietro Perona: Learning Generative Visual Models from Few Training Examples: An Incremental Bayesian Approach Tested on 101 Object Categories. Conference on Computer Vision and Pattern Recognition Workshop(CVPRW2004) Vol. 12.

4. J. Sivic, B. Russell, A.A.Efros, and A. Zisserman: Discovering Objects and Their Location in Images. In Proc. International Conference on Computer Vision(ICCV 2005).
5. Li Fei-Fei, Pietro Perona: A Bayesian hierachical model for learning scene categories. In Proc. International Conference on Computer Vision (ICCV 2005).
6. G. Wang, Y. Zhang, and L. Fei-Fei: Using dependent regions for object categorization in a generative framework. In Proc.IEEE Conference on Computer Vision and Pattern Recognition(CVPR2006).
7. G. Csurka, C. Bray, C. Dance, and L. Fan: Visual Categorization with bags of keypoints. In Workshop on Statistical Learning in Computer Vision (ECCV 2004).
8. P. Felzenszwalb and D. Huttenlocher: Pictorial structures for object recognition. In Proc. the IEEE Conference on Computer Vision and Pattern Recognition (CVPR2000).
9. Berg, T. Berg and J. Malik: Shape matching and object recognition using low distortion correpondence. In Proc. the IEEE Conference on Computer Vision and Pattern Recognition, (CVPR2005).
10. R.Fergus, L. FeiFei, P. Perona, A. Zisserman: Learning Object Categories from Google's Image Search. International Conference on Computer Vision (ICCV 2005).
11. Hofmann, T.: Propabilistic latent semantic indexing. ACM SIGIR(1998).
12. Hofmann, T.: Unsupervised learning by probabilistic latent semantic analysis. Machine Learning 41(2001) 177-196.
13. T. Kadir and M. Brady: Scale Saliency and image description. In International Journal of Computer Vision (2001) 83-105.
14. Heng Liu, Xilin Chen, Wen Gao, Shengye Yan: Rotated Face Detection In Color Images Using Radial Template (Rt) (ICASSP2003) ppIII, 213-216.

## Appendix: RTSI-pLSA EM

The category of an image $d$ is determined by $z^*=\text{argmax}_z(P(z|d))$, and $P(z|d)$ is estimated using EM as follows:

E step
$$P(z_k \mid d_i, w_j, x_l) = \frac{P(w_j, x_l \mid z_k)P(z_k \mid d_i)}{\sum_m P(w_j, x_l \mid z_m)P(z_m \mid d_i)} \tag{5}$$

M step1
$$P(w_j, x_l \mid z_k) = \frac{\sum_i n(d_i, w_j, x_l)P(z_k \mid d_i, w_j, x_l)}{\sum_g \sum_m \sum_i n(d_i, w_m, x_g)P(z_k \mid d_i, w_m, x_g)} \tag{6}$$

M step2
$$P(z_k \mid d_i) = \frac{\sum_l \sum_j n(d_i, w_j, x_l)P(z_k \mid d_i, w_j, x_l)}{\sum_l \sum_j n(d_i, w_j, x_l)} \tag{7}$$

# A Novel Method for Spoken Text Feature Extraction in Semantic Video Retrieval*

Juan Cao[1,2], Jintao Li[1], Yongdong Zhang[1], and Sheng Tang[1]

[1] Institute of Computing Technology, Chinese Academy of Sciences
Beijing 100080, China
[2] Graduate University of the Chinese Academy of Sciences
Beijing 100039, China
{caojuan, jtli, zhyd, ts}@ict.ac.cn

**Abstract.** We propose a novel method for extracting text feature from the automatic speech recognition (ASR) results in semantic video retrieval. We combine HowNet-rule-based knowledge with statistic information to build special concept lexicons, which can rapidly narrow the vocabulary and improve the retrieval precision. Furthermore, we use the term precision (TP) weighting method to analyze ASR texts. This weighting method is sensitive to the sparse but important terms in the relevant documents. Experiments show that the proposed method is effective for semantic video retrieval.

**Keywords:** ASR texts, relevant documents, HowNet, TREVID.

## 1 Introduction

Video is a rich source of information. It includes visual, acoustical and textual content. Among them, the textual information of video mainly includes the texts extracted by optical character recognition (OCR) and the transcripts obtained from automatic speech recognition (ASR). The visual features have been applied widely in the video retrieval [1,2,3], but the text features extracted from ASR didn't be deeply studied . One reason is that the ASR technique has a moderate word error rate. Another reason is that the OCR texts exist in the target shots, while the relevant ASR texts can be spoken in the vicinity near the target shots. However, these reasons can't deny the text feature's superiority to the visual feature, for a semantic gap remains between the low-level visual features that can be automatically extracted and the semantic descriptions that users desire, and the text features free from this problem. The semantic gap has became a significant stumbling block in the semantic video retrieval. Every year's results of the TREC and TRECVID display that the mean average precision(MAP) of text retrieval is far above that of the video retrieval. So taking full advantages of the

---

* This work was supported by Beijing Science and Technology Planning Program of China (D0106008040291), the Key Project of Beijing Natural Science Foundation (4051004), and the Key Project of International Science and Technology Cooperation (2005DFA11060).

Y. Zhuang et al. (Eds.): PCM 2006, LNCS 4261, pp. 270–278, 2006.

video's text resources to support the visual retrieval is imperative and feasible. This is the paper's aim.

## 1.1 Related Work

Information retrieval from speech recognition transcripts has received a lot of attention in recent years in the spoken document retrieval (SDR) track at TREC7, TREC 8 and TREC 9 [4]. But SDR is analyzing the texts independently to the videos, and retrieving the texts on the story level. In this paper we focus on mining the valuable information from the ASR texts as one feature to assist the semantic video retrieval, not retrieve the spoken texts.

Many TRECVID participants have done a lot of work in the video's text information analysis[1.2.3]. In the high-level feature extraction task, most of them used the basic and simple statistic methods to build the concept lexicons. These methods didn't consider the imbalance of concept's relevant documents and irrelevant documents. The calculated weights can only mean the importance degree of the terms to the documents, not the importance degree of the terms to their special concepts.

## 1.2 The Characters of ASR Texts

In the 2005 TRECVID's English development data, the concepts' proportions of the relevant documents to irrelevant ones are 1/1000 to 1/2, and the average proportion is 1/16. This is a problem of data imbalance. In this circumstance, our term weighting method should be more sensitive to the occurrence in relevant documents than in the irrelevant documents. It is a pity that many weighting methods can't make a difference between the relevant documents and irrelevant documents.

ASR texts are transformed from speech. Firstly the spoken language has freer rules than written language. As a previous study noted, only about 50% of the words that appear as written text in the video are also spoken in the audio track [5]. Besides, the outputs of ASR systems contain a moderate word error rate (WER). Therefore, it is important to select the few informative terms without sacrificing the query accuracy of the concept.

These characteristics raise the following two questions:

- How to resolve the problem of sparse data?
  In the experiments, the term precision model performs well.
- How to build a smaller dimension with more informative concept lexicon?

In the later experiment results, we'll found that combining the statistic and rule-based methods can get a good answer.

In the following sections, we'll describe three methods and their improved versions for processing spoken documents in video retrieval in section 2. In section 3 we'll present the experiments and results. In section 4 we'll discuss this paper's major findings. Finally we'll get the conclusion in section 5.

# 2   ASR Text Feature Extracting Methods

## 2.1   The Representation of Extraction of ASR Text Feature

ASR text feature extraction in semantic video retrieval includes three parts:

- Training data: A ASR documents collection labeled with semantic concepts.
- Testing data: A candidate documents collection waiting for labeling with concepts.
- Retrieval list: The candidate documents ranked according their similarity to a semantic concept. Documents that are likely to be relevant to the concept should be ranked at the top and documents that are unlikely to be relevant should be ranked at the bottom of the retrieval list.

We represent a concept's relevant documents collection with a terms collection (Concept Lexicon) D={$t_1$ ,$t_2$ ,..., $t_n$}, each term has it's weight. D is not the simple compounding of the document terms, whose terms are selected by many terms selecting methods, and the terms' weights reflect their importance to the concept.

We represent a shot document in the test data as a query Q: Q={$t_1$ ,$t_2$ ,..., $t_k$}.

Then the ASR text feature extraction in semantic video retrieval is transformed to a text retrieval problem: Computing the similarity between D and Q: similarity (Q, D).

Following we'll introduce three methods realized in our experiments.

## 2.2   TF*IDF Model (Model-TF*IDF)

TF*IDF is the most common and simple method in text retrieval, used by many TRECVID participants [1]. TF is the number of terms in a shot document. DF is the number of documents including the term. IDF is the inverse of DF. In our experiments, we realized the TF*IDF method for comparison, and called it as Model-TF*IDF.

To learn the relationship between the spoken terms and concepts, firstly this method will construct a concept lexicon. We select the lexicon terms based on the DF in the concepts' relevant documents collection. The basic assumption is that rare terms in relevant documents collection are either non-informative for the concept, or not influential in global performance.

To indicate the term's importance to the concept, we weight the terms with TF*IDF. A higher occurrence frequency in a given shot document indicates that the term is more important in that document; at the same time, a lower document frequency indicates that the term is more discriminative.

Finally we represent the ASR text feature as the sparse vectors, whose $i^{th}$ item reflects the weight of the $i^{th}$ term in the concept lexicon.

These ASR feature vectors will be trained by Support Vector Machine(SVM). We rank the shot documents according to the probabilities produced by the SVM model.

## 2.3   BM25 Model (Model-BM25)

Recent TREC tests showed that BM25 was the best known probabilistic weighting schemes in text retrieval[11]. This is a simple effective approximation to the 2-Poisson Model for probabilistic weighted retrieval [8,12]. We realized the Cornell/BM25 algorithm in our experiments to verify whether it performs as good in ASR text feature extraction as in common text retrieval.

The exact formulas for the Cornell version of BM25 method are:

$$similariy(Q,D) = \sum_{k=1}^{l} w_{qk} \bullet w_{dk}$$

$$w_{qk} = tf(t_k, q) \tag{1}$$

$$w_{dk} = \frac{tf(t_k, d)}{2 \cdot (0.25 + 0.75L) + tf(t_k, d)} \bullet \log \frac{(N - df(t_k) + 0.5)}{(df(t_k) + 0.5)}$$

Where $N$ is the total number of documents. $L$ is the normalized document length (i.e. the length of this document divided by the average length of documents in the collection). $df(t_k)$ is the document frequency of term $t_k$. $tf(t_k, d)$ is the occurrence frequency of term $t_k$ in documents collection. $f(t_k, q)$ is the occurrence frequency of term $t_k$ in query.

The comparison of experiments results indicates that the performance of BM25 in ASR text feature extraction is not the best.

## 2.4 Term Precision Model (Model-TP)

In nature both TF*IDF and BM25 weight the terms with DF. The DF weighting method is the simplest method and to some extent has good performance. But a term's high DF value can't tell us the information that it frequently occurs in the relevant documents or in the irrelevant ones. Especially in the training data labeled with semantic concepts, the imbalance between the relevant documents and irrelevant documents is salient. Then we can't treat the DF in relevant documents and the ones in irrelevant documents equally. We apply the TP weighting method [6] to amend the data imbalance problem. TP method respectively computes the DF in relevant documents and irrelevant documents. Moreover, it is more sensitive to the relevant documents. In the common text retrieval, there are not positive and negative samples annotations, so the TP weighting method is rarely applied to the text retrieval. In our experiments, we realized the TP methods, called as Model-TP.

The application of TP weighting method in the Model-TP is as following:

$$similariy(Q,D) = \sum_{k=1}^{l} w_{qk} \bullet w_{dk} + k_2 n_q \frac{1-L}{1+L}$$

$$w_{qk} = \frac{tf(t_k, q)}{k_3 + tf(t_k, q)} \tag{2}$$

$$w_{dk} = \frac{tf(t_k, d)}{k_1 L + tf(t_k, d)} \bullet \log \frac{(A + 0.5)(SumN - B + 0.5)}{(B + 0.5)(SumP - A + 0.5)}$$

Where $k_1, k_2, k_3$ are constants. $A$ is the number of relevant documents containing the term $t_k$. $B$ is the number of non-relevant documents containing the term $t_k$.

*SumP* is the total number of relevant documents. *SumN* is the total number of non-relevant documents. $n_q$ is the length of the query.

According to the speech text's properties, we set the parameters as:$k_1=1$, $k_2=0$, $k_3=1$,$L=1$. The Model-TP performs better than the former two methods in our experiments.

## 2.5 The Models of Integrating Statistical Methods and Rule-Based Methods

Weighting the terms of concept lexicons with the TP method can effectively amend the data's imbalance problem. But the TP method does not perform as well as in selecting terms to build a concept lexicon, for the statistic methods can't effectively and quickly reduce the vocabularies. We try a HowNet-rule-based method to resolve this problem. HowNet is an on-line common-sense knowledge base that provides the inter-conceptual relations and attribute relations of concepts for lexical senses of the Chinese language and their English equivalents [9]. It is the most famous semantic lexical database currently.

We compute the concept relevancy based on the HowNet knowledge dictionary, and build the concept's rule-lexicon based on the values of the relevancy. Simultaneity we build the concept's statistic lexicon separately use the above three statistic weighting methods. The rule-lexicon's terms are correlative with the concept in meaning, and the statistic lexicon's terms are frequently co-occurrence with the concept. We extract the intersections of the rule-lexicons and statistic lexicons as the final concept lexicons, and use them to the semantic concept retrieval experiments. According different weighting methods, we call the models as Model-DF-HN, Model-BM25-HN, and Model-TP-HN correspondingly.

Experiments show that the introduction of the HowNet-rule-based method improved the former three statistic methods.

# 3 Empirical Validation

We choose the TRECVID 2005's English development data as our experimental data, each shot has been labeled with 40 concepts by IBM. We randomly divided the data to two parts according to the proportion of 1 to 2. The training data include 19935 shot documents, while the testing data include 9540 shot documents.

The version of HowNet we used in our experiments includes 158849 words.

## 3.1 Evaluation Method

To determine the accuracy of the methods' retrieval results, we use *average precision*, following the standard in TRECVID evaluations. Let $L^k = \{l_1, l_2, \ldots\ldots, l_k\}$ be a ranked version of the retrieve results set S. At any given rank k let $R_k$ be the number of relevant shots in the top $k$ of L, where R is the total number of relevant shots in a set of size S. Then average precision is defined as:

$$\text{average precision} = \frac{1}{R}\sum_{k=1}^{A}\frac{R_k}{k}f\left(l_k\right) \qquad (3)$$

Where function $f\left(l_k\right) = 1$ if $l_k \in R$ and 0 otherwise. The average precision favors highly ranked relevant shots.

### 3.2 Pre-processing

Firstly, we matched the ASR texts with the shots based on the shot temporal boundaries. At the same time, we expanded the shot boundaries to include up to 3 immediate neighbors on either side to a shot document. This shot expansion results in overlapping speech segments and attempts to compensate for speech and visual misalignment.

Then we removed the words in a standard stop word list which includes 524 terms. Besides, we computed all the terms' document frequency occurred in the whole train data, and add the terms with highest DF to the user-defined stop word list. This preprocessing is a good supplement to the standard stop list.

We also used the Porter's well-established stemming algorithm [10] to unify terms, which allows several forms of a word to be considered as a unique term.

### 3.3 Primary Results

Without losing generality, we choose the following five concepts to experiment: Outdoor(1:3), Building(1:15), Military(1:30), Sports(1:100), Snow(1:250). The numbers in the brackets are the proportions of relevant documents to irrelevant ones.

Fig. 1. displays the performance curves for the retrieval average precisions of "sports" after using Model-TF*IDF, Model-BM25, and Model-TP respectively. From the figure, we found that Model-TP's performance is best.

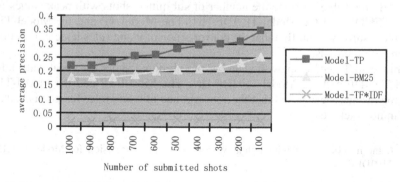

**Fig. 1.** Average precision of Model-TP,Model-BM25,Model-TF*IDF vs. sports

Considering that Model-TF*IDF is the traditional method, and the Model-TP is the best method, we chose the two models to validate the HowNet's rule-based lexicons. Fig.2 and Fig.3 separately displays the compare of the Model-TF*IDF and the

Model-TF*IDF-HN, the Model-TP and the Model-TP-HN. The improvement after using the rule-based lexicons in the Model-TF*IDF and the Model-TP is obvious.

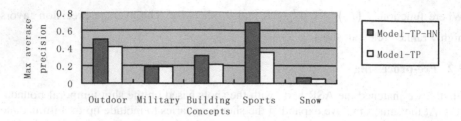

**Fig. 2.** Comparison of the Model-TP and Model-TP-HN

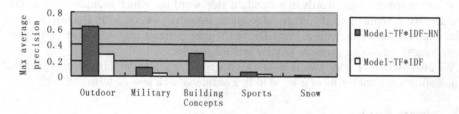

**Fig. 3.** Comparison of the Model-TF*IDF and Model-TF*IDF-HN

We used the value of "Max Average Precision" in Fig. 2 and Fig. 3. In general, the average precision increases as the number of submitted shots. After reaching the peak, then decreases as the number of submitted shots. The above Max Average Precisions are the peak values with the number of submitted shots between 10 and 1000. The number of submitted shots with peak values is small, which reflects that the most likely relevant documents are ranked at the top of the rank lists, vice versa.

Table1 and Table2 display the number of submitted shots with peak values for the Model-TF*IDF and the Model-TF*IDF-HN, The Model-TP and the Model-TP-HN. From the results, we can find that the convergence of using rules lexicon is better than the common methods.

Table1 and Table2 display the number of submitted shots with peak values for the Model-TF*IDF and the Model-TF*IDF-HN, The Model-TP and the Model-TP-HN. From the results, we can find that the convergence of using rules lexicon is better than the common methods.

**Table 1.** the number of submitted shots with max average precision for Model-TF*IDF and Model-TF*IDF-HN

| Concept<br>Model | Outdoor | Military | Building | Sports | Snow |
|---|---|---|---|---|---|
| Model-TF*IDF | 300 | 1000 | 50 | 100 | 50 |
| Model-TF*IDF-HN | 100 | 1000 | 10 | 10 | 30 |

**Table 2.** The number of submitted shots with max average precision for Model-TP and Model-TP -HN

| Concept<br>Model | Outdoor | Military | Building | Sports | Snow |
|---|---|---|---|---|---|
| Model-TP | 1000 | 1000 | 10 | 500 | 300 |
| Model-TP-HN | 10 | 300 | 10 | 500 | 300 |

## 4 Discussion

The weighting algorithms of TF*IDF and BM25 don't distinguish between the relevant documents and irrelevant ones, and suppose that the more rare terms are more valuable. The weight curve with the DF is as Fig.4. The TP method's weight curve with the DF is as Fig.5. The weight firstly increases as the DF, it indicates that the term is frequently occur in the data. After reaching a peak, the weight curve decreases as the DF, it indicates that the term is too frequently occurs in the data to became non-discriminative.

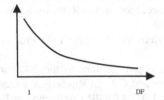

**Fig. 4.** The variation curve of term weight in Model-TF*IDF and Model-BM25

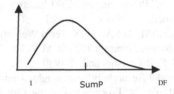

**Fig. 5.** The variation curve of term weight in Model-TP

In our experiments, the size of the intersections of the rule-based lexicon and the statistic lexicon is about 100, which indicates that the rule-based method can rapidly narrow the vocabulary. But there are some concept lexicons with the very small size. E.g. the size of lexicon for "Snow" is only 14, which badly influence the concept retrieval results(The max average precision of Snow in Model-TP-HN is 0.0588 ). We analyze the cause is that the proportion of relevant documents to irrelevant documents is too small (1:250), and few terms correlative with "Snow" are spoken. So we get a conclusion that the ASR text features is not effective to all the semantic concepts. We can weight all kinds of features in feature fusion step.

## 5 Conclusion

In this paper, we propose a method of integrating statistic method and rule-based method to build concept lexicon. The introduction of HowNet rapidly and effectively narrows the vocabulary. Simultaneously we apply the TP weighting method to analyze the ASR texts. Experiments show that this method is more suited to the extraction of the ASR text features. Future work we will study how to use the ASR text features better to support the video semantic concept retrieval.

# References

1. Arnon Amir, Janne Argillander, Murray Campbell, Alexander Haubold, Shahram Ebadollahi, Feng Kang, Milind R. Naphade, Apostol Natsev, John R. Smith, Jelena Te˘si´c, and Timo Volkmer, "Ibm research trecvid-2005 video retrieval system," in *NIST TRECVID-2005 Workshop*, Gaithersburg, Maryland, November 2005.
2. Cees G.M. Snoek, Jan C. van Gemert, Jan-Mark Geusebroek, Bouke Huurnink, Dennis C. Koelma, Giang P. Nguyen, Ork de Rooij, Frank J. Seinstra, Arnold W.M. Smeulders, Cor J.Veenman, and Marcel Worring, The MediaMill TRECVID 2005 Semantic Video Search *Engine*. In Proceedings of the 3rd TRECVID Workshop , Gaithersburg, USA, November 2005.
3. Tat-Seng Chua, Shi-Yong Neo, Ke-Ya Li, Gang Wang, Rui Shi, Ming Zhao and Huaxin Xu "TRECVID 2004 Search and Feature Extraction Task by NUS PRIS" In TRECVID 2004, NIST, Gaithersburg, Maryland, USA, 15-16 Nov 2004.
4. The TREC Video Retrieval Track Home Page,http://www-nlpir.nist.gov/projects/trecvid/
5. Hauptmann, A., Ng, T.D., and Jin, R. "Video Retrieval using Speech and Image Information," Proceedings of 2003 Electronic Imaging Conference, Storage and Retrieval for Multimedia Databases, Santa Clara, CA, January 20-24, 2003
6. K.LAM , G.SALTON, Term Weighting in Information Retrieval Using the Term Precision Model , January 1982 ,ACM Vol29, No 1, pp 152-170
7. S E Robertson and S Walker. Some simple effective approximations to the 2-Poisson model for probabilistic weighted retrieval. In W B Croft and C J van Rijsbergen, editors, SIGIR '94: Proceedings of the 17th Annual International ACM SIGIR Conference on Research and Development in Information Retrieval, pages 345–354. Springer-Verlag, 1994.
8. D. Hiemstra. A probabilistic justification for using tf idf term weighting in information retrieval. International Journal on Digital Libraries, 3(2), 2000.
9. Z. Dong and Q. Dong, HowNet, http://www.keenage.com/
10. M.F. Porter An Algorithm for Suffix Stripping Program, 14 pp. 130-137, 1980
11. TREC 2001 National Institute of Standards and Technology, Text Retrieval Conference web page, http://www.trec.nist.gov/, 2001.

# A Semantic Image Category for Structuring TV Broadcast Video Streams

Jinqiao Wang[1], Lingyu Duan[2], Hanqing Lu[1], and Jesse S. Jin[3]

[1] National Lab of Pattern Recognition
Institute of Automation, Chinese Academy of Sciences, Beijing 100080, China
{jqwang, luhq}@nlpr.ia.ac.cn
[2] Institute for Infocomm Research, 21 Heng Mui Keng Terrace, Singapore 119613
lingyu@i2r.a-star.edu.sg
[3] The School of Design, Communication and Information Technology,
University of Newcastle, NSW 2308, Australia
Jesse.Jin@newcastle.edu.au

**Abstract.** TV broadcast video stream consists of various kinds of programs such as sitcoms, news, sports, commercials, weather, etc. In this paper, we propose a semantic image category, named as Program Oriented Informative Images (POIM), to facilitate the segmentation, indexing and retrieval of different programs. The assumption is that most stations tend to insert lead-in/-out video shots for explicitly introducing the current program and indicating the transitions between consecutive programs within TV streams. Such shots often utilize the overlapping of text, graphics, and storytelling images to create an image sequence of POIM as a visual representation for the current program. With the advance of post-editing effects, POIM is becoming an effective indicator to structure TV streams, and also is a fairly common "prop" in program content production. We have attempted to develop a POIM recognizer involving a set of global/local visual features and supervised/unsupervised learning. Comparison experiments have been carried out. A promising result, F1 = 90.2%, has been achieved on a part of TRECVID 2005 video corpus. The recognition of POIM, together with other audiovisual features, can be used to further determine program boundaries.

## 1 Introduction

The management of large TV broadcast video corpus is a challenging problem. Aiming at effective indexing and retrieval, semantic concepts and ontologies have been proposed to bridge the semantic gap inherent to video content analysis. For example, TRECVID'06 proposed the task of extracting 39 high-level features. In this paper, we focus on the structuring of TV streams. We propose a semantic image category, named as Program Oriented Informative Image Category (POIM), to represent significant visual patterns of images occurring at program boundaries. Referring to Fig. 1 and Fig. 2, POIM can be considered as a visual concept about TV stream structure, an intermediate feature to be combined

Y. Zhuang et al. (Eds.): PCM 2006, LNCS 4261, pp. 279–286, 2006.

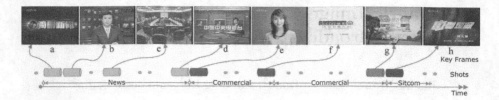

**Fig. 1.** An illustrative example of TV stream structure with POIM images as the anchors of different programs. Shot keyframe a, d, f, g and h are POIM images.

with other audiovisual feature for segmenting different programs and searching for special programs.

In TV broadcast video stream, there are various kinds of programs such as sitcoms, news, sports, commercials, weather, etc. Although different programs are multifarious in video contents, most programs exhibit a prominent structural feature, often in the form of lead-in/-out video shots, at the beginning and/or the end. For example, when we watch a TV program, a sequence of frames marked with the program title can visually indicate the beginning of a program segment after a TV commercial block. On the other hand, a program often comes to the end with frames marked with textual information about its producers and sponsors. Especially in a commercial block, the frames marked with explicit product and company information are often utilized as a prop to highlight what is offered at the end of an individual commercial. Therefore, we generally propose the semantic image category POIM aiming to structure TV streams. In Fig. 2, the functionality of POIM is illustrated by image samples according to different program genres. POIM is a useful concept for distinguishing the transition between different programs in TV streams.

As illustrated in Fig. 2, POIM is generally classified into four categories: news POIM, commercial POIM, sitcom POIM, and others. News POIM displays

**Fig. 2.** Examples of POIM images from different TV programs (From top to bottom: news, commercial, sitcom, and others)

the title of news programs, such as "DECISION 200" and "ELECTION NIGHT 200". Commercial POIM provides the brand name, trademark, address, telephone number, and cost, etc. For example, "GEICO" is a brand name and "XEROX" is a company name. An image of a product might be placed with computer graphics techniques. Sitcom POIM shows the name of sitcoms and the producer information. Others POIM show the title of weather report such as "EARTHWATCH" or TV station logos such as "MSNBC" and "LBC".

Let us investigate the example of structuring TV programs from CCTV4 as shown in Fig. 1. From the key frames listed, we note news and sitcom programs start with FMPI shots for providing the names of TV programs. Two commercials end with FMPI shots to catch users' attention by showing product and trademark information. As introduced above, POIM images are dealt with as a useful anchor to represent the structural characteristics of TV streams.

Generally speaking, POIM is composed of text, graphics, and storytelling images. The text is significant, which explicitly provides the information of corresponding TV programs. The graphics and images create a more or less abstract, symbolic, or vivid description of program contents or propagandize a product. The POIM image somehow serves as an introduction poster, by which users can decide whether to continue watching the program or to switch to other TV channels. Moreover, commercial POIM images give a vivid yet brief description of the product and can be considered as the summary of a commercial.

In this paper, we utilize learning algorithms to model the semantic image category POIM on the basis of local and global visual features. As POIM occurs in a sequence of frames, the detection of POIM is applied to key frames within a video shot. For the convenience of description, we call the shot containing at least one POIM image as a POIM shot. Both unsupervised spectral clustering [1] and supervised SVM learning [2] are employed to distinguish POIM images from Non-POIM images. Comparison experiments are carried out.

The rest of this paper is organized as follows. Section 2 presents the extraction of local and global features. Section 3 discusses the unsupervised and supervised learning for training the POIM recognizer. Experiments results are given in Section 4. Finally, Section 5 concludes our work.

## 2    Feature Extraction

The POIM image can be dealt with as a document image involving text, graphics, and storytelling images. We rely on color, edge, and texture features to represent a POIM image. For an incoming TV stream, we perform video shot boundary detection [3]. Loose thresholding is applied to reduce missed video shots. One key frame is simply extracted at the middle of each shot. The extraction of local and global features are carried out within selected key frames.

### 2.1    Global Features

The text, graphics and storytelling image in a POIM image tends to locate at the central part of a frame, as illustrated in Fig. 2. A simple background is often

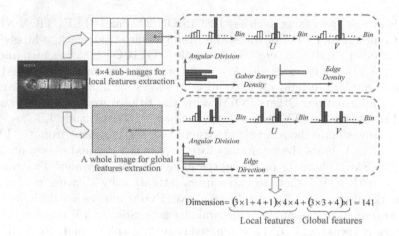

**Fig. 3.** Global feature and local feature extraction for POIM images detection

used to highlight the text, graphics, or storytelling image to draw a TV viewer's attention. For global features we take into account the cues of color and edge. CIE LUV color space is used because of its perceptual uniformity. Dominant colors are applied to construct an approximate representation of color distribution. In terms of color we actually utilize a reduced dominant color descriptor. The percentages of selected color bins are taken into account to represent spatial coherency of color. Each channel is uniformly quantized into 100 bins. Three maximum bin values are selected as dominant color features from L, U, and V channels, respectively. This results in a 9-dimensional color feature vector for a whole image. Edge direction histogram is employed to describe the global statistical property of edges. Using Canny edge detection algorithm [4](with $\sigma = 1$, Gaussion mask $Size = 9$), edges are broadly grouped into $h$ categories of orientation by using the angle quantizer as,

$$A_i = \left[ \left\lfloor \frac{180}{h} \right\rfloor \cdot i, \left\lfloor \frac{180}{h} \right\rfloor \cdot (i+1) \right) \qquad i = 0, ...h - 1 \qquad (1)$$

In our experiment, $h = 4$. Thus 4-dimensional edge direction features are yielded. The total global features are 13 dimensional including color and edge features.

## 2.2 Local Features

As shown in Fig. 2, the spatial distribution is a significant factor in distinguish POIM images. The POIM images first are divided into $4 \times 4$ sub-images, then color, edge and texture features are extracted within each sub-image. The maximum bin value of each channel in the LUV color space is selected as the local dominant color feature. Note that the bin values are meant to represent the spatial coherency of color, irrespective of concrete color values. The edge density feature for each sub-image is calculated as,

$$Edgedensity_i = \begin{cases} \frac{2E_i}{N} & \text{if } \frac{E_i}{N} \leq 0.5 \\ 1 & \text{else} \end{cases} \qquad (2)$$

where $i = 1, \ldots, 16$ is the number of sub-image. $E_i$ is the number of canny edge pixels for sub-image $i$. $N$ is the total number of pixels in sub-image $i$. The local edge density feature are 16 dimensional.

Textures are replications, symmetries and combinations of various basic patterns or local functions, usually with some random variation. Gabor filters [5] exhibit optimal location properties in the spatial domain as well as in the frequency domain, they are used to capture the rich texture in POIM detection. Filtering an image $I(x, y)$ with Gabor filters designed according to [5] results in its Gabor wavelet transform:

$$W_{mn}(x, y) = \int I(x, y) g^*_{mn}(x - x_1, y - y_1) dx_1 dy_1 \qquad (3)$$

where $g_{mn}$ is the gabor filters and $*$ indicates the complex conjugate. Within each sub-image, the mean $\mu_{mn}$ of the magnitude of the transform coefficients is used. One scale and four orientations are selected to represent the spatial homogeneousness for each local region. Different from image retrieval and recognition, our task is to find the mutual property of POIM images. One scale and four orientation can reach more satisfactory results than that by more scales and orientations. The total local texture feature are $4 \times 16 = 64$ dimensional.

A 128-dimensional feature vector involving color, edge, and texture is finally formed to represent local features. With the 13-dimensional global feature (9-dimensional dominant color and 4-dimensional edge direction features), we finally construct a 141-dimensional visual feature vector including 128-dimensional local features.

## 3   Detection of POIM Images

The classification of POIM images can be accomplished in both supervised and unsupervised manners. For unsupervised learning, spectral clustering [1] is used to cluster the keyframes into POIM images and non-POIM images. For supervised learning, determinative SVM is employed.

### 3.1   Unsupervised Approach

Spectral clustering [1] is a data clustering algorithm developed in recent years. Compared with prior clustering approaches, spectral clustering is a piecewise distance based method and does not assume the data in each cluster having a convex distribution. Also spectral clustering is free of the singularity problem caused by high dimensionality. The data points are represented as vertices in a graph, and spectral clustering aims at partitioning a graph into disjointed sub-graphs based on the eigenvectors of the similarity matrix. The algorithm is briefly described in Algorithm 1. The affinity matrix $A$ is directly built from the 141-dimensional global and local features. The features are projected into a 2-dimensional space generated by the two largest eigenvectors.

**Algorithm 1. Spectral Clustering**

1. Form the affinity matrix $A \in R^{n \times n}$, $A_{i,i} = 0$, $A_{i,j} = \exp(-\|s_i - s_j\|^2 / 2\sigma^2)$.
2. Construct the Laplacian matrix $L = D^{-1/2} A D^{-1/2}$, with degree matrix $D_{i,i} = \sum_j A_{i,j}$.
3. Form the matrix $X = [x_1, x_2, ..., x_k]$ by staking the $k$ largest eigenvectors of $L$.
4. Normalize each row of $X$ to unit length.
5. Cluster each row $X$ into $k$ clusters via K-mean.

## 3.2 Supervised Approach

The recognition of a POIM frame is here formulated as a binary classification problem. For supervised learning, SVMs provide good generalization performance and can achieve excellent results on pattern classifications problems. Through a kernel, the training data are implicitly mapped from a low-level visual feature space to a kernel space, and an optimal separating hyperplane is determined therein. This mapping is often nonlinear, and the dimensionality of the kernel space can be very high or even infinite. The nonlinearity and the high dimensionality help SVMs achieving excellent classification performance, especially for linearly nonseparable patterns. Let $\mathbb{R}$ denote the n-dimensional feature space. The training data are $(x_i, y_i), i = 1, \ldots, l$ where $x_i \in \mathbb{R}^n$, $y \in \{-1, +1\}^l$. SVM finds an optimal separating hyperplane that classifies the two classes by the minimum expected test error. The hyperplane has the following form: $\langle w, x_i \rangle + b = 0$, where $w$ and $b$ is the normal vector and bias, respectively. The training feature vectors $x_i$ are mapped into a higher dimensional space by the function $\phi$. The problem of finding the optimal hyperplane is a quadratic programming problem of the following form [2]:

$$\min_{w,\xi} \quad \frac{1}{2} w^T w + C \sum_{i=1}^{n} \xi_i \tag{4}$$

with the constraints $y_i(\langle w, x_i \rangle + b) \geq 1 - \xi_i, \quad i = 1, 2, \ldots, l$. $C$ is the cost controlling the trade-off between function complexity and training error, and $\xi_i$ is the slack variable. The commonly used Gaussian radical basis function (RBF) kernel is optimized to incorporate the prior knowledge of small sample. Gaussian RBF kernel is defined as $exp(-\gamma \|x_i - x_j\|^2), \gamma > 0$. RBF kernel is used in our SVM learning.

## 4 Experiments

To evaluate the performance of POIM recognition, we performed experiments on TRECVID 2005 video database, which is an open benchmark data for video retrieval evaluation. Our training and testing data are taken from 6 general sources: CNN, NBC, MSNBC, NTDTV, LBC and CCTV4. The genres of TV programs include: news, commercial, movie, sitcom, animation, MTV and weather report.

Ground truth of POIM frames was manually labeled. F1 is used to evaluate our algorithm. F1 is defined as follow: $F1 = \frac{2 \times Recall \times Precision}{Recall + Precision}$.

Our POIM image recognizer has achieved an accuracy of $F1 = 81.5\%$ for the unsupervised method, and $F_1 = 90.2\%$ for the supervised method by using 6000 frames comprising 2000 POIM frames and 4000 Non-POIM frames selected from the video database described above. The results of unsupervised spectral clustering are shown in Fig. 4. From Fig. 4, the distribution of POIM images is clearly different from that of Non-POIM images. Moreover, the clustering results shows the effectiveness of our features. For supervised SVMs, this accuracy is

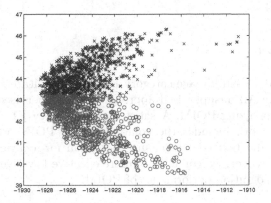

**Fig. 4.** Clustering results of POIM images and non-POIM images. The blue points represent Non-POIM images and the red points represent the POIM images.

calculated by averaging the results of ten different random half-and-half training and testing partitions. Radial basis function (RBF) is used for SVMs learning. We are required to tune four parameters, i.e. gamma $\gamma$, cost $C$, class weight $\omega_i$,

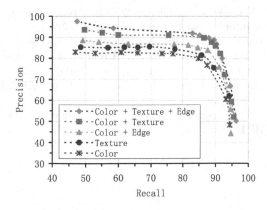

**Fig. 5.** POIM classification performance yielded by using different visual features and different pairs of SVMs parameters $(\gamma, C)$

and tolerance $e$. Class weight $\omega_i$ is for weighted SVM to deal with unbalanced data, which sets the cost $C$ of class $i$ to $\omega_i \times C$. Class weights $\omega_1 = 2$ are set as for POIM and $\omega_0 = 1$ for Non-POIM, respectively. $e$ is set to 0.0001. $\gamma$ is tuned between 0.1 and 10 while $C$ is tuned between 0.1 and 1. As indicated in Fig. 5, "Color" and "Texture" have demonstrated individual capabilities of our color and texture features to distinguish POIM from Non-POIM. Comparatively, texture features play a more important role. The combination of color and texture features results in a significant improvement of performance. An optimal pair $(\gamma, C)$ is selected as $(0.5, 1.0)$ to get an accuracy $F1 = 90.2\%$. By fusing with audio and textual features, POIM can be further utilized to determine the program boundaries.

## 5   Conclusion

We have proposed a useful image category POIM to facilitate structural analysis in TV streams. An unsupervised approach and a supervised one have been compared for recognizing POIM. A satisfactory accuracy F1=90.2% has been achieved. Future work includes the combination of POIM with audio scene change detection and text content change detection for locating boundaries of TV programs. Moreover, we will explore more effective low-level visual features to improve the recognition performance of POIM.

## Acknowledgement

This work is supported by National Natural Science Foundation of China (Grant No. 60475010 and 60121302).

## References

1. Ng, A.Y., Jordan, M.I., Weiss, Y.: On spectral clustering: analysis and an algorithm. Advance in Neural Information Processing Systems (2001)
2. Vapnik, V.: The nature of statistical learning theory. Springer-Verlag (1995)
3. Wang, J., Duan, L., Lu, H., Jin, J.S., Xu, C.: A mid-level scene change representation via audiovisual alignment. In: Proc. ICASSP'06. (2006)
4. Canny, J.: A computational approach to edge detection. IEEE Trans. PAMI 8(6) (1986) 679–698
5. Manjunath, B., Ma, W.: Texture features for browsing and retrieval of image data. IEEE Trans. PAMI 18(8) (1996) 837–842

# Markov Chain Monte Carlo Super-Resolution Image Reconstruction with Simultaneous Adaptation of the Prior Image Model

Jing Tian and Kai-Kuang Ma

School of Electrical and Electronic Engineering, Nanyang Technological University,
Singapore 639798
jingtian@ieee.org, ekkma@ntu.edu.sg

**Abstract.** In our recent work, the *Markov chain Monte Carlo* (MCMC) technique has been successfully exploited and shown as an effective approach to perform super-resolution image reconstruction. However, one major challenge lies at the selection of the hyperparameter of the prior image model, which affects the degree of regularity imposed by the prior image model, and consequently, the quality of the estimated high-resolution image. To tackle this challenge, in this paper, we propose a novel approach to automatically adapt the model's hyperparameter during the MCMC process, rather than the exhaustive, off-line search. Experimental results presented show that the proposed hyperparameter adaptation method yields extremely close performance to that of the optimal prior image model case.

## 1 Introduction

The goal of *super-resolution* (SR) image reconstruction is to fuse a set of low-resolution images acquired from the same scene to produce a single higher-resolution image with more details [1, 2, 3]. In our recent work, a Bayesian approach, together with the *Markov chain Monte Carlo* (MCMC) technique, has been developed and shown its attractive performance in addressing the SR problem [4]. The developed algorithm provides a flexible framework for the incorporation of the prior knowledge of the unknown high-resolution image, as well as for the modeling of the dependence among the observed low-resolution images and the unknown high-resolution image.

One major challenge in the above-mentioned Bayesian SR methods is how to select the hyperparameter of the prior image model, for it intimately affects the degree of the regularity and the quality of the reconstructed high-resolution image. To tackle this problem, some works have been developed to automatically select the hyperparameter [5, 6, 7], rather than the heuristic approach that experimentally determines this hyperparameter [8], [9]. Tipping and Bishop [5] proposed to estimate the hyperparameter by assessing its marginal likelihood function. However, the computational cost of this method is so huge that, in their works, patches from the center of the low-resolution images (these patches

Y. Zhuang et al. (Eds.): PCM 2006, LNCS 4261, pp. 287–294, 2006.

were covered by a $9 \times 9$ window) were used to provide the approximate estimation of the hyperparameter. Woods *et al.* proposed to apply the *Expectation-Maximization* (EM) method to compute the maximum likelihood estimation of the hyperparameter [6]. This method requires that the geometric displacements between the low-resolution images have the globally uniform translations only. He and Kondi [7] proposed to automatically estimate the regularization parameter, which was defined as the ratio of the hyperparameter and the noise variance incurred in the image acquisition process. This method assumes that the geometric displacements between the low-resolution images are restricted to integer displacements on the high-resolution grid. However, both methods are improper to address real-world applications, since their assumptions are fairly strict.

In this paper, we will extend our works in [4] to simultaneously produce the high-resolution image and select the hyperparameter by assessing their joint posterior distribution function, which is developed by the Bayesian inference method. The unknown high-resolution image can be obtained by the mean of the samples, which are generated by the MCMC technique, and distributed according to the above-derived posterior probability distribution.

The paper is organized as follows. Firstly, a Bayesian formulation of the SR problem is proposed in Section 2. Then the MCMC SR algorithm is developed in Section 3. Experimental results are presented in Section 4. Finally, Section 5 concludes this paper.

## 2    Bayesian Inference

### 2.1    Observation Model

Given an original image, it is considered as the high-resolution ground truth, which is to be compared with the reconstructed image from a set of low-resolution images for performance evaluation. To simulate the observed low-resolution images, the original high-resolution image is warped, convolved with a *point spread function* (PSF), downsampled to a lower resolution, and finally added with the zero-mean Gaussian noise. These operations can be formulated as

$$\mathbf{y}^{(k)} = \mathbf{H}^{(k)}\mathbf{X} + \mathbf{V}^{(k)}, \tag{1}$$

where $\mathbf{y}^{(k)}$ and $\mathbf{X}$ represent the $k$-th low-resolution image and the high-resolution image represented in the lexicographic-ordered vector form, with the size of $L_1L_2 \times 1$ and $M_1M_2 \times 1$, respectively. $\mathbf{H}^{(k)}$ is an $L_1L_2 \times M_1M_2$ matrix, representing the above-mentioned warping (e.g., shift and rotation), convolving and downsampling processes, and $\mathbf{V}^{(k)}$ is an $L_1L_2 \times 1$ vector, representing the additive noise, which is generated from a Gaussian distribution with zero mean and the variance $\sigma_v^2$.

With such establishment, the goal of the SR image reconstruction is to produce a single high-resolution image $\mathbf{X}$ based on a few low-resolution observations (say, $\rho$), which are denoted as $\mathbf{y}^{(1)}, \mathbf{y}^{(2)}, \ldots, \mathbf{y}^{(\rho)}$. To simplify the notation, we define $\mathbf{Y} = \{\mathbf{y}^{(1)}, \mathbf{y}^{(2)}, \ldots, \mathbf{y}^{(\rho)}\}$, $L = L_1L_2$, and $M = M_1M_2$, which will be used in the rest of the paper.

## 2.2    Bayesian Inference

In this section, we present a Bayesian inference approach to find the joint posterior density function (pdf) of the unknown high-resolution image and the hyperparameter in the prior image model $p(\mathbf{X}, \lambda|\mathbf{Y})$. To compute the above joint posterior pdf, we firstly apply the Bayes rule to rewrite $p(\mathbf{X}, \lambda|\mathbf{Y})$ as

$$p(\mathbf{X}, \lambda|\mathbf{Y}) = \frac{p(\mathbf{X}, \lambda, \mathbf{Y})}{p(\mathbf{Y})}$$
$$\propto p(\mathbf{X}, \lambda, \mathbf{Y}) = p(\mathbf{Y}|\mathbf{X}, \lambda)\, p(\mathbf{X}, \lambda) = p(\mathbf{Y}|\mathbf{X}, \lambda)\, p(\mathbf{X}|\lambda)\, p(\lambda). \quad (2)$$

In the following presentation, we will describe how to compute the likelihood function $p(\mathbf{Y}|\mathbf{X}, \lambda)$, the prior function on the high-resolution image $p(\mathbf{X})$, and the prior function on the hyperparameter $p(\lambda)$ in (2).

Firstly, assume that the low-resolution images are obtained independently from the high-resolution image and the hyperparameter; according to (1), we can express $p(\mathbf{Y}|\mathbf{X}, \lambda)$ as

$$p(\mathbf{Y}|\mathbf{X}, \lambda) = p(\mathbf{Y}|\mathbf{X}) = \prod_{k=1}^{\rho} p\left(\mathbf{y}^{(k)}|\mathbf{X}\right) \propto \exp\left(-\frac{1}{2\sigma_v^2} \sum_{k=1}^{\rho} \left\|\mathbf{y}^{(k)} - \mathbf{H}^{(k)}\mathbf{X}\right\|^2\right). \quad (3)$$

Secondly, the prior model on the image usually reflects the expectation that the image is locally smooth. In our works, we choose the $\gamma$-neighbourhood MRF model [10], which yields the form as

$$p(\mathbf{X}|\lambda) = \frac{1}{Z(\lambda)} \exp\left\{-\frac{1}{2}\lambda\mathbf{X}^T\mathbf{C}\mathbf{X}\right\}, \quad (4)$$

where $\lambda$ is the hyperparameter and $\mathbf{C}$ is the $M \times M$ matrix, whose entries are given by $C(i,j) = \gamma$, if $i = j$; $C(i,j) = -1$, if $i$ and $j$ both fall in the $\gamma$-neighbourhood; otherwise, $C(i,j) = 0$. The *partition function* $Z(\lambda)$ is the normalizing factor, and is defined as $Z(\lambda) = \int_{\mathcal{X}} \exp\left\{-\lambda U(\mathbf{X})\right\} d\mathbf{X}$, where the *energy function* $U(\mathbf{X})$ is made of $U(\mathbf{X}) = \sum_{c \in C} V_c(\mathbf{X})$, in which $V_c(\mathbf{X})$ is the *potential function* of a local group of pixels $c$ (called the *clique*) and its value depends on the local configuration on the clique $c$.

Thirdly, we choose the *flat prior* (i.e., the uniform distribution) to build up the prior pdf on the hyperparameter $p(\lambda)$, which yields the form as

$$p(\lambda) = \frac{1}{\lambda_{max} - \lambda_{min}}, \quad \text{for} \quad \lambda \in [\lambda_{min}, \lambda_{max}], \quad (5)$$

where $[\lambda_{min}, \lambda_{max}]$ is the dynamic range of the value of $\lambda$.

Finally, substituting (3), (4) and (5) into (2), we have

$$p(\mathbf{X}, \lambda|\mathbf{Y}) \propto \frac{1}{Z(\lambda)} \exp\left\{-\frac{1}{2\sigma_v^2} \sum_{k=1}^{\rho} \left\|\mathbf{y}^{(k)} - \mathbf{H}^{(k)}\mathbf{X}\right\|^2 - \frac{1}{2}\lambda\mathbf{X}^T\mathbf{C}\mathbf{X}\right\} \frac{1}{\lambda_{max} - \lambda_{min}}. \quad (6)$$

However, the direct assessment of (6) is extremely difficult, since the computation of the partition function (i.e., $Z(\lambda)$) is computationally intractable; this computation needs to integrate over all possible values of $\mathbf{X}$ (the size of the space $\chi$ is $N^{M_1 \times M_2}$ for the $N$-bit gray level image with the size of $M_1 \times M_2$). Hence, we resort to the MCMC method, which provides an extremely powerful way to address this problem in the following section.

## 3    The Proposed MCMC Super-Resolution Approach

The goal of the proposed MCMC SR algorithm is to simultaneously estimate the high-resolution image as well as the hyperparameter, by generating $N$ samples from $p(\mathbf{X}, \lambda | \mathbf{Y})$; these samples are denoted as $\mathbf{Z}^{(1)}, \mathbf{Z}^{(2)}, \ldots, \mathbf{Z}^{(N)}$ (each of them is an $M \times 1$ vector, and with the same size as that of $\mathbf{X}$) and $\lambda^{(1)}, \lambda^{(2)}, \ldots, \lambda^{(N)}$, where $N$ is large enough to guarantee the convergence of the MCMC method. Then, the samples generated up to the sample number $T$ are considered unreliable and thus should be discarded. Finally, the high-resolution image is obtained by computing the mean of the rest $(N - T)$ samples; that is

$$\hat{\mathbf{X}} = \frac{1}{N - T} \sum_{i=T+1}^{N} \mathbf{Z}^{(i)}. \tag{7}$$

Also, the optimal hyperparameter can be obtained by

$$\hat{\lambda} = \frac{1}{N - T} \sum_{i=T+1}^{N} \lambda^{(i)}. \tag{8}$$

In (7) and (8), the parameter $T$ was derived in [4] as

$$T = \frac{\ln\left(\frac{\epsilon}{M(\theta_{max} - \theta_{min})}\right)}{\ln\left(1 - \frac{1}{M} \frac{\rho H_{min}^2}{\rho H_{min}^2 + \lambda \gamma \sigma_v^2}\right)}, \tag{9}$$

where $\epsilon$ is the user-defined tolerance, $\theta_{min}$ and $\theta_{max}$ are the minimum and maximum gray values, respectively. $M$ is the dimension of the high-resolution image, $\lambda$ and $\gamma$ are the parameters used in the MRF, $\rho$ is the number of low-resolution observations, $\sigma_v^2$ is the variance of the additive white noise and $H_{min}$ represents the minimum value of all non-zero entries of the matrices $\mathbf{H}^{(1)}, \mathbf{H}^{(2)}, \ldots, \mathbf{H}^{(\rho)}$.

To generate the above samples from $p(\mathbf{X}, \lambda | \mathbf{Y})$, in our works, the *Metropolis-Hastings* (M-H) algorithm [11] is applied for generating $\lambda^{(1)}, \lambda^{(2)}, \ldots, \lambda^{(N)}$, while the Gibbs sampler [11] is used to generate $\mathbf{Z}^{(1)}, \mathbf{Z}^{(2)}, \ldots, \mathbf{Z}^{(N)}$. This is due to the fact that it is difficult to generate a high-dimensional sample by updating its entire components in a single step. On the other hand, the M-H algorithm is efficient enough to address the simple random variable, while the Gibbs sampler is suitable to handle the high-dimensional data [11].

Now, let us look at the process of samples generation in detail as follows. Firstly, both of the above two techniques start from the randomly-generated samples, respectively. Next, at each time step, the M-H algorithm first generates a candidate sample based on a Gaussian distribution, whose mean and variance are the functions of the previous sample. Depending on the *acceptance probability* measured, this candidate sample will be either accepted as the new sample or rejected. In the latter case, the new sample will be the same as the sample of the previous step. On the other hand, the Gibbs sampler generates a new sample, by updating one single component of the sample, according to its conditional distribution given the remaining components, the hyperparameter and the observations. Then, the above-mentioned processing steps will be repeated to generate $N$ samples.

According to the above presentation, we firstly need to compute the conditional distribution used for the Gibbs sampler. Let $X_n$ denote the $n$-th component of $M \times 1$ vector $\mathbf{X}$, and $\mathbf{X}_{-n}$ denote the vector of $\mathbf{X}$ with the $n$-th component omitted; that is, $\mathbf{X}_{-n} = \{X_1, X_2, \ldots, X_{n-1}, X_{n+1}, \ldots, X_M\}$. According to (6), the distribution function of $X_n$ conditional on $\mathbf{X}_{-n}$, $\lambda$, and $\mathbf{Y}$ can be expressed as,

$$p\left(X_n | \mathbf{X}_{-n}, \lambda, \mathbf{Y}\right) \propto \exp\left\{-\frac{1}{2\tau_{X_n}}\left(X_n - \mu_{X_n}\right)^2\right\}, \tag{10}$$

where

$$\mu_{X_n} = \frac{\tau_{X_n}}{2}\left(2\sum_{k=1}^{\rho}\sum_{i=1}^{L}\frac{\psi_i^{(k)}(X_n)H_{i,n}^{(k)}}{\sigma_v^2} - \lambda\phi(X_n)\right), \tag{11}$$

$$\tau_{X_n} = \frac{1}{\sum_{k=1}^{\rho}\sum_{i=1}^{L}\frac{\left(H_{i,n}^{(k)}\right)^2}{\sigma_v^2} + \lambda C_{n,n}}, \tag{12}$$

in which $\psi_i^{(k)}(X_n)$ and $\phi(X_n)$ are defined as $\psi_i^{(k)}(X_n) = y_i^{(k)} - \sum_{j\neq n}H_{i,j}^{(k)}X_j$ and $\phi(X_n) = \sum_{s\neq n}C_{s,n}X_s + \sum_{t\neq n}C_{n,t}X_t$. The proof of (10) was provided in [4].

To summarize this section, the proposed MCMC SR approach can be stated below.

- Initialize $\mathbf{Z}^{(1)}$ and $\lambda^{(1)}$.
- For $t = 1 : N - 1$,
  - generate the $n$-th component of $\mathbf{Z}^{(t+1)}$ by sampling $Z_n^{(t+1)} \sim p\left(Z_n^{(t+1)}|\right.$
  
    $\left.\mathbf{Z}_{-n}^{(t)}, \lambda^{(t)}, \mathbf{Y}\right)$, which is defined as in (10), and $n$ is randomly selected; that is, $n$ is drawn from the discrete uniform distribution over the interval $[1, M]$.
  - the remaining components of $\mathbf{Z}^{(t+1)}$ are the same as that of $\mathbf{Z}^{(t)}$; that is, $\mathbf{Z}^{(t+1)} = \left\{Z_1^{(t)}, Z_2^{(t)}, \ldots, Z_{n-1}^{(t)}, Z_n^{(t)}, Z_{n+1}^{(t)}, \ldots, Z_M^{(t)}\right\}$.
  - generate a candidate $\lambda^{(t+1)^*}$ according to a Gaussian distribution with the mean $\lambda^{(t)}$ and the variance $\alpha \times \lambda^{(t)}$, where $\alpha = 0.05$ in our works.
  - accept the candidate $\lambda^{(t+1)^*}$ as the sample $\lambda^{(t+1)}$ with an acceptance probability $A$, which is given by $A = \min\left\{1, \frac{p(\mathbf{Z}^{(t)}, \lambda^{(t+1)^*}|\mathbf{Y})}{p(\mathbf{Z}^{(t)}, \lambda^{(t)}|\mathbf{Y})}\right\}$. If $\lambda^{(t+1)^*}$ is rejected, $\lambda^{(t+1)}$ will be the the same as $\lambda^{(t)}$.
- Compute $\hat{\mathbf{X}}$ via (7).

# 4   Experimental Results

Experimental results are provided to evaluate the performance of the proposed MCMC SR algorithm. The low-resolution images are generated from the high-resolution (i.e., original) image through a series of operations as follows. We first apply a shift, which is drawn from a continuous uniform distribution over the interval $(-2, 2)$ in the units of pixels, followed by applying a rotation, which is drawn from a continuous uniform distribution over the interval $[-4, 4]$ in the units of degrees. Next, the processed images are convoluted with a point spread function, which is a Gaussian low-pass filter with a size of $4 \times 4$ and the standard derivation of 2, followed by down-sampling by a factor of two in both the horizontal and the vertical directions, respectively. Lastly, the processed image is added with a zero-mean Gaussian noise to yield 20 dB signal-to-noise ratio (SNR); SNR is defined as $10 \times \log_{10}(\sigma_s^2/\sigma_v^2)$, where $\sigma_s^2$ and $\sigma_v^2$ are the variance of the noise-free image and the noisy image, respectively. For our simulation, four such low-resolution images are independently generated for each test image.

The proposed SR algorithm produces the high-resolution image as follows. Firstly, the initial image sample $\mathbf{Z}^{(1)}$ is randomly generated, and the initial hyperparameter sample $\lambda^{(1)}$ is drawn from a continuous uniform distribution over the interval $[1, 50]$. The convergence bound $T$ is computed via (9). In our simulation, the parameter $\epsilon$ is set to 10, $\gamma$ is set to 4; that is, we apply 4-neighbourhood MRF model. Then, the MCMC technique is applied to generate $N$ samples, the parameter $N$ is defined by the user and it should be large enough to meet the statistics of the target distribution. In our simulation, $N$ is selected to be $10 \times T$. Finally, the first $T$ samples are removed, and the remaining $9 \times T$ samples are used to produce the high-resolution image via (7).

In our experiment, we clearly demonstrate that the choice of the hyperparameter is critical to the quality of the reconstructed high-resolution image. Furthermore, we compare the performance of the proposed MCMC SR algorithm with that of the *bi-cubic interpolation* approach and that of the method developed in [4], where the optimal hyperparameter needs to be exhaustively searched offline. The Figure 1 presents the results obtained from the test image *Boat* ($256 \times 256$). The Figure 1 (c) and (d) demonstrate the reconstructed high-resolution image of [4] with the *fixed* hyperparameter $\lambda = 0.1$ and $\lambda = 300$, respectively. One can see that if the hyperparameter value is too small, the high-resolution image will be *under*-regularized (i.e., under-smoothing). On the other hand, if the hyperparameter is too large, it will cause the high-resolution image *over*-regularized (i.e., over-smoothing). Moreover, the Figure 1 (e) present the result of [4] with the optimal hyperparameter, which is exhaustively searched as the integer value in the interval $[1, 50]$. Comparing Figure 1 (e) with that of the proposed MCMC SR method using the simultaneous adaptation of the prior image model (i.e., through the adaptively-updated hyperparameter) as shown in Figure 1 (f), one can see that the performance of the proposed method is fairly close to the case when the optimal prior image model is exploited.

**Fig. 1.** A result of *Boat* image: (a) the original image; (b) the bi-cubic spline interpolation approach (PSNR = 24.00 dB); (c) the method developed in [4] with a fixed hyperparameter $\lambda = 0.1$ (PSNR = 24.65 dB) to demonstrate *under*-smoothing; (d) the method developed in [4] with a fixed hyperparameter $\lambda = 300$ (PSNR = 24.85 dB) to demonstrate *over*-smoothing; (e) the method developed in [4] with the best experimentally-selected hyperparameter $\lambda = 20$ (PSNR = 28.13 dB) to demonstrate *optimal* smoothing; and (f) the proposed MCMC SR algorithm with the automatically-updated hyperparameter (PSNR = 28.02 dB), which is fairly close to the optimal smoothing case as presented in (e)

# 5  Conclusions

A Bayesian MCMC approach was successfully introduced for conducting SR imaging in our recent work [4]. However, the regularization hyperparameter requires the exhaustively search in order to determine the best value for the derived framework. In this paper, we improve this hyperparameter selection aspect by making the prior image model being adaptive through the automatic determination of the hyperparameter. The proposed method consistently yields fairly close performance to that of the optimal prior image model case.

# References

1. Chaudhuri, S.: Super-Resolution Imaging. Kluwer Academic Publishers, Boston (2001)
2. Kang, M.G., Chaudhuri, S.: Super-resolution image reconstruction. IEEE Signal Processing Mag. **20** (2003) 19–20
3. Bose, N.K., Chan, R.H., Ng, M.K. Special Issue on High Resolution Image Reconstruction, International Journal of Imaging Systems and Technology **14**(2-3) (2004)
4. Tian, J., Ma, K.K.: A MCMC approach for Bayesian super-resolution image reconstruction. In: Proc. IEEE Int. Conf. on Image Processing, Genoa, Italy (2005) 45–48
5. Tipping, M.E., Bishop, C.M.: Bayesian image super-resolution. In Becker, S., Thrun, S., Obermeyer, K., eds.: Advances in Neural Information Processing Systems. MIT Press, Cambridge (2002)
6. Woods, N.A., Galatsanos, N.P., Katsaggelos, A.K.: EM based simultaneous registration, restoration, and interpolation of super-resolved images. In: Proc. IEEE Int. Conf. on Image Processing, Barcelona, Spain (2003) 303–306
7. He, H., Kondi, L.P.: Resolution enhancement of video sequences with simultaneous estimation of the regularization parameter. SPIE Journal of Electronic Imaging **13** (2004) 586–596
8. Nguyen, N., Milanfar, P., Golub, G.: Efficient generalized cross-validation with applications to parametric image restoration and resolution enhancement. IEEE Trans. Image Processing **10** (2001) 573–583
9. Bose, N.K., Lertrattanapanich, S., Koo, J.: Advances in superresolution using L-curve. In: Proc. IEEE Int. Symp. Circuits and Systems, Sydney, Australia (2001) 433–436
10. Li, S.Z.: Markov Random Field Modeling in Computer Vision. Springer-Verlag, New York (1995)
11. Winkler, G.: Image Analysis, Random Fields and Markov Chain Monte Carlo Methods: A Mathematical Introduction. Springer, New York (2003)

# Text Detection in Images Using Texture Feature from Strokes

Caifeng Zhu, Weiqiang Wang, and Qianhui Ning

Graduate School of Chinese Academy of Sciences, Beijing, China 100039
{cfzhu, wqwang, qhning}@jdl.ac.cn

**Abstract.** Text embedded in images or videos is indispensable to understand multimedia information. In this paper we propose a new text detection method using the texture feature derived from text strokes. The method consists of four steps: wavelet multiresolution decomposition, thresholding and pixel labeling, text detection using texture features from strokes, and refinement of mask image. Experiment results show that our method is effective.

**Keywords:** text detection, wavelet decomposition, co-occurrence matrix, texture.

## 1 Introduction

Text embedded in images or videos is an important cue for indexing multimedia information. A large amount of research work has been done for text detection in images or videos with complex background. In [4] by Jain et al, color reduction and multi-valued image decomposition are performed to convert a color image to a binary domain, where connected component analysis is employed; Wu et al [10] present a method of four steps: texture segmentation to focus attention on regions where text may occur, stroke extraction based on simple edged detection, text extraction and bounding box refinement; Li et al [6] use a three-layer BP neural network with the first three order moments of wavelet subbands as the main features; Lienhart et al [7] propose a text localization and segmentation system, which utilizes a multilayer forward-feed network with image gradient as input. Chen et al [1] apply edge information to extract candidate text regions and then employs support vector machine (SVM) to identify text in edge-based distance map feature space. Ye [11] first uses edge detection to locate candidate text regions and then verifies candidate regions by SVM which is trained with features obtained from co-occurrence matrixes; [9] [5] also use SVM, with the edge gradient and texture as the main features respectively. Many other methods are surveyed in [9].

In this paper we propose a text detection method based on the texture feature from strokes. Texture has been used in text detection, for example, in [10] [5]. However, they applied texture analysis directly on color or gray level values rather than on strokes. Stroke is one of the most significant features of text, so texture features derived from strokes should be more effective than those from color values.

Y. Zhuang et al. (Eds.): PCM 2006, LNCS 4261, pp. 295–301, 2006.
© Springer-Verlag Berlin Heidelberg 2006

## 2  Text Detection Using Stroke Texture

The following subsections give detailed introduction to the four main steps of our method: wavelet decomposition, thresholding and pixel labeling, texture description, and mask refinement. The example image used for our discussion is shown in Fig1 (a). It has been converted into gray; we assume that all color images have been converted into gray ones. The original color image with detection result is shown in Fig1 (b).

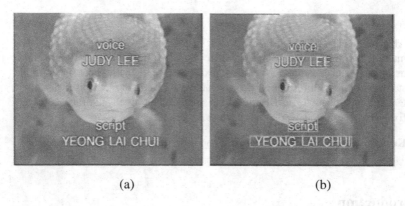

(a)                                                    (b)

**Fig. 1.** (a) Example gray image. (b) Original color image with detection result.

### 2.1  Wavelet Decomposition

Since text usually has different font sizes, the input image should undergo multiresolution processing through wavelet transformation. For its simplicity and computational efficiency, we choose Haar wavelet. Detailed wavelet theory is introduced in [3] [8]. Let $F(x, y)$ represent the original input image, $H_2$ the Haar transformation kernel matrix, and $S_{LL}(x, y), S_{LH}(x, y), S_{HL}(x, y), S_{HH}(x, y)$ four subband images. Then the single-level 2D Haar wavelet transformation is defined by the below equation

$$\begin{bmatrix} S_{LL}(x, y) & S_{LH}(x, y) \\ S_{HL}(x, y) & S_{HH}(x, y) \end{bmatrix} = H_2 F H_2 = H_2 \begin{bmatrix} F(2x, 2y) & F(2x, 2y + 1) \\ F(2x + 1, 2y) & F(2x + 1, 2y + 1) \end{bmatrix} H_2 \quad (1)$$

Here $H_2 = \dfrac{1}{\sqrt{2}} \begin{bmatrix} 1 & 1 \\ 1 & -1 \end{bmatrix}$. Substituting it into the above equation, we get

$$S_{LL}(x, y) = \frac{1}{2}[F(2x, 2y) + F(2x, 2y + 1) + F(2x + 1, 2y) + F(2x + 1, 2y + 1)] \quad (2)$$

$$S_{LH}(x,y) = \frac{1}{2}[F(2x,2y) - F(2x,2y+1) + F(2x+1,2y) - F(2x+1,2y+1)] \quad (3)$$

$$S_{HL}(x,y) = \frac{1}{2}[F(2x,2y) + F(2x,2y+1) - F(2x+1,2y) - F(2x+1,2y+1)] \quad (4)$$

$$S_{HH}(x,y) = \frac{1}{2}[F(2x,2y) - F(2x,2y+1) - F(2x+1,2y) + F(2x+1,2y+1)] \quad (5)$$

Considering normalization, we change the coefficient of $S_{LL}(x,y)$ as 1/4. At the $i$th resolution level ($i$ = base level J, J-1, J-2, $\cdots$), we represent the four sub-bands as $S_{LL}^i(x,y), S_{LH}^i(x,y), S_{HL}^i(x,y), S_{HH}^i(x,y)$, where $S_{LH}^i(x,y)$ is passed down to the ($i$-1)th resolution level as the input image and $S_{LH}^i(x,y), S_{HL}^i(x,y), S_{HH}^i(x,y)$ are processed at the current resolution level to create a mask image as the following subsections describe.

By the properties of the Haar wavelet, we know that $S_{LH}^i(x,y), S_{HL}^i(x,y), S_{HH}^i(x,y)$ are respectively sensitive to the vertical, horizontal, diagonal edges of the original image, and these edges are usually associated with text strokes. Fig2 (a) shows the wavelet transformation result.

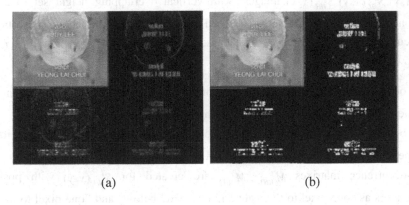

(a)                                        (b)

**Fig. 2.** (a) Wavelet transformation result. (b) The result of thresholding and labeling. The label-2 pixels are represented with white, the label-1 pixels are represented with gray, and the label-0 pixels are represented with black.

## 2.2 Thresholding and Labeling

We utilize boundary characteristics for thresholding and labeling, of which detailed description is presented in [3]. For the subband images $S_{LH}^i(x,y), S_{HL}^i(x,y), S_{HH}^i(x,y)$, we three-level each one by labeling background regions as 0, transition regions as 1 and stroke regions as 2. Then we make minor modifications to transition region labels according to the following rules.

- For $S_{LH}^i(x, y)$, we mark the label of a pixel in transition regions as 1.5 if at least one of its above and below pixels is labeled as 2, trying to restore broken vertical strokes.

- For $S_{HL}^i(x, y)$, we mark the label of a pixel in transition regions as 1.5 if at least one of its left and right pixels is labeled as 2, trying to restore broken horizontal strokes.

- For $S_{HH}^i(x, y)$, we mark the label of a pixel in transition regions as 1.5 if at least one of one of its four diagonal pixels is labeled as 2, trying to restore broken diagonal strokes..

- Finally all the labels with the values 1.5 are changed as 2

Fig2 (b) shows the result after thresholding and labeling. This thresholding and labeling step facilitates the utilization of co-occurrence matrix to describe texture from strokes.

## 2.3   Texture Description and Mask Creation

A sliding window of size $8 \times 16$ is moved over three-leveled $S_{LH}^i(x, y), S_{HL}^i(x, y), S_{HH}^i(x, y)$ images, with vertical overlapping height set to 2 and horizontal overlapping width set to 4. Based on the labeling of the above subsection, a co-occurrence matrix is created for each sub-image on $S_{LH}^i(x, y), S_{HL}^i(x, y), S_{HH}^i(x, y)$ covered by the sliding window. Specifically:

- co-occurrence matrix $M_{LH}^i$ is created for $S_{LH}^i(x, y)$, with the position operator as "one pixel below", corresponding to vertical strokes,

- co-occurrence matrix $M_{HL}^i$ is created for $S_{HL}^i(x, y)$ with the position operator as "one pixel right", corresponding to horizontal strokes, and

- co-occurrence matrixes $M_{HH1}^i$   $M_{HH2}^i$ are created for $S_{HH}^i(x, y)$ with position operators as "one pixel to the right and one pixel below" and "one pixel to the left and one pixel below" respectively, corresponding to oblique strokes

We create a binary mask image for current resolution level, which is initially set to black. As the sliding window moves, if the following conditions are satisfied for the region within the window,

- $M_{LH}^i[2][2] > t_1$,                                                                 // enough vertical strokes

- $M_{LH}^i[2][2] + M_{HL}^i[2][2] + M_{HH1}^i[2][2] + M_{HH2}^i[2][2] > t_2$,   // and other strokes

- $t_3 < entrophy(M_{LH}^i) < t_4$,                                               // neither too flat nor too coarse we consider this region contain text and draw on the mask image a white rectangle of size equivalent to the sliding window.

After the sliding window completes image scanning, the mask image is finished for the current resolution level. It is first refined as next subsection describe, then upsampled (i.e. enlarged) and passed to the upper level recursively, and finally to the top level, where we get a final mask image. Fig3 (a) shows an unrefined mask image.

## 2.4 Mask Refinement

As the above description implies, the mask image is not exactly accurate and may covers a few non-text regions, so we must refine and verify it. The refinement procedure relies on the observation that text lines usually have a large number of (nearly) vertical strokes. We first perform canny edge detection on the sub-image of the input image, which is covered by the corresponding white region on the mask image. Then we detect vertical lines on these edges with the operator described in [3]. These vertical lines are projected on the y-axis and the y-axis projection profile is analyzed using the method in [4] to tighten the text covering region in the mask image. Fig3 (b) shows the refined one of Fig3 (a).

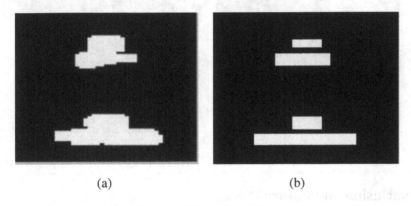

(a)                              (b)

**Fig. 3.** (a) An unrefined mask image. (b) The refined image of (a).

# 3   Experiment Results

We use the same image test set as [Gllavata2], which has 45 video frames extracted from MPEG-7 videos. These video frames all have a resolution of 384*288 pixels, and on the whole have 145 human-readable text boxes. The overall result is listed in Table 1, where recall is defined as the ratio of the number of correctly detected text lines to the number of all text lines and precision as the ratio of the number of correctly detected lines to the number of all detected text lines, including false alarms. The parameters mentioned in subsection 2.3 are set as $t_1 = 0.24$, $t_2 = 0.36$, $t_3 = 1.1$ and $t_4 = 1.9$ in our experiment.

**Table 1.** Experiment result

| Window size | Recall | Precision |
|:---:|:---:|:---:|
| H = 8 , w = 16 | 91.1% | 88.9% |

Four sample detection images are shown in Fig4.

**Fig. 4.** Four images with detection results

## 4   Conclusion and Future Work

In this paper we propose a text detection method by applying wavelet decomposition and analyzing the texture obtained from strokes. The experiment results show that the texture features from strokes are effective for text detection, even our method uses only a few simple decision rules. In the future, we will introduce machine learning techniques to further increase the robustness of text detection.

## References

1. D. T. Chen, H. Bourlard, J-P. Thiran, "Text Identification in Complex Background Using SVM," Int. Conf. on CVPR, 2001.
2. J. Gllavata, R Ewerth, B Frisleben "Text detection in images based on unsupervised classification of high-frequency wavelet coefficients" Proceedings of the ICPR Vol1, pp.425- 428 2004.

3. R. C. Gonzalez, R. E. Woods "Digital Image Processing " 2$^{nd}$ ed, pp.360-363, pp.570-572, pp.608-610 Prentice Hall, Upper Saddle River, N.J. 2001
4. K. Jain and B. Yu, "Automatic text location in images and video frames," Pattern Recognition. vol. 31, No.12, pp. 2055-2076, 1998.
5. K. I. Kim; K. Jung; J. H. Kim "Texture-based approach for text detection in images using support vector machines and continuously adaptive mean shift algorithm" IEEE Trans on Pattern Analysis and Machine Intelligence, Vol25, Issue 12, pp1631 - 1639 2003
6. H. Li, D. Doermann, and O. Kia, "Automatic text detection and tracking in digital video," Maryland Univ. LAMP Tech. Report 028,1998.
7. R. Lienhart and A. Wernicke, "Localizing and segmenting text in images and videos," IEEE trans.on Circuits and Systems for Video Technology,Vol.12, No.4, April, 2002.
8. S. G. Mallat "A theory for multiresolution signal decomposition: the wavelet representation" IEEE Trans on Pattern Analysis and Machine Intelligence, Vol11, Issue 7 pp.674-693,1989
9. C. Wolf, J. M. Jolin, "model based text detection in images and videos: a leaning approach" Technical Report LIRIS RR-2004
10. V. Wu, R. Manmatha, and E. Riseman, "Finding textin images," 20th Int. ACM Conf. Research and Development in Information Retrieval, pp. 3-12,1997.
11. Q Ye, W Gao, W Wang, W Zeng "A robust text detection algorithm in images and video frames" ICICS PCM 2003

# Robust Mandarin Speech Recognition for Car Navigation Interface

Pei Ding, Lei He, Xiang Yan, Rui Zhao, and Jie Hao

Toshiba (China) Research and Development Center
5/F Tower W2, Oriental Plaza, No.1 East Chang An Avenue,
Dong Cheng District, Beijing 100738, China
{dingpei, helei, yanxiang, zhaorui, haojie}@rdc.toshiba.com.cn

**Abstract.** This paper presents a robust automatic speech recognition (ASR) system as multimedia interface for car navigation. In front-end, we use the minimum-mean square error (MMSE) enhancement to suppress the background in-car noise and then compensate the spectrum components distorted by noise over-reduction by smoothing technologies. In acoustic model training, an immunity learning scheme is adopted, in which pre-recorded car noises are artificially added to clean training utterances to imitate the in-car environment. The immunity scheme makes the system robust to both residual noise and speech enhancement distortion. In the context of Mandarin speech recognition, a special issue is the diversification of Chinese dialects, i.e. the pronunciation difference among accents decreases the recognition performance if the acoustic models are trained with an unmatched accented database. We propose to train the models with multiple accented Mandarin databases to solve this problem. The efficiency of the proposed ASR system is confirmed in evaluations.

**Keywords:** Speech Recognition, Accented Mandarin, In-Car Noise, Speech Enhancement, Immunity Learning.

## 1 Introduction

Communication via speech is the most natural and efficient style for human beings, and it is an important application for ASR systems to act as a voice-activated human-machine interface in car navigation devices, consequently. For example, the ASR system recognizes the commands spoken out by the driver, and the results will instruct the operations of navigation system as well as other in-car electrical devices. These embedded ASR engines usually make good balance between usable functionality and system complexity, and provide an ideal input method for in-car applications considering the requirement of both safety and convenience. Therefore, in resent years, such devices become very popular and many kinds of mass-produced cars have been equipped.

Among the difficulties in such in-car speech recognition tasks, the most critical problem is to cope with the background noise, which is incurred by mechanical oscillation of engine, friction between the road and tires, blowing air outside the car,

Y. Zhuang et al. (Eds.): PCM 2006, LNCS 4261, pp. 302–309, 2006.

and etc. Recognition performance tends to be drastically degraded by interfering noise. Noise robustness is the common challenge of ASR systems, and many approaches have been proposed for this issue [1]. Some methods [2-5] aim at designing a robust front-end in which the interfering noise is removed from the speech or representations of acoustic signals are inherently less distorted by noise. Other methods [6-8] are concentrated on online model adaptation technologies which reduce the mismatch between noisy speech features and the pre-trained acoustic models. The robust front-end technologies have the advantage that their less dependency on the recognizer can effectively reduce the complexity of ASR systems.

In the proposed ASR system a noise robust front-end is designed, in which MMSE estimation algorithm [9] is used to suppress the noise in frequency domain. Compared to other conventional speech enhancement algorithms, such as spectral subtraction (SS) [2], the MMSE estimation is more efficient in minimizing both the residual noise and speech distortion. In speech enhancement, some spectrum components at very low signal-to-noise ratios (SNR) tend to be floored by meaningless threshold in Mel-scaled filter binning stage because of the noise over-reduction. Even not floored, these spectrum components are prone to aggressively degrade the recognition performance. We propose to smooth the enhanced spectrum both in time and frequency index with arithmetic sequence weights. Thus, those unreliable spectrum components will be fed with speech energy from neighbors with high local SNRs, and the recognition rate can be efficiently improved.

Besides the front-end, we utilize an immunity learning scheme [10] in offline model training stage, in which several pre-recorded in-car noise are artificially added to the clean training utterances with different SNRs to imitate a similar scenario. If we further consider the noise suppression in front-end, another advantage is that not only the residual noises are absorbed by the acoustic models, but also speech distortion caused by enhancement will be learned in immunity training.

In the context of Mandarin speech recognition, an inevitable problem is the diversification of Chinese dialects. The dialectal pronunciation characteristic will affect the style of uttering Mandarin speech and cause the phonetic and acoustic confusion [11]. If the speaker has a regional accent different from the standard Mandarin on which the acoustic models are trained, the recognition performance will be degraded. Representative methods for this issue include speaker and model adaptation [12-13], accent detection and model selection [14], and pronunciation modeling [13]. In this paper, we propose an acoustic model training scheme that uses multiple accented Mandarin databases, and confirm its efficiency in isolated phrase recognition task.

## 2 Robust Front-End Design

The proposed robust front-end is developed upon the framework of Mel-frequency cepstral coefficients (MFCC) features [15], which is the most commonly used in ASR but very sensitive to background noise. To improve the robustness, two modules, i.e. MMSE enhancement and spectrum smoothing are incorporated in the flowchart as shown in Figure 1.

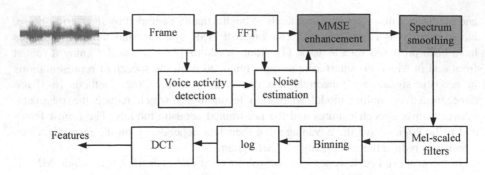

**Fig. 1.** Framework of the proposed ASR front-end

## 2.1  MMSE Speech Enhancement Algorithm

In [9] a short-time spectral amplitude (STSA) estimation algorithm based on a MMSE criterion is proposed to enhance the noise corrupted speech. One advantage is that MMSE estimation algorithm can efficiently suppress the background noise while at the expense of very few speech distortions. Another property of this method is that it can eliminate the residual "musical noise".

We assume that the noise is additive and independent to the clean speech, and after fast Fourier transform (FFT) analysis of windowed speech frames each spectral component is statistical independent and corresponds to a narrow-band Guassian stochastic process. Let $A(k, n)$, $D(k, n)$ and $R(k, n)$ denote the $kth$ spectral component of the $nth$ frame of speech, noise, and the observed signals respectively, the estimation of $A(k,n)$ is given as

$$\hat{A}(k,n) = \frac{1}{2}\sqrt{\frac{\pi\xi_k}{\gamma_k(1+\xi_k)}}M(-0.5;1;-\frac{\gamma_k\xi_k}{1+\xi_k})R(k,n), \quad (1)$$

where $M()$ is the confluent hyper-geometric function, the *a priori* SNR $\xi_k$ and the *a posterior* SNR $\gamma_k$ are defined as :

$$\xi_k \triangleq \frac{E(|A(k,n)|^2)}{E(|D(k,n)|^2)}; \quad \gamma_k \triangleq \frac{|R(k,n)|^2}{E(|D(k,n)|^2)}. \quad (2)$$

In practice, we use a voice activity detection (VAD) based noise estimation method and substitute the estimation of clean speech by enhanced spectra of the previous frame.

## 2.2  Spectrum Smoothing Technology

The MMSE enhancement algorithm can be interpreted as it suppresses or emphasizes the spectrum components according to their local SNRs. The speech signals in those components at very low SNRs are prone to be seriously distorted owing to the noise over-reduction.

In the binning stage of MFCC feature extraction a threshold is usually adopted, which is essential to eliminate the sensitivity of logarithmic transform to very small outputs of the Mel-scaled filters. Thus, after speech enhancement, those low SNR spectrum components tend to be floored by a meaningless threshold in Mel-scaled filter binning stage, which causes the mismatch between the features and the acoustic models. Even over the thresholds, the low SNR components are also prone to aggressively degrade the recognition performance.

In order to compensate the spectrum components distorted by noise over-reduction, we propose to smooth the spectrum both in time and frequency index with symmetrical normalized arithmetical sequence weights. The unreliable spectrum component will be filled with speech energy from neighboring bins whose local SNRs are high and avoid being floored in binning stage, consequently. Thus, the implementation of MMSE enhancement is tamed towards ASR tasks and the recognition performance is efficiently improved further.

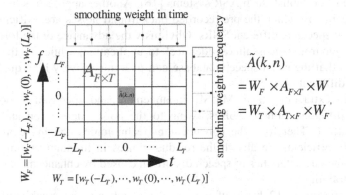

**Fig. 2.** Spectrum smoothing in time and frequency index

At frame $n$ and frequency band $k$, the smoothed spectrum component $\tilde{A}(k,n)$ is obtained as follows:

$$\tilde{A}(k,n) = \sum_{i=-L_F}^{i=L_F} \sum_{j=-L_T}^{j=L_T} w_F(i) \times w_T(j) \times \hat{A}(k+i,n+j)$$

$$\triangleq W_F' \times A_{F \times T} \times W_T = W_T \times A_{T \times F} \times W_F' \tag{3}$$

where $w_F(i)$ is the arithmetic sequence weight in the frequency index with smoothing length $F = 2 \times L_F + 1$:

$$w_F(i) = w_F(-i) = \frac{(1 - w_F(0))(L_F + 1 - i)}{L_F(L_F + 1)}, 1 \le i \le L_F, \tag{4}$$

$W_F = [w_F(-L_F), \cdots, w_F(0), \cdots, w_F(L_F)]'$ and $w_F(0)$ is the weight of current frequency bin. $w_T(j)$ and $W_T$ are the smoothing weights in time index and have the similar definitions. The matrix $A_{F \times T}$ corresponds to the spectrum block that is used for smoothing. As illustrated in Figure 2, in Eq.(3) the expression in matrix multiplication style indicates that we can firstly smooth the spectrum in frequency index and then in time index, or equivalently reverse the order.

## 3  Immunity Learning Scheme

Normally acoustic models are trained on clean speech, thus when there exists background noise in application environments mismatch is introduced between the models and the features, which tends to dramatically degrade the recognition performance. Training the model in similar noisy environments can efficiently reduce the mismatch. One approach for this purpose is to directly use scenario speech data for training. For example, in car navigation application, real in-car speech corpus can be developed to establish such ASR systems [16]. Another approach is the immunity learning scheme, in which the pre-recorded background noises are artificially add to clean training speech at different SNRs. Obviously the advantage of the former is that the training environment is almost identical to application, while for the latter the advantage is that the clean speech database can guarantee a very high quality and is flexible for different task.

In feature extraction stage, MMSE enhancement and spectrum smoothing can reduce the difference among noises owing to the noise suppression and spectrum whitening effect. Therefore, the enhancement technologies can make the acoustic models more efficiently to absorb the residual noises in immunity training. On the other hand, the characteristics of speech distortion caused by enhancement can also be learning in training.

In our experiments,12 kinds of car noises, which are the combinations of the following three conditions, are artificially added to clean training utterances.

(1) Speed (km/h): 40, 60 and 100
(2) Road type: "asf" (asphalt), "tun"(tunnel) and "con" (concrete)
(3) Air-conditioner state: on/off.

## 4  Robust ASR for Accented Mandarin

A major difficulty in Mandarin speech recognition is to cope with various accented pronunciation. In China, there are seven major dialects and each has a particular pronunciation property. For example, /zh/ is usually pronounced as /z/ by speakers in Wu dialect regions, whose representative city is Shanghai. Such phenomena in accented Mandarin cause both phonetic and acoustic confusions. If the ASR system is trained on a standard or a certain dialectal Mandarin database, it will fail to perform well when the speaker has a different regional accent compared to recognizing the matched speech. In real applications diversification of Chinese dialects is unavoidable, thus robustness to accented Mandarin is a critical issue in designing a universal ASR system for all kinds of accents.

In this paper we propose to train the acoustic models by multiple accented Mandarin speech databases. With this training scheme, the acoustic models are capable of covering statistical characteristics of possible accented pronunciations under moderate model size. Evaluations prove its efficiency in isolated phrase recognition task, which is commonly adopted in the scenario of in-car speech recognition. Besides, using a uniform acoustic model trained on multiple dialectal databases has the advantage to make the ASR system flexible and reduce its complexity.

## 5  System Configurations

In the experiments, the speech data are sampled at 11025Hz and 16 bits quantization. The frame length and window shift are 23.2ms and 11.6ms, respectively. In spectra processing, after MMSE speech enhancement and spectrum smoothing, 24 triangle Mel-scaled filters are applied to combine the frequency components in each bank, and the outputs are compressed by logarithmic function. Then the Discrete cosine transform (DCT) decorrelation is performed on the log-spectrum. The final acoustic feature of each frame is a 33 dimensional vector consisting of 11 MFCC and their first and second order derivatives.

For Mandarin speech recognition on isolated phrase task, we adopt the model structure with moderate complexity, in which each Mandarin syllable is modeled by a right-context-dependent INITIAL (bi-phone) plus a toneless FINAL (mono-phone). Totally, there are 101 bi-phone, 38 mono-phone and one silence hidden Markov models (HMM). Each model consists of 3 emitting left-to-right states with 16 Gaussian mixtures.

Seven accented Mandarin speech databases are developed in the representative city of the corresponding dialectal region. The 7 cities include Beijing, Shanghai, Dalian Guangzhou, Tianjin, Xiamen and Chengdu, which are carefully selected according to the coverage of accents as well as economic situation. The speakers are native and the speech data are recorded in quiet environments. Each database includes 50000 utterances in training set and 2000 in testing set. In recognition tasks, the vocabulary includes 500 isolated phrases, which includes addresses, names and commands.

## 6  Evaluation Results and Analysis

### 6.1  Accented Mandarin Recognition Experiments

To improve the robustness for different accented Mandarin speech recognition, we propose to train the acoustic models on multiple accented Mandarin databases, i.e. the seven training sets are merged into one that is denoted as 7in1. Three single accented models each of which is trained on the corresponding dialect Mandarin database are selected for comparison.

Table 1 shows the word error rate (WER) results in clean accented Mandarin recognition experiments. From the results we can find that if the acoustic models are trained on a certain accented Mandarin database, the recognition performance is very

**Table 1.** Experiment results (WER, %) of clean accented Mandarin speech recognition task

| Training Scheme | Accented Testing Set | | | Ave. |
|---|---|---|---|---|
| | Shanghai | Guangzhou | Chengdu | |
| Shanghai | 1.30 | 5.20 | 2.90 | 3.13 |
| Guangzhou | 2.90 | 1.15 | 2.70 | 2.25 |
| Chengdu | 2.65 | 2.65 | 1.70 | 2.33 |
| 7in1 | 1.55 | 2.20 | 2.30 | 2.02 |

high to deal with the same accented speech, but dramatically degrades in the cross testing with another dialectal accent. For example, in Shanghai training scheme, the WER for matched testing set is 1.30% and drastically drops to 5.20% and 2.90% when dealing with the speech from Guangzhou and Chengdu testing set, respectively. The proposed training scheme, 7in1, shows the robustness to the variation of dialectal pronunciation and provides consistent satisfying performance for each accented Mandarin testing set. Compared to the Shanghai, Guangzhou and Chengdu training scheme, the proposed 7in1 scheme achieves the average error rate reduction (ERR) of 35.5%, 10.2% and 13.3%, respectively.

## 6.2  Experiments in Car Noise Environments

12 car noises described in section 3 are used to generate the artificial evaluation noisy speech with the SNRs from –5dB to 20dB. In the experiments, the baseline denotes the common MFCC feature without robust technologies (MFCC_CT).

Figure 3 compares the recognition performance of the baseline and proposed methods. We can observe the robustness of the baseline is poor, e.g. at 20dB the WER is as high as 56.8%. Using immunity learning scheme for MFCC (MFCC_ILS) can efficiently improve the robustness. If we adopt MMSE enhancement and spectrum smoothing, the performance can be further improved. The scheme applied in our proposed ASR system, i.e. MMSE_Smooth_ILS provides the best performance and the average ERR versus baseline is 86.2%.

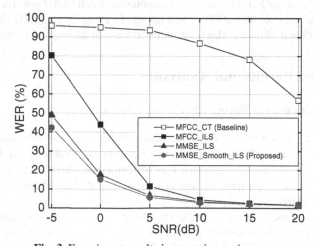

**Fig. 3.** Experiment results in car noise environments

# 7 Conclusions

This paper presents a robust ASR system for car navigation interface. The Noise robust technologies include MMSE enhancement and spectrum smoothing in front-end and immunity learning scheme in model training. To deal with various dialectal pronunciation styles in Mandarin speech, the acoustic model is trained on multiple accented Mandarin databases. Evaluation results confirm that the proposed ASR system is robust to both background in-car noise and accent variation.

# References

1. Y. Gong, "Speech recognition in noisy environments: a survey", Speech Communication, Vol. 16, pp. 261-291, 1995.
2. S. F. Boll, "Suppression of acoustic noise in speech using spectral subtraction", IEEE Trans. Acoust. Speech and Signal Processing, Vol. ASSP-27, pp.113-120, 1979.
3. O. Viikki, D. Bye and K. Laurila, "A recursive feature vector normalization approach for robust speech recognition in noise", in Proc. Of ICASSP, 1998, pp. 733-736.
4. ETSI Standard, "Speech processing, transmission and quality aspects (STQ); Distributed speech recognition; Advanced front-end feature extraction algorithm; Compression algorithms", ETSI ES 202 050 v.1.1.1, October 2002.
5. B. Mak, Y. Tam and Q. Li, "Discriminative auditory features for robust speech recognition", in Proc. Of ICASSP, 2002, pp. 381-384.
6. M. J. F. Gales and S. J. Young, "Robust continuous speech recognition using parallel model combination", IEEE Trans. on SAP, Vol.4, No. 5, pp. 352-359, 1996.
7. P. J. Moreno, B. Raj and R. M. Stern, "A vector Taylor series approach for environment-independent speech recogntion", in Proc. Of ICASSP, 1995, pp. 733-736.
8. H. Shimodaira, N. Sakai, M. Nakai and S. Sagayama, "Jacobian joint adaptation to noise, channel and vocal tract length", in Proc. Of ICASSP, 2002, pp. 197-200.
9. Y. Ephraim and D. Malah, "Speech enhancement using a minimum mean-square error short-time spectral amplitude estimator", IEEE Trans. Acoustic, Speech, and Signal Processing, Vol. ASSP-32, pp.1109-1121, 1984.
10. Y. Takebayashi, H. Tsuboi and H. Kanazawa, "A robust speech recognition system using word-spotting with noise immunity learning", in Proc. Of ICASSP, 1991, pp. 905-908.
11. Y. Liu and P. Fung, "Acoustic and phonetic confusions in accented speech recognition", in Proc. of Eurospeech, 2005, pp.3033-3036.
12. C. Huang, E. Chang, J. Zhou, and K. Lee, "Accent modeling based on pronunciation dictionary adaptation for large vocabulary Mandarin speech recognition," in Proc. of ICSLP, 2000, pp. 818–821.
13. Y. Liu and P. Fung, "State-dependent phonetic tied mixtures with pronunciation modeling for spontaneous speech recognition", IEEE Trans. on SAP, Vol.12, No. 4, pp. 351-364, 2004.
14. Y. Zheng, R. Sproat, L. Gu, I. Shafran and etc., "Accent detection and speech recognition for Shanghai-accented Mandarin", in Proc. of Eurospeech, 2005, pp.217-220.
15. S. B. Davis and P. Mermelstein, "Comparison of parametric representations for monosyllabic word recognition in continuously spoken sentences", IEEE Trans. on ASSP, Vol.28, No. 4, pp. 357-366, 1980.
16. K. Takeda, H. Fujimura, K. Itou and et al, "Construction and evaluation of a large in-car speech corpus", IEICE Trans. Inf. & Syst., Vol. E88-D, No.3, pp. 553-561, 2005.

# GKDA: A Group-Based Key Distribution Algorithm for WiMAX MBS Security

Huijie Li[1], Guangbin Fan[2], Jigang Qiu[1], and Xiaokang Lin[3]

[1] Department of Electronic Engineering, Tsinghua Universtity, Beijing, 100084, China
[2] Intel China Research Center, Beijing, 100080, China
[3] Graduate School at Shenzhen, Tsinghua University, Shenzhen, Guangdong, 518055, China
{geolee97, qiujg03}@mails.thu.edu.cn, guangbin.fan@intel.com,
lxk-dee@tsinghua.edu.cn

**Abstract.** Multicast and Broadcast Service (MBS) is a novel application supported by the currently released IEEE 802.16e. This service can increase the efficiency of WiMAX networks. The key management and distribution is crucial to evolve MBS efficiently and safely. In this paper, we present a group-based key distribution algorithm GKDA to provide a more scalable solution to reduce the key updating overhead, therefore a base station (BS) can support and maintain more MBS users. Theoretical analyses and simulation results have proven the performance and advantage of our algorithm. In addition, GKDA can strengthen the network security.

**Keywords:** WiMAX, IEEE 802.16e, MBS, GKDA, network security.

## 1 Introduction

WiMAX [1, 2] is an emerging wireless metropolitan area network (WMAN) technology based on IEEE 802.16 standards, which provides end users an air interface to access Internet with high data rate among a large cellular area. One popular class of applications that will be widely deployed in future wireless networks is the group-oriented multimedia application, such as pay-per-view broadcasts or communal gaming. Multicast and broadcast are most appropriate to be used to support these applications because they are efficient and power-saving. Since the wireless link is a shared medium, wireless networks naturally support multicast and broadcast services. Similar to Multimedia Broadcast/Multicast Service (MBMS) [3] specified by the 3rd Generation Partnership Project (3GPP), Multicast and Broadcast Service (MBS) [4] is supported in the most recently released IEEE 802.16e.

To enable the multicast service into commercial wireless applications, well designed access admission to multicast data is needed. The problem of controlling access to multicast data requires the distribution and maintenance of the traffic encryption key used to encrypt the multicast content. In IEEE 802.16e, MBS provides users with strong protection from theft of service (ToS) across the broadcast wireless mobile network by encrypting broadcast connections between users and BSs. Multilevel keys are used to protect MBS: GTEK (group traffic encryption key) encrypts the multicast contents, GKEK (group key encryption key) encrypts GTEK, and KEK (key

Y. Zhuang et al. (Eds.): PCM 2006, LNCS 4261, pp. 310–318, 2006.
© Springer-Verlag Berlin Heidelberg 2006

encryption key) encrypts GKEK. However, only an optional multicast and broadcast rekeying algorithm, i.e. MBRA [4], is introduced in IEEE 802.16e. The detailed management mechanism to handle the user join/leave behavior has not been clarified yet. And the current scheme is inefficient when the MBS group size becomes larger.

In this paper we present a new key management mechanism which can significantly reduce the management overhead via a grouping scheme. The rest of this paper is organized as follows: section 2 reviews the MBRA algorithm in IEEE 802.16e. The new algorithm GKDA is specifically presented in section 3. Section 4 depicts the simulation modeling and analyzes the simulation results. Finally, section 5 gives a conclusion.

## 2  MBRA Algorithm

In IEEE 802.16e, MBRA is proposed to refresh traffic keying material for MBS, and it doesn't adapt to the unicast service. The MBRA overall flow is shown in Figure 1.

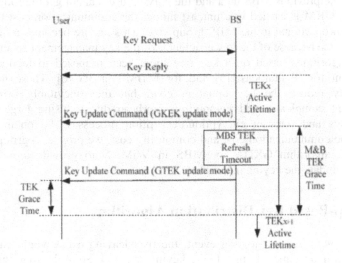

**Fig. 1.** MBRA management

A user should get the traffic keying material before it joins in a specific MBS. The initial GTEK request exchange procedure is executed by using the Key Request message (denoted as KQM) and Key Reply message (denoted as KPM) that are carried on the Primary Management connection, which is a unicast mode. Then the BS updates and distributes the traffic keying material periodically by sending two Key Update Command messages according to the *M&B TEK Grace Time* (MTGT), a parameter used to distribute the new GTEK in time.

Before MTGT starts, a BS transmits the PKMv2 Group Key Update Command message for the GKEK update mode (denoted as GKM) to each user in the MBS group to update GKEK. This message is carried on the Primary Management connection. The BS intermittently transmits this message to each user in order to reduce the BS's load in refreshing traffic key material. GKEK may be randomly generated in a BS or an ASA (authentication and service authorization) server.

After MTGT starts, a BS transmits the PKMv2 Group Key Update Command message for the GTEK update mode (denoted as GTM) carried on the broadcast connection to distribute new GTEK, which is encrypted with already transmitted GKEK, and the other traffic keying material to all users in the MBS group.

If an MBS user receives the valid two Key Update Command messages and shares new valid GKEK and GTEK with a BS before the *TEK Grace Time* (a smaller interval than MTGT maintained by the user) starts, then the user does not need to request a new set of traffic keying material. If it does not receive at least one of GKM or GTM, it sends KQM to initiate the GTEK request exchange procedure again.

MBRA uses the pushing mode instead of the pulling mode to update the keying material, and it can effectively reduce the key updating overhead. MBRA refers how to handle the user joining, but does not mention how to handle the user leaving. Generally speaking, in order to maintain a high security level, the BS should update the keying material whenever an MBS member joins or leaves, so that the joining user cannot get the previous MBS data and the leaving user cannot get the following MBS data. Since GKM is carried in a unicast mode, the communication cost to distribute GKEKs is proportional to the MBS group size. This feature becomes a bottleneck of the MBS scope because of the low efficiency of the key management scheme.

Some algorithms based on a key tree have been proposed to facilitate the key management for IP multicast [5] and for MBMS in 3G [6]. These methods can significantly reduce the key updating cost, but they inevitably bring in high management complexity and computing overhead due to using large amount of interim keys and relevant encryption/decryption processes. To obtain a balance between the communication cost and computing cost, we propose a group-based key distribution algorithm GKDA for MBS in WiMAX to provide a more scalable solution to update the keying material.

# 3 Group-Based Key Distribution Algorithm

Comparing with the user-joining event, the user-leaving event would cause a more complicated management to update the keying material. So in the following sections, we mainly address how to handle the user-leaving event and currently still use Key Request and Key Reply messages to accept new members.

## 3.1 Overview of GKDA

In GKDA, the MBS group is divided into $n$ subgroups, and $n$ GKEKs instead of one common GKEK are used for the subgroups. When a user leaves, only GKEK used in its subgroup needs to be updated. GKEK is still encrypted by the KEK of every user in the subgroup, and sent to the users in a unicast mode. But the total number of these unicast messages is significantly reduced.

The attribute *GTEK-Parameters* in GTM is lengthened, where $n$ GTEK ciphertexts encrypted by different GKEKs are filled. When GTM is broadcasted among the MBS group, every member in subgroup $i$ can recover the GTEK plaintext using the $GKEK_i$. It is assumed that each user knows which subgroup it belongs to so that it can parse the right GTEK ciphertext and decrypt it. This information may be carried in the remained field of the GKM message.

Table 1 lists the main parameters related with the performance of GKDA. In the following description and simulation, it is assumed that: 1) $Ns$ and $n$ are predefined for a certain MBS and $N = Ns{\times}n$; 2) all key management messages can be transferred successfully. For simplicity, MTGT is omitted and only $T$ is used to denote the lifetime of the keying material. Two main functions of GKDA are the subgroup management policy and the key updating policy.

**Table 1.** Main parameters used in GKDA

| Parameter | Content |
|---|---|
| $N$ | Maximum of the MBS group |
| $n$ | Maximum of the subgroup number |
| $Ns$ | Maximum of the subgroup size |
| $T$ | Inherit GKEK/GTEK lifetime |
| $\tau$ | Threshold to update keys |
| $m$ | Total number of members leaving during $\tau$ |

### 3.2 Subgroup Management

The subgroup management policy is mainly to deal with the user-grouping problem when a user joins. The performance of GKDA relies on the grouping number $n$. If $n$ is too small, then there a great deal of users in a subgroup, and the GKEK updating cost becomes large. On the other hand, if $n$ is too large, then there are few members in a subgroup and the GTEK updating cost becomes huge because the length of GTM is proportional to $n$. In fact, as an MAC management message, GTM shouldn't be too long. Therefore two different grouping modes are adopted and we will compare their performances through a series of simulations.

1. *average* mode: an MBS simultaneously maintains $n$ subgroups. When a user joins, the BS adds it into the minimum subgroup among the $n$ subgroups. In this mode, there are usually less than $Ns$ users in a subgroup.

2. *overflow* mode: when a user joins, the BS adds it into one existing subgroup whose size is still less than $Ns$. If all subgroups reach their maximum size, the BS creates a new subgroup for new users. In this mode, there are usually less than $n$ subgroups coexisting.

### 3.3 Key Updating

The key updating policy is mainly to determine the specific mechanism on how to update GKEK and GTEK. When a user leaves MBS, GKEK used in its subgroup should be updated and then GTEK is updated. If no users leave during a fairly long period that GKEK and GTEK reach their lifetimes, the keys need to be updated too. The detailed key updating procedure is:

1. Each subgroup $i$ maintains a timer $T_{ki}$ for its $GKEK_i$, and BS maintains another timer $T_t$ for GTEK.

2. After a time interval $\tau$, every subgroup checks if user-leaving events occur during this period. If yes, its $GKEK_i$ and GTEK are updated. At the same time, $T_{ki}$ and $T_t$ are reset.

3. If a $T_{ki}$ or $T_t$ is overtime, $GKEK_i$ or GTEK is updated and the timer is reset.

The value of $\tau$ is determined by the security requirement of MBS. The higher the security level requires, the smaller the value of $\tau$ is. And the key updating cost is inverse proportional to $\tau$.

### 3.4 Theoretical Analysis

Suppose that there are $n$ subgroups and $Ns$ members in each subgroup, and $m$ users leave during $\tau$ ($m \geq 1$, and $m$ is much less than $Ns$) and their leaving behaviors are totally independent. $X_1, X_2, \cdots, X_n$ are used to denote each subgroup. If no user leaves in the subgroup $i$, we define $X_i = 0$, otherwise $X_i = 1$. Thus the possibility of $X_i$ is:

$$P(X_i = 0) = (\frac{n-1}{n})^m, P(X_i = 1) = 1 - (\frac{n-1}{n})^m. \tag{1}$$

We define $E(X)$ to denote the expectation of the summation of $X_i$ ($i = 0, 1, \cdots, n$). Actually $E(X)$ represents the expectation of the total number of the subgroups where the user-leaving behavior happens. Then

$$E(X) = E(X_1 + X_2 + \cdots + X_n) = n \times E(X_1) = n \times \left[ 1 - \left(\frac{n-1}{n}\right)^m \right]. \tag{2}$$

The total key updating cost of GKDA during $\tau$ is about:

$$C_{GKDA} \approx L_{GKM} \times N_s \times E(X) + L_{GTM} + L_{TEK} \times (n-1). \tag{3}$$

$L_{GKM}$ and $L_{GTM}$ are the message lengths of GKM and GTM. $L_{TEK}$ is the length of an single extra TEK ciphertext.

We define two approaches without grouping derived from MBRA. In one approach (denoted as Simple), GKEK and GTEK are updated immediately whenever a user leaves. In another approach (denoted as Delay), GKEK and GTEK will be updated an interval $\tau$ later after the first user leaves in every round. If Simple is used, the cost is:

$$C_{Simple} \approx \left[ L_{GKM} \times N_s \times n + L_{GTM} \right] \times m. \tag{4}$$

Therefore, we get:

$$\frac{C_{GKDA}}{C_{Simple}} \approx \frac{1}{m} \left[ 1 - \left(\frac{n-1}{n}\right)^m + \frac{n}{N} \times \frac{L_{TEK}}{L_{GKM}} \right]. \tag{5}$$

From Formula (5) we can get some interesting deductions. For example, when $m = 1$,

$$\frac{C_{GKDA}}{C_{Simple}} \approx \frac{1}{n} + \frac{n}{N} \times \frac{L_{TEK}}{L_{GKM}} \propto \begin{cases} 1/n, & n \text{ is small} \\ 1/Ns, & n \text{ is large} \end{cases}. \qquad (6)$$

When $m$ is large and $n$ is small, or when $n = 1$,

$$\frac{C_{GKDA}}{C_{Simple}} \approx \frac{1}{m}\left[1 + \frac{n}{N} \times \frac{L_{TEK}}{L_{GKM}}\right]. \qquad (7)$$

Formula (7) shows in some cases, $C_{GKDA}$ becomes larger than $C_{Delay}$, because $C_{Delay} \leq C_{Simple}/m$.

## 3.5 Security Comparison

Both MBRA and GKDA use a two-level encryption mechanism to protect the distribution of the keying material: GTEK is encrypted by GKEK (Level 1) and GKEK is encrypted by KEK (Level 2). It is defined in IEEE 802.16e that the two key encryptions use the same cipher algorithm and GKEK and GTEK are updated more frequently than KEK. Therefore the most possible theft of service in MBRA is that one user might parse another user's KEK via the same GKEK. In another word, the security level of MBRA is determined by the Level 2 encryption. GKDA brings on another risk that one user may parse another user's GKEK via the same GTEK. But due to the time limitation, it is more difficult to thieve a GKEK than a KEK. Thus the security level of GKDA is also determined by the Level 2 encryption. Furthermore, in GKDA the shared scope of GKEK is smaller because of grouping. As a result, the security level of GKDA is stronger than MBRA.

## 4  Modeling and Simulation

Now we present simulations to validate the theoretical conclusions about the new key distribution schemes: the average mode (denoted as GKDA-a) and the overflow mode (denoted as GKDA-o). They are compared with Simple and Delay. As a new application, we are not aware of any existing research on data traffic for the MBS service. On the other hand, as we can imagine, the join/leave behavior of the MBS members should be similar to the IP multicast [7], and therefore we use IP multicast traffic patterns [8] in our MBS experiments. Without losing the generality, we only consider one multicast service running in the WiMAX network in our simulation scenario.

The inter-arrival time and the membership duration characterize the group join/leave behavior. We adopt the model corresponding to the real measurement of the UCB seminar in [8], where the user join/leave behavior may be modeled as a Poisson Process. We simulate an MBS session lasting for 4000 seconds. The inter-arrival time is modeled using one exponential distribution with the mean of 1 second for the first 180 seconds of the MBS session and another exponential distribution with the mean of 60 seconds for the remainder of the MBS session. The mean membership duration is set as 2700 seconds. In summary, there are much more users joining when the MBS starts, and fewer joining after the first few minutes.

Here we merely care about the communication cost related with the key distributions, so we don't count the MBS flow into the results. Only the overheads of KQM, KPM, GKM and GTM are counted in here. According to the MAC message frames defined in IEEE 802.16e, we set $L_{KQM} = 212$ $bits$, $L_{KQM} = 1592$ $bits$, $L_{GKM} = 716$ $bits$, $L_{GTM} = 412+ L_{TEK}$ ($n'$-1) $bits$. Here $n'$ denotes the number of the existing subgroups and $L_{TEK} = 128$ $bits$. In Simple and Delay, $L_{GTM} = 412$ $bits$. And we set $T = 600s$. Note that these numerical values are only probable values derived from the standard, not absolute values. But they do not affect our general conclusions.

Fig. 2 shows an overview of the performances of these four mechanisms. It is obvious that GKDA-a and GKDA-o are much better than Simple and Delay. Although there are only less than 256 users coexisting during the MBS session, the peak bandwidth of Simple can be more than 1Mb/s, so the delaying and grouping schemes are very important to enhance the scalability of MBS. The bandwidths in the first hundred seconds are much higher because the MBS size is larger during this period due to most users arriving in the first 180 seconds.

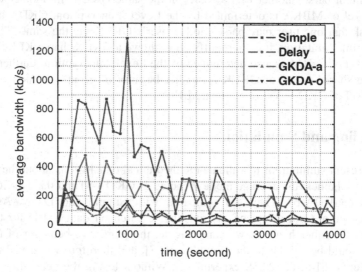

**Fig. 2.** Average bandwidth (kb/s) in four modes, for $n = 8$, $Ns = 32$ and $\tau = 20s$

Fig. 3 shows that Simple and Delay have nothing to do with $n$ because none adopts the grouping method. When $n = 1$, $C_{Delay} < C_{GKDA}$. When $n$ is small, $C_{GKDA} \propto 1/n$. The conclusions of Formula (6) and Formula (7) are verified. When $n$ is excessively large, the overhead of lengthened GTM is significant, consequently both GKDAs' performances become worse and GKDA-o is better than GKDA-a. But in a normal condition as mentioned above, $n$ is not allowed to be too large, so GKDA-a is always better than GKDA-o because it can provide more fairness.

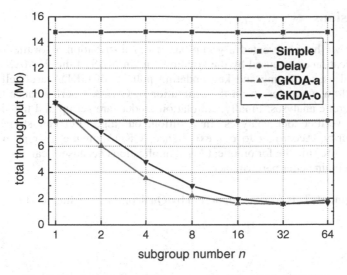

**Fig. 3.** Total throughput (Mb) *vs n*, where $Ns = 256/n$ in GKDA-o

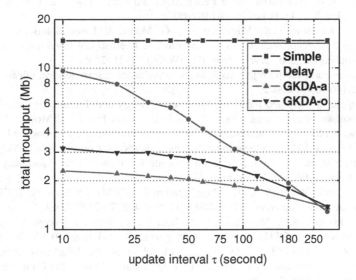

**Fig. 4.** Total throughput (Mb) *vs* $\tau$, for $n = 8$ and $Ns = 32$

Fig. 4 shows that Simple has nothing to do with $\tau$ because it doesn't adopt the delaying method. When $\tau$ becomes larger, less key updating events occur, therefore both $C_{Delay}$ and $C_{GKDA}$ drop. In the meanwhile, $m$ becomes larger and the gap between $C_{Delay}$ and $C_{GKDA}$ becomes smaller. When $\tau = 300s$, $C_{Delay} < C_{GKDA}$. This result verifies Formula (7) again. But from a security perspective, $\tau$ isn't allowed to be excessively large. Hence the performances of GKDA-a and GKDA-o will be much better than Delay and Simple in real applications.

# 5  Conclusions

In this paper we have presented a group-based key distribution algorithm to reduce the communication cost caused by the key updating in MBS of the WiMAX network. First, detailed user grouping and key updating policies of GKDA are well defined. Second, we draw a conclusion on the estimation of GKDA's performance through a series of theoretic analyses. Finally, simulation models are set up and the simulation results have verified our analyses. In addition, our algorithm can strengthen the network security. According to our experience, GKDA on the average mode, i.e. GKDA-a, is more suitable for practical MBS applications because it can provide more fairness and obtain better performance.

**Acknowledgment.** This work is supported by Qualcomm-Tsinghua joint research program.

# References

1. Ghosh, A., Wolter, D.R., Andrews, J.G., Chen, R.: Broadband Wireless Access with WiMax/802.16: Current Performance Benchmarks and Future Potential. Communications Magazine, IEEE, Vol. 43, Issue 2, 129-136. 2005.
2. Santhi, K.R., Kumaran, G.S.: Migration to 4 G: Mobile IP based Solutions. Advanced International Conference on Telecommunications and International Conference on Internet and Web Applications and Services (AICT-ICIW '06), 76-81. 2006.
3. 3rd Generation Partnership Project: Multimedia broadcast/multicast service; release 6. Tech. Rep. TS 22.146 v6.1.0. 2002.
4. IEEE Computer Society and the IEEE Microwave Theory and Techniques Society: Local and metropolitan area networks - Part 16: Air Interface for Fixed and Mobile Broadband Wireless Access Systems; Amendment 2: Physical and Medium Access Control Layers for Combined Fixed and Mobile Operation in Licensed Bands and Corrigendum 1. 2006.
5. Wong, C.K., Gouda, M., Lam, S.S.: Secure Group Communications Using Key Graphs. IEEE/ACM Transactions on Networking, Vol. 8, No. 1, 16-31. 2000.
6. Xu, W.Y., Trappe, W., Paul, S.: Key Management for 3G MBMS Security. IEEE Global Telecommunications Conference / GLOBECOM, Vol. 4, 2276-2270. 2004.
7. Sarac, K., Almeroth, K.C.: Monitoring IP Multicast in the Internet: Recent Advances and Ongoing Challenges. IEEE Communications Magazine, Vol. 43, Issue 10, 85 - 91. 2005.
8. Almeroth, K., Ammar, M.: Collecting and Modeling of the Join/Leave Behavior of Multicast Group Members in the Mbone. High Performance Distributed Computing Focus Workshop (HPDC), 209-216. 1996.

# A Watermarking Algorithm for JPEG File

Hongmei Liu[1,2], Huiying Fu[1,3], and Jiwu Huang[1,2]

[1] Dept.of Electronics and Communication, Sun Yat-sen University,
Guangzhou, 510275, P.R. China
[2] Guangdong province Key Laboratory of Information Security,
Guangzhou, 510275, P.R. China
[3] School of Electronic and Information Engineering, South China University of Technology,
Guangzhou, 510640, P.R. China
isslhm@mail.sysu.edu.cn

**Abstract.** In this paper, we propose a watermarking algorithm working directly on JPEG bit-stream. The algorithm embeds watermark bits by modifying de-quantized DC coefficients. By improving an existing embedding method for watermark bit, the quality of the watermarked image can be improved greatly while keeping the same robustness of the original method. Further more, we analyze the performance of the watermarking algorithm against re-quantization and recompression. We give the relationship among the watermarking strength, the quality factor of JPEG compression and the BER (Bit Error Rate) of the watermark. Experiment results support the analysis. Compared with several JPEG-based algorithms in literature, the robustness to JPEG recompression of the proposed algorithm is better than most of them when recompression quality factor is above 30.

**Keywords:** digital watermark, DC coefficient, quantization.

## 1 Introduction

JPEG is a common file format for digital cameras and the Internet. Although many watermark algorithms were proposed to embed digital watermarks in uncompressed images, those algorithms may not be suitable for embedding watermarks in JPEG-compressed images [1]. For existing JPEG format image, it's more practical to embed watermark in compressed domain [2]. A number of requirements, such as invisibility, recompression robustness, data capacity and computational complexity, are desirable for image watermarking in compressed domain [3]. This is also the objective of this paper.

Differential energy watermarking (DEW) algorithm in [4], which is based on partially discarding quantized DCT coefficients in the compressed image stream, is considered as one of the representative image watermark algorithms in compressed domain. Although DEW algorithm has relatively low complexity and is robust against the recompression of image bit streams, it still has several disadvantages. The performance of DEW highly depends on parameter settings. In [5], a scheme against

Y. Zhuang et al. (Eds.): PCM 2006, LNCS 4261, pp. 319–328, 2006.
© Springer-Verlag Berlin Heidelberg 2006

recompression is given. Low frequency de-quantized DCT coefficients are extracted to form an M-dimensional vector. Watermark bits are embedded by modifying this vector. This scheme is further developed in [6]. A scheme using inter-block correlation of DCT coefficients to embed watermark bits on quantized DCT coefficients are discussed in [7]. This scheme skips inverse quantization, inverse DCT transform and RGB conversion in JPEG decoding procedure. And the embedded watermarks can be detected without the original image. How to determine the threshold value is the main problem of this scheme. In [1], algorithms in [5] and [6] are improved by using a modified approach called Direct JPEG Watermarking Embedding (DJWE). Human Visual System (HVS) model is used to prioritize the DCT coefficients to achieve good visual quality.

In this paper, we propose a compressed domain watermarking algorithm worked in JPEG compressed domain. The watermark bit is embedded in de-quantized DC coefficients. By improving an existing embedding method for watermark bit [8], the quality of the watermarked image can be improved greatly while keeping the same robustness of the original method. Experiment results show that this algorithm has high capacity, good watermarked image quality, low complexity and good robustness to recompression. Compared with several JPEG-based algorithms in literature [4][7][9], the performance of the proposed algorithm is better than most of them when recompression quality factor is above 30.

The proposed algorithm is described in section 2. Section 3 analyzes the performance of the algorithm. Experimental results and discussion are shown in section 4. At the end of this paper, we draw the conclusions for our work.

## 2 The Proposed Algorithm

### 2.1 The General Scheme

The embedding process of the scheme is as follows:

1. Encode the watermarking information using error-correcting code (BCH) and get $X = \{x_j\}, j = \{0, K-1\}$, where $X$ is the BCH-coded watermark vector, and $K$ is the number of bits in $X$.
2. Partly decode the JPEG bit stream, get the de-quantized DCT coefficients of blocks, denoting by $DQ_i$. $B_i$ denotes blocks in JPEG bit stream and $i$ is its number according to its decoding order.
3. From $B_0$, embed one watermarking bit every $M$ blocks, the embedding block is denoted by $B_e$, where $e = M \times j$, where $M$ is variable and could be used for data capacity control, and $j$ is the sequence number of the watermark bit to be embedded, $j = \{0, K-1\}$. Bit $x_j$ is embedded as follows [8]:

$$\begin{cases} A'(i) = A(i) - A(i) \bmod S + \dfrac{3}{4}S, \ if \ x_j = 1. \\ A'(i) = A(i) - A(i) \bmod S + \dfrac{1}{4}S, \ if \ x_j = 0. \end{cases} \tag{1}$$

where $A(i)$ and $A'(i)$ are the absolute value of de-quantized DCT coefficient before and after embedding, respectively. $S$ is the embedding strength.

4. $A'(i)$ has the same sign as $A(i)$.

5. Repeat step 3 until all the watermark bits have been embedded.

The extraction of watermark is the inverse of embedding process, and the watermark bit is extracted as follows [8]:

$$
\begin{cases}
A'(i) \bmod S \ge \dfrac{1}{2}S, \; then \; x'_j = 1. \\[2mm]
A'(i) \bmod S < \dfrac{1}{2}S, \; then \; x'_j = 0.
\end{cases}
\tag{2}
$$

where $x'_j$ is the extracted watermark bit.

## 2.2  Improving the Watermark Bit Embedding Method in [8]

First we analyze the range of change of de-quantized DCT coefficients by watermark bit embedding method in [8]. Then we present the method to improve it. Because $A(i)$ and $S$ are integer, the range of $A(i) \bmod S$ is $[0,S-1]$. We assume $S>4$.

According to equation (1), if the watermark bit is 1 and $A(i) \bmod S$ is 0, after embedding the watermark bit, we can get a new expression $A'(i) = A(i) + 0.75{\times}S$. The change of DCT coefficient introduced by watermarking is $0.75{\times}S$. If the watermark bit is 0 and $A(i) \bmod S$ is $(S-1)$, after embedding the watermark bit, we can get a new expression $A'(i) = A(i) - (0.75{\times}S-1)$. The change of DCT coefficient introduced by watermarking is $-(0.75{\times}S-1)$. So the maximum amplitude of the change of DCT coefficient before and after watermarking is $0.75{\times}S$. When $S$ is large, it may influence the quality of the watermarked image. We propose the following adaptive method to reduce the change of DCT coefficient from $0.75{\times}S$ to $0.5{\times}S$ and improve the quality of watermarked image significantly.

The adaptive method is described as follows:
If the watermark bit is 1, the embedding method is as follows:

$$
\begin{cases}
A'(i) = A(i) - A(i) \bmod S - S + \dfrac{3}{4}S, \; if \; A(i) \bmod S < \dfrac{1}{4}S, A(i) > S. \\[2mm]
A'(i) = A(i) - A(i) \bmod S + \dfrac{3}{4}S, \quad otherwise.
\end{cases}
\tag{3}
$$

If the watermark bit is 0, the embedding method is as follows:

$$
\begin{cases}
A'(i) = A(i) - A(i) \bmod S + S + \dfrac{1}{4}S, \; if \; A(i) \bmod S > \dfrac{3}{4}S. \\[2mm]
A'(i) = A(i) - A(i) \bmod S + \dfrac{1}{4}S, \quad otherwise.
\end{cases}
\tag{4}
$$

According to equation (3) and (4), the maximum amplitude of the change of DCT coefficient before and after watermarking is close to $0.5{\times}S$. On the other hand, because the extraction of watermark bit is based on the modulus operation, add $S$ and minus $S$ in equation (3) and (4) will not affect the equation (2). We can conclude that the adaptive embedding method can improve the quality of the watermarked image while keeping the same robustness of the original method in [8].

We demonstrate the effectiveness of this adaptive scheme in Table 1, where $S$ is 50. The first column represents blocks with watermark embedded in it. Parenthesis indicates the blocks we will focus on. Comparing with its original value, $DQ_i$ in block $B_{22}$ decreases 30 after embedding a bit with method in [8], but increases 20 after embedding a bit with our adaptive method. The change of the de-quantized DCT coefficient by our method is less than by the method in [8]. But during extraction, we can get same watermark bit. Same situations also happen in block $B_{99}$ and $B_{110}$ in Table 1.

**Table 1.** The demonstration of effectiveness of compensation ($S$=50)

| Block | Original $DQ_i$ | $DQ_i$ after embedding by method in [8] | $DQ_i$ after embedding by our method |
|-------|------|-------|-------|
| $B_{22}$ | (40) | (10) | (60) |
| $B_{99}$ | (200) | (240) | (190) |
| $B_{110}$ | (190) | (160) | (210) |

We test the original algorithm in [8] and our adaptive algorithm with 100 JPEG images downloaded from Internet. With $S$ 50, average 2.7dB of PSNR increase can be observed when applying our adaptive algorithm. In Fig.1, we demonstrate the effectiveness of our algorithm in improving the quality of the watermarked image under different watermark strengths. In Fig.1, (a) is the original image; (b), (c) and (d) are the watermarked images with $S$ 200, 100 and 50 by using the original method in [8], respectively; (e), (f) and (g) are the watermarked images with $S$ 200, 100 and 50 by using our adaptive method, respectively; (h),(i) and (j) are the zoomed parts (the rectangles) of (b),(c) and (d), respectively; (k),(l) and (m) are the zoomed parts (the rectangles) of (e),(f) and (g), respectively. We can see that by applying our adaptive method, the subjective and objective quality of the watermarked image can be improved greatly. We can get the following conclusion: under the same requirement of invisibility, our algorithm can have stronger watermark and better robustness than the original algorithm.

## 3   Performance Analysis

For the proposed algorithm, we know that the watermark suffers from re-quantization when the watermarked DC coefficients are written back to the compressed bit-stream. The watermark may also suffer from re-compression. In order to study the performance of the watermarking algorithm, the possible distortions of re-quantization and re-compression are discussed in this section.

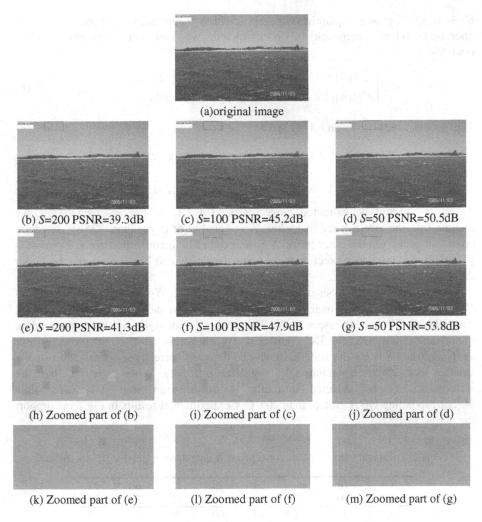

(a)original image

(b) $S$=200 PSNR=39.3dB

(c) $S$=100 PSNR=45.2dB

(d) $S$=50 PSNR=50.5dB

(e) $S$ =200 PSNR=41.3dB

(f) $S$=100 PSNR=47.9dB

(g) $S$ =50 PSNR=53.8dB

(h) Zoomed part of (b)

(i) Zoomed part of (c)

(j) Zoomed part of (d)

(k) Zoomed part of (e)

(l) Zoomed part of (f)

(m) Zoomed part of (g)

**Fig. 1.** Demonstration of compensation

## 3.1  Re-quantization

After embedding watermark, modified de-quantized DCT coefficients are re-quantized when written back to bit-stream. Re-quantization may induce detection error of watermark.

For convenience, we can rewrite equation (1):

$$\begin{cases} A'(i) =0.75\times S+N1\times S \, , \, if \quad x_i =1 \, . \\ A'(i) =0.25\times S+N1\times S \, , \, if \quad x_i =0 \, . \end{cases} \tag{5}$$

where N1 is an integer. Re-quantized DCT coefficient is $[(0.75\times S+N1\times S)/Q1]$ when embedded watermark bit is 1, and is $[(0.25\times S+N1\times S)/Q1]$ when embedded watermark bit is 0. Q1 represents quantization step in JPEG compression, [] represents round operation. When watermark bit is extracted, we first get de-quantized DCT coefficient:

$$\begin{cases} A^*(i) = [(0.75 \times S + N1 \times S)/Q1] \times Q1 \ , \ if \ x_i = 1 \ . \\ A^*(i) = [(0.25 \times S + N1 \times S)/Q1] \times Q1 \ , \ if \ x_i = 0 \ . \end{cases} \tag{6}$$

The error between $A'(i)$ and $A^*(i)$ is:

$$\Delta = \left| A^*(i) - A'(i) \right| = \left| [(0.75 \times S + N1 \times S)/Q1] \times Q1 - (0.75 \times S + N1 \times S) \right| \tag{7}$$

By Equations (2) we know that if $\Delta = \left| A^*(i) - A'(i) \right| \notin (k \times S - S/4, k \times S + S/4)$ , the watermark cannot be extracted correctly, $k=\{0,1,2,3...\}$. For re-quantization, we assume $k=0$, then we can see that when $\Delta$ is equal to or larger than $0.25 \times S$, detection error will occur. On the other hand, $\Delta$ is introduced by quantization error, its range is [0, Q1/2]. In order to protect $\Delta$ from being larger than $0.25 \times S$, $S$ should be larger than $2 \times Q1$.

We test the above analysis on Lena image (512x512). We embedded watermark in JPEG compressed Lena images with quality factors list in Table 2. The watermark strengths are 50 and 80, respectively. The quality factor (QF) and its corresponding quantization step (QS) for DC coefficient are shown in table 2. According to our analysis, when $S$ is 50, the watermark can be detected correctly if quantization step is smaller than 25(corresponding QF is greater than 32). When $S$ is 80, then the watermark can be detected correctly if quantization step is smaller than 40(corresponding QF is greater than 20). Our experimental results in Fig.2 (a) support the above analysis.

**Table 2.** The quality factor and its corresponding quantization step for DC coefficient

| QF | 10 | 15 | 20 | 22 | 25 | 30 | 32 |
|----|----|----|----|----|----|----|----|
| QS | 80 | 53 | 40 | 36 | 32 | 27 | 25 |
| QF | 35 | 40 | 50 | 60 | 70 | 80 | 90 |
| QS | 23 | 20 | 16 | 12 | 10 | 6 | 3 |

## 3.2 Re-compression

If watermarked JPEG compressed image with quality factor $QF_1$(quantization step is Q1) is recompressed by JPEG with $QF_2$, we consider the relationship among BER, $S$ and $QF_2$ (quantization step is Q2). We assume that $S$ is larger than $2QF_1$ according to the analysis in section 3.1.

When watermark bit is extracted from re-compressed image, we first get de-quantized DCT coefficient:

$$A^{**}(i) = [A^*(i)/Q2] \times Q2 \tag{8}$$

The error between $A'(i)$ and $A^{**}(i)$ is:

$$\Delta^* = \left| A^{**}(i) - A'(i) \right| \qquad (9)$$

If Q2 is equal to Q1, according to Equations (6), (8) and (9), we can get $\Delta^* \approx \Delta$, BERs of recompression are similar to BERs of re-quantization. We embed watermark in 512x512 Lena image with QF 50 and $S$ 50. According to the above analysis, recompress the watermarked image with QF 50, BER of watermark will be 0. We recompress the image with QF 60, 50, 40, BERs of detected watermark before recompression are 0, 0, 0 and BERs of detected watermark after recompression are 10.3%, 0, and 10.6%.

If Q2 is not equal to Q1, we find in our extensive experiments that BER of recompression is low when $S$ is larger than 2.5xQ2. The experiments results of Lena image are shown in Fig 2(b), where QF1 is 50, and S are 50 and 80, respectively. The recompression QF is from 10 to 90 (step is 10). From Fig 2(b), we can see that if Q2 is smaller than 20 (QF is 40), BER is low for $S$ 50. And if Q2 is smaller than 32 (QF is 25), BER is low for $S$ 80.

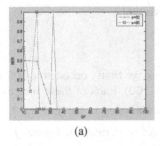    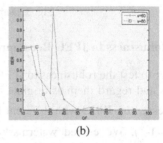

(a)                                      (b)

**Fig. 2.** BERs for re-quantization and recompression

# 4   Experimental Results and Discussion

By applying our adaptive method during embedding process, we test the algorithm with 100 JPEG images downloaded from Internet. The images have different sizes and contents. The watermark is embedded in Y component only. We embed one bit every $M$ block. The larger value $M$ takes, the fewer coefficients will be changed and thus the better invisibility will be obtained. The larger value $M$ takes, the fewer watermark bits may be embedded. In our experiments, $M$ is set as 10. The parameter $S$ controls the robustness and invisibility of the watermark. The larger $S$ will produce the more robust watermark and the more visual decrease in the watermarked image. In the following experiments and comparisons, $S$ is set as 50.

## 4.1   Invisibility

We compare the original image and the watermarked image by putting them together in Fig. 3. We can see that visual degradation is imperceptible.

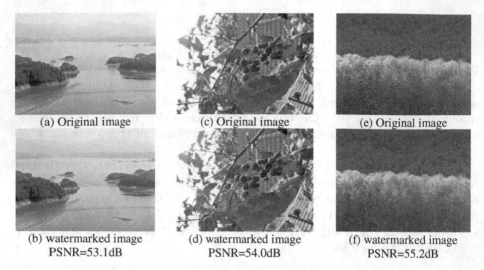

(a) Original image          (c) Original image          (e) Original image

(b) watermarked image       (d) watermarked image       (f) watermarked image
   PSNR=53.1dB                  PSNR=54.0dB                 PSNR=55.2dB

**Fig. 3.** Demonstration of invisibility

## 4.2  Robustness to JPEG Recompression

In order to test the robustness to JPEG recompression, we firstly decode the 100 JPEG images and regard them as original images $f_i$ ($i$ =1-100). Each of these images $f_i$ is compressed by JPEG with different QF from 40 to 100 (step is 10) and get $f_{ij}$ ($i$=1-100, $j$=1-7). We embed watermark into $f_{ij}$ and get watermarked image $f'_{ij}$. The watermarked image $f'_{ij}$ is recompressed by JPEG with different QF from 10 to 100 (step is 10) and get $f'_{ijk}$ ($i$=1-100, $j$=1-7, $k$=1-10). We detect watermark from $f'_{ijk}$ and the average bit error rate of watermark is shown in Fig. 4. Each line represents a group of images with the same original quality factor. X-axis represents the QF used in recompressing the watermarked image. Y-axis represents average BER. The left and right figures in Fig.4 are the BERs before and after BCH decoding, respectively. From Fig.4, we can see that watermark is robust when recompression QF is higher than 30.

## 4.3  Comparison

We compare the recompression robustness of the proposed algorithm with DEW algorithm proposed in [4] in Fig 5(a), where X-axis is the recompressed QF and Y-axis is the BER of watermark. From Fig.5(a), we can see that the performance of the proposed algorithm is close to that of DEW algorithm using optimized settings, and much better than that of DEW algorithm using not-optimized settings. Compared with DEW algorithm using optimized settings, the proposed algorithm has lower complexity and more data capacity.

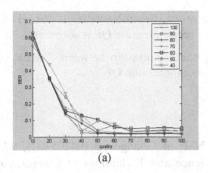
(a)

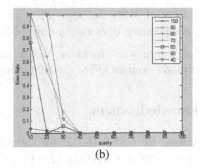
(b)

**Fig. 4.** Average BER after JPEG recompression

We also compare the proposed method with FRW (fast and robust watermarking) algorithm proposed in [9] and the ICW (inter-block correlation watermark) algorithm proposed in [7]. The results are shown in Fig 5(b) and 5(c) respectively, where X-axis is the recompressed QF and Y-axis is the similarity between the original watermark and extracted watermark. The higher the similarity is, the better the robustness is. From Fig.5 (b), we can see that the performance of the proposed algorithm is much better than that of FRW algorithm when quality factor is above 30 and is not as good as FRW algorithm when quality factor is below 30. We think it's more important to have better performance when QF is higher. From Fig 5(c), we can see in that the performance of the proposed algorithm is much better than that of ICW algorithm.

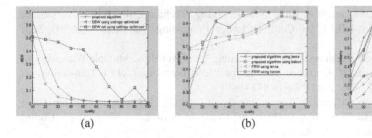
(a)                          (b)                          (c)

**Fig. 5.** Comparison with DEW[4], FRW[9] and ICW[7] algorithm

## 5   Conclusion

The contributions of this paper are as follows:

1. Improve the embedding method in [8]. The quality of the watermarked image can be improved greatly while keeping the same robustness as the original method.
2. Propose an image watermarking algorithm in JPEG compressed domain based on the above embedding method. The algorithm has a low computational complexity and suitable for real-time watermarking; has good quality of watermarked image; has a variable data capacity controlled by $M$ (a parameter of the algorithm).

Compared with the algorithms in the literature, the robustness to the JPEG recompression of our algorithm is better when recompression QF is above 30.

Our future work includes further analyzing the relationship between $S$, BER of watermark, original QF of the JPEG image and recompression QF.

## Acknowledgement

Supported by NSFC (60325208, 90604008), NSF of Guangdong (04205407), 973 Program （2006CB303104), Key Project of Science and Technology of Guangzhou, China (2005Z3-D0391).

## References

1. H.Peter W. Wong, A.Chang, O.-C. Au, "On improving the iterative watermark embedding technique for JPEG-to-JPEG watermarking", In Proc. of ISCAS'04, 2(2): 161-164, May 2004.
2. H. Liu, F.Shao, J. Huang, "A MPEG-2 Video Watermarking Algorithm with Compensation in Bit Stream",
3. C.I. Podilchuk, E.J. Delp, "Digital Watermarking Algorithms and Applications", IEEE Signal Processing Magazine, July 2001, pp. 33-46.
4. G. C. Langelaar, R.L.Lagendijk, "Optimal Differential Energy Watermarking of DCT Encoded Image and Video", IEEE Transactions on Image Processing, Jan. 2001, 10(1): 148-158.
5. P.H.W. Wong, O.C. Au, "A Blind Watermarking Technique in JPEG Compressed Domain", in Proc. of IEEE Int. Conf. on Image Processing, vol. 3, pp. 497-500, Sept. 2002.
6. P.H.W. Wong, Oscar C. Au and Gene Y.M. Yeung, "A Novel Blind Multiple Watermarking Technique for Images", Circuits and Systems for Video Technology, IEEE Transactions on, Volume 13, Issue 8, Aug. 2003 Page(s): 813 – 830
7. Y. Choi, K. Aizawa, "Digital Watermarking using Inter-Block Correlation: Extension to JPEG Coded Domain", in Proc. of IEEE Int. Conf. on Information Technology: Coding and Computing, pp.133-138, Mar. 2000.
8. M.-J. Tsai, K.Yu, Y.Chen, "Joint wavelet and spatial transformation for digital watermarking", IEEE Transactions on Consumer Electronics, Volume 46, Issue 1, Feb. 2000 Page(s):237
9. W. Luoay, G. L. Heilemana, C. E. Pizanob, "Fast and Robust Watermarking of JPEG Files", In Proceedings. Of Fifth IEEE Southwest Symposium on Image Analysis and Interpretation: 158-162, 2002.
10. G. K. Wallace, "The Jpeg Still Picture Compression Standard", IEEE Transactions on Consumer Electronics, 38(1): xviii-xxxiv, Feb. 1992.

# SNR Scalability in H.264/AVC Using Data Partitioning

Stefaan Mys[1], Peter Lambert[1], Wesley De Neve[1],
Piet Verhoeve[2], and Rik Van de Walle[1]

[1] Ghent University – IBBT
Department of Electronics and Information Systems – Multimedia Lab
Gaston Crommenlaan 8 bus 201, B-9000 Ghent, Belgium
{stefaan.mys, peter.lambert, wesley.deneve, rik.vandewalle}@ugent.be
http://www.multimedialab.be
[2] Televic NV,
Leo Bekaertlaan 1, B-8870 Izegem, Belgium
p.verhoeve@televic.com
http://www.televic.com

**Abstract.** Although no scalability is explicitly defined in the H.264/AVC specification, some forms of scalability can be achieved by using the available coding tools in a creative way. In this paper we will explain how to use the data partitioning tool to perform a coarse form of SNR scalability. The impact of various parameters, including the presence of IDR frames and the number of intra-coded macroblocks per frame, on bit rate and bit rate savings and on quality and quality loss will be discussed. Furthermore we will introduce and elaborate a possible use case for the technique proposed in this paper.

**Keywords:** data partitioning, H.264/AVC, scalability, SNR scalability.

## 1 Introduction

The rapidly increasing number of broadband Internet connections allows more and more people to enjoy a wide range of multimedia applications on the Internet. However, although most broadband Internet providers offer enough download capacity to comfortably allow the use of these multimedia applications, upload capacity often is limited. As a result, while *consuming* multimedia applications is feasible for home users, functioning as multimedia content *provider* still remains difficult. However, some applications, e.g., video conferencing, need to be able to function as content provider as well as consumer.

H.264/MPEG-4 Part 10 Advanced Video Coding (H.264/AVC) allows us to encode video at very low rates while still offering acceptable quality [1]. Besides the high coding efficiency, H.264/AVC also comes with a number of additional coding tools, such as Flexible Macroblock Ordering (FMO) [2] and data partitioning [3], two important error resilience tools.

Y. Zhuang et al. (Eds.): PCM 2006, LNCS 4261, pp. 329–338, 2006.

Although no scalability is explicitly defined in the H.264/AVC specification, some forms of scalability can be achieved by using the available coding tools in a creative way [4]. Temporal scalability can be achieved by using hierarchical coding patterns to obtain multi-layered bitstreams [5]. FMO can be used to exploit Region of Interest (ROI) scalability [6].

In this paper we will discuss how we can use data partitioning to obtain a coarse form of SNR scalability. The influence of Instantaneous Decoding Refresh (IDR) pictures, the number of intra-coded macroblocks and the amount of data removed from the bitstream will be investigated in terms of bit rate savings and visual quality loss.

We would like to stress that we do not have the intention to provide an alternative to explicit scalable video codecs, such as the Joint Scalable Video Model (JSVM) currently under development by the Joint Video Team (JVT) [7]. Instead, we are looking for a quick and low-complexity solution that uses, albeit slightly differently than intended, only technologies that are currently available on the market.

This paper is organized as follows. First, in Sect. 2, an in depth overview of the data partitioning tool as defined in the H.264/AVC specification is given. Next, we present a typical use case in Sect. 3. Section 4 contains the results of various experiments. Finally the conclusion of this paper is given in Sect. 5.

## 2    Data Partitioning in H.264/AVC

In H.264/AVC a clear distinction is made between the Video Coding Layer (VCL) and the Network Abstraction Layer (NAL) of the standard. Normally, each slice is separately encoded in the VCL, and then put into a syntactic structure in the NAL, called a NAL Unit (NALU). Such a NALU consists of a one-byte NAL header followed by payload data. In the header, nal_unit_type specifies the type of the NALU and nal_ref_idc can be used to signal the importance of the NALU to the network. When using data partitioning, however, the coded data of each slice is split up into three partitions and each partition is put into a separate NALU. The following partitioning is defined in the specification:

**partition A** contains the slice header, macroblock types, quantization parameters, prediction modes, and motion vectors;
**partition B** contains the residual information of intra-coded macroblocks;
**partition C** contains the residual information of inter-coded macroblocks.

One can easily understand that the information contained in partitions B and C is useless if the corresponding partition A is not present. However, even when partitions B and C are missing, the information in partition A can still be used for error concealment purposes at the decoder.

Two dependencies exist between partitions B and C. First of all, many of the intra prediction modes use pixels from neighboring macroblocks to predict the current macroblock. This possibly makes intra-coded macroblocks dependent on neighboring inter-coded macroblocks for decoding. This dependency can be avoided by using a special option: *constrained intra prediction*. Constrained intra prediction restricts the encoder to use only residual data and decoded samples from other *intra-coded* macroblocks for intra prediction.

A second dependency can be found in the Context-based Adaptive Variable Length Coding (CAVLC). CAVLC uses the number of non-zero transform coefficients in neighboring macroblocks for parsing the number of non-zero transform coefficients in the current macroblock. This introduces a possible dependency between neighboring inter-coded and intra-coded macroblocks. When constrained intra prediction is enabled, the total number of non-zero transform coefficients in neigboring macroblocks that are inter-coded is considered equal to zero when decoding an intra-coded macroblock. Thus, constrained intra prediction removes both dependencies from intra-coded macroblocks on inter-coded macroblocks, making decoding partition B independent of the presence of the corresponding partition C. However, no option exists to make the decoding of partition C independent of partition B. Thus, to conclude, partition A is independent of partitions B and C, and using constrained intra prediction makes partition B independent of partition C.

The goal of data partitioning is to be used as an error resilience tool for the transmission of coded video over channels that allow selective protection of the different partitions. This kind of channels could be implemented, for example, using increased error protection or using a differentiated network such as Diffserv [8]. Obviously, video quality will be optimal if the most important partitions (i.e., A and B) are the better protected ones.

To conclude this section we mention another option in the JVT reference encoder. *Random Intra Macroblock Refresh* (IMBR) forces the encoder to insert a given number of intra-coded macroblocks in P or B slice coded pictures. For example, when IMBR is set equal to 10, besides the macroblocks for which the mode decision algorithm had decided to use intra prediction, at least 10 randomly chosen macroblocks per picture will be intra coded.

# 3  Use Case

The use case we consider in this paper is one of the many possible network-based multimedia applications, namely video conferencing. Note that a video conference can serve for business as well as private purposes. Three important remarks can be made in the context of this use case. Firstly, video conferencing requires low latency. This means that only a very small buffer can be used to store the downloaded video before playing it.

Secondly, although most broadband Internet providers offer enough download capacity to allow video conferencing, often the available upload capacity is still limited. For example, Belgian broadband providers typically offer upload capacities between 128 and 256 kilobits per second.

Finally, note that it is likely that the full upload capacity will not be available all the time. For example, if we want to send a file to our conversation partner, this data transfer will use some of the available upload capacity. This will result in temporarily less bandwidth available to transmit the video images.

Considering these three remarks, we are looking for a way to allow the sender of a video stream to very quickly react to changes in the available upload capacity by adapting the bit rate. One possibility would be to change the settings in the encoder and encode at a different target bit rate. However, dynamically changing the target bit rate might not be possible for some hardware encoders.

Another possibility would be using SNR transcoding to reduce the bit rate at which the video was originally encoded. However, this is a complex and computational expensive solution, and therefore not what we are looking for.

Instead we propose an alternative solution for reducing the bit rate, based on dropping less important parts of the video sequence. To be more precise, in order to decrease the bit rate, we remove C and/or B partitions from the bit stream. This removal can be done very quickly, since we only need to know the type of a NALU – as indicated in its header – to decide whether or not to remove that NALU.

Instead of exploiting SNR scalability, we might also exploit temporal scalability as discussed in [5]. Low frame rates however may cause bad lip synchronization, which has a very negative impact on the user experience.

## 4    Experimental Results

### 4.1    General Remarks

Considering the video conferencing use case, we have chosen test sequences with little or no camera and background movement and little to moderate foreground movement, in particular Akiyo and Silent. Because low bit rates are required, we used a QCIF resolution and a frame rate of 15 frames per second. In order to keep the encoding speed high and preserve low latency, we used no B slices and only one reference frame for inter prediction. Furthermore we used a fixed number of 33 macroblocks per slice, resulting in three slices per picture. Data partitioning and constrained intra prediction were of course enabled, as was rate-distortion optimization.

We chose a target bit rate of 256 kbits/s. Following the methodology described in [9], the initial quantisation parameter was set equal to 10. Each sequence was encoded once with an IDR frame period of 25 frames, and once with only one IDR frame at the beginning of the sequence. Also we encoded each sequence once with each of the following IMBR values: 0, 5 and 10. Each of the resulting sequences can be scaled down to several lower quality versions by removing all or some partitions from the bitstream. We introduce the following notation (with $n$ being a natural number): $n$C (resp. $n$B) stands for the sequence scaled down by removing the C (resp. B and C) partitions from 1 out of $n$ frames. So 1C is the sequence after removing all C partitions, 2B is the sequence after removing the B and C partitions from each even frame, etc... Note that IDR frames are never split up into data partitions, and thus no data is ever removed from IDR frames.

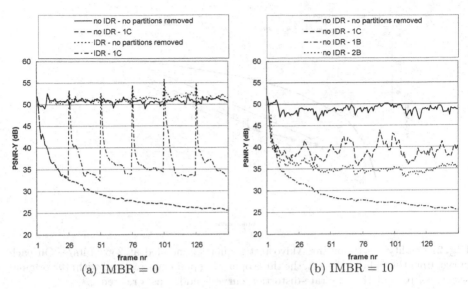

**Fig. 1.** PSNR per frame for the Akiyo sequence encoded at 256 kbits/s. 'IDR' means one IDR frame is inserted every 25 frames; 'no IDR' means only the first frame is an IDR frame.

At the decoder, error concealment must be applied in order to minimize the visible errors due to the removal of partitions from the bitstream. We use a very basic error concealment scheme: when the decoder detects a missing C partition, the residual information for inter-coded macroblocks is assumed to be zero, but besides that the frame is decoded as usual. When the B partition is also missing, intra-coded macroblocks are copied from the previous frame. Inter-coded macroblocks are still decoded as usual (i.e. using motion-compensated prediction), except for the residue, which is assumed to be zero.

### 4.2  Impact of Various Parameters

**Stopping error propagation.** In Fig. 1(a) we see that without using IDR frames, removing all C partitions results in a continuous decrease of the quality of the video. This is caused by the fact that at no point in time the decoder is able to recover from the loss of data. This makes the average quality of the sequence proportional with its length. This is very undesirable, since it means that the quality of the video will inevitably become unacceptable after a certain time.

We examine two possible solutions for this problem. First of all, we can use IDR frames on a regular basis. Since IDR frames are not split up into data partitions, no data is ever removed from the IDR frames. This allows the decoder to recover from previous loss at every IDR frame. Because of that, the average quality of the sequence is no longer dependent on the length of the sequence, but rather on the distance between IDR frames.

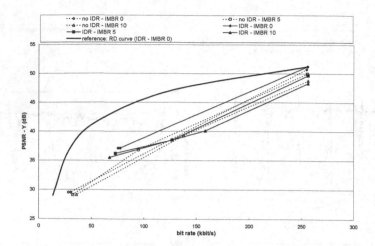

**Fig. 2.** Quality layers for the Akiyo test sequence, encoded at 256 kbits/s. On each curve, from the right to the left, the three operating points correspond with: the original sequence, 1C and 1B. The rate-distortion curve is added as a reference.

**Table 1.** Some interpretations of the charts in Fig. 2

| | using higher IMBR values means | using IDR frames means |
|---|---|---|
| full quality | worse quality | slightly worse quality |
| | more or less the same bit rate | more or less the same bit rate |
| 1C | better quality | slightly better quality |
| | higher bit rates | higher bit rates |
| 1B | slightly worse quality | better quality |
| | slightly lower bit rates | higher rates |

A second possible solution is forcing the encoder to use extra intra-coded macroblocks (Fig. 1(b)). These macroblocks will allow the decoder to recover from the errors caused by the removal of C partitions. However, they do not offer a solution in case we also remove B partitions from the bitstream. Therefore, we could choose not to remove B partitions from every frame, but only from every second frame. This way, the decoder can recover from the loss of data in the frames where no partitions are lost.

**Impact of IDR frames and intra macroblocks.** Table 1 summarizes some characteristics of the charts plotted in Fig. 2. When we increase the IMBR value, and thus the number of intra-coded macroblocks, more information is contained in B partitions and less in C partitions. Therefore, removing C partitions will result in less reduction of the bit rate and quality. The opposite holds true for B partitions. Forcing the encoder to use extra intra-coded macroblocks will result in slightly worse quality of the original sequence, since the encoder is forced to make sub-optimal mode decisions. However, an important advantage of forcing

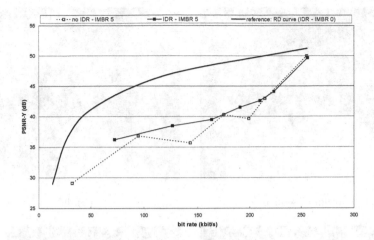

**Fig. 3.** Quality layers for the Akiyo test sequence, encoded at 256 kbits/s. On each curve, from the right to the left, the operating points correspond with: the original sequence, 4C, 4B, 2C, 2B, 1C and 1B. The rate-distortion curve is added as a reference.

intra-coded macroblocks is that the difference between 1C and 1B increases. This means that a wider range of bit rates can be extracted from the original sequence. We conclude that it is good to enforce some intra-coded macroblocks at the encoder. Experiments have shown that values between 5 and 10 percent of the number of macroblocks per frame are good values for sequences with little to moderate movement.

Considering the choice whether or not to use IDR frames, again pros and cons balance each other out when looking at lower quality layers (1C and 1B). An important advantage on using IDR frames is that they keep the quality of the sequences acceptable – and not continuously decreasing over time as discussed above – even when removing all B and C partitions. Therefore we choose to use IDR frames notwithstanding the decrease in quality of the original sequence they cause.

**Impact of the number of partitions that are removed.** Figure 3 shows that we can achieve a finer granularity by removing partitions not from every frame but only from some of them. Remark that in general removing C partitions gives better results than removing B partitions. In the case 'no IDR - IMBR 5' 2C and 1C even have both lower bit rate and higher quality than respectively 4B and 2B, which certainly make them the better options. In Fig. 5 we see that for the Silent test sequence this is even true for both cases. We conclude that we will only remove B partitions (in addition to the C partitions) if we want to obtain the lowest possible bit rate. All B and C partitions will be removed in that case. Some representative screenshots for the Akiyo and Silent test sequences are shown in respectively Fig. 4 and Fig. 6.

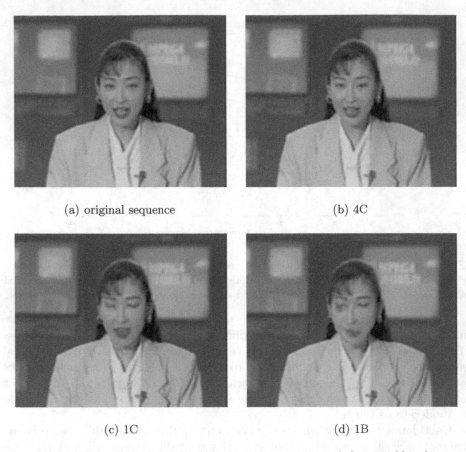

(a) original sequence                    (b) 4C

(c) 1C                                    (d) 1B

**Fig. 4.** Screenshots from the Akiyo test sequence, encoded at 256 kbits/s

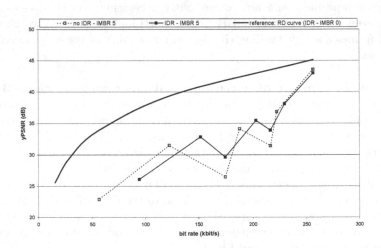

**Fig. 5.** Quality layers for the Silent test sequence, encoded at 256 kbits/s. On each curve, from the right to the left, the operating points correspond with: the original sequence, 4C, 4B, 2C, 2B, 1C and 1B. The rate-distortion curve is added as a reference.

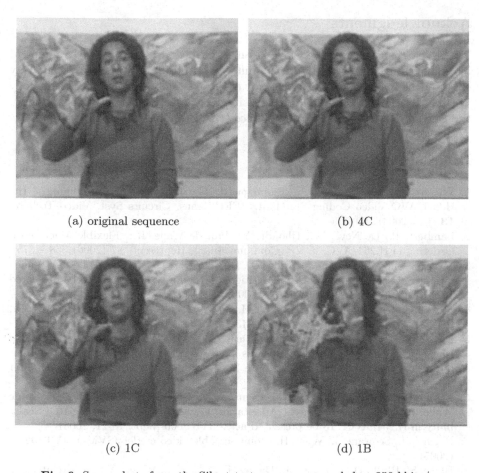

(a) original sequence                    (b) 4C

(c) 1C                                   (d) 1B

**Fig. 6.** Screenshots from the Silent test sequence, encoded at 256 kbits/s

Note that the adaptation engine can decide how many partitions to remove based on the currently available upload capacity and on information about the sizes of the different partitions extracted by the encoder.

## 5   Conclusion

In this paper we introduced a way to achieve a coarse form of SNR scalability in H.264/AVC using the data partitioning tool. Several experiments were conducted to investigate the influence of IDR frames and the number of intra-coded macroblocks on bit rate and quality of the video sequence. Results of those experiments led to the decision to use periodic IDR frames and force 5 to 10 percent of the macroblocks in a frame to be intra coded. Furthermore a possible use case for this form of scalability was introduced and elaborated in this paper.

## Acknowledgments

The research activities that have been described in this paper were funded by Ghent University, the Interdisciplinary Institute for Broadband Technology (IBBT), the Institute for the Promotion of Innovation by Science and Technology in Flanders (IWT), the Fund for Scientific Research-Flanders (FWO-Flanders), the Belgian Federal Science Policy Office (BFSPO), and the European Union.

## References

1. Wiegand, T., Sullivan, G.J., Bjontegaard, G., Luthra, A.:  Overview of the H.264/AVC Video Coding Standard. IEEE Trans. Circuits Syst. Video Technol. **13** (july 2003) 560–576
2. Lambert, P., De Neve, W., Dhondt, Y., Van de Walle, R.:  Flexible Macroblock Ordering in H.264/AVC. J. Vis. Commun. Image Represent. **17** (2006) 358 – 375
3. Mys, S., Dhondt, Y., Van de Walle, D., De Schrijver, D., Van de Walle, R.: A Performance Evaluation of the Data Partitioning Tool in H.264/AVC. To be presented at SPIE Optics East 2006 (Oct. 1-4, 2006)
4. Stockhammer, T., Hannuksela, M.M.: H.264/AVC Video for Wireless Transmission. IEEE Wireless Commun. **12** (2005) 6–13
5. De Neve, W., Van Deursen, D., De Schrijver, D., De Wolf, K., Van de Walle, R.: Using Bitstream Structure Descriptions for the Exploitation of Multi-layered Temporal Scalability in H.264/AVC's Base Specification. Lecture Notes in Computer Science **3767** (2005) 641–652
6. Lambert, P., De Schrijver, D., Van Deursen, D., De Neve, W., Dhondt, Y., Van de Walle, R.: A Real-time Content Adaptation Framework for Exploiting ROI Scalability in H.264/AVC. To be presented at ACIVS 2006 (Sept. 18-21, 2006)
7. Reichel, J., Schwarz, J., Wien, H.: Joint scalable video model JSVM-4. JVT-Q202. (2005)
8. Blake, S., Black, D., Carlson, M., Davies, E., Wang, Z., Weiss, W.: An Architecture for Differentiated Services. RFC 2475. IETF (Dec. 1998)
9. Kim, J., Kim, S., Ho, Y.: A Frame-Layer Rate Control Algorithm for H.264 Using Rate-Dependent Mode Selection. Lecture Notes in Computer Science **3768** (2005) 477–488

# A Real-Time XML-Based Adaptation System for Scalable Video Formats

Davy Van Deursen, Davy De Schrijver, Wesley De Neve, and Rik Van de Walle

Ghent University – IBBT
Department of Electronics and Information Systems – Multimedia Lab
Gaston Crommenlaan 8 bus 201, B-9050 Ledeberg-Ghent, Belgium
{davy.vandeursen, davy.deschrijver, wesley.deneve,
rik.vandewalle}@ugent.be
http://multimedialab.elis.ugent.be

**Abstract.** Scalable bitstreams are used today to contribute to the Universal Multimedia Access (UMA) philosophy, i.e., accessing multimedia anywhere, at anytime, and on any device. Bitstream structure description languages provide means to adapt scalable bitstreams in order to extract a lower quality version. This paper introduces a real-time XML-based framework for content adaptation by relying on BFlavor, a combination of two existing bitstream structure description languages (i.e., the MPEG-21 Bitstream Syntax Description Language (BSDL) and the Formal Language for Audio-Visual Representation extended with XML features (XFlavor)). In order to use BFlavor with state-of-the-art media formats, we have added support for transparent retrieval of context information and support for emulation prevention bytes. These extensions are validated by building a BFlavor code for bitstreams compliant with the scalable extension of the H.264/AVC specification. Performance measurements show that such a bitstream (containing a bitrate of 17 MBit/s) can be adapted in real-time by a BFlavor-based adaptation framework (with a speed of 27 MBit/s).

**Keywords:** BFlavor, content adaptation, H.264/AVC Scalable Video Coding.

## 1 Introduction

People want to access their multimedia content anywhere, at anytime, and on any device. This phenomenon is generally known as Universal Multimedia Access (UMA) [1]. However, the huge heterogeneity in multimedia formats, network technologies, and end-user devices causes problems for content providers. They want to create their content once whereupon they can distribute it to every possible end-user device using every possible network technology. Scalable video coding is a solution for this multimedia diversity problem. It enables the extraction of multiple (lower quality) versions of the same multimedia resource without the need for a complete encode-decode process.

The use of scalable bitstreams implies the need of an adaptation system in order to extract lower quality versions. To support multiple scalable bitstream

Y. Zhuang et al. (Eds.): PCM 2006, LNCS 4261, pp. 339–348, 2006.

formats, a generic approach is needed for the adaptation of these scalable bit-streams. As explained in [2], bitstream structure description languages can be used to build an adaptation system which supports multiple bitstream formats and which can easily be extended for new bitstream formats. A Bitstream Structure Description (BSD), which is typically an XML document containing information about the high-level structure (information about packets, headers, or layers of data) of a bitstream, is generated by a bitstream-to-BSD parser. According to a given set of constraints, the BSD is transformed, resulting in a customized BSD. Because of the high-level nature of the BSD, only a limited knowledge about the structure of a bitstream is required to perform this transformation. Based on an adapted version of the BSD, an adapted bitstream is created with a BSD-to-bitstream parser.

In this paper, special attention is paid to the BSD generation process, which needs the most computations. In Sect. 2, we introduce BFlavor, a new description tool that harmonizes two existing bitstream structure description languages. Section 3 elaborates on some extensions for BFlavor in order to fulfil the short-comings of the previous version of BFlavor. This enables the creation of a BFlavor code for H.264/AVC's scalable extension which is discussed in Sect. 4. Finally, the conclusions are drawn in Sect. 5.

## 2    Using BFlavor to Describe Bitstreams

In this paper, we use BFlavor (BSDL + XFlavor) to create BSDs. BFlavor is a combination of two existing technologies for generating bitstream structure descriptions (i.e., the MPEG-21 Bitstream Syntax Description Language (MPEG-21 BSDL) and the Formal Language for Audio-Visual Representation extended with XML features (XFlavor)).

### 2.1    MPEG-21 BSDL and XFlavor

MPEG-21 BSDL is a tool of part 7 (Digital Item Adaptation, DIA) of the MPEG-21 specification. It is built on top of the World Wide Web Consortium's (W3C) XML Schema Language and is able to describe the structure of a (scalable) bit-stream in XML format [3]. The Bitstream Syntax Schema (BS Schema), which contains the structure of a certain media format, is used by MPEG-21's Binto-BSD Parser to generate a BSD for a given (scalable) bitstream. After the BSD is transformed, an adapted bitstream is created by using the BSDtoBin Parser, which takes as input the BS Schema, the customized BSD, and the original bitstream.

XFlavor is a declarative C++-like language to describe the syntax of a bit-stream on a bit-per-bit basis. It was initially designed to simplify and speed up the development of software that processes audio-visual bitstreams by automatically generating a parser for these bitstreams. By extending this automatically generated parser with XML features, it was possible to translate the syntax of a bitstream in XML format [4]. The XFlavor code, which contains a description

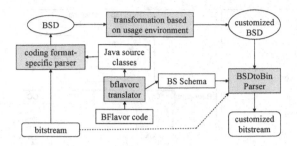

**Fig. 1.** BFlavor-based adaptation chain

of the syntax of a certain media format, is translated to Java or C++ source classes. This set of source classes is compiled to a coding format-specific parser. XFlavor comes with the Bitgen tool for creating an adapted bitstream, hereby guided by the customized BSD.

MPEG-21 BSDL and XFlavor can be used as stand-alone tools [5], but both have pros and contras. XFlavor's bitstream generator (i.e., Bitgen) only uses information from the BSD and thus is independent of the XFlavor code. Hence, the complete bitstream data are actually embedded in the BSD, resulting in potentially huge descriptions. On the contrary, MPEG-21 BSDL makes use of a specific datatype to point to a data range in the original bitstream when it is too verbose to be included in the description (i.e., by making use of the language construct bs1:byteRange). This results in BSDs containing only the high-level structure of the bitstream. The strengths of XFlavor are the fast execution speed and the low and constant memory consumption of the coding format-specific parser, while the BintoBSD Parser of MPEG-21 BSDL struggles with an unacceptable execution speed and increasing memory consumption caused by an inefficient XPath evaluation process. This is due to the fact that the entire description of the bitstream structure is kept in system memory in order to allow the evaluation of arbitrary XPath 1.0 expressions.

## 2.2 BFlavor

As described in [6], BFlavor combines the strengths of MPEG-21 BSDL and XFlavor. As such, BFlavor allows generating a compact high-level BSD at a fast execution speed and with a low memory consumption. The BFlavor-based adaptation chain is illustrated in Fig. 1. The BFlavor code describes the structure of a specific bitstream format in an object-oriented manner. The bflavorc translator uses this code to automatically generate Java source classes. These Java source classes have to be compiled to a coding format-specific parser. This parser generates a BSD which is compliant with the BSDL-1 specification of MPEG-21 BSDL. After the transformation of the BSD, the customized BSD is used by MPEG-21 BSDL's BSDtoBin Parser to create an adapted bitstream, suited for the targeted usage environment. The BSDtoBin Parser needs a Bitstream Syntax Schema (BS Schema). This schema contains the structure of a specific

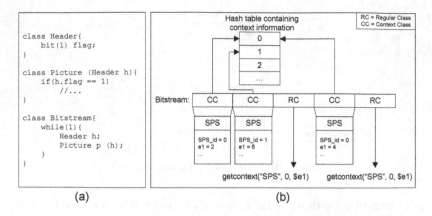

**Fig. 2.** (a) BFlavor code example for the first type of context information. (b) Steps for processing context classes.

bitstream format, analogous to the BFlavor code. Therefore, the bflavorc translator is also able to generate such a BS Schema from the BFlavor code. Thus, the BSDtoBin Parser uses the customized BSD, the generated BS Schema, and the original bitstream to generate an adapted bitstream.

## 3    Extending BFlavor

Although BFlavor outperforms MPEG-21 BSDL and XFlavor in terms of execution time, memory consumption, and BSD size when parsing for example an H.263-compliant bitstream [7], it still contains some shortcomings in order to describe state-of-the-art media formats. In this section, attention is paid to two important problems: the collection of context information and the occurrence of emulation prevention bytes.

### 3.1    Collection of Context Information

When parsing a bitstream of a specific coding format, information about previously parsed bits is often needed to correctly steer the parsing process. This information is called *context information*. There are two types of context information. First, there is context information which is located within a fixed distance of the place in the bitstream where the context information is needed. An example of this type of context information is illustrated in Fig. 2(a). In this figure, a fictive BFlavor code fragment of a sequence of pictures with their headers is shown. The picture can access the context information located in the header by making use of the parameter mechanism in BFlavor. As one can see, access to this type of context information is already supported by BFlavor.

A second type of context information is information not necessarily appearing within a fixed distance of the current parsing position. For example, the header in Fig. 2(a) could be repeated within the bitstream (containing other values). In this case, the parameter mechanism will not work anymore because we do not know which header will be active for the current picture at the time of writing the BFlavor code. A first example of coding formats, which make use of such a context information mechanism, are H.264/AVC and its scalable extension [8] (use of Sequence Parameter Sets (SPS) and Picture Parameter Sets (PPS)) which is further discussed in Sect. 4. A second example is SMPTE's Video Codec 1 (VC-1) (use of Sequence Headers and Entry-point Headers).

We have extended BFlavor to solve the problem of the second type of context information. It is now possible to mark a class in the BFlavor code as a context class (e.g., the SPS class in H.264/AVC). This is done by using the `context` verbatim code, as illustrated on line 5 in Fig. 4. The argument within the verbatim code is the name of the index element of the context class. This index element is used to access a specific instance of the context class. If the context class does not have an index element, no argument is given in the verbatim code. In this case, always the last occurrence of the context class will be active (examples are the Sequence headers and Entry-point headers of VC-1). When a context class is parsed, every syntax element together with its value is stored in a hash table. Based on the value of the index element of the context class, the context class is stored on the right place in the hash table, as illustrated in Fig. 2(b) (the context class SPS is stored in the hash table based on the SPS_id element).

To access a context class from within the BFlavor code, a new built-in function is defined: `getcontext()`. The working is illustrated in Fig. 2(b). This function can only be used in regular classes (i.e., classes that are not context classes). The value of element e1 of context class SPS with index element equal to 0 is obtained by specifying the following arguments to the `getcontext()` function: the name of the context class (as a string), the value of the index element (as an integer), and the name of the actual element (as a variable prefixed with a $). Note that always the last occurence of the context class with the specific index element value will be accessed. When the `getcontext()` function with the same arguments (as shown in Fig. 2(b)) is called for the second time, the value of the element e1 is different (it is first equal to 2; the second time, it is equal to 4). Other examples of the `getcontext()` function are shown in Fig. 4.

## 3.2   Emulation Prevention Bytes

A second problem we have to deal with, is the occurrence of emulation prevention bytes in a bitstream. Coding formats such as MPEG-1/2 Video and MPEG-4 Visual prevent start code emulation by adding restrictions to values of syntax elements (forbidden values). More recent coding formats such as H.264/AVC, VC-1, and the wavelet-based Dirac specification use the mechanism of emulation prevention bytes. When a start code occurs coincidentally in the bitstream, an emulation prevention byte is inserted in order to prevent a start code emulation. For example, when an H.264/AVC coded bitstream contains the start code 0x000001 by accident, the emulation prevention byte 0x03 is inserted resulting in the following bitstream fragment: 0x00000301.

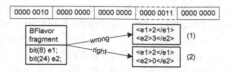

**Fig. 3.** Example of an emulation prevention byte

These emulation prevention bytes cause problems when using BFlavor, as illustrated in Fig. 3. The fourth byte (0x03) is an emulation prevention byte. The given BFlavor code fragment results in a wrong description (1) shown in Fig. 3. This is because the current version of BFlavor does not take into account the occurrence of emulation prevention bytes.

To solve this problem, we have extended BFlavor with two new verbatim codes (i.e., `emulationBytes` and `emulateBytes`) as illustrated on the first two lines of Fig. 4. The `emulationBytes` verbatim code is used by BFlavor to ignore the emulation prevention bytes. A list of couples *(code with emulation prevention byte, code without emulation prevention byte)* is given as an argument to this verbatim code. With this information, BFlavor can now correctly describe the bitstream given in Fig. 3, resulting in description (2). Obviously, the process to construct a bitstream from a given bitstream structure description (i.e., the BSDtoBin Parser of MPEG-21 BSDL) must also support the use of emulation prevention bytes. Therefore, the `emulateBytes` verbatim code tells an enhanced version of the BSDtoBin Parser which codes have to be emulated. The argument of this verbatim code is a list of couples *(code which cannot appear in the bitstream, emulated version of the code)*.

## 4   A BFlavor Code for H.264/AVC Scalable Video Coding

### 4.1   Joint Scalable Video Model

The Joint Video Team (JVT) has started the development of the Joint Scalable Video Model (JSVM), which is an extension of the single-layered H.264/AVC coding format. It is now possible to encode an video sequence once at the highest resolution, frame rate, and visual quality, after which it is possible to extract partial streams containing a lower quality along one or more scalability axes (i.e., the temporal, spatial, and Signal-to-Noise Ratio (SNR) axis).

As discussed above, the scalable extension of H.264/AVC makes use of emulation prevention bytes as well as context classes (i.e., SPSs and PPSs). Therefore, we have created a BFlavor code for JSVM version 5 in order to evaluate the extensions we added to BFlavor. An excerpt of this code is shown in Fig. 4.

### 4.2   BFlavor Code for JSVM-5

A JSVM-5-compliant bitstream is a succession of Network Abstraction Layer Units (NALUs). Next to the slice layer NALU, there are three main categories

```
 1:%emulationBytes{ (000003, 0000); %emulationBytes}
 2:%emulateBytes{ (000000, 00000300); (000001, 00000301);
 3:              (000002, 00000302); (000003, 00000303); %emulateBytes}
 4:
 5:%context{seq_parameter_set_id%context}
 6:class Seq_parameter_set_rbsp{
 7:    bit(8) profile_idc;
 8:    //...
 9:    bit(8) level_idc;
10:    UnsignedExpGolomb seq_parameter_set_id;
11:    if(profile_idc == 83)
12:        //...
13:}
14:
15:%context{pic_parameter_set_id%context}
16:class Pic_parameter_set_rbsp{
17:    UnsignedExpGolomb pic_parameter_set_id;
18:    UnsignedExpGolomb seq_parameter_set_id;
19:    bit(1) entropy_coding_mode_flag;
20:    //...
21:}
22:
23:class Slice_header(int nal_unit_type, int nal_ref_idc){
24:    UnsignedExpGolomb first_mb_in_slice;
25:    UnsignedExpGolomb slice_type;
26:    UnsignedExpGolomb pic_parameter_set_id;
27:    bit(getcontext("Seq_parameter_set_rbsp",
28:    getcontext("Pic_parameter_set_rbsp", pic_parameter_set_id.value, $seq_parameter_set_id),
29:    $log2_max_frame_num_minus4 ) + 4 ) frame_num;
30:    //...
31:}
32:
33:class Nal_unit_header_svc_extension{
34:    bit(6) simple_priority_id;
35:    bit(1) discardable_flag;
36:    bit(1) extension_flag;
37:    if(extension_flag == 1){
38:        bit(3) temporal_level;
39:        bit(3) dependency_id;
40:        bit(2) quality_level;
41:    }
42:}
```

**Fig. 4.** An excerpt of the fine-granulated BFlavor code for JSVM-5

of NALUs: SPSs containing information related to the whole sequence; PPSs containing information related to a set of pictures; Supplemental Enhancement Information (SEI) NALUs containing additional information that is not needed to correctly decode the bitstream. The first NALU in the bitstream is a SEI NALU containing scalability information (i.e., information about the different scalability axes). This NALU is followed by a set of SPSs and PPSs. Every slice refers to a PPS and every PPS refers to an SPS. As a consequence, every SPS and PPS has to be kept in memory during the BSD generation process. In our BFlavor code, both the SPS and the PPS classes are context classes. In the slice header class, values of the SPS and PPS can be obtained by making use of the getcontext() built-in function. One can also see the signalling of emulation prevention bytes on the first two lines of the code.

### 4.3   Performance Results

In order to evaluate the performance of our BFlavor-based adaptation chain, we have generated five encoded scalable bitstreams compliant with the JSVM-5 specification. A part of the trailer *the new world* [1] was used with a resolution

---

[1] This trailer can be downloaded from http://www.apple.com/trailers.

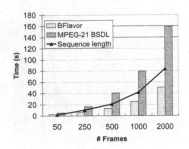

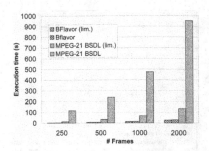

**Fig. 5.** Total execution times for the whole adaptation chain. In this chain, one spatial layer was removed from the JSVM-5-compliant bitstream.

**Fig. 6.** Execution times for the BSD generation of a JSVM-5-compliant bitstream

of $1280 \times 512$ pixels at a frame rate of 24Hz. The encoded bitstreams contain 5 temporal, 4 spatial, and 3 quality levels.

For each bitstream, the corresponding BSD is generated once by making use of BFlavor and once by making use of an optimized version of the BintoBSD Parser of MPEG-21 BSDL, as explained in [9]. The transformation of the BSD is done by making use of Streaming Transformations for XML (STX) [10]. *Joost* (v. 2005-05-21) is used as STX engine. Finally, the adapted bitstream is generated by using an enhanced version of MPEG-21 BSDL's BSDtoBin Parser, using as input the transformed BSD, the BS Schema, and the original bitstream. We also used two BFlavor codes with a different granularity. The first BFlavor code describes the syntax of the JSVM-5 bitstream up to and including the NALU header for the slices. The second BFlavor code describes the syntax of the slices up to and including the slice header. Performance measurements were done on a PC having an Intel Pentium D 2,8GHz CPU and 1GB of RAM at its disposal. Every step was executed five times, whereupon the average was calculated.

As one can see in Fig. 5, the BFlavor-based adaptation chain is executed in real-time (in contrast to the MPEG-21 BSDL-based adaptation chain). Note that in this figure the resolution of the video sequence was rescaled to $640 \times 256$ pixels. Both technologies have a linear behavior in terms of execution time, a constant memory consumption (circa 3 MB for BSD generation), and a relatively compact BSD (26 MB uncompressed or 317 KB compressed with WinRAR 3.0's default text compression algorithm when the size of the bitstream is 176 MB).

Although the optimized version of MPEG-21 BSDL's BintoBSD parser shows the same characteristics in the performance measurements, there is a remarkable difference when we look at the BSD generation time (see Fig. 6). When parsing the JSVM-5-compliant bitstream up to and including the slice header, a lot of information has to be retrieved from the active SPS and PPS. This is not the case when parsing up to and including the NALU header. When parsing up to

**Table 1.** Execution time results of the adaptation chain. *(limited)* points to a description up to and including the NALU header.

| Techniques | #Pic. | BSD generation (s) | STX (s) | Bitstream generation (s) | Total time (s) | Speed (Mbit/s) |
|---|---|---|---|---|---|---|
| BFlavor (limited) | 50 | 0.4 | 1.4 | 0.8 | 2.6 | 2.2 |
| | 250 | 1.7 | 3.0 | 1.2 | 5.9 | 11.2 |
| | 500 | 6.4 | 5.0 | 1.9 | 13.4 | 23.5 |
| | 1000 | 13.3 | 9.0 | 3.0 | 25.4 | 26.2 |
| | 2000 | 27.9 | 17.0 | 5.6 | 50.4 | 27.9 |
| BFlavor | 50 | 0.4 | 1.7 | 1.5 | 3.6 | 1.6 |
| | 250 | 2.1 | 4.0 | 3.7 | 9.8 | 6.8 |
| | 500 | 7.2 | 6.8 | 6.7 | 20.6 | 15.2 |
| | 1000 | 14.7 | 13.4 | 12.3 | 40.4 | 16.5 |
| | 2000 | 30.1 | 26.4 | 23.7 | 80.3 | 17.5 |
| BSDL (limited) | 50 | 3.0 | 1.5 | 0.8 | 5.5 | 1.0 |
| | 250 | 11.8 | 3.3 | 1.4 | 16.5 | 4.0 |
| | 500 | 32.8 | 5.5 | 2.1 | 40.4 | 7.8 |
| | 1000 | 66.2 | 9.8 | 3.2 | 79.3 | 8.4 |
| | 2000 | 134.5 | 18.6 | 5.7 | 158.8 | 8.9 |
| BSDL | 50 | 23.9 | 1.9 | 1.7 | 27.4 | 0.2 |
| | 250 | 114.8 | 5.3 | 4.0 | 124.1 | 0.5 |
| | 500 | 238.6 | 9.5 | 7.2 | 255.3 | 1.2 |
| | 1000 | 474.8 | 17.7 | 13.3 | 505.9 | 1.3 |
| | 2000 | 954.1 | 34.1 | 25.5 | 1013.7 | 1.4 |

and including the slice header with the coding format-specific parser of BFlavor, execution times are almost as good as the execution times when parsing up to and including the NALU header (28 s versus 30 s for 2000 pictures). Therefore, the BFlavor-based adaptation chain can adapt a JSVM-5-compliant bitstream in real-time when parsing up to and including the slice header, as illustrated in Table 1 (80 s needed for a sequence of 83 s). Looking at the MPEG-21 BSDL-based adaptation chain, we see a significant loss of performance when parsing up to and including the slice header (134 s versus 954 s for 2000 pictures).

We can conclude that only BFlavor is able to adapt a JSVM-5-compliant bitstream in real-time (even if we parse up to and including the slice header). It is clear that the use of hash tables by BFlavor performs much better than the XPath evaluation mechanism used in MPEG-21 BSDL for the retrieval of context information.

## 5   Conclusions

In this paper, we have extended BFlavor, which is a combination of the fast BSD generation speed and constant memory consumption of XFlavor and the possibility to create the compact BSDs of MPEG-21 BSDL. Support for the transparent retrieval of context information and support for emulation prevention bytes were added to BFlavor. The transparent retrieval of context information is realized by making use of hash tables. Emulation prevention bytes are signalled on top of the BFlavor code. Both features were needed to create a BFlavor code for the JSVM version 5. Performance measurements have shown that a BFlavor-based adaptation chain for JSVM-5-compliant bitstreams operates in real-time.

## Acknowledgements

The research activities that have been described in this paper were funded by Ghent University, the Interdisciplinary Institute for Broadband Technology (IBBT), the Institute for the Promotion of Innovation by Science and Technology in Flanders (IWT), the Fund for Scientific Research-Flanders (FWO-Flanders), the Belgian Federal Science Policy Office (BFSPO), and the European Union.

## References

1. Vetro A., Christopoulos C., Ebrahimi T.: Universal Multimedia Access. IEEE Signal Processing Magazine 20 (2) (2003) 16
2. Panis, G., Hutter, A., Heuer, J., Hellwagner, H., Kosch, H., Timmerer, T., Devillers, S., Amielh, M.: Bitstream Syntax Description: A Tool for Multimedia Resource Adaptation within MPEG-21. Signal Processing: Image Communication 18 (2003) 721-747
3. Devillers, S., Timmerer, C., Heuer, J., Hellwagner, H.: Bitstream Syntax Description-Based Adaptation in Streaming and Constrained Environments. IEEE Trans. Multimedia 7 (3) (2005) 463-470
4. Hong D., Eleftheriadis A.: XFlavor: Bridging Bits and Objects in Media Representation. Proceedings, IEEE Int'l Conference on Multimedia and Expo (ICME), Lauzanne, Switzerland, August 2002
5. De Neve, W., Van Deursen, D., De Schrijver, D., De Wolf, K., Van de Walle, R.: Using Bitstream Structure Descriptions for the Exploitation of Multi-layered Temporal Scalability in H.264/AVC's Base Specification. Lecture Notes in Computer Science, Volume 3767, pages 641-652, Oct 2005
6. De Neve, W., Van Deursen, D., De Schrijver, D., De Wolf, K., Lerouge, S., Van de Walle, R.: BFlavor: a harmonized approach to media resource adaptation, inspired by MPEG-21 BSDL and XFlavor. Accepted for publication in EURASIP Signal Processing: Image Communication, Elsevier.
7. Van Deursen, D., De Neve, W., De Schrijver, D., Van de Walle, R.: BFlavor: an Optimized XML-based Framework for Multimedia Content Customization. Proceedings of the 25th Picture Coding Symposium (PCS 2006), 6 pp on CD-ROM, Beijing, China, April 2006
8. Reichel J., Schwarz H., Wien M.: Joint Scalable Video Model JSVM-5. Doc. JVT-R202, 2006
9. De Schrijver, D., De Neve, W., De Wolf, K., Van de Walle, R.: Generating MPEG-21 BSDL Descriptions Using Context-Related Attributes. Proceedings of the 7th IEEE International Symposium on Multimedia (ISM 2005), pages 79-86, USA, December 2005
10. De Schrijver D., De Neve W., Van Deursen D., De Cock J., Van de Walle R.: On an Evaluation of Transformation Languages in a Fully XML-driven Framework for Video Content Adaptation. Accepted for publication in proceedings of IEEE ICICIC 2006, China, 2006

# Generic, Scalable Multimedia Streaming and Delivery with Example Application for H.264/AVC

Joseph Thomas-Kerr, Ian Burnett, and Christian Ritz

Whisper Laboratories, University of Wollongong, Northfields Ave. North Wollongong, NSW
2522, Australia
{joetk, i.burnett, chritz}@elec.uow.edu.au

**Abstract.** The ever increasing diversity of multimedia technology presents a
growing challenge to interoperability in as new content formats are developed.
The Bitstream Binding Language (BBL) addresses this problem by providing a
format-independent language to describe how multimedia content is to be delivered. This paper proposes extensions to BBL that enable a generic, scalable
streaming server architecture. In this architecture, new content formats are supported by providing a simple file with instructions as to how the software may
be streamed. This approach removes any need to modify existing software to
provide such support.

## 1 Introduction

The quantity of multimedia content available via the Internet, and the number of formats in which it is encoded, stored and delivered continues to grow rapidly. So too the
number and diversity of the devices and software applications which produce, process
and consume such content. This constantly changing landscape presents an increasing
challenge to interoperability, since more and more software and hardware must be
upgraded as new formats are developed and deployed. The Bitstream Binding Language (BBL) [1] attempts to address this problem, by providing a format-independent
framework for the description of multimedia content delivery. This means that instead
of having to write additional software to deliver new content formats (as is currently
required), support for a new format is provided by a small XML file containing BBL
instructions.

This paper proposes extensions to BBL to extend the scalability and flexibility of the
framework, by integrating support to output the widely-used ISO [2] and Quicktime
(QT) [3] file formats. These are essentially generic multimedia containers, and provide
*hint-tracks* which are used by most multimedia streaming servers to facilitate highly
scalable multi-user streaming (Figure 1 (a)). The hint track allows much of the processing involved in streaming content to be performed offline – by the *hinter* – to generate
*hints*, which are essentially byte-copy instructions. These hints may be processed very
efficiently by the streaming server, and they alleviate any requirement that the server
itself possess detailed knowledge about individual formats. The application of hint
tracks to the BBL-based streaming architecture (Figure 1 (b)) provides a complete

Y. Zhuang et al. (Eds.): PCM 2006, LNCS 4261, pp. 349–356, 2006.

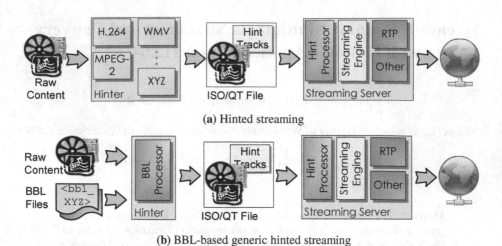

(a) Hinted streaming

(b) BBL-based generic hinted streaming

**Fig. 1.** Streaming architectures

format-independent, scalable streaming architecture, by replacing the individual software modules within the hinter with a BBL processor, which is driven by a data file containing BBL instructions for hinting each particular format.

Other related work is gBSD-based hinting – proposed by Ransburg et al [4]. gBSD – generic Bitstream Syntax Description – is a tool specified by MPEG-21 [5] which describes the structure of multimedia content using a single generic XML grammar, to enable adaptation of scalable codecs. Ransburg et al propose the extension of the gBSD language with markers to specify the temporal parameters of each bitstream structure, providing a hint track-like description. They suggest that the format-independent nature of the language means that the streaming architecture is also format-independent. However, there is no generic application with which to generate the gBSD (the hinter); instead, they propose that "the gBSD for any content which is to be distributed in a multimedia system is produced during content creation" [4] – that is, by the format-specific encoder.

Bitstream Syntax Description Tools – gBSD, the related BSDL (Bitstream Syntax Description Language) [5], and XFlavor [6], are also related to this work. However, as observed by Ranbsurg et al [4], such languages identify only the structure of the content, and do not provide information about how it should be fragmented into packets nor when each packet should be delivered.

## 2   Bitstream Binding Language

The Bitstream Binding Language (BBL) [1] is an XML grammar that describes how to bind multimedia content and metadata into streaming formats (eg RTP or MPEG-2 Transport Streams), and other delivery mechanisms (such as a container file). Figure 2 depicts the operation of the BBL processor that transforms raw content and metadata into a network stream or other delivery format. Figure 4 provides a BBL example.

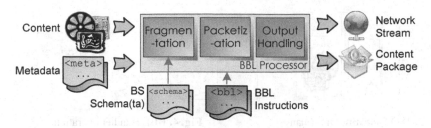

**Fig. 2.** BBL Processor Architecture

The first stage of this process is the *fragmentation* of the input data into semantic units appropriate for the intended delivery. This may be audio frames, slices of video content, scalability layers, or pieces of metadata. This process is format-independent; a BBL processor does not contain detailed knowledge of any particular format. Instead, a Bitstream Syntax (BS) Schema [5] identifies the necessary syntax of the specific format. BS Schemata are an extension of XML schema [7], providing an XML abstraction of the underlying binary data. This abstraction allows BBL to handle binary content using the same XPath-based [8] syntax as native XML (which is increasingly used for metadata markup).

Fragments of data are then *packetized*, by assigning the fragment header data, a delivery timestamp, and potentially other parameters specific to the delivery format (such as a marker bit or timestamp offset for RTP). Syntactically, packets are specified within a BBL description by one or more `<packet>` and/or `<packetStream>` elements, where the latter declares a sequence of packets in a compact format.

Finally, packets are processed by an *output handler* for the particular delivery format. The handler mechanism is extensible – additional handlers may be defined as required. The handler is initialized with global parameters – such as a timescale, payload type code, and/or SDP information in the case of RTP. It is then responsible for outputting each packet according to the parameters which it is provided, in conformance with the standard to which it complies.

## 3   ISO/Quicktime File Output Handler

To implement the format-independent, scalable streaming application scenario outlined in section 1, the BBL processor must be able to output valid ISO format files, including sample tables and hint tracks. As discussed, the BBL architecture is designed to be extensible, via its output handler mechanism, so ISO file output may be provided by specifying an appropriate handler. The following provides an overview of the ISO file handler design. A full specification may be found elsewhere[1], and section 4 (below) presents an example which may aid understanding of the discussion.

In designing the handler, a number of requirements must be observed: the handler must be format-independent – that is, it is able to receive input content of any form and place it within an ISO file. Secondly, the handler must be extensible; it must

---

[1] http://whisper.elec.uow.edu.au/people/jtkerr/index.php?page=html/Research

**Fig. 3.** ISO/Quicktime file (many boxes hidden)                    **Fig. 4.** BBL Handler operation

allow arbitrary ISO file structures to be defined as required, enabling the BBL processor to create ISO files which conform to file formats which may not yet exist (such as the various MAFs). Finally, the handler must be as simple as possible – the BBL author must not be required to describe details which may otherwise be computed automatically (such as the data in sample tables and hint tracks).

ISO files have an object-based structure, via a set of nested "boxes" (Figure 3). Each box has a particular semantic, and contains data fields and/or other boxes. Every ISO file has a *file* box (ftyp), which specifies the type of content within the file, and usually a *movie* box (moov), which contains a large number of boxes for the low-level metadata necessary to understand the raw content. This metadata includes sample tables, timing data, and hint information. Conversely, a *metadata* box (meta) contains high-level metadata such as an MPEG-7 description of the content, or links to related content. The content itself is stored in the *media data* box (mdat).

The handler is able to make some assumptions about the box structure of the file it is to create – for example, certain sub-boxes are mandatory or contingent upon various conditions, including many within the *movie* box. Other aspects of the file structure must be explicitly specified within the BBL description, such as the number and type of tracks within the file, the movie timescale and sample descriptors. These attributes are specified as part of the global parameter set provided when the handler is initialized (Figure 4).

The global parameter set establishes the structure of the output file, provides values for header fields, and initialises sample descriptors. It also provides ids for each track, sample descriptor and/or metadata item to allow packet-level parameters to identify where the packet belongs. Figure 5 shows the schema of this parameter set using XMLSpy-style notation: each box is an XML element, and most elements contain attributes which provide values for various fields in the ISO box structure. The structure of the parameter set is related to the hierarchical box structure of the ISO file format. However only those details which must be parameterized by the BBL description are exposed - many parts of the file, such as sample tables and hint tracks, are created automatically by the handler, and need not be specified by the parameter set.

The handler is designed to be as generic as possible – sample descriptors may be specified by extending the base classes with format-specific information using BSDL. Similarly, a generic box element is provided which may be used to add additional boxes using BSDL syntax. This means that the handler does not need to be modified to support new content formats.

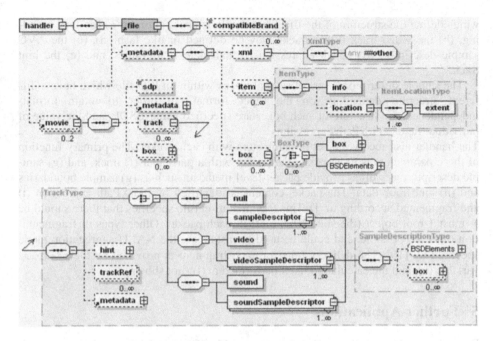

**Fig. 5.** ISO file format handler global parameter set

Once the global structure of the ISO file is defined, the handler is able to process packets of content. Each packet must include parameters associating the content with a particular track, as well as sample-specific information such as a composition time offset and hint track information. The handler uses this information to make appropriate entries in the track sample table, associated hint track, and/or *item location and information* tables (`iloc`/`iinf` – used by certain MAFs [9], see section 1). Figure 6 shows the schema for the packet-level parameters.

## 4  Example – Scalable Generic Streaming of H.264/AVC over RTP

This section presents a detailed example of one of the applications previously outlined – scalable generic streaming. It implements the architecture shown in Figure 1 (b), packaging a raw H.264/AVC [10] stream within an ISO file. This ISO file may then be delivered using any existing streaming server supporting the ISO format – for example, the Darwin Streaming Server[2].

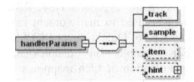

**Fig. 6.** ISO file format handler local parameter set

Figure 8 presents a BBL description for this operation which shows the instructions pertinent to the proposed ISO handler. The handler is registered at the beginning of the file, and provided with global parameters

---

[2] http://developer.apple.com/opensource/server/streaming/index.html

which define the structure of the file. These include declaration of (a) file-type branding, (b) the video track (other tracks may be defined in like fashion), (c) the AVC sample descriptor, (d) XPath expressions to calculate field values, and (e) the hint track.

The sample descriptor is one of several boxes within an ISO file which have a different structure depending on the input format. In order to retain format-independence, the structure of such boxes are specified using BSDL, and the value of individual fields via XPath expressions.

The handler also receives a set of parameters with each packet. The primary function of these parameters is to associate the packet with a particular (f) track, and (g) sample descriptor, as well as provide packet-level metadata such as (g) sample boundaries and (h) hint track data. The packet content is identified by the XPath expression (i) and fragmented according to (j). This fragmentation rule specifies that there should be at most 1 root object (the slice NAL unit) in each packet. Other types of fragmentation rules are possible, and could be used to instantiate the NALU aggregation mode specified by [10]. The delivery time for each fragment is provided by the $delTime variable (k), and the calculation itself performed at (l) (not shown).

## 5   Further Applications

Recently, the Motion Picture Experts Group (MPEG) have begun to define a Multimedia Application Format (MAF) architecture [9]. Traditionally, third parties such as the Digital Video Broadcasting Project (DVB), and the 3rd Generation Partnership Project (3GPP), have been responsible for combining MPEG standards together into application frameworks suitable for their particular domain. In contrast, the MAF architecture attempts to identify domain-neutral application scenarios, and provide complete solutions for each scenario that operate "out of the box". The first formats under development are a (protected) music player MAF and a photo player MAF.

The MAF framework facilitates interoperability by providing generic solutions, but it faces issues similar to those observed in deploying new streaming formats (section 1). That is, existing infrastructure cannot produce nor consume MAF content. Using BBL to transform MAF content into existing formats has been addressed [11]; the ISO handler would allow BBL to also package content *into* MAFs (Figure 7).

As a more general case, BBL may be used to map content into any type of Quicktime or ISO file. For example, this enables the specification of such mappings in a way that may be directly implemented. Consequently, when a new content format is developed, its creators can provide a BBL description which allows any user to package the data into a compliant file format.

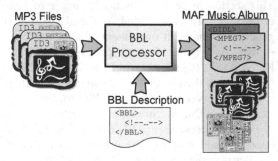

**Fig. 7.** Generic Production of MAF content

```
<bbl>
  <binding>
    <register>
      <handler id="iso" type="ISOFile">
        <mpff:file majorBrand="isom" filename="?$outFile?">       <!-- (a) -->
          <mpff:compatibleBrand>avc1</mpff:compatibleBrand>
        </mpff:file>
        <mpff:movie timeScale="90000">
          <mpff:track id="videoTrack" timeScale="1001">           <!-- (b) -->
            <mpff:video/>
            <mpff:videoSampleDescriptor dimensions="176 144" id="sd"
                                        codingName="avc1">         <!-- (c) -->
              <mpff:box type="avcC" desc="config">
                <avcFF:AVCDecoderConfigurationRecord>
                  <avcFF:ver>1</avcFF:ver>
                  <avcFF:profile>?$sps/avc:profile_idc/text()?</avcFF:profile>
                  <avcFF:compatibility>
                    ?$sps/avc:constraint_set_flags/text()?         <!-- (d) -->
                  </avcFF:compatibility>
                  <!-- ... -->
                </avcFF:AVCDecoderConfigurationRecord>
              </mpff:box>
            </mpff:videoSampleDescriptor>
            <mpff:hint timeScale="90000" type="rtp ">              <!-- (e) -->
              <mpff:sdp>
                <!-- ... -->
              </mpff:sdp>
            </mpff:hint>
          </mpff:track>
        </mpff:movie>
      </handler>
    </register>

    <packetStream handler="iso">
      <handlerParams>
        <mpff:track ref="videoTrack"/>                            <!-- (f) -->
        <mpff:sample sampleDescriptor="sd" firstPacket="?$newAU?"
                     compositionTimeDelta="?$compDelta?"/>         <!-- (g) -->
        <mpff:hint isBframe="false" marker="?$newAU?"/>            <!-- (h) -->
      </handlerParams>
      <contentTemplate>
        <include ref="/avc:h264/avc:slice" depth="-1">            <!-- (i) -->
          <fragmentation>
            <count value="1" bbl:match="."/>                      <!-- (j) -->
          </fragmentation>
          <timing>
            <delTimes bbl:match="." bbl:value="$delTime"/>        <!-- (k) -->
          </timing>
        </include>
        <!-- ... -->
      </contentTemplate>
      <variables>                                                 <!-- (l) -->
        <!-- ... -->
      </variables>
    </packetStream>
  </binding>
</bbl>
```

**Fig. 8.** Abbreviated BBL instructions for scalable generic streaming of H.264/AVC on RTP

# 6 Conclusion

This paper has presented an extension to the BBL framework which allows it to act as a format-independent hinting application. This enables a generic streaming architecture which may support new content formats as they are developed simply by disseminating a data file – a BBL description for delivering content in the new format. Such a solution obviates the need for any modification of existing streaming infrastructure in order to deploy new content formats, and consequently simplifies interoperability with these formats. The paper has detailed the design of the ISO/Quicktime file format handler which comprises the proposed extension to BBL, showing how it can be used to generically produce ISO files containing the content with appropriate hint tracks. Such files may be streamed using existing servers such as the Darwin Streaming Server. We have validated the approach using an example of H.264/AVC packaging for streaming via RTP, and provided details of this example.

# References

[1] ISO/IEC, "FCD 21000-18, IT - Multimedia framework (MPEG-21) -Part 18: Digital Item Streaming," 2006.
[2] ISO/IEC, "14496-12, IT - Coding of audio-visual objects - Part 12: ISO base media file format," 2005.
[3] Apple, *"QuickTime File Format."* http://developer.apple.com/documentation/QuickTime/QTFF/qtff.pdf, 2001.
[4] M. Ransburg and H. Hellwagner, "Generic Streaming of Multimedia Content," presented at *Internet & Multimedia Sys. & Apps.*, 2005.
[5] ISO/IEC, "21000-7:2004 IT - Multimedia framework (MPEG-21) - Part 7: Digital Item Adaptation," 2004.
[6] D. Hong and A. Eleftheriadis, "XFlavor: bridging bits and objects in media representation," presented at *Multimedia & Expo, 2002, IEEE Intl. Conf. on*, 2002.
[7] H. S. Thompson, *et al.*, "XML Schema Part 1: Structures Second Edition," 2004.
[8] A. Berglund, *et al.*, "XML Path Language (XPath) 2.0," in *Candidate Recommendation.* http://www.w3.org/TR/xpath20, 2005.
[9] K. Diepold, *et al.*, "MPEG-A: multimedia application formats," *Multimedia, IEEE*, vol. 12, pp. 34, 2005.
[10] S. Wenger, "H.264/AVC over IP," *Circuits & Systems for Video Technology, IEEE Trans. on* vol. 13, pp. 645, 2003.
[11] J. Thomas-Kerr, *et al.*, "Enhancing interoperability via generic multimedia syntax translation," accepted to *Automated Production of Cross Media Content for Multi-Channel Distribution. AXMEDIS. 2nd Intl. Conf. on* 2006.

# Shape-Based Image Retrieval in Botanical Collections

Itheri Yahiaoui, Nicolas Hervé, and Nozha Boujemaa

Projet IMEDIA, INRIA Rocquencourt, Domaine de Voluceau-Rocquencourt-B.P. 105.
78153 LE CHESNAY Cedex, France
{itheri.yahiaoui, nicolas.herve, nozha.boujemaa}@inria.fr

**Abstract.** Apart from the computer vision community, an always increasing number of scientific domains show a great interest for image analysis techniques. This interest is often guided by practical needs. As examples, we can cite all the medical imagery systems, the satellites images treatment and botanical databases. A common point of these applications is the large image collections that are generated and therefore require some automatic tools to help the scientists. These tools should allow clear structuration of the visual information and provide fast and accurate retrieval process. In the framework of the plant genes expression study we designed a content-based image retrieval (CBIR) system to assist botanists in their work. We propose a new contour-based shape descriptor that satisfies the constraints of this application (accuracy and real-time search). It is called Directional Fragment Histogram (DFH). This new descriptor has been evaluated and compared to several shape descriptors.

**Keywords:** Content-based image retrieval, region-of-interest based visual query, shape descriptor, contour extraction, image segmentation, botanical image processing.

## 1 Introduction

The content-based image retrieval (CBIR) systems have proven to be very useful in many fields to browse and search very huge image databases. Botanists are usually brought to use large collections of plants images. They need automatic tools to assist them in their work. Some very recent initiative in botany can be found in [1][12]. In a recent work Reference [1], we were interested in issues that are specific to the study of the function of genes in plants. These genetic modifications generate visual changes in the visual appearance of the plants. The biologists must find which phenotypes are visually similar; indeed, visual resemblances between phenotypes reflects similarities in the roles of the genes whose expression was blocked when obtaining these phenotypes.

At first time, we use a number of descriptors that were already implemented in our generic CBIR system IKONA [3]. Our existing shape descriptor based on the Hough transform captures the global structural information inside the plant. However, we need to describe more precisely the external shape of the plants to improve the plant characterization.

Y. Zhuang et al. (Eds.): PCM 2006, LNCS 4261, pp. 357–364, 2006.

Different contour based descriptors were proposed in the literature. The well-known *shape contexts* and *curvature scale space* (CSS) descriptors record good performances but use complex and heavy methods to extract descriptors and to compute distances between them. In the case of a large database, with real-time performances issues, as in our application, this could be a bottleneck. As a consequence, we propose a new shape descriptor based on the external outline of a region that addresses these constraints. It is called Directional Fragment Histogram (DFH).

This paper focuses on a new extension of this shape descriptor and on its evaluation against state of the art descriptors. It is organized as follows. In the next section, we overview the related works on shape description. Then we expose in section 3 our proposal for a new contour-based shape descriptor. Section 4 presents the evaluation of this descriptor.

## 2  Related Works

The shape is a very important aspect in the recognition of objects and therefore plays a major role in CBIR systems. It has been widely studied in the past years and many shape descriptors have been proposed. They differ in their ability to be invariant to translation, rotation and scale, and in their computational performances. One generally distinguishes two kinds of shape descriptors: region-based descriptors and contour-based descriptors. For the latter, one can cite the Fourier descriptor [11], the chain code histogram [5], the edge orientation histogram [6], the shape context descriptor [2] or the curvature scale space descriptor [8]. The chain code histogram (CCH) is a simple histogram of the 8 directions of the freeman code computed on the contour of a shape. The contour shape descriptor chosen in the MPEG-7 standard is an extension of the CSS descriptor [7]. It uses a representation of a contour in the curvature scale space and computes a feature vector of the corresponding region by using the maxima of curvature zero-crossing in this space. These maxima, called peaks, correspond to the main inflection points of the contour between its convex and concave portions. The contour is analyzed several times, at different scales after a smoothing process. This brings scale invariance to this descriptor and a good robustness to noise in the contour. In order to compute a similarity measure between two descriptors, a matching algorithm is used. It is designed to ensure a rotation invariance of the descriptor. Additionally, the feature vector includes the overall eccentricity and circularity of the contour.

## 3  Shape Descriptor

We propose a new approach to describe the shape of a region, inspired by an idea related to the color descriptor in [9]. This new generic shape descriptor is computed using the outline of a region. In our case, the region of interest is the plant. We first need to separate each plant from the background of the image. Once this plant mask is extracted, we are able to compute the outline that represents the external shape of the plant.

## 3.1 Directional Fragment Histograms

Our new shape descriptor, called Directional Fragment Histogram (DFH), is computed using the outline of the region. We consider that this contour is composed of a succession of elementary components. An elementary component can either be a pixel or the elementary segment between two neighbour pixels. We associate to each elementary component of the contour a direction information which can take $N$ different values $d_0, d_1,...,d_{N-1}$. A segment of size $s$ is composed of exactly $s$ elementary components.

For example, given a contour $C$ composed of $m$ elementary components:

$$C = ec_1\ ec_2\ ec_3\ ec_4\ ec_5\ ec_6\ ec_7\ ...\ ec_i\ ...\ ec_m$$

The two first segments of size 4 are:

$$\mathbf{Seg}_4 1 = ec_1\ ec_2\ ec_3\ ec_4 \qquad \mathbf{Seg}_4 2 = ec_2\ ec_3\ ec_4\ ec_5$$

The total number of all possible segments is equal to $m$ in the case of a closed contour, and is equal to $m-s+1$ for open contours.

For each possible segment of the external contour, we identify groups of elementary components having the same direction (orientation) in this segment. Such groups are called directional fragments. The DFH codes two kinds of information. At a local level, it codes the relative length of these groups of elementary components within a given segment. This relative length is expressed as a percentage of the segment length. We choose to quantify the percentage axis into $J$ percentiles. At a global level, the DFH codes the elementary components frequency distribution. The length of the segment defines the scale $s$ of the DFH.

A DFH at scale $s$ is a two-dimensional array of values that contains $N \times J$ bins. We illustrate in Figure 1. the extraction procedure of the fragment histogram supposing that we have 8 different directions and 4 different fraction ranges.

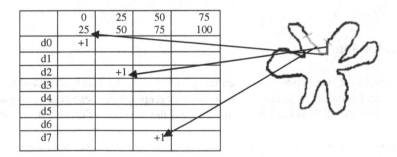

|     | 0 25 | 25 50 | 50 75 | 75 100 |
| --- | --- | --- | --- | --- |
| d0  | +1  |     |     |     |
| d1  |     |     |     |     |
| d2  |     | +1  |     |     |
| d3  |     |     |     |     |
| d4  |     |     |     |     |
| d5  |     |     |     |     |
| d6  |     |     |     |     |
| d7  |     |     | +1  |     |

**Fig. 1.** Extraction of the directional fragment histogram

The direction information associated to elementary components can be absolute with respect to a fixed reference. It can also be relative by deriving the absolute direction information. The use of relative direction information allows this new shape descriptor to be rotation invariant by focusing only on directions changes. As a counterpart, we are, of course, unable to distinguish the global directions. The DFH descriptor is in both cases invariant to translation but not to scale. To decrease the sensitivity of this descriptor to scale, we set a segment length to be proportional to the total length of the global outline of the considered shape. The fragment histogram DFH can also be normalized by the number of all the possible segments. To achieve real-time search, we use a simple L1 distance to compare the descriptors.

### 3.2 Freeman-DFH

A basic version of this new general framework for shape descriptor is to describe the contour of each region by a freeman code using 8 directions. It is a chain code representing a contour by a sequence of orientations of unit-sized line segments. In order to approximate rotation invariance, we compute a chain code derivative using modulo 8 differences code. This new chain code is another numbered sequence that represents relative directions of region boundary elements, measured as multiples of counter-clockwise 45° direction changes.

### 3.3 Gradient-DFH

A contour representation by a freeman chain code (absolute or relative versions) that uses only 8 directions might discretize too roughly the direction space. Thus, the contour coding is too sensitive to low variations of direction. We investigate a more elaborate version of DFH that consists in using a gradient N-directional chain code instead of the 8-connexity freeman chain code. In order to associate this local directional information to each extracted pixel belonging to the external contour, we compute the corresponding gradient angles on the original image. Then we project these angles to a quantified directional space. This quantification is based on a pre-defined parameter equal to N. The outline will then be represented by a string composed of directions resulting from this quantified space. Here again, the directional chain code can be derivated to gain rotation invariance using modulo N differences.

## 4 Evaluation

The Freeman-DFH descriptor has been integrated in the IKONA system and tested on the genetically modified plants database. Our perception of these results is that they are good in general. This has been confirmed by the biologists during a demonstration session.

In order to automatically evaluate the performance of this new shape descriptor we need a larger database, with clear ground truth information (which is not the case with the genetically modified plants database). The shape should be the most pertinent feature to discriminate different classes. We use a Swedish trees leaves database collected by the Swedish Museum of Natural History for a project with Linköping University [10]. It contains 15 different Swedish trees species. Each species is represented by 75 images. All these images represent isolated leaves. We note that although they are from different species, some leaves look very similar to a non specialist user.

**Fig. 2.** Representative leaves of the 15 different species

## 4.1 Leaves Description

Usually the color descriptors are used in CBIR systems because they caraterize well visual similarity. As known, the color of most leaves is green during the spring season. This green hue may vary due to climatic conditions and sun exposure. In addition this color changes to a variety of hot colors in autumn. This happens for allmost all species of trees. When the leaves fall from the trees and decompose, they become dry and brown. This visual aspect modifications affect both the color and the texture of the leaves, as shown in the next figure (Figure 7).

**Fig. 3.** Different colors for the same species leaves

Thus, even is this features vary from one species to an other, we suppose they won't be discriminant enough. This shows that this database is particularly well adapted to be discriminated by shape descriptors.

## 4.2   External Contour Extraction and Coding

As for the INRA database we need the outlines of the leaves to compute our shape descriptor. In this database we have a high contrast between the leaves and the white background. Thus the separation, and consequently the contour pixels, are easily obtained. We distinguish the external contour from all the possible contours (due to small gaps or overlapping in composite leaves) by keeping the longest one.

**Fig. 4.** External contour extraction

## 4.3 Comparison of DFH Versions

We compared the DFH descriptor computed respectively on the absolute and on the relative directional chains codes. Figure 5. represents a comparison of precision curves of both freeman and gradient DFH descriptors computed on absolute chain codes. We included also the combined version (relative + absolute) of gradient DFH.

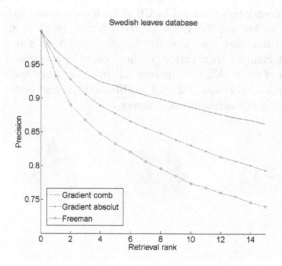

**Fig. 5.** Comparison of DFH versions

The gradient DFH improves the performances of the freeman DFH. This is due to a finer quantization of the angle space that is made available with the use of a gradient directional space instead of the classical freeman chain code. For the gradient DFH version, we notice that the combination of the relative and absolute chain codes provides the best results. In this database, the rotation variance is low. This small variation is corrected by the introduction of the relative directional information in the computation of the DFH descriptor.

## 4.4  Comparison with Other Shape Descriptors

In order to measure the contributions of Gradient-DFH descriptor, we evaluate it jointly with some existing shape descriptors on the Swedish database and compare the relative performances. These shape descriptors are:

- IKONA shape descriptor (Hough transform [4])
- Edge Orientation Histogram (EOH) [6] that we adapted to leaves outlines
- MPEG-7 CSS descriptor
- CCH descriptor

For our descriptor, these results are obtained using 40 quantified directions, 6 quantified percentiles. The segment lengths are fixed to 1.1% of the contour size. These parameters where chosen empirically. We are then using 240 bins histograms. The EOH descriptor was computed on the original gradient space without quantification. For CSS, we use the original MPEG-7 implementation.

These results demonstrate both the good performance and the contribution of the Gradient-DFH shape descriptor to the existing descriptors. The results are slightly better than those obtained with CSS. The Hough transform records average performances because it captures structural information of leaf images. Both CCH and EOH give lower results because they focus only on the global shape without taking into account local distribution of directions.

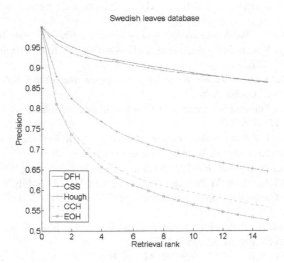

**Fig. 6.** Precision curves

One of the main reasons for introducing this new shape descriptor was the computation performances. We compare the time needed to compute all the possible similarity measures between the 1125 images of the database (about 1.2 million measures computed). On a P4-2.8GHz computer, it takes 0.5 second for the DFH descriptor and 123 seconds for the CSS descriptor. The gain is obvious. In other hand, the CSS descriptor is coded on only 116 bits (average on the entire database), but this is not a critical point for our application.

## 5  Conclusion

In order to build an automatic tool that will help botanists to study the impact of genetic modification on the visual appearance of plants, we propose a new generic shape descriptor. We evaluate the performance of this descriptor using a ground truth leaves database and compare it to known shape descriptors. The results show the effectiveness of this approach for similarity based retrieval.

## References

[1]  P. Belhumeur and al., An Electronic Field Guide: Plant Exploration and Discovery in the 21st Century. http://www.cfar.umd.edu/~gaaga/leaf/leaf.html
[2]  S. Belongie, J. Malik and J. Puzicha. *Shape matching and object recognition using shape contexts*. IEEE transactions. Pattern analysis and machine intelligence. 2002. vol 24 no 24.
[3]  N. Boujemaa, J. Fauqueur, M. Ferecatu, F. Fleuret, V. Gouet, B. LeSaux and H. Sahbi, *IKONA: interactive specific and generic image retrieval*, International workshop on Multimedia Content-Based Indexing and Retrieval (MMCBIR'2001), Rocquencourt, France, 2001
[4]  M. Ferecatu, *Image retrieval with active relevance feedback using both visual and keyword-based descriptors*, PhD thesis, 2005, Université de Versailles Saint-Quentin en Yvelines
[5]  J. Iivarinen and A. Visa. *Shape recognition of irregular objects*. 1996. Intelligent Robots and Computer Vision XV: Algorithms, Techniques, Active Vision, and Materials Handling, Proc. SPIE.
[6]  K. Jain and A. Vailaya, *Image retrieval using color and shape*, Pattern Recognition, 29(8):1233--1244, August 1996.
[7]  B.S. Manjunath, Philippe Salembier and Thomas Sikora, *Introduction to MPEG-7*, Wiley, 2002, ISBN 0-471-48678-7
[8]  F. Mokhtarian, S. Abbasi and J. Kittler, *Robust and efficient shape indexing through curvature scale space*. British Machine Vision Conference, 1996.
[9]  R.J. Qian, P.L.J. van Beek and M.I. Sezan, *Image retrieval using blob histograms*, in IEEE Proc, Int'l. Conf. On Multimedia and Expo, New York City,July 2000.
[10]  O. Söderkvist, *Computer vision classification of leaves from swedish trees*, Master thesis, 2001
[11]  C.T. Zahn and R.Z. Roskies. *Fourier descriptors for plane closed curves*. IEEE Transactions on computers, march 1972
[12]  J. Zou and G. Nagy, Evaluation of Model-Based Interactive Flower Recognition. (ICPR'04), Cambridge, United Kingdom, 2004.
[13]  Yahiaoui and N. Boujemaa, Content-based image retrieval in botanical collections for gene expression studies, (ICIP'05), Genova, Italy, September 2005

# Macroblock Mode Decision Scheme
# for Fast Encoding in H.264/AVC

Donghyung Kim, Joohyun Lee, Kicheol Jeon, and Jechang Jeong

Department of Electrical and Computer Engineering, Hanyang University,
17 Haengdang, Seongdong, Seoul 133-791, Korea
{kimdh, saint81, hobohemia, jjeong}@ece.hanyang.ac.kr

**Abstract.** To improve coding efficiency, the H.264/AVC video coding standard uses new coding tools, such as variable block size, quarter-pixel-accuracy motion estimation, multiple reference frames, intra prediction and a loop filter. Using these coding tools, H.264/AVC achieves significant improvement in coding efficiency compared with existing standards. However, the encoder complexity also increases tremendously. Among the tools, macroblock mode decision and motion estimation contribute most to total encoder complexity. This paper focuses on complexity reduction in macroblock mode decision. Of the macroblock modes which can be selected, inter8×8 and intra4×4 have the highest complexity. We propose three methods for complexity reduction, one for intra4×4 in intra-frames, one for inter8×8 in inter-frames, and one for intra4×4 in inter-frames. Simulation results show that the proposed methods save about 56.5% of total encoding time compared with the H.264/AVC reference implementation.

**Keywords:** H.264/AVC video coding, macroblock mode decision, fast mode decision.

## 1 Introduction

The H.264/AVC standard is a video compression standard that was jointly developed by the ITU-T Video Coding Experts Group and the ISO/IEC Motion Picture Experts Group [1]. To improve coding efficiency, H.264/AVC adopts new coding tools, such as quarter-pixel-accuracy motion estimation (ME), multiple reference frames, a loop filter, variable block size (VBS), etc. [2], [3]. These tools have enabled the standard to achieve higher coding efficiency than prior video coding standards. The encoder complexity, however, increases tremendously.

Several approaches have been proposed to reduce the complexity of the H.264/AVC encoder. Pan et al. proposed the fast mode decision method in intra-frames [4]. They first evaluate the distribution of the edge direction histogram, and then choose the prediction mode candidates according to that result. Through this method, 20% of total encoding time can be reduced. Yin et al. proposed a method to alleviate encoder complexity caused by ME and macroblock mode decision [5]. Their low complexity ME algorithm consists of two steps. First, integer-pixel ME is carried out using enhanced prediction zonal search (EPZS). Then, depending on the result of

Y. Zhuang et al. (Eds.): PCM 2006, LNCS 4261, pp. 365–374, 2006.
© Springer-Verlag Berlin Heidelberg 2006

the integer-pixel ME, sub-pixel ME is carried out within some limited areas. To achieve faster macroblock mode decision, their method simply examines limited modes based on the costs of inter16×16, inter8×8, and inter4×4. Huang et al. proposed an algorithm to reduce the time to search the reference frames for ME complexity reduction [6]. For each macroblock, they analyze the available information after intra prediction and ME from the previous frame to determine whether it is necessary to search more frames. Their method can save about 10-67% of ME computation. Ahmad et al. proposed a fast algorithm for macroblock mode decision based on a 3D recursive search algorithm that takes cost into account as well as the previous frame information [7]. This algorithm leads to a decrease of over 30% in encoding time compared with the H.264/AVC reference implementation. The bitstream length, however, increases by about 15%.

To speed up the H.264/AVC encoding time, we focus on complexity reduction of macroblock mode decision. When an 8×8 DCT is not used, the candidate macroblock modes are SKIP, inter16×16, inter16×8, inter8×16, inter8×8, intra16×16, and intra4×4. An inter8×8 mode can be further partitioned into four sub-macroblock modes: inter8×8, inter8×4, inter4×8, and inter4×4. Among these modes, inter8×8 and intra4×4 modes contribute most to the complexity, especially when rate-distortion optimization (RDO) is used.

In this paper, we propose three algorithms. First is to alleviate intra4×4 complexity in intra-frames by limiting the number of selectable prediction modes. Second reduces the inter8×8 complexity in inter-frames by estimating four sub-macroblock modes within inter8×8 by using the costs of other inter modes with relatively low complexity. Lastly, third reduces the intra4×4 complexity in inter-frames by using the similarity between RD costs of two intra modes.

## 2 Overview of Macroblock Modes in H.264/AVC

### 2.1 Macroblock Modes in H.264/AVC

In intra-frames, the H.264/AVC standard allows three intra-modes as macroblock modes. They are intra4×4, intra8×8, and intra16×16. As shown in Table 1, each intra-mode has the different number of prediction modes, and is applied to the different block size. Four prediction modes are available in intra16×16, and nine prediction modes are available intra8×8 and intra4×4.

In inter-frames, H.264/AVC allows not only intra-modes but also SKIP and four inter macroblock modes: SKIP, inter16×16, inter16×8, inter8×16 and inter8×8. Furthermore, each block within inter8×8 can be divided into four sub-macroblock modes. The allowed sub-macroblock modes are inter8×8, inter8×4, inter4×8, and inter4×4.

An inter16×16 mode has only one motion vector, whereas inter16×8 and inter8×16 have two motion vectors. An inter8×8 mode may have 4-16 motion vectors depending on the selected sub-macroblock modes. A SKIP mode refers to the mode where neither motion vector nor residual is encoded.

**Table 1.** The relationship between prediction modes and prediction directions

| prediction modes | prediction directions | |
| :---: | :---: | :---: |
| | intra4×4 and intra8×8 | intra16×16 |
| 0 | vertical | vertical |
| 1 | horizontal | horizontal |
| 2 | DC | DC |
| 3 | diagonal-down-left | plane |
| 4 | diagonal-down-right | |
| 5 | vertical-right | |
| 6 | horizontal-down | |
| 7 | vertical-left | |
| 8 | horizontal-up | |

## 2.2 Cost Criteria for Mode Decision in the Reference Software

The reference software decides macroblock modes using three cost calculation criteria: motion vector (MV) cost, reference frame (REF) cost, and rate distortion (RD) cost. The MV cost and the REF cost are calculated using a lambda factor and are defined as follows respectively.

$$MVcost = WeightedCost(f, mvbits[(cx << s) - px]$$
$$+ mvbits[(cy << s) - py])$$

$$where \quad f : lambda \ factor$$
$$cx, cy : candidate \ x \ and \ y \ position \ for \ ME$$
$$px, py : predicted \ x \ and \ y \ position \ for \ ME$$

(1)

$$REFcost = WeightedCost(f, refbits(ref))$$
$$where \ f : lambda \ factor$$

(2)

In (1) and (2), *WeightedCost( )* returns the cost for the bits of motion vector and reference frame, respectively. Finally, the RD cost is defined as:

$$RDcost = Distortion + \lambda \cdot Rate$$
$$where \ \lambda : Lagrange \ multiplier$$

(3)

In (3), the distortion is computed by calculating the SNR of the block and the rate is calculated by taking into consideration the length of the stream after the last stage of encoding.

Using these cost criteria, the reference software chooses the mode with the minimum cost value as a macroblock mode [8].

# 3 Proposed Algorithm

In this paper, in order to reduce the complexity of the H.264/AVC encoder, we propose three independent schemes. One of them is the complexity reduction of intra4×4 in intra-frames. The others reduce the complexity of inter8×8 and intra4×4 in inter-frames, respectively.

### 3.1 Complexity Reduction of Intra4×4 in Intra-frames

As described in Section 2, the intra4×4 mode has nine prediction modes per 4×4 block. Therefore 144(9*16) RD cost computations are required altogether, in order to decide prediction modes for sixteen 4×4 blocks, when rate-distortion optimization (RDO) technique is used.

In order to reduce the number of RD cost computations, we restrict the number of prediction mode candidates to five at most, which consist of DC, two candidates based on the edge direction and two candidates based on the context.

**Edge-Based Candidates.** There are two modes for the edge direction-based candidates, which are the primary edge mode (PEM) and the secondary edge mode (SEM). The SEM is chosen between two neighboring modes of the PEM in terms of prediction direction.

We first evaluate edge magnitudes and phase at twelve pixel positions (dark region in Fig. 1) located at 4×4 block boundary to find the PEM by using the Prewitt edge operator which has two convolution kernels. In this process, since the reconstructed image is not available yet, we use the original image data.

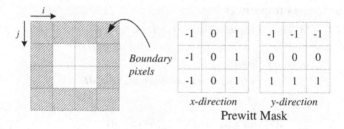

**Fig. 1.** Twelve pixel positions to evaluate edge magnitudes and phases in a current 4×4 block and two convolution kernels of Prewitt mask

For a pixel value, $p_{i,j}$, the degree of difference in each direction, that is, the deviations are as follows:

$$dx_{i,j} = (p_{i-1,j+1} - p_{i-1,j-1}) + (p_{i,j+1} - p_{i,j-1}) + (p_{i+1,j+1} - p_{i+1,j-1})$$
$$dy_{i,j} = (p_{i+1,j-1} - p_{i-1,j-1}) + (p_{i+1,j} - p_{i-1,j}) + (p_{i+1,j+1} - p_{i-1,j+1})$$

(4)

After these deviation calculations, the edge magnitude and phase at the position $(i,j)$ can be obtained by using Eqs. 5 and 6, respectively.

$$mag(i,j) = |dx_{i,j}| + |dy_{i,j}|$$

(5)

$$ang(i,j) = \arctan(\frac{dy_{i,j}}{dx_{i,j}})$$

(6)

In the actual implementation, we can use *nearest()* function, which consists of only adders and comparators, to find the nearest prediction mode (NPM) to the edge phase easily, instead of *arctan()* function. This is because H.264/AVC uses the limited prediction modes. For more details, refer to [4].

$$NPM = nearest(\frac{dy_{i,j}}{dx_{i,j}}) \tag{7}$$

Once the edge magnitudes and the NPMs are obtained at twelve pixel positions, the PEM is decided as the prediction mode which maximizes the sum of the edge magnitudes in each prediction mode.

Then, between the two neighboring prediction modes in terms of prediction direction, the bigger one is chosen as a SEM.

**Context-Based Candidates.** Two context-based candidates, as shown in Fig. 2, are set to the modes of left and upper 4×4 blocks of the current block, provided that every candidate mode included in DC, PEM, or SEM will be excluded.

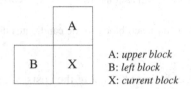

A: *upper block*
B: *left block*
X: *current block*

**Fig. 2.** The upper and left 4×4 blocks to obtain two context-based candidates

**Early Termination Condition.** During calculating the RD cost of candidates in turn, if the current RD cost is 1.2 times smaller than both the RD costs of upper and left blocks, in other words, if the current RD cost satisfies following expression, the calculation will be terminated even though there still remain candidates.

$$RD\,cost_{cur} < \min(RD\,cost\ of\ blockA, RD\,cost\ of\ blockB)/1.2 \tag{8}$$

Therefore our proposed algorithm has 1 to 5 candidates using early termination scheme, and also has 3 to 5 candidates not using early termination scheme. Hence we can save more than 44% of RD cost computations of intra4×4 in intra-frames.

### 3.2 Fast Mode Decision in Inter-frames

The H.264/AVC standard allows many kinds of macroblock modes in inter-frames. They are SKIP, inter16×16, inter16×8, inter8×16, inter8×8, intra16×16, intra8×8, and intra4×4. Furthermore, each block within inter8×8 can be divided into four sub-macroblock modes: inter8×8, inter8×4, inter4×8, and inter4×4.

To improve the fast mode decision in inter-frames, we focus on the complexity reduction of inter8×8 and intra4×4 which occupy the most of mode decision complexity in inter-frames.

**Complexity Reduction of Inter8×8.** As sub-macroblock mode decision of inter8×8 requires additional RD cost computations, inter8×8 has the highest complexity among four inter macroblock modes (i.e. inter16×16, inter16×8, inter8×16, and inter8×8) in inter-frames.

For the complexity reduction of sub-macroblock mode decision, we assume that the costs of inter macroblock modes monotonically increase or decrease according to their partitioned directions. Under this assumption, we choose sub-macroblock mode

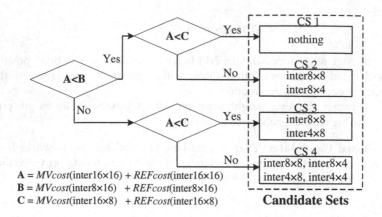

A = *MVcost*(inter16×16) + *REFcost*(inter16×16)
B = *MVcost*(inter8×16)  + *REFcost*(inter8×16)
C = *MVcost*(inter16×8)  + *REFcost*(inter16×8)

**Candidate Sets**

**Fig. 3.** The decision method of sub-macroblock mode candidates using the costs of inter16×16, inter8×16, and inter16×8.

candidates of each 8×8 block in inter8×8 using the costs of inter16×16, inter16×8, and inter8×16. Figure 3 depicts the decision method of sub-macroblock mode candidates.

As shown in Fig. 3, we classify sub-macroblock modes into four different candidate sets (CS) depending upon the sum of MV cost and REF cost of the other macroblock modes, that is, inter16×16, inter8×16, and inter16×8.

In $CS_1$, since the cost of inter16×16 is smaller than both costs of inter16×8 and inter8×16, we may expect that additional block partitions in any directions are not able to reduce the cost. Therefore, in this case, we skip the whole process of sub-macroblock mode decision. In $CS_2$, since the cost of inter16×16 is smaller than that of inter8×16 and is larger than that of inter16×8, we may expect that additional block partition in the vertical direction is able to reduce the cost of macroblock. Therefore, in this case, we consider only inter8×8 and inter8×4 as sub-macroblock modes. In $CS_3$, since the cost of inter16×16 is smaller than that of inter16×8 and is larger than that of inter8×16, we may expect that additional block partition in the horizontal direction is able to reduce the cost of macroblock. Therefore, we consider only inter8×8 and inter4×8 as sub-macroblock modes. In $CS_4$, since the cost of inter16×16 is larger than those of both inter16×8 and 8×16, we may expect that additional partitions in both directions are able to reduce the cost. Therefore, in this case, we consider all allowed sub-macroblock modes.

**Table 2.** the probabilities of each CS selection for several test sequences in QCIF format

| Sequences | $CS_1$ | $CS_2$ | $CS_3$ | $CS_4$ |
|---|---|---|---|---|
| Akiyo | 72.89 | 11.91 | 8.42 | 6.78 |
| Container | 81.45 | 6.53 | 7.74 | 4.28 |
| Mobile | 41.77 | 17.66 | 15.44 | 25.13 |
| Silent | 62.35 | 9.05 | 14.64 | 13.96 |
| Stefan | 49.10 | 16.83 | 12.95 | 21.12 |
| Trevor | 51.16 | 12.15 | 15.64 | 21.05 |

Table 2 represents the probabilities of each CS selection for several test sequences in QCIF(176×144) format. In this result, first 100 frames of each test sequence are encoded into IPPP structure and quantization parameter (QP) is set to 28.

As shown in Table 2, $CS_1$ which skips the whole process of sub-macroblock mode decision is a lot larger than the others, especially for Akiyo and Container sequences.

**Complexity Reduction of Intra4×4 in Inter-frames.** The intra4×4 mode has higher complexity than intra16×16 because it has more prediction modes for finer granularity. Due to this characteristic, intra4×4 generally yields a smaller prediction error than intra16×16. However, most macroblocks have only a little difference between the RD costs of intra16×16 and intra4×4. This is because edges directed in vertical or horizontal directions are dominant in natural images, which are considered in intra16×16. Furthermore, intra4×4 have more overhead bits for encoding prediction modes.

Using similarity between the RD costs of two intra modes, we first find the inter mode with a minimum RD cost. Then we compare the RD cost of the selected inter mode with that of intra16×16. If the RD cost of intra16×16 is much larger, namely if Eq. (9) is true, then the RD cost computation of intra4×4 is skipped. In this formula, $K$ is a proportional constant.

$$RDcost(intra\ 16 \times 16) > min(\ RDcost(\ inter\ modes)\ ) \times K \tag{9}$$

Table 3 describes the missing rate of intra4×4. The missing rate indicates the probability that the skipped intra4×4 has the smallest RD cost. As shown in Table 3, the average missing rate is only about 0.9% for $K = 1.5$.

**Table 3.** Missing rates of intra4×4 according to $K$

| Sequences | Missing Rate (%) | | |
|---|---|---|---|
| | $K=1.3$ | $K=1.5$ | $K=1.7$ |
| Akiyo | 7.7 | 1.5 | 0.0 |
| Container | 2.7 | 1.0 | 0.9 |
| Mobile | 0.4 | 0.0 | 0.0 |
| Silent | 4.7 | 1.7 | 0.4 |
| Stefan | 2.8 | 0.2 | 0.0 |
| Trevor | 9.0 | 0.9 | 0.1 |

# 4   Simulation Results

Since three schemes we proposed are uncorrelated, they can be applied independently or simultaneously. In our simulation, we applied the three proposed algorithms simultaneously to encode test sequences. For the purpose of evaluation, the baseline profile of the public reference encoder JVT Model (JM) v.9.3 was used. The software was tested on an Intel Pentium-IV based computer with 512 MB RAM under the Windows XP Professional operating system.

In this simulation, we adopted full search for ME, used RDO, and set Quantization Parameter (QP) and $K$ in Eq. (9) to 28 and 1.5, respectively. The first 100 frames of six standard video sequences in QCIF (176×144) format were encoded using different frame structure: GOP($N$=0, 30). In case of $N$=0, only the first frame is encoded as an intra-frame and in case of $N$=30, there is an intra-frame for every 30 coded frames.

Tables 4 and 5 represent the number of RD cost computations of inter8×8 and intra4×4 in inter-frames when using GOP($N$=0) and GOP($N$=30), respectively. As described in Section 3, the RD cost computations of intra4×4 blocks in intra-frames are always reduced as much as 44% at least. As shown in these results, we can save 72% and 93% of the RD cost computations in inter8×8 and intra4×4, respectively.

**Table 4.** The number of RD cost computation of inter8×8 and intra4×4 in inter-frames when the coding structure is GOP($N$=30)

| Sequences | Inter8×8 | | | Intra4×4 | | |
|---|---|---|---|---|---|---|
| | Reference Software | Proposed Method | Reduction Ratio (%) | Reference Software | Proposed Method | Reduction Ratio (%) |
| Akiyo | 152,064 | 27,704 | 81.8 | 9,504 | 20 | 99.8 |
| Container | 152,064 | 18,160 | 88.1 | 9,504 | 1,545 | 83.7 |
| Mobile | 152,064 | 63,416 | 58.3 | 9,504 | 105 | 98.9 |
| Silent | 152,064 | 40,688 | 73.2 | 9,504 | 622 | 93.5 |
| Stefan | 152,064 | 55,416 | 63.6 | 9,504 | 840 | 91.2 |
| Trevor | 152,064 | 51,936 | 65.8 | 9,504 | 570 | 94.0 |

**Table 5.** The number of RD cost computation of inter8×8 and intra4×4 in inter-frames when the coding structure is GOP($N$=0)

| Sequences | Inter8×8 | | | Intra4×4 | | |
|---|---|---|---|---|---|---|
| | Reference Software | Proposed Method | Reduction Ratio (%) | Reference Software | Proposed Method | Reduction Ratio (%) |
| Akiyo | 156,816 | 28,832 | 81.6 | 9,801 | 17 | 99.8 |
| Container | 156,816 | 17,288 | 89.0 | 9,801 | 1,862 | 81.0 |
| Mobile | 156,816 | 64,864 | 58.6 | 9,801 | 120 | 98.8 |
| Silent | 156,816 | 40,232 | 74.3 | 9,801 | 613 | 93.8 |
| Stefan | 156,816 | 57,136 | 63.6 | 9,801 | 883 | 91.0 |
| Trevor | 156,816 | 53,592 | 65.8 | 9,801 | 859 | 91.2 |

Tables 6 and 7 compare the bitrates and PSNRs for each test sequence. Since the reference implementation is an exhaustive search for deciding the macroblock mode, the number of encoded bits is the least for each sequence. These results show the average increase of the total bitrates is only about 0.95%, and the average PSNR drop is only about 0.06 dB when using the proposed method.

Finally, Table 8 compares total encoding time from the proposed method with that from the reference software. This result shows a substantial decrease of about 56.5% in total encoding time compared with the reference implementation.

**Table 6.** Comparison of bitrates (Kbits/sec) and PSNRs (dB) when the coding structure is GOP(N=30)

| Sequences | Bitrate (Kbits/sec) | | | PSNR (dB) | | |
|---|---|---|---|---|---|---|
| | Reference Software | Proposed Method | Increase Ratio (%) | Reference Software | Proposed Method | Decrease dB |
| Akiyo | 44.91 | 45.69 | 1.7 | 38.45 | 38.38 | 0.07 |
| Container | 59.39 | 59.88 | 0.8 | 36.31 | 36.28 | 0.03 |
| Mobile | 533.51 | 535.60 | 0.4 | 33.23 | 33.15 | 0.08 |
| Silent | 104.49 | 106.56 | 1.9 | 35.95 | 35.87 | 0.08 |
| Stefan | 409.29 | 412.46 | 0.8 | 34.32 | 34.25 | 0.07 |
| Trevor | 141.03 | 142.49 | 1.0 | 36.63 | 36.56 | 0.07 |

**Table 7.** Comparison of bitrates (Kbits/sec) and PSNRs (dB) when the coding structure is GOP(N=0)

| Sequences | Bitrate (Kbits/sec) | | | PSNR (dB) | | |
|---|---|---|---|---|---|---|
| | Reference Software | Proposed Method | Increase Ratio (%) | Reference Software | Proposed Method | Decrease dB |
| Akiyo | 30.40 | 30.72 | 1.0 | 38.18 | 38.14 | 0.04 |
| Container | 40.16 | 40.23 | 0.2 | 36.07 | 36.03 | 0.04 |
| Mobile | 496.49 | 498.30 | 0.4 | 33.14 | 33.05 | 0.09 |
| Silent | 82.69 | 83.74 | 1.3 | 35.84 | 35.77 | 0.07 |
| Stefan | 379.26 | 382.61 | 0.9 | 34.22 | 34.16 | 0.06 |
| Trevor | 132.49 | 133.86 | 1.0 | 36.40 | 36.39 | 0.01 |

**Table 8.** Comparison of total encoding time (sec) when the coding structure is GOP(N=0, 30)

| Sequences | GOP (N=30) | | | GOP (N=0) | | |
|---|---|---|---|---|---|---|
| | Reference Software | Proposed Method | Reduction Ratio (%) | Reference Software | Proposed Method | Decrease PSNR |
| Coastguard | 103.5 | 45.0 | 56.5 | 105.2 | 45.5 | 56.8 |
| Container | 109.0 | 46.5 | 57.3 | 110.7 | 47.1 | 57.5 |
| Mobile | 140.9 | 57.1 | 59.5 | 142.8 | 58.4 | 59.1 |
| Silent | 112.0 | 49.9 | 55.4 | 113.7 | 50.0 | 56.0 |
| Stefan | 128.8 | 56.0 | 56.5 | 130.5 | 56.2 | 56.9 |
| Trevor | 108.3 | 50.8 | 53.1 | 110.6 | 51.9 | 53.1 |

## 5  Conclusions

We proposed three simple and effective schemes for the quick decision of macroblock modes in H.264/AVC video coding. Using our methods, the RD cost computation of intra4×4 in intra-frames can be reduced as much as 44% at least and the RD cost computations of inter8×8 and intra4×4 were reduced by about 72% and 93%, respectively. The proposed schemes can be applied independently. When three methods are used simultaneously, simulation results show that our methods can save about 56.5% of total encoding time regardless of input sequences, yet the average increased rate of the total bits and average PSNR drop are only about 0.95% and 0.06 dB, respectively. This huge reduction of encoder complexity may be useful in real-time implementation of the H.264/AVC standard.

# References

1. Wiegand, T.: Version 3 of H.264/AVC. Doc. JVT-K051 (2004)
2. Wiegand, T., Sullivan, G. J.: Overview of the H.264/AVC Video Coding Standard. IEEE Trans. Circuits Syst. for Video Technol., Vol. 13. (2003) 560-576
3. Wiegand, T., Schwarz, H., Joch, A., Kossentini, F.: Rate-Constrained Coder Control and Comparison of Video Coding Standard. IEEE Trans. Circuits Syst. for Video Technol., Vol. 13. (2003) 688-703
4. Pan, F., Lin, X., Rahardja, S., Lim, K.P., Li, Z.G., Wu, D., Wu, S.: Fast Mode Decision Algorithm for Intraprediction in H.264/AVC Video Coding. IEEE Trans. Circuits Syst. for Video Technol., Vol. 15. (2005) 813-821
5. Yin, P., Tourapis, H. C., Tourapis, A. M., Boyce, J.: Fast Mode Decision and Motion Estimation for JVT/H.264. ICIP'03, Vol. 3. (2003) 853-856
6. Huang, Y. W., Hsieh, B. Y., Whang, T. C., Chien, S. Y., Ma, S. Y., Shen, C. F., Chen, L. G.: Analysis and Reduction of Reference Frames for Motion Estimation in MPEG-4 AVC/JVT/H.264. ICASSP'03, Vol. 3 (2003) 145-148
7. Ahmad, A., Khan, N., Masud, S., Maud, M.A.: Efficient Block Size Selection in H.264 Video Coding Standard. Electronics Letters, Vol. 40. (2004) 19-21
8. JM9.3: http://bs.hhi.de/~suehring/tml/ download/ jm93.zip.

# A Mathematical Model for Interaction Analysis Between Multiview Video System and User

You Yang[1,2,5], Gangyi Jiang[1,2], Mei Yu[2,3], and Zhu Peng[4]

[1] Institute of Computing Technology, Chinese Academy of Science, Beijing, 100080, China
[2] Faculty of Information Science and Eng., Ningbo University, Ningbo, 315211, China
[3] National Key Laboratory of Machine Perception, Peking University, 100871, China
[4] School of Mining and Safety Engineering, China University of Mining and Technology,
Xuzhou, 221008, China
[5] Graduate School of Chinese Academy of Science, Beijing, 100080, China
{sayu_yangyou, jianggangyi}@126.com

**Abstract.** Multiview video coding (MVC) plays an important role in three-dimensional audio-video (3DAV) systems. Multiview video display systems are built to provide interactive video services and quality of services (QoS) provided by the system is currently under consideration. MVC encoder uses advanced coding schemes and group of GOP (GoGOP) structure to pursue high compressibility. There is a conflict between compressibility and access ability, i.e., QoS of interaction. In this paper, several evaluation functions are proposed to measure the load and access ability of multiview video system. A nonlinear multipurpose mathematical model based on these functions is provided for interaction analysis. On considering the model, the access ability is a factor to be taken into account for encoder when high compressibility is the primary, and so is the compressibility when trying to achieve high access ability.

**Keywords:** Multiview video coding, random access, interaction analysis.

## 1 Introduction

Video services have greatly changed our daily life. With the technical development in various fields, more and more flexibility has been provided. Furthermore, more and more research efforts were exerted than ever before in the field of advanced applications including interactive free viewpoint television (FTV) or other multiview video services. As a natural extension to the monoview video, multiview video or FTV can be widely used in many applications, such as advertisement, educational program, sports, and some important events. Therefore, the QoS problems of multiview video system are emerging.

MPEG has formally begun the research on 3DAV, including MVC and FTV[1]. Along with other technologies, temporal and view random access, i.e., video VCR functionalities, are basic requirements for MVC[2]. Random access requires the decoder to access a frame in a given time and view with minimal decoding frame cost. Since then, experimental interactive multiview video (MV) display systems have been built, including ray-space based communication system[3,4], scalable system[5] and interactive MV display system[6], etc.. It has been shown that smooth in view

Y. Zhuang et al. (Eds.): PCM 2006, LNCS 4261, pp. 375–384, 2006.
© Springer-Verlag Berlin Heidelberg 2006

transition, degree of interaction and handling computational complexity turn out to be the key challenges for FTV and MV applications. Therefore the flexibility in temporal and spatial access is an important evaluation parameter for interaction and QoS. Average processing time and average CPU load are proposed for evaluation, but the scores are video content and environment dependent. So far, advanced MVC schemes were proposed to improve coding efficiency and compressibility[7-9], but the common sense is that the well-compressed MV may be worse in random access[10]. It is challenge to handle the conflict and design an efficient coding scheme while providing flexible interaction.

In this paper, several evaluation functions to measure the MV system load and access ability are proposed, then a nonlinear multipurpose mathematical model is proposed for interaction analysis between system and users. Followed by this model, the encoders will no longer pursue high compressibility without considering the access ability, and vice versa.

## 2  Preliminaries, Definitions and Notations

The model and evaluation functions are based on random graph theory, hyper-space and dynamic programming, and some basic terminologies and notations are presented first as follows.

**Definition 1**[11]. A graph $G$ is defined as a pair of $(V, E)$, where $V$ is a vertex set and $E$ is an edge set that satisfying $e_{ij}=(v_i,v_j)$ if $v_i$ and $v_j$ are joined by an edge. The cardinal of $V$ and $E$ are called order and size of a graph $G$, respectively. All the vertexes connecting to vertex $v_i$ is called the neighborhood of $v_i$, and denoted by $N_{(vi)}$. A complete graph $G$ with order $s$ is denoted by $K_s$. Directed graph means that all edges in the graph are assigned with directions. Furthermore, the edge can be assigned with weight for practical use and then the graph is a directed weight graph.

**Definition 2**[12]. A random graph $G=(V, E, \Omega)$ is a graph $G$ defined in a probability space $\Omega$, in which each edge $e_{ij}$ is assigned with a probability $p_{ij}$, where $0<p_{ij}<1$ and satisfying $\sum p_{ij}=1$. $G$ is called directed weight random graph for the directed weight graph $G$. The path in $G$ is denoted by $\mathcal{P}$.

**Definition 3**[7]. Let $V=\{v_i|1\leq i\leq n\times m\}$ be the finite set of the frames to be encoded in MV sequence, then, hyper-space $H$ is defined as $H=(V, E)$, where $E=(E_i)_{i\in I}$, and $E_i$ is the subset of nodes with the disparity-motion estimation relationship and $I$ is an index set of $H$. $v_i$ and $E_j$ represent node and edge in $H$, respectively.

Let $n$ and $m$ be the number of viewpoints and frames in each view of a MV sequence, $m_1$ be the number of frames in a single view in a GoGoP, respectively. The users receive bit stream from MV system and will control the video freely. Lou et al[6] defined three interaction modes for users and system, as described in Fig.1(a). These modes are convenient for application development, but actually the users can freely control the video and may feel dull with the defined modes. For more practical use, three interaction modes are defined.

(1) Neighbor view switch mode, in which MV users watch the video at normal speed, no fast forward or backward, and the next frame of $V_iT_j$ is $V_{i(\pm 1)}T_{j+1}$.

(2) Random view switch mode, in which the next frame of $V_iT_j$ is $V_{i(\pm k)}T_{(j+1)}$, where $1 \leq i \pm k \leq n$.

These two interaction modes allow users to watch MV from the first frame to the terminal, which form a random directed path $\mathcal{P}$ in $\mathcal{G}$, as shown in Fig.1(b) and (c). The path $\mathcal{P}$ is then called *path view* for the users. Besides the path view, the user may browse MV optionally, then the third mode is defined.

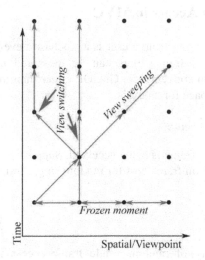

(a) Three interaction modes defined in [6]

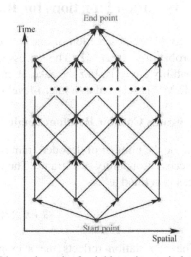

(b) Directed graph of neighbor view switch mode

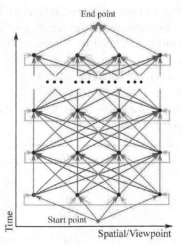

(c) Directed graph of random view switch mode

**Fig. 1.** Three interaction modes and two path view modes defined for multiview video users

(3) Arbitrary view switch mode, in which the user can access any frame in temporal or view axis, forward or backward, at normal or fast speed, any view at any moment. It can be described as a complete graph $K_{n \times m}$, which is the multiview video VCR functionality.

$K_{n \times m}$ can be decomposed into bi-direction strongly complete graph. For more complex interaction, $K_{n \times m}$ can be decomposed into many hyper-spaces which contain mono-direction. Thus, mono-directed graph is enough for analysis.

## 3   Evaluation Functions for Random Access in MVC

For any MV, the selection of one frame for viewing from a user is a stochastic event in probability space $\Omega$. The access ability of frames thus can be measured by probability analysis. For the sake of calculation convenience, GoGOP rather than the whole MV is selected as a micro-level hyper-space for analysis.

### 3.1   Frame Cost for Random Single Frame Access

Let $x_i$ be the number of decoded frames when $i^{th}$ frame is being accessed. Suppose $p_i$ is the access probability of $i^{th}$ frame. The expectation frame cost for random single frame access is defined as[7]

$$E(X_f) = \sum_{i=1}^{n \times m_i} x_i p_i \tag{1}$$

The expectation reflects the average ability of random single frame access in decoder, which is an aspect of interaction. Lower expectation means higher access ability. If $x_i$ is set to be the number of stored reference frames when predicting $i^{th}$ frame, $E(X_m)$ which is the expectation of the number of reference frames stored in system buffer, can be similarly calculated by formula (1). $E(X_m)$ reflects the average buffer cost in video system. $E(X_m)$ and $E(X_f)$ of several advanced MVC encoding schemes as shown in Fig.2(a)-(j) are listed in Table 1.

**Table 1.** Scores of random access and server buffer load for several different MVC schemes and SP frame applied schemes in Fig.2

| GoGoP structure | $F_{0,0}$ | $F_{0,0}/m_1$ | $F_{m-0,0}$ | $F_{m-0,0}/m_1$ | $E(X_f)$ | $E(X_m)$ |
|---|---|---|---|---|---|---|
| All I frame | 5 | 1 | 0 | 0 | 1 | 0 |
| Tree mode | 7.75 | 1.94 | 3.75 | 0.94 | 3.5 | 2.5 |
| Simulcast | 9.13 | 1.83 | 7.53 | 1.51 | 3 | 2 |
| Transposed | 23 | 4.60 | 18.20 | 3.64 | 13 | 12 |
| Improved transposed | 23 | 4.60 | 18.58 | 3.72 | 13 | 12 |
| SP transposed structure (1) | 15 | 3.00 | 10.77 | 2.15 | 5 | 4 |
| SP transposed structure (2) | 13.93 | 2.79 | 9.86 | 1.97 | 5.64 | 4.64 |
| SP transposed structure (3) | 15.45 | 3.09 | 11.35 | 2.27 | 6.28 | 5.28 |
| Improved SP transposed structure (2) | 15.57 | 3.11 | 11.72 | 2.34 | 5.56 | 4.56 |
| Improved SP transposed structure (3) | 13.42 | 2.69 | 9.70 | 1.94 | 6.28 | 5.28 |

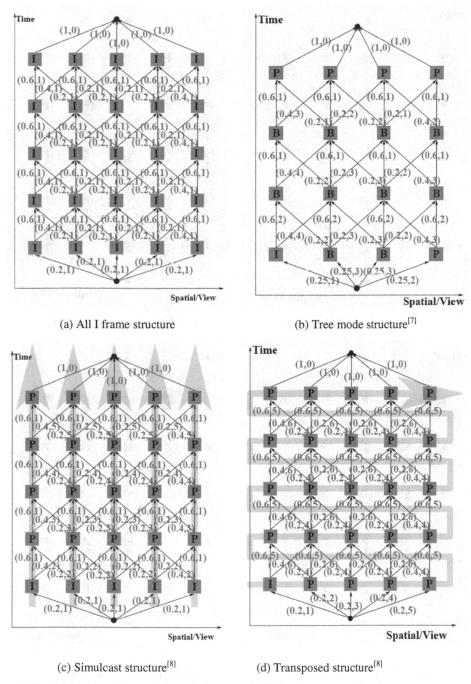

(a) All I frame structure

(b) Tree mode structure[7]

(c) Simulcast structure[8]

(d) Transposed structure[8]

**Fig. 2.** Neighbor view switch mode for several MVC schemes and SP-applied schemes

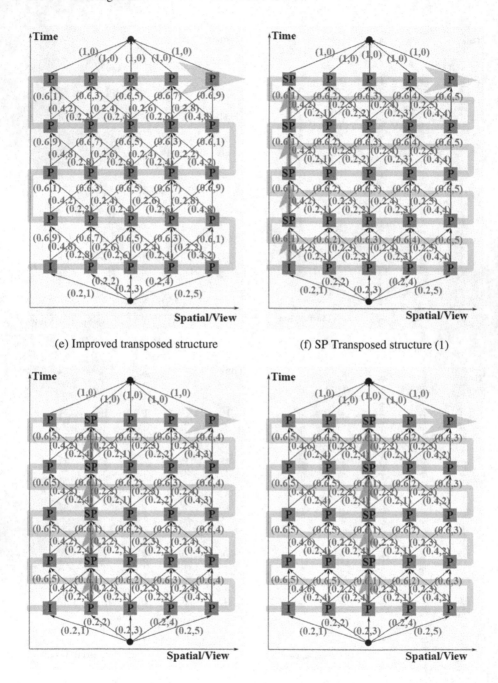

(e) Improved transposed structure        (f) SP Transposed structure (1)

(g) SP Transposed structure (2)        (h) SP Transposed structure (3)

**Fig. 2.** (*continued*)

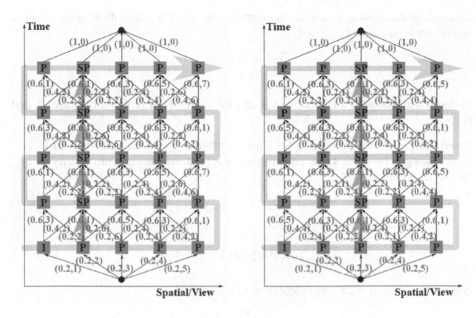

(i) Improved SP transposed structure (2)      (j) Improved SP transposed structure (3)

**Fig. 2.** (*continued*)

## 3.2  Frame Cost for Complex Interaction

The frames continuously viewed by a user are stochastic events in $\Omega$, i.e., a directed path $\mathcal{P}$ in $\mathcal{G}$. It is clear that the probability and weight for path $\mathcal{P} \in \mathcal{G}$ are

$$
\begin{cases}
P_{\mathcal{P}} = \prod_{e_{ij} \in \mathcal{P}} p_{ij} \\
W_{\mathcal{P}} = \sum_{e_{ij} \in \mathcal{P}} w_{ij}
\end{cases}
\tag{2}
$$

It is a common sense that a user will access the next frame in temporal axis in the same view of current frame with higher possibility than switching to other directions. With the knowledge of the statistics and probability theory, it can be supposed that the event of direction selection satisfies standard normal distribution. For the case that normal distribution not satisfied, it can be transformed by the standardized formula.

$$
\frac{X - E(X)}{\sigma} \sim N(0,1)
\tag{3}
$$

On the other hand, frame costs $w$ is defined as the number of further decoded frames before the next selected frame can be accessed after the current one. As shown in Fig.2(a)-(j), several proposed encoding schemes are described as directed weight random graphs. The edges are labeled with $(p,w)$, where $p$ is the probability of the direction to be chosen, and $w$ is the frame costs. Clearly, the following formula is natural for each frame, i.e., $v_i \in \mathcal{G}$.

$$\sum_{j \in N(v_i)} p_j = 1 \tag{4}$$

**Proposition:** The path selection in $\mathcal{G}$ is stochastic events in probability space $\Omega$, and $P(\Omega)=1$.

**Proof:** Let $p_{(i,j),k}$ be the probability for a user selecting $v_{(i+1,k)}$ as the next frame of $v_{(i,j)}$, where $k \in N_{(v(i,j))}$. From the knowledge of dynamic programming and probability theory, the induction function

$$\begin{cases} P_{i,j} = \sum_{k \in N(i,j)} P_{i+1,k} P_{(i,j),k} \\ P_{m_1,j} = 1 \\ j \in [1,n]; i \in [0,m_1] \end{cases} \tag{5}$$

must be satisfied. It is an easy calculation to complete the proof.

$\square$

The proposition is true for any interaction modes defined above, which is a theoretical basis for interaction analysis. From the above procedure of the proof, we can apply the function to evaluate the flexibility for user controlling MV.

**Evaluation function:** The access ability measured by frame costs and probability can be calculated by

$$F_f = E(\Omega) = \sum_{\mathcal{P} \in \mathcal{G}} E(\mathcal{P}) = \sum_{\mathcal{P} \in \mathcal{G}} P_{\mathcal{P}} W_{\mathcal{P}} \tag{6}$$

where $F_f$ is the expectation frame cost for the user to view $m_1$ frames.

Formula (6) can adapt to any defined interaction modes. The differences between these modes are the values of $p_{i,j}$ and $w_{i,j}$. On the other hand, $p_{i,j}$ is relatively stable in a specified application, while $w_{i,j}$ is determined by the structure of GoGoP or MVC coding scheme. Hence, $F_f$ is determined by application requirements and encoding scheme. Furthermore, set $F_m$ to be the average buffer cost of video system, and $w_{i,j}$ is the number of stored reference frames when predicting the next frame. The $F_m$ of MV system can be drawn out similarly by formula (6). $F_f$ and $F_m$ for several MVC coding schemes with 'neighbor view switch mode' in Fig.2(a)-(j) are also listed in Table 1. For convenience of calculation, the probability of forward selection is set to be 0.6, while the neighbor selection is 0.2. The similar calculation can be done for other modes or situations.

## 4   Interaction Mathematical Model

As concluded from Table 1, MVC coding scheme can greatly affect interaction flexibility between video system and users. Different coding schemes have different ability in access ability and compressibility, and scheme design can no longer pursue high efficiency without considering bandwidth, server load and interaction flexibility. Thus, a nonlinear multi-purpose programming model for analyzing these practical interconnected factors is proposed as follows

$$\min z = s_1^+ + s_2^+ + s_3^+ + s_4^+ + s_5^+$$

$$s.t. \begin{cases} B(\overline{w}) + s_1^- - s_1^+ = B \\ F_f + s_2^- - s_2^+ = F_f c \\ F_m + s_3^- - s_3^+ = F_m c \\ E(X_f) + s_4^- - s_4^+ = E_f \\ E(X_m) + s_5^- - s_5^+ = E_m \end{cases} \qquad (7)$$

$$(\overline{w} \in N) \geq 1, \overline{s^-} \geq 0, \overline{s^+} \geq 0$$

where $s_i^+$ and $s_i^-$ are positive and negative difference variables satisfying $s_i^+ \times s_i^- = 0$, $B(\overline{w})$ is the bit rate of a specific MVC coding scheme. The constant $B$, $F_f c$, $F_m c$, $E_f$, $E_m$ are corresponding limitations for bandwidth, random access and server buffer, which are set according to practical conditions. The objective function means that the model is optimized when all constraints are satisfied. Clearly, the model is a multi-solution multipurpose programming model, and each MVC coding scheme that satisfies all the constraints is applicable.

## 5  Applications of Interaction Mathematical Model

The goal of MVC scheme design is high compressibility or efficiency, but rarely takes access ability into consideration. Some of these schemes will not be implemented because of lower interaction ability. The interaction mathematical model can be used to determine whether a scheme is available for a certain application or not.

Several MVC schemes are evaluated by evaluation functions and the score are listed in Table 1. For the purpose of comparison between different GoGOP size, proportion ratio is applied. It can be seen that 'All I frame' performs best in interaction. But evidently, it can not satisfy the bandwidth constraints and is not a suitable solution in almost all applications. 'Simulcast' is similar to 'All I frame'. 'Improved transposed' is better than 'Transposed' in bandwidth limitation, but both of them are inapplicable in real-time systems. 'Tree mode' uses small GoGoP size, and it has better performance in random access than all others excluding 'All I frame' and 'Simulcast'. It is shown that RD result of this mode is also better than the others[7].

SP frame technology is widely used to improve flexibility in interaction[10]. Several 'SP Transposed' and 'SP Improved transposed' schemes are designed, as shown in Fig.2(f)-(j), and the results can be seen in Table 1. Clearly, SP technology can greatly improve random access ability and reduce system buffer load.

## 6 Conclusions

Several evaluation functions are proposed to measure the random access and video system buffer load in this paper. These functions can provide intuitive and objective score for interaction and QoS. Furthermore, a nonlinear multi-purpose programming mathematical interaction model is proposed based on these evaluation functions. The proposed model can be used to determine whether a MVC coding scheme is applicable or not, and point out what aspect should be improved when this scheme is not a practical one. It is also a guide in designing efficient MVC coding schemes.

## Acknowledgment

This work was supported by the Natural Science Foundation of China (grant 60472100), the Natural Science Foundation of Zhejiang Province (grant RC01057, 601017, Y105577), the Ningbo Science and Technology Project of China (grant 2003A61001, 2004A610001, 2004A630002), and the Zhejiang Science and Technology Project (grant 2004C31105).

## References

1. ISO/IEC JTC1/SC29/WG11 N6720, Call for Evidence on Multi-View Video Coding, (2004).
2. ISO/IEC JTC1/SC29/WG11 N7282, Requirements on MVC v.4, (2005).
3. Jiang, G., Fan, L., Yu, M., et al.: Fast ray-space interpolation with discontinuity preserving for free viewpoint video system, Lecture Notes in Computer Science, LNCS 3767, 408-419, (2005).
4. Jiang, G., Shao, F., Yu, M., et al.: Efficient Block Matching for Ray-Space Predictive Coding in Free-Viewpoint Television Systems, Lecture Notes in Computer Science, LNCS 3980, 307-316, (2006).
5. Matusik,W., Pfister, H.: 3DTV: A Scalable System for Real-Time Acquisition, Transmission, and Auto stereoscopic Display of Dynamic Scenes. Proc. of SIGGRAPH/ACM, (2004).
6. Lou, J., Cai, H., Li, J.: A Real-Time Interactive Multiview Video System, 13th ACM International Conference on Multimedia, 161-170, (2005).
7. Yang, Y., Jiang, G., Yu, M., et al.: Hyper-Space Based Multiview Video Coding Scheme for Free Viewpoint Television, Picture Coding Symposium (PCS), Beijing, (2006)
8. ISO/IEC JTC1/SC29/WG11 N6909, Survey of Algorithms used for Multi-view Video Coding (MVC), (2005).
9. Fecker, U., Kaup, A.: H.264/AVC-Compatible Coding of Dynamic Light Fields Using Transposed Picture Ordering, 13th European Signal Processing Conference, Antalya, (2005).
10. Ramanathan, P., Girod, B.: Random Access for Compressed Light Fields Using Multiple Representations, IEEE 6th Workshop on Multimedia Signal Processing, 383-386, (2004).
11. Bollobas, B.: Modern graph theory, vol. 184, Springer, New York, (1998).
12. Bollobas, B.: Random Graphs, Cambridge University Press, 2nd edition, (2001).

# Motion Composition of 3D Video

Jianfeng Xu[1], Toshihiko Yamasaki[2], and Kiyoharu Aizawa[2,1]

[1] Dept. of Electronics Engineering
[2] Dept. of Frontier Informatics
The University of Tokyo
5-1-5 Kashiwano-ha, Kashiwa, Chiba, 277-8561, Japan
{fenax, yamasaki, aizawa}@hal.k.u-tokyo.ac.jp

**Abstract.** 3D video, which is composed of a sequence of mesh models and can provide the user with interactivity, is attracting increasing attention in many research groups. However, it is time-consuming and expensive to generate 3D video sequences. In this paper, a motion composition method is proposed to edit 3D video based on the user's requirements so that 3D video can be re-used. By analyzing the feature vectors, the hierarchical motion structure is parsed and then a motion database is set up by selecting the representative motions. A motion graph is constructed to organize the motion database by finding the possible motion transitions. Then, the best path is searched based on a proposed cost function by a modified Dijkstra algorithm after the user selects the desired motions in the motion database, which are called key motions in this paper. Our experimental results show the edited 3D video sequence looks natural and realistic.

## 1 Introduction

3D video, which consists of a sequence of dynamic 3D mesh models, is generated frame-by-frame with multiple synchronized cameras, which capture real-world in real time from different viewpoints [1,2,3,4,5]. Describing the dynamic scene, 3D video can reproduce not only the 3D spatial information such as shape and color of real-world 3D objects, but also the temporal information such as motion. Therefore, 3D video can provide the user with interactivity since the user can watch it from any viewpoint (not limited to those of cameras in the generation system) as shown in Fig. 1. Thus, the potential of 3D video applications includes movies, gaming, medical system, broadcast, heritage documentation, CAD, and so on.

Most of 3D video generation systems are designed to capture human motions such as sports and dancing [1,2,3,4,5]. Some systems generate model-based 3D video [5], where a prior human model is defined and the human model is fitted by the captured videos. However, those systems [5] are difficult to model such a human model as a dancer wearing Japanese traditional clothes. On the other hand, other systems generate model-free 3D video [1,2,3,4], where no prior human model is defined and each frame is generated independently. Therefore, no

Y. Zhuang et al. (Eds.): PCM 2006, LNCS 4261, pp. 385–394, 2006.

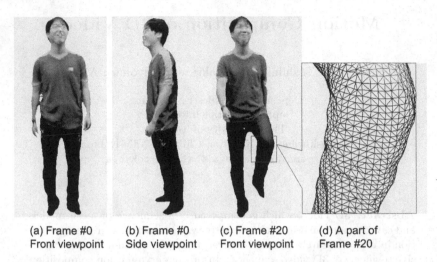

(a) Frame #0          (b) Frame #0          (c) Frame #20          (d) A part of
Front viewpoint       Side viewpoint        Front viewpoint        Frame #20

**Fig. 1.** Two sample frames in 3D video, which is a sequence of mesh models [2]. (a) Frame #0 from a single viewpoint in a "Walk" sequence, (b) another viewpoint of Frame #0, (c) Frame #20, (d) a part of Frame #20 in detail.

structure features are available due to the mesh models. And no kinematic information among frames is available since both the geometry and topology may vary frame by frame. In our generation system with 22 cameras [2], 3D video is represented as triangle mesh models, whose positions, topology, and colors of vertices are given as shown in Fig. 1 (d). Two characteristics of 3D video are that 3D video data are massive, and 3D video generation is time-consuming and rather expensive.

Re-usage of 3D video is necessary due to the cost of 3D video generation. In conventional 2D video, it is demonstrated that video editing is a powerful tool. Many technologies have been developed to (semi)automatically edit the home video such as AVE [6]. In the professional field of film editing, video editing such as montage is surely necessary, which is still implemented mainly by experts using some commercial softwares such as Adobe Premiere. Similarly, video editing is necessary in 3D video. Another merit of 3D video editing is that some impossible motions for human beings can be generated by editing. In this paper, motions in the motion database are composed to edit 3D video with the user's requirements. Since our motion composition is based on motion level instead of frame level, the user can easily edit 3D video. In our system, a motion database is set up after parsing the temporal structure of 3D video by the method in our previous work [7]. Then, a motion graph is constructed to find the possible motion transition. After the user selects the desired motions (called *key frames*) from the motion database, the best paths are searched by Dijkstra algorithm in the motion graph to generate a desired sequence.

The remainder of this paper is organized as follows. We will first introduce some related works in Section 2. In Section 3, we will describe briefly how to set up the motion database, based on our previous work, including parsing the motion structure and selecting representative motions. Then, we will discuss in detail how to define and construct the motion graph from the motion database in Section 4. Motion composition will be presented in Section 5. Experimental results will be reported and analyzed in Section 6. Lastly, our conclusions and future work will be given in Section 7.

## 2   Related Work

3D video editing remains an open and challenging problem until now. Starck *et al.* proposed an animation control algorithm based on motion graph and a motion blending algorithm based on spherical matching in geometry image domain [8]. However, only genus-zero surface can be transfered into geometry image, which limits the adoption in our 3D video sequences. Our previous work proposed a framework for 3D video editing by signal processing method [9], which is suitable for any mesh model sequence. Motions, selected by the user, are directly connected one by one in [9], whose transitions may be not so smooth. In this paper, we propose a new motion composition method based on motion graphs although we share the motion database with [7].

Motion graphs are widely applied in motion capture data editing, which are proposed independently by Arikan *et al.* [10], Lee *et al.* [11], and Kovar *et al.* [12]. A motion graph in motion capture data is a graph structure to organize the motion capture data for editing. In [10,11], the node in motion graph is a frame in motion capture data and an edge is the possible connection of two frames. In [12], the edge is the clip of motion and the node is the transition point which connects the clips. A cost function is also defined as the weight of the edge to reflect how good the motion transition is. Motion blending is also used to smooth the motion transition in [11,12]. The edited sequence is composed in the motion graph with some constraints by some search algorithms. Lai *et al.* proposed a group motion graph by a similar idea to deal with the groups of discrete agents such as flocks [13]. The key requirement for successful application of motion graph is that the motions in motion graphs should be various enough. Therefore, the larger the motion graph is, the better the edited sequence may be. However, the search algorithm will take longer time in a larger motion graph.

A directed motion graph in this paper is defined as $G(V, E, W)$, where the node $v_i \in V$ is a motion in the motion database, the edge $e_{i,j} \in E$ is the transition from the node $v_i$ to $v_j$, and the weight $w_{i,j} \in W$ is the cost to transit from $v_i$ to $v_j$ (detailed in Section 4). A cost function for a path is defined in Section 5. In our system, the user selects some motions he/she expects, which are called *key motions* in this paper. The best path between two neighboring key motions is searched in the motion graph. Therefore, the edited sequence is obtained after finishing the searches.

Obviously, our motion graph is different from those in motion capture data. In our motion graphs, a node is a motion instead of a frame. Therefore, we need to parse the motion structure of 3D video. To balance the size and variance of the motion graph, the best motion is selected into the motion graph in each motion

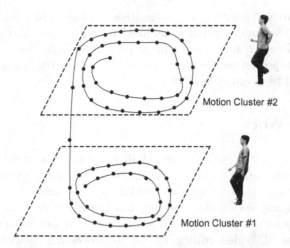

**Fig. 2.** Hierarchical motion structure in 3D video (point denotes a frame, curve denotes the motion trajectory), the objects perform a basic motion (e.g. walking in the bottom) several times and transit into another (e.g. running in the top), where the basic motion is called *motion texton* and the group of textons becomes a *motion cluster*, the redundant motions are removed in motion database

type. The size of motion graph is greatly reduced by selecting only one motion in a motion type and the variance is guaranteed by selecting a motion in every motion type. Therefore, only a part of frames in original 3D video are utilized in our motion graph, which is different from other motion graphs [10,11,12,13]. Also, 3D video is represented in mesh model. Unlike motion capture data, mesh model has no kinematic or structural information. Therefore, it is difficult to track the motion.

## 3   Motion Database

It is observed that our 3D video sequences have a hierarchical motion structure. As shown in Fig. 2, the object performs a basic motion (e.g., walking) several times and transits into another (e.g., running), where the basic motion is called a *motion texton* and the group of textons becomes a *motion cluster*. The detail definitions are in [7].

As mentioned before, 3D video has huge data without kinematic information or structural data, which makes geometry processing (such as model-based analysis and tracking) difficult and time-consuming. On the other hand, strong correlation exists in the statistical point of view. Therefore, statistical feature vectors are preferred. To parse the motion structure, feature vectors, proposed in [14], are extracted in each frame, which are the histograms of vertex coordinates in spherical coordinate system transformed from Cartesian coordinate system. The distance between two frames is defined as the Euclidean distance of feature

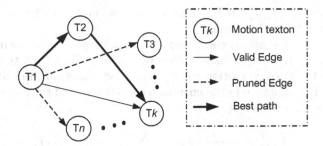

**Fig. 3.** Motion graph (only include the edges for a node), a node is a cyclic motion and an edge is a possible transition between the motions; a complete motion graph is constructed firstly, then the impossible edges are pruned, the best path is searched with two key motions

vectors in the two corresponding frames. To consider both the pose and velocity of the object, a distance between *motion atoms*, which are several frames in fixed-length, is calculated in a Hanning window. By analyzing the distances among motion atoms, the boundaries of motion textons and motion clusters are detected. Since the motion textons in a motion cluster contain identical motions, only a single motion texton is selected from each motion cluster, which is required to be cyclic enough to transit smoothly from the end to the beginning. Therefore, the motion database is composed of those representative motion textons. Compared with the frames of original 3D video, the motion database is much simpler but contains all the motion information, which will benefit the motion graph in the next section. The readers are encouraged to refer to our previous work [7] for detail.

## 4   Motion Graph

To construct a motion graph, we try to find a possible transition between the motion textons in the motion database. A possible transition exists if the transition in the two motion textons (or two nodes in the motion graph) is smooth enough. A complete motion graph is constructed firstly. Then, some impossible transitions, whose costs are large, are pruned to get the final motion graph. Therefore, a reasonable cost definition is a significant issue in motion graph construction, which should be consistent with the smoothness of transition.

Since the node is a motion texton, a transition frame should be chosen in the motion texton. A distance of two textons is defined as the minimal distance of any two frames separately in the two textons as Eq. (1).

$$d_V(T_i, T_j) = \min_{t_i \in T_i, t_j \in T_j} d_f(t_i, t_j) \tag{1}$$

$$\{t_i, t_j\}^* = \arg_{t_i \in T_i, t_j \in T_j} \min d_f(t_i, t_j) \tag{2}$$

where $T_i$ and $T_j$ are two nodes in the motion graph, and $t_i/t_j$ is a frame in the nodes $T_i/T_j$. $d_f(t_i, t_j)$ is the Euclidean distance of their feature vectors, called *frame distance.* $d_V(T_i, T_j)$ is the distance of two nodes, called *node distance*. $\{t_i, t_j\}^*$ are the transition frames.

Another factor that affects the transition smoothness is the motion intensity in the current node. By human visual perception, a large discontinuity in transition is tolerant if the current motion texton has a large motion intensity, and vice versa. An average distance in the current node is calculated to reflect the motion intensity of motion texton $T_i$.

$$\overline{d(T_i)} = \frac{1}{n(T_i) - 1} \cdot \sum_{t_i \in T_i \& t_{i+1} \in T_i} d_f(t_i, t_{i+1}) \tag{3}$$

where $n(T_i)$ is the number of frames in node $T_i$, $d_f(t_i, t_{i+1})$ is the frame distance between two neighboring frames, and $\overline{d(T_i)}$ is the motion intensity of $T_i$. Thus, the ratio of node distance and motion intensity is defined as the weight of the edge $e(i, j)$ in motion graph.

$$w(T_i, T_j) = \begin{cases} \frac{d_V(T_i, T_j)}{\overline{d(T_i)}} & i \neq j \\ \infty & i = j \end{cases} \tag{4}$$

where $w(T_i, T_j)$ is the weight of edge $e_{i,j}$ or the cost of transition. Notice that the motion graph is a directed graph: $w(T_i, T_j) \neq w(T_j, T_i)$.

After calculating the weights for all edges, the complete motion graph will be pruned. Considering a node $v_i$ in the complete motion graph, all the edges for the node $v_i$ are classified into two groups, one includes those possible transitions and another includes those pruned transitions. The average weight of all edges for $v_i$ is adopted as the threshold for the classifier. However, a parameter is given for the user to control the size of motion graph.

$$\overline{w(T_i)} = \frac{1}{N(T_i) - 1} \cdot \sum_{T_j \in E(T_i)} w(T_i, T_j) \tag{5}$$

where $G$ denotes the motion graph, $N(T_i)$ denotes the number of edges who connect with $T_i$, and $E(T_i)$ denotes the set of edges who connect with $T_i$. Then, the edge $e_{i,j}$ will be pruned if

$$w(T_i, T_j) \geq \mu \cdot \overline{w(T_i)} \tag{6}$$

where $\mu$ is the parameter, which controls the size of motion graph.

After pruning the edges, the motion graph is constructed as shown in Fig. 3. It should be mentioned that the IDs of two transition frames are attached to each edge. And the motion graph is constructed in an off-line processing.

## 5   Motion Composition

Motions are composed in an on-line processing after the user selects the desired motion textons in the motion database. Those motion textons are similar to key

**Table 1.** Modified Dijkstra algorithm to search the best path

```
1   function Dijkstra(G, w, s)                    // Modified Dijkstra algorithm
2       for each node v in V[G]                   // Initializations
3           d[v] := infinity
4           previous[v] := undefined
5       d[s] := 0
6       length[s] := 0
7       S := empty set
8       Q := V[G]
9       while Q is not an empty set               // The algorithm itself
10          u := Extract-Min(Q)
11          S := S union u
12          for each edge (u,v) outgoing from u
13              if max(d[u],w(u,v)) < d[v]         //With cost function
14                  d[v] := max(d[u],w(u,v))
15                  length[v] := length[u]+1
16                  previous[v] := u
17              else if max(d[u],w(u,v)) = d[v]    //With shortest path
18                  if length[u]+1 < length[v]
19                      length[v] := length[u]+1
20                      previous[v] := u
```

frames in computer animation and therefore called *key motions*. Between two key motions, there are many paths in the motion graph. A cost function of the path is defined to search the best path. The edited sequence is composed of all the best paths searched in every two neighboring key motions in order.

The quality of a path should depend on the maximal weight in the path instead of the sum of all weights in the path. For example, the quality of a path will become bad if there is a transition with a very large cost even if other transitions are smooth. Therefore, the cost function is defined as

$$cost(p(T_m, T_n)) = max_{e_{i,j} \in p(T_m,T_n)} w(T_i, T_j) \qquad (7)$$

where $p(T_m, T_n)$ is a path from the node $v_m$ to $v_n$, $T_m, T_n$ are two key motions. However, by this definition, some paths have the same costs. The best path is required to be shortest, i.e., it has the least edges. Then, given the motion graph $G(V, E, W)$ and two key motions $T_m$ and $T_n$, the problem of the best path can be represented as

$$p(T_m, T_n)^* = \arg_{p(T_m,T_n) \in G} \min cost(p(T_m, T_n)) \qquad (8)$$
$$\text{s.t. } p(T_m, T_n) \text{ is shortest}$$

Dijkstra algorithm can work in the problem of Eq. (8) after some modifications. Table 1 lists the algorithm, where the part in italic fonts is the difference from the standard Dijkstra algorithm. Line 6, 15, and 17-19 are from the requirement of the shortest path; line 13 and 14 are from the cost function in Eq. (7).

**Table 2.** The number of frames in our 3D video sequences

|          | Person A | Person B | Person C | Person D |
|----------|----------|----------|----------|----------|
| Walk     | 105      | 105      | 117      | 113      |
| Run      | 106      | 107      | 96       | 103      |
| BroadGym | 1981     | 1954     | 1981     | 1954     |

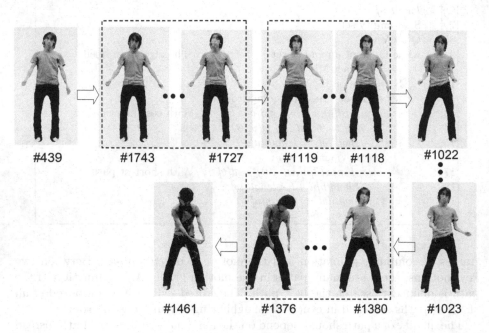

**Fig. 4.** Transitions (denoted by arrows) in two best paths, middle motion textons are searched to smooth the edited sequence as shown in dash rectangles, the numbers are the frame indices in original sequence and the whole sequence is in the attached video

## 6   Experimental Results

As shown in Table 2, the 3D video sequences in the experiments were generated from four persons with the rate of 10 frames per second. In these sequences, the number of vertices in a frame is about 16,000, the number of edges is about 32,000, and the number of colors is the same as vertices. "Walk" sequence is to walk normally for about 10 seconds. "Run" sequence is to run normally for about 10 seconds. And "BroadGym" sequence is to do the broadcast gymnastics exercise, which lasts about 3 minutes. Total time of these sequences lasts 872.2 seconds (i.e., 8722 frames).

As mentioned above, the user selects the desired motions as key motions. At least, two key motions are required. If more than two motions are selected, the best paths will be searched in every two neighboring key motions in order. And the ID indices of motion textons in the best paths and their transition frames are stored in a log file to render the edited sequence, which avoids to restore the mesh models. The edited 3D video sequence is played using OpenGL.

In our experiments, the parameter $\mu$ is set as 0.9. Fig. 4 shows the transitions in the best paths with key motions randomly selected by the authors. Our method achieves natural transitions. In the attached video, the whole edited video is played, where the transition is as fast as possible but every frame in the motion texton is rendered at least once before transition (as mentioned in Section 3, the motion textons are cyclic). It is demonstrated the realistic 3D video is composed.

In our experiments, it is observed that the best path does not exist in some cases due to the key motion is unreachable from the previous key motion. The problem can be solved by selecting a new key motion or a larger $\mu$ in Eq. (4). Although a larger $\mu$ means more edges in the motion graph, the path may include some transitions with large weights so that the motion blending is required, which is our future work. Some extensions are possible in our system. For example, the user can decide some forbidden motions in the edited sequence. For all edges to the forbidden motions, their weights are set as $\infty$. Therefore, the cost of any path including a forbidden motion will be $\infty$.

Another issue is how to evaluate the performance of the system, which is rather subjective. However, it is very difficult to design the metric like PSNR in video coding although it is sure important and meaningful in a research system. No report is founded in the literature as [8,9,10,11,12], leaving it an open question until now. Generally speaking, it depends on the users and applications: different users have different criteria in different applications. What is more, the edited sequence also depends on the key motions. An experienced expert will be expected to improve the results.

## 7  Conclusions and Future Work

In this paper, a motion composition method has been proposed, where the best paths are searched in the motion graph according to the key motions selected by the users. The edited 3D video sequences are composed in our experiments by cutting and pasting the motions in the database. The motion graph in this paper is different from those in the motion capture data [10,11,12] in the meaning of the motion graph definition and construction. In our motion graph, the node is motion texton, which is selected from motion cluster. Therefore, the balance of size and variance of motion graph is achieved. The complete motion graph is pruned by a reasonable weight definition for edges. After the user selects the desired motion textons, the best paths are searched in the motion graph with a path cost by a modified Dijkstra algorithm.

However, some improvements are possible. In the current system, the length of edited sequence is out of control. In Eq. (7), the length error should be considered if necessary. In addition, motion blending at the transitions with large costs will be useful as Kovar *et al.* [12] did, especially when the motion database is relatively small so that there are motion textons which cannot transit to others smoothly. Also, we believe the system should provide the interactivity with the user to improve the result. Another research topic is to classify the motions into subsets by the motion genre when the motion database is large enough.

## Acknowledgments

This work is supported by Ministry of Education, Culture, Sports, Science and Technology, Japan within the research project "Development of fundamental software technologies for digital archives". The generation studio is provided by NHK, Japan. And the volunteers are greatly appreciated to generate 3D video.

## References

1. Kanade, T., Rander, P., Narayanan, P.: Virtualized reality: constructing virtual worlds from real scenes. In: IEEE Multimedia. Vol. 4, No. 1, (1997)34–47
2. Tomiyama, K., Orihara, Y., et al.: Algorithm for dynamic 3D object generation from multi-viewpoint images. In: Proc. of SPIE. Vol. 5599, (2004)153–161
3. Matsuyama, T., Wu, X., Takai, T., Wada, T.: Real–time dynamic3–D object shape reconstruction and high–fidelity texture mapping for 3–D video. In: IEEE Trans. Circuit and System for Video Technology. Vol. 14, No. 3, (2004)357–369
4. Wurmlin, S., Lamboray, E., Staadt, O. G., Gross, M. H.: 3D video recorder. In: Proc. of Pacific Graphics'02. (2002)325–334
5. Carranza, J., Theobalt, C., Magnor, M. A., Seidel, H. P.: Free–Viewpoint Video of Human Actors. In: SIGGRAPH 03. Vol. 22, No. 3, (2003)569–577
6. Hua, X., Lu, L., Zhang, H. J.: AVE-Automated Home Video Editing. In: Proc. of ACM Multimedia. (2003)490–497
7. Xu, J., Yamasaki, T., Aizawa, K.: Motion Structure Extraction for 3D Video Editing. In: ITE Annual Convention. (2006)18–3.
8. Starck, J., Miller, G., Hilton, A.: Video-Based Character Animation. In: Symposium on Computer Animation (SCA'05). (2005)49–58
9. Xu, J., Yamasaki, T., Aizawa, K.: Motion Editing in 3D Video Database. In: Third International Symposium on 3D Data Processing, Visualization and Transmission (3DPVT'06). (2006)
10. Arikan, O., Forsyth, D. A.: Interactive Motion Generation from Examples. In: SIGGRAPH 02. (2002)483–490
11. Lee, J., Chai, J., Reitsma, P. S. A.: Interactive Control of Avatars Animated with Human Motion Data. In: Conference on Computer graphics and interactive techniques. (2002)491–500
12. Kovar, L., Gleicher, M., et al.: Motion Graphs. In: SIGGRAPH 02. (2002)473–482
13. Lai, Y. C., Chenney, S., et al.: Group Motion Graphs. In: Symposium on Computer Animation (SCA'05). (2005)281–290
14. Xu, J., Yamasaki, T., Aizawa, K.: Effective 3D Video Segmentation Based on Feature Vectors Using Spherical Coordinate System. In: Meeting on Image Recognition and Understanding. (2005)136–143

# EKM: An Efficient Key Management Scheme for Large-Scale Peer-to-Peer Media Streaming

Feng Qiu, Chuang Lin, and Hao Yin

Department of Computer Science and Technology, Tsinghua University
Beijing, 100084, P.R. China
{fqiu, clin, hyin}@csnet1.cs.tsinghua.edu.cn
http://www.cs.tsinghua.edu.cn/

**Abstract.** Recently media streaming applications via Peer-to-Peer (P2P) overlay networks are getting more and more significant. However, before these applications can be successfully deployed, it is very important to develop efficient access control mechanisms to ensure that only legitimate members can access the media content. Existing schemes of key management and distribution often fail in facing a large-scale group accessing. In this paper, we propose an efficient key management scheme (EKM) for large-scale P2P media streaming applications. It employs the Distributed Hash Table (DHT) technique to build a key distribution overlay network and incorporates a periodical global rekeying mechanism, which is highly scalable and efficient, and is robust against frequently joining/leaving of members. EKM can cut down the overhead of storage and communication on the server side, which can eliminate potential bottleneck of the server. We demonstrate its scalability, efficiency and robustness properties through simulation. Its performance can be examined under real environments by combining EKM with the existing P2P media streaming protocols.

**Keywords:** P2P, media streaming, key management, DHT.

## 1 Introduction

Recently media streaming applications via Peer-to-Peer (P2P) overlay networks are getting more and more significant. Due to the essential of capitalizing receivers' bandwidth to provide services to other receivers, P2P overlay networks exhibit a high level of scalability and efficiency and several solutions have been proposed [1-5]. However, before these group-oriented media streaming applications can be successfully deployed, it is very important to develop efficient access control mechanisms to ensure that only legitimate members can access the media content. A primary method of access control is through encryption and selective distribution of the keys used to encrypt the communication information, usually called "session key" (SK). There have been many schemes proposed to solve the problems of distributing SK to valid members [7][8]. Whereas, these conventional approaches often fail in

Y. Zhuang et al. (Eds.): PCM 2006, LNCS 4261, pp. 395–404, 2006.

facing a large-scale group accessing, due to high computational or communication overhead, as well as the dynamic properties of members.

In this paper, we propose an efficient key management scheme, named "EKM", aiming at providing highly scalable, efficient and robust key management and distribution for the access control of large-scale P2P media streaming applications. More specially, the unique advantages of our proposed scheme are: 1) EKM employs the Distributed Hash Table (DHT) technique to build a key distribution overlay network, which is highly scalable and efficient, and is also very robust against dynamically joining/leaving of members; 2) due to the distributed and structured properties of DHT, the server does not need to store the whole overlay topology, but it is still very easy to find a certain member; 3) the global session key updating (rekeying) process is carried out by server periodically, which can eliminate potential bottleneck at the server; 4) EKM is independent of any P2P media streaming protocols and can be easily combined with them to protect the media content.

The rest of this paper is organized as follows. Section II presents the background and related work. A detailed description of our proposed key management scheme is in Section III. Section IV demonstrates and discusses the performance of our scheme. Finally, Section V concludes the paper.

## 2  Related Work

### 2.1  Key Management Schemes

As mentioned in [7], key management schemes for multicast are divided into three classes: centralized approach, decentralized approach, and distributed approach. Considering the one-to-many characteristics of video multicast applications, we are especially interested in the centralized approach.

In centralized key management approach, a single entity is employed for controlling the whole group of members, called Key Distribution Center (KDC), in charge of initiating and updating the keys, distributing the rekeying messages. The centralized approaches can be further classified into two groups: Hierarchy Tree Scheme (HTS) and Centralized Flat Scheme (CFS). We only present HTS schemes here because of its relevance. Readers interested to CFS can refer to [9][10]. In HTS, KDC manages all the keys based on a binary tree data structure called Logical Key Hierarchy (LKH) [8]. The main objective of LKH scheme is to decrease the size of rekeying messages, and it is achieved by maintaining all the keys with a balanced binary tree, i.e. the *key tree*, at the KDC. The SK is usually stored at the root node of the key tree. Every legitimate client is associated with a leaf node of the key tree, as well as the keys along the path from its leaf node up to the root. So with $n$ legitimate clients, the average tree height is $O(\log_2 n)$. The beauty of this LKH scheme is that, once a client joins or leaves the group, only $2\log_2 n$ keys in the key tree need to be changed. There are also lots of schemes aiming at improving the performance of LKH, including Efficient Large-group Key Distribution (ELK) [11], One-way Function Tree (OFT) [12], and Hierarchical $a$-ary Tree with clustering [13]. Hierarchical Tree based schemes appear to be very suitable for a group key management. They achieve good overall results without compromising any aspects of security [7].

However, in such schemes, the SK should be changed once a user leaves or joins the group, and this will lead to an extremely high overhead for the KDC to maintain a key tree as the group grows very large. The KDC is likely to become a potential bottleneck and its failures will affect the entire group. Some schemes use clustering or decentralized approaches to minimize the problem of concentrating the work on a single place [7][13]. Commonly, they divide the group into subgroups, and select a leader to take the charge of key management and distribution for each subgroup. Since rekeying messages are relayed by leaders of different subgroups, their leavings or faults will significantly affect their subgroups. In other words, these schemes prevent KDC from becoming a bottleneck at the cost of efficiency and robustness.

## 2.2 Distributed Hash Table

Distributed Hash Table (DHT) is a common technique to overcome such a low scalability of the flooding-based indexing schemes, and it has been applied to many pure P2P systems such as Tapestry [15], Chord [16], and Content Addressable Network (CAN) [17]. Here we focus on the scheme of CAN. CAN assumes a virtual $d$-dimensional coordinate space, and each index of files and documents is mapped onto a point in the space by an appropriate uniform hash function. At any time, the entire coordinate space is dynamically partitioned among all nodes in the system, in such a way that every node owns its individual zone within the whole space, and thus, the store and the retrieval of an index will be realized by routing an inquiry message to the corresponding point, i.e., to the node who owns the point. CAN shows a high level of scalability, fault tolerance and self-organization, and it is a good choice for building large-scale information retrieval system. In this paper, we refer to its key idea and propose our scheme, which is to be discussed in the following section.

## 3 Efficient Key Management Scheme

### 3.1 Overview

As mentioned above, EKM builds its key distribution overlay network by adopting the DHT technique. More concretely, it assumes a 2-d space, as described in CAN [17], but with some differences. All the members are firstly mapped onto points in this space by a uniform hash function, and these points (called position points) stand for the positions where they will stay. The whole space is dynamically partitioned according to the existing members, and each of them owns its zone which covers its position point, as shown in Fig.1. In our scheme, their zones can be overlapped.

The distribution of rekeying messages is carried out not only among neighbors, but also between "Supervisors" and "Supervisees", as shown in Fig. 1. For each member, it can find its supervisor by mapping itself again onto another point (called supervisor point) in the space by a second uniform hash function. Its supervisor should be the owner in whose zone the point lies, and the member itself is called the supervisee, accordingly. In fact, a supervisor may have many supervisees, and so does supervisee, due to the possible overlapped zones.

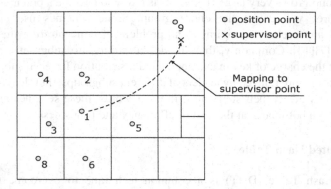

**Fig. 1.** An example for the 2-d coordinate space, $M_9$ is the supervisor of $M_1$

The KDC divides the P2P media streaming procedure into sessions, as shown in Fig. 2. It periodically updates the SK at the beginning of each session, and then sends the new SK for the next session only to a few members via secure channels by unicast. The rekeying message should contain such information: $\{ E_{PKi}(SK \mid E_{CSK}(MD(SK))) \}$, as explained in Sect 3.2. And the entire group will have their SKs updated in a short time. Besides rekeying, the KDC also takes charge of authenticating new members and maintaining the status of the online members.

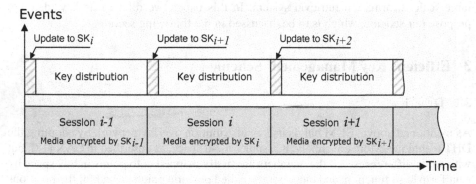

**Fig. 2.** Sessions of updating the SK

## 3.2 Notation

In this section, we give a summary of the notations used in this paper, as shown in Table 1.

**Table 1.** Notation summary

| Notation | Meaning |
|---|---|
| $H_P(m): m \rightarrow (x, y)$ | hash function for mapping members onto position points |
| $H_S(m): m \rightarrow (x, y)$ | hash function for mapping members onto supervisor points |
| $MD(m)$ | digest of message $m$ |
| $E_K(m)$ | asymmetric encryption of message $m$ by using key $K$ |
| $D_K(m)$ | asymmetric decryption of message $m$ by using key $K$ |
| $SK$, $SK_i$ | Session key |
| $MPK_i$, $MSK_i$ | public and secret keys of member $i$, respectively |
| $CPK$, $CSK$ | public and secret keys of the KDC, respectively |
| $ID_i$ | identity number of member $i$ |
| $x \mid y$ | concatenating x and y |

### 3.3 Member Joins

When a user wants to join the P2P media streaming group (shortly called "group" later), it should firstly contact the KDC to be authenticated. Then it can join the space and find its zone, where it can get the future rekeying messages from its neighbors. The detailed procedures of member joining are listed as follows:

1) Before user $i$ joins the group, it generates a pair of keys, i.e., $MPK_i$ and $MSK_i$.

2) User $i$ sends a login request with $MPK_i$ inside to the KDC via a secure channel. After been authenticated, user $i$ becomes a new member and gets some materials from the KDC: { $ID_i$, $E_{CSK}(ID_i \mid MPK_i)$, $E_{MPKi}(SK \mid E_{CSK}(MD(SK)))$, $CPK$ }.

   And also this new member also gets a list of randomly selected members.

3) Member $i$ figures out its position by applying $H_P(ID_i)$ and then sends a request to the listed members, which contains { $H_P(ID_i)$ }. These members forward this request to their neighbors, supervisors or supervisees who are closer to the position point $H_P(ID_i)$, until it reaches the member $j$ in whose zone the point lies, as described in CAN [17]. Then they contact and exchange their identities, i.e., { $E_{CSK}(ID_j \mid MPK_j)$ } and { $E_{CSK}(ID_i \mid MPK_i)$ }. Member $j$ splits its zone and assigns part of it to member $i$. But exceptionally if they are too close, they can own the same zone instead of splitting it, as described in Sect 3.5.

4) Member $i$ establishes the memberships with its new neighbors in the same way.

5) Member $j$ hands member $i$ some of its supervisees to whose supervisor points lie in its zone. At the same time, member i figures out its supervisor point by applying $H_S(ID_i)$ and finds its supervisor similarly as mentioned above. Then it establishes the connections with all its supervisors and supervisees.

## 3.4 Member Leaves

When a member is going to leave the group, it should firstly notify all its neighbors, supervisors and supervisees, and then hand out its zone according to the negotiations already made with them as described in Sect. 3.5. After that, the member contacts the KDC to logout. The detailed procedures are listed as follows:

1)  If member $i$ wants to leave the group, it should firstly send a *LEAVE* message to all its neighbors, which contains { $ID_i$ , $E_{CSK}(ID_i \mid MPK_i)$ }, as well as the information about all of its neighbors. Additionally, member $i$ should hand over its zone to its neighbors, which can be remerged with their zones.

2)  Member $i$ sends a *LEAVE* message only containing { $ID_i$ , $E_{CSK}(ID_i \mid MPK_i)$ } to its supervisors.

3)  Member $i$ should hand its supervisees to the proper neighbors in whose zone the supervisor points lie. And it then sends its supervisees a *LEAVE* message, only containing { $ID_i$ , $E_{CSK}(ID_i \mid MPK_i)$ }.

4)  After that, member $i$ contacts the KDC to logout. The KDC then generates a piece of message, and sends it to a random member. This message contains:

$$\{ E_{CSK}(H_P(ID_i) \mid ID_i \mid MPK_i), E_{CSK}(H_S(ID_i) \mid ID_i \mid MPK_i) \}$$

This message is finally forwarded to the old neighbors of member $i$ and tells them its exiting, in order to prevent possible malicious members from pretending to leave the group.

## 3.5 Zone Splitting and Remerging

In our scheme, the space is a square with side of $2^N$ integer points long, where $N$ is usually set to 32 for the convenience of programming. A zone of the space can be either a square or a rectangle.

**Zone Splitting.** Assuming that member $M_1$ (position point $P_1$) wants to hand over part of its zone to member $M_2$ (position point $P_2$). Here the coordinates of its zone can be denoted as $(x_0, y_0) - (x_1, y_1)$ . Therefore, the problem of zone splitting can be described as: Member $M_1$ tries to find a proper partition of its zone, from horizontal and vertical directions. This partition should split the zone into two parts, which should cover $P_1$ and $P_2$ respectively. In addition, this partition should also satisfy the following two terms:

1)  If the area of the zone is lower than threshold $T_{Area}$ , or the distance between $P_1$ and $P_2$ is lower than threshold $T_{Dist}$ , the zone can not be split. Here we can set $T_{Area} = 4$ and $T_{Dist} = 2$ .

2)  The split line should be horizontal or vertical, and between $P_1$ and $P_2$ . Taking a vertical split line for example, its coordinates can be denoted as $(x, y_0) - (x, y_1)$ ,

where $x \in (x_0, x_1)$ and can be written as $\dfrac{k}{2^n} \cdot 2^N$, where $n \in [1, N]$, $k$ is an odd number and $0 < k < 2^n$. A proper partition should let $n$ to be as small as possible.

**Zone Remerging.** Assuming that member $M_1$ wants to hand over its zone to the neighbors. It should follow the listed procedures:

1) If the member who gave the zone to $M_1$ still exists, $M_1$ simply returns it back.
2) Otherwise, member $M_1$ should split its zones into parts, mainly according to the terms of zone splitting as well as the knowledge of the zones of its neighbors.
3) All the parts generated after splitting should be merged with neighbors' zones to make them become larger valid squares or rectangles.

### 3.6 Maintenance and Failure Recovery

When a member receives a new rekeying message, it immediately forwards this message to its neighbors and supervisees. The forwarded rekeying message is encrypted by the public key of the receiver and sent out by unicast.

Each member maintains its relationships by periodically querying the status of its neighbors, supervisors and supervisees. Within the maintaining procedure, the member negotiates some zone remerging schemes with its neighbors, in case of possible member departures or failures. If a member loses the connection with one of its neighbors silently, it broadcasts a *WARNING* message to its neighbors, for the purpose of telling them to make sure if the member has gone. Then the neighbors of the leaving member remerge its zone with theirs according to the negotiations.

## 4 Simulation

In our simulation, we use a square 2-d space with side of $2^{32}$ integer points long, as mentioned in Sect. 3.5, to build the key distribution network. To map the members into the space as dispersedly as possible, we adopt the MD5 algorithm [18] to construct the two hash functions, i.e., $H_P(m)$ and $H_S(m)$. Also we have simulated the possible failures and abnormal departures of members, denoted by the ratio of member failures, which indicates the percentage of the abnormal members. We simulate a P2P media streaming group with the population ranging from 1,000 to 10,000,000 and with a ratio of member failures from 5% to 35%. And the KDC sends the rekeying message only to randomly 10 members in the group for each key updating. This simulation shows the times of key management and distribution in different situations and mainly demonstrates the performance of our proposed EKM scheme, especially on the efficiency and robustness of key management and distribution.

As shown in Fig. 3, there is a comparison of the efficiency between EKM scheme and general hierarchical tree based schemes. For the tree based schemes, when a single member event occurs, the time complexity of communication is $O(\log_2 N)$, according to the properties of logical key trees. But when multiple member events appear concurrently, the overhead can be increased very fast and the complexity will be likely to get close to $O(N)$. While EKM scheme shows a much better performance with a time complexity of $O(\log_4 N)$ for both single and multiple member events. Events of members only lead to a local overhead for zones maintaining by themselves. The KDC only needs to update the SK and send out a rekeying message periodically, even when facing a very large group of members, which is highly scalable.

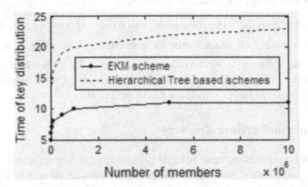

**Fig. 3.** The time of key distribution between EKM scheme and general hierarchical tree based schemes

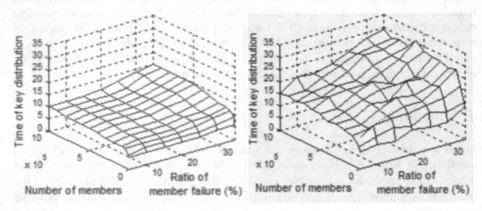

(a) Robustness of EKM scheme     (b) Robustness of hierarchical tree based schemes

**Fig. 4.** The robustness of EKM scheme and hierarchical tree based schemes with clustering. This figure shows the rounds of key distribution as the number of members and the ratio of member failure change.

Clustering-based key management schemes are the most typical ones to solve the problem of efficiency in large-scale group communication. They have a high performance in key distribution, but may have bottlenecks on the cluster leaders. Fig. 4 gives a comparison of the robustness against member failures between our proposed EKM scheme and a general clustering-based scheme. Obviously, higher ratio of member failure and larger population lead to an unstable and disturbed times of key distribution for the clustering-based scheme. On the contrary, EKM has a more peaceful situation, thanks to its multi-path key distribution and the equal status of all the members. In other words, EKM is more robust and stable than these schemes.

## 5 Conclusions

In this paper, we have proposed an efficient key management scheme for large-scale P2P media streaming applications, called the EKM. It employs the DHT technique to build a key distribution overlay network using a 2-d coordinate space, and incorporates the periodical rekeying, which is highly scalable and efficient, and is robust against dynamically member events. EKM can cut down the overhead of storage and communication on the server side, which can eliminate potential bottleneck of the server. We have done some simulation experiments, and the results have demonstrated its scalability, efficiency and robustness properties. It achieves a high performance in key management and distribution in large-scale P2P media streaming systems, for which it is very suitable. In our future work, we will combine it with some existing P2P media streaming protocols to examine its performance under real environments.

**Acknowledgements.** This work is supported by the National Natural Science Foundation of China (No. 90412012, 60429202, 60372019 and 60573144), and the National Grand Fundamental Research 973 Program of China (No. 2003CB314804).

## References

1. E.K. Lua, J. Crowcroft, M. Pias, R. Sharma, and S. Lim, A Survey and Comparison of Peer-to-Peer Overlay Network Schemes, IEEE Communications Surveys & Tutorials, pp. 72-93, Second Quarter 2005.
2. S.A. Theotokis and D. Spinellis, A Survey of Peer-to-Peer Content Distribution Technologies, ACM Computing Surveys, Vol.36, No. 4, pp. 335-371, Dec. 2004.
3. Yang-Hua Chu, Sanjay G. Rao, and Hui Zhang, A Case for End Systems Multicast. In ACM SIGMETRICS, 2000, pp. 1-12.
4. S. Banerjee, B. Bhattacharjee, and C. Kommareddy, Scalable application layer multicast, in Proceedings of ACM Sigcomm, August 2002.
5. D. Tran, K.Hua, and T. Do. ZIGZAG: An Efficient Peer-to-Peer Scheme for Media Streaming. In Proceedings of IEEE INFOCOM'03, San Francisco, CA, USA, April 2003.
6. P. Judge, M. Ammar, Security issues and solutions in multicast content distribution: a survey, Network, IEEE Vol.17, Issue 1, Jan.-Feb. 2003, pp. 30-36.
7. S. Rafaeli, D. Hutchison, A survey of key management for secure group communication, ACM Computing Surveys (CSUR), Vol.35, Issue 3, Sep. 2003, pp. 309-329.
8. C. Wong, M. Gouda, S. Lam, Secure group communication using key graphs, IEEE/ACM Transaction on Networking, vol. 8, pp. 16–30, Feb. 2000.
9. D.M. Wallner, E.J. Harder, and R.C. Agee, Key Management for Multicast: Issues and Architectures, RFC 2627, June 1999.
10. S. Mitta, Iolus: A framework for the scalable secure multicasting, in proceedings of the ACM SIGCOMM'97, September 1997, pp. 277–288.

11. A. Perrig, D. Song, and J.D. Tygar, A New Protocol for Efficient Large-Group Key Distribution, in proceedings of IEEE Symposium on Security and Privacy, Los Alamitos, USA, 2001.
12. R. Canetti, J. Garay, G. Itkis, et al, Multicast Security: A Taxonomy and Some Efficient Constructions, in proceedings of IEEE INFOCOM, pp.708-716, 1999.
13. R. Canetti, T. Malkin, and K. Nissim, Efficient communication-storage tradeoffs for multicast encryption, In Advances in Cryptology-EUROCRYPT'99, J. Stem, Ed. Lectures Notes in Computer Science, vol. 1599. Springer-Verlag, New York, pp. 459–474.
14. S. Banerjee and B. Bhattacharjee, Scalable Secure Group Communication over IP Multicast; IEEE Journal on Selected Areas in Communications, vol.20, no.8, pp.1511-1527, October 2002.
15. B. Zhao, J. Kubiatowicz, and A. Joseph, Tapestry: An Infrastructure for Fault-tolerant Wide-area Location and Routing. Technical Report, UCB/CSD-01-1141, 2000.
16. I. Stoica, R. Morris, D. Karger, F. Kaashoek, and H. Balakrishnan, Chord: A Scalable Peer-to-peer Lookup Service for Internet Applications. In Proc. of SIGCOMM 2001, pp. 149–160, Aug. 2001.
17. S. Ratnasamy, P. Francis, M. Handley, R. Karp, and S. Shenker, A Scalable Content-Addressable Network, in Proceedings of SIGCOMM 2001, pp.161-172, Aug. 2001.
18. R. L. Rivest, The MD5 Message-Digest Algorithm, RFC 1321, April 1992.

# Using Earth Mover's Distance for Audio Clip Retrieval

Yuxin Peng, Cuihua Fang, and Xiaoou Chen

Institute of Computer Science and Technology
Peking University, Beijing 100871, China
{pengyuxin, fangcuihua, cxo}@icst.pku.edu.cn

**Abstract.** This paper presents a new approach for audio clip retrieval based on Earth Mover's Distance (EMD). Instead of using frame-based or salient-based features in most existing methods, our approach propose a segment-based representation, and allows many-to-many matching among audio segments for the clip similarity measure, which is capable of tolerating errors due to audio segmentation and various audio effects. We formulate audio clip retrieval as a graph matching problem in two stages. In the first stage, segment-based feature is employed to represent the audio clips, which can not only capture the change property of audio clip, but also keep and present the change relation and temporal order of audio features. In the second stage, based on the result of the segment similarity measure, a weighted graph is constructed to model the similarity between two clips. EMD is proposed to compute the minimum cost of the weighted graph as the similarity value between two audio clips. Experimental results show that the proposed approach is better than some existing methods in terms of retrieval and ranking capabilities.

**Keywords:** Audio similarity measure, audio retrieval.

## 1 Introduction

With the drastic advances of the audio and music content on the internet, there is an increase in the demand for audio content analysis, retrieval and summarization. In these techniques, content-based similarity measure is a critical fundamental step. In this paper, we propose a new approach for the similarity measure and ranking of audio clips based on Earth Mover's Distance (EMD).

Existing approaches on audio clip retrieval can be classified into two categories: frame-based features [1, 2] and salient-based features [3-5]. In the methods of frame-based features [1, 2], a long audio clip is divided into many frames to catch the short time property. The features are extracted from each frame and their mean and standard deviation are calculated to form the feature vector of the audio clip. However, the frame features in an audio clip usually vary greatly along the time line. The mean and standard deviation of frames cannot give an accurate presentation of such property in audio clips. To complement the drawback, the methods in [3-5] propose to extract the salient characteristics or dominant features to present the change property in audio clips. In [3, 4], structure pattern is proposed for the similarity measure of audio clips, which describes the structural characteristics of

Y. Zhuang et al. (Eds.): PCM 2006, LNCS 4261, pp. 405–413, 2006.

both temporal and spectral features. In [5], dominant feature vectors are extracted from audio clips to represent the multiple salient characteristics of the clip. The methods in [3-5] are reasonable in capturing the change property of audio clip. Nevertheless, the salient characteristics are based on the statistical features of an audio clip, which cannot keep and present the change relation and order of audio clip along the time line.

In audio retrieval task, frame-based representation, in general, is intuitive because audio frame is the basic structure existing in audio. However, due to the excessive number of frames in an audio clip, the mean and standard deviation of frames are then utilized to represent the audio clip for data reduction purpose, which is too rough to describe and represent the content change of audio clips. Similar to frame-based, the salient-based representation cannot solve this problem. In addition, *shot*, as the basic structure composed of frames in video domain, has been proved to be effective for the similarity measure of video clips [6]. In this way, a video clip is composed of shots, while a shot is composed of video frames. Motivated by this idea, we exploit a structural representation, namely *audio segment*, for the similarity measure of audio clips. Similar with shot in video domain, audio segment is a series of audio frames that are acoustically homogeneous, and the clip characteristics are represented by segment-based features. Since an audio clip, although may has the long duration, is divided into few segments according to their content change, which can avoid frame-based representation problem. In addition, because audio segment is acoustically homogeneous, segment-based representation can not only capture the change property of audio clip, but also keep and present the change relation and order of audio features because an audio clip is divided into physical segments along the time line.

Suppose audio clips are divided into several segments, the next problem will be how to measure the clip similarity. Because an audio clip is composed of several audio segments, the similarity between two clips can be measured by their audio segments. Based on the result of segment similarity measure, the similarity between two audio clips will be many-to-many matching among their segments because every segment in an audio clips has the similarity value with every segment in another audio clip. Certain criterion is demanded to measure the similarity between two clips. In addition, we consider the following problems for many-to-many matching demand:

- *Different audio effect.* The content of a long segment in an audio clip may be segmented and appeared as several segments in other clips. For example, a long segment with animal sound may be appeared several short segments in other clips. In addition, the same music sound also has the long and short editions due to the different audio effects.
- *Segment boundary detection error.* One segment may be falsely segmented into several short segments. Several segments may also be incorrectly merged as one segment.

The composition or decomposition of segments, either due to different audio effects or audio partitioning errors, sometime follows the nature of many-to-many scrambling. In this situation, one-to-many or many-to-many matching techniques among segments are needed to guarantee effective matching. In our approach, we model the similarity measure of two clips as a weighted graph with two vertex sets:

one vertex set represents an audio clip, and each vertex represents a segment in an audio clip and is stamped with a signature (or weight) to indicate its significance during matching. The signature symbolizes the duration proportion of a segment in an audio clip. EMD is then employed to compute the minimum cost of the graph, by using the signatures to control the degree of matching under the many-to-many segment mapping. The computed cost reflects the similarity between two audio clips.

## 2  Audio Preprocessing

Preprocessing includes audio segmentation, feature representation and segment similarity measure. Bayesian Information Criterion (BIC) in [7] is employed to locally detect the single changes in the audio clip within a sliding window of variable size. Basically an audio clip is divided into several segments by the detected change points, and every segment is a series of audio frames that are acoustically homogeneous. Let the feature vector of an audio segment $x_i$ be $\{f_{i1}, f_{i2}, ...\}$, the distance between two audio segments $x_i$ and $y_j$ is defined as

$$d(x_i, y_j) = \left( \sum_{p=1}^{n} (f_{ip} - f_{jp})^2 \right)^{\frac{1}{2}} \tag{1}$$

The distance function $d(x_i, y_j)$ is Euclidean Distance of the feature vectors between two audio segments $x_i$ and $y_j$. In the proposed approach, two types of features are computed for each audio frame: (1) log energy; (2) 12 order Mel-Frequency Cepstral Coefficients (MFCC). In this way, an audio frame is represented by a 13-dimensional feature vector. The first dimension feature is log energy, and the others are represented by MFCC features. Because a segment is a series of audio frames that are acoustically homogeneous, the frames in a segment have nearly no change. So we use the mean feature of all frames in the segment to represent every audio segment. Thus, an audio segment is also represented by a 13-dimensional feature vector.

## 3  Clip-Based Similarity Measure

Earth Mover's Distance (EMD) has been successfully employed for image-based retrieval [8]. In this section, we will employ EMD for audio clip similarity measure. A weighted graph is constructed to model the similarity between two audio clips, and then EMD is employed to compute the minimum cost of the weighted graph as the similarity value between two clips.

EMD is based on the *transportation problem*. Suppose some suppliers, each with a given amount of goods, are required to supply some consumers, each with a given limited capacity to accept goods. For each supplier-consumer pair, the cost of transporting a single unit of goods is given. The transportation problem is: Find a minimum expensive flow of goods from the suppliers to the consumers that satisfy the consumers' demand.

Given two audio clips $X$ and $Y_k$, a weighted graph $G_k$ is constructed as follows:

- Let $X = \{(x_1, \omega_{x_1}), (x_2, \omega_{x_2}), ..., (x_m, \omega_{x_m})\}$ as a query clip with $m$ segments, $x_i$ represents a segment in $X$, $\omega_{x_i}$ is the signature (or weight) of audio segment $x_i$ to indicate its significance during matching. In our approach, $\omega_{x_i}$ is defined as

$$\omega_{x_i} = \frac{frame\#(x_i)}{frame\#(X)} \tag{2}$$

   $frame\#(x_i)$ represents the frame number of the segment $x_i$, and $frame\#(X)$ represent the frame number of the audio clip $X$. Eqn (2) is the proportion of the frame number between the segment $x_i$ and clip $X$, which reflect the duration of the audio segment as its significance during matching.
- Let $Y_k = \{(y_1, \omega_{y_1}), (y_2, \omega_{y_2}), ..., (y_n, \omega_{y_n})\}$ as the $k^{th}$ audio clip with $n$ segments in an audio $Y$, $y_j$ represents a segment in $Y_k$. Similar with Eqn (2). $\omega_{y_j}$ is defined as

$$\omega_{y_j} = \frac{frame\#(y_j)}{frame\#(Y_k)} \tag{3}$$

- Let $D = \{d_{ij}\}$ as the distance matrix where $d_{ij}$ is the distance between two segments $x_i$ and $y_j$, which is based on Eqn (1).
- Let $G_k = \{X, Y_k, D\}$ as a weighted graph constructed by $X$, $Y_k$ and $D$. $V_k = X \cup Y_k$ is the vertex set while $D = \{d_{ij}\}$ is the edge set.

In the weighted graph $G_k$, we want to find a flow $F = \{f_{ij}\}$ where $f_{ij}$ is the flow between $x_i$ and $y_j$, that minimizes the overall cost

$$WORK(X, Y_k, F) = \sum_{i=1}^{m} \sum_{j=1}^{n} d_{ij} f_{ij} \tag{4}$$

subject to the following constraints:

$$f_{ij} \geq 0 \quad 1 \leq i \leq m, \ 1 \leq j \leq n \tag{5}$$

$$\sum_{j=1}^{n} f_{ij} \leq \omega_{x_i} \quad 1 \leq i \leq m \tag{6}$$

$$\sum_{i=1}^{m} f_{ij} \leq \omega_{y_j} \quad 1 \leq j \leq n \tag{7}$$

$$\sum_{i=1}^{m} \sum_{j=1}^{n} f_{ij} = \min\left(\sum_{i=1}^{m} \omega_{x_i}, \sum_{j=1}^{n} \omega_{y_j}\right) \tag{8}$$

Constraint (5) allows moving frames from $X$ to $Y_k$ and not vice versa. Constraint (6) limits the amount of frames that can be sent by the segments in $X$ to their weights. Constraint (7) limits the segments in $Y_k$ to receive no more frames than their weights, and constraint (8) forces to move the maximum amount of frames. We call this amount as the *total flow*. Once the transportation problem is solved, and we have found the optimal flow $F$, the earth mover's distance is defined as the resulting work normalized by the total flow:

$$EMD(X,Y_k) = \frac{\sum_{i=1}^{m}\sum_{j=1}^{n} d_{ij} f_{ij}}{\sum_{i=1}^{m}\sum_{j=1}^{n} f_{ij}} \tag{9}$$

The normalization factor is the total weight of the smaller clip as indicated in constraint (8). Finally, the similarity between two clips $X$ and $Y_k$ is defined as:

$$Sim_{clip}(X,Y_k) = \exp(-EMD(X,Y_k)/2) \tag{10}$$

Since $EMD(X,Y_k)$ is the minimum cost of the weighted graph, we can compute the maximum similarity value between two clips and normalize it in the range of [0, 1] by Eqn (10). The higher the value of $Sim_{clip}(X,Y_k)$, the more similar the two audio clips.

## 4   Experimental Results

To evaluate the performance of the proposed approach, we set up a database with 1000 audio clips, which includes the database of Muscle Fish. The Muscle Fish database is extensively employed for the experimental evaluation of audio clip retrieval [3-5], which includes many kinds of sounds, such as *animals, human, vehicles, machines, music, weapon* and so on. In addition, the experimental database also includes some commercial clips. In total, the average time of every audio clip in the experimental database is 9 seconds.

In the database, all audio streams are down-sampled into 44k Hz and mono-channel. Each frame is 512 samples (23ms) with 25% overlapping. In the 1000 audio clips, 500 clips have the relevant clips, while the other 500 clips only appear one time in the database. The relevant clips, although belong to the same kind of sound, have different sound property. Overall, all the 500 clips with one or more relevant clips are selected as the query clips for a comprehensive performance comparison. Four methods are experimented for comparison, including the proposed approach, Gu's approach [5], $L_2$ distance, and Kullback-leibler distance [9]. In the above methods, the frame features are represented by 13 dimensional feature vectors. The first dimension feature is log energy, and the others are represented by MFCC features, as the same with our approach in Section 2 for objective comparison. The major differences among the four approaches are summarized in Table 1.

## 4.1 Clip Retrieval

Recall and precision are adopted to evaluate the retrieval performance of audio clips. The recall and precision for the four methods are shown in Figure 1 and Figure 2. The proposed approach outperforms other three methods in terms of recall and precision. By manually investigating the retrieval results, we find the advantage of our approach is mainly due to: (1) Segment-based features can effectively represent and describe the audio clips, which guarantee the effectiveness of clip-based similarity measure. (2) EMD provides an effective mechanism for the similarity measure among segments between two audio clips by many-to-many matching.

## 4.2 Clip Ranking

In this experiment, our aim is to compare the ranking capability of these approaches. AR (average recall) and ANMRR (average normalized modified retrieval rank) are adopted to evaluate audio clip ranking performance [10]. The values of AR and ANMRR range from 0 to 1. A *high* value of AR denotes the superior ability in retrieving relevant clips, while a *low* value of ANMRR indicates the high retrieval rate with relevant clips ranked at the top [10]. Experimental results on AR and ANMRR for the four methods are shown in Table 2. The proposed approach outperforms other three methods in terms of AR and ANMRR. By tracing the details of experimental results, we found the similarity measure of frame-based or dominant-based features in other three methods can not always give the satisfactory results. In contrast, the proposed similarity measure based on EMD can rank most of relevant audio clips at the top-$k$ ranked list ($k$ depends on the number of relevant clips [10]).

Currently, on a Pentium-4 2.4GHz machine with 512M memory, the average retrieval time for a query by our approach is approximately 0.434 second. By investigation, we found the average number of audio segments is 10 in the experimental database, although many of them have a long duration. Therefore, although EMD is not a linear time algorithm, it is still efficient even in a large database since most of audio clips are divided into few segments according to their content change. This implies that the weighted graphs constructed by audio clips have less vertices, which lead our approach to a fast retrieval speed.

**Table 1.** Comparison among our approach and other three methods

| | Our approach | Gu's approach[5] | K-L distance[9] | $L_2$ distance |
|---|---|---|---|---|
| Representation | segment-based | dominant-based | frame-based | frame-based |
| Measure | EMD | dominant features | K-L distance | $L_2$ distance |

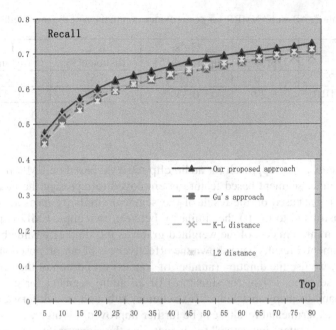

**Fig. 1.** Recall comparison of the four methods

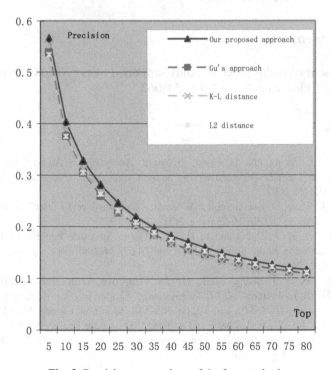

**Fig. 2.** Precision comparison of the four methods

**Table 2.** AR and ANMRR for performance comparison of the four methods

|  | Our approach | Gu's approach[5] | K-L distance[9] | $L_2$ distance |
|---|---|---|---|---|
| AR | 0.70 | 0.66 | 0.67 | 0.66 |
| ANMRR | 0.29 | 0.33 | 0.32 | 0.33 |

## 5 Conclusions

We has presents a new approach for audio clip retrieval based on EMD in two stages. In the first stage, segment-based feature is employed to represent the audio clips. In the second stage, based on the result of the segment similarity measure, a weighted graph is constructed to model the similarity between two clips. EMD is proposed to compute the minimum cost of the weighted graph as the similarity value between two clips. Experimental results have shown the effectiveness of our proposed approach.

Currently, we use the duration (number of frames) proportion of the segment in its clip to represent the weight (or signature) of an audio segment for controlling the degree of many-to-many matching. This scheme, although straightforward and yield encouraging experimental results, can be further improved. In future, we will consider other effective "content indicators" to characterize the signature of an audio segment for EMD-based audio clip retrieval.

## Acknowledgement

The work described in this paper was fully supported by the National Natural Science Foundation of China under Grant No. 60503062.

## References

1. L. Lu, H. J. Zhang and H. Jiang, "Content Analysis for Audio Classification and Segmentation", *IEEE Transactions on Speech and Audio Processing*, Vol.10, No.7, pp.504-516, Oct. 2002.
2. E. Wold, T. Blum, D. Keislar, and J. Wheaton, "Content-based Classification, Search, and Retrieval of Audio", *IEEE Multimedia*, 3(3): 27-36, 1996.
3. R. Cai, L. Lu, H. J. Zhang and L. H. Cai, "Using Structure Patterns of Temporal and Spectral Feature in Audio Similarity Measure", *ACM Multimedia Conference*, pp.219-222, Berkeley, CA, Nov. 2-8, 2003.
4. R. Cai, L. Lu, H. J. Zhang and L. H. Cai, "Improve Audio Representation by Using Feature Structure Patterns", *IEEE International Conference on Acoustics, Speech and Signal Processing (ICASSP)*, Vol. IV, pp. 345-348, Montreal, Canada, May 17-21, 2004.
5. J. Gu, L. Lu, R. Cai, H. J. Zhang and J. Yang, "Dominant Feature Vectors Based Audio Similarity Measure", *Pacific-Rim Conference on Multimedia (PCM)*, 2, pp.890-897, Nov 30-Dec 3, Tokyo, Japan, 2004.

6.  Y. Peng, and C. W. Ngo, "Clip-Based Similarity Measure for Query-Dependent Clip Retrieval and Video Summarization", *IEEE Transactions on Circuits and Systems for Video Technology*, Vol. 16, No. 5, pp. 612-627, May 2006.
7.  M. Cettolo and M. Vescovi, "Efficient Audio Segmentation Algorithms based on the BIC", *IEEE International Conference on Acoustics, Speech and Signal Processing (ICASSP), 2003*.
8.  Y. Rubner, C. Tomasi, and L. Guibas, "The Earth Mover's Distance as a Metric for Image Retrieval", *International Journal of Computer Vision*, Vol. 40, No. 2, pp. 99-121, 2000.
9.  Z. Liu and Q. Huang, "Content-based Indexing and Retrieval-by-Example in Audio", *IEEE International Conference on Multimedia and Expo (ICME)*, 2000.
10. MPEG video group, "Description of Core Experiments for MPEG-7 Color/Texture Descriptors", ISO/MPEGJTC1/SC29/WG11 MPEG98/M2819, July, 1999.

# Streaming-Mode MB-Based Integral Image Techniques for Fast Multi-view Video Illumination Compensation

Jiangbo Lu[1,2], Gauthier Lafruit[2], and Francky Catthoor[1,2]

[1] Department of Electrical Engineering, University of Leuven, Belgium
[2] Multimedia Group, DESICS, IMEC
Kapeldreef 75, B-3001, Leuven, Belgium
{Jiangbo.Lu, Gauthier.Lafruit, Francky.Catthoor}@imec.be

**Abstract.** Multi-view video systems are often faced with brightness variations across the multi-perspective captured images. To tackle this problem and maintain the coding performance, block-based illumination compensation (BBIC) methods are recently proposed, where a first order affine BBIC model, consisting of a multiplicative factor and an additive offset, is often adopted. However, so far little attention has been paid to the fast algorithms that can reduce the computational overhead of BBIC. Therefore, we propose a fast image local statistics computation scheme using the technique of integral images, which can largely ease the process of computing the BBIC parameters for any blocks of interest. Moreover, a fast progressive integral image generation scheme, seamlessly integrated in a streaming-mode macroblock-based video coding system, is proposed. The experimental results show that the proposed technique achieves an average six-fold speedup, in comparison to the traditional computation methods under typical conditions.

**keywords:** Block-based illumination compensation, integral images, weighted prediction, multi-view video coding.

## 1 Introduction

Block-Based Illumination Compensation (BBIC) is an important coding tool to achieve the optimal multi-view video coding performance, when there are noticeable brightness variations across the multi-perspective captured images [1]. In fact, brightness variation or illumination mismatch is not unusual for a practical multi-view video system, which is either caused by inconsistent color responses associated with the cameras, or sometimes by varying reflection and illumination effects exhibiting in different capturing angles [2]. For this reason, BBIC, as a block-level extension of weighted prediction in H.264/AVC, is an active explorative topic in MPEG's 3D audio-visual (3DAV) ad hoc group [3] for multi-view video standardization.

To achieve a good trade-off between coding efficiency and computational complexity, most BBIC algorithms resort to a first order affine model to compensate

Y. Zhuang et al. (Eds.): PCM 2006, LNCS 4261, pp. 414–423, 2006.
© Springer-Verlag Berlin Heidelberg 2006

for the block-level illumination mismatch [1,2,3]. As a consequence, (1) is usually adopted, where $R(x,y)$ and $\hat{R}(x,y)$ are the reference block signals before BBIC and after BBIC, respectively, in a multi-view video coder performing motion/disparity estimation between the current and reference MacroBlock (MB).

$$\hat{R}(x,y) = a_{ic} \cdot R(x,y) + b_{ic} \, . \tag{1}$$

Let the mean and variance values of a reference block (and the current block) be $\mu_R(\mu_C)$ and $\sigma_R(\sigma_C)$ respectively, then the multiplicative factor and additive offset in (1) are given by $a_{ic} = \sigma_C/\sigma_R$ and $b_{ic} = \mu_C - (\sigma_C/\sigma_R) \cdot \mu_R$, respectively. Consequently, mean and variances should be repetitively calculated at the block level. Even for some BBIC algorithms using an intensity offset only, block-level mean values are still needed. Hence, a fast computation technique is desirable for most BBIC algorithms.

In this paper, we propose a local, MB-based image statistics computation scheme for fast BBIC calculation, which remains a little explored topic so far. Our approach is based on the technique known as *integral images*, and it can achieve an average speedup factor of 6 over the straightforward computation method which does not use our optimized implementation of integral images. The key ideas are two-fold, one is the adoption of the integral images for BBIC processing in a multi-view video encoder, and the other is our optimized progressive generation scheme for integral images, as presented in Sect. 2.

## 2   Streaming-Mode MB-Based Integral Images for Fast Illumination Compensation

### 2.1   Baseline Integral Image Techniques for Fast Block-Level Image Statistics Computation

Integral images (or summed-area tables in graphics terms), originally introduced by Crow [4], is a technique of precomputing the integrals (e.g. sum of pixels, sum of squared pixel values) of the image over the defined area and storing the results into look-up tables for fast computation at run-time. This technique is widely accepted in the domain of 3D graphics, but has hardly been considered for video processing purposes. In this paper we adopt integral images as a key technique for fast BBIC algorithms in multi-view video compression, which heavily rely on block-level mean and variance calculations.

Let $S(x,y)$ be the integral sum of the pixels (or squared pixels) to the left-top of (and including) pixel position $(x,y)$, as shown in Fig. 1(a). $S(x,y)$ is often generated pixel-by-pixel in a raster scan order for the entire image. Once the integral image $S(x,y)$ is generated, the sum (or squared sum) of any rectangular $M \times N$ region $F(x_c, y_c, M, N)$ at pixel $(x_c, y_c)$ can rapidly be computed at a constant computational cost, according to (2) and Fig. 1(b),

$$F(x_c, y_c, M, N) = S(x_c + M - 1, y_c + N - 1) - S(x_c - 1, y_c + N - 1) \\ - S(x_c + M - 1, y_c - 1) + S(x_c - 1, y_c - 1) \, . \tag{2}$$

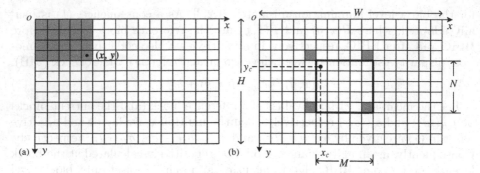

**Fig. 1.** The basic principle of integral images. (a) $S(x,y)$ is the sum of pixels or squared pixel values in the shaded area. (b) To compute the sum of the delineated rectangular region, the integral values of four shaded locations are read and evaluated.

## 2.2    Integral Images Revisited: A Block-Based Streaming Approach

Instead of constructing the integral images only after having a full video frame available, we propose to progressively generate the integral images $S(x,y)$ on a MB basis: for each new incoming pixel $(x,y)$ of current reconstructed MB, $S(x,y)$ is calculated, out of which the mean and variance of the MB at position $(x_c, y_c)$ can be calculated according to (2) at a later stage.

This streaming-mode generation of integral images brings two clear advantages over the frame-based generation method, such as the *cvIntegral* function implemented in open source computer vision (OpenCV) library [5]: (i) its data locality processing solicits only local buffers/caches achieving processing speedups in commonly used processors, and (ii) the MB-level processing for fast BBIC can be seamlessly embedded into the conventional video coding structure, as a MB-level post-processing task (shown in Fig. 2). It is clear from Fig. 2 that, the proposed modules can progressively construct integral images by reusing the reconstructed MB data, so a separate frame-level generation pass is avoided.

To further reduce the computational cost of MB-level integral image generation, we maintain an array of cumulative sums along each scanline within the image stripe that the current MB belongs to, so the integral value for a certain pixel position is the sum of current pixel value, cumulative sum for the current row, and the integral value of the above pixel position, as shown in Fig. 3 and Listing 1.

```
GenerateIntegralImage(
   int*    IntegralTable, unsigned char* CurrentMBData,
   int     IntegralTableWidth, bool IsRowStart)
begin
   const  int MB_SIZE = 16;
   static int CumulativeRowSum[MB_SIZE];
   if (IsRowStart)
     ResetArrayToZero(CumulativeRowSum);
```

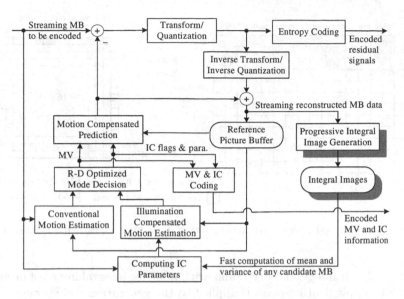

**Fig. 2.** The proposed modules of streaming-mode MB-based integral images techniques (*the blocks with shadows*) for BBIC in a conventional video coding framework

```
   end
   for Row = 0 : MB_SIZE-1, step = 1
     for Col = 0 : MB_SIZE-1, step = 1
        CumulativeRowSum[Row] += CurrentMBData[Col];
        IntegralTable[Col] = CumulativeRowSum[Row]
                        + IntegralTable[Col-IntegralTableWidth];
     end
        CurrentMBData += MB_SIZE;
        IntegralTable += IntegralTableWidth;
   end
   end.
```

Listing 1: Pseudo-code of streaming-mode integral image generation.

### 2.3  Optimization and Application of the Proposed Technique on a Commodity CPU

We have attempted at accelerating and exploring the proposed streaming-mode integral images from a few specific aspects, on a commodity CPU platform.

**Data Type Selection.** Based on the numerical precision requirements of the BBIC and Motion Estimation (ME) processing in the multi-view video codec, we have selected the appropriate data type for minimal data storage and execution time saving.

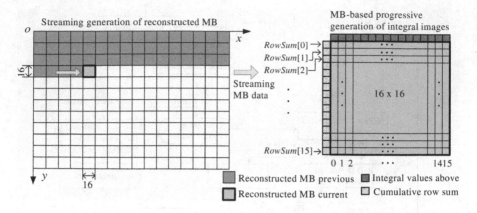

**Fig. 3.** The proposed progressive generation of integral images using streaming MB data

We use 32-bit integer data type and arithmetic for integral image of mean values, while 32-bit floating-point is applied to the generation and storage of integral images for variance values. Additionally, a static table storing precomputed squared pixel values with 255 entries is created to avoid computing the squared values at run-time. Different from *cvIntegral* in OpenCV, where double-precision floating-point is used as the data type to generate variance integral images, our proposed variance integral image generation relies on single-precision floating-point arithmetic to reach a good trade-off among storage size, execution speed and computational precision loss.

**Parallelization Possibilities and Data Packing Overhead.** It is a common practice to pack different data values into a wide data value for parallel processing, by leveraging Single Instruction Multiple Data (SIMD) paradigms, e.g. the Streaming SIMD Extension 2 (SSE2) supported on Intel Pentium 4 processors, the GPU (Graphics Processing Unit) SIMD processing. In [6], a parallel computing technique, called *recursive doubling*, is adopted to construct the integral images with much reduced number of passes on a GPU. However, our similar implementation on a CPU cannot achieve a pronounced gain in the execution speed, because the overhead of packing and unpacking the wide data for parallel processing at different passes actually results in a severe overall slow-down. We speculate that the GPU has specially optimized texture pipelines and the internal computation is performed automatically in the unified floating-point arithmetic, which make GPU more suitable for this type of parallel computing than CPU.

Similarly, we find that SSE2 supported on Intel Pentium 4 processors cannot accelerate the straightforward method for this addition-centric computation, because of the dominant overhead in preparing the 128-bit data and also the data type conversion involved. However, if we unroll the loops to leverage the compiler to manage the floating-point registers for optimal execution, the straightforward computation method can achieve a 4-fold speedup on Intel Pentium 4 processors.

**Trade-off between Sliding Window Data Reuse and Integral Images.**
Block matching in ME typically compares the current MB with a number of
candidate reference MBs in a search window of the previous frame. In a classical
BBIC implementation, the mean and variance values over each candidate MB
have to be calculated in accordance with (1), yielding 255 additions over the
$16 \times 16$ pixels of that MB. Nevertheless, if a high probability of overlapping candidate MBs exists (this probability depends on the searching technique used), a
potentially large portion of computations can be saved by reusing the immediate
previous sum computed for the same overlapping area, and hence a good BBIC
processing speedup is enabled.

On the other hand, with the integral images approach of (2) – besides the
cost of calculating the integral image with adequate cache behavior in streaming
mode – only 3 additions per candidate MB have to be calculated, albeit at the
cost of loading these 4 integral values into the data cache. No data reuse of
$S(x, y)$ in (2) is possible between successive candidate MB.

Hence, there exists a trade-off point – determined by the number of visited
candidate MBs and their degree of overlapping – in which our integral image
technique outperforms the straightforward method and associated BBIC processing. The results in Sect. 3.3 clearly indicate that it is highly advantageous to
choose the proposed technique under practical operating conditions.

## 3   Simulations and Experimental Results

Since the proposed integral image based local statistics computation method
is a generally applicable kernel to most BBIC algorithms, we have chosen to
simulate and evaluate it in a stand-alone test model instead of implementing it
into any particular BBIC algorithms. Based on this clean test model, we can more
precisely measure the speedup of the execution time for this specific portion of
the processing. More precisely, we explicitly model the reference frame buffer at
different resolutions, with the current reconstructed MB in a small local buffer,
and with motion search processes as existing in real video encoders.

Throughout our experiments, we set the search range of illumination compensated motion estimation to $\pm 16$, surrounding the zero motion vector (MV)
position. To effectively simulate illumination adaptive motion search paths and
memory access pattern of integral images, spiral motion search pattern and
Gaussian distributed random search pattern are adopted, where the latter is
used to statistically simulate the peaky histogram of best MV distribution observed in some fast motion search heuristics [7].

To clearly investigate the impact of image resolutions on the overall execution
speed, we take following test images: *Lena* $(256 \times 256)$ and *Peppers* $(512 \times 512)$,
as standard test images, *Ballet* $(1024 \times 768)$, as a multi-view image sequences,
and *Galaxy* $(1024 \times 1024)$ from the internet. The *QueryPerformanceFrequency*
function is used to query the high-resolution processor performance counter, to
precisely measure the execution time. All the experiments are performed on a
3.2GHz Intel Pentium 4 processor with 1GB RAM.

## 3.1   Integral Images Generation Speed Comparison

The proposed MB-based streaming integral image generation speed is compared to that of OpenCV's *cvIntegral* function. Table 1 shows the generation time of mean integral image, the generation time of mean and variance integral images, and the corresponding speedup ratio for different images. A speedup factor of up to 2.79 and 2.19 can be achieved by the proposed MB-based streaming generation method to create mean integral image, and the mean and variance integral images, respectively.

**Table 1.** Mean (and variance) integral images generation time comparison between our proposed streaming-mode generation method and the scanline-mode generation method adopted in OpenCV

|  | Generation time (ms) | $256 \times 256$ | $512 \times 512$ | $1024 \times 768$ | $1024 \times 1024$ |
|---|---|---|---|---|---|
| Mean | OpenCV's *cvIntegral* | 0.78 | 2.42 | 5.94 | 7.74 |
| integral | Streaming generation | 0.28 | 0.98 | 2.75 | 3.46 |
| image only | Speedup ratio | **2.79** | **2.47** | **2.16** | **2.24** |
| Mean+var. | OpenCV's *cvIntegral* | 1.88 | 4.85 | 15.53 | 20.67 |
| integral | Streaming generation | 0.86 | 2.53 | 8.19 | 11.57 |
| images | Speedup ratio | **2.19** | **1.92** | **1.90** | **1.79** |

## 3.2   Quantitative Computational Precision Evaluation of Our Single-Precision Floating-Point Based Variance Computation

We evaluate the precision loss of our proposed variance computation with regard to the reference variance obtained from the straightforward computation. In fact, when the variance of a MB is computed straightforwardly, the single-precision floating-point element type will be sufficient, since the maximum summed-area values cannot exceed 24 bits ($\log_2(256 \times 256 \times 256)$). The distribution percentages of different level of precision loss are shown in Table 2 for different image sizes of the reference test set, where the absolute precision loss ratio ($E_{abs}$) is defined as $\|Var_{proposed} - Var_{straightforward}\| / Var_{straightforward}$. We can observe that both the maximum $E_{abs}$ and the percentages of variances with small precision loss are safely negligible.

## 3.3   Overall Execution Time Tests on Fast and Full Motion Search

To validate that our proposed scheme of streaming MB-based integral images is consistently better than the straightforward computation method under typical operating conditions, we have performed speed tests to identify the aforementioned trade-off point in Sect. 2.3, under different fast motion search techniques, and also for full motion search.

**Overall Execution Time Tests on Fast Motion Search Patterns.** We have measured the overall execution time speedup of our proposed method over the optimized straightforward method with loop unrolling, based on both spiral

**Table 2.** The distribution percentages of different level of computational precision loss observed in our proposed single-precision floating-point variance computation method with regard to the reference variance obtained from the straightforward computation method

| Percentage | $E_{abs} \geq 0.20\%$ | $E_{abs} \geq 0.15\%$ | $E_{abs} \geq 0.10\%$ | $E_{abs} \geq 0.05\%$ | $\text{Max}(E_{abs})$ |
|---|---|---|---|---|---|
| $256 \times 256$ | 0.0000% | 0.0000% | 0.0000% | 0.0001% | 0.087% |
| $512 \times 512$ | 0.004% | 0.005% | 0.008% | 0.015% | 2.343% |
| $1024 \times 768$ | 0.005% | 0.007% | 0.012% | 0.030% | 0.998% |
| $1024 \times 1024$ | 0.001% | 0.002% | 0.005% | 0.016% | 0.893% |

motion search pattern and Gaussian distributed random search pattern. Due to the limited space, only the results of spiral search pattern are reported here. Figure 4 and Table 3 present the speedup factors for block-level mean (and variance) computation under different average spiral search candidate numbers per MB. The speedup figures tested on Gaussian distributed random search pattern demonstrate the similar performance.

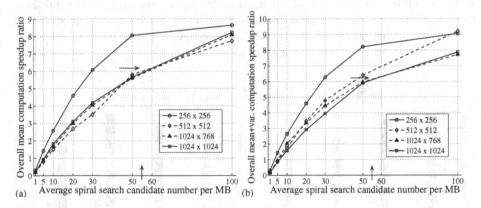

**Fig. 4.** Overall (a) mean (b) mean and variance computation speedup of the proposed scheme over the straightforward method under different average spiral search numbers per MB

It can be clearly observed that, when the search candidate number is close to and larger than 10, our proposed computation method based on integral images (with the generation overhead included) is consistently better than the optimized straightforward method, because the gain in the run-time complexity saving greatly outweighs the overhead of integral image generation. The experiments in [8] indicate that for most reasonably good fast ME algorithms, the candidate MB search number is typically ranging from 13 to 190. Our experiments on multi-view video coding using UMHexagonS [9], as a fast ME algorithm adopted in H.264 JM model, show that on average 50–60 candidate blocks will be checked for one MB, which corresponds to an overall speedup factor of about 6 in average cases, as marked by the arrows in Fig. 4.

**Table 3.** Overall mean (and variance) computation speedup of the proposed scheme over the straightforward method under different average spiral candidate numbers per MB (Cand#)

| Resolutions | Cand#1 | Cand#5 | Cand#10 | Cand#20 | Cand#30 | Cand#50 | Cand#100 |
|---|---|---|---|---|---|---|---|
| | **Overall mean computation time speedup** | | | | | | |
| 256 × 256 | 0.31 | 1.42 | 2.59 | 4.59 | 6.07 | 8.05 | 8.63 |
| 512 × 512 | 0.19 | 0.79 | 1.50 | 2.68 | 3.51 | 5.80 | 7.73 |
| 1024 × 768 | 0.19 | 0.87 | 1.69 | 3.00 | 4.04 | 5.60 | 8.08 |
| 1024 × 1024 | 0.21 | 0.92 | 1.82 | 3.11 | 4.18 | 5.65 | 8.21 |
| | **Overall mean and variance computation time speedup** | | | | | | |
| 256 × 256 | 0.31 | 1.44 | 2.64 | 4.59 | 6.27 | 8.21 | 9.05 |
| 512 × 512 | 0.20 | 0.94 | 1.74 | 3.47 | 4.78 | 6.39 | 9.20 |
| 1024 × 768 | 0.18 | 0.94 | 2.03 | 3.34 | 4.44 | 5.96 | 7.71 |
| 1024 × 1024 | 0.16 | 0.85 | 1.58 | 2.92 | 3.94 | 5.90 | 7.86 |

The cumulative contributions of our proposed technique for speeding BBIC computing can be easily examined through Fig. 5, where the average spiral search candidate number per MB is fixed to 50. Under such a typical condition, the adoption of baseline integral image techniques in block-level image statistics computation, can gain a speedup factor of more than 3.2. The further MB-based integral image optimization can lead to an extra complexity saving up to 1.9.

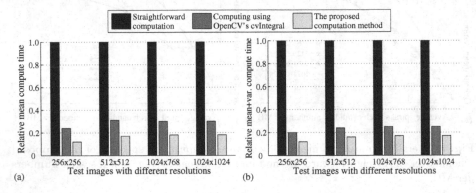

**Fig. 5.** Relative execution time for three different techniques in computing block-level (a) mean (b) mean and variance, when the average spiral search candidate number per MB is fixed to 50

**Overall Execution Time Tests on Full Motion Search.** When the full search is performed in a fixed search window, the straightforward computation method can be further optimized by using the "sliding column" technique in [10] to avoid the computation redundancies. Table 4 shows that our proposed computation method with the same row-by-row search order can still reach a speedup factor of more than 2.9, compared to the optimized straightforward method with the "sliding column" scheme.

**Table 4.** Image local statistics computation speedup of the proposed scheme over the optimized straightforward method using "sliding column", for full motion search

|                        | $256 \times 256$ | $512 \times 512$ | $1024 \times 768$ | $1024 \times 1024$ |
|------------------------|------------------|------------------|-------------------|--------------------|
| Mean speedup           | 2.92             | 4.34             | 5.03              | 5.03               |
| Mean+variance speedup  | 3.59             | 4.61             | 4.73              | 4.74               |

## 4   Conclusion

A fast image local statistics computation technique is proposed to accelerate most popular block-based illumination compensation algorithms in multi-view video coding using streaming-mode integral images. It can reduce the generation overhead by half compared with the scanline-based technique in OpenCV. Eventually, an overall computation speedup factor of about 6 can be achieved by our proposed technique over the straightforward method under typical conditions.

Future work will be focused on the reduction of the memory storage overhead and the speedup validation of this technique on a wider range of platforms.

## References

1. J. López., J.-H. Kim, A. Ortega, G. Chen: Block-Based Illumination Compensation and Search Techniques for Multi-view Video Coding. Picture Coding Sym. (2004)
2. A. Ilie, G. Welch: Ensuring Color Consistency across Multiple Cameras. Tenth IEEE Conference on Computer Vision (ICCV), Vol. 2 (2005) 1268–1275
3. ISO/IEC JTC1/SC29/WG11: Description of Core Experiments in MVC. W8019 (2006)
4. F. C. Crow: Summed-Area Tables for Texture Mapping. ACM SIGGRAPH, Vol. 18 (1984) 207-212
5. OpenCV Library. http://www.intel.com/technology/computing/opencv/index.htm
6. J. Hensley, T. Scheuermann, G. Coombe, M. Singh, A. Lastra: Fast Summed-Area Table Generation and its Applications. EUROGRAPHICS, Vol. 24 (2005) 547-555
7. K.-K. Ma, G. Qiu: Unequal-Arm Adaptive Rood Pattern Search for Fast Block-Matching Motion Estimation in the JVT/H.26L. IEEE ICIP (2003) 901-904
8. A. Chimienti, C. Ferraris, D. Pau: A Complexity-Bounded Motion Estimation Algorithm. IEEE Tran. on Image Processing, Vol. 11 (2002) 387-392
9. Z.B. Chen, P. Zhou, Y. He: Fast Integer Pel and Fractional Pel Motion Estimation for JVT. JVT-F017 (2002)
10. O. Faugeras, et al. Real Time Correlation-Based Stereo: Algorithms, Implementations and Applications. Technical Reports 2013, INRIA (1993)

# A Motion Vector Predictor Architecture for AVS and MPEG-2 HDTV Decoder

Junhao Zheng[1,3], Di Wu[1], Lei Deng[2], Don Xie[4], and Wen Gao[1,2,3]

[1] Institute of Computing Technology, Chinese Academy of Sciences,
100080 Beijing, China
[2] Department of Computer Science, Harbin Institute of Technology,
150001 Harbin, China
[3] Graduate University of Chinese Academy of Sciences
[4] Grandview Semiconductor (BeiJing) Corporation
{jhzheng, ldeng, dwu, wgao}@jdl.ac.cn, don.xie@grandviewsemi.com

**Abstract.** In the advanced Audio Video coding Standard (AVS), many efficient coding tools are adopted in motion compensation, such as new motion vector prediction, direct mode matching, variable block-sizes etc. However, these features enormously increase the computational complexity and the memory bandwidth requirement and make the traditional MV predictor more complicated. This paper proposes an efficient MV predictor architecture for both AVS and MPEG-2 decoder. The proposed architecture exploits the parallelism to accelerate the speed of operations and uses the dedicated design to optimize the memory access. In addition, it can reuse the on-chip buffer to support the MV error-resilience for MPEG-2 decoding. The design has been described in Verilog HDL and synthesized using 0.18µm CMOS cells library by Design Compiler. The circuit costs about 62k logic gates when the working frequency is set to 148.5MHz. This design can support the real-time MV predictor of HDTV 1080i video decoding for both AVS and MPEG-2.

**Keywords:** Motion compensation, Motion vector prediction, AVS, MPEG, VLSI architecture.

## 1 Introduction

Chinese Audio Video Coding Standard [1] is a new national standard for the coding of video and audio which is known as AVS. The first version of AVS video standard [2] has been finished in Dec. 2003. AVS defines a hybrid block-based video codec, similar to prior standards such as MPEG-2 [3], MPEG-4 [4] and H.264 [5]. However, AVS is an application driven coding standard with well-optimized techniques. By adopting many new coding features and functionality, AVS [6] achieves more than 50% coding gains over MPEG-2 and similar performance with lower cost compared with H.264.

The traditional block-based motion compensation (MC) is improved in the AVS standard. In the prior video standard, the simple MV prediction schemes are applied. For example, in H.264 [5] the predicted MV is just equal to the median value selected

Y. Zhuang et al. (Eds.): PCM 2006, LNCS 4261, pp. 424–431, 2006.
© Springer-Verlag Berlin Heidelberg 2006

from three decoded MVs of the spatial neighborhood. However, for AVS, the complicated algorithm based on the vector triangle which consists of a series of multiplier and division operations is adopted, as further described in section 2.2. Besides, AVS supports variable block sizes, new motion vector (MV) prediction, multiple reference pictures, direct and symmetric prediction modes etc. All new features require higher calculation capacity and more memory bandwidth which directly affect the cost effectiveness of a commercial video decoder solution. For HDTV 1080i application, the time budget is so tight that pure software implementation cannot provide real-time decoding if just depending on a simple or low-end CPU. So for the high-end application such as Set Top Box etc., it is necessary for the dedicated hardware accelerators. In [7], [8] some kinds of dedicated MC architectures had been proposed which were based on prior specific video standards. However AVS is a new standard, its own features associated with the new requirements make the old designs unsuitable.

In this paper, we propose an efficient MV predictor architecture which can fully support the MV prediction algorithms of both AVS and MPEG-2. The proposed design employs the pipelined structure to exploit the parallelism for the AVS's special median prediction algorithm, adopts the line buffer to store the neighboring motion data and uses the specific FIFO to smooth the memory accessing. For AVS, the data of the line buffer are used in the spatial prediction. For MPEG-2, the on-chip line buffer is reused and can provide the neighboring motion data to help conceal the error.

The remainder of the paper is organized as follows. The MV prediction algorithms applied by AVS and MPEG-2 are described in Section 2. Section 3 describes the details of the implemented architecture. Simulation results and VLSI implementation will be shown in Section 4. Finally, we draw a conclusion in Section 5.

## 2 MV Prediction Algorithm

The aim of MC is to exploit temporal redundancy to obtain the higher coding performance. The prediction for an inter-coded macroblock (MB) is determined by the set of MVs that are associated with the MB. Since significant gains in efficiency can be made by choosing a good prediction, the process of MV prediction becomes quite complicated. In this section, some special functional blocks of the MV prediction algorithm will be explained.

### 2.1 Temporal Prediction of AVS

AVS can support rich MB coding schemes with more than 30 kinds of MB types and tree structure MB partition (16×16 to 8×8). The predictive modes include intra, skip, forward, backward, spatial direct, temporal direct and symmetric. AVS adopts its own particular way to specify the symmetric and direct mode [2].

For the symmetric prediction, only the forward MV is transmitted for each partition. The backward MV is conducted from the forward one by a symmetric rule.

For the direct prediction, both the forward and backward MVs are derived from the MV of the collocated inter-coded block in the backward reference picture.

To support the temporal direct MV prediction, all MVs in the latest P-picture need to be stored in the memory as the collocated MV buffer. However, for AVS 1080i video the total bits of all motion data in one picture is about 118KB. It is so huge that all data must be stored to the external memory rather than the on-chip one.

## 2.2  Spatial Prediction of AVS

For the spatial prediction, AVS employs a novel median selector. The edge with the median length is selected from the vector triangle [2]. The scaled MVs make up of the triangle which is illustrated in Fig. 1.

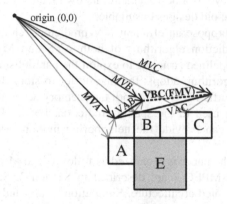

**Fig. 1.** MV spatial prediction

Firstly, calculate the scaled *MVA*, *MVB* and *MVC* using equation (1).

$$MVX = \frac{\frac{512}{BlkDistX} \times mvX \times BlkDistE + 256}{2^9} \qquad (1)$$

*X* denotes the block A, B or C and *mv* for the origin MVs of the neighboring block. *BlkDist* is the distance differences between the reference pictures of the neighboring blocks. The vectors with double arrow are the scaled MVs in Fig. 1.

Secondly, calculate the spatial distances between two scaled MVs. *M* and *N* denote the block A or B or C.

$VMN = Abs(MVM\_x–MVN\_x) + Abs(MVM\_y–MVN\_y)$

Thirdly, the temporary parameter *FMV* is given by the median of the corresponding spatial distances. The dashed line denotes the *FMV* in Fig. 1.

$FMV$=Median ($VAB$, $VBC$, $VAC$).

Finally, obtain the *MVP* using the scaled value from the corresponding vertex. For example, if the *FMV* is the *VAB*, thus the *MVP* is the *MVC*.

Three vertexes (see Fig. 1) need to be calculated so as to get only one MVP value which totally needs 3 divisions, 12 multiplications and 15 additions. Furthermore, AVS can support the 8×8 partition thus the maximum number of MVP value in one MB is 5 (three blocks with unidirectional prediction and one block with spatial direct prediction). The special method needs to be applied to accelerate the process which is described further in the subsection 3.2.

In addition, because the motion data from the upper and left neighbor are required, a specific buffer is involved to store all relative neighboring data.

### 2.3 Concealment MVs of MPEG-2

MPEG-2 can support the concealment MVs [3] which are carried by intra MBs. For the normal decoding, these MVs are useless and can be discarded. However, when the data errors occur in the MB which lies vertically below the intra MB, these MVs can be used as the candidate MVs to conceal the visual error.

Because the neighboring MBs have high correlation, it is reasonable that the lost block is very likely to have similar movement in the spatial domain. The more correct data are provided, the better quality can be achieved through the error-concealment. So the motion data from the neighboring MB should be stored including the concealment MVs of the intra MB and the real MVs of the inter MB.

## 3 MV Predictor Architecture

MV predictor module is responsible for generating all motion data (MVs and reference picture indices). The module consists of the Input/Output Interface, the Main Controller, the public Line Buffer, the MPEG sub-module and the AVS sub-module. Fig. 2 shows the implemented architecture of the MV predictor. The real lines indicate the data flow, and the dash lines for control messages.

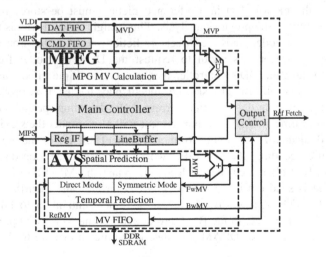

**Fig. 2.** MV Predictor block diagram

Main controller unit firstly parses the commands sent by MIPS which contain the stream type and the MB information such as mb_type, the available flag for neighboring MBs etc. Then the controller invokes the corresponding sub-module working according to the current MB mode. For example if the controller finds the mb_type is equal the AVS symmetric mode, the Symmetric Prediction module will be activated through the handshake protocol.

For the AVS side, the Spatial and Temporal Predictions perform the spatial and temporal MV predictive operations respectively. The motion data from or to the external memory are stored to the MV FIFO firstly to avoid trivial memory accessing request. The MV data read from MV FIFO are used by the Direct Prediction as the reference motion data. Output controller manages the final motion data to output to the reference fetch module and updates the Line Buffer whose data is used in the spatial prediction. Besides, in order to support the variable prediction blocksize, the MV predictor unit transfers all block modes to the uniform 8×8 block which is the minimum blocksize to simplify the operations in the downstream stages.

For the MPEG-2 side, the MVs are generated in the MV Calculation unit according to the motion type and the MB type. The final motion data each MB is stored into the Line Buffer. The firmware can read back all motion data in the Line Buffer through the Register Interface when the error occurs. Then the firmware can use some specific error concealment algorithms to select or re-calculate the MVs and send them to the CMD FIFO. These special MVs will directly be outputted as the final MVs to the downstream stages (See the Mux unit in Fig. 2). So the MV predictor can provide the error concealment scheme.

Due to the limit space, only the spatial prediction, the MV FIFO and the Line Buffer units are described in detail.

### 3.1  MV FIFO

Direct mode needs to use the reference MVs from the backward reference picture. It is known that the motion data in a reference picture must be stored into the DDR SDRAM according to the previous analysis. The straightforward way is to access the memory once the decoder finds the direct prediction mode in the process of current MB decoding. However, it's awful to request the DDR controller frequently and irregularly. Because the DDR controller has to serve multiple clients and guarantee the schedulability of all critical tasks, i.e. the display feeder, it is probable that the request for the motion data in the current MB decoding period could not be acknowledged in time and the irregular request will also impact the services for other clients. So a dedicated FIFO is built to improve the efficiency of the memory access. In the P-picture decoding, the MV FIFO works as a cache. Motion data are written into the MV FIFO after each MB is decoded. When the MV FIFO is half full, the writing request is send out to inform the DDR controller and then the data are read from the MV FIFO successively. At the same time, send them to DDR SDRAM through the DDR interface. In the B-picture decoding, the MV FIFO pre-fetches the motion data from the DDR SDRAM. The data flows are shown in Fig. 3.

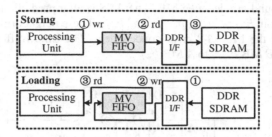

**Fig. 3.** Data flows for the MV FIFO

## 3.2  Pipelined Spatial Prediction

The algorithm is described in section 2.2. The pipelined architecture for the spatial MV prediction is shown in Fig. 4. It contains 5 stages for *FMV* calculation.

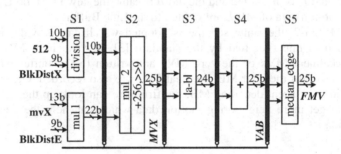

**Fig. 4.** Pipelined spatial prediction

S1. Division and 1st multiplication;
S2. 2nd multiplication,
    successive addition and shift;
S3. Absolute value
S4. Addition
S5. Median value

The 10b/9b division costs 2 cycles in our design. So it takes only 15 cycles to finish all operations for the calculation of one MV prediction including preparing the input data. So for the worse case the total cycle is 15×5 = 75 cycles.

Because the scaling technique is also applied to the direct and symmetric prediction in the AVS standard, the similar pipelined structures are implemented in the temporal prediction unit (see Fig. 2).

## 3.3  Line Buffer

All motion data which had been decoded are stored to the Line Buffer which is illustrated in Fig. 5. There are $n$ MBs in the horizontal direction and $b_{x,y}$ denotes the MB with (x,y) coordinates. $E$ is the current MB with bold block edge and the MBs with gray background are decoded MB. The AVS spatial prediction for MB $b_{x,y}$ need the motion data from $b_{x-1,y-1}$, $b_{x,y-1}$, $b_{x+1,y-1}$ and $b_{x-1,y}$. These neighboring motion data are also important for the MPEG-2 error concealment. The Line Buffer is composed of motion data from $B$ MB $b_{x,y-1}$ to $A$ MB $b_{x-1,y}$.

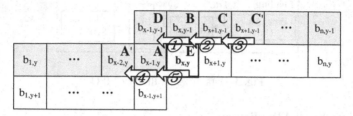

**Fig. 5.** Data flow for the Line buffer

After finished the MV calculation for one MB, the data flow is beginning as shown in Fig. 5. The old $D$ is discarded and the old $B$ became the new $D$. So do $C$ and others. The current motion data of MB $E$ are written to the Line Buffer.

For the MPEG-2, the same scheme is adopted which can provide more useful motion data than one specified by the standard [3]. For the intra MB, either the existed concealment MVs or the zero MVs are written to the buffer based on the bitstream syntax. For the inter MB, the final MVs are also recorded. Once the motion data is lost in the current decoding MB, the firmware can look up the buffer for any positions and get more neighboring motion data which can help the decoder make better decision.

## 4   Implementation Results

We have described the design in Verilog HDL at the RTL level. According to AVS verification model [9] and MPEG2 reference codec [10], a C-code model of MV predictor is also developed to generate the simulation vectors. By testing with 52 HD (including AVS and MPEG-2) bitstreams, Synopsys VCS simulation results show that our Verilog code is functionally identical with the MV prediction module of the verification model for two standards.

The validated Verilog code is synthesized using TSMC 0.18-μm CMOS cells library by Synopsys Design Compiler. The circuit totally costs about 62K logic gates exclusive the SRAM when the working frequency is set to 148.5MHz. Table 1 is our

**Table 1.** Synthesized Results

| Technology | TSMC 0.18μm |
|---|---|
| Working Frequency | 148.5 MHz |
| Gate Count (without SRAM) | 62K |
| SRAM | 34K |
| Cycles/MB | Max. 310 |
| Processing Capacity | 1920×1088,HD interleave, 60 field/s AVS Jizhun Profile 6.2, MPEG-2 MP@HL |

synthesized result. The logic gates for SRAM are about 34K. The line buffer occupies 18K logic gates which can store the 1,830 Bytes for the maximum 1920 pixel width.

The implemented architecture costs at most 310 cycles to perform the MV calculation operation for each MB, which is sufficient to realize the real-time MV prediction process for AVS Jizhun Profile 6.2 bit streams. The proposed design can also meet the real-time requirement of MPEG-2 MP@ HL bit streams.

# 5  Conclusion

In this paper, we contribute an efficient VLSI architecture for MV predictor of AVS and MPEG-2 standard. Firstly, we described the algorithm of MV prediction. Then the architecture was proposed. Our main idea is to employ the pipelined structure to accelerate the process for the new median prediction algorithm and use the dedicated MV FIFO to smooth the memory accessing. Besides, the special line buffer is adopted to store the motion data which can provide either the neighboring motion information for AVS or the error concealment MVs for MPEG-2. Finally, we gave out the simulation results. The architecture was synthesized using TSMC 0.18μm CMOS cells library. The synthesized results show that our design can support the real-time MV prediction calculation of HDTV 1080i AVS and MPEG-2 video. The proposed design can easily embedded into the AVS and MPEG-2 CODEC SoC.

**Acknowledgments.** This work has been supported by National Hi-Tech Development Programs (863) of China under grant No. 2003AA1Z1290.

# References

1. AVS working group official website. http://www.avs.org.cn
2. Information technology — Advanced coding of audio and video – Part 2: Video. AVS-P2 Standard draft (2005)
3. Information technology — general coding of moving picture and associated audio information: video. ITU Recommendation H.262 I ISO/IEC 13818-2 (MPEG-2) Standard draft (1994)
4. Information technology — coding of audio-visual objects - Part 2: visual. ISO/IEC 14496-2 (MPEG-4) Standard (2001)
5. Advanced video coding for generic audiovisual services. ITU-T Recommendation H.264 I ISO/IEC 14496-10 AVC Standard draft (2005)
6. Liang Fan, Siwei Ma, Feng Wu: Overview of AVS Video Standard. In: 2004 IEEE International Conference on Multimedia and Expo. Taibei China (2004) 423-426
7. He Wei-feng, Mao Zhi-gang, Wang Jin-xiang, Wang Dao-fu: Design and implementation of motion compensation for MPEG-4 AS profile streaming video decoding. In: Proceedings. 5th International Conference on ASIC, Beijing China (2003) 942-945
8. Chih-Da Chien, Ho-Chun Chen, Lin-Chieh Huang, Jiun-In Guo: A Low-power Motion Compensation IP Core Design for MPEG-1/2/4 Video Decoding. In: IEEE International Symposium on Circuits and Systems, Kobe Japan (2005) 4542-4545
9. AVS1.0 part 2 reference software model. RM52r1 (2004)
10. MPEG2 codec, V1.2a. MPEG Software Simulation Group (1996)

# Inter-camera Coding of Multi-view Video Using Layered Depth Image Representation

Seung-Uk Yoon[1], Eun-Kyung Lee[1], Sung-Yeol Kim[1], Yo-Sung Ho[1],
Kugjin Yun[2], Sukhee Cho[2], and Namho Hur[2]

[1] Department of Information and Communications
Gwangju Institute of Science and Technology (GIST)
1 Oryong-dong, Buk-gu, Gwangju, 500-712, Republic of Korea
{suyoon, eklee78, sykim75, hoyo}@gist.ac.kr
[2] Broadcasting System Research Group
Electronics and Telecommunications Research Institute (ETRI)
161 Gajeong-dong, Yuseong-gu, Daejeon, 305-700, Republic of Korea
{kjyun, shee, namho}@etri.re.kr

**Abstract.** The multi-view video is collection of multiple videos, capturing the same scene at different viewpoints. If we acquire multi-view videos from multiple cameras, it is possible to generate scenes at arbitrary view positions. It means that users can change their viewpoints freely and can feel visible depth with view interaction. Therefore, the multi-view video can be used in a variety of applications including three-dimensional TV (3DTV), free viewpoint TV, and immersive broadcasting. However, since the data size of the multi-view video linearly increases as the number of cameras, it is necessary to develop an effective framework to represent, process, and display multi-view video data. In this paper, we propose inter-camera coding methods of multi-view video using layered depth image (LDI) representation. The proposed methods represents various information included in multi-view video hierarchically based on LDI. In addition, we reduce a large amount of multi-view video data to a manageable size by exploiting spatial redundancies among multiple videos and reconstruct the original multiple viewpoints successfully from the constructed LDI.

**Keywords:** multi-view video coding, layered depth image, MPEG.

## 1 Introduction

The multi-view video is a collection of multiple videos capturing the same scene at different camera locations. If we acquire multi-view videos from multiple cameras, it is possible to generate video scenes from any viewpoints, which means that users can change their views within the range of captured videos and can feel the visible depth with view interaction. The multi-view video can be used in a variety of applications including free viewpoint video (FVV), free viewpoint TV (FTV), three-dimensional TV (3DTV), surveillance, and home entertainment.

Although the multi-view video has much potential for a variety of applications, one big problem is a huge amount of data. In principle, the multi-view video data

Y. Zhuang et al. (Eds.): PCM 2006, LNCS 4261, pp. 432–441, 2006.
© Springer-Verlag Berlin Heidelberg 2006

are increasing linearly as the number of cameras; therefore, we need to encode the multi-view video data for efficient storage and transmission. Hence, it has been perceived that multi-view video coding (MVC) is a key technology to realize those applications.

ISO/IEC JTC1/SC29/WG11 Moving Picture Experts Group (MPEG) has been recognized the importance of MVC technologies, and an ad hoc group (AHG) on 3-D audio and visual (3DAV) has been established since December 2001. Four main exploration experiments (EE) on 3DAV were performed from 2002 to 2004: EE1 on omni-directional video, EE2 on FTV, EE3 on coding of stereoscopic video using multiple auxiliary components (MAC), and EE4 on depth/disparity coding for 3DTV and intermediate view interpolation. In response to the Call for Comments issued in October 2003, a number of companies have expressed their interests for a standard that enables FTV and 3DTV. After MPEG called interested parties to bring evidences on MVC technologies in October 2004 [1], some evidences were recognized in January 2005 [2] and a Call for Proposals (CfP) on MVC has been issued in July 2005 [3]. Then, the responses to the CfP has been evaluated in January 2006 [4].

In this paper, we propose representation and inter-camera coding methods of multi-view video using the concept of layered depth image (LDI) [5], which is an efficient image-based rendering (IBR) technique. Based on the proposed framework [6], we generate LDI frames from the natural multi-view video, which is different from the previous LDI generation methods mainly using 3-D synthetic objects. We also describe coding methods for the number of layer (NOL) and residual data of the constructed LDI.

The paper is organized as follows. In Section 2, we review our framework [6] for representing multi-view video and explain the generation procedure of LDI from the natural multi-view video. Then, we describe encoding methods of NOL and residual data in Section 3. After experimental results and analysis are presented in Section 4, we draw conclusions in Section 5.

## 2 Representation of Multi-view Video Based on LDI

An important aim of the multi-view video is to provide view-dependant scenes from the pre-captured multiple videos. This goal is similar to the functionality of image-based rendering (IBR) techniques; the novel view generation using 2-D input images.

Traditionally, IBR has been mainly applied to static objects, architectures, and sceneries. However, there have been several approaches to extend it to the dynamic scenes [7], which are called video-based rendering. Kanade et al. [8] extract a global surface representation at each time frame using 51 cameras (512 x 512) in a geodesic dome. They tried to construct 3-D objects from captured images and render them at interactive rate. Matusik et al. [9] use the images from four calibrated cameras (256 x 256) to compute and shade visual hulls. They could render 8000 pixels of the visual hull at about 8 fps. Carranza et al. [10] used seven inward looking synchronized cameras (320 x 240) distributed around a room to capture 3D human motion. They used a 3-D human model as a prior to compute 3D shape at each time frame. Yang et al. [11] designed an 8 x 8 camera array (320 x 240) for capturing dynamic scenes. Instead of storing and rendering the data, they transmit only the rays necessary to compose the desired virtual view. In their system, the camera capture rate is 15 fps, and the interactive viewing rate is 18 fps. In 2004, Zitnick et al. [7] proposed efficient view interpolation and rendering methods using multiple videos acquired from eight cameras. However, these approaches are mainly focusing on the real-time rendering rather than the representation and encoding of a huge amount of input video data.

Inspired by these ideas, we have proposed a framework for representation and encoding of multi-view video using the concept of LDI [6]. In our framework, we have obtained LDI frames from natural multi-view video test sequences by 3-D warping using the given depth images. As the concept of LDI, it is possible to generate LDI by storing intersecting points with color and depth. However, this method can only be applied to 3-D computer graphics (CG) models because rays cannot go through the real object. Therefore, we have exploited multiple color and depth images to construct LDI for natural scenes [5][6] and have used the modified LDI data structure [12].

In the previous work [6], the following incremental 3-D warping equation [5] has been used in the warping stage. When $C_1 = V_1 \cdot P_1 \cdot A_1$, $C_2 = V_2 \cdot P_2 \cdot A_2$, the transform matrix $T_{1,2} = C_2 \cdot C_1^{-1}$. C is a camera matrix, V is the viewport matrix, P is the projection matrix, and A is the affine matrix.

$$T_{1,2} \cdot \begin{bmatrix} x_1 \\ y_1 \\ z_1 \\ 1 \end{bmatrix} = \begin{bmatrix} x_2 \cdot w_2 \\ y_2 \cdot w_2 \\ z_2 \cdot w_2 \\ w_2 \end{bmatrix} = T_{1,2} \cdot \begin{bmatrix} x_1 \\ y_1 \\ 0 \\ 1 \end{bmatrix} + z_1 \cdot T_{1,2} \cdot \begin{bmatrix} 0 \\ 0 \\ 1 \\ 0 \end{bmatrix} \qquad (1)$$

where $(x_1, y_1)$ is the pixel location in $C_1$, $z_1$ is the depth at $(x_1, y_1)$. $(x_2, y_2)$ is the warped pixel location in $C_2$.

However, the problem is that these matrices are designed for 3-D graphics models; there is no clear definition of them for real scenes or objects. Since the camera matrix C was only appropriate for 3-D synthetic scenes, we have calculated a new camera matrix from the given camera parameters contained in multi-view video test sequences. In this paper, we have modified the previous camera matrix C because it does not properly consider the intrinsic characteristics of multiple cameras. It has only considered affine transformations of each camera. The modified camera matrices and the 3-D warping equation are as follows.

$$\dot{C}_1 = \dot{A}_1 \cdot \dot{E}_1, \dot{C}_2 = \dot{A}_2 \cdot \dot{E}_2, \dot{T}_{1,2} = \dot{C}_2 \cdot \dot{C}_1^{-1} \qquad (2)$$

$$\dot{A} = \begin{bmatrix} -f_{s_x} & \theta & t_x \\ 0 & -f_{s_y} & t_y \\ 0 & 0 & 1 \end{bmatrix}, \dot{E} = \begin{bmatrix} R_{11} & R_{12} & R_{13} & T_1 \\ R_{21} & R_{22} & R_{23} & T_2 \\ R_{31} & R_{32} & R_{33} & T_3 \end{bmatrix} \qquad (3)$$

$$T_{1,2}^{\cdot} \cdot \begin{bmatrix} x_1 \\ y_1 \\ z_1 \\ 1 \end{bmatrix} = \begin{bmatrix} x_2 \cdot w_2 \\ y_2 \cdot w_2 \\ z_2 \cdot w_2 \\ w_2 \end{bmatrix} = T_{1,2}^{\cdot} \cdot \begin{bmatrix} x_1 \\ y_1 \\ 0 \\ 1 \end{bmatrix} + z_1 \cdot T_{1,2}^{\cdot} \cdot \begin{bmatrix} 0 \\ 0 \\ 1 \\ 0 \end{bmatrix} \qquad (4)$$

where $f_{s_x}$, $f_{s_y}$ are focal length, $s_x$, $s_y$, are scaling factors, $t_x$, $t_y$, are positions of the focal center, and $\theta$ is the skew angle. $\dot{A}$ defines the intrinsic camera parameters and $\dot{E}$ is an affine transform matrix expressing a rotation and a translation. Finally, we add an additional row to make a homogeneous 4 x 4 camera matrix $\dot{C}$, because $\dot{A} \cdot \dot{E}$ becomes a 3 x 4 matrix.

# 3    Inter-camera Coding of Multi-view Video Using LDI

## 3.1    Color and Depth Components

After generating LDI frames from the natural multi-view video with depth, we separate each LDI frame into three components: color, depth, and the number of layers (NOL). Specifically, color and depth component consists of layer images, respectively. The maximum number of layer images is the same as the total number of views. In addition, residual data should be sent to the decoder in order to reconstruct multi-view images. Color and depth components are processed by data aggregation/layer filling to apply H.264/AVC. NOL could be considered as an image containing the number of layers at each pixel location. Since the NOL information is very important to restore or reconstruct multi-view images from the decoded LDI, it is encoded by using the H.264/AVC intra mode. Finally, the residual data, differences between the input multi-view video and reconstructed ones, are encoded by using the H.264/AVC intra mode.

The data aggregation or layer filling is used in the preprocessing stage [12]. Although H.264/AVC is powerful to encode rectangular images, it does not support shape-adaptive encoding modes. Therefore, we need to aggregate each layer image and then fill the empty locations with the last pixel value of the aggregated image [13]. One problem of the data aggregation is that the resultant images have severely different color distributions. It leads to poor coding efficiency because the prediction among aggregated images is difficult.

The second method is called the layer filling. In order to solve the above problem, we can fill the empty pixel locations of all layer images using pixels in the first layer. Since the first layer has no empty pixels, we can use same pixels in the first layer to fill the other layers. This increases the prediction accuracy of H.264/AVC, therefore data size could be reduced further. We can eliminate the newly filled pixels in the decoding process because the information of NOL is sent to the decoder. It is an eight bit gray scale image that each pixel contains an unsigned integer number representing how many layers there are.

## 3.2    Coding of Number of Layers (NOL)

For color and depth components, we have applied two kinds of preprocessing algorithms. Still remaining important data to encode are the NOL and residual data. Therefore, we describe a coding method of NOL and an algorithm to reduce the residual information in this section.

NOL could be considered as an image containing the number of layers at each pixel location. Figure 1 illustrates an example of the NOL image. Usually, the maximum number of layers is the same as the number of cameras used to capture the scene. If we use eight cameras to acquire eight-view video, then the maximum number of layers is eight. The minimum number of layers is one because there always exists more than one layer. In other words, there are no empty pixels in the first layer of LDI.

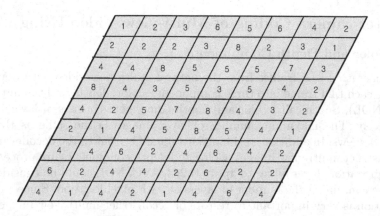

**Fig. 1.** An example of the NOL image

The physical meaning of the NOL is that it represents the hierarchical structure of the constructed LDI in the spatial domain. Assuming the NOL is known, we can efficiently use empty pixel locations to increase the coherency between pixels. We can freely change the pixel orders, add dummy pixels in the empty locations, and remove them after the decoding because we know where those pixels are.

Since the NOL information is very important to restore or reconstruct multi-view images from the decoded LDI, it is encoded by using the H.264/AVC intra mode. However, if we treat the NOL image as a direct input to the codec, we cannot assure the restoration accuracy. Since the dynamic range of the values of NOL is small, quantization noises can contaminate the reconstructed values. Consequently, it is difficult to restore the original NOL image.

In order to solve this problem, we change the dynamic range of the pixel values of the NOL image by considering both the encoding bits required for the changed dynamic range and the accuracy of restored NOL value.

$$\alpha \cdot nMinLayer \leq \alpha \cdot V_{NOL} \leq \alpha \cdot nMaxLayer, \alpha(\in N) \leq 255/V_{NOL} \quad (5)$$

where $nMinLayer$ is the minimum number of layers, $nMaxLayer$ is the maximum number of layers, and $\alpha$ is the scaling factor.

## 3.3    Reduction of Residual Information Using Pixel Interpolation

Theoretically, one way of reducing residual data is to reconstruct multi-views without using the information from the original images. It means that we should maximally exploit depth pixels (DPs) in back layers of LDI, neighboring pixels within a layer image, and spatial relationships between multiple images for the same scene.

In our reconstruction algorithms, there are three steps such as, inverse 3-D warping, reconstruction without residual information, and reconstruction with residual information [12]. In order to reduce residual information, we exploit the neighboring reconstructed images in the second reconstruction stage. We can get intermediate reconstruction results after applying inverse 3-D warping and depth ordering of the back layer pixels. As shown in Fig. 2, we can get intermediate reconstruction results after applying the inverse 3-D warping and depth ordering of the back layer pixels.

(a)                    (b)                    (c)                    (d)

**Fig. 2.** Reconstruction using back layers: (a) view 0, (b) view 1, (c) view 4, (d) view 7

Our approach is to use the neighboring pixels and reconstructed images for interpolating empty pixels of the current reconstructed image. There are mainly two factors influencing the interpolation result: one is spatially located neighboring pixels within the current reconstructed image and the other is temporally located pixels in neighboring reconstructed images. We define the following equation to perform the pixel interpolation.

$$I_S(x,y) = \frac{1}{k} \cdot \sum_{i=0}^{W} \sum_{j=0}^{W} I(R_{(i,j)}) \qquad (6)$$

$$I_V(x,y) = \sum_{n=0}^{N-1} a_n \cdot I(R_n), \sum_{n=0}^{N-1} a_n = 1 \qquad (7)$$

$$I_E(x,y) = \alpha \cdot I_S(x,y) + (1-\alpha) \cdot I_V(x,y), 0 \le \alpha \le 1 \qquad (8)$$

where $I_S(x,y)$, $I_V(x,y)$ is the intensity value of the interpolated pixel at the (x, y) position of the current image, respectively, $I_E(x,y)$ is the final interpolated pixel value, $k$ is the valid number of pixels within a $W$ x $W$ window, $a_n$ and $\alpha$ are the weighting factors, $N$ is the number of cameras, and $R$ means the reconstructed image. These equations are only applied to interpolate the empty pixels of the current image. The weighting factors have been determined by experiments.

Figure 3 shows the reconstruction results after performing the interpolation using the above equations. We can observe that most holes except left-most and right-most sides are recovered with much less visual artifacts compared to the results in Fig. 2.

(a)          (b)          (c)          (d)

**Fig. 3.** Reconstruction results using the pixel interpolation: (a) view 0, (b) view 1, (c) view 4, (d) view 7

## 4   Experimental Results and Analysis

In our experiments, we have used the "Breakdancers" sequence provided by Microsoft Research. It includes a sequence of 100 images captured from eight cameras; the camera arrangement is 1-D arc with about 20cm horizontal spacing. Depth maps computed by stereo matching algorithms are provided for each camera together with the camera parameters: intrinsic parameters, barrel distortion, and rotation matrix. The exact depth range is also given [7][14].

### 4.1   Generation of LDIs from Natural Multi-view Video

The main part of generating LDI frames from the natural multi-view video is the incremental 3-D warping. Figure 4 shows the results of 3-D warping using the modified camera matrices. We can observe that actors are slightly rotating as the camera number changes. In order to identify the warping results clearly, we did not interpolate holes. White pixels in each image represent the holes, which are generated by the 3-D warping. Among eight cameras, the fifth camera is the reference LDI view and the warping has been performed from other camera locations to the reference LDI view. When the warping is carried out from the left cameras (view 0, 1, 2, and 3) to the reference camera (view 4), major holes are created along the right side of the actors. On the other hand, holes are mainly distributed in the left side of the actors as the warping is done from the right cameras (view 5, 6, and 7) to the LDI view.

The generated LDI has several layers and the maximum number of layer is the same as the camera number. For the test sequence used in our experiments, each LDI frame can therefore have eight layers in maximum. The layer images (color components) of the constructed LDI frame with depth threshold 3.0 is presented in Fig. 5.

**Fig. 4.** Results of the incremental 3-D warping: (a) view 0 to view 4, (b) view 1 to view 4, (c) view 7 to view 4

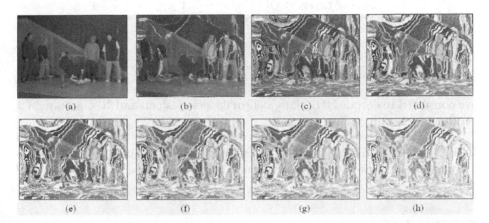

**Fig. 5.** Layer images of the first LDI frame: (a) 1st layer; (b) 2nd layer, (c) 3rd layer, (d) 4th layer, (e) 5th layer, (f) 6th layer, (g) 7th layer, (h) 8th layer

## 4.2 Inter-camera Coding of Multi-view Video Using LDI

In Table 1, we have compared the data size between the sum of frames of the test sequence and the generated LDI frame. In Table 1, the sum of frames means the summation of eight color and depth images of the test sequence without encoding. Simulcast using H.264/AVC (color + depth) means the summation of data size calculated by the independent coding of color and depth images.

Table 1 shows the data size by changing the depth threshold value from 0.0 to 5.0, but the data size has not been decreased much as the threshold value is over 3.0 from the experiments. The depth threshold means the difference among actual depth values. The given depth range was from 44.0 to 120.0. The size of NOL data is varying to the encoding condition, mainly by the dynamic range of NOL and quantization parameters. In addition, the depth threshold could affect to the size of them. In Table 1, the size of NOL is computed by using the fixed alpha value of one. From our experiments, about 60 to 70% of the total bitrates

**Table 1.** Data size for the "Breakdnacers" sequence [kbytes]

|  | 1st 8 Frames | 2nd 8 Frames |
|---|---|---|
| Sum of frames | 25,166 | 25,166 |
| Simulcast (color+depth) | 137.7 | 132.5 |
| LDI frame (threshold=0.0) | 24,520 | 24,644 |
| Encoded LDI (Layer filling) | 71.4 | 72.9 |
| Number of Layers (NOL) | 6.3 | 6.4 |
| LDI frame (threshold=3.0) | 13,924 | 13,803 |
| Encoded LDI (Layer filling) | 48.4 | 48.2 |
| Number of Layers (NOL) | 5.1 | 5.0 |
| LDI frame (threshold=5.0) | 13,808 | 13,723 |
| Encoded LDI (Layer filling) | 46.3 | 47.0 |
| Number of Layers (NOL) | 4.2 | 4.4 |

are consumed to encode NOL data as near-lossless fashion and 10% are used for residual data coding.

Still remaining issues of the LDI-based approach are how to select the proper back layer pixels to fill out the current pixel location and how to dynamically adjust bitrates per each component, e.g., color, depth, NOL, and residual data.

## 5   Conclusions

In this paper, we have described a procedure to generate layered depth images (LDIs) from the natural multi-view video and encoding methods for the number of layers (NOL) and residual data. Incremental 3-D warping has been modified to consider intrinsic characteristics of multiple cameras. For the inter-camera coding of multi-view video, we have applied two kinds of preprocessing algorithms to encode color and depth components of the constructed LDI based on our framework. The number of layers (NOL) and residual data are coded by changing the dynamic range and exploiting pixel interpolation techniques. We have reduced a large amount of multi-view video data to a manageable size by combining the proposed encoding techniques and reconstructed the original multiple viewpoints successfully. Finally, we will investigate temporal prediction structures of the constructed LDI frames in the future.

**Acknowledgements.** This work was supported by the Ministry of Information and Communication (MIC) through the Realistic Broadcasting Research Center (RBRC) at Gwangju Institute of Science and Technology (GIST).

# References

1. ISO/IEC JTC1/SC29/WG11 N6720: Call for Evidence on Multi-view Video Coding. October (2004)
2. ISO/IEC JTC1/SC29/WG11 N6999: Report of the Subjective Quality Evaluation for Multi-view Coding CfE. January (2005)
3. ISO/IEC JTC1/SC29/WG11 N7327: Call for Proposals on Multi-view Video Coding. July (2005)
4. ISO/IEC JTC1/SC29/WG11 N7779: Subjective Test Results for the CfP on Multi-view Video Coding. January (2006)
5. Shade, J., Gotler, S., Szeliski, R.: Layered Depth Images. Proc. of ACM SIGGRAPH, July (1998) 291-298
6. Yoon, S.U., Kim, S.Y., Lee, E.K., and Ho, Y.S.: A Framework for Multi-view Video Coding using Layered Depth Images. Lecture Notes in Computer Science (LNCS), 3767 (2005) 431-442
7. Zitnick, C.L., Kang, S.B., Uyttendaele, M., Winder, S., and Szeliski, R.: High-quality Video View Interpolation using a Layered Representation. Proc. of ACM SIGGRAPH, August (2004) 600-608
8. Kanade, T., Rander, P.W., and Narayanan, P.J: Virtualized Reality: Constructing Virtual Worlds from Real Scenes. IEEE Multimedia Magazine, Vol. 1, No. 1, (1997) 34-47
9. Matusik, W., Buehler, C., McMillan, L., and Gortler, S.J.: Image-based Visual Hulls. Proc. of ACM SIGGRAPH, (2000) 369-374
10. Carranza, C., Theobalt, C., Magnor, M.A., and Seidel, H.-P.: Free-viewpoint Video of Human Actors. ACM Trans. on Graphics, Vol. 22, No. 3, (2003) 569-577
11. Yang, J.C., Everett, M., Buehler, C., and McMillan, L.: A Real-time Distributed Light Field Camera. Eurographics Workshop on Graphics, (2002) 77-85
12. Yoon, S.U., Lee, E.K., Kim, S.Y., Ho, Y.S., Yun, K., Cho, S., and Hur, N.: Coding of Layered Depth Images Representing Multiple Viewpoint Video. Proc. of Picture Coding Symposium (PCS) SS3-2, April (2006) 1-6
13. Duan, J. and Li, J.: Compression of the LDI. IEEE Trans. on Image Processing, Vol. 12, No. 3, (2003) 365-372
14. Interactive Visual Media Group at Microsoft Research, http://research.microsoft.com/vision/InteractiveVisualMediaGroup/ 3DVideoDownload/

# Optimal Priority Packetization with Multi-layer UEP for Video Streaming over Wireless Network

Huanying Zou, Chuang Lin, Hao Yin, Zhen Chen,

Feng Qiu, and Xuening Liu

Dept. of Computer Science and Technology, Tsinghua University,
Beijing, 100084, China
{hyzou, clin, hyin, zhenchen, fqiu,
xliu}@csnet1.cs.tsinghua.edu.cn

**Abstract.** Most of current packetization schemes consider only bit error or packet erasure, both of which are common in wireless networks. This paper addresses these two problems together, and proposes an optimal packetization scheme for video streaming over wireless network, which is independent of video coding method. To combat the packet erasure, priority packetization combined with multi-layer unequal error protection (UEP) is applied on video frames. Multi-layer UEP contains low-complexity duplication of high-priority packet in application layer and different retransmission limit in media access control layer. Content-aware rate-distortion optimization is also introduced in order to countermine the distortion caused by bit errors. Simulations show that our scheme gains 2.17 dB or more compared with the conventional scheme.

**Keywords:** Priority packetization, rate-distortion optimization, multi-layer unequal error protection, video streaming, wireless network.

## 1 Introduction

With the rapid growth of wireless networks and great success of internet video, wireless video services are expected to be widely deployed in the near future. However, packet loss and bit error in wireless video service is inevitable due to the limited bandwidth and error-prone channel. In order to improve the quality of service (QoS) of the wireless video service, many error control algorithms have been proposed. For well-designed packetization scheme can not only significantly improve the error resilience of streaming video but also reduce the overhead of compressing coding, there are many researches focusing on the error-resilient packetization.

However, most current works only considers either the packet erasure or bit errors. Lots of researches focus on alleviation of video distortion caused by packet erasure. X.Wu et al. [1] study various packetization schemes, and propose globally optimal and sub-optimal packetization algorithms for embedded multimedia bitstream. H. Cai et al. propose an rate-distortion (R-D) optimized packetization scheme for fine granularity

Y. Zhuang et al. (Eds.): PCM 2006, LNCS 4261, pp. 442–449, 2006.

scalability (FGS) bitstream streaming with inter-packet dependence completely removed [2, 3], and unequal error protection (UEP) is adopted to enhance error resilience in [4]. P. A. Chou et al. [5] study the packetization method against packet-loss network in an R-D optimized way for general scalable video transmission. A source-adaptive packetization scheme [6, 7] with intra-frame packet interleaving and fixed forward error correction coding is proposed to combat the severe packet losses over wireless channels. On the other hand, some researches focus on the packetization against transmission bit error over error-prone networks. S.T. Worrall et al. in [8] propose a motion-adaptive scheme by dynamically changing the length of video packets. A scheme with smallest possible video packet size and compressed header in [9] is proposed for MPEG-4 video over 3G. An R-D optimized packetization in [10] is studied for FGS over error-prone channel.

In this paper, we propose an R-D optimized packetization scheme for wireless video streaming. More specially, the multifold advantages of our scheme are: 1) it provides error resilience for bit error and packet erasure simultaneously; 2) the framework is independent of video coding method, making it suitable for various coding standards; 3) priority packetization with multi-layer UEP remarkably improves packet loss resilience compared with other schemes; 4) it is R-D optimized based on content information, trying to minimize the distortion caused by bit errors; 5) a prototype system of proposed scheme is implemented, and the experimental results show that it gains 2.17 dB or more than the conventional packetization scheme.

The rest of this paper is organized as follows. Section 2 lists the notations used in the other sections. The framework of our packetization scheme is introduced in Section 3, and the content-aware R-D optimization for our scheme is presented in Section 4. Simulations and results are described in Section 5, followed by the conclusion in Section 6.

## 2  Notations

The table below shows the description of notations used in the following sections.

**Table 1.** Notations

| Notation | Description |
|----------|-------------|
| $VOP_i$ | i-th visual object plane (VOP) in a frame |
| $VP_{i,j}$ | j-th video packet in $VOP_i$ |
| $MB_{i,j,k}$ | k-th macro-block in $VP_{i,j}$ |
| $VP^h_{i,j}$ | High-priority partition of $VP_{i,j}$ |
| $VP^l_{i,j}$ | Low-priority partition of $VP_{i,j}$ |
| $D_{i,j,k}$ | Distortion caused by lost $MB_{i,j,k}$ |
| $D'_{i,j,k}$ | Distortion caused by $MB_{i,j,k}$ decoded with error concealment |
| $P_e$ | Bit error rate |
| $P^h_{i,j}$ | Corruption possibility of $VP^h_{i,j}$ |
| $P^l_{i,j}$ | Corruption possibility of $VP^l_{i,j}$ |

## 3  Framework of Proposed Packetization Scheme

Content-aware R-D optimization tries to mitigate the influence of bit errors. Priority packetization with multi-layer UEP is achieved according to the different importance of compressed video data, aiming to combat bursty packet-erasure. The framework is independent of coding method. We take the MPEG-4 coding standard for example, as shown in Fig. 1. One can easily extend this framework to other coding methods.

### 3.1  Priority Packetization

During encoding, a video frame is segmented into several visual object planes (VOP). Optimal video packets are then generated through content-aware R-D optimization. The details will be discussed in next section.

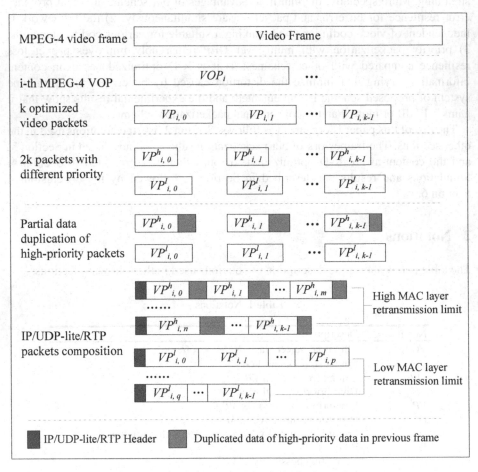

**Fig. 1.** Framework of proposed packetization scheme

Data in video packet are divided into high-priority and low-priority partitions according to their different importance in video decoding. According to MPEG-4 standard in [11], video packet header and motion data are necessary for decoding, while the loss of texture data can be partially recovered by error concealment method. Therefore, header and motion data will be in high-priority packet with the texture data in low-priority packet. As shown in Fig.1, $VOP_i$, is packed into k optimal video packets, i.e. $VP_{i, j}$ ($0 \le j < k$), which is further split into a high-priority packet $VP^h_{i, j}$ and a low-priority packet $VP^l_{i, j}$.

Then these packets are assembled into real-time transport protocol (RTP) packets. To reduce the header overhead, packets with same-priority will be tried to fill into an RTP packet as long as there are enough space. As shown in Fig.1 m+1 high-priority packets $VP^h_{i,j}$ (m<k, $0 \le j \le m$) are stored in an RTP packet, and p+1 low-priority packets $VP^l_{i,j}$ (p<k, $0 \le j \le p$) are in another RTP packet. RTP packets will be further encapsulated with UDP-lite and IP header. Note that the UDP-lite protocol in [13] is adopted in order to pass the corrupted packets to application layer other than drop them in transport layer. To futher reduce the bandwidth consumption, IP/UDP-lite/RTP header can be compressed [14] and transmitted with IP tunneling method [15].

### 3.2 Multi-layer Unequal Error Protection

UEP in multi-layer contains high-priority data duplication in application layer and different retransmission limit in media access control (MAC) layer.

We improve the loss-resilient packet duplication method proposed in [12] to achieve UEP in application layer. An additional interlacing method is introduced in order to improve resilience against bursty packet erasure. As shown in Fig. 1, only high-priority data will be duplicated, and the duplicated data will be attached as a piggyback to high-priority packets of video packets in next frame.

In MAC layer, UEP is achieved by adopting different retransmission limit in order to alleviate the loss of high-priority packets. High-priority IP/UDP-lite/RTP packets are sent with high retransmission limit in MAC layer, while low-priority packets has low retransmission limit.

## 4   Content-Aware Rate Distortion Optimization

In our packetization scheme, distortion caused by bit errors is minimized through dynamically determining the number of macro-blocks for every video packet in a VOP based on the content information, while overhead can be limited by fixing the number of video packets per frame. A similar R-D optimization method is also adopted in 10. The optimization is formulated as below.

Assume that a frame has $L$ macro-blocks and $M$ VOPs. $VOP_i$ has $N_i$ video packets, and $VP_{i, j}$ has $N_{i,j}$ macro-blocks. To limit the overhead of packet header, $N$ video packets are generated for every frame. The average distortion of a video frame can be formulated as below:

$$D = \sum_{i=0}^{M-1} \sum_{j=0}^{N_i-1} (P^h_{i,j} \times \sum_{k=0}^{N_{i,j}-1} D_{i,j,k} + P^l_{i,j} \times \sum_{k=0}^{N_{i,j}-1} D'_{i,j,k}) \qquad (1)$$

$$\text{with } \sum_{i=0}^{M-1} N_i = N, \sum_{i=0}^{M-1} \sum_{j=0}^{N_i} N_{i,j} = L, \tag{2}$$

The corruption possibility of a packet depends on its length and bit error rate. Especially, $P^h_{i,j}$ denotes the possibility that both the high-priority packet and its duplication are corrupted. Assume that the length of $VP^h_{i,j}$ and its duplication are $L^h_{i,j}$ and $L^{h,d}_{i,j}$, $L_{hdr}$ is the length of IP/UDP-lite/RTP header, and $L^l_{i,j}$ is the length of $VP^l_{i,j}$. We get:

$$P^h_{i,j} = (1 - (1 - P_e)^{L_{hdr} + L^h_{i,j}}) \times (1 - (1 - P_e)^{L_{hdr} + L^{h,d}_{i,j}}) \tag{3}$$

$$\text{and } P^l_{i,j} = 1 - (1 - P_e)^{L_{hdr} + L^l_{i,j}} \tag{4}$$

Besides, the distortion of a macro-block can be given by the number of its non-zero bits, which can be easily got during the encoding procedure.

The optimization is to find the appropriate $\{N^*_i, N^*_{i,j}: 0 \le i < M, 0 \le j < N^*_i\}$ to minimize the average distortion $D$. Dynamic programming can be used to solve this optimization problem with $O(N*L)$ time [10].

# 5 Simulations

We have implemented a prototype system of our packetization scheme, and its performance is evaluated based on NS-2 with the extensions implemented in [16]. Two quarter common intermediate format (QCIF) video test sequences, Foreman and Suzie are encoded with MPEG-4 standard. Only the first frame is I-frame while the others are P-frames, and I-frame is assumed to be error free. Simple error concealment mechanism is adopted. If high-priority data are corrupted, the whole video packet will be dropped, and the image of the same position in previous frame will be used instead. If low-priority data are lost, the video packet will be decoded with motion compensation mechanism. In this simulation, power signal-to-noise ratio (PSNR) is adopted to evaluate the objective video quality. The performance evaluation considers both the packet loss rate (PLR) and bit error rate (BER) and every simulation are run 30 times. Performance is evaluated between our optimal scheme and the scheme adopted by MPEG-4 standard.

## 5.1 Performance Against Packet Loss Rate

We evaluate the performance at different PLR (0%, 5%, 10%, 20%), while BER is fixed at $10^{-4}$. Results of the two sequences are shown in Fig. 2. While PLR equals to 0%, i.e. no packet is lost during transmission, our scheme gets a higher PSNR than traditional scheme with 2.66 dB and 2.72 dB gain for Foreman and Suzie respectively. We can see that the R-D optimization reduces the distortion caused by bit errors. Besides, UEP in application layer also improves video quality against bit errors. As PLR increases, the value of PSNR of both the two schemes decrease. However, performance of our scheme drops much slower than the traditional scheme. As shown in Fig.2, our scheme gains 4.22 dB for Foreman and 3.05 dB for Suzie at 20% of PLR.

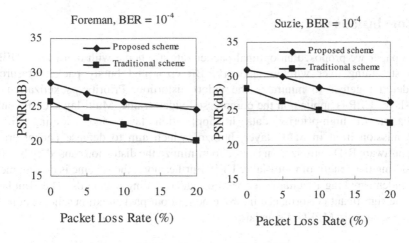

**Fig. 2.** Performance against PLR

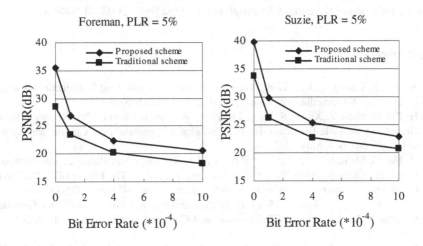

**Fig. 3.** Performance against BER

## 5.2 Performance Against Bit Error Rate

The evaluation is performed with various BER ($0$, $10^{-4}$, $4*10^{-4}$, $10^{-3}$), while PLR is fixed at 5%. Fig. 3 illustrates the simulation results of Foreman and Suzie. Our scheme gets much higher PSNR than traditional scheme when no bit error happens. That is because multi-layer UEP effectively reduces the erasure of high-priority data. BER increment remarkably deteriorates corruption possibility of both high-priority and low-priority data, leading PSNR to descend sharply. When BER equals to $10^{-3}$, our scheme has 2.26 dB and 2.17 dB gain for Foreman and Suzie respectively.

# 6  Conclusions

In this paper we proposed an optimal packetization scheme with multi-layer UEP for video streaming over wireless network. Bit error and bursty packet erasure are considered together to minimize the video distortion. Priority packetization with multi-layer UEP is applied on the compressed video frame. Multi-layer UEP contains duplication of high-priority data in application layer and adopting different retransmission limit in MAC layer, both of which aim to defense packet erasure. Content-aware R-D optimization is used to minimize the distortion caused by bit errors, considering the benefit of multi-layer UEP. Furthermore, the scheme is coding method independent, making it suitable for various video coding standards. The simulations show the significant performance improvement of our packetization scheme compared with the scheme in MPEG-4 standard.

**Acknowledgements.** This work is supported by the National Natural Science Foundation of China (No. 90412012, 60429202 and 60372019), and the National Grand Fundamental Research 973 Program of China (No. 2003CB314804).

# Reference

1. X. Wu, S. Cheng, and Z. Xiong. On Packetization of Embedded Multimedia Bitstreams. IEEE Trans. Multimedia, vol. 3, no. 1, pp. 132-140, March 2001.
2. H. Cai, G. Shen, Z. Xiong, S. Li, and B. Zeng. An Optimal Packetization Scheme for Fine Granularity Scalable Bitstream. IEEE International Symposium On Circuits and Systems, vol. 5, pp. 641-644, May 2002.
3. H. Cai, G. Shen, S. Li, and B. Zeng. A Novel Low-Complexity Packetization Method For Fine-Granularity Scalable (FGS) Video Streaming. Proc. of The Fourth IEEE Pacific-Rim Conference on Multimedia, Singapore, vol. 3, Dec. 15-18, 2003, pp. 1375-1379.
4. H. Cai, B. Zeng, G. Shen, and S. Li. Error-Resilient Unequal Protection of Fine Granularity Scalable Video Bitstreams. IEEE International Conference on Communication, vol. 3, pp. 1303-1307, 2004.
5. P. A. Chou, Z. Miao. Rate-Distortion Optimized Streaming of Packetized Media. IEEE Transactions On Multimedia, VOL. 8, NO. 2, APRIL 2006, pp. 390-404
6. Q. Qu, Y. Pei, X. Tian, J. Modestino, Y. Chan. Motion-based interactive video coding and delivery over wireless IP networks. IEEE International Conference on Communications, 16-20, May, 2005 Vol. 2, pp. 1195-1199.
7. Q. Qu, Y. Pei and J. W. Modestino. Robust H.264 Video Coding and Transmission over Bursty Packet Loss Wireless Networks. in Proc. of IEEE VTC2003, Orlando, Oct. 2003.
8. S.T.Worrall, A.H.Sadka, PSweeney and A.M.Kondoz. Optimal packetisation of MPEG-4 using RTP over mobile networks. IEE Proc. Commun., Vol. 148, No. 4, August 2001.
9. Z. Ahmad, S. Worrall, A.H. Sadka, A. Kondoz. A novel packetisation scheme for MPEG-4 over 3G wireless systems. Fifth IEE International Conference on 3G Mobile Communication Technologies, 2004, pp. 302-306.
10. B. Zhu, Y. Yang, C. Chen, S. Li. Optimal packetization of fine granularity scalability codestreams for error-prone channels. IEEE International Conference on Image Processing, 11-14, Sept., 2005, vol. 2, pp. 185-188.

11. Coding of moving pictures and audio. ISO/IEC 14496-2:2004/Amd 1:2004, 24-05-2004.
12. Man-Keun Seo, Yo-Won Jeong, Jae-Kyoon Kim, and Kyu-Ho Park. A New Packet Loss-Resilient Duplicated Video Transmission. 2005 Asia-Pacific Conference on Communications, pp.1063-1067, Perth, Western Australia, 3 - 5 October 2005.
13. L.A. Larzon, S. Pink, G. Fairhurst. The Lightweight User Datagram Protocol (UDP-Lite). RFC 3828, July, 2004.
14. S. Casner, V. Jacobson, "Compressing IP/UDP/RTP Headers for Low-Speed Serial Links", RFC 2508, Feb. 1999.
15. W. Simpson. IP in IP Tunneling. RFC 1853, Oct. 1995.
16. C. Ke, C. Lin, C. Shieh, W. Hwang. A Novel Realistic Simulation Tool for Video Transmission over Wireless Network. The IEEE International Conference on Sensor Networks, Ubiquitous, and Trustworthy Computing, June 5-7, 2006, Taichung, Taiwan.

# A Multi-channel MAC Protocol with Dynamic Channel Allocation in CDMA Ad Hoc Networks

Jigang Qiu[1], Guangbin Fan[2], Huijie Li[1], and Xiaokang Lin[1]

[1] Department of Electronics Engineering, Tsinghua University, Beijing, China
[2] Intel China Research Center, Beijing, China
{qiujg03, geolee97}@mails.thu.edu.cn, guangbin.fan@intel.com,
lxk-dee@ tsinghua.edu.cn

**Abstract.** It is a challenging task to design an efficient MAC protocol in Ad Hoc networks due to the lack of central control equipments. In this paper, a new multi-channel MAC protocols with dynamic channel allocation in CDMA Ad Hoc networks, MMAC-DCA, is presented. In MMAC-DCA, the wireless channel is divided into one common sub-channel and L service sub-channels by CDMA mechanism. All the nodes exchange RTS and CTS on the common sub-channel to reserve the service sub-channels for transmission. Different from the MACA/C-T and C-T, the service sub-channels are allocated dynamically in the distributed mode only when a node has a package to transmit. The protocol can reduce the number of spreading codes required and increase the throughput normalized by available bandwidth. In addition, a Markov mode is presented to analyze the performance of this protocol in theory including the normalized throughput and the transfer delay of data packages.

**Keywords:** Ad Hoc networks, dynamic channel allocation (DCA), CDMA, multi-channel MAC.

## 1 Introduction

Because there are no central control equipments such as AP in Ad Hoc networks, it is a challenging task to design an efficient medium access control (MAC) protocol. The existing MAC protocols can be classified into the single-channel MAC protocols and the multi-channel MAC protocols. The single-channel MAC protocols include multiple access with collision avoidance (MACA) [1], MACAW [2], IEEE 802.11 DCF [3], etc. In MACA [1], before the data transmission, the transmitting node and the destination node exchange RTS and CTS to resolve the hidden terminal problem and the exposed terminal problem. In MACAW [2], a five-way handshake mechanism RTS-CTS-DS-DATA-ACK is presented to ensure that the data package can be transferred successfully. IEEE 802.11 DCF [3] adopts carrier sense medium with collision avoidance (CSMA/CA) mechanism whose contention window is calculated by the binary exponential back-off algorithm.

To utilize the wireless resource more efficiently, some multi-channels protocols are presented in recent years. MMAC [4] directly applies the single-channel MAC protocol onto each of sub-channels. In HRMA [5], all the nodes follow the same

Y. Zhuang et al. (Eds.): PCM 2006, LNCS 4261, pp. 450–458, 2006.

frequency-hopping graph with each hop duration equivalent to the time of transmitting RTS and CTS. Two spread-spectrum protocols called Common-Transmitter-Based (C-T) protocol and Receiver-Transmitter-Based (R-T) are proposed in [6]. In C-T, a single spreading code is used by all the nodes. In addition, each node is pre-assigned a unique transmitter-based code. The addressing information is transferred on common spreading code and data packages are transferred using a transmitter-based spreading code. In R-T, each node is pre-assigned two unique spreading codes. The addressing information is transmitted on the destination node's receiver-based spreading code and the data packet is sent on the transmitting node's transmitter-based spreading code. In MACA/C-T and MACA/R-T [7], a RTS-CTS dialogue is used to improve R-T and C-T to resolve the hidden terminal problem and the exposed terminal problem.

However, a common drawback of C-T, R-T, MACA/C-T and MACA/R-T is that each node must be assigned at least one spreading code whether the node has a data package to send (or receive) or not, which impose a severe penalty on the bandwidth utilization. To improve the bandwidth utilization, in [8] a cross layer design for medium access control with dynamic channel allocation is presented. However, in [8] a complex Neyman-Pearson detector is needed and the transmission of Query packages may cause the interference on service spreading sub-channels. So we propose a new multi-channel MAC protocol with DCA mechanism, MMAC-DCA.

## 2  Multi-channel MAC with Dynamic Channel Allocation

It is assumed that all the nodes are equipped with one half-duplex transceiver and the transceiver can switch among sub-channels quickly. The system is assumed to be slotted and a RTS-CTS dialogue can complete in one time slot. It is assumed that there are $N$ nodes and $L+1$ spreading codes available for transmission where $L < N/2$. The spreading codes have good correlation properties and each code identifies a unique sub-channel. The transmission of the packages on different spreading nodes doesn't interfere with each other. One of spreading codes is used to transmit RTS and CTS and other $L$ spreading codes are used to transmit data packages.

Every node maintains a "code-occupation-status" table to conserve the information of the service spreading codes. When receiving RTS/CTS, nodes update the table.

When idle, each node stays on the common sub-channel (the common spreading code) to monitor. If an idle node (e.g. A) attempting to transmit data package to its immediate neighbors (e.g. B), it look-ups the code-occupation-status table to calculate out the idle spreading codes which is not occupied by its neighbor nodes (Idle-Spreading-Code-Set A), and broadcasts a RTS on the common spreading code. The following information is encapsulated in the RTS: the transmitting node identifier (A), the destination node identifier (B), the status of the local spreading code.

If node B receives the RTS, it look-ups the local code-occupation-status table to calculate out the idle spreading codes (Idle-Spreading-Code-Set B). Node B randomly selects an idle spreading code (e.g. Code-X) from the intersection of Idle-Spreading-Code-Set A and Idle-Spreading-Code-Set B. Node B transmits the CTS on the common spreading code carrying the ID of Code-X and turns the transceiver onto the Code-X. If node B cannot find an idle service spreading code, it doesn't transmit the CTS and turns the transceiver onto the common spreading code.

If node A receives the CTS, it turns the transceiver onto the Code-X and begins to transmit the data package. If node B receives the data package successfully, it immediately transmits ACK as a response and returns back onto the common spreading code. When node A receives the ACK, it returns back onto the common spreading code. The process of data transmission is illustrated in figure 1.

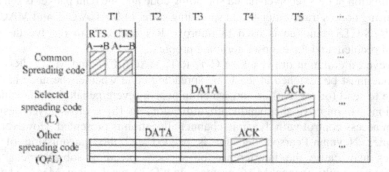

**Fig. 1.** The process of data transmission in MMAC-DCA

# 3   Performance Analysis of MMAC-DCA

Although the Ad Hoc networks posses the characteristic of multi-hop, the current researches mostly assume that the system is fully connected due to the trouble of mathematical analysis. This means is proved to be effective via simulation and practice, and then we adopt this means to evaluate the performance of MMAC-DCA.

## 3.1  Normalized Network Throughput

The network throughput ( $S_{total}$ ) is defined as the average number of packages in one time slot within the whole network. Assuming that the spreading gain is $G$ which is the ration of the chip rate to the symbol rate, the normalized throughput ( $S_{normalized}$ ) can be defined as the ration of the network throughput to the spreading gain. If the spreading codes are such codes as Walsh codes, the spreading gain is equal to the number of the spreading codes $L+1$. We have,

$$S_{normalized} = S_{total} / G = S_{total} /(L+1) \qquad (1)$$

The length of data packages is assumed to be geometrical distribution with parameter $q$ per time slot, and then the probability of a package with length $z$ is $(1-q)q^{z-1}$ . So the average length of data package is $1/(1-q)$ .

It is assumed that the service type of data packages is unicast, which means that the packages of transmitting nodes only address to one destination nodes and vice versa. The total number of the networks nodes is sum of three parts: the number of idle nodes which don't transmit and receive packages; the number of nodes transmitting packages; the number of nodes receiving packages. In MMAC-DCA, the nodes suspend transmitting the data package if the RTS-CTS dialogue fails, so that the number of transmitting nodes is equal to the number of receiving nodes.

When the node is idle, it is assumed to transmit a new package in one time slot with probability $p$. The system state is presented as the number of communication pairs $m$. let $P_m$ denotes the probability of the steady state $m$, and the normalized network throughput in mini-packets per time slot can be calculated as

$$S_{normalized} = \sum_{m=0}^{L} P_m.m/(L+1) \qquad (2)$$

Let $p_{k,m}$ denote the transition probability from state $k$ to state $m$, i.e., the probability from $k$ communicating pairs to $m$ communicating pairs. Only when one RTS-CTS dialogue occurs on the common spreading code, the RTS-CTS dialogue can succeed. Otherwise, multiple RTS-CTS dialogues at the given time slot will collide with each other.

If $k < L$ at the slot $t$-$1$, once the RTS-CTS dialogue succeeds, the transmitting node always discovers at least one idle spreading for the transmission at the time slot $t$.

It is conditioned that at the beginning of slot $t$, the number of communicating pair of nodes becoming idle is $i$. And then the number of nodes that are available to receive or transmit is $N' = N - 2k + 2i$. It is assumed that at the beginning of slot $t$, there are $x'$ nodes which transmit RTS packets. Let $n'$ and $m'$ denote the number of nodes attempting to send RTS packets but failing to receive CTS packets and the number of nodes that successfully send RTS packets and receive CTS packets, respectively. $m'$ is equal to $m - k + i$, and $n'$ is equal to $x' - m'$.

Since at any time slot, at most, one RTS-CTS dialogue can succeed, a transition state $k$ to state $m$ is possible only if $m' = 1$ or $m' = 0$.

Let $\Phi$ denote the event that one transition from state $k$ to state $m$ occurs; let $\Omega^I$ denote the event that exactly one transmission occurs and it is addressed to a idle node; let $\Omega^B$ denote the event that exactly one transmission occurs and it is addressed to a busy node. The transition probability can be calculated as follows.

$$
\begin{aligned}
P_{k,m} &= \sum_{i=0}^{k} \left\{ P\binom{i \text{ pairs}}{\text{become idle}} [P(\Phi \cap \Omega^I) + P(\Phi \cap \Omega^B) + P(\Phi \cap \binom{0 \text{ or} >1}{\text{transmission}})] \right\} \\
&= \sum_{i=0}^{k} B(k,1-q,i) * \{ \delta(m'-1)\delta(n')B(N',p,1)\frac{N'-1}{N-1} + \delta(m')\delta(n'-1)B(N',p,1)\frac{N-N'}{N-1} \\
&\quad + \delta(m')(1-\delta(n'-1))B(N',p,n') \}
\end{aligned} \qquad (3)
$$

Where $\delta(k)=1$ when $x=0$, $\delta(k)=0$ when $x \neq 0$; where $B(n,p,k)$ is binomial distribution, and then can be expressed as $B(n,p,k)=\binom{n}{k}p^k(1-p)^{n-k}$.

When $k < L$, (3) can be simplified as

$$
\begin{cases}
P_{k,m}=q^{m-1}(1-q)^{k-m}\{\binom{k}{m-1}(1-q)p(1-p)^{M+1}\dfrac{M^2+3M+2}{N-1} -\binom{k}{m}qp(1-p)^{M-1}\dfrac{M^2-M}{N-1} \\
\quad +\binom{k}{m}q\} & \text{where } 0<m\le k<L. \\[2mm]
P_{k,m}=q^{m-1}(1-q)^{k-m}\binom{k}{m-1}(1-q)p(1-p)^{M+1}\dfrac{M^2+3M+2}{N-1} & \text{where } m=k+1. \\[2mm]
P_{k,m}=0 & \text{where } m>k+1 \\[2mm]
P_{k,m}=(1-q)^k[1-(N-2k)p(1-p)^{N-2k-1}\dfrac{N-2k-1}{N-1}] & \text{where } m=0 \\[2mm]
\text{Where } M=N-2m
\end{cases}
\tag{4}
$$

If $k=L$, the node attempting to send data packet discovers that there is no idle spreading code in the network, and then it suspends the RTS-CTS dialogue. In such a case, the probability that the idle node becomes into communication node is zero. The transition probability can be calculated as follows:

$$
P_{L,m}=P\left(\begin{array}{c}L-m \text{ pairs} \\ \text{become idle}\end{array}\right)=B(L,1-q,L-m)
\tag{5}
$$

$$
\text{where } m=0,1,...,L-1
$$

Because the above Markov chain is ergodic, the steady state distribution $p_m$ can be calculated from transition probability $p_{k,m}$. And $S_{normalized}$ can be obtained by (2).

### 3.2  The Average Transfer Delay of Data Packages

Let $Z_m$ denote the transfer delay of the data package due to the back-off and collision when the system state is $m$. We have,

$$
\begin{aligned}
Z_m &= P(\Omega')*1+\left[1-P(\Omega')\right]\sum_{i=0}^{m}[1+P\left(\begin{array}{c}i \text{ pairs} \\ \text{become idle}\end{array}\right)*Z_{m-i}] \\
&= B(N'-1,p,0)\dfrac{N'-1}{N-1}*1+\left\{1-B(N'-1,p,0)\dfrac{N'-1}{N-1}\right\}*\sum_{i=0}^{m}[1+B(m,1-q,i)*Z_{m-i}]
\end{aligned}
\tag{6}
$$

Where $m=0,1,2...L-1$

When $m=L$, since there is not an idle spreading code, then $p(\Omega')=0$. We have,

$$
Z_L=1+B(L,1-q,i)*Z_{L-i}
\tag{7}
$$

Combining (6) and (7), the numerical value of $Z_m$ can be obtained. And then the average transfer delay of data package can be calculated as follows:

$$Z_{average} = \sum_{m=0}^{L} Z_m P_m \qquad (8)$$

## 4   Result and Performance Evaluation

Fig.2 shows the normalized throughput versus the probability of transmission $p$ at a fixed number of service spreading codes $L = 8$, where the parameter of data packages' length $q$ is 0.98. Under both MMAC-DCA and MACA/C-T, the normalized throughput increases firstly, and decreases as the probability of transmission $p$ increases from 0 to 0.9. It can be seen that the normalized throughput under MMAC-DCA is larger than that under MACA/C-T, especially when the number of nodes is greater than the number of service spreading codes. For example, when $N = 40$ and $p = 0.06$, the normalized throughput under MACA/C-T and under MMAC-DCA is 0.226 and 0.7585, respectively.

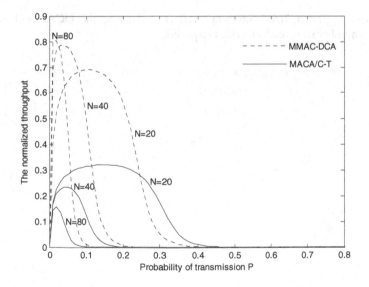

**Fig. 2.** The normalized throughput versus probability of transmission $P$ at a fixed number of service spreading codes $L = 8$

Fig.3 shows the normalized throughput versus the probability of transmission $p$ at a fixed number of nodes $N$ is equal 40, where the parameter of data packages' length $q$ is 0.90. Likewise, the normalized throughput under MMAC-DCA is larger than that under MACA/C-T. In addition, the less the number of service spreading codes $L$

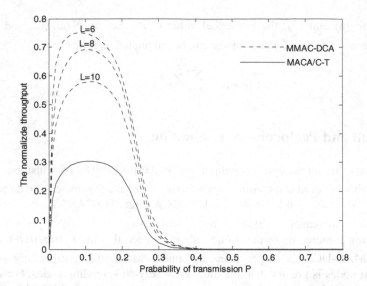

**Fig. 3.** The normalized throughput versus probability of transmission $P$ at a fixed number of nodes $N = 40$

is, the more the normalized throughput is. It is because the DCA mechanism can reduce the number of spreading codes required.

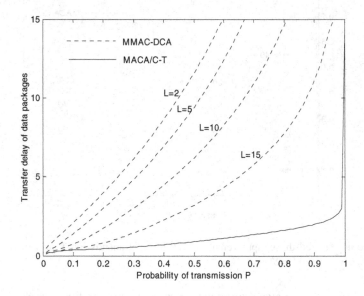

**Fig. 4.** The transfer delay of data packages versus the probability of transmission $P$ When $q = 0.90$ and $N = 40$

Fig.4 shows the average transfer delay of data packages $Z_{average}$ versus the probability of transmission $p$ with a fixed $q = 0.90$ and $N = 40$, when the number of service spreading code $L$ is equal to 2, 5, 10 and 15, respectively. Under MACA-DCA, the average transfer delay of data packages increases when $p$ increases, because the higher probability of transmission causes the more frequent package's collision on the common sub-channel. When the number of service spreading codes decreases, the transmitting nodes have a smaller probability of finding out an idle spreading code when implementing RTS-CTS dialogue, so that the average transfer delay of data packages increases. Thus, the transfer delay of data packages under MMAC-DCA is greater than that under MACA/C-T.

# 5  Conclusion

A new multi-channel MAC protocol with DCA mechanism, MMAC-DCA, is proposed in this paper. Different from the traditional protocol such as MACA/C-T, MACA/R-T, R-T, C-T, in MMAC-DCA only when a node has a data package to transmit, the node is assigned a service spreading code by the RTS-CTS dialogue on the common spreading code. In addition, a Markov mode is proposed to analyze the performance of MMAC-DCA. The result shows that the average transfer delay of data packages under MMAC-DCA is greater than that under MACA/C-T. However, the throughput normalized by available bandwidth under MMAC-DCA is remarkably greater than that under MACA/C-T, especially when the number of nodes is greatly bigger than the number of spreading codes.

## Acknowledgement

The research work is supported by Qualcomm Corporation.

## References

1. P.Karn, "MACA - a new channel access method for packet radio," ARRL/CRRL Amateur Radio 9th Computer Networking Conf., 1990, pp. 134-140.
2. V. Bharghavan, A. Demers, S. Shenker and L. Zhang, "MACAW: a media access protocol for wireless LAN's," ACM SIGCOMM'94, 1994, pp. 212-225.
3. IEEE 802.11e/ D5. 0, Draft Supplement to Part 11: Wireless Medium Access Control (MAC) and physical layer (PHY). Enhancements for Quality of Service (QoS), specifications: Medium Access Control [S], 2002
4. J. So, "A Multi-channel MAC Protocol for Ad Hoc Wireless Networks", UIUC report, 2003
5. A.Tzamaloukas and J.J. Garcia-Luna-Aceves, "Channel-hopping multiple access", in Proc. IEEE ICC 2000, vol. 1, pp. 415-419, 2000.
6. E.S.Sousa and J.A. Silvester, "Spreading code protocols for distributed spread-spectrum packet radio networks", IEEE Trans. Communications, vol 36, pp. 272-281, March 1988.

7.  M. Joa-Ng and I-Tai Lu, "Spread-spectrum medium access protocol with collision avoidance in mobile ad hoc wireless network", in Proc. IEEE INFOCOM 1999, vol. 2, pp. 776-783, 1999.
8.  Amit Butala, Lang Tong, "Dynamic Channel Allocation and Optimal Detection for MAC in CDMA Ad hoc Networks", 36th Asilomar Conference on Signals, Systems and Computers, November 2002.

# Fuzzy Particle Swarm Optimization Clustering and Its Application to Image Clustering

Wensheng Yi[1,2], Min Yao[1,2], and Zhiwei Jiang[1,2]

[1] College of Computer Science of Zhejiang University, Hangzhou, P.R. China
[2] State Key Lab of Software Engineering, Wuhan University
{snks, myao, j_z_w}@zju.edu.cn

**Abstract.** Image classification and clustering is a challenging problem in computer vision. This paper proposed a kind of particle swarm optimization clustering approach: FPSOC to process image clustering problem. This approach considers each particle as a candidate cluster center. The particles fly in the solution space to search suitable cluster centers. This method is different from previous work in that it employs fuzzy concept in particle swarm optimization clustering and adopts attribute selection mechanism to avoid the 'curse of dimensionality' problem. The experimental results show that the presented approach can properly process image clustering problem.

**Keywords:** image clustering, particle swarm optimization, fuzzy.

## 1 Introduction

Image classification and clustering is a challenging problem in computer vision. The existed image classification and clustering methods can be roughly divided into two kinds. One is to classify images with the combination of some assistant annotations and the low-level features [1-4]. Platt [1] successfully got the clusters of photographs using timestamps by events. Boutell and Luo [2] solved the indoor-outdoor image classification and the sunset detection problems by employing Bayesian network to fuse camera metadata cues and visual features. Tian et al [3] classified web images using link context as well as low-level features. These methods effectively processed image classification problem with the additional information. But they are more complex than those without assistant information. In addition, how to obtain the assistant information and how to combine them with the visual features are still problems.

Another common method is content-based image classification [5-8]. Wan and Chowdhury [8] improved the method of Chapelle et al. [7] by incorporating the color, texture, and edge histograms features. It showed that assembled feature performed more effective than single feature. Nevertheless the dimension of feature vector will be high if many features are extracted, which will lead to so-called 'curse of dimensionality' problem. In order to solve this problem, Sheikholeslami and Chang [6] presented a clustering method named SemQuery. They clustered images according to every feature respectively, and then merged each result as the final result.

Y. Zhuang et al. (Eds.): PCM 2006, LNCS 4261, pp. 459–467, 2006.

Particle swarm optimization (PSO) algorithm is a kind of evolutionary computation technique developed by Kennedy and Eberhart in 1995 [9, 10]. It is similar to other population-based evolutionary algorithms in that the algorithm is initialized with a population of random solutions. Unlike most of other population- based evolutionary algorithms, however, each candidate solution (called particle) is associated with a velocity and 'flies' through search space. PSO algorithm rapidly attracted researchers' attention and has been applied in neural network optimization [11], image quantization[12], data clustering [13, 14], etc. van der Merwe and Engelbrecht proposed a method to find cluster centers by PSO algorithm [13], and Omran and Engelbrecht applied it on image clustering [14]. Shi and Eberhart adopted fuzzy system to dynamically determine the inertia parameters of PSO algorithm [15].

This paper presents a kind of fuzzy PSO clustering method (FPSOC) and its variation FPSOCS, and applies them to image clustering. In these methods, particles search the optimal cluster centers in solution space, and images are classified according to the membership degree of images to cluster centers. Our methods are different in two ways. First they combine the fuzzy concept with the PSO algorithm. The feature vectors of images in different classes may be very close in feature space [6], so to introduce fuzzy into image PSO clustering is reasonable. Second, to solve the 'curse of dimensionality' problem, we introduce feature weights, which are dynamically determined during clustering, to represent the importance of features.

The rest of this paper is arranged as follows. In section 2 we discuss the proposed fuzzy PSO clustering algorithm. The fuzzy PSO based image clustering method is described in section 3. And section 4 gives the experimental results. At last a conclusion is drawn in section 5.

## 2 Fuzzy Particle Swarm Optimization Clustering Method

### 2.1 Particle Swarm Optimization Algorithm

In PSO, each particle corresponds to a potential solution. It has its velocity, its position, and a fitness value determined by a fitness function. Particles update their velocity and position through tracing two kinds of 'best' value. One is its personal best ( *pbest* ), which is the location of its highest fitness value. In global version, another is the global best ( *gbest* ), which is the location of overall best value, obtained by any particles in the population. In local version, in addition to *pbest* , each particle keeps track of a local best value( *lbest* ), obtained within a local topological neighborhood of particles. For global version, particles update their positions and velocities according to equation (1) and (2):

$$v_{id}^{k+1} = v_{id}^{k} + c_1 rand_1^{k}(pbest_{id}^{k} - x_{id}^{k}) + c_2 rand_2^{k}(gbest_{d}^{k} - x_{id}^{k}) \qquad (1)$$

$$x_{id}^{k+1} = x_{id}^{k} + v_{id}^{k+1} \qquad (2)$$

where $v_{id}^k$ is the velocity of the $d$ th dimension of the $i$ th particle in the $k$ th iteration, $x_{id}^k$ is the corresponding position, and $pbest_{id}^k$ and $gbest_d^k$ are the corresponding personal best and global best respectively. $c_1$ and $c_2$ are the accelerate parameters, which respectively adjust the maximal steps particles flying to the personal best and the global best. $rand_1$ and $rand_2$ are two random numbers in [0, 1].

## 2.2  Fuzzy PSO Clustering Algorithm

A particle $\mathbf{x}_i$ can be expressed as a $K$-dimension vector $\mathbf{x}_i = (\mathbf{m}_{i1}, \mathbf{m}_{i2}, ..., \mathbf{m}_{iK})$ [13, 14], in which $\mathbf{m}_{ij}$ means the $j$ th cluster center vector of the $i$ th particle, and $K$ is the number of clusters. So a swarm represents a set of candidates of cluster centers. The fitness value of the $i$ th particle is computed to follow equation (3).

$$f_m(\mathbf{x}_i, \mathbf{z}_j) = \alpha_1 d_{in}^m(\mathbf{x}_i, \mathbf{Z}) + \alpha_2 (d_{out}(\mathbf{x}_i, \mathbf{Z}))^{-1} \tag{3}$$

Where $z_j$ is the $j$ th object, $m$ is the fuzzy number, and $\alpha_1$ and $\alpha_2$ are constant more than 0. And

$$d_{in}^m(\mathbf{x}_i, \mathbf{Z}) = \sum_{j=1}^{N} \sum_{k=1}^{K} \mu_{ijk}^m d(\mathbf{m}_{ik}, \mathbf{z}_j) \tag{4}$$

is the sum of the weighted distances of objects, where $\mu_{ijk}^m$ is the element of fuzzy division matrix $U$, which is the membership degree of the $j$ th object to the $k$ th cluster centers of the $i$ th particle. Here the distance uses the Euclidean distance. And

$$d_{out}(\mathbf{x}_i, \mathbf{Z}) = \sum_{\forall j, k, j \neq k} d(m_{ij}, m_{ik}) \tag{5}$$

is the sum of any pair of cluster centers of a particle.

So this fitness function minimizes the intra-distance between objects in a cluster, as quantified by $d_{in}^m(\mathbf{x}_i, \mathbf{Z})$, and maximizes the inter-distance between any pair of clusters, as quantified by $d_{out}(\mathbf{x}_i, \mathbf{Z})$.

The fuzzy division matrix $U$ is updated according to equation (6):

$$\mu_{ijk}^m = 1 \Big/ \sum_{p=1}^{K} (d(\mathbf{m}_{ik}, \mathbf{z}_j) / d(\mathbf{m}_{ip}, \mathbf{z}_j))^{2/(m-1)} \tag{6}$$

The fuzzy particle swarm optimization clustering (FPSOC) algorithm is summarized as follows. First we randomly initialize the positions X and velocities V of all particles. Then, calculate the fitness value of each particle according to the fitness function in equation (3) and update the division matrix $U$ to follow equation (6). For each particle, if the fitness value is better than the global best or its personal best, replace them. Then equations (1) and (2) is used to change the positions X and velocities V of all particles. This process will be iterated until a stop condition is satisfied or a predefined number of iterations is reached.

## 3 Image Clustering Based on Fuzzy Particle Swarm Optimization

In this section, we propose an image clustering approach based on fuzzy particle swarm optimization clustering algorithm. The structure is shown in figure 1. First we extract visual features of images in image database. Then the fuzzy PSO clustering algorithm is implemented to classify these images and the results are obtained.

However, it will cause 'curse of dimensionality' problem if the dimensions of features are too high. It will sometimes lower the accuracy of the clustering results. In order to avoid this, we assign a weight to each feature to specify the importance of each feature in clustering. The weight is dynamically changed during clustering. We call this fuzzy PSO clustering method with feature selection FPSOCS.

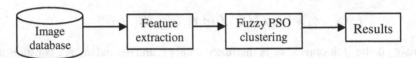

**Fig. 1.** The structure of image Clustering approach based on FPSOC

Suppose the feature vector of an image is L-dimension, then a particle $\mathbf{x}_i$ is redefined as $\mathbf{x}_i = (\mathbf{m}_{i1}, \mathbf{m}_{i2}, ..., \mathbf{m}_{iK}, \mathbf{m}_{i,K+1})$, where $\mathbf{m}_{ij}$ means the same as it is in section 2.2. And $\mathbf{m}_{i,K+1} = \{w_{i1}, w_{i2}, ..., w_{iL}\}$, $(0 \le w_{ij} \le 1)$ is the additional feature weight vector, where $w_{ij}$ is the feature weight of the $j$ th feature of the $i$ th particle. $w_{ij} = 0$ means that the $j$ th feature of the $i$ th particle is not selected, and $w_{ij} = 1$ means that the feature very important. Thus, the fitness function of the $i$ th particle is redefined as equation (7) and the new intra-distance is redefined as equation (8):

$$f_m(\mathbf{x}_i, \mathbf{z}_j) = \alpha_1 d_{in}^{m,w}(\mathbf{x}_i, \mathbf{Z}) + \alpha_2 (d_{out}(\mathbf{x}_i, \mathbf{Z}))^{-1} \tag{7}$$

$$d_{in}^{m,w}(\mathbf{x}_i, \mathbf{Z}) = \sum_{j=1}^{N} \sum_{k=1}^{K} \mu_{ijk}^m d_w(\mathbf{m}_{ik}, \mathbf{z}_j) \tag{8}$$

where the distance function is

$$d_w^2(\mathbf{m}_{ik}, \mathbf{z}_j) = \| \mathbf{m}_{i,K+1} \cdot (\mathbf{m}_{ik} - \mathbf{z}_j) \|^2 \tag{9}$$

However, in the processing of clustering, most of the feature weights tend to be zero, and this is not what we expect. So we give a limit:

$$\sum_{j=1}^{L} w_{ij} \ge \beta \cdot L, (0 \le \beta \le 1) \tag{10}$$

where parameter $\beta$ is a predefined constant. If $\beta = 0$, there is no constrain to feature weight. If $\beta = 1$, it means all features are forced to select. Usually set $\beta = 0.5$, which means at least half of the features should be selected.

In general, the proposed image clustering approach are described as follows:

Step 1: Extract visual features of images;
Step 2: Randomly initialize the positions $X$ and velocities $V$ of all particles;
Step 3: Calculate the fitness value of each particle according to equation (7);
Step 4: Update the value of the division matrix $U$ following equation (6). And assign image $z_j$ to cluster $C_{ik}$ iff

$$\mu_{ijk}^m \leq \mu_{pjq}^m, \quad \forall p,q, \quad i \neq p, k \neq q \tag{11}$$

Step 5: For each particle $i$, update $pbest_i$ if the current value is better than it;

Step 6: For each particle $i$, replace $gbest$ with the current value if the current value is better than it;

Step 7: Update the positions $X$ and corresponding velocities $V$ of all particles according to equations (1) and (2).

Step 8: Repeat step 3 - step 7 until a stop condition is satisfied or a predefined number of iterations is reached.

## 4   Experimental Results

### 4.1   Experiment 1: Clustering for Some Test Datasets

This section compares the results of the fuzzy c-means (FCM), basic PSO clustering algorithm, fuzzy PSO clustering algorithms (FPSOC) and FPSOCS on three datasets downloaded from the UCI website. The first one is Iris plant database (Iris), which has 150 instances in 3 classes with 4 attributes. The second is wine recognition database (Wine), which contains 178 instances with 13 attributes. The last is ionosphere database(Ionosphere) with 2 classes, 351 instances, and 34 numeric attributes. The quality of the respective clustering is measured by using two criteria: the information entropy and the cluster purity (or called accuracy). The information entropy is defined as equation (12)

$$Entropy = \sum_{i=1}^{k} \frac{n_i}{N} (-\frac{1}{\log q} \sum_{j=1}^{q} \frac{n_i^j}{n_i} \log \frac{n_i^j}{n_i}) \tag{12}$$

and the cluster purity is defined as equation (13)

$$Purity = \sum_{i=1}^{k} \frac{1}{N} \max_j (n_i^j) \tag{13}$$

where $q$ is the number of classes in the image set, and $n_i^j$ is the number of images of the $j$ th class that are assigned to the $i$ th cluster.

Table 1 summarizes the results obtained from these four clustering algorithms. The values are averages about 20 simulations. For the information entropy, the FPSOCS algorithm had the smallest information entropy on all three database, while the PSO clustering algorithm had the largest one both for Iris and for Ionosphere. The entropy of the FPSOC algorithm was similar to that of the FCM algorithm. Also the cluster purities of these two algorithm were close. The cluster purities of the FPSOCS algorithm for Iris and Ionosphere were higher than those of the other three algorithms, though for Wine database its cluster purities was a bit lower than that of the FPSOC. However the PSO algorithm had the lowest cluster purities of all. To introduce fuzzy into PSO clustering can greatly improve the performance.

**Table 1.** Comparison of four clustering algorithms

| Dataset | Algorithm | Entropy | Cluster purity |
|---|---|---|---|
| Iris | FCM | $0.2497 \pm 0.0001$ | $0.8933 \pm 0.0021$ |
| | PSO | $0.4206 \pm 0.0005$ | $0.6667 \pm 0.0005$ |
| | FPSOC | $0.2536 \pm 0.0078$ | $0.9000 \pm 0.0033$ |
| | FPSOCS | $0.1873 \pm 0.0231$ | $0.9267 \pm 0.0035$ |
| Wine | FCM | $0.5621 \pm 0.0002$ | $0.9182 \pm 0.0040$ |
| | PSO | $0.5598 \pm 0.0249$ | $0.8904 \pm 0.0261$ |
| | FPSOC | $0.3818 \pm 0.0111$ | $0.9338 \pm 0.0089$ |
| | FPSOCS | $0.3908 \pm 0.0120$ | $0.9413 \pm 0.0121$ |
| Ionosphere | FCM | $0.8232 \pm 0.0001$ | $0.7094 \pm 0.0071$ |
| | PSO | $0.9248 \pm 0.0376$ | $0.6524 \pm 0.0392$ |
| | FPSOC | $0.8070 \pm 0.0204$ | $0.7436 \pm 0.0018$ |
| | FPSOCS | $0.7642 \pm 0.0397$ | $0.7593 \pm 0.0199$ |

Figure 2 illustrates the convergence behavior of the four algorithms for Iris and Wine. For Iris, the FCM algorithm exhibited a fast convergence with a small quantization errors. The FPSOCS algorithm was slower than the FCM algorithm but had a bit lower errors than FCM algorithm. The FPSOC algorithm was slower than

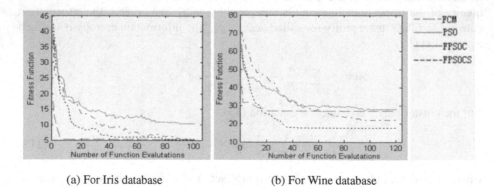

(a) For Iris database          (b) For Wine database

**Fig. 2.** The convergence of three algorithms

FPSOCS and its errors was closed to that of the FPSOCS algorithm. The PSO algorithm exhibited a slower convergence to a higher errors. For Wine, the FCM algorithm still exhibited a fastest, but premature convergence to a large error, while the FPSOCS had slower convergence to lower errors.

## 4.2  Experiment 2: Image Clustering

We adopt an image database with 528 images in it to evaluate our approach. These images are downloaded from web, including 209 sunset/sunrise images, 186 beach images and 133 grassland images. The image features extracted are color histogram in hsv space, color auto-correlograms, wavelet texture feature, moment invariant, and edge direction histogram. The performance is listed in Table 2, and some of the image clustering results are illustrated in Figure 3.

(a) The images clustered as sunset/sunrise

(b) The images clustered as sea and beach

(c) The images clustered as grassland

**Fig. 3.** Partial results of image clustering based on fuzzy particle swarm optimization

The results in Table 2 were consistent with those in Table 1. The FPSOCS algorithm had the highest average accuracy and was much faster than FPSOC. The average accuracy of FPSOC was higher than that of FCM but its speed was much slower than that of FCM.

**Table 2.** The performance of the four algorithms when to process image classification

| Algorithm | Accuracy | | | |
|---|---|---|---|---|
| | Sunset/sunrise | Beach | Grassland | Avg. |
| FCM | 85.17% | 82.48% | 63.65% | 77.10% |
| PSO | 77.99% | 91.01% | 53.38% | 74.13% |
| FPSOC | 83.30% | 87.77% | 64.41% | 78.49% |
| FPSOCS | 89.00% | 85.53% | 66.91% | 80.48% |
| Avg. | 83.87% | 86.70% | 62.09% | -- |

In three classes of images, beach images had the highest average accuracy while grassland images had the lowest. Some grassland images had been incorrectly classified into beach images because these two kinds of images is very similar in that most of them consist of two main regions: blue sky, and sea/beach (beach images) or grassland (grassland images), that is, they have the similar edge features and color features.

## 5  Conclusion

This paper proposed two new PSO clustering algorithms: FPSOC and its variation FPSOCS, and applied them on image classification. Results showed that these approaches are effective. These methods have two main characteristics:

First, it introduces fuzzy concept into PSO clustering algorithm. For a given image, it contains rich information, so it is hard to exactly classify which class the image belongs to, i.e. the image classification problem is fuzzy. We adopt the division matrix to describe such fuzzy characteristic.

Second, in order to avoid the 'curse of dimensionality' problem, which is brought by too high dimension in feature space, we employ a feature selection method. For each feature, a feature weight is added to represent the importance of the feature. So during clustering, we not only obtain the final clusters and cluster centers, but also dynamically adjust the importance of every feature.

Future studies will extend the clustering algorithm to video stream. Another extension is to improve the speed of these algorithms.

**Acknowledgement.** This work is supported by the Natural Science Foundation of Zhejiang Province under Contract Z104267.

## References

1. Platt, J.: Autoalbum: Clustering Digital Photographs Using Probabilistic Model Merging. in IEEE Workshop on Content-based Access of Image and Video Libraries: Hilton Head Island, SC. (2000). 96-100.
2. Boutell, M. and Luo, J.: Bayesian Fusion of Camera Metadata Cues in Semantic Scene Classification. in Proceedings of the 2004 IEEE Conference on Computer Vision and Pattern Recognition (CVPR'04): Dept. of Comput. Sci., Rochester Univ., NY, USA. Vol. 2. (2004). 623-630.
3. Tian, Y.-H., Huang, T.-J. and Gao, W.: Exploiting Multi-Context Analysis in Semantic Image Classification. in Journal of Zhejiang University SCIENCE. Vol. 6A. (2005). 1268-1283.
4. Yin, X., Li, M., Zhang, L., et al.: Semantic Image Clustering Using Relevance Feedback. in IEEE International Symposium on Circuits and Systems (ISCAS'03) Vol. 2. (2003). 904-907.
5. Szummer, M. and Picard, R. W.: Indoor-Outdoor Image Classification. in Proceedings of IEEE Workshop on Content-based Access of Image and Video Databases: Bombay, India. (1998). 42-51.

6. Sheikholeslami, G., Chang, W. and Zhang, A.: Semquery: Semantic Clustering and Querying on Heterogeneous Features for Visual Data. in IEEE Transactions on Knowledge and Data Engineering. Vol. 14. (2002). 988-1002.
7. Chapelle, O., Haffner, P. and Vapnik, V.: Svms for Histogram-Based Image Classification. in IEEE Transactions on Neural Networks. Vol. 10. (1999). 1055-1065.
8. Wan, H. L. and Chowdhury, M. U.: Image Semantic Classification by Using Svm. in Journal of Software. Vol. 14. (2003). 1891-1899.
9. Kennedy, J. and Eberhart, R. C.: Particle Swarm Optimization. in Proceeding of IEEE International Conference on Neural Networks. IEEE Press: Perth, WA. Vol. 4. (1995). 1942-1948.
10. Eberhart, R. C. and Kennedy, J.: A New Optimizer Using Particle Swarm Theory. in Proceeding of the Sixth International Symposium on Micro Machine and Human Science: Piscataway, NJ, Nagoya, Japan. (1995). 39-43.
11. Eberhart, R. C. and Shi, Y.: Evolving Artificial Neural Networks. in Proceeding of International Conference on Neural Networks and Brain: Beijing, P.R.C. . (1998). 5-13.
12. Omran, M. G., Engelbrecht, A. P. and Salman, A.: A Color Image Quantization Algorithm Based on Particle Swarm Optimization. in Informatica Journal. Vol. 1. (2005). 261-269.
13. van der Merwe, D. W. and Engelbrecht, A. P.: Data Clustering Using Particle Swarm Optimization. in Proceedings of IEEE Congress on Evolutionary Computation (CEC): Canberra, Australia. (2003). 215-220.
14. Omran, M. G., Engelbrecht, A. P. and Salman, A.: Particle Swarm Optimization Method for Image Clustering. in International Journal on Pattern Recognition and Artificial Intelligence. Vol. 19. (2005). 297-321.
15. Shi, Y. and Eberhart, R. C.: Fuzzy Adaptive Particle Swarm Optimization. in Proceedings of the IEEE Conference on Evolutionary Computation: Seoul, Korea. (2001). 101-106.

# A New Fast Motion Estimation for H.264 Based on Motion Continuity Hypothesis

Juhua Pu[1], Zhang Xiong[1], and Lionel M. Ni[2]

[1] School of Computer Science, Beijing University of Aeronautics and Astronautics, Beijing, China, 100083
[2] Department of Computer Science, Hong Kong University of Science and Technology
[1]{Pujh, Xiongz}@buaa.edu.cn, [2]ni@cs.ust.hk

**Abstract.** H.264 video standard, in spite of its high quality, is too time-consuming for widespread acceptance in video applications, mainly due to its computationally complex motion estimation (ME). To reduce this complexity, we propose motion continuity hypothesis, which means that all motion vectors (MVs) of a block are usually located in a small area. This area is formalized as modified valid region (MVR), an improved version of valid region which is proposed by the present authors in a previous paper. Then, this paper develops a new fast ME algorithm for H.264, called MVR-based fast ME (MVRF), which searches only a much smaller area in reference frames(RFs) for motion estimation than full search *H*.264 does, so it reduces up to 43% search pixels. MVRF is so deliberately chosen that on average, up to 98% MVs determined by MVRF coincide with those by full search H.264, therefore keeping the recovery quality and bit-rate almost the same as those of full search H.264.

## 1 Introduction

As a new video standard, H.264 is expected to lead video applications to brilliant future, because of its dominant advantages over other video standards in compression ratio, recovery quality, and network friendliness, etc.[1,2]. The advantages come from many novel strategies used in H.264, which however bring about formidable computational complexity at the same time. This complexity is now a challenging obstacle to the victory of H.264, so how to minimize it while maximizing the advantages is an important and urgent task both in theory and in practice.

Take motion estimation as an example. H.264 introduces such heavy-weighted strategies as *multiple RFs* (MRFs), fractural pixel precision search, and quad-tree sub-partition. The ME of a macro block can be sketched as follows:

(i) Given an arbitrary sub-partition of this macro block, estimate motion for each sub-block in each legal RF to get its best MV, and the frame where the best MV lies is called the best RF.
(ii) Check total cost of all sub-blocks of this sub-partition.
(iii) Select the sub-partition whose total cost is the least, and the corresponding estimation is the final result.

Y. Zhuang et al. (Eds.): PCM 2006, LNCS 4261, pp. 468–476, 2006.

In this process, all the sub-blocks of all sub-partitions have to be checked against all legal RFs. This complexity is intolerable in practice, especially when the number of reference frame of a block is large. Thus, many fast motion estimation (FME) algorithms for H.264 have been proposed, some of which are suitable for Intra-prediction[3,4], some for the quad-tree sub-partition[5-8], some for the fractural pixel precise search[9,10], and some for the MRFs[11,12]. This paper is focused on MRFs.

In the related literature, The basic idea is to do a coarse search first to find the best RF, followed by a fine one to obtain the ultimate MV in the best RF. Chung[11] uses a lower resolution version of the frame, whose size is only ¼ of the normal, to acquire coarse MV. The best RF is then selected such that the coarse MV in it is the best, and ME is done in this RF under the actual resolution. Ting[12] claimed that the center-biased characteristic is preserved in MRFs, with approximately 78% MVs located in the area of $w=\pm2$ in the search window. Thus he used a center-biased path to run 3SS in each RF, aiming to get the best RF. Finally a full search is employed in the best RF.

These methods work well in reducing computational complexity. Please note that they calculate independently the MVs of one block in multiple RFs, so it's possible to improve their efficiency if there is some relationship among these MVs. In fact, as claimed in [13], motion continuity hypothesis holds, i.e. the MVs in different RFS of the same block usually lie in a small area. [13] shows that the valid region of the MV in the nearest RF is such an area, and thus adapting the algorithm in [12] by restricting the 3-step search only in that region.

This hypothesis is not a surprise. Full search H.264 only search each RF within the search window, which is far smaller than the whole frame, so it implicitly hypothesizes the above motion continuity, except that its small area is the whole search window rather than our valid region. Due to the motion continuity, the algorithm VRF in [13] reduces up to 82% search pixels of full search H.264, with PSNR-Y only decreased 0.24dB and bit-rate increased 8.81%, far better than other FME algorithms such as that in [12]. However, can its performance be further improved?

This is the task of the present paper. We present modified-valid-region-based FME algorithm, which differs from VRF mainly in two aspects. First, a new valid region, MVR, is defined, which is in some cases smaller than the valid region defined in [13]. Second, full search is done in each search window to estimate the motion of a block B, but only in MVR when the frame is not the first RF of B.

This paper is organized as follows. The motion continuity hypothesis of video sequences is formulated in terms of MVR in Section 2, followed by detailed description of the proposed algorithm in Section 3. The performance of the algorithm is evaluated in Section 4, and Section 5 concludes this paper.

# 2 Motion Continuity Hypothesis and MVR

In this paper, only previous frames can be referenced to encode a frame, so, without loss of generality, assume that all the video sequences are of the form $\{F_k\}_{k=-N}^M$, where $F_0$ is the current frame being encoded, each $F_i\,(i>0)$ a future frame to be encoded, and $F_{-i}\,(i>0)$ a previous frame that has been encoded.

In H.264, more than one frame can be referenced to encode a block. Then, a question arises: is there any relationship among the MVs in different RFs?

**Notation:** Given a block $B$ of $F_0$, let $MV(B,-j)$ denote its MV in $F_{-j}$, and $MV_{-k}(B,-j)$ the pixel in $F_{-k}$, $k \neq j$, which shares the coordinates with $MV(B,-j)$.

Intuitively, a video sequence has the property that the closer two frames are, the more similar they are likely to be. This property was first claimed in [13] as motion continuity and was formulated and tested in terms of valid regions. In fact, in the implementation of many video standards, only $F_{-1}$ is referenced for the sake of simplicity and low latency in video display. Their practical success also supports our observation of motion continuity. Now we formulate this hypothesis in terms of MVR. First, recall the notion of valid region.

**Valid region:** the valid region of a vector $v=(x,y)$ is defined as the set $VR(v)=\{(z,w)|zx\geq0 \wedge wy\geq0\}$ of pixels in the search window. See Figure 1, where the black dot represents $v$, and the shaded area depicts its valid region $VR(v)$.

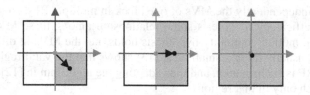

**Fig. 1.** Valid regions in motion coordinate systems

When the MV lies at the origin, the valid region is so large that it occupies the whole search window, so it's desirable to choose only a small area in this case. This leads to MVR, as illustrated in Figure 2.

*Modified valid region* (MVR): the MVR of a vector $v$, denoted by $MVR(v)$, is the same as $VR(v)$ except that it is only the square of size $\left\lceil \frac{w}{2} \right\rceil$ when the vector is at the origin, where $w$ is the size of the entire search window.

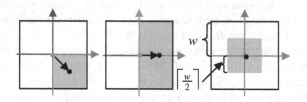

**Fig. 2.** Modified valid regions in motion coordinate systems

**Motion continuity hypothesis:** $P(MV(B,-j)\in MVR(MV_{-j}(B,-1)))\approx1$ for any block $B$ on $F_0$ and $j>1$, where $P(X)$ means the probability of event $X$.

To test this hypothesis by experiments, the notion of hit-ratio is introduced.

**Hit-ratio:** Given a finite video sequence $\{F_k\}_{k=-N}^M$, let $B_{ik}$ denote the $i^{th}$ block in frame $F_k$. If $F_j$ ($j<k-1$) is a RF of $B_{ik}$ and $MV(B_{ik}, j)$ lies in $MVR(MV(B_{ik}, k-1))$, $MV(B_{ik}, j)$ is said to be a *hit*. Define two functions $f$, $g$: $S^3\rightarrow\{0,1\}$ where $S=\{i|-N\leq i\leq M\}$,

$f(i,k,j)=1$ if and only if $F_j$ is a RF of $B_{ik}$, and $g(i,k,j)=1$ if and only if $f(i,k,j)=1$ and $MV(B_{ik}, j)$ is a hit. The *hit-ratio* of $\{F_k\}_{k=-N}^M$ is:

$$hit-rate = \frac{\sum_k \sum_i \sum_{j \neq i-1} g(i,k,j)}{\sum_k \sum_i \sum_{j \neq i-1} f(i,k,j)}$$

Intuitively, the hit-ratio of a sequence is the frequency that a MV is located in the valid region. Hence, $P(MV(B,j) \in VR(MV_{jk}(B,-1)))$ can be approximated by the hit-ratio of the sequence, where $j<-1$ is such that $F_{-j}$ is a RF of $F_0$.

Experiments are done on the hit-ratios of seven standard video sequences, as shown in Table 1. Since the average hit-ratio here is no less than 97%, the motion continuity hypothesis is justified. Thus, in estimating motion of a block $B$ in $F_0$, if $MV(B,-1)$ is known, the search in any other RF $F_{-j}$ can be done only in $VR(MV_j(B, -1)$. This search area is much smaller than the entire search window, so the computational complexity of motion estimation may be dramatically reduced.

Please note that all experiments hereafter are on these seven standard sequences. Most of the sequences are of QCIF format (only Flower is of CIF format since it includes fast motion with camera panning), with 30fps frame frequency. 200 consecutive frames of every sequence are used in the experiments, with the 1st and 100th frames being encoded as I-frames and the others as P-frames.

**Table 1.** Hit ratios of typical video sequences

| Sequences | Un-hit Ratio | Hit Ratio |
|---|---|---|
| Coastguard | 3.80% | 96.20% |
| Forman | 6.20% | 93.80% |
| Mother | 0.77% | 99.23% |
| Mobile | 1.46% | 98.54% |
| Tennis | 5.25% | 94.75% |
| Hall | 0.24% | 99.76% |
| Flower(CIF) | 2.37% | 97.63% |
| Average | 2.87% | 97.13% |

# 3   Modified-Valid-Region Based Fast Motion Estimation Algorithm

## 3.1   Specification of the Algorithm

By the motion continuity hypothesis, given a block $B$ in $F_0$, if $MV(B, -1)$ is known, its reasonable to do ME only in the area $MVR (MV_{-j}(B, -1))$ of $F_{-j}$ to calculate $MV(B, -j)$, $j>1$. Since $MVR(MV_{-j}(B, -1))$ is only 1/2 or 1/4 as large as the whole search window, even full search in this area takes much less time than the full search H.264, and hence is practically feasible. On this ground, we propose MVRF, a fast motion estimation algorithm based on modified valid regions.

MVRF estimates the motion of a block $B$ on $F_0$ in five steps;

**Step 1:** do full search in the entire search window on $F_{-1}$ to calculate $MV(B,-1)$;
**Step 2:** calculate $MVR(MV_{-j}(B, -1))$ for each reference frame $F_{-j}$, $j>1$;
**Step 3:** perform full search in each $MVR(MV_{-j}(B, -1))$, $j>1$;
**Step 4:** select the best reference frame according to some cost measurement;
**Step 5:** perform fractural pixel precision search in the best reference frame to calculate the final MV.

**Remark 1.** Full search is performed in Step 1 and Step 3. Compared with VRF proposed in [13] which takes 3SS to calculate the best reference frame, this strategy is helpful to improve the pixel precision search.

### 3.2 Fractural Pixel Precision Estimation

Unlike other fast motion estimation algorithm such as 3-step search, in the pixel precision search process, MVRF performs full search in the modified valid region which covers a rectangle area, even though not in the whole search window. As a result, any pixel precision search fast algorithm that's based on full search in the whole search window can also be applied to MVRF.

The following strategy is taken in Step 5 of MVRF:

**Case 1:** the best MV calculated in the pixel precision search lies inside the corresponding MVR. Any fast pixel precision search algorithm can be applied, just as in the case of full search in the whole search window.

**Case 2.** the pixel precision best MV lies on the boundary of the MVR. Then some algorithms in Case 1 may be not applicable. As far as compression ratio and recovery quality is concerned, normal pixel precision search algorithm is taken.

**Remark 2.** We take the normal pixel precision search algorithm in our experiments, in order to make a satisfactory trade-off between computational complexity and performance.

## 4 Analysis and Evaluation

### 4.1 Computational Complexity

Since full search H.264 (FS) , FFS in [12], VRF in [13] and MVRF all adopt the same MB sub-partitions and quarter-pixel- precision ME, we can approximate their computational complexities of ME by the number of search pixels per block. The pixels involved in the ME for one block include those in the search windows for pixel-precision search, half-pixel-precision search and quarter-pixel-precision search. For a block $B$, the number of pixels for half-pixel-precision search and that for quarter-pixel-precision search are both 9, and that for pixel-precision search depends on whether $MV(B, -1)$ is at the origin, in a quadrant, or on an axis. Let $\alpha_q$, $\alpha_o$ and $\alpha_a$ denote the frequencies that $MV(B, -1)$ lies in a quadrant, at the origin, and on an axis respectively. Experiments are done to calculate $\alpha_q$, $\alpha_o$ and $\alpha_a$, with the results listed in Table 2. For each of these parameters, it is reasonable to take the average over standard sequences as its expectation.

**Table 2.** MV distribution in MVRF algorithm

| Sequences | Origin($\alpha_o$) | Axes($\alpha_a$) | Quadrant($\alpha_q$) |
|---|---|---|---|
| Coastguard | 25.27% | 53.50% | 21.23% |
| Forman | 21.64% | 33.61% | 44.75% |
| Mother | 68.51% | 24.98% | 6.51% |
| Mobile | 6.92% | 54.94% | 38.14% |
| Tennis | 49.75% | 20.27% | 29.98% |
| Hall | 81.91% | 15.77% | 2.33% |
| Flower(CIF) | 24.94% | 30.50% | 44.56% |
| Average | 39.85% | 33.37% | 26.78% |

Thus, the following formula holds, in which $T_X$ represents the computational complexity of algorithm X in terms of the number of search pixels. $N_F$ is the number of reference frames. $w$ is the size of the search windows. In the experiments, the values of $N_F$ and $w$ are 5 and 7 respectively as in [12] and [13].

$$T_{MVRF} = (2w+1)^2 + (N_F - 1)[\alpha_o (2\lceil \tfrac{w}{2} \rceil + 1)^2 + \alpha_q (w+1)^2 + \alpha_a (w+1)^2] + N_F * 16$$
$$= 15*15 + 4(81*0.40 + 64*0.27 + 120*0.33) + 4*16 = 646.12$$

As calculated in [13], $T_{VRF}$=198.69, $T_{FS}$=1141, and $T_{FFS}$=326.
We have

$$\frac{T_{FS} - T_{VRF}}{T_{FS}} = \frac{1141 - 198.69}{1141} = 82.59\%$$

$$\frac{T_{FS} - T_{FFS}}{T_{FFS}} = \frac{1141 - 326}{1141} = 71.43\%$$

$$\frac{T_{FS} - T_{MVRF}}{T_{FS}} = \frac{1141 - 646.12}{1141} = 43.37\%$$

So, it's safe to draw the conclusion that MVRF works well in reducing the computing complexity of full search H.264, though not so well than VRF and FFS.

### 4.2 Performance Evaluation

JM73 software is referenced to test the recovery quality and compression ratio of full search H.264, FFS, VRF, and MVRF. In the experiments, 5 RFs are used for estimating each block, with four sub-block partitions allowed (16x16, 16x8, 8x16, and 8x8). The search window size is 7, and QP here is 32. CAVLC is used for entropy coding here. The experiments ignore Hadamard transformation and the error robustness strategies.

PSNR-Y and Bit-rate are used respectively measure the compression ratio and the recovery quality of these algorithms. As can be seen from the experimental results shown in Table 3, the PSNR-Y of MVRF is almost the same as that of full search H.264, and is much higher than those of FFS and VRF. Meanwhile, Table 4 shows that the bit-rate of MVRF is also almost equal to that of full search H.264, and is much lower than those of FFS and VRF, except that it's a little higher than the bit-rate of VRF for the sequences Mother and Hall.

As a result, a conclusion can be drawn that MVRF considerably outperforms FFS and VRF and is almost optimized in performance.

**Table 3.** PSNR-Y of FS, FFS, VRF, and MVRF (dB)

| Sequences / Algorithm | Coast | Forman | Mother | Mobile | Tennis | Hall | Flower |
|---|---|---|---|---|---|---|---|
| FS | 30.91 | 32.93 | 33.44 | 29.56 | 33.04 | 34.45 | 31.06 |
| FFS | 30.78 | 32.69 | 33.34 | 29.32 | 32.94 | 34.33 | 30.88 |
| VRF | 30.75 | 32.54 | 33.23 | 29.23 | 32.87 | 34.19 | 30.91 |
| MVRF | 30.91 | 32.90 | 33.49 | 29.57 | 33.04 | 34.47 | 31.06 |
| MVRF-FS | 0 | -0.03 | 0.05 | 0.01 | 0 | 0.02 | 0 |
| MVRF-FFS | 0.13 | 0.21 | 0.15 | 0.25 | 0.1 | 0.14 | 0.18 |
| MVRF-VRF | 0.16 | 0.36 | 0.26 | 0.34 | 0.17 | 0.28 | 0.15 |

**Table 4.** Bit-rates of FS, FFS, VRF, and MVRF (Kbps)

| Sequences / Algorithm | Coast | Forman | Mother | Mobile | Tennis | Hall | Flower |
|---|---|---|---|---|---|---|---|
| FS | 106.91 | 71.97 | 33.12 | 209.42 | 88.32 | 35.59 | 912.58 |
| FFS | 122.25 | 84.99 | 35.15 | 247.42 | 104.13 | 38.68 | 1088.06 |
| VRF | 117.58 | 80.02 | 32.71 | 238.92 | 100.54 | 34.88 | 1056.65 |
| MVRF | 106.98 | 72.25 | 32.94 | 209.75 | 89.03 | 35.65 | 914.18 |
| (MVRF–FS)/FS(%) | 0.065 | 0.389 | -0.543 | 0.158 | 0.804 | 0.169 | 0.175 |
| (MVRF–FFS)/FFS(%) | -12.491 | -14.990 | -6.287 | -15.225 | -14.501 | -7.834 | -15.981 |
| (MVRF–VRF)/VRF(%) | -9.015 | -9.710 | 0.703 | -12.209 | -11.448 | 2.208 | -13.483 |

### 4.3   Analysis of the Matching Ratio of MVRF

Now we try to interpret why MVRF parallels full search H.264 in performance.

**Matching ratio:** Given a block, if its MV calculated by MVRF coincides with that by full search H.264, this vector is said to be a *matching* one. The ratio of all matching MVs to all MVs for a video sequence is called the *matching ratio* of this sequence.

Obviously, how MVRF performs compared with full search H.264 depends on the probability that a MV is a matching one. This probability, called *matching probability* of MVRF, can be approximated by average matching ratio of MVFR over some standard video sequences.

To estimate this probability, we start by analyzing the location of the MV of a block on $F_0$ calculated by MVRF. There are three possibilities.

(i)   The MV is in the first reference frame $F_{-1}$.
(ii)  It is in reference frame $F_{-i}$, $i>1$, and in the corresponding MVR.
(iii) It is in reference frame $F_{-i}$, $i>1$, but not in the corresponding MVR.

One can see that if and only if in cases (i) and (ii), the MV is a matching one. Let $E_1$ denote the event that the MV isn't in $F_{-1}$, and $E_2$ the event that the MV isn't in the corresponding MVR. Then the matching probability $P_{mat}$ can be approximated by $1-P(E_1 \cap E_2)=1-P(E_1)*P(E_2|E_1)$. As Chi showed in [12], the probability that a MV lies in the first RF is about 48.83% when 5 RFs are used and the search window size is $w=7$. Hence, $P(E_1) \approx 1-48.83\%$. On the other hand, $P(E_2|E_1) \approx 1$-hit ratio=2.87%. As a result, $P_{mat} \approx 1-2.87\% \times (1-48.83\%) = 98.53\%$.

The matching probability of MVRF is up to 98%, which accounts for the low bit-rate and high com recovery quality of MVRF, even though the number of search pixels is decreased dramatically.

## 5 Conclusion

An important topic of H.264 is to reduce its time consumption in motion estimation. This paper observes and makes good use of a desirable property of video sequences—motion continuity. Modified valid regions for MVs are introduced, based on which a fast motion estimation algorithm, MVRF, is proposed. The reasonability of this algorithm is guaranteed by the motion continuity hypothesis.

Formal analysis and experiments show that MVRF reduces the search pixels of full search H.264 up to 43% while it keeps the bit-rate and PSNR-Y almost intact. Compared with two other fast motion estimation algorithms FFS and VRF, our MVRF achieves much higher PSNR-Y and lower bit-rate, though at the cost of an increase in the number of search pixels. To sum, it's reasonable to say that MVRF makes a better trade-off between computational complexity and performance in optimizing H.264.

A possible future direction is to further reduce the modified valid region, especially in the case where the MV in the nearest reference frame is on an axis.

## Acknowledgements

The authors wish to thank Mr. Zhenxing Wu for preparing the experiments. The thanks also go to Dr Xingwu Liu for his proofreading this paper and many technique suggestions.

## References

1. Gianluca Bailo, Ivano Barbieri, Massimo Bariani, and Marco Raggio. Search Window Estimation Algorithm for Fast and Efficient H.264 Video Coding with Variable Size Block Configuration. http://www.ee.bilkent.edu.tr/~signal/defevent/papers/cr1132.pdf
2. T. Wiegand, G. J. Sullivan, G. Bjontegaard, and A. Luthra. Overview of the H.264/AVC Video Coding Standard. IEEE Transactions on Circuits and Systems for Video Technology, 2003, 13(7):560-576.
3. Liu Qiong, Hu Rui-min, Zhu Li, Zhang xin-chen and Han Zhen. Improved fast intra prediction algorithm of H.264/AVC. Journal of Zhejiang University SCIENCE A, 2006, 7(Suppl. I):101-105.
4. Feng Pan, Xiao Lin, Susanto Rahardja, Keng Pang Lim, Z. G. Li, Dajun Wu, and Si Wu. Fast Mode Decision Algorithm for Intra prediction in H.264/AVC Video Coding. IEEE Transactions on Circuits and Systems for Video Technology, 2005, 15(7): 813-822.

5. M. Yang, W. S. Wang. Fast Macroblock Mode Selection Based on Motion Content Classification in H.264/AVC. International Conference on Image Processing, 2004: 741-744.
6. Woong Il Choi, B. Jeon, and Jechang Jeong. Fast Motion Estimation with Modified Diamond Search for Variable Motion Block Sizes. Proceedings of 2003 IEEE International Conference on Image Processing, 2003: 371-374.
7. Andy Chang, Peter H. W. Wong, Y. M. Yeung, Oscar C. Au. Fast Multi-block Selection for H.264 Video Coding. ISCAS, 2004, Vol. III: 817-820.
8. Yang Libo, Yu Keman, Li Jiang and Li Shipeng. An Effective Variable Block-Size Early Termination Algorithm for H.264 Video Coding. IEEE Transactions on Circuits and Systems for Video Technology, 2005, 15(6):784-788.
9. X. C. Zhang, H. J. Ai, R. M. Hu, and D. R. Li. A Novel Algorithm for Sub-pixel Block Motion Estimation. Proceedings of 2004 International Symposium on Intelligent Multimedia, Video and Speech Processing, 2004: 587-590.
10. W. D. Wang, Q. D. Yao, P. Liu. Fast Algorithm of Fractional Pixel Accurancy Motion Estimation. Journal of China Institute of Communications, 2003, 24(4): 128-132.
11. H. Chung, D. Romacho, and A. Ortega, Fast Long-term Motion Estimation for H.264 Using Multiresolution Search. Proceedings of 2003 International Conference on Image Processing, 2003: 905 - 908.
12. C. W. Ting, L. M. Po and Ch. H. Cheung, Center-biased Frame Selection Algorithms for Fast Multi-Frame Motion Estimation in H.264, Proceedings of the 2003 International Conference on neural networks & Signal Processing. 2003, Vol. 2: 1258 - 1261.
13. Juhua Pu, Zhang Xiong, Yongli Liu. Fast Motion Estimation Algorithm for H.264 with Multi-references, Journal of Aeronautics and Astronautics, 32(5), 2006: 617-620.

# Statistical Robustness in Multiplicative Watermark Detection*

Xingliang Huang and Bo Zhang

Department of Computer Science and Technology
Tsinghua University, Beijing 100084, P.R. China
hxliang98@mails.tsinghua.edu.cn,
dcszb@mail.tsinghua.edu.cn

**Abstract.** The requirement of robustness is of fundamental importance for all watermarking schemes in various application scenarios. When talking about watermark robustness, we usually mean that the receiver performance degrades smoothly with the attack power. Here we look from another angle, i.e., robustness in statistics. A new detector structure which is robust to small uncertainties in host signal modeling for multiplicative watermarking in the discrete Fourier transform (DFT) domain is presented. By relying on robust statistics theory, an $\epsilon$-contamination model is applied to describe the magnitudes of the DFT spectrum, based on which we are able to derive a minimax detector that is most robust in a well-defined sense. Experiments on real images demonstrate that the new watermark detector performs more stably than classical ones.

## 1 Introduction

As a potential solution to the increasingly prominent issues of intellectual piracy and data security, digital watermarking has been continuously gaining interest from both academia and industry. Although the requirements that are necessary to provide useful and effective watermarking schemes may vary considerably in different application scenarios, it is no doubt that the requirement of robustness, i.e., recovering the watermark with a high degree of reliability, is of fundamental importance for all practical applications [1].

The technique of watermark detection has advanced from the early heuristic correlation detector to the optimum detectors based on classical hypothesis testing theory [2] and some typical probability distribution models [1],[3],[4]. These optimum watermark detectors rely on perfect modeling of the host signals. However, as pointed out in [5], there are always uncertain deviations of the actual situation from the idealized theoretical models due to inherent modeling errors and various attack distortions. Although usually small, these deviations may lead to a small minority of "bad" observations, which can override the evidence of the majority and thus fool the optimum detectors. A preliminary conceptual

---

* This work is supported by National Nature Science Foundation of China (60135010, 60321002) and Chinese National Key Foundation R & D Plan (2004CB318108).

Y. Zhuang et al. (Eds.): PCM 2006, LNCS 4261, pp. 477–484, 2006.

example was given by Huber [6]: a single factor $p_1(y_i)/p_0(y_i)$ equal (or almost equal) to 0 or $\infty$ may upset the test statistic $L(\mathbf{y}) = \prod_{i=1}^{N} p_1(y_i)/p_0(y_i)$. Thus, we need a robust watermark detector that is insensitive to small model deviations from the idealized assumptions. The robust optimum detectors proposed by Cheng and Huang [4] are not the robust detector mentioned here, but actually the locally optimum (LO) detectors [2], which also imply the assumption of perfect modeling of host signals and thus may be sensitive to small model uncertainties as well. As to our knowledge, robust detector structure for watermarking application was first presented in [5], where the robust hypothesis testing theory was employed and robust detection of additive watermarks incorporating the the generalized Gaussian distribution (GGD) model was discussed.

This paper presents our investigations on statistical robustness in detection of multiplicative spread spectrum (SS) watermarking in the discrete Fourier transform (DFT) domain. The magnitude-of-DFT domain is often used in watermarking applications, since it is invariant to image translations [1]. Multiplicative watermarking is very attractive because proportional embedding automatically adapts to the content of the host signals [4]. For the problem of watermark detection, most of the proposed algorithms are based on the SS idea [1],[3],[4]. Another track is the quantization-based (QB) method [7], which makes use of side information and brings huge improvements in watermark decoding. Actually, the proportional embedding can also be seen as a way to take into account of side information, as the embedded signal depends on the host content [8]. It was also shown that the multiplicative SS scheme reduces the gap between QB and SS methods: although its performance is worse than that of the QB approach for low noise level, the multiplicative SS scheme outperforms QB watermarking at heavy attack noise [9]. So our studies may help to explore the interesting point of integrating robust statistics theory and side informed embedding.

The rest of this paper is organized as follows. In Section 2, robust modeling of the magnitudes of DFT spectrum is presented and the corresponding robust watermark detector is derived. A few considerations closely relating to the robust model for watermark detection are discussed in Section 3. Experimental results are given in Section 4 to show the effectiveness of the proposed detector. Section 5 concludes the paper.

## 2    Robust Detection of Multiplicative Watermarks

Based on the theory of robust statistics, we use a contaminated version of the Weibull distribution to model the DFT spectrum and derive a minimax detector that is most robust in a well-defined sense. Although there are always uncertainties in modeling the host signals, we may feel confident in using the new scheme since it is designed to be robust over a broad class of host signal distributions.

### 2.1    Multiplicative Embedding Rule and Robust Detection Model

The commonly used multiplicative embedding rule is:

$$y_i = x_i(1 + \theta_i s_i), \qquad i = 1, \ldots, N, \qquad (1)$$

where $x_i$ and $y_i$ are the original host and the watermarked signals, respectively, $s_i$ is the watermark signal, $\theta_i$ is the watermark strength, and $N$ denotes the watermark length. In the DFT domain, watermarks are usually carried by the magnitudes of DFT spectrum with approximately Weibull-distributed features [4]-[6]. The Weibull probability density function (pdf) is defined by

$$w(x; \alpha, \beta) = \frac{\beta}{\alpha} \left(\frac{x}{\alpha}\right)^{\beta-1} \exp\left[-\left(\frac{x}{\alpha}\right)^{\beta}\right], \tag{2}$$

where $\alpha$ and $\beta$ are positive constants controlling the mean, variance and shape of the distribution.

The goal of watermark detection is to verify whether or not a given watermark $\mathbf{s} = (s_1, \ldots, s_N)$ is present in the observation signal $\mathbf{z} = (z_1, \ldots, z_N)$. For the multiplicative rule and the Weibull model, the watermark detection problem can be formulated as the binary hypothesis test, with the hypothesis $H_0$ that the watermark $\mathbf{s}$ is not present and the alternative $H_1$ that it is present:

$$H_j: \quad p(\mathbf{z}) = \prod_{i=1}^{N} w_{ji}(z_i), \qquad j = 0, 1, \tag{3}$$

where $w_{0i}(x) \triangleq w(x; \alpha_i, \beta_i)$, $w_{1i}(x) \triangleq (1 + \theta_i s_i)^{-1} w(x(1 + \theta_i s_i)^{-1}; \alpha_i, \beta_i)$, and $\theta_i$, $\alpha_i$ and $\beta_i$ are parameters for the $i$th component. Denote the cumulative distribution function (cdf) of $w_{ji}$ as $W_{ji}$, then the hypothesis testing problem (3) can be rewritten compactly in terms of $W_{ji}$ as

$$H_j: \quad \{W_{ji}\}, \qquad j = 0, 1, \tag{4}$$

where the sequences of cdfs, $\{W_{ji}\} \triangleq \{W_{ji}\}_{i=1}^{N}$, $j = 0, 1$, represent the two possible marginal distributions of every component of the observation signal under the simple hypothesis and the simple alternative, respectively.

As discussed above, the actual marginal distributions of the observation samples are very likely not to be exactly $\{W_{0i}\}$ or $\{W_{1i}\}$ but rather are only approximately $\{W_{0i}\}$ or $\{W_{1i}\}$. In order to formalize the uncertain deviations in these marginal distributions, they are blown up into composite hypothesis and alternative sets by using the $\epsilon$-contamination model [6],[10]:

$$H_j: \quad \mathscr{F}_j = \{\{F_{ji}\} | F_{ji} = (1 - \epsilon) W_{ji} + \epsilon G_{ji}, \ i = 1, \ldots, N\} \quad j = 0, 1, \tag{5}$$

where $\{F_{ji}\} \triangleq \{F_{ji}\}_{i=1}^{N}$, $j = 0, 1$, denote the sequences of the actual distributions, in respect of the nominal distributions $W_{0i}$ and $W_{1i}$, $G_{ji}$'s are unknown and arbitrary "contaminating" distributions, and $\epsilon \in [0, 1)$ is a small fixed number representing the degree of contamination. In order to obtain nontrival solution to the problem, we shall always assume that $\mathscr{F}_0$ and $\mathscr{F}_1$ do not overlap, i.e., the hypothesis and alternative distributions are disjoint for all $i$'s [10]. (This condition will be made more specific in Section 3).

Let $\phi$ be any test between $\mathscr{F}_0$ and $\mathscr{F}_1$, and let $P_{FA}(\phi, \{F_{0i}\})$ and $P_{MI}(\phi, \{F_{1i}\})$ denote the false-alarm and the miss probabilities associated with $\phi$ and individual elements of $\mathscr{F}_0$ and $\mathscr{F}_1$. Then our goal is to determine the minimax test $\phi^*$ that attains the best worst-case performance among all possible tests [10]:

$$\phi^* = \arg\min_{\phi} \max_{\{F_{1i}\}\in\mathscr{F}_1} P_{MI}(\phi, \{F_{1i}\})$$

$$\text{subject to} \tag{6}$$

$$\max_{\{F_{0i}\}\in\mathscr{F}_0} P_{FA}(\phi, \{F_{0i}\}) \leqslant \lambda,$$

where $0 \leqslant \lambda \leqslant 1$ is the false-alarm level of the test.

## 2.2   Robust Watermark Detector

It follows from [10] that the solution to (6) is the corresponding probability ratio test for the simple hypothesis testing problem (4) when the pair $\{W_{0i}\}$ and $\{W_{1i}\}$ are replaced by a pair of *least favorable* hypothesis and alternative distributions $\{F_{0i}^*\} \in \mathscr{F}_0$ and $\{F_{1i}^*\} \in \mathscr{F}_1$, which can be given in terms of their densities by

$$f_{0i}^*(x) = \begin{cases} (1-\epsilon)w_{0i}(x) & r_i(x) < c_i'' \\ c_i''^{-1}(1-\epsilon)w_{1i}(x) & r_i(x) \geqslant c_i'', \end{cases}$$

$$f_{1i}^*(x) = \begin{cases} (1-\epsilon)w_{1i}(x) & r_i(x) > c_i' \\ c_i'(1-\epsilon)w_{0i}(x) & r_i(x) \leqslant c_i', \end{cases} \tag{7}$$

where $r_i(x) \triangleq w_{1i}(x)/w_{0i}(x)$, and the constants $c_i'$ and $c_i''$ are determined by

$$\int_{r_i(x)>c_i'} w_{1i}(x)\mathrm{d}x + c_i' \int_{r_i(x)\leqslant c_i'} w_{0i}(x)\mathrm{d}x = (1-\epsilon)^{-1}$$

$$\int_{r_i(x)<c_i''} w_{0i}(x)\mathrm{d}x + c_i''^{-1} \int_{r_i(x)\geqslant c_i''} w_{1i}(x)\mathrm{d}x = (1-\epsilon)^{-1}. \tag{8}$$

Define the constants relating to the total embedded signal $\theta_i s_i$ and the Weibull model parameter $\beta_i$ as

$$D_i = (1 + \theta_i s_i)^{\beta_i},$$

$$A_i = (D_i^{-1} - 1)^{-1},$$

$$B_i = D_i^{A_i/D_i} - D_i^{A_i}.$$

Then after some developments on the first equation of (8), we obtain $c_i'$ as

$$\begin{cases} c_i' + B_i c_i'^{A_i/D_i} = (1-\epsilon)^{-1} & s_i > 0 \\ c_i' = \left[\dfrac{-\epsilon}{B_i(1-\epsilon)}\right]^{D_i/A_i} & s_i < 0, \end{cases} \tag{9}$$

In other words, $c_i'$ is given explicitly by the second expression of (9) for $s_i < 0$ and is determined implicitly when $s_i > 0$. It was shown that for the case of

$s_i > 0$, $c_i'$ can be easily obtained by numerical methods [10]. Similarly, $c_i''$ is given by

$$\begin{cases} c_i'' = \left[ \dfrac{\epsilon}{B_i(1-\epsilon)} \right]^{1/A_i} & s_i > 0 \\ c_i''^{-1} - B_i c_i''^{A_i} = (1-\epsilon)^{-1} & s_i < 0. \end{cases} \tag{10}$$

Define the light-limiter function as

$$l(x; c_1, c_2) \triangleq \begin{cases} c_2 & x \geqslant c_2 \\ x & c_1 < x < c_2 \\ c_1 & x \leqslant c_1. \end{cases}$$

Then, once $c_i'$ and $c_i''$ are obtained, the minimax test (the robust watermark detector) based on the log-likelihood ratio for the least favorable densities will be given by

$$L^*(\mathbf{z}) = \sum_{i=1}^{N} \log \frac{f_{1i}^*(z_i)}{f_{0i}^*(z_i)} = \sum_{i=1}^{N} l\left( -A_i^{-1}\left(\frac{z_i}{\alpha_i}\right)^{\beta_i}; C_i', C_i'' \right) \underset{H_1}{\overset{H_0}{\lessgtr}} T, \tag{11}$$

where $C_i' = \log c_i' + \log D_i$, $C_i'' = \log c_i'' + \log D_i$, and the threshold $T$ is set to satisfy $T = P_{FA}(\phi^*, \{F_{0i}^*\})$.

Note that $\delta_i(z_i) \triangleq -A_i^{-1}(z_i/\alpha_i)^{\beta_i}$ is the optimum nonlinearities and that $\delta_i^*(z_i) \triangleq l(\delta_i(z_i); C_i', C_i'')$ is the robust nonlinearities of (11). Thus it turns out that the robust nonlinearities are a "censored" version of the optimum ones. Specifically, we have $|\delta_i^*(z_i)| \to \infty$ as $z_i \to \infty$. However, for the robust test, $|\delta_i^*(z_i)|$ is bounded away from $\infty$, which prevents the detector from being disturbed by very large $z_i$.

## 3  Relevant Considerations

### 3.1  The Non-overlapping Condition

As mentioned above, when applying the $\epsilon$-contamination model, we need to ensure that the two neighborhoods $\mathscr{F}_0$ and $\mathscr{F}_1$ do not overlap. It can be shown that if $\mathscr{F}_0$ and $\mathscr{F}_1$ overlap, then $c_i' = c_i'' = 1$ and, consequently, $F_{0i}^* \equiv F_{1i}^*$ for some $i$'s, i.e., the robust test simply ignores these observation samples and guesses at the hypothesis [2]. Here we shall make this condition more clear.

Define the functions:

$$\tilde{D}_i(x) = (1+x)^{\beta_i},$$
$$\tilde{A}_i(x) = (\tilde{D}_i(x)^{-1} - 1)^{-1},$$
$$\tilde{B}_i(x) = \tilde{D}_i(x)^{\tilde{A}_i(x)/\tilde{D}_i(x)} - \tilde{D}_i(x)^{\tilde{A}_i(x)}.$$

Then the non-overlapping condition for the $\epsilon$-contaminated Weibull model can be specified by the following theorem.

**Table 1.** Typical values of $\tau_i^+$ and $\tau_i^-$

|  | $\beta = 1.5$ | $\beta = 2.0$ | $\beta = 2.5$ |
|---|---|---|---|
| $\epsilon = 0.001$ | 0.0018 | 0.0014 | 0.0011 |
|  | $-0.0018$ | $-0.0014$ | $-0.0011$ |
| $\epsilon = 0.01$ | 0.0185 | 0.0138 | 0.0110 |
|  | $-0.0181$ | $-0.0136$ | $-0.0109$ |

**Theorem 1.** *Consider a given $\epsilon \in [0, 1/2)$ and a pair of hypothesis and alternative distributions $F_{0i}$ and $F_{1i}$ for the $i$th component, as defined in (5), for the $\epsilon$-contaminated Weibull model. Then it holds that $F_{0i} \neq F_{1i}$ for arbitrary contaminating distributions $G_{0i}$ and $G_{1i}$, provided that*

$$\theta_i s_i > \tau_i^+ > 0 \quad or \quad \theta_i s_i < \tau_i^- < 0, \tag{12}$$

*where $\tau_i^+$ and $\tau_i^-$ are the two solutions of the equation*

$$|\tilde{B}_i(\tau_i)| = \epsilon(1 - \epsilon)^{-1}. \tag{13}$$

The proof, which mainly involves constructing a pair of $G_{0i}^*$ and $G_{1i}^*$ that makes $F_{0i} \equiv F_{1i}$ when the conditions (12) and (13) are not satisfied, is omitted here due to space limit. Typical values of $\tau_i^+$ and $\tau_i^-$ are listed in Table 1.

### 3.2   The Contamination Factor

For watermark detection, the contamination factor is designed to account for the deviations caused by inherent modeling errors and possible attack distortions. However, in most practical situations, we have no idea what kind of attack was imposed and how much the attack power was. This accentuates the difficulty in determining the appropriate $\epsilon$.

In light of these difficulties, we may simply choose to fix $\epsilon$ at a certain level in order to impart a degree of robustness, with which the robust detector may not always attain the best performance (in respect of the optimal $\epsilon$) but performs fairly well over a broad range of situations. It is observed from experimental results that $\epsilon = 0.001$ can be an appropriate setting for multiplicative watermarking, with which the robust watermark detector performs at least as well as and in some cases much better than both the optimum and the LO detectors.

## 4   Experimental Results

Typical embedding approaches, as proposed in [1], are adopted for tests. The watermark consists of a pseudorandom sequence that takes value $+1$ or $-1$ with equal probabilities and is embedded in the magnitudes of DFT coefficients belonging to the diagonals which are divided into different subregions (see [1] for more details). The embedding strength is set to 0.2, which is in accordance with

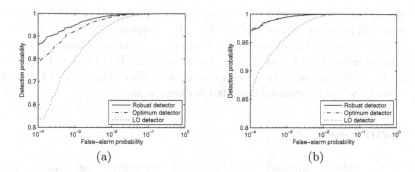

(a)    (b)

**Fig. 1.** ROCs when no attack is imposed for (a) subregion 4 of Lena with $N = 200$ and (b) subregion 11 of Goldhill with $N = 200$

the settings in [1]. We vary the watermark signal and the detection threshold to obtain empirical receiver operating characteristics (ROCs) of the robust, the optimum [1] and the LO detectors [4] for comparisons.

Some results when no attack is imposed are shown in Fig. 1. We can see that although there are no attack distortions, the robust detector performs significantly

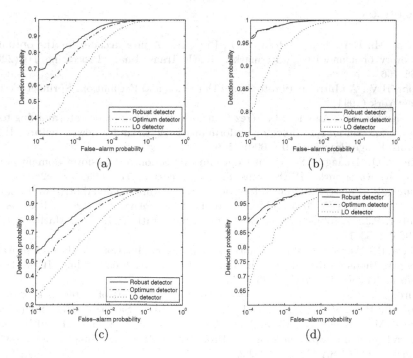

**Fig. 2.** ROCs after general image processing operations: JPEG coding (70%) for (a) subregion 4 of Lena with $N = 200$ and (b) subregion 11 of Goldhill with $N = 200$, and median filtering ($3 \times 3$) for (a) subregion 4 of Lena with $N = 200$ and (b) subregion 11 of Goldhill with $N = 200$

better that of the optimum ones in some cases. This demonstrates the robustness of the proposed detector against inherent modeling errors. We also evaluate the detector performance in the presence of general image processing operations, such as lossy compression (JPEG) and image smoothing (median filtering). As shown in Fig. 2, the performance of all detectors degrades after attacks, but the robust detector displays better resistance to attack distortions.

## 5    Conclusions

A statistically robust approach to detecting multiplicative watermarks in the magnitude-of-DFT domain is proposed. Instead of the original Weibull distribution, an $\epsilon$-contaminated version of it is adopted to capture the uncertainties in host signal modeling, based on which the robust detector structure is determined by a least favorable distribution pair and turns out to be a censored version of the optimum probability ratio test. Experiments on real images show that the proposed detectors perform more stably than both the optimum and the LO detectors, which provide another good example of the benefits achievable by casting the watermark problem into the framework of robust detection.

## References

1. Barni, M., Bartolini, F., Rosa, A.D., Piva, A.: A new decoder for the optimum recovery of nonadditive watermarks. IEEE Trans. Image Processing 10 (2001) 755–766
2. Poor, H.V.: An Introduction to Signal Detection and Estimation. Springer-Verlag, New York (1994)
3. Hernández, J.R., Amado, M., Pérez-González, F.: Dct-domain watermarking techniques for still images: detector performance analysis and a new structure. IEEE Trans. Image Processing 9 (2000) 55–68
4. Cheng, Q., Huang, T.S.: Robust optimum detection of transform domain multiplicative watermarks. IEEE Trans. Signal Processing 51 (2003) 906–924
5. Huang, X., Zhang, B.: Robust detection of transform domain additive watermarks. In: Proc. of IWDW 2005. Volume 3710 of LNCS., Siena, Italy (2005) 124–138
6. Huber, P.J.: A robust version of the probability ratio test. Ann. Math. Stat. 36 (1965) 1753–1758
7. Chen, B., Wornell, G.W.: Quantization index modulation: A class of provably good methods for digital watermarking and information embedding. IEEE Trans. Inform. Theory 47 (2001) 1423–1443
8. Furon, T., Josse, J., Squin, S.L.: Some theoretical aspects of watermarking detection. In: Proc. SPIE-IS&T Elec. Imag. Volume 6072., San jose, CA, USA (2006)
9. Barni, M., Bartolini, F., Rosa, A.D.: Advantages and drawbacks of multiplicative spread spectrum watermarking. In: Proc. SPIE-IS&T Elec. Imag. Volume 5020., San jose, CA, USA (2003) 290–299
10. Martin, R.D., Schwartz, S.C.: Robust detection of a known signal in nearly gaussian noise. IEEE Trans. Inform. Theory IT-17 (1971) 50–56

# Adaptive Visual Regions Categorization with Sets of Points of Interest*

Hichem Houissa[1], Nozha Boujemaa[1], and Hichem Frigui[2]

[1] INRIA-Rocquencourt, Domaine de Voluceau, BP 105 - 78153 Le Chesnay
{hichem.houissa, nozha.boujemaa}@inria.fr
[2] CECS Dept, University Of Louisville, Louisville, KY 40292
h.frigui@louisville.edu

**Abstract.** The Query By Visual Thesaurus (QBVT) paradigm has strongly contributed to the visual information retrieval objective when no starting example is available. The Visual Thesaurus is a representative summary of all the visual patches in the database. Its reliable construction helps the user expression a "mental image" by composing the visual patches according to the details he has in mind. In this paper, we introduce a relational clustering algorithm (CARD) to build the Visual Thesaurus from regions finely described by variable signature dimensions. The resulting visual categories depict the variability of regions based on local color points of interest. Therefore, we extend first the notion of image matching to regions using non-traditional metrics suitable for the multi-dimensional variables. We also, introduce an appropriate relational clustering for regions categorization using the similarity matrix induced by the latter metrics. Moreover, we propose an efficient method to speed up distance computation and reduce the feature representatives based on adaptive clustering. Our approach was tested on generic images and gives perceptually relevant visual categories.

**Keywords:** Visual Thesaurus, region categorization, points of interest.

## 1 Introduction

Most Content-Based Image Retrieval (CBIR) systems are based either on global image or region-based query by example. Those approaches have significantly proven their efficiency in cases where the user can provide starting image/region example. Unfortunately, several retrieval scenarios lack this starting example and the user is asked to compose a mental image query according to vague details. The Query By Visual Thesaurus paradigm [1] relies on a panel of visual patches representing the summary of the regions in the database. These categories -similar from a photometric and a structural point of view- stand for a reliable overview of the different regions and constitute the "page zero" from which the user selects several patches to compose his mental image. In this paper, we present a novel method for building the Visual Thesaurus (VT) that relies on a dual description of regions. Those are roughly extracted by coarse segmentation,

* This work was supported by the European Commission under Contract FP6-001765 aceMedia, partial support of this research was provided by an NSF-INRIA international collaboration award No. OISE-0528319.

Y. Zhuang et al. (Eds.): PCM 2006, LNCS 4261, pp. 485–493, 2006.

but finely described using Points of Interest. In our context, points of interest are used to describe the local variability inside visually coherent regions. The advantage of this approach is that it outcomes the single description that stresses on several features and omits many others. The Visual Thesaurus is a novel query alternative that offers the possibility to the user to combine multiple visual patches in order to retrieve the target mental image. VT is obtained by regions clustering in visual patches that are the representative of similar regions from a photometric as well as a structural point of view. An earlier formulation of a texture thesaurus was introduced by Ma et al. [2] combining learning similarity and hierarchical vector quantization for aerial photographs indexing. The idea of describing images through Points of Interest was mainly exploited for image matching [3] and object recognition [4]. Points of interest are of a great stability regarding illumination and point of view changes; they are also of a complementary use with global attributes (mean colors, histograms, adaptive distribution...) since each description focuses on specific parts: large visually relevant regions for global features and small patches denoting the local photometric variations for Points of Interest. This paper is organized as follows: In Section 2, we describe distance measures that can compare sets of points with different cardinalities. These points are the local descriptors for each region. In order to cluster these multi-dimensional descriptors, the relational clustering algorithm is explained in details in Section 3. Section 4 presents our visual categories representatives composing the Visual Thesaurus. We will conclude with some remarks and perspectives of this work.

## 2 Comparing Variable Sets of Points

Region description and point-based description are dual representation of local image content. Indeed, points of interest could not be detected on smooth or low variability subpart of a given image. Thus, its local description could not be available. The Harris detector [5] was adapted to color version for object retrieval [6]. A coherence criterion based on the spatial distribution of points of interest was derived in [7] in order to distinguish between homogenous and textured regions. Once the regions are binarily categorized (homogenous/textured), specific metrics are used in order to compare them. In fact, the idea is to use suitable approaches according to the region complexity; indeed, there is no need to use points of interest in case of homogenous regions since few points are detected over such regions. As the point detection process provides a variable number of points for each region, standard metrics such as Minkowski, Mahalanobis, Kullback-Leibler Divergence,... are not suitable for they are based on bin-by-bin matching and they tackle descriptors in a fixed-dimension space. Notice here that although the feature space is the same for all regions, comparing sets of points with different cardinalities requires non-traditional metrics to tackle the descriptors with the variable number of attributes. In fact, each region is described by the set of its detected points of interest features. We have used two suitable distances: the Hausdorff distance [8] and the Earth Mover's distance [9]. Both distances as well as the Harris color points descriptor are revisited in details in the following sections.

## 2.1  Harris Color Points of Interest

We have used the Color version of the Harris detector [6] and the descriptor involves the combination of Hilbert's invariants at different derivative orders. The description vector at order 1 ($DV_1$) is an 8-dimension vector given by:

$$DV_1(x, \sigma) = (R, \| \nabla R \|^2, G, \| \nabla G \|^2, B, \| \nabla B \|^2, \nabla R . \nabla G, \nabla R . \nabla B) \quad (1)$$

$DV_1$ is stable under image rotation and noise induced by high order derivatives and numerical complexity of invariants computation[6]. In this paper, we stress on the metrics rather than the description schema itself.

## 2.2  The Hausdorff Distance

Given two sets $A = \{a_1, a_2, ..., a_p\}$ and $B = \{b_1, b_2, ..., b_q\}$ with a finite number of points. $A$ and $B$ include the points of interest that describe two regions $R_p$ and $R_q$ respectively. The Hausdorff distance between $A$ and $B$ is defined by:

$$H(A, B) = \max(h(A, B), h(B, A)), \quad (2a)$$

$$where \qquad h(A, B) = \max_{a \in A} \min_{b \in B} \| a - b \| . \quad (2b)$$

In (2b), $\| . \|$ is an underlying norm on the points of $A$ and $B$, typically the Euclidean norm. Hausdorff distance measures the degree of mismatch between two sets, through the *maximum distance of a set to the nearest point of the other set*. Unlike most traditional distances, there is no explicit pairing of points of $A$ with those of $B$; the similarity inferred between two regions is that each point of $A$ is at most at distance $h(A, B)$ to some point of $B$ and vice versa. The advantages of Hausdorff distance, compared to the shortest distance, is that it is not applied to one single point irrespective of all others points. Thus, ensuring more stability and efficiency in computing the mutual proximity between two sets of points [8]. Another concern is that Hausdorff distance is quite sensitive to the affine transformations of regions. Unfortunately, the point-to-point matching of Hausdorff may results in biased distances as it doesn't take into account the neighbors of a current point. Hence, the computed distances may not represent the dissimilarity between regions adequately.

## 2.3  The Earth Mover's Distance (EMD)

Several advantages of the EMD have been outlined in [9]. We can briefly list the following: the EMD handles variable-size structures and can extend the point-to-point matching to subsets partial matching. EMD is a true metric if the ground distance is metric and the signatures have the same total weight. Computing the EMD is based on solving transportation problem; intuitively, the EMD is the minimum amount of "work" required to transform one signature into the other. Let $P = \{\mathbf{p}_1, w_{p_1}, ..., \mathbf{p}_m, w_{p_m}\}$ and $Q = \{\mathbf{q}_1, w_{q_1}, ..., \mathbf{q}_n, w_{q_n}\}$ be two signatures where $(\mathbf{p}_i, \mathbf{q}_j)$ are the representatives and $(w_{p_i}, w_{q_j})$ are their respective weights, the EMD is defined by:

$$EMD(P, Q) = \frac{\sum_{i=1}^{m} \sum_{j=1}^{n} d_{ij} f_{ij}}{\sum_{i=1}^{m} \sum_{j=1}^{n} f_{ij}} \quad (3)$$

where $d_{ij}$ and $f_{ij}$ are the ground distance and the flow between $\mathbf{p}_i$ and $\mathbf{q}_j$ respectively. Note that $\mathbf{F} = [f_{ij}]$ is obtained through the minimization of the overall cost:

$$WORK(P, Q, \mathbf{F}) = \sum_{i=1}^{m} \sum_{j=1}^{n} d_{ij} f_{ij} \tag{4}$$

The pending issue of EMD is its computational complexity due to the algorithm used (simplex, interior points, bipartite graph...) to minimize (4). In order to decrease the computation time when regions are composed of a large number of points, we introduce a clustering step in order to summarize the whole set of points by a small subset of prototypes that stand for the best representatives of the points of interest extracted on each region. This approach is described in the following section.

### 2.4 Clustering-Based EMD

The variable and increasing number of points of interest detected on regions is a major computational burden. Furthermore, the comparison between deeply unbalanced sets of points (for e.g. $w_{p_i} \ll w_{q_j}$) induces non perceptually coherent dissimilarity measure. To overcome this problem, we use an adaptive robust fuzzy clustering algorithm [10] for two purposes: $(i)$ speeding up the computation of the EMD; and $(ii)$ handling representative points of interest instead of the entire set of points that are often redundant. The algorithm is based on the minimization of the following objective function:

$$J = \sum_{j=1}^{C} \sum_{i=1}^{N} u_{ji}^2 d^2(x_i, \beta_j) - \sum_{j=1}^{C} \alpha_j \left[ \sum_{i=1}^{N} u_{ji} \right] \tag{5}$$

under the constraint: $\sum_{j=1}^{C} u_{ji} = 1$ for $i \in \{1, ..., N\}$ where $X = \{x_i | i \in \{1, ..., N\}\}$ is a set of $N$ 8-dimension vectors ($\mathbf{DV}_1$) describing the image, $B = \{\beta_s | s \in \{1, ..., C\}\}$ is the set of prototypes of the $C$ clusters and $u_{si}$ is the membership of data $x_i$ to cluster $s$. Let $N_j$ be the number of points of interest extracted in region $j$. The number of points $N_j$ related to region $j$ is automatically reduced to $n_j$ clusters where each cluster encapsulates similar points according to their features (eq. 1). $\alpha_j$ is an agglomerative factor that ensures adaptive cluster dependent agglomeration mechanism. The clustering process keeps the visual information of the region in an aggregate representation and avoids redundancy for it groups all similar points of interest -in the sense of their Hilbert invariants descriptor (eq. (1))- and "replace" them by their representatives. Notice also that for the computation of the similarity measure using EMD, we replace the respective weights of each signature ($w_i$) by the cardinality of the cluster representing the underlying visual category. Figure 1 shows the final categories of points of interest obtained by clustering. The computational cost is considerably reduced without loss of information.

## 3    Relational Clustering Using EMD Similarity Matrix : CARD Algorithm

We previously used EMD to compute the similarity between two regions. The obtained similarity matrix illustrates the distance between each pair of regions. We have compared

(a) Original extracted Points of Interest

(b) Points of Interest after competitive agglomeration clustering

**Fig. 1.** Points clustering for redundancy reduction

EMD to Hausdorff distance and we have figured out that EMD is much more robust and gives more perceptual similarity. Moreover, as we are interested in generating representative categories that reliably summarize the content of the region database, we used the relational clustering approach. The clustering identifies representative patches composing the "page zero" of the VT, according to their mutual implicit relationships depicted by their similarity.

### 3.1 Similarity Matrix

We compute the similarity matrix $R = [R_{ij}]$ from the EMD matrix $D = [D_{ij}]$ so that $R_{ij}$ represents the similarity between regions $R_j$ and $R_i$.

We use $R_{ij} = \frac{e^{-D_{ij}/\sigma^2}}{\sum_{k=0}^{Regions} e^{-D_{ij}/\sigma^2}}$ where $\sigma$ is the standard deviation of the smoothing gaussian. The gaussian stresses mainly on the regions surrounding the query region and avoids the biasing effect of far regions where EMD is not discriminant enough. Notice that the dimension of the problem is an issue because as the database size grows, the storage should grow accordingly. For our evaluations, we have considered a reasonable database in order to first validate our approach. Further partitioning techniques are to be considered in our future work.

### 3.2 CA Relational Clustering

The EMD cannot be used in an object-based clustering because regions are described by multi-dimensional features. Thus, defining iteratively prototypes is meaningless. Hence, relational clustering takes into account the implicit relations (similarity measures) between regions given by the EMD computation. The relational clustering was first introduced in [11] to adapt the Fuzzy C-Means algorithm to $n$ objects described in terms of relational data i.e. a set of $n^2$ measurements of similarities between pairs of objects. We used the relational formulation of the Competitive Agglomeration (CA) algorithm [12]; prototypes are no longer updated but only memberships $u_{ij}$ are computed iteratively.

Let $X = \{x_i | i \in \{1, ..., N\}\}$ be a set of $N$ regions, $B = \{\beta_s | s \in \{1, ..., C\}\}$ the set of $C$ clusters and $u_{si}$ is the membership of region $x_i$ to cluster $s$. The membership vector $v_s$ and the distance $d_{si}$ from region $x_i$ to cluster $\beta_s$ can be respectively written using the relation matrix $\mathbf{R}$ as follows:

$$d_{si}^2 = (\mathbf{R}v_s)_i - \frac{v_s \mathbf{R} v_s}{2} \quad \text{and} \quad v_s = \frac{(u_{s1}^m, ..., u_{sN}^m)^t}{\sum_{i=1}^N u_{si}^m} \tag{6}$$

The update steps are explained in details in [12], we summarize below the CA Relational Data (CARD) algorithm.

---

**Algorithm 1.** Competitive Agglomeration Relational Data

---

Fix the maximum number of clusters $C_{max}$
Initialize $k = 0$; $\beta = 0$; $\mathbf{U}^{(0)}$; $N_i$
**repeat**
    Compute memberships $v_i$ for $1 \leq i \leq C$ using (6)
    Compute $d_{ik}^2 = (\mathbf{R}v_i)_k - v_i \mathbf{R} v_i / 2$ for $1 \leq i \leq C$
    If $(d_{ij}^2 < 0$ for any $i$ and $k)$ then $\{$
        Compute $\Delta_\beta = \max_{i,k}\{-2d_{ik}^2 \parallel v_i - e_k \parallel^2$
        Update $d_{ik}^2 \leftarrow d_{ik}^2 + (\Delta_\beta / 2) * \parallel v_i - e_k \parallel^2$ for $1 \leq i \leq C$ and $1 \leq k \leq N_s$
        Update $\beta = \beta + \Delta_\beta \}$
    Update $\alpha_k = \eta_0 e^{-\frac{k}{\tau}} \frac{\sum_{j=1}^C \sum_{i=1}^N u_{ji}^2 d^2(x_i, \beta_j)}{\sum_{j=1}^C [\sum_{i=1}^N u_{ji}]^2}$
    Update $U^{(k)}$ using $u_{st} = u_{st}^{FCM} + u_{st}^{Bias}$
    Update $N_i = \sum_{j=1}^N u_{ij}$
    If $(N_i < \epsilon_1)$ Discard $i^{th}$ cluster and update $C$
    $k = k + 1$;
**until** (memberships stabilize)

---

The CARD algorithm is the best alternative for clustering multidimensional features according to their similarity instead of their features distances. Notice that the EMD provides a reliable similarity between regions in a reasonable computational time, providing that we previously cluster points of interest of every region.

## 4   Evaluation and Results Interpretation

For our experiments, we consider a generic professional database (Images Du Sud[1]) containing about 2700 images representing natural landscapes, indoor scenes and some human portraits. The segmentation process provides on average 5 regions per image, hence the actual region database contains about 13000 regions. Notice that the segmentation is coarse and the contours may have few irregularities and overlaps; but the overall visual aspect is catched. We extract for each region no more than 500 points of interest using Harris color detector. Those regions are then divided into 2 distinct categories: homogenous and textured. For this purpose, we used the coherence criterion introduced

---

[1] www.imagedusud.fr

in [7]. The EMD metric is computed over the textured category since the robustness of EMD implies comparing sets of points with comparable cardinalities i.e. it does not make sense to define a similarity measure between 2 regions containing respectively few and hundreds points of interest because the overall descriptor weight will emphasize the big dimensional signatures at the expense of low dimensional ones. As a matter of fact, EMD is computed for the sets of prototypes and no longer for the points of interest themselves in order to ensure perceptually reliable similarity measures between considered regions. The similarity matrix is built using EMD distance; the relational clustering is applied using this matrix and starting from an overestimation of the number of clusters.

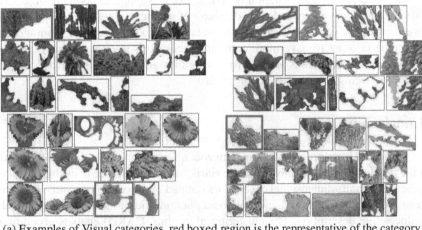

(a) Examples of Visual categories, red boxed region is the representative of the category

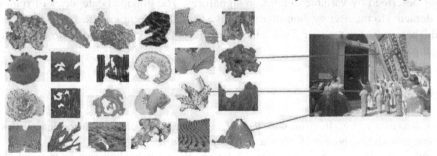

(b) Starting "page zero" with some categories representative (left) used for composition with visual patches (right)

**Fig. 2.** *(a)* Examples of categories obtained with relational clustering; the representative region is defined by the red box, following regions are sorted by decreasing memberships, *(b)* Example of mental image query using Visual Thesaurus and user selection of visual patches

CARD algorithm has the major advantage to determine the optimal number of final clusters automatically according to a convergence criterion that evaluates the stability of memberships from an iteration to another. Fig (2) (a) shows examples of categories obtained by relational clustering. Similar regions are clustered together thanks to EMD-based similarity matrix. In fact, as the EMD gives perceptual similarities between regions described by points of interest, the relational clustering induces the same perceptual similarity. Notice that the "page zero" is the set of representatives resulting from the relational clustering: a representative is defined as the region with the highest membership degree toward the cluster it belongs to. These representatives could be used to guide the user in formulating his mental query image by arranging visual patches. For e.g. the user want to retrieve a target image he has already seen. This mental image could be of type "procession in front of a church". VT let him select several visual patches he has in mind, as shown in Fig 2 (b).

It is important to notice that these results are preliminary and need further refinements. Moreover, as far as evaluation is concerned, it is tough to compare objectively our experiments since no ground truth database of segmented regions is available. We are investigating the construction of a reliable large database of regions (homogeneous and textured) in order to have more convincing comparison curves. Finally, our VT adaptive construction enables proper processing of regions regarding their "complexity" defined in terms of homogeneity or texture.

## 5 Conclusion

In this paper, we have presented a new approach for automatic region categorization using the relational clustering. We used the Earth Mover's Distance to evaluate the similarity between multi-dimensional descriptors defined by Harris color points of interest. The resulting region signature focuses on local photometric variability of visual patches and induces fine description. The clustering algorithm (CARD) enables grouping regions described by variable dimension signatures. The obtained categories of regions are depicted to the user by their representatives and they compose the visual panel (Visual Thesaurus) for the user from which he selects those corresponding to his mental target picture.

## References

1. J. Fauqueur and N. Boujemaa, "Mental image search by boolean composition of region categories," *to appear in Multimedia Tools and Applications*, 2005.
2. Wei-Ying Ma and B.S. Manjunath, "A texture thesaurus for browsing large aerial photographs," *Journal of American Society for Information Science*, 49(7):633–648, 1998.
3. J. Sivic and A. Zisserman, "Video google: A text retrieval approach to object matching in videos," In *In Proc. of ICCV*, pages 1470–1477, 2003.
4. A. Opelt, M. Fussenegger, A. Pinz, and P. Auer, "Generic object recognition with boosting," *IEEE Trans. on PAMI*, 28(3), March 2006.
5. C. Harris and M. Stephens, "A combined corner and edge detector," In *Alvey Vison Conference*, pages 147–151, 1988.
6. V. Gouet and N. Boujemaa, "Object-based queries using color points of interest." *In Workshop on Content-Based Access of Image and Video Libraries (CVPR)*, 2001.
7. H. Houissa and N. Boujemaa, "Region labelling using a point-based coherence criterion," *To appear in IS&T/SPIE conference on Multimedia Content Analysis, Management and Retrieval*, 2006.

8. D. Huttenlocher, G. Kanderman, and W. Rucklidge, "Comparing images using the hausdorff distance," *IEEE Trans. on PAMI*, 15(9):850–863, September 1993.
9. Y. Rubner, C. Tomasi, and L. Guibas, "The earth mover's distance as a metric for image retrieval," *IJCV*, 40(2):99–121, November 2000.
10. B. Le Saux and N. Boujemaa, "unsupervised robust clustering for image database categorization," *In Proc. ICPR'2002*, 2002.
11. R.J. Hathaway, J.W. Davenport, and J.C. Bezdek, "Relational duals of the c-means clustering algorithms," *Pattern Recognition*, 22(2):205–212, 1989.
12. O. Nasraoui, H. Frigui, R. Krishnapuram, and A. Joshi, "Extracting web user profiles using relational competitive fuzzy clustering," *IJAI Tools*, 9(4):509–526, 2000.

# A Publishing Framework for Digitally Augmented Paper Documents: Towards Cross-Media Information Integration

Xiaoqing Lu and Zhiwu Lu

Institute of Computer Science and Technology, Peking University,
Beijing 100871, China
xiaoqing@founder.com, zhiwu.lu@yahoo.com.cn

**Abstract.** Paper keeps as a key information medium and this has motivated the development of new technologies for digitally augmented paper (DAP) that enable printed content to be linked with multimedia information. Among those technologies, one simplest approach is to print some visible patterns on paper (e.g., barcodes in the margin) as cross-media links. Due to the latest progress in printing industry, some more sophisticated methods have been developed, that is, some kinds of patterns printed on the background of a page in a high resolution are almost invisible and then we are affected little when reading. For all these pattern-embedding based approaches to integrate printed and multimedia information, we aim to present a unified publishing framework independent of particular patterns and readers(e.g., cameras to capture patterns) used to realize DAP. The presented framework manages semantic information about printed documents, multimedia resources, and patterns as links between them and users are provided with a platform for publishing DAP documents.

## 1 Introduction

Paper remains a pervasive resource in everyday settings such as classrooms, museums, galleries and the like. In general, a range of characteristics of paper seem critical to human communication and collaboration. Some of these are well known but it is perhaps helpful to mention one or two. Paper is mobile, portable between different spaces and regions and it can be positioned in delicate ways to support mutual access and collaboration [1]. Paper retains a persistent form and preserves the layout and character of art work that is produced on its surface, which can be pictured, navigated, and even scanned with ease. These characteristics and many more not only support complex individual activities but also perhaps provide a firm foundation to many forms of collaboration whether it is synchronous or asynchronous, co-located or distributed.

This pervasive nature of paper has motivated the development of new technologies for digitally augmented paper (DAP) that enables printed content to be linked with multimedia information. Some researchers focus on the capabilities

Y. Zhuang et al. (Eds.): PCM 2006, LNCS 4261, pp. 494–501, 2006.

that paper has as a display and develop some paper-like substances extremely thin and flexible. For example, some kind of display sheets are produced with the electronics printed using conductive organic materials, which can affect changes in color. More recently are the electro-wetting surfaces patented by Philips, which enable colored oils to cover or expose white surfaces under the influence of an electric field [2]. These devices all produce a two-color display (often using blue and white), but with more complex electronics they are, in principle, capable of a full-color output. Although prototypes of each of these technologies exist, few of these products, if any, have reached large-scale commercialization.

More cost-effective approaches are to consider paper as an input device and then print on it some visible patterns, of which the most familiar are barcodes. The familiarity of the mechanism and the common availability of barcode readers has meant that several researchers have explored simple applications where barcodes can link paper documents with digital resources [3]. More sophisticated methods are to encode linking information within locations on the paper. This may be realized by printing visible patterns such as CyberCodes [4] or RFID tags [5] on a page and detecting them from cameras or some other reading devices. Relying on barcodes or other visible patterns does reveal the augmented functionality to the users, but it may spoil the displayed image and text of a page. Hence, some invisible or at least non-obtrusive patterns are then designed to track the position of a pen or reader over the paper surface, such as the fine dots used in [6] to record a large amount of data on the backgrounds of pages without deteriorating the appearance. Furthermore, we can take on a group of fine dots as a pattern, such as the Clevercodes designed by our cooperator Clevercode Corp. in Hong Kong which are just a series of $64 \times 64$ bitmaps with $4 \times 4$ fine dots (each pattern has slight shift of dot position) printed on paper in a high resolution and then seem transparent or non-obtrusive for the users.

In this paper, we would like to discuss this seemingly simple solution for DAP that the cross-media integration of printed and multimedia information is realized in such a pattern-embedding way. The solution resorts to augmenting paper to support systematic links with digital content whatever that might be, rather than replacing paper with a paper-like substance. The solution is primarily concerned with reading, rather than writing, and enabling people to access connections between any paper document and digital resource. This simple solution could be exemplified by considering the enhancement of an educational book associated with a PDA or TV. Such a book could be augmented to enable the reader to point to pictures or texts on the page and gain associated audio information and the like.

For all these approaches to integrate printed and multimedia information in a pattern-embedding way, we aim to present a unified publishing framework independent of particular patterns and readers(e.g., cameras to capture patterns) used to realize DAP. The presented framework manages semantic information about printed documents, multimedia resources, and patterns as links between them and users are provided with a platform for publishing DAP documents.

## 2    Pattern Embedding for Integrating Printed and Multimedia Information

In this paper, only some kind of non-obtrusive patterns are considered in our publishing framework, which can be modified slightly to process other visible patterns such as barcodes. We first embed the pattern into the print area of certain content on a page which is to be connected with multimedia information, and then recognize it from the page as an index to search in the multimedia database.

Actually, any kind of almost invisible patterns (i.e., bitmaps) of fine dots can be used as our non-obtrusive patterns. In order to not be obtrusive for readers after printed out, these patterns must be limited in a small print region with a high resolution at the same time. As shown in Fig.1, we present two kinds of these patterns. Fig.1(a) is the self-clocking pattern DataGlyph proposed in [7], which consists of three black pixels along a 45-degree line as a bitmap pattern, tilted to the left to represent a data value one and tilted to the right to represent a data value zero. Moreover, Fig.1(b) is the pattern designed by our cooperator Clevercode Corp., which is a $64 \times 64$ bitmap with $4 \times 4$ fine dots printed in a region approximatively $1.0mm \times 1.0mm$ in a high resolution 1200dpi. In the following, we only show this kind of patterns as a example in our publishing framework.

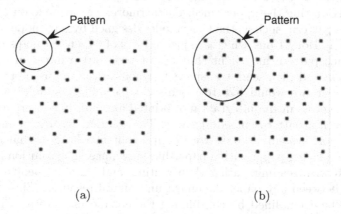

(a)                                        (b)

**Fig. 1.** Two kinds of non-obtrusive patterns

Since the Clevercode patterns have so high a resolution and at the same time are limited in such a small region, they seem almost transparent after printed out and then outperform barcodes [3] in the literature. As shown in Fig.2, we are affected little by these extra embedded patterns during reading, which is just the reason why we call them non-obtrusive patterns. Obviously, there are some OCR methods to extract text (i.e., the content of interest) from one page of printed document just as [8], and we can also connect the content of interest with its corresponding multimedia information without any pattern embedded. However,

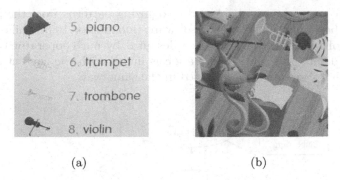

(a)                          (b)

**Fig. 2.** Two samples of printed documents with non-obtrusive patterns embedded

the OCR method can easily be disturbed by the background of the content of interest, while our approach almost always succeeds in this case. Moreover, our approach can be used to connect the region of interest in a picture with multimedia information, while the OCR method is helpless.

**Fig. 3.** A word embedded with 56 copies of one pattern

Given a region of the content to be linked with multimedia information, one pattern is embedded repeatedly until this region is filled up, and finally this region consists of a few copies of the pattern. We expect to identify the pattern more reliably by embedding it repeatedly. As shown in Fig.3, the word "China" is embedded with 56 copies of one non-obtrusive pattern.

## 3   A Publishing Framework for Digitally Augmented Paper Documents

In this section, we give out the publishing framework for DAP documents based on our software BookMaker 10.0, one of the most famous publishing softwares. Though we aim to present a unified framework independent of particular patterns and readers, we have to first know what hardware is also necessary to realize DAP documents. As shown in Fig.4, the DAP system contains two parts: embedding patterns into one page of a book and recognizing patterns from the page. The former can be implemented by our software BookMaker 10.0, while the latter is the task of some kind of magic pen designed by our cooperator Clevercode Corp. As a demo, only audio information is linked with the content of a page, and other digital resources can be used in the same way.

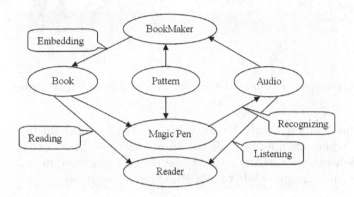

**Fig. 4.** The DAP system including hardware and software parts

The integration of cross-media information in the DAP system is also shown in Fig.4. In the following, we will explain it in detail. To publish a DAP document, in the similar way just as the above section has given out, the non-obtrusive patterns are continually embedded in the print areas of the words or pictures and act as indexes to further link these contents with corresponding audio information. For example, we can embed a single pattern in the print region of the word "China" as shown in Fig.3, and further connect this word with audio files about China. Once the DAP system has identified the embedded pattern via the magic pen, the detail information about China can be provided by using the detected pattern as an index, and readers can then expect to get a deep impression of China with the audio information. Hence, the DAP system just acts as a guide for those who plan a tour of China in this case.

Now we consider the software part of the DAP system, that is, the publishing framework for DAP documents. As shown in Fig.5, the publishing framework consists of four steps: separating text into words, searching patterns for words, embedding patterns when outputting PS file, and printing the PS file. The pictures in a page can be processed in the same way. Note that our publishing software BookMaker 10.0 can work fluently to print a book, we just need to improve it to support pattern embedding. Of course, we can do this just manually word by word. However, there are usually so many words in a book that this is not an efficient method. Hence, we resort to BookMaker 10.0. With a markup language specially designed for BookMaker, the non-obtrusive patterns can be embedded automatically just when the layout of one page of a book is being arranged. Note that the markup language is similar to the well-known Latex

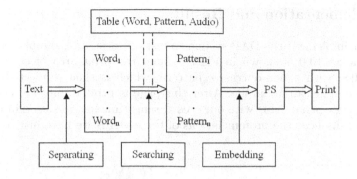

**Fig. 5.** A publishing framework for DAP documents

and HTML, and some tags are shown in Fig.6. With the mapping table of words (or sentences), audio files and non-obtrusive patterns, which is actually managed by BookMaker, the content of a page can be embedded with non-obtrusive patterns as follows. We first search for sentences in the table. If the content of the page consists of a sentence which is also in the table, the print area of this sentence is embedded with the corresponding pattern. Otherwise, we search for words in the table and the following step is just the same.

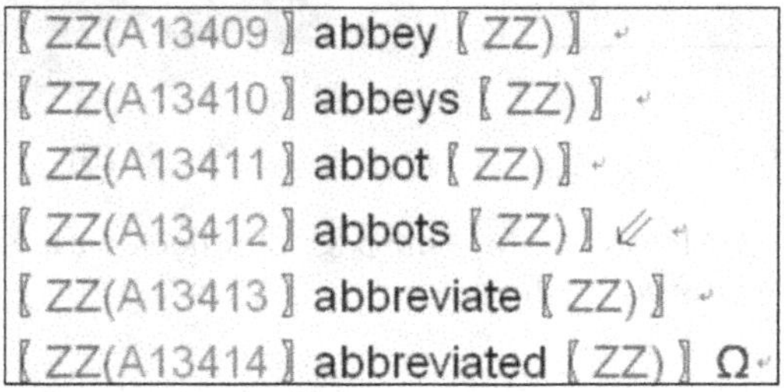

```
[ ZZ(A13409] abbey [ ZZ)]  ·
[ ZZ(A13410] abbeys [ ZZ)]  ·
[ ZZ(A13411] abbot [ ZZ)]  ·
[ ZZ(A13412] abbots [ ZZ)]  ⫙ ·
[ ZZ(A13413] abbreviate [ ZZ)]  ·
[ ZZ(A13414] abbreviated [ ZZ)]  Ω·
```

**Fig. 6.** Some tags of the markup language for BookMaker to embed patterns on the background of English words

Though one page of a book is usually printed out with four colors, i.e., cyan (C), magenta (M), yellow (Y), and black (K), the first three colors are enough for printing. Hence, we can use the color K only to print non-obtrusive patterns in order not to make the magic pen disturbed by the corresponding contents. That is, all the contents of a page except non-obtrusive patterns are rendered only by C, M, and Y. We can easily finish this task with BookMaker 10.0. Moreover, in this way, the non-obtrusive patterns embedded in the region of pictures can successfully be recognized by the magic pen since only they are really black.

## 4    Implementation and Results

We further implement the DAP system to test our design. A sample page made by BookMaker 10.0 is shown in Fig.7(a), and the print area of each Chinese word is filled with a non-obtrusive pattern, which is then connected with its pronunciation, i.e, an audio file. After this page is printed out, we read it and make the magic pen moving with our eyes at same time just as shown in Fig.7(b). We successfully hear the pronunciations of these words we have just read.

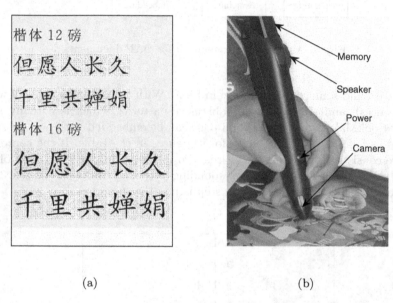

(a)                                                     (b)

**Fig. 7.** A test for the DAP system. (a) One page of a book with embedded patterns; (b)The magic pen used during reading.

We also attempt to embed non-obtrusive patterns into pictures in a book. For each picture of one page, there may be different objects. We can draw out the region of each object, and then embed a pattern. Just as shown in Fig.7(b), each object of a picture is also connected with multimedia information.

## 5    Conclusions

We concentrate on introducing a publishing framework for DAP documents and expect a renovation of the printing industry. Though we give a example to show the publishing framework just based on some kinds of non-obtrusive patterns, our design can be easily modified to process other patterns (e.g., barcodes). Moreover, we can use a separation color space to output the non-obtrusive patterns specially, while the origin contents of a page are still rendered by CMYK color space and then affected little by the extra embedded patterns.

We can also expect many potential applications of the DAP documents. For example, the DAP system can perform as a teacher for children who are just beginning to learn a language. Such an application may have a great impact on language learning. Moreover, we can take advantage of DAP to protect the copyright of documents, since the DAP reader (e.g., pen) just acts as a hard key and we can learn about associated multimedia information only using the unique reader for this document.

# References

1. Luff, P., Heath, C.: Mobility in Collaboration. In: Proceedings of ACM Conference on Computer Supported Cooperative Work (1998) 305–314
2. Seyrat, E., Hayes, R.A.: Amorphous Fluoropolymers as Insulators for Reversible Low-Voltage Electrowetting. Journal of Applied Physics **90** (3) (2001) 1383–1386
3. Lange, B., Jones, M., Meyers, J.: Insight Lab: An Immersive Team Environment Linking Paper, Displays, and Data. In: Proceedings of ACM Conference on Human Factors in Computing Systems (1998) 550–557
4. Rekimoto, J., Ayatsuka, Y.: CyberCode: Designing Augmented Reality Environments with Visual Tags. In: Proceedings of Designing Augmented Reality Environments (2000) 1–10
5. Harrison, S.R., Minneman, S.L., Balsamo, A.M.: Methods & Tools: How to XFR: "Experiments in the Future of Reading". Interactions **8** (3) (2001) 31–41
6. Kise, K., Miki, Y., Matsumoto, K.: Background as Information Carriers for Printed Documents. In: Proceedings of International Conference on Pattern Recognition (2000) 592–596
7. Hecht, D.L.: Printed Embedded Data Graphical User Interfaces. Computer **34** (2001) 47–55
8. Arai, T., Aust, D., Hudson, S.E.: PaperLink: A Technique for Hyperlinking from Real Paper to Electronic Content. In: Proceedings of ACM Conference on Human Factors in Computing Systems (1997) 327–334

# Web-Based Semantic Analysis of Chinese News Video

Huamin Feng [1], Zongqiang Pang [2], Kun Qiu [2], and Guosen Song [2]

[1] Key Laboratory for Security and Secrecy of Information, BESTI,
Beijing100070, China
[2] The school of Information Science and Engineering, YanShan University,
Qin Huangdao 066004, China
{fenghm, zq_pang, qiukun.songgs}@besti.edu.cn

**Abstract.** The semantic analysis of the Chinese news video with the help of World Wide Web is proposed. First, we segment the news video into a series of story units. Second, we extract the key phrases from the corresponding ASR transcript of news story, and optimize the key phrases through computing both the correlation among key phrases and the correlation between key phrases and event. Finally, we get the news Web-page corresponding to the event from World Wide Web via the search engine, and obtain the information of news video through analyzing the news Web-page. In order to extract effectively the searching key phrases from the ASR transcription containing mistakes, this paper also presents a novel method of optimizing key phrase for searching, the experiment result with the set of Chinese news video (CCTV4_NEWS) from the TRECVID2005 shows that our approach is effective.

**Keywords:** Semantic Analysis   Video Segmentation   Page Layout analysis Text Filtering.

## 1   Introduction

Video content analysis and indexing is the most active area of international multimedia research [1], [2], [3]. Generally, the video structure is analyzed firstly in the video content analysis. For example, video shot segmentation [4] and the story segmentation based on the shot [5]; and then video semantics is analyzed for each story unit. Qi et al [14] integrated video, audio, text on the news video analysis and demonstrated an intelligent highlight player and a HTML-based complete browser. However, there are many mistranslated errors (especially names and place, proper noun) in general ASR, and the results of ASR have no format features (such as the title, paragraph and punctuation, etc.). With the development of network technology and the establishment of news websites, a news video story usually corresponds with some news websites in the Word Wide Web. However, these news web-pages are error free, and preserve a lot of additional information (such as accurate classification artificially, the news title, the related links and the relevant pictures). Through comparing the keywords voice the keywords of the related website will replace the mistaken keywords of the video transcript [16]. If the corresponding Web-page with the video is found, the website information will help us better in news video content analysis, and will play an important role in forming semantic web. Dowman produced

Y. Zhuang et al. (Eds.): PCM 2006, LNCS 4261, pp. 502–509, 2006.

the Rich News system that can automatically annotate radio and television news with the aid of resources retrieved from the World Wide Web [6].

A lot of work in the area of news video structure analysis [5] [7] and news website analysis [8] has been done in our multimedia lab. Aiming at the Chinese news video, based on the video shot segmentation and story segmentation, we propose a framework to obtain the news semantics. We extract precisely the searching key phrases from the transcript containing mistakes, and use search engine to search the news website, then use coordinates tree model [8] to extract the topical content from the web page. Finally, through the text filtering, we reach to the most relevant website to the news video and get the satisfactory result for news video.

The rest of the paper is organized as following. We segment news video into story units in section 2. In section 3, we divide the transcript into paragraphs according to story units. Searching keywords are extracted by using an improved *TFIDF* algorithm in section 4. In section 5, we remove the mistranslated searching keywords by calculating the correlation among the keywords and the correlation between the keywords and event. The relevant web pages are obtained with the help of Google search engine in section 6. In section 7 and 8, we extract the topical content of web page and filter out the most relevant one to the news story. Section 9 is the initial experiment result. Finally, we conclude our work and outlook at section 10.

## 2 News Video Story Segmentation

For the news video semantic analysis, news video will be segment into story units in general.

Our framework employs the two-level approach for news story segmentation [5]. The process is achieved at two levels, the bottom (shot level): using the decision tree for shot classification; and the top (story level): using the HMM (hidden-Markov models) for story unit segmentation. First ,we use IBM "VideoAnnEx" [17] to segment news video into a series of shot, and then we use semi-automatically extract features, more about features, please refer to research work [5], and employ SVM (Support Vector Machine) to get the following high-level audio features: pure music, pure speech, speech and background noise, speech and the background music, and silence. For visual features, we use face features (number of faces, face size, face position), motion features (minor, intermediate, intense and static activity), caption features (topic caption and centralized video text), temporal features (shot duration). Based on these features, the decision tree is used to classify the video shot into the following: Intro/Highlight, One Anchor, Two Anchor, Speech/Interview, Meeting, Normal Report, Theme Report, Still Image, Text Scene, Weather and commercial, a total of 11 categories. Considering that one anchor shots often confuse with Speech/Interview shots, we further calculate the color histogram of background region to reduce the error-rate. We also use pre-partition module based on heuristic rule to merge the short shots, and enhance Intro/Highlight and Speech/Interview resolution.

# 3  News Stories Transcript

After news story segmentation, the story transcripts are extracted according to each
story unit. Fig 1 shows video story transcripts.

**Fig. 1.** Video Story Transcripts

We employ ASR software to obtain the transcript from the news video, for
example, one section of transcript is given as following:

Transcript 1：

ｎ n、回收百姓节目浇灌着阿拉法特的病情时好刚刚在法国巴黎的戏剧院看望了阿拉法特的巴赞宗教领袖
弹力米对手或在剧院门口的记者说阿拉法特目前的情况很不好但是他依然活着被扒开龙虾万难应该有外来
客关于娃娃穿越热，娃娃他又说，台湾是爱那抹微有瓦尔多萨班爱我来给那我该在哪还有诺，我们的老师
把我带来一木呐的说没事干了又看看那诺瓦约阿木好比你知道天上午抵达巴黎的财产是阿拉法特拒绝好的
电视剧远？对新闻界降耗、．．．．．，我，．．．。瓦特还有一所历史上很久没去成。不说那叫把他们的介
绍的脸事实上了所有做法纷纷发表文章在

Note that there exist many errors in the transcript.

# 4  Searching Keywords Extraction

Once the story transcript is extracted, it is necessary to determine some keywords in
order to use search engine to look for the corresponding news web-pages in the Word
Wide Web. We call these keywords searching keywords. There is a certain distinction
between the searching keywords and general keywords. In general, searching
keywords often contain time, place, character and event that occurred in the news
story. We use HLSplitWord software [12] to split words in the transcript and then
count the rate of words, and identify POS (Part-of-Speech) (name, place, organization
and the general term).

For the individual word weight, we consider not only the presentation of the
information within the transcript, but also the efficiency of different words in the
searching. Although there are many algorithms [9] [10] for extracting keywords, they
require a lot of pre-identified keywords of the articles, therefore, identifying the
searching keywords is an extremely large workload. We use the *TFIDF* algorithm to
extract searching keywords. In the video transcript, named entities (name of person
and place, organization) can reduce error rate through manual calibration, and named
entities in the search process are very useful compared with the general search terms.
Then we proposed the improved *TFIDF* algorithm.

$$w_{ij} = \alpha_j TF_i * IDF_i = \alpha_j TF * \log_2 (1 + N/n_i) \tag{1}$$

Where $w_{ij}$ denotes the word weight; $TF_i$ denotes frequency that the word appear in the transcript; $N$ is the total number of transcripts in training sets, $n$ is the number of transcripts that include the term, $j$ denotes the POS of words, different POS have different coefficient $_j$. We use the Google search engine API googleapi [12]. Because the number of using Google search engine is limited to 1,000 times a day, we only collect the names of persons and places, organizations name, the idiom and noun. By experiment, we assign $_j$ to be 0.3, 0.2, 0.3, 0.1, 0.1. Finally, the keywords are arranged by measuring score, and choose the top 20 keywords as a group of candidate keywords.

For example, the candidate searching keywords of news story transcript which is mentioned above are given as following:

"阿拉法特" "瓦尔多萨班" "诺瓦约" "巴赞" "巴黎" "娃娃" "台湾" "法国" "做法" "新闻界" "戏剧" "万难" "门口" "龙虾" "剧院" "电视剧" "弹力" "财产" "文章" "事实上"

## 5  Searching Keyword Optimization

After we get the keyword score through the improved TFIDF algorithm, we found that the mistranslated keywords are assigned high value because the wrong identified words generally are uncommon words that rarely occur in other transcripts, moreover, the wrong identified words by ASR identification is irrelevant to the news event. If we do not remove searching keywords, the search results will be poor. Here we remove such irrelevant keywords via calculating the relevance among the words and the relevance between words and event. In order to make statistics more reliable, we focused on one Chinese news website and adding "site:www.cctv.com/news." in the front of each searching group in Google search. The following is an example of a group of searching keywords:

"site:www.cctv.com/news "阿拉法特" "瓦尔多萨班" "

So we obtain a phrase correlative matrix $C^{n \times n}$ ($n$ is the number of candidate searching keywords)

$$C^{n \times n} = \begin{pmatrix} c_{1,1} & c_{1,2} & \cdot & \cdot & \cdot & c_{1,n} \\ c_{2,1} & c_{2,2} & \cdot & \cdot & \cdot & c_{2,n} \\ \cdot & & \cdot & & & \cdot \\ \cdot & & & \cdot & & \cdot \\ \cdot & & & & \cdot & \cdot \\ c_{n,1} & c_{n,2} & \cdot & \cdot & \cdot & c_{n,n} \end{pmatrix} \tag{2}$$

Where $c_{i,j}$ is the number of both $i$th phrase and $j$th phrase appear in the same web page at the news website "site:www.cctv.com/news". Big $c_{i,j}$ implies that the more web-pages contain the two words, and the correlation between words is higher. Conversely, the correlation between words is lower. If the number of non-zero elements in the $i$th column of Correlative matrix $C$ is bigger, we think the $i$th word is irrelevant to the news event.

Taking into account the effect of website noise (such as advertisement or related links) in web-related statistics, we need to set correlation threshold $p$ between two searching keywords. Due to the error-rate of the ASR, we need to set thresholds $e$

between searching keywords and event. Two-step process of calculating condition is given as following.

Condition 1: if $c_{i,j}$ less than the minimum correlation threshold $p$, we think between the two words are irrelevant with each other.

Condition 2: counting the number of relative words in $i$th column. If the number is less than the minimum event correlation threshold $e$; we think that the $i$th keyword have nothing to do with the event.

Then we remove those words satisfying the condition 1 and 2, and obtain the good searching keywords. For example, the searching keywords optimized of news story transcript mentioned above are given as following:

"阿拉法特" "巴黎" "台湾" "法国" "做法" "新闻界" "戏剧" "门口" "剧院" "电视剧" "弹力" "财产" "文章" "事实上"

# 6　Web Search Using Searching Keywords

We use the searching keywords to search with the help of Google search engine. Our search focuses on the Chinese authority news website "www.cctv.com", and adding the term "site:www.cctv.com" before each searching keywords. To improve the accuracy of search, we also get the date that news story occurred at from the transcript. Sometimes video news website information will be posted later. So we use two dates as a term, for example, "'2004□11□10□'OR'2004□11□11□'". Google search engine requires that the number of keywords is no more than 10, therefore, we arrange searching keyword by measuring score. For example, the searching terms of transcript mentioned before:

"site:www.cctv.com "2004年12月01日" OR" 2004年12月02日" "阿拉法特" "巴赞" "台湾" "巴黎" "法国" "做法" "新闻界" "

In order to search accurately and automatically, we use a greedy searching method. The number of web addresses Google search engine returns limited to 10. If no website satisfied the terms, most right keyword will be removed from the term list until we have websites returned. If the number of website returned is less than 10, the most right keyword will also be removed in the order, and then withdraw the front addresses from the next search results, so that we obtain about 10 websites that most likely to meet the terms.

# 7　Topical Content Extraction

The "noise content" in web-pages is a critical factor that impact on the quality of web content analysis. Rapidly and accurately identifying of the topical content is one of the key technologies for improving semantic analysis quality. We extract the topical content by using the method based on coordinate tree [8], and the method introduces a coordinate tree model containing information on the nodes of web. Firstly, use CyberNeko HTML Parser [11] transform HTML documents into Coordinate tree, and then, calculate the location coordinates and width and height of the nodes in Coordinate tree. On the one hand, we will divide the web page into blocks, and table□TD and DIV label as sub-nodes, then judge if the nodes are top or bottom or left or right region. If the sub-node is any one of these region, it will be deleted. On the other hand, use coordinate tree to create a web map (Graph) model, which designates coordinate tree all leaf nodes in the Graph as the basic elements of Graph, and then analyzing the borders between adjacent basic elements. In one word, with the help of web layout analysis, we extract the topic content. More detail, please refer to [8].

# 8  News Text Filtering

The purpose is to determine whether the news pages are relevant with news transcript. After we obtain the news topical content in section 7, web filtering completes similarity measurement between web-pages and news story transcript. We use a generic cosine formula to determine the degree of similarity, and select the topical contents with the higher similarity score. To avoid the impact of mistaken words by ASR, we use the optimized keyword to calculate the cosine value. Thus we attempt to remove the impact of mistaken words of ASR on the similarity measurement. Then we obtain the news website that can describe the video semantics correctly.

# 9  Initial Experimental Result

The initial experiment use the Chinese news video set CCTV4_NEWS in TRECVID2005. We choose 17-day concise news reports about 145 minutes. First, we segment video into story units and obtain 115 story units. Then, searching keywords are extracted from the corresponding news transcripts. Searching keywords are optimized using our method. Finally, we input the search keywords into Google search engine, and the returned results are input to text filter to obtain the most similar website to news video.

As judging whether the website is relevant or irrelevant to the news video is subjective, we use manual method to evaluate the results. We assign returned news web-page to the "good, general and bad" three classes. If both the video news and the website have the same figures, time, location, events, the score is "good". If video news and website both describe the event that has related content, or the same event, such as press comments and news analysis, the score is "general". If the events are not same or irrelevant with each other, the score is "poor".

We randomly choose 8 test persons to evaluate 115 video news and website, and then calculate the average, so achieve the initial result as show in table 1.

**Table 1.** Initial Result

| Story units | good | general | bad |
|---|---|---|---|
| ×100% | 26.6 | 17.5 | 55.9 |
| ×100% | 44.1 | | 55.9 |

Experimental process has four steps: step 1, video segmentation; step 2, searching keyword extraction and optimization; step 3, network searching; step 4, the topical website content extraction and text filter. A good system needs each step to complement with each other. 1) If the story segment misidentifies the boundary and put two stores together into one, the keywords will extracted from the two different story transcripts. This leads to the failure of searching web. 2) In the step of searching keywords extraction, the wrong keywords which are commonly used terms in web can not be removed in optimizing process, such as, in the above transcript, an Arabic phrase is wrongly translated into "台湾". Because the frequency of "台湾" is very high in news websites, thus keywords can not be removed in the process of optimizing. 3) As for searching keywords, if the first word is the wrong word, we will obtain the irrelevant website. 4) Error in web topical extracted process is also an important factor which affects the search results. We sometimes can not filter out web "noise", or even filter out topical content mistakenly. 5) In this experiment, we only use the corrected nouns and idioms in calculating the text similar degree, and ignore other words (such as verb and adjective etc) result in failure. For example, if the searching terms are only the name of country, the international sport event schedule will be achieved, because they contain a large number of related names. 6) The difference organization between web-page news and video news stories is one of reasons that affect the performance of the system. For example, the website is composite with more than two news events. 7) Since there are no clear named entities prepared in some financial reports, the search results are worse. On the contrary, meetings with the obvious named entities, the results will be relatively well. Unlike other types, the results of weather and sports are better.

## 10   Conclusion and Future Work

We attempt to analyze Chinese news video semantics with the help of web search. Via Word Wide Web, we statistically calculate the correlation among words and the correlation between the words and events. Based on the correlation matrix, we remove mistranslated words of video transcript and obtain the text from the Word Wide Web similar to the news video. The initial experiments on CCTV4_NEWS of TRECVID2005 show that our approach is effective. In the future, many aspects need to be improved: (1) Effective algorithms for automatically determining the threshold to remove mistranslated words; (2) A more flexible searching method, which searches more websites, such as "news.xinhuanet.com". (3) Improving the quality of news by filtering.

**Acknowledgments.** This research is supported in part by National Natural Science Foundation [Grant No. 60472082], Beijing Natural Science Foundation [Grant No. 4062031] and Key Lab Foundation of Beijing Electronic Science and Technology Institute [Grant No. YZDJ0430]. The author would also like to thank to Google, IBM and Tianjin Hailiang technology development Corporation for providing software.

## References

1.  Alan Hanjalic, Reginald L. Lagendijk and Jan Biemond, Recent Advances in Video Content Analysis: From Visual Features to Semantic Video Segments. International Journal of Image and Graphics, p63-81.2001.1.

2. Nicu Sebe, Michael S.Lew, Xiang Zhou, et al. The State of the Art in Image and Video Retrieval. International Conference on Image and Video Retrieval. Springer-Verlag Heidelberg. 2003.
3. Yao Wang, Zhu Liu and Jin-Cheng Huang. Multimedia Content Analysis. IEEE Signal Processi-Ng Magazine, 2000.12-36.
4. Huamin Feng, et al; "A New General Framework for Shot Boundary Detection Based on SVM", The 2nd ICNN&B--International Conference on Neural Networks and Brain--Oct.13-15, Beijing, China.
5. Huamin Feng , Xiaofei Zhai , et al ; "story segmentation in news video", 2nd ICNN&B—International Conference on Neural Network and Brain.
6. Mike Dowman, et al; Web-Assisted Annotation, Semantic Indexing and Search of Television and Radio News ,www2005.org/cdrom/docs/p225.pdf\.
7. Fang Wei, et al; "A New General Framework for Shot Boundary Detection and Key-Frame Extraction", MIR05--2005 International Multimedia Information Retrieval Conference--Nov.11-13, Singapore.
8. Huamin Feng et al; A New Framework of Web Page Analysis and Content Extraction; The 2nd ICNN&B—International Conference on Neural Networks and Brain——Oct.13-15, Beijing, China.
9. Dumais S., Platt J., Heckerman, D.and Sahami, M. Inductive learning algorithms and representations for text categorization. Proceedings of the Seventh International Conference on Information and Knowledge Management, 148-155. ACM, 1998.
10. Turney, P.D. Learning algorithms for key phrase extraction. Information Retrieval, 2, 303-336, 2000
11. CyberNeko HTML Parser. http://www.apache.org/~andyc/neko/doc/html/index.html
12. Hailiang software introduction: http://www.hylanda.com.
13. Googleapi: http://www.google.com/apis.
14. Wei Qi, Lie Gu, Hao Jiang, Xiang-Rong Chen and Hong-Jiang Zhang," INTEGRATING VISUAL, AUDIO AND TEXT ANALYSIS FOR NEWS VIDEO(Invited Paper)", 7th IEEE Intn'l Conference on Image Processing (ICIP 2000), Vancouver, British Columbia, Canada,10-13 September 2000.
15. www-nlpir.nist.gov/projects/tv2005/tv2005.html
16. Hui Yang, Lekha Chaisorn, Yunlong Zhao, Shi-Yong Neo, Tat-Seng Chua.VideoQA:Question Answering on News Video.In proceedings of the ACM conference on Multimedia (Multimedia'03),Berkeley, CA, November 2-8.
17. VideoAnnEx: http://www.research.ibm.com/VideoAnnEx.

# A Quality-Controllable Encryption for H.264/AVC Video Coding

Guang-Ming Hong[1], Chun Yuan[1], Yi Wang[2], and Yu-Zhuo Zhong[1]

[1] Division of Information Technology, Graduate School at Shenzhen,
Tsinghua University, Shenzhen 518055, Guangdong Province, China
[2] Department of Computer Science and Technology,
Tsinghua University, Beijing 100084, China
hgm@mails.tsinghua.edu.cn,
yuanc@mail.sz.tsinghua.edu.cn,
wangy01@mails.tsinghua.edu.cn,
zhongyz@mail.sz.tsinghua.edu.cn

**Abstract.** During the boosting of networking multimedia applications
in recent years, secure transmission of video streams becomes highly demanded by many hot applications, such as confidential video conference
and pay-TV. In this paper, we present a quality-controllable encryption
method for H.264 coded video streams. Our goal has been to provide an
efficient way to scramble the video streams to prevent illegal users from
plagiarizing. By making use of the property of H.264 specification that
Intra coded blocks are divided into three different types with different
sizes, our algorithm provides the flexibility of scrambling the video up
to certain level, which may be manually specified by the user or automatically determined by the system according to the networking traffic
condition. Our design ensures that even the deepest scrambling level adds
trivial performance overhead to the standard H.264 encoding/decoding
process.

**Keywords:** Quality-Controllable Encryption, Partial Encryption,
H.264/AVC.

## 1 Introduction

During the development of multimedia and Internet technology and the steadily
boosting of digital communication and entertainment, the secure transmission
of multimedia data, in particular, the video streams, gains great attention from
both the end users and the multimedia content providers. However, the Internet is still far from a secure transmission medium, especially its wireless part.
It is necessary to use encryption technologies to protect the multimedia data
from being plagiarizing during transmission. Unfortunately, the huge amount
of multimedia data usually grabs most networking bandwidth and computing
power and makes the adding of encryption protection even more challenging.
This situation is particularly serious for the video streaming, which may be the
far most intriguing multimedia service on the Internet.

Y. Zhuang et al. (Eds.): PCM 2006, LNCS 4261, pp. 510–517, 2006.

In this paper, we present a highly efficient approach to encrypt H.264 video. Our goal is to hide part of the information from unauthorized users with low computational requirement and little bit-rate overhead. We achieve this goal, without losing the compression efficiency, by encrypting only the most critical part of the H.264 video stream. By making use of the property of H.264 that Intra coded blocks are divided into three different types with different sizes, our approach uses a high performance encryption method, the AES [1], to scramble the video content from low security level up to certain security level, which may be manually specified by the user or automatically determined by the system adapting to the networking traffic situation.

According to the literature, our work is among the first attempts to provide quality-controllable video protection for H.264 video streaming. H.264 is the newest international video coding standard published by the ITU-T VCEG and the ISO/IEC MPEG. It aims at enhancing the compression performance and providing a network-friendly video representation [2]. In addition, H.264 has a lot of features in details to improve the compression efficiency and to make the video streams more robust to channel errors, such as variable block-size, multiple reference, weighted prediction and so on [8] [9] [10]. However, the standard does not include any guidelines about video encryption.

This paper is organized as follows. Section 2 gives a brief introduction about previous work done in video encryption. Section 3 provides an analysis of the H.264 standard and figures out which features can be used to provide different security levels. The main introduction of our quality-controllable video encryption algorithm is presented in Section 4, and the experimental results are provided and discussed in Section 5. Section 6 in the last place gives the conclusion and future work.

## 2   Previous Work in Encrypting Video

Although, because H.264 is newly proposed, most previous work on video encryption are for MPEG1, MPEG2 and MPEG4 video, a commonality that can be found from the following review is that, to achieve both of the effective encryption and efficient performance, all the encryption methods have to make good use of the features of video encoding schemes. Our method inherits this feature by selectively encrypting parts of the H.264 video streams.

In [3], Tang presents a method of MPEG video encryption. By making use of the property of MPEG encoding, this method provides the flexibility of four levels of encryptions: (1) encrypting all headers, (2) encrypting all headers and I frames, (3) encrypting all I frames and all I blocks in P and B frames, and (4) encrypting all frames. Our method also provides multiple levels of encryption, but by exploiting other features of the video encoding scheme of H.264, in particular, the types and sizes of Intra coded blocks.

In [4], Qiao and Nahrstedt present another encryption method for MPEG video, the VEA algorithm, which depends on the statistical features of the compressed video data. The VEA algorithm divides the video streams into chunks, which are further separated into lists. Light weighted operation, the XOR operation, and highly efficient encryption algorithm, the DES algorithm, are used to compress certain parts of the lists.

A third method for encrypting MPEG video was proposed by Shi and Bhargava in [5], whose basic idea is to use a secret key to randomly change the sign bits of all the DCT coefficients of MPEG video. Although, using very light weighted encryption, this methods does not provide high security, however, the algorithm is highly efficient for scrambling the video stream in real-time.

In [6], Zhu et. al. discussed the scalable protection for MPEG4. By making use of the mechanism of fine granularity scalability (FGS), the authors proposed two novel encryption algorithms to adapt to the varying network traffic conditions. The first algorithm encrypts an FGS stream into a single access layer and preserves the original scalability and error resilience performance. The second algorithm encrypts an FGS stream into multiple quality layers divided according to PSNR and bit rates. Both the two algorithms enable intermediate stages to process encrypted data directly without decryption, so the algorithm preserves most adaptation capabilities of FGS.

In [7], Shi et. al. proposed two techniques of selective encryption for the H.264 video. The first technique, the SEH264Algorithm1, groups the video data into five blocks: a block of the Sequence Parameter Set (SPS) and the Picture Parameter Set (PPS) of H.264, a block of intra coded frames, a block of the slice headers and the macro block headers of P slice and the DC coefficients, a block of all the ac coefficients and a block of motion vectors, and then encrypts the first three blocks only. The second technique, which is called SEH264Algorithm2, has the main idea of encrypting all the start codes in the bitstream which are used for synchronization.

## 3   H.264 Overview

In this section, we introduce the necessary background knowledge about the H.264 standard that is closely related to video encryption work.

The general coding structure of H.264, similar with earlier standards,uses the hybrid DPCM/DCT video codec model, which has also been used in H.261, H.263, MPEG1, MPEG2, MPEG4 Part2. Details about the hybrid DPCM/DCT model can be found in Figure 2 and 3 of [8] and Figure 3.50 and 3.51 in [10]. In this model, video encoding is applied sequentially, picture by picture, and for each picture, which is partitioned into one or more slices, encoding is applied to the slices independently. Each slice consists of a set of macroblocks, where, each is composed of one $16 \times 16$ luminance sample (Y) and two $8 \times 8$ chrominance samples (Cb and Cr) in the 4:2:0 chroma format [8] [9] [10].

Slices are categorized into three types: I (Intra) slice, P (Predictive) slice, and B (Bi-predictive) slice. In H.264/AVC standard, the macroblocks in I slices are compressed without any motion prediction which is similar in earlier standards. In P slices and B slices, the macroblocks can be compressed with or without motion prediction. When using motion prediction, the macroblocks in P slices use one prediction, and, the macroblocks in B slices may use two predictions. For the decoding of Inter coded blocks need correctly decoded reference blocks, we can see that the Intra blocks which are compressed without motion predictions are the most important part in the H.264 bitstreams. If we encrypt all the Intra blocks, the Inter blocks (blocks with motion prediction) would result in incorrect decoding. Although the motion vectors and residual coefficients are unsecured, the adversary is still inadequate to construct the original picture because the reference blocks are not correct.

For Intra macroblocks, spatial prediction is performed in H.264. To minimize the difference between the current block and previously encoded reference block, the $16 \times 16$ macroblocks are divided into three different block sizes: $16 \times 16$, $8 \times 8$, $4 \times 4$. Generally, blocks with smaller size, for example, $4 \times 4$, will offer better prediction efficiency than blocks with larger size, for example, $16 \times 16$, but will bring more overhead for mode decision bits. So it is suitable to use $16 \times 16$ blocks for smooth macroblocks while $4 \times 4$ blocks for fragmented ones. The $8 \times 8$ blocks are used as a compromise and they are newly added to the standard (see 8.3 in [9] for more details). For the chroma components of an intra coded macroblock, the two $8 \times 8$ blocks are also predicted from the previously encoded chroma samples and both use the same prediction mode. It is concluded that all the Intra blocks consists of four types of blocks: the Intra $16 \times 16$, $8 \times 8$, $4 \times 4$ luma blocks and $8 \times 8$ chroma blocks. We can encrypt different parts of them to gain different security levels.

# 4   The Quality-Controllable Encryption Method of H.264

Basing on the discussion in Section 3, we can see that different parts of Intra blocks in H.264 can be encrypted to achieve the flexibility of different security levels. Although the motion vectors and residual coefficients of Inter blocks are not encrypted, the decoders still can not reconstruct the original block because the base data used as reference block can not be decoded correctly. However, the adversary may be able to tell the motion nature whether there is high or low motion from frame to frame.

After studying the statistical behavior of the encoded H.264 bitstreams (c.f. Table 1), we can see that the frequency of occurrence of Intra_$16 \times 16$ is much less than Intra_$8 \times 8$ in most bitstreams, and the frequency of Intra_$4 \times 4$ is the highest of all the three block types. Furthermore, the Intra coded chroma blocks are not critical, because the chroma component is not very important to HVS (Human Vision System). So we put Intra coded chroma blocks and Intra $16 \times 16$ blocks in a same group, and, Intra $8 \times 8$ and Intra $4 \times 4$ blocks are also organized as individual groups.

The selection of encryption algorithm is another important issue in the framework of video encryption. There are several encryption algorithms that we can choose to encrypt video streams. In this paper, we select the AES algorithm and the ZIGZAG algorithm. The former one treats the pre-encoded data as bitstream and encrypts each 128 bits with a key, and the latter one applies random permutation

**Table 1.** Statistical Analysis of H.264 bitstreams

| H.264 Video Name | Size | Length | Intra16 × 16 | Intra8 × 8 | Intra4 × 4 |
|---|---|---|---|---|---|
| foreman_qcif.264 | 176 × 144 | 400 frames | 3.0% | 15.7% | 81.3% |
| container_qcif.264 | 176 × 144 | 300 frames | 9.6% | 30.3% | 60.1% |
| highway_qcif.264 | 176 × 144 | 2000 frames | 7.8% | 28.5% | 63.6% |
| silent_qcif.264 | 176 × 144 | 300 frames | 2.0% | 2.5% | 95.5% |
| akiyo.264 | 352 × 288 | 300 frames | 19.2% | 40.6% | 40.2% |
| container.264 | 352 × 288 | 300 frames | 15.3% | 34.5% | 50.3% |
| highway.264 | 352 × 288 | 2000 frames | 14.4% | 49.3% | 36.3% |
| silent.264 | 352 × 288 | 300 frames | 4.7% | 15.3% | 80.1% |

to the pre-encoded data before encryption. We develop our quality-controllable encryption method to provide four security levels:

- **Level 0:** no encryption;
- **Level 1:** encrypt all the Intra16 × 16 blocks and the DC coefficients of Intra coded chroma blocks with AES algorithm or ZIGZAG algorithm;
- **Level 2:** encrypt all the Intra8 × 8 blocks with the same algorithm additionally;
- **Level 3:** encrypt all the Intra4 × 4 blocks with the same algorithm additionally;

Compared with the selective encryption algorithm developed for H.264 in [7], our quality-controllable encryption algorithm features the following advantages:

- All the standard decoders can decode the bitstreams without crashing, but the picture quality depends on the encryption level. So only the decoder which has been modified according to the encryption algorithm and equipped with the encryption key can perform the decoding correctly. This is applicable to many applications.
- The algorithm provides different security levels. This can be chosen and changed easily at the encoder. This feature enables the encoder to provide different picture qualities and is useful in some special application areas.
- The algorithm brings little overhead in cost and efficiency. The results are presented in Section 5. This is useful when the decoder is running with limited computing capability and limited bandwidth.

## 5   Experimental Results

We use JM (version 10.2) and x264 to test our algorithm. JM is the reference software of H.264 (see [11]), but the encoding speed of JM is quite slow, so we use x264, another open source encoder of h.264 whose encoding speed is much more faster (about 500 times generally), as a substitute (see [12]). Both the encoder and decoder are modified to apply the encryption and decryption algorithm.

The two QCIF sized sequences, Foreman, and Container, were compressed with the default parameters of the encoder except that −8x8dct was added to enable Intra_8 × 8 blocks. Figure 1 to Figure 4 show the results of encrypting foreman with AES algorithm at different security levels. Table 2 lists the summary of overhead in that condition. Figure 5 to 8 show the results of encrypting container with ZIGZAG algorithm at different security levels. Table 3 tells the summary of overhead in that condition.

**Table 2.** Overhead of encrypting <u>Foreman</u> with AES algorithm

| foreman | original | level 1 | level 2 | level 3 |
|---:|---:|---:|---:|---:|
| PSNR(average) | 37.64 | 35.84 | 34.74 | 29.92 |
| Bit-rate(Kbps) | 172.39 | 183.55 | 206.36 | 232.01 |
| Encoding Time(fps) | 75.64 | 61.08 | 57.97 | 52.42 |

Fig. 1. The original frame of foreman

Fig. 2. The level 1 encrypted with AES

Fig. 3. The level 2 encrypted with AES

Fig. 4. The level 3 encrypted with AES

From Figure 1 to Figure 8, we found that, the higher secure level reveals less information, both for AES and ZIGZAG algorithms. This is because that in most sequences the amount of Intra 4 × 4 blocks is much more than the other two types. So we should use level 1 and 2 to scramble the video sequences because the visual quality is still tolerable, and level 3 if we want to get the best encryption result. Accordingly, the overhead increases with the encryption level, that is another factor we should consider.

Furthermore, by comparing the AES and ZIGZAG algorithms, we found that the former gives better results while losing much in the compression efficiency.

This is because that the correlation of DCT coefficients is heavily destroyed by the AES algorithm, whereas, it is only disturbed slightly by the ZIGZAG algorithm. However, from Table 2 we can see that the AES algorithm in level 3 brings 34% overhead in bit rate, which, may be not suitable for some applications with extreme requirement of real-time performance.

**Table 3.** Overhead of encrypting Container with ZIGZAG algorithm

| Container | original | level 1 | level 2 | level 3 |
|---|---|---|---|---|
| PSNR(average) | 38.844 | 38.809 | 38.799 | 37.702 |
| Bit-rate(Kbps) | 56.18 | 56.93 | 57.30 | 57.62 |
| Encoding Time(ms) | 115.70 | 113.94 | 106.32 | 102.41 |

From Table 3 we can see that ZIGZAG in all encryption levels brings little overhead, measured by both bit rate and encoding time. So we suggest using ZIGZAG in applications that requires more on real-time performance but less on the extent of encryption, such as video conference and Video-On-Demand (VOD).

**Fig. 5.** The original frame of Container   **Fig. 6.** The level 1 encrypted with ZIGZAG

**Fig. 7.** The level 2 encrypted with ZIGZAG   **Fig. 8.** The level 3 encrypted with ZIGZAG

## 6   Conclusion and Future Work

In this paper, we present a quality-controllable encryption method for H.264 video streams. By making use of the feature of H.264 that the Intra coded blocks are divided into three types with different block size, Intra_16 × 16, Intra_8 × 8, Intra_4 × 4, our algorithm provides the flexibility of three different extents of encryption. In particular, we encrypt only the Intra_16 × 16 blocks and the DC coefficients of chroma blocks as the lowest security level, level 1, put also with the Intra_8 × 8 blocks under encryption results in level 2, encrypt all the three types of Intra blocks and the DC coefficients of chroma blocks in level 3.

From the experiments results, we are confident with the adaptivity and applicability of the algorithm. The detailed qualitative experimental results listed in Section 5 are valuable on instructing the deployment of the algorithm on various applications with different requirements on the extent of encryption and encryption performance.

Future work may include: encrypting more part of the bitstream to gain better security, extending our method to SI frames in the extended profile, reducing the overhead of the encryption algorithm.

# References

1. M. Bishop, Computer Security: Art and Science, Addison Wesley. (2002)
2. Thomas Wiegand, Gary J. Sullivan, Gisle Bjontegaard, and Ajay Luthra: Overview of the H.264/AVC Video Coding Standard, IEEE Transactions on Circuits and Systems for Video Technology, Vol. 13, No. 7, pp. 560-576, July 2003.
3. L. Tang: Methods for Encrypting and Decrypting MPEG Video Data Efficiently, the ACM International Multimedia Conference and Exhibition, pp.219-229, Boston, MA, USA, 1996.
4. L. Qiao, K. Nahrstedt: A New Algorithm for MPEG Video Encryption, International Conference on Imaging Science, Systems, and Technology, pp. 21-29, Las Vegas, NV, June, 1997.
5. C. Shi, B. Bhargava: A Fast MPEG Video Encryption Algorighm, the ACM International Multimedia Conference and Exhibition, pp.81-88, Bristol, UK, 1998.
6. B. Zhu, Chun Yuan, Yidong Wang and Shipeng Li: Scalable Protection for MPEG-4 Fine Granularity Scalability, IEEE Transactions on Multimedia, Vol. 7, No. 2, April 2005.
7. Tuo Shi, Brian King, and Paul Salama: Selective Encryption for H.264/AVC Video Coding, the Society of Photo-Optical Instrumentation Engineers Vol. 6072, pp. 461-469, Feb, 2006.
8. Atul Puri, Xuemin Chen, Ajay Luthra: Video coding using the H.264/MPEG-4 AVC compresion standard, Signal Processing: Image Communication Vol. 19, No. 99, pp. 793-849, 2004.
9. ITU-T Recommendation H.264 Advanced video coding for generic audiovisual services, March, 2005.
10. Iain E. G. Richardson: H.264 and MPEG-4 Video Compression: Video Coding for Next-generation Multimedia, John Wiley and Sons, Dec, 2003.
11. http://iphome.hhi.de/suehring/tml/index.htm.
12. http://developers.videolan.org/x264.html.

# Texture Synthesis Based on Minimum Energy Cut and Its Applications

Shuchang Xu, Xiuzi Ye, Yin Zhang, and Sanyuan Zhang

Department of Computer Science, Zhejiang University, China
xusc@cgimlab.cn, yxz@zju.edu.cn, yinzh@zju.edu.cn,
syzhang@zju.edu.cn

**Abstract.** In this paper, a simple but efficient texture synthesis algorithm is presented. New image is synthesized by a patch-based approach. Motivated by energy equation, the method can manipulate the overlap region perfectly. After the most reasonable cut path through overlap regions is found, satisfying resultant images whose size specified by user can be produced. As a general method, our algorithm is also applied to image composition and texture transfer— rendering a target image with given source texture image. Experiments show that our algorithm is very efficient and easy to implement....

## 1 Introduction

A common method to add realism to 3D objects or computer-generated images is texture mapping. Distortions can appear on surfaces in texture mapping [1]. Unlike texture mapping, procedure texture synthesis (PTS) can produce seamless results [2-4]. But PTS requires the user to define different parameters for different texture types (e.g. cloud, sky, fur), and this interaction may make the user feel inconvenient. Alternatively, the notation of texture synthesis, where a sample image is given to generate arbitrarily sized texture, is developed and is gaining more and more popularity in recent years. In texture synthesis, desired and tillable textures are available from a small sample image. Unfortunately, it is very difficult to develop a robust and general algorithm for texture synthesis. Here, we give a brief review on the work done in texture synthesis.

**Pixel-based texture synthesis:** Motivated by communication theory of Claude Shannon, Efros and Leung [5] proposed a non-parametric method to "grow" a texture one pixel at a time. A Markov random field (MRF) is assumed and conditional distribution of a pixel is built by performing an exhaustive search through the sample image. Also based on MRF, Wei and Levoy [6] (abbreviated as WL below) proposed optimizations to Efros's and presented an efficient algorithm using multi-resolution image pyramid. Their approach uses a tree-structured vector quantization (TSVQ) to accelerate the synthesis process, and works remarkably well for various textures. However, the WL algorithm performs poorly in some nature textures such as talus fields, leafs and blossoming flowers. Ashikhmin [7] developed a simpler straightforward algorithm that is well suited for special natural textures. The algorithm significantly reduces

Y. Zhuang et al. (Eds.): PCM 2006, LNCS 4261, pp. 518–526, 2006.
© Springer-Verlag Berlin Heidelberg 2006

search space by constraining output candidate pixels in several L-shaped neighborhoods. However, Ashikhmin algorithm doesn't work well when structure textures are considered. One common disadvantage of pixel-based texture synthesis is that the process is relatively time-consuming. Alternatively, patch-based texture synthesis can run in real-time which preserving local structures.

**Patch-based texture synthesis:** A group of Microsoft Research Asia has done lots of work on patch-based sampling [8-9]. The algorithm presented by Liang et al. [9] is very fast. It makes high-quality texture synthesis a magnitude faster than existing algorithms. Overlap region feathering then is applied to avoid mismatching across patch boundaries, but which may on the other hand result in losing some high frequency con-tents. The paper appeared in SIGGRAPH 2001, proposed by Efros and Freeman [10], introduced the image quilting concept. Their Minimal Error Boundary Cut (MEBC) can lead to good blending results between overlap regions. Compared with [9], MEBC doesn't have any acceleration optimizations. Cohen et al. [11] generated non-periodical textures with a small set of Wang Tiles. This novel algorithm allows Wang Tiles to share the efficiency of reusing sample tiles to create a large arrangement of plants. Therefore, the method can be applied to create 3D geometry textures. But Wang tiles also introduces corner problem which can't be solved.

In addition to above mentioned algorithms, Nealen [12] presented an approach that can produce high quality overlap regions while using the KNN (k-Nearest Neighborhood) data structure to save run time. Zelinka's [13] Jump Map is a good idea but difficult to implement. Besides 2-D texture synthesis, some surface texture synthesis methods [14-16] have also been developed with the extensions of pixel-based or patch-based algorithms.

In this paper, we present a novel algorithm based on energy equation to perfectly handle overlap region. It is not only easy to implement, but can produce results in real time. Most important is our general algorithm can be applied in other applications (see section 3).

## 2 The Texture Synthesis Algorithm

In this section, our texture synthesis method is described in detail. More efficient but simpler algorithm is proposed to find cut between overlap regions. Our algorithm works very well not only for texture synthesis. In section 3 we give other applications based on our minimum energy cut. We start with the energy equation which our algorithm based on.

### 2.1 The Energy Equation

Let S be a site set

$$S = \{1, \ldots, m\} \tag{1}$$

In which $1 \ldots, m$ is indices. A site can represent a point in the 2D space such as an image pixel. Sites on a lattice are considered as spatially regular. A rectangular lattice for a 2D image of size $n \times n$ can be denoted by

$$S = \{(i,j)|1 \leq i, j \leq n\} \tag{2}$$

For an $n \times n$ image, pixel $(i, j)$ can be re-indexed by $k$ where $k$ takes values in $\{1, 2,...,m\}$ with $m=n \times n$. The relationship between sites is represented by a neighborhood system:

$$N = \{N_p \mid \forall p \in S\}, \ N_p = \{q \in S \mid D(p,q) \leq r, q \neq p\} \tag{3}$$

Here function $D(.)$ denotes the Euclidean distance between pixels and $N_p$ is the set of sites neighboring to $p$. There are two common neighborhood systems: 4-neighborhood (also known as first order neighborhood system) and 8-neighborhood system (also known as second order neighborhood system). In our algorithm, however, we use only ordered 2-neighborhood system. A clique $c$ for $(S, N)$ is defined as a subset of sites in S. It is composed of single, or pair of, or triple of $N_i$, and so on. We use $C_k$ to show the collections of $k$-site clique, e.g.:

$$C_1 = \{p \mid p \in S\}, C_2 = \{\{p,q\} \mid q \in N_p, p \in S\} \tag{4}$$

Energy function can be written as a sum of clique potentials $V_c(P)$ ($P$ denotes a pixel):

$$E = \sum_{c \in C} V_c(P) \tag{5}$$

As mentioned before, we consider only $C_2$, and hence the above equation can be rewritten as (subscript of $V$ is omitted for simplicity):

$$E = \sum_{c \in C_2} V(P) \tag{6}$$

## 2.2  The Minimum Energy Cut

Let us define patch unit $B_i$ to be a squared block with a user-defined size. In each step of synthesis process, the neighboring block that will be sampled from the input texture is constrained by the overlap with existing synthesized regions. How to sew overlap regions between the new block and the existing region (denoted by $B_i^{new}$, $B_i^{old}$ respectively in figure 1(a)) is essential in the patch-based texture synthesis process. Our target is to find a cut through the overlap region, as mentioned in [10]. We define $V(P)$ in equation (6) as a penalty for a discontinuity between $p$, $q$ in the overlap region $B_i^{old}$, $B_i^{new}$ respectively (The red dashed lines in Figure 1(b) represent the penalty strength). The penalty function can be written as:

$$V(P) = L2(p,q) \mid (p \in B_i^{old}, q \in B_i^{new}, \{p,q\} \in C_2)$$
$$L2(p,q) = sqrt(\sum_{\alpha=R,G,B} (p_\alpha - q_\alpha)^2) \tag{7}$$

Here $L2(.)$ means L2 distance. A possible cut is defined by equation (8):

$$E = \begin{cases} V_{i,j} & i=0 \\ E + \min(V_{i,j-1}, V_{i,j}, V_{i,j+1}) & i>0 \end{cases} \tag{8}$$

Here, *(i, j)* denotes pixel coordinates in 2D space. We choose *Min(E)* as our vertical cut path. In figure 1(b), the black vertical line denotes a possible vertical cut. Similar process can be applied to horizontal overlaps. The 2-neighborhood system is shown by dashed line frame on top right in Figure 1 (b).

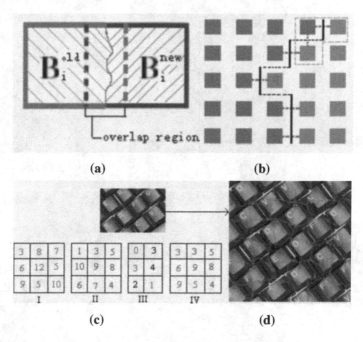

**Fig. 1.** Overlap cut based on minimum energy. (**a**) The overlap region between the new block and the existing block. (**b**) The pixel presentation of the overlap region in (a). (**c**) Demo of choosing minimum energy cut. (**d**) A resultant example. The red lines show the minimum energy cut.

The instance in Figure 1 (c) shows the process of finding the desired vertical cut. I and II represent overlap regions. III is the energy table calculated by equation (8). The red number shows the minimum energy path. IV denotes the synthesized result. The same process can be applied when horizontal cut is considered.

## 2.3 The Texture Synthesis Process

Our texture synthesis algorithm can be described as follows. First, we pick a new block from the sample texture and put it into the image to be synthesized in raster scan order. Unlike the exhausting search method used in [10], we only randomly pick

**Fig. 2.** Compare texture synthesis results produced by Efros' algorithm and by our algorithm. The left columns are the original input texture images. The middles are results produced by Efros' algorithm and right are our results.

*SelNum* (in our experiments set to be 200) blocks and choose the one who has the highest similarity with its neighbors along the overlap region. The similarity function could be L2 distance between the neighboring blocks in the overlap region. Initially, a new block is randomly selected from a sample with no constraint. We then manipulate the overlap region by finding out the cut in the overlap region, and picking an appropriate region from the new block to patch into the result image.

The above process is repeated until the resultant image with user-specified size is fully filled. In our algorithm because the texture image can be modeled as MRF [5-6], we randomly choose a limited number of blocks to be matched but perform a full search. Even without specific code optimization, the proposed algorithm can still produce high-quality resultant images with a run-time far less than [10].In Figure 2, it takes 69s,  65s,  79s to produce the middle three images respectively. Using our algorithm, only 2s, 1s, 2s are taken respectively. Based on the texture database (size  96×96)  from  following  website  http://www.vision.ee.ethz.ch/~rpaget/ pwp_texture.htm, to synthesize resultant image (size 200×200), it takes about 40s and 1.8s by [9] and our algorithm respectively. More results are listed at the end of the paper (see Figure 5).

# 3  Other Applications

## 3.1  Texture Transfer

Two input images called source texture image and target image are required to recreate the target image by replacing some high-frequency information with the source

**Fig. 3.** Examples of Texture Transfer. The left columns are source images. The middle columns are target images and the right column are resultant images.

**Fig. 4.** An example of image composition

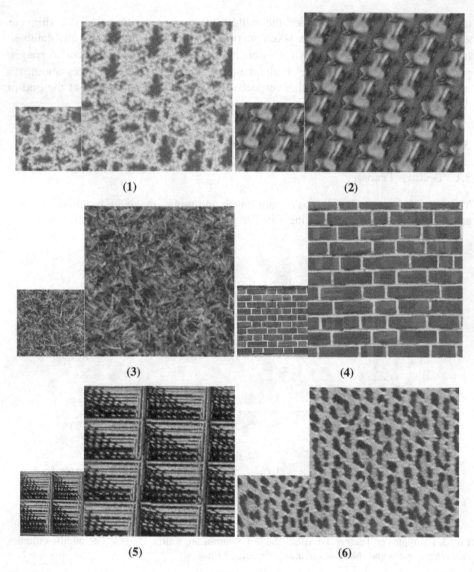

**Fig. 5.** Texture synthesis results of various kinds of images by our proposed algorithm. In every pair of images (1) ~ (6), the left image is the input sample and the right is the synthesized image. (1), (3) are stochastic textures, (4), (5) are structured textures, and (2), (6) are semi-structured textures.

texture. Therefore, the resultant image has identical size with the target image. Applying our proposed texture synthesis algorithm to texture transfer, we can obtain images similar to the target image in shape and to the source image in texture.

We extend the synthesis algorithm by adding constraints to match the corresponding intensity information in target image. Each new block is picked to meet two re-quirements: texture synthesis requirements described in the above sections and corresponding intensity requirements on the target image. So we modify our similarity function in texture synthesis algorithm using weight value $\lambda$:

$$e = \lambda M_{L2}(B_i^{old}, B_i^{new}) + (1 - \lambda)M_{lumi}(B_i^{trg}, B_i^{new}) \tag{9}$$

Here function $M$ (.) denotes L2 distance. To generate a satisfactory resultant image, we use the same strategy described in [10] and repeat the transfer algorithm several times. Figure 3 gives some texture transfer examples.

### 3.2 Image Composition

The algorithm we propose to find the most reasonable cut between overlap regions can be used to compose image. Here we demonstrate a simple example by jointing two images seamlessly.

## 4 Conclusions

In this paper we present a new algorithm for texture synthesis and extend our algorithm to texture transfer and image composition. It is shown that the cut based on minimum energy equation can remarkably eliminate the artifacts in the overlap region. Compared with existing algorithms, our algorithms are much more efficient and can create images with better quality. We intend to extend our methods to image synthesis with multi-sample inputs in the future and other concerning research fields.

**Acknowledgement.** The authors would like to thank the support from the China NSF under Grant #60473106, #60333010.

## References

1. Bruno L., Mallet J. L.: Non-distortion texture mapping for sheared triangulated meshes. In: proc of ACM SIGGRAPH, ACM Press, Orlando (1998) 343-352
2. Witkin A., Kass M.: Reaction-diffusion textures. In: Proc of ACM SIGGRAPH, ACM Press, Las Vergas (1991) 299-308
3. Perlin K.: An image synthesizer. In: Proc of ACM SIGGRAPH, ACM Press, San Francisco (1985) 287-296
4. Neyret F., Cani M.P.: Pattern-based texturing revisited. In: Proc of ACM SIGGRAPH, ACM Press, LOS Angeles (1999) 235-242
5. Efros A., Leung T.: Texture synthesis by non-parametric sampling. In: International Conference on Computer Vision, Sep, Vol. 2, (1999) 1033-1038
6. Wei L.Y., Levoy M.: Fast texture synthesis using tree-structured vector quantization. In: Proc of ACM SIGGRAPH, ACM Press, New Orleans (2000) 479-488
7. Ashikhmin M.: Synthesizing Natural Textures. Proc ACM Symposium on Interactive 3D Graphics, (2001) 217-226
8. Xu Y. Q., Guo B., Shum H. Y.: Chaos Mosaic: Fast and Memory Efficient Texture Synthesis. In: Microsoft Research Technical Report MSR-TR-2000-32, April, (2000)
9. Liang L., Liu C., Xu Y., Guo B., Shum H.-Y.: Real-time texture synthesis by patch-based sampling. In: ACM Transactions on Graphics, Vol. 20(3), (2001) 127-150

10. Efros A., Freeman W.T.: Image Quilting for texture synthesis and transfer. In: Proc of ACM SIGGRAPH, ACM Press, Los Angeles (2001) 341-346
11. Cohen M. F., Shade J., Hiller S., Deussen O.: Wang tiles for image and texture generation. In: Proceedings of ACM SIGGRAPH, ACM Press, San Diego (2003) 287-294
12. Nealen A., Alexa M.: Hybrid texture synthesis. In: Rendering Techniques 2003, 14th Eurographics Workshop on Rendering, Eurographics Association, (2003) 97-105
13. Zelinka S., Garland M.: Towards real-time texture synthesis with the jump map. In: Proceedings of the 13th Eurographics workshop on Rendering, Eurographics Association, (2002) 99-104
14. Turk G.: Texture Synthesis on Surfaces. In: Proc of ACM SIGGRAPH, ACM Press, LOS Angeles (2001) 347-354
15. Wei L.Y, Levoy M.: Texture Synthesis over Arbitrary Manifold Surfaces. In: Proc of ACM SIGGRAPH, ACM Press, LOS Angeles (2001) 355-360
16. Emil P., Adam F., Hugues H.: Lapped textures. In: Proc of ACM SIGGRAPH, ACM Press, New Orleans, (2000) 465–470

# Unifying Keywords and Visual Features Within One-Step Search for Web Image Retrieval*

Ruhan He, Hai Jin, Wenbing Tao, and Aobing Sun

Cluster and Grid Computing Lab
Huazhong University of Science and Technology, Wuhan, 430074, China
{ruhanhe, hjin, wenbingtao, absun}@hust.edu.cn

**Abstract.** The multi-modal characteristics of Web image make it possible to unify keywords and visual features for image retrieval in Web context. Most of the existing methods about the integration of these two features focus on the interactive relevance feedback technique, which needs the user's interaction (i.e. a two-step interactive search). In this paper, an approach based on association rule and clustering techniques is proposed to unify keywords and visual features in a different manner, which seamlessly implements the integration within one-step search. The proposed approach considers both *Query By Keyword* (QBK) mode and *Query By Example* (QBE) mode and need not the user's interaction. The experiment results show the proposed approach remarkably improve the retrieval performance compared with the pure search only based on keywords or visual features, and achieve a retrieval performance approximate to the two-step interactive search without requiring the user's additional interaction.

## 1 Introduction

To efficiently and effectively retrieve the images available on the Web, the multi-modal characteristics of the Web image, i.e. the textual and visual features of the Web images, bring information that are complementary and that can disambiguate each other, due to the low-level visual features addressing the more detailed perceptual aspects and high-level semantic features (which can be represented by keywords) underlying the more general conceptual aspects of visual data [1]. The integration of *text-based image retrieval* and *content-based image retrieval* techniques for Web image retrieval is an evitable trend. Neither of these two types of features is sufficient to retrieve or manage visual data in an effective or efficient way [1].

A number of approaches have been proposed to integrate keywords and visual features[2-6]. Most of them use the interactive relevance feedback technique to integrate the keywords and visual features, which needs the user's interaction and carries out the two-step search in an interactive manner. However, a recent analysis has shown that a typical user of a Web search engine uses only about two words on the average for a query and views only 1-3 results pages, without feedback to system

---

* This paper is supported by China Next Generation Internet (CNGI) project under grant No.CNGI-04-15-7A.

Y. Zhuang et al. (Eds.): PCM 2006, LNCS 4261, pp. 527–536, 2006.

[7-9]. Therefore, the approach that can improve the retrieval accuracy of a search engine without any user feedback is valuable.

In this paper, different from the relevance feedback method, a new approach is proposed to seamlessly integrate keywords and visual features. It not only improves the retrieval performance by the integration of the two features, but also satisfies most of the Web users for image search within one-step search (i.e. without any user feedback).

The remaining part of this paper is organized as follows: section 2 introduces the related works about the integration of the keywords and visual features. In section 3, we propose our approach that unifies keywords and visual features without user's interaction. The QBK and QBE mode of the proposed approach are presented in detail. In section 4, we provide experimental results that evaluate two modes of the proposed approach. Finally, we draw conclusion and give future works in section 5.

## 2  Related Works

Some representative works have been done to integrate keywords and visual features in image retrieval. The framework proposed in [2] used a semantic network and relevance feedback based on visual features to enhance keyword-based retrieval and update the association of keywords with images. In [3] and [4], *Latent Semantic Indexing* (LSI) was used to exploit the underlying semantic structure of web images, and the new hybrid query including keywords and visual features was obtained by relevance feedback. Zhou [5] applied relevance feedback based on keywords and visual features in image retrieval. Jing et al [6] integrated visual and keywords by online learning process for relevance feedback and offline learning for keyword propagation. In addition, some Web image retrieval systems, such as WebMars [10], WebSeek [11], ImageRover [12] and Cortina [13], also used the relevance feedback to integrate keywords with visual features.

It can be seen that these previous works use the interactive relevance feedback technique to integrate the keywords and visual features, which needs the user's interaction and carries out the two-step search in an interactive manner. Moreover, QBE is ignored except for [6].

The approach we propose implements the integration of keywords and visual features in a different manner, which needs not the user additional interaction. Moreover, both QBK and QBE query modes are considered.

## 3  The Proposed Approach

We use the data mining technology to construct semantic rules between keywords and visual features if they really exists strong relationship. Otherwise, based on the majority rule, clustering technology is used to obtain the visual features or keywords in QBK or QBE respectively. Therefore, new hybrid query including keywords and visual features is obtained. An overview of the approach is shown in Fig.1.

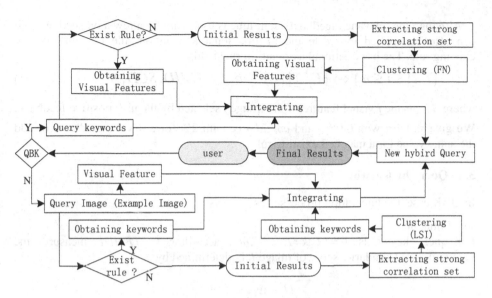

**Fig. 1.** The overview of the proposed approach

Our approach supports both QBK and QBE query scenarios. The detail steps for QBK and QBE are described at the following section 3.2 and section 3.3, respectively. In section 3.1, we simply introduce the extraction of keyword and visual features, as well as the creation of the semantic rules for the later work.

### 3.1  Keyword, Visual Feature, and Semantic Rule

The collected Web images are indexed in both keyword and visual feature spaces. The keywords are extracted by the text related to Web image, including ALT tag, image name, URL address, page title, and surrounding text. They are ranked by the *TF*IDF* measure. Two visual feature types from the MPEG-7 standard, i.e. the *edge histogram descriptor* (EHD) and the *scalable color descriptor* (SCD), are applied in a global manner to the image.

Like *Cortina* system [13], the semantic rules between text and visual features are firstly extracted based on the *frequent itemset mining* and *association rules* techniques. They are under the *support-confidence* framework and the *min_support* and *min_confidence* are 1% and 5%, respectively. Therefore, the simple mono-directional semantic association rules, which associate a single keyword with the low level visual clusters, are as following:

$$\{T_q\} \rightarrow \{C_i^f \mid 1 \le i \le n, f \in \{EHD, SCD\}\} \tag{1}$$

where $T_q$ represents the textual keyword $q$ and $C_i^f$ is the $i$-th cluster for visual feature $f$. Furthermore, other association rules are inferred as follows:

$$\{T_q\} \rightarrow \{F_i^f \mid 1 \le i \le n, f \in \{EHD, SCD\}\} \tag{2}$$

where $F_i^f$ is the centroid of the cluster $C_i^f$.

Although the relevance feedback technique is used only by a few advanced users, it can also be applied to create the bi-directional association rule or reinforce the existing rule. The bi-directional association rule is like:

$$\{T_i \mid 1 \le i \le m\} \leftrightarrow \{F_j^f \mid 1 \le j \le p, f \in \{EHD, SCD\}\} \tag{3}$$

where $F_i^f$ is the $f$ visual feature of the image $j$ selected by the user positive feedback. We give *support* with 0.05% and *confidence* with 2% for a new created rule or add the same value for a matched existing rule.

### 3.2 Query by Keyword

In QBK case, the integration process is as follows:

1) Initial query
For query keywords $T_q = \{T_k \mid k=1, \ldots, m\}$, according to *TF\*IDF* measure, the keyword-based similarity score of image $I_i$ is determined by:

$$Sim_{q,i}^T = 1 - (\frac{\sum_{k=1}^{m}(1 - w_{k,i})}{m}) , 1 \le i \le N \tag{4}$$

where $N$ is the number of initial retrieved images and $w_{k,i}$ is the rank of the keyword $T_k$ in document $j$ and $w_{k,i} = tf_{k,i} \times idf_k / \max_{j \le N}(idf_j)$. The $tf_{k,i}$ is the normalized frequency of keyword $T_k$ in document $i$ and $idf_j$ is the inverse document frequency for keyword $T_j$. Thus we get an initial ordered query result $I(Q) = \{I_i \mid 1 \le i \le N\}$.
2) Obtain the visual features
For $T_q$, if there exists the association rule similar to the equation (2), the visual features are $V_q = \{F_i^f\}$. If there does not exist the association rule, a strong relation set of $I(Q)$ is defined as $I_s(Q) = \{I_j \mid j=1,\ldots,M, M \le min(N, 60)$ and $Sim_{q,j}^T > H_s\}$, where $H_s$ is set 0.7 by default. Based on the $L_1$ distance, images in $I_s(Q)$ are clustered by the *farthest neighbor* method. The clustering process repeats merging clusters until all distances between them are more than $H_d$ or the image number in the maximal cluster is more than $H_n$, where $H_d$ and $H_n$ are set 0.08 and 8 by default in our system. After clustering, the centroid of the largest cluster is the visual feature $V_q$.
3) Search again by the new hybrid query
To unify $T_q$ and $V_q$ for search again, the visual similarity score for $V_q$ is determined by the linear combination of the $L_1$ distance of EHD and SCD descriptor:

$$Sim_{q,i}^V = 1 - D_{q,i}^V \tag{5}$$

where $D_{q,i}^V$ is the normalized $L_1$ distance between visual feature $V_q$ and $V_i$.

Therefore, from the equation (4) and (5), the combined similarity is calculated:

$$Sim_{q,i}^{ALL} = \alpha Sim_{q,i}^T + (1-\alpha)Sim_{q,i}^V , 0 \le \alpha \le 1 \tag{6}$$

where $\alpha$ is a factor and set 0.7 based on experience in QBK scenario.

### 3.3 Query by Example

Similar to QBK scenario, the integration process in QBE scenario is as follows:

1) Initial query

For a query example image $V_q$, the visual similarity score of image $I_i$ is $Sim_{q,i}^V$ by equation (5) and an initial ordered query result $I(Q)=\{I_i|1\leq i\leq N\}$ is obtained, where $N$ is the number of initial retrieved images.

2) Obtain the keywords

Like in the QBK scenario, if there exists the association rule, we use the bi-directional association rules as equation (3) to automatically get the keywords $T_q$ for $V_q$. If there does not exist the association rule, a strong relation set of $I(Q)$ for $V_q$ is defined $I_s(Q)=\{I_j|j=1,...,M, M<=min(N,60)$ and $Sim_{q,j}^V >H_v\}$, where $H_v$ is set 0.8 by default.

A term-image matrix $A$ is constructed from the set $I_s(Q)$. Then, we use the LSI method to get the semantic similarity between the images of set $I_s(Q)$.

First, a *Singular Value Decomposition* (SVD) is performed on the term-image matrix $A$. The result comprises three matrices, namely, $U$, $\Sigma$, and $V$, where $A = U\Sigma V^T$. A rank-$k$ approximation, $A_k$ is defined by $A_k=U_k\Sigma_kV_k^T$, where $k=4$. We define two matrices: $A_k=[a_{i,j}]_{m\times n}$ and $B=[b_{i,j}]_{n\times n} =A_k^T\times A_k =V_k\times\Sigma_k^2\times V_k^T$. The correlation between the keyword $T_i$ and image $I_j$ is $a_{i,j}$. The similarity between image $I_i$ and $I_j$ is $b_{i,j}$. Based on the similarity $b_{i,j}$, the semantic distance of image $I_i$ and $I_j$ is defined as $D_{i,j}^T =1-((b_{i,j} -\mu)/\sigma+1)/2$, where $\mu$ and $\sigma$ are the mean and variance of matrix $B$, respectively. The images in $I_s(Q)$ are clustered by the *farthest neighbor* method. The clustering processes repeats merging clusters until all distances between them are more than $H_d$ or the image number in the maximal cluster is more than $H_n$, where $H_d$ and $H_n$ are set 0.08 and 8 by default in our system.

After clustering, we select the largest cluster $C_m$ and get the keywords $S=\{T_i|i=1, ... ,n\}$, the top $k$ representative keywords are selected according to the order of $S(T_i)= \sum_{I_j\in C_m}a_{i,j}$ . Then, we get the most related keywords $T_q=\{T_i|i=1, ... ,k\}$.

3) Search again by new query

Similar to QBK case, the combined similarity is calculated by equation (6) to unify $T_q$ and $V_q$ for search again, but the factor $\alpha$ in equation (6) is 0.5 here based on experience.

## 4 Performance Evaluation

### 4.1 Experiment Setup

We evaluate the proposed approach in a prototype of web image retrieval system, called *VAST* (VisuAl & SemanTic image search) [14], with a database of about 100,000 Web images collected from the domain ".*edu.cn*", starting from the website *http://www.hust.edu.cn/*.

To evaluate the effectiveness of the proposed approach in retrieval performance, we adopt the measurement in literature [13], which is suitable for web system. This measurement defines the precision $P=C/A$, where $C$ is the number of the relevant retrieved images (which is judged by user) and $A$ is the scope of judgment. The measurement evaluates the precision of the top-$A$ returned images. The relevance feedback method used in the following for comparison is same as WebMars [10] system with one iteration for feedback.

In QBK scenario, the set of query keywords is {*bridge, car, cloud, dog, flower, grass, the Great Wall, lake*}, while in QBE scenario, the set of query example images is shown as Fig.2. In addition, there are association rules in knowledge base for keywords {*cloud, flower, grass, lake*} and images {*cloud.jpg, flow.jpg, grass.jpg, lake.jpg*}.

**Fig. 2.** Query example images for QBE case

### 4.2  Comparison and Analysis

Based on the aforementioned data preparation, the proposed approach is evaluated as follows. First, the integration in QBK case is evaluated. The average precision $P$ versus scope $A$ graph is shown in Fig.3. It is observed that, the retrieval precision of QBK-P is remarkably better than that of QBK-T, and is close to that of QBK-RF, which suggests the effectiveness of QBK-P.

Second, the integration in QBE case is evaluated similar to QBK case. It can be seen from Fig.4 that, QBE-P improves the precision in contrast to QBE-V and achieves precision approximate to QBE-RF with different scopes.

From Fig.3 and Fig.4, we can see two facts. One is that the combination of keyword and visual features is necessary because it is more effective than using each feature alone. The other is that the proposed scheme for integrating the keywords and visual features does not reduce much the retrieval accuracy comparing the scheme of integration by interactive feedback. The two facts suggest the effectiveness of the proposed approach.

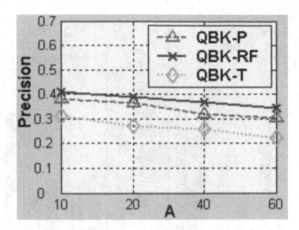

**Fig. 3.** Precision for different QBK modes. QBK-P (the proposed approach in QBK), QBK-RF (QBK with relevance feedback), QBK-T (text-only QBK).

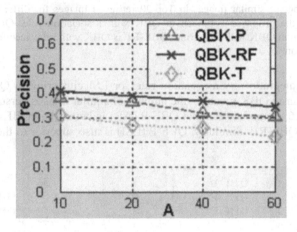

**Fig. 4.** Precision for different QBE modes. QBE-P (the proposed approach in QBE ), QBE-RF (QBE with relevance feedback), QBE-V (pure QBE).

Third, the integration by association rules or clustering algorithm in QBK scenario is evaluated at the scope of 20. The number of similar images versus query keyword graph is shown in Fig.5. It can be seen that QBK-P (AR) is superior to QBK-T, and is almost equal to QBK-RF. At the same time, QBK-P (CL) is better than QBK-T and close to QBK-RF for most of times. One exception is the keyword "dog", in which QBK-T is better than both QBK-P (CL) and QBK-RF. It maybe the keyword "dog" is enough to describe the user needed image or the selected visual features extraction method is not suitable for the type of "dog" images. In addition, from Fig.5, QBK-P (AR) is closer to QBK-RF than QBK-P (CL), which suggests the association rules are more trustable than the clustering algorithm.

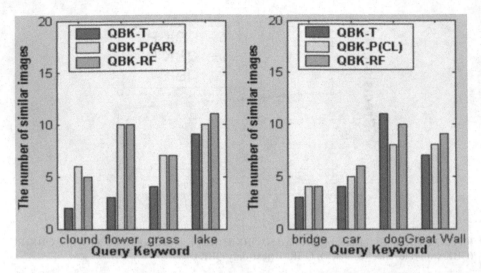

**Fig. 5.** The number of similar images in Top-20 retrieved images for different QBK modes. QBK-P (AR) is the proposed approach in QBK with association rule, QBK-P(CL) is the proposed approach in QBK with clustering, QBK-RF is QBK with relevance feedback, QBK-T is QBK with text only.

Finally, the integration by association rules or LSI clustering in QBE scenario is evaluated. Similar to QBK scenario, the number of similar images versus query images is shown in Fig.6. It can be seen that QBE-P (AR) is better than QBE-V and is close, even exceed to QBE-RF. Similarly, QBE-P (LSI) is also superior to the QBE-V, even

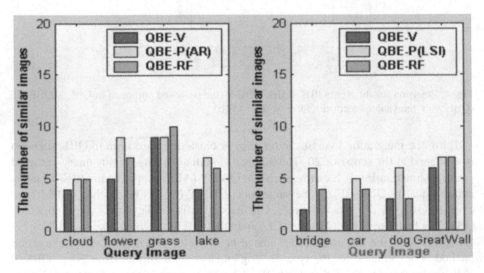

**Fig. 6.** The Number of Similar Images in Top-20 Retrieved Images for different QBE modes. QBE-P (AR) is the proposed approach in QBE with association rule, QBE-P (LSI) is the proposed approach in QBE with LSI clustering, QBE-RF is QBE with relevance feedback, QBE-V is the pure QBE.

QBE-RF. The proposed approach performs excellent in QBE scenario. The reason may be that the proposed approach introduces the semantic concepts to the submitted query, while both QBE-V and QBE-RF consider the visual features only. It is noticed that the second step search of QBE-RF is also based on the visual features of user selected images.

The above evaluations illustrate that, compared with pure QBK or pure QBE, the proposed approach is remarkably superior in retrieval precision, while compared with the relevance feedback method, it achieves approximate retrieval precision. However, our approach does not need user additional interaction and thus satisfies the behavior of most of Web users.

We notice that our approach is effective in most of the case, but in a few worst cases, it is even inferior to the pure QBK or pure QBE. It is possibly due to the initial retrieval result is too sparse, we expect to adjust the threshold $H_d$ and $H_n$ to make the query regress to the pure QBK or pure QBE in these worst case in the future work. In addition, the proposed approach is slower than the pure QBK and QBE. But the delayed time is very little because the target collection for clustering is small, the clustering algorithm is simple and the dimension of the LSI is also relatively small.

## 5  Conclusions and Future Work

We present an approach for Web image retrieval by unifying the keyword and visual feature within one-step search, which is a different manner compared with the common relevance feedback method. Although the integration of keyword and visual feature is novel, this paper emphasizes the successful use of one-step search to both improve image retrieval performance and satisfy most of the Web users' need. Two classical query scenarios, i.e. QBK and QBE, are considered. In the QBK scenario, association rules or clustering algorithm are applied to obtain the visual features corresponding to the query keywords. In the QBE scenario, association rules or LSI technique are used to get the keywords related to the query image. The experiments results show the effectiveness of the proposed approach.

While the results are still far from satisfactory, the integration within one-step search is promising for Web image retrieval. Some future works of this approach include investigating the effect of different clustering algorithms and exploring better combination strategies than a simple linear combination of the textual and visual features, as well as mining the association between high concepts and low-level visual features.

## References

[1]  A. W. M. Smeulders, M. Worring, S. Santini, A. Gupta, and R. Jain, "Content-Based Image Retrieval at the End of the Early Years", *IEEE Transactions on Pattern Analysis and Machine Intelligence*, Vol.22, No.12, 2000, pp.1349-1380

[2]  Y. Lu, C. Hu, X. Zhu, H. Zhang, and Q. Yang, "A unified framework for semantics and feature based relevance feedback in image retrieval systems", *Proc. ACM Int. Multimedia Conf.*, 2000, pp.31-38

[3]  R. Zhao and W. I. Grosky, "Narrowing the semantic gap - Improved text-based web document retrieval using visual features", *IEEE Trans. Multimedia*, Vol.4, No.1, 2002, pp.189-200

[4]  W. I. Grosky and R. Zhao, "Improved Text-Based Web Document Retrieval Using Visual Features", *Proceedings of The First International Conference on Integration of Multimedia Contents*, Gwangju, Korea, 2001

[5]  X. S. Zhou and T. S. Huang, "Unifying keywords and visual contents in image retrieval", *IEEE Trans. Multimedia*, Vol.4, No. 1, 2002, pp.23-33

[6]  F. Jing, M. Li, H. Zhang, and B. Zhang, "A Unified Framework for Image Retrieval Using Keyword and Visual Features", *IEEE Transaction on Image Processing*, Vol.14, No.7, 2005, pp.979-989

[7]  B. Jansen, A. Spink, J. Bateman, and T. Saracevic, "Real Life Information Retrieval: A Study Of User Queries On The Web", *SIGIR FORUM Spring 98*, Vol.32, No.1, 1998, pp.5-17

[8]  C. Silverstein, M. Henzinger, H. Marais, and M. Moricz, "Analysis of a Very Large Web Search Engine Query Log", *SIGIR FORUM Fall 99*, Vol.33, No.1, 1999, pp.6-12

[9]  M. W. Berry, P.Wang, and Y. Yang, "Mining longitudinal Web queries: Trends and patterns", *J. Amer. Soc. Inform. Sci. Tech.*, Vol. 54, 2003, pp.743-758

[10]  M. Ortega-Binderberger, S. Mehrotra, K. Chakrabarti, and K. Porkaew, "WebMARS: A multimedia search engine", *Proceedings of the SPIE Electronic Imaging 2000: Internet Imaging*, San Jose, CA, 2000

[11]  J. R. Smith and S. F. Chang, "Visually searching the Web for content", *IEEE Multimedia*, Vol.4, No.3, 1997, pp.12-20

[12]  S. Sclaroff, M. LaCascia, S. Sethi, and L. Taycher, "Unifying textual and visual cues for content-based image retrieval on the World Wide Web", *Computer Vision and Image Understanding*, Vol.75, 1999, pp.86-98

[13]  T. Quack, U. Monich, L. Thiele, and B. S. Manjunath, "Cortina: A System for Large scale, Content-based Web Image Retrieval", *Proc. of MM'04*, New York, USA, 2004

[14]  H. Jin, R. He, Z. Liao, W. Tao, and Q. Zhang, "A Flexible and Extensible Framework for Web Image Retrieval System", *Proceedings of International Conference on Internet and Web Applications and Services (ICIW 2006)*, Guadeloupe, French Caribbean, 2006

# Dynamic Bandwidth Allocation for Stored Video Under Renegotiation Frequency Constraint

Myeong-jin Lee[1], Kook-yeol Yoo[2], and Dong-jun Lee[3]

[1] Dept. of Electrical Engineering, Kyungsung University, Busan, 608-736, Korea
mjlee@ieee.org
[2] School of EECS, Yeungnam University, Gyeongsanbuk-do, 712-749, Korea
kyoo@yu.ac.kr
[3] School of Electronics, Telecomm. and Computer Engineering, Hankuk Aviation
University, Gyeonggi, 412-791, Korea
ldj@hau.ac.kr

**Abstract.** In this paper, a dynamic bandwidth allocation algorithm is proposed for stored video transmission with renegotiation interval constraint. It is to handle the problem of short renegotiation intervals in optimal smoothing algorithms[4,5], which may increase the renegotiation cost or cause renegotiation failures. Based on the transmission rate bounds derived from buffer constraints, a transmission segment is calculated based on the optimal smoothing algorithm[5]. If the length of the segment is less than the minimum renegotiation interval, it is merged to the neighboring segment considering the relation between the transmission rates of neighboring segments by allowing encoder buffer underflows. From the simulation results, the proposed algorithm is shown to keep the renegotiation intervals larger than the minimum and the renegotiation cost is greatly reduced with slight decrease in the channel utilization.

## 1 Introduction

Most of current and future video applications may require the playback of stored video over a high-speed network. Also, with the development of quality of service(QoS) provisioning technologies, there exist increasing demand of high-quality video services for stored video contents, e.g. high quality video-on-demand or broadcasting over premium network services. For high-quality or constant-quality video services, there have been studies on the dynamic bandwidth allocation methods by considering the inherent multiple-time-scale burstiness of VBR video[1,2,4,5,6]. Most of the researches have focused on the traffic smoothing of pre-recorded VBR video traffic for bandwidth renegotiation, where the transmission scheduler knows the bit-rates of all frames[4,5].

Jiang[4] proposed a dynamic programming algorithm to compute the optimal renegotiation schedule given the relative cost of renegotiation and client buffer size. But, the algorithm has high peak rates and frequent renegotiations. Salehi[5] proposed an optimal smoothing algorithm to minimize the rate variability and evaluated the impact of optimal smoothing on the network resources needed

Y. Zhuang et al. (Eds.): PCM 2006, LNCS 4261, pp. 537–546, 2006.

for video transport under renegotiated constant-bit-rate(RCBR) service; it will be referred by Minimum Variance Smoothing(MVS) algorithm hereafter. However, the optimal algorithms cannot handle the problem of short renegotiation intervals. Lee[6] showed that more than half of the bandwidth renegotiations in MVS occurred with renegotiation intervals less than 20 frame times. The bandwidth renegotiation request rightly after the recent renegotiation may not be accepted by networks. Because the renegotiation failure may cause delay violations of video frames or the re-scheduling of the remaining video traffic, it should be prevented by the transmission scheduler by generating transmission schedule conforming to the service policies of networks.

In this paper, we address the problem of dynamic bandwidth renegotiation for stored video applications. Firstly, we state the problem of short renegotiation intervals in the optimal smoothing algorithm[5]. Secondly, we propose a transmission rate decision algorithm for stored video which can keep renegotiation intervals larger than the minimum required. It first finds a transmission segment by the optimal smoothing algorithm, then the segment of short interval is merged into the neighboring segment by considering the relation between the rates of the segments and by allowing encoder buffer underflows. The rest of this paper is organized as follows. In section 2, we discuss the transmission rate constraint for stored video and state the problem of short renegotiation intervals in the optimal smoothing algorithm. In section 3, we propose a transmission rate decision algorithm for stored video which can keep the renegotiation interval larger than the minimum required. In section 4 and 5, we present simulation results and conclusion, respectively.

## 2   Dynamic Bandwidth Allocation for Stored Video

### 2.1   Transmission Rate Constraint for Video Communication Systems

In lossless video transmission systems, encoder and decoder buffers should not have underflow and overflow states[1]. Encoder and decoder buffer overflows can be prevented by placing sufficiently large buffers. Also, encoder buffer underflow does not have any serious effect on the operation of video communication systems except low channel utilization. However, decoder buffer underflow is the condition that sufficient video frame data has not arrived by its decoding time, which may stop the decoding process. Thus, it should be prevented by controlling encoding process or by renegotiating new transmission rate.

The encoder buffer occupancy at the $n^{th}$ frame time is given by

$$B^e(n) = B^e(n-1) + e(n) - r(n),\qquad(1)$$

where $e(n)$ and $r(n)$ are the encoder output rate and the effective transmission rate, respectively.[1] The decoder buffer occupancy is also given by

---

[1] If the transmission rate is set to $R$, the effective transmission rate is given by $r(n) = \min\{B^e(n-1) + e(n), R\}$.

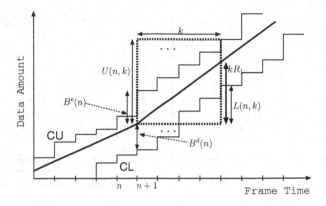

**Fig. 1.** Constraints on the accumulated transmission rate for stored video

$$B^d(n) = \begin{cases} \sum_{j=1}^{n} r(j) - \sum_{j=1}^{n-D} e(j), & \text{if } n \geq D \\ \sum_{j=1}^{n} r(j), & \text{if } n < D \end{cases} \tag{2}$$

where $D$ is the end-to-end delay through the video transmission system.

If the transmission rate is changed to a new value $R_1$ at the $(n+1)^{th}$ frame time and it is assumed that no encoder and decoder buffer overflow and underflow occurs[2], the accumulated transmission rate $kR_1$ during $k$ frame intervals from the $(n+1)^{th}$ frame time has the constraint which is given by

$$L(n, k) \leq kR_1 \leq U(n, k), \tag{3}$$

where $L(n, k)$ and $U(n, k)$ are the lower and the upper bounds of the accumulated transmission rate and are given by Eq. 4 and Eq. 5.

$$L(n, k) = \max \left\{ B^e(n) + \sum_{i=n+1}^{n+k} e(i) - B^e, \sum_{i=1}^{n-D+k} e(i) - \sum_{i=1}^{n} r(i) \right\}. \tag{4}$$

$$U(n, k) = \min \left\{ B^e(n) + \sum_{i=n+1}^{n+k} e(i), \sum_{i=1}^{n-D+k} e(i) - \sum_{i=1}^{n} r(i) + B^d \right\}. \tag{5}$$

Fig. 1 illustrates the constraints of the accumulated transmission rate during $k$ frame interval from the $(n+1)^{th}$ frame time. The upper and the lower lines, $CU$ and $CL$, represent the cumulative data transmitted by the encoder and consumed by the decoder, respectively. They do not include the data which may be lost in encoder buffer and decoder buffer overflow states, and the transmission rate should be decided not to have data loss due to buffer overflow. The lower line $CL(n)$ and the upper line $CU(n)$ can be represented by $CL(n) = L(0, n)$ and $CU(n) = U(0, n)$, respectively.

---

[2] The encoder and decoder buffer constraints are given by $0 \leq B^e(n) \leq B^e$ and $0 \leq B^d(n) \leq B^d, \forall n$, where $B^e$ and $B^d$ are encoder and decoder buffer sizes, respectively.

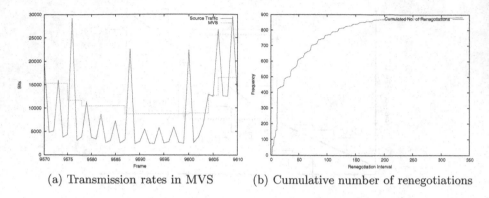

(a) Transmission rates in MVS          (b) Cumulative number of renegotiations

**Fig. 2.** Problem of short renegotiation intervals in the MVS algorithm. 'bond', $D = 10$.

## 2.2   Problem in Video Traffic Smoothing Algorithms for Dynamic Bandwidth Allocation

There have been so many studies on the traffic smoothing for live and stored video transmission [4,5,6]. The smoothed rates are all constrained by the lower and the upper bounds of the accumulated transmission rate to meet the end-to-end delay constraint of video transmission systems. Difference exists in the objectives of optimization. Jiang[4] focused on the cost of renegotiation and Salehi[5] on the rate variability. However, they did not consider or handle the problem of short renegotiation intervals, which is the main focus of our research.

Salehi[5] proposed an optimal smoothing algorithm(MVS) to minimize the rate variability and evaluated the impact of optimal smoothing on the network resources needed for video transport under RCBR service. Fig. 2 shows the transmission scheduling result of the 'bond' trace. We used the MPEG traces in [3] for our simulation. Fig. 2(a) shows that MVS requests new transmission rates only to catch out the changes in the source traffic with the objective of minimum rate variability. Fig. 2(b) shows the cumulative number of renegotiations for the renegotiation interval. Half of the total renegotiations occurred with the renegotiation interval less than 12 frames. Such a short renegotiation interval increases the number of renegotiations and the corresponding renegotiation cost. Also, there may exist minimum renegotiation interval allowed by networks which depends on the service policies of networks. If enough time has not elapsed after the recent renegotiation, new renegotiation request by the transmission scheduler may not be accepted by networks. Because renegotiation request failures may cause delay violations of video frames or the re-scheduling of the remaining video traffic, it is needed to develop a transmission algorithm to meet the condition of minimum renegotiation interval while minimizing the rate variability and the channel resources used.

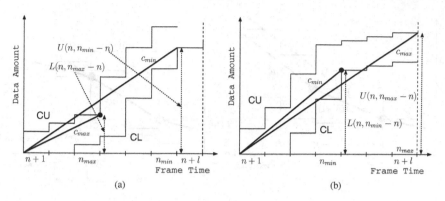

**Fig. 3.** Traffic smoothing variables for transmission rate change points. (a) Transmission rate increase(convex point). (b) Transmission rate decrease(concave point).

## 3   Traffic Smoothing Algorithm for Stored Video Under Renegotiation Interval Constraint

### 3.1   Description of Variables for Video Traffic Smoothing

Before describing the proposed algorithm, we define the following variables shown in Fig. 3 for increasing and decreasing cases of transmission rate.[3] :

– $c_{max}$ : the maximum transmission rate at which the encoder may transmit over a given interval $[n, n + l]$ without decoder buffer overflow and encoder buffer underflow.

$$c_{max} = \min_{1 \le k \le l} \frac{U(n, k)}{k} \tag{6}$$

– $n_{max}$ : the latest time at which the decoder buffer is full or the encoder buffer is empty when the encoder transmits at $c_{max}$ over $[n, n + l]$.

$$n_{max} = n + \max_{1 \le k \le l} \left\{ k : \frac{U(n, k)}{k} = c_{max} \right\}. \tag{7}$$

– $c_{min}$ : the minimum transmission rate at which the encoder may transmit over a given interval $[n, n + l]$ without decoder buffer underflow and encoder buffer overflow.

$$c_{min} = \max_{1 \le k \le l} \frac{L(n, k)}{k} \tag{8}$$

– $n_{min}$ : the latest time at which the decoder buffer is empty or the encoder buffer is full when the encoder transmits at $c_{min}$ over $[n, n + l]$.

$$n_{min} = n + \max_{1 \le k \le l} \left\{ k : \frac{L(n, k)}{k} = c_{min} \right\}. \tag{9}$$

---

[3] By referring the MVS algorithm[5], the change point of transmission rate is said to be *convex*(or *concave*), if the rate is increased(or decreased).

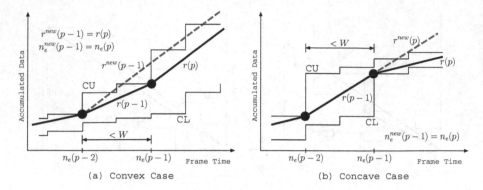

(a) Convex Case                (b) Concave Case

**Fig. 4.** Merging a short transmission segment with the neighboring segment to meet the minimum renegotiation interval

The parameter $l$ represents the range for the calculation of the variables and could be increased to the end of the video sequence.

### 3.2  Traffic Smoothing Algorithm Under Renegotiation Interval Constraint

The proposed traffic smoothing algorithm is based on the optimal MVS algorithm [5]. Based on the transmission rate bounds derived in section 2, a transmission segment is calculated using the MVS algorithm. To solve the problem of short renegotiation intervals in MVS, if the length of the segment is less than the minimum renegotiation interval, then it checks the relations of the transmission rates between the previous and the current transmission segments, and determines whether to merge the segments into one or not. To simplify the problem, the encoder and the decoder buffer sizes are assumed to be large enough to completely remove out buffer overflows. The assumption is feasible due to the low cost of memory for high-quality video transmission systems.

Fig. 4 shows the possible two cases of transmission segment merging. Fig. 4(a) shows the case of segment merging for increasing rate. While decoder buffer underflow should be prevented completely for high quality video services, encoder buffer underflow does not cause any effect on the operation of video transmission systems except for the decrease in the channel utilization. Thus, by allowing encoder buffer underflow, the two transmission segments can be merged into one. Fig. 4(b) shows the case of segment merging for decreasing rate. Encoder buffer underflow is also allowed to merge two segments into one.

Fig. 5 is the pseudo-code of the proposed algorithm. In the double loops, the optimal smoothing algorithm extracts the $p^{th}$ transmission segment by calculating the transmission rate($r(p)$) and the end point of the segment($n_e(p)$)(line 5~11). If the length of the $(p-1)^{th}$ transmission segment is less than the minimum renegotiation interval($W$) required, the segment is merged with the neighboring $p^{th}$ segment according to the rate increasing and decreasing conditions(line 12~17).

```
 1 FUNCTION VTS_MRI
 2     p = 0
 3     WHILE n ≤ N
 4        WHILE k ≤ N − n
 5           Update c_max, c_min, n_max, n_min over [n, n + k]
 6           IF c_min > c_max
 7              IF n_min < n_max
 8                 r(p) = c_min, n_e(p) = n_min
 9              ELSE IF n_min ≥ n_max
10                 r(p) = c_max, n_e(p) = n_max
11              END IF
12              IF n_e(p − 1) − n_e(p − 2) < W
13                 IF r(p) > r(p − 1)
14                    r(p − 1) = r(p), n_e(p − 1) = n_e(p)
15                 ELSE IF r(p) < r(p − 1)
16                    n_e(p − 1) = n_e(p)
17                 END IF
18              ELSE
19                 p = p + 1
20              END IF
21              BREAK
22           END IF
23           k = k + 1
24        END WHILE
25        n = n_e(p)
26     END WHILE
27 END FUNCTION
```

**Fig. 5.** Video traffic smoothing algorithm guaranteeing the minimum renegotiation interval(VTS_MRI)

## 4    Experimental Results

In this section, we show some experimental results for the proposed traffic smoothing algorithm. We used four MPEG video traces in [3]. They are 40,000 frames long each and the GOP pattern is IBBPBBPBBPBB. Because we focus on the performance of video traffic smoothing algorithms under renegotiation interval constraint, we assumed that the renegotiation request is always accepted by networks if the renegotiation interval is larger than the minimum presented by networks.

For performance comparison, the MVS algorithm for offline optimal smoothing [5] and a simple window-based smoothing(WBS) algorithm is implemented. The WBS algorithm sets the window size as the minimum renegotiation interval($W$) and periodically determines the transmission rate by dividing the average rate over the window by the channel utilization factor($U$).

Fig. 6 shows the traffic smoothing results of the MVS and the proposed algorithms. There exist renegotiation requests with short intervals in the MVS algorithm, which cannot be accepted by networks. The proposed algorithm shows

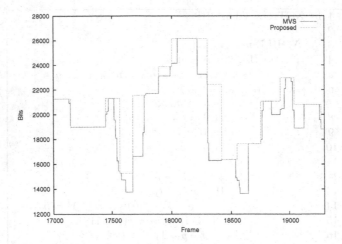

**Fig. 6.** Transmission scheduling of the MVS and the proposed algorithms. 'bond', $W = 100$, $D = 10$.

the same scheduled results as MVS for the segments larger than the minimum renegotiation interval. Also, it can completely remove out short segments by merging them appropriately.

Fig. 7 shows the cumulative renegotiation frequency for the renegotiation interval. For the same parameter set of the end-to-end delay and the minimum renegotiation interval, the proposed algorithm is shown to greatly reduce the number of renegotiations by completely removing short transmission segments less than the minimum required. But, in the MVS algorithm, more than half of the renegotiations occur at the intervals less than the minimum.

Fig. 8 shows the average renegotiation interval, number of decoder buffer underflows, and the channel utilization for the proposed, the MVS and the WOS algorithms. Channel utilization factors of 1.0, 0.9, and 0.7 are used to compare the performance for different minimum renegotiation intervals. The channel utilization of the proposed algorithm decreases as the minimum renegotiation interval increases. It is because that the proposed algorithm merges short segments into larger one by allowing encoder buffer underflows. Larger minimum renegotiation interval means that more number of short segments are merged into one, which causes the channel utilization to be decreased. The average renegotiation interval of the proposed is larger than the MVS and the WBS algorithms, which means that the renegotiation cost is the minimum among the algorithms. Also, there is no decoder buffer underflow in the proposed while the WBS algorithm has a lot of decoder buffer underflows. Though the MVS algorithm does not have decoder buffer underflow, there may exist renegotiation failures and the renegotiation cost is much higher than the proposed. Because the WBS algorithm does not consider the end-to-end delay constraint, it cannot completely remove the decoder buffer underflows even for low channel utilizations.

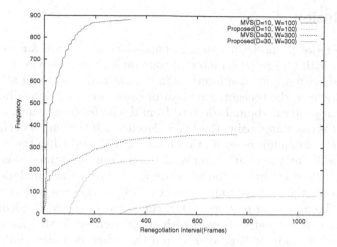

**Fig. 7.** Comparison of renegotiation cost between the MVS and the proposed algorithms

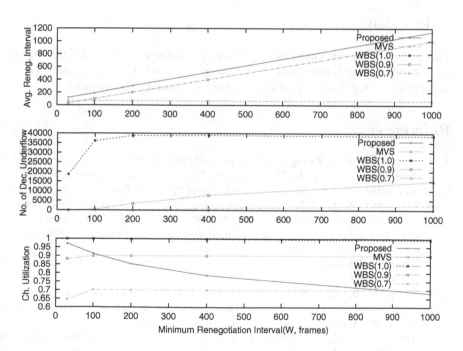

**Fig. 8.** Traffic Smoothing Performance. 'lambs' trace, $D = 20$.

In summary, the proposed traffic smoothing algorithm can completely remove renegotiations with short renegotiation intervals less than the minimum required at the expense of channel utilization. With the slight decrease in the channel utilization, the proposed algorithm can decrease the number of renegotiations greatly without decoder buffer underflows.

# 5  Conclusion

In this paper, we proposed a dynamic bandwidth allocation for stored video transmission with renegotiation interval constraint. It is designed to handle the problem of short renegotiation intervals in the optimal smoothing algorithm[5], which may increase the renegotiation cost or cause renegotiation failures. Based on the transmission rate bounds derived from the buffer constraints, a transmission segment is calculated using the MVS algorithm. If the length of the segment is less than the minimum renegotiation interval, it is merged to the neighboring segment considering the relation between the transmission rates of neighboring segments by allowing encoder buffer underflows. From the simulation results, it is shown that the proposed algorithm could keep the renegotiation intervals larger than the minimum required. Also, compared to the MVS algorithm, the renegotiation cost is greatly reduced with slight decrease in the channel utilization. For further study, it is needed to find the reference renegotiation interval which minimizes the overall cost for renegotiation and bandwidth allocated.

## Acknowledgements

This research was supported by the Ministry of Information and Communication, Korea, under the Information Technology Research Center support program supervised by the Institute of Information Technology Assessment.

## References

1. T. V. Lakshman, A. Ortega, and A. R. Reibman, *VBR Video: Tradeoffs and Potentials*, Proceedings of the IEEE, Vol. 86, No. 5, pp. 952-973, May. 1998.
2. M. Grossglauser, et al, *RCBR : A Simple and Efficient Service for Multiple Time-Scale Traffic*, IEEE/ACM Trans. Networking, Vol. 5, No. 6, pp. 741-755, 1997.
3. O. Rose, *Statistical Properties of MPEG Video Traffic and Their Impact on Traffic Modeling in ATM Systems*, 20^{th} Conference on Local Computer Networks, Oct. 1995.
4. Z. Jiang, L. Kleinrock, *A General Optimal Video Smoothing Algorithm*, IEEE Infocomm, 1998.
5. J. Salehi, Z. Zhang, J. Kurose and D. Towsley, *Supporting stored video: reducing rate variability and End-to-End Resource requirements through optimal smoothing*, IEEE/ACM Trans. Networking, Vol. 6, No. 4, Aug. 1998.
6. M. Lee, *Video Traffic Prediction Based on Source Information and Preventive Channel Rate Decision for RCBR*, IEEE Trans. Broadcasting, Vol. 52, No. 2, pp. 173-183, June 2006.

# Online Selection of Discriminative Features Using Bayes Error Rate for Visual Tracking

Dawei Liang[1], Qingming Huang[2], Wen Gao[3], and Hongxun Yao[1]

[1] School of Computer Science and Technology, Harbin Institute of Technology,
Harbin, 150001, China
[2] Graduate School of Chinese Academy of Sciences, Beijing, 100080, China
[3] School of Electronic Engineering and Computer Science, Peking University,
Beijing, 100871, China
{dwliang, qmhuang, wgao}@jdl.ac.cn, yhx@vilab.hit.edu.cn

**Abstract.** Online feature selection using Bayes error rate is proposed to address visual tracking problem, where the appearances of the tracked object and scene background change during tracking. Given likelihood functions of the object and background with respect to a feature, Bayes error rate is a natural way to evaluate discriminating power of the feature. From previous frame, object and background pixels are sampled to estimate likelihood functions of each color feature in the form of histogram. Then, all features are ranked according to their Bayes error rate. And the top $N$ features with the smallest Bayes error rate are selected to generate a weight map for current frame, where mean shift is employed to find the local mode, and hence, the location of the object. Experimental results on real image sequences demonstrate the effectiveness of the proposed approach.

**Keywords:** Feature Selection, Bayes Error Rate, Visual Tracking.

## 1 Introduction

Visual tracking has been extensively studied in the past decade, since it is a crucial step in many computer vision tasks, such as visual surveillance [1], human computer interaction [2], robotics [3], etc. Tracking algorithms can be roughly classified into two major groups, namely, stochastic filtering algorithms (e.g. particle filter [4]) and deterministic location algorithms (e.g. mean shift [5]). In particle filter, object tracking is modeled as a Bayesian filtering problem and a set of weighted samples is used to approximate and propagate the filtering distribution. Particle filter has been proved to be robust to background clutter and partial occlusion. In mean shift, object is represented by kernel-weighted histogram and is located by maximizing similarity function derived from object histogram and target image histogram. Mean shift tracking is computationally efficient and robust to object deformation.

Although these methods have achieved some success, visual tracking is still a challenging topic, especially when the appearances of the tracked object and

Y. Zhuang et al. (Eds.): PCM 2006, LNCS 4261, pp. 547–555, 2006.

scene background change during tracking. Recently, treating tracking as a binary classification problem has gained much attention. Collins and Liu [6] propose to online select discriminative tracking features from color feature spaces. Features are ranked according to variance ratio and the top $N$ features are selected with each producing a weight map. Then, mean shift is used to locate object on each weight map. Finally, object is located by selecting the median location. Nguyen and Smeulders [7] treat tracking as a texture discrimination problem, where Gabor filter is used to obtain texture representations of the object and background. Wang et al. [8] select a subset of Harr-like features using particle filter and use them to construct a binary classifier. Avidan [9] propose to combine weak classifiers trained and updated online into a strong classifier using AdaBoost and use the strong classifier to label pixels in the next frame. Hence, a confidence map is generated and the local mode is found by mean shift. These methods have achieved some success when the appearances of the object and background change during tracking.

Motivated by Collins and Liu's work, online feature selection using Bayes error rate is proposed in this paper. As opposed to variance ratio, we choose to use Bayes error rate to select features. Given likelihood functions of the object and background with respect to a feature, Bayes error rate is a natural way to evaluate discriminating power of the feature. Firstly, for each feature Bayes error rate is estimated from object and background pixels sampled in previous frame. Secondly, all features are ranked according to their Bayes error rate, and the top $N$ features with the smallest Bayes error rate are selected. Thirdly, the log likelihood ratio is back-projected to produce a weight map for each selected feature in current frame, and then all weight maps are combined to generate a final weight map. Finally, mean shift is employed to find the local mode, and hence, the object location in the weight map.

The rest of the paper is organized as follows. Section 2 introduces the proposed approach in detail. Section 3 provides some experimental results on real image sequences. Section 4 concludes the paper.

## 2   The Proposed Approach

In this section, we first review the estimation of Bayes error rate, then describe the feature selection method and weight map generation, and finally present the tracking algorithm.

### 2.1   Bayes Error Rate

Let's consider pattern classification involving two classes $\omega_1$ and $\omega_2$. Given one dimensional feature $x$, we want to determine from which class the feature is drawn from. According to the Bayes decision theory, if a posteriori probabilities $P(\omega_1|x)$ and $P(\omega_2|x)$ are known and if $P(\omega_1|x) > P(\omega_2|x)$, $x$ belongs to $\omega_1$, and vice versa. According to the Bayes rule

$$P(\omega_i|x) = \frac{p(x|\omega_i)P(\omega_i)}{p(x)} \quad i = 1, 2. \tag{1}$$

Substituting (1) into the inequality, the decision rule can be rewritten as: if $p(x|\omega_1)P(\omega_1) > p(x|\omega_2)P(\omega_2)$, $x$ belongs to $\omega_1$, and vice versa. Providing that the feature space is partitioned into two disjoint intervals $R_1$ and $R_2$ by Bayes optimal decision boundary with $R_1$ corresponding to the interval where $p(x|\omega_1)$ $P(\omega_1) > p(x|\omega_2)P(\omega_2)$ and with $R_2$ corresponding to the one where $p(x|\omega_2)P(\omega_2)$ $> p(x|\omega_1)P(\omega_1)$, Bayes error rate is as follows [10]:

$$P(e) = \int_{R_2} p(x|\omega_1)P(\omega_1)dx + \int_{R_1} p(x|\omega_2)P(\omega_2)dx \qquad (2)$$

In general, the analysis of Bayes error rate is very complicated. However, by using histogram approximation to the unknown likelihood functions and averaging appropriately, it is possible to estimate Bayes error rate. Suppose that the two classes are equally likely a priori and the feature space can be partitioned into $m$ disjoint bins $B_1, \ldots, B_m$. Let $p_i = P(x \in B_i|\omega_1)$ and $q_i = P(x \in B_i|\omega_2)$. Since we have assumed that $P(\omega_1) = P(\omega_2) = 1/2$, the vectors $\mathbf{p} = (p_1, \ldots, p_m)^T$ and $\mathbf{q} = (q_1, \ldots, q_m)^T$ fully determine the probability structure of the problem. If $x$ falls in $B_i$, the Bayes decision rule is to decide $\omega_1$ if $p_i > q_i$ and vice versa. The resulting Bayes error rate is given by [10]

$$P(e|\mathbf{p}, \mathbf{q}) = \frac{1}{2} \sum_{i=1}^{m} \min(p_i, q_i) \qquad (3)$$

## 2.2   Feature Selection

Feature selection is commonly used to discard irrelevant or redundant features in pattern classification, where an optimal subset of features is chosen from a feature set according to a certain criterion. As for tracking task considered here, the criterion involves evaluation of discriminating power of the selected feature subset. The size of the optimal subset is usually unknown; hence, for a feature set containing $n$ elements, the size of search space is $2^n - 1$, which is a very large number for the feature set considered here. For online application, speed is favored over optimality; hence, like [6], we rank the features first and then select $N$ top-ranked features.

To begin with, the feature set should be provided. Color has been proved to be successful in visual tracking [5], [6], [11], [12]. Here, we adopt color feature set proposed in [6]. Color feature set consists of linear combinations of RGB channels, and the coefficients of RGB are given by 3-tuple set $\{(c_1, c_2, c_3)^T | c_1, c_2, c_3 \in \{-2, -1, 0, 1, 2\}\}$. There are totally 125 features in the feature set; however, by discarding coefficients where $(c'_1, c'_2, c'_3)^T = k(c_1, c_2, c_3)^T$ and by disallowing $(c_1, c_2, c_3)^T = (0, 0, 0)^T$, only 49 features are left. Hereinafter, we use this feature set for feature selection and denote it as $F$. All features are scaled into the range from 0 to 255 and further uniformly partitioned into histograms with $2^b$ ($b$ is the bit number of resolution) bins to defeat the curse of dimensionality that occurs while estimating feature distribution with small sample size.

The center-surround approach [6] as shown in Fig. 1a is used to sample pixels from the object and background. Pixels within a rectangle of size $h \times w$ pixels which covers the object denote samples from the object, while pixels within a surrounding ring of width $0.5 \times \max(h, w)$ pixels denote samples from background. Given a feature $f \in F$, denote $p_f$ as the feature histogram of the object, and denote $q_f$ as the feature histogram of background. Both histograms are normalized to make them probability distributions.

(a)                                              (b)

**Fig. 1.** Illustration of center-surround approach. (a) the original image. (b) corresponding weight map.

We use formula (3) to evaluate a feature's discriminating power and rank all the features according to Bayes error rate. The top $N$ features with the smallest Bayes error rate are selected. Intuitively, smaller Bayes error rate demonstrates better discriminating power. Compared with the two-class variance ratio [6], Bayes error rate has several advantages. First, Bayes error rate can deal with arbitrary probability distributions. While variance ratio fails to work when the feature distributions are multi-modal. To tackle this problem, the authors [6] propose to apply variance ratio to the log likelihood ratio of feature distributions of the object and background. Second, given the feature distributions, Bayes error rate is easy to compute. only several comparison and addition operations are needed. Third, Bayes error rate has a good theoretical foundation as pointed out in section 2.1.

### 2.3   Weight Map Generation

Each feature $f \in F$ corresponds to a weight map of the same size as current image $I$. We denote the weight map as $W_f$. Each pixel value $W_f(u)$ is computed by first projecting feature value $(I(u), f)$ ($I(u)$ denotes RGB vector of pixel u, and $(\cdot)$ denotes inner product of two vectors) to obtain the bin index $n$, and then deriving the pixel value from the log likelihood ratio

$$W_f(u) = \max\left(-\delta, \min\left(\delta, \log\left(\frac{p_f(n) + \epsilon}{q_f(n) + \epsilon}\right)\right)\right), \tag{4}$$

where $\epsilon$ ($\epsilon = 0.001$ in our experiment) is a small positive value to avoid dividing by zero or taking log of zero, and $\delta=7$ in our experiment. The final weight map is computed as the weighted sum of weight maps corresponding to the top $N$ selected features. Denote $\tilde{\omega}_f = 1 - P(e|\mathrm{p}_f, \mathrm{q}_f)$ and $\omega_f = \tilde{\omega}_f / \sum_f \tilde{\omega}_f$ (hence, $\sum_f \omega_f = 1$), the final weight map as shown in Fig. 1b is

$$W(\mathrm{u}) = \sum_f \omega_f W_f(\mathrm{u}). \tag{5}$$

### 2.4   Tracking Algorithm

We summarize the tracking algorithm in Algorithm 1. From previous frame, object and background pixels are sampled, given the tracked object location. For each feature in the feature set, object and background feature histograms are constructed and Bayes error rate is computed. All features are ranked according to their Bayes error rate and the top $N$ features with the smallest Bayes error rate are selected to generate the final weight map. Then, mean shift is employed to locate the object in current frame.

Online feature selection also introduces model drift problem [6], [13], which builds up as misclassified background pixels begin to pollute the object feature histogram, resulting in further misclassification and final tracking failure. To avoid this problem, we simply average current object feature histogram and the one in the first frame.

---

**Algorithm 1.** The proposed tracking algorithm

---

**Input:** Video frames $I_1, I_2, \ldots, I_T$, and initial object location.
**Output:** Object locations of $I_2, \ldots, I_T$.

**Initialization:** Generate object feature histogram $\tilde{\mathrm{p}}_f$ for each feature $f \in F$;

For $t = 2, \ldots, T$
1. Sample object and background pixels from $I_{t-1}$;
2. For each feature $f \in F$
   (a) Compute object histogram $\mathrm{p}_f$ and background histogram $\mathrm{q}_f$;
   (b) Compute Bayes error rate $P(e|\mathrm{p}_f, \mathrm{q}_f) = \frac{1}{2} \sum_{i=1}^{m} \min(\mathrm{p}_f(i), \mathrm{q}_f(i))$;
3. Rank all the features $f \in F$ according to Bayes error rate and select the top $N$ features with the smallest Bayes error rate;
4. For each selected feature $f$
   (a) Assign $(\tilde{\mathrm{p}}_f + \mathrm{p}_f)/2$ to $\mathrm{p}_f$;
   (b) Compute bin index $n$ of feature value $(I_t(\mathrm{u}), f)$;
   (c) Compute weight map $W_f(\mathrm{u}) = \max(-\delta, \min(\delta, \log(\frac{\mathrm{p}_f(n)+\epsilon}{\mathrm{q}_f(n)+\epsilon})))$;
   (d) Compute $\tilde{\omega}_f = 1 - P(e|\mathrm{p}_f, \mathrm{q}_f)$;
5. Compute final weight map $W(\mathrm{u}) = \sum_f \omega_f W_f(\mathrm{u})$, where $\omega_f = \tilde{\omega}_f / \sum_f \tilde{\omega}_f$ ;
6. Locate object in $W(\mathrm{u})$ using mean shift;

---

# 3  Experiment

We perform experiments on several image sequences, which are publicly available [14]. In all experiments, the number of histogram bins is set to be 32, and the top 3 features are selected. The selected image sequences are very challenging, where the appearances of the objects and background change almost all the time. The initial location of the object can be determined by object detection algorithm. Here, the tracker is initialized manually, since the focus of this paper is object tracking. To enhance the efficiency of tracking, feature selection is performed every ten frames in the following experiments.

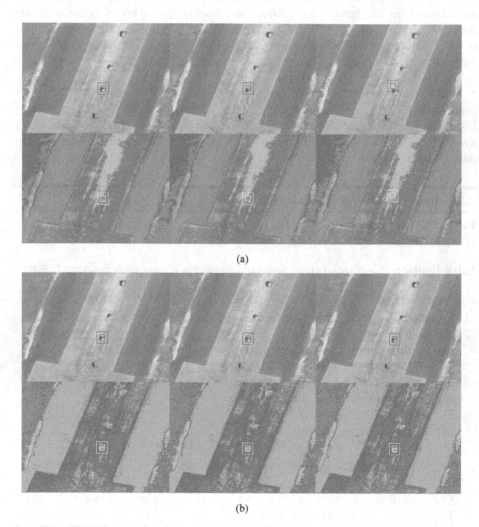

(a)

(b)

**Fig. 2.** (a) Tracking results without online feature selection. (b) Tracking results with online feature selection. Bottom rows in (a) and (b) correspond to weight maps.

The first experiment compares tracking results between trackers with online feature selection and without online feature selection as shown in Fig. 2. The tracking results of Fig. 2a are obtained by selecting features in the first frame only and keeping them unchanged during tracking. As can be seen in Fig. 2 that without online feature selection the tracker finally drifts from the car when surrounding background shows similar appearance to the car, while the proposed tracker successfully locks on the car via online selection of discriminative features. The bottom rows in Fig. 2a and Fig. 2b are the corresponding weight maps. Note that these weight maps are presented here just for the purpose of visualization. In practice, only the weight map of a small local region needs to be computed, which makes the proposed tracking algorithm computationally efficient.

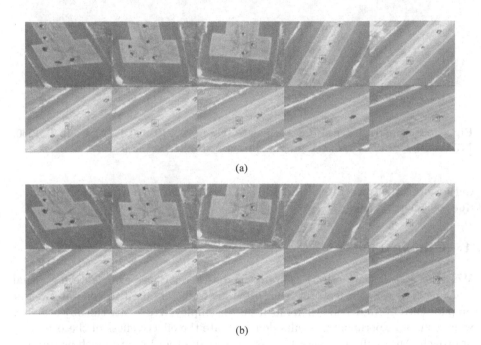

(a)

(b)

**Fig. 3.** Tracking results on *egtest01* sequence (Frames 0, 200, 400, 600, 800, 1000, 1200, 1400, 1600, and 1820). (a) The proposed tracker. (b) Tracker in [6].

The second experiment compares tracking results between the proposed tracker and the tracker in [6] which is implemented by the authors themselves [14]. Note that both trackers are initialized with the same conditions (i.e., location, the number of histogram bins, and the number of selected features) and also the tracker in [6] performs feature selection every ten frames. Two image sequences with each having nearly 2, 000 images are used. The proposed tracker successfully tracks the cars in both sequences from beginning to end. The tracking results are shown in Fig. 3 and Fig. 4. As can be seen from Fig. 3, the proposed tracker achieves comparable results with the tracker in [6]. In Fig. 4 we can see that the proposed tracker

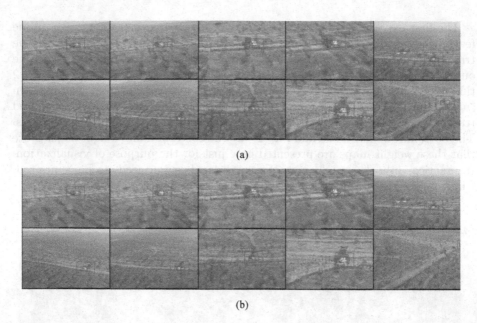

(a)

(b)

**Fig. 4.** Tracking results on *redteam* sequence (Frames 0, 210, 420, 630, 840, 1050, 1260, 1470, 1680, and 1917). (a) The proposed tracker. (b) Tracker in [6].

outperforms the tracker in [6]. Actually, it loses the car from frame 1886 probably due to camera zooming.

## 4    Conclusion

We propose a feature selection approach based on Bayes error rate for visual tracking. The selected features from previous frame are used to generate weight map for current frame, and then mean shift is employed to locate the object in the weight map. Experimental results demonstrate the effectiveness of the proposed approach. Although only color features are used, other features such as texture, edge, and motion, also can be applied as long as they can be represented by histograms.

**Acknowledgments.** This work is partly supported by NEC Research China, "Science 100 Plan" of Chinese Academy of Sciences, and the Natural Science Foundation of Beijing, China (4063041).

## References

1. Stauffer, C., Grimson, W.: Adaptive background mixture models for real-time tracking. In: Proceedings of IEEE Computer Society Conference on Computer Vision and Pattern Recognition. Volume 2. (1999) 246–252

2. Bradski, G.: Real time face and object tracking as a component of a perceptual user interface. In: Proceedings of IEEE Workshop on Applications of Computer Vision. (1998) 214–219

3. Papanikolopoulos, N., Khosla, P., Kanade, T.: Visual tracking of a moving target by a camera mounted on a robot: a combination of control and vision. IEEE Transactions on Robotics and Automation **9** (1993) 14–35

4. Isard, M., Blake, A.: Condensation–conditional density propagation for visual tracking. International Journal of Computer Vision **29** (1998) 5–28

5. Comaniciu, D., Ramesh, V., Meer, P.: Kernel-based object tracking. IEEE Transactions on Pattern Analysis and Machine Intelligence **25** (2003) 564–577

6. Collins, R., Liu, Y.: On-line selection of discriminative tracking features. In: Proceedings of Ninth IEEE International Conference on Computer Vision. Volume 1. (2003) 346–352

7. Nguyen, H., Smeulders, A.: Tracking aspects of the foreground against the background. In: Proceedings of European Conference on Computer Vision. Volume 2. (2004) 446–456

8. Wang, J., Chen, X., Gao, W.: Online selecting discriminative tracking features using particle filter. In: Proceedings of IEEE Computer Society Conference on Computer Vision and Pattern Recognition. Volume 2. (2005) 1037–1042

9. Avidan, S.: Ensemble tracking. In: Proceedings of IEEE Computer Society Conference on Computer Vision and Pattern Recognition. Volume 2. (2005) 494–501

10. Duda, R., Hart, P., Stork, D.: Pattern Classification, 2nd edition. New York: Wiley-Interscience (2001)

11. Perez, P., Hue, C., Vermaak, J., Gangnet, M.: Color-based probabilistic tracking. In: Proceedings of European Conference on Computer Vision, Lecture Notes in Computer Science. Volume 2350. (2002) 661–675

12. Zivkovic, Z., Krose, B.: An em-like algorithm for color-histogram-based object tracking. In: Proceedings of the IEEE Computer Society Conference on Computer Vision and Pattern Recognition. Volume 1. (2004) 798–803

13. Matthews, I., Ishikawa, T., Baker, S.: The template update problem. IEEE Transactions on Pattern Analysis and Machine Intelligence **26** (2004) 810–815

14. Collins, R., Zhou, X., Teh, S.: An open source tracking testbed and evaluation web site. In: Proceedings of IEEE International Workshop on Performance Evaluation of Tracking and Surveillance. (2005)

# Interactive Knowledge Integration in 3D Cloth Animation with Intelligent Learning System

Chen Yujun, Wang Jiaxin, Yang Zehong, and Song Yixu

State Key Laboratory of Intelligent Technology and System,
Department of Computer Science and Technology
Tsinghua University, Beijing, China, 100084
chenyujun03@mails.tsinghua.edu.cn,
wjx@mail.tsinghua.edu.cn,
zehong@263.net, songyixu@sohu.com

**Abstract.** In this paper, we focus on the parameter identification problem, one of the most essential problems in the 3D cloth animation created by multimedia software. We present a novel interactive parameter identification framework which integrates the industry knowledge. The essential of this paper is that we design a hybrid intelligent learning system using statistical analysis of kawabata evaluation system(KES) data from fabric industry database, fuzzy system and radial basis function(RBF) neural networks. By adopting our method the 3D cloth animator can interactively identify the parameters of cloth simulation with subjective linguistic variables while in the past decades it is very difficult for cloth animators to tune the parameters. We solve the 3D cloth parameter problem using the intelligent knowledge integration method for the first time in the multimedia and graphics research area and our method is applied to the most popular 3D tool Maya. The experimental results illustrate the practicability and expansibility of this method.

**Keywords:** Interactive parameter identification, 3D Cloth Animation, Kawabata evaluation system, Fuzzy system, RBF Neural network.

## 1 Introduction

In recent years 3D simulations and animations, especially the cloth animations are becoming a potential research area in computer graphics and virtual reality [6]. Some of the professional softwares have also provided the cloth simulation model, such as Maya. One of the most essential problems in cloth animation is how to use knowledge to identify the parameters of the cloth and make the simulation and animation vivid and natural. These animations are difficult to tune due to so many parameters that must be adjusted to achieve the look of a particular fabric and the lack of fabric knowledge makes the problem a difficult one. In the actual animation production, such as in the 3D animation software Maya , this problem becomes more sensitive and important to the animators. This paper focuses on this important practical problem to the animators and developers of the multimedia tool.

Y. Zhuang et al. (Eds.): PCM 2006, LNCS 4261, pp. 556–563, 2006.

Cloth animation researches have got the public concerns since Terzopoulos [6] did the pioneer work in 1987. Parameter identification is an important aspect of the 3D cloth animation which highly influence the vision effects. Recently some researchers carried out some studies about parameter identification. Bhat [2] uses simulated annealing to estimate the spring constants in a cloth mesh, using video of real cloth as their reference for comparison. Bianchi[3] uses a genetic algorithm to identify spring constants as well as mesh topology in a volumetric mass-spring system. While such methods work well in the specific domain, they are computationally expensive and their reference learning data are synthetic. Besides, their works are not interactive to the animator which means that they only identify some specific parameters and models. Moreover, very few of these papers have validated their techniques on experts' knowledge and real data. Therefore in this paper, we exert our utmost to derive a general method which can combine the fabric industry data and integrate the knowledge beneath these data together with representing the knowledge into practical implementation in Maya by using the intelligent learning system.

The contribution of this paper is that we solve the parameter identification problem of 3D software using intelligent method for the first time. The animator of Maya can easily identify the parameters of the animation with interactive user interface and retrain the RBF neural network to update the model. We apply this knowledge integration to the practical software Maya and get the experimental results that can testify the practicability by the 3D graphical cloth animation. It is valuable for the practical animation production and multimedia software development.

## 2 Knowledge Integration Framework

We divide our interactive knowledge integration framework into three parts: data analysis of the KES fabric database data [1], knowledge integration based on fuzzy system and RBF neural network, and the knowledge representation in the cloth animation in Maya by means of parameter variety. The whole structure of our interactive knowledge integration framework in cloth simulation is show in figure 1. In the following parts we will describe the details of each module.

The input of our framework is the KES data from web database, and then the data are analysis by the statistic analysis module using main factor analysis and other statistic method. After finding the relationship between the fabric data, we obtain the fuzzy rules and build the original fuzzy system to represent the relationship between fabric knowledge and actual animation parameters. In order to make the method more expansible and efficient, we combine the RBF neural network to the framework. The initial learning data of the neural network are obtained from the fuzzy system which integrates the industry knowledge. In the application stage, the users input the subjective linguistic variables to the system and the RBF neural network computes the parameters of the 3D cloth animation and the parameters can reflect the knowledge of fabric industry.

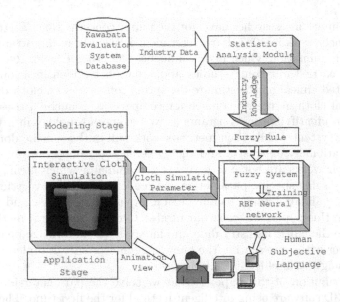

**Fig. 1.** Framework structure of interactive knowledge integration

# 3   Relationship Analysis of the KES Data

Kawabata evaluation system is a standard set of fabric measuring equipments that can measure the bending, shearing and tensile properties of cloth. The equipment measures what force or moment as is required to deform a fabric sample of standard size and shape, and produces plots of force or moment as a function of measured geometric deformation and it can measure 16 parameters that reflect the deformations. First of all, we acquire the data from a fabric database in [1]. We analysis the data using statistic methods, for example, the relativity of the 185 data. The KES parameters and their meanings are illustrated in table 1:

**Table 1.** Statistic Data of Kawabata Evaluation System Parameters

| Symbol | Description | Symbol | Description |
|--------|-------------|--------|-------------|
| $B$ | Bending rigidity (gf.$cm^2$/cm) | $2HB$ | Hysteresis of bending moment (gf.cm/cm) |
| $MIU$ | Mean frictional coefficient | $MMD$ | Deviation of frictional coefficient |
| $SMD$ | Surface roughness (Micron) | $G$ | Shearing rigidity (gf/cm.degree) |
| $2HG$ | Hysteresis of shear force at $0.5°$ (gf/cm) | $2HG5$ | Hysteresis of shear force at $5°$ (gf/cm) |
| $LT$ | Linearity of tensile curve | $WT$ | Tensile energy (gf.cm/$cm^2$) |
| $RT$ | Tensile resilience (%) | $LC$ | Linearity of Compression thickness curve |
| $WC$ | Compressional energy (gf.cm/$cm^2$) | $RC$ | Compressional resilience (%) |
| $T$ | fabric thickness (mm) | $W$ | fabric weight (gr/$m^2$) |

From these KES data, we can then calculate other statistic. In the fabric industry the style of a fabric is also determined using the quantitative analysis. The industry experts measures the style including stiffness, smoothness and fullness which related to the human intuition. In Kawabata evaluation system, the style of the fabric is computed by the performance value mentioned above using linear regression function. The equation of the style is

$$Y = C_0 + \sum_{i=1}^{16} C_i X_i \tag{1}$$

where $C_0$ and $C_i$ is the constant gained from the experts knowledge of style such as stiffness, smoothness and fullness. $X_i$ is the standardization of the 16 parameters.

$$X_i = \frac{x_i - \bar{x}_i}{\sigma_i} \tag{2}$$

where $\bar{x}_i$ is the mean value of the parameters described in table 1, $\sigma_i$ is the standard deviation of the parameters. After obtaining the KES data, the most important thing is to find the relationship between the parameters, in purpose of mapping the experts knowledge to the cloth simulation system using the most related parameters.

In order to find the relation between the parameters and get the main factors that can be mapped to the cloth animation, we adopt the correlation analysis and the regression analysis. Figure 2 shows the correlation coefficient of the KES parameters. Figure 3 is the diagram of $B$ and $2HB$ and indicates that $B$ and $2HB$ has a close relationship such as linear relation.

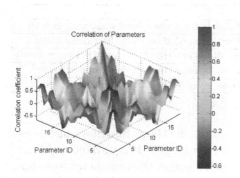
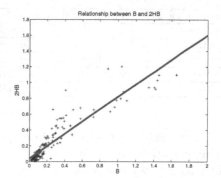

**Fig. 2.** Relationship between the Parameters using the correlation analysis

**Fig. 3.** Relationship between the KES Parameters B and 2HB using linear regression analysis

Using these analysis, we can find out the main factors that related to the expert knowledge of stiffness, smoothness and fullness using regression function. Through our analysis we find that bend, stretch, shear and friction influence these human intuition of cloth animation. Therefore we can use the expert knowledge and the cloth animation data to build the fuzzy system.

# 4  Integration Using Fuzzy System and RBF Neural Network

## 4.1  Construction of Fuzzy System

The input of the fuzzy system $X$ is the animator's subjective variables: *stiffness, smoothness, fullness*, which are converted to the fuzzy variables. The output of the fuzzy system is the cloth simulation parameters $Y$: *Bend Resistance, Stretch Resistance, Shear Resistance, Friction, Thickness, Density, Static Friction, Dynamic Friction.* Fuzzy logic includes 3 steps: fuzzifier, fuzzy inference and defuzzifier[4]. In fuzzy inference, we use the Mamdani method [5] for calculating the output inferred by a set of $m$ fuzzy rules as follows:

*If U  is $B_i$  then V  is $D_i$*

where the $B_i$ and $D_i$ are the fuzzy subsets of the universes of the input $X$ and the output $Y$, and U and V are fuzzy variables corresponding to $X$ and $Y$, respectively. These fuzzy rules are extracted from the KES data and the relationship between KES data and experts' style. The detail of the fuzzy system can be found in [5].

The fuzzy system used for the initialization of the physical model parameters describes the relations between vague knowledge of the cloth object. For example "very hard," "middle stiff", "soft" can be used to describe the stiffness of a cloth. The details of the fuzzy system can be seen in the reference. Some sample rules are described in Table2.

**Table 2.** Sample rules of cloth parameter identification

| Input Linguistic | Output Parameter | Rule |
| --- | --- | --- |
| Stiffness | bend resistance | if stiffness is hard then bend resistance is high |
| Stiffness | cloth friction | if stiffness is hard then cloth friction is small |
| smoothness | cloth friction | if smoothness is hard then cloth friction is small |
| fullness | cloth friction | if fullness is large then cloth friction is large |
| fullness | density | if fullness is large then density is large |

The membership function in this paper adopts the Gauss function which is used in many statistics applications. The last step of using the fuzzy system to identify the parameters is the scale translation, which changes the parameter from fuzzy system ranging from 0 to 1 to the real parameter scale in the cloth simulation.

## 4.2  RBF Neural Network

Although the fuzzy system can compute the parameter output, the fuzzy system is fixed and can not be adjusted during the application process. An RBF network is a type of feed forward neural network that learns using a supervised training technique. It has been shown that RBF networks are able to approximate any reasonable continuous function mapping with a satisfactory level of accuracy.

Thus the RBF neural network has the ability to replace the fuzzy system and reflect the affiliation between the input and the output.

RBF neural networks consist of three layers: the input layer, the hidden layer and the output layer. The input layer collects the input information and formulates the input vector. The hidden layer consists of L hidden nodes, which apply nonlinear transformations of the input vector. The output layer is the liner mapping to the final output. A typical node in the hidden layer is described by a basis function. For instance the number $j$ hidden node is often defined by a Gaussian exponential function as follows:

$$\alpha_i(x) = exp(-\frac{\|x - c_i\|^2}{\sigma_i^2}) \tag{3}$$

Where $\sigma_j$ denotes the width of number $j$ hidden node and $\| x - c_i \|$ is the Euclidean norm of the distance between the input and the neuron center $c_j$. The network output $Y$ is formed by a linearly weighted sum of the number of basis functions in the hidden layer. The output nodes value can be calculated as follows:

$$y(i) = \sum_{j=1}^{m} w_{ji}\alpha_j(x); i = 1, 2, \ldots, r \tag{4}$$

where $m$ presents the number of the hidden layer neuron and $r$ is the number of the output neuron. $w_{ji}$ stands for the weight from the number $i$ hidden layer neuron to the number $j$ output layer neuron. In this structure only the neurons whose centers are close to the input pattern will produce nonzero activation values to the input stimulus for a given input pattern. Thus the learning algorithm of RBF network could be extremely fast. As the other neural network, the RBF network has two operating modes: training and testing. The training methods had been widely researched in the recent years. The training data in this paper is the data from the fuzzy system. The RBF weights parameters can be adjust along the descent gradient direction.

$$w_{ij}(l+1) = w_{ij}(l) - \eta_1 \frac{\partial(RMS)}{\partial(w)} = w_{ij}(l) + \eta_1 [y_i^d - y_i(l)]\alpha_j(x)/\alpha^T(x)\alpha(x) \tag{5}$$

Where $RMS$ is the root mean squared error as the error function and $\eta_1$ is the learning rate, $y_i^d$ is the ideal output of node $i$. After the parameters of the neural network are learned it is easy to calculate the result of a new input. Moreover, the animation user can adjust the RBF neural network by adding the new train data in order to make the model more adaptive and interactive.

## 5    Experimental Results

In order to testify our framework, we give the human subjective knowledge and get the parameters of the cloth animation and then animate the cloth using the different parameters computed by the framework in Maya.

The human subjective knowledge is quantitatively combined in the three linguistic variables: stiffness, smoothness and fullness. The linguistic variables are quantified to $[0 \ldots 1]$. 0 means it is less stiff, smooth and full, while 1 means it is more stiff, smooth and full. Table 3 gives 4 examples of the animator demand. Animation of example1 and example2 are carried out for comparison.

**Table 3.** Sample Results of the fuzzy system parameter identification

| Symbol | Input/Output | Example1 | Example2 | Example3 | Example4 |
|---|---|---|---|---|---|
| *Stiffness* | input | 0.322 | 0.805 | 0.96 | 0.572 |
| *Smoothness* | input | 0.455 | 0.856 | 0.995 | 0.569 |
| *Fullness* | input | 0.358 | 0.748 | 0.752 | 0.495 |
| *BendResistance* | output | 50.0372 | 63.9718 | 78.5359 | 52.7307 |
| *StrechResistance* | output | 109.6961 | 137.1609 | 161.3248 | 115.6874 |
| *ShearResistance* | output | 107.6837 | 139.6328 | 163.1226 | 116.4126 |
| *Density* | output | 0.0054 | 0.0061 | 0.0061 | 0.0055 |
| *Friction* | output | 0.3543 | 0.2783 | 0.2266 | 0.3491 |
| *StaticFriction* | output | 0.4505 | 0.3618 | 0.3016 | 0.4489 |
| *DynamicFriction* | output | 0.4006 | 0.2941 | 0.222 | 0.3987 |

Figure 4 is the comparison between data example exmaple1 and exmaple2 in table 3. Both of the animations use the same 3D physical model in Maya, but they use different parameters derived from the framework of this paper. The graphics in the first line uses exmaple1 parameters which input variables mean the animator wants to make the cloth animation a little softer, smoother and less fullness than exmaple2 parameters in the second line of figure 4.

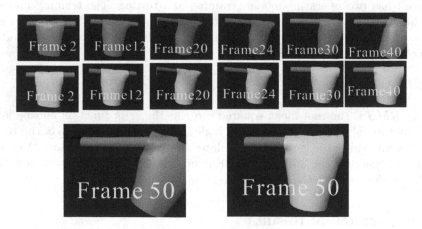

**Fig. 4.** Cloth simulation comparison result between exmaple1 and exmaple2.Both of the animation use the same 3D physical model in Maya, but they use different parameters derived from the framework of this paper. The graphics in the first line uses exmaple1 parameters which input variables mean the animator wants to make the cloth animation a little softer, smoother and less fullness than exmaple2 parameters in the second line.

We compare the same frame of these two animation and the results of the two animation illustrate the effect of the different parameters which embody the human knowledge. The model of the animation is a cloth in a rotate pillar which rotate at frame 10 and gradually rotate back. In figure 4, at the beginning of the animations the two animation result is basically similar, but as the pillar rotates the first line animation slide to the end of the pillar because it is smoother than the second line. Frame 50 obviously exhibits this difference. If we take a close look at each animation, we can also find that the first line animation wafts while second line animation does not because the second line is harder. Therefore, we can draw the conclusion that the knowledge have been integrated in the fuzzy system and RBF neural network. Besides, it can be represented by the cloth animation. The results verify the practicability of this method.

## 6 Conclusion

We have attempted to propose a novel interactive knowledge integration framework in the cloth animation using statistic analysis to find the knowledge in industry fabric KES data, the fuzzy system to represent the knowledge in cloth animation and the RBF neural network to learn and adjust the model in terms of the urgent problem of parameter identification. From the experiment results we can draw the conclusion that KES data is a potential industry data set for 3D cloth animation because it reflects the physical parameters of the cloth. Besides, it is worthful to investigate the method to apply the knowledge in more general way especially in the multimedia software. The framework proposed in this paper solves the problem in a new prospect and gets excellent result. Based on this framework some further research can be carried out as to find more congruous human liturgistic variables for different application.

## References

1. Ayse G. : An online fabric database to link fabric drape and end-use properties. Louisiana State University and Agricultural and Mechanical College. Master Thesis, (2004)
2. Bhat K., Twigg C., HodginssJ etc. : Estimating cloth simulation parameters from video. ACM Siggraph/ Eurographics Symposium on Computer Animation. (2003)
3. Bianchi G., Solenthaler B., Harders M. : Simultaneous topology and stiffness identification for mass-spring models based on fem reference deformations. LNCS, Int .Conf. on Medical Image Computing and Computer Assisted Intervention. (2004) 293–301
4. Chen, Y., Wang, J., Jia, P., etc. : Research on dynamic scheduling approach of construction machinery group based on layered fuzzy logic. Chinese High Technology Letters 15 (9), 53-57.
5. Sun Zeng Qi, Zhang ZaiXing, Deng ZhiDong. : Theory and Technology of Intelligent Control, Beijing. Tsinghua University Publishing Ltd. (1997) 16–24
6. Terzopoulos D., Platt J., Barr A., FleischerK. : Elastically deformable models. Siggraph 1987. (1987) 205–214
7. Yu WeiD., Chu CaiY.: Textile Physics, Shanghai. Donghua University Publishing Ltd. (2002) 378–396

# Multi-view Video Coding with Flexible View-Temporal Prediction Structure for Fast Random Access

Yanwei Liu[1], Qingming Huang[1,2], Xiangyang Ji[1], Debin Zhao[3], and Wen Gao[4]

[1] Institute of Computing Technology, Chinese Academy of Science, Beijing, China
[2] Graduate School of Chinese Academy of Science, Beijing, China
[3] Department of Computer Science, Harbin Institute of Technology, Harbin, China
[4] School of Electronics Engineering and Computer Science, Peking University
{ywliu, qmhuang, xyji, dbzhao, wgao}@jdl.ac.cn

**Abstract.** Multi-view video is becoming increasingly popular, as it provides users greatly enhanced viewing experience. Multi-view video coding (MVC) focuses on exploiting not only the temporal correlation among the adjacent pictures for each view, but also inter-view correlation. Though the coding efficiency is a key target for MVC, the view-temporal prediction structure for improving the compression efficiency usually results in the decoding delay and limits the random access ability. Random access ability is an important feature in MVC because it provides the view switching, temporal frame sweepingly browsing and other interactive abilities for the client users in multi-view video streaming. In this paper, we propose an algorithm to flexibly regulate the view-temporal prediction structure. It is able to achieve a good trade-off between compression performance and random access ability.

**Keywords:** Multi-view video coding, random access, view-temporal prediction structure.

## 1 Introduction

Multi-view video is a 3-D extension of the traditional video sequence. Compared with mono-view video, the ideal multi-view video system allows viewers to navigate freely within a visual scene to change their viewpoint and view direction and thus, offers a similar interactive look-around capability. With these features it will be used for various services, such as entertainment, education, surveillance, 3D-TV (3D television), and Free Viewpoint Video (FVV) communication [1]. The available and emerging technologies for modeling, coding, and rendering of dynamic real world scenes for these interactive applications have been reviewed at the convergence point of computer graphics, computer vision, and classical media in [2]. Generally, video data are tremendous because multiple cameras are used. To be able to transmit these video sequences with available bandwidth, high efficiency data compression technique is needed. So far, some related work has been done on Multi-view Video Coding (MVC). The compression of multi-view video aiming at exploiting inter-view

Y. Zhuang et al. (Eds.): PCM 2006, LNCS 4261, pp. 564–571, 2006.

redundancy due to high correlation between the multiple views was done by Michael.E at first [3]. Recently, different view-temporal prediction structures were proposed to exploit both temporal and view redundancies in response to the CfP on MVC in 3DAV group of the MPEG community and these results show that higher coding performance is able to be achieved by inter-view prediction compared with independent coding of all views [4].

Though the compression efficiency is very important, the interactive feature of multi-view video requires the ability to randomly access the different views and different time-instant frames in the same view from the compressed bit stream. Random access ability means that the decoder can access one frame at a given time with minimal decoding of frames. The decoder can search the bit steam for an IDR-picture or recover point SEI (Supplemental Enhancement Information) message before the frame to be accessed and then decode the minimal needed frames from the point until the desired frame is decoded. Multi-view video applications require three kinds of random access abilities including random access to different views, random access to different temporal frames and random access to different interested regions in the same picture (spatial random access)[4]. Because all views are compressed into one bit stream in MVC, there only exists the efficient random access to arbitrary frame in the compressed bit stream including random access to different views and different time-instant frames of the same view. Fast random access not only provides flexible view switching ability but also increases the transmission robustness and synchronization. Since inter-view prediction introduces more view dependencies which limit the flexible random access ability in MVC bit stream, the random access in multi-view streaming is tightly dependent on view-temporal structure in MVC.

In this paper, we propose a flexible approach, to select the optimal hierarchical-B based view-temporal prediction structure, which is able to fulfill a given random access constraint while providing a good compression performance. The rest of the paper is organized as follows: in Section 2, we outline the relation between prediction structure and corresponding random access ability. In Section 3, we describe how to adaptively regulate the view-temporal prediction structure to increase the random access ability while keeping relatively optimal coding performance. That also means reducing the prediction structure enabled delay with flexible regulating scheme. Section 4 illustrates, by experiment results, how to achieve an efficient trade-off relation between the prediction structure and coding performance for different random access constraints. Finally, we conclude the paper in Section 5.

## 2   Prediction Structure and Random Access Analysis

Of all multi-view video coding solutions the simple scheme is to encode all views independently (simulcast coding). In this coding scheme the user can switch views among different view bitstreams directly. The decoder can initiate random access to another view sequence from the current view by quitting decoding the current view sequence. So the random access ability is related to the length of temporal group of pictures (GOP). In [6] some interactive visual effects of multi-view video services are described with independent coding for all views. In MVC, inter-view prediction is adopted to exploit the spatial redundancy between the views and the solutions with inter-view prediction exhibit better compression performance than simulcast coding scheme. Though inter-view prediction improves the compression performance, random access ability is limited by inter-frame and cross-view prediction in MVC.

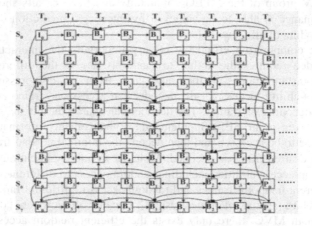

**Fig. 1.** View-temporal prediction structure using dyadic hierarchical B pictures

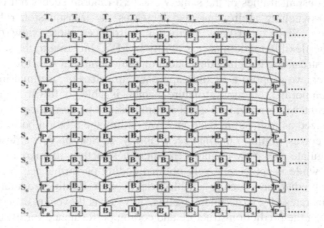

**Fig. 2.** View-temporal prediction structure using non-dyadic hierarchical B pictures

Specially, the prediction structure using Hierarchical B pictures proposed by Fraunhofer HHI [7] has achieved good compression performance. Its coding solution based on the H.264/AVC codec, as shown in Fig.1, uses prediction structure with hierarchical B pictures for each view and inter-view prediction is applied to every second view. In [7] there is an equation to derive the maximum number of delay frames for decoding some one B frame within a GOP according to the prediction structure from Fig. 1. However, the equation does not hold true when the prediction structure changes though it reflects the random access ability of current prediction structure. It is obvious that the temporal level number of hierarchical B picture decomposition significantly affects the compression performance. In Fig. 1 the dyadic hierarchical B structure is used. We also can adopt the non-dyadic hierarchical B structure to improve the coding efficiency as shown in Fig. 2. The maximum decomposition level ascends in the non-dyadic hierarchical B prediction structure and the random access ability of the whole structure is deteriorated on the contrary.

## 3   Enhancing Random Access Ability with Flexible Prediction Structure

In the multi-view streaming operation, random access point is very arbitrary. If the requested frame is an intra-coded frame, the server side only needs to transmit this frame. In the current multi-view coding solution the prediction structure with hierarchical B pictures decomposition supports cross-GOP prediction which means a frame in one GOP can refer a frame in next GOP. When random access point is a B frame, the server side needs to find the previously nearest and the subsequently nearest I frame to this requested frame, then transmits all the necessary dependent frames between the two I frames. Therefore, compression efficiency improvement by inter-view or inter-frame prediction is at the cost of degrading the random access ability. In order to increase the random access ability involved in the prediction structure, we consider removing some dependency induced by inter-view or inter-frame prediction while providing a relatively optimal coding efficiency. According to the prediction structure where hierarchical B pictures are used in temporal prediction, though generalized B pictures are used in the view direction, view frames are formed in hierarchy levels. We find that when the decoder decodes the current frame, the minimal number of decoding frames required is strongly associated with the temporal hierarchy level, view hierarchy level and the deepest dependency in view hierarchy level 0 of the current view in which the current frame situates. The deeper the hierarchy level in which the current frame situates is, the more the needed decoding of frames is. We build a formula parameterized by $(V_0, P_V, L_V, L_T)$ to characterize the relation between prediction structure and random access ability.

$$N_{decode} = \begin{cases} 2 \cdot \{(V_0+1)+L_V\}+L_T \cdot (P_V+1)-1, & L_{V\_MAX}>0, L_{T\_MAX}>0 \ and V_{0\_MAX} \geq 0 \\ 2 \cdot (V_0+1)+L_T \cdot (V_0+1)-1, & L_{V\_MAX}=0, L_{T\_MAX}>0 \ and V_{0\_MAX}>0 \\ 0, & L_{V\_MAX}=0, L_{T\_MAX}=0 \ and V_{0\_MAX}=0 \end{cases} \quad (1)$$

where $N_{decode}$ denotes minimal number of the frames to be decoded when the decoder decodes the current frame from the IDR-pictures or recovery point. The other parameters are explained as follows:

$V$ is the view number of current frame to be decoded and $V_0$ is the deepest dependency from anchor view in the view hierarchy level 0 if the V view will be decoded. $V_0 = 0,1,\cdots,V_{0\_MAX}$, and $V_{0\_MAX} < N$. For example, in Fig.1 if the decoder wants to decode the frame $S_3T_2$, it has to find that V is equal to 3 and $V_0$ is equal to 2 (from anchor view $S_0$, the decoder must decode $S_0$, $S_2$, $S_4$ successively). $V_{0\_MAX}$ is the maximal value of $V_0$. We define anchor view is the view with intra frame, e.g. $S_0$ in Fig. 1. $L_V$ is the view hierarchy level that the current frame situates along view direction. $L_{V\_MAX}$ is the maximal view hierarchy level in prediction structure. $L_T$ is the temporal hierarchy level that current frame situates along temporal direction. We also define $P_V$ as a view prediction flag. The value of $P_V$ is 0 when the current view is encoded independently; the value of $P_V$ is 1 when the current view is encoded with one view unidirectional prediction; the value is 2 when the current view is encoded with two view bidirectional prediction.

When $L_{V\_MAX}$, $L_{T\_MAX}$ and $V_{0\_MAX}$ are fixed on a set of values, the corresponding view-temporal prediction structure is uniquely definite. Here we define $N\_decodeCost$ as the maximal $N_{decode}$ in one GoGOP (Group of GOPs of all views, such as the picture matrix formed by 8 views with temporal GOP length of 8 frames in Fig.1) under the definite prediction structure to evaluate the random access ability.

$$N\_decodeCost = Max\{N_{decode}\} \tag{2}$$

The prediction structure can be parameterized under a given random access constraint. By playing on the parameter $L_{T\_MAX}$, $L_{V\_MAX}$ and $V_{0\_MAX}$, we can reduce the prediction dependency and therefore improve the random access ability. In some circumstances, several groups of parameters ($L_{T\_MAX}$, $L_{V\_MAX}$, $V_{0\_MAX}$) which depict different view-temporal prediction structure provide the same $N\_decodeCost$. We select the prediction structure with larger $L_{T\_MAX}$, because the efficiency of inter-view prediction is less than the one of inter-frame (temporal) prediction in the case of the same $N\_decodeCost$. We can also limit $V_{0\_MAX}$ via putting anchor view into the center of all views to decrease the prediction distance.

According to Equation (1), we propose a level-adaptive approach to adaptively choose the view-temporal prediction structure based on hierarchical B pictures while with the trade-off between random access ability and coding performance. The algorithm is described as follow:

---

**Step 1:** Compute the corresponding delay frames according to the end-user's random access time constraints.

**Step 2:** Find the maximum and minimum values of $L_{T\_MAX}$, $L_{V\_MAX}$, $V_{0\_MAX}$ and $P_V$. Traverse all combination sets of the parameters $L_{T\_MAX}$, $L_{V\_MAX}$, $V_{0\_MAX}$ and $P_V$ and compute the $N\_decodeCost$ according to Equation (1). If we obtain the same value of $N\_decodeCost$ with different combination parameter combinations, we choose the parameter set with larger $L_{T\_MAX}$.

**Step 3:** According to Formula (1), the smaller is $V_{0\_MAX}$ if $N\_decodeCost$ is smaller. For limiting $V_{0\_MAX}$, we exchange the position of Anchor View with other view and set the middle view to Anchor view. With the above result received from

Step 2, if $V_{0\_MAX}$ and other parameters are identical and $N\_decodeCost$ is also equal, we choose the parameter set whose Anchor view situates in the middle of views.

**Step 4:** Choose the matching optimal parameter set which depicts the optimal view-temporal prediction structure at the given random access constraint from Step 1.

From the above approach, we obtain the optimal parameters which depict corresponding view-temporal prediction applied to multi-view video sequence with frame rate f=25 and temporal GOP length =12, for several given random access constraints. Table 1 provides the detailed result.

**Table 1.** Optimal parameters ( $L_{T\_MAX}$ , $L_{V\_MAX}$ , $V_{0\_MAX}$ ) to depict an optimal prediction structure for MVC solution within several given random access constraints. Video sequence frame rate f=25 and temporal GOP =12.

| Random access(s) | Decoding(frames) $N\_decodeCost$ | Optimal parameters ( $L_{T\_MAX}$ , $L_{V\_MAX}$ , $V_{0\_MAX}$ ) | (View dependency structure, Anchor View position) |
|---|---|---|---|
| 1.2 | 30 | (4,1,4) | (IBPBPBPP,0) |
| 0.8 | 20 | (3,1,4) | (IBPBPBPP,0) |
| 0.65 | 17 | (3,1,2) | (IBPBIPBP,5) |
| 0.5 | 13 | (3,0,1) | (IBPBPBPP,0) |
| 0.3 | 8 | (2,0,1) | (IPIPIPIP,0,2,4,6) |
| 0.15 | 4 | (3,0,0) | Simulcast |
| 0.05 | 2 | (1,0,0) | Simulcast |
| 0 | 0 | (0,0,0) | All intra |

## 4   Experiment Result

To investigate the effect of the proposed algorithm and evaluate the trade-off between coding performance and random access ability, we do some MVC experiments with standard multi-view video sequence "Ballroom" from MERL[8]. The simulations are conducted based on the reference MVC solution from HHI [7]. The coding conditions are shown in Table 2. Table 3 provides the performance data comparison of different prediction structure within different random access constraints. The rate-distortion curves comparisons are showed in Fig. 3. The coding solution with optimal random access ability is all intra coding which behaves the worst coding efficiency of all solutions. Fig.3 shows that, when the random access ability is more than 0.65s, the coding performance is improved slowly with small gains. The coding efficiency of the solutions whose random access ability exceeds 0.15s is better than the anchor's. The anchor is independent coding of all views with IBBP prediction structure. We also observe from Fig. 3 that the proposed method could provide the optimal prediction structure to fulfill the best coding efficiency within the given random access ability constraint.

**Table 2.** Coding parameters in the experiment

| Temporal GOP | 12 |
|---|---|
| Search range | 96 (full pixel) |
| BasisQP | 29 |
| Entropy coding | CABAC |
| Encoded frames(all views) | 2000 |

**Table 3.** Rate-distortion (Rate in kbps, PSNR in dB) data comparison of the different view-temporal hierarchical prediction structure with corresponding maximum random access processing ability for Ballroom sequences

| Random access(s) | Coding performance | | Random access(s) | Coding performance | |
|---|---|---|---|---|---|
| | Rate | PSNR | | Rate | PSNR |
| 1.2 | 488.8851 | 35.7046 | 0.3 | 689.9949 | 36.3144 |
| | 382.8994 | 34.7180 | | 545.4027 | 35.2844 |
| | 262.4944 | 33.1115 | | 374.0297 | 33.6136 |
| 0.8 | 497.4 | 35.7 | 0.15 | 590.3635 | 35.1732 |
| | 387.9 | 34.7 | | 465.0941 | 34.1419 |
| | 267.1 | 33.1 | | 369.9456 | 33.0418 |
| 0.65 | 521.7455 | 35.7663 | 0.05 | 780.559 | 35.5233 |
| | 407.8060 | 34.7761 | | 553.8277 | 33.929 |
| | 280.3118 | 33.1769 | | 438.3625 | 32.8331 |
| 0.5 | 632.8811 | 36.0862 | 0 | 931.6871 | 30.0702 |
| | 497.3211 | 35.0579 | | 743.2127 | 28.8396 |
| | 343.5179 | 33.3999 | | 582.5565 | 27.7826 |

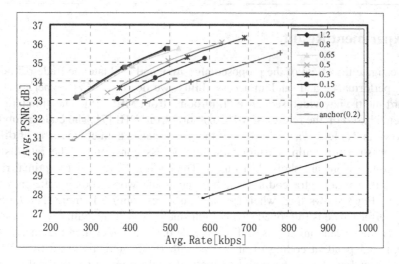

**Fig. 3.** Rate-distortion comparison curves of different prediction structures with corresponding random access ability constraints for Ballroom sequences

# 5 Conclusion

In this paper we have discussed an adaptive approach to improve the random access ability with relatively optimal coding performance in hierarchical-B pictures based multi-view video coding. We also illustrated the trade-off between compression efficiency and random access ability via a series of simulations. When the end user gives a random access constraint, we can adopt the proposed approach to fulfill its requirement and keep the relatively optimal coding performance. It was shown by experimental results that the proposed scheme is effective in enhancing the random access ability. In the future work we will consider optimizing the coding efficiency with new frame type, such as SP frame, to support fast random access.

**Acknowledgments.** The research of this paper has been supported by the National Natural Science Foundation of China (No.60333020) and the Natural Science Foundation of Beijing, China (No.4041003). The authors would like to thank MERL Lab for providing sequences used in the simulation and also would like to thank HHI for providing MVC reference solution.

# References

1. Hideaki Kimdta. Free-viewpoint video communication using Multiview Video Coding . NTT Technical Review. Vol.2 No.8 Aug.2004.
2. A. Smolic, P. Kauff, "Interactive 3-D video representation and coding technologies," Proc. IEEE, vol. 93, no. 1, pp. 98-110, Jan. 2005.
3. Michael E Predictive coding of multi-viewpoint image sets .In Proc. ICASSP'86 pages 521-524, Oct, 1986
4. ISO/IEC JTC1/SC29/WG11, "Subjective test results for the CfP on Multi-view Video Coding", Doc.N7779, Bangkok, Thailand, January 2006.
5. ISO/IEC JTC1/SC29/WG11, "Multiview Video Coding Requirements",Doc.N8064, Montreux, Switzerland, April, 2006
6. J. Luo, H. Cai, J. Li, "A Real-Time Interactive Multi-view Video System", in Proc. of the 13th ACM International Conference on Multimedia(MM2005), Singapore, Nov. 2005.
7. Müller, K., Merkle, P., Smolic, A., Wiegand, T.,"ISO/IEC JTC1/SC29/WG11, Multiview Coding using AVC", Doc. m12945, Bangkok, Thailand,January 2006.
8. ISO/IEC JTC1/SC29/WG11, "Multiview Video Test Sequences from MERL", Doc.M12077, Busan.Korea,April 2005.

# Squeezing the Auditory Space: A New Approach to Multi-channel Audio Coding

Bin Cheng[1], Christian Ritz[2], and Ian Burnett[3]

Whisper Laboratories, School of Electrical Computer and Telecommunications Engineering,
University of Wollongong, Wollongong, Australia
[1] bcheng@titr.uow.edu.au, [2] chritz@elec.uow.edu.au,
[3] i.burnett@elec.uow.edu.au

**Abstract.** This paper presents a novel solution for efficient representation of multi-channel spatial audio signals. Unlike other spatial audio coding techniques, the solution inherently requires no additional side information to recover the surround sound panorama from a two-channel downmix. For a typical five-channel case, only a stereo downmix signal is required for the decoder to reconstruct the full five-channel audio signal. In addition to the bandwidth saved by transmitting no side information, the technique has significant advantages in terms of computational complexity.

**Keywords:** Audio Signal Processing, Multi-Channel Audio, Spatial Audio, Surround Sound Scene.

## 1 Introduction

Very low bit-rate coding of multi-channel audio signals has recently been an area of significant research interest. In particular, solutions aiming at the representation of multi-channel audio channels using a downmixed signal with fewer channels plus a very compact set of side information have been proved to be successful. Examples of such algorithms are *Binaural Cue Coding* (BCC) [1] and *Parametric Stereo* (PS) [2]. Basically, these techniques exploit the cross-channel relationships, including *inter-channel level difference* (ICLD), *inter-channel time difference* (ICTD) and *inter-channel coherence* (ICC), to form a set of spatial cues so that a decoder is able to recover the full channel signal by applying the inter-channel relationships contained in these cues to the downmixed signal. For instance, a classical 5.1-channel audio signal can be downmixed into stereo or mono audio with an additional side information file less than 10 kBytes, and the downmixed stereo or mono audio can be further coded by conventional audio codecs, such as MP3 or AAC [9]. Thus, with a bit-rate only slightly higher than the normal stereo signal, the decoder can recover a full 5.1-channel audio signal and provide the audience with a surround sound panorama. Furthermore, backward compatibility can be easily achieved since the stereo/mono downmix has no difference between any other conventional stereo/mono audio formats. Due to the impressive performance of these coders,

Y. Zhuang et al. (Eds.): PCM 2006, LNCS 4261, pp. 572–581, 2006.

the MPEG Audio standardization group developed a new technology called "MPEG Surround" [3].

Although these surround compression techniques, based on a "downmixing + cues" framework, have been reported to have satisfactory performance in terms of significant bit-rate reduction and near- transparent perceptual audio quality [1, 2, 3], they have a major drawback. This is that an additional side information file (either incorporated into the binary format or as a separate transmission) is essential for the precise recovery of the spatialized auditory events and the full surround sound scene. This results in increased computational complexity for cue synthesis, as well as increasing storage and transmission requirements.

In this paper, we present a new approach to coding multi-channel audio signals, called *Spatial Squeezing Surround Audio Coding* (S³AC); this requires no additional side information to recover the full channel signal from a stereo downmix. Instead of exploiting the arithmetic relationships between audio channels, this solution achieves the compression of a 5-channel surround sound by representing it with a smaller sound field, typically, a stereo sound field, which contains every auditory event in the full surround sound scene with a corresponding position in a 'squeezed' space. In this approach, a 5-channel audio signal is firstly assumed to be rendering a 360° circle surround sound scene and channels are separated into different pairs based on their physical positions and the common way of multi-channel audio mixing. Frequency domain coefficients of each channel pair are then analysed and virtual sources and their positions estimated in the frequency domain. Subsequently, these virtual sources and their corresponding positions are mapped from the 360° to 60° auditory field, which can be typically rendered using only 2 speakers. Since this mapping is unique, the decoder is able to remap the virtual sources from the 60° stereo field back into the 360° circle correctly, thus recovering the full 5-channel audio signal and complete auditory scene.

This paper is structured as follows. Section 2 presents the rationale of S³AC in more detail and section 3 describes a *short-time Fourier transform* (STFT) implementation of S³AC. In Section 4, the complexity of S³AC is discussed and listening test results reviewed. Conclusions are drawn in section 5.

## 2 Theory

### 2.1 Background

Ideally, a typical 5-channel speaker setup can provide an audience, standing at or near the centre "sweet-point" of the imaginary circle, with a full 360° surround sound scene. However, psychoacoustics shows that human hearing has a limited resolution in locating sound objects; this is known as *localization blur* [4]. Researchers have shown that although different features may result from altering the frequency properties of the perceived sound, localization blur does not drop below 0.5° [4]. For the horizontal plane alone, the perceptual resolution could sometimes be even lower.

This means that displacement of an auditory event of up to 0.5° is theoretically unnoticeable for human listeners [4]. Nevertheless, when mixing music to stereo or multi-channel speakers using classical amplitude panning laws, the precision of a panned source direction can be much higher than 0.5°, since the numerical calculation is only limited by the algorithm's numerical precision. For the reverse mixing case where it is necessary to estimate a source's direction from a pair of audio channels, the inverse amplitude panning laws can be applied and high precision source localization achieved.

Based on these assumptions, this paper proposes that a small sound field with high computational level precision of virtual source localization is theoretically sufficient to represent and be recovered to a much larger auditory space for listening purposes. Typically, a 360° sound panorama rendered by a 5-channel speaker setup can be squeezed into a 60° stereophonic sound field and recovered back to the full surround sound circle without losing perceptual localization information. Initially, since distance information is not considered, the position of an auditory source in the 5-channel 360° horizontal plane is only represented by azimuth. However, planned future work will allow the algorithm to also consider radial information.

## 2.2 Amplitude Panning and Inverse Panning

The theory and performance of various amplitude panning laws have been extensively studied in literature [5, 6]. In our application, we utilise the "sin law" pan-pot [5, 7], which is the simplest pan-pot law that considers the angle between the speakers. It is given by:

$$\frac{\sin(\theta)}{\sin(\varphi)} = \frac{L-R}{L+R} \tag{1}$$

where $\theta$ and $\varphi$ are the angles of the source direction and loudspeakers respectively. Fig. 1 illustrates a typical stereophonic case where the two speakers are placed at ±30° and a virtual sound source is to be panned to $\theta$. $L$ and $R$ are the magnitudes of the left and right speakers, and should satisfy the following relationship such that the total energy of the source is maintained:

$$|L|^2 + |R|^2 = |S|^2 \tag{2}$$

where $S$ is the magnitude of the source to be panned.

Conversely, when estimating the direction of a virtual source from a pair of speakers, we can simply the inverse relationship to (1) and get:

$$\theta = \arcsin\left[\frac{L-R}{L+R} \cdot \sin(\varphi)\right] \tag{3}$$

Since we only consider angles within ±90°, the inverse sin function is monotonic.

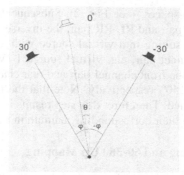

**Fig. 1.** Stereophonic Amplitude Panning: An auditory object can be placed anywhere between two speakers using the amplitude pan-pot law and conversely a virtual auditory object can be derived from the two speaker signals

### 2.3 Five Channel Virtual Source Direction Analysis

Considering a typical 5-channel loudspeakers setup where the speakers are placed at the horizontal plane according to the ITU BS.775 recommendation [8], as illustrated in Fig. 2, the front and rear speaker pairs are symmetrically placed at ±30° and ±110°, respectively.

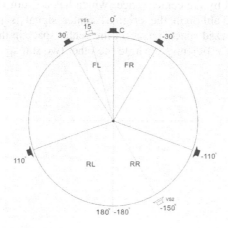

**Fig. 2.** 5-Channel Surround Speakers and Virtual Sound Sources Estimation: Assuming that 5 speakers are placed according to the ITU recommendation, Virtual Source 1 (VS1) and Virtual Source 2 (VS2) then can be estimated from the front and rear speaker pairs respectively

The 5-channel signal is first divided into three groups: front-left (FL) front-right (FR) pair, rear-left (RL) rear-right (RR) pair, and the center channel; this is a very common mixing method for 5-channel music synthesis. The channels in these pairings are more likely to have strong correlation than channels between pairs, and thus may represent one source, while the center speaker is usually comparatively independent from any other channel. As a result, the 360° sound field is effectively separated into several sub-spaces, (see Fig. 2). Subsequently, for the front and rear sub-spaces, i.e. the FL-FR pair and RL-RR pair, the inverse panning law is applied on each pair of FFT points resulting in a virtual source with a certain azimuth between the two speakers of a channel pair, e.g. virtual source 1 (VS1) and virtual source 2 (VS2) are estimated from the front channel pair and rear channel pair, and resulting in the azimuths of 15° and -150°, respectively. Note that the total energy of the virtual sources should be maintained. Therefore, this step results in a set of virtual sources in the frequency domain with their corresponding azimuth in the space.

### 2.4    360-60 Down Mapping and 60-360 Up Mapping

Following the estimation of virtual sources and their azimuths across the whole frequency band, a 360° to 60° space mapping is performed. 60° squeezed space was chosen since it can be effectively rendered by a stereo signal, hence a multi-channel to stereo downmix achieved. It is also worth mentioning here that the downmix signal for our solution must have at least two channels, since we still need a sound field in the downmix signal and this cannot be represented by a mono audio signal.

Fig. 3 shows a typical 360° to 60° down mapped sound field corresponding with the system in Fig. 2. It can be seen that VS1 and VS2 are mapped to their corresponding position in the squeezed space. Furthermore, in order to decrease the localization ambiguity during the decoding, the sub-sound-fields in the squeezed space should be separated by a certain distance. For example, the FL-FR sub-space and RL-RR sub-space are discriminated by the center space, which has a width of about 10°. Thus, in the squeezing process, although the original center signal is mapped to the exact center point in the squeezed space, i.e. at 0°, the center space in the squeezed field still needs a certain width to efficiently separate the other two sub-spaces.

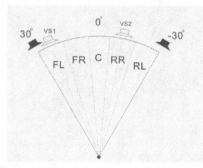

**Fig. 3.** Squeezed Sound Field: The two virtual sound sources at 15° and -150° in Fig. 2 are mapped into the corresponding locations in the compressed stereophonic sound field

A stereo downmix can now be generated. Like other state-of-the-art spatial audio coding downmix streams, this downmix file can also be further compressed using other conventional audio codecs, such as MP3 and AAC. The resulting bit-rate will be the same as a classical stereo MP3 or AAC file, and there is no additional requirement for spatial side information as all the source localization information is contained in the downmix signal. With this downmix signal, the decoder will perform a 60° to 360°

up mapping after estimating the virtual sources' positions in the squeezed space from the stereo downmix file. Intuitively, the sub-spaces in the squeezed sound field will be extended and virtual sources in this 60° space will be assigned new positions in the full 360° circle, which should approximate their original azimuths before coding. These virtual sources are then amplitude panned to appropriate speaker pairs with respect to their azimuths. Therefore, the 5-channel full 360° surround sound scene is recovered.

## 3  Implementation

In this section, we describe a *short-time Fourier transform* (STFT) implementation of $S^3AC$. Given a block of time domain signal $x(n)$ with length N (n=0, 1, ... , N-1), the STFT representation is given by:

$$X(k) = \sum_{n=0}^{N-1} x(n)w(n)W_N^{kn} \tag{4}$$

for k=0, 1, ... , N-1, where $w(n)$ is the window function with the same length as $x(n)$ and $W_N^{kn} = e^{-j2\pi kn/N}$. In practice, we use a 1024-point FFT with 50% overlapping between adjacent blocks and a "Kaiser-Bessel Derived" (KBD) analysis/synthesis window, which is given in [9, 10].

Next, the virtual source estimation is carried out on each pair of the generated frequency domain coefficients as described in Section 2.3, and we assign the phase of the left channels to the estimated sources, while maintaining the overall energy. For example, for the front channel pair, the virtual sources and their related azimuths are calculated by:

$$S_F(k) = \sqrt{FL^2(k) + FR^2(k)} \cdot e^{j\theta_{FL}} \tag{5a}$$

$$A_F(k) = \arcsin\left[ \frac{|FL(k)| - |FR(k)|}{|FL(k)| + |FR(k)|} \cdot \sin(30^o) \right] \tag{5b}$$

for k = 0, 1, 2, ... ,N-1.

The resulting source azimuths then need to be mapped from the 360° circle to a 60° arc. According to Fig. 3 and Section 2.4, this mapping can be done by:

$$A_F'(k) = \frac{5}{12} \cdot A_F(k) + 17.5 \tag{6a}$$

$$A_R'(k) = \begin{cases} -[A_R(k) - 180] \cdot \dfrac{5}{28} + 17.5 & \text{if } 110 \le A_R \le 180 \\[2mm] [A_R(k) + 110] \cdot \dfrac{5}{28} - 5 & \text{if } -180 \le A_R \le -110 \end{cases} \tag{6b}$$

And this mapping effectively maps [-30° 30°] to [5° 30°] and [110° 180°] ∪ [-180° - 110°] to [-30° -5°], respectively.

The downmixing to the stereo is subsequently performed using amplitude panning of the virtual sources to their new azimuths in the squeezed space. That is, according to (1) (2):

$$L_{DM}(k) = S(k) \cdot \left|\sin(\varphi) + \sin(A'(k))\right| / K \tag{7a}$$

$$R_{DM}(k) = S(k) \cdot \left|\sin(\varphi) - \sin(A'(k))\right| / K \tag{7b}$$

where $K$ is a coefficient for maintaining the overall energy given by $K = 2 \cdot \sin(\varphi)$, and $\varphi$ is 30° since in the downmix signal, left and right speakers are placed at ±30°. The centre channel of the 5-channel original signal will be mapped to the 0° point by equally panning it to both channels in the stereo downmix.

The resulting frequency domain stereo downmix is then transformed back to time domain using the IFFT:

$$x(n) = \frac{1}{N}\sum_{k=0}^{N-1} X(k)W_N^{-kn} \tag{8}$$

and recombined by synthesis windowing and an overlap-add method.

Since all sources from the original 5-channel audio signal are now mixed into the 2-channel signal, if the original channels are strongly correlated, the resulting virtual sources from different processing sub-spaces affect each other during the down mapping and consequently result in ambiguous sources between the correct positions. In other words, if the front channels and rear channels were rendering similar content, the generated virtual sources in the downmix signal would have incorrect azimuths. Although the decoder can still successfully recover the full 5-channel signal, the re-rendered sound scene may have auditory localization that differs from the original surround scene. This error can be avoided by intelligently choosing the correlated channels for virtual source estimation and adaptively performing the azimuth mapping. However, this is beyond the scope of this initial paper.

The decoding process is similar to the encoding. First, the virtual source estimations have to be carried out again in the frequency domain on the stereo downmix using equation (5). Then the resulting azimuths are up-mapped to the 360° circle by the inverse functions of (6):

Next, the virtual sources have to be panned to corresponding speaker pair regarding their up-mapped azimuths. Equations (7a) and (7b) are used, where $\varphi$ should be chosen as either 30° or 70° according to the speaker pair where the source is to be panned. Finally, all 5 channels are transformed back to the time domain and the full surround panorama is recovered.

# 4   Evaluation

## 4.1   Complexity

As shown in the previous sections, the $S^3AC$ scheme only involves very simple algorithms such as classical amplitude panning laws; as a result, the complexity of $S^3AC$ codec is relatively low. In this section, we compare the complexity of $S^3AC$ and the Binaural Cue Coding [1], which is the fundamental theory of MPEG Surround [3] and MP3 Surround [11]. Assuming that the same time-frequency transform is used for both schemes and not perceptual band implementation is involved, Table 1 gives the number of calculations required by $S^3AC$ and BCC for each frequency coefficient during the 5-channel to stereo downmixing/encoding and upmixing/decoding processes. These results are generated based on the equations described in [1] for BCC and the equations presented in Section 3 for $S^3AC$. Note that for $S^3AC$, two channel pairs are processed by the frequency-azimuth analysis and azimuth mapping during the encoding, while BCC needs to carry out the downmixing 4 times if a stereo downmix is used. And it can be found out in this table that $S^3AC$ has a much lower complexity than BCC.

**Table 1.** Encoding/Decoding complexity of $S^3AC$ and BCC. The table below shows the number of calculations required for one set of frequency dowmain components of all five channels. While assuming that the compuational cost of summations can be ignored, only the numbers of multiplications of both algorithms are considered.

|  |  | $S^3AC$ | BCC |
|---|---|---|---|
| Encoding | Multiplications | 28 | 48 |
| Decoding | Multiplications | 14 | 42 |

## 4.2 Subjective Evaluation

This section presents the results from a listening test comparing the $S^3AC$ scheme and other two state-of-the-art spatial audio codecs, the MPEG Surround [3] and MP3 Surround [11]. The listening test employed the MUSHRA [12] methodology and included a hidden reference and a 3.5 kHz low-pass filtered anchor with the three candidate codecs. 11 multi-channel sound recordings were selected for the test (3 immersion recordings, 4 pop music, 3 classical music, 1 movie sound track) and 8 subjects including both expert and none expert listeners participated in the test. In this test, for direct comparison with $S^3AC$, the MPEG Surround codec used NonGuided blind up-mixing, which means that no side information was used for decoding; the MP3 Surround was the only codec that used spatial side information. All codecs downmixed the 5-channel audio signal into a stereo pair. The MPEG Surround and $S^3AC$ downmix files were compressed using 128kbps AAC and the MP3 Surround used 192kbps MP3 for further compression of the stereo downmix. Fig. 4 shows the results of this listening test with mean and 95% confidence intervals indicated for each test item.

As can be seen, the proposed $S^3AC$ algorithm performs competitively with the two state-of-the-art spatial audio coding techniques, in terms of both bit rate efficiency and decoding quality. While the MPEG Surround codec provides the highest quality performance in most items due to its usage of additional spatial cues and higher compressed bit rate for the downmix signal, the $S^3AC$ provides a very close performance to the MPEG Surround NonGuided codec. The quality of the $S^3AC$ coded signals was mostly rated around a grade of 80%, which corresponds to "good" or "excellent' quality according to the ITU MUSHRA recommendation [12]. During

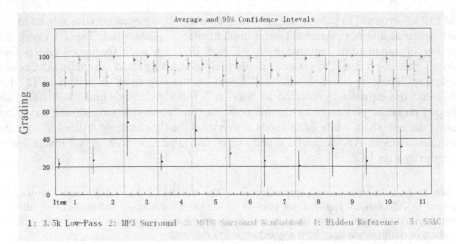

Fig. 4. The listening test results with mean value and 95% confidence intervals. Five conditions for each item including: 3.5 kHz low-pass filtered, MP3 Surround at 192kbps+cues, MPEG Surround NonGuided at 128kbps, hidden reference and $S^3AC$ at 128kbps.

the test, listeners reported that the $S^3AC$ codec achieved more accurate localization recoverability; while the MPEG Surround NonGuided seemed to be upmixing the sound sources to all the channels in most cases. However, listeners claimed that the monophonic perceptual quality of $S^3AC$ is not as good as the other candidates and that resulted in lower marks than MPEG Surround NonGuided in some trials. It should be noted that the $S^3AC$ codec used in this test was only a preliminary version, including only the basic algorithms presented in Section 2 and 3 of this paper; we expect significant improvements in performance once perceptual quality tuning algorithms can be incorporated. Moreover, as discussed in Section 4.1, its computational cost is much lower than the other two codecs.

## 5  Conclusions

A new method for efficient compression of multi-channel audio signals called $S^3AC$ is presented in this paper. This uses a smaller spatial sound field to represent a large surrounding sound field by employing an amplitude panning law and its inverse for analyzing virtual objects in the frequency domain and assigning new locations to these objects in a squeezed space. Therefore, multi-channel audio rendering of a full circle surround sound panorama can be compressed into a stereophonic sound scene and efficiently recovered. As a consequence, the need for spatial cue side information is inherently avoided.

A Short-Time Fourier implementation of $S^3AC$ scheme is also described in this paper and its algorithm is compared with the BCC scheme in terms of computational complexity. The implemented $S^3AC$ codec has been subjectively tested and compared with other spatial audio codecs. In these tests $S^3AC$ compares favourably with other spatial compression approaches. In comparison with MP3 Surround and MPEG

Surround, $S^3AC$ provides very similar coding efficiency and perceptual quality while having the advantages of a significantly simpler algorithm and lower computational cost.

# References

1. Faller. C, Baumgarte F.: Binaural Cue Coding – Part II: Schemes and Applications, IEEE Trans. on Speech and Audio Proc., vol. 11, No.6, Nov. 2003.
2. Schuijers E., Breebaart J., Purnhagen H., Engdegard J.: Low Complexity Parametric Stereo Coding, Proc. 116th AES Convention, Berlin, Germany, 2004.
3. Breebaart J., Herre J., Faller C., Roden J., Myburg F., Disch S., Purnhagen H., Hotho G., Neusinger M., Kjorling K., Oomen W.: MPEG Spatial Audio Coding/MPEG Surround: Overview and Current Status, Proc. 119th AES Convention, New York, USA, 2005.
4. Blauert J.: Spatial Hearing: the Psychophysics of Human Sound Localization, Revised Edition, MIT Press, Cambridge, MA, USA, 1996.
5. Neoran I. M.: Surround Sound Mixing using Rotation, Stereo Width, and Distance Pan-Pots, Proc. 109th AES Convention, Los Angeles, USA, 2000.
6. Pulkki V.: Virtual Sound Source Positioning Using Vector Base Amplitude Panning, J. Audio Eng. Soc., vol. 45, No.6, June 1997.
7. A. D. Blumlein, U.K. Patent 394,325, 1931.
8. ITU-R BS.775-1: Multichannel stereophonic sound system with and without accompanying picture, 1994.
9. Bosi M., Goldberg R.E.: Introduction to Digital Audio Coding and Standards, Springer, New York, USA.
10. Bosi M., Brandenburg K., Quackenbush S., Akagiri K., Fuchs H., Herre J., Fielder L., Dietz M., Oikawa Y., Davidson G.: ISO/IEC MPEG-2 Advanced Audio Coding, J. Audio Eng. Soc., 51, 780-792, Oct. 1997.
11. Herre J., Faller C., Ertel C., Hilpert J., Hoelzer A., Spenger C.: MP3 Surround: Efficient and Compatible Coding of Multi-Channel Audio, Proc. 116th AES Convention, Berlin, Germany, 2004.
12. ITU-R: Method for the Subjective Assessment of Intermediate Quality Level of Coding Systems (MUSHRA), ITU-R Recommendation. BS. 1534, 2001.

# Video Coding by Texture Analysis and Synthesis Using Graph Cut

Yongbing Zhang[1], Xiangyang Ji[2], Debin Zhao[1], and Wen Gao[1,2]

[1] Department of Computer Science and Technology, Harbin Institute of Technology,
Harbin 150001, P.R. China
[2] Institute of Computing Technology, Chinese Academy of Sciences, Beijing 100080,
P.R. China
{ybzhang, xyji, dbzhao, wgao}@jdl.ac.cn

**Abstract.** A new approach to analyze and synthesize texture regions in video coding is presented, where texture blocks in video sequence are synthesized using graph cut technique. It first identifies the texture regions by video segmentation technique, and then calculates their motion vectors by motion vector (MV) scaling technique like temporal direct mode. After the correction of these MVs, texture regions are predicted from forward and/or backward reference frames by the corrected MVs. Furthermore, Overlapped Block Motion Compensation (OBMC) is applied to these texture regions to reduce block artifacts. Finally, the texture blocks are stitched together along optimal seams to reconstruct the current texture block using graph cuts. Experimental results show that the proposed method can achieve compared visual quality for texture regions with H.264/AVC, while spending fewer bits.

**Keywords:** texture, analysis and synthesis, video coding, graph cut, optimal seam.

## 1 Introduction

Texture regions, such as grass, flower, sand, and cloud, appear in many video sequences. However, viewers are not sensitive to these texture regions which usually spend a lot of coding bits. In [1], it is assumed that for these highly textured regions, viewers perceive the semantic meaning of the displayed textures rather than the specific details. Thus it is not necessary to code these texture regions at the expense of high bit rate. In [2], a scheme of texture analyzer and synthesizer is presented. The aim of texture analyzer is to segment video frames and identify the texture regions in them. The texture synthesizer warps the identified texture regions by the warping parameters sent in the bit stream. The non-textured regions are encoded using traditional methods. Their method can save the bit rate up to 19.4% [2] without significant loss of visual performance. It achieved good results for rigid objects. However, it had to consider the neighborhood of the texture regions for non-rigid textures.

Y. Zhuang et al. (Eds.): PCM 2006, LNCS 4261, pp. 582–589, 2006.

Analysis-synthesis-based codec has already been introduced for object-based video coding applications, e.g. see [3]. However, the purpose of the analyzer and synthesizer modules in this case is usually the identification and appropriate synthesis of moving objects, rather than texture regions. A similar wavelet-based analysis-synthesis for still image and video coding approach was introduced by Yoon and Adelson [4]. Whereas, the algorithm presented is optimized for still images.

Graph cut was introduced for image and video synthesis in [5]. In their approach textures are generated by copying input texture patches. It first searches for an appropriate location to place the patch, and then uses a graph cut technique to find the optimal region of the patch to paste in the output. This algorithm can generate textures perceptually similar to the example ones.

In this paper, the input sequences are classified into key frames (frames used as reference) and non-key frames (frames that are not used as reference). The non-key frames are first segmented and then the texture regions are synthesized using graph cut. As there is no bit for the MVs of the texture regions, the MVs of the texture regions are derived by direct mode. Due to the unreliable characteristic of the direct mode MVs, MV correction is required after the direct mode MVs are got. In most cases, translation mode is not suitable for texture regions, which present random distribution, thus OBMC [6] is applied when the MV correction is finished. After OBMC, block artifacts are greatly reduced. Texture regions processed by the aforementioned stages seem close to the natural ones. Next, each texture macroblock is divided into 4 overlapped patches. Each patch has three candidates, which are forward, backward, and bi-directional predictions. The best candidate patch is chosen according to the mismatch of pixels in the overlapped region between the new and old patches. Then graph cut is processed by finding an optimal seam in the overlapped regions, and the existing pixels in the old patches are maintained or updated on the different side of the seam. Textures processed by graph cut seem to be smoother, more natural and the spatial accuracy remain unchanged. So, it will be hard for viewers to find detail differences between synthesized and original texture regions.

The remainder of this paper is organized as follows. In Section 2 we introduce the MV derivation and MV correction in texture regions. In Section 3, we compensate the texture regions utilizing OBMC. And in Section 4 graph cut synthesis is presented. Experimental results are given in Section 5. Finally, conclusions are drawn in Section 6.

## 2  MV Derivation and MV Correction in Texture Regions

In order to achieve better visual performance, some preprocessing techniques are required. The first is to identify texture regions in a frame, which can be finished by image segmentation. In this paper, we utilize a similar segmentation method as [2]. As there is no bit for MVs of texture blocks in bitstream, the MVs of texture blocks are derived by direct mode [7]. As is shown in Fig. 1, for each texture block, the forward motion vector $MV^{fw}$ and backward motion vector $MV^{bw}$ are calculated as

$$MV_{b1}^{fw} = \frac{TD_B}{TD_D} \times MV_{B4} \tag{1}$$

$$MV_{bw}^{b1} = \frac{(TD_B - TD_D)}{TD_D} \times MV_{B4} \tag{2}$$

If the co-located block in the backward reference frame was coded in intra mode, we got the spatial direct MV to replace the corresponding temporal one. As the MVs derived by direct mode may be sometimes unreliable, the MVs of adjacent blocks are used to correct or smooth the unsatisfied MVs because of the spatial correlation as described in [8]. The aim of the MV correction is to smooth the isolated MVs. If an MV has a weak spatial correlativity with adjacent MVs, it is considered as an isolated MV. The isolated MVs make motions unreliable and cause block artifacts. So it is necessary to correct the isolated MVs by smoothing or median filtering using MVs of adjacent blocks.

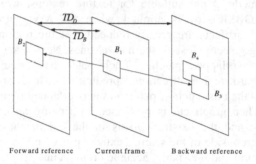

Fig. 1. MV Derivation of current block

Let Block($x,n$) be the block in frame $n$ and $x=x(i,j)$ denotes the spatial position at $(i,j)$ in one frame and $n$ is the frame number. Similarly, set MV($x,n$) to be the MV at position $x$ in frame $n$. To detect the isolated MV of Block($x,n$), the distance (MVD) between MV($x,n$) and its surroundings are calculated and the maximum MVD is selected as

$$MaxMVD(x,n) = \underset{x \in s(x)}{Max} \left\| MV(x,n) - MV(x^{'},n) \right\| \tag{3}$$

where $s(x)$ denotes the set of adjacent blocks. $x^{'}$ is in the same frame as $x$. A threshold T by averaging the adjacent block MVs is computed to determine whether the MV($x,n$) is isolated. If $MaxMVD(x,n)$ is larger than T, MV($x,n$) is isolated and should be corrected by MVs of adjacent blocks. In this paper, median filter is utilized for its good performance in removing noises. After MV correction, the MV of texture block becomes more reliable, and the block artifact is reduced.

## 3   Reduction of Block Artifacts by OBMC

Block artifacts reduced by just MV correction are not enough. Assign each block an MV is under the assumption that the corresponding block is undergoing translational movement. However, for texture regions, the pixel is unstructured and the movement is irregular. Thus, translational mode is not very suitable for texture regions. However, we find that OBMC is very suit for texture regions. As is shown in Fig.2, each pixel in the current block is predicted by a weighted average of several corresponding pixels in the reference frame. The corresponding pixels are determined by the MVs of the current block as well as adjacent blocks. The final pixel value is computed as

$$\Psi p(x) = \sum h_k(x)\Psi r(x + d_{m,k}), x \in B_m \qquad (4)$$

where $h_k(x)$ is the weight of corresponding pixel in neighboring block $B_m$ and should be inversely proportional to the distance between $x$ and the center of $B_{m,k}$. For each 4x4 block, OBMC is used after MV correction is finished. The block artifacts are greatly reduced when OBMC is applied and the texture regions seem smoother and more natural.

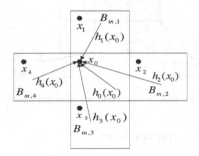

**Fig. 2.** OBMC with 4 neighborhood MVs

## 4   Texture Synthesis Using Graph Cut

In [5], texture is synthesized by copying irregularly shaped patches from the sample image into output image. The patch copying process is performed in two stages. Firstly, a candidate rectangular patch is selected by performing a comparison between the candidate patch and the patches already in the output image. Secondly, an optimal (irregularly shaped) portion of this rectangle is computed and only these pixels are copied into the output image. The portion to copy is determined by using a graph cut algorithm.

### 4.1   Selection of the Best Candidate Patch

Combining with H.264, we divide each texture macroblock into 4 non-overlapped 8x8 blocks. As is shown in Fig.3, the patch size is set to be 12x12. Each patch contains two parts: an 8x8 block and its overlapped regions. So, each macroblock can be synthesized by stitching 4 patches together. As each texture block has forward and backward MVs, it has 3 candidate patches, i.e. forward, backward and bi-direction patches. In order to determine which candidate patch is chosen, we first compute the sum of square error (SSE) in the overlapped region□ where $OV$ means overlapped

$$Dif = \sum_{x \in OV} \left( I_N(x) - I_O(x) \right)^2 \tag{5}$$

region $A$ and region $B$, $I_N(x)$ and $I_O(x)$ means the pixel value of position $x$ in the new and old patches respectively. Using formula 5, we compute the forward, backward and bi-directional $Dif$, and find the minimum. Then, we set the direction of the chosen patch to be the corresponding direction of the minimum $Dif$. Once the direction is determined, we get the best candidate patch.

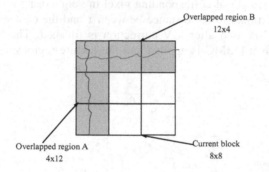

**Fig. 3.** A patch and its overlapped regions

## 4.2 Determination of the Optimal Seam

The heart of the patch based synthesis is to determine an optimal seam in the overlapped regions. When the optimal seam is determined, the pixels on the opposite side of the seam are processed differently. For example, in the overlapped region $A$, the pixels on the left of the optimal seam (red line) maintains the same, while the pixels on the right of the red line are updated by the pixels in the current patch. In the same way, the pixels above the green line are unchanged, whereas the pixels below the green line are replaced by the pixels in the current patch. It can be easily seen that the up left corner of the patch is processed twice, which is because it is contained in both region $A$ and region $B$. Pixel values in the right and bottom part of the current 8x8 block may be changed in the following steps, and it is just the basic idea of the patch synthesis.

In order to find an optimal seam in the overlapped region, we have to choose a matching quality measure for pixels from the old and new patch. In this paper, we choose the simplest quality measure, the luminance difference between pixels in the overlapped regions. Let $s$ be the pixel position in the overlapped region, and let $N(s)$

and $O(s)$ be the luminance at position $s$ in the new and old patches, respectively. The matching quality cost $M$ between pixels, which come from patches $N$ and $O$, is defined to be

$$M(s,N,O) = (N(s) - O(s))^2 \qquad (6)$$

We then use this matching quality to solve the path finding problem. Considering the overlapped region $A$ shown in Fig.3, from the top to the bottom, we find a minimum cost path, and record the minimum cost pixels in the path. For the pixels in the path and the pixels in the left of the path, pixel values remain the same, whereas pixels on the right of the path are replaced by the corresponding ones in the new patch.

## 5   Experimental Results

In this paper, we synthesized two well known sequences: *flowergarden* and *coastguard* with 30fps. *Flowergarden* contains rigid textures and *coastguard* contains non-rigid textures. All the experiments are implemented based on the H.264/AVC reference software JM98. Fig.4 shows results of the traditional methods in H.264 and proposed method used for texture regions in sequence *coastguard* and *flowergarden*. From Fig.4, we can see that the proposed method achieves similar visual performance as H.264, while saving the bits above 20%.

(a) H.264 296 bits                    (b) proposed method 224 bits

(c) H.264 5672 bits                   (d) proposed method 4528 bits

**Fig. 4.** Visual comparisons between different methods. (a),(b),(c) and (d) illustrate the results for H.264 encoded and the proposed for sequences *coastguard*(QCIF) and *flowergarden*(CIF)

Table. 1 shows that our proposed method outperforms the skip mode in H.264 for texture regions at the same bit rate. The maximum PSNR gain is up to 0.34dB for sequence *coastguard* in CIF format compared with the skip mode. And the maximum PSNR gain is up to 0.25dB for sequence *flowergarden* in QCIF format. As texture regions only take up a small fraction of the whole frame, and the proposed method is only applied to texture regions, the PSNR gain is relatively large compared with the whole frame. The detailed information about the bit saving of the proposed method compared with H.264 is shown in Table 2. The maximum saving of bits can be up to 36.29% compared with H.264 for sequence *coastguard* in CIF format. The maximum saving of bits can be up to 21.83% compared with H.264 for sequence *flowergarden* in CIF format.

Fig.5 shows the rate-distortion curves of the proposed method for sequences *coastguard* and *flowergarden* compared with the skip mode. It can be easily seen that the proposed method can significantly improve the coding efficiency compared with the skip mode when spending the same bits.

**Table 1.** PSNR comparison between the proposed method and the skip mode

| Video Sequence | Format | Average PSNR gain | | | |
|---|---|---|---|---|---|
| | | QP=30 | QP=32 | QP=34 | QP=36 |
| flower | CIF | 0.2363db | 0.2757db | 0.1847db | 0.1589db |
| | QCIF | 0.2514db | 0.1167db | 0.0926db | 0.0736db |
| coastguard | CIF | 0.2186db | 0.241db | 0.343db | 0.2353db |
| | QCIF | 0.1563db | 0.1557db | 0.1649db | 0.085db |

**Table 2.** Bit rate comparison between the proposed method and H.264

| Video Sequence | Format | Average bits saving | | | |
|---|---|---|---|---|---|
| | | QP=30 | QP=32 | QP=34 | QP=36 |
| flower | CIF | 21.83% | 18.06% | 20.02% | 11.54% |
| | QCIF | 10.45% | 9.3% | 3.53% | 6.48% |
| coastguard | CIF | 36.29% | 34.97% | 29.45% | 19.94% |
| | QCIF | 15.55% | 21.91% | 28.6% | 2.1% |

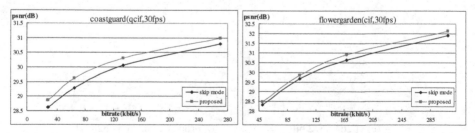

**Fig. 5.** Rate-distortion curves for skip mode and proposed method for texture regions in sequences *coastguard* and *flowergarden*

# 6 Conclusions

In this paper, we propose a video texture analysis and synthesis approach using graph cut. It is composed of three steps. Firstly, it segments a frame into texture macroblocks and non-texture macroblocks. Secondly, it carries on some preprocessing for texture macroblocks, which include MV derivation, MV correction and OBMC. Thirdly, optimal texture candidates are determined and stitched together. Experimental results show that the proposed method achieves better object and visual performances than that when encoded by skip mode for texture regions. Furthermore, the proposed method achieves similar visual performance compared with H.264, while saving bit rate up to 36% at most. Besides, the proposed method is suitable for both rigid and non-rigid textures, which approves its robustness.

# References

1. P.Ndjiki-Nya, T. Hinz, A. Smolic, and T. Wiegand.: A Generic Automatic Content-based Approach for Improved H.264/AVC Video Coding. ICIP 2005, Genoa, Italy, September 2005
2. P.Ndjiki-Nya, T. Wiegand: Video Coding using texture analysis and synthesis. PCS 2003, Saint-Malo, France, April 2003
3. M.Wollborn Prototype Prediction for Clour Update in Object-Based Analysis-Synthesis Coding. IEEE Trans. Circuits Syst. Video Technol., vol.4, no.3,pp.236-245, June. 1994
4. S.-Y. Yoon and E.H. Adelson. Subband texture-synthesis for image coding. Proceedings of SPIE, Human vision and Electronic Imaging III (1998) 489-497
5. V.Kwatra, A.Schödl, I.Essa, G. Turk, A. Bobick: Graphcut Textures: Image and Video Synthesis using Graph Cuts. ACM Transactions on Graphics, SIGGRAPH 2003
6. T. Kuo, and C.-C. Jay Kuo. Fast Overlapped Block Motion Compensation with Checkerboard Block Partitioning. IEEE Trans. Circuits Syst. Video Technol, vol.8, no.6, pp 705-712, October, 1998
7. A.M.Tourapis, Feng.Wu, Shipeng Li. direct mode coding for bipredictive slices in the H.264 Standard. IEEE Trans. Circuits Syst. Video Technol, vol.15, no.1, pp 119-126, Jan. 2005
8. H. Sasai, S. Kondo and S.Kadono. frame-rate up-conversion using reliable analysis of transmitted motion information. Proc. of IEEE Conference on Acoustics, Speech, and Signal processing, vol.5, pp 257-260, May, 2004
9. J.Zhang, L.Sun, S.Yang.: Position Prediction Motion-compensated interpolation for frame rate up conversation using temporal modeling. ICIP 2005
10. Jiefu Zhai, Keman Yu, Jiang Li, Shipeng Li.: A Low Complexity Motion Compensated Frame Interpolation Method. ISCAS 2005, May 2005
11. A.Schödl, R. Szeliski, David H. Salesin, and Irfan Essa. Video Textures. Proceedings of the 27th annual conference on computer graphics and interactive techniques.(2000) 489-498

# Multiple Description Coding Using Adaptive Error Recovery for Real-Time Video Transmission

Zhi Yang, Jiajun Bu, Chun Chen, Linjian Mo, and Kangmiao Liu[1]

College of Computer Science, Zhejiang University, Hangzhou, China
{yangzh, bjj, chenc, molin, lkm}@zju.edu.cn

**Abstract.** Real-time video transmission over packet networks faces several challenges such as limited bandwidth and packet loss. Multiple description coding (MDC) is an efficient error-resilient tool to combat the problem of packet loss. The main problem of MDC is the mismatch of reference frames in encoder and decoder, when some descriptions are lost during transmission. This paper presents an adaptive error recovery (AER) scheme for multiple description video coding. The proposed AER scheme, which is based on statistical analysis, can adaptively determine the nearly optimal error recovery (ER) method among our predefined ER methods such as interpolation, block replacement and motion vector (MV) reusing. The AER scheme has three advantages. First, it efficiently reduces the mismatch error. Second, it is completely based on pre- post-processing which requires no modification of the source coder. Third, it has low computational complexity, which is suitable for real-time video applications. Simulation results demonstrate that our proposed AER scheme achieves better performance compared with MDC with fixed error recovery (FER) scheme over lossy networks.

## 1 Introduction

With the rapid development of wired and wireless networks, more and more real-time video communication services are coming into being. However, for video streaming over error-prone networks (e.g. Internet), there are many challenging problems such as limited bandwidth and packet loss. The existing video coding standards, such as MPEG-2/4 and H.263/264, adopt predictive coding which is suitable for nearly error-free environment. In other words, packet loss may cause great quality degradation and error drift. Thus, many error resilient techniques have been introduced into video coding [1].

Multiple description coding (MDC) [2] is an efficient error resilient tool to combat the packet loss without requiring feedback and retransmission. The principle of multiple description (MD) video coding is to encode the source video data into several sub-streams, called descriptions. Each description can be decoded independently and reconstructs video with acceptable quality. More descriptions together can reconstruct higher quality video. Many techniques can be used to generate MD for video, such as polyphase down-sampling MD [3], MD quantization [4] and MD transform coding [5], etc.

---

[1] The work was supported by National Grand Fundamental Research 973 Program of China (2006CB303000), Key Technologies R&D Program of Zhejiang Province (2005C23047).

Y. Zhuang et al. (Eds.): PCM 2006, LNCS 4261, pp. 590–597, 2006.

The fundamental design issue of these MD generation methods is to balance the mismatch and redundancy. Many efficient error recovery (ER) schemes have been proposed to reduce the mismatch when packet loss occurs during transmission. The ER in [6] uses multihypothesis motion prediction to estimate lost content and the ER in [7] uses multiple reference frames to generate side information to control the mismatch. Most of ER schemes adopt fixed error recovery (FER), which is not compliant to various video motion scenarios. Drift-free MDC for video is also investigated [8], but more redundancy is required.

In this paper, we proposed a novel adaptive error recovery (AER) scheme for MD video coding. The AER scheme completely depends on pre- post-processing, so that it is compatible with existing video coding standards. Furthermore the AER scheme can efficiently reduce the mismatch and behave finer flexibility for different video contents. Simulation is designed to compare the performance of our proposed AER and existing FER for MD video coding in different loss rate environment. Experimental results also demonstrate that in error-prone networks, the AER outperforms the FER with various video motion scenarios. Moreover, the low computational-complexity feature makes the AER feasible for real-time video applications.

The rest of the paper is organized as follows. In Section 2, we present the proposed scheme and describe details about the MDC framework and the process of AER. Experimental results are shown in Section 3 and conclusions are drawn in Section 4.

## 2 Proposed Scheme

### 2.1 Codec-Independent MD Framework

The proposed MD framework is composed of three parts and Fig.1 shows that. The encoding part uses pre-processing to generate $N$ descriptions and encode each description independently. Then the transmission part sends the $N$ descriptions through $M$ paths. Finally the decoding part decodes $W$ received descriptions respectively and use post-processing to merge all descriptions reconstructing the video sequence. It should be mentioned that the number of received descriptions $W$ is equal to or less than the number of sent descriptions $N$ because of packet loss or

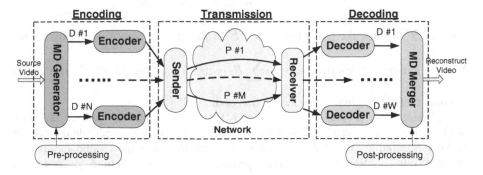

**Fig. 1.** Framework of codec-independent MD video coding ($D$ denotes the description; $P$ denotes the transmitting path; $N, M, W$ are integer number)

congestion in the networks. Thus, an additional function of MD merger is error recovery. The framework has two advantages. First, it adopts MDC which can provide error resilient feature. Second, the MD generation is completely depending on pre- post-processing, which is low complexity and coding standards compatible. Next sub-sections will present the MD generation and AER scheme in detail.

## 2.2 MD Generation

To generate MD, there are two sub-sampling methods, namely, spatial sub-sampling and temporal sub-sampling. In spatial sub-sampling MD, each frame is sub-sampled along rows. Fig.2 (a) is an example of spatial sub-sampling MD, which generates 2 descriptions. In temporal sub-sampling MD, the frame sequence is divided into odd and even frame sub-sequences. Fig.2 (b) is an example of temporal sub-sampling MD, which generates 2 descriptions.

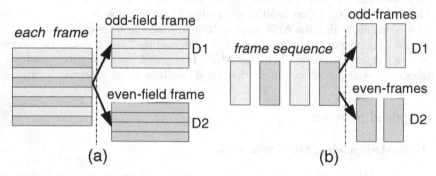

**Fig. 2.** MD generation through (a) Spatial sub-sampling and (b) Temporal sub-sampling

Different MD generation scheme leads to different redundancy rate. Redundancy rate is defined by Equation 1.

$$R_r = \frac{(\sum_{i=1}^{N} B_i) - B_s}{B_s} \qquad (1)$$

Where $R_r$ denotes the redundancy rate; $B_i$ is the coding bits of descriptions $i$ and $N$ is the number of description; Thus $\sum_{i=1}^{N} B_i$ is the coding bits of MDC; $B_s$ denotes the coding bits of original single description coding (SDC).

Fig.3 describes the relationship between MD generation and redundancy rate with different quantization parameters (QP). It can be seen that the redundancy rate of spatial sub-sampling MD decreases while QP increasing. But the redundancy rate of temporal sub-sampling MD gets the opposite result. For real-time video coding applications such as video phone and video conference, low bit-rate video coding is

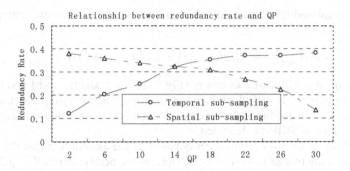

**Fig. 3.** Redundancy rate comparison of MD generation methods (codec - MPEG4 simple profile, test sequences - *News, Foreman* and *Coastguard*, resolution - CIF, frame rate - 30fps, search range - 16×16)

more suitable. Spatial sub-sampling MD induces lower redundancy rate in low bit-rate coding scenario, so we choose spatial sub-sampling MD (Fig.2 (a)) as the MD generation method.

## 2.3 Adaptive Error Recovery

### 2.3.1 Introduction of Error Recovery Methods

Since all descriptions are encoded independently in our proposed framework (Fig.1), the decoding process is straightforward. After each received description is decoded independently, all descriptions are merged to reconstruct the displaying video. If all sent descriptions are received correctly, the only thing need to do is merging these descriptions into one video sequence. If some descriptions are lost, ER method will be introduced into the merging process.

The fundamental of ER is to retrieve the lost descriptions according to the received descriptions, because the descriptions have correlations in spatial and temporal domain. Fig.4 shows three ER methods in both domains.

The interpolated ER (Fig.4 (a)) uses spatial correlation to reconstruct the missed block in one description according to the corresponding block in another description. Since spatial sub-sampling is adopted to generate MD and original video frames are separated into odd-field frames and even-field frames, the spatial correlation between descriptions is strong. Thus linear interpolation can recover the missed content, e.g. if

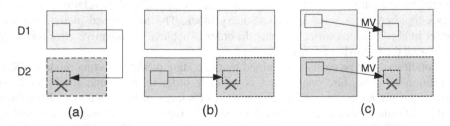

**Fig. 4.** Error recovery schemes (a) Interpolation (b) Direct block-replacement (c) MV reused

even-field is missed then two odd-fields can be used to achieve the interpolation as Equation 2.

$$field_{even}(i) = (field_{odd}(i) + field_{odd}(i+1))/2 \qquad (2)$$

The ER of direct block-replacement (Fig.4 (b)) is straightforward and depends on temporal correlation. If one block is error, then the corresponding block in previous frame is used to replace the faulted block. This method is suitable for the scenario that the faulted block is SKIP-mode coded.

The motion vector (MV) reused ER is based on the assumption that the motions of the corresponding blocks in different descriptions are nearly identical. Fig.5 shows the distribution of the difference between MVs of corresponding blocks in two descriptions. The data is acquired through three test sequences *News*, *Foreman* and *Coastguard*. The difference presents normal distribution (Equation 3) and the mean $\mu_h = 0, \mu_v = 0$, the variance $\sigma_h^2 = 0.53, \sigma_v^2 = 0.24$. According to the feature of normal distribution, the probabilities will reach 94% and 99% respectively when the range of MV difference is [-1, +1]. Thus when motion exists in video contents, MV reused ER is better than that of direct block replacement.

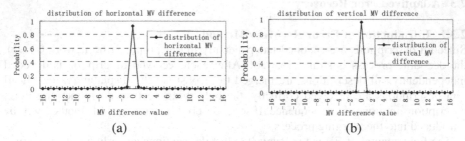

**Fig. 5.** The distribution of MV difference in (a) horizontal direction (b) vertical direction

$$P(x) = \frac{1}{\sigma\sqrt{2\pi}} e^{-(x-\mu)^2/(2\sigma^2)} \qquad (3)$$

### 2.3.2 The Design of Adaptive Error Recovery

The aforementioned three ER methods can adapt to different environment. The interpolation is suitable for video contents with strongly spatial correlation. The direct block-replacement is suitable for stationary block. The MV reused method behaves better in block with motorial contents. In order to achieve the adaptive error recovery, we define the following process (Fig.6).

Condition 1 can be easily determined by the coding mode. If coding mode is SKIP, condition 1 is true, else condition 1 is false. In order to determine condition 2, we investigate the relationship between recovery efficiency of the other two ER methods and SAD (sum of absolute difference) values. The recovery efficiency is measured by average MSE (mean square error) per-pixel and the sample data, 2000 macroblocks,

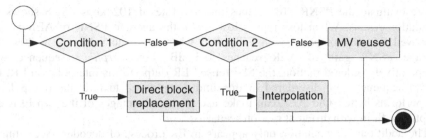

**Fig. 6.** Adaptive error recovery process

is randomly chosen from *News*, *Foreman* and *Coastguard*. Fig.7 shows the result. The recovery efficiency of interpolation is comparatively little interfered by SAD value and we simply set $y = b_1$ as its fitting curve. $b_1$ is a constant value and equal to 120 which is the average MSE value by interpolated recovery. The recovery efficiency of MV reused method is strongly related to SAD value and the correlation value is up to 0.75. So we use linear function $y = a_2 x + b_2$ as its fitting curve. Through linear regression analysis, we get $a_2 = 0.1, b_2 = -50$. The intersection point of the two fitting curves is (1700, 120) (Fig.7 (b)). Thus the condition 2 is defined as follows. If SAD > 1700, the condition 2 is true, else the condition 2 is false.

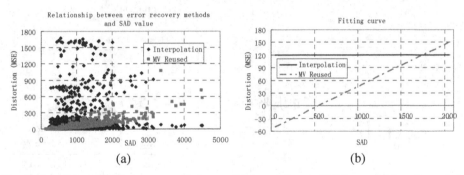

**Fig. 7.** Comparison of the recovery efficiency of interpolation and MV reused (a) scatter points (b) fitting curve

## 3 Experimental Results

To evaluate the proposed scheme, we set up the experiment as follows. MPEG-4 [9] simple profile is chosen as the video codec. Other two standard sequences *Carphone* and *Basket* of CIF resolution at 30 fps are used as our test set, which contains various motion scenarios. Interval of I frame is 30. We design three testing cases which are (a) MDC with interpolated ER; (b) MDC with MV reused ER and (c) MDC with AER. The comparison is based on different packet loss rate: 5%, 10% and 20% respectively. We assume that one description occurs packet loss and the packet loss is randomly generated on macroblocks of P frames.

We evaluate the PSNR (dB) values under a rate of 1024kbps. Fig.8 shows the simulation results. When loss rate is low (5%), the average PSNR of AER is only improved 0.2 dB compared with FER. But when loss rate increases to 20%, the average PSNR gain of AER reaches 0.5 dB. For *Carphone* sequence with comparatively ordered motion, the MV reused ER outperforms interpolation ER. For *Basket* sequence with disordered motion and complicated texture, the interpolation ER performs better. Our AER can make use of the advantages of the two FER and adaptively fit in with different motion scenarios.

The additional computation only appears in ER process of decoder. According to experiment, when loss rate is 5%, the increase of computational complexity is negligible. When loss rate is up to 20%, the average increase of computational complexity is below 2%. Low computational complexity makes the AER scheme suit for real-time video applications.

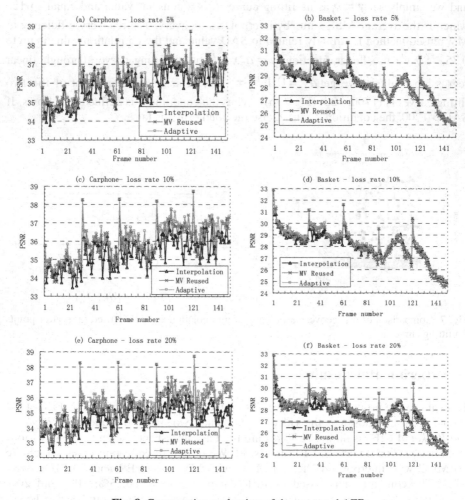

**Fig. 8.** Comparative evaluation of the proposed AER

# 4 Conclusions

In this paper, we proposed a novel adaptive error recovery (AER) scheme for real-time multiple description (MD) video coding. The codec-independent MD framework is presented, which not only provides error resilience for video communication in error-prone networks, but also achieves low-complexity and flexibility so that it is compatible with all existing video coding standards. AER scheme can achieve better recovery efficiency than fixed ER scheme. Simulation results have proved the good performance of the AER.

Also, we believe that recovery efficiency can be improved by dynamic threshold in condition 2. In our future work, we will design the distributed MD transmission scheme to farther improve the error-resilience for real-time video applications.

# References

1. Wang, Y., Wenger, S., Wen, J.T., Katsaggelos A.K.: Error Resilient Video Coding Techniques, IEEE Signal Processing Magazine, Vol. 17, (2000), 61-82
2. Groyal, V. K.: Multiple Description Coding: Compression Meets the Network, IEEE Signal Processing Magazine, Vol. 18, (2001), 74-93
3. Arsura, E., Fumagalli, M., Lancini, R.C.: Multiple Description Coding Approach for Internet Video Delivery, Visual Communications and Image Processing (VCIP), (2002), 69-79
4. Vaishampayan, V.A.: Design of Multiple Description Scalar Quantizer, IEEE Transaction on Information Theory, Vol.39, (1993) 821-834
5. Goyal, V.K., Kovacevic, J.: Generalized Multiple Description Coding with Correlating Transforms, IEEE Transaction on Information Theory, Vol. 47, (2001), 2199-2224
6. Zhang, G.J., Stevenson, R.L.: Efficient Error Recovery for Multiple Description Video Coding, IEEE International Conference on Image Processing, Vol. 2, (2004), 829-832
7. Zheng, J.H., Chau, L.P.: Multiple Description Coding Using Multiple Reference Frame for Robust Video Transmission, IEEE International Symposium on Circuits and Systems, Vol. 4, (2005), 4006-4009
8. Boulgouris, N.V., Zachariadis, K.E., Leontaris, A.N., Strintzis, M.G.: Drift-free Multiple Description Coding of Video, IEEE Workshop on Multimedia Signal Processing, (2001), 105-110
9. Xvid core library source code 1.1.0, http://download.xvid.org/downloads/xvid-core-1.1.0.zip

# An Improved Motion Vector Prediction Scheme for Video Coding

Da Liu[1], Debin Zhao[1], Qiang Wang[1], and Wen Gao[2]

[1] Department of Computer Science, Harbin Institute of Technology, Harbin 150001, China
[2] Institute of Computer Technology, Chinese Academy of Science, Beijing 100080, China
{dliu, dbzhao, qwang, wgao}@jdl.ac.cn

**Abstract.** The motion vector prediction (MVP) is an important part of video coding. In the original median predictor, if the neighbor blocks of current block are intra-mode coded, their motion vectors (MVs) will be set to zeros for MVP of current block. This is not very precise for sequences with strong motion. This paper propose an improved motion vector prediction (MVP) scheme for H.264. In the proposed scheme, when there are intra-mode macroblocks beside current block, more MV of the neighbor inter-mode block is utilized instead of zero MVs of intra-mode macroblocks for MVP of current block. The experimental results show that the improved scheme achieves better coding efficiency than the original median predictor. Meanwhile the point obtained by the proposed MVP scheme is closer to the global minimum point, the following fast motion estimation (FME) computation complexity is reduced.

**Keywords:** motion vector prediction, video coding.

## 1 Introduction

The MVP plays an important role in the video coding standard. A good MVP can give a good starting point for following fast motion estimation (FME) in inter-prediction. FME would like to obtain the best matching block for current block from the reference frames by searching a few points. The majority of FME algorithms often fall into local optimal point which may not be really optimal MV for current block. If the MVP predicts a point closer to the global optimal point, a high quality reference block for current block is obtained, the coding performance of the picture is improved, and the computation complexity of FME is reduced. The MVPs of neighbor blocks can influence current block's MVP. MVP of current block use MVs of neighbor blocks as reference MV, the MVP accuracy of current block is influenced by the accuracy of neighbor blocks' MV. A good MVP of neighbor block can obtain a good estimated MV for itself and can give a good reference MV for current block's MVP. Then, the coding performance of whole picture is improved if a few influencing blocks obtain more accurate MVs.

At present, the median predictor is widely used in many important coding standards, such as H.263/H.264 [1][2]. It obtains the median values from the MVs of neighbor blocks. As can be seen form Fig. 1, MV of block E is predicted using MVs of block A B C when all the blocks are available. The scheme is simple, but when meeting

Y. Zhuang et al. (Eds.): PCM 2006, LNCS 4261, pp. 598–605, 2006.
© Springer-Verlag Berlin Heidelberg 2006

inhomogeneous motion scene, its efficiency is not very good. Besides the median prediction, the weighted mean prediction is employed in [3]. It assigns every neighbor block a weighted factor. [4] adds the temporal prediction in MVP to compensate the insufficiency of spatial prediction. [5] joins a predefined threshold to guarantee the validate MVs to be used for median predictor. In [6], [7] and [8], S. D. Kim and J. B. Ra introduce a flag indicating which neighbor MVs are used to predict the current MV in bitstream. All the proposed MVP methods following the median predictor want to improve MVP accuracy in inhomogeneous motion scene and can achieve a good MVP value. But when there are intra-mode macroblocks beside current block, all the proposed MVP methods look the reference MVs of the intra-mode macroblocks as zero when predicting MV of current block. However some other useful reference MVs of neighbor inter-mode blocks have not been utilized, this is a waste of surrounding inter MV information, and the MVP accuracy of current block will be influenced.

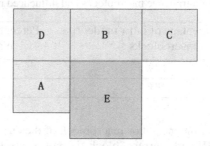

**Fig. 1.** Block E and the neighbor blocks

The influence of intra-mode macroblocks to the MVPs of other macroblocks in the picture is large. Four surrounding macroblocks will be influenced by one intra-mode macroblock. Fig. 2 give an illustration, block I are separately at up-right, up, up-left, left of macroblocks F, G, H, J. When predicting MVs of macroblocks F, G, H, J, MV of block I will be used as a reference MV. If block I is intra-mode macroblock, MV of macroblock I will be looked as zero, MVPs of macroblocks F, G, H, J are all influenced. The more the intra-mode macroblocks in a picture, the more the macroblock's MVPs will be influenced. Table 1 shows in the sequences with strong motion, the percentage of intra-mode macroblocks is not small. In sequence stefan and foreman, it is separately up to 12% and 9% in all kinds of macroblocks. The percentage of macroblocks, whose MVPs are directly influenced by the intra-mode macroblocks, is separately about 48% and 36%. In this condition, lots of macroblocks' MVPs are not accurate enough, its following FMEs can not fall into global optimal point then can not bring the optimal MV and the best matching block for current macroblock. The MVPs accuracy of some other macroblocks in the picture will be influenced too because of poor MVs accuracy of the macroblocks beside intra-mode macroblocks. The coding performance of whole picture will be greatly influenced by the intra-mode macroblocks.

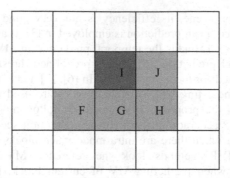

**Fig. 2.** The location of macroblock I (intra-mode macroblock) and the macroblocks influenced by macroblock I

**Table 1.** Percentage of intra-mode macroblocks and influenced macroblocks(QP=32)

|  | Percentage of intra-mode macroblocks | Percentage of influenced macroblocks |
|---|---|---|
| Stefan | 12% | About 48% |
| Foreman | 9% | About 36% |

As mentioned in [9], if one neighbor macroblock of the current block is intra coded, the motion vector (MV) of current block is not easy to predict and greater computation cost is needed. In this case, [9] will select one between two FME methods according to whether there are intra-mode macroblocks beside current block. But [9] has not considered how to improve the MVP accuracy to reduce the computation complexity of FME for current block when there are intra-mode macroblocks in surrounding area.

In this paper, we propose an improved MVP scheme. When there are intra-mode macroblocks beside current block, some abundant MV of neighbor inter-mode block is utilized instead of the zero MVs of intra-mode macroblocks for MVP of current block. More inter-mode MV information is utilized to achieve a better prediction performance and bring less FME computation complexity. The coding efficiency is enhanced, the computation complexity is reduced.

The remainder of the paper is organized as follows. In Section 2, the detailed description of the method is given, when there are intra-mode macroblocks beside current block, the original zero MVs of intra-mode macroblocks can be optionally replaced by MV of block D (see Fig. 1) in different cases for MVP of current block. Section 3 provides the experimental results and performance comparison. Finally, section 4 concludes this paper.

## 2  Improved MVP Scheme

To give clearer illustration, some average performance comparisons are showed in two typical sequences "Stefan" and "foreman", which have strong motion scene. They are both 300 frames CIF sequences with the frame rate of 30f/s. The experiment conditions are showed in Table 4, depicted in section 3. QP is set to 32.

There are four macroblocks beside the intra-mode macroblock as shown in Fig.2, its MVPs are influenced by the MV of intra-mode macroblock. We name this kind of areas as intra-mode macroblock areas. The average performance of the intra-mode macroblock areas and average performance of all macroblocks in the sequence are compared. Table 2 shows that, the average PSNR of intra-mode macroblock areas is smaller than the average PSNR of all macroblocks in sequence.

**Table 2.** PSNR comparison (QP=32)

|  | Average PSNR of intra-mode macroblock areas(dB) | Average PSNR of all macroblocks in sequence(dB) |
|---|---|---|
| Stefan | 32.20 | 32.44 |
| Foreman | 34.61 | 34.82 |

The computation complexity can not be simply evaluated by the count of search points, it is because that the block matching size in H.264 is variable and the partial SAD (sum of absolute difference) computation is used. The computation of a SAD is early terminated when the partially accumulated SAD has exceeded the minimum known SAD. So we use the count of AD (absolute difference) operations as the evaluation of a ME algorithm's complexity. An AD operation includes the subtracting between one pixel in the current block and corresponding pixel in the candidate block, getting the absolute value of difference, adding the absolute value to the SAD.

Table 3 shows the mean AD counts per macroblock in intra-mode macroblock areas is greater than the mean value of all the macroblocks in the sequence. This means larger computation is needed for macroblocks in the neighbor of intra-mode macroblocks.

**Table 3.** AD counts comparison (QP=32)

|  | Mean AD counts of intra-mode macroblock areas($*10^3$) | Mean AD counts of all macroblocks in sequence($*10^3$) |
|---|---|---|
| Stefan | 124.82 | 94.43 |
| Foreman | 33.54 | 25.47 |

All the blocks have the same coding method, the reason of small PSNR and high computation complexity in macroblocks beside intra-mode macroblocks is that its MVPs are influenced by the MVs of intra-mode macroblocks. Based on the above analysis, the details of the proposed algorithm can be depicted as follows:

In the first case, there is only one intra-mode macroblock beside the block E. When predicting the MV of block E, the MV of the intra-mode macroblock will be looked as zero in the original median predictor. In our proposed scheme, if block D is the intra-mode macroblock, the MV of block D is looked as zero. MVs of blocks A, B, C are used for MVP of block E, the proposed method is the same as the original median predictor. If block A is the intra-mode macroblock (see Fig. 3), the MV of macroblock A will be set to the MV of block D. If macroblock B or macroblock C is the intra-mode block, the proposed scheme is the same as the condition when block A is the intra-mode macroblock (see Fig. 3).

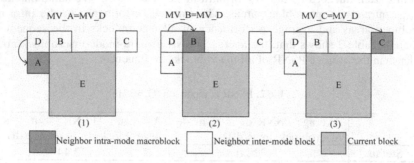

Fig. 3. Only one intra-mode macroblock beside block E

In the second case, there are two intra-mode macroblocks beside the block E. When predicting the MV of block E, the MVs of the two intra-mode macroblocks will be looked as zero in the original median predictor. In our proposed scheme, if block A and block D (or block B and block D, or block C and block D) are the intra-mode macroblocks, MVs of block A and block D (or block B and block D, or block C and block D) are still zero, the same as original median predictor. Because there are always one block D in the two intra-mode blocks. MV of block D is looked as zero. No more redundant neighbor MV can be used. When block A and block B are the intra-mode macroblocks(see Fig. 4), block D and block C are inter-mode blocks. In predicting MV of block E, MV of block D can be utilized by setting its MV to the MV of block A or MV of block B. In the two intra-mode macroblocks, only one macroblock's MV can be set to MV of block D, the other macroblock's MV is still zero. Which intra-mode macroblock's MV remained zero have no influence on the MVP value in the median predictor. When block A and block C (or block B and block C) are intra-mode macroblocks, the proposed scheme is the same as the condition when block A and block B are intra-mode macroblocks (see Fig. 4).

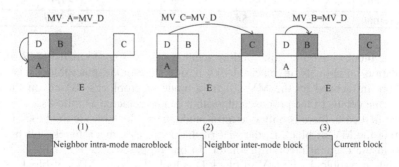

Fig. 4. Two intra-mode macroblocks beside block E

In the third case, there are three intra mode macroblocks beside the block E. In the original median predictor, there are at least two zero reference MVs in the surrounding blocks of block E, MV of block E is zero. In the proposed scheme, when block D is located in the three intra-mode macroblocks, the proposed method is the same as the original median predictor. When block D is not located in the three intra-mode macroblocks (see Fig. 5), blocks A, B, C are intra-mode macroblocks. The MVP value of block E is set to the MV of the block D, which is not intra-mode macroblock and have an inter MV.

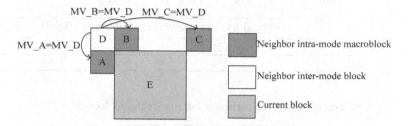

**Fig. 5.** Three intra-mode macroblocks beside block E

## 3 Experimental Results

To evaluate the coding efficiency, our experiments compare the performance of the proposed MVP scheme with that of median predictor, which is widely used in current video coding standards. The proposed method is implemented based on the H.264/AVC reference software JM76. The two test sequences, stefan and foreman, are both 300 frames CIF sequences with the frame rate of 30f/s. The test conditions are showed in Table 4.

**Table 4.** Test conditions

| MV resolution | 1/4 pel |
|---|---|
| Hadamard | ON |
| RD optimization | ON |
| Search Range | ±16 |
| Reference Frames | 2 |
| GOP structure | IBPBP |

Table5 shows that the number of intra-mode macroblocks is reduced by about 28% using proposed MVP scheme than before in the sequences. It is thought that after implementation of the proposed MVP scheme, less macroblocks fall into intra-mode than before.

As shown in table 6, for macroblocks in the neighbor of intra-mode macroblocks, the average coding efficiency of our scheme is better than median predictor, the maximum PSNR gain is up to 0.19dB (QP=32).

The test results of two predictors in different QPs are compared in Table 7. PSNR and bitrate of sequences are showed in the two tables. A comparison can be observed that the proposed predictor achieves better performances than median predictor in most of QPs. Especially at low bit rate, the luma PSNR gain is up to 0.18dB.

Table8 shows that the computation complexity of the proposed algorithm is reduced. In blocks beside intra-mode macroblocks, the speeding up ratio is about 24%. In the whole sequence, the speeding up ratio is about 12%.

**Table 5.** Percentage of intra mode macroblocks (QP=32)

|  | Original median predictor | Proposed MVP scheme |
|---|---|---|
| Stefan | 12% | 9.5% |
| Foreman | 9% | 7.1% |

**Table 6.** Average PSNR comparison in intra-mode macroblock areas(QP=32)

|  | Original median predictor | Proposed MVP scheme |
|---|---|---|
| Stefan | 32.20 | 32.39 |
| Foreman | 34.61 | 34.79 |

**Table 7.** The test results of two predictors for sequences in CIF (300 frames)

| Sequence | QP | Original median predictor | | Proposed MVP scheme | |
|---|---|---|---|---|---|
|  |  | PSNR(dB) | Bitrate(bps) | PSNR(dB) | Bitrate(bps) |
| Stefan | 24 | 38.71 | 1861.80 | 38.77 | 1859.65 |
|  | 28 | 35.63 | 1002.00 | 35.69 | 1000.20 |
|  | 34 | 31.05 | 358.10 | 31.13 | 354.05 |
|  | 40 | 26.72 | 143.38 | 26.83 | 138.43 |
|  | 44 | 23.99 | 81.47 | 24.17 | 76.74 |
| Foreman | 28 | 37.22 | 376.34 | 37.27 | 374.32 |
|  | 34 | 33.69 | 165.23 | 33.75 | 163.34 |
|  | 40 | 30.33 | 76.47 | 30.42 | 73.53 |
|  | 44 | 28.11 | 48.67 | 28.21 | 46.35 |
|  | 48 | 25.59 | 30.73 | 25.76 | 28.43 |

**Table 8.** AD counts comparison(QP=32)

|  |  | Mean AD counts of intra-mode areas($*10^3$) | Mean AD counts of all blocks($*10^3$) |
|---|---|---|---|
| Stefan | Median predictor | 124.82 | 94.43 |
|  | Proposed predictor | 98.23 | 83.57 |
| Foreman | Median predictor | 33.54 | 25.47 |
|  | Proposed predictor | 26.32 | 22.42 |

# 4 Conclusion

In this paper, we firstly review the median predictor and other MVP schemes proposed by researchers before. Then we propose an improved MVP scheme for H.264. For the block whose MV is to be predicted, the scheme exploits its more neighbor MV information and uses these information adaptively. The proposed MVP method is simple, but it is effective. It gives a better coding efficiency and brings less FME computation complexity. It can be applied in current wireless video communication. In the future, the proposed method can further exploit the spatial-temporal MV information, in that it gets the more accurate derivation of MVP than original median predictor.

## Acknowledgements

The study work has been supported in part by the National Natural Science Foundation of China under grant No.60333020.

## References

[1] ITU-T Recommendation H.263: Video Coding for Low Bitrate Communication (June 1996)
[2] Draft ITU-T recommendation and final draft international standard of joint video specification (ITU-T Rec.H.264/ISO/IEC 14 496-10 AVC). In Joint Video Team (JVT) of ISO/IEC MPEG & ITU-T VCEG, JVT-G050 (2003)
[3] Y. Lee, F. Kossentini, R. Ward, M. Smith: Prediction and Search Techniques for RD-Optimized Motion Estimation in a Very Low Bit Rate Video Coding Framework. ICASSP-97, vol.4 (Apr 1997) 2861-2864
[4] Ismaeil. I., Docef, A., Kossentini, F., Ward, R.K.: Efficient Motion Estimation Using Spatial and Temporal Motion Vector Prediction. Proc. of the IEEE Inter. Conf. on Image Proc.. Koke, Japan (October 1999)
[5] J. B. Xu, L. M. Po and C. K. Cheung: Adaptive motion tracking block matching algorithms for video coding. IEEE Trans. Circuits and Syst. Video Technol., vol. 97 (Oct. 1999) 1025-1029
[6] Sung Deuk Kim, Jong Beom Ra: A New Motion Vector Coding Technique. 39th MPEG meeting, m2100. Bristol, UK (Apr. 1997)
[7] S. D. Kim and J. B. Ra: An efficient motion vector coding scheme based on minimum bitrate prediction. IEEE Trans. Image Processing, vol. 8 (Aug. 1999) 1117-1120
[8] Sung Deuk Kim, Jong Beom Ra: Improved Motion Vector Coding Scheme. 38th MPEG meeting, m1748. Sevilla, Spain (Feb. 1997)
[9] Li Zhang, Wen Gao: Hybrid Algorithm with Adaptive Complexity for Interger Pel Motion Estimation of H.264. Conference of ICME (Mar 2005)

# Classifying Motion Time Series Using Neural Networks

Lidan Shou, Ge Gao, Gang Chen, and Jinxiang Dong

College of Computer Science, Zhejiang University, Hangzhou, 310027, P.R. China
{should, cg, djx}@cs.zju.edu.cn, gggrace@126.com

**Abstract.** This paper proposes an effective time-series classification model based on the Neural Networks. Classification under this model consists of three phases, namely *data preprocessing, training,* and *testing*. The main contributions of the paper are described as following: We propose a feature extraction algorithm, which involves computation of finite difference of sequences, for preprocessing. We employ two different types of Neural Networks for training and testing. The results of the experiments on real univariate motion capture data and synthetic data show that our approach is effective in providing good performance in terms of accuracy. It is therefore a promising method for classifying time-series, in particular for univariate human motion capture data.

## 1 Introduction

Time-series data are widely available in numerous applications. Exchange rate, audio signals, medical equipment records are all examples of time-series. Recently, with the wide-spread proliferation of multimedia technology, more and more new types of domain-specific time-series data have appeared. These include motion capture data, video sequences, animation, facial expressions, and many others. Classifying such multimedia time-series data is regarded one of the most important problems for time-series retrieval, especially in pattern recognition applications. As an example, in a typical gesture recognition system, a gesture sequence has to be analyzed efficiently and a target pattern has to be recognized to activate a user command.

The problem of time-series classification/clustering has been extensively studied. Most previous methods for time-series clustering are characterized by three common steps, namely *data preprocessing, distance calculation,* and *clustering*. Classification is handled a bit differently. First, a training sequence set must be processed to generate a classifier. Second, the distances between a testing sequence and the *centroids* of classes are evaluated. The class label with the smallest distance is regarded as the one that the testing sequence belongs to.

In this paper, we look at the classification problem from a machine-learning perspective. Similar to the above approaches, we firstly preprocess the time-series to produce feature vectors in a high-dimensional space. Secondly, we employ *neural network* to address the classification issue. The main contributions of this paper are as follows:

Y. Zhuang et al. (Eds.): PCM 2006, LNCS 4261, pp. 606–614, 2006.

1. We propose a novel feature extraction technique, which involves a non-uniform segmentation algorithm, for preprocessing the data. This segmentation algorithm splits sequences according to the *finite difference* of the data, which is computationally inexpensive. We use local features extracted from the segments, instead of global features computed from the sequence, to produce more accurate representations for the original data.

2. We present a model based on the Neural Network (NN) for classifying time-series. We treat the time-series as feature vectors, which will be fed to the NN for training. Unlike conventional time-series methods, our model does not require definition of distance metric and lower-bound function. We report the experimental results of our classification model using two distinct types of NN.

The rest of the paper is organized as following. Section 2 discusses the related works in time-series clustering/classification and neural networks. Section 3 proposes our NN-based classification method. Section 4 discusses the technique to extract features from the sequences. Section 5 presents the experimental results and evaluation. In the end, we conclude the paper in section 6.

## 2  Related Works

In this section, we review the related works in the area of time-series clustering/classification, and NN-based classification approaches.

There have been quite many approaches proposed to address the classification/clustering problem of time-series. Many of these approaches involve the usage of piecewise linear segmentation, the extraction of local features[2] or a combination of both local and global features[8], the definition of a distance measure [4,7], the deployment of a multi-dimensional spatial index [7], and various scaling techniques such as discrete time warping [1].

The most essential parts of these research works are focused on feature extraction, and similarity computation. In an early work [2], Faloutsos et al. propose a method to decomposed a time-series into *windows*. Features are extracted from each window, in the form of local spectral coefficients, and efficient matching is then performed using an $R^*$-tree structure. Similarity is defined as the distance in the feature space. Keogh et al. [6] use linear segments to represent the shape of the sequence, and a weight vector to represent the relative importance of each segment. The weight vector of a query is adjusted based on relevance feedback. Geurts proposes to solve multi-variate time-series with a certain kind of pattern extraction algorithm and to integrate it with decision trees [3]. In [7], Keogh et al. present a global scaling approach for searching human motion capture data. The search performance is expedited by employing a lower bound of the query and the sequences.

Kehagias et al. applied *predictive modular neural networks* for time-series classification based on Bayesian or non-probabilistic decision rules [5]. Our method is different from theirs in that we employ different types of NN, and we use a novel scheme to extract features.

# 3    Neural Network Classification of Time-Series

In this section, we propose a model of time-series classification based on the neural networks. We also describe how the training and the testing processes are handled in our method.

## 3.1    Model of NN for Time-Series Classification

The processing of the NN-based classification can be divided into three steps, namely *preprocessing, training* and *testing*. In the preprocessing step, the "significant" features are extracted for each time-series to generate a corresponding *feature vector*. This step is critical for the classification problem, as the output from it would have considerable impact on the effectiveness of our approach. For the training dataset, we feed the output from the preprocessing to the neural network to generate (train) a time-series classifier. For the testing time-series, we also extract the feature vectors and use the classifier to verify the efficiency of the NN model. The detailed feature extraction(preprocessing) technique is elaborated in section 4.

## 3.2    The Training Algorithms

We employ two types of training algorithms in our NN-based model, namely the back-propagation (BP) algorithm, and the functional link algorithm. The first one is the simplest and most widely used algorithm, while the second is known for its high training speed. Due to space limit, we will not discuss the BP algorithm in detail here. Readers are referred to [11] for details of the BP algorithm. We use a three-layer BP network in our model.

The functional link training algorithm simulates a mapping between the input and the class labels (output) using an artificially augmented single-layer network, namely *functional link neural network* (FLNN) [9]. Functional link network is able to handle linearly non-separable classes due to the additional dimensions of the inputs, such as the products of the original input vectors and functions of them. In our approach, we use the additional input dimensions that are calculated from the trigonometric functions of the original input vectors, as shown in the following:

$$x_1, \ldots, x_f, sin(\pi x_1), cos(\pi x_1), \ldots, sin(\pi x_f), cos(\pi x_f), \ldots, sin(k\pi x_f), cos(k\pi x_f).$$

It should be noted that we consider generic classification problems where the output class could have more than two possible values. Therefore, we build a multi-output network for multiple class labels. For example, when running experiments on the Gun-Point dataset, where the possible classes are *Draw*, and *Point*, we create a 2-output BP network (and a 2-output FLNN) for these classes.

### 3.3   Training and Testing

After the preprocessing, we perform the training to generate the time-series classifier. For each class in a dataset, e.g. the "Draw" class in the Gun-Point dataset, we generate an array of feature vectors for it. When a training sample is fed to the NN, the class label of "Draw" is "1" for a "Draw"-sequence, and "0" for a "Point"-sequence. We use the error back-propagation algorithm and the functional link algorithm for the training, and the weights of the trained networks are saved when the training finishes. We use cross validation process to obtain the best training results for the dataset. The training set is split into 4 disjoint parts randomly. In each fold, one part is used as the validation set while the others are used for training.

In the testing phase, we run the same feature extraction algorithm on the testing sequence to obtain the feature vector. Then we use the classifier to compute the output of the testing sequence on each class label. The one with the largest output score will be regarded as the class that the sequence belongs to.

We note that our training method is not restricted to univariate time-series classification. In a real-world application, such as a multi-variate motion classification system, the input feature vector may contain extracted information from multiple time-series. Training with the NN can still proceed on the feature vectors with the only change in the length of the vectors. That is, feature vectors for the multi-variate case would certainly contain more elements.

## 4   Feature Extraction

Feature extraction is an important stage in the design of a classifier, as the extracted features will determine the effectiveness of the classification. As the sequences in the datasets are high-dimensional, we have to select the most significant components of the features so that the classifier could achieve high learning rate without compromising the classification performance.

Research in previous work reported that both global and local features are useful for classifying time-series [8]. We can simply use the Discrete Fourier Transform (DFT) for extracting the global feature. Meanwhile, we need to design a technique to extract local features from a sequence.

### 4.1   Sequence Segmentation

To compute local features of a time-series, we need to break it into a few pieces, namely *segments*, so that local features would be computed on each segment. As the extracted feature vectors are uniformly fed to the NN for training, the number of segments for each sequence should be same. A naive solution is to segment the whole sequence into a number of fixed-length sub-sequences.

We propose a segmentation technique involving the computing of *finite difference*(FD). Given a sequence $\{S_i\}$ where $i = 1, \ldots, n$, we compute its first order finite forward difference as

$$D_i = S_{i+1} - S_i, \quad (i = 1, \ldots, n-1). \tag{1}$$

$D_i$ indicates how rapidly the sequence varies at point $i$. Intuitively, the sequence varies drastically at points where the $|D_i|$ value is large, while subsequences with small $|D_i|$ values are relatively more invariant. Motivated by this observation, we define a *local maximal absolute difference* to be a point $M$, if there exists an interval $[n_1, n_2]$ containing $M$ ($M \neq n_1, n_2$ and $n_2 \leq n - 1$), so that for each $N \in [n_1, n_2]$, we have

$$0 < |D_N| \leq |D_M|. \tag{2}$$

According to the theory of mathematical analysis, when the first order finite difference of a function $f(x)$, $\Delta f(x_0)$, equals to 0, $x_0$ might be a *local maximum*, or a *local minimum*, or an *inflection point*. Similarly, in a sequence, if $|D_i| < \epsilon$, where $\epsilon$ is a small positive quantity, $S_i$ can be approximately regarded a local maximum/minimum or an inflection point.

In our datasets, to minimize the impact of the signal noises, we use the *moving average* operator as a smoothing method. This step is optional regarding different datasets.

Based on the above discussions, we propose the segmentation algorithm as following. Given a sequence of length $n$, the main purpose of the algorithm is to find a set of split points on which the sequence would be segmented.

1. For the input sequence, initialize an (*id, finite_difference*)-tuple array $\{T_i\} = \{(i, D_i)|i = 1, 2, \ldots, n\}$. Initialize an empty set for the output, $O = \phi$.
2. For a given small constant $\epsilon > 0$, find the maximum $|D_i|$ value greater than $\epsilon$, denoted as $|D_m|$, in $\{T_i\}$.
3. Find the largest *neighborhood* of $m$, denoted as $[L_m, U_m]$, so that either inequation (3) or (4) holds for all points in the neighborhood:

$$\forall i \in [L_m, U_m] : \epsilon \leq D_i \leq D_M \tag{3}$$

or

$$\forall i \in [L_m, U_m] : -\epsilon \geq D_i \geq D_M. \tag{4}$$

The above description implies that point $L_m - 1$ and $U_m + 1$ do not satisfy either inequation (3) or (4).

4. If $U_m - L_m + 1$ is smaller than a specified threshold value $\eta$, the local maximum/minimum FD is regarded as a disturbance, and the tuples on the neighborhood, namely $(L_m, D_{L_m})$, $\ldots$, $(U_m, D_{U_m})$ will be removed from $\{T_i\}$. Otherwise, point $L_m$ and $U_m$ are added to the output set $O$. All the records on the neighborhood are then removed from $\{T_i\}$.
5. Goto step 2 until $\{T_i\} = \phi$ or all $D_i$ values in $\{T_i\}$ are in $(-\epsilon, \epsilon)$.

Our feature extraction technique has slight similarity to [2] in the *adaptiveness*. However, the segmented objects of our work are different: we segment the sequences directly, while Faloutsos splits the trails in the feature space. The problem that we look at is also different: We try to classify entire sequences instead of sub-sequences.

Figure 1 shows the difference of the real output of our segmentation scheme and that of a naive uniform segmentation scheme. It is apparent that our scheme can produce more meaningful segmentation compared to the naive one.

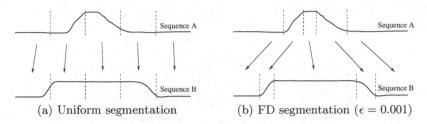

| (a) Uniform segmentation | (b) FD segmentation ($\epsilon = 0.001$) |

**Fig. 1.** The non-uniform segmentation technique based on Finite Difference

## 4.2 Computing Feature Vectors

After obtaining the segments, we use the Discrete Fourier Transform (DFT) algorithm to compute the feature components for each sequence. We can change the algorithm to other alternatives, such as wavelet transformation and so on, with trivial efforts. In each segment, we compute the first few coefficients, for example $f$ numbers. Suppose we have $NS$ segments for each sequence, we obtain a $NS \cdot f$ dimensional feature vector, which contains the local features of all segments.

## 5   Experimental Results

We use a real motion capture dataset, the Gun-Point (GP) dataset [10], and the well-known synthetic Cylinder-Bell-Funnel (CBF) dataset in our experiments. The software is implemented on Windows NT using the C language. The total number of sequences in the GP dataset is 200, with 100 labeled for each class. The CBF dataset generated by us contains 1800 sequences, with 600 for each class. By default, we use the BP network. The system error of the neural networks is set to 0.001 for the training.

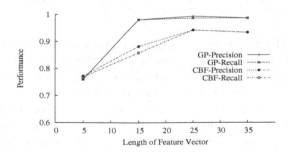

**Fig. 2.** Effect of the length of feature vectors

Figure 2 shows the effect of changing the length of the feature vectors. Generally, when the length of the feature vector increases, the accuracy of the generated classifier improves. This is expected, as more information is added to the input of the NN. However, as the newly added coefficients are less significant compared

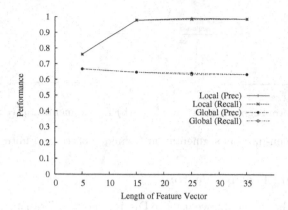

**Fig. 3.** Testing results using local features vs. global features

to the earlier ones, the performance improvement is small when the length of the feature vector is greater than 25.

Figure 3 illustrates the results using local-only feature vectors and global-only feature vectors for one dataset. It is apparent that the local features achieve better performance compared to the global ones.

**Table 1.** The performance of BP and functional link network

| Features | BP network | | | FLNN | | |
|---|---|---|---|---|---|---|
| | precision(%) | recall(%) | cycles | precision(%) | recall(%) | cycles |
| 6 | 91.8 | 91.9 | 62137 | 93.5 | 87.2 | 112 |
| 8 | 97.5 | 97.3 | 9156 | 97.1 | 96.3 | 986 |
| 10 | 98.3 | 98.1 | 6148 | 98.3 | 88.3 | 678 |
| 12 | 98.8 | 98.8 | 4849 | 98.3 | 87.2 | 923 |
| 14 | 98.9 | 98.8 | 1703 | 98.3 | 83.8 | 847 |

Table 1 shows the performance comparison between the BP network and the functional link network. Column *cycles* indicates the number of training cycles needed. The accuracy of the FLNN, in terms of recall, is not as good as the BP network. However, the FLNN has at least one-order faster convergence speed with acceptable accuracy. As the training time of BP is just in a few minutes for a training set containing hundreds of samples, we consider BP as a better solution for small datasets. However, the FLNN could be a better choice when the training time becomes critical.

Figure 4 shows the effectiveness of the FD segmentation algorithm. We compare the testing results with the naive uniform segmentation algorithm. Generally, the FD segmentation algorithm produces better results than the uniform algorithm. This is because the segments generated from our method is more meaningful for the feature representation. The result confirms our discussion in section 4.1.

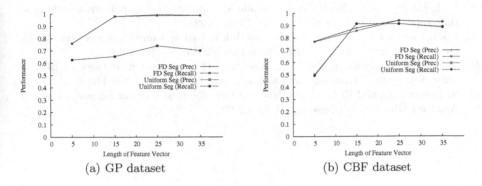

(a) GP dataset                    (b) CBF dataset

**Fig. 4.** FD segmentation vs. naive segmentation

## 6    Conclusion

This paper presented a model for time-series classification using Neural Networks. Compared to conventional time-series classification methods, our NN-based approach does not require definition of a distance metric or a lower-bound function. We discussed the deployment of two types of networks, namely BP and functional link network, in our classification model. We also proposed a novel feature extraction algorithm based on computation of finite differences. The experiments showed that our method achieved good performance in classifying univariate motion capture time-series and synthetic data.

For future work, we plan to extend our proposed classification method to handle multi-variate motion capture data. We would also look at indexing techniques using finite-difference-based feature extraction method.

## References

1. D. J. Berndt and J. Clifford. Using dynamic time warping to find patterns in time series. In *KDD Workshop*, pages 359–370, 1994.
2. C. Faloutsos, M. Ranganathan, and Y. Manolopoulos. Fast subsequence matching in time-series databases. In *SIGMOD*, pages 419–429, 1994.
3. P. Geurts. Pattern extraction for time series classification. In *PKDD*, pages 115–127, 2001.
4. K. Kalpakis, D. Gada, and V. Puttagunta. Distance measures for effective clustering of arima time-series. In *ICDM*, pages 273–280, 2001.
5. Ath. Kehagias and V. Petridis. Predictive modular neural networks for time series classification. *Neural Networks*, 10:31–49, 1997.
6. E. Keogh and M. Pazzani. An enhanced representation of time series which allows fast and accurate classification, clustering and relevance feedback. In *KDD*, pages 239–243, 1998.
7. E. J. Keogh, T. Palpanas, V. Zordan, D. Gunopulos, and M. Cardle. Indexing large human-motion databases. In *VLDB*, pages 780–791, 2004.

8. E. J. Keogh and P. Smyth. A probabilistic approach to fast pattern matching in time series databases. In *KDD*, pages 24–30, 1997.
9. Y.-H. Pao and Y. Takefuji. Functional-link net computing: theory, system architecture, and functionalities. *IEEE Computer*, 25(5):76–79, 1992.
10. C. A. Ratanamahatana and E. Keogh. The gun-point dataset. http:// www.cs.ucr.edu /˜eamonn/ time_series_data/. UCR Time Series Data.
11. S. Theodoridis and K. Koutroumbas. *Pattern Recognition (2nd Edition)*. Elsevier Academic Press, San Diego, CA, USA, 2003.

# Estimating Intervals of Interest During TV Viewing for Automatic Personal Preference Acquisition

Makoto Yamamoto, Naoko Nitta, and Noboru Babaguchi

Graduate School of Engineering, Osaka University
2–1 Yamadaoka, Suita, Osaka, 565–0871 Japan
{m-yamamoto, naoko, babaguchi}@nanase.comm.eng.osaka-u.ac.jp

**Abstract.** The demand for information services considering personal preferences is increasing. In this paper, aiming at the development of a system for automatically acquiring personal preferences from TV viewers' behaviors, we propose a method for automatically estimating TV viewers' intervals of interest based on temporal patterns in facial changes with Hidden Markov Models. Experimental results have shown that the proposed method was able to correctly estimate intervals of interest with a precision rate of 86.6% and a recall rate of 80.6%.

**Keywords:** Personalized Services, Personal Preferences, TV Viewer's Behaviors, Estimating Intervals of Interest.

## 1 Introduction

Recently, the demand for information services considering personal preferences has been increasing. In order to realize such services, it is essential to prepare personal preferences beforehand. There is some previous work to automatically acquire personal preferences from human behaviors. Web browsing histories[1], selections of TV programs[2], and operation records of remote controls[3] have been used as sources to analyze human behaviors. Because Web is mainly composed of text information, detailed personal preferences can be acquired easily. However, since the Web browsing is an intentional action such as retrieval based on key words or categories with clear purposes, such a method can acquire only personal preferences that he has already been aware of.

On the other hand, when a person turns on a TV, the TV programs are broadcasted one-sidedly regardless of whether he watches TV or not. Therefore, even personal preferences which he is still unaware of are expected to be acquired through the TV viewing. However, preferences extracted by using electronic program guide (EPG) are limited in comparison with using the Web browsing histories. Moreover, the browsing/viewing behaviors need to be observed for a long time to estimate how much the viewer is interested in each content.

We are now developing a system that automatically acquires personal preferences from TV viewer's behaviors and the metadata attached to the videos

Y. Zhuang et al. (Eds.): PCM 2006, LNCS 4261, pp. 615–623, 2006.

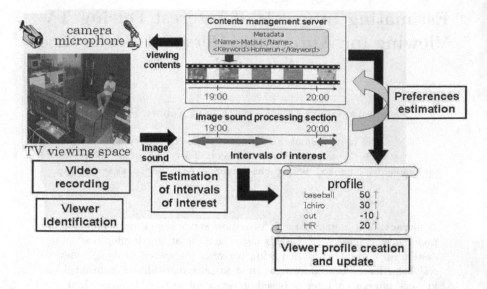

**Fig. 1.** Schematic diagram of our system

that are broadcasted at that time[4][5]. Our system tries to acquire detailed personal preferences by examining TV viewer's behaviors against video segments and considering the degrees of interest inferred by emotional differences in the viewer's behaviors such as laughing and crying. To acquire personal preferences, our system needs to estimate when the viewer shows his interest. In this research, the features that represent facial expressions are extracted, and the intervals of interest are estimated based on temporal patterns learned beforehand in assumption that facial expression changes when the viewer is interested in what he/she sees.

## 2   Personal Preference Acquisition System

Fig.1 shows a schematic diagram of our system. We assume that all videos have the MPEG-7 metadata which describes their content in a text form.

We describe a flow of the process of the system.

**(1) Video Recording.** Viewers watching TV are recorded with cameras and microphones.

**(2) Identification.** Viewers to acquire preferences are identified.

**(3) Interval of Interest Estimation.** Intervals of interest are estimated by video and audio processing.

**(4) Preference Estimation.** Personal preferences of each viewer are estimated by associating estimated intervals of interest with content information described in the metadata of the watched program.

**(5) Viewer Profile Creation and Update.** The viewer profile is created for each viewer and updated over time.

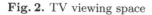

**Fig. 2.** TV viewing space

(a) Camera1      (b) Camera2

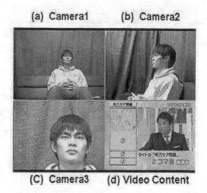

(C) Camera3     (d) Video Content

**Fig. 3.** Image of TV viewing

Fig.2 shows our experimental setup of the TV viewing space. There is a sofa in front of a TV and three cameras are installed to record viewers on the sofa. Cameras 1 and 3 are installed in front of the sofa and Camera 2 is installed on the left side of the sofa. Camera 1 records the entire sofa and Camera 3 records a viewer's face in close-up. Fig.3 shows the example images recorded by these cameras. Fig.3 (a), (b), and (c) are images recorded by Cameras 1, 2, and 3 respectively. Fig.3 (d) is an image which the viewer is watching. These four images are integrated into an image by a multiplexer. The system obtains a sequence of these integrated images as the input video. The frame rate of the input video is 10fps and the image resolution is $352 \times 240$. In this paper, only the image by camera 3 is cut out from the input image and used for the estimation of intervals of interest. In the following, this image is called a face image.

## 3   Estimating Intervals of Interest During TV Viewing

In this section, we proceed to describe a method of estimating intervals of interest. We assume that characteristic changes appear in a face in intervals of interest. We focus on the changes of facial expressions for the estimation of intervals of interest. We use features obtained from a face based on the existing method in the field of facial expression recognition. The process of facial expression recognition can be divided into two steps: (1) detecting changes in a face from a face image sequence[6][7]; and (2) associating changes in the face with a facial expression[8][9].

Similarly, the process of estimation of intervals of interest is divided into two steps: (1) detecting changes in a face from a face image sequence; and (2) determining whether the viewer is interested based on changes in the face. At the first step, we employ a simple method which extracts distances between points in the face as features. At the second step, we employ HMM that can adjust to the time sequence data because facial changes should have temporal patterns.

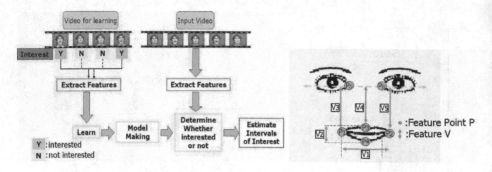

**Fig. 4.** A concept of estimation    **Fig. 5.** Extracted features

Fig.4 shows the outline of the estimation of intervals of interest. Feature points representing facial changes are extracted from each frame of sample videos. Next, features representing facial changes are calculated from feature points. An interest model and a no-interest model are obtained by learning the HMM with the sequential features extracted respectively from intervals of interest and other intervals, which are called intervals of no-interest. Moreover, sequential features are similarly generated from input videos. For each frame, whether the viewer is interested is determined by examining which of the two models an interval around the frame corresponds to. A set of consecutive frames conforming to the interest model is determined as the interval of interest.

### 3.1 Extraction of Feature Points

Fig.5 shows a set of feature points. We focus on six points. $P_1, ..., P_4$ are on the mouth, while $P_5$ and $P_6$ are on the right and left eye area, respectively. Here, the areas of eyes in the left and the right of the image are described as a right eye area and a left eye area, respectively.

In this case, feature points are extracted by using template matching. The positions of feature points are roughly specified to prevent miss-extraction and to shorten the calculation time before matching. Template $T_1, ..., T_6$ ($n \times n$ images) that centers on each feature point $P_1, ..., P_6$ are created beforehand. The flow of feature point extraction is shown below.

(1) **The first frame** Positions of feature points are roughly specified based on the extraction of eye areas and mouth area using color features. A point which gives the minimum $f_k(x, y)$ is set as the feature point. $f_k(x, y)$ is defined as

$$f_k(x, y) = \sum_{i=-\frac{n-1}{2}}^{\frac{n-1}{2}} \sum_{j=-\frac{n-1}{2}}^{\frac{n-1}{2}} \sum_{c=1}^{3} (|I_c(x+i, y+j) - I_{c,T_k}(x+i, y+j)|) \quad (1)$$

where $I_{1,2,3}(x, y)$ are R, G, and B value of a point $(x, y)$ in the face image, $I_{c,T_k}(x, y)$ are R, G, and B value of a point $(x, y)$ in $T_k (k = 1, ..., 6)$. In addition, $x$ and $y$ satisfy the following conditions: $x_r - r_1 \leq x \leq x_r + r_1$ and $y_r - r_1 \leq y \leq y_r + r_1$, where $x_r$ and $y_r$ are the points of the rough positions.

**(2) After the second frame** Templates created from the previous frame are used in addition to the templates used for the first frame in order to improve the extraction accuracy. The feature points in the previous frame are set as the rough positions of feature points. Template $T_7, ..., T_{12}$ ($n \times n$ images) that centers on the rough position of each feature point of the previous frame is created. Eq. (1) is calculated using both $T_1, ..., T_6$ and $T_7, ..., T_{12}$ as the templates. The point which minimizes the total of $f_k(x, y)$ is set as the feature point. Here, $r_2$ is used instead of using $r_1$.

Next, the method of specifying rough positions of feature points is described.

**[Face area extraction]**

**(1)** $I$ component of the $YIQ$ color space is calculated from the image, skin areas tend to have large $I$ component.

**(2)** This image is binarized. A minimum rectangular area including the maximum white area in this binary image is determined as a face area.

**[Position specification of mouth feature points]**

**(1)** The pixels whose $R$, $G$ and $B$ components satisfy the following conditions are set to white and others are set to black: $(R > 150) \wedge (G/R < 0.5) \wedge (B/R < 0.5)$.

**(2)** The maximum white area in this binary image is considered to be a mouth area. The most left, right, top, and bottom pixels in this area are determined as feature points $P_1$, $P_2$, $P_3$, and $P_4$ respectively.

**[Position specification of eye feature points]**

**(1)** $Y$ component of the $YIQ$ color space is calculated from the image.

**(2)** The edges of $Y$ component image are emphasized by Laplacian filter. This emphasized $Y$ component image is binarized.

**(3)** Two areas that are the right eye area and the left eye area are extracted by considering the positions of eyes.

**(4)** The most right pixel of the right eye area and the most left pixel of the left eye area are set to be $P_5$ and $P_6$ respectively.

## 3.2   Calculation of Features

Five features $V_1, ..., V_5$ shown in Fig.5 are calculated. At first, coordinates of each feature point are converted into the coordinate system based on $P_5$ and $P_6$ by the following expression.

$$\begin{pmatrix} x'_k \\ y'_k \end{pmatrix} = \frac{1}{l^2} \begin{pmatrix} x_6 - x_5 & y_6 - y_5 \\ -y_6 + y_5 & x_6 - x_5 \end{pmatrix} \begin{pmatrix} x_k - x_5 \\ y_k - y_5 \end{pmatrix} \tag{2}$$

where $(x_5, y_5)$, $(x_6, y_6)$, $(x_k, y_k)$, and $(x'_k, y'_k)$ represent the coordinates of $P_5$, $P_6$, $P_k$, and $P'_k$ respectively. $P'_k$ corrsponds to $P_k$ after revision and $l$ is the distance between $P_5$ and $P_6$. As a result, the size and inclination of the face can be corrected. Five features are calculated from coordinates of each feature point in the converted coordinate system.

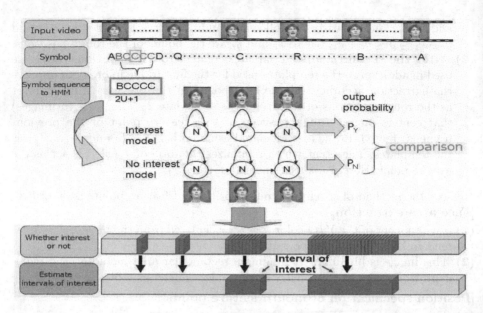

**Fig. 6.** A flow of the estimation of intervals of interest

## 3.3 Generation of Sequence of Features

It is undesirable to use five features in respect of the computational complexity. There should be correlations between the features. We reduce them to $m$-dimensions by using Principal Component Analysis (PCA).

Moreover, the values obtained by using PCA are changed from continuous values to discrete values to make them easily usable with HMM. At first, the maximum value $t_{k,max}$ and the minimum value $t_{k,min}$ are obtained in the $k$-th principal component. Each value of the $k$-th principal component is divided equally in $d_k$ between $t_{k,max}$ and $t_{k,min}$. The vectors of the discrete value are obtained by performing this processing in each principal component. A vector of these discrete values representing each frame is called a symbol.

## 3.4 Estimation of Intervals of Interest Using HMM

Fig.6 shows a flow of the estimation of intervals of interest. The two HMMs of the interest model and the no-interest model are prepared to learn temporal patterns of symbol in intervals of interest and intervals of no-interest. HMM is a model with a finite set of states, transitions among the states is described by a set of probabilities $A = \{a_{ij}\}$, where $a_{ij}$ indicates the transition from state $i$ to $j$. At each state there are observation probabilities $B = \{b_j(O)\}$, where $b_j(O)$ indicates the occurrence of symbol $O$ in state $j$. The initial state is determined by the initial state distribution $\pi = \{\pi_i\}$. We suppose that viewer's state changes in the order of no-interest / interest / no-interest in the intervals of interest, and set the number of states of the HMM as three in order to associate each condition with the state of the HMM. The left-to-right HMM is used to appropriately model these temporal patterns. The parameters of the HMMs are estimated with the BaumWelch algorithm[10].

The input to the HMMs for each frame is the sequence of symbols obtained from the sequence of frames which consist of total $2U + 1$ frames, i.e. the former and the latter $U$ frames. The likelihood of the symbols being observed from both models is calculated by the Forward algorithm[10]. If the likelihood for the interest model is higher than the likelihood for the no-interest model, the viewer is determined to be interested during the frame. If the viewer is determined to be interested during consecutive $S$ frames, the interval is regarded as an interval of interest.

## 4    Experiments and Evaluations

We experimented our proposed method on three viewers in their twenties. We showed viewers entertainment programs because the viewers should frequently show their interests in watching such programs. After they had watched the videos of about 90 minutes that consist of two programs, intervals of interest were specified by themselves.

Table 1 shows the parameters determined experimentally for feature points extraction and intervals of interest estimation. The parameters of initial state probability $\pi$ of left-to-right HMM were set to be $\pi_1 = 1$ and $\pi_{2,3} = 0$. The initial values of parameters for $A$ and $B$ are determined by equally dividing the probability into the number of the possible transitions from each state and observable symbols at each state respectively as follows.

$$A = \begin{bmatrix} 1/2 & 1/2 & 0 \\ 0 & 1/2 & 1/2 \\ 0 & 0 & 1 \end{bmatrix} \qquad B = \begin{bmatrix} 1/36 & 1/36 & \cdots & 1/36 \\ 1/36 & 1/36 & \cdots & 1/36 \\ 1/36 & 1/36 & \cdots & 1/36 \end{bmatrix} \qquad (3)$$

The extraction accuracy of six feature points is almost 100 for 10000 frames for each of three viewers. Whether or not the feature points were able to be extracted correctly was subjectively evaluated because the accurate feature points were not able to be determined objectively.

Next, 30 intervals were randomly selected from the intervals specified by each viewer, and were used as the sample data for the interest model. 30 intervals consisting of 100 frames were also extracted from other parts of the recorded video and were used as sample data for the no-interest model. Fig.7 and Table 2 show the experimental results of the estimation of intervals of interest for the input videos excluding the sample data that was used for the two HMMs. The definitions of the precision rate and the recall rate are $Precision = I/II$ and $Recall = I/III$, where $I, II$, and $III$ are the number of correctly estimated intervals of interest, the number of estimated intervals of interest, and the number of correct intervals of interest, respectively.

**Table 1.** Parameters for examination

| n | $r_1$ | $r_2$ | h | m | $d_1$ | $d_2$ | $d_3$ | U | S |
|---|---|---|---|---|---|---|---|---|---|
| 21 | 50 | 10 | 10 | 3 | 6 | 3 | 2 | 24 | 5 |

**Table 2.** A result of estimation

| viewer | precision(%) | recall(%) |
|---|---|---|
| A | 90.0(126/140) | 72.4(126/174) |
| B | 80.9(38/47) | 86.7(38/44) |
| C | 84.0(68/81) | 97.1(68/70) |
| total | 86.6(232/268) | 80.6(232/288) |

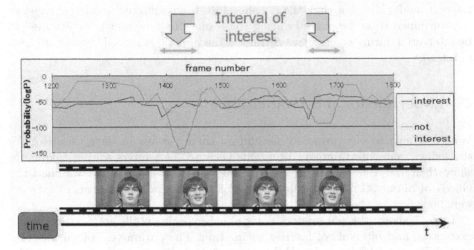

**Fig. 7.** An example of the result of estimation

We consider that the estimated interval is correctly estimated if the interval contains a part of intervals of interest and the total time of intervals of no-interest is shorter than 5 seconds at the same time. Moreover, when an estimated interval contains two or more intervals of interest, We consider the estimated interval is correctly estimated if the gaps between any two intervals of interest are shorter than 5 seconds while the total time of the intervals of no-interest excluding these gaps is shorter than 5 seconds. Although the time of the interval of interest varied from 1 to 25 seconds, using HMM succeeded in robust estimation. Good results were obtained for all three viewers. The reason for the false detections can be considered as follows: The viewer was smiling slightly in the intervals of no-interest even though the facial expression did not change in the sample videos for the no-interest model. The sample videos of the no-interest model needs to include intervals of no-interest where the viewer's facial expression changes for more accurate estimation. However, in that case, the recall rate would decrease because the sample videos for the no-interest model will be similar to those for the interest model. How to select the sample videos should be examined. On the other hand, the reason for the miss detections is considered as follows: The face did not change even though the viewer was interested. In this case, other features such as changes in the postures or the sound should be added because it is difficult to estimate viewer's interests only with the features in faces.

Most of the viewer's facial expression changes in intervals of interest was caused by laughter because they watched the entertainment programs in these experiments. Therefore, further experiments by using videos of other genres are necessary.

## 5 Conclusion

This paper proposed a system for acquiring personal preferences from TV viewer's behaviors. We proposed a method for automatically estimating intervals of interest based on temporal patterns in facial changes with HMM. As a result of the experiments with three viewers, the proposed method was able to correctly estimate intervals of interest with a precision rate of 86.6% and a recall rate of 80.6%. Examining how to select the sample videos, conducting experiments by using videos of various genres, and introducing other features will be our future work. Moreover, how to specify whether the viewer is interested and how to estimate the degree of interest from the viewer's behaviors should be examined. This work was partly supported by HBF Inc.

## References

1. N. Miura, K. Takahashi, and K. Shima, "A User-models construction Method for Presonal-adaptive WWW", *The IEICE Transactions on infomation and system*, Vol.39, No.5, pp.1523-1535, 1998.
2. T. Taka, T. Watanabe, and H. Taruguchi, "A TV Program Selection Support Agent with History Database", *The IEICE Transactions on infomation and system*, Vol.42, No.12, pp.3130-3143, 2001.
3. K. Masumithu, and T. Echigo, "Personalized Video Summarization Using Importance Score", *J. of IEICE*, Vol.J84-D-II, No.8, pp.1848-1855, 2001.
4. T. Yao, Y. Ohara, F Shibata, N. Babaguchi, and Y. Yagi, "Recognizing Actions for Automatically Acquiring Personal Preferences from TV Viewer's Behabiors", *Technical Report of PRMU 2003-209*, pp.65-70, 2004.
5. H. Tanimoto, N. Nitta, and N. Babaguchi, "TV Viewing Interval Estimation for Personal Preference Acquisition", *ICME2006*.
6. H. Gu, G. Su, and C. Du, "Feature Points Extraction from Face", *Image and Vision Computing*, Vol.9, pp.154-158, 2003.
7. K. Mase, "Recognition of facial expression from optical flow", *the IEICE transactions*, Vol.E74, No.10, pp.3474-3483, 1991.
8. H. KobayashiCand F. Hara, "Dynamic Recognition of Basic Facial Expressions by Discrete-time Recurrent Neural Network", *Proceedings of International Joint Conference on Neural Network*, No.10, pp.155-158, 1993.
9. I. Cohen, N. Sebe, L. Chen, A. Garg, and T. S. Huang, "Facial Expression Recognition from Video Sequences: Temporal and Static Modeling", *Computer Vision and Image Understanding*, Vol.91, Issues 1-2, 2003.
10. Lawrence. R. Rabiner, "A Tutorial on Hidden Markov Models and Selected Applications in Speech Recognition", *Proceeding IEEE*, Vol.77, pp.257-285, 1989.

# Image Annotations Based on Semi-supervised Clustering with Semantic Soft Constraints

Rui Xiaoguang, Yuan Pingbo, and Yu Nenghai*

MOE-Microsoft Key Laboratory of Multimedia Computing and Communication
University of Science and Technology of China
Hefei, Anhui, China
davidrui@mail.ustc.edu.cn,
{ypb, ynh}@ustc.edu.cn

**Abstract.** An efficient image annotation and retrieval system is highly desired for the increase of amounts of image information. Clustering algorithms make it possible to represent images with finite symbols. Based on this, many statistical models, which analyze correspondence between visual features and words, have been published for image annotation. But most of these models cluster only using visual features, ignoring semantics of images. In this paper, we propose a novel model based on semi-supervised clustering with semantic soft constraints which can utilize both visual features and semantic meanings. Our method first measures the semantic distance with generic knowledge (e.g. WordNet) between regions of the training images with manual annotations. Then a semi-supervised clustering algorithm with semantic soft constraints is proposed to cluster regions with semantic soft constraints which are formed by semantic distance. The experiment results show that our model improves performance of image annotation and retrieval system.

**Keywords:** image annotation, semi-supervised clustering, soft constraints, semantic distance.

## 1 Introduction

With the rapid development of digital photography, digital image data has increased tremendously in recent years. Consequently image retrieval has drawn the attention of many researchers. Content-based image retrieval (CBIR) computes relevance based on the visual similarity of low-level image features. However there is a gap between low-level visual features and semantic meanings. The so-called semantic gap is a major problem that needs to be solved for most CBIR approaches. Consequently, image annotation which can settle this problem has received extensive attention recently.

One approach to automatically annotate images is to look at the probability of associating words with image regions. Mori et al. [1] proposed a co-occurrence model in which they looked at the co-occurrence of words with image regions created using a regular grid. Duygulu et al [2] proposed to describe images using a vocabulary of

---

* Corresponding author.

Y. Zhuang et al. (Eds.): PCM 2006, LNCS 4261, pp. 624–632, 2006.

blobs. First, regions are created using a segmentation algorithm like normalized cuts. For each region, features are computed and then blobs are generated by **clustering** the image features for these regions across images. Each image is generated by using a certain number of these blobs. Their Translation Model (TM) applies one of the classical statistical machine translation models to translate from the set of keywords of an image to the set of blobs forming the image. Jeon et al [3]used a cross-media relevance model (CMRM) to perform both image annotation and ranked retrieval.

Since most of above approaches rely on clustering as the basis for automatic image annotation, the performance of annotation is strongly influenced by the quality of clustering. However, most approaches perform region clustering only based on low-level visual features, ignoring semantic concepts of images. Thus regions with different semantic concepts but share similar appearance may be grouped, leading to a poor clustering performance.

To address this problem, we first measure the correlations of annotations based on semantic distance. Next, we select some of the semantic distance of annotations as soft constraints, and then develop a semi-supervised clustering with these semantic soft constraints when clustering the regions to blobs. So the new approach comprehensively uses both semantic concepts and low-level features.

In the previous research some efforts have been made to cluster using a semi-supervised method. The prior knowledge was provided at the instance level in the form of positive (must-link) and negative (cannot-link) pairwise constraints in [4-5]. Soft constraints were introduced in the dissertation of Wagsta [6]. [7] proposed a principled probabilistic framework based on Hidden Markov Random Fields (HMRFs) for semi-supervised clustering.

Our clustering approach can be seen as an extend work by [7] whose method gets a good performance, but only copes with the hard constraints. To account for soft constraints, we use a more complex objective function.

The main contribution of this paper is as follows: we propose an image annotation model based on semi-supervised clustering which can make use of the semantic meanings of images, and develop an image annotation and retrieval system.

This paper is organized as follows: Section 2 explains semantic distance measure and how it forms the soft constraints, and presents our proposed approach of the semi-supervise clustering which can utilize these semantic soft constraints. Section 3 presents experiment setup and results of our approach. Section 4 presents conclusion and a comment on future work.

## 2   Region Clustering with Semantic Soft Constraints

Most approaches perform image regions clustering merely based on visual features. Thus regions with different semantic concepts but similar appearance may be easily grouped, which will lead to poor clustering performance.

In TM & CMRM model, each training image is represented by a set of keywords and visual tokens, and every visual token inherits all the concepts from its image.

That is to say, we can get the semantic meanings of training images as prior knowledge in an image annotation task. So by using the structure and content of WordNet or any other thesaurus, similarities between tokens can be calculated not only using visual token feature but also semantic concepts.

A natural way to use these semantic similarities is to impose constraints on the processing of clustering. Then we develop a semi-supervised clustering approach with semantic soft constraints which consist of soft must-link / cannot-link constraints.

So, the task contains the following parts:

- Measure semantic distance between visual tokens.
- Form soft constraints
- Develop a semi-supervised clustering using these constraints

## 2.1 Measuring Semantic Distance

We will use the structure and content of WordNet for measuring semantic similarity between two concepts. Current state of the art can be classified to different categories such as: Node-Based [8-10], Distance-Based [11].

In our system, we choose LIN measure. Lin et al. [9] used the first Information Content (IC) notion and took into account the similarity between selected concepts. Lin used Corpus to get the probabilities of each concept and computed how many times the concept appears in the Corpus. Next, the probabilities of each concept were calculated by the relative frequency. So the Information Content (IC) is determined.

With regard to semantic similarity between two concepts, Lin used the IC values of these concepts along with the IC value of lowest common subsumer (lcs) of these two concepts.

$$similarity(c_1, c_2) = \frac{2 \times IC(lcs(c_1, c_2))}{IC(c_1) + IC(c_2)} \tag{1}$$

Furthermore, we can get semantic distance between visual tokens:

$$D(t_1, t_2) = \begin{cases} -1 & t_1.image = t_2.image \\ 1 - \underset{min(p,q)}{average}[\underset{max(p,q)}{min} \ similarity(t_1.keyword_p, t_2.keyword_q)] & t_1.image \neq t_2.image \end{cases} \tag{2}$$

Where $t_1$, $t_2$ refer to visual tokens, $t_1.image$ means the image which $t_1$ belongs to, $t_1.keyword_p$ means the p-th keyword with which $t_1.image$ is manually annotated. When $t_1$, $t_2$ belong to the same image, it is no use to calculate the semantic distance between them for their keywords are the same, so we set its value -1.

## 2.2 Form Soft Constraints

By using semantic distances between visual tokens, constraints can be formed. There are two common constraints: must-link constraints and cannot-link constraints.

A cannot-link/ must-link constraint means two data (in our work, it is a token) cannot/ must be put in the same cluster. They are always "hard" constraints, while in our work we can define a constraint with an additional strength factor which is called a "soft" constraint.

Compared with a hard constraint [12], a soft constraint has many advantages in our task. For example, there are two certain tokens: token A in the image"sky trees" and token B in another image"sky grass'. It is hard to use hard must-link constraints to say that token A and token B must in the same cluster, but it can be described by a soft must-link constraint with a strength factor s. If the semantic distance D between token A and B is smaller than the down-threshold, we think they have a soft must-link constraint with a strength factor s = D. So, a soft constraint can better utilize known knowledge than a hard constraint, and can easily cope with semantic distance.

Constraints can be listed using the following expression:

$$S = \begin{cases} -D & if \ up\text{-}threshold < D < 1 \\ 1-D & if \ 0 < D < down\text{-}threshold \end{cases}$$ (3)

$(A, B, S)$: define a constraint; $A, B$: tokens; $S$:strength factor

If semantic distance is out of threshold, a constraint will be formed. When S>0, (A, B, S) defines a soft must-link constraint; When S<0, (A, B, S) defines a soft cannot-link constraint.

## 2.3 Clustering with Soft Constraints

After forming soft constraints between regions from different images, we perform clustering with these constraints to generate region clusters/blobs.

### 2.3.1 HMRF-Kmeans
HMRF-Kmeans [7] motivates an objective function derived from the posterior energy of the HMRF framework.

$$J_{obj} = \sum_{x_i \in X} D(x_i, \mu_{l_i}) + \sum_{(x_i, x_j) \in M} w_{ij} D(x_i, x_j) I(l_i \neq l_j)$$
$$+ \sum_{(x_i, x_j) \in C} \overline{w_{ij}} (D_{max} - D(x_i, x_j)) I(l_i = l_j)$$ (4)

Where M is the set of must-link constraints, C is the set of cannot-link constraints, $w_{ij} / \overline{w_{ij}}$ is the penalty cost for violating a must-link/cannot-link constraint between $x_i$ and $x_j$, and $l_i$ refers to the cluster label of xi. $\mu_{l_i}$ refers to the representative of cluster $l_i$. I is an indicator function (I[true] = 1, I[false] = 0). The first term in this objective function is the standard Kmeans' objective function; the second term is a penalty function for violating must-link constraints; while the third term is a penalty function for violating cannot-link constraints.

The algorithms developed to find a minimal value of this objective function, using an iterative relocation approach like Kmeans.

### 2.3.2 Soft HMRF-Kmeans

But HMRF-Kmeans can only cope with hard constraints. We achieve clustering with soft constraints by modifying HMRF-Kmeans' objective function to deal with a real-valued penalty for violating constraints. Two methods are proposed:

- Indicator method

In the original objective function, Indicator function $I(a)$ is a two-value function. $((I(true) = 1, I(false) = 0))$

In order to deal with soft constraints, Indicator function can be modified to a real function $I'(a)$ range from 0 to 1. And the value of real indicator function $I'(a)$ equals the absolute value of the strength factor S when a is true. $((I(true) = |S|, I(false) = 0))$ So in the modified objective function, the penalty is proportional to the absolute value of the strength factor S.

- MVS method

$MVS(x_i, \mu_h)$ means in all soft constraints ($x_i$ ,B,S) if $x_i$ in cluster $h$ calculating the maximum strength of the violated constraints. $MVS(x_i, \mu_h)$ can be calculated as follows:

$$MVS(x_i, \mu_h) = \frac{nViol}{nConst} \times \max_{\text{violate constraints}} |S| \qquad (5)$$

Where $nConst$ is the times when $|S|$ gets maximum value, $nViol$ is the times when $|S|$ gets maximum value and constraint is violated.

New objective function combines MVS with old objective function in the following way:

$$J_{obj}^{MS}(x_i, \mu_h) = \frac{J_{obj}(x_i, \mu_h)}{1 - MVS(x_i, \mu_h)} \qquad (6)$$

When MVS gets a value which is near to 1, $J_{obj}^{MS}$ will reach a very high value. In this case, $x_i$ will not choose cluster $h$. Therefore, the new objective function can show how strong constraints are.

Finally, we combine these two methods, and get the soft objective function:

$$J_{obj}^{SOFT}(x_i, \mu_h) = [D(x_i, \mu_h) + \sum_{S>0} w_{ij} D(x_i, x_j) I'(l_i \neq l_j)$$
$$- \sum_{S<0} \overline{w_{ij}} D(x_i, x_j) I'(l_i = l_j)] / (1 - MVS(x_i, \mu_h)) \qquad (7)$$

Note that we remove $D_{max}$ for accelerating the processing of the algorithm and it will not alter the meaning of objective function.

Soft HMRF-Kmeans aims to minimize the penalty of violating the soft constraints, which can be achieved by minimizing the new objective function. In detail, Soft HMRF-Kmeans is also an EM-like algorithm:

- In the E-step, given the current cluster representatives, every data point is re-assigned to the cluster which minimizes its contribution to $J_{obj}^{SOFT}$. Iterated conditional mode (ICM) [13] is applied to reduce $J_{obj}^{SOFT}$.

- In the M-step, the cluster representatives $\{\mu_n\}_{h=1}^{K}$ are re-estimated from the cluster assignments to minimize $J_{obj}^{SOFT}$ for the current assignment. Also the clustering distance measure D is updated to reduce the objective function by transforming the space. We define L2 distance measure D = A*|X-Y|, every weight $a_m$ in A would be updated using the update rule:

$$a_m = a_m + \mu \frac{\partial J_{obj}^{SOFT}}{a_m}$$

## 3   Experiment and Result

### 3.1   Dataset and Model Parameter

We use the dataset in Duygulu et al[2]. The dataset consists of 5,000 images from 50 Corel Stock Photo cds. Each cd includes 100 images on the same topic. Segmentation using normalized cuts followed by quantization ensures that there are 1-10 blobs for each image. Each image was also assigned 1-5 keywords. Overall there are 374 words in the dataset. Dataset is divided into 2 parts - the training set of 4500 images and the test set of 500 images.

Two thresholds need to be defined to form constraints, and we choose up-threshold = 0.9, down-threshold = 0.3 which are tuned according to the experiment. Unit constraint costs W and $\overline{W}$ are used for all constraints, since indicator function already provides individual weights for the constraints. Other parameter such as constraints can be automatically handled by our model.

### 3.2   Results and Discussion

We perform image annotations based on CMRM model [3] and compare Soft HMRF-Kmeans/CMRM with Hard HMRF-Kmeans/CMRM as well as Kmeans/CMRM.

- Soft HMRF-Kmeans/CMRM: use Soft HMRF-Kmeans in CMRM model.
- Hard HMRF-Kmeans/CMRM: use Hard HMRF-Kmeans in CMRM model. And it only uses cannot-link constraints because it is difficulty to form hard must-link constraints according to the Section 2.2.
- Kmeans/CMRM: only use unsupervised Kmeans in CMRM model.

Fig. 1 shows some annotation results based on these three models. Fig. 2 is a precise-recall graph and demonstrates the performance of the retrieval system.

Comparing these three image annotation models, system performance enhances when using a semi-supervised clustering method. And soft HMRF-Kmeans/CMRM gets the best performance.

| Image | 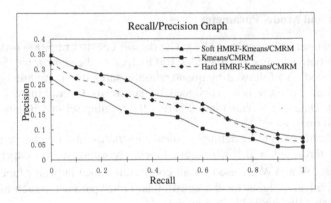 | | |
|---|---|---|---|
| Original annotation | boats horizon shops water | mountain people road | beach people sand water |
| Kmeans/CMRM | water sky man people clouds | tree temple buddha people sky | sky sand hills dunes water |
| Hard HMRF-Kmeans/CMRM | water sky clouds pillar buildings | tree people buildings street swimmers | sand sky dunes people water |
| Soft HMRF-Kmeans/CMRM | boats ships water sky vehicle | people street road grass mountain | sand beach dunes people water |

**Fig. 1.** Automatic annotations (best five words) compared with the original manual annotations

**Fig. 2.** Performance of the three model

We can see more detail in Fig. 1. The automatic annotations of Kmeans/CMRM often contain some irrelevant keywords, e.g. "man", "people" in first image. And the semi-clustering/CMRM can remove some of them, e.g. "people" (first image), "sky" (second image), "hills" (third image). Comparing with Hard HMRF-Kmeans/CMRM, Soft HMRF-Kmeans/CMRM can remove more irrelevant keywords (e.g. "sky" in third image) and extend the existed keywords (e.g. "boats" in the first image is extended with "ships" and "vehicle"; "street" which is the automatic annotations of Hard HMRF-Kmeans/CMRM in the second image is extended with "road", and the same is to "sand" in the third image). Therefore, when apply Soft HMRF-Kmeans to cluster regions to blobs, our system naturally have the ability of "removing" and "extending" when using semantic constraints.

Manual annotations are not always true, e.g. "shops" (first image). But In the Soft HMRF-Kmeans/CMRM model, it is corrected with "ships". So this may be a useful approach in checking the accuracy of manual annotations.

Fig.3 shows that blobs formed by Kmeans are not well described. The test image and the training image are 5 blobs in common while they have not any semantic relation. But blobs formed by Soft HMRF-Kmeans are described better. The two images have little blobs in common. So blobs formed by Soft HMRF-Kmeans are better descriptors of images.

| Left: training image<br>Right: test image | | |
|---|---|---|
| Soft HMRF-Kmeans | Blobs:  56 95 259 458 62 56<br>106 256 | Blobs: 362 507 159 20 64<br>92 106 |
| Kmeans | Blobs: 83 419 186 8 33 33 250<br>142 142 199 | Blobs: 449 145 8 484 33<br>142 145 142 269 |

**Fig. 3.** different clustering method to form blobs

# 4 Conclusions and Future Works

We have shown a semi-supervised clustering can help existed region-based image annotation model improve the performance of annotating and retrieving image. Using semantic meanings of regions, soft constraints can be formed to get better results.

Obtaining large amounts of labeled training and test data is difficult but we believe this is needed for improvements in both performance and evaluation of the algorithms proposed here. Better feature extraction will probably improve the results. Other areas of possible research include the use of captions in the World Wide Web. We believe that this is a fruitful area of research for applying semi-supervised learning method in image or video annotation.

# Acknowledgement

This work is supported by MOE-Microsoft Key Laboratory of Multimedia Computing and Communication Open Foundation (No.05071804). The authors wish to thank Prof. Li Mingjing for his contributions in this work.

# References

1. Mori Y, Takahashi H, Oka R. Image-to-word transformation based on dividing and vector quantizing images with words. First International Workshop on Multimedia Intelligent Storage and Retrieval Management, 1999
2. Duygulu P, Barnard K, De F N, et al. Object recognition as machine translation: Learning a lexicon for a fixed image vocabulary. Seventh European Conference on Computer Vision (ECCV), 2002, 4: 97~112
3. Jeon J, Lavrenko V, Manmatha R. Automatic image annotation and retrieval using cross-media relevance models. Toronto, Canada: ACM Press, 2003. 119~126P

4. Wagstaff K, Cardie C, Rogers S, et al. Constrained k-means clustering with background knowledge. Proceedings of the Eighteenth International Conference on Machine Learning, 2001, 577～584
5. Wagstaff K, Cardie C. Clustering with instance-level constraints. Proceedings of the Seventeenth International Conference on Machine Learning, 2000, 1103～1110
6. Wagstaff K et al. Intelligent Clustering with Instance-Level Constraints, Proceedings of the Seventeenth International Conference on Machine Learning, 2000, 1103～1110.
7. Basu S, Bilenko M, Mooney R J. A probabilistic framework for semi-supervised clustering. Proceedings of the 2004 ACM SIGKDD international conference on Knowledge discovery and data mining, 2004, 59～68
8. Jiang J J, Conrath D W. Semantic similarity based on corpus statistics and lexical taxonomy. Proceedings of International Conference on Research in Computational Linguistics, 1997, 19～33
9. Lin D. Using syntactic dependency as local context to resolve word sense ambiguity. Proceedings of the 35th Annual Meeting of the Association for Computational Linguistics, 1997, 64～71
10. Resnik P. Using information content to evaluate semantic similarity in a taxonomy. Proceedings of the 14th International Joint Conference on Artificial Intelligence, 1995, 1: 448～453
11. Leacock C, Chodorow M. Combining local context and WordNet similarity for word sense identification. WordNet: An Electronic Lexical Database, 1998, 265～283
12. Shi R, Wanjun J, Tat-seng C. A Novel Approach to Auto Image Annotation Based on Pairwise Constrained Clustering and Semi-Naive Bayesian Model. 2005. 322～327P
13. Besag J. On the statistical analysis of dirty pictures (with discussion). Journal of the Royal Statistical Society, Series B, 1986, 48(3): 259～302

# Photo Retrieval from Personal Memories Using Generic Concepts

Rui M. Jesus[1,2], Arnaldo J. Abrantes[1], and Nuno Correia[2]

[1]Multimedia and Machine Learning Group, Instituto Superior de Engenharia de Lisboa
Rua Conselheiro Emídio Navarro, n°1, 1940-014 Lisboa, Portugal
[2]Interactive Multimedia Group, DI/FCT, New University of Lisbon
Quinta da Torre, 2825 Monte da Caparica, Portugal
+351 212948536
rjesus@deetc.isel.ipl.pt, nmc@di.fct.unl.pt

**Abstract.** This paper presents techniques for retrieving photos from personal memories collections using generic concepts that the users specify. It is part of a larger project for capturing, storing, and retrieving personal memories in different contexts of use. Semantic concepts are obtained by training binary classifiers using the Regularized Least Squares Classifier (RLSC) and can be combined to express more complex concepts. The results that were obtained so far are quite good and by adding more low level features, better results are possible. The paper describes the proposed approach, the classifier and features, and the results that were obtained.

**Keywords:** multimedia retrieval, personal memories, classification based on kernel.

## 1 Introduction

Humans like to keep information about their lives in order to later remember important moments or to create personal histories. One way of doing this is by collecting photos or videos. With the technological advances, multiple devices including phones, PDA's, digital stills cameras or digital video cameras are being increasingly used. The storage capacity of these devices has also increased a lot in the last few years, thus providing a very convenient way to store materials in digital form. The success of the WWW as a global platform for sharing information also promoted the media exchange process. Digital pictures are easier to capture and collect than the traditional pictures and for this reason many people have large collections of personal photos and videos.

The traditional way of organizing pictures in directories with suitable names for their content will not be enough to search and browse for personal pictures in an easy and fruitful way. One possible solution is the manual annotation with keywords of all the images, but this is not an easy task for large databases. Moreover, home users lack the expertise, the tools and, most of all, the time to perform this task. Automatic annotation is generically done using low-level features [1] or context metadata

Y. Zhuang et al. (Eds.): PCM 2006, LNCS 4261, pp. 633–640, 2006.

obtained at the capture time [2]. The combination of these two sources of information [3] improves the performance of the retrieval but the systems based on low-level features (CBIR) still have some limitations [4]. The performance of these systems depends essentially of the low-level features, and for this reason, sometimes, these systems present a low performance because it is hard to capture semantic concepts (semantic gap [5]). These difficulties can be overcome by the previous training of semantic models and then, automatically associate textual descriptions to the images [6]. However, the image perception of the user must be the same of the annotator. Other solution is the use of relevance feedback [7, 8], including the user in the search process. The user interacts with the system by providing additional information in the retrieval task. The main difficulty of this solution is related with the initial results presented to the user. If they are not relevant and many different results are provided the relevance feedback will not work properly. Querying the system with just a few images samples will never be good for relevance feedback. However, relevance feedback is the best way to annotate images.

The tools and techniques that we are presenting here are part of a larger project to capture, store, and retrieve personal memories in different contexts and with different devices and user interfaces.

This paper presents an image retrieval system that uses previously trained generic concepts that are suitable to search in a personal picture collection. These generic concepts have the ability to provide relevant and distinctive images that could be used in the relevance feedback process. The models of the generic concepts are obtained by training binary classifiers using the Regularized Least Squares Classifier (RLSC) proposed in [9] and used in our previous work in relevance feedback [10, 11]. To combine several generic concepts the sigmoid function is applied to the output of RLSC.

The paper is structured as follows. Section 2 presents the related work, section 3 describes the features used and how the RLSC and the sigmoid function are used to rank the database. Section 4 presents the results obtained and the last section presents some conclusions and directions for future work.

## 2   Related Work

To manage personal memories with pictures several commercial applications (e.g., Adobe Photoshop Album, Paint Shop Pro, Picasa, Photofinder) and online sites like www.flickr.com or www.phlog.net are available. All of them use directories to organize pictures and some of them allow visualizing the directories chronologically. Most of these applications use the manual annotation for search photos. In fact, annotation is very important in order to explore personal collections. The manual annotation is the most effective way but it is time consuming. The MyAlbum [12] system use a semi-automatic strategy to annotate picture based on low-level features and in relevance feedback. In [13] camera phone users can annotate their photos instants after the capture, some annotations are done automatically (data and location) and then users can interact with the system to do some corrections. Automatic systems rely on context metadata [14] or in visual content [2, 3, 15, 16]. Most of these systems use CBIR techniques that were used in other contexts different from the personal memories and combine them with context metadata. Other important aspect in multimedia retrieval is the user, in [17] several factors are discussed.

Concerning the problem of associating semantic concepts with low-level features, one of the first approaches proposed is described in [6]. They divided the images into rectangular regions and applied a co-occurrence model to words and regions. Following this work several proposals were made, some of them also associating words to images [16] and others, words to image regions [18, 19]. Naphade and Huang [19] proposed a probabilistic framework based on Bayesian Belief Networks. They segment the images in blob regions to create *multijetcs* (probabilistic multimedia objects) and to build a network of concepts. Recently, it was proposed a method in the domain of personal memories [16] that explores context metadata and visual content. The visual part of this work is similar to ours, but they use SVMs.

# 3 Query by Generic Concepts

This section describes the method proposed to query the database for pictures that belong to generic concepts. A set of generic concepts that were previously trained is available and the user can defines the query by combining them. These concepts are trained using the Regularized Least Squares Classifier for binary classification and the sigmoid function to convert the output of the classifier in a pseudo probability.

## 3.1 Low-Level Features

The low-level features that were used are the Marginal HSV color Moments [10] and Gabor Filter [20] to represent texture.

To extract the color feature, first each image is divided in 9 tiles (3x3) and for each tile individual histograms for the three color channels are computed. Then, the mean and the second central moment of each histogram are calculated. The color feature of each image is represented by a vector of 54 values.

The texture feature is extracted by applying to each picture a bank of 6 orientations and 4 scales sensitive filters that map each image pixel to a point in the frequency domain. The feature consists of the mean and standard deviation of the modulus of the filtering results. Each image is represented by a vector of 48 values.

## 3.2 Training the Generic Concepts

Useful concepts (e.g., people, indoor, outdoor, beach and snow) to search things in a personal collection are trained using the Regularized Least Squares Classifier. The images used to train were obtained from some CD's of the Corel Stock Photo, from the TRECVID2005 database and from www.flickr.com, in order to build a more generic training set.

Given the training set $S_m = \{(x_i, y_i)_{i=1}^m\}$ where labels $y_i \in \{-1,1\}$, the decision boundary between the two classes (e.g., indoor, outdoor) is obtained by the discriminant function,

$$f(x) = \sum_{i=1}^{M} c_i K(x_i, x) \tag{1}$$

where $K(x, x')$ is the Gaussian Kernel $K(x, x') = e^{-\frac{\|x - x'\|^2}{2\sigma^2}}$ , $m$ is the number of training points and $c = [c_1, ..., c_m]^T$, is a vector of coefficients estimated by Least Squares [9],

$$(m\gamma I + K)c = y \tag{2}$$

where $I$ is the identity matrix, $K$ is a square positive definite matrix with the elements $K_{i,j} = K(x_i, x_j)$ and $y$ is a vector with coordinates $y_i$. To choose the optimal $\sigma$ for the Gaussian kernel the cross-validation method is used. Training the classifier is equivalent to solve a linear system with $m$ equations.

The points $\{x_i\}$ with $f(x_i) \leq 0$, are classified in non relevant class $(y_i = -1)$, and the points with $f(x_i) > 0$ are classified in relevant class $(y_i = 1)$.

### 3.3 Ranking the Database

The output of the classifier is used to rank the database, however when several concepts are combined we need to convert the output in a pseudo probability $p$. Assuming $w$ is a class (concept), given the output of the RLSC, the probability $p(w/x)$ is obtained by the sigmoid function in a similar manner of [21],

$$p(w/x) = \frac{1}{1 + e^{-f(x)}} \tag{3}$$

Given a query formed with $k$ concepts $Q = \{w_1, w_2, ..., w_k\}$ and using $f$ features the rank of each image is obtained by the probability,

$$p(w_1, w_2, ..., w_k/x) = \sum_{j=1}^{f} a_j \prod_{i=1}^{k} p(w_i/x) \tag{4}$$

where $a_j$ is the weight of each features and $\sum_{j=1}^{f} a_j = 1$.

## 4   Experimental Results

The proposed method to query the database was tested using the personal collection of one person (Rui Jesus) with 818 images and a set of pictures shared by his friends in a total of 2582 photos. These pictures were manually annotated in order to evaluate the results obtained.

Personal memories are essentially composed by pictures of people, nature or urban scenes, holidays and parties. Five binary classifiers for concepts suitable to search in a personal collection were trained: people versus no people; indoor versus outdoor; snow versus no snow; beach versus no beach; party versus no party.

Figure 1 shows a simple interface that was implemented to evaluate the method. The left panel shows toggle buttons labeled with the trained concepts. By selecting some of these buttons the user defines the query. Then, all the pictures are ranked and the top 30 images are presented in the central panel from top left corner to bottom right corner. For the query, "outdoor+beach", only 3 pictures are incorrect.

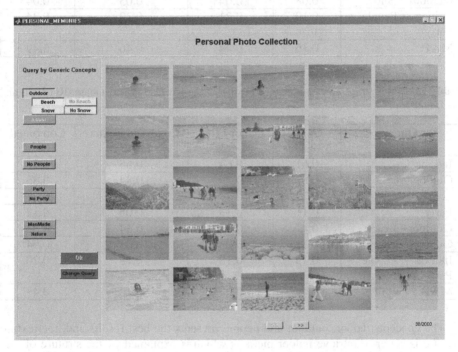

**Fig. 1.** Interface with the results obtained for the query Outdoor + Beach combining the 2 features

To evaluate the system seven queries (see tables below) were performed in Rui Jesus collection and in the entire database. The features were evaluated individually, joined together in a vector obtained by concatenation of the color and texture feature, and by combining the ranks obtained by each feature individually. Mean average precision (MAP) was used to measure the performance of the system.

Tables 1 and 2 show the results obtained by the proposed method. As expected the results obtained by the Rui Jesus personal collection were slightly better than in the entire database, but only because the number of pictures. The combination of the rank of the two features presents the best results in both tables.

**Table 1.** Mean Average Precision obtained using the personal collection of one person (Rui Jesus)

| Query | Color Moments | Gabor Filter | Color and Texture Feature | Combined Feature |
|---|---|---|---|---|
| Indoor | 0,69 | 0,76 | 0,76 | 0,82 |
| Outdoor | 0,92 | 0,92 | 0,94 | 0,96 |
| People | 0,78 | 0,77 | 0,73 | 0,80 |
| Party | 0,05 | 0,06 | 0,03 | 0,05 |
| Outdoor+ Beach | 0,51 | 0,34 | 0,44 | 0,48 |
| Outdoor + Snow | 0,08 | 0,04 | 0,03 | 0,04 |
| Indoor + People + Party | 0,19 | 0,21 | 0,29 | 0,34 |
| **MAP** | 0,46 | 0,44 | 0,46 | 0,49 |

**Table 2.** Mean Average Precision obtained using all the images in the database (Rui Jesus and his friends)

| Query | Color Moments | Gabor Filter | Color and Texture Feature | Combined Feature |
|---|---|---|---|---|
| Indoor | 0,61 | 0,64 | 0,65 | 0,70 |
| Outdoor | 0,82 | 0,79 | 0,84 | 0,86 |
| People | 0,77 | 0,77 | 0,76 | 0,78 |
| Party | 0,11 | 0,13 | 0,05 | 0,12 |
| Outdoor+ Beach | 0,41 | 0,17 | 0,34 | 0,36 |
| Outdoor + Snow | 0,11 | 0,03 | 0,03 | 0,04 |
| Indoor + People + Party | 0,15 | 0,18 | 0,18 | 0,20 |
| **MAP** | 0,42 | 0,39 | 0,40 | 0,48 |

The concepts indoor, outdoor and people presents the best results and, the texture feature is better to retrieve indoor pictures which is explained by the struture of the manmade objects.

The query "Indoor + People+Party" presents better results than the query "Party" and this illustrates the main idea of the paper.

## 5  Conclusions and Future Work

This paper presents a method to retrieve images from personal memories based on generic concepts trained using the Regularized Least Squares Classifier. To combine several concepts in a query the sigmoid function was applied to the output of the classifier. The method proposed was tested with 2582 pictures of a personal collection with a performance measured by a mean average precision of 0,48 when combining the rank of the two features. In the future, more generic concepts for querying personal memories will be trained and specific features for some concepts (party, face, snow) will be developed and evaluated.

We are currently building a complete environment to capture images and videos and additional contextual data, annotate, browse and search the collections. A previous project provided some of the scientific guidelines for this effort. We have implemented a mobile storytelling project (InStory) in a cultural and historical site [22] that uses PDAs to navigate narratives in a physical space. Users can navigate the story threads that are provided but they can also contribute with their own materials. The environment that we are building includes a PDA client that allows to capture the images along with GPS data and user annotations. We are also researching the way people use digital memories. Clients for browsing are also envisaged for different target platforms, including desktop/laptop PC, PDA, and augmented reality devices. The developed system will target to main types of users: (1) people engaged in tourism activities; (2) and also people that have difficulties to remember past events or are away from their natural environment, e.g., when in a hospital. In this case special care has to taken when designing the interfaces and we are planning to repurpose the stored materials, using techniques such as the ones reported in this paper and access them in other devices including mobile phones, TV sets and even paper or other custom made physical objects.

# References

1. Veltkamp, R., and Tanase, M., *Content-Based Image Retrieval Systems: A Survey.* Technical Report UU-CS-2000-34, October, 2000.
2. Hori, T., and Aizawa, K., *Context-based video retrieval system for the life-log applications.* In Proceedings of the Fifth ACM SIGMM International Workshop on Multimedia Information Retrieval (Berkeley, CA, Nov. 7, ). ACM Press, New York, 2003: p. 31-38.
3. O'Hare, N., Jones, G., Gurrin, C., and Smeaton, A., *Combination of content analysis and context features for digital photograph retrieval.* IEE European Workshop on the Integration of Knowledge, Semantic and Digital Media Technologies, London, 2005.
4. Lew, M., Sebe, N., Djeraba, C., and Jain R., *Content-based Multimedia Information Retrieval: State-of-the-art and Challenges.* ACM Transactions on Multimedia Computing, Communication, and Applications, 2006. 2(1).
5. Smeulders, A., Worring, M., Santini, S., Gupta, A., and Jain, A., *Content-based image retrieval at the end of the early years.* IEEE Trans. Pattern Analysis and Machine Intelligence, 2000. 22(12): p. 1349 -1380.
6. Mori, Y., Takahashi, H., and Oka, R., *Image-to-word transformation based on dividing and vector quantizing images with words.* In Proceedings of the International Workshop on Multimedia Intelligent Storage and Retrieval Management, 1999.
7. Yong, R., Huang, T., and Mehrotra, S., *Relevance feedback techniques in interactive content-based image retrieval.* In Storage and Retrieval for Image and Video Databases (SPIE), 1998: p. 25-36.
8. Zhou, X., and Huang, T., *Relevance feedback in image retrieval: A comprehensive review.* Multimedia Systems, 2003. 8(6): p. 536-544.
9. Poggio, T., and Smale, S., *The mathematics of learning: Dealing with data.* Notice of American Mathematical Society, 2003. 50(5): p. 537-544.
10. Jesus, R., Magalhães, J., Yavlinsky, A., and Rüger, S., *Imperial College at TRECVID.* TREC Video Retrieval Evaluation (TRECVID), Gaithersburg, MD, Nov, 2005.

11. Jesus, R., Abrantes, A. , and Marques, J., *Relevance feedback in CBIR using the RLS classifier.* In 5th EURASIP Conference focused on Speech and Image Processing, Multimedia communications and Services, Bratislava, Junho, 2005.
12. Wenyin, L., Sun, Y., and Zhang H., *MiAlbum-A System for Home Photo Management Using the Semi-Automatic Image Annotation Approach.* ACM Multimedia, 2000.
13. Wilhelm, A., Takhteyev, Y., Sarvas, R., Van House, N., and Davis, Marc, *Photo Annotation on a Camera Phone.* Proc. ACM CHI 2004: p. 1403-1406.
14. *World-Wide Media eXchange.* http://wwmx.org, 2005.
15. Cooper, M., Foote, J., and Girgensohn, A., *Automatically organizing digital photographs using time and content.* In Proc. of the IEEE Intl. Conf. on Image Processing (ICIP 2003), 2003.
16. Jiebo, L., Boutell, M., and Brown, C., *Pictures are not taken in a vacuum - an overview of exploiting context for semantic scene content understanding.* Signal Processing Magazine, IEEE, 2006. 23(2): p. 101-114.
17. Jaimes, A., *Human Factors in Automatic Image Retrieval System Design and Evaluation.* Proceedings of SPIE, Internet Imaging VII, San Jose, CA, USA, 2006. 6061.
18. Cusano, C., Ciocca, G., and Schettini, R., *Image annotation using SVM.* Proceedings of the SPIE, Internet Imaging V 2003. 5304: p. 330-338
19. Naphade, M.R., and Huang, T.S., *A probabilistic framework for semantic video indexing, filtering, and retrieval.* IEEE Transactions on Multimedia, 2001. 3(1): p. 141-151.
20. Manjunath, B.S., and Ma, W. Y., *Texture features for browsing and retrieval of image data.* IEEE Trans. Pattern Anal. Machine Intell., 1996. 18: p. 837-842.
21. Platt, J.C., *Probabilistic Outputs for Support Vector Machines and Comparisons to Regularized Likelihood Methods,* in *Advances in Large Margin Classifiers,* P.B. A. Smola, B. Schölkopf, D. Schuurmans, Editor. 1999, MIT Press. p. 61-74.
22. Correia, N., Alves, L., Correia, H., Morgado, C., Soares, L., Cunha, J., Romão, T., Dias, A. E., and Jorge, J., *InStory: A System for Mobile Information Access, Storytelling and Gaming Activities in Physical Spaces.* ACE2005 - ACM SIGCHI International Conference on Advances in Computer Entertainment Technology, Universidade Politècnica de Valencia (UPV), Spain, 15 - 17 June, 2005.

# PanoWalk: A Remote Image-Based Rendering System for Mobile Devices

Zhongding Jiang[1], Yandong Mao[1], Qi Jia[1], Nan Jiang[1], Junyi Tao[1], Xiaochun Fang[1], and Hujun Bao[2]

[1] Computer Graphics Lab, Software School, Fudan University, Shanghai, China
[2] State Key Lab. of CAD&CG, Zhejiang University, Hangzhou, China
zdjiang@fudan.edu.cn, bao@cad.zju.edu.cn

**Abstract.** Real-time rendering of complex 3D scene on mobile devices is a challenging task. The main reason is that mobile devices have limited computational capabilities and are lack of powerful 3D graphics hardware support. In this paper, we propose a remote Image-Based Rendering system for mobile devices to interactively visualize real world and synthetic scenes under wireless network. Our system uses panoramic video as building block of representing scene data. The scene data is compressed with one MPEG like encoding scheme tailored for mobile device. The compressed data is stored on remote server. Our system carefully partitions the rendering task between client and server. The server is responsible for determining the required data for rendering novel views. It streams the required data to client in server pushing manner. After receiving data, mobile client carries out rendering locally using image warping and displays the resultant images onto its small screen. Experimental results show that our system can achieve real time rendering speed on mainstream mobile devices. It allows multiple mobile clients to explore the same or different scenes simultaneously.

## 1 Introduction

Mobile devices, such as PDA and smart phone, become popular among billions of users. In addition to audio communication, they can run interactive applications, including mobile games, virtual tour, digital navigation, and so on.

For these applications, real-time rendering of complex 3D scene on mobile devices is one of the key techniques. Currently, mobile devices have less memory and weaker processing capabilities than their PC counterparts. The mainstream mobile graphics processing units (GPUs) are not powerful due to its chip size, manufacture cost and power consumption. Hence, interactive rendering of complex scenes is still challenging on mobile devices.

One solution is using scene simplification techniques [9] to reduce datasize. If the simplified scene contains much polygons and texture details, client can selectively prefctch data from server [14, 4]. For large scale scene, however, the reduced datasize is still unmanageable and impractical for networked rendering.

Remote rendering scheme is another solution. It employs high performance server to render 3D scene, compresses the resultant images, and streams the

Y. Zhuang et al. (Eds.): PCM 2006, LNCS 4261, pp. 641–649, 2006.

compressed data to mobile client [2,7,11,5,1]. After receiving compressed data from server, mobile client can directly display decompressed data [11,7,5] or perform rendering novel images by warping decoded images using local computation resource [2,1].

3D Image warping used in [2,1] is a well established technique in Image-Based Rendering (IBR) community [13]. IBR is an alternative to traditional geometry based rendering approach [14,4]. It can generate photo-realistic novel images using recorded images captured from real-world or rendered from synthetic scenes.

Previous work on remote IBR systems for mobile device [2,1] only deal with synthetic scene, without considering real world data. Furthermore, they are difficult to support multiple mobile clients simultaneously when 3D scene is very complex.

For supporting multiple mobile clients and handling real world scenes, we propose one remote IBR system called PanoWalk. Our system adopts panoramic video with associated camera pose information as building block to represent real world and synthetic scenes. We design one MPEG like compression scheme tailored for mobile device for reducing datasize. An interactive data transmission scheme between client and server is devised for reducing influence of network latency.

The remainder of the paper is organized as follows. Section 2 describes the related work. The details of our system are presented in Section 3. The experimental results are shown in Section 4. We draw conclusions and point out the future work in Section 5.

## 2    Related Work

Remote rendering has received much attention in recent years [14,4,2,7,11,1, 5,10,15]. The system proposed by Teler *et al.* can selectively transmit parts of scene and lower quality representations of objects from server to client [14]. The transmitted information is determined based on user's viewing parameters and network bandwidth. Chim *et al.* [4] implement a distributed walkthrough environment using on-demand transmission strategy. Clients render virtual scenes by fetching geometry data from server. A multi-resolution caching mechanism is employed for reducing influence of network latency.

Instead of transmitting 3D scene data to client, images can be rendered by high performance server on demand [2,7,11,1]. Before being sent to mobile client, the rendered images are usually compressed using image/video encoder. Chang *et al.* propose one remote IBR system that can generate novel views by warping depth images sent by server [2]. Bao and Gourlay propose one remote rendering framework [1] similar to [2], which compresses residual depth images before sending to mobile client. The system proposed by Lamberti *et al.* allows interaction with remote 3D model on PDAs [7]. The PDAs only decode and display images received from network. Noimark and Cohen-Or design a remote rendering system [11] which uses MPEG-4 encoder for compressing images before sending to mobile client. Instead of transferring images to client, Diepstraten *et al.*

propose one remote system that renders 3D scene into feature lines, and sends 2D line primitives to mobile client [5]. The aforementioned remote rendering systems only deal with synthetic scene and are not scalable well to support multiple mobile clients simultaneously. Our system has good scalability and support rendering of real world scenes.

The systems in [10, 15] can handle real world data like ours. The panoramic video encoding scheme [10] uses MPEG-2 like compression algorithm for reducing data volume. However, it is not tailored for mobile device and need more computation resource for decoding. Zhang and Li design one IBR system for remote wandering over internet [15]. Since the system transfers the required data segments in client pulling manner, its rendering speed is limited by round trip time of network. Using server pushing scheme, our system can offer higher rendering speed by transferring data in pipeline manner.

## 3   The Remote Image-Based Rendering System

### 3.1   System Architecture

Our system can achieve interactive rendering of real world and synthetic scenes under wireless network. It allows multiple mobile clients to explore the same or different scenes simultaneously. Figure 1 illustrates its architecture.

In our system, panoramic video serves as building block of representing scene data. The scene data is compressed with our MPEG like encoding scheme tailored for mobile device. The compressed data is stored on remote server. Our system carefully partitions the rendering task between client and server. The server is responsible for determining the required data for rendering novel views. It streams the required data to client in server pushing manner. After receiving data, client carries out rendering locally using image warping and displays the resultant images onto its small screen. The details are described in the following subsections.

### 3.2   Scene Representation

There are many image-based representations that can be used to represent a scene. LightField/Lumigraph [8, 6], and Concentric Mosaics [12] are well known IBR representations. However, capturing them is not an easy task and usually requires specific devices. Therefore, we choose panoramic video as rendering primitive of our system. Panoramic video is a sequence of panoramic images. It can be directly captured from real world using omnidirectional camera. It can also be generated by stitching multiple captured perspective images [3]. For scene navigation, camera pose information is recovered using computer vision algorithm.

Using camera pose information, one panoramic video can be represented as a path in the navigation map. For authoring a complex scene, many panoramic videos are used. Multiple panoramic videos can form path network in the navigation map. Since each panorama is associated with camera pose information,

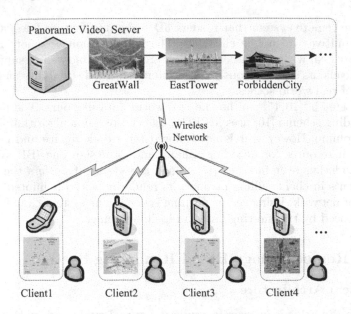

**Fig. 1.** System architecture

user can move freely along paths in the navigation map. At branching point between paths, the next-navigation-path can be automatically chosen based on user's viewpoint and paths' definitions.

Rendering panorama only involves image warping and it is cheap on common PC. For mobile device, it need more effort to optimize source code due to the absence of floating-point unit. We first compute mapping from each pixel of rendered image to its corresponding pixel position of source panorama. The mapping can be represented with integer part and fractional part. Four weight values are calculated from the fractional part for bilinear interpolation of pixel colors. These weight values are represented as fixed-point values. They are stored in lookup table along with integer part for fast rendering. On mobile device, fixed-point arithmetics can be implemented with integer operation of mobile CPU. Hence, our optimized warping scheme with lookup table can execute very fast. When computing the pixel mapping between rendered image and source panorama, we choose cylindrical projection to represent the source panorama. With cylindrical projection, the integer parts of lookup table are fixed. Only integer increments are added to them when user rotates the virtual camera. This can significantly reduce the size of lookup table.

**Fig. 2.** Partitioning panoramic video into tiles

### 3.3   Data Compression

The raw data of panoramic videos are huge. Compression algorithms must be employed for reducing storage space and bandwidth requirement for network rendering. Since field-of-view (FOV) of the virtual camera is limited, only parts of one panoramic image are required for rendering a novel view. Similar to [10], we divide each panorama into several disjoint tiles. Consequently, panoramic video are divided into several image sequences (Figure 2).

Established video compression standards, such as MPEG-1/2/4, H.263/264, do not support random access [13] and must be modified for IBR data compression. Previous panoramic video compression method [10] is based on MPEG-2. It drops P frames from Group of Pictures (GOP) structure for reducing frame dependencies. With the new GOP structure, it provides fast random access with good compression ratio. Since decoding one B picture requires two neighboring frames, this method is still complicated for mobile device equipped with weak CPU.

For further reducing decoding cost on mobile device, we design one panoramic video compression method in the same spirit of [10]. Our method makes three major modifications of MPEG GOP structure (Figure 3). First, we remove B frame from GOP structure. Second, all P frames are predicted from I frame instead of neighboring P frame. This reduces frame dependency to only one frame. Third, I frame is put in the middle position of GOP frames. This scheme provides more compression ratio than keeping I frame at the head of GOP. When compressing image sequences of one panoramic video are completed, all bitstreams are rebinned into one final file. Meanwhile, one index file is created for random access, which records the offset of each frame in the final bitstream.

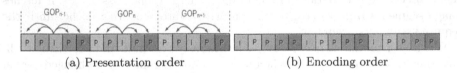

(a) Presentation order                    (b) Encoding order

**Fig. 3.** GOP structure for panoramic video compression. The frame number of GOP is chosen to be 5 for illustration.

### 3.4   Interactive Data Transmission

In our system, user manipulates the virtual camera of mobile client using stylus. The virtual camera can move forward and backward, rotate or pause at one position, or jump to positions linked by hot spots. These interaction events are sent from client to server through one command channel (Figure 4). The other communication channel in Figure 4 is used to transmit the required compressed data from server to mobile client for rendering novel views. In the following paragraphs, we refer these required compressed data as image segments.

The image segments are determined by server according to parameters of client status. These parameters include user's viewpoint, wandering manner, and *simulating cache*, which are maintained by server. The change of viewpoint and wandering manner are mainly due to user's interaction. Server will be notified and update these parameters if user interaction event occurs.

Simulating cache is a unique component of our system, which is unavailable in previous remote IBR systems [10, 15]. It does not hold compressed data sent to client. Instead, it records which parts of bitstream are sent and still available on client. It *simulates* the behavior of *rendering cache* resident on mobile client. Using TCP protocol, both caches are kept consistent with the same data replacement scheme. For reducing bandwidth requirement, server only transmits image segments, which are unavailable on simulating cache.

Rendering cache is the counterpart of simulating cache resident on mobile client. It is designed for improving the rendering performance on client. It caches the received compressed data from receive buffer for avoiding data retransmission. It also stores the decompressed version of received data for fast rendering. Rendering cache is always kept consistent to simulating cache resident on server.

Our system works in server pushing manner while previous remote IBR system [15] employs client pulling scheme. In client pulling system, client is responsible for determining the image segments and sends request to server before rendering each frame. As response, server sends the required data to client. After the required data is available, client decodes it and carries out rendering. The whole process takes at least one round trip time of network.

In our system, server is responsible for determining the image segments for rendering novel views and streaming those that are unavailable in simulating cache to client. After transmitting each image segment, simulating cache is updated for keeping consistence with rendering cache. As local rendering, mobile client directly fetches data from rendering cache. If cache miss occurs, it fetches image segments from receive buffer, put them into rendering cache, until the required segments occur.

When user motion is fixed, server continuously transmits data to client without communication overhead. When user's wandering manner is changed, server

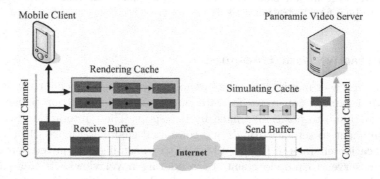

**Fig. 4.** Interactive data streaming between client and server

will send one tag package to client as response of interaction event, then send image segments using the updated client's status parameters. Meanwhile, client stops rendering novel image until receiving the tag package.

## 4    Experimental Results

We have implemented our remote image-based rendering system in an IEEE 802.11b wireless network with 11Mbps bandwidth. The server process runs on Dell laptop with Intel Pentium IV 1.8GHz CPU, 1GB memory, and Microsoft Windows XP operating system. Two HP iPAQ hx2750 PocketPC and one BenQ P50 PDA phone are used as mobile clients. These mobile devices are equipped with Intel PXA270 XScale CPU and Microsoft PocketPC 2003 SE operating system. The maximum screen size is 320 × 240 in pixel resolution.

We captured panoramic video clips of GreatWall and FobbidenCity, which are world famous spots of China. The camera pose information was recovered using computer vision algorithms. When generating synthetic dataset, one virtual scene showing EastTower (Shanghai) is used. Figure 5(a) shows one snapshot of our client-server system, which supports three mobile clients simultaneously. Figure 5(b) is the screen of mobile client wandering in ForbiddenCity. With GUI, user can jump to his/her interesting places by clicking hot spots using stylus. Figure 5(c) illustrates our system can be interacted using bluetooth gamepad.

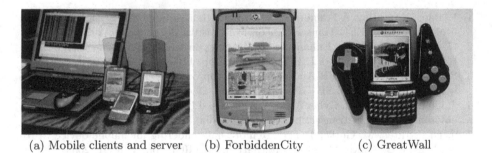

(a) Mobile clients and server      (b) ForbiddenCity          (c) GreatWall

**Fig. 5.** Experimental results

We use Intel IPP library to optimize the source code. Interactive rendering performance is achieved on mobile clients. When user conducts translation, the average rendering speed is about 16 fps. Rotation action is faster than translation, and the average frames per second is 30. The reason is that the required image segments for rotation are located at one position, and they can be directly found in rendering cache without data transmission from server. The compression ratio of these datasets is about 13 when JPEG format is used with image quality is set to be 75%. Using our MPEG like encoding scheme, the compression ratio is above 50. The required network bandwidth for each mobile client is about 350 kbps.

## 5   Conclusions and Future Work

In this paper, we propose one remote IBR system for mobile devices. It can achieve interactive rendering of real world and synthetic scenes under wireless network. In our system, panoramic video serves as building block of scene data stored at server. For mobile device, we design one MPEG like encoding method to compress panoramic video. Our system works in sever pushing manner. It uses server to compute and transmit the required image segments according to client's status parameters. After receiving image segments, client caches them and carries out rendering locally. Our system allows multiple mobile clients to explore the same or different scenes simultaneously. In the future, we will implement method which provides better QoS to mobile clients. Our system will be further optimized and tested under 3G wireless network.

## Acknowledgements

This work is supported in part by Microsoft Research Asia, NSFC (No.60021201), 973 Program of China (No.2002CB312104), and the Key Scientific and Technical Innovation Project, Ministry of Education of China (No.705027). Thanks to Lei Yu for his startup work in this project.

## References

1. P. Bao, D. Gourlay. A Framework for Remote Rendering of 3-D Scenes on Limited Mobile Devices. IEEE Transactions on Multimedia, 8(2):382-389, 2006.
2. C.-F. Chang, S.-H. Ger. Enhancing 3D Graphics on Mobile Devices by Image-Based Rendering. Proceedings of IEEE PCM 2002, pp. 1105-1111, 2002.
3. S.E. Chen. QuickTime VR-An Image-based Approach to Virtual Environment Navigation. Proccedings of SIGGRAPH 1995, pp. 29–38, August 1995.
4. J. Chim, R.W.H. Lau. CyberWalk: A Web-Based Distributed Virtual Walkthrough environment. IEEE Transactions on Multimedia, 5(4):503–515, 2003.
5. J. Diepstraten, M. Gorke, T. Ertl. Remote line rendering for mobile devices. Proceedings of Computer Graphics International (CGI04), pp. 454-461, 2004
6. S.J. Gortler, R. Grzeszczuk, R. Szeliski, M.F. Cohen. The lumigraph. Proceedings of SIGGRAPH 1996, pp.43–54, August 1996.
7. F. Lamberti, C. Zunino, A. Sanna, A. Flume, M. Maniezzo. An accelerated remote graphics architecture for PDAs. Proceeding of the eighth international conference on 3D web technology, pp. 55-61, 2003.
8. M. Levoy, P. Hanrahan. Light field rendering. Proceedings of SIGGRAPH 1996, pp.31–42, August 1996.
9. D. Luebke, M. Reddy, J. Cohen, A. Varshney, B. Watson, R. Huebner. Level of Detail for 3D Graphics. Morgan Kaufmann Publishing, 2002.
10. K.-T. Ng, S.-C. Chan, H.-Y. Shum. Data Compression and Transmission Aspects of Panoramic Video. IEEE Transactions on Circuits and Systems for Video Technology, 15(1):82-95, 2005.

11. Y. Noimark, D. Cohen-Or. Streaming Scenes to MPEG-4 Video Enabled Devices. IEEE Computer Graphics and Applications, 23(1):58–64, 2003.
12. H.-Y. Shum, L.-W. He. Rendering with concentric mosaics. Proceedings of SIG-GRAPH 1999, pp. 299–306, August 1999.
13. H.-Y. Shum, S.B. Kang, S.-C. Chan. Survey of Image-Based Representation and Compression Techniques. IEEE Transactions on Circuits Systems for Video Technology, 13(11):1029–1037, 2003.
14. E. Teler, D. Lischinski. Streaming of Complex 3D Scenes for Remote Walkthroughs. Computer Graphics Forum, 20(3):17-25, 2001.
15. C. Zhang, J. Li. On the Compression and Streaming of Concentric Mosaic Data for Free Wondering in a Realistic Environment over the Internet. IEEE Transactions on Multimedia, 7(6):1170-1182, 2005.

# A High Quality Robust Watermarking Scheme

Yu-Ting Pai[1], Shanq-Jang Ruan[1], and Jürgen Götze[2]

[1] Department of Electronic Engineering,
University of Science and Technology, Taiwan, China
{M9302101, sjruan}@mail.ntust.edu.tw
http://lps.et.ntust.edu.tw
[2] University of Dortmund, Germany
juergen.goetze@uni-dortmund.de
http://www-dt.e-technik.uni-dortmund.de

**Abstract.** In recent years, digital watermarking has become a popular technique for hiding information in digital images to help protect against copyright infringement. In this paper we develop a high quality and robust watermarking algorithm that combines the advantages of block-based permutation with that of neighboring coefficient embedding. The proposed approach uses the relationship between the coefficients of neighboring blocks to hide more information into high frequency blocks without causing serious distortion to the watermarked image. In addition, an extraction method for improving robustness to mid-frequency filter attacks is proposed. Our experimental results show that the proposed approach is very effective in achieving perceptual invisibility with an increase in the peak signal to noise ratio (PSNR). Moreover, the proposed approach is robust to a variety of signal processing operations, such as compression (JPEG), image cropping, sharpening, blurring, and brightness adjustments. In those experimentation, the robustness is especially evident under the attack of blurring.

## 1 Introduction

The development of digital services has created new requirements for multimedia security and copyright protection techniques. One of the more popular techniques is digital watermarking, which secretly embeds information in ordinary binary images (e.g., scanned text, figures, and digital signatures). In general, changing the image pixel value by a small amount is imperceptible to the naked eye. The hidden data can then be detected or extracted later on by secret keys for copyright verification.

In the literature, several researchers have investigated digital watermarking. Cox *et al.* argued that inserting a watermark in the DCT domain would make it robust to signal processing operations [1]. Fei *et al.* proposed an algorithm for improving resistance to compression [2]. Kii *et al.* used patchwork to endure cropping of the image [3]. Wu and Hsieh used zerotree of DCT to extract embedded watermarks from images without the need for the original image [4]. Tang *et al.* developed a robust watermarking scheme that combines the advantages of feature extraction and image normalization to simultaneously resist image geometric distortion and reduce watermark synchronization problems [5]. Kang *et al.* proposed a DWT-DFT composite watermarking scheme that embeds messages in the DWT domain and templates in the DFT domain to resist both affine transformations and JPEG compression [6].

Y. Zhuang et al. (Eds.): PCM 2006, LNCS 4261, pp. 650–657, 2006.

In order to realize perceptual invisibility, block-based permutation mapping is proposed in several researches. Lin and Chen achieved the permutation mapping by computing the number of non-zero DCT coefficients in each block [7]. Hsu and Wu used variance of each block in spatial domain to perform the permutation mapping [8]. Furthermore, Hsu's approach improved the robustness by embedding the watermark according to the relationship between neighboring blocks. However, this combined method, decreases the image quality making differences between the original and the watermarked images easily discernible by the human eye.

In this paper, we develop an effective watermark embedding method, which improves the invisibility of watermarks without seriously distorting the image. Furthermore, our approach is extremely robust to signal processing, and therefore, attempts to remove watermarks by methods, such as JPEG compression, cropping, sharpening, blurring, and brightness adjustment will be unsuccessful. The experimental results verify that our approach improves imperceptibility of watermarks and robustness (NC value increased from 0.3 to 0.8 under the attack of blurring).

## 2    The Relationship Between Block-Based Permutation and Neighboring Block

Block-based permutation is a mechanism for hiding watermark information into higher frequency blocks. Since high frequencies are inconspicuous to the human eye, using block-based permutation can improve the quality of the watermarked image. Furthermore, hiding the coefficients of neighboring blocks is an approach that uses similar yet disordered data instead of using a binary pattern watermark. Although this embedding method can improve the robustness of watermarked images, it is difficult to obtain similar data from neighboring blocks after block-based permutation. Since the coefficient's distribution in the high frequency block differs from the distribution in the neighboring block, we can conclude that there is serious noise and distortion in the high frequency blocks of the watermarked image. For example, Fig. 1 (a) and (b) show the middle-frequency coefficients picked up from a high frequency block and the neighboring block, respectively. We can see that the distributions in these two blocks are extremely different. On the other hand, Fig. 1 (d) and (e) show the middle-frequency coefficients picked up from a low frequency block and the neighboring block, respectively. In this case the coefficients of the low frequency block are close to the coefficients of the neighboring block. The fact that coefficients of neighboring blocks in high frequencies are dissimilar confirms that hiding most of the data in high frequency blocks causes serious distortion to the watermarked image. 1 (c) and (f) illustrate the watermarked results of the high and low frequency blocks, respectively. The modified coefficients are shaded in the figures. Obviously, the variation in the high frequency block is larger than in the low frequency block. For this reason, differences between the original and the watermarked image can be distinguishable by the human eye. Fig. 2 shows a closeup of the eyes from the famous test image, Lena, where we can easily observe degradation to the left eye.

Hsu and Wu proposed the use of a threshold to preserve the quality of an image but did not define a method to process data that are higher than the threshold. Since most data hidden in high frequency blocks are dissimilar, a lot of embedded data exceed the

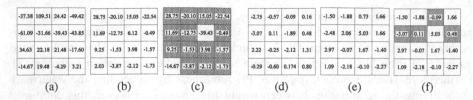

**Fig. 1.** The embedded process of high and low frequency blocks. (a) the neighboring high frequency block, (b) the high frequency block, (c) the embedded result of high frequency block obtained by Hsu's approach, (d) the neighboring low frequency block, (e) the low frequency block, and (f) the embedded result of low frequency block obtained by Hsu's approach.

lower threshold, producing a watermark that is not very robust. However, setting a higher threshold allows serious noise to pass through the threshold filter. To solve the problem of a mismatch between block-based permutation and neighboring block embedding, we propose a new method to hide irregular data with high quality in the next section.

## 3 Proposed Method

Before describing the proposed algorithm, we make some assumptions. Let $H$ be the original gray-level host image of size $N_1 \times N_2$, which is divided into blocks of size $8 \times 8$ pixels. The original image $H$ is represented as follows:

$$H = \left\{ h_n(i, j),\ 0 \leq i < 8,\ 0 \leq j < 8,\ 0 \leq n < \frac{N_1 N_2}{64} \right\}. \tag{1}$$

The $M_1 \times M_2$ watermark $W_o$ is treated as a visually recognizable binary pattern where $M_1 \times M_2 \leq (N_1 \times N_2)/4$. The embedding and extracting methods are described in the following subsections.

### 3.1 Embedding Process

We adopt the pseudo-random permutation and the block-based permutation proposed by Hsu and Wu [8] in the first stage. The original watermark $W_o$ is first permuted by a predetermined key to generate the permuted watermark $W_p$. Then, the block-based permutation and mapping perform the corresponding relationship between $W_p$ and $H$. Thus, we can obtain a sorted watermark $W_b$ according to the blocks of host image $H$. The block-based $W_b$ is represented as follows:

$$W_b = \{ w_n(u, v),\ 0 \leq u < 4,\ 0 \leq v < 4 \}. \tag{2}$$

After completing the preceding steps, each block of the host image is transformed independently by forward discrete cosine transform (FDCT) [9], i.e.

$$Y = \text{FDCT}(H),$$

is obtained by applying FDCT to each block $h_n$:

$$y_n = \text{FDCT}(h_n).$$

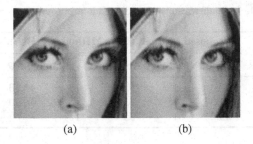

(a)                    (b)

**Fig. 2.** The eyes part of (a) original Lena image and (b) watermarked Lena image obtained by Hsu's approach

(a)              (b)              (c)              (d)              (e)

**Fig. 3.** (a) The test image "lena" of size $512 \times 512$, (b) the watermark, (c) the watermarked image obtained by our approach (PSNR=43.23), (d) the extracted watermark under no attacks (NC=1), and (e) the eyes part of watermarked Lena image obtained by proposed approach

Since the human eye is more sensitive to noise in lower-frequency coefficients and the noise in the high-frequency range might be discarded after quantization operations of lossy compression, the middle-frequency coefficients are extracted and $W_b$ is embedded in the middle-frequency coefficients. The selected coefficients are collected to compose a reduced image of size $4 \times 4$, i.e.

$$y'_n(u, v) = \text{Reduce}(y_n).$$

Here we apply our embedding method. In order to create similar embedding coefficients, we reduce the range of the neighboring block $y'_{n-1}$ to $y''_{n-1}$:

$$y''_{n-1} = \left[ \lfloor y'_{n-1} \rfloor \bmod \alpha \right] + \left[ y'_{n-1} - \lfloor y'_{n-1} \rfloor \right] + \beta, \tag{3}$$

where $\alpha$ and $\beta$ are positive integer constants defined by the user and $\alpha + \beta > y''_{n-1} > \beta$. The choice of $\alpha$ and $\beta$ allows a trade-off between image quality and robustness. Next, we use $y''_{n-1}$ instead of $y'_n$ to perform the hiding process, and we have the following equation:

$$\hat{y}_n = y'_n + \lambda \times \gamma \times y''_{n-1} \tag{4}$$

where

$$\lambda = \begin{cases} 1, & y_n(u, v) < y_{n-1}(u, v) \\ -1, & \text{otherwise} \end{cases} \tag{5}$$

**Table 1.** Quality results of original and proposed algorithms

| Embedded bits | Proposed Method PSNR | NC value | Hsu's Method PSNR | NC value | Hsieh's Method [10] PSNR | NC value |
|---|---|---|---|---|---|---|
| 1024 | 60.45 | 1 | 53.36 | 1 | 45.10 | 1 |
| 8192 | 52.37 | 1 | 43.59 | 1 | 44.20 | 0.982 |
| 65536 | 43.23 | 1 | 35.45 | 1 | | |

and

$$\gamma = \begin{cases} 1, \ w_n(u, v) \text{ is black point} \\ 0, \text{ otherwise.} \end{cases} \tag{6}$$

Therefore, the embedded image $\hat{Y}$ can be obtained from the modified middle frequnecy coefficients $\hat{y}_n$ together with the original high- and low-frequency coefficients. Finally, we can obtain the watermarked image $\hat{H}$ after inverse discrete cosine transform (IDCT) of $\hat{Y}$.

It is clear that the maximal difference between $y'_n$ and $\hat{y}_n$ is limited by the value $\alpha + \beta$, and we can still keep the embedded data disordered. Since the modifications required are relatively small, the watermarked data is more similar to the original data, and therefore, the quality of watermarked image can be improved effectively.

### 3.2 Extracting Process

Extraction is done by retrieving watermarked information from the DCT domain and therefore requires that both the original image $H$ and the watermarked image $\hat{H}$ be transformed to the DCT domain.

$$Y = \text{FDCT}(H)$$
$$\hat{Y} = \text{FDCT}(\hat{H}).$$

The extracted watermark represented by $w'_n$ can be obtained by a comparison of the middle frequency coefficients:

$$w'_n = \begin{cases} 1, \ |y_n - \hat{y}_n| \geq \beta \\ 0, \text{ otherwise.} \end{cases} \tag{7}$$

Finally, the extracted watermark $W'_o$ can be obtained by performing an inverse permutation operation.

When this approach is attacked by an image process, a white point can be extracted correctly if the modification is smaller than $\beta$, and a black point can be extracted correctly if the modification is larger than $\alpha + 2\beta$. Thus, we can be sure that some of the extracted points must be correct. Moreover, we can increase the robustness by hiding some information to low-frequencies with a little quality damage. Therefore, our proposed method is more resistant to an attack filter than the original algorithms, in particular, to a middle-frequency filter.

**Table 2.** The PSNR and NC under JPEG compression

| 65536 bits watermark ($256 \times 256$) | | | | | | 1024 bits watermark ($32 \times 32$) | | | | | |
| Hsu's Method | | | Proposed Method | | | Hsieh's Method | | | Proposed Method | | |
| JPEG Rate | PSNR | NC value | JPEG Rate | PSNR | NC value | JPEG Rate | PSNR | NC value | JPEG Rate | PSNR | NC value |
|---|---|---|---|---|---|---|---|---|---|---|---|
| 7.81 | 32.07 | 0.830 | 7.5 | 42.423 | 1 | 9.58 | 38.0 | 1 | 9.6 | 43.333 | 1 |
| 8.46 | 31.75 | 0.726 | 8.5 | 41.700 | 1 | 13.3 | 36.5 | 1 | 14.1 | 40.615 | 0.998 |
| 9.05 | 31.47 | 0.661 | 14 | 37.554 | 0.945 | 18.3 | 34.9 | 0.997 | 21.5 | 38.414 | 0.978 |
| 9.81 | 31.41 | 0.493 | 26 | 36.574 | 0.896 | 26.2 | 32.7 | 0.910 | 27.2 | 37.235 | 0.940 |

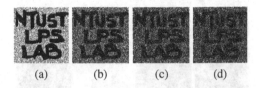

(a)        (b)        (c)        (d)

**Fig. 4.** The $256 \times 256$ extracted watermark after JPEG lossy compression with compression ratio (a) 9.2, (b) 14, (c) 16.1, and (d) 17.5

## 4  Experimental Results

To estimate the quality of our method, we used the peak signal to noise ratio (PSNR) to evaluate the distortion of the watermarked image.

$$\text{PSNR(db)} = 10 \log_{10} \frac{255^2}{\text{MSE}} \tag{8}$$

where MSE is the mean square error between a watermarked image and its original. Since the extracted watermark is a visually recognizable pattern, we define a normalized correlation (NC) as a similarity measure between the referenced watermark $W_o$ and extracted watermark $W_o'$.

$$NC = \frac{\sum_x \sum_y W_o(x,y)W_o'(x,y)}{\sum_x \sum_y [W_o(x,y)]^2} \tag{9}$$

where $0 < NC \leq 1$. This provides an objective measure of the extracting performance.

To evaluate and compare the performance of our proposed approach, the $512 \times 512$ "Lena" image was used. The different size of "NTUST LPS LAB" pattern were used as the watermarks. The $256 \times 256$ bits watermark is the largest size watermark image for a $512 \times 512$ gray level image for our algorithm. That is, we also considered the worst case to test our algorithm. Table I shows the PSNR and NC values without any attacks for the original algorithms and the proposed method. Fig. 3 shows the result of $256 \times 256$ bits embedding for proposed method. We can see that a close-up of the eyes of watermarked Lena image as shown in Fig. 3 (e) is very similar to the original image as shown in Fig. 1 (a)

**Table 3.** The PSNR and NC under image operations

| Attacks | 1024 bits watermark | | | | 16384 bits watermark | | | |
| | Hsu's Method | | Proposed Method | | Hsieh's Method | | Proposed Method | |
| | PSNR | NC | PSNR | NC | PSNR | NC | PSNR | NC |
|---|---|---|---|---|---|---|---|---|
| Sharpening | 30.586 | 0.957 | 33.204 | 0.952 | 35.1 | 0.91 | 34.197 | 0.963 |
| Blurring | 33.754 | 0.270 | 26.151 | 0.825 | 36.5 | 0.885 | 26.187 | 0.945 |
| Cropping | 5.636 | 0.098 | 5.636 | 0.107 | | | 18.522 | 0.102 |
| Brightness | 7.130 | 0.537 | 7.134 | 0.783 | | | 7.135 | 0.895 |

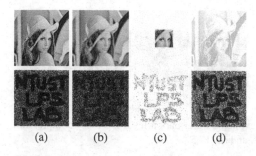

(a)          (b)          (c)          (d)

**Fig. 5.** The watermarked images after various attacks and the 256 × 256 extracted watermarks; (a) sharpening, (b) blurring, (c) cropping, and (d) brightness increasing

Table 2 shows the watermark extraction results after JPEG lossy compression with different compression ratios. As the compression ratio increases, the PSNR decreases. However, for all compression ratios, the NC values are improved with the proposed method. Fig. 4 shows the 256 × 256 bits extracted watermarks from each compressed image.

Table 3 shows the results of applying sharpening, blurring, cropping, and brightness adjustment attacks to the watermarked image. It is interesting to note that the proposed approach can resist the attack of blurring very effectively. Fig. 5 shows the attacked version of the watermarked images and the corresponding extracted watermarks, which are all still distinguishable from the original watermark. Although the Hsu's algorithm has a higher NC value under the attack of sharpening, the result of our approach is very close. It is noteworthy that for all other attacks, the proposed method outperforms the original scheme. In particular, we can see that the NC value is significantly improved under a blurring attack. Therefore, the proposed method not only delivers higher quality watermarked images but is also more robust to attacks.

## 5   Conclusion

In this paper, a high quality robust embedding and extracting method for digital watermarking is proposed. This proposed method overcomes the problem between block-based permutation and embedding method and is robust to many attacks, especially blurring. Simulation results verify the imperceptibility and robustness of the proposed watermarking scheme with substantial increase in PSNR and improved NC value under various attacks. In future work, we plan to apply the proposed approach to other transform domain watermarking methods, such as wavelet and Fourier transform domain, that disorderly hide data with block-based operations,.

# References

1. Cox, I.J., Kilian, J., Leighton, F.T., Shamoon, T.: Secure spread spectrum watermarking for multimedia. IEEE Trans. on Image Processing **6** (1997) 1673–1687
2. Fei, C., Kundur, D., Kwong, R.H.: Analysis and design of watermarking algorithms for improved resistance to compression. IEEE Trans. on Image Processing **13** (2004) 126–144
3. Kii, H., Onishi, J., Ozawa, S.: The digital watermarking method by using both patchwork and dct. IEEE International Conference on Multimedia Computing and Systems **1** (1999) 7–11
4. Wu, C.F., Hsieh, W.S.: Digital watermarking using zerotree of dct. IEEE International Conference on Consumer Electronics **46** (2000) 87–94
5. Tang, C.W., Hang, H.M.: A feature-based robust digital image watermarking scheme. IEEE Trans. on Signal Processing **51** (2003) 950–959
6. Kang, X., Huang, J., Shi, Y.Q., Lin, Y.: A dwt-dft composite watermarking scheme robust to both affine transform and jpeg compression. IEEE Transactions on Circuits and Systems for Video Technology **13** (2003) 776–786
7. Lin, S.D., Chen, C.F.: A robust dct-based watermarking for copyright protection. IEEE Transactions on Consumer Electronics **46** (2000) 415–421
8. Hsu, C.T., Wu, J.L.: Hidden digital watermarks in image. IEEE Trans. on Image Processing **8** (1999) 58–68
9. Cho, N.I., Lee, S.U.: Fast algorithm and implementation of 2-d discrete cosine transform. IEEE Trans. on Circuits and Systems **38** (1991) 297–305
10. Hsieh, M.S., Tseng, D.C., Huang, Y.H.: Hiding digital watermarks using multiresolution wavelet transform. IEEE Trans. on Industrial Electronics **48** (2001) 875–882

# An Association Rule Mining Approach for Satellite Cloud Images and Rainfall*

Xu Lai[1], Guo-hui Li[1], Ya-li Gan[1], and Ze-gang Ye[2]

[1] Department of System Engineering, School of Information System and Management,
National University of Defense Technology,
Yanwachi St.47, 410073, Changsha, Hunan, China
boy_lailai@sina.com.cn
[2] Hydrology Bureau of Hunan Province,
410007, Changsha, Hunan, China
yzg@163.com

**Abstract.** This paper aims at discovering useful knowledge from a large collection of satellite cloud images and rainfall data using image mining. The paper illustrates how important the data conversion is in building an accurate data mining architecture. Most of data about image features and rainfall data are values or vectors, which are not fit for mining directly. We present two approaches to implement the conversion of data: a clustering algorithm and a fuzzy clustering method (FCM). The clustering algorithm is used to map the numerical value to categorical value. The FCM implements the conversion of feature vector. Finally, the association rules are determined using the Apriori algorithm. The experiment results show that the acquired association rules are consistent with the fact and the results are satisfying.

**Keywords:** Association rules mining, satellite cloud image, clustering partition.

## 1 Introduction

The satellite cloud images are acquired by remote sensing technology. They include rich information, such as the cloud ceil temperature, the cloud distribution and so on. The information assists experts to analyze and forecast rainfall instance. During these years, the satellite cloud images have become an important tool to prevent blood and fight drought. In the past, people analyzed the satellite cloud images mainly depending on the domain experts' knowledge and experience. The working is a kind of manual mode, which led the problem of short of quantitative account.

After realizing the disadvantage, people study new techniques of analyzing the satellite cloud images. The method proposed in [2] input the features extracted from the images into the neural network (NN). The NN can accomplish forecasting the rainfall in the next hours. The method in [4] used the co-occurrence matrix to classify the cloud

* Supported by the National Natural Science Foundation of China under Grant No.60473116.

Y. Zhuang et al. (Eds.): PCM 2006, LNCS 4261, pp. 658–666, 2006.

class. There are many other people established the regression model to analyze the satellite cloud images in [1] and [3].

However, the methods above mentioned can't deal with the volumes of satellite cloud images with great efficiency. Data mining is an intelligent analysis technique adapting to large dataset [8]. This new technique consists of many methods that can extract hidden knowledge from data volume, and it also incorporates many tasks. Association rule mining is one of the important tasks. In this work, we use association rule mining to acquire the relation between the satellite cloud images and rainfall data. These relations will serve for the short duration forecast in the future. The remainder of the paper is organized as follows. Section 2 describes the concept of association rule. The following section describes the feature extraction and presents two methods used to partition the value intervals. Section 4 introduces the data collection and the experimental results obtained, while in the last section we summarize our work.

## 2  Association Rule

The association rule mining focuses on discovering the relations between two or more items in the database [9]. Let $I = \{i_1, i_2, ..., i_m\}$ be a set of items. $A$ is a $K - itemset$, if $A \subseteq I$ and $|A| = K$ .An association rule is an expression $A \Rightarrow B$ , where $A$ and $B$ are itemsets that satisfy $A \cap B = \Phi$ . Lets $D = \{t_1, t_2 ..., t_n\}$ as a set of transactions, where $t_i$ is an itemset such that $t_i \subseteq I$ . Transaction $t_i$ supports an itemset $A$ if $A \subseteq t_i$ . The following four types of measurements are currently used to evaluate the association rules from different aspects:

(1) *Support* measures statistical significance of an association rule. It indicates how typical the rule is in all transactions. The bigger *support* is, the rule is more typical.

$$Support\ P(A \cup B) = \frac{|\{T \in D \mid A \subseteq T\}|}{|D|} \tag{1}$$

(2) *Confidence* is a strength measure of association rule.

$$Confidence = P(B \mid A) = \frac{|\{T \in D \mid A \subseteq T \wedge B \subseteq T\}|}{|\{T \in D \mid A \subseteq T\}|} \tag{2}$$

(3) *Expected confidence* denotes the *support* of B while neglecting the attributes A.

$$Expected\ confidence = P(B) = \frac{|\{T \in D \mid B \subseteq T\}|}{|D|} \tag{3}$$

(4) *Lift* is a degree to which A influences B. Only when the *confidence* is bigger than the *expected confidence*, it illuminates that the occurrence of A promotes the

occurrence of B and that they are correlative. If *lift* is not bigger than 1, the rule is meaningless.

$$Lift = P(B \mid A)/P(B) \tag{4}$$

Support and Confidence are the most important in the four measures. If they are not considered, too many association rules will be found. In fact, a majority of them are useless for people. In order to find significant association rules, two thresholds need to be given in advance, which are *Minsup(R)* and *minconf(R)*. When the rules meet the conditions: $\sup(R) \geq \min \sup(R)$ and $conf(R) \geq \min conf(R)$, they can be called strong rules.

Association Rule mining consists of two steps: firstly, the algorithm finds out all frequent itemsets. Secondly, the association rule is built based on the frequent itemset. In this paper, we use the *Apriori* algorithm to find the frequent itemset. The *Apriori* algorithm can produce the candidate itemset $C_{k+1}$ based on the frequent itemset $L_k$. The method improves the efficiency by reducing the number of scanning database.

# 3   Conversion of Data

In this paper, we define the problem of mining association rules over quantitative and categorical attributes. Categorical attribute has a few values. It is easy for the mining algorithm to deal with categorical attributes. However, the amount of quantitative value is large and it is not suitable for association rule mining algorithm. People refer to this problem as the *quantitative association rules* problem. Converting the quantitative attribute into categorical attribute is the main method solving the problem at present. People should partition the numerical value into some intervals and then map each interval to an *id*. The disposal accomplishes the conversion of data attribute. Then we can use any algorithm for finding categorical association rules to find *quantitative association rules*.

## 3.1   Feature Extraction

The satellite cloud images contain many kinds of features, such as color, texture and shape, etc. When confirming which features to be extracted, we propose making use of the domain experts' experience and knowledge. The suitable features should be quite relevant to rainfall. Another problem is diversity about granularity between rainfall data and cloud images. The granularity of rainfall data is six hours interval, however the granularity of cloud image is one hour interval. It means that one piece of rainfall data is corresponding to six satellite cloud images.

We solve the above problems by extracting two features: the gray mean $\overline{g}$ and gray variance vector $\overrightarrow{V_g}$ . The gray mean direct reflects the ceil cloud temperature. The gray variance vector is another important feature. The gray variance can reflect the changing degree of the cloud system during six hours. Firstly, each image is divided into many 3*3 blocks, in which the rainfall stations locate in the center. After partitioning into blocks, we calculate the gray mean value of the image block using the formula (5). To correspond to the rainfall data, we use the mean of the six image blocks as the extracted feature, as shown in formula (6).

$$g_t = \sum_{i,j} I(X_i, Y_j) \Big/ 9, \ i,j=1,2,3,....9 \tag{5}$$

$$\overline{g} = g_t / 6 \ t=1, 2, 3,...6 \tag{6}$$

The gray variance can be calculated based on the gray mean, as shown in formula (7). The variance vector $\overrightarrow{V_g}$ consists of six variances of cloud images: $\overrightarrow{V_g} = (V_1, V_2, ..., V_6)$.

$$v_t = \sum_{i,j} [I(x_i, y_j) - g_t]^2 \ i,j=1, 2, 3,....9 \tag{7}$$

## 3.2 A Clustering Algorithm

The weather department has strict provision that partition the rainfall data into 5 intervals, as showed in Tab1. People have no difficulty in accomplishing partition following these standards.

Table 1. The interval of rainfall data

| No. | Identifier | Interval |
|-----|------------|----------|
| 1 | no rain | $(-\infty, \ 0.1mm)$ |
| 2 | light rain | $(0.1mm, \ 4.9mm)$ |
| 3 | moderate rain | $(5mm, \ 14.9mm)$ |
| 4 | heavy rain | $(15mm, \ 29.9mm)$ |
| 5 | rainstorm | $(30mm, \ +\infty)$ |

However, the partition of gray range has no standard rule. At present, many methods about the range's partition have been studied. The biggest problem among these methods is that it is overly influenced by people and the partition can not reflect the data characteristic in nature. This paper proposes *clustering partition method* to implement partitioning the gray mean into intervals. The adopted method is completely based on the characteristic of data distribution, so it can reflect the essential of data.

The *"Rainfall times—Gray value"* curve in the Fig.1 is the object which the *clustering partition method* analyzes. The abscissa represents the gray value and the ordinate represents rainfall times. Each value of rainfall times is corresponding with a gray value.

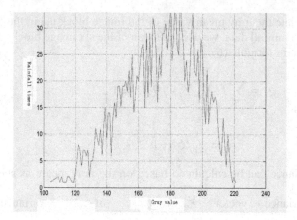

**Fig. 1.** Rainfall times-gray value

The clustering partition algorithm includes 8 steps:

(1) Account the times of rainfall $C_i$ corresponding with each gray value.

(2) Search all of the local maximum($Max_i$). The minimum on the left of Maxi is called $MinL_i$ and the minimum on the right of Maxi is called $MinR_i$.

(3) Account the times of rainfall($Sum_i$) between each $MinL_i$ and $MinR_i$.

(4) If $Sum_i$ meets the combining condition, we should combine the neighboring two intervals.

(5) $S=\Sigma Sum_i - max\{Sum_i\} - min\{Sum_i\}$.

(6) $S_{ave}=S/(K-2)$.

(7) Search all of the $Sum_i(Sum_i >C\times S_{ave})$, the result of the interval is recorded in $Stmp$.

(8) For each interval($Sum_i$) recorded in $Stmp$ do

**if** $Sum_i/(MinR_i-MinL_i) > S/(MinR-MinL)$ **then** record the interval in the $S_{res}$.

The result is the $S_{res}$ that saves the valued intervals. If some $Sum_i$ is too large or too small, the representative of $S_{ave}$ will be affected. The value of $S_{ave}$ should not near to $max\{Sum_i\}$ or $min\{Sum_i\}$ . The 5$^{th}$ step solves the problem. It can make the final mean more representative. If we throw away all of intervals in which the times of rainfall is lower than $S_{ave}$, there would be so many information to be lost. The 4$^{th}$ step solves the problem by combining the neighbor intervals. If the width of the interval is too narrow and the distance with the neighbor interval is short, people can combine these two intervals. If each $Sum_i$ is near to $S_{ave}$, people have difficulty in distinguishing which interval is more valued. The 8$^{th}$ step solves the problem. If the $Sum_i$ meet the inequality in the 8$^{th}$ step, we regard the interval as valued.

Based on *the clustering partition methods*, we partition the gray mean into five intervals. Each interval is given an identifier easily understood by people. The Tab2 shows the partition results.

**Table 2.** Interval of the average gray

| No | Identifier | Interval |
|----|-----------|----------|
| 1 | deep gray | [0,  126] |
| 2 | gray | [127,  148] |
| 3 | light gray | [149,  169] |
| 4 | white | [170,  193] |
| 5 | special white | [194,  255] |

## 3.3  A Fuzzy Clustering Method (FCM)

The variance vector reflects the extent of the cloud changing during the 6 hours. The vector is not appropriate to the rule mining algorithm. Therefore, we use the *FCM* [7] to implement mapping the vector to a certain identifier. The identifier collection includes: *the greatly change, moderate change* and *light change*. Using these identifiers it can solve the problem that the association rule mining algorithm can not deal with the vector date.

The *FCM* is an unsupervised clustering method. It can implement data clustering by minimizing the objective function. When the data contains fuzziness and uncertainty, the *FCM* is adaptive to solve these problems. The objective function is described as follows,

$$J_m(U,V) = \sum_{j=1}^{n}\sum_{i=1}^{c} u_{ij}{}^{m} d_{ij}{}^{2} ,1 \leq m < \infty \tag{8}$$

In the above formula, $u_{ij}$ represents the degree of the sample $x_j$ subjecting to the class $v_i$. $u_{ij}$ meets the requirement $\sum_{i=1}^{c} u_{ij} = 1$ ,j=1,2,...,n. There is an important weight coefficient $m$ in the Eq.(8). The bigger m is, the larger the degree of classifying matrix is. Define $d_{ij}$ as the distance between $x_j$ and the $i^{th}$ cluster center.

The algorithm of FCM is outlined as follows:

(1) Initialization: In the initialization step, we should confirm some values, including the amount of class $c$ , weight coefficient $m$ , threshold $\varepsilon$ , and iterative numbers $loop$ .

(2) Confirming initial subjective matrix $U$ based on the apriori knowledge.

(3) Calculating the $u_{ij}, v_i$ during the iterative process based on the formula (9).

$$U_{ij} = \frac{1}{\sum_{k=1}^{c} \left(\dfrac{d_{ij}}{d_{kj}}\right)^{\frac{2}{m-1}}} , \quad V_i = \frac{\sum_{j=1}^{n} u_{ij}{}^{m} x_j}{\sum_{j=1}^{n} u_{ij}{}^{m}} \tag{9}$$

If $\max_{ij} \left\| u_{ij} - \hat{u}_{ij} \right\| < \varepsilon$ or the iterative number exceed *loop,* the iterative process is over.

## 4 Experiment Results and Remarks

In the experiments, we collect 1434 satellite cloud images around the Hunan province range from April to August in 1996. These images are taken by the Japanese weather satellite GMS-5. Plenty of rainfall records are simultaneously archived from 262 rainfall stations. After pre-processing and converting of the feature data, we use the *Apriori* algorithm to discover association rules among the conclusive datasets consisting of 316 pieces of data records. In the paper, we specify the *minsup* and *minconf* respectively: *minsup*=10%, *minconf*=20%. Tab3,4 showed the association rules results. In our approach, we constrained the association rules such that the antecedent of rules is composed of a conjunction of features from the satellite cloud images while the consequent of rules is always the level to which the rainfall belongs to.

Based on the measurement of association rules described above, we can obtain the following hidden knowledge from eight association rules listed in the Table3,4.

The first rule shows that if the change degree of the gray is *light* in the former six hours, it will be *moderate rain* in the following 7$^{th}$ hour with the 36% probability. The value 1.06 of *lift* indicates the appearance of the condition promote the result occurring.

The 4$^{th}$ rule shows that if the gray average is mapped to *white* in the former six hours, it will be *heavy rain* in the following 7$^{th}$ hour with the 42% probability. The value 1.07 of *lift* indicates the appearance of the condition promote the result occurring.

The 6$^{th}$ rule shows that if the two conditions meet the requirements in the former six hours: the change degree of the gray is *light*, moreover the gray average is mapped to *special white*, and it will be a *rainstorm* in the following 7th hour with the 33.7% probability. The value 1.41 of *lift* indicates the appearance of the two conditions promote the result occurring.

**Table 3.** One- dimension association rules result

| No. | Association Rules | Support | Confidence | Expected confidence | Lift |
|-----|-------------------|---------|------------|---------------------|------|
| 1 | The changing degree of cloud during 6 hours: light ➜ Moderate rain. | 23.77% | 32.04% | 30% | 1.06 |
| 2 | The changing degree of cloud during 6 hours: light ➜ Heavy rain. | 28.69% | 38.67% | 39% | 0.98 |
| 3 | The changing degree of cloud during 6 hours: light ➜ Rainstorm. | 16.80% | 22.65% | 24% | 0.92 |
| 4 | The vision characteristic of gray average during 6 hours : white ➜ Heavy rain. | 14.34% | 42.17% | 39% | 1.07 |

**Table 4.** Two-dimension association rules result

| No. | Association Rules | Support | Confidence | Expected confidence | Lift |
|-----|-------------------|---------|------------|---------------------|------|
| 5 | The vision characteristic of average gray: special white and the changing degree of cloud: light during 6 hours ➔ Heavy rain. | 11.48% | 36.36% | 39% | 0.93 |
| 6 | The vision characteristic of average gray: special white and the changing degree of cloud: light during 6 hours ➔ rainstorm. | 10.66% | 33.77% | 24% | 1.41 |
| 7 | The vision characteristic of average gray: white and the changing degree of cloud: light during 6 hours ➔ moderate rain. | 15.98% | 37.5% | 30% | 1.25 |
| 8 | The vision characteristic of average gray: white and the changing degree of cloud: light during 6 hours ➔ Heavy rain. | 18.85% | 44.23% | 39% | 1.13 |

**Table 5.** Validation of association rules

| No. | Association Rules | Accuracy1 | Accuracy2 | Accuracy3 | Accuracy4 | Average |
|-----|-------------------|-----------|-----------|-----------|-----------|---------|
| 1 | The changing degree of cloud during 6 hours: light ➔ Moderate rain. | 24.5% | 38.5% | 27.1% | 30.5% | 30.15% |
| 2 | The vision characteristic of gray average during 6 hours : white➔Heavy rain. | 44.4% | 26.6% | 65.2% | 39.2% | 43.8% |
| 3 | The vision characteristic of average gray: white and the changing degree of cloud: light during 6 hours ➔ Heavy rain. | 52.9% | 31.5% | 70.5% | 40% | 48.7% |
| 4 | The vision characteristic of average gray: white and the changing degree of cloud: light during 6 hours ➔ moderate rain. | 11.7% | 47.3% | 17.6% | 15% | 22.9% |

The 7th rule shows that if the two conditions meet the requirements in the former six hours: the change degree of the gray is *light*; the gray average is mapped to *white* , it will be *moderate rain* in the following 7th hour with the 38% probability. That the lift is 1.25 indicates the appearance of the two conditions promote the result occurring.

The 8th rule makes it clear that if the two conditions meet the requirements in the former six hours: the change degree of the gray is *light*, moreover the gray average is mapped to *white*, it will be *heavy rain* in the following 7th hour with the 44% probability. The value 1.13 of *lift* indicates the appearance of the two conditions promote the result occurring.

In the experiment, we adopt the *n-dimension cross validating* method to test the correctness of rules. The *n-dimension cross validating* can make use of the entire data. We randomly partition the data into four parts. The first part used as test dataset that are not participated in the production of association rules, then the left three parts are used as training collection to produce the association rules. Each part has chance to act as the test dataset. Therefore, we get four accuracies of the rules and the conclusive value is the average of the four accuracies, as showed in Tab5.

## 5  Conclusions

In conclusion, the accuracy of rain forecast is barely 38% in the traditional weather domain. Some rules' accuracy in this work has exceeded 40%, which is better than the average accuracy of the weather domain. The reality specifies that the association rules are believable and the rules are consistent with the domain experts' knowledge. We find that the values of support and confidence are not very large. We can solve the problem by archiving more sufficient satellite cloud images and rain records. Although, the association rules acquired in the paper can not be directly used in the rain forecasting at present, we hope the rules will serve for the short duration forecasting of the rain soon.

## References

1. Flaviana D.Hilario: Short Duration Rainfall Estimation Using GMS IR and VIS Images. CAB, PAGASA,DOST: ACRS 1998 Water Resources.
2. Abe, Yoshiyki (1990): Precipitation Intensity Derived from GMS Imagery. Report of Meteorological Satellite Center. JMA.
3. Goodman, B., W.P. Menzel, E.C. Cutrim and D.W. Martin (1993): A Non-linear Algorithm for Estimating 3-hourly Rain Rates over Amazonia from GOES/VISSR Observations. Remote Sensing Reviews.
4. Dvorak, Vernon F., 1975: Tropical Cyclone Intensity Analysis and Forecasting from Satellite Imagery. Monthly Weather Review: Vol. 103, No. 5, 420-464.
5. T. Nakazawa: TRMM and NSCAT/QuikSCAT Applications for Tropical Cyclones Studies. The Fifth International Workshop on Tropical Cyclones.
6. Chi-Farn, Jyh-Ming Lee: The Validity Measurement of Fuzzy C-means Classifier for Remotely Sensed Images. 22nd Asian Conference on Remote Sensing,5-9 November 2001.
7. U. M. Fayyad, G. Piatetsky-Shapiro, P. Smyth, et al: Advances in Knowledge Discovery and Data Mining. AAAI/MIT Press, 1996.
8. Zajane O.R, et al. Multimediaminer: A System Prototype: for Multimedia Data Mining, Proc of ACM SIGMOD Conf on Management of Data, Seattle, 1998: 581-583.
9. Jianning Dong,William Perrizo,Qin Ding and JingKai Zhou: The Application of Association Rule Mining on Remotely Sensed Data, ACM SAC,Italy,2000.

# AVAS: An Audio-Visual Attendance System

Dongdong Li, Yingchun Yang[*], Zhenyu Shan, Gang Pan, and Zhaohui Wu

Department of Computer Science and Technology,
Zhejiang University, Hangzhou, P.R.China, 310027
{lidd,yyc, shanzhenyu, gpan, wzh}@zju.edu.cn

**Abstract.** Biometric identification technology is being applied to physical and information access control in some workplace with the improvements in the accuracy of biometric devices and declining price. This paper describes a multimodal biometric identification system for time and attendance application called AVAS (Audio-Visual Attendance System). This system takes users' voice and face characteristics as their badge. The motivation behind using multimodal biometrics is to improve availability and accuracy of the system. The score differences between the genuine speaker class and the mistaken identified speaker class labeled by each classifier are taken into account, and Score Difference Weighted Sum rule (SDWS) is introduced to fuse the individual expert. We describe the functions of the AVAS in detail from three aspects, the interaction with users, the authentication implementation and the data management. The practical tests conducted on staff working environment gain distinct improvement about 9.8% with the proposed system.

**Keywords:** multimodal, speaker recognition, time and attendance system.

## 1 Introduction

Initially time-and-attendance systems were based on punch cards, which required employees to punch in, as well as managers to manually compile time cards information. Some alternative solutions are developed based on badges, but still couldn't eliminate "buddy punching". Biometrics technologies are introduced to construct a more powerful version of time and attendance tracking devices, which is not token-based identification techniques, but recognizes unique and unalterable features [1]. The popular attendance devices recognize user's fingerprint or hand geometry, making access as easy as swiping your hand [2, 3]. However, these biometric systems require very specialized hardware and are not well accepted by users for their unfriendliness and insanitariness. What's more, a single physical characteristic or behavioral trait of an individual sometimes fails to be sufficient for user's authentication [4, 5].

Multimodal Biometrics technologies with voiceprint and face characteristics could achieve both acceptable level of distinctiveness and user friendliness[6]. In our former work, a novel decision-level fusion method, Score Difference Weighted Sum rule

---

[*] Corresponding author.

Y. Zhuang et al. (Eds.): PCM 2006, LNCS 4261, pp. 667–675, 2006.

(SDWS) [7] is introduced to fix the weights of each biometric trait. This algorithm takes the degree of support (e.g. score) delivered by the component experts into account, learns the score difference between the genuine speaker class and the mistakenly identified speaker class labeled by each classifier and gives the weights. Compared with other classical fusion methods, the SDWS shows its superiority in multimodal fusion [7, 8].

In this paper, we apply the SDWS to constructing a new type of time and attendance system based on multimodal biometrics technologies, called AVAS (Audio-Visual Attendance System). The AVAS aims at attendance controlling, buddy-punching eliminating and payroll accuracy improving for modern workplaces.

The remainder of the paper is organized as follows: in Section 2 we give a brief introduction of the architecture of the AVAS through three core modules. We introduce the functions of the AVAS through the user interface module in Section 3. In Section 4, the implementation of the authentication center module is discussed in detail. We describe the database management module in Section 5. The practical application is presented in Section 6. Finally, we give a conclusion in Section 7.

## 2   System Description

The AVAS is an intelligent system, which provides attendance solutions and working time record for workplaces management. It also achieves user friendliness and easy operation at the same time.

Fig.1 shows the architecture of the proposed identification system based on the fusion of multimodal recognizer at the decision level where the matching scores obtained from multiple matchers are combined. The system relies on 3 modules:

- The user interface is an intelligent client and provides users with a series of attendance and query functions.
- The authentication center processes the voiceprint signal and face images, makes the final decision (i.e. reject or accept person) and records the check-in or check-out time at the same time.
- The database stores the information of genuine users and their models and gives abundant data for system further improvement.

Although the presented work combines only two modalities, it can be extended to any number of modalities.

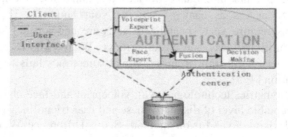

**Fig. 1.** The Architecture of the AVAS

## 3 User Interface

We meant to build a widely acceptable and friendly user interface for the AVAS. The intelligent functions of the interface are introduced below according to its access-right.

### 3.1 User Right

There are two main processes for users to interact with the AVAS, enrollment and attendance.

The enrollment is implemented at a central personnel department and consists of two steps. The interface is shown in Fig.2.

- **Personal information and face image collection:** The users are expected to provide their information such as name, birthday and telephone number as well as a photo of frontal face.
- **Voiceprint collection:** The voiceprint consists of a 50 sec of neutral speech with discretionary content as well as utterances of birthday and phone number for three times respectively.

These physical characteristics are used for training the speakers' personal biometric model when users register before their first check-in.

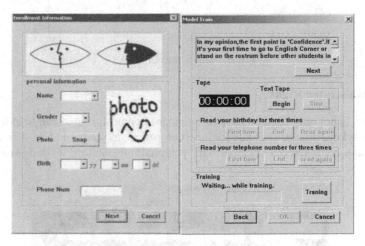

**Fig. 2.** The interface of enrollment part

As daily attendance, the employees begin and end their shift use the AVAS as the follows. The main screen of the AVAS is shown on Fig. 3.

- **Face image and voice collection:** Users are asked to record some utterances that are longer than 1 sec and get their faces shot into a PC which is equipped with microphones and cameras. Then the system starts the biometric characteristic analysis by inserting them into the Authentication Center.

- **User ID confirmation:** Based on the decision derived from the Authentication Center, the AVAS user interface immediately shows the user's photo whose biometric features best match the input ones if the person is genuine, otherwise it rejects the request. If the system gives a right response, the person should click 'yes' to check in or out. Users usually have three chances at most to get it right.
- **Advance voice collection:** This process is rarely needed and only happens in the case that the system gives wrong identification for three times continuously. Utterances of birthday and phone number are asked to provide, which have the same content as the ones collected in the enrollment process. Text-dependent speaker identification is implemented.

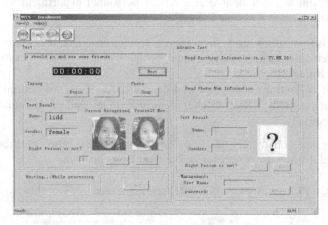

**Fig. 3.** Main Screen of AVAS

## 3.2 Administrator Right

The AVAS is not only used to provide attendance control, it also can help to account the total working time of the staff for a certain period, as shown in Fig. 4. The system administrator could not only browse staff' personal information, working status, detail

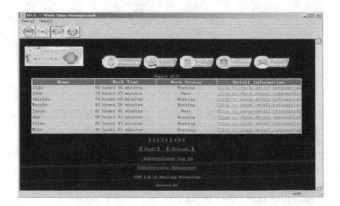

**Fig. 4.** Administrator Management Interface

of working hours and total working hours on the net, but also control the database, including helping the staff to check in, counting mistaken identification, and so on.

## 4 Authentication Center

The authentication center is the kernel of the AVAS, which coordinates both voiceprint and face biometric experts, fuses individual results and gives the final decisions.

### 4.1 Voiceprint Recognition Part

The utterances are recorded with a sampling rate of 16 bits of resolution at 8 KHz. The acoustic speech is processed using a 32ms Hamming window, with the frame period set at 16ms. The silent and unvoiced segments are discarded under a certain energy threshold. A pre-emphasis filter whose constant $\alpha$ value is 0.94 is generally used before spectral analysis. The feature vectors are composed by 16 MFCC and their delta coefficients.

A 16th order diagonal covariance Gaussian Mixture Model (GMM) is applied to our system because of its advantage in computational efficiency. In model training, the Expectation-maximization (EM) algorithm [9] iteratively refines the GMM parameters to monotonically increase the likelihood of the estimated model for the observed feature vector. Generally, five iterations are sufficient for parameter convergence.

During attendance, a maximum log-likelihood classification rule is used to identify the speaker of the input utterances. Each model has a score with the attendance utterance.

### 4.2 Face Recognition Part

As we know, a face recognition system includes face detection, preprocessing feature extraction and match [10]. The first two steps are based on a machine learning approach for rapid objective detection using a boosted cascade of simple features [11]. The face feature extraction method is based on standard Principal Component Analysis classifier (PCA). The 32 largest eigenvectors are taken from the list of eigenvectors. The Eigenface method is used as the face matcher. Images are then compared by means of their corresponding feature vectors.

### 4.3 Decision Fusion

The decision fusion function combines the outputs of the component classifiers to reach a more reliable decision to accept or reject the users. We give each classifier a weight to exhibit its importance or confidence.

The face expert always gives distinct discriminate support to different classes, while the voiceprint expert labels each class with almost the same score. We introduce SDWS algorithm to utilize this character. This fusion method aims at learning the score difference between the genuine speaker class and the mistakenly identified speaker class that is labeled by either classifier.

The identification problem using a combination of classifiers can be formulated as follows. Classify an input sample **x** to one class form $\Omega$. $\Omega = \{\omega_1,...,\omega_c\}$ is a set of class labels. c is the number of classes, and represents the number of people in the system.

Let $D_1$ and $D_2$ be the component classifiers representing voiceprint expert and face expert respectively. $X = \{x_1, x_2,..., x_N\}$ is the training data set with N elements. We demote the output of $X$ after classified as

$$H(X) = [\begin{matrix} h_{1,1}(X),...,h_{1,N}(X) \\ h_{2,1}(X),...,h_{2,N}(X) \end{matrix}] \tag{1}$$

where $h_{i,j} = D_i(x_j)$, i=1, 2 be the class labels assigned to $x_j$ by expert $D_i$ in the identification process. Here, j=1,..., N is the number of the training data.

The genuine class labels of X are $L(X) = [m_1,...,m_N]^T$ i.e., $L : \mathfrak{R}^n \rightarrow \Omega$.

For classifier $D_i$, if the identified class label is different from the genuine one, e.g. $h_{i,j} \neq m_j$, the score difference between these two labels is taken into account. We treat the $d_{i,k}(x)$ as the degree of support (e.g. score) given by classifier $D_i$ to the hypothesis that **x** comes from class $\omega_k$, k=1,..., c

Here, $d_{i,k}(x) \in \{0,1\}$, $\sum_{k=1}^c d_{i,k}(x) = 1$.

The score difference $SD_i(X)$ between the mistaken identified class label $h_{i,j}$ and the genuine class label $m_j$ of expert i can be calculated as follows:

$$SD_i(X) = \sum_{j=1}^N SD_i^j(x_j) = \sum_{j=1}^N h_{i,j} \neq m_j | d_{i,m_j}(x_j) - d_{i,h_{i,j}}(x_j) | \tag{2}$$

Here, we set the weights according to the score difference with different classifiers. That is,

$$W_i = \frac{SD_i(X)^{-1}}{\sum_{i=1}^2 SD_i(X)^{-1}} \tag{3}$$

where $W_i$ is the weight assigned to classifier $D_i$.

Since SDWS is based on the inaccurate classification, the weights are set according to the experimental value obtained in [7] initially and retained with the accumulative data in the AVAS.

## 4.4  Decision Making

The task of identification is to determine whether the speaker is a specific one in the group of N known speakers given his utterance and face image. As in all other biometric techniques, tolerances and probabilities should be used for such comparison. The differentiation is typically done by the maximum membership rule to determine the person whose features best match the features of the person to identify. Then the most probability is compared with a predetermined threshold to make the assurance that the person is enrolled in the system.

## 5  Database and Management

The database provides user information to the user interface module and user biometric model to the authentication center. The utterances of employees are also recorded in the database.

- **Enrolment Information Storage.** In the enrolment process, the biometric models representing the user's voiceprint and face are saved to the template file. This file also contains the relevant personal information mentioned in Chapter 3.1. Each authorized user is assigned with an index. Through the management of the attendance information database, we can get various working time information, which is beneficial to the management.
- **Further System Improvement.** We find that the recognition rate is becoming lower as the time goes by. For better user acceptance, the test data of genuine users are recorded when each time they come to check in or out. These data are stored for statistic purpose. The further function that the biometric models are retrained to adapt to the change of user's physical features will be developed as future work.

## 6  Practical Application

In this section, the performance of the proposed system to control accuracy is evaluated practically.

The robustness of the AVAS is test in CCNT lab of Zhejiang University, China. 18 persons are involved in the survey including 12 males and 6 females. The AVAS is used to record the attendance time of each person. The performance of AVAS is shown in Fig. 5, compared with biometric system using voiceprint or face character only. The above three methods are tested at three months interval, one for each.

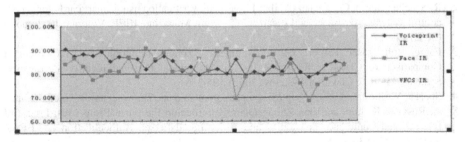

**Fig. 5.** The daily-change performance of the AVAS compared with single-biometric system, and each method is tested at one-month interval. The X-axis represents the date of the running system.

This figure shows the Identification Rate (IR) for either modality independently, as well as for the combined system AVAS. All the curves are of interest since the threshold is determined with an evaluation population separated from the test population. As illustrated in the figure, the AVAS outperforms either of the single modality and compensates the performance degradation problem of the audio modality as the time goes by. An improvement of 10.23% and 11.98% is gained compared with voiceprint and face recognition experts respectively.

The performance of the AVAS fluctuates from time to time, which is probably caused by the sensitivities of both experts to the environment and the variability of users themselves. We aim at investigating the robustness of either expert as well as a balanced period with respect to the weights adaptation according to the performance fluctuation of the individual modality as our future work.

## 7  Conclusion

This paper presents a new multi-modal biometric system that achieves high availability, usability and acceptability by combining the voiceprint and face experts in speaker identification for time and attendance application. The Score Difference-Based Sum rule (SDWS) algorithm is applied to multi-modal decision fusion to calculate the weight of the sum rule for each expert. We evaluated the ability of the system in real staff working environment practically, and showed encouraging results.

**Acknowledgments.** This work is supported by National Science Fund for Distinguished Young Scholars 60525202, Program for New Century Excellent Talents in University NCET-04-0545 and Key Program of Natural Science Foundation of China 60533040.

## References

1. Kenta Takahashi, Masahiro Mimura, Yoshiaki Isobe, and Yoichi Seto.: A secure and user-friendly multi-modal biometric system. Biometric Technology for Human Identification Proceedings of SPIE. Vol. 5404 (2004) 12-19
2. R. Sanchez-Reillo, C. Sanchez-Avila,: Fingerprint verification using smart cards for access control systems. Aerospace and Electronic Systems Magazine, IEEE, Volume: 17, Issue: 9 (2002) 12 - 15
3. Fabio Roli. Josef Kittler. Giorgio Fumera. Daniele Muntoni.: An Experimental Comparison of Classifier Fusion Rules for Multimodal Personal Identity Verification Systems. Multiple Classifier Systems (2002) 325-336
4. Speaker Verification Library: http://www.patni.com/innovate/innovate_prods_voicesafe.htm
5. A. Ross. A. K. Jain. and Jian Zhong Qian.: Information Fusion in Biometrics. Proc. 3rd International Conference on Audio- and Video-Based Person Authentication (AVBPA). Sweden. (2001) 354-359
6. S. Ben-Yacoub. Y. Abdeljaoued. and E. Mayoraz.: Fusion of face and speech data for person identity verification. IEEE Transactions on Neural Networks. (1999) 1065-1074.

7. D.D. Li, Y.C. Yang and Z.H. Wu.: Combining Voiceprint and Face Biometrics for Speaker Identification Using SDWS. Proceedings of the 9th Eurospeech, (2005) 1209-1212.
8. Y.M. Wang, G. Pan, Y.C. Yang, D.D. Li and Z.H. Wu.: Enhancing 3D Face Recognition by Combination of Voiceprint. ICCS 2006, Part I, LNCS 3991, (2006) 435–442
9. D.A. Reynolds,: A Gaussian Mixture Modeling Approach to Text-Independent Speaker Identification. IEEE Trans. Speech Audio Process.3 (1995) 72-83
10. Y. Wang. T. Tan and A. K. Jain.: Combining Face and Iris Biometrics for Identity Verification. Proc.of 4th Int'l Conf.on Audio- and Video-Based Biometric Person Authentication (AVBPA). Guildford. UK. (2003) 805-813.
11. P. Viola, M. Jones,: Rapid object detection using a boosted cascade of simple features. Computer Vision and Pattern Recognition. Volume:1 (2001) 511- 518

# Improved POCS-Based Deblocking Technique Using Wavelet Transform in Block Coded Image

Goo-Rak Kwon[1], Hyo-Kak Kim[1], Chun-Soo Park[1], Yoon Kim[2], and Sung-Jea Ko[1]

[1] Department of Electronics Engineering, Korea University
5 Ga, Anam-Dong, Sungbuk-ku, Seoul 136-701,Korea
{grkwon, hkkim, cspark, sjko}@dali.korea.ac.kr
http://dali.korea.ac.kr

[2] Department of Electrical and Computer Engineering, Kangwon national University
192-1 Hyoja 2-Dong, Chunchon, Kangwon-Do, 200-701, Korea
yooni@ieee.org

**Abstract.** This paper presents a improved POCS-based deblocking technique, based on the theory of the projection onto convex sets (POCS) to reduce the blocking artifacts in decoded images. We propose a new smoothness constraint set (SCS) and its projection operator in the wavelet transform (WT) domain to remove unnecessary high-frequency components caused by blocking artifacts. In order to eliminate the blocking artifacts component while preserving the original edge component, we also propose a significant coefficient decision method (SCDM)for fast and efficient performance. Experimental results show that the proposed method can not only achieve a significantly enhanced subjective quality but also increase the PSNR improvement in the reconstructed image.

## 1 Introduction

One of the most annoying artifacts introduced by video coding is blocking. Since human vision is naturally sensitive to edges, these distortions are very noticeable especially in uniform areas. Blocking artifacts are produced when large images are broken into sub-images of a smaller size and compressed independently.

This approach inevitably causes two primary visual artifacts in tile-based decompressed images. One is the ringing noise that distorts edge shapes. The other is the grid noise in monotone areas. There are two typical methods for the reduction of blocking artifacts in block-coded images: the spatial low-pass filtering algorithms using the human visual system [1], and the iterative method based on projections onto convex sets (POCS's) [2]. The simplest approach among the post-processing algorithms is low-pass filtering. It is somewhat simple to implement but might blur real edges at block boundaries. To solve these problems, a more sophisticated nonlinear space-variant filter was proposed in [3], where image blocks were classified and each was processed through a proper filter. And also the algorithms of the POCS-based method require nearly ten or more iterations of alternating projections over an entire image. The iterative

Y. Zhuang et al. (Eds.): PCM 2006, LNCS 4261, pp. 676–685, 2006.
© Springer-Verlag Berlin Heidelberg 2006

approaches based on the theory of POCS can be thought of as special cases of image restoration [4].

Zakhor [5] first tried to apply the theory of POCS to the reduction of blocking artifacts of tile-based coding images and proposed an iterative algorithm. The iterative algorithm can be proved as a method of the steepest descent iteration in a constrained minimization problem. There were two constraints on the coded image; SCS ($C_s$), which denotes the set including the images free from blocking artifacts, and QCS ($C_q$), which denotes the set including the images close to the original image. Notice in Fig. 1 that the $P_q$ and $P_s$ are the projection operators onto $C_q$ and $C_s$, respectively.

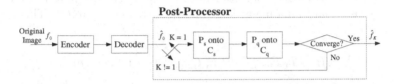

**Fig. 1.** Block diagram of the post-processing method on POCS

Various POCS-based algorithms have been proposed that are effective in alleviating blocking artifacts [2,5,6,8]. These methods perform the projections onto the SCS's in the pixel domain and the projections onto the QCS's are performed in the DCT domain. These algorithms have some drawbacks. First, they require the DCT and the IDCT operations with heavy computational burden. Second, it is difficult to distinguish the original edge component from the blocking artifacts in the reconstruction image since DCT coefficients cannot exactly divide each band in a transformed block.

In this paper, we propose a improved POCS-based deblocking technique based on the theory of POCS to alleviate the blocking artifacts in video coding. Our algorithm uses a new SCS and its projection operator in the WT domain to remove the unnecessary high-frequency components caused by the blocking artifacts. Moreover, the proposed method converges within a few iterations while the conventional POCS-based post-processing requires heavy computational complexity.

The paper is organized as follows. In the next section, the conventional POCS-based post-processing method is briefly reviewed. The proposed post-processing scheme is presented in Sect. 3. Sect. 4 presents and discusses the experimental results. Finally, our conclusion is given in Sect. 5.

## 2   Iterative Approaches Based on the Theory of POCS and Analysis of Blocking Artifacts

In image processing, POCS was first used to solve the problem of image restoration or enhancement. Assume that every known property of the original image $f$

can be formulated into a corresponding closed convex subset in Hilbert space $H$ [4]. For example, $n$ known properties of original $f$ generates $n$ well-defined closed convex sets $C_i$, $i = 1, 2, \cdots, n$, and necessarily, should be included in all the $C_i$'s and also the intersection of all the $C_i$'s $C^*$, i.e.,

$$f \in C^* = \bigcap_{i=1}^{n} C_i, \tag{1}$$

then by picking an arbitrary initial image and following an iterative scheme of projections onto each convex set, the original image can be restored. The intersection $C^*$ is a closed and convex set, and any element in $C^*$ satisfies $n$ given properties. Moreover, the problem of restoring the original image from its n properties is equal to finding at least one point belonging to $C^*$. This iterative equation

$$f_k = P_n P_{n-1} \cdots P_2 P_1 f_{k-1}, \quad k = 1, 2, \cdots, m \tag{2}$$

will converge to a limiting point $f^*$ of the intersection $C^* = \bigcap_{i=1}^{n} C_i$, as $k \to \infty$, for an arbitrary initial element $f_0$ in $H$ where $P_i$ ,the projection operator onto $C_i$ , is given by

$$\|f - P_i f\| = \min_{g \in C_i} [[f - g]]. \tag{3}$$

The theory of projections onto convex sets (POCS) is a special case of the composite mapping algorithms for image restoration. It is known that the post-processing techniques based on the theory of POCS satisfy two requirements: First, the closed convex sets, which have the properties of the image free from the blocking artifacts and close to the original image, should be defined. Second, the projection operators onto them are derived. As shown in Fig. 1, the projection $P_s$ onto SCS bandlimits the image in the horizontal and vertical directions so as to reduce directional blocking artifacts. On the other hand, the projection onto QCS requires N×N point DCT/IDCT operations.

# 3   Proposed Post-processing Method Using WT

## 3.1   Proposed New SCS and Its Projection Operator

In this section, we first examine the blocking artifacts by analyzing frequency characteristics of the original 8×8 block in the WT domain. Then, we introduce a smoothness constraint set and its projection operator in the WT domain to reduce the blocking artifacts.

Denote an $nN \times mN$ input image and its pixel by $\boldsymbol{f}$ and $f$ (a, b), respectively, where (a, b) is the pixel coordinate. Also, let $\boldsymbol{f}_{ij}$ be $N \times N$ vectors, representing $N \times N$ elements in each block, given by

$$\boldsymbol{f}_{ij} = \{f_{ij}(0,0), \cdots, f_{ij}(N-1, N-1)\} \tag{4}$$

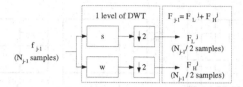

**Fig. 2.** 1-D DWT: The symbol ↓denotes the decimation by two

Let $F^j$ be the WT of signal $f^{j-1}$. In Fig. 2, $s$ is low-pass filter and $w$ is high-pass filter. One dimensional (1-D)Discrete Wavelet Transform (DWT) [7] can be implemented by using multilevel decomposition technique. Each decomposition level $j$ can be seen as the further decomposition of the sequence $f^{j-1}$ having $N_{j-1}$samples into two subbands $F_L^j$ and $F_H^j$, both $N_{j-1}/2$ having samples. Such decomposition can be implemented by two convolutions followed by a decimation by two, as follow:

$$F_L^j = \sum_{i=0}^{K-1} s_i \cdot f_{2n-i}^{j-1}, \ 0 \leq n < N_j, \tag{5}$$

$$F_H^j = \sum_{i=0}^{K-1} w_i \cdot f_{2n-i}^{j-1}, \ 0 \leq n < N_j, \tag{6}$$

where $s_i$ and $w_i$ denote coefficients of forward low-pass and high-pass K-tap filters, respectively.

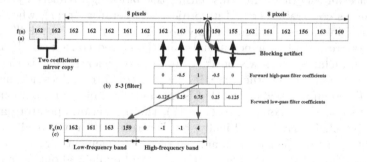

**Fig. 3.** 5-3 filter processing for extracting the blocking artifact: (a) 1-D 8 pixels with the blocking artifact (b) 5-3 filter (c) 1-D wavelet transformed signal

In the decoded image, to find the undesired high frequency components, we analyze the characteristics of $F^j$. Fig. 3 shows the example of WT by the 1-D 5-3 filtering process in the blocking boundary. As shown in Fig. 3 (c), the blocking components in the boundary of neighboring blocks are mostly located on the $4^{th}$ coefficients of the high frequency band's $4^{th}$ coefficients. And Fig. 4 shows the 2-D WT and the positions of blocking artifact components in $HL_1$ and $LH_1$. In fact, as shown in Fig. 4(c), the original edge and the blocking artifact components

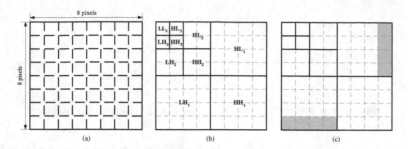

**Fig. 4.** $P_s$ onto $C_s$: (a) 8×8 sub-image, (b) Each sub-band in 2-D WT, (c) Gray region with original edge and blocking components

appear in the gray region. We tend to propose smoothness constraint sets and their projection operators as follow: Denote a closed convex set $C_{ij}$ as

$$
\begin{aligned}
C_{ij} &= \{f | f_{ij} \subset f, F^2 \geq F^2 - \alpha \cdot HL_1(F^2_{4^{th} column}) - \beta \cdot LH_1(F^2_{4^{th} row})\}, \\
\alpha &= \begin{cases} 1 \; if \; T \leq \; any \; of \; coefficients \; in \; HL_1 \\ 0 \; otherwise \end{cases}, \\
\beta &= \begin{cases} 1 \; if \; T \leq \; any \; of \; coefficients \; in \; LH_1 \\ 0 \; otherwise \end{cases}
\end{aligned}
\tag{7}
$$

where $HL_1(\cdot)$ and $LH_1(\cdot)$ represent $4^{th}$ row's and $4^{th}$ column's coefficients of the vertical and the horizontal band in the WT, respectively. And $T$ will be obtained by using the SCDM in the next section. Based on the above equation, we produce an algorithm for eliminating the blocking artifacts by proposing a smoothness constraint set and its projection operator. In (7), whether those coefficients have an original edge component or not, $4^{th}$ row's and $4^{th}$ column's coefficients are included or not included in the closed convex set. If $\alpha$ or $\beta$ is equal to 0, includes $4^{th}$ row's or $4^{th}$ column's coefficients, that is the original edge components. In the other case, if $\alpha$ or $\beta$ is equal to 1, does not include $4^{th}$ row's or $4^{th}$ column's coefficients, that is the undesired blocking components. By observing smoothness constraint set in (7), the projection operator onto those sets can be efficiently found. Finally, by discarding $4^{th}$ row's or $4^{th}$ column's coefficients, we can efficiently obtain the projected element $F^2_{4th\_clumn, 4th\_row}$, as shown in Fig. 5(b)-(c). In next section, we will explain about $\alpha$ and $\beta$ value decision using the SCDM.

### 3.2   Proposed SCDM

In block-based coding, the decoded image includes the blocking artifacts. To eliminate the undesired high frequency component, we convert it to the frequency domain. The high frequency area of the transformed contains the blocking artifacts as well as the original edge components. Therefore, in this section, we propose as improved SCS to remove the blocking artifacts while maintaining the original edge component. In a hierarchical sub-band system, with the exception of the highest frequency sub-bands, every coefficient at a given scale can

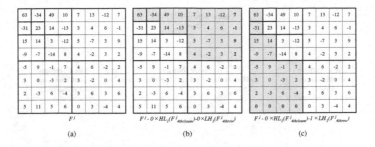

**Fig. 5.** For example: SCDM in each band

be related to a set of coefficients at the next finer scale of similar orientation. The coefficient at the coarse scale is called the parent, and all coefficients corresponding to the same spatial location at the finer scales of similar orientation are called children. In [9], a wavelet coefficient $x$ is to be significant with respect to a given threshold $T$ if $|x| > T$. A significant coefficient is closely related to original image quality. Therefore, to improve the decoded image quality, we preserve a sub-band with a significant coefficient rather than discarding it. Here, we propose a SCDM using the concept of the EZW algorithm. The flow chart for the decisions made at each coefficient is shown in the Fig. 6. Consider the simple 3-level WT of an $8\times8$ decoded image (see Fig. 6). The convex set of coefficients is shown in Fig. 6(a). Since the largest coefficient's magnitude is 63, we choose a threshold to by anywhere in (31.5, 63]. Let $T = 32$. In Fig. 5, if any of $LH_1$ band's coefficients are greater than $T$, the $4^{th}$ row's coefficients of are preserved. However, if one of them is less than $T$, it is discarded. In the same manner, if any of $LH_1$ band's coefficients are greater than $T$, the $4^{th}$ column's coefficients of $HL_1$ are preserved. If all of them are less than $T$, it is discarded. $T$ is determined by using the coefficient in $LL_3$ band. For example, if $\alpha = 0$ and $\beta = 1$, we can define a closed convex set $C_{ij}$ as

$$C_{ij} = \{f | f_{ij} \subset f, F^2 \geq F^2 - LH_1(F^2_{4^{th} row})\}. \tag{8}$$

Finally, the $4^{th}$ column or row coefficients are preserved or discarded. In general, the thresholds does not need to be powers of two. However, the starting $T$ can be expressed in terms of a threshold that is a power of two,

$$T = 2^{\lfloor \log_2 x_{\max} \rfloor}, \tag{9}$$

where $x^{max}$ is the largest wavelet coefficient.

# 4 Experimental Results

In this section, to evaluate the performance of our blocking artifact reduction and the maintenance of an original edge component, a computer simulation was performed for $256\times256$ images of [0, 255] gray-level range. And the performance has

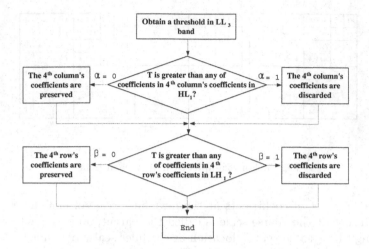

**Fig. 6.** The flow chart for SCDM

been evaluated for JPEG coded with about 30:1 compression ratio. The coded image for the experiment was obtained by applying JPEG with the quantization table shown in Table 1. The performance of four post-processing techniques, Zakhor's, Kim's, Paek's and our proposed algorithm are evaluated on various still images. As an objective measure of image quality, PSNR is used.

**Table 1.** Quantization Table

| 50  | 60  | 70  | 70  | 90  | 120 | 255 | 255 |
|-----|-----|-----|-----|-----|-----|-----|-----|
| 60  | 60  | 70  | 96  | 130 | 255 | 255 | 255 |
| 70  | 70  | 80  | 120 | 200 | 255 | 255 | 255 |
| 90  | 96  | 120 | 145 | 255 | 255 | 255 | 255 |
| 90  | 130 | 200 | 255 | 255 | 255 | 255 | 255 |
| 120 | 255 | 255 | 255 | 255 | 255 | 255 | 255 |
| 255 | 255 | 255 | 255 | 255 | 255 | 255 | 255 |
| 255 | 255 | 255 | 255 | 255 | 255 | 255 | 255 |

In Fig. 7, with increasing iteration, the PSNR performance of the proposed algorithm is compared with that of Zakhor's, Paek's, and Kim's algorithm. One iteration of post-processing is processed by applying two projection operators, that is, first $P_s$ on $C_s$ and next $P_q$ on $C_q$.

Note that the Zakhor's method fails to converge in order to the theory of POCS. The performance of the proposed method is better than that of Paek's and Kim's methods in terms of PSNR. Moreover, as shown in Fig. 7, the proposed method was shown to be robust in the original image, in terms of convergence and high performance.

To make a comparison of the subjective quality more clear, we also present whole and enlarged image of the details of BARBARA in Fig. 8. As is observed

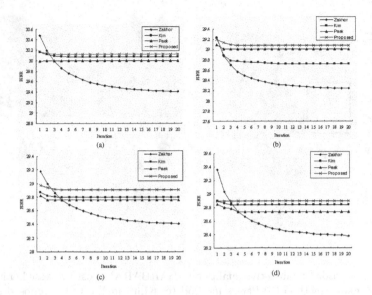

**Fig. 7.** PSNR performance variations on four decoded images (a) ZELDA image. (b) PEPPER image (c) FACE image (d) BARBARA image.

**Table 2.** Converged PSNR For the Different Post-Processing Methods

| Methods | Test images | | | |
|---|---|---|---|---|
| | Zelda | Pepper | Face | Barbara |
| JPEG | 29.81 | 28.84 | 28.61 | 28.43 |
| Zakhor's method | 29.41 | 28.25 | 28.41 | 28.38 |
| Paek's method | 30.00 | 29.02 | 28.76 | 28.76 |
| Kim's method | 30.05 | 28.80 | 28.84 | 28.87 |
| Proposed | 30.12 | 29.09 | 28.91 | 28.91 |

in Fig. 8, even though Zakhor's and Kim's methods reduce the blocking artifacts component in these figures, it produces a blurring image owing to the use of a global low-pass filter. For Paek's and Kim's method, although the edges are well preserved, the blocking artifacts are still observed in smooth areas. On the other hand, the blocking artifacts component is reduced more effectively by the proposed method than the other three methods. It is also observed that the original edge component is better preserved by the proposed method as compared with the result of the conventional ones. In Table 2, the PSNR performance of the proposed technique is compared with that of Zakhor's, Paek's, and Kim's technique. Note that the proposed algorithm is superior to Zakhor's, Peak's, and Kim's in terms of the converged PSNR performance. Hence, the proposed method provides good performance in terms of both subjective quality and the PSNR. It is also observed that the convergence of the proposed method is faster than the other methods.

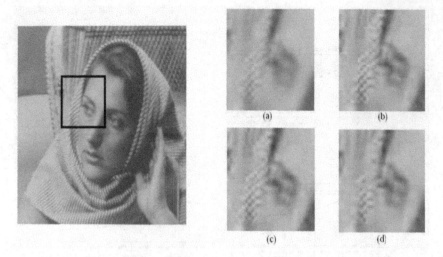

**Fig. 8.** Comparison of subjective quality on "BARBARA". Post-processed enlarge images (a) Zahkor's method (b) Paek's method (c) Kim's method (d) Proposed method.

## 5    Conclusions

In this paper, we proposed a new post-processing method, based on the theory of the projection onto convex sets to reduce the blocking artifacts in HDTV decoded images. We propose a new SCS and its projection operator in the WT domain to remove unnecessary high-frequency components caused by blocking artifacts. We also propose the SCDM to preserve effectively the original edge component. Experimental results show that the proposed method can achieve not only an objective quality of about 0.5-0.8 dB, but also subjective quality nearly free of the blocking artifacts and edge blur. Finally, owing to the non-repetitive conception of the proposed method, it can be efficiently applied for the post-processing of HDTV decoded images.

## Acknowledgments

This research was supported by Seoul Future Contents Convergence (SFCC) Cluster established by Seoul Industry-Academy-Research Cooperation Project.

## References

1. Reeve, H. C., Lim, J. S.: Reduction of the blocking effects in image coding, Opt. Eng., vol. 23 (1984) 34–37
2. Yang, Y., Galatsanos,N. P., Katsaggelos, A. K.: Projection-based spatially adaptive reconstruction of block-transform compressed images. IEEE Trans. Image Processing, vol. 4 (1995) 896–908

3. Ramamurthi, B., Gersho, A.: Nonlinear space-variant post-processing of block coded images. IEEE Trans. Acoustics, Speech, and Signal Proc., vol. ASSP-34 (1986) 1258–1267

4. Youla, D., Webb, H.: Image restoration by the method of convex projections: part i-theory. IEEE Trans. Med. Imag., vol. MI-1 (1982) 81–94

5. Zakhor, A.: Iterative procedures for reduction of blocking effects in transform image coding. IEEE Trans. on Circuits Syst. Video Technol., vol. 2 (1992) 91–95

6. Paek, H., Kim, R. C., Lee, S. U.: On the pocs-based post-processing technique to reduce the blocking artifacts in transform coded images. IEEE Trans. on Circuits Syst. Video Technol., vol. 8 (1998) 358–367

7. Antonini, M., Barlaud, M., Mathieu, P., Daubechies, I.: Image coding using wavelet transform. IEEE Trans. Image Proc., vol. 1 (1992) 205–218

8. Kim, Y., Park, C. S., and Ko, S. J.: Fast POCS Based Post-processing Technique for HDTV. IEEE Trans. on Consumer Electronics. vol. 49 (2003) 1438–1447

9. Shapiro, J. M.: Embedded Image Coding Using Zerotrees of Wavelet Coefficients. IEEE Trans. On Signal Proc., vol. 41 (1993) 3445–3462

# Sketch Case Based Spatial Topological Data Retrieval

Yuan Zhen-ming, Zhang Liang, and Pan Hong

Institute of Information Engineering, Hangzhou Teachers College
310036 Hangzhou, China
{zyuan, zhl, chin}@hztc.edu.cn

**Abstract.** A large proportion of the information can be regarded as spatial data which is spatial position related. For accessing spatial databases, different query specification techniques have been proposed. But traditional query methods are tedious and cannot realize fuzzy query. A content-based spatial data retrieval system is presented to afford users a sketch interface which has the ability to accept fuzzy retrieval. Firstly the retrieval algorithm builds the spatial topological vector by refining the 9-intersection model metrically. Then the independent topological relations are extracted by training ICA assisted fuzzy SVMs, which can remove redundancy among the binary relations and reduce the dimension in complex spatial scene. In query processing the *tf×idf* model is referenced, and the similarity is calculated by cosine distance function on the weight vectors of the query scene and each of spatial scenes in database. The experimental results show the recall factor and precision factor are improved compared with the query method without ICA and SVM.

**Keywords:** Data Retrieval, ICA, SVM, Topological Invariant.

## 1 Introduction

Traditional spatial data retrieval technologies have many limits: (1) The query methods and procedure are tedious when using the Zoom In , Zoom Out, and Pan tools only [1][2], (2) The common queries are based on keywords and places, but the keywords and the names of places are always confusing[3], (3) The spatial queries based on SQL can not be used to realize the fuzzy query for the spatial data[4] [5], (4) The recognition of complicated nature query language still has hard difficulty. At present, many new information retrieval methods appear in the multimedia retrieval field. Content based image retrieval uses the color, texture, or shape as query characters [6]. Sketch based graph and CAD retrieval use the structures of graph to retrieve CAD/CAM data [7]. Spatial-query-by-sketch [8] uses spatial relations to retrieve GIS data. This paper introduces the sketch interface and the content based query into the spatial retrieval system, which accords with the query habit of people, and can afford fuzzy information query.

One of the most significant characters between the spatial data query and normal multimedia data query is that the users are concerned more about the spatial position and the spatial topological relations of the spatial data. So in the content based spatial retrieval the topological attributes are the important query keys. Considering the

Y. Zhuang et al. (Eds.): PCM 2006, LNCS 4261, pp. 686–694, 2006.

uncertainty nature in the matching processing of the content based retrieval, this paper uses the independent component analysis (ICA) to build the independent topological relationship space for the spatial scene, identifies the topological relationship vector by SVM, and sorts and retrieves the spatial data by using $tf{\times}idf$ model.

The remainder of this paper is structured as follows. Section 2 presents the topological invariants to describe the spatial scenes. Section 3 proposes the ICA assisted SVM to learn the topological relations. Section 4 presents the $tf{\times}idf$ retrieval model to retrieval the spatial data. Finally, section 5 presents the experimental results and conclusion.

## 2  Measurements of Formalized Topological Relationships

The topological relation is the characters of the geometrical object invariably under the homeomorphism transform which can produce the qualitative difference, and is one of the basic problems of reasoning in the qualitative space. And the topological invariant is the value which is unchanged under the topological equivalence. The topological invariants in this paper are based on Egenhofer's 9-intersection model [9], which characterizes the topological relation $t$ between two point sets, $A$ and $B$, by the set intersections of $A$'s interior( $A^{\circ}$ ), boundary( $\partial A$ ), and exterior( $A^{-}$ ) with the interior, boundary, and exterior of $B$.

$$I(A,B) = \begin{pmatrix} A^{\circ} \cap B^{\circ} & A^{\circ} \cap \partial B & A^{\circ} \cap B^{-} \\ \partial A \cap B^{\circ} & \partial A \cap \partial B & \partial A \cap B^{-} \\ A^{-} \cap B^{\circ} & A^{-} \cap \partial B & A^{-} \cap B^{-} \end{pmatrix} \qquad (1)$$

However, the 9-intersection model cannot completely describe the topological relation [10]. So it can only be used to take qualitative analysis. In order to analysis the topological relation by quantitative method, some topological invariants are defined in the content based spatial retrieval as followings [8].

### 2.1  The Invariants of Topological Components

The invariant $\phi_1^{CC}$ is the component counting (CC) defined as the number of components in two point sets. A component of set $Y$ is a largest connected subset of $Y$.

The dimension of component (DC) is another invariant $\phi_2^{DC}$ of topological components. It is defined as the usual definition from topology, which means the dimension of empty set being -1, and the arbitrarily small neighborhoods whose boundaries have dimension less than $n$. Thus, a point has dimension 0, the dimension of line is 1, and the dimension of region is 2.

### 2.2  The Invariants of Metrical Topological Relation

Representing the spatial relations only by 9-intersection model is insufficiently. For the instance of overlapping of regions, the intersections of regions are regarded as the most important value. In [8], the invariants as Inner Area Splitting (**IAS**), Outer Area Splitting (**OAS**), Exterior Splitting (**ES**), are calculated by the normalized proportion of overlapped region areas as Fig.1.

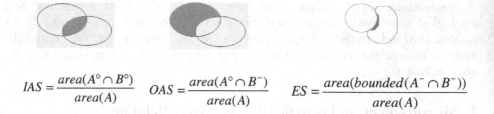

$$IAS = \frac{area(A° \cap B°)}{area(A)} \qquad OAS = \frac{area(A° \cap B^-)}{area(A)} \qquad ES = \frac{area(bounded(A^- \cap B^-))}{area(A)}$$

**Fig. 1.** Three region Invariants

Though those invariants are independent on scales, it is obviously the redundancy exists in IAS and OAS, and only the area is considered without considering the shape of intersections. In this paper, invariant moments are introduced into those invariants, and the metrical region invariants are defined as the second-order, and third-order moments of IAS, OAS, and ES respectively. Let $I(i,j)$ be the intersections of IAS, OAS, or ES. The central moments of IAS are defined as

$$\mu_{pq}^{IAS} = \sum_i \sum_j (i - \bar{x})^p (j - \bar{y})^q \tag{2}$$

where $\bar{x}$ and $\bar{y}$ are the center of gravity of the intersections, $p$ and $q$ define the order of moment. Then the second-order IAS moment is defined as

$$\phi_3^{IAS} = \frac{1}{\mu_{00}^{IAS4}} [(\mu_{20}^{IAS} - \mu_{02}^{IAS})^2 + 4\mu_{11}^{IAS2}] \tag{3}$$

Other five metrical topological invariants (from $\phi_4^{IAS}$ to $\phi_8^{ES}$) are also defined as above.

For the instance of having overlapping boundary, the metrical boundary invariants can be calculated based on the normalized proportion of lengths of overlapped boundaries. The invariants are Inner Traversal Splitting ($\phi_9^{ITS}$), Outer Traversal

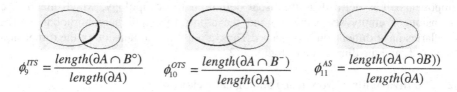

$$\phi_9^{ITS} = \frac{length(\partial A \cap B°)}{length(\partial A)} \qquad \phi_{10}^{OTS} = \frac{length(\partial A \cap B^-)}{length(\partial A)} \qquad \phi_{11}^{AS} = \frac{length(\partial A \cap \partial B))}{length(\partial A)}$$

**Fig. 2.** Two Metrical Boundary Invariants

Splitting ( $\phi_{10}^{OTS}$ ), Alongness Splitting ( $\phi_{11}^{AS}$ ), which represent the proportion between the inner boundary, the outer boundary and meeting boundary to the whole boundary.

For the instance of disjoint, an invariant called by Outer Closeness ( $\phi_{12}^{OC}$ ) can be calculated by proportion between the area of Maximum Boundary Rectangle of both regions and the area of one region.

Then a 1×12 spatial topological vector

$$\Phi = [\phi_1, \phi_2, \phi_3, \phi_4, \phi_5, \phi_6, \phi_7, \phi_8, \phi_9, \phi_{10}, \phi_{11}, \phi_{12}]$$  (4)

can be defined to represent the relation between two spatial objects, which will be used to topological classification. But there is corresponding relation between the invariants of metrical topological relation and intersections, and it is obvious that the dimension of the complex spatial scene with $n$ objects is much high, and the elements in the vector is not independent and have redundancies. So an ICA assisted Support Vector Machine is used to reduce the dimension, to extract the eigenvectors, and to implement the topological classification and retrieval [12].

# 3   Learning Topological Relation Using ICA Assisted SVM

## 3.1   Constructing the Spatial Scene Independent Topological Relation

Supposing $N$ objects in a spatial scene in $R^2$, there are $\dfrac{N(N-1)}{2}$ binary spatial relationships among $N$ objects. Each relationship between two objects can represented by 1×$M$ row vector composed of $M=9$ topological invariants defined as previous. The $\dfrac{N(N-1)}{2}$ vectors comprise $\dfrac{N(N-1)}{2} \times M$ sample matrix $x$ (assuming $\dfrac{N(N-1)}{2} > M$), and $x$ can be regarded as the result of a linear mixture model in ICA:

$$x = As$$  (5)

where components of $s$ are independent sources and unknown, $A$ is unknown, and $x$ is the observation. ICA tries to estimate the matrix $W$ in the reconstruction model:

$$y = Wx$$  (6)

Applying the natural gradient algorithm [13] to minimize the Kullback-Leibler divergence between the source signal vector and its estimate, the statistically independent topological relations can be found and the spatial scene can be represented by the coefficients of the projection on those independent topological relations. To control the number of independent topological relations, the first $m$ eigenvectors of the training topological relations of spatial scene are used, instead of the original spatial scene to train ICA [14]. The independent topological relations can be obtained by following:

At first each spatial scene is regarded as the observation value of random vector; the eigenvector of $x$ are computed, eigenvectors corresponding to the maximum $m$

eigenvalues are taken as a matrix $P_m$, and then each eigenvector is the column vector of $P_m$. Then replace $x$ with $P_m^T$ and apply the ICA algorithm as followings:

$$WP_m^T = y \Rightarrow P_m^T = W^{-1}y \tag{7}$$

where each row of $y$ represents an independent topological relation.

From $P_m$, a minimum squared error approximation of $x$ is obtained by

$$x_{rec} = xP_m P_m^T \tag{8}$$

Substituting equation (16) into equation (17), we get

$$x_{rec} = xP_m W^{-1}y \tag{9}$$

The rows of $xP_m W^{-1}y$ are the coefficients for the linear combination of independent topological relation in $y$. Thus for the representation of a spatial scene, which is a row vector $I_{1 \times N}$, the ICA representation is:

$$c = IP_m W^{-1} \tag{10}$$

where $P_m W^{-1}$ is obtained during the ICA training procedure.

## 3.2  Topological Relation Classification Based on Fuzzy SVM

After getting the ICA features, the goal of training the sample spatial data using SVM [11] is to output the subjection values between the query topological vector and the independent topological relations when giving a spatial scene input. In traditional SVM with the training set $\{c_i, d_i\}_{i=1}^l$, the classification results are $d_i = \{1, -1\}$, where $l$ is the size of training set. So it can only be applied to binary classification problems. In spatial scene, each independent topological relation needs one SVM to training. It is possible that one spatial scene is labeled as 1 by two or more SVM. So a fuzzy SVM is introduced to support transforming the output of SVM to probability, which can be used to estimate the SVMs owned by the spatial scene.

To carry out the fuzzy SVM, a sigmoid function maps the SVM of each independent topological relation to posterior probability [15]:

$$P(S_i \mid X) = \frac{1}{1 + \exp(A_i X_{out} + B_i)} \tag{11}$$

where $A_i$ and $B_i$ is the Sigmoid parameters of each SVM, $X_{out}$ is the distance between any topological relation eigenvector $X$ and SVM. Then a membership functions:

$$\mu_{indkey}(X) = \max_{S_i} P(S_i \mid X) \tag{12}$$

is used to judge one topological relation feature $X$ belong to which independent topological relation. A threshold $\varepsilon$ is proposed, and if $\mu_{indkey}(X) \le \varepsilon$, then the topological relation feature is not belonging to any independent topological relation.

## 4  Retrieval the Spatial Data Based on *tf×idf* Model

The *tf×idf* model [16] is used to process the content based spatial scene retrieval. Let $X_{indkey}(k)$ $(k=1,...,12n)$ be all the independent spatial relations contained in the spatial scene database which have $n$ scenes, $\omega_{i_k}$ be the weight of spatial scene $S_i$ corresponding to the $k$th independent topological relation. Then spatial scene $S_i$ can be represented by weighting vector:

$$I_i = [\omega_{i_1},...,\omega_{i_k},...,\omega_{i_n}]$$  (13)

The weight of each independent topological relation in spatial scene can be computed by document frequency and inversed document frequency. Here let $tf_{ij}$ be the frequency of the $j$th independent topological relation presented in spatial scene $S_i$. $df_j$ be the number of spatial scenes containing the $j$th independent topological relation. It implies $tf_{ij}$ is in inverse proportion to $df_j$, and $tf_{ij}$ increase with the frequency.

$$tf_{ij} \approx \frac{df_j}{N_{scene}}$$  (14)

But if one independent topological relation appears in almost every spatial scene, it has no ability to distinguish one spatial scene from others. So an inversed frequency $u$ is introduced, which is in inverse proportion to the number of scenes containing this independent topological relation. $u$ is defined as follows:

$$u = \log_2 \frac{N_{scene}}{df_j} + 1$$  (15)

where $N_{scene}$ is the number of scenes in the spatial scene database. Then the weight $\omega_{i_k}$ of the independent topological relation in the scene $S_i$ is defined as the product of $tf_{ij}$ and $u$. The independent topological vector of a sample spatial scene $Q$ is extracted by SVM, which then can be represented by the weight vector:

$$Q = [\omega_{q_1},...,\omega_{q_k},...,\omega_{q_n}]$$  (16)

At last, the similarity between $Q$ and each of spatial scenes is defined by cosine distance function:

$$S(I,Q) = \frac{I_i Q}{\| I_i \| \| Q \|}$$  (17)

## 5  Experimental Results and Future Works

The framework of the experimental system is illustrated in Fig.3. In the preprocessing, a few manually annotated spatial scene samples are used to train the ICA assisted SVM for learning each independent topological relation. By projecting the scene to independent topological relations, the spatial database is indexed by the topological eigenvector corresponding to each scene. A sketch interface is provided to support users draw their query scene by using object-oriented graph tools. After topological invariants of the query were extracted, the weights of independent topological relation are calculated by the trained SVMs, and the results are sorted according to the similarities computed by *tf×idf* model.

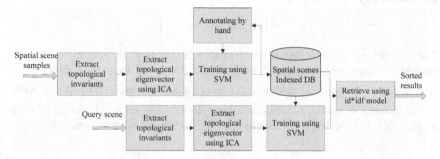

**Fig. 3.** The framework of content based spatial data retrieval

The experimental database is composed of two kinds of spatial scenes. The first database includes 1050 spatial scenes obtained from [8], in which the similarity scenes are produced by transforming spatial position of objects continuously. The second database includes 2000 actual spatial scenes obtained from 1:500 building GIS data of Hangzhou City. The retrieval method (method I) using *tf×idf* model with ICA assisted SVM is compared with the one (method II) only using *tf×idf* model. To analysis the performances of the classifiers under different sizes of training samples, four training sample groups are extracted from datasets, the numbers of which are respectively 10, 20, 40 and 60. The precision and recall factors are calculated by averaging the results of 20 queries in the first whole database, because the first database is more objective on the measurement than the second one.

**Table 1.** Correct Rate of retrieval

| Results | Samples | Group1 | Group2 | Group3 | Group4 |
|---------|---------|--------|--------|--------|--------|
| Precision factor (%) | Method I | 70.3 | 85.1 | 92.21 | 94.7 |
| | Method II | 64.2 | 72.4 | 77.76 | 75.31 |
| Recall factor (%) | Method I | 72.1 | 87.6 | 93.44 | 96.12 |
| | Method II | 66.5 | 73.86 | 89.34 | 90.1 |

Table 1 shows that Method I with ICA assisted SVM has significant improvement in comparison with Method II, which means ICA has established exact independent topological vectors and fuzzy SVM has good classification ability. At the same time, when the number of samples is 10, the precision and recall factors are low, which means few samples result in few topological characters and insufficient to describe scenes. By increasing the number of training samples, the two factors (precision and recall) are improved significantly, which means the number of topological characters is increasing highly for SVM. Although the relativities are also high, the ICA topological vectors have high-order independent after mapped through fuzzy SVM. By increasing numbers of training samples continuously, the two factors improve with lower speed, which means SVM has good learning and classification abilities under enough number of samples.

**Table 2.** Examples of spatial query and results. The first two rows show the retrieval results in the first database, and the query results in the second database are listed in the third row.

| Query Example | Sorted Results | | | |
|---|---|---|---|---|
| | | | | |
| | | | | |
| | | | | |

The first two rows in Table 2 show the retrieval results in the first database, which give the right order according to the matching degree. The experimental results in the second database are listed in the third row, which show that the retrieval results are similar to the query scene in shapes, topological relations and overlapping of spatial objects. And the result scenes are similar to the query scene on large scale, which suggests the algorithm can afford fuzzy retrieval.

The future works about the content based spatial data retrieval are: (1) constructing an efficient spatial index mechanism to support the statistic learning based retrieval, (2) embedding in large GIS database to implement practical spatial query, (3) designing a relevance feedback fitted for our spatial query algorithm.

# References

1. Goodchild, M.: Integrating GIS and spatial data analysis: Problems and possibilities. International Journal of Geographical Information Systems, 6(5):407--423, 1992
2. Morehouse, S.: The ARC/INFO geographic information system. Computers and Geosciences: An international journal, Vol. 18, No. 4, pp. 435-443, 1992

3. Ooi, B.C.: Efficient Query Processing in Geographic Information Systems. Springer Verlag, 1990
4. Medeiros, C.B. and Pires, F.: Databases for GIS. SIGMOD Record, Vol. 23, No. 1, pp. 107-115, March 1994
5. Egenhofer, Max J.: Spatial SQL: a query and presentation language. IEEE Transactions on Knowledge and Data Engieering, 6(1), pp.86-95, 1994
6. Flickner, M., Sawhnewy, H., Niblack, W., et al: Query by image and video Content: The QBIC System. IEEE Computer, 1995, 28(9): 23-32
7. Rosenthal, A., Heiler, S., and Manola, F.: An example of knowledge-based query processing in a CAD/CAM DBMS. Proceedings of 10th International Conference on Very Large Data Bases, Singapore, 1984, pp.363-370
8. Egenhofer, Max J.: Query Processing in Spatial-Query-by-Sketch. Journal of Visual Languages and Computing, Vol.8, No.4, pp. 403-424, 1997
9. Egenhofer, MJ, Sharma, J: Topological relations between regions in R2 and Z2. In: Abel D, Ooi BC, eds. Advances in Spatial Databases, the 3rd International Symposium, SSD'93. LNCS 692, Berlin: Springer-Verlag, 1993. 316~336.
10. Egenhofer, MJ.: On the Equivalence of Topological Relations. International Journal of Geographical Information Systems, Vol. 8, No. 6, pp.133-152, 1994
11. Vapnik, V.: The Nature of Statistical Learning Theory.Springer. New York, 1995
12. Qi, Y., DeMenthon, D., and Doermann, D.: Hybrid Independent Component Analysis and Support Vector Machine Learning Scheme for Face Detection. International Conference on Acoustics, Speech, and Signal Processing (ICASSP01), May 2001, Salt Lake City,Utah
13. A. Cichocki S. Amari and H. H. Yang: A new learning algorithm for blind signal separation. In NIPS 8, pp.752–763, Cambridge, MA, 1996. MIT Press
14. Bartlett, M.S., Lades, H.M., and Sejnowski, T.J.: Independent component representations for face recognition. In SPIE Conf. on Human Vision and Electronic Imaging III, vol. 3299, pp. 528–539, 1998
15. Platt, JC.: Probabilistic outputs for support vector machines for pattern recognition, Smola A, Barlett P, Scholkopf B Editor, In: Advances in Large margin Classifiers, Boston: Kluwer Academic Publishers, 1999
16. Salton, G., Buckley, C.: Term Weighting approaches in automatic text retrieval, Information Processing and Management, 1997, 24(5):513-523

# Providing Consistent Service for Structured P2P Streaming System*

Zhen Yang and Huadong Ma

Beijing Key Lab of Intelligent Telecommunications Software and Multimedia,
School of Computer Sci. & Techno., Beijing University of Posts and Telecommunications,
Beijing 100876, China
mhd@bupt.edu.cn

**Abstract.** In decentralized but structured peer-to-peer (P2P) streaming system, when a node is overloading, the new incoming requests will be replicated to its neighboring nodes in the same session, and then the requesting nodes will receive the streams from these neighboring nodes. However, the replication of the requests might result in the service inconsistency due to no-zero replicated time. In general, there is a tradeoff between the system performance and the service consistency. In this paper, we focus on how to provide the service consistency for decentralized but structured P2P streaming system, under the precondition of no obvious degrading at the system performance. We propose a service update algorithm (SUA) which iteratively adjusts the actual read delay at these neighboring nodes, and thus converges to the desired misread probability. The analytic and simulated results show that the algorithm achieves a good tradeoff between the service consistency and the system performance.

**Keywords:** peer-to-peer, service consistency, streaming system.

## 1 Introduction

Over the past few years, peer-to-peer (P2P) technologies have rapidly evolved and become an important part of the existing Internet. The P2P network is constructed by application-layer multicast routing protocol [1-5,10]. Currently, there are several different architectures for P2P network: centralized, decentralized but structured, and decentralized but unstructured. In this paper, we focus on decentralized but structured P2P streaming system.

One of the most widely used applications in P2P network is P2P live streaming service [1,2]. The characteristics of live streaming services are likely to be fundamentally different from those of pre-recorded, stored media services. Live streaming services exhibit stronger temporal patterns that may not be present (or may be significantly weaker) in stored media services. For stored media, when QoS degrades below a certain threshold, the under-provisioned resource may choose to simply "reject"

---

* This work reported in this paper is supported by NSFC under Grant No. 90612013, the Specialized Research Fund for the Doctoral Program of Higher Education under Grant No. 20050013010, and the NCET of MOE, CHINA.

Y. Zhuang et al. (Eds.): PCM 2006, LNCS 4261, pp. 695–703, 2006.

new requests. The "admission control" solution may be acceptable since a user can be expected to come back at a later time to request the stored content. For live streams, users do not have the option of revisiting the content again in the future, since the content is in its liveness. Thus, admission control is not a viable alternative for live streaming providers. In the P2P live streaming service, when a node is overloading, the new incoming request will be replicated to its some neighboring nodes in the same session (we define session in sec 3.1). And then the requesting node will receive the media streams from the node chosen among these neighboring nodes. The replicated operation improves the availability of the live streams. However, due to no-zero time of replicated operation, it might result in that some neighboring nodes read an obsolete session state and thus forward the wrong streams to the requesting node. This problem is particularly critical for P2P live content delivery. In this paper, we called this problem as service inconsistency, which isn't still answered well.

In general, there is a tradeoff between the system performance and the service consistency. Service consistency can be improved at the expense of service response time and vice versa. In other words, strong service consistency requires high overhead and thus limits the performance of system.

The goal of this paper is to provide service consistency for decentralized but structured P2P streaming system, under the precondition of no obvious degrading at the system performance. We adopt the continuous consistency model [8] and apply it to structured P2P streaming system. We propose a service update algorithm (SUA) which iteratively adjusts the actual read delay, and thus converges to the desired misread probability.

The remainder of this paper is organized as follows. In section 2, we review the related works. In section 3, we present the SUA algorithm in detail. Section 4 presents the simulated results. Finally, we conclude in section 5 with a summary of our findings and give some discussion about future works.

## 2  Related Works

In this section, we will overview the related works about P2P streaming system, and service consistency.

### 2.1  Live P2P Streaming System

Live P2P streaming system has been an active research area in the recent years. Three architectures have been proposed. There are centralized, decentralized but structured, and decentralized but unstructured architecture.

ALMI [3] and other similar systems employ a centralized solution. In a centralized scheme, a central controller is used to compute and instruct the construction of the delivery tree based on the information of metrics (e.g. distances, degree bounds) provided by the overlay members. Nodes in the P2P network issue queries to the central controller to find which other nodes hold the desired files. Thus, such centralized approaches do not scale well and have single points of failure.

CAN [4] and some other systems are based on a decentralized but structured solution. These systems have no central directory server, but they have a significant amount of structure. By "structure", we mean that the P2P overlay topology is tightly controlled. Structured P2P overlays are highly resilient. Structured P2P streaming system usually assume existence of a distributed has table (DHT). But current overlays don't provide good service consistency; even a small fraction of failed nodes can prevent correct live content delivery throughout the overlay. This problem is particularly serious in open P2P systems.

Decentralized but unstructured system [5] is neither a centralized control nor any precise control over the network topology. The overlay network is formed by nodes joining the network following some loose rules. These unstructured designs are extremely resilient to nodes entering and leaving the system. In most unstructured P2P systems, whenever a new peer wishes to join the system, it connects to an existing peer randomly selected from a list of known peers. However, this approach has the drawback that it does not take into account the content of the peers and thus, the current routing mechanisms are extremely un-scalable, generating large loads on the network participants.

In this paper, we focus on decentralized, structured live P2P streaming systems. We do so because (1) these systems are actively used by a large community of Internet users, and (2) these systems have not yet been solved well about service consistency.

## 2.2 Service Consistency

Service consistency is an important index for the live streaming QoS. Many studies focused on the streaming scheduler (such as [5,9]) to provide good QoS. Those studies have improved our understanding of the nature of live streaming service.

The tradeoffs between consistency, performance, and availability are well understood. Traditionally, however, designers of P2P live streaming systems have been forced to choose from either strong consistency guarantees or none at all. S. Susarla [11] described a new consistency model for P2P sharing of mutable data called composable consistency, and outlined its implementation in a wide area middleware file service. However, this model doesn't adapt to the live system. H.Yu [8] developed a conit-based continuous consistency model to capture the consistency spectrum using three application-independent metrics, numerical error, order error, and staleness. This model is good for real-time system. In this paper, we adopt the conit-based continuous consistency model. Some optimistic consistency techniques have been proposed to support availability and performance at the expense of weak consistency. The authors of [6,7] proposed an update commit algorithm for adaptive consistency control based the conit-based continuous consistency model.

P2P streaming service can tolerate the occurrence rate of misreading streaming up to a certain predefined level. This feature simplifies the design of consistency control. In fact, the maximum acceptable level of service inconsistency can be predefined at the overlay routing protocol. And thus end hosts are guaranteed that their services can be correctly completed with a certain probability.

## 3  SUA Algorithm

In this section, we will study how to provide service consistence for P2P live stream-ing service. We present an algorithm which we call Service Update Algorithm.

### 3.1  Problem Description

Session is the key concept in P2P streaming applications. For instance, a session is a set of senders, receivers and the data streams flowing from senders to receivers. P2P streaming service encapsulates the entire process of providing a kind of media to users. A session may support various services simultaneously, such as audio, video, whiteboard, application sharing. We now define the P2P session formally.

**Definition 1:** A **P2P session** can be defined as a tuple: *Session = (Services, Users, Streams)*, where *Services* is a set of services that the session can provide, and *Services = (s1, s2, ..., sn)*; *Users* is a set of users who attend the session, and *Users = (u1, u2, ..., um)*; *Streams* is a set of streams in the session, and *Streams ⊆ Users× Users× Services*.

In decentralized but structured P2P streaming system, certain nodes are likely to be far more frequently accessed than others. It might result in the overloading of those nodes. To solve the overloading problem, overlay routing protocols [1-3] adopt the replication techniques commonly applied to web. When a node is overloading, it can replicate the new incoming requests at some of its neighboring nodes belonging to the same session. According to the routing protocol, a neighboring node holding a replica of a request can, with a certain probability, choose to either satisfy the request or forward it on its way. The requesting node will receive the media streams from the chosen node. We can see the overloading node (sender) and its neighboring nodes belonging to the same session as *a resource set*. The nodes in the set can provide the same functionality by running a state-sharing mechanism [2,6].

The state-sharing mechanism running in each node distributes the state-update messages to its neighbor nodes in the same resource set. A state-update message is committed by the state-sharing mechanism only when the new incoming request ar-rives at a node. The state update message can be stored at a queue in a simple round-robin fashion. The operation of reading the state can be allowed if and only if the state-update message is committed, otherwise reading a correct state is impossible. Apparently, there are two types of state-update message: local and remote. A local state-update message is generated locally in the node, whereas, a remote state-update message is generated by any other peer node in the same resource set. In this paper, we assume that only the arrivals of remote state-update message affect the misread probability.

However, the replication of message might make the node that send the requesting message read an outdate state. We now give the definition of a **correct P2P session**.

**Definition 2:** A P2P session is correctly completed if the request returns a response with the consistent state information.

If the probability of a session correctly completed is over a certain threshold, service consistency can be guaranteed. In others words, service consistency is figured by the probability that a request read a correct response. Correspondingly, P2P service inconsistency can be described by the probability that a request reads an obsolete state. Thus, we can identify the P2P service inconsistency with misread probability.

### 3.2 SUA Algorithm for Service Consistency

In this subsection, we will describe the service update algorithm (SUA) in detail.

The misread probability is the probability of which a request reads an obsolete state. Due to the misread probability mainly caused by the read delay, it can be denoted as a function of the read delay. A non-zero misread probability can be achieved in a P2P live streaming system if the system chooses an appropriate read delay. Apparently, the zero misread probability cannot be guaranteed in the current live system.

We adopt the continuous consistency model [8] and apply to P2P streaming system. Our SUA algorithm uses an update function to iteratively correct the read delay value. The SUA algorithm can converge to a given misread probability. The SUA algorithm can be regarded as a part of any overlay routing protocol, which run at each node. The SUA is triggered when a request arrives at a node, which will read a state of given P2P session.

We now define some parameters relevant for the SUA algorithm. For a node $S_i \in S$, we use $P_i$ to denote the streaming misread probability at node $S_i$, where $S$ denote the resource set and is a subset of *Users*. Let $d_i$ be the read delay at node $S_i \in S$ and let $d_{max}$ be the maximum allowed value of the read delay. Read delay is the interval between the time that a request arrives at the node $S_i$ and the time that read processing start. In other words, the read delay $d_i$ is the response time of node $S_i$. The delay for the $n$th read request and the $(n+1)$th read request at node $S_i$ are denoted as $d_i(n)$ and $d_i(n+1)$, respectively. Let $P_{i,b}$ be the predefined misread probability value. $R_i(n-1)$ and $R_i(n)$ are the misread rate after the $(n-1)$th and the $n$th read access, respectively.

The update function applied to the nth read delay is defined as follows.

$$d_i(n+1) = \begin{cases} d_i(n) + d_{max} * abs\{(R_i(n) - P_{i,b})^{\alpha}\}, & \text{if } R_i(n) - P_{i,b} > 0 \\ d_i(n) - d_{max} * abs\{(R_i(n) - P_{i,b})^{\alpha}\}, & \text{if } R_i(n) - P_{i,b} < 0 \end{cases}. \tag{1}$$

Where, *abs()* is the absolute value, and the factor $\alpha > 0$ has an impact on the convergence speed.

If there are $N$ nodes $S_i$ $(i=1,...,N)$ in the source set $S$, we assume that the process of remote state-update message arrival obeys the Poission process with mean rate $\lambda_i$. We define the update distribution time $t_d$ as the interval between the time of the state-update message sent by the overloading node and the time of it arrival at a neighbor node. In fact, $t_d$ can be considered as a function of the QoS parameters (delay, bandwidth, packet loss rate) of overlay edge linking two nodes in the set $S$. We assume that the dissemination process of the state-update message is reliable and the state update message is not lost. We model the update distribution time $t_p$ as a random variable defined by the general exponential probability density function (pdf). According to the consistency model described in [6-8], the expression of probability density function is described as follows.

$$P_{\sigma,T_p}(t_p) = \begin{cases} \exp[-\dfrac{(t_p-T_p)}{\sigma}]*s(t_p-T_p)/\sigma, & if\ \sigma>0 \\ \delta(t_p-T_p), & if\ \sigma=0 \end{cases}. \tag{2}$$

Where, $s(x)$ and $\delta(x)$ are the unit step function and Dirac delta function, respectively. $T_p$ and $T_p+\sigma$ are the minimum and mean value of the state distribution time, respectively. The parameter $\sigma$ is the mean deviation of the update distribution time from the minimum value. The probability density function is enough to cover fluctuations of the propagation time caused by node failures. From the expression (2), we can see that the state-update message can arrive at the destination node for some finite delay.

As described above, the misread probability can be denoted as a function of read delay. The misread probability at the node $S_i \in S$ is the probability that at least one remote state-update message arrives after the read processing finished.

We assume that only the remote state-update message can affect the misread probability. For fixed $t_p$, we define the conditional misread probability as $P_i(d_i|\ t_p=t)$. Thus, the misread probability of node Si is denoted as follows.

$$P_i(d_i) = \int_0^{\infty} P_i(d_i\ |\ t_p=t)P_{\sigma,T_p}(t)dt. \tag{3}$$

By considering the assumed update distribution time as given in (2), the misread probability at node $S_i$ is given as follows.

$$P_i(d_i) = \begin{cases} 1-\dfrac{1}{1+\lambda'_i\sigma}\exp(-\lambda_i(T_p-d_i)), d_i \le T_p \\ \dfrac{\lambda_i}{1+\lambda_i\sigma}\exp(-(d_i-T_p)/\sigma), d_i > T_p \end{cases}. \tag{4}$$

For the expression (4), we can see that the misread probability of the node $S_i \in S$ can be denoted by a function of the read delay $d_i$, the total mean rate of remote state-update message arrivals $\lambda_i$, the minimum distribution time $T_p$ and the parameter $\sigma$.

## 4   Simulation

In the simulation, we used the [12] simulator and the topology in Fig. 1. Where, $d$ denotes the new incoming node. For any two nodes, there is an overlay link. In this topology, a number of flows enter the overloading node $S_l$ and traverse randomly some other nodes in the resource set. In order to simulate the P2P streaming system truly, external traffic was injected at every node. For overlay links, we set the bandwidth to 160 Mb/s. The traffic was generated by using the Pareto ON/OFF distribution [13], which can simulate long-range dependencies and is known to be suitable for a large volume of traffic. For each flow, we set the packet size to 1000 B, the hop count to 15 and the flow rate to 32 Kb/s.

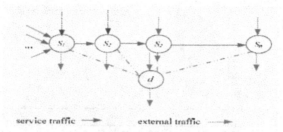

**Fig. 1.** Simulation topology

We assume that the minimum update distribution time is 0.2s ($T_p$=0.2s). Fig. 2 shows the impacts of an update distribution time when $\sigma= T_p/2$, $\sigma= T_p/4$ and $\sigma= 0$, respectively. Note that when $\sigma$=0, the node misread probability is zero if the $d_i \geq T_p$. This is the ideal case. In fact, the value of $\sigma$ is always larger than zero. When $\sigma$>0, the misread probability can never be zero. From the fig. 2, we can see that for any $\sigma$>0, the misread probability rapidly decreases with the read delay.

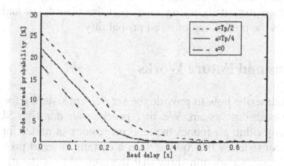

**Fig. 2.** Misread probability v.s. the read delay, where $T_p$=0.2s , $1/\lambda^\gamma$=1s and $\sigma$(denoted by $a$ in figure ) is variable

Now, we look at the performance of our SUA algorithm. In Fig. 3 and Fig. 4, we set the parameter value as follows: $P_{i,b}$=0.2%, $T_p$=0.2s, $\sigma$=0.05s, $1/\lambda_i$=3s, $d_{max}$=1s. It

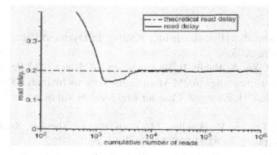

**Fig. 3.** Read delay v.s. cumulative number of read message

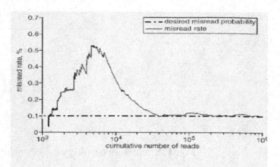

**Fig. 4.** Misread rate v.s. cumulative number of read message

is well noted that a real P2P streaming system is expected to run thousands of sessions in parallel. Thus, the SUA convergence based on the total traffic statistics in the system can be accepted widely. Fig. 3, the read delay approaches the theoretical value 0.2s after about 6500 reads. Fig. 4, we can see that the misread rate is close to the desired misread probability 0.001 after 40000 reads. The results of simulation show that the algorithm is iteratively trying to correct the read delay and the misread rate converges towards the predefined misread probability.

## 5  Conclusions and Future Works

In this paper, we describe how to provide the service consistency for decentralized but structured P2P streaming system. We first propose an iterative SUA algorithm for read delay. Our algorithm postpones the read processing at nodes for a short time, and thus the service consistency is acquired with a certain misread probability level. The results of analytic and simulation show that the algorithm is iteratively trying to correct the read delay and the misread rate converges towards the predefined misread probability.

For the future works, dynamic and online algorithms should be studied. We also will explore general ways to find statistical service consistency for all P2P streaming system.

## References

1. Y. Cui, K. Nahrstedt.: High-Bandwidth Routing in Dynamic Peer-to-Peer Streaming. In ACM Multimedia 2005.
2. M. Herfeeda, D. Xu, A. Habib, B. Bhargava, and B. Botev.: "Collectcast: A peer-to-peer service for media streaming". ACM Multimedia Systems Journal, 2005.
3. Y. Chu, S. G. Rao, H. Zhang: A Case for End System Multicast. In ACM SIGMETRICS 2000.
4. Ratnasamy, S., Francis, P., Handley, M., Karp, R., and Shenker, S.: A Scalable Content-Addressable Network. In ACM SIGCOMM 2001, pp.161-172.
5. Gnutella [Online]. Available: http://gnutella.wego.com.

6.  Bozinovski, M., Renier, T., Schwefel, H.-P., and Prasad, R.: Transaction consistency in replicated SIP call control systems. 4th IEEE Pacific-Rim Conf. on Multimedia, 2003, December 2003.
7.  M. Bozinovski, H.-P. Schwefel and R. Prasad.: Algorithm for controlling transaction consistency in SIP session control systems. Electron. Lett. 2004.
8.  Yu, H., and Vahdat, A.: Design and Evaluation of a Conit-based Continuous Consistency Model for Replicated Services. ACM Trans. Comput. Syst. (TOCS), 2002, 20, (3), pp. 239–282.
9.  M Zhang, L Zhao, Y Tang, J Luo, and S Yang.: Large-Scale Live Media Streaming over Peer-to-Peer Networks through Global Internet. ACM Multimedia, 2005, pp. 21-28.
10. Reza Rejaie, Shad Stafford.: A framework for architecting peer-to-peer receiver-driven overlays. In Proceedings of NOSSDAV 2004, June 2004.
11. Sai Susarla, John Carter.: Flexible Consistency for Wide Area Peer Replication. Proceedings of the 25th IEEE International Conference on Distributed Computing Systems (ICDCS'05), Jun. 2005.
12. ns2 Simulator [Online]. Available: http://www.isi.edu/nsnam/ns/
13. A. Popescu.: Traffic Self-Similarity. Blekinge Institute of Technology, Karlskrona, Sweden, white paper, 1999.

# Adaptive Search Range Scaling
# for B Pictures Coding

Zhigang Yang[1], Wen Gao[1,2], Yan Liu[1], and Debin Zhao[1]

[1] Department of Computer Science and Technology,
Harbin Institute of Technology, Harbin 150001, China
[2] Institute of Computing Technology, Chinese Academy of Science,
Beijing 100080, China
{zgyang, wgao, liuyan, dbzhao}@jdl.ac.cn

**Abstract.** This paper presents a frame-level adaptive search range scaling strategy for B pictures coding for H.264/AVC from the hardware-oriented viewpoint. After studying the relationship between search range of P and B picture, a simple search range scaling strategy is proposed at first, which is efficient for normal or low motion video. After that, this strategy is extended to high motion video by using the information of intra prediction and motion vector of each P picture to restrict the search range of adjacent B pictures. This adaptive search range scaling strategy can not only reduce approximate 60% search area of B pictures, but also keep almost the same coding performance as the reference software.

**Keywords:** Video coding, adaptive search range scaling, B pictures, high motion video, H.264/AVC.

## 1 Introduction

In hybrid video coding, B pictures are encoded using both future and past pictures as references [1]. In the recent H.264/AVC standard [2], there are usually five prediction modes in B pictures coding, including forward prediction, backward prediction, bi-prediction, direct prediction and intra modes. The prediction signals of direct and bi-prediction modes are obtained by a linear combination of forward and backward prediction values based on motion compensation. The usage of such various modes is able to exploit the temporal correlation more efficiently between reference pictures and current B picture, especially for uncovering areas caused by zooming, non-linear motion etc. Therefore, B pictures can achieve higher compression ratio than P pictures. B pictures can also be coarsely quantized in some applications as B picture does not propagate errors when it is not used as a reference. In other words, B pictures become a substantial part in video coding in terms of both coding performance and video transmissions, especially in some real-time video transmissions services [3].

The high performance of B pictures is on the basis of various motion compensation predictions and complex motion estimation. In order to accelerate B pictures encoding for real-time applications, fast block-matching algorithm might be used. However, in hardware implementation, for example by means of application specified integrated circuits (ASIC) or field programmable gate arrays (FPGA), full search (FS) is usually adopted [4], [5] after comparing with other fast block-matching algorithms, because the specific hardware is usually designed for pipelines but not for uncertain condition branch operations. Another efficient way to reduce the computational complexity is search range adjustment for different motion-level video. When full search is adopted, the search range mainly determines the time spent. Furthermore, the processor can only deal with the data which have already been loaded into the high speed cache from outside. Therefore the size of search area also affects the cache hit rate and the data exchange rate between on-chip and extended memory [6]. In one word, a reasonable search range should not only reduce the encoding time but also keep the encoding performance.

The existing search range adjustment algorithms like [7], [8], [9], [10] are mainly focused on marcoblock level. That is to say, the motion information from four adjacent blocks (left, up-left, up, up-right) is used to estimate the current block's search range. Such methods can achieve good efficiency under the framework of general purpose processor, but they can not work well with full hardware design. Because these kinds of search range prediction bring serious correlations between the current block and its adjacent blocks, the current block's search area can not be determined until the prior blocks finish motion estimation. These correlations limit wide usages of background transfer and force the hardware architecture to process block serially. The actually efficient algorithm for hardware implementation is frame-based search range adjustment. Although [7] and [8] have mentioned some frame-level search range adjustment algorithms, they are not suitable for B pictures coding. In [7], the mean and variance of the entire motion vector in one frame are adopted to characterize the global motion activity, which is a part of whole search strategy. This frame-level algorithm is simply to help the macroblock-level algorithm to be more precise, and it can not give a good performance when working separately. In [8], the sum of absolute vector values and the sum of prediction errors in one frame are calculated to decide search range, which is based on fixed thresholds. In fact, using fixed thresholds is not practical, because the thresholds vary a lot on different video content, and even different coding tools can also affect the thresholds. Moreover, all the existing algorithms have not considered the relationship between P and B pictures.

The purpose of this paper is to find out a hardware-oriented search range scaling algorithm for B pictures coding based on the H.264/AVC to reduce the computational complexity while keeping the coding performance. The rest of this paper is organized as follows. In Section 2, the relationship between P and B pictures is first studied, and then simple search range scaling method is introduced. After analyzing the proposed simple method, an improved efficient adaptive search range scaling algorithm is presented in Section 3. Simulated results are demonstrated in Section 4 to show its effectiveness. Finally, the paper is concluded in Section 5.

## 2  Search Range Scaling (SRS)

The proposed strategy is on the basis of on the relationship between P and B pictures, so we first study the motion feature in P and B pictures.

## 2.1 Motion Feature in P and B Pictures

Based on H.264/AVC standard, we assume that MV is the motion vector of the current block, PredMV is the motion vector prediction of the current block, and MVD is the difference between MV and PredMV. The search center in the reference picture is pointed by PredMV, so MVD is actually restricted by the search range.

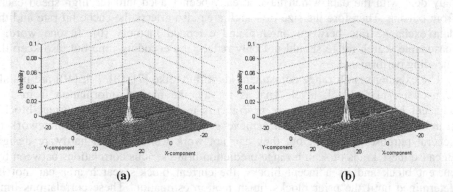

(a)                                                        (b)

**Fig. 1.** MVD joint probability distributions of *bus* (condition: CIF, 150 frames, IBBPBBP, 2 reference, QP=24, full search ±32). (a) Distribution of P pictures. (b) Distribution of B pictures.

In order to get MVD statistic, *bus* sequence in CIF format was tested on conditions of full search in ±32 window and constant QP=24. Comparing the two typical MVD joint probability distributions of P and B pictures, respectively shown in Fig. 1(a) and Fig. 1(b), we can see that P pictures seem more "active" than B pictures. This is mainly because the temporal distance between B picture and its forward/backward reference picture is smaller than the distance between the forward and backward reference picture. Suppose that there is an object M moving from point A to point B, and the corresponding position in B picture is point C, shown in Fig. 2. Then

$$CA : CB : BA = tb : -tp : td \qquad (1)$$

where *tb and tp* denote the temporal distance between the current B picture and the forward/backward reference picture respectively, and *td* denotes the temporal distance

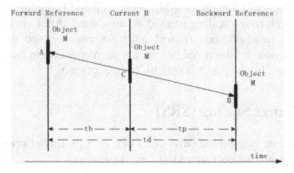

**Fig. 2.** Demonstration of different motion degree in P/B pictures

between the forward and backward reference picture. *CA* and *CB* represent the forward/backward motion vector of the blocks in object M in current B picture, and *BA* represents the motion vector of the blocks in object M in backward P picture.

## 2.2 Search Range Scaling (SRS) and Its Performance

Equation (1) indicates that the object's motion degree of B picture is lower than that of P picture. That is to say, the search range of B picture needs not to be as large as that of P picture. A simple search range scaling (SRS) algorithm for B picture can be obtained as follows:

$$SR_F = \lceil SR_{max} \times tb/td \rceil \text{ (for the latest forward reference picture)} \qquad (2)$$
$$SR_F = SR_{max} \qquad \text{(for other forward reference picture)}$$

$$SR_B = \lceil SR_{max} \times tp/td \rceil \text{ (for the latest backward reference picture)} \qquad (3)$$

where $SR_F$ denotes the forward search range of B picture, $SR_B$ denotes the backward search range of B picture, and $SR_{max}$ denotes the max search range of P picture.

Six sequences with 30fps in CIF format are selected to evaluate SRS algorithm, including two high motion sequences *stefan* and *foreman*, two normal motion sequences *bus* and *mobile*, and two low motion sequences *news* and *paris*. The test conditions are listed in Table 1. Because this scaling method only focuses on the latest forward reference picture, so we only choose one forward reference which can show the changes of coding performance more clearly.

Table 2 shows the average PSNR gain and the average bit rate saving for only B pictures comparing with the original reference software. SRS algorithm works very

**Table 1.** Test conditions

| Reference Software | H. 264/AVC JM10. 2 |
|---|---|
| MV Resolution | 1/4 pixel |
| RD Optimization | OFF |
| P References Number | 2 |
| B References Number | 1 Forward, 1 Backward |
| Search Range | 24 |
| Motion Estimation | Fast Full Search |
| GOP Structure | IBBPBBP |
| QP | 24, 28, 32, 36 |
| Loop Filter | ON |

**Table 2.** Performance comparisons between SRS and the reference software

| Sequences | | stefan | foreman | bus | mobile | news | paris |
|---|---|---|---|---|---|---|---|
| B pict-ures | PSNR gain | −0. 049 | −0. 011 | 0 | −0. 001 | 0 | 0 |
| | BR saving | −26. 29% | −3. 315% | 0. 183% | 0. 105% | −0. 016% | 0. 010% |

Note: BR denotes bit rate.

well on normal and low motion sequences, but for high motion sequences, the performance losses quite a lot. Especially for *stefan* sequence, the bit rate of B pictures even increases more than 26%. So in the next part, we will analyze this phenomenon and improve the SRS algorithm.

## 3  Adaptive Search Range Scaling (ASRS)

In this section, we are going to find out why the bit rate increase so much, and then extend SRS algorithm to high motion video by adaptive prejudgment.

### 3.1  SRS Algorithm Analysis

SRS algorithm is based on the assumption that all the motion vectors of P pictures are restricted in the maximum search range. However, this requirement is not reachable all the time for high motion video; for example, there are two sudden camera motions in *stefan* sequence, and our experiments show that the peak difference between two P picture during the camera motion could be more than 100 pixels. Under such

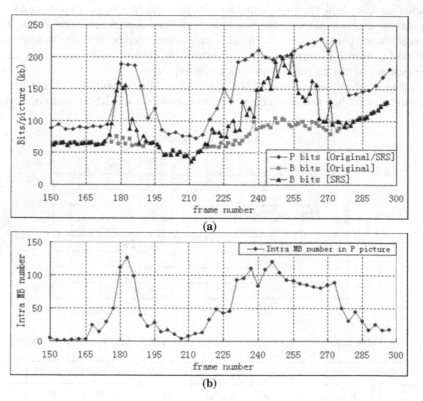

**Fig. 3.** SRS algorithm testing on *stefan* sequence when QP=24. (a) Coding bits comparisons between SRS algorithm and the original reference software. (b) Intra mode usage statistic for P pictures.

circumstance, still using SRS to cut down the search range of B pictures would only result in worse and worse coding performance. As shown in Fig. 3(a), coding bits per picture of *stefan*, there are two obvious bits increment of B pictures in SRS' curve, which happen at frame 176-191 and 220-278. These two parts exactly match the two periods of sharp motion in the original sequence.

In order to perform SRS under the proper condition, the encoder should decide whether the initial search range suits the motion level of current coded P picture or not. That is to say, if most of the blocks in current P picture can not find enough matched blocks in its references, the adjacent B pictures should avoid processing SRS.

The intra macroblock (MB) number of P picture is an efficient judgment. Generally speaking, the initial search range is suitable for most of the pictures, so intra MB does not often appear during P picture coding; but when the initial search range is too small, inter mode can not find the right matched block, then intra mode is selected for many MB. Fig. 3(b) shows the intra mode statistic for P pictures. Since the search range of P pictures is not changed during the tests in Section 2, the intra MB numbers of each P picture in two corresponding tests are the same all the time. Comparing the coding bits in Fig. 3(a) with the intra mode statistic in Fig. 3(b), we can find that the trend of bits per B picture coded with SRS is as same as the trend of the intra MB number of P picture. So according to the intra MB number of P picture, the encoder can make the decision that whether to perform SRS for next B pictures.

In next part, we are going to elaborate on how to decide the threshold of the intra MB number.

## 3.2 Adaptive Threshold Decision

First, we define some symbols shown in Fig. 4. $w$ and $h$ ($w \geq h$) are the width and height of the picture; $w_{mb}=w/16$ and $h_{mb}=h/16$ are the MB width and MB height of the picture. $\Delta w$ and $\Delta h$ are picture offsets in horizontal and vertical direction caused by the motion. OLD is the remained area from last P picture, and NEW is the new area of the picture caused by the motion. $SR_{init}$ is the initial search range.

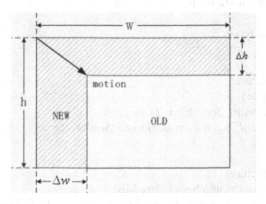

**Fig. 4.** Demonstration of picture division caused by motion

Then, we assume that all the MBs in NEW area are intra coded because there are no matched blocks in OLD area for them. The number of intra MB in NEW area is *intras*.

Next, we classify the motion into three cases:

(1) $CASE1 = (\Delta w \geq 2SR_{init})$ or $(\Delta h \geq 2SR_{init})$

$intras \geq min(h_{mb} \times \Delta w/16, w_{mb} \times \Delta h/16)$

$\geq min(h_{mb} \times 2SR_{ini}/16, w_{mb} \times 2SR_{ini}/16)$

$\geq h_{mb} \times \lfloor SR_{init}/8 \rfloor = Threshold1$

In this case, the motion exceeds duple search range, so the right matched position can not be found.

(2) $CASE2 = (CASE1 = FALSE)$ and

$((SR_{init} \leq \Delta w < 2SR_{init})$ or $(SR_{init} \leq \Delta w < 2SR_{init}))$

$intras < Threshold1$, and

$intras \geq min(h_{mb} \times \Delta w/16, w_{mb} \times \Delta h/16)$

$\geq min(h_{mb} \times SR_{ini}/16, w_{mb} \times SR_{ini}/16)$

$\geq h_{mb} \times \lfloor SR_{init}/16 \rfloor = Threshold2$

In this case, the motion is less than duple search range but more than search range, so there must exist some MBs whose motion vector $(mv_x, mv_y)$ satisfies $mv_x \geq SR_{ini}$ or $mv_y \geq SR_{ini}$ (motion vector could exceed search range in H.264/AVC, because MV=PredMV+MVD, PredMV and MVD are restricted by search range). We suppose that the number of such MB is at least $h_{mb}$ (*Threshold3*). It should also be one important rule for the algorithm.

(3) $CASE3 = (CASE1 = FALSE)$ and $(CASE2 = FALSE)$

SRS algorithm can work well in this case.

Last, we can restrict the search range of B pictures in terms of *Threshold1*, *Threshold2* and *Threshold3*.

### 3.3 Adaptive Search Range Scaling (ASRS)

As a summary, the algorithm description of adaptive search range scaling (ASRS) for B pictures coding is shown below.

```
SWITCH (image type):
{
  CASE I:
    Coding I picture;
    IF (first frame)
    THEN Backward_Scalable = TURE;
    ELSE Forward_Scalable = Backward_Scalable;
    BREAK;
  CASE P:
    Coding P picture;
    Stat. Num_intra : the number of intra MB;
    Stat. Num_mv : the number of MB whose MV exceeds the initial search range
            SR_init;
```

*Forward_Scalable = Backward_Scalable*;
IF $(Num_{intra} \geq h_{mb} \times \lfloor SR_{init} / 8 \rfloor)$
THEN *Backward_Scalable = FALSE*;
ELSE

      IF $(Num_{intra} \geq h_{mb} \times \lfloor SR_{init} / 16 \rfloor$ and $Num_{mv} \geq h_{mb})$

      THEN *Backward_Scalable = FALSE*;

      ELSE *Backward_Scalable = TURE*;

BREAK;
CASE B:
  IF (*Forward_Scalable = TRUE* and *Backward_Scalable = TRUE*)
  THEN $SR_F = \lceil SR_{init} \times tb / td \rceil$, for the latest forward reference picture;

      $SR_F = SR_{init}$    , for other forward reference picture;

      $SR_B = \lceil SR_{init} \times tp / td \rceil$ , for the latest backward reference picture;

  ELSE $SR_F = SR_B = SR_{init}$;
  Coding B picture;
  BREAK;
}

One more attention, we have another reason for collecting $Num_{mv}$ to co-judge with $Num_{intra}$. There are some MBs coded with intra mode not due to the great motion, however $Num_{mv}$ statistic can reduce such effect.

## 4  Simulated Results

To evaluate the performance of ASRS and also compare ASRS with SRS, we still choose the same sequences mentioned in Section 2, with 30fps in CIF (352x288) format, including *stefan, foreman, bus, mobile, news,* and *paris*. The test conditions are listed in Table 1. Fig. 5 shows that ASRS can make a right decision whether to

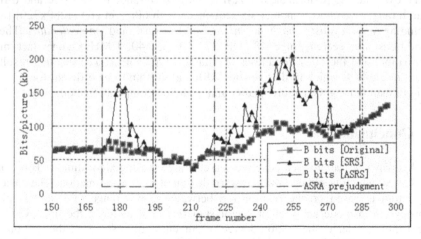

**Fig. 5.** ASRS vs. SRS testing on *stefan* sequence when QP=24

**Table 3.** Performance comparisons between ASRS and the reference software (CIF)

| Sequences | | stefan | foreman | bus | mobile | news | paris |
|---|---|---|---|---|---|---|---|
| All pict-ures | PSNR gain | -0.002 | 0 | 0 | 0 | 0 | 0 |
| | BR saving | -0.354% | 0.011% | 0.254% | 0.094% | 0.038% | 0.019% |
| B pict-ures | PSNR gain | -0.004 | 0 | -0.001 | 0 | 0 | 0 |
| | BR saving | -0.724% | 0.022% | 0.484% | 0.172% | 0.081% | 0.032% |
| | SA saving | 47.84% | 41.68% | 68.83% | 71.30% | 68.50% | 71.30% |

Note: BR denotes bit rate, and SA denotes search area.

**Table 4.** Performance comparisons between ASRS and the reference software (HD)

| Sequences | | city | cyclists | harbour | night | shuttl-estart | spinca-lendar |
|---|---|---|---|---|---|---|---|
| All pict-ures | PSNR gain | -0.001 | -0.001 | 0 | 0 | 0 | 0.001 |
| | BR saving | 0.062% | 0.065% | 0.015% | 0.021% | 0.009% | 0.071% |
| B pict-ures | PSNR gain | -0.001 | -0.001 | 0 | 0 | 0 | 0.001 |
| | BR saving | 0.110% | 0.115% | 0.034% | 0.043% | 0.023% | 0.120% |
| | SA saving | 71.76% | 52.11% | 71.76% | 25.12% | 55.98% | 71.61% |

Note: BR denotes bit rate, and SA denotes search area.

scale the search range for each B picture or not. And Table 3 shows that ASRS has almost the same performance with the original reference software, however it can reduce average 61.6% search area. When comparing with Table 2, the results of SRS, ASRS improves the performance of high motion sequences a lot, such as for *stefan* and *foreman*.

To evaluate the performance of ASRS under difference picture size and different search range, we choose another six sequences with 60fps in HD (1280x720) format, including *city*, *cyclists*, *harbour*, *night*, *shuttlestart*, and *spincalendar*. The test conditions are: search range 48, QP 27, 30, 35, 40, UMHexagonS fast motion estimation, and the other conditions are same with Table 1. The detailed results are listed in Table 4, which further verifies ASRS algorithm to be efficient for B pictures in both maintaining the picture quality and reducing computational quantity.

# 5  Conclusions

In this paper, a frame-based adaptive search range scaling algorithm for B pictures is presented, which is suitable for hardware-designed motion estimation. The basic SRS algorithm is based on the relationship between search range of P and B picture. Through intra mode and motion vector statistics of P pictures, the improved ASRS algorithm can detect the motion degree of current coding status. If the motion is not exceed the expected range, search range of the following B pictures can be scaled.

This prejudgment can efficiently both keep the coding performance and reduce the computational complexity. Simulated results show the average search area can be reduced by about 60% from the original reference software.

The future work is to apply the adaptive search range scaling algorithm to the VLSI architecture of our designing real-time HD encoder for further optimization.

# References

1. Markus Flierl and Bernd Girod, "Generalized B pictures and the draft H.264/AVC video-compression standard", *IEEE Trans. Circuits Syst. Video Technol.*, Vol. 13, No. 7, pp. 587-597, July 2003.
2. "Draft ITU-T recommendation and final draft international standard of joint video specification (ITU-T Rec. H.264/ISO/IEC 14 496-10 AVC," in Joint Video Team (JVT) of ISO/IEC MPEG and ITU-T VCEG, JVTG050, 2003.
3. Xiangyang Ji, Debin Zhao, Wen Gao, Qingmin Huang, Siwei Ma, and Yan Lu, "New bi-prediction techniques for B pictures coding", *ICME 2004*.
4. Jun-Fu Shen, Tu-Chih Wang, and Liang-Gee Chen, "A novel low-power full-search block-matching motion estimation design for H.263+", *IEEE Trans. Circuits Syst. Video Technol.*, Vol. 11, No. 7, pp. 890-897, July 2001.
5. Lei Deng, Wen Gao, Ming Zeng Hu, and Zhen Zhou Ji, "An efficient hardware implementation for motion estimation of AVC standard", *IEEE Trans. Consumer Electron.*, Vol. 51, No. 4, pp. 1360-1366, Nov. 2005.
6. Zhigang Yang, Wen Gao, and Yan Liu, "Performance-Complexity Analysis of High Resolution Video Encoder and Its Memory organization for DSP Implementation", *ICME2006*, pp. 1261-1264, July 2006.
7. Prabhudev Irappa Hosur, "Motion adaptive search for fast motion estimation", *IEEE Trans. Consumer Electron.*, Vol. 49, No.4, pp. 1330-1340, Nov. 2003.
8. Toru Yamada, Masao Ikekawa, and Ichiro Kuroda, "Fast and accurate motion estimation algorithm by adaptive search range and shape selection", *ICASSP2005*, Vol. 2, pp. ii/897-ii/900, Mar. 2005.
9. Kuo-Liang Chung and Lung-Chun Chang, "A new predictive search area approach for fast block motion estimation", *IEEE Trans. Image Processing*, Vol. 12, No. 6, pp. 648-652, June 2003.
10. Yu-Chan Lim, Kyeong-Yuk Min, and Jong-Wha Chong, "A pentagonal fast block matching algorithm for motion estimation using adaptive search range", *ICASSP2003*, Vol. 3, pp. 669-672, Apr. 2003.

# Video QoS Monitoring and Control Framework over Mobile and IP Networks*

Bingjun Zhang[1], Lifeng Sun[2], and Xiaoyu Cheng

[1] Department of Computer Science and Technology,
Tsinghua University, Beijing, 100084, China
zbj02@mails.tsinghua.edu.cn
[2] sunlf@tsinghua.edu.cn

**Abstract.** With the development of network technology, multimedia applications in various video forms are widely used in network services. In order to leverage video QoS, it becomes a pressing problem to monitor and control video QoS during network transmission of video. In this paper, we propose a monitoring and control framework for video QoS over IP and mobile network. Also, we develop a low computational complexity and more effective video quality assessment (VQA) method based on human visual system (HVS), Improved Human Visual Model (I-HVM), and propose Adaptive and Dynamic Sampling Strategy (ADSS) of video feature, to monitor video quality at both ends of our framework. The experimental results show that our framework can monitor well video QoS over IP and mobile network. Consequence, to leverage video QoS, dynamic control can be applied to transmission decision of video service according to the monitoring results of video QoS by our framework.

**Keywords:** QoS, Video Quality Assessment, HVS, Sampling Strategy.

## 1 Introduction

As the progress of Web2.0 and 3G-Mobile network, more and more multimedia applications in large quantities of video forms are being introduced into industries and people's daily use. Widely applied video services require reliable ways to monitor and control the video QoS level over IP and mobile network.

To monitor video QoS, the critical work is to do VQA. VQA methods can be classified into subjective and objective methods. Taking computer's advantages, objective VQA methods were focused by many researchers and lots of methods have been proposed [3,4,5,6], aiming to get high correlation with human perception. During VQEG's test in 2000 [7], PDM [6] performed the best. Taking the advantage of HVS, PDM can capture all kinds of video distortion caused by codec or transmission errors, but with the drawback of high computational complexity. In 2003, ANSI made its standard on objective VQA [9]. It focuses on certain distortion artifacts that may be caused by quantization, encoding and

---

* Supported by the National Natural Science Foundation of China under Grant No.60503063 and No.60432030 and by 973 Project under Grant No. 2006CB303103.

Y. Zhuang et al. (Eds.): PCM 2006, LNCS 4261, pp. 714–721, 2006.

so on. It works well among the majority of video sets except the videos with certain artifacts caused by packet loss or other channel noise during network transmission.

Having VQA methods, an appropriate monitoring system should be founded to monitor and control video service system. Past, many monitoring and control frameworks for video QoS usually choose one particular VQA method to understand video quality only at user end, such as [10,11]. In [10], Lu applied VQA method [9] with feedback mechanism to monitor video quality at user end and try to provide control advice for video data transmission. But VQA in [9] is not suitable for computing perceptual video quality degradation caused by packet loss. In [11], rPSNR was proposed to predict video degradation with network status parameters. It can well compute video degradation caused by packet loss, but can not correlate well with human perception especially when different kinds of distortions were introduced by encoding at transmitting end.

In this paper, we propose a video QoS monitoring framework with two critical points, ECP and DCP, to compute video degradation during video encoding, transmitting and decoding process. We improve PDM to be Improved Human Visual Model (I-HVM) to do VQA at ECP. While at DCP, similar to [10], we use feedback mechanism to transmit back limited video feature data to transmitting end and compute the video quality degradation by transmission. We propose an adaptive and dynamic sampling strategy (ADSS) to sample limited video feature data. And in order to get high correlation with human perception, it should be dynamic and adaptive to parameters of video quality and network status. With the monitoring results, dynamic control can be applied to video encoding rate and transmission bandwidth for video service system to leverage video QoS.

The rest of the paper is organized as follows: Section 2 presents an overview of our proposed video quality monitoring and control framework; In section 3, we will discuss how to improve PDM to be I-HVM; Section 4, detailed description of ADSS will be given; Section 5 shows the experimental results to evaluate the performance of the proposed techniques; Finally, section 6 concludes the paper and presents future research direction.

## 2    Overview of the Proposed Framework

During the whole process of video service system, video sequence will generally undergo three steps, encoding, transmitting and decoding. So the original video sequence will be processed into four forms including original, encoded, transmitted and decoded video, Fig. 1. As generally accepted, video service provider may apply different compressing rates to encode original video when facing different available bandwidth and various demands from video service users. Therefore, different degradation of the original video sequence may be introduced by encoding before transmitting. The next step of service, video transmitting, will also result considerable degradation of encoded video due to packet loss and other channel noises. When facing the largely degraded transmitted video, decoder at user end will lightly upgrade its quality when decoding with error concealment technologies. The whole process can be presented as Fig. 1.

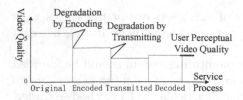

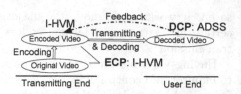

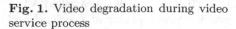

**Fig. 1.** Video degradation during video service process

**Fig. 2.** Proposed video QoS monitoring framework

With the analysis above, there are mainly two video quality degradation steps, encoding and transmitting. In order to understand video quality during whole service process, two critical points can be set to compute video degradation. The first point is between original and encoded video, called encoding critical point (ECP). And the other is after decoded video, named decoding critical point (DCP). At ECP and DCP, we can easily get perceptible video data, i.e., video frame sequence. And taking the advantages of I-HVM, we can compute video degradation caused by various reasons. At ECP, as the original and encoded videos are both available, I-HVM can be used to do reduced-reference VQA, to understand video degradation resulted by encoding. At DCP, we propose ADSS to sample necessary and limited video feature data to feedback to transmitting end. Then with the availability of encoded video feature and transmitted video feature, we apply I-HVM again to accomplish reduced-reference VQA, to understand decoded video degradation mainly resulted by transmission. Fig. 2 illustrates our novel proposed video QoS monitoring framework.

## 3   Improved Human Visual Model (I-HVM)

In [6], Winkler proposed PDM, a VQA model based on HVS. And PDM performed best in VQEG test 2000 [7]. According to psychological contribution of HVS, PDM consists of color space conversion, spatiotemporal decomposition, masking and pooling [6]. In the following, we will propose a new feature contrast method during spatial decomposition, feature contrast in frequency spectrum. And we develop PDM to be I-HVM, which can save much computational complexity and hold higher correlation with human perception.

In PDM, Winkler takes steerable pyramid to do spatial decomposition in frequency spectrum. Then, PDM transforms spatial channels from frequency spectrum back to spatial field. And it contrasts corresponding spatial channels of reference and distorted video to compute spatial degradation, Fig. 3(a).

One Discrete Fourier Transformation (DFT) and many Inverse Discrete Fourier Transformation (IDFT) are needed to do spatial decomposition. If spatial channel can contrast directly in frequency spectrum, only 1 DFT will be needed, Fig. 3(b). And computational complexity will be much lower.

Let's illustrate that contrast in frequency spectrum is feasible. Here is an assumption that left side and right side distortion of an object hold nearly equal human perception. As Fig. 4, human will consider the two eye blurred pictures,

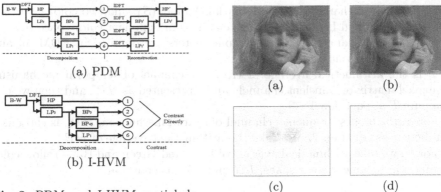

(a) PDM

(b) I-HVM

**Fig. 3.** PDM and I-HVM spatial decomposition, $HP$ indicates high pass channel in frequency spectrum, $BP_0$ indicates band pass channel with $0°$ orientation in frequency spectrum, so is $BP_{45}$, and $LP$ for low pass channel [6]

(a)                                (b)

(c)                                (d)

**Fig. 4.** Spatial contrast proof: (a) Left eye blurred, (b) Right eye blurred, (c) PDM contrast result, (d) I-HVM contrast result

Fig. 4(a) and Fig. 4(b), have equal distortion. However, contrast method in spatial field of PDM presents that the two blurred pictures have considerable spatial difference which is quite obvious in Fig. 4(c). On the contrary, our proposed contrast method in frequency spectrum gives the result that two blurred pictures have nearly equal spatial feature, nearly no difference can be seen in Fig. 4(d).

As illustration above, with the spatial frequency contrast method, not only computational complexity can be saved, but also higher correlation with human perception will be accomplished. That, we improve PDM to be I-HVM, which performs much faster and holds higher correlation with human perception.

## 4 Adaptive and Dynamic Sampling Strategy (ADSS)

The critical matter of DCP is to compute video degradation mainly caused by transmission. Similar to [10], feedback mechanism is adopted by our monitoring framework. However, limited bandwidth of feedback channel forces to sample human perception highly related and limited video feature data, which should be able to capture video degradation caused both by encoding and transmitting.

Under these demands, we propose ADSS to sample human perception highly related and limited video frames, and then apply I-HVM to extract video data to feedback. When reaching the transmitting end, fed back video data and available encoded video data can be used to compute video degradation of transmission. In order to do that, we should know video quality parameters and network noise parameters and their relationship with human perception.

As mentioned in PDM [6], parameters of video quality are color, temporal and spatial channels. According to research in [2], human holds higher sensitivity to higher frequency part of spatiotemporal channels. Consequence, to construct sampling strategy, the chosen video quality parameters include high frequency part of temporal channels $(T)$ and spatial channel $(S)$, and two color channels, i.e., Red-Green and Blue-Yellow color channels in opponent color space $(C)$.

The original channels of all these parameters are detailed in PDM [6] and I-HVM. Let's present how to compute $T$, $S$, $C$.

$T$ is the arithmetical average of transient channel of temporal mechanism. The pixel matrix of transient channel can be presented as $HP_t$, and then we can compute $T$ as equation 1.

For $S$, the highest frequency channel of spatial mechanism, $HP_s$, is chosen. $S$ can be got as equation 2, also take the arithmetical average of $HP_s$.

For $C$, we take arithmetical average of both Red-Green and Blue-Yellow color channels in opponent color space, $RG$ and $BY$, as equation 3.

$$T = \frac{\sum HP_t}{|HP_t|} \qquad (1) \qquad\qquad S = \frac{\sum HP_s}{|HP_s|} \qquad (2)$$

$$C = \frac{\sum RG + \sum BY}{|RG| + |BY|} \qquad (3) \qquad\qquad P = \frac{L}{\alpha} \qquad (4)$$

The main network parameter for video degradation is packet loss. So we set packet loss rate $(P)$ for the latest $\alpha$ packets as the network parameter to construct sampling strategy. We can monitor packet sequence number to calculate the number of lost packets $(L)$ among the latest $\alpha$ packets. $P$ can be computed as equation 4. Higher of $P$ is, more degradation of the latest frame will be introduced. Therefore, in order to capture degradation caused by packet loss, we should sample more when $P$ is getting larger.

As generally accepted, frames just after shot boundary of video sequence will attract much more human attention. Therefore, we consider $k$ consecutive frames just after shot boundary as the critical frames. All the critical frames should be sampled to reflect higher human perception sensitivity. In this paper, we choose the shot boundary detection method, SM AIM in [8], to detect shot boundary. If a shot boundary meets, we set $k$ consecutive frames from boundary to be critical frames, and set value $K$ of these frames as 1. Others are 0.

The definition of sampling distance, $SD$, initial sampling distance, $ISD$, and sampling descending step, $SDS$, give the details of ADSS as follows:

Each frame holds its own $SD$ and $SDS$. If $SD$ of certain frame equals to zero, this frame should be sampled, in the mean time, an initial sampling distance decision should be made to compute a new $ISD$, and $SD$ of this frame will be reset as $ISD$. If $SD$ of certain frame doesn't equal to zero, it should subtract $SDS$ and the reduced $SD$ is for next frame to go on subtracting.

$ISD$ is computed in initial sampling distance decision, equation 5, representing the number of frames to subtract. It will be set to $SD$ of current frame when generated. When $SD$ becomes zero at certain frame, the frame should be sampled, and a new initial sampling distance decision should be made.

$$ISD = \lceil [1 - Nor\,(P \cdot T \cdot S \cdot C)] \cdot N \rceil \cdot (1 - K) \qquad (5)$$

Where the operation $Nor(x)$ is normalization, constant $N$ is the largest $ISD$.

$SDS$ is the sampling descending step for each frame to decrease $SD$. $SDS$ is computed as equation 6.

$$\begin{cases} SDS = \begin{cases} 1 & , \ if \quad Ratio < 1 \\ \lfloor SD \cdot (Ratio - 1) \rfloor + 1 & , \ if \quad 1 \leqslant Ratio \leqslant 1.5 \\ \left\lfloor \dfrac{SD}{2} \right\rfloor + 1 & , \ if \quad Ratio > 1.5 \end{cases} \\ Ratio = \dfrac{T \cdot S \cdot C \cdot P}{T' \cdot S' \cdot C' \cdot P'} \end{cases} \tag{6}$$

Where $T$, $S$, $C$ and $P$ is the parameters of current frame, and $T'$, $S'$, $C'$ and $P'$ is of the former frame.

Because human holds higher sensitivity to $T$, $S$, $C$, larger value are these parameters of certain frame, higher attention will be paid by human. So $ISD$ should be decided smaller and $SDS$ larger in order to sample more frames. So is the same of $ISD$ and $SDS$ when $P$ gets larger, to capture degradation caused by transmission. When critical frame meets, that is $K$ equals to 1, it should be sampled directly, and compute a new $ISD$ to reset $SD$.

After sampling, we apply I-HVM to extract video feature from sampled frames and feedback the feature data to transmitting end. Finally contrast with encoded video data will tell degradation of decoded video resulted by transmission. Until now, with I-HVM and ADSS we accomplish the whole video QoS monitoring framework.

# 5   Experimental Results and Discussions

To validate I-HVM monitoring at ECP, we carried out objective VQA experiment using video database founded by VQEG [7]. This database contained 320 video sequences with different types of distortion. More, each distorted video holds a reliable subjective difference mean opinion score (DMOS). Experimental results are shown as Fig. 5. As illustration, with proposed spatial frequency contrast technique, I-HVM performs higher correlation with human perception than PDM. Further, I-HVM saves much more computational complexity.

To validate the monitoring mechanism at DCP, H.263 codec is introduced to regenerate distorted video sequence resulted by packet loss under two compressing rates (10 and 20 for quantization parameter of codec). We use Gilbert-Elliott model [1] to simulate packet loss distribution over mobile network (1024 bytes for packet size) and IP network (4096 bytes for packet size) transmission under 5 packet loss rates (0.01, 0.03, 0.05, 0.07 and 0.10). Then the simulated packet loss distributions are input into H.263 codec to regenerate distorted video sequences. In this way, we establish a video database with 20 sets of video sequences distorted by encoding and packet loss, each set with 20 video sequences. In all, 400 video sequences are available in our video database, publicly available in [12].

Then for each distorted video sequence, we apply ADSS to sample certain frames and then apply I-HVM to extract video feature to feedback to original

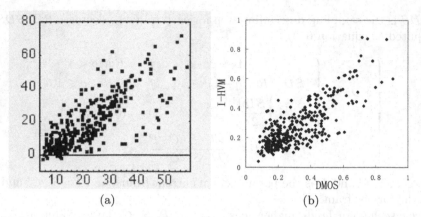

(a)                          (b)

**Fig. 5.** Correlation with subjective DMOS. (a) PDM [7], (b) I-HVM

undistorted video, which should be available at ECP, to do VQA. Next, only I-HVM is applied to assess video degradation contrast with original undistorted video. For each distorted video sequence, we compare the two scores obtained by ADSS and I-HVM, as Fig. 6(a). As seen, ADSS holds high correlation with scores of I-HVM, which is highly correlated with human perception. In order to compare ADSS with unadaptive sampling strategy, we sample one frame every four consecutive frames to compute video degradation. The correlation of the scores computed by unadaptive sampling strategy with I-HVM's is illustrated as Fig. 6(b), which does not correlate well with human perception. Therefore, Fig 6 shows ADSS can do effective sampling to get critical and limited video feature data which captures video degradation caused by encoding and packet loss, i.e., ADSS can do effective sampling to highly correlate with human perception.

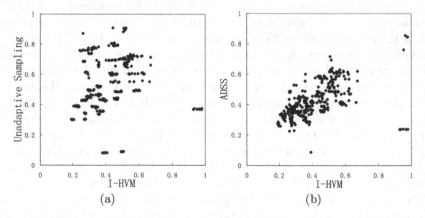

(a)                          (b)

**Fig. 6.** Correlation with I-HVM scores which is highly correlated with subjective DMOS. (a) Unadaptive Sampling Strategy, (b) ADSS.

# 6  Conclusions and Future Work

In this paper, we have presented a novel monitoring and control framework for video QoS over IP and mobile network. Based on PDM, we have developed I-HVM to do VQA at ECP with low computational complexity, and it correlates highly with human perception. In addition, we have proposed a low complexity video feature sampling strategy, ADSS, to monitor video quality at DCP. The experimental results reveal that ADSS can do effective sampling to correlate highly with human perception. With our monitoring framework and VQA methods I-HVM and ADSS, effective monitoring can be achieved during the whole video service process. As a result, to leverage video QoS, dynamic control can be applied to transmission decision of video service.

However, in VQA method at DCP, packet loss parameter is introduced only in sampling distance decision of ADSS. To fully investigate packet loss parameter, combined VQA method both with HVS and network parameters is expected in our future work, which would be more computational efficient and better correlated with human perception.

# References

1. E. O. Elliott, *A model of the switched telephone network for data communications.* Bell Syst. Tech. J., vol. 44, pp. 89–109, Jan. 1965.
2. D. H. Kelly, *Spatiotemporal variation of chromatic and achromatic contrast thresholds.* Journal Opt. Soc. Amer. A,vol. 73, pp. 742-750, 1983.
3. A. A. Webster et al., *An objective video quality assessment system based on human perception.* in Proc. SPIE, vol. 1913, pp. 15-26, San Jose, CA, 1993.
4. Sarnoff Corp. *Sarnoff JND Vision Model Algorithm Description and Testing.* VQEG, Aug. 1997.
5. A. Watson. *Toward a perceptual video quality metric.* In Human Vision and Electronic Imaging III, pp. 139–147. Proceedings of SPIE Vol. 3299, 1998.
6. Winkler S., *A Perceptual Distortion Metric for Digital Color Video.* Proc. SPIE Human Vision and Electronic Imaging Conference, vol. 3644, pp. 175-184, San Jose, California, January 23-29, 1999.
7. VQEG, *Final report from the video quality experts group on the validation of objective models of video quality assessment.* http://www.vqeg.org/, Mar. 2000.
8. Y. Yusof, W. Christmas, and J. Kittler, *Video shot cut detection using adaptive thresholding.* In Proceedings of the 11th British Machine Vision Conference, pp. 362–371, September 2000.
9. ANSI T1.801.03, *American National Standard for Telecommunications - Digital transport of one-way video signals. Parameters for objective performance assessment.* American National Standards Institute, 2003.
10. X. Lu, R. O. Morando, and M. ElZarki, *Understanding video quality and its use in feedback control.* in Proceedings of Packet Video Workshop, Pittsburgh, PA, 2002.
11. Shu Tao et al., *Real-Time Monitoring of Video Quality in IP Networks.* Proceedings of the International Workshop on Network and Operating System Support for Digital Audio and Video 2005 (NOSSDAV 2005), pp. 129-134, 2005.
12. Bingjun Zhang et al., *ADSS test video database.* ftp://166.111.247.12:21, Department of Computer Science and Technology, Tsinghua University, 2006.

# Extracting Moving / Static Objects of Interest in Video

Sojung Park and Minhwan Kim

Dept. of Computer Engineering, Pusan National Univ., Busan, Korea
{sjpark, mhkim}@pusan.ac.kr

**Abstract.** Extracting objects of interest in video is a challenging task that can improve the performance of video compression and retrieval. Usually moving objects in video were considered as objects of interest, so there were many researches to extract them. However, we know that some non-moving (static) objects also can be objects of interest. A segmentation method is proposed in this paper, which extracts static objects as well as moving objects that are likely to attract human's interest. An object of interest is defined as the relatively large region that appears frequently over several frames and is not located near boundaries of the frames. A static object of interest should also have significant color and texture characteristics against its surround. We found that the objects of interest extracted by the proposed method were well matched with the objects of interest selected manually.

**Keywords:** object of interest, visual attention, content-based video retrieval.

## 1 Introduction

In content-based image/video retrieval, it is a very important subject to reduce the semantic gap between what user-queries represent and what the users think. Many researchers have studied the region- or object-based image retrieval [1,2] to overcome the semantic gap, which needs to extract the objects that attract human's interest. In video, moving objects attract human's attention and they tend to be objects of interest. That is, human is much interested in moving objects in video. So the moving objects can be effectively used in representing content of the video and in reducing the semantic gap. There are several approaches to extracting the moving objects by using motion information and color information, the region-based approach [3,4], the motion-based approach [5], and the combined method [6].

On the one hand, human's *interest* in some objects of images or videos needs to be differentiated from *visual attention*. While the visual attention stands for the behavior and the neuronal architecture of the early primate visual system [7], the interest in images or videos is related to what their producer wants to show or what we want to represent in content-based retrieval. The visual attention shows local conspicuity that is related to the focus of attention and the eye movement on images or visual scenes. So the visual attention is useful in analyzing scenes, coding images and videos, and automatically finding regions of attention [8]. Meanwhile, clearly specifying our interest is very difficult, because the interest is related to higher-level processing in

Y. Zhuang et al. (Eds.): PCM 2006, LNCS 4261, pp. 722–729, 2006.

human visual system and it tends to depend on individual subjective decision. Osberger and Maeder [9] tried to determine the perceptual importance of different regions by considering the higher-level factors, location and size information, as well as the visual attention. Kim *et al.* [10] argued that a relative big object near image center was closely related to the object of interest in the image.

Fortunately, moving objects in videos tend to arrest attention and to be of interest, if they are not too small or are not located near border of video frames. Small moving objects might not attract human's interest, even though they draw attention. Moving objects not near image center might not be of interest too, because video producers intend to locate near center a protagonist or what plays an important role in a scene. On the one hand, non-moving (static) objects in video might also be objects of interest, even though they arrest less attention than moving objects, as shown in Fig. 1. For example, we are more interested in the new car staying near center in a motor show video than the moving people around the car. We also think that the young girl is an object of interest in the second video sequence even though moving people are behind her. Han and Ngam [11] suggested a unified framework for segmenting automatically objects of interest in video. They actually extracted moving objects or *attentional static objects* by using the saliency map [7] that showed attention degree well in still images but did not represent human's interest well. Examples of the saliency map are shown at the bottom row of Fig. 1, where the new car, the young girl, and the jumping man have low attention degree even though they are objects of interest.

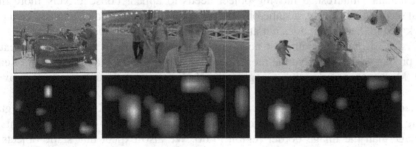

**Fig. 1.** Examples of images including objects of interest and their saliency map [7] are shown. Even though the new car, the young girl, and the jumping man are objects of interest, they have low attention degree.

In this paper, a segmentation method is proposed, which extracts not only moving objects but also static objects that are likely to attract human's interest. An object of interest is defined as the relatively large region that appears frequently over several frames and is not located near border of the frames. A static object of interest is defined to have also significant color and texture characteristics against its surround. Moving objects of interest are determined by filtering out meaningless (small or adjacent to frame border) ones among the moving objects extracted by the AMOS [4]. Static objects of interest are extracted using the central object extraction method [10], when there is no moving object of interest and no frequently occurring moving objects in center 25% of frame. On a test with 45 video sequences, the proposed method extracted almost all (moving or static) objects of interest chosen manually.

## 2  Defining Objects of Interest in Video

Objects of interest in images or videos are very useful for representing what their producer wants to show and what users want to search in content-based image/video retrieval. However, defining the objects of interest is a difficult and ambiguous problem. Kim *et al.* [10] discussed well the difficulty and the ambiguity of defining objects of interest in images. Fortunately, objects of interest in a video can be defined more easily than in an image, because the video contains temporal information as well as spatial information. It is probable that a relatively big moving object is an object of interest. However, we need to define static objects of interest in videos more carefully, as in still images [10].

An object of interest in video is defined as the region that satisfies the following conditions.

(1) It appears frequently,
(2) Its size is relatively big,
(3) It is not located near border of frame, and
(4) It has significant motion against its background, or has significant color and texture characteristics near center of frame

Objects of interest need to appear frequently over entire frames. A moving object appearing for a time can be an attentional object but not an object of interest. To attract human's interest, a moving object needs to appear consecutively more than several seconds. Similarly, a static object appearing over few frames tends to be a part of background, because it does not attract visual attention or human's interest.

The size of objects of interest needs to be relatively big in each frame, because video producers tend to have the most interesting object occupy a large extent of each frame. Moreover, people tend to neglect small objects even though those are moving ones.

Objects of interest need to be located near center of frame. Kim *et al.* [10] argued that the region of center 25% of an image was more effective to represent contents of the image than the image border region to do. We also expect that static objects of interest in video are located near center of frame, because video producers tend to locate the protagonist or the most interesting object at center of frame. Sometimes moving objects of interest can be located a little far from the center, because those objects can attract human's attention and can appear (disappear) from (to) a frame edge.

Finally, moving objects of interest need to have significant motion against its background and static ones significant color and texture characteristics near center of frame against those at surround region of frame. However, both objects of interest cannot appear simultaneously near center of frame. Therefore static objects of interest will be searched and extracted only when there is relatively low motion activity near center of frame.

Here we should note that the above conditions are selected empirically. We believe that human's interest is closely related to higher-level processing in brain and tends to depend on individual subjective decision. So we were interested in just usefulness of the conditions from an engineering point of view.

# 3  Extracting Objects of Interest in Video

## 3.1  Overview

Fig. 2 shows the block diagram of our segmentation method to extract objects of interest in video. Moving objects are first extracted by using the AMOS [4] and moving objects of interest are determined by filtering out meaningless moving objects that do not satisfy the conditions in section 2.

Then static objects of interest are searched and extracted when there is no significant motion activity near center of frame. In this paper, central motion activity is defined by considering occurrence frequency of moving objects and their occupying ratio in center 25% of frame. The higher the central motion activity is, the less probable a static object of interest occurs near center. The static objects of interest satisfying the conditions in section 2 are segmented by a modified version of the central object extraction method [10].

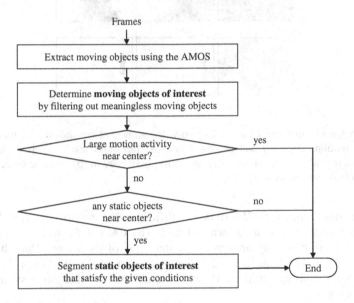

**Fig. 2.** The block-diagram of the proposed segmentation method is shown. Moving objects of interest are first determined by filtering out meaningless moving objects. Then static objects of interest are searched and extracted when there is little motion activity near center of frame.

## 3.2  Central Motion Activity

The central motion activity (CMA) is to measure degree of motion near center of frame. Let $MO_f$ be the motion occurrence array that represents location of moving objects at frame $f$. The element $MO_f(i,j)$ is set by 1 if there exists any moving object at pixel $(i,j)$ in frame $f$. Otherwise, it is reset by 0. Then the motion frequency $MF(i,j)$ at each pixel location $(i,j)$ can be computed by accumulating all the motion occurrence arrays $MO_f(i,j)$'s, as shown in Eq. 1 where $N$ is the number of frames in a given video sequence.

$$MF(i, j) = \sum_{f=1}^{N} MO_f(i, j)$$

$$MO_f(i, j) = \begin{cases} 1, & (i, j) \in moving\ object \\ 0, & otherwise \end{cases}$$

(1)

Fig. 3(a) shows an example of the motion frequency for a boxing video sequence. The motion frequency value is high near center, because a boxer moves from the left to the center. Fig. 3(b) shows another example of the motion frequency for a motor show video sequence. We can expect to find a static object of interest, because there is very low motion activity near center.

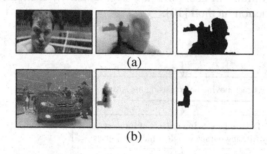

(a)

(b)

**Fig. 3.** Examples of motion frequency for two video sequences are shown. The second column shows the motion frequency and the third one the threshold result. There is high motion frequency near center in (a), while very low motion frequency in (b). A static object of interest is expected to occur near center in (b).

The motion frequency $MF(i,j)$ is simplified to the motion activity $MA(i,j)$ by thresholding appropriately as shown in Eq. 2. The $CMA$ is defined as the proportion of the high motion activity area in the center 25% of the frame (Default Attention Window, DAW). The $S_{DAW}$ in Eq. 2 indicates area of the DAW. When there are few moving objects near center, the $CMA$ is low and it is probable that a static object of interest occurs.

$$MA(i, j) = \begin{cases} 1, & MF(i, j) > threshold \\ 0, & otherwise \end{cases}$$

$$CMA = \frac{1}{S_{DAW}} \sum_{(i,j) \in DAW} MA(i, j)$$

(2)

### 3.3 Finding Significant Static Objects

In a frame of video, a static object of interest is conceptually identical with the central object in [10]. That is, the conditions (2)-(4) in section 2 for defining static objects of interest are the same as the conditions for the central object. The core object region

(COR) in [10] is the primary region that satisfies the conditions (2)-(4). Therefore, a significant static object that satisfies also the condition (1) in section 2 can be determined by testing the occurrence frequency of the COR. That is, if a significant color and texture region $r$ exists near center over several frames, it is probable to be a part of static objects of interest. The occurrence frequency $OF(r)$ can be computed as shown in Eq. 3. In this paper, when there is a region whose $OF$ is greater than 0.6, a static object of interest in a frame is segmented by using a modified version of the central object extraction method [10].

$$OF(r) = \frac{1}{N} \sum_{f=1}^{N} COR_f(r)$$

$$COR_f(r) = \begin{cases} 1, & r \in core\ object\ regions\ in\ frame\ f \\ 0, & otherwise \end{cases} \tag{3}$$

## 4 Experimental Results and Discussions

We tested the proposed method with 45 video sequences in 10 videos. Fig. 4 shows examples of the moving objects (at right column to the frame image column) extracted by the AMOS [4] and the (moving and static) objects of interest by our method. Some meaningless moving objects are filtered out well, but there still remain non-interesting moving objects.

**Fig. 4.** Examples of objects of interest extracted by the proposed method: moving objects by the AMOS [4] at $2^{nd}$ and $5^{th}$ columns and (moving and static) objects of interest by our method at $3^{rd}$ and $6^{th}$ columns

Table 1 shows the confusion matrix [13] for experimental results with the 45 video sequences that include 47 objects of interest (OOIs) selected manually. All 27 moving OOIs are extracted correctly, while three static OOIs are missed. However, many wrong OOIs (false positives) are also extracted, so the precision is relatively low (0.77 in Table 2). We see that almost wrong OOIs are moving ones as shown in Fig. 4.

Even though we got relatively high F-measure, the precision for moving OOIs needs to be improved. We expect to improve the precision by using another powerful tool for extracting moving objects instead of the AMOS or developing more intelligent method for filtering out meaningless moving objects. The wrong static OOIs shown in Fig. 5 are also expected to be removed by using the image classification method [12] that can filter out the images not including any object of interest in accuracy of 84.2%.

**Table 1.** The confusion matrix for experimental results with 45 video sequences in 10 videos that include 27 manually-selected moving objects of interest and 17 static ones

| OOI (moving, static) | Positive | Negative |
|---|---|---|
| True | 44 (27, 17) | 3 (0, 3) |
| False | 13 (11, 2) | - |

**Table 2.** Evaluation of the proposed method based on the precision, recall, and F-measure [13]

|  | Recall | Precision | F-measure |
|---|---|---|---|
| All OOIs | 0.94 | 0.77 | 0.86 |
| Moving OOIs | 1.00 | 0.71 | 0.86 |
| Static OOIs | 0.85 | 0.89 | 0.87 |

**Fig. 5.** Typical examples of wrong static objects of interest in our experiment with 45 video sequences

On the one hand, we can see in Fig. 4 that the static objects of interest are extracted inaccurately. We believe that this inaccuracy problem causes from the inaccurate segmentation in the AMOS. We expect to solve the problem by using the JSEG segmentation method [14] that is used in the central object extraction method [10].

## 5   Conclusions

An object of interest extracting method is proposed in this paper, which can extract static objects of interest as well as moving ones. Through experiments with 45 video sequences in 10 videos, we found that it worked well (recall 0.94, precision 0.77, F-measure 0.86). Further research will be focused on improving the precision for moving objects of interest and refining the concept of object of interest in video. The proposed method can be effectively used in video analysis and content-based video retrieval.

**Acknowledgments.** This work was supported by the Regional Research Centers Program (Research Centers for Logistics Information Technology), granted by the Korean Ministry of Education & Human Resources Development.

# References

1. Kam, A.H., Ng, T.T., Kingsbury, N.G., Fitzgerald, W.J.: Content Based Image Retrieval through Object Extraction and Querying. IEEE Workshop on Content-Based Access of Image and Video Libraries. (2000) 91-95
2. Wang, W., Song, Y., Zhang, A.: Semantics Retrieval by Region Saliency. Int'l Conf. on Image and Video Retrieval. (2002) 29-37
3. Salembier, P., Marques, F.: Region-based Representations of Image and Video: Segmentation Tools for Multimedia Services. IEEE Transaction on Circuits and Systems for Video Technology. **9(8)** (1999) 1147-1169
4. Zhong, D., Chang, S.F.: An Integrated Approach for Content-Based Video Object Segmentation and Retrieval. IEEE Trans. on Circuits and Systems for Video Technology. **9(8)** (1999) 1259-1268
5. Babu, R.V., Ramakrishnan, K.R., Srinivasan S.H.: Video Object Segmentation: A Compressed Domain Approach. IEEE Transaction on Circuits and Systems for Video Technology. **14(4)** (2004) 464-474
6. Porikli, F., Wang, Y.: Automatic Video Object Segmentation Using Volume Growing and Hierarchical Clustering. EURASIP Journal on Applied Signal Processing. **6** (2004) 814-832
7. Itti, L., Koch, C., Niebur, E.: A Model of Saliency-Based Visual Attention for Rapid Scene Analysis. IEEE Trans. on Pattern Analysis and Machine Intelligence. **20(11)** (1998) 1254-1259
8. Serra, J.R., Subirana, J.B.: Texture Frame Curves and Regions of Attention Using Adaptive Non-cartesian Networks. Pattern Recognition. **32** (1999) 503-515
9. Osberger, W., Maeder, A.J.: Automatic Identification of Perceptually Important Regions in an Image. IEEE Int'l Conf. on Pattern Recognition. **1** (1998) 701-704
10. Kim, S., Park, S., Kim, M.: Central Object Extraction for Object-Based Image Retrieval. Lecture Notes in Computer Science, Vol. 2728. (2003) 39-49
11. Han, J., Ngan. K.N.: Automatic Segmentation of Objects of Interest in Video: a Unified Framework. Proc. Int'l Symposium on Intelligent Signal Processing and Communication Systems. (2004) 375-378
12. Kim, S., Park, S., Kim, M.: Image Classification into Object / Non-object Classes. Lecture Notes in Computer Science, Vol. 3115. (2004) 393-400
13. Witten, I.H., Frank, E.: Data Mining. Academic Press. (2000)
14. Deng, Y., Manjunath, B.S., Shin, H.: Color Image Segmentation. IEEE Conf. on Computer Vision and Pattern Recognition. **2** (1999) 446-451

# Building a Personalized Music Emotion Prediction System

Chan-Chang Yeh[1], Shian-Shyong Tseng[1,2], Pei-Chin Tsai[1,*], and Jui-Feng Weng[1]

[1] Department of Computer Science,
Chiao Tung University, 30099 Hisnchu, Taiwan, China
[2] Department of Information Science and Applications,
Asian University, Taiwan, China
gis93617@cis.nctu.edu.tw, sstseng@cis.nctu.edu.tw,
kotoco@cis.nctu.edu.tw, roy@cis.nctu.edu.tw

**Abstract.** With the development of multimedia technology, research on music is getting more and more popular. Nowadays researchers focus on studying the relationship between music and listeners' emotions but they didn't consider users' differences. Therefore, we propose a Personalized Music Emotion Prediction (P-MEP) System to assist predicting listeners' music emotion concerning with users' differences. To analyze listeners' emotional response to music, the P-MEP rules will be generated in the analysis procedure consisting of 5 phases. During the application procedure, the P-MEP System predicts the new listener's emotional response to music. The result of the experiment shows that the generated P-MEP rules can be used to predict emotional response to music concerning with listeners' differences.

**Keywords:** Personalized Music Emotion Prediction, Data Mining, Classification, Clustering.

## 1 Introduction

With the development of multimedia technology, digital music has been widespread used. To find out some useful information or knowledge from such huge amount of music files has become an important issue. In current researches, most of them focused on music structure analysis, music classification or implementing music recommendation system [1][2][11]. Besides, few researches studied perceived emotion when a person listens to music. The system proposed could predict the emotion of listeners by studying the relationship between music patterns and emotion. However, the listeners will get the same emotion in the system even though they have different backgrounds. In fact, listeners' backgrounds will affect the emotion to music.

In this paper, we propose a Personalized Music Emotion Prediction (P-MEP) System based on the user profiles and the music attributes to predict a listener's emotion when

---

* Corresponding author.

Y. Zhuang et al. (Eds.): PCM 2006, LNCS 4261, pp. 730–739, 2006.

listening to music. In this system, there are personalized music emotion prediction rules which are obtained from P-MEP analysis procedure and then used to predict the music emotion.

The analysis procedure of P-MEP includes five phases: *1) Data Preprocessing Phase, 2) User Emotion Group Clustering Phase, 3) User Group Classification Phase, 4) Music Emotion Classification Phase*, and *5) Personalized Music Emotion Prediction Rules Integration Phases.*

During the application procedure, the P-MEP System predicts the new listener's emotional response to music. The result of the experiment shows that the generated P-MEP rules can be used to predict emotional response to music concerning with listeners' differences.

## 2 Related Work

Traditional researches studied music classification, music recommendation and music analysis over digital music. However, they didn't discuss the issue of emotion. For the music emotion analysis, Kuo et al. [7] proposed a music recommendation system and Feng et al. [3] proposed the music retrieval by detecting mood. Lu et al. [8] proposed a music classification system according to listener's emotion. However, only a music classification or recommendation model could be obtained in their system which assumed that everybody should have the same emotional response to music. Accordingly, these models are not suitable to predict music emotion concerning with listeners' differences. In order to consider users' differences, Wang et al. [13] predicted the emotion in a user-adaptive way, but everyone assumingly has his/her owned prediction model before prediction. It will be an overhead and the trained model cannot be reused for other people. Since listeners with similar backgrounds may have similar emotional response to music, the trained prediction rules should be reused to predict new listener's emotion.

## 3 Personalized Music Emotion Prediction (P-MEP)

To analyze the listeners' music emotion with music patterns and their backgrounds, we have two assumptions: Firstly, for the same music, listeners with different user profiles may have different emotions to music. Secondly, music with different music attribute values may have different emotion to listeners.

The input data includes user profiles obtained from a designed questionnaire, music attributes extracted from music midi file and music emotion tagged by listeners. The features of data are described as follows.

(1) User Profiles Vector:
As described in Table 1, the tuples of user profile vector which were selected based on expert's suggestion represent listeners' backgrounds.

**Table 1.** The User Profiles of a Listener

| Category | Attribute |
|---|---|
| | Gender (GN) |
| | Age (AG) |
| Background | Education Status (ES) |
| | Constellation (CS) |
| | Geographical Location (GL) |
| Personality | Containing 19 binary tuples: Placid or Vivid, Like to stay alone or Like to socialize, Like physical exercise or Like brainstorming, Expansive or Shy, Unambitious or Ambitious, Confident or Unconfident, Self-centered or Sensitive to others, Pedantry or Creative, Patient or Inpatient, Despotic or Like to be led, Amiable or Severe, Mild or Combative, Unpredictable tempered or Stable tempered, Serious or Humorous, Cold or Enthusiastic, Responsible or Irresponsible, Moderate or Irritable, Obstinate or Like to be guided, Self-restraint or Easy-going |

(2) Music Attributes Vector:

We are concerned with polyphonic music and choose the track with the highest pitch density to be the main track [2]. The tuples of music attributes extracted from the music midi file are listed in Table 2 where the PM, PS, IM, IS, PE, PD, TD, LM and LS are numerical attributes and the TB, MD and TD are categorical attributes and were proven to have the effect in listener's emotional response in [6].

**Table 2.** Music Attributes

| Category | Attributes |
|---|---|
| | Pitch Mean (PM) |
| | Pitch Standard Deviation (PS) |
| Pitch | Interval Mean (IM) |
| | Interval Standard Deviation (IS) |
| | Pitch Entropy (PE) |
| | Pitch Density (PD) |
| Rhythm | Tempo Degree (TD) |
| Velocity | Loudness Mean (LM) |
| | Loudness Standard Deviation (LS) |
| Timber | Timber (TB) |
| Mode | Mode (MD) |
| | Tonality (TN) |

(3) Music Emotion Vector:

Music emotion vector describes the music emotion vector tagged by listeners for music. Here a music emotion concept hierarchy based upon two emotion models proposed by Thayer [12] and Reilly [10] is proposed to describe the listeners' emotional response to music and shown in Fig. 1. The first layer (root) has one element named *Emotion*. There are two elements named *Positive (A1)* and *Negative (A2)* in the second layer named Layer A. In the third layer named Layer B, *Exuberance (B1)* and *Contentment (B2)* have the AKO relation to *Positive (A1)*, while *Anxious/Frantic (B3)* and *Depression (B4)* have the AKO relation to *Negative (A2)*. This layer is referred to Thayer's two dimensional model of mood. Finally, in the fourth layer named Layer C, there are 30 elements referred to Reilly's emotion model. They also have the AKO relation to *B1, B2, B3* and *B4.*

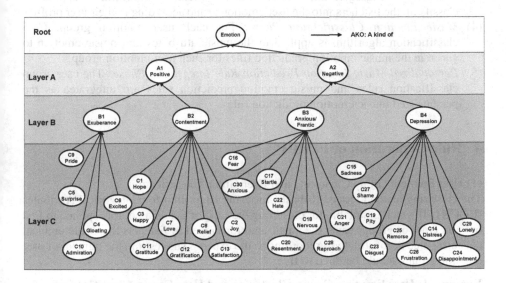

**Fig. 1.** Music Emotion Concept Hierarchy

To predict the music emotion concerning with listeners' differences, we propose a Personalized Music Emotion Prediction (P-MEP) Analysis Procedure consisting of a series of data mining techniques to extract the P-MEP rules.

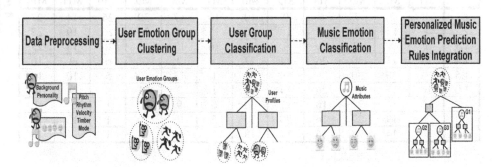

**Fig. 2.** Analysis Procedure of Personalized Music Emotion Prediction

Fig.2 shows a five-phase analysis procedure.

(1) *Data Preprocessing Phase:* In this phase, the user profiles, music attributes and music emotion are collected and preprocessed into vectors.

(2) *User Emotion Group Clustering Phase:* Music emotion tagged by listeners to music is transformed into music emotion vectors. Then the Robust Clustering Algorithm for Categorical Attributes (ROCK) method is applied to music emotion vectors to cluster listeners into several user emotion groups.

(3) *User Group Classification Phase:* ID3 classification algorithm is applied to classify all the listeners into the user emotion group according to their user profiles

(4) *Music Emotion Classification Phase:* For each user emotion group, C4.5 classification algorithm is applied to the music attributes and music emotion to generate the music emotion prediction rules for each user emotion group.

(5) *Personalized Music Emotion Prediction Rule Integration Phase:* The user group classification rules and music emotion prediction rules are integrated as the personalized music emotion prediction rules.

# 4 Rule Generation of P-MEP

(1) User Emotion Group Clustering and User Group Classification
The clustering method named Robust Clustering Algorithm for Categorical Attributes (ROCK) [4] which is suitable for clustering the categorical data point is applied to find out user emotion groups using the music emotion tagged by listeners then a hierarchical clustering tree is constructed. According to the expert's suggestion, the number of user emotion groups should be three to five.

**Example 1: User Emotion Group Clustering and User Group Classification**
Table 3 shows the emotion tagged by listeners to music and the hierarchical clustering tree generated by ROCK is shown in Fig. 3. Three user emotion groups are chosen.

**Table 3.** Music Emotion Tagged by Listeners

|    | M1 | M2 | M3 | M4 | M5 | M6 | M7 | M8 | M9 | M10 | M11 | M12 |
|----|----|----|----|----|----|----|----|----|----|-----|-----|-----|
| L1 | 1  | 2  | 7  | 6  | 9  | 10 | 16 | 17 | 30 | 26  | 14  | 27  |
| L2 | 1  | 13 | 7  | 5  | 10 | 10 | 16 | 20 | 30 | 26  | 19  | 27  |
| L3 | 1  | 2  | 11 | 5  | 9  | 10 | 16 | 17 | 18 | 26  | 14  | 23  |
| L4 | 16 | 17 | 30 | 26 | 14 | 27 | 1  | 2  | 7  | 6   | 9   | 10  |
| L5 | 16 | 20 | 30 | 26 | 19 | 27 | 1  | 13 | 7  | 5   | 10  | 10  |
| L6 | 16 | 17 | 18 | 26 | 14 | 23 | 1  | 2  | 11 | 5   | 9   | 10  |
| L7 | 26 | 14 | 27 | 16 | 17 | 30 | 6  | 9  | 10 | 1   | 2   | 7   |
| L8 | 26 | 19 | 27 | 16 | 20 | 30 | 5  | 10 | 10 | 1   | 13  | 7   |
| L9 | 26 | 14 | 23 | 16 | 17 | 18 | 5  | 9  | 10 | 1   | 2   | 11  |

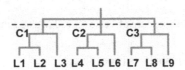

**Fig. 3.** Hierarchical Clustering Tree of Listeners

Next, the ID3 decision tree algorithm [5] is applied to find out the relationship between user profiles and user emotion groups. The analysis result is represented as User Group Classification Tree (Fig. 4).

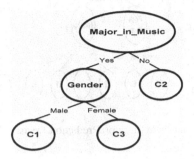

**Fig. 4.** User Group Classification Tree

(2) Music Emotion Classification
C4.5 classification method proposed by Quinlan [9] is now used to generate the music emotion prediction rules. The emotion center of each user emotion group is determined as the majority of all listeners' music emotion in every user emotion group. Then C4.5 classification algorithm is applied to music attributes and emotion center of each emotion group to generate the Music Emotion Prediction Tree.

**Example 2: Music Emotion Classification**
The emotion center of each group is represented by the elements in Layer C. Then the C4.5 algorithm is applied to music attributes and the music emotion of each user emotion group in Table 4 and we get the music emotion prediction tree for each user emotion group which is shown in Fig. 5.

**Table 4.** Music Attributes and Emotion Center of Group

| Music | Pitch Mean | Tonality | Mode | Center of G1 | Center of G2 | Center of G3 |
|-------|-----------|----------|-------|--------------|--------------|--------------|
| M1 | 60 | C | Major | 2 | 3 | 4 |
| M2 | 72 | C | Major | 2 | 3 | 4 |
| M3 | 61 | C | Major | 2 | 3 | 4 |
| M4 | 52 | C | Major | 1 | 4 | 3 |
| M5 | 43 | C | Major | 1 | 4 | 3 |
| M6 | 56 | D | Major | 1 | 4 | 3 |
| M7 | 23 | F | Minor | 3 | 2 | 1 |
| M8 | 25 | G# | Minor | 3 | 2 | 1 |
| M9 | 29 | G# | Minor | 3 | 2 | 1 |
| M10 | 37 | F | Minor | 4 | 1 | 2 |
| M11 | 56 | F | Minor | 4 | 1 | 2 |
| M12 | 21 | F | Minor | 4 | 1 | 2 |

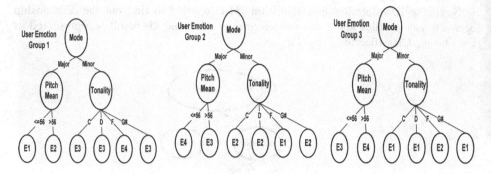

**Fig. 5.** Music Emotion Prediction Decision Tree

(3) Personalized Music Emotion Prediction Rules Integration

Finally, the group nodes in decision tree of user group classification tree are expanded with music emotion prediction trees to be the personalized music emotion prediction rules to perform the music emotion prediction concerning with user differences. An example of the personalized music emotion prediction tree is shown in Fig. 6.

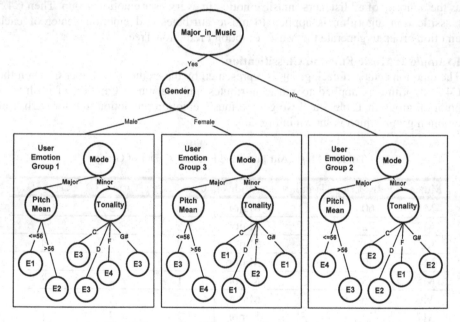

**Fig. 6.** Personalized Music Emotion Prediction Tree

## 5   System Implementation and Experiment

During the application procedure, the new user should fill in the user profiles and the P-MEP System inferences user emotion group of the user. Then the user could input a

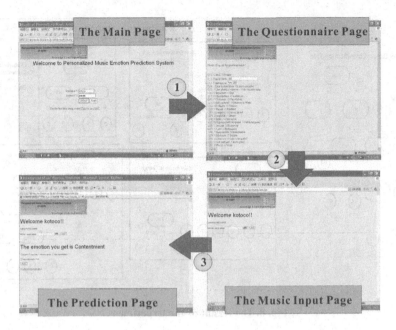

**Fig. 7.** The P-MEP System

midi file and the system predicts the emotional response to music according to the music prediction rules.

For the experiment, 20 pieces of representative music midi file clips were selected and 24 listeners with different backgrounds joined this experiment to annotate the music emotion. Another 10 listeners are invited to annotate 5 different music clips.

The results of the experiments are shown in Fig. 8. For example, a new listener with user profiles that gender is female, and personality is enthusiastic, she is clustered into user emotion group G3. If she listens to music with music attributes that standard deviation of interval is 50.3 and tonality is C, then the P-MEP system predicts that she will get *Exuberance* emotion. Compared with the predicted results, it shows that rules generated above could be used to predict music emotion.

In Fig. 8, there are four listeners in user emotion group 1 (G1) and they are all male. There are five listeners in user emotion group 2 (G2), while 2 are male and 3 are female. There are seven listeners in user emotion group 3 (G3), while 2 are male and 5 are female. Finally, there are eight listeners in user emotion group 4 (G4), while 1 is female and the rest are male. Listeners in G1 have the personality that is vivid, listeners in G2 have the personality that is shy and cold, listeners in G3 have the personality that is enthusiastic if the listener is female and creative if the listener is male, and finally listeners in G4 have the personality that is pedantry or straightforward.

The listeners in G1 have positive emotion to music when the pitch density of the music is greater than 0.094 and the tonality is C, D, D#, G# and A, and have negative emotion when the pitch density of the music is less that 0.094 or the pitch density is greater that 0.094 and the tonality is B. The listeners in G2 have positive emotion when the standard deviation of pitch of music is greater than 28.33 and have negative

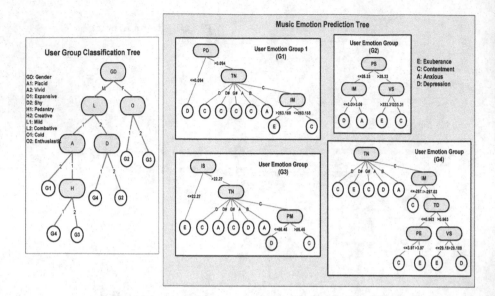

**Fig. 8.** The Result of the Experiment

emotion when it is less than 28.33. The listeners in G3 have positive emotion when the standard deviation of interval is less than 22.27 or when it is greater than 22.27 and the tonality is D, G# or B and have negative emotion in the rest cases. The listeners in G4 have negative emotion when the tonality of music is A or B and when mean of interval is greater than 297, tempo degree is greater than 0.96 and velocity standard deviation is greater than 29.18 and have positive emotion for the rest cases.

# 6   Conclusion

The personalized music emotion prediction rules are generated from the proposed analysis procedure. And the result of the experiment shows that our personalized music emotion prediction system could be used to predict music emotion of listeners concerning with their different backgrounds. In the future, the music emotion ontology could be modified and the user profiles or the music attributes could be added, so that the system could be further improved.

# References

1. Chai, W., Vercoe, B.: Folk Music Classification Using Hidden Markov Models. Proc. Intl. Conf. Artificial Intelligence. (2001)
2. Chen, H.C., Chen, A.L.P.: A Music Recommendation System Based on Music and User Grouping. J. Intelligent Information Systems, Vol. 24. (2005) 113-132
3. Feng, Y., Zhuang, Y., Pan, Y.: Popular Music Retrieval by Detecting Mood. Proc. of the 26th annual international ACM SIGIR conference. (2003) 375-376

4. Guha, S., Rastogi, R., Shim, K.: ROCK: A Robust Clustering Algorithm for Categorical Attributes, Information Systems, Vol. 25. (2000) 345-366
5. Han, J., Kamber. M.: Data Mining : Concepts and Techniques. San Francisco: Morgan Kaufmann Publishers. (2001) pp. 550
6. Juslin, P.N., Sloboda, J.A.: Music and Emotion :Theory and Research. Oxford ;New York: Oxford University Press (2001)
7. Kuo, F.F., Chiang, M.F., Shan, M.K., Lee, S.Y.: Emotion-Based Music Recommendation by Association Discovery from Film Music. Proceedings of the 13th Annual ACM International Conference on Multimedia. (2005) 507-510
8. Lu, L., Liu, D., Zhang, H.J.: Automatic Mood Detection and Tracking of Music Audio Signals," IEEE Trans. Audio, Speech and Language Processing, Vol. 14. (2006) 5-18
9. Quinlan, J.R.: C4.5 :Programs for Machine Learning. San Mateo, Calif.: Morgan Kaufmann Publishers. (1993)
10. Reilly, W.S.N.: Believable Social and Emotion Agents. PhD. Dissertation. (1996)
11. Shan, M.K., Kuo, F.F., Chen, M.F.: Music Style Mining and Classification by Melody. Proc. 2002 IEEE ICME. (2002) 97-100.
12. Thayer, R.E.: The Biopsychology of Mood and Arousal. Oxford University Press. (1989)

# Video Segmentation Using Joint Space-Time-Range Adaptive Mean Shift

Irene Y.H. Gu[1], Vasile Gui[2], and Zhifei Xu[3]

[1] Dept. of Signals and Systems, Chalmers Univ. of Technology, Gothenburg,41296, Sweden
irenegu@chalmers.se
[2] Dept. of Electronics and Communications, Technical Univ.Timisoara, 1900,
Timisoara, Romania
gui@etc.utt.ro
[3] Institute of Image Processing and Pattern Recognition,
Shanghai Jiao Tong University, Shanghai, 200030, China
zfxu@sjtu.edu.cn

**Abstract.** Video segmentation has drawn increasing interest in multimedia applications. This paper proposes a novel joint space-time-range domain adaptive mean shift filter for video segmentation. In the proposed method, segmentation of moving/static objects/background is obtained through inter-frame mode-matching in consecutive frames and motion vector mode estimation. Newly appearing objects/regions in the current frame due to new foreground objects or uncovered background regions are segmented by intra-frame mode estimation. Simulations have been conducted to several image sequences, and results have shown the effectiveness and robustness of the proposed method. Further study is continued to evaluate the results.

**Keywords:** video segmentation, image segmentation, mean shift, joint space-time-range mean shift, inter-frame mode matching, intra-frame mode estimation, kernel density estimation.

## 1 Introduction

There has been an increasing interest in object-based video segmentation largely due to multimedia applications, MPEG video coding, video surveillance and tracking. It is desirable that image and video segmentation generates partitions of images consisting of semantically meaningful entities such as regions, objects (e.g. balls, flowers, persons, cars) or, object parts. Comparing with 2D image segmentation, additional information such as object motion (e.g., homogeneity in speed, direction and acceleration) and temporal correlations may be explored in video segmentation. Strategies for video segmentation can roughly be divided into 3 types: The 1st type uses 2D spatial segmentation followed by temporal directional tracking. In the 2nd type, temporal trajectories of points are extracted based on the motion similarities. These trajectories are then grouped according to, e.g., similarity in motion, constraints in the spatial location and the lengths of trajectories. In the 3rd type, segmentation is

Y. Zhuang et al. (Eds.): PCM 2006, LNCS 4261, pp. 740–748, 2006.
© Springer-Verlag Berlin Heidelberg 2006

directly applied to 3D spatiotemporal pixel volumes of video without favoring one dimension over another [1,2].

Much of the recent development in mean shift filters is motivated by multimedia applications [3]. For example, video segmentation may be performed by first applying 2D mean shift segmentation, followed by motion tracking and spatial temporal integration [6]. In video paintbox [7] 2D mean shift segmentation is performed on some key image frames. Associations are then created between segments according to the color, shape and location of segments to obtain video segmentation and painting. However, such spatial segmentation followed by temporal tracking may lead to favoring one dimension over another. Apart from this, 2D mean shift segmentation may yield rather noisy results along the temporal direction. Alternatively, video segmentation may employ a mean shift filter to video volume so as to mitigate these problems. In [1], 7D feature vectors were proposed including color, time, motion and position-related features. Each video volume is then considered as a collection of three feature vectors, and clustered to obtain a consistent moving object by using a hierarchical mean shift filter. While mean shift segmentation of video volume seems somewhat attractive, the computational cost increases significantly, as the size of data set under video volume becomes large. Motivated by the above, we propose in this paper a novel joint space-time-range mean shift filter for video segmentation. The segmentation method combines the process of inter-frame mode matching and intra-frame mode estimation in the joint space-time-range domain, which is designed to segment objects/regions and to handle newly appeared objects/regions from removed occlusion [10].

The remainder of the paper is organized as follows. In Section 2, theory for mean shift image segmentation is briefly reviewed. In Section 3, a space-time-range adaptive mean shift filter is proposed. The detailed algorithm is also included. Section 4 shows some simulation results from segmented image sequences using the proposed method. Finally, conclusions are given in Section 5.

## 2  Mean Shift and Image Segmentation

Mean shift is a method for seeking mode (local maximum) in a density estimate without requiring the density estimate itself [8]. Let a given set of L-dimensional feature vectors be $S = \{ \mathbf{x}_i,\ i = 1, \cdots, n \}$. Assuming the estimated kernel density of $\mathbf{x}$ has the following form:

$$\hat{p}_K (\mathbf{x}) = \frac{1}{n|\mathbf{H}|^{1/2}} \sum_{i=1}^{n} K\left( \mathbf{H}^{-1/2} d\left(\mathbf{x},\ \mathbf{x}_i,\ \mathbf{H}\right)\right) \tag{1}$$

where $K$ is a $L$-dimensional kernel, $\mathbf{H}$ is a bandwidth matrix of size $L$, and $d$ is a distance function defined between features $\mathbf{x}$ and $\mathbf{x}_i$. For *radial symmetric* kernels and $L_2$ norm, (1) has the general form

$$\hat{p}_K(\mathbf{x}) = \frac{c_k}{nh^L} \sum_{i=1}^{n} k\left(\left\|\frac{\mathbf{x} - \mathbf{x}_i}{h}\right\|^2\right)$$

where $K(\mathbf{x}) = c_k k(\|\mathbf{x}\|^2)$ and $c_k$ is a normalization constant.

The mode of $\hat{p}_K(\mathbf{x})$ is obtained by setting $\nabla \hat{p}_K(\mathbf{x}) = 0$, yielding:

$$\frac{1}{2}h^2 c \frac{\nabla \hat{p}_K(\mathbf{x})}{\hat{p}_G(\mathbf{x})} = \frac{\sum_{i=1}^{n} \mathbf{x}_i g\left(\left\|\frac{\mathbf{x} - \mathbf{x}_i}{h}\right\|^2\right)}{\sum_{i=1}^{n} g\left(\left\|\frac{\mathbf{x} - \mathbf{x}_i}{h}\right\|^2\right)} - \mathbf{x} \tag{2}$$

where $G(\mathbf{x}) = c_g g(\|\mathbf{x}\|^2)$, $c = \frac{c_g}{c_k}$ is a constant, $K$ is the shadow kernel of $G$, and

$g(x) = -k'(x)$. The right hand side of (2) is defined as the mean shift $m_G(\mathbf{x})$ of kernel $G$. Since the shadow kernel of Gaussian is also a Gaussian kernel, further, a Gaussian kernel is known to have a better segmented image after convergence as compared to that of Epanechnikov kernel, only Gaussian kernels are considered in this paper.

A spatial-range mean shift filter is frequently used for image segmentation. If the feature vector is defined as $\mathbf{x} = [\mathbf{x}^d \quad \mathbf{x}^r]^T$, where the domain feature is defined as the spatial location of pixel $\mathbf{x}^d = [s_x \quad s_y]^T$ and the range feature is set as $\mathbf{x}^r = \mathbf{f}(\mathbf{x}^d)$, then one may compute mean shift (in the right hand side of (2)) in the *spatial-range* domain. For a Gaussian kernel, $g(\mathbf{x})$ in (2) becomes,

$$g(\|\mathbf{x}\|^2) = \exp\left(-\frac{\|\mathbf{x}^d\|^2}{2\sigma_d^2}\right) \exp\left(-\frac{\|\mathbf{f}(\mathbf{x}^d)\|^2}{2\sigma_r^2}\right) \tag{3}$$

or, $g(\mathbf{x}) = g_d(\mathbf{x}^d) g_r(\mathbf{f}(\mathbf{x}^d))$, where $h_d = 2\sigma_d^2$, $h_r = 2\sigma_r^2$ are the spatial and range kernel bandwidths, respectively. A joint spatial-range mean shift filter takes into account both the geometrical closeness and photometric similarity in an image. Such a mean shift filter can be used as a nonlinear edge-preserving smoothing filter when the range is set to be the image intensity. When the differences of pixel intensities are small, the mean shift filter acts as a lowpass filter in a local image region. However, if the intensity differences are large (e.g. around edges), then the range filter kernel is close to zero value, hence no filtering is actually applied to these pixels. It is worth to notice that a joint spatial-range mean shift filter is closely related to nonlinear diffusions and bilateral filters [4,5]. However, a significant difference to a bilateral filter is that the kernel in a mean shift filter uses different feature sets { $\mathbf{x}_i$ } during the iterations - the kernel moves in both the spatial and the range domain. While in a bilateral filter, the filter kernel uses features from a fixed spatial area. This makes a spatial-range mean shift more robust than a bilateral filter.

## 3 Joint Space-Time-Range Adaptive Mean Shift Filter for Video Segmentation

Video segmentation includes segmenting (static/moving) objects and background, where motion areas in images are associated with the movement of some foreground (or background) objects (or regions), e.g., a part of an object such as foreground persons, background trees, roads when a camera is moving with a car. Since each object or a distinct part of object is associated with a pdf containing certain mode(s), video segmentation can be obtained by tracking the trajectories of objects/regions that share these particular modes along the temporal direction. It is worth to notice that these objects/regions are likely to be non-rigid, and experience some degree of deformation. If we model the joint pdf of a video volume as a product of two independent pdfs for spatial and temporal domain, then mode seeking by 3D mean shift can be simplified as seeking the modes in the component pdfs. Inspired by this, we propose a novel joint space-time-range mean shift filter for video segmentation. The segmentation method is based on inter-frame mode matching in consecutive image frames combined with dynamically generating new regions by intra-frame mode estimation.

### 3.1  Inter-frame Local Mode Matching by Mean Shift

The main purpose of inter-frame mode matching is to segment moving/static objects/regions between consecutive image frames. Video segmentation through *mode matching* is based on the idea that the mode of a pixel(s) in the current frame should be coincident with the mode of a subset of data (or, region) representing the same object or region. Let the feature vector be $\mathbf{x}(t) = [\mathbf{x}^d(t) \quad \mathbf{x}^r(t)]^T$. For a given image sequence $\mathbf{f}(s_x, s_y, t) \triangleq \mathbf{f}(\mathbf{x}^d(t))$, (e.g., $\mathbf{f} = [R \quad G \quad B]^T$ for color images), let the domain and range features be defined as $\mathbf{x}^d(t) = [s_x(t) \quad s_y(t)]^T$ and $\mathbf{x}^r(t) = \mathbf{f}(\mathbf{x}^d(t))$ from the current frame $t$, and the set of sample features be taken from the previous $(t$-$1)$-th frame, $\{ \mathbf{x}_i(t-1), \ i=1,\cdots,n \}$. We assume that the motion is slow compared with the video frame rate so that two consecutive frames are highly correlated. The mean shift in the joint space-time-range domain is defined as,

$$m(\mathbf{x}(t); \{\mathbf{x}_i(t-1)\}) = \frac{\displaystyle\sum_{l=1}^{n} \mathbf{x}_l(t-1) g\left(\left\|\frac{\mathbf{x}(t) - \mathbf{x}_l(t-1)}{h}\right\|^2\right)}{\displaystyle\sum_{l=1}^{n} g\left(\left\|\frac{\mathbf{x}(t) - \mathbf{x}_l(t-1)}{h}\right\|^2\right)} - \mathbf{x}(t) \tag{4}$$

where (see (3)),

$$g = g_d\left(\left\|\frac{\mathbf{x}^d(t) - \mathbf{x}_l^d(t-1)}{h_d}\right\|^2\right) g_r\left(\left\|\frac{\mathbf{f}(\mathbf{x}^d(t)) - \mathbf{f}(\mathbf{x}_l^d(t-1))}{h_r}\right\|^2\right)$$

It is important to emphasize that the sample feature set used in mean shift iteration is taken from the previously segmented image frame while the feature vector for the initial center of the kernel $\mathbf{x}=\mathbf{x}(t)$ is taken from the current image frame. During the mean shift iterations, the feature set from the previous frame changes as the location of kernel center shifts. The mode matching process continues until $\mathbf{x}(t)$ converges to a mode in the previous frame that matches, or when all feature subsets are exhausted in the previous frame. A feature vector $\mathbf{x}(t)$ is defined to match an object/region in the previous frame if the convergence point $\mathbf{y}_c(t-1)$ has a small range distance to $\mathbf{x}(t)$, i.e., $\left\| \mathbf{x}^r(t) - \mathbf{y}_c^r(t-1) \right\|^2 \le h_r$ . Otherwise, it is assumed that the pixel belongs to a new object or region in the current frame (e.g. from removing an occlusion or introducing a new object/region), and *intra-frame local mode estimation* is then applied. To decide whether a region is associated with a static, or a moving object, one may examine the displacement of mode position after the convergence, i.e., using the motion vector $(\mathbf{x}_c^d - \mathbf{x}_0^d)$, where $\mathbf{x}_0^d$ is the centre of the region in frame $t$, and $\mathbf{x}_c^d$ is the centre of the region in frame ($t$-$1$) at which $\mathbf{f}(\mathbf{x}_0^d)$ converges. If the magnitude of the motion vector is large, then it is recognized as a motion region. Further, to save the computation, instead of mode matching over all possible image area one can limit the search to a smaller area as being the maximum expected object movement.

### 3.2  Intra-frame Local Mode Estimation for Newly Appearing Objects / Regions

For those pixels that have no matched modes from the previous frame, segmentation is switched back to intra-frame local mode estimation. This can be the result of removing an occlusion or introducing a new object/region. In such a case, new objects / regions are estimated by exclusively using the 2D information from the unmatched pixels in the current frame, i.e., by intra-frame segmentation.

### 3.3  Mean Shift-Based Segmentation

Pixels that have found their matching modes in the previously segmented frame are grouped into regions. One can also determine whether an object/background region is static or with motion. If a region has a large displacement as compared with the region in the previous frame having a similar mode, then it is an object/background region with motion. Otherwise, it is a static background/object region.

Pixels that have not found correct mode matching and hence switched back to using space-range mean shift in the current frame are then filtered and intra-frame segmented. However, whether these new regions are associated with static or motion objects/regions can only be estimated in the subsequent image frames.

The final step in the current frame segmentation consists of region mode re-evaluation using data from the current frame. This allows tracking illumination changes and other variations of regional features. It is also beneficial in terms of segmentation stability, along with a temporal mean shift filter (see algorithm in Section 3.4).

## 3.4  Algorithm Description

The proposed video segmentation algorithm is summarized below:

1. Initialize: set frame number $t=1$, apply 2D spatial-range mean shift to segment the $1^{st}$ image frame.
2. Set frame number $t \leftarrow t+1$.
3. For each pixel $\mathbf{x}^d(t) = [s_x(t) \quad s_y(t)]^T$ in the image $\mathbf{f}(\mathbf{x}^d(t))$, do:
4. Set the domain feature vector as $\mathbf{x}^d = [t \quad \mathbf{f}(\mathbf{x}^d(t))]^T$, apply a 1D range mean shift filter with a kernel bandwidth $h_t$ along the temporal direction (to regularize the data along $t$).
5. Apply joint space-time-range adaptive mean shift filtering and segmentation as below:

   5.1. Set kernel center at $\mathbf{x} = [\mathbf{x}^d(t) \quad \mathbf{f}(\mathbf{x}^d(t))]^T$ drawn from a pixel in frame $t$, and set    $j=1, \mathbf{y}_1 = \mathbf{x}$;

   5.2. Assign $\{ \ \mathbf{x}_i = [ \ \mathbf{x}_i^d(t-1) \quad \mathbf{f}(\mathbf{x}_i^d(t-1)) \ ]^T, i = 1,\cdots,n \ \}$ centered at $\mathbf{x}$ (within $h_d$);

   5.3. Iteration for compute the mean shift $j \leftarrow j+1$:

$$
\mathbf{y}_{j+1} = \frac{\displaystyle\sum_{l=1}^{n} \mathbf{x}_l g_d\left(\left\|\frac{\left\|\mathbf{y}_j^d - \mathbf{x}_l^d\right\|^2}{h_d}\right\|\right) g_r\left(\left\|\frac{\left\|\mathbf{f}(\mathbf{y}_j^d) - \mathbf{f}(\mathbf{x}_l^d)\right\|^2}{h_r}\right\|\right)}{\displaystyle\sum_{l=1}^{n} g_d\left(\left\|\frac{\left\|\mathbf{y}_j^d - \mathbf{x}_l^d\right\|^2}{h_d}\right\|\right) g_r\left(\left\|\frac{\left\|\mathbf{f}(\mathbf{y}_j^d) - \mathbf{f}(\mathbf{x}_l^d)\right\|^2}{h_r}\right\|\right)}
$$

   Shift the window centre to $\mathbf{y}_{j+1}$, compute the mean shift $m(\mathbf{x}) = \mathbf{y}_{j+1} - \mathbf{y}_j$, and assign a new set $\{ \ \mathbf{x}_i = \mathbf{x}_i(t-1) \ \}$ ;

   5.4. Repeat the Step 5.3 until $\|m(\mathbf{x})\| = \|\mathbf{y}_{j+1} - \mathbf{y}_j\| < \varepsilon$;

   5.5. Case 1. Inter-mode mode matching:

   If $\|\mathbf{x}^r(t) - \mathbf{y}_c^r\|^2 \le h_r$, where $\mathbf{y}_c = [ \ \mathbf{x}_c^d(t-1) \quad \mathbf{f}(\mathbf{x}_c^d(t-1)) \ ]^T$,

   $\Rightarrow$ a similar mode is found, set filtered pixel as $\mathbf{F}(\mathbf{x}^d(t)) \leftarrow \mathbf{f}(\mathbf{x}_c^d(t))$;

   5.6. Case 2. Intra-frame mode estimation:

   If no similar mode in $(t-1)$ frame that matches $\mathbf{x}(t)$, then set

   $\{ \ \mathbf{x}_i = [ \mathbf{x}_i^d(t) \quad \mathbf{f}(\mathbf{x}_i^d(t)) \ ]^T, i = 1,\cdots,n \ \}$ and apply the joint spatial-range mean shift to $\mathbf{x}(t)$ until converge. Assign filtered value as $\mathbf{F}\left(\mathbf{x}^d\left(t\right)\right) \leftarrow \mathbf{f}\left(\mathbf{x}_c^d\left(t\right)\right)$,

where $\mathbf{y}_c = [\ \mathbf{x}_c^d\left(t\right)\ \ \mathbf{f}(\mathbf{x}_c^d(t))\ ]^T$.

6. Repeat Steps 3-5 until all pixels in the frame t are processed.

7. Segment the mean shift filtered image $\mathbf{F}(\mathbf{x}^d(t))$ and assign the segmented results to $\tilde{\mathbf{F}}(\mathbf{x}^d(t))$.

8. Link similar regions between $(t\text{-}1)$ and t frames.

9. Repeat Steps 2-8 until all N frames are processed.

10. Output the segmented video $\tilde{\mathbf{F}}(\mathbf{x}^d(t))$, $t = 1, .., N$.

It is worth to mention that in Step 4, the 1D range filter along $t$ is applied before joint space-time-range mean shift, which brings additional regularity to the segmentation that otherwise could be instable (e.g., small variations of the pixel values in next frame may lead to different partitions). Temporal directional mean shift filter alleviates such a potential problem.

## 4   Simulations and Results

The proposed video segmentation scheme has been tested for several image sequences. Fig.1 shows 6 image frames extracted from the segmented sequence "tennis" and "flowers", respectively.

For "tennis" sequence perceptually relevant L*u*v* color images were used, while for "flowers" sequence RGB color images were used as the range features. For video "tennis", the bandwidths used were $2\sigma_r^2 = 512$, $2\sigma_d^2 = 16$, the Gaussian kernel was truncated to finite size of $19 \times 19$ pixels in spatial domain, and truncated to 5 in the temporal direction, the threshold for merging small regions in segmentation was $M=25$ pixels. From the results, one can see that the "pin-pong" ball is well matched, although there is an extra region in the 39th frame probably caused by the shadow of ball. One can also observe some over-segmentation in the body of the person. Such type of over-segmentation is unavoidable in low level image processing, however, over-segmentation from mean shift can be significantly reduced by exploring the convergence frequency of mean shift at each pixel location [9]. The region boundaries appear rather sharp.

Since the video "flowers" contain many small regions, e.g., flowers with different colors, and are rich in textures, $2\sigma_r^2 = 1024$, $2\sigma_d^2 = 28$, $2\sigma_t^2 = 36$ were used as the bandwidths. The Gaussian kernel in the spatial domain was truncated to $11 \times 11$ due to narrower spatial bandwidth in this case. Also, since flowers contain many small regions with different colors, a smaller region merging threshold $M=5$ pixels was applied. Results of segmented "flowers" images have shown robustness in matching the moving tree and flowers, and re-generate new regions (e.g. uncovered window in the house).

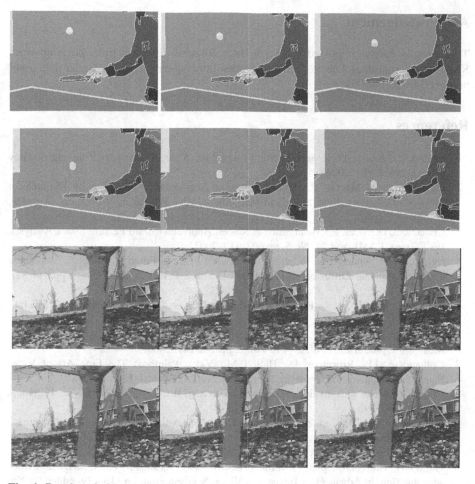

**Fig. 1.** Results of video segmentation using the proposed method. Rows 1-2 (left to right): 6 frames (#35-40) extracted from the segmented "tennis" image sequence. Rows 3-4: 6 frames from segmented "flowers" image sequence (#32-37).

## 5   Conclusions

We have proposed a joint space-time-range adaptive mean shift video segmentation scheme. The combination of inter-frame mode matching and intra-frame mode estimation is shown to be robust and computationally efficient from our video segmentation results applied on several image sequences. The proposed scheme also has the potential for tracking moving objects in videos by examining the displacement of corresponding modes through frames. Further studies on moving object tracking and evaluation are being continued.

## Acknowledgement

This work is partly supported by the ASIAN-Swedish research links program from Swedish International Development Co-operation Agency (SIDA) under the grant number 348-2005-6095.

## References

1. Megret, R., Jolion, T.: Representation of Dynamic Video Content by Tracking of Grey Level Blobs, RFIA, 2002 Cheng,
2. DeMenthon, D., Megret, R.: Spatial-Temporal Segmentation of Video by Hierarchical Mean Shift Analysis, Proc. Statistical Methods in Video Processing Workshop, Denmark, 2002
3. Comaniciu, D., Meer, P.: Mean Shift: A Robust Approach toward Feature Space Analysis, IEEE Trans. PAMI, Vol.24, No.5, pp.603-619, 2002
4. Barash, D.: A Fundamental Relationship between Bilateral Filtering, Adaptive Smoothing and the Nonlinear Diffusion Equation, IEEE Trans. PAMI, Vol.24, No.6, pp.844-847, 2002.
5. Tomasi, C., Manduchi, R.: Bilateral Filtering for Gray and Color Images, Proc. IEEE Int't Conf. ICCV, India, 1998
6. Comaniciu, D., Ramesh, V., Meer, P.: Real-Time Tracking of Non-Rigid Objects using Mean Shift, proc IEEE Conf. CVPR Vol. 2, pp.142-149. 2000
7. Collomosse, J.P., Rowntree, D., Hall, P.M.: Video Paintbox: The Fine Art of Video Painting, Computers and Graphics, Special Edn. on Digital Arts, Elsevier, 2005
8. Cheng, Y.: Mean shift, mode seeking, and clustering, IEEE Trans. PAMI, Vol. 17, No. 8, pp. 790-799, 1995
9. Song, N., Gu, I.Y.H., Cao, Z., Viberg, M.: Enhanced spatial-range mean shift color image segmentation by using convergence frequency and position, in Prof. of 14th European Signal Processing Conference (EUSIPCO 2006), Florence, Italy, Sept. 4-8, 2006
10. Gu, I.Y.H., Gui, V.: Chapter VI: Joint space-time-range mean shift-based image and video segmentation, in Advances in Image and Video Segmentation, pp.113-139, edited by Yu-Jin Zhang, Idea Group Inc. Publishing, 2006.

# EagleRank: A Novel Ranking Model for Web Image Search Engine

Kangmiao Liu, Wei Chen, Chun Chen, Jiajun Bu, Can Wang, and Peng Huang[*]

College of Computer Science and Engineering, Zhejiang University, Hangzhou, P.R. China
{lkm, chenw, chenc, bjj, wcan, oiabm6211}@zju.edu.cn

**Abstract.** The explosive growth of World Wide Web has already made it the biggest image repository. Despite some image search engines provide convenient access to web images, they frequently yield unwanted results. Locating needed and relevant images remains a challenging task. This paper proposes a novel ranking model named EagleRank for web image search engine. In EagleRank, multiple sources of evidence related to the images are considered, including image surrounding text passages, terms in special HTML tags, website types of the images, the hyper-textual structure of the web pages and even the user feedbacks. Meanwhile, the flexibility of EagleRank allows it to combine other potential factors as well. Based on inference network model, EagleRank also gives sufficient support to Boolean AND and OR operators. Our experimental results indicate that EagleRank has better performance than traditional approaches considering only the text from web pages.

**Keywords:** EagleRank, inference network, image search engine, World Wide Web, relevance feedback.

## 1 Introduction

With the explosive growth of World Wide Web, massive amount of images are now accessible from Internet. Despite the existing commercial image search engines like Google can provide convenient access to these images, locating the images accurately is still a challenging work. With millions of relevant images returned in a user query, it becomes difficult to determine the most relevant images among these initial results. Thus, to design a good ranking model is a key issue in the web image search engine.

After collecting images from the Web, a search engine has to extract features which are from images themselves or the textual context of images in the web page to index the images. People may be interested in high-level attributes of an image, which is difficult to be derived from the image content directly. However, such high-level semantics can be derived from the text accompanying the images in most cases. For example, Google claims that "it analyzes the text on the page adjacent to the image,

---

[*] The work was supported by National Grand Fundamental Research 973 Program of China (2006CB303000), Key Technologies R&D Program of Zhejiang Province (2005C23047).

Y. Zhuang et al. (Eds.): PCM 2006, LNCS 4261, pp. 749–759, 2006.
© Springer-Verlag Berlin Heidelberg 2006

the image caption and dozens of other factors to determine the image content" [16]. Many other works [5][8][10][14] use similar technique.

In this paper, a novel ranking model named EagleRank is proposed for web image search engine. EagleRank is based on inference network model. It considers not only the textual context of an image in web page, but also many other factors such as the importance of the web page, the relevance feedback of user queries and so on. Named entity recognition [21] and dependency grammar [20] are used to extract most descriptive terms in a web page. Our work provides a useful insight for future work on web image search engine, the model proposed is flexible enough to allow the inclusion of other factors in ranking images.

The rest of the paper is organized as follows. In Section 2, we introduce the existing work on web image retrieval. Section 3 discusses the evidence of web images used to rank. Section 4 presents a brief introduction to inference network. In section 5, the detail of EagleRank model is further described. In Section 6, we show some experimental results of the prototype system, and a brief discussion will be included. Finally, we conclude our work in Section 7.

## 2  Related Work

There are two basic image retrieval approaches: content-based retrieval and text-based retrieval. Content-based image retrieval (CBIR) systems developed quickly since 1990s. Most of them were based on low-level visual features such as color, texture or shape. They usually allowed users providing sample images or sketches to carry out the retrieval, and worked well when users sought images with a particular appearance. However, we note that they were always performed using closed databases whose contents were under the direct control of the researchers [8].

Due to too large amount of web images, it's not easy to implement CBIR approaches for web image retrieval. Especially, general users usually find it difficult to search or query images by using features directly. They usually prefer textual or keyword-based queries since they are easier and more intuitive to represent their information needs [22]. Much more work [5][8][9][10][13][14][15] are being done to integrate present techniques on the fly to facilitate effective image retrieval and management.

One obstacle in designing a web image search engine is to index images so that they can be queried using keywords. WebSeek [8] classifies images and videos by subject. By analyzing pages' URLS, image name and directory are extracted, which will be used through a combination of automated and semi-automated procedures, to build the catalog. WebSeer [14] uses several kinds of HTML metadata including the file names of images, the text of the ALT attribute of IMG tag to help identify relevant images. Other commercial image search engines [16] like Google, AltaVista base their indexing on the same text, and refinements are added to make a difference, although most of the sites don't go into much detail about how they create their indexes.

T.A.S. Coelho [1] introduces an image retrieval model based on Bayesian belief networks, and considers multiple textual sources of evidence related to the images, their results indicate that retrieval using an image surrounding text passages is as effective as standard HTML tags based retrieval.

A. Ghoshal [11] proposes a novel model for automatic annotation of images with keywords from a generic vocabulary of concepts or objects. Based on a set of manually annotated images, each image is automatically annotated with a posteriori probability of concepts present in it. G. Carneiro [12] uses probabilistic formulation that poses annotation and retrieval as classification problems, and produces solutions that are optimal in the minimum probability of error sense. Unfortunately, these works all need training set and are not easily applied to web image search engines.

Y.T. Zhuang [18] proposes a hybrid approach combining key-word based query selection and CBIR with users' relevance feedback. The query selection process allows the user to filter out many subject-irrelevant images, the result of which serves as good starting point for subsequent content-based retrieval. However, this approach may be inconvenient for web image search engine. M. Lei [7] introduces a ranking approach considering user feedback in their web search engine which has been proved pretty useful.

The named entity recognition is to identify all named locations, named persons, named organizations, dates, times, monetary amounts, and percentages in text[21]. Dependency parsing is the technique used to analyze the syntactic structure of a sentence [20]. They are ongoing research points in Natural Language Processing and perform well in some situations.

However, few work has been done combining various aspects such as the web page's importance, user relevance feedback, image surrounding text passages etc. into a single ranking model for web image search engine. We also use named entity recognition and dependency parsing to extract the most descriptive terms and improve recall and precision of EagleRank Model.

## 3   Evidences for Web Images

World Wide Web documents contain lots of information which are useful for web image retrieval, although they may be very irregular. For example, the ALT attribute in the HTML IMG tag provides alternate description for images, but actually in most cases it is empty. The filename of the images is not always right. People often name images as 'a.jpg' or 'tmp.jpg' and so on for convenience.

In order to find the words that describe the images better, we introduce named entity recognition and dependency parsing approaches to extract this information. In our system, we extract index terms from the image tags, the page titles, the image file names, the image captions, the alternative text, the image hyperlinks, and the body text around the image using named entity recognition and dependency parsing. However, they are not our focus here.

World Wide Web is a huge directed graph. The link structure of the Web is an important resource to rank web pages. Google and IBM invented the famous PageRank [6] and HITS algorithms respectively several years ago. They use the link structure to evaluate the importance of web pages. Many variations of these algorithms are proposed, they are used widely in search engines nowadays. In this paper, we use the link information to estimate the importance of images in web pages.

Unfortunately, there are always a variety of inconsistencies between user textual queries and image descriptions, because an image is different to different people in terms of their viewpoints. And it also changes to the same person over time. Some works investigate user term feedback in interactive text-based image retrieval. However, C. Zhang [19] shows that term feedback is not as effective as what we originally expect. According to M. Lei [7], we capture images which are most often selected by users in response to a particular search, and use it to improve relevance to the search over time. Because the web crawlers pull images day after day, some important images may be newly fetched and few are visited by users. It's better to improve the relevance of these new images by giving them a default relevant factor.

We integrate all the factors mentioned above into our EagleRank model based on inference network. It effectively improves the quality of the set of images retrieved.

## 4   The Inference Network Model

Inference Network Model is the theoretical basis for the retrieval engine Inquery system [4]. Its success has attracted attention to the use of Bayesian networks[3] with information retrieval systems.

Inference Network Model associates random variables with documents, index terms and user queries. As in Fig. 1, index terms and documents variables are represented by nodes in the network, and the arcs between index terms and documents nodes indicate that observation of the document yields improved belief on its term nodes. The user query variables model the event that the information request specified by the query has been met. The belief in query node is a function of the beliefs in the node associated with the index terms.

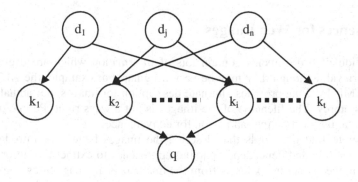

**Fig. 1.** An example of a Basic Inference Network

The ranking of a document $d_j$ with respect to a query q is a measure of how much evidential support the observation of $d_j$ provides to the query q. The ranking of a document $d_j$ is computed as P(q, $d_j$) in the reference network[3].

$$P(q,d_j) = \sum_{\forall K} P(q,d_j \mid K) \times P(K) = \sum_{\forall K} P(q \mid K) \times P(K \mid d_j) \times P(d_j) \tag{1}$$

K is a t-dimensional vector defined by $K=(k_1, k_2, ..., k_t)$ where $k_1, k_2, ..., k_t$ are binary random variables associated with index terms, $d_j$ and q are random variables associated with the document and the user query respectively. $P(d_j)$ is the prior probability for the inference network, it reflects the probability associated with event of observing a given document. The conditional probability $P(K|d_j)$ computes the probability of observing index terms K given that the document $d_j$ was observed. $P(q|K)$ is the conditional probability of observing the user query q in the index terms K.

## 5  EagleRank: A Novel Ranking Model

Now, let's explain how to rank images in web image search engine. We replace $d_j$ in equation 1 with $I_j$, namely, we are now searching images instead of documents, as follows.

$$P(q, I_j) = \sum_{\forall K} P(q, I_j \mid K) \times P(K) = \sum_{\forall K} P(q \mid K) \times P(K \mid I_j) \times P(I_j) \tag{2}$$

$P(I_j)$ represent the prior probabilities for EagleRank, which means the probability of observing image $I_j$. $P(K|I_j)$ is the conditional probability of observing index terms K given that the image $I_j$ was observed, these index terms are extracted from the web pages corresponding to the image.

### 5.1  Prior Probabilities of EagleRank

Suppose an important web page has an image that has more importance, we consider the web page as the source of the EagleRank's prior probabilities. The best-known approach to estimate the importance of a web page is PageRank [6] which is used in Google Search Engine. Besides this, we also think that some web sites that provide professional images play a more important role. So we can prefetch these domains or sub-domains, images from these web sites will have a much higher prior probabilities.

When user retrieves the query results, only a few images best meeting the user's needs are clicked. It is a good practice to change the order of the result list to reflect user behaviors. Once an image is clicked, we record it and upgrade the prior probability of the image periodically. Because some newly fetched images have no chance to be clicked by users, it's better to give these images some compensation. More relevant works refers to M. Lei [7].

Then we compute the prior probability of an image as follows.

$$P(I_j) = k_{pr} \times PR(d_j) + k_{type} \times TYPE(d_j) + k_{hit} \times \text{WH}(I_j) \tag{3}$$

And

$$k_{pr} + k_{type} + k_{hit} = 1 \tag{4}$$

$PR(d_j)$ is the PageRank of a web page where the image $I_j$ belongs to, $TYPE(d_j)$ is the weight of the domain or sub-domain from which the image was crawled. $\text{WH}(I_j)$ reflects the hit rate of the image. All of them are normalized between 0 and 1.

Further, we can also take into account the images themselves such as the sizes, the ratio of length and width etc. and add these to equation 3. We should notice that these factors must be carefully defined. Because they are closely related to the user's requirements (e.g., user may need an image of special size.). Many search engines always filter out small images.

In a word, the prior probabilities of EagleRank really give us a way to integrate various factors conveniently.

## 5.2 Ranking Image

According to R. Baeza-Yates[3], we can write equation 2 as follows:

$$P(q, I_j) = \sum_{\forall \vec{k}_i} P(q \mid \vec{k}_i) \times P(k_i \mid I_j) \times \left( \prod_{\forall l \neq i} P(\overline{k}_l \mid I_j) \right) \times P(I_j) \tag{5}$$

Where $\vec{k}_i$ is a vector given by

$$\vec{k}_i = K \mid k_i = 1 \wedge \forall_{j \neq i} k_j = 0 \tag{6}$$

K is a t-dimensional vector defined by $K = (k_1, k_2, ..., k_t)$ where $k_1, k_2, ..., k_t$ are binary random variables associated with index terms as mentioned in section 4.2. We then define

$$P(q \mid \vec{k}_i) = \begin{cases} idf_i & \text{if } q_i = 1 \\ 0 & \text{if } q_i = 0 \end{cases} \tag{7}$$

The user query q is an instance of the t-dimensional vector K, $q_i$ means the $i^{th}$ binary random variables in K. TF(i.e., term frequency) and IDF(i.e., inverse document frequency)[3][9] are widely used indicators weighting the relevance of a term to a document. In equation 7, $idf_i$ represents the inverse document frequency for the index term $k_i$, which is normalized between 0 and 1.

To compute TFs and IDFs, as T.A.S. Coelho [1] mentioned, we take into account three different sources of evidential information. Description tags: composed of the terms found in the filename of the image, in the ALT attribute of the IMG tag, between the anchor tags <A> and </A>; Meta tags: composed of the terms located between the tags <TITLE> and </TITLE> and in the META of the page; Text passages: composed of the terms located close to the image. That is, given an image, we consider the text in the web page to represent the image. Then, we define

$$P(k_i \mid I_j) = f_{i,j}$$
$$P(\overline{k}_i \mid I_j) = 1 - f_{i,j} \tag{8}$$

Where $f_{i,j}$ is the term frequency of the index term $k_i$ which is extracted to describe image $I_j$, and $f_{i,j}$ is also normalized. Especially, we use the named entity recognition and dependency parsing techniques to extract the index terms. So the most descriptive words are used to represent the images. Further, we can define the weights of different HTML tags as M. Lei [7] to tune $f_{i,j}$. By applying equations discussed above, we rewrite equation 5 as follows.

$$P(q, I_j) = \left( \prod_{\forall i} P(\overline{k_i} \mid I_j) \right) \times P(I_j) \times \left( \sum_{\forall k_i} P(k_i \mid I_j) \times P(q \mid \overrightarrow{k_i}) \times \frac{1}{P(\overline{k_i} \mid I_j)} \right)$$

$$= \left( \prod_{f_{i,j} > 0} (1 - f_{i,j}) \right) \times P(I_j) \times \left( \sum_{q_i = 1 \wedge f_{i,j} > 0} f_{i,j} \times idf_i \times \frac{1}{1 - f_{i,j}} \right) \quad (9)$$

The EagleRank model above allows us to consistently combine evidence from distinct sources to improve the final ranking. Further, because EagleRank is based on inference network model, it can support AND operator and OR operator easily [3].

## 6  Experimental Results and Discussions

In this section, we describe the prototypical system that we developed based on the techniques discussed in previous sections. We perform tests to prove the effectiveness of EagleRank. Finally, we discuss the characteristics of this model.

### 6.1  Experimental Prototype

We have implemented a prototype system named EAGLE(wEb imAGe retrievaL systEm) using EagleRank as its ranking model. Our search engine provides keyword-based search and supports Boolean AND, Boolean OR and exact phrase queries. 1.2 million web pages with their images have been downloaded already. Table 1 shows the statistics of our system.

**Table 1.** Statistics of our system used for tests

| Collection Size(GB) | 48.6 |
|---|---|
| Web Page Number | 1,214,946 |
| Image Number | 434,573 |
| Sampled Image Number | 113,387 |

In our experiments, we used equation 3 to compute the prior probability of the EagleRank model. All sub-domains were classified into three categories according to its type and given weight as 0.3, 0.6, and 0.9. To avoid involving too much subjective judgment, user feedback was not considered here. In addition, we filtered out small images with a size no larger than 50 pixels, and other factors such as the images traits were not taken into account for the moment.

### 6.2  Experimental Results and Discussions

According to T.A.S. Coelho [1], we sampled 113,387 images from our system to do the experiments and invited volunteers to do relevance evaluations. We used 40 test queries and retrieved 40 highest ranked images using EagleRank considering different factors, and pooled into unique images set. Then, the volunteers labeled these images in the pool as relevant or not, independent of how they were retrieved. Based on these relevant images in the pool, we computed the precision and recall. The recall is 100% if all relevant images are retrieved in the pool. The average number of relevant images in the pool is 15.2.

### 6.2.1 Evaluation of Text Evidence in Web Pages

Similar to T.A.S. Coelho [1], we performed a test to determine the best size for the passages surrounding the images first. We tested 10-term, 20-term, 30-term, 40-term, 50-term extracted from passages around the image as index terms. Differently, our prototype system is based on Chinese, and we use named entity recognition and dependency parsing. We considered 40 top images for our 40 test queries, and the average precision is showed in Table 2. The results showed that 30-term performed best. So we extracted 30 index terms in following tests.

**Table 2.** Average precision for distinct index terms

| 10 Terms | 20 Terms | 30 Terms | 40 Terms | 50 Terms |
|----------|----------|----------|----------|----------|
| 0.3245   | 0.3687   | 0.3812   | 0.3482   | 0.3039   |

Then, we do precision-recall test using different sources of evidence in text, following are four different combinations:

1. Description tag: terms in ALT attribute of IMG tag, filenames and between A tags.
2. Meta tag: terms in HTML TITLE and META tags.
3. Passage: 30 index terms around images
4. Description + Meta + Passage

The results in Fig. 2 indicate that the meta tags and description tags do not have as many informative terms as passages around the images. We observed that there were always not many useful words in meta tags. People prefer to name images using simple letters and leave the ALT attribute of IMG tags empty. We found that the passages around images were the major sources describing images, a slightly different from T.A.S. Coelho [1]. The reason for this maybe lies in the difference between Chinese and English web image search engine.

### 6.2.2 Evaluation of Retrieval Effectiveness

In this section, we compute the precision-recall metrics to characterize the retrieval effectiveness of our system. Four ranking approaches are considered:

1. Consider both the web site type and PageRank of the prior probability.
2. Consider only the web site type of the prior probability.
3. Consider only the PageRank of the prior probability.
4. Not consider the prior probability, that is, $P(I_j)$ in equation 9 is always 1.

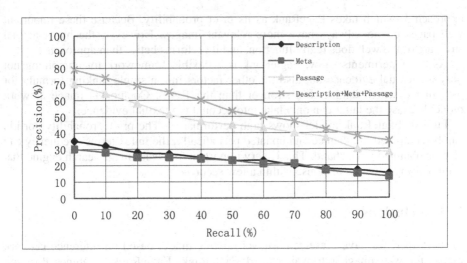

**Fig. 2.** Average precision-recall using four sources of evidence for 40 test queries

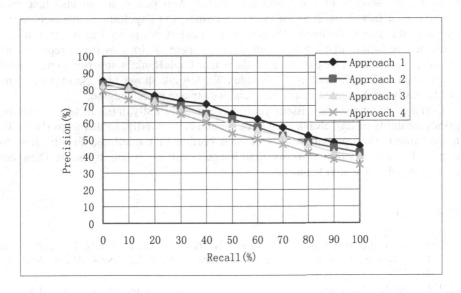

**Fig. 3.** Average precision-recall using our four ranking approach for 40 test queries

The precision-recall curves of the tests using four EagleRank approaches are showed in Fig. 3. We observed that approaches considering the web site type and PageRank did really improve the precision in certain recall level. That is, the prior probability portion in EagleRank model does really have benefits.

We now examine the results obtained using four different approaches. Approach 1 that considers both the PageRank and web site type have the best result. Approach considering only web site type presents a slightly better retrieval performance than approach 3, which takes PageRank as its prior probability. Because these important web pages do not always have more relevant images. However, the hyper-textual structure of the web does really function, and it performs better than approach 4.

As the experiments show, EagleRank is a flexible framework for combining not only the textual evidence but also the other factors into a single ranking formula for web image search engine. It's stronger than the T.A.S. Coelho [1] image network model because the latter can only take into account the textual evidence.

Further, EagleRank model shows high performance. The prior probability portion can be computed in advance and updated periodically, the index terms' frequency can also be obtained beforehand. This is very important to a web image search engine that should always give its response within a few seconds.

## 7  Conclusions

In this paper, we have presented a novel ranking model based on inference network model for web image retrieval, named EagleRank. EagleRank combines different sources to compute the rank according to a query. That is, it can combine information from distinct sources of text-based evidence in web pages; It can also take into account other factors, such as the type of websites, the PageRank of the web pages, and also the user's feedback; What's more, EagleRank is so flexible that it can combine any factors that we have not discussed here, as long as it can represent an image's importance. Our experiments show that EagleRank is superior to traditional model such as T.A.S. Coelho [1]. Besides, EagleRank shows high performance and can be easily implemented in a commercial web image search engine.

Certainly, there are a few issues yet to be resolved. Firstly, more factors impact the prior probability of EagleRank need to be found out. Secondly, further steps should be taken towards the optimal weights of each portion in EagleRank. Finally, how to extract the most descriptive words of an image is still a challenging work. These are all our on-going research focuses.

## References

[1] T.A.S. Coelho, P.P. Calado, L.V. Souza, B. Ribeiro-Neto, R. Muntz, Image Retrieval Using Multiple Evidence Ranking, IEEE Trans. KDE, Vol.16, No.4, APRIL 2004, pp. 408-417.

[2] D. Metzler, R. Manmatha, An Inference Network Approach to Image Retrieval, Proceedings LNCS 3115 Springer 2004, pp. 42-50.

[3] R. Baeza-Yates, B. Ribeiro-Neto, Modern Information Retrieval, China Machine Press, 2004.

[4] J.Broglio, J.P. Callan, W.B. Croft, D.W. Nachbar. Document Retrieval and Routing Using the INQUERY System, In D.K. Harman, editor, Overview of the TREC-3, pp.29-38, 1995.

[5] Y. Tsymbalenko, E.V. Munson. Using HTML Metadata to Find Relevant Image on the World Wide Web. Proc. Internet Computing 2001, Vol II, LasVegas, pp. 842-848. CSREA press, June 2001.

[6] S. Brin and L. Page, The Anatomy of a Large-Scale Hypertextual Web Search Engine. Proc. 7th WWW Conference, Elsevier Science, Amsterdam, 1998, pp. 107-117.

[7] M. Lei, J.Y. Wang, B.J. Chen, X.M. Li, Improved Relevance Ranking in WebGather, Journal of Computer Science and Technology, Vol.16, No.5, Sep 2001, pp.410-417.

[8] M.L. Kherfi, D. Ziou, A. Bernardi, Image Retrieval from the World Wide Web: Issues, Techniques, and Systems, ACM Computing Surveys, Vol. 36, No.1, Mar 2004, pp.25-67.

[9] Y.T. Zhuang, Y.H. Pan, F. Wu, Web-based Multimedia Information Analysis and Retrieval. TsingHua University Press, 2002.

[10] E. V.Munson, Y. Tsymbalenko, To search for Images on the Web, Look at the Text, Then Look at images, Proc. 1st Int'l workshop on web document analysis, Sept.2001.

[11] A. Ghoshal, P. Ircing, S. Khudanpur, Hidden Markov Models for Automatic Annotation and Content-Based Retrieval of Images and Video, Proc. 28th Int'l ACM SIGIR conf. on Research and development in IR, 2005, pp. 544-551.

[12] G. Carneiro, N. Vasconcelos, A Database Centric View of Semantic Image Annotation and Retrieval, Proc. 28th Int'l ACM SIGIR conf. on Research and development in IR, 2005, pp. 559-566.

[13] K. Stevenson, C. Leung, Comparative Evaluation of Web Image Search Engines For Multimedia Applications, IEEE Int'l Conf. on Multimedia and Expo, 2005.

[14] C. Frankel, M. Swain, and V. Athitsos, Webseer: An Image Search Engine for the World Wide Web, IEEE Conf. on CVPR, 1997.

[15] V. Rathi, A.K.Majumdar, Content based image search over the World Wide Web, Indian Conf. on Computer Vision, Graphics and Image Processing, 2002.

[16] R.Entlich, FAQ-Image search engine, http://www.rlg.org/preserv/diginews/ diginews5-6.html#faq.

[17] QBIC Home Page, http://wwwqbic.almaden.ibm.com.

[18] Y.T. Zhuang, Q. Li, R. W.H. Lau, Web-Based Image Retrieval: a Hybrid Approach, Proc. Computer Graphics Int'l 2001, pp. 62-69.

[19] C. Zhang, J.Y. Chai, R. Jin, User Term Feedback in Interactive Text-based Image Retrieval, Proc. SIGIR 2005, pp.51-58.

[20] J. Nivre, Dependency Grammar and Dependency Parsing, MSI report 05133, Växjö University: School of Mathematics and System Engineering.

[21] D.M. Bikel, R. Schwartz, R.M. Weischedel, An Algorithm that Learns What's in a Name, Machine Learning 34, 1999, pp.211-231.

[22] Y. Choi, E.M. Rasmussen, Searching for Images: The Analysis of Users' Queries for Image Retrieval in American History, Journal of the America Society for Information Science and Technology, Vol. 54, No.6, 2003, pp. 498–511.

# Color Image Enhancement
# Using the Laplacian Pyramid

Yeul-Min Baek[1], Hyoung-Joon Kim[1], Jin-Aeon Lee[2],
Sang-Guen Oh[2], and Whoi-Yul Kim[1]

[1] Division of Electrical and Computer Engineering, Hanyang University
Haengdang-dong, Seongdong-gu, Seoul, Korea 133-791
{ymbaek, khjoon}@vision.hanyang.ac.kr, wykim@hanyang.ac.kr
[2] Samsung Electronics,
Giheung-eup, Yongin-si, Gyeonggi-do, Korea 449-712
{jalee, stephen.oh}@samsung.com

**Abstract.** we present a color image enhancement method. The proposed method enhances the brightness and contrast of an input image using the low pass and band pass images in Laplacian pyramid, respectively. For color images, our method enhances the color tone by increasing the saturation adpatively according to the intensity of an input image. The major parameters required in our method are automatically set by the human preference data, therefore, the proposed method runs fully automatically without user interaction. Moreover, due to the simplicity and efficiency of the proposed method, a real time implementation and the enhanced results of the image quality was validated through the experiments on various images and video sequences.

## 1 Introduction

Due to wide use of various multimedia devices such as digital cameras, DMB players, and portable multimedia players recently, the need for techniques to enhance images has been increasing recently. The popular enhancement methods are based on histogram equalization (HE) [1][2], Multi Scale Retinex with Color Restoration (MSRCR) [3], and unsharp masking [4][5], to name a few.

The HE method that makes an image with uniform distributions is widely used because of simplicity. However, it tends to make images unnatural and produces flickering effect in video sequences owing to stretching intensities excessively. To prevent these problems, the BUBO (HE with Bin Underflow and Bin Overflow) method is proposed [2]. The BUBO method uses the clipped histogram of an image and thus prevents excessive stretching. Even with the clipping histogram of the BUBO method, however, suffers from flickering effect when the scenes change gradually in a video sequence.

Since the MSRCR method enhances an image by removing the illumination component, the results of the MSRCR method are usually better than those from the HE method. However, the enhanced results are too sensitive to the parameters and

Y. Zhuang et al. (Eds.): PCM 2006, LNCS 4261, pp. 760–769, 2006.
© Springer-Verlag Berlin Heidelberg 2006

often look very unnatural. Besides, the computational complexity is too high to apply for video sequences.

In this paper, we propose a color image enhancement method. The proposed method enhances the global brightness with the low resolution image and the local contrast with the band-passed images in the Laplacian pyramid. For color images, the color restoration is additionally performed by increasing the saturation according to the intensity values of the input image. Especially, the major parameters required in the proposed method are automatically set using the human preference data.

## 2   Enhancement onto Decomposed Images

In the proposed method image is first decomposed into the Laplacian pyramids. Then steps for brightness, contrast and color enhancement are applied to the decomposed counter parts in the Laplacian pyramids in sequence.

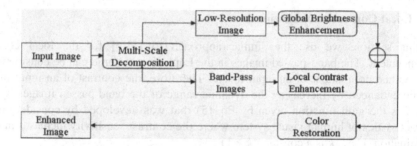

**Fig. 1.** Block diagram of the proposed method

### 2.1   Multi-scale Decomposition Using the Laplacian Pyramid

The proposed method consists of the global brightness enhancement and the local contrast enhancement for the intensity channel. Therefore, we must separate the brightness and contrast components from an input image.

The brightness component is generally characterized by slow spatial variations, while the contrast component tends to vary abruptly [10].Therefore, the brightness component has a low frequency while the contrast component tends to have a relatively high frequency. Using this idea, several similar methods adjust the brightness and contrast components using FFT, the Laplacian pyramid and FWT, etc.

In our method, the Laplacian pyramid is used for separating the brightness and contrast components from an input image. The Gaussian pyramid needed to build the Laplacian pyramid can be computed by Eq. (1). Then the Laplacian pyramid is computed by Eq. (2). In Eqs. (1) and (2), $n$ denotes the $n^{th}$ layer of the pyramid, $S \downarrow$ is a down-sampling operator, and $S \uparrow$ is a up-sampling operator, where $F$ is a Gaussian mask.

$$LP_{n+1} = S \downarrow (F * LP_n) \tag{1}$$

$$BP_n = LP_n - S \uparrow LP_{n+1} \tag{2}$$

## 2.2 Global Brightness Enhancement

The low resolution image of the top layer in the Laplacian pyramid means the brightness component of an input image. Therefore, the brightness of an input image can be enhanced by transforming the low resolution image as Eq. (3), which is a transform function as illustrated in Fig. 2(a). As the figure indicates, Eq. (3) makes the intensity values of dark region increased while the values in very bright region decreased. In Eq. (3), $a$ is a constant between 0 and 1.

$$LP_{Top}'(x, y) = -\left\{-0.2\ln\left(LP_{Top}(x, y)\right)\right\}^a + 1 \tag{3}$$

## 2.3 Local Contrast Enhancement

In this section, we use the similar approach to [5][6] for the local contrast enhancement. The band-passed images in the Laplacian pyramid can be considered as the contrast component of an input image. Therefore, the contrast of an input image can be enhanced by increasing the dynamic range of the band-passed images by Eq. (4). $G$ is the gain function given by Eq. (5) that was developed by considering the characteristics of human visual system where the contrast sensitivity increases in dark illumination. Here, $k$ is a constant ($k \geq 1$).

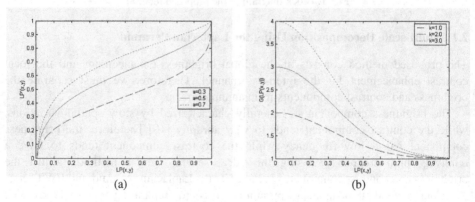

(a)                                          (b)

**Fig. 2.** (a) is the transform function for the global brightness enhancement and (b) is the gain function for the local contrast enhancement

$$BP_n' = G\left(S \uparrow LP_{n+1}(x, y)\right) \times BP_n \tag{4}$$

$$G(I) = k \exp\left(-I^2 / 0.2\right) + 1 \tag{5}$$

## 2.4  Color Restoration

As mentioned above, the global brightness and local contrast enhancements operate only on the intensity channel. For color images, the color restoration is additionally needed. Eq. (6) is the color restoration method widely used [6] . In Eq. (6), $C$ is the color channel value of R, G, and B. $I_{in}$ and $I_{out}$ denote the original and the enhanced intensity values. In [6], $s$ is a constant determined by experiments. Although Eq. (6) is widely used, colors restored by the equation tend to look unnatural because the fixed parameter $s$ increases the saturation of the low saturation region.

In our method, to prevent the problem, we set the parameter $s$ in accordance with the intensity value of an input image by Eq. (7). Then the determined parameter $s$ suppresses the saturation from increasing in the low saturation region, resulting in colors restored in more natural look. Fig. 3(c) shows that the proposed method prevents the colors being restored in the low saturation region look unnatural. In Eq. (7), $\alpha$ and $\beta$ are constants between 0 and 1.

$$C_{out} = \left( \frac{C_{in}}{I_{in}} \right)^{s} I_{out} \tag{6}$$

$$s = I_{in}^{\alpha} + \beta \tag{7}$$

(a)                                    (b)                                    (c)

**Fig. 3.** The effectiveness of parameter $s$: (a) original color image. (b) the result of color restoration with the fixed parameter $s = 1.2$, the blue color in the red circle indicates the restored color look unnatural in the low saturation region. (c) the result of the restored color with the proposed adaptive parameter $s$.

## 3  Automatic Parameter Setting

As our experimental results indicate, when the parameter $a$ is set to 0.5 in Eq. (3) and $k$ is 2.0 in Eq. (5), the proposed method shows good enhancement results in most test images. However, as the Fig. 4 indicates, the change of parameters is needed

(a)

(b)

**Fig. 4.** The effectiveness of parameters $a$ and $k$: the left column images are the origin images, the middle column images are the enhanced results of proposed method with the parameters $a = 0.3$, $k = 3.0$ and the right column images are the enhanced results of proposed method $a = 0.5$, $k = 2.0$

according to an input image for the best enhancement result. That is, the parameters $a$ and $k$ in Eq. (3) and (5) must be set automatically. This is essential for the proposed method to run fully automatically without user interaction.

### 3.1 The Brightness Measure

The parameter $a$ in Eq. (3) indicates the degree of the global brightness enhancement. That is, as the parameter $a$ gets closed to 1, the intensity of a dark region gets more stretched. Therefore, to set the optimal parameter $a$, we need a measure for the brightness of an input image. In this paper, we call this measure the brightness measure $m_a$ as defined in Eq. (8). As Eq. (8) indicates, we use the low resolution image in the Laplacian pyramid that corresponds to the brightness component. Note that $L$ is the number of intensity level in Eq. (8).

$$m_a = \frac{The\ number\ of\ pixels\ with\ LP_{Top}(x, y) < (L-1)/3}{The\ total\ number\ of\ pixels\ in\ LP_{Top}} \tag{8}$$

### 3.2 The Contrast Measure

The parameter $k$ in Eq. (5), determine the strength of the local contrast enhancement. That is, as the parameter $k$ increases, so does the strength of local contrast. Therefore, to set the optimal parameter $k$, we define a measure for the contrast of an input image or the contrast measure $m_k$. For that, we simply use the standard deviation of normalized intensity in the input image.

### 3.3  The Human Preference Data

We can infer the fact that $m_a$ is directly proportional to the parameter $a$, while $m_k$ is inversely proportional to the parameter $k$. Now, we must decide the parameter $a$ and $k$ in accordance with $m_a$ and $m_k$, respectively.

Since the goal of an image enhancement is to increase the perceptual visual quality, the optimal parameters must be set for the enhanced result that is visually pleasing most. Based upon this idea, we made the questionnaire form to find the optimal parameters according to our measures. The questionnaire form has 16 enhanced results of proposed method with different parameters ($a$ = 0.3, 0.4, 0.5, 0.6; $k$ = 1.0, 2.0, 3.0, 4.0) per each of 30 input images collected from various types of input devices such as camera phone or digital cameras. Then, we asked the participants to select the best enhanced resulting images per input image. The participants in this survey were 13 people consist of 4 women and 9 men, and we use the mean value of selected parameters as the human preference parameter. As obvious in the results shown in Fig. 5, $m_a$ is directly proportional to the human preference parameter $a$, while $m_k$ is inversely proportional to the human preference parameter $k$ as we expected. For the optimal parameters, we use a least squared line fitting method to the human preference data, resulting in Eq. (10) and (11) for the parameters $a$ and $k$, respectively.

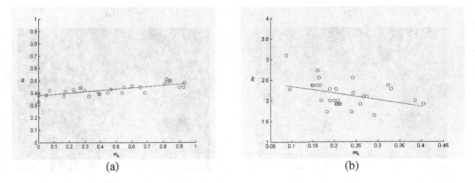

(a)                                    (b)

**Fig. 5.** The human preference data: (a) the human preference parameter $a$ corresponding to $m_a$. (b) the human preference parameter $k$ corresponding to $m_k$. The red line is the fitted line.

$$a = 0.1050m_a + 0.3777 \tag{10}$$

$$k = -1.6366m_k + 2.5079 \tag{11}$$

## 4  Experimental Result

To verify the enhancement performance, we compared our method with the histogram equalization and MSRCR method. The histogram equalization method is applied to the intensity component in HSI model for color images. When tested onto video sequences, the BUBO method instead of the MSRCR method is compared because the MSRCR method has too high computational complexity.

The results with some still images are shown in Figures 6, 7 and 8. Fig. 6(a) shows an image with locally bright and dark regions, Figures 6(b) and 6(c) show the enhanced result of HE and MSRCR, respectively. As the Fig. 6 indicates, the results of HE and MSRCR show the poor contrast in the bright face region of a baby. On the other hand, however, Fig. 6(d) shows the enhanced results of the image: the brightness and contrast look more natural in the dark background region. Moreover, it does not degrade the contrast in the bright face region of the baby.

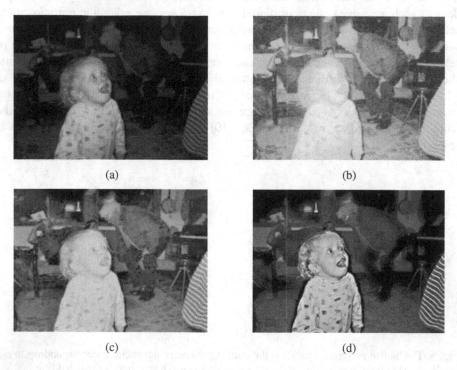

(a)                                              (b)

(c)                                              (d)

**Fig. 6.** Comparison of enhancement algorithms with an image - a small bright object with dark background in large area: (a) original color image. (b) the result of HE. (c) the result of MSRCR. (d) the result of the proposed method. In (d), the parameters $a$ and $k$ were set to 0.47 and 2.18 automatically by Eq. (10) and (11), respectively.

Fig. 7(a) shows the original image which is almost dark. The results of HE and MSRCR are shown in Fig. 7(b) and (c), respectively. Although the enhanced results of HE and MSRCR show better contrast, the result of the proposed method reveals the best performance among them as shown in Fig. 7(d). Also, Fig. 8(a) shows another example that is almost bright both in foreground and background. The result of HE shown in Fig. 8(b) shows the object of interest, the baby in this case, is too dark to be a memorable picture due to the excessive contrast, while the result of MSRCR is shown in Fig. 8(c) with very poor contrast. The result of proposed method shown in Fig. 8(d) shows a well balanced picture in terms of both brightness and contrast. In terms of color restoration, the results of proposed method show far better enhancement results than those of HE and MSRCR in all situations.

Fig. 9 shows the experimental results of a video sequence. In Fig. 9, the images in sequence are captured with every two frames interval while the video scene is changing gradually. As Fig. 9(d) shows, the proposed method does not produce any flickering effect in the video sequence. In addition, with a video (320×240) sequence in QVGA resolution, the processing time of the proposed method process takes 31*ms/frame* by a PC with 2.0GHz Pentium VI, regardless of automatic parameter setting. Therefore, the proposed method can be implemented for the real time processing.

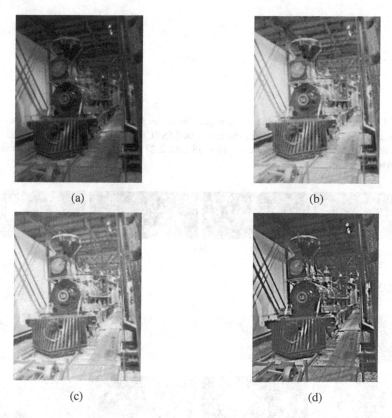

(a)  (b)

(c)  (d)

**Fig. 7.** Comparison of enhancement algorithms with an almost dark image: (a) original color image. (b) the result of HE. (c) the result of MSRCR. (d) the result of proposed method. In (d), the parameters $a$ and $k$ were set to 0.47 and 2.26 automatically by Eq. (10) and (11), respectively.

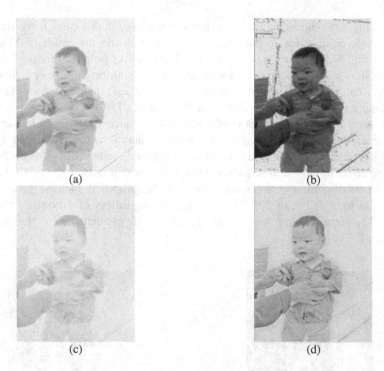

**Fig. 8.** Comparison of enhancement algorithms with an almost bright image: (a) the original color image. (b) the result of HE. (c) the result of MSRCR. (d) the result of proposed method. In (d), the parameters $a$ and $k$ were set to 0.38 and 2.27 automatically by Eq. (10) and (11), respectively.

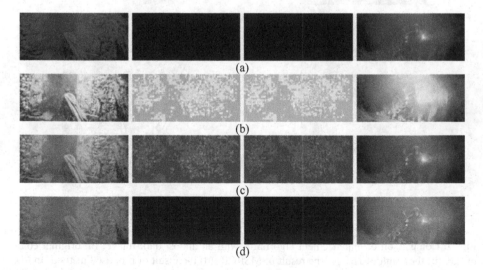

**Fig. 9.** Comparison of enhancement algorithms with the video sequence: (a) the original frames within the gradual cut (fade in/out). (b) the result HE. (c) the result of BUBO. (d) the result of proposed method does not show any flickering effect.

# 5  Conclusion

In this paper, we proposed a color image enhancement method. After the input image is decomposed using the Laplacian pyramid, the global brightness and the local contrast are enhanced using the low resolution image and the band-passed images of the pyramid, respectively. For a color image, the color restoration is also performed by increasing saturation in accordance with the intensity of the input image. Meanwhile, the major parameters required in our method were automatically set by the human preference data. That is, our method runs fully automatically without any user interaction. In the experimental results, our method showed better enhancing performance than conventional methods such as the histogram equalization and MSRCR method. In addition, our method enhances video sequences in real time without flickering effect.

# References

1. Forrest, A. K.: Colour Histogram Equalisation of Multichannel Images. IEE Proceedings on Vision, Image and Signal Processing, Vol. 152, No. 6 (2005) 677–686
2. Yang, S., Oh, J. H., Park, Y.: Contrast Enhancement using Histogram Equalization with Bin Underflow and Bin Overflow. International Conference on Image Processing, Vol. 1 (2003) 881–884
3. Rahman, Z., Jobson, D. J., Woodell, G. A.: A Multiscale Retinex for Color Rendition and Dynamic Range Compression. SPIE Applications of Digital Image Processing XIX, Vol. 2847 (1996) 183–191
4. Dippel, S., Stahl, M., Wiemker, R., Blaffert, T.: Multiscale Contrast Enhancement for Radiographies: Laplacian Pyramid versus Fast Wavelet Transform. IEEE Transaction on Medical Imaging, Vol. 21, No. 4 (2002) 343–353
5. Huang, K., Wang, Q., Wu, Z.: Color Image Enhancement and Evaluation Algorithm based on Human Visual System," IEEE International Conference on Acoustics, Speech, and Signal Processing, Vol. 3 (2004) 721–724
6. Pattanaik, S. N., Ferwerda, J. A., Fairchild, M. D., Greenberg, D. P.: A Multiscale Model of Adaptation and Spatial Vision for Realistic Image Display. ACM Special Interest Group on Computer Graphics and Interactive Techniques (1998) 287–298
7. Rahman, Z., Jobson, D. J., Woodell, G. A.: Retinex Processing for Automatic Image Enhancement. Journal of Electronic Imaging, Vol. 13, No. 1 (2004) 100–110
8. Tao, L., Tomkins, R., Asari, V. K.: An Illuminance-Reflectance Model for Nonlinear Enhancement of Color Images. Computer Vision and Pattern Recognition, Vol. 3 (2005) 159–159
9. Huber, P. J., Robust Statistics. Wiley, New York, (1981)
10. Gonzalez, R. C., Woods, R. E., Digital Image Processing, 2$^{nd}$ ed., Prentice Hall, (2002)

# 3D Mesh Construction from Depth Images with Occlusion

Jeung-Chul Park[1], Seung-Man Kim[2], and Kwan-Heng Lee[3]

[1] Computer Graphics Research Team, Electronics and Telecommunications Research Institute,
161 Gajeong-dong, Yuseong-gu, Daejeon, 305-700, Korea
jucpark@etri.re.kr
[2] CIS Gr., Digital Media Lab., LG Electronics Inc. Korea
sman2000@gmail.com
[3] Intelligent Design and Graphics lab., Gwangju Institute of Science and Technology (GIST),
1 Oryong-dong, Buk-gu, Gwangju, 500-712. Korea
khlee@gist.ac.kr

**Abstract.** The realistic broadcasting is a broadcasting service system using multi-modal immersive media to provide clients with realism that includes such things as photorealistic and 3D display, 3D sound, multi-view interaction and haptic interactions. In such a system, a client is able to see stereoscopic views, to hear stereo sound, and even to touch both the real actor and virtual objects using haptic devices. This paper presents a 3D mesh modeling considering self-occlusion from 2.5D depth video to provide broadcasting applications with multi-modal interactions. Depth video of a real object is generally captured by using a depth video camera from a single point of view such that it often includes self-occluded images. This paper presents a series of techniques that can construct a smooth and compact mesh model of an actor that contains self-occluded regions. Although our methods work only for an actor with a simple posture, it can be successfully applied to a studio environment where the body movement of the actor is relatively limited.

**Keywords:** occlusion, depth camera, Delaunay triangulation, depth video.

## 1 Introduction

As the need for realistic digital broadcasting is rapidly increasing, generation of 3D contents becomes more important than before. 2D stream media with the conventional video and audio-based contents still prevail in the broadcasting industry. But the end-users want to see realistic media contents, such as three-dimensional and multi-modal media. To realize more realistic multi-modal interactions, dynamic objects in the real scene should be modeled accurately using 3D meshes [1].

With the development of 3D depth sensors such as the ZCam[TM] depth camera [2], per-pixel depth information of a dynamic real object can be captured in real time. For example, for a flat black-and-white object that we capture by the depth camera, the white part shows a high depth value, while the black part shows a relatively low depth value although the white and black region are in the same plane. But the depth images usually contain quantization errors and optical noise, due to the reflectance properties and environmental lighting conditions.

Y. Zhuang et al. (Eds.): PCM 2006, LNCS 4261, pp. 770–778, 2006.

Depth image-based modeling method proposed by Kim [3] shows the construction of a 3D mesh model from the depth images. This method uses a series of techniques that successfully generates a smooth 3D mesh model from a raw depth image. This method, however, has restrictions in terms of providing multi-modal interactions since it did not take into account self-occluded regions of the actor.

In this paper, we present a 3D mesh modeling method which does take into account the self-occluded regions of a real actor in which the occluded arm can be modeled separately from the body of the actor. In our method, we first segment the foreground object and apply the median-filtering technique to reduce noise. Then, we separate the occluded region (e.g., arm) using a thresholding method in the original depth image. We adaptively sample feature points of two separated depth images which take into account depth variation using 1st gradient analysis, since depth variation greatly affects the quality of a reconstructed surface. We basically use three types of points for the reconstruction of the model: feature points from the previous step, points from the model silhouette contour and some uniformly sampled points from the inside of the model [3]. We additionally interpolate new feature points using contour points of a restored region for geometry restoration. The feature points using the Delaunay triangulation technique are triangulated. After triangulation, we merge separated objects. Since initial 3D meshes still contain local noises that produce jagged surfaces, we apply Gaussian smoothing to enhance the smoothness of the surface. Finally, we map the texture image onto the refined 3D meshes, where the texture image is taken from the color frame captured together with the corresponding depth image.

The self occlusion of the model is occurred by the motion of the actor. It is difficult to consider all different types of the occlusion occurred by the motion of the actor. This research is limited to the occlusion with the following assumptions:

1. Single self-occluded region.
2. Enough depth difference between an occluded region and the rest.
3. Excludes the occluded region which has a complex shape such a face with hair.

## 2 Depth Image Preprocessing and Separation of Occluded Region

### 2.1 Data Acquisition and Pre-processing

High quality depth and RGB image sequences are acquired using commercial broadcasting equipment, ZCam$^{TM}$ manufactured by 3DV Systems (Fig. 1).

**Fig. 1.** Depth and RGB image sequences acquired by ZCam$^{TM}$

This equipment generates depth images of objects using IR-sensor with 30fps. It enables us to generate 3D mesh of the model from the image since the each image contains depth information.

The raw depth image acquired from ZCam$^{TM}$ usually contains significant noise and artifacts. If we use feature points extracted directly from the original depth image, jagged triangular mesh will be generated as shown in Fig. 2(a). The median filter is applied for generating a smoother shape model shown in Fig. 2(b). Smoothing is performed to create smoother triangular mesh but also to extract good silhouette points for later use.

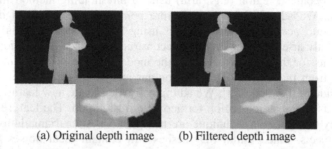

(a) Original depth image    (b) Filtered depth image

**Fig. 2.** Shape smoothing using median filter

## 2.2 Separation of Occluded Region

A thresholding method [4][9] is applied to separate an occluded region from the depth map enhanced by median filter. The center of gravity of a depth image for different depth level and its mean and standard deviation are utilized for searching the threshold value to identify the occluded region. Fig. 3 shows a series of depth images for different levels of depth value.

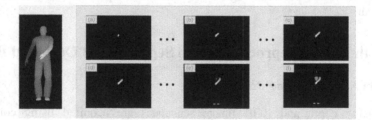

**Fig. 3.** Depth images for different levels of depth value

The center of gravity of the object in each image is calculated by the mean of the pixel coordinates of the object in each image. The threshold value is determined by observing the standard deviation of distance of all the pixels of the object contained in the depth images. The mean distance indicates the average distance between the center of gravity of the depth image and all the pixel values of the image. As we lower the depth level as shown in Fig. 3, more and more of the body region appears in the depth image starting from the occluded region which in this case is the arm.

A small variation of standard deviation occurs in depth images in which some pixels of the image are located closely as shown in Fig. 3(a) to (c). But a sudden change of standard variation occurs for a depth image in which some pixels of the image are located further apart as shown in Fig 3(d).

Fig. 4 shows the change standard deviation of depth images for decreasing depth levels. The standard deviation changes sharply at the threshold depth value of 152. The threshold depth value of 152 is the standard deviation of the depth image shown in Fig. 3(d) and it is determined as the threshold value of the entire depth image.

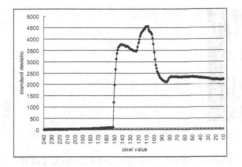

**Fig. 4.** Standard deviation of depth image for decreasing depth levels

Two depth images are then obtained by applying this threshold value. Fig. 5 (center) shows the depth image without occluded region, and Fig. 5 (right) shows the depth image of the occluded region.

**Fig. 5.** Depth image separated by threshold value

## 3  Texturing of 3D Mesh Model

### 3.1  Extraction of Feature Points

After the occluded region is separated, the point data for each depth image is used to generate 3D mesh. However, a point sampling process is required since each depth image consists of extremely heavy and dense points. Algorithms extracting feature points are needed, and this paper uses the method proposed by Kim [3].

Three main steps are needed to extract feature points as shown in Fig. 6. After the noise and artifacts of raw depth image are removed, an adaptive sampling process is performed to extract more data for the region with greater depth variation, as shown by Fig. 6(b). Next, a uniform sampling process is performed for the region that does not produce any feature points during adaptive sampling. It uniformly extracts data points that may otherwise leads to holes and overlarge triangles during the triangulation stage as shown in Fig. 6(c). Finally, silhouette points are extracted from the boundary of the model as shown in Fig. 6(d). The silhouette points play an important role in refining triangular mesh and restoring the occluded region. The silhouette points should be ordered for these operations, and the chain code algorithm is used for this purpose.

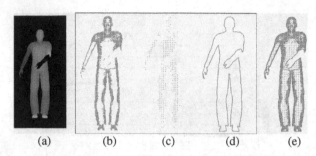

     (a)       (b)       (c)       (d)       (e)

**Fig. 6.** The process of feature point sampling: (a) Original depth image (b) Adaptively sampled points (c) Uniformly sampled points (d) Silhouette points (e) Integration of these points

Additional feature points are also needed to restore the occluded region, for example, the region of the body occluded by the arm. Since no point data exists for this region, we approximated the region using a linear interpolation scheme that takes into account the 3D boundary contour. Then the feature points for the occluded region are extracted from this approximated surface. Fig. 7 shows the process of restoring the occluded region.

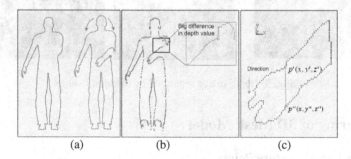

     (a)         (b)         (c)

**Fig. 7.** The restoration scheme using linear interpolation

When we search for two end points to restore the occluded region, different positions can be obtained by comparing the silhouette points extracted from an original depth image with the silhouette points with the occluded region removed as shown in Fig. 7(a). If we observe the silhouette points near the occluded region in 3D space, we can find a point that has a big difference in depth value as illustrated in Fig. 7(b). The lower point in Fig. 7(a) and the point in Fig. 7(b) with a smaller depth value are selected for restoring the occluded region using linear interpolation. Upon completion of interpolation, a 3D closed contour for the occluded region is obtained. Linear interpolation for filling inside the contour is needed to create point data, and it is performed by interpolating corresponding points in y-direction (Fig. 7(c)). The linear interpolation using only y-direction interpolation gives a good result for the body area that does not show big depth variation.

### 3.2   Generation of 2D Mesh

Delaunay triangulation is used to generate triangular mesh in a two-dimensional space. The Delaunay triangulation [5] was invented in 1934 by the Russian mathematician Boris Nikolaevich Delaunay. It provides the most efficient way to generate irregular triangular mesh from unorganized point data. Each point is connected by lines to its closest neighbors, in such a way that all line parts form triangles, and do not intersect and no triangles overlap. Fig. 8 shows the result of triangular mesh of an actor using Delaunay triangulation algorithm. The Delaunay triangulation basically generates triangular mesh for the convex hull shape so that it also generates some unnecessary triangles. Some web-like external triangles of the model should be removed for a precise shape. The external triangles which contain silhouette points can be easily removed.

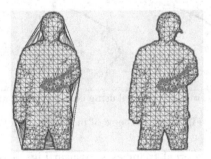

**Fig. 8.** 2D Delaunay triangulation

However, all the triangles with silhouette points are not external triangles as illustrated in Fig. 9(a). Internal triangles are maintained by distinguishing the inside and outside of the shape using the cross product of ordered silhouette points and two edges as described in Fig. 10(a).

When silhouette points are sampled for triangulation, it is possible to have some external triangles that are not removed as shown in Fig. 9(b). The constrained Delaunay triangulation is applied to solve this problem [6]. The silhouette line generated by silhouette points extracted from the depth image is given as a constraint.

Fig. 10(b) shows the process of generating irregular triangular mesh considering the constraint. When a new point is inserted, triangle A, B and C which have a circumscribed circle encompassing the point are searched. The triangle A and B are removed except the triangle C with a silhouette line, and then new triangles are formed between the new edges and the new point. The purpose of this method is to

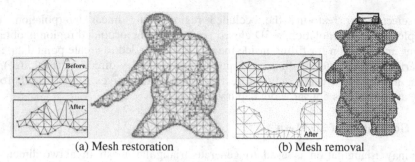

(a) Mesh restoration                                 (b) Mesh removal

**Fig. 9.** Mesh refinement

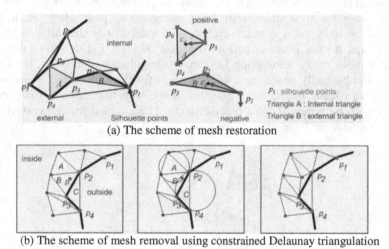

(a) The scheme of mesh restoration

(b) The scheme of mesh removal using constrained Delaunay triangulation

**Fig. 10.** The scheme of mesh refinement

prevent generating the external triangles shown in Fig. 9(b) which do not contain silhouette points.

### 3.3 Recovery of the Texture

The RGB frame obtained by ZCam$^{TM}$ is utilized for texture mapping. Since the coordinate of an object in RGB frame and the depth frame match, a normalized x- and y-coordinate in the image plane corresponds to texture coordinate of the object. The size of an image is 720 x 486. The normalized x-coordinate of the point of the object for texture mapping is calculated by dividing the coordinate value by 720, and in the same manner the normalized y-coordinate is obtained by dividing it by 486.

However, texture recovery of the occluded region needs special treatment since it has no texture information. The texture of the occluded region is recovered by applying the image completion algorithm for texture recovery given in [7][8]. The image completion method is composed of structure propagation and texture propagation. Fig. 11 shows the result of recovered texture using this algorithm.

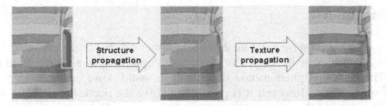

**Fig. 11.** Texture recovery of the occluded region

# 4 Results

Finally, 3D mesh is generated by projecting 2D mesh model to z-direction. Then the textured 3D mesh is generated by mapping an original texture image and the recovered texture image as shown by Fig. 12.

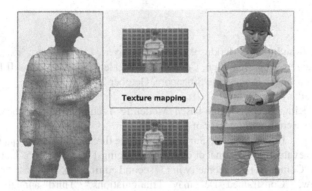

**Fig. 12.** Textured 3D mesh

We compared our results with the depth image-based modeling method proposed by Kim [3]. When we want to see the actor from a different angle in a 3D video, the processing of the occluded region becomes crucial in providing a natural view. While Kim's method (Fig. 13 left) show unnatural view of the actor for the occluded region, our proposed method shows a clean view.

**Fig. 13.** Comparison with Kim's method

# 5  Conclusion

In this paper, we propose a 3D mesh modeling method that considers occlusion. The modeling algorithm is developed to work with depth images acquired from a single view. The occlusion phenomenon is difficult to avoid if we capture a depth image from a single view. However, it is possible to solve the occlusion problem when we deal with model with a simple shape. The actor in a studio environment is modeled with textured mesh. The usability of the proposed system is verified by applying view and haptic interaction to experimental results.

**Acknowledgements.** This research was supported by RBRC at GIST under the ITRC support program supervised by the IITA (IITA-2005-C1090-0502-0022) and funded by the Ministry of Information and Communication in Korea and by ICRC at GIST funded by the Ministry of Science and Technology.

# References

1. Smolic, A., Mueller, K., Merkle, P., Rein, T., Eisert, P., Wiegand, T., "Free Viewpoint Video Extraction, Representation, Coding, and Rendering". ICIP 2004, IEEE International Conference on Image Processing, Singapore, October 24-27. (2004)
2. http://www.3dvsystems.com
3. Seung-man Kim, "Depth Image-based Modeling Techniques for Generating 3D Video Contents". Dissertation for doctor of philosophy
4. Mehmet Sezgin, Bulent Sankur, "Survey over image thresholding techniques and uantitative performance evaluation". Journal of electronic imaging 13(1), 146-165, January 2004
5. J. o'rourke, "Computational geometry in C" second edition, pp. 161-164.
6. L. P. Chew, "Constrained Delaunay Triangulations," Third annual symposium on Computational geometry, Waterloo, Ontario, Canada, pp.215 - 222, 1987.
7. A. Criminisi, P. Perez and K. Toyama, "Region filling and object removal by exemplar-based image inpainting", IEEE transactions on image processing, vol. 13, no. 9 sep 2004
8. Jian Sun, Lu Yuan, Jiaya Jia, Heung-Yeung Shum : Image completion with structure propagation, siggraph , 861-868, 2005
9. C. V. Jawahar, P. K. Biswas, and A. K. Ray, "Investigations on fuzzy thresholding based on fuzzy clustering," Pattern Recogn. 30(10), 1605-1613

# An Eigenbackground Subtraction Method Using Recursive Error Compensation

Zhifei Xu[1], Pengfei Shi[1], and Irene Yu-Hua Gu[2]

[1] Institute of Image Processing and Pattern Recognition
Shanghai Jiao Tong University, Shanghai 200240, P.R. China
zfxu@sjtu.edu.cn, pfshi@sjtu.edu.cn
[2] Department of Signals and Systems
Chalmers University of Technology, SE-412 96, Gothenburg, Sweden
irenegu@chalmers.se

**Abstract.** Eigenbackground subtraction is a commonly used method for moving object detection. The method uses the difference between an input image and the reconstructed background image for detecting foreground objects based on eigenvalue decomposition. In the method, foreground regions are represented in the reconstructed image using eigenbackground in the sense of least mean squared error minimisation. This results in errors that are spread over the entire reconstructed reference image. This will also result in degradation of quality of reconstructed background leading to inaccurate moving object detection. In order to compensate these regions, an efficient method is proposed by using recursive error compensation and an adaptively computed threshold. Experiments were conducted on a range of image sequences with variety of complexity. Performance were evaluated both qualitatively and quantitatively. Comparisons made with two existing methods have shown better approximations of the background images and more accurate detection of foreground objects have been achieved by the proposed method.

## 1 Introduction

Detection of foreground objects in video often requires robust techniques for background modeling. The basic idea of background modeling is to maintain an estimation of the background image which should represent the scene with no foreground objects and must be kept updated frame by frame so as to model both static and dynamic pixels in the background. Moving objects can then be detected by a simple subtraction and threshold procedure.

Recently, many background modeling methods for background subtraction have been proposed. Most background models are pixel-based and very little attention is given to region-based or frame-based methods. Typical models, among many others, include Kalman filters [1], Gaussians [2], mixture of Gaussians (MoG) [3, 4] and kernel density estimation [5]. Despite being capable of solving many background maintenance issues, pixel-based models are less efficient and effective in handling light switching and time-of-day problems [6]. Rather, frame-based background models may potentially handled such a problem more

Y. Zhuang et al. (Eds.): PCM 2006, LNCS 4261, pp. 779–787, 2006.

efficiently. Eigenbackground method proposed in [7] is one of such kind of models. However, this model lacks the mechanism of selective updating, hence foreground objects may be absorbed into the background model. In improve this, [8, 9, 10] proposed an incremental and robust subspace learning method. In the method, principal component analysis (PCA) is used to represent the foreground regions in the reconstructed background image. This may lead to errors that are spread over the entire reconstructed background image, resulting in quality degradation in the background image. As a result, background subtraction with such a reconstructed background image can lead to inaccurate and imprecise moving object detection.

Motivated by the above issues, we propose a recursive error compensation method in this paper. The method is designed to compensate the detected foreground objects, hence may result in a better reference background image leading to a more accurate foreground object detection. The proposed method is inspired by the idea in [11] where a recursive error compensation process is used to remove the glasses. However, in their method the location of glasses must be given in advance by another detection process. In the proposed method, this constraint is removed. Our experiments were conducted over a wide range of image sequences containing scenarios with different complexity, results have shown that a better approximation of the reconstructed background image is reconstructed and more accurate foreground object detection.

The rest of this paper is organized as follows. In Section 2, Eigenbackground learning based on PCA is briefly reviewed. In Section 3, the proposed background model using improved recursive error compensation is described. The experiments are described and some results on several different environments are shown in Section 4. Further, the performance of the proposed method is evaluated quantitatively, and compared with an existing method. Finally, conclusions are given in Section 5.

## 2    Eigenbackground

Background modeling based on eigenvalue decomposition was firstly proposed by Oliver et al [7]. By applying PCA on a training set of images, the background can be represented by the mean image and $p$ significant eigenbackgrounds. Once eigenbackgrounds are found, an input image is projected onto the eigenbackground space and an reference background image can be reconstructed. The foreground pixels can then be obtained by computing the difference between the input image and the reconstructed image. The method, consisting of a learning phase and a testing phase, can be summarized as below.

### 2.1    Learning Phase

Let the column scanned vectors of $n$ training images be $\gamma_1, \gamma_2, \gamma_3, \cdots, \gamma_n$ and the mean vector be $\varphi$. Each image differs from the mean background by $\psi_i = \gamma_i - \varphi$. Principal Component Analysis is then applied to this set of large vectors.

PCA seeks a set of $p$ orthonormal eigenvectors $\mu_k$ and eigenvalues $\lambda_k$ from the covariance matrix

$$\mathbf{C} = \frac{1}{n} \sum_{i=1}^{n} \psi_i \psi_i^T = \mathbf{A}\mathbf{A}^T, \qquad (1)$$

where the matrix $\mathbf{A}$ can be define as $\mathbf{A} = [\psi_1 \psi_2 \psi_3 \cdots \psi_n]$.

When the size of matrix $\mathbf{C}$ is large, the computation of eigenvectors and eigenvalues is intensive. The computation can be reduced by computing the orthonormal vectors of $\mathbf{C}^T$ [12].

Let $\mathbf{C}^T = \mathbf{A}^T\mathbf{A}$, and vectors $v_k$ and $\xi_k$ be the orthonormal vectors and eigenvalues of the covariance matrix $\mathbf{C}^T$, respectively. Then $\mu_k$ and $\lambda_k$ can be computed as follows

$$\mu_k = \frac{\mathbf{A}v_k}{\sqrt{\xi_k}}, \qquad \lambda_k = \xi_k. \qquad (2)$$

## 2.2 Testing Phase

Once the eigenbackground and the mean background are trained, the input image ($\gamma_i$) with foreground objects can be approximated by the mean background ($\varphi$) and weighted sum of the eigenbackgrounds $\mu_k$. Defining an Eigenbackground matrix as $\mathbf{\Delta} = [\mu_1, \mu_2, \mu_3, \cdots, \mu_p]$. it follows that the coordinate (weight) in eigenbackground space of input image $\gamma_i$ can be computed as follows

$$\mathbf{w} = (\gamma_i - \varphi)^T \mathbf{\Delta}. \qquad (3)$$

When $\mathbf{w}$ is back projected onto the image space, a reference background image is created:

$$\gamma_i^R = \mathbf{\Delta}\mathbf{w}^T + \varphi. \qquad (4)$$

Noting that since the eigenbackground matrix describes the general background appearances well however not the small moving objects, $\gamma_i^R$ does not contain small objects. By computing and thresholding the Euclidean distance (distance from the feature space DFFS [13]) between the input image and the reconstructed background image, one can detect the (small) moving objects in the scenes:

$$\mathbf{d}_i = \left|\gamma_i - \gamma_i^R\right| > \delta, \qquad (5)$$

where $\delta$ is a given threshold.

## 3   Recursive Error Compensated Eigenbackground

In this section, we describe the proposed method in details. Since the method in Section 2 only holds for small foreground objects, our aim is to find an improved effective method that is able to handle some general foreground objects of any size. Noting that the limitation of the traditional PCA in Section 2 is caused by seeking the best projections that approximate the original data under the least mean square sense. When the size of foreground objects is large, the eigenback-ground space may not well represent the foreground objects. This leads to errors which are spread over the entire reconstructed reference image. As a result, the degradation in the constructed background may lead to an inaccurate moving objects detection.

We extend the eigenbackground model by introducing a recursive error com-pensation procedure for reducing the degradation hence improving the detection accuracy. The main idea is to recursively compensate the input image by using a recursively reconstructed image through PCA. The detected object area is compensated by the mean background in the first iteration and the recursively reconstructed image in the later iterations.

In the method, the standard eigenbackground method in Section 2 is first employed to detect foreground objects. The detected foreground object areas are then recursively compensated. Instead of using a fixed threshold $\delta$, an online adaptive threshold $\delta$ is utilized according to the difference between the input image and the reconstructed image in order to achieve more robust detection of foreground objects,

$$\delta = \frac{\alpha \sum_{i=1}^{l} |\gamma_i - \gamma_i^R|}{l} \tag{6}$$

where $l$ is the size of the column scanned image vector, and $\alpha$ is an empirically determined number ($\alpha = 3.2$ was used in our tests).

After detecting the foreground objects, the corresponding foreground object areas of the input image or the reconstructed image can be replaced by the mean background image ($\varphi$), or the previously reconstructed background image ($\gamma^R$). This image is used to reconstruct a new background image that is "nearer" to the real background in the eigenbackground space. That is

$$\gamma_t^C = \begin{cases} d \cdot \varphi + (1-d) \cdot \gamma, & t = 1 \\ d \cdot \gamma_t^R + (1-d) \cdot \gamma, & t > 1 \end{cases} \tag{7}$$

where $t$ is the iteration number used for the recursive error compensation process, and $d$ indicates the detected pixel in foreground objects. $d(i) = 1$ implies that the input region $\gamma(i)$ is regarded as foreground objects, otherwise $d(i) = 0$ means that $\gamma(i)$ belongs to the background. The regions of the detected foreground objects are then compensated recursively by the mean background $\varphi$, or the previously reconstructed background $\gamma^R$.

The iteration stops when the difference between the two consecutive recon-structed background images is less than a given threshold $\varepsilon$,

$$\left\| \gamma_t^C - \gamma_{t-1}^C \right\| \le \varepsilon \tag{8}$$

Using such recursive PCA reconstruction and error compensation approach, one can observe a more accurately reconstructed background image without generating foreground object estimates. Fig. 1 and Fig. 2. show some images containing foreground objects that were detected using such a method. One can observe that a "ghost" appears in the background image. However, the background image reconstructed using recursive error compensation looks more natural (see Fig.1(e)), and higher detection accuracy is obtained. Fig. 2 shows three iterations of the foreground object detection procedure using the proposed method. The reconstructed foreground images do not change much after $2^{nd}$ iteration indicating that the recursive error compensation process converges very quickly.

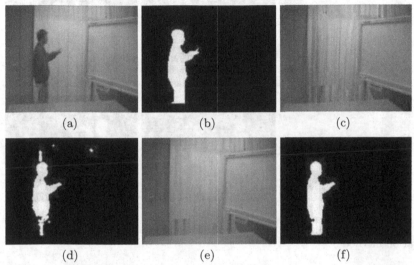

(a)                    (b)                    (c)

(d)                    (e)                    (f)

**Fig. 1.** Advantages of the recursive error compensated eigenbackground. (a) Input image with foreground object, (b) ground truth, (c) reconstructed background using PCA, (d) detected object using PCA, (e) recursive error compensated background, and (f) detected object using recursive error compensated background.

## 4   Experiment Results and Evaluation

Experiments were conducted for a range of image sequences with different complexity in order to test the effectiveness of the method. The performance of the method is then evaluated both qualitatively and quantitatively. To further evaluate the method, comparisons are made with some existing methods. Image sequences used performance evaluation and comparisons contained the sequences captured by ourselves as well as from [14]. For image sequences from provided by [14], ten test sequences together with the "ground truths" are used. Since our method lacks the bootstrapping ability, only five test sets are fit for our tests. They are: "meeting room with moving curtain (MR)", "campus with wavering tree branches" (CAM), "lobby in an office building with switching on/off lights" (LB), and "water surface" (WS) and "fountain" (FT). These five test sequences were used for our tests. During the tests, the first 200 frames of the sequences without foreground objects were used for the training process.

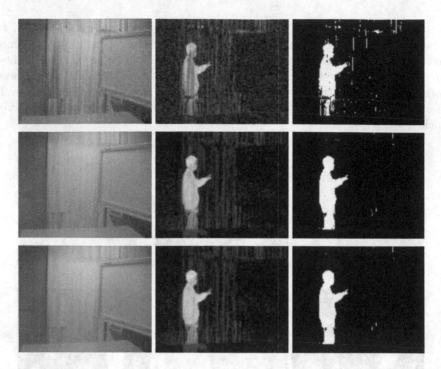

**Fig. 2.** Foreground objects detection process using the proposed recursive error compensation method

## 4.1 Qualitative Evaluation

When reconstructing the background images using the conventional eigenbackground model, a "ghost" areas could appear in the reconstructed background especially when the size of foreground objects is large. Degradation in the constructed background image may also occur leading to false or imprecise foreground object detection. However, the reconstructed images using the proposed recursive error compensated method look more natural, and more similar to the true background. Fig. 3 shows some experimental results on several different kind of image sequences. Each row (from left to right are original image), contains the reconstructed images using the conventional PCA, the image reconstructed images using the proposed method, the "ground truth", the detected objects from the conventional PCA, and the detected objects from the proposed recursive error compensation, respectively. All our experimental results have shown that more natural background images were reconstructed and better performance in object detection was achieved.

## 4.2 Quantitive Evaluation

To obtain a systematic evaluation of the proposed method, the performance was evaluated quantitatively on randomly selected frames taken from image

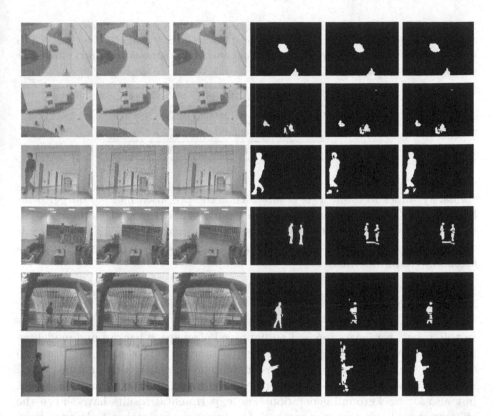

**Fig. 3.** Experimental results on home made image sequences and image sequences in [14]. From top to bottom are the frames from five examples captured from one crossing and second crossing in the campus of Shanghai Jiao Tong University, a corridor, a lobby environment, a fountain environment and a meeting room environment.

sequences in [14]. We used the similarity measure proposed in [14] for evaluating the results of foreground segmentation. Let $A$ be a detected region and $B$ be the corresponding "ground truth", then the similarity measure between the regions $A$ and $B$ is defined as

$$S(A, B) = \frac{A \cap B}{A \cup B}. \tag{9}$$

In the measure, $S(A, B)$ has a maximum value 1.0 if $A$ and $B$ are the same, 0 when the two regions are least similar. Further, $S(A, B)$ is a monotonically increasing function according to the similarity. It integrates the false positive and negative errors in one measure. One drawback of the measure is that it is a nonlinear measure. The similarity measure for the foreground masks detected by the proposed method is computed on all the five test sequences. The results by the proposed method are then compared with the results from the MoG method in [3] and conventional eigenbackground method [7]. Table 1 includes the similarity values measured from these 3 different methods. By comparing the

**Table 1.** Quantitative evaluation and comparison result from the test sequences. The sequences are Meeting Room, Lobby, Campus, Fountain and Water Surface from left to right. EB represents eigenbackground method and MoG represents method of mixture of Gaussians.

|          | MR    | LB    | CAM   | FT    | WS    | Average |
|----------|-------|-------|-------|-------|-------|---------|
| Proposed | 0.769 | 0.675 | 0.460 | 0.496 | 0.793 | 0.679   |
| EB       | 0.652 | 0.667 | 0.455 | 0.493 | 0.775 | 0.608   |
| MoG      | 0.445 | 0.421 | 0.480 | 0.663 | 0.536 | 0.509   |

similarity values in Table 1, it is shown that the proposed method outperforms both the MoG method and the conventional eigenbackground method. It also showed that similarity value has increased by approximately 7.1% as the result of introducing the recursive error compensation procedure to the convectional eigenbackground method.

## 5   Conclusions

In this paper, we have proposed an improved eigenspace background model using a recursive error compensation that is more accurate than the standard eigenbackground method. The reconstructed background is more natural which means that our method not only can be used for foreground object detection, but also for background generation. The experimental results have shown the effectiveness of the proposed method. Quantitative evaluation and comparison with 2 existing methods have shown that the proposed method has provided an improved performance for foreground object detection in complex background.

## Acknowledgment

This work is partly supported by the ASIAN-Swedish research links program from Swedish International Development Co-operation Agency (SIDA) under the grant number 348-2005-6095.

## References

[1] Koller, D., Weber, J., Huang, T., Malik, J., Ogasawara, G., Rao, B., Russell, S.: Towards robust automatic traffic scene analysis in real-time. In: Proceedings of the International Conference on Pattern Recognition, Israel (1994) 126–131
[2] Wren, C.R., Azarbayejani, A., Darrell, T., Pentland, A.P.: Pfinder: Real-time tracking of the human body. IEEE Transactions on Pattern Analysis and Machine Intelligence 19(7) (1997) 780–785
[3] Stauffer, C., Grimson, W.E.L.: Learning patterns of activity using real-time tracking. IEEE Transactions on Pattern Analysis and Machine Intelligence 22(8) (2000) 747–757

[4] Lee, D.S.: Effective gaussian mixture learning for video background subtraction. IEEE Transactions on Pattern Analysis and Machine Intelligence **27**(5) (2005) 827–832

[5] Elgammal, A., Duraiswami, R., Harwood, D., Davis, L.S.: Background and foreground modeling using non-parametric kernel density estimation for visual surveillance. Proceedings of the IEEE **90**(7) (2002) 1151–1163

[6] Toyama, K., Krumm, J., Brumitt, B., Meyers, B.: Wallflower: Principles and practice of background maintenance. In: ICCV (1). (1999) 255–261

[7] Oliver, N.M., Rosario, B., Pentland, A.: A bayesian computer vision system for modeling human interactions. IEEE Transactions on Pattern Analysis and Machine Intelligence **22**(8) (2000) 831–843

[8] Li, Y.: On incremental and robust subspace learning. Pattern Recognition **37** (2004) 1509–1518

[9] Skočaj, D., Bischof, H., Leonardis, A.: A robust PCA algorithm for building representations from panoramic images. In: ECCV 2002. Volume IV. (2002) 761–775

[10] Skocaj, D., Leonardis, A.: Weighted and robust incremental method for subspace learning. In: ICCV 2003. (2003) 1494–1501

[11] Park, J.S., Oh, Y.H., Ahn, S.C., Lee, S.W.: Glasses removal from facial image using recursive error compensation. IEEE Transactions on Pattern Analysis and Machine Intelligence **27**(5) (2005) 805–811

[12] Turk, M., Pentland, A.: Eigenfaces for recognition. Journal of Cognitive Neuroscience **3**(1) (1991) 71–86

[13] Moghaddam, B., Pentland, A.: Probabilistic visual learning for object detection. In: International Conference on Computer Vision (ICCV'95). (1995) 786–793

[14] Li, L., Huang, W., Gu, I.Y.H., Tian, Q.: Statistical modeling of complex backgrounds for foreground object detection. IEEE Transactions on Image Processing **13**(11) (2004) 1459–1472

# Attention Information Based Spatial Adaptation Framework for Browsing Videos Via Mobile Devices

Yi Wang[1], Houqiang Li[1], Zhengkai Liu[1], and Chang Wen Chen[2]

[1] Dept. of EEIS, Univ. of Sci. and Tech. of China, Hefei, 230027, P.R. China
[2] Wireless Center of Excellence Dept. of ECE, Florida Institute of Technology Melbourne, FL 32901 USA

`wy1979@mail.ustc.edu.cn`, {`lihq`, `Zhengkai`}`@ustc.edu.cn`,
`cchen@fit.edu`

**Abstract.** The limited display size of the mobile devices has been imposing significant barriers for mobile device users to enjoy browsing high-resolution videos. In this paper, we present a novel video adaptation scheme based on attention area detection for users to enrich browsing experience on mobile devices. During video compression, the attention information which refers to as attention objects in frames will be detected and embedded into bitstreams using the supplement enhanced information (SEI) tool. In this research, we design a special SEI structure for embedding the attention information. Furthermore, we also develop a scheme to adjust adaptive quantization parameters in order to improve the quality on encoding the attention areas. When the high-resolution bitstream is transmitted to mobile users, a fast transcoding algorithm we developed earlier will be applied to generate a new bitstream for attention areas in frames. The new low-resolution bitstream containing mostly attention information, instead of the high-resolution one, will be sent to users for display on the mobile devices. Experimental results show that the proposed spatial adaptation scheme is able to improve both subjective and objective video qualities.

**Keywords:** Video adaptation, attention model, video browsing, transcoding, SEI.

## 1 Introduction

Recent advances in mobile devices and wireless networks have enabled a new array of applications in image and video over wireless networks beyond traditional applications in voice and text. Real time multimedia applications, such as video streaming, have become feasible in the wireless environment, especially with the emergency of 3G network. In a video streaming system, a video server pre-stores encoded video streams and transmits them to clients for decoding and playback. In wired networks, those pre-stored videos may be encoded at high bitrate and high resolution (HR) to guarantee users' browsing experiences. However, it is difficult to directly use those videos in wireless video streaming because of lower bandwidth of wireless networks. Another critical constraint is the limited display size of mobile

Y. Zhuang et al. (Eds.): PCM 2006, LNCS 4261, pp. 788–797, 2006.

devices. This constraint often hinders the users to fully enjoy the video scene. It remains a critical factor affecting the browsing experiences even though the network bandwidth and computation power of the mobile devices have been greatly improved recently. It is very much desired for mobile users to access videos with current display size but with an enhanced viewing experience.

Video adaptation [1] is an emerging research field that offers a rich set of techniques to handle all kinds of adaptation problems. Previous adaptation solution to such problem is through spatial transcoding [2][3]. Through simply downsizing HR videos into low resolution (LR) ones by a factor of two or power of two, users may be able to browse video scenes with limited display size. The bitrates can also be reduced. However, considering perceptual results, excessive resolution reduction will cause significant loss in the perception of desired information. This is because the simple downsizing will result in unacceptable reduction of the region of interest (ROI) within the video frames. In our previous work [4], a ROI based transcoding scheme has been proposed to address this problem. The proposed transcoding can be placed on a gateway. When the video server transmits a HR video to the client, the system will first crop the attention area in each frame and assembles them into a new video sequence containing as much the desired information as possible. Then, it performs compression on the new sequence and generates a bitstream by a technique of fast mode decision which utilizes the motion and residue information included in the original bitstream. The size of attention area can be adaptively adjusted according to different display sizes of mobile devices.

In this research, we first design a special supplemental enhancement information (SEI) structure [5] for embedding the detected attention information into the encoded video bitstreams. With the SEI structure, the module of attention area detection can be applied in the process of video content production using the transcoding algorithm we have recently developed. The embedded attention information enables the transcoding system to complete bitstream generation without additional processing. This will greatly facilitates the implementation of real-time adaptation process for mobile devices. Furthermore, based on the pre-detected attention information, we develop an approach to improve both coding performance and visual quality by adjusting bit allocation strategy for attention and non-attention areas within a video frame.

The rest of this paper is organized as follows. Section 2 presents the reviews of the spatial adaptation based on ROI transcoding we have recently developed. Section 3 introduces the proposed SEI structure for attention information and the algorithm of adaptive quantization parameter (QP) adjustment. Section 4 describes several experiments to demonstrate that the proposed algorithm is indeed able to improve the video browsing experience of mobile users. Section 5 concludes this paper with a summary.

## 2  Spatial Adaptation System Based on ROI Transcoding

In our previous work [4], we have developed a spatial adaptation system based on ROI transcoding. We assume that a video server pre-stores high quality videos and serves various terminals, including PCs, smart phone, PDA etc. When a mobile user client requests for a service, the server sends a video to the client. We assume that this system is placed on a server or a proxy and will adapt the HR video to generate a LR video suitable for the display size and the bandwidth of the user's mobile device. The adaptation will improve the user's perceptual experiences by appropriately transcoding the HR video to generate LR video. For different users, the modification for the video resolution can be different and will be decided by the real display sizes of mobile devices. The system consists of three main modules: *decoder, attention area extractor* and *transcoder*. The module of decoder is to decode the HR bitstream. Decoded information will be transmitted to the module of attention area extractor and transcoder. The module of attention area detector includes several sub-modules: motion, face, text and saliency detectors to extract attention objects and the combiner to output smooth attention areas for the following transcoder. Based on the output areas, the last module, transcoder, will produce the LR bitstream. The transcoding module is composed of three sub-modules: mode decision, motion vectors adjustment and drifting error removal.

A visual attention model [6][7][8] is adopted to find the region that is usually attracting the users' attention in the decoded video frames. As shown in Definition 1, a set of information carriers – attention objects (*AOs*) are defined as:

$$Definition1 : \{AO_i\} = \{(SR_i, AV_i, MPS_i)\}, 1 \le i \le N \tag{1}$$

Each *AO* consists of three attributions: *SR*, *AV* and *MPS*. SR is referred as a spatial region corresponding to an *AO*. The attention value (*AV*) indicates the weight of each *AO* in contribution to the information contained in the image. Since the delivery of information is significantly dependent on the dimension of presentation, minimal perceptible size (*MPS*) is introduced as an approximate threshold to avoid excessively sub-sampling during the reduction of display size. Four types of attention objects are taken into account in our model: motion objects, face objects, text objects and saliency objects. Given detected user attention objects in one frame, the module attention area extractor decides the best region which contains most attention information and that is also suitable for the target devices.

In the transcoder module, a fast mode decision method is adopted. For each macroblock, the best mode and motions are decided by the motion and residue information in the original bitstream rather than by full motion search. So the encoding complexity is significantly reduced.

## 3   Attention-Information-Based Spatial Adaptation Framework

In the video adaptation system we developed earlier [4], four types of attention objects are defined in order to accurately detect the attention areas. For each frame, the detection of four types of attention objects will be performed separately, which is a heavy burden for either the server or the proxy. Moreover, the same detection process may be repeated for different users every time they request video services. This further increases the computational load.

As we know, the generation of videos stored in the video server is off-line and its computational complexity is not a great concern. On the other hand, the assumption that attention objects in each frame may not change even for different mobile users is reasonable. This is because the attention model we adopted is quite generic for a variety of users. Therefore, we can move the complexity loaded attention detection operation from the transcoding process to the encoding process. The attention information detected can be stored along with the bitstream for the video content.

Based on the above analysis, we propose a new spatial adaptation framework as shown in Fig. 1. During the process of video content production, the encoder also detects the attention information and then embeds such information into the video bitstreams. This way, we will be able to accomplish fast attention model based video adaptation for a variety of mobile device users.

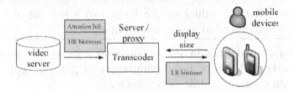

**Fig. 1.** A new spatial adaptation framework

## 3.1 SEI-Based Attention Information

The proposed video adaptation framework requires the generated bitstreams to contain attention information, while still conform to the video coding standard. Therefore, we adopt the tool of SEI to fulfill such requirements. SEI is a technique developed in H.264 Standard and assists in the processes related to decoding, display or other re-purpose of video signals. H.264 has defined some SEI messages for special purposes, such as spare picture, buffering period, picture timing etc. More details of SEI messages can be found in [5]. In this research, a new SEI message is designed to signal the attention information as shown in Fig. 2.

| attention_information( PayloadType, PayloadSize ) { | Descriptor |
|---|---|
| **attention_object_number** | ue(v) |
| if(attention_object_number > 0 ) { | |
| for( i = 0; i < attention_object_number; i++ { | |
| **attention_value** | ue(v) |
| **left_top_x** | ue(v) |
| **left_top_y** | ue(v) |
| **right_bottom_x_minus_left_top_x** | ue(v) |
| **right_bottom_y_minus_left_top_y** | ue(v) |
| } | |
| } | |
| } | |

**Fig. 2.** Proposed SEI structure for attention information

The SEI message we defined contains several items: *attention_object_number*, *attention_value*, *left_top_x*, *left_top_y*, *right_bottom_x_minus_left_top_x*, and *right_bottom_y_minus_left_top_y* for the desired attention information. They are all coded by ue(v) which is unsigned integer Exp-Golomb-coded syntax element. The meanings of these items are explained as follows:

> *attention_object_number*: the number of attention objects in a frame;
> *attention_value*: the attention value of an object;
> *left_top_x*,    *left_top_y*,    *right_bottom_x_minus_left_top_x*    and *right_bottom_y_minus_left_top_y*: the coordinates of each attention object. It should be noted that the values of the latter two terms are the differences between the left-top point and the right-bottom one.

With these parameters defined in SEI message, the transcoding module of the video adaptation can make full use of these parameters to generate appropriate LR and proper region of attention for mobile device users.

## 3.2 Adaptive QP Adjustment for Attention Areas

During the process of transcoding, reconstructed frames after decoding are regarded as the input video. The better the quality of the reconstructed frames, the higher coding performance the transcoder will achieve. In this research, the new video sequence generated by the transcoding and suitable for the target mobile device will consist of mostly attention areas in each frame. Therefore, if we can adjust the bit allocation strategy in the original encoding for attention and non-attention areas, we shall be able to improve the quality of transcoded videos. That is to say, if it is known to us that the majority of the clients are mobile device users, we can move some bits allocated for non-attention areas to attention areas when we encode the original video.

We expect that, at the same bit rate, the quality of attention areas will be improved if we apply the attention area-aware bit allocation strategy. Since the true display size of mobile devices is known only when the video server receives the request from the mobile users, the information is unavailable at the time of encoding original video. In this case, the attention area we extract in each frame will need to be the one that covers all attention objects in the whole frame rather than the one which is restricted by the true display size.

We have also carried out some preliminary bit allocation experiments in an attempt to uncover the relationship between the performance of bit allocation and motion characteristics of the video sequences. We found that excessively increasing the mount of bits allocated for attention areas will cause obvious coding performance loss especially when for the video sequences with low motion. For high-motion sequences, such loss is negligible since traditional coding of such sequences also allocates more bits to high motion areas within each frame. Based on the results of these experiments, we propose a frame-level adaptive QP adjusting approach according to the motion characteristics of a given frame.

When encoding for possible mobile device browsing, the encoder searches optimal motion vectors for each macroblock in frames during motion estimation. Motion vectors will indicate the displacement of one macroblock relative to the reference frame. The more complicated motion the frame has, the greater the values of motion vectors are. Therefore, we can measure the motion characterics of a frame by its motion intensity defined as follows:

$$I = \frac{1}{MN} \sum_{j=0}^{M-1} \sum_{i=0}^{N-1} \sqrt{(mvx_{j,i})^2 + (mvy_{j,i})^2} ,$$  (2)

where $M$ and $N$ are the height and width of a frame, $mvx_{i,j}$ and $mvy_{i,j}$ are two components of the motion vector for the pixel (i, j). Here, we assume pixel (i, j) has the same motion vector as the macroblock to which it belongs. A frame can be classified into three types, *High, Medium, Low*, by its motion intensity $I$. However, since motion information is unavailable before encoding; we may adopt the motion intensity of previous frame to predict the type of current frame,

$$Type_i = \begin{cases} High & I_{i-1} > T_h \\ Medium & T_l < I_{i-1} < T_h \\ Low & I_{i-1} < T_l \end{cases} ,$$  (3)

where $T_h$ and $T_l$ are two thresholds. It is known in the video coding community that, for a frame, the rate-distortion optimization (RDO) adopted by H.264 will affect the motion intensity when the video is coded at different bitrates. Therefore, $T_h$ and $T_l$ may vary with different bitrate. Because all videos are encoded at high bitrate in our application scenario, we can train the two thresholds using small QP (such as 20). Extensive experiments based on many various training sequences lead to the conclusion that we may set the two parameters: $T_h = 10$ and $T_l = 3$.

Given any type of video frame, the encoding QP for attention areas will be adjusted by:

$$QP_{attention} = \begin{cases} QP - 3 & Type = High \\ QP - 2 & Type = Medium \\ QP - 1 & Type = Low \end{cases} .$$  (4)

where QP is the quantization parameter for non-attention areas.

### 3.3    Summary of the Proposed Algorithm

With proposed SEI structure and adaptive QP adjustment algorithm, the attention-based adaptation bitstream for a video sequence can be easily generated. In the process of encoding a given frame, the encoder firstly decides its motion type by the motion intensity of the previous frame. Then the QP value will be adjusted according to the type and applied to the encoding process of this frame. After the encoder finishes the encoding process, the information including the motion field, the residue, the original frame etc. will be collected and imported into the module of attention area extractor [4]. Finally, the attention information output from the extractor is encapsulated by the proposed SEI structure and stored along with the bitstream of this frame that also conforms to the H.264 standard. When the bitstream of the sequence is sent to mobile users, the transcoder proposed in [4] will generate more suitable bitstreams for the clients by making full use of the attention information embedded in the bitstream.

# 4 Experimental Results

In this section, we present some experiments to evaluate the performance of our video adaptation framework. The system has been implemented based on the reference software of H.264, jm61e [9]. Four sequences, foreman, coastguard, football and table (CIF 90 frames, 30HZ), are selected as the test sequences. We apply the method we developed earlier to detect the attention information [4] during the encoding process. We then encapsulate the attention information with the proposed SEI structure and embedded into video bitstreams.

## 4.1 Overhead of Attention Information

Attention information may be seen as a type of metadata. We calculate the bits spent on attention information and show them in Table 1. Original bitrate refers to bits for motion and residue. As shown in Table 1, comparing with the amount of bits for motion and residue, the overhead of attention information is negligible.

**Table 1.** Overhead of Attention Information

| Sequences | Original Bitrate (kb/s) | Attention Information Bitrate(kb/s) |
|---|---|---|
| Foreman | 512 | 2.5 |
| Table | 1024 | 6.6 |
| Coastguard | 1034 | 3.1 |
| Football | 2048 | 11.4 |

## 4.2 Performance Comparison With and Without QP Adjustment

It is anticipated that the QP adjustment shall not degrade the encoding performance. Given the thresholds $T_h=10$ and $T_l=3$, the four sequences are encoded with several QPs. The encoding results of adaptive QP adjustment have been shown in Fig. 3, and compared with that of without QP adjustment, i.e. fix-QP encoding. For sequences of table and football, there are virtually no performance loss with our approach while for the sequences of foreman and coastguard, the performance loss has been consistently less than 0.2dB. The results prove that adaptive adjusting QP for attention area has little effect on the encoding performance.

## 4.3 Comparison of Transcoding Performance

We anticipate that the QP adjustment shall improve the transcoding performance since the attention areas are encoded with higher quality. We compare the proposed attention-information-based adaptation framework with QP adjustment against our previous framework without such adjustment. In this experiment, four sequences are firstly encoded at different bitrates: foreman 512k/s, coastguard 1024kb/s, table 1024kb/s and football 2048kb/s. For the proposed framework in this research, attention information is included in bitstreams and adaptive QP adjusting has been performed. We apply the same transcoding algorithm for both frameworks. Without loss of generality, we may set the target display size as QCIF. Then the original CIF bitstreams are transcoded into QCIF bitstreams containing attention areas at a variety of bitrates. As shown in Fig. 4, comparing with previous framework, the proposed framework in this research is able to obtain R-D performance improvement at all bitrates. Especially for the video sequence foreman at high bitrate, the gain can be up to 0.5dB.

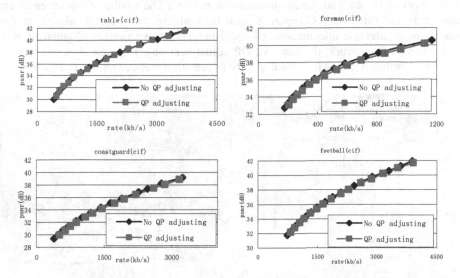

**Fig. 3.** Encoding performance comparison between with and without QP adjusting

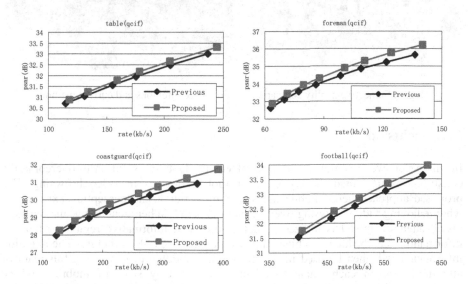

**Fig. 4.** Transcoding performance comparison between with and without QP adjusting

### 4.4  Visual Quality Comparison

We expected that the visual quality of the video adaptation will also be improved. Fig. 5 gives an example of visual quality comparison. The first line is the results of simple downsizing. By directly downsizing video sequences from CIF into QCIF, videos are adapted to the display size. However, the details in frames, for example, the boat and the man, are too small to be recognized. The second line is the results of our previous framework in [4] with adaptation to attention regions. The results of this research are shown in the third line. Comparing with downsizing method, our algorithm can supply more attention information and better perceptive experiences. Comparing with our previous framework, the adaptive QP adjustment based on attention information is able to further improve the visual quality of attention areas as shown in Fig. 5.

**Fig. 5.** Subjective quality comparison of downsize, previous and current method

## 5  Conclusion

In this paper, we have developed a novel video adaptation solution to overcome the constraint from limited display sizes of mobile devices in video browsing. The proposed approach helps mobile users to gain better visual perception experiences when enjoying video browsing over wireless channel. When generating bitstreams, a visual attention model is utilized to detect the most informative regions. Attention information is embedded into bitstreams by the proposed SEI structure. The attention information will then be used in the transcoding module to generate a bitstream of attention areas in each frame to adapt to the display sizes of mobile devices. Furthermore, based on detected attention information, we also propose an adaptive QP adjustment method for attention areas. Experimental results have proven that both subjective and objective quality improvements have been noticeable comparing with the passive approach we have developed earlier. The improvements are significant when comparing with the simple downsizing method.

## Acknowledgments

This work is supported by NSFC under contract No. 60333020, Open Fund of MOE-Microsoft Key Laboratory of Multimedia Computing and Communication under contract No. 05071803, and Florida Institute of Technology Allen Henry Endowment Fund.

## References

1. S.-F. Chang and A. Vetro, "Video adaptation: Concepts, technologies, and open issues", *Proc. IEEE*, vol. 93, no. 1, pp. 148-158, Jan. 2005.
2. J. Xin, C.–W. Lin, and M.–T. Sun, "Digital Video Transcoding", Proceedings of the IEEE, Vol. 93, No. 1, Jan 2005.
3. A. Vetro, C. Christopoulos, H. Sun, "An overview of video transcoding architectures and techniques," IEEE Signal Processing Magazine, Vol.20, No.2, p18-29, Mar. 2003.
4. Y. Wang, H. Q. Li, X. Fan and C. W. Chen, "An attention based spatial adaptation scheme for H.264 videos over mobiles," *IJPRAI special issue on Intelligent Mobile and Embedded Systems*, Vol. 20, No. 4, p565-584, 2006.
5. "Draft ITU-T recommendation and final draft international standard of joint video specification (ITU-T Rec. H.264/ISO/IEC 14496-10 AVC," in Joint Video Team (JVT) of ISO/IEC MPEG and ITU-T VCEG, JVT-GO50, 2003.
6. L.Q. Chen, X. Xie, X. Fan, W.Y. Ma, H.J. Zhang, and H.Q. Zhou, "A visual attention model for adapting images on small displays", ACM Multimedia Systems Journal, Springer-Verlag, Vol.9, No.4, pp. 353-364, 2003.
7. X. Fan, X. Xie, H.-Q. Zhou and W.-Y. Ma, "Looking into Video Frames on Small Displays," Proceedings of the eleventh ACM international conference on Multimedia, pp. 247-250, Berkeley, CA, USA, Nov. 2003.
8. Y.-F. Ma and H.-J. Zhang, "Contrast-Based Image Attention Analysis by Using Fuzzy Growing," Proceedings of the eleventh ACM international conference on Multimedia, pp. 374-381, Berkeley, CA, USA, Nov. 2003.
9. "JVT reference software official version," Image *Processing Homepage*, http://bs.hhi.de/~suehring/tml/.

# Style Strokes Extraction Based on Color and Shape Information

Jianming Liu[1], Dongming Lu[1,2], Xiqun Lu[1], and Xifan Shi[1]

[1] College of Computer Science and Technology, Zhejiang University
[2] State Key Lab. of CAD and CG, Zhejiang University
310027, Hangzhou, Zhejiang, China
stoneliu1981@gmail.com, ldm@zju.edu.cn, xqlu@zju.edu.cn

**Abstract.** Taking Dunhuang MoGao Frescoes as research background, a new algorithm to extract style strokes from fresco images is proposed. All the pixels in a fresco image are classified into either the stroke objects or the non-stroke objects, and the strokes extraction problem is defined as the process of selecting pixels that forms stroke objects from a given image. The algorithm first detects most likely ROIs (Region-Of-Interest) from the image using stroke color and shape information, and produces a stroke color similarity map and a stroke shape constraint map. Then these two maps are fused to extract style strokes. Experimental results have demonstrated its validity in extracting style strokes under certain variations. This research has the potential to provide a computer aided tool for artists and restorers to imitate and restore time-honored paintings.

## 1 Introduction

DunHuang frescoes located in Gansu Province are the invaluable civilization legacies of the world. Unfortunately these invaluable frescoes have been severely damaged by both human and nature factors through thousands of years. One of the most important traditional preservation methods is to imitate those precious frescoes. The traditional manual imitation procedure involves laborious work of artists. Moreover, for this manual imitation, it is extremely inconvenient to undo a slip of the pen. Advanced image analysis techniques enable the computers to improve the efficiency of imitation work greatly. In [1], an interactive sketch generation method is presented. The algorithm first got the contour of a fresco image which is composed of many connected curves, and then rendered the strokes by learning styles from examples. Since the most important of the fresco imitation is to make sure that the final imitated artwork is identical to the original one as far as possible, it's still time-consuming to get the whole style sketch only by rendering the strokes and very difficult to make the imitated strokes the same as the original strokes on the fresco. On the other hand, there are still a lot of visible style strokes on the fresco images and extracting these style strokes from a fresco image is very useful and challenging. In this paper, we propose a style strokes extraction algorithm from fresco images using the color and shape information.

Y. Zhuang et al. (Eds.): PCM 2006, LNCS 4261, pp. 798–807, 2006.

## 1.1 Major Challenges

Undergone thousands of years, the qualities of many frescoes have been degraded severely. In order to improve the image quality for the following processing, special image enhancement techniques, such as histogram equalization and contrast adjustment, are applied to some local regions of the input image during the preprocessing stage. Furthermore it should be pointed out that the sketches of frescoes are different from the edge maps of frescoes. For example, the eyebrow of the Buddha in a fresco is drawn by one stroke, but the general edge detection operators will detect two lines around the eyebrow: the upper line and the bottom line, and we call this phenomenon in the edge map as "**ShangGou lines**", as shown in fig.4.

To extract style strokes from a fresco image, we classify pixels of the fresco image into two classes: stroke objects and non-stroke objects. Then the style strokes extraction can be defined as the process of selecting which pixels of a given fresco image correspond to stroke object. Let $I$ be an image, $p$ be a pixel of the image $I$ and $x_p$ be value of the pixel $p$ in the color space $\zeta$, A style stroke detector $D(x_p)$ in $\zeta$ is defined as follow:

$$
D(x_p) = \begin{cases} 1 & if \quad p \in stroke \quad objects \\ 0 & if \quad p \notin stroke \quad objects \end{cases}
\tag{1}
$$

So the style strokes extraction problem is equal to find an optimal detector $D(x_p)$.

## 1.2 Related Work

The research is related to several technical fields including edge detection techniques, image enhancement techniques, stroke-based rendering techniques and classification techniques in computer vision.

Edge detection for an image significantly reduces the amount of data and filters out useless information, while preserving the important structural properties in an image. And the Canny edge detection algorithm [2] is known to many people as the optimal edge detector. However, in most cases, it extracts the contour of style strokes rather than strokes, because they usually have certain widths. An automatic human facial strokes generated system based on the learning samples is studied in [3]. There are also some papers [4, 5, 7] about artistic strokes rendering techniques. All these approaches are studied to create non-photorealistic imagery by placing discrete elements such as paint strokes or stipples to mimic different styles of paintings based on an input natural color image. However, the above algorithms cannot detect strokes of different styles from an input image. The skin color detection problem is very similar to our problem. A lot of research works [8][9][10] have been done. Most of mentioned approaches are based on the same pixel-wise processing paradigm, in which each image pixel is individually analyzed. In [11], context information is incorporated in the skin detection process by using neighborhood information. Following this idea, a style strokes extraction approach that uses color and shape information is presented in this article.

The rest of the paper is organized as follows: in Section 2 we will describe the style strokes detection algorithm for frescoes in detail. Section 3 shows some results, and compares with general edge detection algorithms. Finally, Section 4 concludes the paper and discusses our future works.

## 2  Style Strokes Extraction

Like the skin, the style strokes have their own special colors, mostly dark red or black. So we can utilize the color information to extract the remaining strokes. Since most of the frescoes are severely deteriorated by human and natural factors, the colors of some non-stroke objects become black too. As a result, it's very difficult to distinguish stroke objects from non-stroke objects only by color information.

Additionally, all strokes share some characteristic. For example, the path of a stroke is a smooth curve and the width is less than a threshold $W_T$. These shape constraints can be used to decide whether a pixel belongs to a stroke object or not. Both the shape information and the color information can be employed to detect the style strokes. The processing flow of the whole system is illustrated in Fig. 1. Since most of the frescoes are severely deteriorated by human and natural factors, the first step is to apply some enhancement techniques on some local regions of the input image to improve the region quality for the ensuing detection. Then color similarity map and shape constraint map are computed. In the color similarity map, a useful morphological filter known as the top-hat transformation [12] is used. A threshold operation is performed to identify the ROIs (Region-Of-Interest) potentially containing style strokes. In shape constraint map, the relationship between curves and points can be used to judge whether a pixel belongs to stroke objects or not. At last, these two maps are fused to get the detector $D(x)$. The fusion operation is as follows:

$$D(x) = D_c(x) \wedge D_s(x) \tag{2}$$

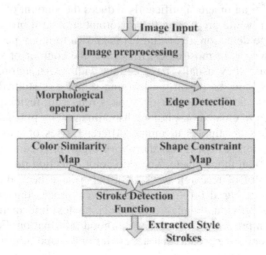

**Fig. 1.** Architecture of the System

where $D_c(x)$ is CSM (Color Similarity Map), and $D_s(x)$ is SCM (Shape Constraint Map). This system also provides some ancillary tools for interactive modification to improve the quality of the final digital sketch.

## 2.1 Color Similarity Map

In ancient time, the artists always used special color to draw strokes, mostly black or reddle. So the color information can be applied to extract the style strokes. Style strokes can be detected with the implementation of a very useful morphological filter known as the top-hat transformation developed by Meyer [12]. The closing top-hat operator is designed to detect dark details, which is defined as:

$$CTH_S^e = \varphi_S^e(A) - A \tag{3}$$

Where $\varphi_S^e(A)$ is the morphological closing operator. The top-hat operator can be tuned for the detection of specific features by modifying two important parameters:

- The type and the size of the structuring element. A square-shaped or disk-shaped structuring element may be used. The size of the element depends on the thickness of the stroke to be detected. In our experiments, we set the size to 5 pixels.
- The number of times in which erosion or dilation is performed.

After doing the closing top-hat operator, a threshold operator is required to segment the image to separate the stroke patterns from the background. To automatically obtain an optimal threshold that is adaptive to the image contents, the entropic thresholding method [13, 14] is used. Given a threshold $T$, the probability distributions for stroke pixels and non-stroke pixels can be defined as $p_s(i)$ and $p_n(i)$.

$$p_s(i) = \frac{f_i}{\sum_{h=T+1}^{M} f_h}, T < i \le M \tag{4}$$

$$p_n(i) = \frac{f_i}{\sum_{h=0}^{T} f_h}, 0 \le i \le T \tag{5}$$

Where $f_i$ indicates the number of pixels whose gray values are equal to $i$. The entropies for these two pixel classes are then given as:

$$H_s = -\sum_{i=T+1}^{M} p_s(i) \log p_s(i) \tag{6}$$

$$H_n = -\sum_{i=0}^{T} p_n(i) \log p_n(i) \tag{7}$$

The optimal threshold $\bar{T}$ has to satisfy the following criterion function:

$$H(\bar{T}) = \max_{T=0,1,2...,M} \{H_n(T) + H_s(T)\} \qquad (8)$$

The global optimal threshold $\bar{T}$ can be found in $O(n)$ time by calculating the re-normalized part repeatedly [14]. Figure 2 shows the results after doing the closing top-hat operator (middle) and threshold operator (right).

**Fig. 2.** The results after doing the closing top-hat operator and threshold operator

Then we use morphological erosion operator to remove isolated pixels, and dilation operator to fill the holes. Some isolated small pixel regions which are not stroke regions maybe still exist. We compute the perimeter $l_r$ of each region, and if $l_r$ is less than a threshold (In our experiment, it is 20 pixels and the result is quite satisfactory.), the region is removed.

The color information of style strokes can also be applied to remove noise. The color difference measure is used to distinguish noise from style strokes. Since Vector angle can distinguish colors of different hues regardless of their intensities, and Euclidean Distance can distinguish colors of different intensity very well. So a combination of them is defined as the new color difference measure via the following formula [6]:

$$D(\mathbf{c}_1, \mathbf{c}_2) = \alpha(1 - (\frac{c_1^T c_2}{\|c_1\| \cdot \|c_2\|})^2)^{1/2} + (1-\alpha)\|\mathbf{c}_1 - c_2\| \qquad (9)$$

where $\alpha$ is varying from patch to patch in the input image.

Finally, we get the most likely stroke regions or ROIs (Region-Of-Interest) from the fresco image and produce the color similarity map $D_c(x)$.

## 2.2 Shape Constraint Map

In order to extract as many edges as possible, we first apply the Canny algorithm to the luminance component of the input image. The right of Fig. 3 shows the final edge map detected by the Canny algorithm.

**Fig. 3.** An edge map by Canny

Unlike the general edge, the style stroke has a certain width, such as the eyebrows and the circles behind the Buddha. The ordinary edge detection operators will detect two lines around the stroke, and we call this phenomenon in the edge map as **"ShangGou lines"**, such as the eyebrows in Fig.3. The shape constraint map can be produced using the distance between the detected edge curves and pixels. Fig.4 shows the magnified part near the eyebrow of Fig.3.

We define the up line of the eyebrow in Fig.4 as $L_2$, and the bottom line of the eyebrow as $L_1$. From Fig.4 we can find that the pixel $P_1$ is on the eyebrow, and $P_2$, $P_3$ is away off the eyebrow. The largest distance between these two curves is defined as $W_{stroke}$. To judge whether a pixel belongs to stroke object or not, our approach consists of two steps:

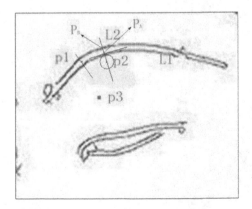

**Fig. 4.** The magnified edge of an eye

**Step 1.** To decide whether a pixel $p$ is located near the stroke or not: a circle is drawn centered on $p$, and the radius is set as $W_{stroke}/2$, as shown in Fig.4. If any part of stroke is located within this circle, then this point $p$ is located near the stroke; otherwise this point is far away from the stroke, and we do not consider this point anymore, such as the point $p_3$ in Fig. 4. If the point is positioned near the stroke, the coordinations of all the edge pixels located in the circle are kept in a list.

**Step 2.** To produce the shape constraint map $D_s(x)$: Since the edge pixels located in the circle have been recorded in a list in step 1, we can choose the edge pixel which is the nearest to the point $p$. In Fig. 4, the ray $\overline{p_2 p_A}$ intersects curve $L_2$ at $p_B$. Because $p_2$ is not within the line segment $\overline{p_A p_B}$, $p_2$ is off the stroke; otherwise $p_2$ is on the stroke, such as the point $p_1$ in Fig. 4. The stroke shape constraint map is produced as follows: for each pixel $p$, if $p$ is on the stroke, then $D_s(x_p)=1$, else $D_s(x_p)=0$.

## 3 Results

To show the performance of the proposed algorithm, we report a set of experiment results. All fresco images are captured through a high resolution digital camera in Dunhuang MoGao Cave and classified into three categories by quality of strokes: good, marginal, poor. The final digital sketch in Fig. 5 is extracted from a fresco image of good quality. Most of the style strokes are detected and form the Chinese line drawing, some manual operations had been done to improve the quality of final digital sketch. Fig. 6 and 7 show the style strokes detected from a marginal quality image. Only parts of strokes can be extracted. Since the style strokes in the poor quality

**Fig. 5.** The final digital sketch results

fresco images are almost invisible, very few style strokes are extracted. It's pointed out that the proposed algorithm is effective only if the style strokes of fresco images are visible.

The general edge detection algorithms only find the edge by taking the gradient of the input image and cannot extract the style strokes as a whole because the style strokes usually have certain widths. Since most of frescoes are degraded severely, it is impractical to extract all style strokes automatically. It is necessary to provide some interactive modification ancillary tools for artists to improve the final digital sketches. This system is applied in the digital imitation procedure for artists in the DunHuang Research Institute to preserve precious frescoes now.

**Fig. 6.** Another example of digital sketch by our algorithm

**Fig. 7.** Third example of digital sketch by our algorithm

# 4 Conclusions and Future Work

In this paper, we present a style strokes detection algorithm for frescoes based on color and shape information. Combining the shape and color information, the style strokes can be extracted more efficiently compared with the edge detection algorithms of state of the art. However, there are still some improvements to be explored. First, as a lot of the skin color detection techniques have been put forward, some of them can be used to extract style strokes of fresco images, such as statistical models for solving the skin/non-skin classification problem. Second, the extracted style strokes are pixel-based image and not scale-invariant, they need to be vectorized. For some parts of these frescoes have been stripped, we plan to restore the missing strokes or parts based on statistical example learning algorithms too. But what we need to do first is to analyze and classify the different styles of strokes appeared in the Dun-Huang frescoes.

**Acknowledgments.** The research was partially funded by National Basic Research Program of China (No.2002CB312106), National High-tech R&D Program (No. 2003AA119020) and Key Technologies R&D Program (No. 2004BA810B), The Program for New Century Excellent Talents in University (NCET-04-0535).

# References

1. Jianming Liu, Dongming Lu, Xifan Shi: Interactive Sketch Generation for Dunhuang Frescoes. LNCS 3942, First International Conference, Edutainment 2006: 943-946.
2. J. Canny, "A Computational Approach to Edge Detection," IEEE Trans. ON Pattern Analysis and Machine Intelligence, vol. 8, no. 6, pp. 679-698, Nov. 1986.
3. H. Chen, Y. Q. Xu, H. Y. Shum, S. C. Zhu, and N. N. Zheng. "Example-based facial sketch generation with non-parametric sampling," in Proc. Of ICCV01, vol.2, pp.433-438, 2001.
4. S. L. Su, Y. Q. Xu, H. Y. Shum and F. Chen, "Simulating artistic brushstrokes using interval splines," in Proc. Of the 5th IASTED International Conference on Computer Graphics and Imaging (CGIM'2002), pp.85-90, Kauai, Hawaii, Aug. 2002.
5. A. Hertzmann, "A survey of stroke-based rendering," IEEE Computer Graphics and Applications, vol.23, no.4, pp.70-81, July/Aug. 2003.
6. R. D. Dony and S. Wesolkowski, "Edge detection in RGB using jointly Euclidean distance and vector angle," in Proc. Vision Interface'99, Canada, 1999.
7. Der-Lor Way and Zen-Chung Shih, "The Synthesis of Rock Textures in Chinese Landscape Painting." EUROGRAPHICS, Vol.20, No.3, 2001.
8. Vezhnevets V., Sazonov V., Andreeva A., "A Survey on Pixel-Based Skin Color Detection Techniques". Proc. Graphicon-2003, pp. 85-92, Moscow, Russia, September 2003.
9. J. Brand and J. Mason, A Comparative Assessment of Three Approaches to Pixel-Level Human Skin Detection, Proc. IEEE Int'l Conf. Pattern Recognition, vol. 1, pp. 1056-1059, Sept. 2000.
10. Son Lam Phung, Abdesselam Bouzerdoum, Douglas Chai, "Skin Segmentation Using Color Pixel Classification: Analysis and Comparison," IEEE Transactions on Pattern Analysis and Machine Intelligence, vol. 27, no. 1, pp. 148-154, Jan., 2005.

11. Javier Ruiz-del-Solar, Rodrigo Verschae, "Skin Detection using Neighborhood Information," fgr, p. 463, Sixth IEEE International Conference on Automatic Face and Gesture Recognition, 2004.
12. F. Meyer, "Iterative image transformations for an automatic screening of cervical smears," J. Histoch. Cytochem, vol. 27, 1979.
13. T. Pun, "Entropic thresholding: A new approach" , Comput. Vision Graphics Image Process. 16, 210-239,1981.
14. J. Fan, DKY Yau, AK Elmagarmid, and WG Aref. "Automatic image segmentation by integrating color-edge extraction and seeded region growing". IEEETrans. Image Process, 10:1454--1466, 2001.

# Requantization Transcoding of H.264/AVC Bitstreams for Intra 4 × 4 Prediction Modes

Stijn Notebaert, Jan De Cock, Koen De Wolf, and Rik Van de Walle

Ghent University – IBBT
Department of Electronics and Information Systems – Multimedia Lab
Gaston Crommenlaan 8 bus 201, B-9050 Ledeberg-Ghent, Belgium
{stijn.notebaert, jan.decock, koen.dewolf, rik.vandewalle}@ugent.be
http://multimedialab.elis.ugent.be

**Abstract.** Efficient bitrate reduction of video content is necessary in order to satisfy the different constraints imposed by decoding devices and transmission networks. Requantization is a fast technique for bitrate reduction, and has been successfully applied for MPEG-2 bitstreams. Because of the newly introduced intra prediction in H.264/AVC, the existing techniques are rendered useless. In this paper we examine requantization transcoding of H.264/AVC bitstreams, focusing on the intra 4×4 prediction modes. Two architectures are proposed, one in the pixel domain and the other in the frequency domain, that compensate the drift introduced by the requantization of intra 4×4 predicted blocks. Experimental results show that these architectures perform approximately equally well as the full decode and recode architecture for low to medium bitrates. Because of the reduced computational complexity of these architectures, in particular the frequency-domain compensation architecture, they are highly suitable for real-time adaptation of video content.

**Keywords:** bitrate reduction, H.264/AVC, requantization, transcoding.

## 1 Introduction

More and more video content is coded using the state-of-the-art H.264/AVC video coding standard. This content has to be made available to a large number of devices with varying network characteristics and network connectivity. In order to meet the different constraints, elegant solutions are needed for fast adaptation of the video content to a lower bitrate. Architectures for bitrate adaptation have been discussed in the past, more specifically for MPEG-2 coded video content [1,2]. Requantization transcoding is a fast technique for bitrate reduction, and is able to approximate the quality of a full decoder-recoder with large reduction in computational complexity [3]. The problem of requantization of intra-coded frames in MPEG-2 has been examined in [4].

Due to the increased complexity of the encoding process and the newly introduced intra prediction in H.264/AVC, these results no longer apply as such. The augmented number of dependencies in the coded pictures no longer allow straightforward open-loop requantization.

Y. Zhuang et al. (Eds.): PCM 2006, LNCS 4261, pp. 808–817, 2006.

Since intra prediction in H.264/AVC is performed on 4×4 and 16×16 , a clear distinction has to be made between both. We have described requantization techniques for intra $16 \times 16$ prediction in [5], hence this discussion is omitted here. In this paper, we tackle the problem of requantization for the intra $4 \times 4$ prediction modes of H.264/AVC, and propose two architectures that compensate the errors due to drift propagation, resulting in highly improved visual quality of the transcoded stream.

The remainder of this paper is organized as follows. An overview of the relevant H.264/AVC coding tools is given in Sect. 2. In Sect. 3, we revisit the open-loop requantization architecture, applying it to H.264/AVC, and introduce two drift-compensating architectures. The results of the implementation of the transcoders are given in Sect. 4. Finally, conclusions are given in Sect. 5.

## 2    H.264/AVC Tools

### 2.1    Intra Prediction

Intra prediction is used to exploit the spatial redundancy between neighbouring pixels. A block is predicted using previously encoded and reconstructed pixels of surrounding blocks. In H.264/AVC, a macroblock can be predicted using a combination of nine $4 \times 4$ or one of four $16 \times 16$ intra prediction modes. The intra prediction, which was not present in, for example, MPEG-2 Video, results in an improved compression efficiency. However, it also introduces a number of dependencies. As we will see, this has an important impact on the perceptual quality of the transcoded video sequences. In this paper, we focus on the intra 4×4 prediction.

### 2.2    H.264/AVC Transform and Quantization

The integer transform in the H.264/AVC specification [6,7] is based on the Discrete Cosine Transform, and is applied on 4×4 blocks. The forward transform of a 4×4 block $X$ is represented by

$$Y = (C_F X C_F^T) \otimes E_F ,$$

where $C_F$ represents the kernel transformation matrix. $E_F$ is the post-scaling matrix. For efficiency reasons, the post-scaling operation of the transformation is postponed and integrated in the quantization process. After the core transformation $W_{ij} = (C_F X C_F^T)_{ij}$, with $i, j = 0, \ldots, 3$, the coefficients $W_{ij}$ are quantized. H.264/AVC provides 52 values for the Quantization Parameter (QP), which can vary on a macroblock basis. The values of QP were defined in such a way that, if QP is increased with a value of 6, the quantization step is doubled and the bitrate is approximately halved. This non-linear behaviour results in the possibility to target a broad range of bitrates. The forward quantization can be implemented as

$$|Z_{ij}| = (|W_{ij}| \cdot M_{ij} + f) \gg qbits$$

where $qbits = 15 + \lfloor QP/6 \rfloor$, and $f$ represents the dead zone control parameter [6]. The multiplication factor $M_{ij}$ is determined by $QP$ mod 6 and the position in the $4 \times 4$ block. At the decoder side, the process is defined as follows. The inverse quantization process is defined as

$$W'_{ij} = Z_{ij} \cdot V_{ij} \cdot 2^{\lfloor QP/6 \rfloor} .$$

The values of $M_{ij}$ and $V_{ij}$ result in the coefficients $W'_{ij}$ that exceed the pre-quantized values $W_{ij}$ by a factor $64 \cdot E_{F_{ij}} \cdot E_{I_{ij}}$, hence including the post-scaling of the forward transform along with the pre-scaling of the inverse transform:

$$X' = C_I^T (Y \otimes E_I) C_I .$$

The factor 64 is introduced to avoid rounding errors in the inverse transformation that follows. We refer to [6,7] for more information about the intertwined transformation and quantization.

## 3   Requantization Transcoder Architectures

### 3.1   Open-Loop Transcoder

The most straightforward method for requantization is the open-loop requantization transcoder, as shown in Fig. 1. This type of transcoder consists of a dequantization step $Q_1^{-1}$, followed by a requantization step $Q'_2$ with a coarser quantization parameter (QP).

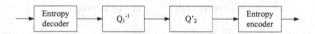

**Fig. 1.** Open-loop requantization transcoder

The implementation of this type of requantization transcoder was rather straightforward in MPEG-2 [4]. However, in H.264/AVC, special attention has to be paid to the requantization $Q'_2$. The multiplication factors have to be adapted in order to bring into account the scaling factors $E_{F_{ij}}$ and $E_{I_{ij}}$ of the H.264/AVC integer transform [5,8]. Since these scaling factors are already applied in the original quantization, they may not be repeated in the requantization. As a result, the multiplication factors for the integer transformation have to be downscaled by the factors 4, 2.56 and 3.2, depending on their position $(i, j)$ in the $4 \times 4$ block of coefficients. The downscaling factors arise from:

$$(M_{ij} \cdot V_{ij}) \gg 15 = 64 \cdot E_{F_{ij}} \cdot E_{I_{ij}} = \begin{cases} 4, & r = 0 \\ 2.56, & r = 1 \\ 3.2, & r = 2 \end{cases}$$

where the factor 64 is introduced to avoid rounding errors during the inverse transform[1], and

$$r = \begin{cases} 0, & (i,j) \in \{(0,0),(0,2),(2,0),(2,2)\} \\ 1, & (i,j) \in \{(1,1),(1,3),(3,1),(3,3)\} \\ 2, & \text{otherwise} \end{cases}$$

The quality loss due to open-loop requantization in MPEG-2 intra frames remains limited, and is caused only by requantization noise [3]. In H.264/AVC, due to the introduction of intra prediction, drift arises and accumulates the requantization differences throughout the pictures. As will be seen in Sect. 4, this results in unacceptable quality of the transcoded video.

## 3.2 Requantization Transcoder with Pixel-Domain Compensation (PDC)

In order to avoid drift, a full decoder-recoder (FDR) might be used. The resulting sequence will have the highest achievable quality, but clearly, this concatenation will be too time-consuming to be used in real-time adaptation engines. An important bottleneck consists in searching the optimal prediction mode. This is especially true for rate-distortion optimized mode search, which includes entropy coding of every examined prediction mode. An alternative is to re-use the coding mode decisions from the incoming bitstream. This eliminates the mode search, and gives a good approximation of the quality of the FDR architecture. For MPEG-2, this was described in [1]. The architecture for a requantization transcoder with mode re-use (MR) in H.264/AVC is shown in Fig. 2, where $\Im_p(.)$ denotes the pixel-domain intra prediction operator.

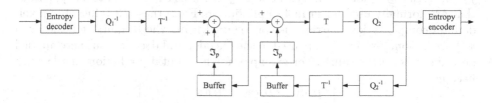

**Fig. 2.** Requantization transcoder with mode re-use

For low-delay applications, it is useful to further reduce the computational complexity of the transcoder. In this context, we here introduce a requantization transcoder with pixel-domain compensation. This architecture is shown in Fig. 3. When compared to the open-loop requantization transcoder, the PDC architecture restrains the drift of accumulated errors by compensating the dequantized 4×4 block of pixels in the pixel domain by a mode-dependent matrix $\phi$. The computational advantage of this architecture over the MR transcoder is that intra prediction has to be performed only once. Additionally, in the MR

---

[1] After the inverse transform, the residual values are downscaled by 64.

transcoder, one buffer has to be maintained at the decoder side, and one at the encoder side. The PDC architecture halves the required memory, and the corresponding memory allocation and load and store operations.

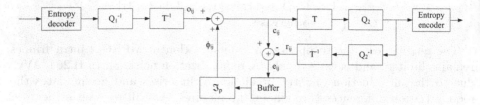

**Fig. 3.** Requantization transcoder with pixel-domain compensation

In order to obtain the compensation matrix $\phi$, we first define the error values $e_{ij}$ as the difference between the incoming residual information after inverse quantization, inverse transformation and drift compensation, and the corresponding requantized residual values after inverse quantization and inverse transformation, i.e., $e_{ij} = c_{ij} - r_{ij}$, for $i, j = 0, \ldots, 3$ (see Fig. 3). These quantization errors are stored in memory, and are used to compensate drift in the 4×4 blocks that depend on the current block.

The compensation matrix $\phi$ for a given $4 \times 4$ block is then constructed as follows. We select from the buffer the error values $e_{B,i,j}$, $e_{C,i,j}$, $e_{D,i,j}$, and $e_{E,i,j}$. By these, we denote the stored quantization errors $e_{ij}$ of the 4×4 blocks B (top), C (upper-right), D (left), and E (upper-left), that surround the current $4 \times 4$ block A. For clarity, we only mention the error values that are required for the construction of the compensation, namely the error values $e_{B,3,j}$ and $e_{C,3,j}$ for $j = 0, \ldots, 3$, $e_{D,i,3}$ for $i = 0, \ldots, 3$, and $e_{E,3,3}$. These correspond to the positions that are normally used for intra 4×4 prediction. From these 13 values, the pixel-domain compensation matrix $\phi$ is constructed using the formulas for the intra 4×4 prediction, just as they are used in the encoder and decoder, but here applied on the smaller error values. For example, for horizontal prediction (mode 1), $\phi$ becomes:

$$\phi = \begin{bmatrix} e_{D,0,3} & e_{D,0,3} & e_{D,0,3} & e_{D,0,3} \\ e_{D,1,3} & e_{D,1,3} & e_{D,1,3} & e_{D,1,3} \\ e_{D,2,3} & e_{D,2,3} & e_{D,2,3} & e_{D,2,3} \\ e_{D,3,3} & e_{D,3,3} & e_{D,3,3} & e_{D,3,3} \end{bmatrix}.$$

In fact, $\phi$ is the difference of the intra prediction matrix of the original (unquantized) values, $P$, and the intra prediction matrix of the requantized values, $P'$, i.e.,

$$\phi = \Im_p(\mathbf{e}) = \Im_p(\mathbf{c} - \mathbf{r}) = \Im_p(\mathbf{c}) - \Im_p(\mathbf{r}) = P - P' \quad,$$

where $\mathbf{c}$ and $\mathbf{r}$ denote the compensated and requantized vectors of 13 prediction pixels used for prediction of the current 4×4 block. This equality holds exactly for prediction modes 0 and 1 (horizontal and vertical prediction). For modes 2 through 8, the right shift used for calculating the prediction may result in rounding errors.

### 3.3   Requantization Transcoder with Transform-Domain Compensation (TDC)

The transcoder with pixel-domain compensation as described in the previous section tries to overcome the quality-related problems of the open-loop requantization transcoder or the computational disadvantages of the MR transcoder. The question remains if it possible to further reduce the computational complexity of the PDC architecture. This reduction is possible by eliminating forward and inverse transforms, hence working as much as possible in the transform domain. This requantization transcoder with transform-domain compensation is visualized in Fig. 4.

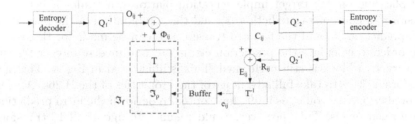

**Fig. 4.** Requantization transcoder with transform-domain compensation

This architecture is obtained, starting from the PDC architecture, through the following two steps. In the first step, forward and inverse transforms are moved to the feedback loop. This results in the elimination of one inverse transform. In the second step, we propose to combine the pixel-domain intra prediction $\Im_p$ and the forward transform $T$ as indicated by the dashed line in Fig. 4. This results in transform-domain intra prediction $\Im_f$, which is for most of the prediction modes more efficient than the combination of the pixel-domain intra prediction $\Im_p$ and the forward transform $T$.

In order to achieve this, we need to obtain the transform-domain compensation matrix $\Phi$, which can be obtained through the forward transform of the pixel-domain compensation matrix $\phi$, i.e., $\Phi = C_f \phi C_f^T$. Because of the linear nature of the H.264/AVC integer transform, this matrix can also be written as the difference between the intra prediction matrices $P$ and $P'$ after transformation, i.e.,

$$\Phi = C_f \phi C_f^T = C_f (P - P') C_f^T = C_f P C_f^T - C_f P' C_f^T \quad .$$

Depending on the used prediction mode, the transformed coefficients will be compensated in a number of frequency-dependent positions. Using the above equation, in the case of the horizontal prediction (mode 1), we obtain:

$$\Phi = 4 \begin{bmatrix} e_{D,0,3} + e_{D,1,3} + e_{D,2,3} + e_{D,3,3} & 0 & 0 & 0 \\ 2e_{D,0,3} + e_{D,1,3} - e_{D,2,3} - 2e_{D,3,3} & 0 & 0 & 0 \\ e_{D,0,3} - e_{D,1,3} - e_{D,2,3} + e_{D,3,3} & 0 & 0 & 0 \\ e_{D,0,3} - 2e_{D,1,3} + 2e_{D,2,3} - e_{D,3,3} & 0 & 0 & 0 \end{bmatrix} \quad .$$

For the vertical prediction (mode 0), $\Phi$ is constructed in a similar way. In the case of the DC prediction (mode 2), only the DC frequency position has to be compensated:

$$\Phi = 2 \begin{bmatrix} \sum_{j=0}^{3} e_{B,3,j} + \sum_{i=0}^{3} e_{D,i,3} & 0 & 0 & 0 \\ 0 & 0 & 0 & 0 \\ 0 & 0 & 0 & 0 \\ 0 & 0 & 0 & 0 \end{bmatrix}.$$

For the diagonal predictions (modes 3 and 4), $\Phi$ is a symmetric matrix, and thus can be calculated very efficiently. For the other predictions (modes 5 through 8), a larger number of multiplications is required. Depending on the cost of the multiplication on the target implementation platform, a trade-off between the transform-domain intra prediction $\Im_f$ and the combination of the pixel-domain intra prediction $\Im_p$ and the forward transform $T$ can be made for these modes.

In order to calculate the prediction errors $e_{ij}$, one inverse integer transform for every 4×4 block is still performed. This is illustrated in Fig. 4. The inverse transform is kept to take full advantage of the properties of the H.264/AVC intra 4×4 prediction. We could, as in [9], have opted to perform the intra prediction on transformed pixels. This, however, would require storage of all 16 transformed coefficients $E_{ij}$. Because of the inverse transform, we only have to store 7 pixels for every 4×4 block. Apart for the lower memory requirements, it also has positive implications on the inverse transform, which now requires only 46 addition and 19 shift operations, instead of the complete inverse transform, which uses 80 addition and 32 shift operations. Another drawback of [9] is that the complete transform-domain intra prediction involves extensive floating-point multiplication, whereas the calculation in our architecture can be performed with integer arithmetic only.

The calculation of the compensation in the frequency domain should have no impact on the quality when compared to the PDC architecture. However, the frequency-domain operations are performed on inverse quantized values, which are upscaled by a factor 64 [6]. The non-linearity of the downscaling operation, which is performed after the inverse transform, introduces rounding errors, which could result in small quality differences between both architectures.

## 4   Experimental Results

In this section, we describe the results for the software implementation of our transcoding architectures for H.264/AVC bitstreams. The different transcoding architectures are tested using the video sequences Container and Stefan, both in CIF resolution. The objective quality and the bitrate of the transcoded bitstreams, using the PDC and TDC transcoding architectures, are compared with the results obtained through the FDR transcoder, the MR transcoder and the open-loop requantization transcoder.

The initial bitstreams were encoded using the JVT reference software (Joint Model 9.8), restricted to the intra 4×4 modes only. The bitstreams were then transcoded from the initial $QP_1$ to a higher $QP_2$ ($\Delta QP = QP_2 - QP_1$), using the five architectures. The rate-distortion performance for the transcoded Container video sequences is depicted in Fig. 5.

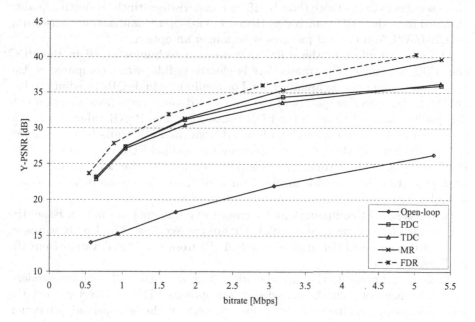

**Fig. 5.** Rate-distortion performance ($\Delta QP = 12$, Container sequence)

For completeness, the PSNR values (dB) and the bitrates (Mbps) for the different transcoding architectures using the video sequence Container are shown in Table 1 ($\Delta QP = 12$). The results obtained for the video sequence Stefan are similar, and are omitted here due to place constraints.

**Table 1.** PSNR [dB] and bitrate [Mbps] results (Container, $\Delta QP = 12$)

| Original | | FDR | | MR | | PDC | | TDC | | Open-loop | |
|---|---|---|---|---|---|---|---|---|---|---|---|
| $QP_1$ | bitrate | PSNR | Bitrate | PSNR | Bitrate | PSNR | Bitrate | PSNR | Bitrate | PSNR | Bitrate |
| 11 | 10.1 | 40.3 | 5.01 | 39.6 | 5.36 | 35.9 | 5.36 | 36.2 | 5.35 | 26.3 | 5.26 |
| 17 | 6.61 | 36.0 | 2.90 | 35.3 | 3.18 | 34.4 | 3.18 | 33.6 | 3.17 | 22.0 | 3.06 |
| 23 | 4.04 | 32.0 | 1.62 | 31.3 | 1.84 | 31.2 | 1.84 | 30.4 | 1.84 | 18.3 | 1.72 |
| 29 | 2.33 | 27.9 | 0.88 | 27.4 | 1.04 | 27.4 | 1.04 | 27.2 | 1.04 | 15.3 | 0.94 |
| 35 | 1.35 | 23.7 | 0.54 | 23.1 | 0.64 | 23.2 | 0.64 | 22.9 | 0.64 | 14.1 | 0.57 |

The FDR architecture generates qualitatively the best transcoded sequences over the full range of QPs. This architecture defines an upper bound for the objective quality of transcoded video sequences and will serve as reference in this section. For practical use, this type of transcoder is not feasible due to its high computational complexity, mainly originating from the exhaustive comparison of the prediction modes.

Although open-loop requantization transcoding of MPEG-2 bitstreams results in acceptable quality [1], the intra prediction in the H.264/AVC standard makes an open-loop architecture not suitable. The objective quality of the transcoded video sequences drops more than 10 dB in comparison with the objective quality obtained from the FDR transcoder. Hence, open-loop requantization transcoding of H.264/AVC intra coded pictures is no longer an option.

The positive effect of the drift compensation techniques used in the PDC and TDC requantization transcoders is clearly visible, when compared to the open-loop requantization architecture. For medium to high QPs (medium to low bitrates), the objective quality of the transcoded video sequences approximates the quality obtained through the FDR transcoder. The PSNR values vary little (less than 2 dB) from the quality obtained from the FDR transcoder. For lower QPs (high bitrates), the PSNR gap between the optimal FDR transcoder and the PDC and TDC architectures increases. This is caused by the non-linearity of the intra prediction formulas for modes 2 through 8, which become more dominant at higher bitrates.

In the case that complexity and memory requirements are not an issue, the MR transcoder can be used for high bitrate transcoding. The PSNR values of the MR transcoder differ approximately 1 dB from the PSNR values from the FDR architecture.

Table 1 also presents the bitrates originating from the different transcoders. The difference between the rate-distortion optimal FDR architecture and the four transcoder architectures is mainly caused by the suboptimal prediction modes for the target bitrate. The open-loop transcoder generates bitstreams with a bitrate which is approximately 5% larger than the bitstreams generated by the FDR architecture. The other three transcoding architectures, the MR transcoder and both the PDC and TDC transcoders generate bitrates which are between 5% and 10% larger than the optimal bitrates from the FDR architecture, due to the addition of new coefficients in the feedback-loop.

## 5    Conclusions

In this paper, requantization techniques for H.264/AVC bitstreams were discussed, focusing on the intra 4×4 prediction. Two architectures were presented that solve the problem of drift propagation, as encountered for the more traditional open-loop requantization transcoder. Results show that both architectures perform approximately equally well, and are able to approach the visual quality of a full decode and recode within 2 dB for medium to high QPs. Because of the reduced computational complexity of the proposed architectures over the FDR and MR architectures, they are highly suitable for on-the-fly rate reduction operations. As mentioned before, the TDC architecture is less complex than the PDC architecture, and therefore we suggest to use the former architecture.

# Acknowledgements

The described research activities were funded by Ghent University, the Interdisciplinary Institute for Broadband Technology (IBBT), the Institute for the Promotion of Innovation by Science and Technology in Flanders (IWT), the Fund for Scientific Research-Flanders (FWO-Flanders), the Belgian Federal Science Policy Office (BFSPO), and the European Union.

# References

1. Sun, H., Kwok, W., Zdepski, J.W.: Architectures for MPEG compressed bitstream scaling. IEEE Transactions on Circuits and Systems for Video Technology **6** (1996) 191–199
2. Vetro, A., Christopoulos, C., Sun, H.: Video transcoding architectures and techniques: an overview. IEEE Signal Processing Magazine (2003) 18–29
3. Nakajima, Y., Hori, H., Kanoh, T.: Rate conversion of MPEG coded video by requantization process. In: Proceedings of the 1995 International Conference on Image Processing, Washington, D.C. (1995)
4. Werner, O.: Requantization for transcoding of MPEG-2 intraframes. IEEE Transactions on Image Processing **8** (1999) 179–191
5. De Cock, J., Notebaert, S., Lambert, P., De Schrijver, D., Van de Walle, R.: Requantization transcoding in pixel and frequency domain for intra 16x16 in H.264/AVC. In: Proceedings of ACIVS 2006 (Advanced Concepts for Intelligent Vision Systems). (2006) Accepted for publication
6. Malvar, H., Hallapuro, A., Karczewicz, M., Kerofsky, L.: Low-complexity transform and quantization in H.264/AVC. IEEE Transactions on Circuits and Systems for Video Technology **13** (2003) 598–603
7. Wiegand, T., Sullivan, G., Bjøntegaard, G., Luthra, A.: Overview of the H.264/AVC video coding standard. IEEE Transactions on Circuits and Systems for Video Technology **13** (2003) 560–576
8. Lefol, D., Bull, D., Canagarajah, N.: Performance evaluation of transcoding algorithms for H.264. IEEE Transactions on Consumer Electronics **52** (2006) 215–222
9. Chen, C., Wu, P.H., Chen, H.: Transform-domain intra prediction for H.264. In: Proceedings of the 2005 IEEE International Symposium on Circuits and Systems, Kobe, Japan (2005)

# Prediction Algorithms in Large Scale VOD Services on Grid Infrastructure

Bo Li and Depei Qian

School of Computer Science and Engineering,
Beijing University of Aeronautics & Astronautics,
Beijing, China
{libo, depeiq}@buaa.edu.cn

**Abstract.** VOD (Video on Demand) is one of significant services for next generation networks. Commonly large scale VOD services mean local networks to provide VOD services to communities about 500 to 1000 users accessing simultaneously. VOD services on grid infrastructure make resources sharing and management easy, which leads substantial cooperation among systems distributed in many places. This paper presents prediction algorithms trying to reduce the cost of external communications among large VOD nodes in a grid community. Basic algorithms can reduce overall costs about 30% and well trained ANN can provide extra 10% performance.

**Keywords:** VOD, Predication, Grid.

## 1 Introduction

VOD systems have been implemented in market for nearly ten years. In early years, it started from KTV discs based system, which was operated by a PC to provide single video clip through local Ethernet networks. Video clips were compressed in RM or MPEG1 standards with a CIF resolution, the quality was very close to VCD. The services could be delivered to tens of customers if there were enough PCs available. The second generation VOD services were implemented in hotels for customers to enjoy personal TV programs. Some of them were provided in 2M TS stream with MPEG2 standards similar to DVD quality. Single service cost 2Mbps bandwidth and it was difficult to provide the service out of the hotel. And the rapid popularizing is expected when IPTV and HDTV enter families. From now on, VOD not only is an engineering term, but raises some academic interests.

It is very clear that for each local area, and local networks, to provide VOD, a server or a server group is required and it transfer video clips from storage to customers. There are lots works done on the single VOD system [1][2][3][4][5]. Most of them concentrated on the efficiency of local server group or local bandwidth and tried to reduce the latency for a single requirement. Now VOD system can be implemented in community scale and it is not difficult and not expensive to run a VOD system to serve 1,000 users simultaneously. Recent works concern more on mobile devices and large scale VOD problems [6][7][8][9].

Y. Zhuang et al. (Eds.): PCM 2006, LNCS 4261, pp. 818–826, 2006.

Grid computing is a technology really hot in recent years. At its early age, it was supposed to be consisted of many highly autonomy and distributed systems sharing their resources. Ideal grid in this way was very difficult to monitor, to manage and even to use. With grid entering into business area, high quality services become the most important issue to be considerate for not only operators but also solution provider. Big grid nodes cooperating on grid infrastructure to provide kinds of services becomes an obvious solution for reliable services and good cooperation. It is also a very good architecture for VOD systems to share their media resource and sometimes computing resources. GFTP can be very efficient for a grid system to transfer files and for VOD system similar protocol can do very well comparing to GFTP for FTP.

For VOD system collaborations, there are two kinds of basic sharing strategies. The first is all sharing are not cached and each customer can require video clips from external accessing. Obviously, it costs bandwidth a lot and it avoids any problems invoked by copying from one networks to another. The second methods assume two or more networks belong to the same group and there is nothing wrong to cache programs from one. For any single requirement, it makes a copy of required video clip and transfers it to customers locally. This method avoids some unnecessary transferring but gets another kind of unnecessary transferring when the user just wants to skim those clips. In most cases, it is difficult to say which method is better.

This paper presents a few prediction algorithms for VOD systems to cooperate and it also presents predicting methods based on the working mode. With prediction, systems could know if the transferring is necessary or in which cases it is necessary. The prediction also could show the probabilities for each transferred copy to be used in short future, which is very important for server groups to optimize the performance of whole system. Following sections will presents cooperative architecture of VOD, predicting approaches. At the end of this paper, some simulation results will be presented to indicate the performance of prediction.

## 2   Cooperative VOD Nodes Architecture

For a single VOD system, it works in following way:

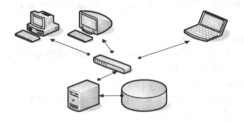

**Fig. 1.** VOD nodes

The video clips are stored in a SAN or similar device. A server or server group get clips from storage and transferred to terminal devices. In the testbed for this paper, the video clips follow H.264 and enhanced AAC+ standard, packed into TS stream format, which can be implemented in general broadcasting devices. For video stream with a resolution of 640 by 360 at 30 FPS, it can provide a DVD quality video with 512Kbps bandwidth. In this case, the overall performance is much better than most of VOD systems.

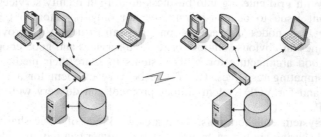

**Fig. 2.** Cooperative VOD nodes

Commonly, two VOD nodes are connected through internet, and for special reason, they can be connected through a dedicated cable. For the first case, the internet bandwidth is also shared by other purposes and costs considerable expensive. This is why to optimize cooperative methods for VOD nodes.

The testbed for this paper can serve about 500 VOD request simultaneously. The main obstacle to serve more customers is the effective local bandwidth and server groups output capability. Assuming there are about 2,000 users in a communities use this kind of VOD services, 3% programs are not available in local VOD system, each programs lasts about half an hour, getting all clips from external system needs about 54G bits each day. For some new and hot programs, the costs can be great. The person in Charge of those services can manage it in this way: for some clips they think hot and popular, get them from external and serve them locally, and this solution leads to the prediction methods described in following section.

## 3    Prediction Algorithms for VOD Nodes

It is not difficult for human to decide which clip is hot or not, but it is not easy for computer system to know about it. A clip is required by a user, maybe in different conditions:

- User want to watch it from beginning to end
- User want to know about the story of it, he will skip most of details
- User want to know if he had watched or not
- User want to know if there is any player he likes
- User want to continue watching from last time position
- User make a mistake to click on it
- ......

Generally, different conditions show different signal to system, and system could analyze what the original intention of the user.

If each user's intention is clear, system could get an overall trends for users to a video clips. Operators can provide preview clips and detailed information for each clip to help users to find what to watch and how to watch. It is very important for systems to know well about users' intentions.

For each video program, there are also many conditions different from each other:

- New video program never being required
- New video program required many times
- Old video program required many time recently
- Old video program required many time, but last requirement was made a year ago
- Old video program seldom being required, but until now there still some requirements made for it
- ......

Generally, system could make a rank list for each video program to be evaluated, if the rank higher than a threshold, it could be a hot program and of course, for any external requirement, it is better to get the full video and put it in local storage.

The statistics of video requirements and user access log can help external visitor know about the programs and ranked list can help it decide what to do next. For prediction methods is to find what will happen next, especially for video program without a clear future. And all the predictions are based on statistics and rules produced by the system.

In a VOD node, for a user's single requirement, assume $A$ represents all operations for this requirement, each $A_i$ represents a single operation and its timestamp like watching from position a to position b. Then a user operation model $U(A)$ can be implemented to decide the type of this requirement.

For a video program, $R$ represents all requirements since it put into the storage. $R_i$ represents a single requirement for this video program. Then a video program usage model $V(R, U(R_1), ...U(R_n))$ can be implemented to decide the type of this video program.

When $U(A)$ and $V(R, U(R_1), ...U(R_n))$ are available, a prediction can be made through $P(V(R, U(R_0), ..., U(R_n), U_P))$, where $U_p$ means current requirement type.

The main problem for the prediction is that the model is not easy to build. For different user group, user models are much different from each other. A young people model can not be used on old people. Another problem is how to estimate time factor in the models. Time factors will vary from different. Two basic factors can not be ignored: one is strategy of operator, and another one is internet tariff standard, both of them can affect models above greatly. If tariff is higher enough, the cooperative transferring can be ignored. If the system can provide detailed introduction, the users can decide if to require the program before send requirement. Any way, it is possible to estimate user behavior and program accessing pattern, which lead to a prediction to show how much probabilities this program can be required by other users in a short time.

An ANN was implemented to estimate video program model as figure 3. The input is video program properties and a single requirement, with parameters as time, operation, duration, time to previous requirement and time to next requirement. The ANN is trained with real data from system and could output a popular rate.

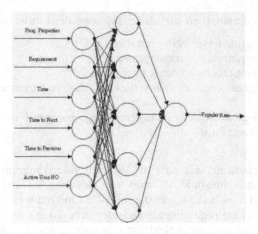

**Fig. 3.** ANN to produce program model

For a few cooperative VOD nodes, it is not difficult to evaluate a program's popular rate in each network. Overall result can be used to calculate the related probabilities.

There are three prediction models for program popular rate compared in the testbed. The first one is simple fuzzy logic model. Preset the rules and formulas to calculate the probabilities. For example, rules can be in this way:

- If the same type of program is hot, this program with a middle above popular rate, the probability is high
- If the program is new and the type is popular and the topic is OK, the probability is middle
- If the program is old, and recent usage is not bad, the probability is middle
- ......

The performance of this prediction depends on the rules very much. For different system, rules should be adjusted to adapt new system, boring and low efficient.

The second prediction method is by Monte-Carlo methods and Bayesian methods. The main problem is the observed result is not probabilities what the prediction produced. In this case, another parameter was used to evaluate usage of supposed to be transferred video programs, the time span to next requirement in local networks. The prediction algorithm needs to use requirement recodes in required nodes to estimate the time span and it is very difficult to make a right estimation for new programs while there are not enough data to be used in perdition.

The third method is ANN. ANN methods can also be implemented in predicting the time span.

It is recommended to combine different methods at same time to achieve better performance.

User behaviors should be also predicted based on the user profiles and user operation. The basic ideas are the same with program popular rate predictions. And other affective issues are more than popular rate predictions. For instance, the time of a requirement affects not only the number of simultaneous requirements, but also accessing patterns of users. And prediction for a user's accessing operations in his own pattern can be done analyzed individually.

Two VOD node cooperation is not enough to provide highly cooperative environment. For more than three nodes, sharing their model and prediction ANN will be also very efficient to improve the overall performance.

## 4  Experimental Results and Explanation

It is still difficult for our testbed to simulate a real VOD system provides 500 programs simultaneously. So a simulation program developed to evaluate the performance of prediction algorithms.

The simulation was set in following way:

- Video clips are compressed with H.264 and Enhance AAC+, resolution 640 by 360, 30 fps, stereo audio, packed in TS stream, 512Kbps
- Storage is an 30T raid5 SAN, connected with Fiber Channel Card to VOD server
- VOD server is about 32 CPU and 64GB RAM, maximal capability to serve 1,000 users simultaneously
- Local connection is 1000M Ethernet to desktop
- Users are classified into eight group, by age and sex
- Video clips are classified into ten type, some subtypes are stressed like cartoons and hot movies, all clips can be downloaded in seconds.

Figure 4 compare external bandwidth usage for three strategies. Here, prediction strategy is combination of fuzzy logic and ANN.

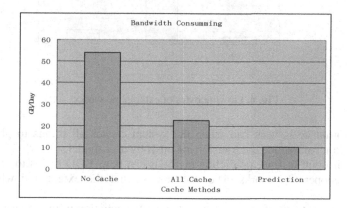

**Fig. 4.** External bandwidth consuming

The data in Figure 4 stresses more hot programs to share and the share rate is about 3%. Figure 5 shows in mirror mode, the performance of the prediction methods.

In a short time the prediction methods allow only very popular programs to be transferred, in the experiment, it ranged from 3% to 5%. There may be some in future, about 10% to 15% to be transferred. For a huge program warehouse, most of them are ignored by most of users.

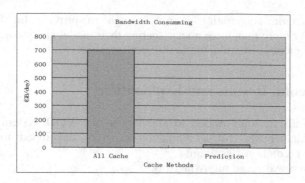

**Fig. 5.** External bandwidth consuming for mirror mode

For some requirements just to watch no more than 10 minutes. Figure 6 shows the external bandwidth consuming in a simulation process.

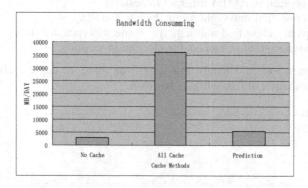

**Fig. 6.** Flowing bytes of external networks

The performance is very bad when the system caches all things to play. In this case, prediction can reduce the transferring costs by user model.

It is not difficult to find, prediction methods can help VOD nodes to reduce costs invoked in cooperative works. The question is what the extent and where is the limitation.

Figure 7 shows the performance curve for ANN prediction trained to achieve better performance. It was improved with extra fuzzy based rules and it can be improved with more training samples and more rules.

ANN can be trained to close the reality, but it can't get too close. It affected the performance of prediction algorithms. Before a good model to describe prediction and user behaviors in VOD area, ANN could be used for a good balance system performance.

Figure 8 shows Monte-Carlo prediction performance. Fixed PDFs were implemented in these experiments. Because the PDFs is preset and can't describe system very well, the performance is a bit poor compared to ANN results.

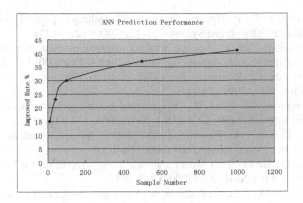

**Fig. 7.** Trained ANN prediction performance

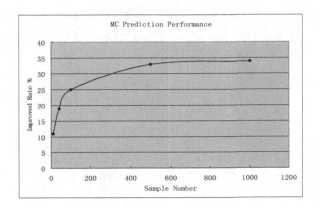

**Fig. 8.** Monte-Carlo prediction performance

## 5  Conclusion and Future Work

Some starting works in prediction algorithm for VOD nodes to cooperative presented in this paper. A testbed to VOD service and VOD nodes to cooperate is build. During the development of VOD system, we found it very important to do some preparation for future cooperative works. For VOD cooperation, cooperative learning and remote learning will be our future work to do. The VOD based grid frameworks are being studied for next step. A VOD on grid protocol will be proposed. Hopefully, there will be a common service grid for people to enjoy high quality VOD services in a few years.

## References

1. Allen, R.J., Heltai, B. L., Koenig, A. H., Snow, D. F., Watson, J. R.: VCTV: a video-ondemand market test. AT&T Technical Journal, 72(1) (1993) 7–14
2. Chou, C. F., Golubchik, L., Lui ,J. C. S.: Striping doesn't scale: how to achieve scalability for continuous media servers with replication. In Proc. IEEE ICDCS'00 (2000) 64–71

3. Lee, Y. B.,Wong, P. C.: Performance analysis of a pullbased parallel video server. IEEE Trans. on Parallel andDistributed Systems, 11(12) (2000) 1217–1231
4. Zhou, X., L¨uling, R., Xie, L.: Solving a media mapping problem in a hierarchical server network with parallel simulatedannealing. In Proc. 29th ICPP (2000) 115–124
5. Zink, M., Griwodz, C., Steinmetz, R., KOM Player-A Platform for Experimental VoD Research, In Proc. ISCC 2001 (2001)
6. Sato K., Katsumoto, M., Miki, T.,: Fragmented Patching: New VOD Technique That Supports Client Mobility, in Proc. Of AINA 2005 (2005) 527-532
7. Bellavista, P., Corradi , A., Foschini, L.: MUMOC: An Active Infrastructure for Open Video Caching, In Proc. Of DFMA2005 (2005) 64-71
8. Chen, Y., Dai, Q.: Research on Model and Scheduling Algorithm for Double-Mode VoD Servers, In Proc. Of ICCNMC 2003 (2003) 297-304
9. Bruneo, D., Villari, M., Zaia, A., Puliafito, A.: VOD services for mobile wireless devices, in Proc. Of Eighth IEEE International Symposium on Computers and Communications (2003) 602-609

# A Hierarchical Framework for Fast Macroblock Prediction Mode Decision in H.264

Cheng-dong Shen and Si-kun Li

School of Computer Science, National University of Defense Technology, ChangSha, China
shencd@163.com

**Abstract.** Many intra and inter prediction modes for macroblock are supported in the latest video compression standard H.264. Using the powerful Lagrangian minimization tool such as rate-distortion optimization, the mode with the optimal rate-distortion performance is determined. This achieves highest possible coding efficiency, but total calculation of cost for all candidate modes results in much higher computational complexity. In this paper, we propose a hierarchical framework for fast macroblock prediction mode decision in H.264 encoders. It is based on hierarchical mode classification method which assists fast mode decision by pre-selecting the class for macroblock using the extracted spatial and temporal features of macroblock. Since tests for many modes of non-selected classes will be skipped, much computation of rate-distortion optimization can be saved. Experimental results show that the proposed method can reduce the execution time of mode decision by 85% on the average without perceivable loss in coding rate and quality.

**Keywords:** Mode decision, rate-distortion optimization, video coding, H.264.

## 1 Introduction

The newest H.264 video coding standard [1] can achieve much higher coding efficiency than the previous standards such as H.263 and MPEG-4. This is mainly due to more complicated approaches employed by H.264 encoder, especially the advanced prediction method supporting various inter and intra prediction mode. For the inter prediction, H.264 allows blocks of 7 different motion-compensation sizes and shapes which are 16×16, 16×8, 8×16, 8×8, 8×4, 4×8 and 4×4. And for intra prediction, H.264 offers 9 prediction modes for 4×4 luminance blocks and 4 prediction modes for 16×16 luminance blocks. To achieve as highest coding efficiency as possible, H.264 encoder uses complex mode decision technique based on rate-distortion optimization (RDO) that requires high computational complexity. Using RDO, all possible coding modes are undergone exhaustively resulting in dramatically increased computational complexity compared to previous standards. This makes H.264 difficult for real-time applications with low computational capability, such as mobile devices.

To reduce computational complexity of mode decision, recently many attempts have been made in developing fast intra mode prediction algorithms and fast inter mode prediction algorithms. F. Pan, et al. [2] proposed a fast intra-mode decision scheme with a pre-processing technique, which measures the edge direction of a given block

Y. Zhuang et al. (Eds.): PCM 2006, LNCS 4261, pp. 827–834, 2006.

using Sobel operator and their histogram and thus adopts the edge direction to predict the possible mode, so as to reduce the number of modes to be checked. It assumes high correlation between the edge direction and intra mode but this assumption of edge direction is not always true. Kim et al. [3] uses two features, i.e. the sum of absolute residual coefficients (SATD) and the sum of absolute gradients (SAG), and a simplified RDO method to determine the best mode for 4x4 blocks. Some other works consider fast inter mode decision to speed up the variable block size motion estimation and RDO mode decision in H.264. Lim [4] selected several possible inter modes based on the texture homogeneity of the macroblock or sub-block. The performances of these methods highly depend on the threshold used and the video contents. Tu [5] proposed a method by first doing full search on four 8x8 sub-blocks. Two sub-blocks may then be merged according to the estimated error surface by experiments, which however is under the unimodal assumption and may vary sequence by sequence.

Different from the above mentioned methods, which individually develop fast intra or inter mode decision algorithms, this paper proposed a hierarchical framework for macroblock prediction mode decision which is based on hierarchical mode classification using the spatial and temporal feature of macroblock. According to some extracted feature parameters the most possible class can be selected before RDO mode decision is done. By skipping testing for prediction modes of the non-selected classes the computational complexity of mode decision can be reduced significantly while maintaining similar coding performance. The rest of the paper is organized as follows. In Section 2, we present the proposed hierarchical framework for fast macroblock prediction mode decision. The simulation results are shown in Section 3 and conclusions are made in Section 4.

## 2   Proposed Hierarchical Framework for Mode Decision

The reason for that H.264 supports so many prediction modes as introduced above is to adapt different temporal and spatial correlations that exist in various macroblocks, frames and video sequences, so as to better exploit these correlations and achieve smallest RDO cost. According to some features which are defined to represent the temporal and spatial correlations, all of the modes can be hierarchically classified by three levels. At each level, one class can be selected for the current macroblock by evaluating some extracted feature parameters. Finally, only modes in selected class should be tested in the RDO mode decision procedure instead of full modes test. This section will elaborate the mode classification method, the selection and extraction of feature parameters and the fast mode decision algorithm. These three parts form the proposed framework for fast mode decision.

### 2.1   Macroblock Prediction Mode Classifications

Since different modes will be used to exploit different temporal and spatial correlations, intuitively they can be classified in term of temporal and spatial features. We define five features to help mode classification, that is, three motion feature (MF) and two texture feature (TF), which represent temporal and spatial correlations respectively, denoted as MF1~MF3 and TF1~TF2. As depicted in Fig.1, the whole modes can be hierarchically classified by three levels using these defined features. At the first level joint motion and texture feature, namely MF1&TF1, is used to divide all the modes into two classes (Class0 and Class1) which correspond to intra prediction mode and inter prediction mode respectively. At the second level, the classification for Class0 and Class1 continues. For Class0, modes of intra type are further divided into Class00 (INTRA16) and Class01 (INTRA4) using texture feature TF2. And for Class1, modes of inter type are further divided into Class11 and Class10 using motion feature MF2, which will be used for macroblocks with stationary or global motion (SGM) and macroblocks without stationary or global motion (NON-SGM) respectively. Ultimately, modes of Class10 (NON-SGM) are classified as two classes using motion feature MF3: Class100 which includes modes used for macroblock with simple motion (SMM, simple motion mode) and Class101 which includes modes for macroblock with complex motion (CMM, complex motion mode). Modes belong to class INTRA16, INTRA4, SGM, SMM, and CMM are listed in Fig.1. The goal of mode classification is that macroblock to be encoded can be assigned to one certain class before full mode decision by evaluating the motion feature and/or texture feature parameters of macroblock, so that only partial modes should be tested and lots of computation of RDO can be saved. Details about the selection and extraction of feature parameters will be presented in the following subsection.

## 2.2 Extraction of Motion and Texture Feature Parameters

The key problem for mode classification-based fast mode decision algorithm is to select the appropriate feature parameters which are used to decide an appropriate mode class for current macroblock during the mode decision procedure. Good feature parameters should be easily computed with little computation overhead whereas spatial and/or temporal correlation is well captured. Based on this rule, we proposed the extraction method of parameters for texture features (TF1 and TF2) and motion features (MF1, MF2 and MF3), which are described respectively as follows.

*MF1*: To get the feature to reflect the temporal domain correlation for Class1, motion search using 8×8 macroblock partition mode is performed to get four best matched blocks. To be more specific, four motion vectors are obtained using EPZS [7] algorithm with the quarter pixel accuracy. The four prediction residual blocks are 1/2 down sampled to 4×4 arrays and then Hadamard transform of 4×4 matrix size is applied to them. The reason for using Hadamard transform to due to its simplicity. The sums of absolute transform difference (SATD) of the four prediction residual blocks are computed respectively and the sum of them is defined as parameter for MF1, denoted as $f_1$.

*TF1*: To characterize the spatial domain correlation for Class0, we compute the sum of SATD of intra prediction residual using Hadamard transform. Representative modes from Class00 and Class01 are selected respectively to perform intra predictions and get the mode with the smallest prediction error. For Class00, three mode (DC, vertical and horizontal) are selected; and for Class01, five modes including DC, vertical, horizontal, diagonal down-left and diagonal down-right are selected. The sum of 16 SATD values for each 4*4 prediction residual blocks of one macroblock is computed as the TF1 parameter, denoted as $f_2$.

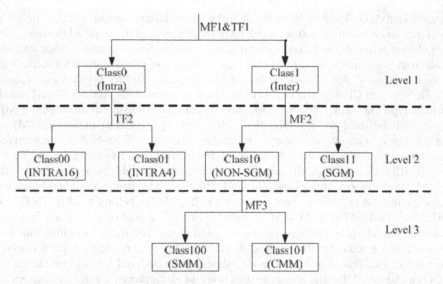

INTRA16={Vertical, Horizontal, DC, Plane};
INTRA4={Vertical, Horizontal, DC, Diagonal down-left, Diagonal down-right,
              Vertical-right, Horizontal-down, Vertical-left, Horizontal-up};
SGM={SKIP, INTER16×16 (MV=0 or MV=PMV)};
SMM={INTER16×16, INTER16×8, INTER8×16};
CMM={INTER8×8, INTER8×4, INTER4×8, INTER4×4}

**Fig. 1.** Macroblock mode prediction classification

*TF2*: Based on the above test results of representative modes for Class00 and Class01, the texture features for mode decision between Class00 and Class01 are extracted as follows. From the test results of three modes of Class00, the mode with the smallest prediction error is selected and the sum of 16 SATD values of macroblock prediction residual is computed, denoted as $f_3$, which is used to reflect the prediction accuracy of Class00 and regarded as one texture feature parameter of TF2. In the same way another texture feature parameter $f_4$ is obtained from test result of Class01.

*MF2*: The motion features used to discriminate between class SGM and class NON-SGM can be extracted by computing the cost of SKIP mode and the cost of zero MV for 16*16 inter prediction mode, which are denoted as $f_5$ and $f_6$ respectively.

*MF3*: During the extraction of parameters for MF1, fast motion estimation is carried out for 8×8 macroblock partition mode. The resulting four motion vectors can be used to determine whether the motion of current macroblock is simple or complex. As depicted in Fig.2, the four motion vectors are MV1, MV2, MV3 and MV4, the distance of neighboring MVs is computed, denoted as MVD1, MVD2, MVD3 and MVD4. Then parameters for MF3 can be represented by $f_7$ and $f_8$, which are computed as the sum of horizontal neighboring MVs' distances and that of vertical neighboring MVs' distances respectively.

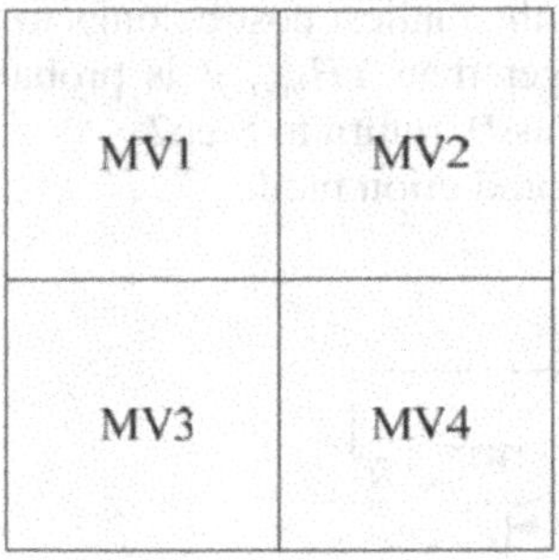

| | |
|---|---|
| MV1 | MV2 |
| MV3 | MV4 |

$$MVD1 = |MV1_x - MV2_x| + |MV1_y - MV2_y|$$

$$MVD2 = |MV3_x - MV4_x| + |MV3_y - MV4_y|$$

$$MVD3 = |MV1_x - MV3_x| + |MV1_y - MV3_y|$$

$$MVD4 = |MV2_x - MV4_x| + |MV2_y - MV4_y|$$

$$f_7 = MVD1 + MVD2$$

$$f_8 = MVD3 + MVD4$$

**Fig. 2.** Extraction of motion feature (MF3)

### 2.3 Fast Mode Decision Algorithm

Based on the feature-based mode classification, the most probable modes can be hierarchically determined by evaluating some motion and texture feature parameters prior to full search of all modes. This is the key idea of our proposed hierarchically framework for fast macroblock mode decision. This subsection will discuss a fast mode decision algorithm which is based on mode classification. As depicted in Fig.3, the critical part of fast mode decision algorithm is hierarchically selecting the proper mode class for current macroblock. The main process of the fast mode decision algorithm is summarized as follows.

*Step1*: Using the joint motion and texture feature, $f_1$ and $f_2$, to discriminate between Class0 and Class1. Generally, the cost of inter mode is comparative smaller than that of intra mode. If $f_1$ is smaller than one threshold (denotes as *TH1*) Class1 is selected and goto Step3; otherwise, compare $f_2$ with threshold *TH2*, if $f_2$<*TH2*, Class0 is selected and goto Step2, otherwise, Class1 is again selected and goto Step3.
*Step2*: Continue to select the class that the intra modes belong to. Compare $f_3$ with $f_4$, if the former is smaller Class00 is selected, goto Step5; otherwise, choose Class01 and goto Step6.
*Step3*: Compare $f_5$ and $f_6$ with one threshold (denoted as *TH3*), if one of them is smaller than *TH3* the macroblock can be treated as stationary or with global motion and Class11 is selected, goto Step7; otherwise, select Class10 and continues.
*Step4*: Compare $f_7$ and $f_8$ with one threshold (denoted as *TH4*), if one of them is smaller than *TH4* Class100 is selected; otherwise Class101 is selected, goto Step7.
*Step5*: Select the mode with smallest cost during extraction of $f_3$ and DC mode as the candidate intra prediction modes; compute their RDO costs and goto Step8. It should be noted that if the mode with $f_3$ is DC then only DC mode should be checked.
*Step6*: Select the mode with $f_4$, two modes adjacent to it and the DC mode as the candidate intra prediction modes; compute their RDO costs and goto Step8. Here note that if the mode with $f_4$ is DC then only DC mode should be checked.
*Step7*: The modes with regard to the class selected are chosen; compute their RDO costs and continues.
*Step8*: If the mode with smallest cost belongs to Class1, compare it with one threshold $TH_{Intra}$, if it is larger than $TH_{Intra}$ it is probable that selecting Class1 (Inter) is erroneous

and reselect Class0, return to Step2. If the mode with smallest cost belongs to Class0, compare it with one threshold $TH_{Inter}$, if it is larger than $TH_{Inter}$ it is probable that selecting Class0 (Intra) is erroneous and reselect Class0, return to Step2.

*Step9*: The mode with the smallest cost is the final prediction mode.

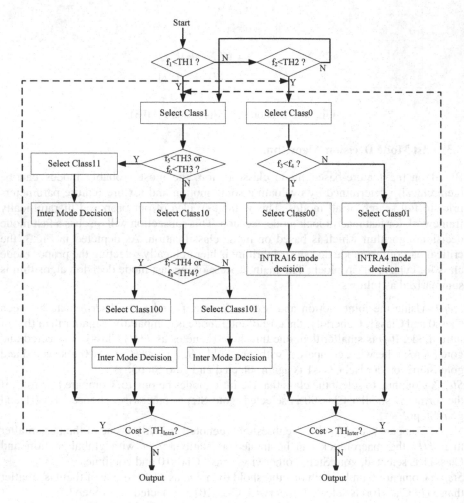

**Fig. 3.** Framework for macroblock prediction mode decision

It should be noted that fast mode decision for Intra prediction is performed in Step 5 and Step 6, due to heavy computation load of RDO mode decision for Intra modes.

In Step 8, we employ class switch scheme for Class0 and Class1. The use of this scheme can effectively alleviate the influence of erroneous class decision at first level.

Essentially, the above fast mode decision process is a demonstration of proposed framework for fast macroblock mode decision. In the practical application of the framework, mode classification can be made at any level and other fast mode decision schemes can be utilized on selected mode class. For instance, mode classification is applied only on first level and fast mode decision algorithms proposed in other literatures for Class0 or Class1 are used.

## 3 Experimental Results

Our proposed mode decision framework has been integrated with the reference JVT software JM8.6 [6]. Test sequences and major encoding options are shown in Table 1. We compare proposed mode decision method with the RDO mode decision of JM8.6 in terms of computational complexity which is counted by encoding time for mode decision routine. The time saving results are given in Table 2. To demonstrate the encoding performance in terms of PSNR and bitrate, we also give the average PSNR gain (BDPSNR) and bitrate reduction (BDBR), which are recommended by [8]. The result is listed in Table 2.

From these results we observe that proposed method is very effective in reducing the RDO mode decision time. 78.32% to 91.35% (average 85.41%)complexity reduction can be achieved versus the reference software, while its compression efficiency loss in terms of BDBR and BDPSNR [8] is very negligible, which are only 1.83% and 0.09dB, respectively.

**Table 1.** Test sequences and encoding conditions used in experiments

| Test Sequence (QCIF, 300 frames) | Encoding Options |
|---|---|
| Foreman | QP: 28, 32, 36, 40 |
| Stefan | Search Range: 16 |
| Mobile | Number of Reference: 5 |
| Container | Coding Structure: IBBPBBPBB |
| News | Others: RDO, CABAC, Hadamard transform |

**Table 2.** Performance of proposed method

| Sequence | BDBR (%) | BDPSNR (dB) | Time Saving (%) |
|---|---|---|---|
| Foreman | 2.36 | -0.11 | 89.13 |
| Stefan | 1.55 | -0.09 | 85.78 |
| Mobile | 3.12 | -0.12 | 78.32 |
| Container | 0.88 | -0.06 | 91.35 |
| News | 1.25 | -0.08 | 82.46 |
| Average | 1.83 | -0.09 | 85.41 |

## 4 Conclusions

In this paper we developed a hierarchical framework for fast macroblock prediction mode decision based on mode classification. This framework can be effectively used in fast macroblock mode algorithms. Experimental results demonstrate that the fast mode decision method using the proposed framework can reduce the execution time significantly while maintaining coding efficiency.

# References

1. Joint Video Team (JVT) of ISO/IEC MPEG & ITU-T VCEG, "Draft ITU-T Recommendation and Final Draft International Standard of Joint Video Specification (ITU-T Rec. H.264 I ISO/IEC 14496-10 AVC)", ITU-T ISO/IEC , 2003.
2. Feng Pan and Xiao Lin et. al., "Fast mode decision for intra prediction", ISO/IEC JTC1/SC29/WG11 and ITU-T SG16 Q.6, JVT 7th Meeting Pattaya II, Thailand, March 2003.
3. C. Kim, H. Shih, and C. Kuo, "Multistage mode decision for intra prediction in H.264 codec," in Proc. SPIE Symp. Visual Communications and Image Processing 2004, 2004, p 355-363
4. K.P. Lim, S. Wu, D.J. Wu, S. Rahardja, X. Lin, F. Pan, and Z.G. Li, "Fast Inter Mode Selection", JVT-I020, Joint Video Team (JVT) of ISOIIEC MPEG & ITU-T VCEG, 9th meeting, 2003
5. Y.K.Tu, J.F.Yang, Y.N.Shen, M.T.Sun, "Fast variable size block motion estimation using merging procedure with an adaptive threshold", Proc. Int. Conf. Multimedia and Expo, Vol.2, pp.789-792, Jul. 2003.
6. H.264 JVT reference software, http://bs.hhi.de/~suehring/tml/download.
7. A. Tourapis, O. C. Au, and M. L. Liou, "Highly efficient predictive zonal algorithm for fast block-matching motion estimation," IEEE Trans. Circuits Syst. Video Technol., vol. 12, pp. 934-947, Oct. 2002.
8. G. Bjontegaard, "Calculation of Average PSNR Differences between RD-curves," Doc. VCEG-M33, Apr. 2001.

# Compact Representation for Large-Scale Clustering and Similarity Search

Bin Wang[1], Yuanhao Chen[1], Zhiwei Li[2], and Mingjing Li[2]

[1] University of Science and Technology of China
[2] Microsoft Research Asia
{binwang, yhchen04}@ustc.edu,
{zli, mjli}@microsoft.com

**Abstract.** Although content-based image retrieval has been researched for many years, few content-based methods are implemented in present image search engines. This is partly bacause of the great difficulty in indexing and searching in high-dimensional feature space for large-scale image datasets. In this paper, we propose a novel method to represent the content of each image as one or multiple hash codes, which can be considered as special keywords. Based on this compact representation, images can be accessed very quickly by their visual content. Furthermore, two advanced functionalities are implemented. One is content-based image clustering, which is simplified as grouping images with identical or near identical hash codes. The other is content-based similarity search, which is approximated by finding images with similar hash codes. The hash code extraction process is very simple, and both image clustering and similarity search can be performed in real time. Experiments on over 11 million images collected from the web demonstrate the efficiency and effectiveness of the proposed method.

**Keywords:** similarity search, image clustering, hash code.

## 1 Introduction

Image is one of the most popular media types in our daily life. With the profusion of digital cameras and camera cell phones, the number of images, including personal photo collections and web image repositories, increases quickly in recent years. Therefore, people will find desired images on the web. To meet those needs, many image search engines have been developed and are commercially available. For instance, both Google Image Search [1] and Yahoo [2] have indexed over one billion images.

Present image search engines generally accept only keyword-based query, while very few simple content-based methods are supported recently. Google and Yahoo allow the categorization of images according to their sizes (large, middle and small) or colors (black/white vs. color images). Fotolia [3] provides limited support to search images based on their colors, which is rough and far insufficient for the images.

With the fact that image is a kind of visual medium, content-based image retrieval (CBIR) has been well studied and many CBIR algorithms have been proposed. ImageRover, RIME and WeebSeer are among the early content-based image retrieval

Y. Zhuang et al. (Eds.): PCM 2006, LNCS 4261, pp. 835–843, 2006.
© Springer-Verlag Berlin Heidelberg 2006

systems [4]. These CBIR systems are restricted to small or medium size datasets. Cortina [5] is a CBIR system which indexes about three million images and exploits the clustering method to avoid high-dimension indexing. [5] also states that the clustering process of millions of images is very time-consuming. A more comprehensive list of CBIR systems can be found in [4], and [6] surveys the related topics about CBIR systems for large datasets.

Although content-based methods are demonstrated to be effective in improving users' search experiences, one of the main difficulties in scaling up the traditional methods to process large-scale dataset is how to index and search in high-dimensional image feature space, as images are usually represented as high dimensional features. The dimensionality of typical image features ranges from tens to hundreds. Building efficient index structure for high-dimension data remains an open research topic in database field. Another companying effect of high dimension features is the storage cost. For an image search engine collecting billions of images, the storage cost will be huge, which prevents the system from efficiently processing the images.

To alleviate those problems which hamper the application of CBIR methods, we propose a very effective method to build a compact representation of image content, which is called "hash code" in this paper and can be regarded as special keyword. The "hash code" of an image is a string of bits built from its visual characteristics and packed into only few bytes. This representation facilitates the index and search process in that the keyword based index and search methods can be similarly applied. In addition, such a compact representation greatly reduces the storage cost. These "hash codes" can be applied in many ways to extend a system's functionality on large-scale image datasets [7]. [8] uses similar quantization method in indexing images but original features are still required for the nearest neighbor search. [9] exploits the integer representation of DCT coefficients of video frames for duplicate video detection. Based on these hash codes, we first address the problem of clustering images on large-scale datasets, which could be very useful for data organization and presentation. Furthermore, interactively finding visually similar images is also discussed. The experimental results on a dataset of over 11 million images suggest the effectiveness of proposed method and the application of content-based image retrieval on large scale datasets is promising.

The rest of the paper is organized as follows. In section 2 we present our algorithm to generate the compact hash-code representation for a given image. Following that, the implementation and evaluation of image clustering are presented in section 3. Section 4 further details the similarity search which exploits the image cluster. At last, we conclude the paper in section 5 and the future work is presented.

## 2 The Hash Code of Image Content

The core part of the proposed method is to build a compact representation of an image's content, which helps apply content-based methods in web image search engines. Figure 1 shows the framework of calculating the hash codes. First, appropriate image features are extracted. The proposed method is independent on the type of the feature. Second, the high-dimension features are projected into a subspace with much lower dimensionality while maintaining most information. This will facilitate the future manipulation and calculation on the features. Third, bit allocation and vector quantization techniques are leveraged to convert the float feature values to integer values. Finally, we packed the quantization results into few bytes. So, we get the hash code ($K$ bits) for an image. In following subsections, we'll discuss the dimension reduction and quantization process.

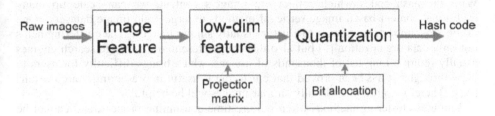

**Fig. 1.** The framework of calculating hash codes of images' contents

## 2.1 Dimension Reduction

Usually, the extracted image features are in very high dimensional space. A typical kind of image feature has tens of dimensions, which is hard for either indexing or searching. Thus we need to reduce the feature dimensions first. Many dimension reduction methods are available. Among all the methods, PCA (principle component analysis) is a simple and technically sound one, and is adopted in this paper. In PCA, the data in original high dimensional space are projected into a lower dimensional subspace which retains the largest variances.

## 2.2 Vector Quantization and Hash Code Generation

The hash code generation is essentially a vector quantization (VQ) process. The projected feature vector $G_i$ is a point in $R^M$ space. To further facilitate the search process, the low-dimension image feature $G_i$ will be mapped into a multi-dimensional integer space $Z^M$. The mapping function is obtained from the statistical analysis of a large image database:

$$H_i = f(G_i) \quad f: R^M \rightarrow Z^M. \tag{1}$$

The simple method is to quantize each dimension separately. If the final quantized vector has $K$ bits, how to allocate the bits to each dimension is an important issue [10, 11]. The bits could be allocated among dimensions according to their variances, or fixed number of bits to few most significant dimensions. We assign 1 bit to each of the most significant 32 dimensions, and the quantized value is determined by whether the feature value is larger than the mean value, 1 for yes and 0 for no. In this way, we convert the original float feature values to a long bit string.

Suppose each dimension in $H_i$ is represented using $L_k$ bit and the total number of bits is $K = \sum L_k$ ($L_k=1$ for all $k$ by now). This is similar to the digitalization of analog signals. Thus $K$ can impact the system performance such as precision and recall. We constrain $K$ to be no more than 32, because most of the present computers are of 32-bit. Therefore, the whole hash code can be packed into one integer type of the computer. Both the data manipulation (such as read and write) and calculation can be quickly performed.

# 3  Image Clustering

With the hash codes which reflect the image's content, we can scale up many traditional content-based image retrieval methods to large-scale image datasets. One of the most important issues is to cluster visually similar images. The clustering helps not only data organization [5] but also the image presentation. Image search engines usually return a long list of thousands of images, which brings difficulty for users to view through. It has been proved that clustering is useful in presenting search results [12]. Therefore, grouping visually similar images will be helpful.

Previous clustering methods often require time-consuming process, and cannot be applied for interactive search process. In this section, we introduce the process to cluster visually similar images based on the proposed hash code. Comparing to the traditional methods, only hash codes are needed during the clustering process. Therefore, the speed is very fast.

---

Input: image hash codes
Parameters: $L_s$, $L_i$, $T_c$, $T_d$
Cluster:
1.  Remove $L_i$ least significant bits of each hash code
2.  Split the images set into groups using most $L_s$ most significant bits
3.  For each group
    a)  Initialize: the images with identical hash codes ($L_i$ least significant bits removed) form one cluster
    b)  If the number of clusters is less than $T_c$, go to 3 for next group
    c)  Find the minimum distance between clusters $min(d_{set}(m,n))$
    d)  If $min(d_{set}(m,n)) > T_d$, go to 3 for next group
    e)  Merge two clusters $m$ and $n$
    f)  Go to b)
4.  Output the clustering results

---

**Fig. 2.** Clustering process

According to the nature of the hash codes which is generated using PCA, the most information is retained in few most significant dimensions. So the clustering can be conducted in these dimensions while some least significant bits are omitted because they represent small values. A hierarchical clustering method is used and Figure 2 shows the detail of the clustering process.

As hash codes are bit strings, the distance $d(h_i, h_j)$ between two images represented by hash codes $h_i$ and $h_j$ is defined as the Hamming distance of $h_i$ and $h_j$, i.e., the number of different bits.

In Figure 2, $d_{set}(m,n)$ denotes the distance between two clusters $m$ and $n$. It is defined as the complete-link distance between two sets

$$d_{set}(m,n)=max(d(h_i,h_j)). \tag{2}$$

where $h_i$ is a member of set $m$ and $h_j$ is a member of set $n$. All the processes are done using only the hash codes and no original high dimension features are required. This implies that those features need not to be stored and save huge amount of storage spaces.

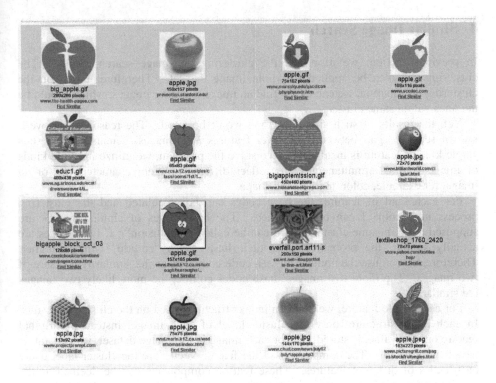

**Fig. 3.** An example of image clustering

**Table 1.** Clustering time

| Query | # of images | # of clusters | Time(second) |
|---|---|---|---|
| britney spears | 1367 | 32 | 0.0028 |
| tiger | 1742 | 37 | 0.0038 |
| saturn | 1228 | 33 | 0.0027 |
| apple | 1586 | 34 | 0.0032 |
| computer | 1771 | 35 | 0.0037 |
| flower | 1793 | 34 | 0.0038 |
| car | 1564 | 34 | 0.0039 |
| football | 1996 | 38 | 0.0042 |
| sport | 1821 | 39 | 0.0039 |
| dragon | 1782 | 39 | 0.0038 |
| Avg: | | | 0.0036 |

Table 1 shows the average clustering time of 11 queries. The number of images varies depending on query words and we adjust the clustering parameter to set the final number of clusters to be around 30. Either too many or too few clusters will be annoying to users. From Table 1, it can be seen that the clustering process can be conducted very fast for thousands of images. Thus the user-interactive operation can be supported. Figure 3 shows an example of clustering result.

## 4  Similar Image Search

In previous section, we discussed the clustering on image search results. The clustering can also be applied to whole image dataset. Therefore, based on the clustering information, we can easily find an image's similar images, which should be the ones within same cluster.

Yet, the results of such simple method won't be good. The reason is the well-known semantic gap between low-level features and images' semantics, and thus single kind of feature is insufficient. To solve the problem, we utilize multiple kinds of image features simultaneously to reflect different content characteristics of an image, for example, color, textual, and shape.

For each kind of feature, the hash codes can be calculated and the clustering process in Section 3 can be performed. The hash codes of similar images are supposed to be in same cluster, which can be called a "collision". If two images are actually similar, the probability that their hash codes "collide" will be higher. Therefore, we can use the number of hash code collisions as the similarity measure of two images. The more two images' hash codes collide, the more likely two images are similar.

For each single feature, we build an index structure based on the clustering results. In each index structure, only the cluster label of each image, instead of original feature or hash value, is stored. So for each image in the image dataset, we generate a new feature vector. The components of the feature vector are the cluster label using hash codes of different features. These feature components can be deemed as the special "keywords" of an image in that similar images share same such "keywords". Then, we can utilize the traditional text-based index and search methods to get one image's similar images list and corresponding similarity measure (by the number of "collisions").

With the returned image list, the similarity measure as well as the images' contrast, colorful blur and other image quality measures are combined to rank the returned images [14]. So the images with the highest quality and most similar to the query image are ranked in the top, which can further improve search experience.

The experiments are conducted on the same dataset as in Section 3. Figure 4 presents the average search time of 20 queries. The X-axis is the number of similar images returned and Y-axis is the consumed time in seconds. It can be seen that the operation is very fast to complete the search over 11 million images. Even for finding 10,000 similar images, the system can complete the work in less than 0.5 second. But we should be aware that the similar images are found in decreasing similarity, so the value in X-axis should not be too large. We ever asked some people to label the

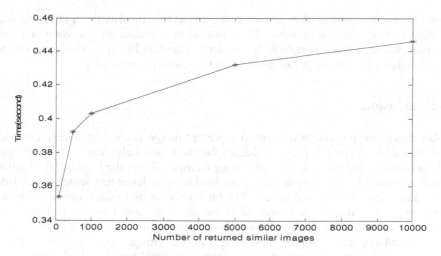

**Fig. 4.** Speed of similar image search

**Fig. 5.** An examples of similarity search based on the images hash codes

retrieval result so as to calculate the precision measure, which is defined as the number of correct retrieved images over total number of retrieved images. During labeling, there is great inconsistency between people on what images are similar. This is because "similar" is a very vague notation without clear definition. While some people judge the similarity using colors and textures (such as face presentation), others depend on some semantics in the process. Thus, instead of calculate the precision or recall measures, we present an example of the similarity search in Figure 5. The image on the top left is the query image. It can be seen that the results are satisfying.

## 5 Conclusion

In this paper, we propose a method to represent image content in a very compact form, called "hash code". Then we discuss the methods to efficiently cluster images and find similar images for large-scale image dataset. To get the hash codes, original high dimensional image features, which are hard to be indexed and searched, are first mapped to a low dimensional space. The bit allocation and vector quantization are further applied. Finally, the quantized values are organized together to form hash codes. With the compact form of hash codes, the clustering process can be performed very fast and applied to improve the presentation of image search results. Further more, finding similar image can also be quickly conducted based on hash codes. The performances of proposed methods on a large-scale dataset of more than 11 million images are encouraging. It is proved that the generated compact representation can help the application of content-based image retrieval in large image datasets.

At present, we use PCA for dimension reduction. LSA and ICA are both promising methods. Besides, joint quantization of multiple dimensions may improve the performance. Those will be interesting future work.

## References

1. Google Image Search, http://images.google.com
2. Yahoo Image Search, http://images.search.yahoo.com
3. Fotolia, http://www.fotolia.com
4. Veltkamp, R. C., Tanase, M.: Content-Based Image Retrieval Systems: A Survey. Technical Report UU-CS-2000-34, Dept. of Computing Science, Utrecht University (2000).
5. Quack, T., Mönich, U., Thiele, U., Manjunath, B.S.: Cortina: a system for large-scale, content-based web image retrieval, In Proceedings of the 12th annual ACM international conference on Multimedia(2004), pp. 508 - 511
6. Kherfi, M.L., Ziou, D., Bernardi A.: Image Retrieval from the World Wide Web: Issues, Techniques and Systems. ACM Computing Surveys(2004)
7. Wang, B., Li Z., Li M.: Large-Scale Duplicate Detection for Web Image Search. In International Conference on Multimedia & Expo. (2006)
8. Böhm, K., Mlivoncic, M., Schek, H.-J., Weber, R.: Fast Evaluation Techniques for Complex Similarity Queries, In Proceedings of the 27th International Conference on Very Large Data Bases, pp. 211-220 (2001)
9. Naturl, X., Gros, P.:A Fast Shot Matching Strategy for Detecting Duplicate Sequences in a Television Stream, Proceedings of the 2nd ACM SIGMOD international workshop on Computer Vision meets DataBases, 2005
10. Ferhatosmanoglu, H., Tuncel, E., Agrawal, D., Abbadi, A.: Vector Approximation based Indexing for Non-uniform High Dimensional Data Sets. Proceedings of 9th CIKM, McLean, USA(2000), pp 202-209,

11. Riskin, E.A.: Optimal Bit Allocation via the Generalized BFOS algorithm. IEEE Trans. on Information Theory, Vol. 37, No. 2, pp. 400-402, (1991)
12. Zeng, H., He, Q., Chen, Z., Ma, W.-Y., Ma, J.:Learning to cluster web search results, Proceedings of the 27th annual international ACM SIGIR conference on Research and development in information retrieval(2004)
13. Li, Z., Xie, X., Liu H., Tang, X., Li, M., Ma, W.-Y.: Intuitive and effective interfaces for WWW image search engines, Proceedings of the 12th annual ACM international conference on Multimedia(2004)
14. Tong, H., Li M., Zhang, H.-J., Zhang, C., He, J., Ma, W.-Y.: Learning No-Reference Quality Metric by Examples. In Proceedings of the 11th International Multimedia Modeling Conference 05 (2005)

# Robust Recognition of Noisy and Partially Occluded Faces Using Iteratively Reweighted Fitting of Eigenfaces

Wangmeng Zuo[1], Kuanquan Wang[1], and David Zhang[2]

[1] School of Computer Science and Technology, Harbin Institute of Technology
Harbin 150001, China
wangkq@hit.edu.cn
[2] Department of Computing, Hong Kong Polytechnic University
Kowloon, Hong Kong
{cswzuo, csdzhang}@comp.polyu.edu.hk

**Abstract.** Robust recognition of noisy and partially occluded faces is essential for an automated face recognition system, but most appearance-based methods (e.g., Eigenfaces) are sensitive to these factors. In this paper, we propose to address this problem using an iteratively reweighted fitting of the Eigenfaces method (IRF-Eigenfaces). Unlike Eigenfaces fitting, in which a simple linear projection operation is used to extract the feature vector, the IRF-Eigenfaces method first defines a generalized objective function and then uses the iteratively reweighted least-squares (IRLS) fitting algorithm to extract the feature vector by minimizing the generalized objective function. Our simulated and experimental results on the AR database show that IRF-Eigenfaces is far superior to both Eigenfaces and to the local probabilistic method in recognizing noisy and partially occluded faces.

**Keywords:** Eigenfaces, Principal Component Analysis, Iteratively Reweighted Least Squares, Noise, Partial Occlusion, Face Recognition.

## 1 Introduction

An automated face recognition system should be able to automatically capture, detect and recognize faces, making it inevitable that facial images will sometimes be noisy, partially occluded, or inaccurately located. The capture and communication of facial image, however, may introduce noise; some accessories, such as scarf or sunglasses, will cause the partial occlusion. In particular, such a face recognition system should be able to robustly recognize of noisy images and images in which faces are partially occluded by accessories such as scarves or sunglasses. This issue has received considerable research attention. In [1], Zhao tested the robustness of appearance-based method (e.g., Eigenfaces [2, 3]) against small degree of noise or partial occlusion. Most appearance-based methods are robust in the presence of low levels of small noise or partially occlusion [1]. Further increases in the extent of occlusion, however, would cause a severe deterioration in the recognition performance of the Eigenfaces method [4]. Analogous to partial occlusion, the further increase of noise would also cause an immediate decrease in the recognition performance.

Y. Zhuang et al. (Eds.): PCM 2006, LNCS 4261, pp. 844–851, 2006.
© Springer-Verlag Berlin Heidelberg 2006

To address the partial occlusion problem, Martinez proposed a local probabilistic (LocProb) approach where each face is divided into six local areas [4]. In the recognition stage, each local area is projected into its eigenspace to compute the local match probability, and then the weighted sum of these six local probabilities is used to make a final decision. Most recently, Tan et al propose another local approach, multiple SOM-Face to recognize partially occluded faces which uses the self-organizating map instead of a mixture of Gaussians to learn the local subspace representation [5]. These local approaches, however, cannot be used to weaken the unfavorable influence of noise because noise is always globally distributed. Further, the local approaches, which divide face into a number of different parts, neglect the global correlation of image pixels.

In this paper, we propose an iteratively reweighted fitting strategy of the Eigenfaces method for addressing the noise and partial occlusion problem. The iteratively reweighted fitting strategy (IRF-Eigenfaces) first defines a generalized objective function and then uses the iteratively reweighted least squares (IRLS) algorithm to extract the feature vector by minimizing the generalized objective function. The IRF-Eigenfaces method is a robust estimation of the coefficients of Eigenfaces, thus is a global appearance-based method and less sensitive to the effect of image noise.

The organization of this paper is as follows: Section 2 presents the procedure of the IRF-Eigenfaces algorithm. We begin by presenting a definition of the generalized objective function and then go on to describe how IRF-Eigenfaces is used to extract the feature vector by minimizing the generalized objective function. This section also discusses the convergence of the IRF-Eigenfaces method. Section 3 presents and discusses the results of experiments using the AR face database. Finally, Section 4 gives our conclusion.

## 2   Iteratively Reweighted Fitting of Eigenfaces

Iteratively reweighted fitting of Eigenfaces (IRF-Eigenfaces), which calculate the feature vector $\mathbf{y}$ by minimizing a generalized objective function, is a generalization of Eigenfaces projection. Given a set of principal components $\mathbf{W} = [\mathbf{w}_1, \mathbf{w}_2, \cdots, \mathbf{w}_d]$ and a $mn$-dimensional face vector $\mathbf{x}$, the classical Eigenfaces projection method calculates the feature vector $\mathbf{y}$ by

$$\mathbf{y} = \mathbf{W}^T \mathbf{x} . \tag{1}$$

The feature vector $\mathbf{y}$ obtained by Eq. (1) can also be calculated by minimizing the 2-norm objective function

$$J_1(\mathbf{y}) = \left\| \mathbf{x} - \mathbf{W}\mathbf{y} \right\|_2^2 = \sum_{i=1}^{mn} (x_i - \mathbf{W}_i \mathbf{y})^2 , \tag{2}$$

where $\mathbf{W}_i$ is the $i$th row of $\mathbf{W}$. From Eq. (2), the feature vector $\mathbf{y}$ corresponds to

$$\frac{\partial J_1(\mathbf{y})}{\partial \mathbf{y}} = 2\mathbf{W}^T\mathbf{W}\mathbf{y} - 2\mathbf{W}^T\mathbf{x} = 0. \tag{3}$$

$\mathbf{W}$ is a set of orthogonal basis, $\mathbf{W}^T\mathbf{W} = \mathbf{I}_d$, where denotes a $d{\times}d$ identity matrix. It is simple to see that $\mathbf{y} = \mathbf{W}^T\mathbf{x}$.

In the development of robust PCA, it has been found that outliers would cause significant deterioration in the performance of the PCA algorithm because the 2-norm is sensitive to the outlier [6, 7]. This can also be used to explain the sensitivity of the Eigenfaces method against noise and partial occlusion because the feature vector $\mathbf{y}$ is extracted by minimizing Eq. (2) where the 2-norm is adopted.

Unlike Eigenfaces, we next propose an IRF-Eigenfaces method which calculates the feature vector $\mathbf{y}$ by minimizing the generalized objective function

$$J(\mathbf{y}) = \sum_{i=1}^{mn} \Psi\left((x_i - \mathbf{W}_i\mathbf{y})^2\right), \tag{4}$$

where the function $\Psi(z)$ could be defined as

$$\Psi(z) = \log\frac{1}{1 + \exp(-\beta(z - \eta))}, \tag{5}$$

where the inverse temperature $\beta$ and saturation value $\eta$ are two tuning parameters. In this paper, we set the inverse temperature to $\beta = 0.1$ and saturation value to $\eta = 100$. Other definitions of the function $\Psi(z)$ can also be found in related literature [10]. We then use the iterative reweighted least squares (IRLS) algorithm to calculate the optimum feature vector $\mathbf{y}$ which minimizes the function $J(\mathbf{y})$ by iteratively performing the next two steps:

**Weighting-Step.** Given $\mathbf{y}^{(t)}$, update the weighted vector $\boldsymbol{\omega}^{(t)} = [\omega_1^{(t)}, \omega_2^{(t)}, \cdots, \omega_{mn}^{(t)}]$ by

$$\omega_i^{(t)} = \varphi\left(z_i^{(t)}\right) = \frac{\exp\{-\beta(z_i^{(t)} - \eta)\}}{1 + \exp\{-\beta(z_i^{(t)} - \eta)\}}, \tag{6}$$

$$z_i^{(t)} = (x_i - \mathbf{W}_i\mathbf{y}^{(t)})^2. \tag{7}$$

**Least-Squares-Step.** Given the weighted vector $\boldsymbol{\omega}^{(t)}$, update $\mathbf{y}^{(t+1)}$ by

$$\mathbf{y}^{(t+1)} = \left(\sum_{i=1}^{mn} \omega_i^{(t)}\mathbf{W}_i^T\mathbf{W}_i\right)^{-1} \sum_i^{mn} \omega_i^{(t)}\mathbf{W}_i^T x_i. \tag{8}$$

In this way, the weight- and least squares-steps are alternated repeatedly until the value of $\mathbf{y}^{(t)}$ converges or $t$ arrives at the pre-determined threshold $t_{max}$.

We next discuss the convergence of the IRF-Eigenfaces method. Because the function $\Psi(z)$ is strictly concave in $z$, we have $\Psi''(z) < 0$. We then calculate the Taylor series expansion of the function $\Psi(z)$ around $z_1$, i.e.,

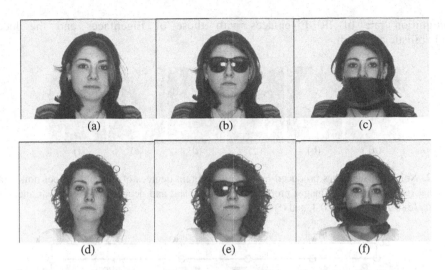

**Fig. 1.** Six images of one person in the AR database. The images (a) through (c) were captured during one session and the images (d) through (f) at a different session.

$$\Psi(z_2) = \Psi(z_1) + \beta\varphi(z_1)(z_2 - z_1) + \Psi''(z^*)(z_2 - z_1)^2 / 2,\tag{9}$$

where $z^*$ lies between $z_1$ and $z_2$. Since $\Psi''(z^*) < 0$, it is obvious to see that $\Psi(z_2) - \Psi(z_1) < \beta\varphi(z_1)(z_2 - z_1)$. We can further get

$$J(\mathbf{y}^{(t+1)}) - J(\mathbf{y}^{(t)}) < \beta\left(\sum_{i=1}^{mn}\varphi(z^t)z^{t+1} - \sum_{i=1}^{mn}\varphi(z^t)z^t\right).\tag{10}$$

Because the procedure of the least-squares-step is to minimize $\sum_{i=1}^{mn}\varphi(z^t)z$ with respect to the feature vector $\mathbf{y}$, it is obvious that $\sum_{i=1}^{mn}\varphi(z^t)z^{t+1} < \sum_{i=1}^{mn}\varphi(z^t)z^t$ and that the generalized objective function decreases strictly,

$$J(\mathbf{y}^{(1)}) > \cdots > J(\mathbf{y}^{(t)}) > J(\mathbf{y}^{(t+1)}) > \cdots.\tag{11}$$

From the definition of $J(\mathbf{y})$, $J(\mathbf{y}^{(t)}) > 0$ and $J(\mathbf{y}^{(t+1)}) < J(\mathbf{y}^{(t)})$, we can therefore guarantee that $\mathbf{y}^{(t)}$ will converge to the local optimal feature vector $\mathbf{y}$. For further discussions on the convergence of the iteratively reweighted least-squares algorithms, please refer to the related literature [8, 9, 10].

## 3 Experimental Results and Discussion

In this section, we use the AR face database [11] to evaluate the performance of the IRF-Eigenfaces method against noise and partial occlusion, and compare the recognition rate of IRF-Eigenfaces with those of Eigenfaces and the local probabilistic approach.

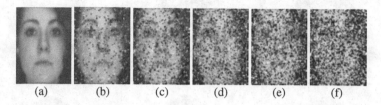

(a)          (b)          (c)          (d)          (e)          (f)

**Fig. 2.** Noisy facial images produced by adding different degrees of salt and pepper noise: (a) original image, and noisy images produced by adding salt and pepper noise with variances of (b) 0.1, (c) 0.2, (d) 0.3, (e) 0.4, and (f) 0.5

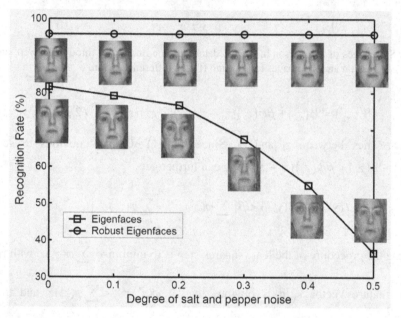

**Fig. 3.** The effect of salt and pepper noise on the recognition performance

The AR face database contains over 4,000 color frontal facial images corresponding to 126 people (70 men and 56 women).There are 26 different images of each person and these were captured in two sessions separated by two weeks. In our experiments, we only use a subset of 720 images of 120 persons. There are six images of each person. Three images were captured in the first session (one neutral, one with sunglasses, and one with a scarf) and the remaining three images were captured in the second session (one neutral, one with sunglasses, and one with a scarf), as shown in Fig. 1. In our experiments, all the images were cropped according to the location of their eyes and mouths, and the 120 neutral images in the first session were used for training Eigenfaces. We set the number of principal components $d_{PCA}=100$ and use the whitened cosine distance measure [12].

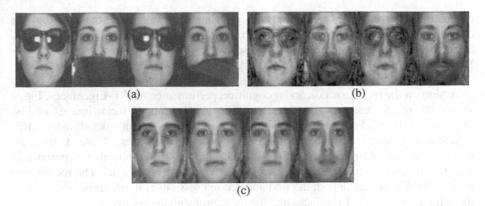

**Fig. 4.** Reconstructed images using Eigenfaces and robust Eigenfaces. (a) original partially iccluded images; (b) reconstructed images using Eigenfaces; (c) reconstructed images using robust Eigenfaces.

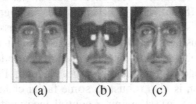

(a)          (b)          (c)

**Fig. 5.** The reconstruction performance of robust Eigenfaces for partially occluded face in the second session. (a) neutral face in the first session; (b) face with sunglasses in the second session; (c) the reconstructed image of (b) using robust Eigenfaces.

**Table 1.** Font sizes of headings

| Methods | Session 1 | | Session 2 | |
|---|---|---|---|---|
| | Sunglasses | Scarf | Sunglasses | Scarf |
| Eigenfaces | 40 | 35 | 26.67 | 25 |
| LocProb [4] | 80 | 82 | 54 | 48 |
| IRF-Eigenfaces | 87.50 | 91.67 | 82.50 | 84.17 |

Using all the neutral images in the second session as a test set, we investigate the construction and recognition performance of IRF-Eigenfaces against different degree of noise. Fig. 2 shows an original facial image and the same image after the addition of various amounts of salt and pepper noise. The largest degree of noise in our test is 50%, which is a seriously contaminated example, as shown in Fig. 2 (f). We then present the recognition rates of Eigenfaces and IRF-Eigenfaces against different degrees of noise contamination, as shown in Fig. 3. Fig. 3 also shows the reconstructed noisy images obtained using Eigenfaces and IRF-Eigenfaces. From Fig. 3, the addition of 50% salt and pepper noise caused the recognition rate of Eigenfaces to fall from 81.67% to 36.67%, but the recognition rate of IRF-Eigenfaces remained unchanged (95.83%). We can also observe from Fig. 3 that the quality of the images reconstructed using IRF-Eigenfaces is consistently better than those using the classical Eigenfaces method. Because both the recognition rate and the reconstructed image are robust against variation of noise, we can validate the robustness of IRF-Eigenfaces against noise.

Using the images with sunglasses or scarves, we tested the influence of partial occlusion on the reconstruction and recognition performance of IRF-Eigenfaces. Fig. 4 shows the reconstructed images corresponding to the cropped facial images of Fig. 1(b), (c), (e), (f). From Fig. 4, the quality of images reconstructed using IRF-Eigenfaces is consistently better than those using Eigenfaces. Table 1 lists the recognition rates of Eigenfaces, IRF-Eigenfaces and the local probabilistic approach in recognizing faces partially occluded with either sunglasses or a scarf. The recognition rate of IRF-Eigenfaces in both the first and second sessions is much higher than that of the other two methods, Eigenfaces and the local probabilistic approach.

Another interesting point to be noted from Table 1 is that robust Eigenfaces is also more robust against the variation of ageing time. Eigenfaces's recognition rate in the second session (25.83%) is much lower than in the first session (37.5%). The local probabilistic approach's recognition rate in the second session (51%) is much lower than in the first session (81%). But IRF-Eigenfaces' recognition rate in the second session (83.34%) is only slightly lower than in the first session (89.58%). There are two reasons for the robustness of IRF-Eigenfaces against ageing time. First, IRF-Eigenfaces uses the whitened cosine distance, which can reduce the adverse effect of global illumination change of the facial image. Second, IRF-Eigenfaces, which is robust to partial occlusion, is also robust to some facial change, such as the presence of a beard. Compare Fig. 5 (a), showing a neutral face captured in the first session, with Fig. 5 (b), showing a face with sunglasses captured in the second session. The image in Fig. 5 (b), captured in the second session, has a heavier beard. Fig. 5(c) shows the image in Fig. 5(b) reconstructed using IRF-Eigenfaces. IRF-Eigenfaces can detect parts of the beard as a partial occlusion and thus its reconstructed image is more consistent with Fig. 5(a).

# 4   Conclusion

In this paper we propose an IRF-Eigenfaces method for recognizing noisy and partially occluded facial image. Unlike Eigenfaces, in which a simple linear projection operation is used to extract the feature vector, the IRF-Eigenfaces method first defines a generalized objective function and then uses the iterative reweighted least-squares fitting algorithm to extract the feature vector which corresponds to the minimum of the generalized objective function. The AR face database is used to evaluate the proposed method. Our simulated and experimental results show that, in recognizing noisy and partially occluded faces, IRF-Eigenfaces is much superior to both Eigenfaces and to the local probabilistic method.

Despite the success of IRF-Eigenfaces in recognizing noisy and partially occluded facial images, it is still very necessary to further study this issue by investigating the influence of the initialization approaches, robustness against illumination and ageing. In the future, we'll further investigate these problems and try to generalize the proposed method to solve the robustness problem against noise, partially occlusion, ageing, and illumination in one uniform framework.

**Acknowledgments.** The work is supported in part by the UGC/CRC fund from the HKSAR Government, the central fund from the Hong Kong Polytechnic University and the National Natural Science Foundation of China (NSFC) under the contracts No. 60332010 and No. 90209020.

# References

1. Zhao, W., Chellappa, R., Phillips, P.J., and Rosenfeld, A.: Face Recognition: a Literature Survey. ACM Computing Surveys, 35(2003) 399-458.
2. Kirby, M., and Sirovich, L.: Application of the KL procedure for the characterization of human faces. IEEE Trans. Pattern Analysis and Machine Intelligence, 12(1990) 103-108.
3. Turk, M., and Pentland, A.: Eigenfaces for recognition. J. Cognitive Neuroscience, 3(1991) 71-86.
4. Martinez, A.M.: Recognizing Imprecisely Localized, Partially Occluded, and Expression Variant Faces from a Single Sample per Class. IEEE Trans. Pattern Analysis and Machine Intelligence, 24(2002) 748-763.
5. Tan, X., Chen, S., Zhou, Z.H., and Zhang, F.: Recognizing partially occluded, expression variant faces from single training image per person with SOM and soft k-NN ensemble. IEEE Trans. Neural Network, 16(2005), 875-886.
6. Higuchi, I., and Eguchi, S.: Robust Principal Component Analysis with Adaptive Selection for Tuning Parameters. Journal of Machine Learning Research, 5(2004) 453-471.
7. Xu, L., and Yuille, A.: Robust principal component analysis by self-organizing rules based on statistical physics approach. IEEE Trans. Neural Networks, 6(1995), 131-143.
8. Dempster, A.P., Laird, N.M., and Rubin, D.B.: Iteratively reweighted least squares for linear regression when errors are normal/independent distributed. In Krishnaiah, P.R.(Ed.), Multivariate Analysis – V, North-Holland, Amsterdam, (1980) 35-57.
9. McLachlan, G.J., and Krishnan, T.: The EM algorithm and extensions. John Wiley & Sons, New York, NJ (1997).
10. Li, G.: Robust regression. In Hoaglin, D.C., Mosteller, F., and Tukey, J.W.: Exploring Data, Table, Trends and Shapes, John Wiley & Sons, New York, (1985).
11. Martinez, A.M. and Benavente, R.: The AR Face Database. CVC Technical Report #24, Robot Vision Lab, Purdue University (1998).
12. Phillips, P.J., Flynn, P.J., Scruggs, T., Bowyer, K.W., Chang, J., Hoffman, K., Marques, J., Min, J., Worek, W.: Overview of the face recognition grand challenge. Proc IEEE Int'l Conf. Computer Vision and Pattern Recognition 2005, 1(2005), 947-954.

# Pitching Shot Detection Based on Multiple Feature Analysis and Fuzzy Classification

Wen-Nung Lie[1], Guo-Shiang Lin[2], and Sheng-Lung Cheng[1]

[1] Dept. of Electrical Engineering, Chung Cheng University, Taiwan
wnlie@ee.ccu.edu.tw
[2] Dept. of Computer Science and Information Engineering, Da Yeh University, Taiwan
khlin@mail.dyu.edu.tw

**Abstract.** Pitching-shot is known to be a root-shot for subsequent baseball video content analysis, e.g., event or highlight detection, and video structure parsing. In this paper, we integrate multiple feature analysis and fuzzy classification techniques to achieve pitching-shot detection in commercial baseball video. The adopted features include color (e.g., field color percentage and dominant color), temporal motion, and spatial activity distribution. On the other hand, domain knowledge of the baseball game forms the basis for fuzzy inference rules. Experiment results show that our detection rate is capable of achieving 95.76%.

**Keywords:** Pitching shot, Fuzzy classification, Baseball video, Video content analysis.

## 1 Introduction

With the rapid increasing of sports videos in our daily life entertainment, automatically analyzing and managing their video contents in an efficient manner become an important issue in this modern era. For instances, structures of the sports video can be analyzed and indexing of them could be established in advance so that quick and personalized browsing of the video sequences can be allowed; events or highlights familiar to audients in the sports video can be identified and recorded so that later search and retrieval of them can be convenient; a summary of the sports video will be also helpful to busy people in modern society. Since the baseball game is very popular in many countries, many researches have been focused on it. A pitching-shot is considered as the "root" shot [1] in baseball videos, meaning that many semantic events (such as "Infield ground out or fly out", "Infield hit", "Infield double play", "Infield hit with wild throw", "Outfield fly out", "Outfield hit", "Sacrifice fly", "Homerun", etc.) will follow in subsequent shots. Once the guiding pitching-shots are detected and located, following semantic events can be easily detected [7] and structure of the whole video is thus easily established. This motivates us to develop an efficient and effective pitching-shot detection scheme.

Pei et al. [2] proposed a pitching-shot verification algorithm. After detecting field color to obtain a binary map, two histograms via projections are measured. Then a

Y. Zhuang et al. (Eds.): PCM 2006, LNCS 4261, pp. 852–860, 2006.

pitching scene can be verified when the statistics of these two histograms satisfy the given conditions. However, their algorithm is unstable for close-up scenes. Bach et al. [6] proposed an algorithm which uses low-level features and hidden Markov models (HMM) to extract highlights for baseball videos. This algorithm can be used to detect pitching shots. However, it is complicated and will be practically unstable, due to many possible events in baseball games. Shia [3],[7] proposed a pitching-shot detection algorithm in his thesis. His algorithm is based on 5 color and motion features extracted from each frame, which are then fed to a SVM (Support Vector Machine) classifier, after a shot change is identified. For shots containing above a certain percentage of pitching frames, they will be identified as the pitching shots.

Expectedly, multiple features will be powerful in distinguishing pitching shots from non-pitching shots. Our detection process is decomposed into two sub-processes of shot segmentation and shot classification. Fuzzy classifier, known to be simple and powerful in integrating human's domain knowledge, is used to classify a frame according to features extracted therein. By combining the classification results of frames in a shot, pitching shots can then be identified.

## 2  Pre-processing – Shot Detection and Feature Extraction

Figure 1 illustrates the block diagram of pitching shot detection.

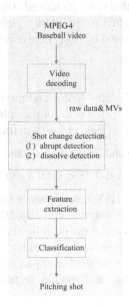

**Fig. 1.** The block diagram of pitching shot detection

In our system, the MPEG-4 compressed video is accepted as the input. Since our algorithm is established in the image domain, the MPEG-4 video should be first decoded to yield the MV information and the RGB image data. Clearly, the shot change boundaries should be first identified. Our system is capable of managing abrupt and dissolve changes. After shot segmentation, shot features are extracted and fed to the fuzzy classifier for classification (pitching shot or non-pitching shot).

## 2.1 Shot Change Detection

Three methods are integrated for abrupt change detection: (A) color histogram difference, (B) linear regression analysis, and (C) field color difference.

For method (A), Haar-wavelets analysis [8] is used to decompose each R, G, or B color histogram to multiple levels, which are then matched between successive frames to indicate the probability of scene change. For method (B), the difference image between successive frames is calculated and a block of interest (BOI) [9] is found out therein. For two pairs of BOIs from 3 successive frames, a 2-D scatter plot is analyzed to obtain a regression line. Behaviors of this line indicate the chance of abrupt shot change. On the other hand, method (C) recognizes the fact of strong color correlation between baseball video shots. Hence, field-color (red for the sand and green for the grass) percentage difference can be used to complement methods (A) and (B). Any frame satisfying one of these three criteria would be recognized to be at an abrupt shot change.

For dissolved (gradual transitions) shot change detection, the method proposed by [10] is used to detect all kinds of dissolved shot change. This algorithm is advantageous of its capability of discriminating global motions caused by camera movement and local motions caused by object movement from a real dissolve.

## 2.2 Feature Extraction

Here we extract two kinds of features (color and motion) to distinguish pitching and non-pitching shots. Dissimilar to [3], we select the color features from the HSV color space. Referring to [2], the range of field colors is defined as

Grass color: $0.16 < H < 0.46$ and $0.16 < S < 0.7$ and $V > 0$

Sand color: $0.022 < H < 0.11$ and $0.25 < S < 0.8$ and $V > 0$

The main reason of selecting HSV color space is that the performance of detecting pixels with the field color using color features in HSV is more stable than that in RGB. Figure 2 shows a comparison of the detection results obtained in HSV and RGB spaces, where the black pixels represent the fields detected. Clearly, the fields (red sands and green grass) cluster around the lower part of the image.

In the following, other color and motion features adopted in our system are introduced.

1. **Field color percentage** ( $x_1$ )

   Expectedly, the variance of field color percentages will be smaller for pitching frames than for non-pitching frames.

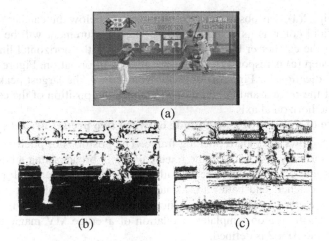

**Fig. 2.** (a) Original frame and results of field color detection in (b) HSV space, (c) RGB space

2. **Dominant color:** H and V components in HSV ($x_2$ and $x_3$)

In [3], the dominant color is measured from fixed regions in a frame. However, this measuring may be only useful for specific kinds of baseball programs. To be general for more kinds of baseball programs, measurement of the dominant color is modified as follows.

a. Project the pixels of non-field color to the horizontal axis.
b. Find local peaks of the resulting curve after projection.
c. Select the third (empirically from a large set of pitching frames) local peaks in according to the projection value. The height of the third peak is used to determine a horizontal line for dominant color calculation.
d. Calculate the dominant color below the horizontal line derived above.

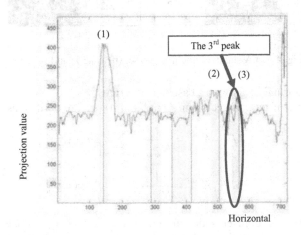

**Fig. 3.** Result of projecting pixels of non-field color to the horizontal axis and the positions of local peaks

From Fig. 2(a), it is observed that the image part below the catcher or batter will have the field color as its dominant color. This measurement will be stable if the position of the catcher or bitter is identified. Clearly, the horizontal line derived in the above step (c) is responsible for indicating this information. Figure 3 shows the result of projection for Fig. 2(a). As seen from Fig. 3, the largest peak reveals the position of the pitcher and the third one indicates the position of the catcher or the batter in the horizontal axis.

3. **Difference of average MV magnitude between two pre-set areas** ($x_4$)

Figure 4(a) shows a standard pitching frame. The positions of pitcher, catcher, and batter are normally fixed, due to the fixed camera in broadcasting a baseball game. Significant motions expectedly occur within the rectangled areas in Fig.4(a), where the pitcher, catcher, and batter are located. However, to deal with more possible situations, we consider two possible region templates, as shown in Fig.4(b) and (c). According to the region templates, a relation of average MV magnitude between two *Area1* and *Area2* is defined.

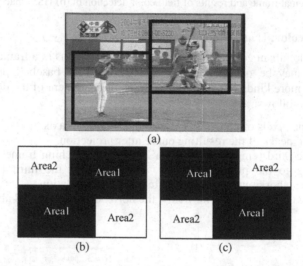

**Fig. 4.** (a) A standard pitching frame, (b) case 1, and (c) case 2

a.  Case 1: (normal in Taiwan's baseball program)
    The averages of motion vectors in *Area1* and *Area2* are defined as

$$MV\_A_1^{Case1} = \frac{1}{N_{Area1}} \sum_{(x,y) \in Area1} \|mv(x,y)\| \tag{1}$$

$$MV\_A_2^{Case1} = \frac{1}{N_{Area2}} \sum_{(x,y) \in Area2} \|mv(x,y)\| \tag{2}$$

where $mv(x, y)$ represents the motion vector at the coordinate $(x, y)$. *Area1* mostly covers the regions of the pitcher, catcher, and batter, and *Area2* is normally the background or field. $N_{Area1}$ and $N_{Area2}$ are the numbers of pixels in *Area1* and *Area2*, respectively.

b. **Case 2:**
Similar to case 1, we calculate $MV\_A_1^{Case2}$ and $MV\_A_2^{Case2}$ via Eqs. (1) and (2).

After obtaining { $MV\_A_1^{Case1}$, $MV\_A_2^{Case1}$ } and { $MV\_A_1^{Case2}$, $MV\_A_2^{Case2}$ }, the feature is computed as

$$Max\{(MV\_A_1^{Case1} - MV\_A_2^{Case1}),\ (MV\_A_1^{Case2} - MV\_A_2^{Case2})\}. \tag{3}$$

4. **Direction of activity ($x_5$)**

This feature is characterized by the major direction of MVs. Here we quantize MV directions into 8 slots and make a histogramming of them. If a major direction exists, its orientation index is recorded. Otherwise, "zero" is selected. For most pitching shots, since there is little camera motion and object motion, the direction of activity is also zero.

5. **Intensity of activity ($x_6$)**

This feature denotes the standard deviation of amplitudes of MVs in a frame.


## 3  Fuzzy Classifier

A fuzzy system is based on both human knowledge and mathematical models. If the human knowledge can be effectively included, the system performance can be raised. Since a trained fuzzy system is simple in computation it is advantageous to adopt fuzzy classifier for pitching shot detection.

Actually, the 5 features derived from Section 2 are different in nature and complementary in performance. Their corresponding membership functions, when properly adjusted, raise the performance of our proposed scheme. According to experiences, direction of activity, field color percentage, H component, and V component are most useful in distinguishing pitching shots from non-pitching ones. Based on this fact, higher weights are assigned to them. A total of 192 fuzzy rules are devised in our system. They are not listed here to save the page space.

Referring to [4],[5], a fuzzy system with a product inference engine, singleton fuzzifier, and center-average defuzzifier is adopted. The fuzzy output is calculated as:

$$y = \frac{\sum_{j=1}^{M} y_c^j \prod_{i=1}^{N} \mu_i^j(x_i)}{\sum_{j=1}^{M} \prod_{i=1}^{N} \mu_i^j(x_i)} \tag{4}$$

where $x_i$ and $y$ are the input and output variables of the fuzzy system, respectively, $y_c^j$ is the center value of the output fuzzy set for the $j$th rule, and $\mu_i^j(x_i)$ ($j$=1,..., $M$, $i$=1, ..., $N$) is the membership value of $x_i$. The membership functions of $x_i$ and $y$ are defined in Fig. 5 and 6, respectively. To classify a frame, the decision rule is described as follows: when $y$ is bigger then *Thd* (set to be 0.65 in current implementation), then this frame is classified as a pitching frame.

After classifying pitching frames, we adopt the majority voting to identify whether a shot is a pitching shot:

If $N_{pitching} \geq 0.5 \cdot N_{test}$, it is a pitching shot; otherwise, it is a non-pitching shot, where $N_{pitching}$ denotes the number of pitching frames involved in the test shot and $N_{test}$ is the number of frames in the test shot.

## 4   Experimental Results

To evaluate the performance of the proposed system, we recorded 305 video clips of Taiwan's baseball game. Each video clip whose frame size is 720×480 pixels contains 4~12 shots (one of them is the pitching shot). From these 305 video clips, we select 75 pitching shots and 468 non-pitching shots for test. $N_{test}$ is set to be 30. That means after shot boundary detection, we select the first 30 frames for pitching shot classification. The detection rate is defined as follows:

$$\text{detection rate} = \frac{\text{total shots} - (\text{missing} + \text{false alarm})}{\text{total shots}} \qquad (5)$$

The higher the detection rate, the better performance the pitching shot detection.

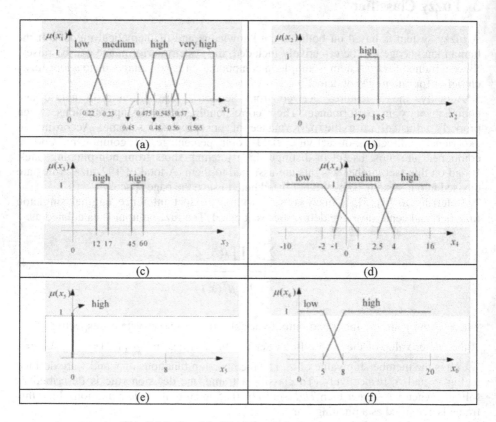

**Fig. 5.** Membership functions of six features, $x_1 \sim x_6$

To compare the performances between the SVM-based [3],[7] and fuzzy-based approaches, the same features are calculated and classified. The detection rates are 95.76% and 94.48%, respectively, for our proposed and the SVM-based method. This result demonstrates that our fuzzy classifier based on the domain knowledge can achieve a higher detection rate though more features are adopted in the SVM-based method.

False alarms of our proposed scheme mostly come from the reason that the features, $x_2$, $x_3$, and $x_4$, extracted from close-up scenes are similar to those extracted from the pitching frames.

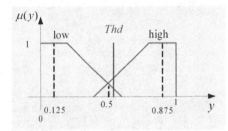

**Fig. 6.** Membership function of output $y$

# 5 Conclusions

In this article, a scheme for pitching shot detection is proposed. Several features of color, motion, and spatial activity, are used for classification. A fuzzy classifier with human knowledge is also developed here. From experimental results, a detection rate of 95.76% demonstrates that our proposed scheme effectively identifies the pitching shots.

# References

1. X. Gao and X. Tang,: Unsupervised Video-Shot Segmentation and Model-Free Anchorperson Detection for News Video Story Parsing. IEEE Trans. on Circuits and System for Video Technology, 12 (2002) 765-776.
2. S.-C. Pei and F. Chen,: Semantic Scenes Detection and Classification in Sports Videos. IPPR Conf. Computer Vision, Graphics and Image Processing, (2003) 210-217.
3. Sheng-Hsiung Shia,: Combining Caption and Visual Features for Semantic Event Detection and Classification of Baseball Video. Master thesis, National Chung Cheng University, Taiwan (2004).
4. L.-X. Wang,: A Course in Fuzzy System and Control. Prentice Hall PTR (1997).
5. D. H. K. Tsang, B. Bensaou, and S. T. C. Lam,: Fuzzy-based Rate Control for Real-Time MPEG Video. IEEE Trans. on Fuzzy Systems, 6 (1998) 504-516.
6. N. H. Bach, K. Shinoda, and S. furui,: Robust Highlight Extraction Using Multi-stream Hidden Markov Models for Baseball Video. IEEE Int'l Conf. on Image Processing, (2005) III - 173-6.

7. Wen-Nung Lie and Sheng-Hsiung Shia,: Combining Caption and Visual Features for Semantic Event Classification of Baseball Video. IEEE Int'l Conf. on Multimedia and Expo, (2005) 1254-1257.
8. Jyrki Korpi-Anttila,: Automatic Color Enhancement and Scene Change Detection of Digital Video. Licentiate thesis, Helsinki University of Technology (2002).
9. Seung-Hoon Han and In-So Kweon,: Detecting Cuts and Dissolves Through Linear Regression Analysis. Electronics Letters, 39 (2003) 1579-1581.
10. C. W. Su, H. R. Tyan, H. Y. Mark Liao, and L. H. Chen,: A Motion-Tolerant Dissolve Detection Algorithm. IEEE Int'l Conf. on Multimedia and Expo, (2002) 26-29.

# Color Changing and Fading Simulation for Frescoes Based on Empirical Knowledge from Artists*

Xifan Shi[1], Dongming Lu[1,2], and Jianming Liu[1]

[1] College of Computer Science and Technology, Zhejiang University
[2] State Key Lab. of CAD and CG, Zhejiang University,
310027, Hangzhou, Zhejiang, China
zjufan@hotmail.com, ldm@cs.zju.edu.cn, stoneliu1981@hotmail.com

**Abstract.** Visualizing the color changing and fading process of ancient Chinese wall paintings to tourists and researchers is of great value in both education and preservation. But previously, because empirical knowledge from artists was not introduced, it is infeasible to simulate the color changing and fading in the absence of physical and chemical knowledge of color changing and fading of frescoes. In this paper, however, empirical knowledge from artists is formalized. Since the improved system can reflect knowledge from artists in addition to the previous physical and chemical modeling, the simulation results are faithful to the color aging process of frescoes. In this article, first, the former related works is reviewed. Then, the formalization of empirical knowledge from artists is narrated. After that, the simulation results are shown and discussed. And finally, future research is suggested.

## 1 Introduction

Visualizing the color changing and fading process of ancient Chinese wall paintings to tourists and researchers is of great value in both education and preservation. It is a hot research area in the past decade [1-12]. The simulation results are demonstrated in the form of video clips either from the past to the present (showing the deterioration process that frescoes have haunted) or from the present to future (predicting the aging process that frescoes will probably suffer) since they are more vivid than the static pictures. The literatures mainly focused on physical or chemical based modeling or image processing techniques. For the latter, since these techniques are not tailored to the restoration of wall paintings, the effects they can achieve will not be better than those for other type of images. And for the former, for instance, in literature [1], modeling color changing due to chemical changing of pigment is presented and the conclusion is drawn by showing an impressive modeling result. And the dust accumulation algorithm is proposed in literature [2] and the system was capable of simulating color changing due to chemical changing of pigment and dust accumulation. But it is not always possible to model the aging process physically

---

* The research was partially funded by National High-tech R&D Program (No. 2003AA119020), the Program for New Century Excellent Talents in University (NCET-04-0535) and Key Technologies R&D Program (No. 2004BA810B).

and/or chemically. Except to some pigments such as red lead [13][14], most color changing mechanism of the pigments is still under intense research and a neat, clean theory has not yet been established. This is where empirical knowledge from artists can be used as a useful complement to the physical or chemical based modeling. In addition, previously, physical and/or chemical experts and artists cannot share their findings or knowledge efficiently because the experts only have the chemical data which reflects the oxidation process of the pigment used for drawing the frescoes while the artists have their own understandings which can only be expressed by painting. The chemical data is too abstract for the artists and the understandings of the artists are not easy to express or quantify. With the help of computer aided simulation, they can sit down before the screen, input either data or models and knowledge, discuss and modify them according to the resultant simulation. As a result, it is urgent to develop a system featuring combining both empirical knowledge from artists and chemical data.

In this paper, the color changing and color fading simulation algorithm for Frescoes based on empirical knowledge from artists is proposed in Chapter 2. Then, the simulation results are presented and discussed in Chapter 3. And finally, further works are elucidated in Chapter 4. As expected, by integrating the empirical knowledge, the improved system boasts a versatile deterioration simulation which can reflect both the knowledge from artists and the quantified chemical data and stimulates information sharing on aging rule of frescoes between different sections.

## 2   Color Changing and Fading Simulation Based on Empirical Knowledge from Artists

The simulation can be divided into two sub-problems: the computable model, namely, the colorimetric modeling based on the previous research outcomes in [1] and formalization of empirical knowledge from artists based on key point based uniform B-Spline color interpolation.

### 2.1   The Computable Model: The Colorimetric Modeling

It is beyond doubt that once the color of pigments and percentage of each pigment are determined for any area of fresco, the resultant color of that area is determined by the following formula as proved in [2]:

$$\left(R_m, \quad G_m, \quad B_m\right) = \left(\sum_{i=1}^{n} P_i R_i, \quad \sum_{i=1}^{n} P_i G_i, \quad \sum_{i=1}^{n} P_i B_i\right), \tag{1}$$

where the color of ingredient $i$ in RGB color space is $(R_i, G_i, B_i)$ and the area proportion of ingredient $i$ in the mixture is $P_i$. Thus, at arbitrary time, if the ingredient of a pixel is only composed of that pixel from the initial and ending, the only thing that is needed to compute the intermediate color is to identify its proportion in the initial and ending. This formula can also be applied to color fading because for color fading, the ending is the color of the background. So both color changing and color fading can be described by formula (1). Or in formula form, let $i(x, y)$ and $e(x, y)$ denote the initial and ending appearance of a fresco at position (x, y) respectively and

$p(x, y, t)$ denote the proportion of initial at position $(x, y)$ at arbitrary time $t$, then the corresponding color $c(x, y, t)$ can be computed by using the following formula provided that the ingredient of any pixel at any time is only composed of its counterpart in the initial and ending:

$$c(x,y,t) = p(x,y,t)i(x,y) + [1 - p(x,y,t)]e(x,y). \qquad (2)$$

If not, for instance, red lead first becomes white lead, and then white lead becomes black lead dioxide, then the whole color changing and fading can be divided into several stages and in each stage formula (2) still holds, which can be formularized as:

$$c(x,y,t) = p(x,y,t)i_i(x,y) + [1 - p(x,y,t)]e_i(x,y), \qquad (3)$$

where $t \in [t_i, t_{i+1}]$ (Time $t$ belongs to the $i^{th}$ stage, and $t_i$ is the starting time of stage $i$ and $t_{i+1}$ is the ending time of stage $i$ and also the starting time of stage $i+1$.) and $e_i(x, y) = i_{j+1}(x, y)$ (The ending appearance of a stage is the same as the starting appearance of the next stage.). This paper focuses on the simulation composed of only one stage since it is not difficult to generalize to the simulation consisting of several stages. Or to put it in detail, the simulation composed of several stages can be done in three phases:

I.    Divide the simulation into several sub simulations, each of which composed of only one stage.

II.   Generate the video clips for these sub simulations.

III.  Merge these video clips in proper order.

The simulation shown in Fig. 4 is indeed composed of two stages, which is created by this three-phase method.

In brief, the aging simulation result only relies on three requisites, i.e., the appearance of initial in each pixel ($i(x, y)$), the appearance of ending in each pixel ($e(x, y)$) and the proportion of initial in each pixel at arbitrary time ($p(x, y, t)$).

## 2.2 Formulation of Empirical Knowledge from Artists

Since appearances are easy to acquire, such as by taking photos or composed by software, say, Photoshop, the attention is paid to the last requirement ($p(x, y, t)$), which reflects the empirical knowledge from artists and chemical data. The chemical data can be either obtained from chemical modeling as in [2] or from simulation experiments.

Evidently, it is theoretically possible and practically impossible for an artist to directly designate $p(x, y, t)$ of each pixel because this task is boring and time-consuming. However, this designating process can be simplified both temporally and spatially.

**Spatial Simplification.** As is known to all, the component of adjacent pixels are correlated, or in other words, a region may use the same pigment, thus it is reasonable that some adjacent pixels with similar color will share the same $p(x, y, t)$. So instead of designating $p(x, y, t)$, it is equivalent and more efficient to designating $g(x, y)$ and $p(g, t)$, where $g(x, y)$ means classifying the pixels according to the aging rule (It is more likely that pixels share the same pigment will share the same rule, as illustrated in Fig. 1. They are named as Aging Classification Map (ACM) since they reflect the aging classification.) and $p(g, t)$ is the aging rule that a group of pixels conform. In Fig. 1, the left ACM has three colors: orange, green and black. It means all the pixels sharing the same color in ACM will have the same aging rule. Or as the following formula form:

$$g(x, y) = \begin{cases} 1 & if \quad c(x, y) = c_1 \\ 2 & if \quad c(x, y) = c_2 \\ 3 & if \quad c(x, y) = c_3 \end{cases}, \tag{4}$$

where $c(x, y)$ represents the pixel color at position $(x, y)$ in ACM, and $c_1$, $c_2$ and $c_3$ are orange, green and black, respectively. The color in ACM is only for distinguishing the different aging rules. If you change all the orange pixels into blue, $g(x, y)$ is still the same because $c_1$ is changed into blue. Of course, ACM can be arbitrarily designated as shown in the right ACM, which means the gowns on the Buddhas do not share the same aging rule because of other factors such as humidity or ultraviolet. Obviously, different ACM will lead to different simulation effect, and by this means, ACM gives the freedom to artist to express his / her own understanding of aging simulation. Generally speaking, the area using the same pigment will have the same aging rule if other factors are almost equal, which is the reason why ACM often looks like the initial or ending appearance.

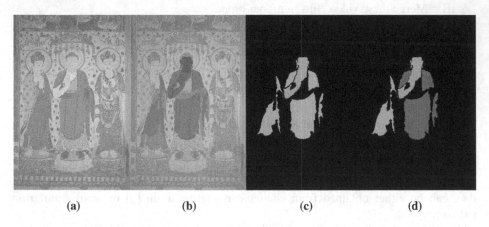

| (a) | (b) | (c) | (d) |

**Fig. 1.** User input. The initial (a) and ending (b) appearance along with two ACMs (c) & (d).

**Temporal Simplification.** $p(x, y)$ can be graphically represented by a curve in a coordinate frame whose x-axis is time and y axis is percentage of the contribution of the initial painting. This curve must be smooth to disallow the presence of sudden color change of any pixels, which from the view of artists is the harmony that they pay a high attention to. Needless to say, $p(x, y)$ must be discretized since computer is inherently discreted. Moreover, the video of the simulated result is composed of frames, so $t$ is discretized to represent the time of each frame and the time that the appearance of fresco is sampled. For a video sampled 250 times (consisting of 250 frames), giving $p(g)$ for each times is theoretically possible and practically impossible because of the tediousness of the task. It is more acceptable to give only a few key points of $p(g, t)$ and the whole $p(g, t)$ is approximated to an extent that error is undetectable. Hence the key points are connected by cubic B-Spline, which boasts $C^2$ continuity, to guarantee the smoothness of the curve of $p(g, t)$, or the harmony of color changing or fading in the opinion of artists. This problem can be formularized as follows [15]:

**Given:** A knot sequence $u_1, \ldots, u_k$ and a degree $n$, also a set of data points $p_1 \ldots p_L$ with $L = k-n$.

**Find:** A set of B-spline controls point $d_1, \ldots, d_L$, such that the resulting curve $x(u)$ satisfies

$$x(\xi_i) = p_i \,; i = 1, \ldots, L.$$

This problem is solved in [15], and for uniform cubic B-spline, Jiaguang [16] has given a simpler solution as the following:

$$
\begin{bmatrix}
6 & & & & & \\
1 & 4 & 1 & & & \\
& 1 & 4 & 1 & & \\
& & \bullet & \bullet & \bullet & \\
& & & \bullet & \bullet & \bullet \\
& & & 1 & 4 & 1 \\
& & & & & 6
\end{bmatrix}
\begin{bmatrix}
d_1 \\ d_2 \\ \bullet \\ \bullet \\ \bullet \\ d_{L-1} \\ d_L
\end{bmatrix}
= 6
\begin{bmatrix}
p_1 \\ p_2 \\ \bullet \\ \bullet \\ \bullet \\ p_{L-1} \\ p_L
\end{bmatrix}.
\tag{5}
$$

This tri-diagonal matrix equation can be solved by using Thomas algorithm, that is, forward elimination and backward substitution [17]. To ensure the resulting curve passing $p_1$ and $p_n$, two additional control points $d_0$ and $d_{L+1}$ are added, where $d_0=2d_1-d_2$ and $d_{L+1}=2d_L-d_{L-1}$. If the generated video is deviated from the thoughts, it can be interactively modified and improved.

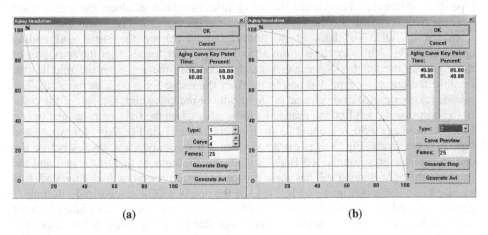

(a)                                                    (b)

**Fig. 2.** Aging curve key points designation after importing Fig. 1(d)

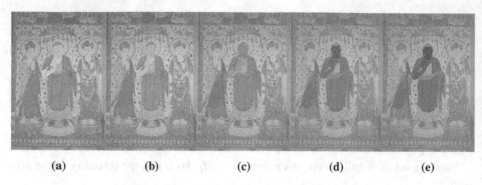

**Fig. 3.** The resultant aging simulation of Fig. 2

Fig. 2 shows a typical aging curve key points designation process. The green curve represents $p(g, t)$, which expresses the empirical knowledge from artists and/or the experiment results or chemical modeling in [1]. For the latter, the key points are experiment results at discreted time or generated by selecting some discreted time and computing from the chemical modeling in [1] at these time. Because ACM in Fig. 1(d) has 4 different colors, so all the pixels are classified into 4 aging types (see the *Type* Combo Box in Fig. 2(a)) and type 1, type 2, type 3 and type 4 correspond to red, orange, green and black respectively. The red dot in the curve represents the key points, which can be dragged or directly modified or input in the *Time* and *Percent* Edit Boxes in *Aging Curve Key Point* Group Box. The curve and Edit Boxes are correlated, which means modifying one will change the other. Since the aging simulation video clip must start from the initial and finish with the ending, two data points, (0, 100) and (100, 0), are implicitly included and only the key points between them is needed to be specified. The user can select the aging type by the *Type* Combo Box and input the curve for each type. The *Frames* Edit Box specifies the length of the whole video clip and 250 frames means 10 seconds in PAL system. As can be seen from Fig. 2, the curve for type 1 and type 2 are different, which means the aging rules are different albeit the pigment for drawing the two gowns are the same. The result is illustrated in Fig. 3 and the aging is from left to right. The leftmost (a) and rightmost (e) are the initial and ending appearance. Fig. 3(b) is extracted from a frame only a few frames after the start, part of the gown on the left Buddha changes much more than the gown on the middle one because the curve for type 1 drops faster than the curve for type 2 at the start. The middle (c) is extracted from a frame in the middle of the video clip, and part of the color of the gown on the left Buddha changed a lot while that on the right one changed only a little, because at $t = 50$, $p$ is about 23 (in Fig. 2(a)) and 77 (in Fig. 2(b)) for type 1 and type 2, respectively. Fig. 3(d) is extracted from a frame only a few frames before the end, part of the gown on the left Buddha is almost the same as that of the end and the gown on the right Buddha still has some noticeable difference from that of the end. It is manifest that if the user imports Fig. 1(c), all the pixels will be categorized into only 3 aging types and the gowns of the two Buddhas will not have the huge variance in color as in shown in Fig. 3. It should be pointed out that the aging rules in Fig. 2 are not created by artists and is only used for illustration. The real aging rules are much more complex, but if the user (artist) inserts sufficient key points, our approach is still applicable to express the rules or thumb from the artists.

## 3 Simulation Results

At present, the algorithm is realized and integrated into color changing and fading simulation system for Dunhuang frescoes. After the user has input an initial and ending image, specified the aging type that each pixel belongs to by importing ACM, designated the aging rule of each type by inputting some key points and finally given the duration of video clip, an AVI clip is generated. The user can make amendments on aging rule and ACM until the result is satisfactory and conveys his / her own understandings or knowledge.

| (a) | (b) | (c) | (d) | (e) |

**Fig. 4.** Color changing simulation of a Buddha

**Fig. 5.** Color fading simulation of fresco

Fig. 4. is extracted from a generated AVI file illustrating a typical color changing of Dunhuang Frescoes, and (a) and (e) are the initial and ending (current) appearance of a Buddha from the south wall of cave 205, respectively. The video clip is created by artists from Fine Arts Institute of Dunhuang Academy by using the software which realizes the approaches presented in this paper. Since parts of the face of Buddha once became white and white cannot be expressed by a combination of red and black (In fact, white lead is a new compound rather than a mixture of red lead and black lead dioxide.), Fig. 4(c) is manually added to force the occurrence of the white face in the video. The whole video clip is generated in two steps (The step of dividing the simulation into two sub simulations is done in mind and consequently this step can be omitted.). First, generate one clip by inputting (a) and (c) as the initial and ending and generated the other clip by inputting (c) and (e) as the initial and ending. Then combine these two video clips into one. Fig. 5. is extracted from a generated AVI file demonstrating the color fading of a small portion from the south wall of cave 260, which is also created by artists from Fine Arts Institute of Dunhuang Academy by using our software.

## 4  Conclusion and Future Work

In this article, the algorithm to simulate color changing and fading for frescoes based on empirical knowledge from artists is brought forward. The algorithm is implemented and integrated into the color changing and fading simulation system for Dunhuang frescoes. The system is put into service in Dunhuang Academy and more simulation results are underway for the forthcoming art exhibition.

This system can be used for at least three purposes. Firstly, the researchers can generate video clips showing the typical diseases that causing the deterioration of the frescoes. These video clips will greatly educate the visitors and authorities and raise their awareness of the magnitude of fresco conservation. Secondly, based on this system, the researchers from Conservation Institute of Dunhuang Academy can discussed the mechanism of the deterioration of the frescoes and the effectiveness if some protective measures are taken because with given parameters (The absence and presence of various protective measures will change the parameters.), a video clip embodying the simulated effect can be produced and viewed, making it possible for the protectors to choose the best steps to carry out. Finally, the experts from Conservation Institute of Dunhuang Academy and the artists from Fine Arts Institute of Dunhuang Academy can share their findings or knowledge in the color aging of frescoes and generate simulation video clips which embody both the empirical knowledge from artists and the quantified chemical data. Admittedly, for some frescoes, it's hard to reach a consensus. In this case, our system can generate several video clips to demonstrate the divergence and let other experts to vote, discuss and comment on these possible scenarios, which will give birth to a more scientific simulation result.

Meanwhile, it raises more questions. First and foremost, the simulation is mainly on the aspect of color changing and fading. But there's another important disease for the frescoes, namely, surface layer turning crisp which changes the surface shape of the frescoes, must also be analyzed, quantified and finally simulated. Second, in addition to the chemical reaction, there are ultraviolet (Ultraviolet indeed leads to chemical reactions, but since they defy the modeling in [1], it must be remodeled.) together with the microbe effects. These two must also be taken into consideration. Last but not least, more and more tourists come to Dunhuang to pay a visit to these cultural relics. It cannot be denied that the carbon dioxide they exhale and the temperature variation they cause will do no good to the Frescoes. Therefore, this side-effect must be analyzed, quantified and visualized so that the authorities can make their decision scientifically based on the principle of both maximizing the social and educational value and not sacrificing this invaluable World Cultural Heritage, which is proposed to and accepted by the National People's Congress.

**Acknowledgement.** We would like to express our sincere gratitude for our research partner, Dunhuang Academy in their providing us the necessary data and dedication in using and making suggestions on our system, especially for the artists from Fine Arts Institute of Dunhuang Academy for their creation of the striking simulation results in this paper. This work cannot be accomplished without their generous help.

# References

1. Xifan Shi, Dongming Lu, Colorimetric and Chemical Modeling Based Aging Simulation of Dunhuang Murals, The Fifth International Conference on Computer and Information Technology, CIT 2005 (2005) 570–574
2. Xifan Shi, Dongming Lu, Jianming Liu, Yunhe Pan: An Integrated Color Changing Simulation System Based on Colorimetric and Chemical Modeling. Edutainment 2006 (2006) 1037–1046
3. Soo-Chang Pei, Yi-Chong Zeng, Ching-Hua Chang, Virtual restoration of ancient Chinese paintings using color contrast enhancement and lacuna texture synthesis, IEEE Transactions on Image Processing, Vol. 13, Issue: 3 (2004) 416–429
4. Baogang Wei, Yonghuai Liu, Yunhe Pan, Using hybrid knowledge engineering and image processing in color virtual restoration of ancient murals, IEEE Transactions on Knowledge and Data Engineering, Vol. 15, Issue: 5 (2003) 1338–1343
5. Barni M, Bartolini F, Cappellini V, Image processing for virtual restoration of artworks IEEE Multimedia, Vol. 7, Issue: 2 (2000) 34–37
6. Stanco F., Tenze, L, Ramponi G, de Polo A, Virtual restoration of fragmented glass plate photographs, Proceedings of the 12th IEEE Mediterranean Electrotechnical Conference, Vol. 1, (2004) 243–246
7. De Rosa, A., Bonacehi A.M., Cappellini V., Barni M., Image segmentation and region filling for virtual restoration of artworks, International Conference on Image Processing, Vol. 1, (2001), 562–565
8. Palamidese P., Betro M., Muccioli G., The virtual restoration of the Visir tomb, Visualization '93, Proceedings., IEEE Conference on Visualization, (1993) 420–423
9. Lin Yi, Lu Dongming, Technical Research on Virtual Color Shading of Dunhuang Fresco, Application Research of Computers, Vol.17 No.12 (2000) 12-14 (In Chinese)
10. Hua Zhong, Lu Dongming, Research on Virtual Color Restoration and Gradual Changing Simulation of Duhuang Fresco Journal of Image and Graphics Vol.7 No.2 (2002) 181-185 (In Chinese)
11. Lin Yi, Lu Dongming, Pan Yunhe, Image Processing for Virtual Recovery of Murals Proceedings of CAD/GRAPHICS'2001 Vol. 2 (2001) 539–542
12. Lin Yi, Lu Dongming, Pan Yunhe, Knowledge-based Virtual Restoration for Artworks Proceedings of CISST 2001 Vol. 2 (2001) 437–443
13. Li Zuixiong, Analysis and Research on the Pigment Used in Fresco and Painted Sculpture of Dunhuang Mogao cave, Art Gallery, Vol. 1 (In Chinese)
14. Li Zuixiong, Crottoes Conservation, Gansu Ethnic Press, (1994) (In Chinese)
15. Gerald Farin, Curves and Surfaces for CAGD A Practical Guide, Fifth Edition, Morgan Kaufmann, (2001) 147–148
16. Jiaguang Sun, Computer Graphics, Third Edition, Tsinghua University Press, (1998) 317
17. William H. Press, Saul A. Teukolsky, William T. Vetterling, Brian P. Flannery, Numerical Recipes in C++: The Art of Scientific Computing Second Edition, Cambridge University Press, (2002)

# A Novel Spatial-Temporal Position Prediction Motion-Compensated Interpolation for Frame Rate Up-Conversion*

Jianning Zhang, Lifeng Sun, and Yuzhuo Zhong

Department of Computer Science and Technology,
Tsinghua University,
Beijing 100084, China
zjn01@mails.tsinghua.edu.cn, sunlf@mail.tsinghua.edu.cn,
zyz-dcs@mail.tsinghua.edu.cn

**Abstract.** In this paper, a novel spatial-temporal position prediction motion-compensated interpolation method (MCI) for frame rate up-conversion is proposed using the transmitted Motion Vectors (MVs). Based on our previous proposed GMPP algorithm, the new method uses the motion vectors correction (MVC) first. Then joint spatial-temporal position prediction algorithm is applied on the transmitted MVs to predict more accurately the positions the interpolated blocks really move to, which makes the MVs used for interpolation more nearer to the true motion. Then the weighted-adaptive spatial-temporal MCI algorithm is used to complete the final interpolation. Applied to the H.264 decoder, the new proposed method can achieve significant increase on PSNR and obvious decrease of the block artifacts, which can be widely used in video streaming and distributed video coding applications.

**Keywords:** Motion-compensated interpolation, spatial-temporal position prediction, weighted-adaptive interpolation.

## 1 Introduction

Frame rate up-conversion (FRC) method can be applied widely in low bit-rate video coding and distributed video coding. In order to reduce the bit-rate, a number of frames are skipped at the encoder and then missing frames are interpolated at the decoder using FRC. Otherwise, the recent popular video coding systems use more complex computations to achieve higher coding performance such as H.264 [1]. Using FRC at the decoder can reduce not only the bit-rate but also the computation complexity at the encoder. The recent popular distributed video coding methods make the complexity balance between encoder and decoder. The frame rate up-conversion interpolation is very important to generate estimation side-information [2].

* This work has been supported by the National Natural Science Foundation of China under Grant No. 60503063 and No. 60432030 and supported by 973 Project under Grant No. 2006CB303103.

Y. Zhuang et al. (Eds.): PCM 2006, LNCS 4261, pp. 870–879, 2006.

Many FRC methods are developed. The simple methods use frame repetition or frame averaging without considering motions. These methods will produce motion jerkiness and object blurring of moving areas. To overcome the problems, the MCI methods have been studied in recent years.

The MCI methods can be divided into two categories. The first category uses motion estimation (ME) at the decoder to achieve the MVs [3][4][5]. The second category uses transmitted MVs from the encoder [6][7][8].

In the former category, bi-directional ME algorithm is proposed in [3][4]. Multiple motions estimation and weighted-adaptive interpolation methods are considered in [5]. But the ME-based methods require much calculation for ME at the decoder.

In order to reduce the computation complexity in the decoder, transmitted MVs are used in MCI instead of MVs from ME [6]. But the transmitted MVs are unreliable such that the block artifacts will occur. The motion vector correction is applied to reduce the failed MVs using the spatial correlation in [7][8]. However, in these methods based on transmitted MVs, the MV used for interpolating a block in the interpolated frame is the MV of the block at the same position in current decoded frame. The decoded frame block is not the true block that the interpolated block moves to. Furthermore, the temporal correlation of MVs is not considered. To solve the problems, we have proposed GMPP-MCI algorithm in [9]. The GMPP-MCI algorithm uses generative model to estimate the temporal dynamic of previous frame MVs and to generate the temporal-predicted MVs for the current frame. Position prediction method is proposed to predict the position that current block moves to. So the MVs used for interpolation are nearer to the true block motion vectors. The main problem of the GMPP algorithm is that the algorithm focuses on the temporal correlation and continuity in MVs field. The spatial correlation and continuity among the MVs of the adjacent blocks are not considered.

In this paper, a novel spatial-temporal position prediction motion-compensated interpolation method (STPP-MCI) on the basis of GMPP-MCI using transmitted MVs is proposed. After MVC, joint spatial-temporal position prediction method is applied on the transmitted MVs to predict more accurately the positions the interpolated blocks really move to. Then in the interpolation step, the weighted-adaptive MCI (WAMCI) proposed in [5] is adopted to deal with the spatial-temporal multiple MVs. So the weighted-adaptive spatial-temporal MCI algorithm is used to complete the final interpolation.

The paper is organized as follows. The GMPP-MCI algorithm is overviewed in Section 2. The proposed STPP-MCI algorithm will be illustrated in Section 3. In Section 4, simulation results and discussions are given. Finally, the conclusions are presented in Section 5.

## 2 The Overview of GMPP-MCI

The GMPP-MCI algorithm has been proposed in [9]. The GMPP-MCI algorithm can be simply illustrated in the following steps: motion vector correction, temporal modeling, position prediction and interpolation using the best MVs selected from the temporal predicted MVs. The details of the algorithm can be found in [9].

1) Motion Vector Correction. MVC is the necessary step applied on the unreliable transmitted MVs at the beginning of MCI algorithm. The MVs of adjacent blocks are commonly used to correct or smooth the unsatisfied MVs because of the spatial correlations. The situations of intra MB and isolated MVs are considered for H.264 video coding. The MVs of these intra MBs should be interpolated using the average of the MVs of adjacent MBs surrounding it. The isolated MVs make motions unreliable and cause block artifacts, which can be corrected by smooth or median filter using MVs of adjacent blocks.

2) Temporal Modeling. The MVs used for interpolation have spatial and temporal correlation. In order to describe the temporal correlation and dynamics, temporal-predicted MVs (PMV) derived from previous frame MVs are used to approximate and correct transmitted MVs (TMV) of current decoded frame. The linear generative model is used to estimate the MVs in the past frames and generate the best predict MVs in the present frame. The temporal model can make the best estimation by least square errors.

3) Position Prediction. The conventional MCI algorithm interpolates each block by using the MV of the same position block in current decoded frame as shown in Fig. 1.

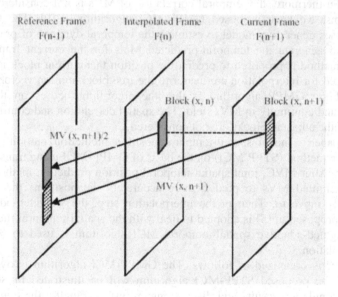

**Fig. 1.** The MVs for interpolation in conventional MCI algorithm. To interpolate Block(x,n) at position x in F(n), the MV(x,n+1) of the same position block, Block(x,n+1) in F(n+1) is used.

The interpolation can be done by the following equation. For each pixel f(x,n):

$$f(x,n) = \frac{f(x+v/2, n-1) + f(x-v/2, n+1)}{2} \tag{1}$$

where f(x,n) means pixel value at position x in F(n). v denotes MV(x,n+1) at the position x in F(n+1).

The problem is that Block(x,n+1) at the same position with interpolated Block(x,n) is not the true block which Block(x,n) moves to. So the MV(x,n+1) of Block(x,n+1) is not the true MV that the interpolated block owns.

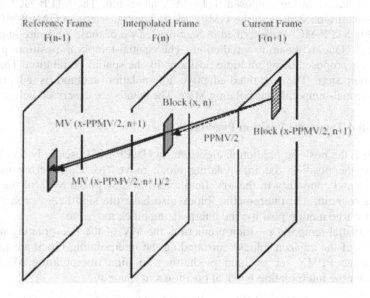

**Fig. 2.** The MVs for interpolation in position prediction MCI algorithm. The interpolated Block(x,n) at position x moves to Block(x-PPMV/2,n+1) at new position x-PPMV/2 in F(n+1). The MV used for interpolation of Block(x,n) becomes MV(x-PPMV/2,n+1) instead of MV(x,n+1).

To overcome this problem, the position prediction method uses position predicted MV (PPMV) to predict the new position x' where the interpolated Block(x,n) moves to in F(n+1). So the MV of Block(x',n+1) is the most similar with the MV owned by the interpolated block as shown in Fig. 2.

If $v'$ denotes MV(x-PPMV/2,n+1), the position prediction interpolation equation can be derived from (1).

$$f(x,n) = \frac{f(x+v'/2, n-1) + f(x-v'/2, n+1)}{2} \tag{2}$$

4) Interpolation using the best selected MVs. First, position prediction is applied on the first candidate MVs derived from the temporal MVs by the generative modeling. Then the second candidate MVs transmitted from the encoder for the current frame are also processed by position prediction. The SAD values are calculated for both the candidate MVs. The best interpolating MVs can be selected from the two position prediction results by the minimal SAD values. The interpolated frame is generated using equation (2).

## 3  The Proposed STPP-MCI Algorithm

On the basis of the GMPP-MCI algorithm, the spatial correlation and continuity are considered further in the proposed STPP-MCI algorithm. The STPP-MCI algorithm has the same framework with the GMPP-MCI. The four steps in GMPP-MCI are all accepted in STPP-MCI as described in Section 2. Two of these steps are improved in STPP-MCI. One is position prediction. The spatial-temporal position prediction algorithm is proposed using multiple positions by the spatial correlation. The other is interpolation step. The weighted-adaptive interpolation method is adopted using multiple spatial-temporal interpolating MVs. The details are described below.

### 3.1  Spatial-Temporal Position Prediction

From Fig.2, the position prediction algorithm in GMPP-MCI uses only one PPMV to prediction the position the interpolating block moves to. Considering the spatial correlation and continuity in the MV field after MVC step, the MVs of the adjacent blocks surrounding the interpolating block also have the significant probabilities to indicate the true motion position the interpolating block moves to.

In the spatial-temporal position prediction, the MV of the interpolating block and eight MVs of the adjacent blocks surrounding the interpolating block are used to be the candidate PPMV for position prediction. So nine interpolating MVs can be achieved for the interpolating block at position x in frame n.

$$IMV_i = MV(x - PPMV_i / 2, n + 1), i \in B \tag{3}$$

B denotes the block set including the interpolating block and the eight adjacent blocks. The best position predicted interpolating MV must be selected from these nine IMVs. The measurement of SAD values between the reference frame and current decoding frame using the IMVs can be used. The IMV with the minimal SAD value is selected to be the final position prediction results as shown in equation (4).

$$PPMV_{best} = \arg\min_{PPMVi}(SAD_{IMVi}), i \in B \tag{4}$$

### 3.2  Weighted-Adaptive Spatial-Temporal Interpolation

After position prediction, the MV in the new position block is used as IMV for interpolation. In the GMPP-MCI, the temporal correlation is only considered. The IMVs derived from the temporal predicted MVs and from the current frame MVs are selected adaptively. The similar idea of the spatial-temporal position prediction can be applied in the interpolating step. The spatial information is also concerned in STPP-MCI algorithm.

Block(x-PPMV/2,n+1) denotes the resulting block in current decoding frame after position prediction. So eight adjacent blocks surrounding the Block(x-PPMV/2,n+2) are selected. Then multiple MVs owned by these nine blocks are all used to interpolate the pixels in the interpolating block if these blocks are available. If the blocks are not available at the edge of the frame, the MVs of the blocks can be set to (0,0). So we can get nine f(x,n) values using equation (2). Weighted-adaptive algorithm is adopted to calculate the interpolating result from these nine f(x,n) values. The detail of weighted-adaptive MCI algorithm is described in [5].

The accuracy function can be presented as:

$$\Phi(v') = \frac{1}{\sum_i \left| f(x+i+v'/2, n-1) - f(x+i-v'/2, n+1) \right|}, \qquad (5)$$

where i denotes each pixel in the Block(x,n) at position x, and $v'$ means one of the multiple MVs illustrated above. If the denominator in equation (5) equals zero, the MV is with maximal accuracy function value and is selected to be the only MV for interpolating. The weighted-adaptive interpolation will not be used. So the final interpolation result f(x,n) can be calculated using the accuracy function values.

$$f(x,n) = \frac{\sum_{i=0}^{M} \Phi(v_i') f_i(x,n)}{\sum_{i=0}^{M} \Phi(v_i')}, \qquad (6)$$

where M = 8 and i = 0 to 8 which means the indexes of the Block(x-PPMV/2,n+1) and the eight adjacent blocks surrounding it. $f_i(x,n)$ values can be calculated by equation (2).

The total STPP-MCI algorithm process steps are simply illustrated in the following.

1) The motion vectors correction for transmitted MVs is first applied as described in Section 2.

2) Spatial-temporal position prediction algorithm is applied on the first candidate MVs derived from the temporal generative modeling to achieve up to nine candidate positions. For each position, the PPMV is derived and the weighted-adaptive MCI is done using equation (6) for the interpolating block. The measurement for selecting the position prediction result in equation (4) must be modified using maximal sum of the accuracy function values instead of minimal SAD value. So the equation (4) becomes:

$$PPMV_{best} = \underset{PPMVi}{\arg\max} (\sum_{i=0}^{M} \Phi(v_i')) \qquad (7)$$

The results of interpolating value and sum of the accuracy function values for the first candidate temporal predicted MVs are saved.

3) Spatial-temporal position prediction is then applied on the second candidate MVs transmitted from the encoder for the current frame. The same processing is done with the above step.

4) The final interpolating result is selected by the maximal sum of the accuracy function values from the results calculated by these two candidate MVs.

## 4  Simulation Results

The experiments are based on H.264 video coding standard with the baseline profile. The version of reference software is JM73. The test sequences include high motion sequences such as foreman, coast guard, and low motion ones such as akiyo and silent. The video format is CIF. The encoded frame rate is 15Hz and the up-conversion frame rate is 30Hz. We compare our proposed STPP-MCI algorithm with the conventional MCI algorithm, the GMPP-MCI proposed in [9] and the WAMCI derived from [5] which only concerns the spatial correlation and continuity. The motion vector correction (MVC) step is added on the WAMCI algorithm in the experiments to make the WAMCI algorithm more efficiency by more continuous MV field. Table 1 shows the results of PSNR comparisons and PSNR gains. The QP used in the experiments in Table 1 is 20, which represents the situation of the common bitrate and the good video quality.

**Table 1.** PSNR(dB) Comparisons and Gains

| Seqs. | MCI (dB) | GMPP (dB) | WAMCI +MVC (dB) | STPP (dB) | Gain from MCI (dB) | Gain from GMPP (dB) | Gain from WAMCI+ MVC (dB) |
|---|---|---|---|---|---|---|---|
| Coastg. | 27.64 | 28.72 | 29.69 | 30.10 | +2.46 | +1.38 | +0.41 |
| Foreman | 29.04 | 29.40 | 29.40 | 30.01 | +0.97 | +0.61 | +0.61 |
| News | 32.13 | 32.76 | 33.24 | 33.45 | +1.32 | +0.69 | +0.21 |
| Silent | 33.09 | 33.59 | 33.82 | 34.17 | +1.08 | +0.58 | +0.35 |
| Akiyo | 38.45 | 38.64 | 39.36 | 39.44 | +0.99 | +0.80 | +0.08 |
| MotherD. | 37.33 | 37.54 | 37.93 | 38.06 | +0.73 | +0.52 | +0.13 |

The Table 1 shows that the STPP-MCI algorithm can achieve higher PSNR than the other algorithms for comparisons. For high motion situations, the STPP-MCI algorithm can achieve average 1.7dB PSNR increase compared with conventional MCI algorithm, average 1dB increase with GMPP-MCI and average 0.5dB increase with WAMCI+MCI. For low motion situations, the average PSNR gain is 1dB compared with conventional MCI, 0.6dB compared with GMPP-MCI and 0.2dB compared with WAMCI+MVC.

In the high motion situation, the motion vectors are large (such as CoastG.) or complex changing (such as Foreman). In this situation, the position prediction algorithm is more efficient than that in the low motion situation. In the low motion situation, the motions are low and the spatial correlation is evident in the MV field. So the weighted-adaptive interpolation for the spatial MVs is efficient. So the proposed STPP-MCI algorithm makes the balance of performances between position prediction (temporal) and weighted-adaptive interpolation (spatial). The simulation results show that the proposed STPP-MCI is more efficient than the other algorithms in all the situations. The PSNR gain is up to 1.38dB compared with GMPP-MCI and up to 0.61dB with WAMCI+MVC.

Fig. 3 and Fig. 4 show the Rate-Distortion (RD) curves of foreman and silent sequences. From these figures we can see that the STPP-MCI algorithm can achieve evident improvement compared with the other algorithms in the figures, for the situations from low bitrate to high bitrate, using both high motion sequence and low motion sequence. In the high bitrate situation, the improvement is much higher than that in the low bitrate situation. This is because that in high bitrate situation, the decoded video quality is much higher and the MVs from the encoder are more accurate and smooth with more correlations in space and time. It also can be seen that the STPP-MCI algorithm is more efficient in the high motion situation than that in the low motion situation compared with the other algorithms for the reason of more efficiency of the position prediction algorithm applied to the transmitted MVs.

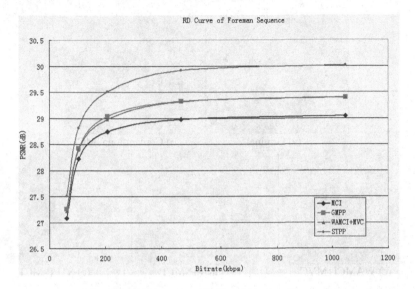

**Fig. 3.** Rate-Distortion Curve of Foreman Sequence

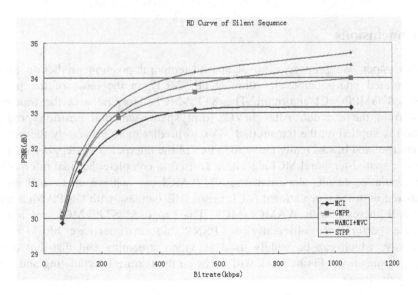

**Fig. 4.** Rate-Distortion Curve of Silent Sequence

The block artifacts can be decreased obviously compared with the other algorithms as shown in Fig. 5. This figure shows the 15th frame comparison results of the Foreman sequence. The block artifacts are evidently shown in the interpolated frames for the conventional MCI algorithm and for the WAMCI algorithm for the reason of no position prediction technology. The GMPP algorithm is much better by using position prediction before interpolation. Finally for the STPP-MCI algorithm, there are nearly no block artifacts in the interpolated frame as shown in (e) of Fig. 5.

(a) Original    (b) Conventional MCI

(c) WAMCI+MVC    (d) GMPP-MCI    (e) STPP-MCI

**Fig. 5.** Comparison of block artifacts for Foreman sequence at Frame 15

## 5  Conclusions

In this paper, we propose a novel spatial-temporal position prediction motion-compensated interpolation algorithm (STPP-MCI) on the basis of the previous proposed GMPP-MCI algorithm. The STPP-MCI algorithm uses the transmitted MVs from the encoder. After MVC, joint spatial-temporal position prediction method is applied on the transmitted MVs to predict more accurately the positions the interpolated blocks really move to. Then in the interpolation step, the weighted-adaptive spatial-temporal MCI algorithm is used to complete the final interpolation. The simulation results show that the STPP-MCI can achieve up to 2dB increase compared with the conventional MCI, up to 1dB increase with GMPP-MCI and up to 0.6dB increase with WAMCI+MCI. The proposed STPP-MCI can not only increase performance efficiently on PSNR but also decrease block artifacts obviously, which can be widely used in video streaming and distributed video coding applications. Future work will focus on the texture interpolating and objects moving modeling.

# References

1. Joint Video Team (JVT) of ISO/IEC MPEG & ITU-T VCEG: Draft ITU-T Recommendation and Final Draft International Standard of Joint Video Specification, JVT-G050r1. Geneva, May, 2003.
2. Artigas, X, Torres, L.: Iterative generation of motion-compensated side information for distributed video coding. IEEE International Conference on Image Processing, Genova, Italy, September 11-14, 2005.
3. Chen, T.: Adaptive temporal interpolation using bidirectional motion estimation and compensation. Proc. of IEEE Conference on Image Processing, Vol. II, pp 313-316, Sept. 2002.
4. Chol, B.T., Lee, S.H., Ko, S. J.: New frame rate up-conversion using bi-directional motion estimiation. IEEE Trans. on Consumer Electronics, Vol. 46, No. 3, Aug. 2000.
5. Lee, S.H., Kwon, O., Park, R.H.: Weighted-adaptive motion-compensated frame rate up-conversion. IEEE Trans. on Consumer Electronics, Vol. 49, No. 3, Aug. 2003.
6. Kuang, C.Y., Vetro, A., Huifang, S., Kung, S.Y.: Frame-rate up-conversion using transmitted true motion vectors. Multimedia Signal Processing, 1998 IEEE Second Workshop on, pp. 622-627, Dec. 1998.
7. Sasai, H., Kondo, S., Kadono, S.: Frame-rate up-conversion using reliable analysis of transmitted motion information. Proc. of IEEE Conference on Acoustics, Speech, and Signal Processing, Vol. 5, pp. 257-260, May, 2004.
8. Dane, G., Nguyen, T.Q.: Motion vector processing for frame rate up conversion. Proc. of IEEE Conference on Acoustics, Speech, and Signal Processing, Vol. 3, pp. 309-312, May, 2004.
9. Zhang, J.N., Sun, L.F., Yang, S.Q., Zhong, Y.Z.: Position prediction motion-compensated interpolation for frame rate up-conversion using temporal modeling. IEEE International Conference on Image Processing, Genova, Italy, September 11-14, 2005.

# Web Image Clustering with Reduced Keywords and Weighted Bipartite Spectral Graph Partitioning

Su Ming Koh and Liang-Tien Chia

Centre for Multimedia and Network Technology
School Of Computer Engineering, Nanyang Technological University
Block N4, Nanyang Avenue, Singapore 639798
{SMKoh, ASLTChia}@ntu.edu.sg

**Abstract.** There has been recent work done in the area of search result organization for image retrieval. The main aim is to cluster the search results into semantically meaningful groups. A number of works benefited from the use of the bipartite spectral graph partitioning method [3][4]. However, the previous works mentioned use a set of keywords for each corresponding image. This will cause the bipartite spectral graph to have a high number of vertices and thus high in complexity. There is also a lack of understanding of the weights used in this method. In this paper we propose a two level reduced keywords approach for the bipartite spectral graph to reduce the complexity of bipartite spectral graph. We also propose weights for the bipartite spectral graph by using hierarchical term frequency-inverse document frequency (*tf-idf*). Experimental data show that this weighted bipartite spectral graph performs better than the bipartite spectral graph with a unity weight. We further exploit the *tf-idf* weights in merging the clusters.

**Keywords:** Image Clustering, Spectral Graph Partitioning, term frequency-inverse document frequency, Image Clustering, Search Result Organization.

## 1 Introduction

The amount of web data and images available is ever expanding, there is therefore a imminent need to cluster and organize the images for better retrieval, understanding and access. In this paper we are keen to investigate clustering for better user access. Current search engines such as Google and Yahoo return their results based on the relevance to the user's query. A user might enter a query that is not specific enough, thus, obtaining results that might be mixed with other semantically different images, but still pertaining to the user's query.

A look at the top 50 results for "apple" from Google image in figure 1 shows several different semantic concepts. We can visually identify "apple fruit", "Apple Macintosh", "apple Ipod" and so on. The user might want to search for images which are related to the query in a specific sense semantically, such as to search for "Apple Computer" when querying "apple". Results returned are not organized, and hence, the user needs to take more time in understanding the result and finding what he wants.

Y. Zhuang et al. (Eds.): PCM 2006, LNCS 4261, pp. 880–889, 2006.

**Fig. 1.** Top 50 results for the query "apple" from Google Image Search (correct as of June 16, 2006)

A method of organizing the retrieval results would be to cluster them accordingly. Active research is being carried out in this area [1][2][3][5]. In this paper we focus on the bipartite spectral graph partitioning method of image clustering and propose a method to reduce the number of vertices for keywords, as well as introduce weights to be used for the graph edges. There has been a lack of discussion regarding the number of keywords as well as the weights used. The traditional term frequency – inverse document frequency (*tf-idf*) is used in a hierarchical manner and applied as the weights for the graph as well as to obtain a more compact, reduced set of keywords.

The rest of the paper is organized as follows. Section 2 reviews the related work done in this area while section 3 introduces the background knowledge on the bipartite spectral graph partitioning. The novel weights and the reduced keywords method for the bipartite spectral graph are introduced in section 4. Section 5 gives structure of the framework used and experimental results are discussed in Section 6. Concluding remarks and future work are discussed in section 7.

## 2   Related Work

Hierarchical clustering of web images for search results organization has been proposed as early as 2004 [1][5] stemming out from the ambiguity of text query [5]. Web images, containing both the image itself and text from the document that contains the image, could benefit from two wide areas where clustering had been long practiced: Image clustering [8][9] and text clustering [10][11]. In [5], images are clustered based only on labels created using the web text. These labels were formed after evaluating their number of appearance with the main keyword in a phrase, or by the percentage of co-occurrence with the main keyword. However, no mention was made to what clustering algorithm was used. Spectral techniques were mentioned and used in [1] for its image clustering based on textual features, by solving the generalized eigenvalue problem $Ly = \lambda Dy$. Essentially a bipartite spectral graph consisting of two disjoint sets represents the keywords and images, and clustering is done by solving the minimum cuts problem. However, each image/document has its own set of keywords, leading to a large number of vertices in the bipartite spectral graph, which slowed down the clustering process.

Dhillon in [4] proposes the use of a spectral clustering technique called bipartite spectral graph partitioning to simultaneously co-cluster keywords and text documents. This method is able to solve a real relaxation to the NP-complete graph bipartitioning problem and is able to cluster both documents and words simultaneously [4]. The use of Singular Value Decomposition (SVD) also improves performance over the method as used in [1]. Gao et al in [5] extends this method to a tripartite graph consisting of keywords, images and low level features. However, these two papers deal with clustering only, and not with hierarchical clustering.

Works have also been reported in the area of reducing the dimension of the words used in text clustering [7][11]. Beil in [7] introduced a frequent term-based text clustering method, which uses frequent terms instead of all keywords for text clustering. However, this method was not applied to the bipartite spectral graph partitioning.

## 3   Bipartite Spectral Graph Partitioning

This section gives a brief overview of the bipartite spectral graph partitioning.

### 3.1   Bipartite Spectral Graph

A bipartite spectral graph is a set of graph vertices decomposed into two disjoint sets such that no two vertices within the same set are adjacent. This graph as shown in Figure 2 models well the relation between web images and their corresponding keywords where web images (and their corresponding web text) and keywords are two disjoint sets.

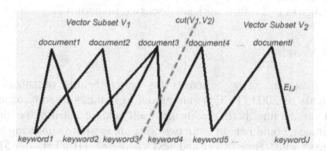

**Fig. 2.** Bipartite graph representation of documents and keywords

A partition, or a cut of the vertices $V$ into two sub sets $V_1$ and $V_2$ is represented by the cut between $V_1$ and $V_2$. Formally

$$cut(V_1, V_2) = \sum_{i \in V_1, j \in V_2} M_{ij}$$

where $M_{ij}$ is the adjacency matrix of the graph, which is defined by

$$M_{ij} = \begin{cases} E_{ij} & \text{if there is an edge } \{i,j\} \\ 0 & \text{otherwise} \end{cases}$$

where $E_{ij}$ is the weight of the edge. Intuitively, when we partition the vertices of $V$, obtaining two sets of distinct classes is done by minimizing the cut. This will ensure that the 2 separated vertices set will have the least in common together. In this paper, we focus on the multipartitioning algorithm using SVD [4].

### 3.2 Multipartitioning Algorithm

The following are the steps for the multipartitioning algorithm. A detailed description of the method can be found in [4]. Consider a $m \times n$ keyword by image matrix $A$.

1. Given $A$, find $D_1$ and $D_2$, where $D_1(i,i) = \sum_j A_{ij}$ and $D_2(j,j) = \sum_i A_{ij}$.

   Both $D_1$ and $D_2$ are diagonal matrices where $D_1$ corresponds to the sum of weights of connected images to a keyword while $D_2$ corresponds to the sum of weights of related keywords to an image.

2. Determine $A_n$ where $A_n = D_1^{-1/2} A D_2^{-1/2}$

3. Compute $l = \lceil \log_2 k \rceil$ where $k$ is the number of intended clusters

4. Compute the singular vectors of $A_n$, $U = u_2 \ldots u_{l+1}$ and $V = v_2 \ldots v_{l+1}$

5. Form $Z$ where $Z = \begin{bmatrix} D_1^{-1/2} U \\ D_2^{-1/2} V \end{bmatrix}$

6. Run K-means on $Z$ to obtain the bipartition.

## 4  Reduced Keywords Method and Hierarchical *tf-idf* Weights for Bipartite Spectral Graph

This section explains the reduced keywords method and the hierarchical *tf-idf* weights used for the bipartite spectral graph as discussed in section 3.

### 4.1  Term Frequency – Inverse Document Frequency

The *tf-idf* weight is a statistical measure used to evaluate how important a word is to a document. The inverse document frequency on the other hand is a measure of the general importance of the term. *tf-idf* is then

$$tf\text{-}idf = tf \log idf$$

A keyword with a higher *tf-idf* weight means that it is a prominent and important word in the document.

### 4.2  Hierarchical Clustering Using the Reduced Keyword Method and Hierarchical *tf-idf*

A typical text based image retrieval system would store the web page's corresponding top keywords generated from *tf-idf*. When a user queries the database, it returns a list of results according to the keywords in the database. A image-document that has the query keyword as one of the top keywords and high *tf-idf* value is returned and ranked higher then images-documents that contain the query keyword, but with a lower *tf-idf* value.

Upon obtaining a set of retrieval results (images and their respective top keywords) for the query keyword, the system could then run through the list of keywords for this particular result set, to again determine the top $m$ keywords in this set using *tf-idf*. These top $m$ keywords could potentially be sub classes.

By nature of *tf-idf*, these second level keywords represent the most prominent and frequent words used for this set of images-documents. These keywords may form semantically different concepts when grouped together with the original keyword, e.g. "Tiger Woods" from the main keyword "tiger". Therefore we can use this set of keywords in the bipartite spectral graph model. The edges between keyword and document would be the image's web document's *tf-idf* weight of the keyword.

The use of the reduced keywords method is also able to focus the clustering on prominent sub-concepts. This helps in removing the set of less important clusters which contains only 1 or 2 members, and "returning" these images back to the main cluster.

We can now construct the $m \times n$ keyword-by-document matrix $A$ as such. $A$ is a $m \times n$ matrix, representing $m$ keywords and $n$ documents/images.

$$A_{ij} = \begin{cases} w_{ij} & \text{if there is an edge } \{i,j\} \\ 0, & \text{otherwise} \end{cases}$$

Where $w_{ij}$ is the *tf-idf* value of the corresponding keyword $i$ in document $j$.

# 5   Hierarchical Clustering Structure and Framework

This section describes the entire hierarchical clustering system that incorporates the use of hierarchical *tf-idf* weighted bipartite spectral graph partitioning method.

### 5.1   The Image and Document Database

A web image repository is to be available and the database contains the *tf-idf* based top keywords and their *tf-idf* weights for each of the images. The *tf-idf* weight calculation is to be based on the full text with emphasis is given to the surrounding text of the image, as well as the page title, image name and alternate text (tool tip text). This would return a set of more related results as a web page might mention about the corresponding image only in sections of the text that are near to the image itself. Stop words removal and the Porter Stemmer [6] were also used to avoid general keywords.

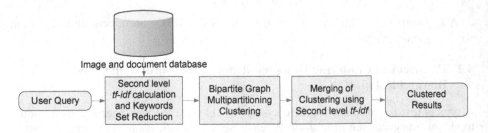

**Fig. 3.** Image Retrieval and Clustering Flowchart

## 5.2  Result Retrieval and Keywords Set Reduction

Upon receiving a user query $q$, the system retrieves images that contain $q$ as one of the top keywords. The result from the database to the system is a list of keywords (corresponding to images) that contains the keyword $q$ and its *tf-idf* value.

A second level *tf-idf* calculation is applied to determine the top $m$ number of keywords in this set of results. A list of $m$ keywords and its *tf-idf* weight is obtained.

## 5.3  Bipartite Spectral Graph Multipartition Clustering

The list of $m$ number of keywords are used to construct the $m \times n$ keyword by image matrix $A$, where the weight of the edges are defined as

$$W_{ij} = tf\text{-}idf \text{ weight of the keyword } i, \text{ to the image } j$$

The system then proceeds to run through the multipartitioning algorithm as described in Section 2.2. For the K-means clustering algorithm, we performed preliminary clustering on a random 10% of the sub sample to choose the initial cluster centriod positions. When all the members leave a cluster we remove that particular cluster. This would prevent us from getting unintentional but forced clusters.

The results of the clustering are $m$ or less than $m$ number of clusters. Due to the nature of the algorithm, the keywords are treated in the same feature space as the images. Therefore, there might be cases where a cluster has only images but no keywords. Such clusters are dropped at this stage and the images are returned to the main class.

## 5.4  Merging and Ranking of Clusters

The set of clusters obtained from Section 5.3 then goes through a merging process. Give two clusters $A$ and $B$, where $K_A$ represents the top keywords for the cluster $A$ and $K_{Ai}$ represents the top keywords for image $i$ in cluster $A$. Cluster $A$ is a sub cluster of cluster $B$ iff the number of keyword match between the keywords for each document in $A$ and the keywords of cluster B is greater than $c$.

$$\sum_i (K_{Ai} = K_B) > c$$

where $c > 0$. The value of $c$ will determine the level of closeness between 2 clusters. The merging algorithm, which also uses the keywords, is as follows:

1. Take clusters $A$ and $B$.
2. For all the images in $A$, check their top 10 keywords and determine if they contain the top keywords of cluster $B$.
3. If 60% (this is the value of $c$) of images of cluster $A$ contains the top keywords of cluster $B$ and size of cluster $A$ is smaller than cluster $B$, merge $A$ and $B$. The value of 60% was obtained empirically.
4. Repeat from step 1 until all is compared.

# 6  Experimental Results

The system was tested with 6 classes of images. Section 6.1 explains the data preparation while Section 6.2 explains the results and Section 6.3 gives a case study of the clustering done.

## 6.1  Data Preparation

A total of 6 classes were used as experimental data. 3 classes (Sony, Singapore, Michelangelo) were directly taken from Google Image's Top 250 results for a given query. Note that the number of images obtained was less than 250 for the classes; this is due to some dead links for the pages. 3 classes (Apple, Mouse, Tiger) contain images that have substantial proportions of images of different semantic meaning.

The system retrieves all the images that contain the user's query in their top 10 keywords, and then proceeds to find the top 20 keywords of the image classes.

## 6.2  Clustering Results

Results for the 6 classes were obtained and tabulated in the tables below. Table 1 shows the ground truth set for comparison; Table 2 shows the clusters formed for each class using the weighted graph.

**Table 1.** Ground Truth set for comparison

| Main Class | Sub Classes | Un-related | Total images |
|---|---|---|---|
| Apple(75) | computer-OS (35), Fiona (16), fruit (27), Ipod (13), juice (10), logo (13), Beatles (3), pie (16), | 25 | 232 |
| Mouse(41) | Mickey (19), animal (21), ear (5), Mighty (8), Minnie (9) | 35 | 201 |
| Tiger(46) | Woods (30), animal (37), Esso (16), OS (26), shark (5), beer (22), gemstone (5) | 51 | 238 |
| Sony(70) | camera (24), phone (30), Vaio (5), Playstation (23), Walkman (5), Blue-ray (7), TV (3) | 42 | 209 |
| Singapore(19) | Map (32), People (18), Places (59), Zoo (5), Currency (4) | 35 | 172 |
| Michelangelo(18) | painting (72), sculpture (27), hotel (18), portrait (14) | 31 | 180 |

**Table 2.** Clusters formed for weighted graph

| Class Name | Weighted |
|---|---|
| Apple | (Mac, window), (tree), (art), (fruit), (Fiona, wallpaper, gallery), (itunes, music), (ipod), (juice), (logo), (Beatles, web), (pie, cook, album), (blog) |
| Mouse | (Mighty), (Mickey, art), (Cartoon, Disney, Minnie), (rat), (mice), (wireless, Logitech, optic, scroll, USB), (button, keyboard), (Ear), (dog), (zip), (love) |
| Tiger | (panthera, siberian, tigris, zoo), (gallery, wild, wildlife), (beer), (Esso), (Apple, desktop, Mac, online, stripe,), (shark), (PGA, tour, Woods, golf) |
| Sony | (Blue, Ray), (camera, Cyber, Shot, DSC, ISO, pro), (Photography), (phone, Ericsson, Nokia), (game, console, Playstation, PSP), (VAIO), (DVD, media) |
| Singapore | (Asia, hotel, map, orchard, subway, tel, walk), (album), (Beach, description), (garden, Raffles, travel), (island, Malaysia), (zoo, park, fax), (view) |
| Michelangelo | (Florence), (hotel), (Adam, creation, painting), (art, artist, Buonarotti, Sistine, chapel, gallery, portrait, renaissance), (David, sculpture), (Vatican), (auml, ein, uuml) |

A look at the results show good clustering for all classes except for "Singapore". High numbers of meaningful classes were obtained in the cases of "Michelangelo", "Sony", "Apple", "Tiger" and "Mouse" indicate the presence of a list of prominent and semantically different second tier keywords. For example, sub keywords for "Michelangelo" would be "Sistine Chapel" and "hotel" while sub keywords for "Tiger" would be "Tiger Woods", "Tiger Beer" etc. The poor results shown in the case of "Singapore" suggest that there is a lack of prominent second level keywords.

Table 3 below shows the precision and recall ratios for both weighted and unity graphs. The weighted graph performs generally better for precision while it also performs well for recall when the retrieved keywords are semantically different, specific and meaningful. The system did not manage to retrieve the "portrait" cluster for the class "Michelangelo", thus affecting its recall and precision percentages when a 0% was observed and taken into account for the average precision and recall percentages.

Table 4 shows the time taken to complete the multipartitioning of the bipartite spectral graph. It is clear that the reduced keywords method used is faster than the conventional method. An average increase in speed of about 5 times is observed.

Take the example of "apple" where there are a total of 232 documents. By using the multiple keyword method and selecting the top 3 keywords for each image to be represented in the graph, a total of 361 keywords were used. This number will increase along with the number of documents and thus, the reduced keywords method provides an alternative by using only the top 20 keywords in the whole cluster.

**Table 3.** Precision-Recall comparison for weighted and unity graph

| Class Name | Weighted | | Unity | |
|---|---|---|---|---|
| | Recall Ratio w.r.t. Ground Truth (%) | Precision Ratio w.r.t. Ground Truth (%) | Recall Ratio w.r.t. Ground Truth (%) | Precision Ratio w.r.t. Ground Truth (%) |
| Apple | 82.6 | 69.6 | 81.0 | 68.8 |
| Mouse | 82.1 | 82.0 | 68.5 | 71.9 |
| Tiger | 72.3 | 77.4 | 71.0 | 71.1 |
| Sony | 73.7 | 65.5 | 69.5 | 64.0 |
| Singapore | 34.9 | 36.3 | 36.6 | 42.3 |
| Michelangelo | 45.9 | 60.8 | 44.25 | 56.15 |

**Table 4.** Time taken for the Multipartitioning of the bipartite spectral graph

| Name of Class | Time Taken for Multiple Keywords Method (seconds) | Time Taken for Reduced Keywords Method (seconds) |
|---|---|---|
| Apple | 2.640 | 0.703 |
| Mouse | 1.610 | 0.297 |
| Tiger | 2.953 | 0.391 |
| Sony | 2.219 | 0.297 |
| Singapore | 1.438 | 0.282 |
| Michelangelo | 1.266 | 0.282 |
| Average | 2.021 | 0.375 |

## 6.3 Case Study: Mouse

Figure 4 shows the resulting clusters for the images with the keyword "Mouse". Table 5 shows a summary of the recall and percentage ratio for each of the clusters formed.

**Table 5.** Summary of Recall and Precision Ratios for the class "Mouse"

| Ground Truth (Human Judgement) Cluster Name | Weighted | | | Unity | | |
|---|---|---|---|---|---|---|
| | Cluster Name | Recall Ratio w.r.t. Ground Truth (%) | Precision Ratio w.r.t. Ground Truth (%) | Cluster Name | Recall Ratio w.r.t. Ground Truth (%) | Precision Ratio w.r.t. Ground Truth (%) |
| Mighty | Mighty | 75.0 | 66.7 | Mighty | 75.0 | 66.7 |
| Mickey | Mickey, art | 84.2 | 69.6 | art, Disney, Mickey, Minnie | 92.9 | 83.9 |
| Minnie | Cartoon, Disney, Minnie | 100.0 | 81.8 | | | |
| animal | rat mice | 80.9 | 89.5 | rat, gallery | 14.3 | 33.3 |
| computer | wireless, Logitech, optic, scroll, USB | 52.4 | 84.6 | mice, optic, scroll, USB, wireless | 60.3 | 76.0 |
| | button, keyboard | | | keybaord button | | |
| ear | Ear | 100.0 | 100.0 | Ear | 100.0 | 100 |
| | **Average** | 82.1 | 82.0 | | 68.5 | 71.9 |

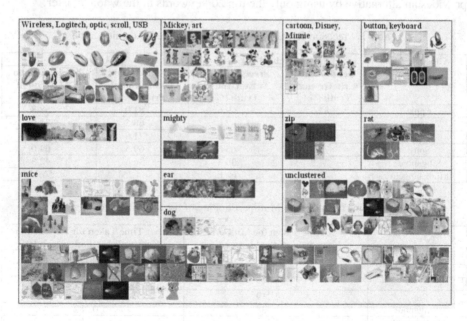

**Fig. 4.** Results for all clusters in "Mouse" class

From Figure 4, it can be seen that the first cluster is a product related class. Several meaningful clusters were obtained including "Mighty Mouse", "Mickey Mouse" etc. Cluster "zip" is a representative of a non-meaningful cluster, mainly because it covers too wide a scope due to the general term selected as a keyword.

A simple way to present more meaningful clusters to the user would be to present only the clusters with higher number of images. Smaller clusters might indicate that the keyword used is too general as in the case of "zip" and "love".

## 7 Conclusions and Future Work

In this paper, a novel method to reduce the number of keywords to be used in the bipartite spectral graph is introduced. A reduction in dimension and complexity is achieved and observed. This method enables a reduction of 5 times the processing time taken to multipartition the bipartite spectral graph. A way to determine the keywords as vertices of the weighted bipartite spectral graph for partitioning of image clusters has been proposed. Besides a novel weight for the graph edges has also been proposed and have proven to outperform those of unity weight. This comes with a tradeoff of processing memory. This has helped to improve clustering of web images, and thus have helped in organizing the search results.

## References

1. Deng Cai, Xiaofei He, Zhiwei Li, Wei-Ying Ma, Ji-Rong Wen : Hierarchical Clustering of WWW Image Search Results Using Visual, Textual and Link Information. MM'04, October 10-16 ACM
2. Xin-Jing Wang, Wei-Ying Ma, Lei Zhang, Xing Li : Iteratively Clustering Web Images Based on Link and Attribute Reinforcements. MM '05 November 6-11 ACM
3. Bin Gao, Tie-Yan Liu, Xin Zheng, Qian-Sheng Cheng, Wei-Ying Ma : Web Image Clustering by Consistent Utilization of Visual Features and Surrounding Texts. MM '05, November 6-11 ACM
4. Inderjit S. Dhillon : Co-clustering documents and words using Bipartite Spectral Graph Partitioning. KDD 2001 ACM
5. Wataru Sunayama, Akiko Nagata, Masashiko Yachida : Image Clustering System on WWW using Web Texts. Proceedings of the Fourth International Conference on Hybrid Intelligent Systems 2004 IEEE
6. M.F.Porter : An Algorithm for Suffix Stripping. Program '80.
7. Florian Beil, Martin Ester, Xiaowei Xu : Frequent Term-Bsaed Text Clustering. SIGKDD 02 ACM
8. Sanghoon Lee, Melba M Crawford : Unsupervised Multistage Image Classification Using Hierarchical Clustering with a Bayesian Similarity Measure. IEEE Transactions on Image Processing March 05, IEEE
9. Yixin Chen, James Z Wang, Robert Krovetz : Content Based Image Retrieval by Clustering. MIR 03 ACM.
10. ST Dumais, GW Furnas, TK Landauer, S Deerwester : Using Latent Semantic Analysis to improve information retrieval. CHI 88 ACM
11. Jian-Suo Xu, Li Wang : TCBLHT: A New Method of Hierarchical Text Clustering. International Conference on Machine Learning and Cybernetics 05, IEEE
12. Yanjun Li, Soon M. Chung : Text Document Clustering Based on Frequent Word Sequence CIKM 05, ACM

# An Architecture to Connect Disjoint Multimedia Networks Based on Node's Capacity

Jaime Lloret, Juan R. Diaz, Jose M. Jimenez, and Fernando Boronat

Department of Communications, Polytechnic University of Valencia
Camino Vera s/n, Valencia, Spain
{jlloret, juadasan, jojiher, fboronat}@dcom.upv.es

**Abstract.** TCP/IP protocol suite allows building multimedia networks of nodes according to nodes' content sharing. Some of them have different types of protocols (some examples given in unstructured P2P file-sharing networks are Gnutella 2, FastTrack, OpenNap, eDonkey and so on). This paper proposes a new protocol to connect disjoint multimedia networks using the same resource or content sharing to allow multimedia content distribution. We show how nodes connect with nodes from other multimedia networks based on nodes' capacity. The system is scalable and fault-tolerant. The designed protocol, its mathematical model, the messages developed and their bandwidth cost are described. The architecture has been developed to be applied in multiple types of multimedia networks (P2P file-sharing, CDNs and so on). We have developed a general-purpose application tool with all designed features. Results show the number of octets, the number of messages and the number of broadcasts sent through the network when the protocol is running.

**Keywords:** P2P, Architecture, content distribution, groups.

## 1 Introduction and Motivation

Today, the grouping of nodes in multimedia networks is more and more extended in Internet. They could be grouped based on content sharing, or according to similar characteristics, functionalities or even social trends. Many researchers try to find the best application layer protocol and architecture to organize and join nodes in a multimedia network [1], [2]. Once they are grouped, data are kept inside the multimedia network and only nodes joined to the network can download or stream data shared inside. Let's consider a set of autonomous multimedia networks. All nodes in the multimedia networks run their application layer protocol. Each node shares or streams content using the application layer protocol. All application layer protocols can be translated to other protocols and they are not encrypted using signatures or private keys. An interconnection system over those multimedia networks will give some benefits for the whole system such as: (1) Content availability will be increased. (2) It will facilitate data or content replication in other multimedia networks. (3) When a new multimedia network is added to the system, existing desktop applications will not be changed. (4) Network measurements could be taken from any multimedia network. (5) Desktop applications could search and download from every multimedia network using only one open service.

Y. Zhuang et al. (Eds.): PCM 2006, LNCS 4261, pp. 890–899, 2006.
© Springer-Verlag Berlin Heidelberg 2006

Once the interconnection system is working, when a node looks for some data, first it will try to get it from its network. In case of no result, the search could be sent to other networks. If it is found, the data can be downloaded or transferred to the first network. Once the node has that data, it will act as a cache for its network sharing the data. The existing systems are based on a desktop application which knows several protocols and is able to join several networks. Examples are Shareaza [3], MLDonkey [4], giFT [5], Morpheus [6] and cP2Pc [7]. To use those solutions, taking "search for a file" as an example, the user has to be permanently connected to all networks. The computer that joins all networks needs a lot of processing capacity. In addition, if a new P2P file sharing network is developed, a new plugin is required to support the new architecture; and, all users will have to update their clients to join the new network. On the other hand, this solution allows a node to join several multimedia networks, but those networks will not be interconnected.

This paper is structured as follows. Section 2 describes our proposal architecture, the mathematical model, its components and its parameters. Section 3 explains the protocol and recovery mechanisms. Messages designed and their bandwidth are shown in section 4. Section 5 shows an application tool developed using our protocol and measurements taken for different events. Related works and differences with them are explained in section 6. Finally, section 7 gives the conclusions.

## 2  Mathematical Description

When a node joins the proposed architecture, it has the following parameters previously defined: (1) A multimedia network identifier (networkID). All nodes in the same network have the same networkID. (2) Upstream and downstream bandwidth. (3) Maximum number (Max_num) of supported connections from other nodes. (4) Maximum % of CPU load used for joining the architecture by the desktop application (Max_load). (4) What kind of content or data shared are in its network.

Nodes could have 2 types of roles. Nodes with first role (Dnodes) establish connections with Dnodes from other networks as a hub-and-spoke. Dnodes are used to send searches and data transfers between networks. Nodes with second role (Onodes) are used to organize connections between Dnodes from different networks. For scalability reasons, Onodes could have 2 roles: to organize Dnodes in zones (level-1 Onodes) and to have connections with Onodes from other networks (level-2 Onodes). This paper considers only one type of Onode which has both roles. More details about an interconnection system using two levels of Onodes are shown in [8].

First node, from a new multimedia network, will be Onode and Dnode. New nodes will be Dnodes, but they could acquire higher roles because of some parameters discussed later. A node identifier (nodeID) is assigned sequentially, using a timestamp by the Onode, to every new node. Then, the new node calculates 2 parameters:

-   $\delta$ parameter. It depends on the node bandwidth and its age in the system. It is used to know which node is the best one to have a higher role. A node with higher bandwidth and older is preferred, so it will have higher $\delta$. The number of nodes needed to promote a node depends on the type of multimedia network. Equation 1 gives $\delta$ parameter.

$$\delta = (BW_{up} + BW_{down}) \cdot K_1 + (32 - age) \cdot K_2 \tag{1}$$

Where $age=log_2(nodeID)$, so age varies from 0 to 32. $K_1$ and $K_2$ adjust the weigh of the bandwidth and the node's age. We can see that older nodes will have more architecture functionalities than new ones unless they have low bandwidth. Nodes with high bandwidth and relatively new ones could have higher $\delta$ values.

- $\lambda$ parameter. It represents the node capacity, and depends on: the node's upstream and downstream bandwidth (in Kbps), its number of available connections (Available_Con) and its maximum number of connections (Max_Con) and its % of available load. It is used to determine the best node. It is given in equation 2.

$$\lambda = \frac{int\left[\frac{(BW_{up}+BW_{down})}{256}+1\right]\cdot Available\_Con\cdot(100-load)+K_3}{Max\_Con} \qquad (2)$$

Where $0 \leq$ Available_Con $\leq$ Max_Con. Load varies from 0 to 100. A load of 100% indicates the node is overloaded. $K_3$ give $\lambda$ values different from 0 in case of a 100% load or Available_Con=0.

Dnodes take the Onode election based on $\delta$ parameter. There could be more than one Onode per network. It depends on the number of Dnodes in the multimedia network. From a practical point of view, we can consider a big multimedia network, which is split into smaller zones (different multimedia networks). Every node has 5 parameters (networkID, nodeID, $\delta$, $\lambda$, role) that characterize the node. The following describes how every node works depending on its role.

## 2.1 Onodes Organization

We have chosen the routing algorithm SPF to route searches for providing Dnodes adjacencies. The cost of the ith-Onode ($C_i$) is based on the inverse of the $i^{th}$-Onode $\lambda$ parameter. It is given by equation 3.

$$C=\frac{K_4}{\lambda} \qquad (3)$$

With $K_4=10^3$, we obtain C values higher than 1 for $\lambda$ values given in equation 2. Nodes with Available_Con=0 and/or load=100 will give C=32.

The metric, to know which is the best path to reach a destination, is based on the number of hops to the destination and the cost of the Onodes involved in that path. It is given by equation 4.

$$Metric = \sum_{i=1}^{n} C_i \qquad (4)$$

Where $C_i$ is the $i^{th}$ node virtual-link cost and $n$ is the number of hops to a destination.

Given G = (V, C, E), an Onodes network, where $V$ is a set of Onodes V= {0, 1,..., n}, $C$ is a set of costs ($C_i$ is the cost of the $i^{th}$-Onode and $C_i{\neq}0$ $\forall$ i-Onode) and E is a set of their connections. Let $D=[M_{ij}]$ be the metric matrix, where $M_{ij}$ is the sum of the costs of the Onodes between $v_i$ and $v_j$. We assume $M_{ii}=0$ $\forall$ $v_i$, i.e., the metric is 0 when the source Onode is the destination. On the other hand, $v_i$ and $v_j \in V$, and $M_{ij}$ $=\infty$ if there is not any connection between $v_i$ y $v_j$. So, supposing $n$ hops between $v_i$ and $v_j$. The Onode $M_{ij}$ matrix is given by equation 5.

$$
M_{ij} = \begin{cases} \min(\sum_{k=1}^{n} \cos t(v_k)) & \text{When } \exists \text{ a path between } v_i \text{ and } v_j \\ \\ \infty & \text{In other case} \end{cases} \tag{5}
$$

In order to calculate the number of messages sent by the whole network, we consider that the $i^{th}$-Onode has $CN(i)$ neighbours, where $CN(i)=\{j \mid \{i,j\} \in E\}$. On the other hand, every Onode calculates $M_{ij} \ \forall j$ and builds its topological using Dijkstra algorithm. Then, every $i$ Onode sends its topological database to its $CN(i)$ neighbours and they to their neighbours until the network converges. Finally, all Onodes can calculate their lower metric paths to the rest of the Onodes, i.e., $M_{ij}$ [9]. When there is a fixed topology where all Onodes have to calculate the lower metric path to the others, the number of messages sent by every Onode is $O(V{\cdot}D+E)$, where $D$ is the network diameter. In the proposed system, Onodes can join and leave the topology any time, so the metric matrix is built as the Onodes join and leave the topology. When a new Onode joins the system, it will build its topological database and its neighbours will send the update to its neighbours except to the new Onode. Neighbour Onodes will send the update to all their neighbours except to the one from who has received the update. In addition, the update is sent only if the update is received from the Onode in the lower metric path to the one who has started the update (Reverse Path Forwarding [10]).

Taking into account considerations aforementioned, given $n=|V|$ Onodes in the whole network, $m=|E|$ the number of connections in the network, $d$ the diameter of the network and supposing that the $i^{th}$-Onode has $CN(i)$ neighbours, we obtain results shown in table 1 ($t_p$ is the average propagation time).

**Table 1.** Results for Onodes organization

| | |
|---|---|
| **Number of messages sent by an Onode because an update** | CN(i)-1 |
| **Number of updates sent in the whole network** | n |
| **Time to converge** | $d{\cdot}t_p$ |
| **Metric** | $\sum_{i=1}^{n} \frac{1}{\lambda(i)}$ |
| **Number of messages sent by an Onode because an update** | CN(i)-1 |

## 2.2 Dnodes Organization

Given $G = (V, \lambda, E)$ a network of nodes, where $V$ is a set of Dnodes, $\lambda$ is a set of capacities ($\lambda(i)$ is the i-Dnode capacity and $\lambda(i)\neq0 \ \forall$ i-Dnode) and $E$ is a set of connections between Dnodes. Let $k$ be a finite number of disjoint subsets of $V$, $\forall V=Union(V_k)$. Given a Dnode $v_{ki}$ (Dnode $i$ from the $k$ subset), there is not any connection between Dnodes from the same subsets ($e_{ki-kj}=0 \ \forall V_k$). Every $v_{ki}$ Dnode has a connection with one $v_{ri}$ from other subset ($r\neq k$). Let $D=[M_{ki}]$ be the capacity matrix, where $M_{ki}$ is the capacity of the i-Dnode from the $k$ subset. Let's suppose $n=|V|$ and $k$ the number of subsets of $V$, then we obtain equation 6.

$$
n = \sum_{i=1}^{k} |V_k| \tag{6}
$$

On the other hand, the number of connections $m=|E|$ depends on the number of subsets $(k)$, the number of Dnodes in each subset $(km)$ and the number connections that a Dnode has with Dnodes from other subsets (we will suppose that a Dnode has $k-1$ connections). Equation 7 gives $m$ value.

$$m = \frac{1}{2}\sum_{i=1}^{k}\sum_{j=1}^{k_m}\sum_{l=1}^{k-1} v_{km}(l)$$

(7)

Where $v_{km}(l)$ is the l-connection from the m-Dnode from the $k$ subset.

Let's suppose there are $n$ multimedia networks and only one Onode per multimedia network. When a Dnode sends a request to its Onode, it broadcasts this request to all other Onodes, so, taking into account results from subsection B, there will be n messages. When this message arrives to the Onode from other network, it will elect its two connected Dnodes with higher $\lambda$ and they acknowledge the message, so, it is needed 2 messages. Then, Dnodes from other networks will send a connection message to the requesting Dnodes and they confirm this connection, so it is needed 2 messages more (it is explained in section 3). This process is done in every network. The sum of all messages, when a Dnode requests adjacencies, is shown in equation 8.

$$messages = 1 + 5 \cdot n$$

(8)

## 3 Protocol Description and Recovery Algorithms

When a Dnode joins the interconnection system, it sends a discovery message with its networkID to Onodes known in advance or by bootstrapping [11]. Only Onodes with the same networkID will reply with their $\lambda$ parameter. Dnode will wait for a hold time and choose the Onode with highest $\lambda$. If there is no reply for a hold time, it will send a discovery message again. Next, Dnode sends a connection message to the elected Onode. This Onode will reply a welcome message with the nodeID assigned. Then, the Onode will add this information to its Dnodes' table (it has all Dnodes in its area). Onodes use this table to know Dnode's $\delta$ and $\lambda$ parameters. Finally, Dnode will send keepalive messages periodically to the Onode. If an Onode does not receive a keepalive message from a Dnode for a dead time, it will erase this entry from its database. Steps explained can be seen in figure 1.

First time a Dnode establishes a connection with an Onode, it will send to that Onode a requesting message to establish connections with Dnodes from all other networks. This message contains destination networkID, or a 0xFF value (broadcast), sender's networkID, sender's nodeID and its network layer address. When the Onode receives the request, it will broadcast the message to all Onodes from other networks. The message is propagated using Reverse Path Forwarding Algorithm. Only Onodes from other networks will process the message. When an Onode receives this message, it will choose its two connected Dnodes with higher $\lambda$ and it will send them a message informing they have to establish a connection with a Dnode from other network. This message contains the nodeID and the requesting Dnode's network layer address. When these Dnodes receive that message, they will send a message to connect with the Dnode from the first network. When the connection is done, Dnodes from the second network will send a message to its Onode to inform they have established a connection with the requesting Dnode. If Onode does not receive this message for a hold time, it will send a new message to the next Dnode with highest $\lambda$. This process will be repeated until Onode receives both confirmations. When the requesting Dnode receives these connection messages, it will add Dnode with highest $\lambda$ as its first neighbor and the second one as the backup. If the requesting Dnode does not receive any connection from other Dnode for dead time, it will send a requesting message again. Then, both Dnodes will send keepalive messages periodically. If a Dnode does not receive a keepalive message from the other Dnode for a dead time, it will erase this entry from its database. Every time a Dnode receives a search or data transfer for other networks, it looks up its Dnodes' distribution table to know to which Dnode send the search or data. Figure 2 shows all steps explained.

When an Onode receives a new networkID, it will send a message to all Dnodes in its zone. Subsequently, Dnodes will begin the process to request Dnodes from the new network. Dnode with highest $\delta$ will be the backup Onode and it will receive Onode backup data by incremental updates. This information is used in case of Onode failure. Onode sends keepalive messages to the backup Dnode periodically. When an Onode fails, backup Onode will check it because of the lack of keepalive messages for a dead time, so, it will start Onode functionalities using the backup information. When an Onode leaves the architecture voluntarily, it will send a message to the backup Dnode. The backup Dnode will send it an acknowledgement, and, when it receives the ack message, it will send a disconnection message to its neighbours and leave the architecture. Then, the Dnode that is the backup Onode starts Onode functionalities using the backup information.

When a Dnode leaves the architecture voluntarily or fails down, Onode and adjacent Dnodes will ckeck it because they do not receive a keepalive message for a hold time. They will delete this entry from their Dnodes' database and adjacent Dnodes will request a new Dnode for this network as explained in figure 2.

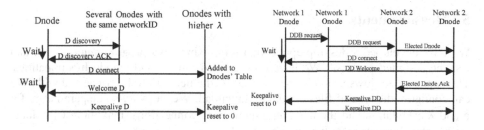

**Fig. 1.** Messages when a new Dnode joins the architecture

**Fig. 2.** Messages to request Dnode's connections

## 4 Messages Bandwidth

We have developed 31 messages for the interconnection system. They can be classified in 2 classes: (1) Fixed size messages. (2) Messages which size depends on the number of neighbours, the size of the topological database or the backup information (O neighbors, ODB, Backup O in table 2).

In order to know the bandwidth consumed by those messages, let's suppose they are sent using TCP/IP over Ethernet headers. The sum of those headers is 58 Bytes (as is has been considered for other P2P protocols [12]). We have considered that networkID, nodeID, $\lambda$ and $\delta$ parameters use 32 bits and, in order to calculate messages that depends on other parameters, every Onode has 4 neighbors, Dnode's table has 28 entries and the topological database may use the available TCP/IP over Ethernet payload. On the other hand, the limit of the TCP/IP over Ethernet payload is 1460 Bytes. Table II shows messages classified taking into account their number of bits. Figure 3 shows their bandwidth (we have used the numbers shown in table 2).

**Table 2.** Message classification

| N° Messages |
| --- |
| 1  D discovery, D connect y O request |
| 2  D discovery ACK, Elected Dnode ACK, O discovery, Failed O, Failed O ACK, New O, Change nodeID, O disconnect, O conversion. |
| 3  New Network, O discovery ACK, O connect. |
| 4  Welcome D, Keepalive D, DDB Request, DD connect, Welcome DD, Keepalive DD, Keepalive O, O reply. |
| 5  Elected Dnode, Welcome O, O replace. |
| 6  O neighbors |
| 7  ODB |
| 8  Backup O |

**Fig. 3.** Messages bandwidth consumption

Messages with higher bandwidth are the ones that send the topological database and the backup information. Because of it, we have designed the system in such a way that these are only sent when changes take place. First time, both messages send the whole information, next times only updates are sent.

# 5  Measurements

We have developed a desktop application tool, using Java programming, to run and test the designed protocol. We have programmed Dnode and Onode functionalities. The application allows us to choose the multimedia network to be connected with. We can configure the type of files or data to download. We can vary some parameters for $\delta$ and $\lambda$ calculation and the maximum number of connections, maximum CPU load, upstream and downstream bandwidth, keepalive time and so on.

We have used 24 Intel ® Celeron computers (2 GHz, 256 RAM) with Windows 2000 Professional © OS to know the protocol bandwidth consumption. They were connected to a Cisco Catalyst 2950T-24 Switch over 100BaseT link. One port was configured in a monitor mode (receives the same frames as all other ports) to be able to capture data using a sniffer application. We have tested three scenarios:

1. First scenario has only one group. It has only one Onode and there are 23 Dnodes in the group. We began to take measurements before we started the Onode.
2. Second scenario has two groups. Every group has one Onode. There are 11 Dnodes in each group. We began to take measurements before we started 1st

Onode. We started a Onode from 1ˢᵗ group, 20 seconds later we started a Onode from the 2ⁿᵈ group, 20 seconds later we started 11 Dnodes from the 1ˢᵗ group and 20 seconds later we started 11 Dnodes from the 2ⁿᵈ group.

3. Third scenario has three groups. Every group has one Onode. There are 7 Dnodes each group. We began to take measurements before we started the Onodes. We started a Onode from 1ˢᵗ group, 10 seconds later we started 7 Dnodes from the 1ˢᵗ group, 10 seconds later, we started a Onode from the 2ⁿᵈ group, 10 seconds later, we started 7 Dnodes from the 2ⁿᵈ group, 10 seconds later, we started a Onode from the 3ʳᵈ group, finally, 10 seconds later, we started 7 Dnodes from the 3ʳᵈ group.

Figure 4 shows the bandwidth consumed inside one group (1ˢᵗ scenario). There are some peaks because of the sum of joining discovery and keepalive messages (every 60 seconds) between Dnodes and the Onode. There are also DDB Request messages from Dnodes to other groups. Figure 5 shows the number of messages per second sent in the 1ˢᵗ scenario. Figure 6 shows the bandwidth consumed in the 2ⁿᵈ scenario. First

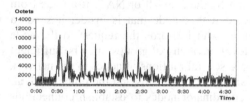

**Fig. 4.** 1ˢᵗ scenario bandwidth

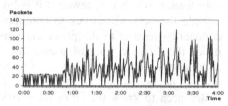

**Fig. 7.** 2ⁿᵈ scenario # of messages

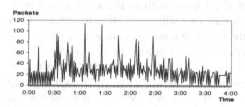

**Fig. 5.** 1ˢᵗ scenario # of messages

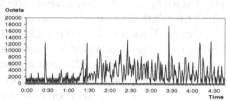

**Fig. 8.** 3ʳᵈ scenario bandwidth

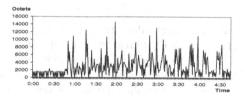

**Fig. 6.** 2ⁿᵈ scenario bandwidth

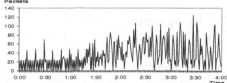

**Fig. 9.** 3ʳᵈ scenario # of messages

peak (around 1 minute) shows when we joined 11 Dnodes from the $2^{nd}$ group. Since this point, the number of octets in the network is higher because of keepalive messages. Figure 7 shows the number of messages per second sent in the $2^{nd}$ scenario. Figure 8 shows the bandwidth consumed in the $3^{rd}$ scenario. First peak (around 30 seconds) shows when we joined 7 Dnodes from the $2^{nd}$ group. Once the $3^{rd}$ group is started the bandwidth consumed is higher, but peaks are just bit higher than other scenarios. Figure 9 shows the number of messages per second in the $3^{rd}$ scenario.

## 6   Related Works

A. Wierzbicki et al. presented Rhubarb [13] in 2002. Rhubarb organizes nodes in a virtual network, allowing connections across firewalls/NAT, and efficient broadcasting. The nodes could be active or passive. This system has only one coordinator per group and coordinators could be grouped in groups in a hierarchy. The system uses a proxy coordinator, an active node outside the network, and Rhubarb nodes inside the network make a permanent TCP connection to the proxy coordinator, which is renewed if it is broken by the firewall or NAT. If a node from outside the network wishes to communicate with a node that is inside, it sends a connection request to the proxy coordinator, who forwards the request to the node inside the network. Rhubarb uses a three-level hierarchy of groups, may be sufficient to support a million nodes but when there are several millions of nodes in the network it could not be enough, so it suffers from scalability problems. On the other hand, all nodes need to know the IP of the proxy coordinator nodes to establish connections with nodes from other virtual networks.

Z. Xiang et al. presented a Peer-to-Peer Based Multimedia Distribution Service [14] in 2004. The paper proposes a topology-aware overlay in which nearby hosts or peers self-organize into application groups. End hosts with in the same group have similar network conditions and can easily collaborate with each other to achieve QoS awareness. When a node in this architecture wants to communicate with a node from other group, the information is routed through several groups until it arrives to the destination. In our proposal, when a Dnode wants to communicate with a particular node from other group, it sends the information to the adjacent Dnode from that group which will contact with the node of that group, so there will be fewer hops to reach a destination (Onodes' network is used to organize Dnodes' connections only).

## 7   Conclusions

We have presented a protocol to join multimedia networks that are sharing the same type of resources or content. It is based on two layers: Organization and distribution layer. First one joins all multimedia networks, organizes nodes in zones and helps to establish connections between Dnodes. Second one allows send searches and data transfers between networks. Once the connections are established, content or resource searches and data transfer could be done without using organization layer nodes. We have defined several parameters to know the best node to promote to higher layers or to connect with. The recovery algorithm when any type of node leaves the architecture or fails down is also described. We have shown that messages with more bandwidth are the backup message and the one which sends the topological database, so, they are maintained by incremental updates and we have designed taking into account that only first message will have all information. Measurements taken, for 2 and 3 multimedia networks interconnection, show the time needed when a Dnode fails. The protocol does not consume so much bandwidth.

A multimedia network can be split into smaller zones to support a large number of nodes. The architecture proposed could be applied easily in that kind of networks. This system has several adaptabilities such as CDNs [15] and railway sensor networks [16]. Now we are trying to interconnect P2P file-sharing networks using protocol signatures instead of the use of network identifiers. In future works we will adapt the architecture to sensor networks, using very short keepalive and dead time intervals, in order to have a fast recovery algorithm for critical systems.

# References

1. E. K. Lua, J. Crowcroft, M. Pias, R. Sharma and S. Lim, "A Survey and Comparison of Peer to-Peer Overlay Network Schemes". IEEE Communications Survey and Tutorial. 2004.
2. A. Vakali, G. Pallis, "Content delivery networks: status and trends". Internet Computing, IEEE, Vol. 7, Issue 6. Pp. 68-74. 2003.
3. Shareaza, available at, http://www.shareaza.com/
4. MLDonkey, at http://mldonkey.berlios.de/
5. Morpheus, available at, http://www.morpheus.com
6. The giFT Project, at http://gift.sourceforge.net/
7. Benno J. Overeinder, Etienne Posthumus, Frances M.T. Brazier. Integrating Peer-to-Peer Networking and Computing in the AgentScape Framework. Second International Conference on Peer-to-Peer Computing (P2P'02). September, 2002
8. J. Lloret, F. Boronat, C. Palau, M. Esteve, "Two Levels SPF-Based System to Interconnect Partially Decentralized P2P File Sharing Networks", International Conference on Autonomic and Autonomous Systems International Conference on Networking and Services. 2005.
9. Edsger W. Dijkstra and C. S. Scholten. Termination detection for diffusing computations. Info. Proc. Lett., ll(1):1-4, August 1980.
10. Yogen K. Dalal y Robert M. Metcalfe, "Reverse path forwarding of broadcast packets", Communications of the ACM. Volume 21, Issue 12  Pp: 1040 – 1048. 1978.
11. C. Cramer, K. Kutzner, and T. Fuhrmann. "Bootstrapping Locality-Aware P2P Networks". The IEEE International Conference on Networks, Vol. 1. Pp. 357-361. 2004.
12. Beverly Yang and Hector Garcia-Molina. Improving Search in Peer-to-Peer Networks. Proceedings of the 22nd International Conference on Distributed Computing Systems (ICDCS'02). 2002.
13. Adam Wierzbicki, Robert Strzelecki, Daniel Świerczewski, Mariusz Znojek, Rhubarb: a Tool for Developing Scalable and Secure Peer-to-Peer Applications, Second IEEE International Conference on Peer-to-Peer Computing, P2P2002, Linköping, Sweden, 2002.
14. Xiang, Z., Zhang, Q., Zhu, W., Zhang Z., and Zhang Y.: Peer-to-Peer Based Multimedia Distribution Service, IEEE Transactions on Multimedia, Vol. 6. No.2, (2004)
15. J. Lloret, C. Palau, M. Esteve. "A New Architecture to Structure Connections between Content Delivery Servers Groups". 15th IEEE High Performance Distributed Computing. June 2006.
16. J. Lloret, F. J. Sanchez, J. R. Diaz and J. M. Jimenez, "A fault-tolerant protocol for railway control systems". 2nd Conference on Next Generation Internet Design and Engineering. April 2006.

# Quantitative Measure of Inlier Distributions and Contour Matching for Omnidirectional Camera Calibration

Yongho Hwang and Hyunki Hong

Dept. of Image Eng., Graduate School of Advanced Imaging Science, Multimedia and Film, Chung-Ang Univ.
hwangyh@wm.cau.ac.kr, honghk@cau.ac.kr

**Abstract.** This paper presents a novel approach to both the calibration of the omnidirectional camera and the contour matching in architectural scenes. The proposed algorithm divides an entire image into several sub-regions, and then examines the number of the inliers in each sub-region and the area of each region. In our method, the standard deviations are used as quantitative measure to select a proper inlier set. Since the line segments of man-made objects are projected to contours in omnidirectional images, contour matching problem is important for more precise camera recovery. We propose a novel contour matching method using geometrical information of the omnidirectional camera.

## 1 Introduction

Camera recovery and 3D reconstruction from un-calibrated images have long been one of the central topics in computer vision. Since the multi-view image analysis is based on establishing correspondence of image, matching features—points, lines, contours—is an important process.

Straight line features are prominent in most man-made environments, and they provide a great deal of information about the structure of the scene. Additionally, since edge features have more image support than point features, they can be localized more accurately. When the motion between two images is large, however, the line matching problem could become very difficult.

This paper aims at both the calibration of omnidirectional camera and the line (contour) matching in architectural scenes. Contours are more general primitives than points or line segments, and they contain more information about the image. However, most of previous calibration researches of omnidirectional images are based on not the contour correspondence but the point. In addition, although the contour matching using epipolar geometry was proposed [1], there is no method to solve the contour matching problem in omnidirectional images up to now [2,3].

Since the fisheye lens has a wide field of view, it is widely used to capture the scene and illumination from all directions from far less number of omnidirectional images. First, we estimate one parametric non-linear projection model of the omnidirectional camera by considering a distribution of the inlier set. Our method uses the standard deviation which represents the degree of the point distribution in each

Y. Zhuang et al. (Eds.): PCM 2006, LNCS 4261, pp. 900–908, 2006.

sub-region relative to the entire image. After deriving projection model of the camera, we can compute an essential matrix of unknown camera motions, and then determine the relative rotation and translation.

The line segments of man-made objects are projected to contours in omnidirectional images. The initial estimation of the essential matrix from the point correspondence is used for contour matching. Then, the matched contour is applicable for more precise multi-view estimation. The experimental results showed that the proposed method can estimate omnidirectional cameras and achieve more precise contour matching.

The remainder of this paper is structured as follows: Sec. 2 reviews previous studies on calibration of omnidirectional camera and line/contour matching. Sec. 3 discusses the quantitative measure of inlier distributions for omnidirectional camera calibration, and a contour matching using the initial estimation is detailed in Sec. 4. Finally, the conclusion is described in Sec. 5.

## 2  Previous Studies

Many researches for self-calibration and 3D reconstruction from omnidirectional images have been proposed up to now. Xiong et al register four fisheye lens images to create the spherical panorama, while self-calibrating its distortion and field of view [4]. However, camera setting is required, and the calibration results may be incorrect according to lens because it is based on equi-distance camera model. Sato et al simplify user's direct specification of a geometric model of the scene by using an omnidirectional stereo algorithm, and measure the radiance distribution. However, because of using the omnidirectional stereo, it is required in advance a strong camera calibration for capturing positions and internal parameters, which is complex and difficult process [6].

Although previous studies on calibration of omnidirectional images have been widely presented, there were few methods about estimation of one parametric model and extrinsic parameters of the camera [7~9]. Pajdla et al just metntioned that one parametric non-linear projection model has smaller possibility to fit outliers, and explanied that simultaneous estimation of a camera model and epipolar geometry may be affected by sampling corresponding points between a pair of the omindirectional images [10]. However, it requires further consideration of a quantitative measure to select a proper inlier set. This paper presents a robust calibration algorithm for the omnidirectional camera by considering the inlier distribution.

Previous studies on contour/line matching are classified into two classes according to whether the geometric information was used. Some researches using the multi-view geometry enables to cope with the occlusion problem of the contour points on several views, in spite of high computational complexity. On the contrary, since another approach assumes generally the continuity of contours in bright and shape over successive frames, it is difficult to solve the occlusion problem. In addition, although the contour matching using epipolar geometry was proposed [1], there is no method to solve the contour matching problem in omnidirectional images based on the estimated camera information.

**Table 1.** Previous studies on omnidirectional calibration and contour/line matching

| Calibration of Omnidirectional Camera | | |
|---|---|---|
| | Image Acquisition | Methods |
| UC Berkeley / Y. Xiong [4] | self-calibration of fisheye lens and capturing the spherical panorama with 3~4 images | - restricted camera parameters: by rotating the camera 90 degrees<br>- based on equi-distance camera model |
| Columbia Univ. / S. K. Nayar [5] | using planar, ellipsoidal, hyperboloidal and paraboloidal mirrors for stereo | - modeling catadioptric system by pre-calibrated camera |
| Univ. of Tokyo / I. Sato [6] | using omnidirectional pairs for scene modeling & scene radiance computing | - 3D reconstruction and lighting<br>- strong pre-calibration and scene constraints |
| Univ. of Amsterdam / B. Krose [7] | using omnidirectional sensor on the mobile robot for scene reconstructionz | - using robot odometry for camera poses estimation and tracking<br>- calibrated catadioptric sensors |
| Czech Tech. Univ. / T. Pajdla [8, 9] | automatic estimation of projection model of dioptric lens without calibration objects and scene constraints | - no optimal method to estimate projection model<br>- no consideration of image sequence |
| | automatic reconstruction of uncalibrated omnidirectional images | - application problems in image sequence: correspondence, frame grouping |
| Contour and Line Matching | | |
| | Methods | |
| Pohang Univ. / J. Han [1] | contour matching using epipolar geometry, the parameterized contour property and intensity correlation values | |
| Univ. of Oxford / A. Zisserman [2] | short and long range motion: the correlation for the points of the line based on the fundamental matrix and the planar homography | |
| Univ. of Arizona/ R.N.Strickland [3] | contour matching using smoothness constraints on the second derivative of velocity | |

## 3   Omnidirectional Camera Model Estimation

### 3.1   One-Parametric Projection Model

The camera projection model describes how 3D scene is transformed into 2D image. The light rays are emanated from the camera center, which is the camera position, and determined by a rotationally symmetric mapping function $f$.

$$f(u,v) = f(\mathbf{u}) = r / \tan\theta \tag{1}$$

where, $r = \sqrt{u^2 + v^2}$ is the radius of a point $(u, v)$ with respect to the camera center and $\theta$ is the angle between a ray and the optical axis.

The mapping function $f$ has various forms by lens construction [11]. The precise two-parametric non-linear model for Nikon FC-E8 fisheye converter as follows:

$$\theta = \frac{ar}{1+br^2}, \quad r = \frac{a - \sqrt{a^2 - 4b\theta^2}}{2b\theta}, \tag{2}$$

where $a$, $b$ are parameters of the model. On the assumption that the maximal view angle $\theta_{max}$ is known, the maximal radius $r_{max}$ corresponding to $\theta_{max}$ can be obtained from the normalized view field image. It allows to express the parameter $b$ with the radius $r_{max}$ and the angle $\theta_{max}$ (= 91.5°). In addition, $r_{max}$ is normalized as 1, and the one-parametric model is derived as follows:

$$\theta = \frac{ar}{1 + r^2(a/1.597 - 1)} .$$ (3)

In order to estimate one parametric non-linear projection model, we use two omnidirectional images with unknown relative camera direction and translation. 97 corresponding points between images are established by MatchMover pro3.0 [12] in Fig. 1. After the correspondences are obtained, the essential matrix is estimated by quadratic eigenvalue problem and epipolar geometry [8].

**Fig. 1.** Input images and corresponding points between two views

The rotation matrix and translation can be determined by the singular value decomposition. There are 4 possible combinations of rotation and translation which result in the same essential matrix. The correct combination can be found by recovering the depths to each tracked point according to the relative poses implied by each combination. The angle between a ray and an epipolar plane is used as the error function, instead of the distance of a point from its epipolar curve [13].

## 3.2 Camera Pose Estimation by Using the Inlier Distribution

One of the main problems is that the essential matrix is sensitive to the point location errors. In order to cope with the unavoidable outliers inherent in the correspondence matches, our method is based on 9-points RANSAC that calculates the point distribution for each essential matrix [14]. Since the essential matrix contains relative orientation and position of the camera, the inliers represent the depths of the scene points and change of the image due to camera motion. By considering the point distribution, we can select effectively the inlier set that reflects the structure and the camera motion, so achieve more precise estimation of the essential matrix.

The standard deviation of the point density in the sub-region and that in an entire image can be used to evaluate whether the points are evenly distributed. First, 3D patches are segmented by the same solid angle in the hemi-spherical model and then they are projected into image plane as shown in Fig. 2.

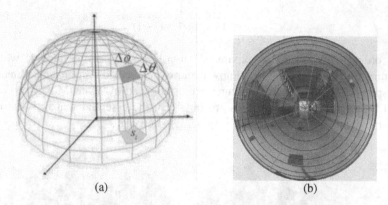

(a)                                        (b)

**Fig. 2.** Segmented sub-regions by proposed method. (a) Segmented 3D patch by uniform solid angle in hemi-spherical model, (b) 2D projected sub-regions and inlier set.

$$\Delta\theta = 0.5\pi \big/ int\big(\sqrt{N}\big), \ \ \Delta\phi = 2\pi \big/ int\big(\sqrt{N}\big) \tag{4}$$

where $N$ is the number of the inliers, and $int(\cdot)$ means conversion to integer. The proposed method computes the standard deviation of two densities that represents a degree of the point distribution in each sub-region relative to the entire. The obtained information is used as a quantitative measure to select the evenly distributed point sets. The standard deviation of the point density is defined as:

$$\sigma_p = \sqrt{\frac{1}{N_S} \sum_{i=1}^{N_S} \left(P_{S_i} - \frac{N}{N_S}\right)^2} \tag{5}$$

where $N_S$ is the number of sub-regions, $N$ and $P_{Si}$ are the number of inliers and that in the $i$-th sub-region, respectively.

The proposed method chooses each inlier set by using the standard deviation of distribution of each inlier set by Eq. 5. Then we find the inlier set with the least standard deviation. In the final step, we estimate the essential matrix from the selected inlier set by minimizing the cost function that is the sum of the distance error of the inliers.

Our method is compared with previous method using 9-poins RANSAC. The regions for selecting inlier sets are showed in Fig. 3. Since points near the center have no special contribution to the final fitting, the center region is omitted [10]. Fig. 4 shows the computed epipole distance error. The results show our method gives relatively better results over the previous method as the iteration number increases.

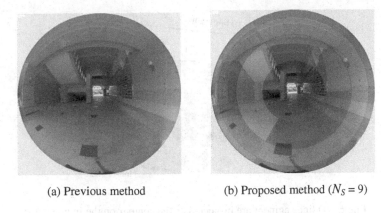

(a) Previous method                (b) Proposed method ($N_S = 9$)

**Fig. 3.** Segmented regions for selecting inlier sets

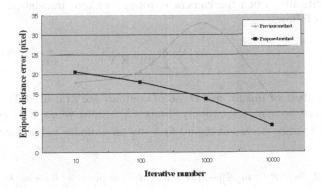

**Fig. 4.** Experimental results on the omnidirectional image pair

## 4 Pose Refinement with Contour Matching

In the case of wide-baseline multi views, the camera pose might not be estimated well with the method in section 3. In this section, a contour matching algorithm is presented for more precise camera pose refinement by using the initial estimated camera pose.

Fig. 5 shows how a straight line segment which can be represented in terms of 3D line vector **v** and the perpendicular vector to the origin **d**, is projected as the contour on the image plane. 3D line vector equations are estimated by the geometry of straight lines, and then we can predict 2D projected contour on another view by using the initial camera pose; rotation matrix **R** and translation **T**. Our method applies the structure and motion estimation from line segments [15] to contour matching in omnidirectional images.

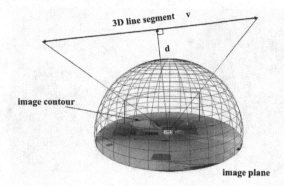

**Fig. 5.** 3D line segment are projected as the contour on the image plane

More specifically, when the camera is rotated without translation, the objective function $C_1$ as follows:

$$C_1 = \sum_{j=1}^{m}\sum_{i=1}^{n}\left(\hat{\mathbf{m}}_{ij}^{\prime T}\mathbf{R}_j\hat{\mathbf{v}}_i\right)^2 \qquad (6)$$

where the numbers of images and those of contours are $j$ (at least 3) and $i$, and $\hat{\mathbf{m}}'$ is the measured normal, respectively. Since $C_1$ is zero when $\mathbf{R}$ is estimated precisely, Eq. (6) can be solved in regard to $\hat{\mathbf{v}}$ by the singular value decomposition as follows:

$$\begin{pmatrix} m_{jx}R_{j1}+m_{jy}R_{j4}+m_{jz}R_{j7} & m_{jx}R_{j2}+m_{jy}R_{j5}+m_{jz}R_{j8} & m_{jx}R_{j3}+m_{jy}R_{j6}+m_{jz}R_{j9} \\ \cdot & \cdot & \cdot \\ \cdot & \cdot & \cdot \end{pmatrix}\begin{pmatrix} v_{ix} \\ v_{iy} \\ v_{iz} \end{pmatrix} = \mathbf{0} \quad (7)$$

In order to obtain $\mathbf{d}$ and the translation vector $\mathbf{t}$, we use the function $C_2$ as follows:

$$C_2 = \sum_{j=1}^{m}\sum_{i=1}^{n}\left(\hat{\mathbf{m}}_{ij}^{\prime T}\mathbf{R}_j(\mathbf{d}_i-\mathbf{t}_j)\right)^2 \qquad (8)$$

In the same manner, when above parameters are obtained precisely, Eq. (8) is zero. Because the normalized translation vector is estimated in Sec. 3, the scale parameters $(\alpha, \beta, \gamma)$ [15] have to be computed as follows:

$$\begin{bmatrix} m_{ijx}(R_{j1}v_{ix}^x+R_{j2}v_{iy}^x+R_{j3}v_{iz}^x)+m_{ijy}(R_{j4}v_{ix}^x+R_{j5}v_{iy}^x+R_{j6}v_{iz}^x)+m_{ijz}(R_{j7}v_{ix}^x+R_{j8}v_{iy}^x+R_{j9}v_{iz}^x) \\ m_{ijx}(R_{j1}v_{ix}^y+R_{j2}v_{iy}^y+R_{j3}v_{iz}^y)+m_{ijy}(R_{j4}v_{ix}^y+R_{j5}v_{iy}^y+R_{j6}v_{iz}^y)+m_{ijz}(R_{j7}v_{ix}^y+R_{j8}v_{iy}^y+R_{j9}v_{iz}^y) \\ \hat{t}_{jx}(m_{ijx}R_{j1}+m_{ijy}R_{j4}+m_{ijz}R_{j7})+\hat{t}_{jy}(m_{ijx}R_{j2}+m_{ijy}R_{j5}+m_{ijz}R_{j8})+\hat{t}_{jz}(m_{ijx}R_{j3}+m_{ijy}R_{j6}+m_{ijz}R_{j9}) \end{bmatrix}^T \cdots \begin{bmatrix} \alpha_i \\ \beta_i \\ \gamma_i \end{bmatrix} = 0 \quad (9)$$

In final, we can compute 3D line equation using the obtained parameters, and predict the candidate contours in another image.

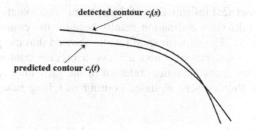

detected contour $c_i(s)$

predicted contour $c_i(t)$

**Fig. 6.** Predicted and detected contours in the image

Fig. 6 shows a typical situation in the image plane, and we define the contour distance error $D$ as follows:

$$D = \sum_{i=1}^{n} D_i, \quad D_i = \int \|c_i(s) - c_i(t)\| ds \qquad (10)$$

where $i$ and $n$ are the subscribe of the contour and the number of contours, and $t(s)$ are monotonic non-decreasing function with $t(0)=0$ and $t(1)=1$. $D$ is dependent on the scale of the initial camera translation vector $\mathbf{T}$. In final, the scale of $\mathbf{T}$ can be refined by minimizing $D$.

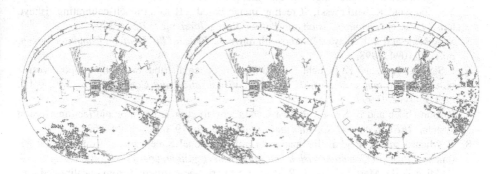

**Fig. 7.** Extracted contours by Canny's in the three views

16896, 18768 and 17184 contours in three views were extracted by Canny's [16] in Fig. 7, respectively. Among them, the contours are discarded when their the distance errors are higher than the constant value. The contour selection process is continued until the average distance is less then a predefined threshold value. 30 contour pairs were remained finally, and then the initial camera pose was refined by the translation vector's scale which has minimum $D$.

## 5   Conclusions

This paper presents a quantitative measure of inlier distributions for omnidirectional camera calibration. In addition, we present a novel contour matching algorithm using the estimated geometrical information of the camera. The matched contour is applicable to refine the multi-view estimation results because the contours are more general primitives than points. The experimental results showed that the proposed method can estimate omnidirectional cameras and achieve a precise contour matching. In near future, we will derive a mathematical relation of the estimated camera model and 3D line segments, and then present a guided contour matching based on the geometrical constraints.

**Acknowledgments.** This research was supported by Seoul Future Contents Convergence (SFCC) Cluster established by Seoul Industry-Academy-Research Cooperation Project.

# References

1. J. Han and J. Park, "Contour matching using epipolar geometry," *IEEE Transactions on Pattern Analysis and Machine Intelligence*, vol.22, no.4, pp.358-370, 2000.
2. C. Schmid and A. Zisserman, "Automatic line matching across views," *In proc. of the IEEE Conference on Computer Vision and Pattern Recognition* (1997), pp. 666-672.
3. R. N. Strickland and Z. Mao, "Contour motion estimation using relaxation matching with a smoothness constraint on the velocity field," *Computer Vision, Graphics, and Image Processing: Image Understanding*, vol.60, no.2, pp.157-167, 1994.
4. Y. Xiong and K. Turkowski, "Creating image based VR using a self-calibrating fisheye lens," *Proc. of Computer Vision and Pattern Recognition*, pp.237-243, 1997.
5. S. A. Nene and S. K. Nayar, "Stereo with mirrors," *Proc. of Int. Conf. on Computer Vision*, pp.1087-1094, 1998.
6. I. Sato, Y. Sato, and K. Ikeuchi, "Acquiring a radiance distribution to superimpose virtual objects onto a real scene," *IEEE Trans. on Visualization and Computer Graphics*, vol.5, no.1, pp.1-12. 1999.
7. R. Bunschoen and B. Krose, "Robust scene reconstruction from an omnidirectional vision system," *IEEE Trans. on Robotics and Automation*, vol.19, no.2, pp.358-362, 2003.
8. B. Micusik and T. Pajdla, "Estimation of omnidiretional camera model from epipolar geometry," *Proc. of Computer Vision and Pattern Recognition*, pp.485-490, 2003.
9. B. Micusik, D. Martinec, and T. Pajdla, "3D Metric reconstruction from uncalibrated omnidirectional Images," *Proc. of Asian Conf. on Computer Vision*, pp.545-550, 2004.
10. B. Micusik and T. Pajdla, "Omnidirectional camera model and epipolar estimateion by RANSAC with bucketing," *IEEE Scandinavian Conf. Image Analysis*, pp. 83-90, 2003.
11. J. Kumler and M. Bauer, "Fisheye lens designs and their relative performance," http://www.coastalopt.com/fisheyep.pdf.
12. http://www.realviz.com
13. J. Oliensis, "Extract two-image structure from motion," *IEEE Transactions on Pattern Analysis and Machine Intelligence*, vol.24, no.12, pp.1618-1633, 2002.
14. R. Hartley and A. Zisserman: Multiple View Geometry in Computer Vision, Cambridge Univ., 2000.
15. C. J. Taylor, D.J. Kriegman, "Structure and motion from line segments in multiple images," *IEEE Transactions on Pattern Analysis and Machine Intelligence*, vol.17, no.11, pp.1021-1032, 1995.
16. J. Canny, "A computational approach to edge detection," *IEEE Transactions on Pattern Analysis and Machine Intelligence*, vol.8, no.6, pp.679-698, 1986.

# High-Speed All-in-Focus Image Reconstruction by Merging Multiple Differently Focused Images

Kazuya Kodama[1], Hiroshi Mo[1], and Akira Kubota[2]

[1] National Institute of Informatics,
Research Organization of Information and Systems
2–1–2 Hitotsubashi, Chiyoda-ku, Tokyo 101–8430, Japan
{kazuya, mo}@nii.ac.jp
[2] Interdisciplinary Graduate School of Science and Engineering,
Tokyo Institute of Technology
4259–G2–31 Nagatsuta, Midori-ku, Yokohama 226–8502, Japan
kubota@ip.titech.ac.jp

**Abstract.** This paper deals with high-speed all-in-focus image reconstruction by merging multiple differently focused images. Previously, we proposed a method of generating an all-in-focus image from multi-focus imaging sequences based on spatial frequency analysis using three-dimensional FFT. In this paper, first, we combine the sequence into a two-dimensional image having fine quantization step size. Then, just by applying a certain convolution using two-dimensional FFT to the image, we realize high-speed reconstruction of all-in-focus images robustly. Some simulations utilizing synthetic images are shown and conditions achieving the good quality of reconstructed images are discussed. We also show experimental results of high-speed all-in-focus image reconstruction compared with those of the previous method by using real images.

## 1  Introduction

In order to generate a certain image such as an all-in-focus image by using multiple differently focused images, conventional methods[1,2,3,4,5,6,7,8] usually analyze each acquired image independently and merge them into a desired image. These methods are not easy to extend for merging very many images, for example, to restore textures of complex scenes. Therefore, we deal with a method of integrating the multiple differently focused images into desired images directly[9,10].

Previously, we proposed a method of all-in-focus image reconstruction by applying a three-dimensional filter to the multi-focus imaging sequences[9]. However, the cost of such a three-dimensional filtering is not inexpensive, if the number of multiple differently focused images or the image size increases. In this paper, we derive a novel two-dimensional relation between the multi-focus imaging sequence and the desired image. Based on the relation, high-speed all-in-focus image reconstruction is realized robustly even just by using a two-dimensional filter instead of the previous three-dimensional one.

Y. Zhuang et al. (Eds.): PCM 2006, LNCS 4261, pp. 909–918, 2006.

We show experimental results of high-speed all-in-focus image reconstruction compared with those of the previous method by utilizing synthetic and real images. The novel proposed method realizes both high-speed and robustness.

## 2  Geometrical Features of Our Blurring Model

In our method, first, we assume that images are acquired with an ideal geometrical blurring model as Fig.1. We define $r_{ij}$ as a radius of the blur on the image plane $P_j$ produced from objects that are focused on the image plane $P_i$. The radius $r_{ij}$ can be expressed with the radius of the lens ($L$) and the distance between the lens plane and the image plane $P_i, P_j$ ($v_i, v_j$, respectively) as follows:

$$r_{ij} = \frac{|v_i - v_j|}{v_i} L . \tag{1}$$

Here, we correct the size of the acquired image to be fit to the image acquired on a certain image plane $P_b$[7]. Using the distance between the lens plane and the plane $P_b$ ($v_b$), the corrected radius of the blur $\bar{r}_{ij}$ can be expressed as follows:

$$\bar{r}_{ij} = \frac{v_b}{v_j} r_{ij} = \frac{v_b}{v_j} \frac{|v_i - v_j|}{v_i} L . \tag{2}$$

On the other hand, a radius of the blur on the plane $P_i$ produced from objects that are focused on the plane $P_j$ is expressed as follows:

$$\bar{r}_{ji} = \frac{v_b}{v_i} r_{ji} = \frac{v_b}{v_i} \frac{|v_i - v_j|}{v_j} L . \tag{3}$$

Therefore, we obtain the following relation:

$$\bar{r}_{ji} = \bar{r}_{ij} . \tag{4}$$

In the same way, each radius of the blur produced between three image planes $P_i, P_j, P_k$ (the distance from the lens plane is denoted by $v_i \geq v_j \geq v_k$, respectively) is expressed as follows:

$$\bar{r}_{ik} = \frac{v_b}{v_k} \frac{v_i - v_k}{v_i} L , \quad \bar{r}_{ij} = \frac{v_b}{v_j} \frac{v_i - v_j}{v_i} L , \quad \bar{r}_{jk} = \frac{v_b}{v_k} \frac{v_j - v_k}{v_j} L . \tag{5}$$

Therefore, we also obtain the following relation:

$$\bar{r}_{ik} = \bar{r}_{ij} + \bar{r}_{jk} . \tag{6}$$

Based on the relations above, by setting $v_0 \sim v_{N-1}$ appropriately, we can acquire multiple differently focused images under the condition using a certain $r (\geq 0)$ as follows:

$$\bar{r}_{ij} = |j - i| r . \tag{7}$$

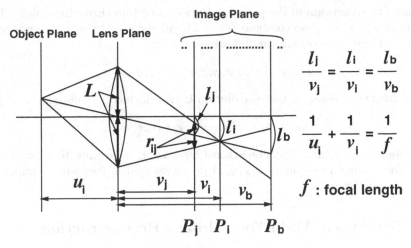

$$\frac{l_j}{v_j} = \frac{l_i}{v_i} = \frac{l_b}{v_b}$$

$$\frac{1}{u_i} + \frac{1}{v_i} = \frac{1}{f}$$

$f$ : **focal length**

**Fig. 1.** A geometrical blurring model

## 3   Scene Analysis Using a Multi-focus Imaging Sequence

We correct the size of the acquired images under the condition described in the previous section and create a multi-focus imaging sequence. Then, we line the sequence up along the orthogonal axis ($z$–axis) to image planes ($x, y$) as Fig.2. The acquired image on the image plane $P_i$ is put at $z = i$ after the size correction. This three-dimensional structure that consists of a multi-focus imaging sequence is denoted by $g(x, y, z)$.

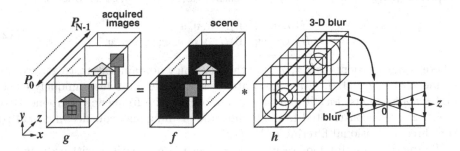

**Fig. 2.** A three-dimensional blur combines the scene and the acquired images

And here, let us introduce images that consist of only focused regions of each acquired image. The other regions are set to 0. When the size of these images is corrected and they are lined up in the same way as $g(x, y, z)$, we can define the three-dimensional structure denoted by $f(x, y, z)$, which represents spatial information of the scene. If the scene is corrected in the manner derived from a perspective imaging, it equals $f(x, y, z)$ except occluded regions.

Under the condition in the previous section, a certain three-dimensional blurring filter $h(x, y, z; r)$ can combine $f(x, y, z)$ and $g(x, y, z)$ by using a convolution as Fig.2. Finally, we obtain the following relation:

$$g(x, y, z) = h(x, y, z; r) * f(x, y, z) . \qquad (8)$$

In the frequency domain, the convolution is transformed as follows:

$$G(u, v, w) = H(u, v, w; r)F(u, v, w) . \qquad (9)$$

Therefore, by analyzing characteristics of $H(u, v, w)$, we are able to know how the multi-focus imaging sequence $g(x, y, z)$ preserves spatial frequency components of the scene $f(x, y, z)$.

## 4    High-Speed All-in-Focus Image Reconstruction

Let 1-D and 2-D Gaussian blurs with the variance of $\sigma^2$ be denoted by $p(x; \sigma)$ and $p(x, y; \sigma)$, respectively (we define $\lim_{\sigma \to 0} p = \delta$). Here, we replace a geometrical blur, the radius of which is $R$, with a Gaussian blur of $\sigma = R/\sqrt{2}$ [6]. Then, the three-dimensional blur can be expressed as follows:

$$h(x, y, z; r) = p(x, y; r|z|/\sqrt{2}) , \qquad (10)$$

$$H(u, v, w; r) = Np(w; r|s|/\sqrt{2}) , \qquad (11)$$

where $s^2 = K_x{}^2u^2 + K_y{}^2v^2$, if the corrected size of images is denoted by $(N_x, N_y)$ and $(K_x, K_y) = (N/N_x, N/N_y)$. We previously proposed a method of generating an all-in-focus image $a(x, y, z)$ (any $z$ will do) from the multi-focus imaging sequence $g(x, y, z)$ without any scene estimation of $f(x, y, z)$ as follows:

$$\begin{aligned}A(u, v, w) &= H(u, v, w; 0.0)F(u, v, w) \\ &= H(u, v, w; 0.0)H^{-1}(u, v, w; r)G(u, v, w) ,\end{aligned} \qquad (12)$$

where $A(u, v, w)$ denotes $a(x, y, z)$ in the frequency domain. Interestingly, we can define $H(u, v, w; 0.0)H^{-1}(u, v, w; r)$ above as a single filter that uniquely exists and remains robust for all $(u, v, w)$. Therefore, all the frequency components of $a(x, y, z)$ are reconstructed from the multi-focus imaging sequence $g(x, y, z)$ by the three-dimensional filtering of Eq.(12).

The method obtains good results very robustly in comparison with ordinary all-in-focus image reconstruction from a single degraded image by a two-dimensional deconvolution. However, the cost of such a three-dimensional filtering is not inexpensive, if the number of multiple differently focused images or the image size increases. In order to reduce the cost, here, we introduce a novel method of replacing the three-dimensional filtering of Eq.(12) with a certain two-dimensional one. First, we define two-dimensional information as follows:

$$a(x, y) = \int f(x, y, z)dz , \quad b(x, y) = \int g(x, y, z)dz , \quad c(x, y) = \int h(x, y, z)dz . \ (13)$$

Then, we obtain the following relation from Eq.(8):

$$b(x,y) = c(x,y) * a(x,y) , \tag{14}$$
$$B(u,v) = C(u,v)A(u,v) , \tag{15}$$

where, for example, $B(u,v)$ denotes $b(x,y)$ in the frequency domain. We notice that $a(x,y)$ equals an all-in-focus image having ordinary quantization step size and, on the other hand, $b(x,y)$ is a degraded image having fine quantization step size of $N$ times. We show the characteristics of $h(x,y,z)$ and $c(x,y)$ in the frequency domain for $r=0.2$ and $N_x = N_y = 128, N = 64$ in Fig.3. Since $C(u,v)$ is always larger than 1 as shown in Fig.3(b), we can fast reconstruct an all-in-focus image $a(x,y)$ as follows:

$$A(u,v) = C^{-1}(u,v)B(u,v) , \tag{16}$$

where $C^{-1}(u,v)$ uniquely exists and remains robust for all $(u,v)$.

This two-dimensional inverse filter suppresses lower frequency components of $B(u,v)$ to obtain $A(u,v)$. It differs from ordinary unstable inverse filters of all-in-focus image reconstruction that emphasize degraded higher frequency components. The emphasis causes artifacts introduced from noise on acquired images and gaps between image edges. Our method does not need Wiener filters or any window function for suppressing these artifacts. The difference of quantization step size between $a(x,y)$ and $b(x,y)$, and relatively preserved high frequency components on $b(x,y)$ enable such simple and robust reconstruction as Eq.(16) in comparison with ordinary two-dimensional deconvolution from a single degraded image.

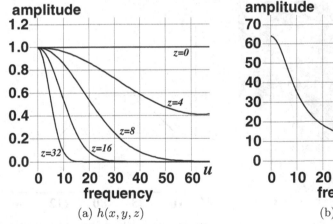

(a) $h(x,y,z)$

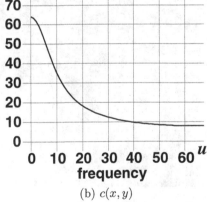

(b) $c(x,y)$

**Fig. 3.** Characteristics of $h(x,y,z)$ and $c(x,y)$ in the frequency domain ($r = 0.2$ and $N_x = N_y = 128, N = 64$)

## 5  Simulations Using Synthetic Images

We assume a scene that has a certain texture and various depths as shown in
Fig.4 in order to synthesize a multi-focus imaging sequence $g(x, y, z)$ in Fig.5(a)-
(c), where the center regions in acquired images are far from a viewpoint. The
sequence consists of 64 images having 128×128 pixels and it is structured with
$r = 0.2$.

We reconstruct an all-in-focus image in Fig.5(d) by applying the previous
three-dimensional filter to the sequence as Eq.(12). Based on the novel two-
dimensional filtering of Eq.(16), we can also reconstruct an all-in-focus image
in Fig.5(f) after combining the multi-focus imaging sequence $g(x, y, z)$ into a
degraded image $b(x, y)$ in Fig.5(e). Of course, the degraded image has fine quantization step size of 64 times. In order to estimate the quality of reconstructed
images, we compare them with the original texture to calculate PSNR. Actually,
64×64 pixles in the center are used for the comparison.

By using Pentium-III 866MHz on IBM ThinkPad X23, the previous three-
dimensional filtering spends 7.80 seconds with given $H(u, v, w; 0.0)H^{-1}(u, v, w; r)$
to gain 36.77dB, and the novel two-dimensional filtering spends 0.21 seconds with
given $C^{-1}(u, v)$ to gain 34.86dB. The results show that the novel method realizes
all-in-focus image reconstruction much faster than the previous one and gains almost the same quality without any visible artifacts.

We notice that both methods adopt just simple inverse filters. They can reconstruct all-in-focus images very robustly without Wiener filters and do not use
any window function. All the frequency components of any regions on the scene
texture are preserved well in reconstructed all-in-focus images.

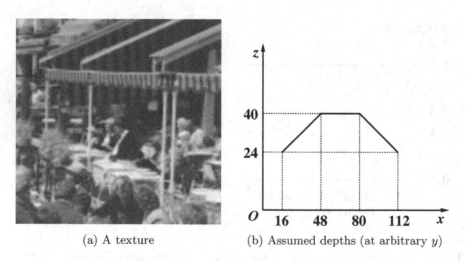

(a) A texture                    (b) Assumed depths (at arbitrary $y$)

**Fig. 4.** A texture and assumed depths for the simulation

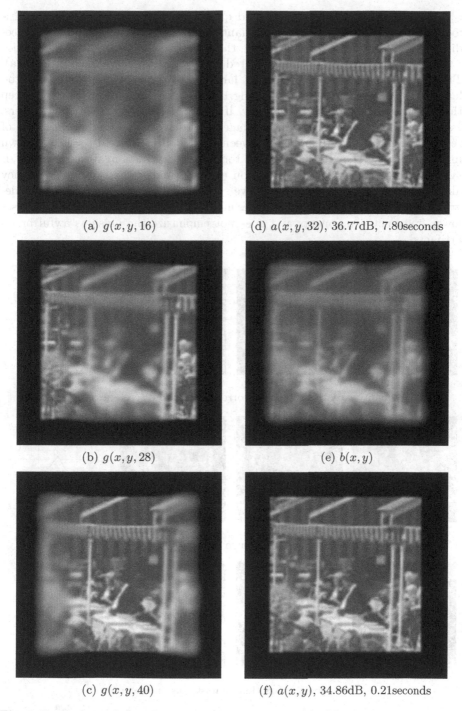

(a) $g(x, y, 16)$

(d) $a(x, y, 32)$, 36.77dB, 7.80seconds

(b) $g(x, y, 28)$

(e) $b(x, y)$

(c) $g(x, y, 40)$

(f) $a(x, y)$, 34.86dB, 0.21seconds

**Fig. 5.** Simulations of all-in-focus image reconstruction: (a)∼(c) a synthetic multi-focus imaging sequence, (d)∼(f) reconstruction results of 3-D and 2-D filtering methods

We also discuss conditions for good quality of reconstructed images. Multi-focus imaging sequences having fine quantization step size and the original three-dimensional filter are used to estimate the robustness of our approach itself.

The quality variation of reconstructed images against $r$ is shown in Fig.6(a). They are not clearly focused against larger $r$. To prevent $r$ from getting too large, we should set image planes in Fig.1 closely enough and, for example, keep the condition of $r \leq 1.0$. By the way, if we do not know camera parameters, we must estimate $r$ from acquired images themselves. The quality variation of reconstruction against difference between estimated $r$ and real $r = 1.0$ is shown in Fig.6(b). They have insufficient or too strong contrasts against smaller $r$ or larger $r$, respectively. If the estimation error is smaller than about 20%, they almost preserve the quality. Finally, we show how noise on acquired images degrades the quality of reconstructed ones in Fig.6(c). Our approach just suppresses lower frequency components and does not emphasize the noise as awful broad artifacts.

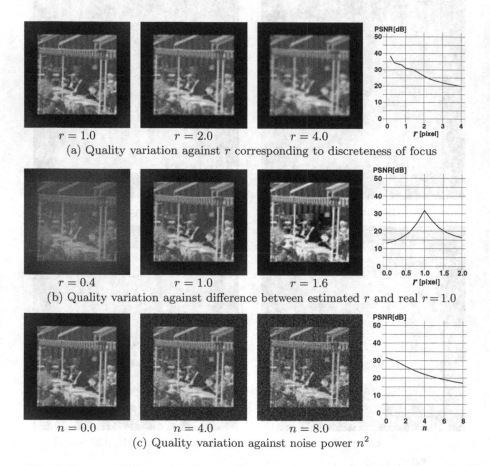

(a) Quality variation against $r$ corresponding to discreteness of focus

(b) Quality variation against difference between estimated $r$ and real $r = 1.0$

(c) Quality variation against noise power $n^2$

**Fig. 6.** Some conditions achieving good quality of reconstructed all-in-focus images

# 6   Experiments Using Real Images

We experiment using a multi-focus imaging sequence of real images as shown in Fig.7(a)-(c). Each image has 512×256 pixels and the sequence consists of 64 images. Based on our previously proposed method[7], we correct the size of actually acquired images to be fit to the condition described in Sect.2 and estimate $r = 0.36$. If we can know camera features and control camera parameters well, such pre-processing can be realized very easily without any estimation.

We reconstruct an all-in-focus image in Fig.7(d) by applying the previous three-dimensional filter to the sequence. By combining the sequence $g(x, y, z)$ into a degraded image $b(x, y)$ in Fig.7(e), we can also reconstruct an all-in-focus image in Fig.7(f) with the novel two-dimensional filtering. The previous method spends 257.16 seconds and the novel one spends 5.88 seconds. The novel method realizes all-in-focus image reconstruction much faster without visible artifacts.

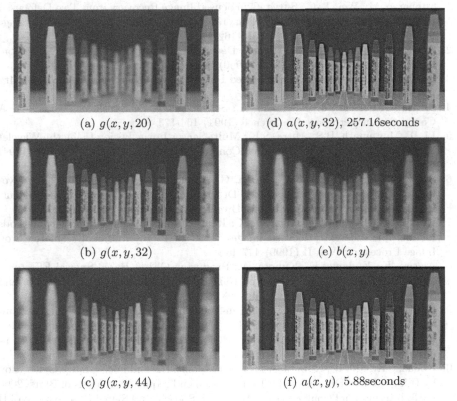

(a) $g(x, y, 20)$              (d) $a(x, y, 32)$, 257.16seconds

(b) $g(x, y, 32)$              (e) $b(x, y)$

(c) $g(x, y, 44)$              (f) $a(x, y)$, 5.88seconds

**Fig. 7.** Reconstruction of an all-in-focus image from real images: (a)∼(c) an acquired multi-focus imaging sequence, (d)∼(f) results of 3-D and 2-D filtering methods

# 7 Conclusion

In this paper, we proposed a novel method of high-speed all-in-focus image reconstruction based on the transformation integrating multiple differently focused images into a single degraded image having fine quantization step size. By applying a stable two-dimensional filter to the integrated image, an all-in-focus image can be robustly reconstructed much faster than the previously proposed three-dimensional filtering[9].

In the future, we would like to extend the method for high-speed reconstruction of more various images such as free viewpoint images from multi-focus imaging sequences[8,10]. In addition, we will consider the possibility of hardware implementation to realize our proposed method with real-time speed for all-in-focus video[11].

# References

1. Subbarao, M., Wei, T.-C., Surya, G.: Focused Image Recovery from Two Defocused Images Recorded with Different Camera Settings. IEEE Transactions on Image Processing, Vol.4, No.12 (1995) 1613-1627
2. Sezan, M.I., et al.: Survey of Recent Developments in Digital Image Restoration. Optical Engineering, Vol.29, No.4 (1990) 393-404
3. Burt, P.J., Kolczynski, R.J.: Enhanced Image Capture Through Fusion. Proc. 4th ICCV (1993) 173-182
4. Pavel, M., Larimer, J., Ahumada, A.: Sensor Fusion for Synthetic Vision. AIAA Computing in Aerospace Conference (1991) 164-173
5. Li, H., Manjunath, B.S., Mitra, S.K.: Multi-Sensor Image Fusion Using the Wavelet Transform. 1994 IEEE International Conference on Image Processing, Vol.I (1994) 51-55
6. Subbarao, M., Agarwal, N.B., Surya, G.: Application of Spatial-Domain Convolution/Deconvolution Transform for Determining Distance from Image Defocus. Computer Vision Laboratory, Stony Brook, Tech.Report 92.01.18 (1992)
7. Kubota, A., Kodama, K., Aizawa, K.: Registration and blur estimation methods for multiple differently focused images. 1999 IEEE International Conference on Image Processing, Vol. II (1999) 447-451
8. Aizawa, K., Kodama, K., Kubota, A.: Producing Object-Based Special Effects by Fusing Multiple Differently Focused Images. IEEE Transactions on Circuits and Systems for Video Technology, Vol.10, No.2 (2000) 323-330
9. Kodama, K., Mo, H., Kubota, A.: All-in-Focus Image Generation by Merging Multiple Differently Focused Images in Three-Dimensional Frequency Domain. Pacific-Rim Conference on Multimedia 2005 (PCM 2005), Part I, Lecture Notes in Computer Science 3767, Springer (2005) 303-314
10. Kodama, K., Mo, H., Kubota, A.: Free Viewpoint, Iris and Focus Image Generation by Using a Three-Dimensional Filtering based on Frequency Analysis of Blurs. 2006 IEEE International Conference on Acoustics, Speech, and Signal Processing, Vol.II (2006) 625-628
11. Ohba, K., Ortega, J.C.P., Tanie, K., Tsuji, M., Yamada, S. : Microscopic vision system with all-in-focus and depth images. Machine Vision and Applications, Vol.15, No.2 (2003) 55-62

# A Real-Time Video Deinterlacing Scheme for MPEG-2 to AVS Transcoding

Qian Huang, Wen Gao, Debin Zhao, and Cliff Reader

Institute of Computing Technology, Chinese Academy of Sciences, Beijing 100080, China
Graduate University of the Chinese Academy of Sciences, Beijing 100039, China
{qhuang, wgao, dbzhao}@jdl.ac.cn, cliff@reader.com

**Abstract.** Real-time motion compensated (MC) deinterlacing is defined to be deinterlacing at the decoder in real-time at low cost using the transmitted motion vectors. Although the possibility of this was shown ten years ago, unfortunately few such studies have been reported so far. The major difficulty is that motion vectors derived from video decoders, which generally refer to average motion over several field periods instead of motion between adjacent fields, are far from perfect. In this paper, a real-time MC deinterlacing scheme is proposed for transcoding from MPEG-2 to AVS, which is the Audio Video coding Standard of China targeting at higher coding efficiency and lower complexity than existing standards for high definition video coding. Experimental results show that the presented scheme is more insensitive to incorrect motion vectors than conventional algorithms.

**Keywords:** Deinterlacing, MPEG-2, AVS, transcoding.

## 1 Introduction

In the future progressive scan will be the major format for video. However, many valuable video archives are still interlaced, which gives birth to deinterlacing [1]. Over the last thirty years, deinterlacing was mainly studied for display purposes and was allowed to be extremely complex, e.g. the Teranex PixelComp$^{TM}$ algorithm [2]. However, as suggested in [3] and [4], deinterlacing can also be used to enhance the performance of interlaced coding, in which case the subjective deinterlacing effects are not of the main concern since subjectively better deinterlacing does not necessarily lead to better coding efficiency. Therefore, in an interlaced-to-progressive transcoding system, the deinterlacing algorithm should cater for the video encoder at the cost of some visual quality.

Motion estimation (ME) is indispensable for high-quality deinterlacing algorithms. However in an efficient transcoding system, the ME procedure of deinterlacing should typically be omitted due to the availability of derived motion vectors. (If the derived ones are too poor, motion vectors can be re-estimated.) Unfortunately, conventional motion vector (MV) mapping/refinement strategies for transcoding are often not applicable when deinterlacing is involved, because many motion vectors recovered from video decoders are not accurate and indicate only average motion over several field periods rather than motion between adjacent fields [5]. How to take

Y. Zhuang et al. (Eds.): PCM 2006, LNCS 4261, pp. 919–926, 2006.

advantage of these motion vectors is a challenging problem for real-time motion compensated (MC) deinterlacing, which is defined to be deinterlacing at the decoder in real-time at low cost using the recovered motion vectors. Although the possibility of developing a real-time MC deinterlacing without ME has already been shown ten years ago, a review of available literature shows that few such studies have been reported. DCT domain deinterlacing was described in [6-8], but the deinterlacing algorithms were too simple and were not motion compensated. A motion compensated interlaced-to-progressive transcoder was introduced in [9], however it talked only about how to perform MV mapping, without any deinterlacing details. Actually, the MV mapping scheme in [9] was not very reliable, as analyzed in [10].

In this paper, a real-time video deinterlacing scheme is proposed for MPEG-2 to AVS [11] transcoding. Before transcoding, IBBP mode is used as the basic coding structure for the Main Profile, Main Level MPEG-2 encoder. Interlaced coding is employed for interlaced source videos according to the experimental results of [12]. An edge-based line averaging (ELA) algorithm [13] is used for the first field in order to eliminate interlacing artifacts entirely. As for other fields, we should discriminate between I, B, and P frames and take the macroblock prediction (MBP) types into account in order to take full advantage of the MPEG-2 encoder. Moreover, the frame reordering characteristic should be considered.

The rest of this paper is organized as follows. Section 2 depicts the real-time deinterlacing scheme for MPEG-2 to AVS transcoding in detail. Section 3 presents and discusses the experimental results. Finally we draw our conclusion in Section 4.

## 2   Real-Time Deinterlacing for MPEG-2 to AVS Transcoding

Before transcoding, interlaced coding is performed in the MPEG-2 encoder as stated in Section 1. Thus only three possible MBP types will be taken into account, namely simple field predictions (SFP), 16X8 motion compensation (16X8 MC) mode and dual prime (DP) mode. Before real-time deinterlacing, more accurate motion vectors based on sub-blocks sized 8 by 8 should be derived first according to the MBP types. The sub-block refinement (SBR) proposed in [14] is used for motion consistency and more accurate motion information.

For clarity, real-time deinterlacing for I, B, and P fields will be discussed separately in the following subsections.

### 2.1   Real-Time Deinterlacing for I Fields

Only the first two fields of the source videos are coded as I fields. Typically, the first field is not specially talked about when we describe a deinterlacing algorithm. Sometimes the line averaging (LA) method is simply used [15]. In our scheme, the ELA algorithm introduced in [13] is used for the first field, as mentioned above. The second I field is regarded as a P field since motion vectors from subsequent P fields to it can be made use of due to the frame reordering characteristic of video codec, as illustrated in Fig. 1.

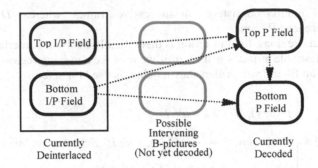

**Fig. 1.** The second I field can be regarded as a P field because motion vectors from subsequent P fields to it can be reversed. Note that intra-field interpolation is applied to the first I field as we want to eliminate interlacing artifacts completely. Here we assume that the first field output by the decoding process is a top field.

## 2.2  Real-Time Deinterlacing for B Fields

If the field to be deinterlaced is from a B frame, motion vectors can be used directly. However, instead of reserving only one MV for each block, in this case we might have at most four predictions (at most two motion vectors will be reserved) for each block in a B field, as shown in Fig. 2 [16]. Therefore analysis on MBP types is required to determine the usage of recovered motion vectors.

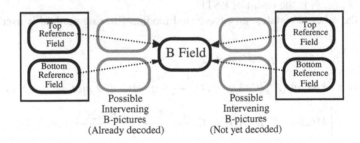

**Fig. 2.** Possible motion vectors for each block in a B field. MBP types should be analyzed to determine the usage of recovered motion vectors.

For B field pictures, there are in total two possible MBP types: SFP and 16X8 MC. In either case each block has at least one MV and at most two motion vectors. Note that a skipped block, which is considered to be stationary, also has motion vectors. Therefore we can apply the directional adaptive motion detection (DAMD) algorithm proposed in [4], which has four possible output states: stationary, horizontally moving, vertically moving, and undirectionally moving.

In the following text, we will use $A$, $B$, $C$, and $D$ to represent the values of the spatially above, spatially below, forward referenced and backward referenced pixels, respectively. Here $C$ is taken from the last deinterlaced frame based on the assumption of motion consistency in successive frames, whereas $D$ is from the backward referenced P frame.

For stationary regions, field insertion is theoretically the best deinterlacing method. However, undesirable artifacts will occur if we mistake a moving region as stationary. Thus the median filtering algorithm shown below is used for safety.

$$F_n(x, y) = \begin{cases} f_n(x, y), & if \ y\%2 = n\%2 \\ Median(A, B, \dfrac{A+B}{2}, C, D), & else \ if \ 2 \ motion \ vectors, \\ Median(A, B, \dfrac{A+B}{2}, C, \dfrac{3A+3B+2C}{8}), & o.w. \end{cases} \quad (1)$$

where $(x, y)$ designates the spatial position. $f_n(x, y)$ and $F_n(x, y)$ are the input and output of deinterlacing, respectively.

For horizontally moving blocks, after the linear spatio-temporal filtering (LSTF) [17], another median filter should be applied as follows.

$$F_n(x, y) = \begin{cases} f_n(x, y), & if \ y\%2 = n\%2 \\ Median(A, B, C, D, LSTF_n(x, y)), & else \ if \ 2 \ motion \ vectors, \\ Median(A, B, C, LSTF_n(x, y), \dfrac{A+B+C+LSTF_n(x, y)}{4}), & o.w. \end{cases} \quad (2)$$

where $LSTF_n(x, y)$ is the result of LSTF.

As for the other two states, an edge-based median filtering method is used:

$$F_n(x, y) = \begin{cases} f_n(x, y), & if \ y\%2 = n\%2 \\ Median(A', B', A, B, C, D, \dfrac{C+D}{2}), & else \ if \ 2 \ motion \ vectors, \\ Median(A', B', A, B, C, C, \dfrac{A'+B'+A+B+2C}{6}), & o.w. \end{cases} \quad (3)$$

where $A'$ and $B'$ are values of the above and below pixels in the edge direction, respectively [18].

## 2.3 Real-Time Deinterlacing for P Fields

For P fields, motion vectors currently recovered from the MPEG-2 bitstream cannot be used immediately due to the frame reordering characteristic. That is to say, the currently decoded frame is not actually the frame for deinterlacing. Hence motion vectors from the current P field to its previous I/P fields should be reserved and reversed, which will lead to the fact that the $C$ value in the last subsection is from the currently decoded frame instead of the last deinterlaced one, as can be seen in Fig. 1.

P field pictures differ from B field pictures in that there is one more MBP type: the DP mode, and that the skipped blocks have no motion vectors. For skipped blocks, a simple ELA method is utilized:

$$F_n(x, y) = \begin{cases} f_n(x, y), & if \ y\%2 = n\%2 \\ \dfrac{A' + B'}{2}, & o.w. \end{cases}$$    (4)

For simplicity, only the first recovered MV of each block will be taken into account with regard to the other cases. The real-time deinterlacing method is the same as that for B field pictures, except that the median filter after LSTF should be redefined as:

$$F_n(x, y) = \begin{cases} f_n(x, y), & if \ y\%2 = n\%2 \\ Median(A, B, C', LSTF_n(x, y), \dfrac{A + B + C' + LSTF_n(x, y)}{4}), & o.w. \end{cases}$$    (5)

where $C'$ is the co-located pixel in the last deinterlaced frame.

Fortunately, this kind of processing does not result in many interlacing artifacts although the currently decoded P frame is not progressive. Furthermore, we can reduce error propagations effectively by means of this scheme.

## 3   Experimental Results

The effects of real-time MC deinterlacing and the subsequent encoding will be shown separately for a MPEG-2 to AVS transcoder.

### 3.1   Effects of Real-Time MC Deinterlacing

Fig. 3 shows an image from the progressive QCIF sequence *Foreman* and the MPEG-2 real-time deinterlacing result on the top field, which is different from the top field of the source image due to the MPEG-2 encoding process. Although there are still some artifacts in the areas of hat and clothes, we get good results most of the time.

Several conventional approaches are also implemented for an objective evaluation. Five progressive sequences with different resolutions are used to generate interlaced sequences for real-time deinterlacing. Table 1 shows the PSNR (dB) comparisons between original progressive sequences and deinterlaced sequences. *Foreman* (300 frames) and *News* (300 frames) are in CIF format, whereas *Coastguard* (300 frames) is in QCIF format. *Crew* (200 frames) and *Night* (200 frames) sized 720 by 576 are down-sampled from high definition (HD) progressive sequences.

It can be seen that the proposed real-time MC deinterlacing outperforms all of the conventional methods, especially MC ones. That is to say, the proposed real-time MC deinterlacing is more robust to inaccurate motion vectors than existing MC ones. Here the PSNR values are lower than those provided in [4] for two main reasons. Firstly, there is a considerable loss during the MPEG-2 interlaced coding process. Secondly, motion vectors used for deinterlacing are far from perfect.

(a) Source Progressive Image    (b) Real-time Deinterlacing Result

**Fig. 3.** Real-time MC deinterlacing result on *Foreman*. Note that the top field for deinterlacing is different from the top field of (a), because there is a degradation in the MPEG-2 encoder.

**Table 1.** PSNR (dB) comparisons

|  | *Coastguard* | *Foreman* | *News* | *Crew* | *Night* |
|---|---|---|---|---|---|
| LA | 26.33 | 32.52 | 34 | 36.39 | 30.34 |
| LSTF | 26.63 | 31.62 | 27.23 | 36.78 | 32.44 |
| AR [17] | 30.46 | 30.91 | 35.18 | 33.85 | 29.79 |
| Proposed | 30.36 | 33.72 | 39.28 | 37.17 | 33.32 |

## 3.2 Efficiency of AVS Coding

An AVS encoder (version RM52C) is employed here to show the coding efficiency before and after real-time MC deinterlacing, as shown in Fig. 4.

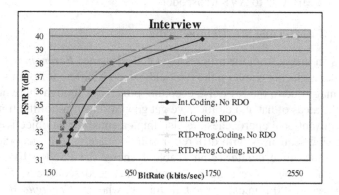

**Fig. 4.** AVS coding efficiency on *Interview*, which is in D1 format. The coding performance can possibly be improved, despite that the video data are doubled.

If the rate-distortion optimization (RDO) is not used, the curve with triangles (CWT) that represents the progressive coding efficiency after real-time deinterlacing is below the one with diamonds (CWD) which denotes the interlaced coding efficiency. This is reasonable since the video data for progressive compression are doubled and the vertical coordinates of CWT explained in [4] are smaller than actual progressive coding PSNR values. When RDO is performed in both interlaced and progressive coding, the coding efficiency after real-time deinterlacing (the curve with crosses, CWC) is higher than that of interlaced coding (the curve with squares, CWS).

Similar experiments have been carried out on several other sequences. It seems that the coding efficiency for interlaced sequences can really be improved due to the spatio-temporal increased correlations within and between frames, especially at low bit-rates.

## 4 Concluding Remarks

In this paper, a real-time MC deinterlacing scheme less sensitive to incorrect motion vectors than conventional approaches is proposed for MPEG-2 to AVS transcoding. Firstly, IBBP mode is used as the basic MPEG-2 interlaced coding structure before transcoding. Then real-time MC deinterlacing for I, B, and P fields are discussed separately, taking full advantage of the Main Profile, Main Level MPEG-2 encoder.

At present, the proposed real-time MC deinterlacing scheme cannot perform as well as the corresponding offline deinterlacing due to the lack of accurate motion estimation. But it is robust to compensate for incorrect motion vectors. The real-time MC deinterlacing on H.264/AVC or AVS is likely to be much better.

**Acknowledgment.** This work is partially supported by the National Natural Science Foundation of China under grant No. 60333020 and the Natural Science Foundation of Beijing under grant No. 4041003. The authors would like to thank Libo Fu for his support on ELA.

## References

1. De Haan, G., Bellers, E.B.: Deinterlacing—An Overview. Proceedings of the IEEE, Vol. 86, No. 9, pp. 1839-1857, Sept. 1998
2. Deame, J.: Motion compensated de-interlacing: The Key to the Digital Video Transition. Proceedings of the SMPTE 141st Technical Conference in New York, Nov. 1999
3. Benzler, U.: Skalierbare Videocodierung mittels Teilbandzerlegung. Dr.-Ing. genehmigte Dissertation, University of Hannover, 2002
4. Huang, Q., Gao, W., Zhao, D.B., Sun, H.F.: Adaptive Deinterlacing for Real-Time Applications. Advances in Multimedia Information Processing—PCM 2005. Lecture Notes in Computer Science, Vol. 3768. Springer-Verlag, Berlin Heidelberg (2005) 550-560
5. Thomas, G.A.: A Comparison of Motion-Compensated Interlace-to-Progressive Conversion Methods. BBC Research and Development Report, Sept. 1996
6. Song, J., Yeo, B.L.: Fast Extraction of Spatially Reduced Image Sequences from MPEG-2 Compressed Video. IEEE Transactions on Circuits and Systems for Video Technology, Vol. 9, No. 7, pp. 1100-1114, Oct. 1999
7. Guo, W.X., Lin, L.J., Ahmad, I.: MPEG-2 Profile Transcoding in MC-DCT Domain. Proceedings of IEEE ICME2001, pp. 333-336
8. Kato, H., Nakajima, Y., Sano, T.: Integrated Compressed Domain Resolution Conversion with De-interlacing for DV to MPEG-4 Transcoding. Proceedings of IEEE ICIP2004, pp. 2809-2812

9.  Wee, S.J., Apostolopoulos, J.G., Feamster, N.: Field-to-frame Transcoding with Spatial and Temporal Downsampling. Proceedings of IEEE ICIP1999, pp. 271-275

10. Xin, J., Sun, M.T., Choi, B.S., Chun, K.W.: An HDTV-to-SDTV Spatial Transcoder. IEEE Transactions on Circuits and Systems for Video Technology, Vol. 12, No. 11, pp. 998-1008, Nov. 2002

11. Liang, F., Ma, S.W., Wu, F.: Overview of AVS Video Standard. Proceedings of IEEE ICME2004, pp. 423-426

12. Guillotel, P., Pigeon, S.: Progressive Versus Interlaced Coding. Proceedings of European Workshop on Image Analysis and Coding for TV, HDTV and Multimedia Applications, Rennes, France, pp. 181-186, Feb. 1996

13. Lee, H.Y., Park, J.W., Bae, T.M., Choi, S.U., Ha, Y.H.: Adaptive Scan Rate Up-conversion System Based on Human Visual Characteristics. IEEE Transactions on Consumer Electronics, Vol. 46, No. 4, pp. 999-1006, Nov. 2000

14. De Haan, G., Biezen, P.W.A.C., Huijgen, H., Ojo, O.A.: True-Motion Estimation with 3-D Recursive Search Block Matching. IEEE Transactions on Circuits and Systems for Video Technology, Vol. 3, No. 5, pp. 368-379, Oct. 1993

15. Wang, F.M., Anastassiou, D., Netravali, A.N.: Time-Recursive Deinterlacing for IDTV and Pyramid Coding. Signal Processing: Image Communications 2, pp. 365-374, 1990

16. ISO/IEC: 13818-2 Information Technology—Generic Coding of Moving Pictures and Associated Audio Information: Video (MPEG-2), 1996

17. De Haan, G., Bellers, E.B.: Deinterlacing of Video Data. IEEE Transactions on Consumer Electronics, Vol. 43, No. 3, pp. 819-825, Aug. 1997

18. Huang, Q., Gao, W., Zhao, D.B., Huang, Q.M.: An Edge-based Median Filtering Algorithm with Consideration of Motion Vector Reliability for Adaptive Video Deinterlacing. Proceedings of IEEE ICME2006, pp. 837-840, Jul. 2006

# Persian Text Watermarking

Ali Asghar Khodami and Khashayar Yaghmaie

School of Electrical and Electronic Engineering
University of Semnan, Iran
a_khodami@semnan.ac.ir, khyaghmaie@semnan.ac.ir

**Abstract.** Digital watermarking applies to variety of media including image, video, audio and text. Because of the nature of digital text, its watermarking methods are special. Moreover, these methods basically depend on the script used in the text. This paper reviews application of digital watermarking to Farsi (Persian) and similar scripts (like Arabic, Urdu and Pashto) which are substantially different from English and other western counterparts, especially in using connected alphabets. Focusing on the special characteristics of these scripts, application of common methods used for text watermarking is studied. By comparing the results, suitable methods which results in the highest payload will be presented.

**Keywords:** text watermarking, line-shift coding, word-shift coding, character coding.

## 1 Introduction

Rapid development of computer networks and especially the internet has enabled people to access different information sources easily. Digital multimedia sources are commonly the most popular source of information among the internet users. However, the easy access to such media sources has created concerns about copyright and the problem of illegal media copies. In fact making a copy of a digital file is very easy while it is very difficult, if not possible, to recognize between the original and the copy. This is why Digital Rights Management (DRM) is known to be the most important problem in digital distribution.

Watermarking is a method to embed a form of digital signature in the desired information source and hence to discourage illegal copy of it [1]. In this technique particular information (the watermark) is embedded imperceptibly into original data which can be later extracted or detected for variety of purposes including identification and authentication. Among different media information, text has the least capacity to hide information. In contrast to image and video which enjoy rich grayscale and color information and hence enable hiding large amount of data, the binary nature of digital texts limits the amount of covert data substantially [2]. Moreover, the need for imperceptibility of the hidden data restricts the size of this data in text watermarking, particularly, since the number of basic blocks (characters, words and lines) in text files on which watermarking can be imposed is very limited. This, however, shows that the amount of the covert data also depends on the script

Y. Zhuang et al. (Eds.): PCM 2006, LNCS 4261, pp. 927–934, 2006.

used in text [3]. A few different approaches have been proposed for text watermarking such as Line-shift coding, Word-shift coding and Character coding.

This paper studies and compares the application of text watermarking methods on Farsi (Persian) and similar scripts (like Arabic, Urdu and Pashto) which are essentially different from western scripts. The basic difference which is the focus of this paper is the use of connected characters in these scripts. In section 2 the major techniques used in text watermarking are introduced briefly. This is followed by a review of characteristics of Farsi script compared with Latin text in section 3. Application of the common text watermarking techniques to Farsi text is presented in section 4. The paper concludes with discussing suitable methods for Farsi text watermarking making use of its special characteristics in section 5.

## 2  Profiles and Marking

### 2.1  Profiles

Upon digitization, a text image is represented by a 2-dimensional array with elements:

$$f(x, y) \in \{0,1\} \qquad x = 1,2,3,..., w \qquad y = 1,2,3,..., l \qquad (1)$$

where $f(x, y)$ represents the intensity of the pixel at position $(x, y)$. For a black and white image $f(x, y) \in \{0,1\}$. Here $w$ and $l$ are the width and length of the image in pixels, respectively and their values depend on the image resolution.

The first stage in text watermarking is the extraction of lines, words or characters as blocks. For this the horizontal and vertical profiles are used. A profile is a projection of 2-dimensional array onto a single dimension. The horizontal profile of the text line

$$h(y) = \sum_{x=1}^{w} f(x, y) \qquad y = b, b+1,..., e \qquad (2)$$

is the sum of array elements along each row $y$. The vertical profile of the text line is:

$$v(x) = \sum_{y=b}^{e} f(x, y) \qquad x = 1,2,..., w \qquad (3)$$

i.e. the sum of array elements along each column $x$.

In these terms, $b$ and $e$ are the beginning and ending row of the text lines, respectively. Horizontal profile can be employed to extract lines in text where vertical profile can be applied to the each detected line in order to recognize words and then characters in that line. This is simply done by noticing that for spaces between adjacent lines $h(y) = 0$ and for spaces between adjacent words or characters $v(x) = 0$. However, it should be noticed that the accuracy in extracting characters depends on the script of the text and for example for scripts which uses connected characters such as Farsi and Arabic many of the characters may not be recognized by applying this method.

## 2.2 Marking and Detection Techniques

In this section we describe the methods for text coding and decoding.

**Line-Shift Coding.** In this approach a mark is embedded by vertically displacing an entire text line. The line which is selected to carry the watermark bit is slightly moved up or down correspond to the value of watermark bit, While the lines immediately above and below are left unmoved. These unmoved adjacent lines are called control lines and are used for detection process as reference locations [4], [5], [6]. There are three major methods for detection process:

*Baseline Detection.* Most documents are formatted with uniform spacing between adjacent lines. In this method detector measures the distance between the base of adjacent lines and decides whether the middle line has been shifted up or down [5]. The principle advantage of baseline detection is that operates on just the watermarked copy and it does not require original document. This type of detection is called "Blind" detection.

*Centroid Detection.* In this method, detection decision is based on the distance of the centroid of the middle line to the centroids of the two control lines [5]. Compared with baseline detection it is more reliable [7]. However, since it requires the centroids of the unmarked document, the original text is needed at the decoder side. Such detection methods are called "Non Blind" methods. The centroid of a text line is:

$$Line \ \ Centroid \ = \frac{\sum_{y=b}^{e} yh(y)}{\sum_{y=b}^{e} h(y)} \tag{4}$$

*Correlation Detection.* Correlation detection uses document profiles directly for detection. In this approach correlation between horizontal profiles of original document and watermarked document is calculated. The decision is based on the maximum likelihood that chooses the direction of the shift [5].

**Word-Shift Coding.** In this technique a mark is embedded by horizontally shifting the location of a word within a text line. The word is displaced left or right while the words immediately adjacent are left unmoved. These unmoved words are called control words and can serve as reference locations in the decoding process [6], [8].

In some new methods, control blocks are not used and watermarking is just based on the space pattern within the text. In these techniques, which are also called *"Space Coding"* the size of inter-word spaces are modified according to the watermark bits. Watermarking documents using Spread Spectrum technique [9] or sine wave [10], [11] are examples of this method.

## 3   Comparison

### 3.1   Farsi and Latin Texts

The most prominent difference between Farsi (and also Arabic, Urdu, Pashto) and English texts is the arrangement of characters in words. In a Standard English text, words are made of distinct characters whereas in Farsi words, characters are mostly connected.

Fig. 1 and Fig. 2 show vertical profiles of an English and a Farsi text line, respectively. As described earlier, valleys in vertical profile correspond to spaces between words and also separate characters within words. Therefore, wider valleys in Fig. 1 indicate separation of words while thin valleys show the space between characters. It can be seen that there is almost no thin valley in Fig. 2 indicating that most of characters within Farsi words are not separate.

The limited number of separate (not connected) characters within Farsi words means that text watermarking methods which rely on space between characters are not suitable for Farsi texts especially that robust watermarking based on character shifting, usually employ a group of inter-character spaces to insert one bit [12], [13] and hence need a large number of separate characters to embed a few number of bits.

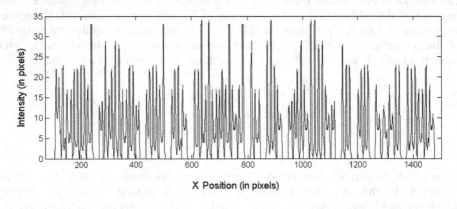

**Fig. 1.** Vertical profile of a Latin text line. (the line contains 12 words and 55 characters.)

Another noticeable difference between English and Farsi is in their horizontal profiles. Fig. 3 shows horizontal profiles of an English and a Farsi texts. Fig. 3(a) demonstrates that the horizontal profile of each line in the Latin text has two prominent peaks. These peaks correspond to the high number of black pixels in the middle and base of the text line. The baselines in English texts are visually distinguishable too since in English script most characters stand over the line.

Fig. 3(b) shows just one peak for each line of Farsi text. It is also seen that this peak does not show that there is concentration of black pixels at the lowest part of

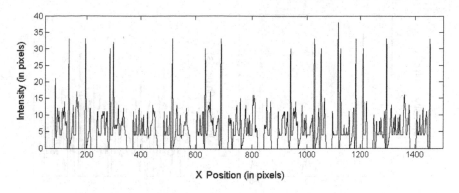

**Fig. 2.** Vertical profile of a Persian text line. (the line contains 13 words and 63 characters.)

lines. In other words in Farsi and similar scripts, the baseline has a position that is visually hidden. This makes "line shifting" a very suitable method for watermarking Farsi texts. In fact presence of baseline in English text, limits the amount of imperceptible shifting to a line. In contrast Farsi text lines can be shifted a few number of pixels without being visually detected.

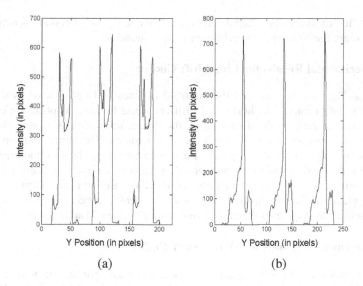

|     |     |
| --- | --- |
| (a) | (b) |

**Fig. 3.** Horizontal profile of (a) Latin text and (b) Persian text. Each text contains three lines.

## 3.2 Arabic and Other Similar Texts

As we described earlier, our experience is not limited to Persian texts and the results is practical for other similar scripts such as Arabic, Urdu and Pashto. It is resulted by comparing profiles of these texts with the profiles of Persian text. As an example, the horizontal and vertical profiles of an Arabic text are shown in Fig. 4.

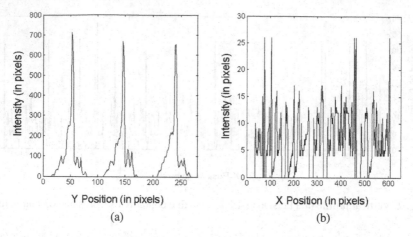

Y Position (in pixels)                    X Position (in pixels)

(a)                                        (b)

**Fig. 4.** (a) Horizontal profile of a typical Arabic text containing three lines and (b) vertical profile of an Arabic text line containing five words. It can be seen that Arabic profiles are very similar to Persian profiles.

## 4 Experiments and Results

In order to examine the capabilities and capacity of Persian script in text watermarking, the following experiments were conducted:

### 4.1 Experimental Results for Line-Shift Coding

Looking at Fig. 3, it is seen that the centroid of lines in English texts is somewhere between the two peaks of its horizontal profiles while because of presence of just one peak in the horizontal profile of Farsi lines, the line centroid should be very close to that peak. Several experiments revealed that for Farsi texts the line centroid differs from this maximum by one or at most two pixels. Further experiments showed that replacing this centroid by the peak of the horizontal profile results in no noticeable error in centroid detection. Furthermore, this peak can also be used as baseline in techniques which uses baseline detection. This means that this horizontal peak can be used as centroid as well as the baseline for Farsi texts which demonstrates a noticeable advantage.

### 4.2 Experimental Results for Word-Shift Coding

Since this method uses word spacing, it is not suitable for scripts with little space between words e.g. Chinese, Japanese and Thai [3], [13]. The inter-word spaces in Farsi and English are very similar and hence no one has advantage over the other when word shift coding is used. Due to the changing the size of inter-word spaces in space coding techniques, the length of lines in watermarked text are different from original and justification is required. This is performed by expanding or shrinking some words in such lines. To expand or shrink a word, vertical lines of equal intervals in the word are duplicated or removed respectively [10]. When justification process is applied to text, a basic difference between the two scripts appears. However, because of the use of connected characters in Farsi texts, the effect is less noticeable comparing to English texts. Fig. 5 shows an example for this case. It can be seen that, the expanded Latin word seems Bold and the shrunk word is deformed while the effect of scaling in Farsi words are less noticeable. This enables Farsi texts to embed more bits when space coding techniques are used.

numbers needed to precisely describe the satellite

قبلاً بیان شد ماهواره‌ها از ساعتهای اتمی برای تولید کلاک

**Fig. 5.** Sample of expansion and shrink in Latin and Persian words. In both lines the words labeled "**I**" are shrunk and the words labeled "**II**" are expanded.

### 4.3 Experimental Results for Character Coding

As quoted earlier, because of low number of distinct characters in Farsi scripts, it is less suitable for watermarking techniques which use inter-character spacing as the basic element for watermarking.

### 4.4 Other Techniques

Because of the characteristics of Farsi script explained above, the space between words in justified text lines is noticeably more uniform in Farsi texts. Fig. 6 shows a profile of variance of space width between words for a Farsi and an English text.

It can be noticed that the variance of spaces size between words are less for Farsi text lines. This characteristic which can be exploited to increase the accuracy of the detection process in methods based on use of spread spectrum is another advantage of Farsi and similar scripts.

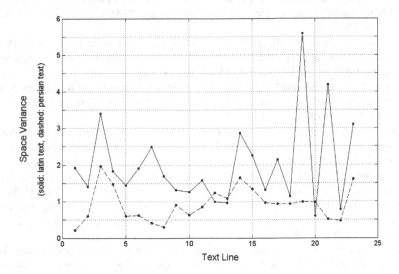

**Fig. 6.** Variance of inter-word spaces width for lines in Latin and Persian texts

# 5 Conclusion

This paper showed the capabilities of Farsi (Persian) and similar scripts such as Arabic, Urdu and Pashto which uses connected characters in view of text watermarking. Explaining the basic methods in text watermarking, the advantages and disadvantages of Farsi script were described and some experiments for demonstrating the capacity of Farsi texts to embed watermark bits were presented. The early results seem very promising and new approaches are being investigated to include robustness while maintaining the good capacity of bit hiding.

# References

1. N. F. Maxemchuk, "Electronic Document Distribution," AT&T Technical Journal, September1994, pp. 73-80.
2. A. Bhattacharjya and H. Ancin, "Data embedding in text for a copier system," Proceedings of ICIP, Vol. 2, pp. 245–249, 1999.
3. N.Chotikakamthorn, "Document image data hiding technique using character spacing width sequence coding," Image Processing, 1999. ICIP 99. Proceedings. 1999 International Conference, Volume 2, Issue, 1999 Page(s):250 - 254 vol. 2.
4. J. Brassil, S. Low, N. Maxemchuk, and L. O'Gorman, "Electronic Marking and Identification Techniques to Discourage Document Copying," IEEE Journal on Selected Areas in Communications, vol.13, no. 8, pp. 1495-1504, October 1995.
5. J. T. Brassil, S. Low, and N. F. Maxemchuk, "Copyright Protection for the Electronic Distribution of Text Documents," Proceedings of the IEEE, vol. 87, no. 7, July 1999, pp.1181-1196.
6. S. H. Low, N.F. Maxemchuk, J.T. Brassil, and L.O'Gorman, "Document Marking and Identification Using Both Line and Word Shifting," Proc. Infoncom'95, Boston, MA, April 1995, pp. 853-860.
7. N. F. Maxemchuk, S. H. Low, "Performance Comparison of Two Text Marking Methods," IEEE Journal of Selected Areas in Communications (JSAC), May 1998. vol. 16 no. 4 1998. pp. 561-572.
8. J. Brassil, S. Low, N. Maxemchuk, L. O'Gorman, "Hiding Information in Document Images," Proceedings of the 29th Annual Conference on Information Sciences and Systems, Johns Hopkins University, March 1995 Page(s): 482–489.
9. Adnan M. Alattar, Osama M. Alattar, "Watermarking electronic text documents containing justified paragraphs and irregular line spacing," San Jose California;June 22, 2004, p.685-695; ISBN / ISSN: 0-8194-5209-2.
10. Ding Huang, Hong Yan, "Interword Distance Changes Represented by Sine Waves for Watermarking Text Images," IEEE Transactions on Circuits and Systems for Video Technology, vol. 11, no. 12, pp. 1237 -1245, Dec 2001.
11. Hyon-Gon Choo, Whoi-Yul Kim, "Data-Hiding Capacity Improvement for Text Watermarking Using Space Coding Method," IWDW 2003, LNCS 2939, pp. 593–599, 2004.
12. Huijuan Yang and Kot. A.C., "Text document authentication by integrating inter character and word spaces watermarking," IEEE International Conference, Volume 2, 27-30 June 2004 Page(s):955 - 958 Vol. 2.
13. N. Chotikakamthorn, "Electronic document data hiding technique using inter-character space," The 1998 IEEE Asia-Paci_c Conf. on Circuits and Systems, 1998, pp. 419-422.

# Three Dimensional Reconstruction of Structured Scenes Based on Vanishing Points[*]

Guanghui Wang[1,2], Shewei Wang[1], Xiang Gao[1], and Yubing Li[1]

[1] Department of Control Engineering, Aviation University of Airforce,
Changchun, 130022, P.R. China
[2] National Laboratory of Pattern Recognition, Institute of Automation, Chinese
Academy of Sciences, Beijing, 100080, P.R. China
ghwanghk@gmail.com

**Abstract.** The paper is focused on the problem of 3D reconstruction of structured scenes from uncalibrated images based on vanishing points. Under the assumption of three-parameter-camera model, we prove that with a certain preselected world coordinate system, the camera projection matrix can be uniquely determined from three mutually orthogonal vanishing points that can be obtained from images. We also prove that global consistent projection matrices can be recovered if an additional set of correspondences across multiple images is present. Compared with previous stereovision techniques, the proposed method avoids the bottleneck problem of image matching and is easy to implement, thus more accurate and robust results are expected. Extensive experiments on synthetic and real images validate the effectiveness of the proposed method.

## 1 Introduction

Three Dimensional Reconstruction from uncalibrated images is a central problem in computer vision community. Examples and applications of this task include robot navigation and obstacle recognition, augmented reality, architectural surveying, forensic science and others. The classical method for this problem is to reconstruct the metric structure of the scene from two or more images by stereovision techniques [8]. However, this is a hard task due to the problem of seeking correspondences between different views. In addition, the errors introduced by matching and calibration may propagate along the computational chain and cause a loss of accuracy to the final results. In recent years, attentions are focused on using geometric constraints arising from the scenes to optimize the reconstruction, especially for architecture scenes [15][12]. Such constraints may be expressed in terms of parallelism, orthogonality, coplanarity and other special inter-relationship of features and camera constraints.

For a wide variety of man-made object, we can usually obtain three vanishing points that correspond to three mutually orthogonal directions in space [1]. Caprile and Torre [4] propose a method for camera calibration from these

---

[*] The work is supported by the National Natural Science Foundation of China under grant no. 60575015.

vanishing points computed from the projected edges of a cuboid. Following this idea, several approaches that make use of vanishing points and lines have been proposed for either cameras calibration or scene reconstruction [9][13]. Most of the studies are usually under the assumption of square pixels. Wilczkowiak *et.al.* [15] expand the idea to general parallelepided structures, and use the constraints of parallelepipeds for camera calibration. Criminisi *et.al.* [6] propose to compute 3D affine measurement from a single image based on the vanishing line of a reference plane and the vertical vanishing point. A similar technique is also studied in [11]. Most of these methods are based on a single view and only part of the structure or some metrical quantities can be inferred with the prior knowledge of geometrical scene constraints.

When multiple images are present, Werner and Zisserman [14] present a coarse-to-fine strategy to reconstruct buildings. The planar model of the principal scene planes is generated by plane sweeping and used as a basis to estimate more details around the plane. Baillard and Zisserman [2] use inter-image homographies to validate and estimate the plane models. Bartoli and Sturm [3] describe the geometric relationship between points and planes as multi-coplanarity constraints, and a maximum likelihood estimator that incorporates the constraints and structures is used in a bundle adjustment manner. Wang *et.al.* [12] propose to refine the space plane homographies recursively by combining the point and line correspondences. Most of these methods are rely on the initial matching or a relatively good projective or metric reconstruction of points and lines, which may not be available in some situations. Some commercial systems, such as Facade [7] and Photobuilder [5] can produce very realistic results. However, these systems usually require a lot of human interactions.

The work in this paper is targeted on man-made structures that typically contain three orthogonal principal directions. The remaining parts of the paper are organized as follows: In section 2, some preliminaries on projection matrix and the camera calibration are reviewed. Then the method to recover the projection matrix from vanishing points is elaborated in detail in section 3. The test results with simulated data and real images are presented in section 4 and 5 respectively. Finally, the conclusions of this paper are given in section 6.

## 2 Some Preliminaries

In order to facilitate our discussions in the subsequent sections, some preliminaries on projection matrix and camera calibration are presented here. Readers can refer to [8] and [13] for more detail.

Under perspective projection, a 3D point $\mathbf{x} \in \mathbb{R}^3$ in space is projected to an image point $\mathbf{m} \in \mathbb{R}^2$ via a rank 3 projection matrix $\mathbf{P} \in \mathbb{R}^{3 \times 4}$ as

$$s\tilde{\mathbf{m}} = \mathbf{P}\tilde{\mathbf{x}} = \mathbf{K}[\mathbf{R}, \mathbf{t}]\tilde{\mathbf{x}} = [\mathbf{p}_1, \mathbf{p}_2, \mathbf{p}_3, \mathbf{p}_4]\tilde{\mathbf{x}} \qquad (1)$$

where, $\tilde{\mathbf{x}} = [\mathbf{x}^T, 1]^T$ and $\tilde{\mathbf{m}} = [\mathbf{m}^T, 1]^T$ are the homogeneous forms of points $\mathbf{x}$ and $\mathbf{m}$ respectively, $\mathbf{R}$ and $\mathbf{t}$ are the rotation matrix and translation vector from the world system to the camera system, $s$ is a non-zero scalar, $\mathbf{K}$ is the camera calibration matrix. For most CCD cameras, we can assume square pixels, then the camera becomes a simplified one with only three intrinsic parameters.

**Lemma 1.** *The first three columns of the projection matrix are images of the vanishing points corresponding to the $X, Y$ and $Z$ axes of the world system respectively, and the last column is the image of the origin of the world system.*

The absolute conic $\mathbf{C}_\infty = \mathbf{I} = diag(1, 1, 1)$ is a conic on the plane at infinity, which is a conic composed of purely imaginary points on the infinite plane. Under perspective projection, we can easily obtain the image of the absolute conic (IAC) as $\omega = (\mathbf{KK}^T)^{-1} = \mathbf{K}^{-T}\mathbf{K}^{-1}$, which is an invisible imaginary point conic in an image. The dual image of the absolute conic (DIAC) is referred as $\omega^* = \omega^{-1} = \mathbf{KK}^T$, which is a dual conic of $\omega$.

It is clear that both the IAC and the DIAC depend only on the camera calibration matrix $\mathbf{K}$. If the value of the matrix $\omega$ or $\omega^*$ is known, then the intrinsic parameters of the camera $\mathbf{K}$ can be recovered straightforwardly by Cholesky decomposition. Thus we often refer camera calibration as the computation of the IAC or the DIAC.

**Lemma 2.** *The camera can be calibrated linearly from a set of three orthogonal vanishing points if it is of square pixels or other three-parameter-model.*

## 3   Recovery of Projection Matrix

From Lemma 1, we know that $\mathbf{P} = [s_x\tilde{\mathbf{v}}_x, s_y\tilde{\mathbf{v}}_y, s_z\tilde{\mathbf{v}}_z, s_o\tilde{\mathbf{v}}_o]$, where $\tilde{\mathbf{v}}_x, \tilde{\mathbf{v}}_y, \tilde{\mathbf{v}}_z$ are the homogeneous form of the three vanishing points, $\tilde{\mathbf{v}}_o$ is the image of the world origin, $s_x, s_y, s_z, s_o$ are four unknown scalars. In the following, we will show how to determine the unkowns for a specific world coordinate system.

### 3.1   Projection Matrix with a Single View

**Proposition 1.** *Given a set of three orthogonal vanishing points $\mathbf{v}_x$, $\mathbf{v}_y$ and $\mathbf{v}_z$ under a certain world coordinate system, then the scalars $s_x$, $s_y$ and $s_z$ can be uniqully determined if the camera is of three-parameter-model.*

Instead of prove the proposition directly, we will give an analysis on how to compute these scalars in the following.

Let $\mathbf{M} = [s_x\tilde{\mathbf{v}}_x, s_y\tilde{\mathbf{v}}_y, s_z\tilde{\mathbf{v}}_z] = [\tilde{\mathbf{v}}_x, \tilde{\mathbf{v}}_y, \tilde{\mathbf{v}}_z]diag(s_x, s_y, s_z)$ be the first three columns of the projection matrix, and let $\mathbf{C} = \mathbf{MM}^T$, then we have:

$$\mathbf{C} = \mathbf{MM}^T = [\tilde{\mathbf{v}}_x, \tilde{\mathbf{v}}_y, \tilde{\mathbf{v}}_z]\begin{bmatrix} s_x^2 & & \\ & s_y^2 & \\ & & s_z^2 \end{bmatrix}[\tilde{\mathbf{v}}_x, \tilde{\mathbf{v}}_y, \tilde{\mathbf{v}}_z]^T \tag{2}$$

On the other hand, we know that $\mathbf{M} = \mathbf{KR}$ from eq.(1). Thus

$$\mathbf{C} = \mathbf{MM}^T = \mathbf{KRR}^T\mathbf{K}^T = \mathbf{KK}^T = \omega^* \tag{3}$$

The dual of the image of absolute conic $\omega^*$ can be obtained from the three vanishing points via Lemma 2. So the three scalars can be obtained by incorporating eq.(2) and eq.(3).

$$\begin{bmatrix} s_x^2 & & \\ & s_y^2 & \\ & & s_z^2 \end{bmatrix} = [\tilde{\mathbf{v}}_x, \tilde{\mathbf{v}}_y, \tilde{\mathbf{v}}_z]^{-1} \omega^* [\tilde{\mathbf{v}}_x, \tilde{\mathbf{v}}_y, \tilde{\mathbf{v}}_z]^{-T} \qquad (4)$$

However, the so computed scalars are not unique, since $-s_x$, $-s_y$ and $-s_z$ are also hold true to eq.(4). Thus there are altogether 8 solutions corresponding to different selections of the signs of the world coordinate axes. The ambiguity can be solved in practice as follows.

**Proposition 2.** *The signs of the scalars $s_x$, $s_y$ and $s_z$ correspond to the signs of the axial directions $X, Y$ and $Z$ of the world coordinate system respectively.*

*Proof.* Suppose point $\mathbf{m} = [u, v]^T$ is the image of a space point $\mathbf{x} = [X, Y, Z]^T$, then from eq.(1) and Lemma 1 we have

$$s \begin{bmatrix} u \\ v \\ 1 \end{bmatrix} = [s_x \tilde{\mathbf{v}}_x, s_y \tilde{\mathbf{v}}_y, s_z \tilde{\mathbf{v}}_z, s_o \tilde{\mathbf{v}}_o] \begin{bmatrix} X \\ Y \\ Z \\ 1 \end{bmatrix} \qquad (5)$$

Obviously, the same image point can be obtained if we reverse the sign of $\{X, s_x\}, \{Y, s_y\}$ or $\{Z, s_z\}$ simultaneously.                    □

**Proposition 3.** *The ambiguity of the signs of the scalars can be reduced from 8 to 4 if right-handed world system is assumed.*

The proof of this proposition is obvious. We usually adopt the right-handed system in practice. Suppose $\{X, Y, Z\}$ is the correct selection of the world system, then $\{-X, -Y, Z\}, \{-X, Y, -Z\}$ and $\{X, -Y, -Z\}$ are also satisfy the right-handed rule and result the same vanishing points in the image, since the vanishing point of an axial direction is unaffected by the sign of the axis.

**Proposition 4.** *The ambiguity of the scalars can be reduced from 4 to 2 if we further assume that the object lie in front of the camera.*

It is easy to verify that only half of the above 4 selections of the world system in Proposition 3 can assure the reconstructed object lie in front of the camera, which may be seen by the camera. One can also verify that the vector directed towards the front of the camera along the principal axis may be computed from $\mathbf{v} = \det(\mathbf{M})\mathbf{m}^3$, where $\mathbf{M}$ is the first three columns of the projection matrix, $\mathbf{m}^3$ is the third row of $\mathbf{M}$.

**Proposition 5.** *Suppose $\mathbf{p}_4$ is known, then the signs of the scalars may be uniquely determined in practice for a given object under certain world system.*

*Proof.* The ambiguity is reduced to 2 in Proposition 4, thus we have 2 projection matrices, say $\mathbf{P}_1$ and $\mathbf{P}_2$. Let us choose a space point $\mathbf{S}_a = [X_a, Y_a, Z_a]^T$ on the positive direction of $X$ axis, suppose its corresponding image point is $\mathbf{m}_a$, then from $s\tilde{\mathbf{m}}_a = \mathbf{P}_1[X_a, 0, 0, 1]^T$, we can obtain the estimation of $\mathbf{X}_a$. The solution of the projection matrix $\mathbf{P}$ can be uniquely determined from the sign of $\mathbf{X}_a$. If $\mathbf{X}_a$ is positive, then $\mathbf{P} = \mathbf{P}_1$, otherwise, $\mathbf{P} = \mathbf{P}_2$. $\quad\square$

**Remark 1:** In Proposition 5, we assume the last column of the projection matrix $\mathbf{p}_4$ is known. Actually, from eq.(1) and Lemma 1 we have that $\mathbf{p}_4 = \mathbf{KT} = s_o\tilde{\mathbf{v}}_o$, which corresponds to the translation vector of the camera to the world origin. Since there is no absolute measurement about the scene geometry, the projection matrix is then only defined up to scale, thus the value of $s_o$ may be set freely. In practice, we may choose $s_o$ such that $(\mathbf{P}_4)_3 = 1$, which means the third element of the translation vector $(\mathbf{t})_3 = 1$.

## 3.2   Projection Matrix of Two or More Views

We have now proven the uniqueness of the first three columns of the projection matrix under a given world coordinate system. For a single view, the scalar of the last column of the projection matrix may be choose freely as noted in Remark 1. However, when we have two or more views, the scalars corresponding to the projection matrices of these views must be consistent so as to obtain a global reconstruction consistently.

**Proposition 6.** *Given one set of corresponding points in two or more views, the scalars associated with the translation terms of the projection matrices can be consistently determined.*

*Proof.* Without loss of generality, suppose we have two views, $\mathbf{S}_c = [X_c, Y_c, Z_c]^T$ is a reference space point with $\mathbf{m}_{c1}$, $\mathbf{m}_{c2}$ the corresponding image points in the two views. Let $\mathbf{P}_1 = [\mathbf{M}_1, s_{o1}\tilde{\mathbf{v}}_{o1}]$, $\mathbf{P}_2 = [\mathbf{M}_2, s_{o2}\tilde{\mathbf{v}}_{o2}]$ be the two projection matrices, where $\mathbf{M}_i(i = 1, 2)$ have been determined in the previous section, $\tilde{\mathbf{v}}_{o1}$ and $\tilde{\mathbf{v}}_{o2}$ are the images of the world origin in the two views. Then from

$$\begin{cases} s_1\tilde{\mathbf{m}}_{c1} = \mathbf{P}_1\tilde{\mathbf{S}}_c = \mathbf{M}_1\mathbf{S}_c + s_{o1}\tilde{\mathbf{v}}_{o1} \\ s_2\tilde{\mathbf{m}}_{c2} = \mathbf{P}_2\tilde{\mathbf{S}}_c = \mathbf{M}_2\mathbf{S}_c + s_{o2}\tilde{\mathbf{v}}_{o2} \end{cases} \tag{6}$$

we have

$$s_1\tilde{\mathbf{m}}_{c1} - s_2\mathbf{M}_1\mathbf{M}_2^{-1}\tilde{\mathbf{m}}_{c2} + s_{o2}\mathbf{M}_1\mathbf{M}_2^{-1}\tilde{\mathbf{v}}_{o2} = s_{o1}\tilde{\mathbf{v}}_{o1} \tag{7}$$

where $s_1$, $s_2$, $s_{o1}$ and $s_{o2}$ are four unknowns. If we select the first view as a reference, $s_{o1}$ can be predetermined, thus a consistent value of $s_{o2}$ can be computed from eq.(7). The same is true for more views. $\quad\square$

After retrieving the projection matrices, one may compute the 3D structure of any pair of correspondence that are tracked automatically or given interactively. Most structured object usually composed of many pieces of planar surfaces, thus the structure is easy to obtain with minimal human interactions of the corners of surfaces across two or more views.

## 4   Experiments with Synthetic Data

During the simulations, we generate a cube in the space, whose dimension is of $20 \times 20 \times 20$ with 40 evenly distributed points on each visible side. As shown in Fig.1(a), there are three parallel lines corresponding to each direction of the world axes. We simulated two images of the cube using the following setup of cameras: $f_u = f_v = 700$, $s = 0$, $u_0 = 310$, $v_0 = 300$, image size is of $600 \times 600$. For the first view, rotation $\mathbf{r}_1 = [-0.2, -0.6, -0.5]$, translation $\mathbf{t}_1 = [-8, -4, 110]$; For the second view, $\mathbf{r}_2 = [-0.1, 0.5, 0.6]$, $\mathbf{t}_2 = [3, -6, 100]$. Gaussian image noise (with mean zero) is added on each imaged point, and the corresponding image lines are fitted from these points using the least squares fitting. The vanishing point is computed as the intersection of each set of parallel lines.

We reconstructed the simulated cube using the proposed algorithm. Since the reconstruction is defined up to a 3D similarity transformation with the ground truth, for convenience of evaluation, we compute the transformation matrix by virtue of the point correspondences between the recovered structure and its ground truth, then transform the reconstructed cube to the coordinate system of the ground truth, and calculate the distances between all the corresponding point pairs. Fig.1(b) and Fig.1(c) show the means and standard deviations of the distances at different noise level. The results at each noise level are evaluated by 200 independent tests so as to obtain more statistically meaningful results. For comparison, we calibrated the cameras via the three vanishing points and reconstructed the cube using typical stereovision technique. The results are also shown in Fig.1. One may see that the proposed technique outperforms the stereovision method in the tests. This is because the proposed algorithm directly uses the vanishing points information to recover the projection matrices that may avoid error propagation along the computation chain.

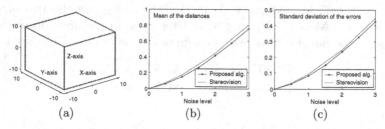

(a)                          (b)                          (c)

**Fig. 1.** (a) the simulated cube in the test; (b) means of the distances between the recovered structure and the ground truth at different noise level; (c) the corresponding standard deviations of the distances

## 5   Experiments with Real Images

We have tested the proposed method on several sets of real images. Here we will only show two results due to space limitation, all test images are downloaded from the Visual Geometry Group of the University of Oxford. The first test is two images of the Wadham College of Oxford, as shown in Fig.2. The image resolution is 1024 × 768. We apply the Canny edge detector and orthogonal regression algorithm to fit the line segments in images [10], and compute the vanishing points from the parallel lines using maximum likelihood estimation [9]. Fig.2(b) shows the detected line segments of the two images. We select the world coordinates and a pair of corresponding points $m_1$ and $m_2$ as shown in Fig.2(a), then use the proposed algorithm to compute the projection matrices, and reconstruct the object by interactively selecting the corner points of each planar surface. Fig.2(c) shows the reconstructed model from different viewpoints with texture mapping. There are three mutually orthogonal planes in the scene: the ground plane, the left and the right walls. The reconstructed angle between these planes are 89.87°, 90.30° and 90.38° respectively.

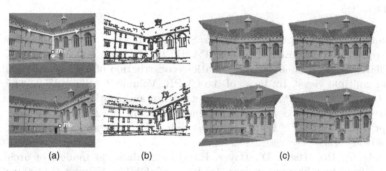

(a)                          (b)                                    (c)

**Fig. 2.** (a) Two images of the Wadham College of Oxford; (b) the detected line segments; (c) the reconstructed model under different viewpoints with texture mapping

The second test is on two images of a church in Valbonne. The image resolution is 512 × 768. Fig.3(a) shows one of the image with the preselected world coordinate system and one reference point. Fig.3(b) and Fig.3(c) give the detected line segments and reconstructed 3D model under different viewpoints respectively. The angle between the reconstructed two orthogonal surfaces of the chimney is 90.32°. We can see from the reconstructions that they are largely consistent with the real cases, and seem very realistic.

(a)               (b)                                 (c)

**Fig. 3.** (a) One of the two images of Valbonne church; (b) the detected line segments; (c) the reconstructed model under different viewpoints with texture mapping

# 6  Conclusions

In this paper, under the assumption of three-parameter-camera model, we have proven the uniqueness of projection matrix from three orthogonal vanishing points with a certain preselected world coordinate system. The method avoids the bottleneck problem of image matching and is easy to implement. It is suitable to reconstruct photo-realistic and accurate model of structured scenes, especially those contain three dominate directions. However, more human interactions may be needed if we want to reconstruct more details of the scene. In practice, one may combine the method with classical stereovision technique so as to obtain better results with minimal interactions.

# References

1. Almansa, A., Desolneux, A., Vamech, S.: Vanishing point detection without any a priori information. IEEE Trans. on PAMI. 25(4) (2003) 502–507
2. Baillard, C., Zisserman, A.: Automatic reconstruction of piecewise planar models from multiple views. In: Proc. of the CVPR. Volume 2. (1999) 2559–2665
3. Bartoli, A., Sturm, P.: Constrained structure and motion from multiple uncalibrated views of a piecewise planar scene. IJCV. 52(1) (2003) 45–64
4. Caprile, B., Torre, V.: Using vanishing points for camera calibration. IJCV. 4(2) (1990) 127–140
5. Cipolla, R. Robertson, D., Boyer, E.: Photobuilder-3d models of architectural scenes from uncalibrated images. In: Proc. of ICMCS. Volume 1. (1999) 25–31
6. Criminisi, A., Reid, I., Zisserman, A.: Single view metrology. IJCV. 40(2) (2000) 123–148
7. Debevec, P. Taylor, C., Malik, J.: Modeling and rendering architecture from photographs: a hybrid geometry-and image-based approach. In: Proc. of SIGGRAPH. (1996) 11–21
8. Hartley, R.I., Zisserman, A.: Multiple View Geometry in Computer Vision. Second edn. Cambridge University Press, ISBN: 0521540518 (2004)
9. Liebowitz, D., Criminisi, A., Zisserman, A.: Creating architectural models from images. In: Proc. of Eurographics. (1999) 39–50
10. Schmid, C., Zisserman, A.: Automatic line matching across views. In: Proc. of IEEE Conference on CVPR. (1997) 666–671
11. Wang, G.H., Hu, Z.Y., Wu, F.C., Tsui, H.T.: Single view metrology from scene constraints. Image Vision Comput. 23(9) (2005) 831–840
12. Wang, G.H., Tsui, H.T., Hu, Z.Y.: Reconstruction of structured scenes from two uncalibrated images. Pattern Recognition Lett. 26(2) (2005) 207–220
13. Wang, G.H., et.al.: Camera calibration and 3d reconstruction from a single view based on scene constraints. Image Vision Comput. 23(3) (2005) 311–323
14. Werner, T., Zisserman, A.: New techniques for automated architecture reconstruction from photographs. In: Proc. of ECCV. Volume 2. (2002) 541–555
15. Wilczkowiak, M. Boyer, E., Sturm, P.: 3d modeling using geometric constraints: a parallelepiped based approach. In: Proc. of ECCV. Volume IV. (2002) 221–237

# Parallel Processing for Reducing the Bottleneck in Realtime Graphics Rendering

Mee Young Sung[1], Suk-Min Whang[1], Yonghee Yoo[1],
Nam-Joong Kim[1], Jong-Seung Park[1], and Wonik Choi[2]

[1] Department of Computer Science & Engineering, University of Incheon,
Incheon 402-749, South Korea
{mysung, hsm0477, yhinfuture, water09z, jong}@incheon.ac.kr
[2] School of Information and Communication Engineering, Inha University,
Incheon 402-751, South Korea
wichoi@inha.ac.kr

**Abstract.** The rendering process of graphics rendering pipeline is usually completed by both the CPU and the GPU, and a bottleneck can be located either in the CPU or the GPU. This paper focuses on reducing the bottleneck between the CPU and the GPU. We are proposing a method for improving the performance of parallel processing for realtime graphics rendering by separating the CPU operations into two parts: pure CPU operations and operations related to the GPU, and let them operate in parallel. This allows for maximizing the parallelism in processing the communication between the CPU and the GPU. Some experiments lead us to confirm that our method proposed in this paper can allow for faster graphics rendering. In addition to our method of using a dedicated thread for GPU related operations, we are also proposing an algorithm for balancing the graphics pipeline using the idle time due to the bottleneck. We have implemented the two methods proposed in this paper in our networked 3D game engine and verified that our methods are effective in real systems.

**Keywords:** Parallel processing, Realtime graphics rendering, Optimization, Bottleneck, Distribution of rendering operations, Multithreading.

## 1 Introduction

Realtime rendering pipeline usually consists of three conceptual stages: application, geometry, and rasterizer. The application stage, implemented in software, may contain collision detection, acceleration algorithms, physics algorithms, character animation with artificial intelligence, etc. The next step implemented either in software or in hardware, depending on the architecture, is the geometry stage, which deals with transforms, projections, lighting, etc. This stage computes what is to be drawn, how it should be drawn, and where it should be drawn. Finally, the rasterizer stage draws (renders) an image with use of the data that the previous stage generated including the interpolation of pixels for shading and the calculation of pixels such as z-buffer testing to appear on the display [1].

Y. Zhuang et al. (Eds.): PCM 2006, LNCS 4261, pp. 943–952, 2006.

In the past, the CPU (Central Processing Unit) had taken charge of the operations in both phases of application and geometry, and the graphics card does the operations of the rasterizer phase. However, the development of graphics cards has made it possible for the GPU (Graphics Processing Unit) to take charge of more operations from the geometry phase and allow the CPU to calculate other useful operations [2]. Now, a series of operations executed in these three phases (application, geometry, rasterizer) is divided into two devices (the CPU and the GPU) and pipelined, therefore, a bottleneck occurs as one device must wait until the other device finishes its operations. That bottleneck hinders the performance of realtime rendering [3].

This paper is proposing an efficient parallelization for reducing the bottleneck and ameliorating the rendering speed. Also, we propose a method for dynamically checking the devices where a bottleneck can be located (the CPU or the GPU) and balancing the pipeline using the bottleneck. Some related work presented in the next section and our methods for minimizing the rendering time and the use of bottleneck are examined in section three. Some experiments for validating our idea are then described in section four, while section five concludes our work.

## 2 Related Works

At the beginning of the development of graphics technology, most of the operations were assigned to the CPU and the GPU only took charge of the rasterizing phase of the display. In those days, we only needed to make the CPU faster for accelerating the graphics rendering speed. However, as graphics accelerators have evolved, the operations of the CPU have migrated to the GPU. Currently, many of the operations which were performed by the CPU in the past have come to be performed by the GPU.

Table 1 illustrates the evolution of the distribution of rendering operations in 3D graphics devices according to years.

**Table 1.** Evolution of 3D (3-Dimensional) graphics devices

|  | 1996 | 1997 | 1998 | 1999 | 2000 | 2001~ |
|---|---|---|---|---|---|---|
| Animation | CPU | CPU | CPU | CPU | CPU | CPU/*GPU* |
| Physics | CPU | CPU | CPU | CPU | *GPU* | *GPU* |
| AI | CPU | CPU | CPU | CPU | *GPU* | *GPU* |
| Lighting | CPU | CPU | CPU | *GPU* | *GPU* | *GPU* |
| Transform | CPU | CPU | CPU | *GPU* | *GPU* | *GPU* |
| Triangle setup and Clipping | CPU | *GPU* | *GPU* | *GPU* | *GPU* | *GPU* |
| Rasterizing | *GPU* | *GPU* | *GPU* | *GPU* | *GPU* | *GPU* |

In the past, the CPU has calculated animations, transforms, lighting, triangle setup, clipping, etc., and then passes the calculated data to the GPU which performs the rasterization of them. This processing structure is linear and the GPU usually waits until the CPU finishes the calculation. Currently, more parallelization of operations has been achieved through the migration of the operations from the CPU to the GPU. The change of the GPU's role allows the CPU to use its idle time for calculating AI algorithms, map algorithms and it generally improves the rendering speed and quality.

On the contrary, the need for faster graphics rendering incessantly increases and many algorithms are designed for reducing the GPU's charge with the aide of the CPU's operations [4]. Fig. 1 illustrates some representative examples of this approach. Fig. 1 (a) presents the View Frustum Culling which does not allow for rendering vertexes outside the camera view. It compares the bounding volume (a volume that encloses a set of objects) of each object to the view frustum. If the bounding volume is outside the frustum, then the geometry it encloses can be omitted from rendering. Fig. 1 (b) depicts an Octree, which is relevant to the Quadtree algorithm. The result of this algorithm is a two-dimensional version of an Octree. A bounding box enclosing all of the objects which are to be present, is recursively divided into four equal-sized boxes until each box is empty or contains one object. Both of these algorithms allow for passing less data to the GPU and improving the rendering speed.

(a)                                          (b)

**Fig. 1.** View Frustum Culling and Octree

## 3   Parallel Processing for Reducing the Bottleneck and Its Use

The objective of our study is to speed up the rendering process, which is the same as that of those algorithms mentioned above. However, our method is much different from those algorithms. The View Frustum Culling and Quadtree algorithms can directly reduce the amount of GPU operations by eliminating the unnecessary vertexes, while our method reduces the idle time between the CPU and the GPU by parallelizing the CPU operations. Therefore, the combined use of our methods and those algorithms for reducing the total number of drawing primitives that have to pass through the pipeline, can allow for the better rendering performance.

Previously, the CPU took charge of most of the rendering operations, except for the rasterization process. The CPU and GPU operations were completed in a linear fashion as shown in Fig. 2 (a). However these days, operations such as transform, lighting, etc., have migrated from the CPU to the GPU. This operation migration allows for better parallelism as presented in Fig. 2 (b). Fig. 2 (b) also displays a time gain of 1 time unit which has resulted from the migration of the CPU operations and parallel processing.

Note that a rendering cycle is defined as the time interval from the end point of the flip operation of a frame to the end point of the flip operation of the next frame. A flip operation corresponds to the swapping of the contents of the front buffer with the contents rendered in the back buffer.

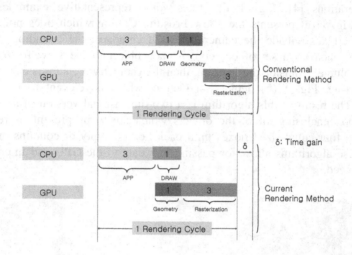

**Fig. 2.** (a) Linear formation of the CPU and the GPU and (b) parallel formation of the CPU and the GPU

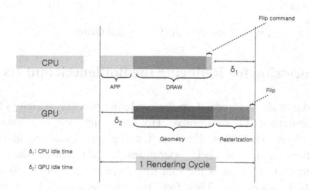

**Fig. 3.** Possible idle time incurred during parallel processing of the CPU and GPU operations using the conventional method

Fig. 3 shows the idle time incurred when we use the CPU and the GPU in parallel. In each rendering cycle, the CPU starts first, and then the GPU starts its operations when the CPU initiates a function in it. Then the GPU finally finishes its operation with the flip operation. In this situation, the CPU usually awaits the completion of the flip operation, and this corresponds to the bottleneck stage of rendering pipeline [5]. In order to minimize this idle time and to improve the rendering performance, we propose a method for maximizing the parallelism among the CPU and the GPU and minimizing the idle time in the rendering pipeline.

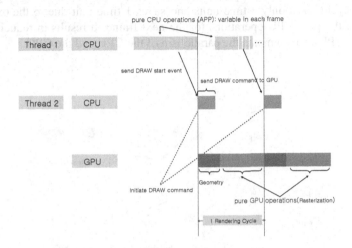

**Fig. 4.** Proposed method for improving the parallel processing of the CPU and GPU, using a separate thread exclusively for the DRAW operations

Fig. 4 demonstrates our mechanism for improving the parallelism among the CPU and the GPU. The main idea is based on the asynchronization of the CPU and GPU operations. The application stage can be further pipelined for obtaining more parallelism. Therefore, the application stage is divided into three stages: APP, CULL, and DRAW [6]. The APP and CULL stages are CPU operations and the DRAW stage is an operation which uses both of the CPU and the GPU. As presented in Fig. 4, we've distinguished the CPU operations into two parts: pure CPU operations and GPU related operations. Each part is assigned to a different thread. The first thread focuses on the APP stage, CULL stage, and parts of the DRAW stage. The second thread is dedicated to the operations concerning the flipping in the DRAW stage. The second thread initiates the flip operation, awaits the completion event which results from flipping, and passes that event to the first thread.

If the rendering system is configured as proposed in Fig. 4, three different results (Fig. 5, Fig. 6, and Fig. 7) can occur. Remember that the flip time is the resulting time interval from after the DRAW command is executed by the CPU to the termination of the display of the corresponding frame.

As shown in Fig. 5, if the flip time is longer than the pure CPU operation time (APP, CULL, and DRAW), it means that a bottleneck is located in the GPU. The example in Fig. 5 is set with the CPU operations taking 2 time units, the GPU operations taking 3 time units, and the DRAW command being executed after 1 time unit of the CPU operations. Fig. 5 (a) illustrates an example of a bottleneck located in the GPU when the rendering is executed in a conventional manner. In this case, we find that the rendering cycle for a frame takes 4 time units, and we also find that 2 time units in the CPU are idle and 1 time unit in the GPU is idle. However, when its rendering is performed using the method proposed in this paper as presented in Fig. 5 (b), a rendering cycle takes only 3 time units and saves 1 time unit due to the execution in advance of the pure CPU operations for the next frame. It results in reducing the idle time of the CPU and augments the parallelism of the CPU and the GPU.

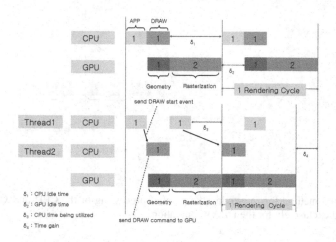

**Fig. 5.** Bottleneck in the GPU

Fig. 6 corresponds to the ideal case and the flip time is equal to the pure CPU operation time. The example in Fig. 6 is set with the CPU operations taking 3 time units, the GPU operations taking 3 time units, and the DRAW command being executed after 2 time units of the CPU operations. This case never causes the bottleneck. In Fig. 6 (a), which illustrates an example of ideal case executed in conventional manner, the rendering cycle time for a frame is 5 time units. However, a rendering cycle takes only 3 time units with this ideal case using our method as shown in Fig. 6 (b).

The figure (Fig. 7) illustrates the case where the bottleneck is located in the CPU. The example is set with the CPU operations taking 4 time units, the GPU operations taking 3 time units, and the DRAW command being executed after 3 time units of the CPU operations. The flip time is shorter than the pure CPU operation time. In the example of a bottleneck occurring in the CPU and rendered in a conventional manner as shown in Fig. 7 (a), we find that the rendering cycle for a frame takes 6 time units. We also find that 2 time units in the CPU are idle and 3 time units in the GPU are idle. On the other hand, if we render using our method, as presented in Fig. 5 (b), a rendering cycle takes only 4 time units and we save 2 time units by executing the pure CPU operations in advance for the next frame.

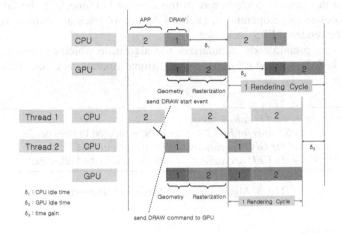

**Fig. 6.** Ideal case

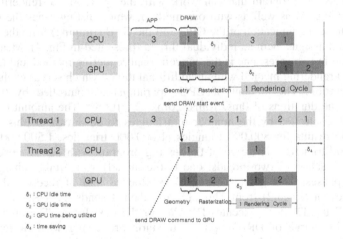

**Fig. 7.** Bottleneck in the CPU

In addition to our method for reducing the bottleneck interval using an independent thread for DRAW operations, we also propose an algorithm for using the bottleneck. As examined above, if we can recognize the device where a bottleneck is located and the bottleneck time of that device when rendering each frame, we can allocate additional operations for as long as the duration of the bottleneck into the non-bottleneck device to achieve a more optimized and higher quality rendering. We use the unit FPS (Frames per Second) for measuring the performance of rendering.

If the CPU operations are increased and the rendered FPS (Frames per Second) decreases, it corresponds to the case of a bottleneck in the CPU, and the GPU can calculate more operations, such as calculating delicate lighting, until the rendered FPS increases again. On the contrary, if the CPU operations are increased and the rendered

FPS does not decrease, it corresponds to the case of bottleneck in the GPU and the CPU can calculate more operations, such as AI and physics algorithms, for the next frame until the rendered FPS decreases.

The following pseudo code summarizes the algorithm which examines in realtime the bottlenecked device and allocates the additional operations to the device without the bottleneck.

```
Increase the amount of calculations;
if ( previous FPS > current FPS )     /* FPS: Rendered Frames per Second */
    then Increase the GPU operations;  /* Bottleneck in the CPU case */
    else Increase the CPU operations;  /* Bottleneck in the GPU case */
```

**Fig. 8.** Algorithm for evaluating a bottleneck

# 4   Experiments

We performed some experiments to validate the effectiveness of our method. We developed a testing program that can work with the conventional rendering method (presented in Fig. 3) as well as with our method, which distinguishes the operations concerning the communication of the CPU and the GPU (flipping) from the pure CPU operations and assigns them an individual thread (presented in Fig. 4). Measurements are performed in two cases: one is the conventional rendering method and the other is our proposed rendering method with an additional thread which serves exclusively for DRAW operation. The amount of CPU operations is controlled by the Sleep() function for the durations of 0ms, 10ms, 20ms, ..., 100ms. The amount of the GPU operations is controlled by the number of triangles to be drawn. In this test we've evaluated the results for 800,000 triangles, 1,000,000 triangles, 1,500,000 triangles, and 2,000,000 triangles. The core of the testing program with our proposed method includes the creation of two threads: one is the thread1 which takes charge of APP and CULL phases. This thread (Thread1) is blocked until it receives the DRAW completion event (Event2) from Thread2, and then it sends the DRAW start event (Event1) to Thread2 which executes DRAW for the next frame. The other thread is exclusively in charge of DRAW phase. It starts processing when it receives the DRAW start event (Event1) from Thread1 and then it sends the command to start DRAW to the GPU. It also sends the DRAW completion event (Event2) to Thread1 for releasing the blocking of Thread1 when the GPU completes its DRAW operation. Our testinf program also includes the creation of two events: The first one corresponds to the DRAW start event sent from Thread1 to Thread2. This makes Thread2 initiate the DRAW command to the GPU. The other event corresponds to the DRAW completion event sent from Thread2 to Thread1 for unblocking Thread1. This refreshes Thread1 and enables it to begin calculating for the next frame.

Fig. 9 illustrates the results of the rendered FPS according to the increases of the CPU time and the number of triangles. The results in each of the four cases were similar. Generally, the FPS measurement was higher when we used our method with the thread dedicated exclusively to the DRAW operation than in the case of the conventional method. All of the four cases showed the similar transition flow: each experiment started with the situation of the bottleneck in the GPU (shown in Fig. 5). It then moved to the ideal case (shown in Fig. 6), and it finally moved to the case with the bottleneck in the CPU (shown in Fig. 7). The point of time for decreasing the rendered FPS retards on the temporal axis as the number of triangles increases. For example, the rendered FPS starts to decrease around 20ms for drawing 800,000 triangles, it starts to decrease around 30ms for drawing 1,000,000 triangles, it start to decrease around 40ms for drawing 1,500,000 triangles, and it starts to decrease around 50 ms for drawing 2,000,000 triangles. This phenomenon can be explained by the fact that the increased number of triangles augments the amount of GPU operations, and it may augment the CPU idle time. Additionally, that phenomenon leads us to conclude that our bottleneck use algorithm can allow for more efficient use of the CPU idle time and is more useful in the case of a heavy bottleneck in the GPU.

We applied a variation of the bottleneck use algorithm described in Fig. 8 to an actual avatar based 3D network game engine (shown in Fig. 10) implemented in our previous work. In our networked 3D game engine, the FPS is checked periodically and the amount of operations both in the CPU and the GPU are controlled according to the way described in section 3. In the case of a bottleneck in the GPU, our 3D avatar system additionally assigns AI and physics algorithms to the CPU, which are useful for our system (such as, collision detection algorithm or kinematics algorithms). In the case of a bottleneck in the CPU, advanced lighting and shading algorithms, such as, Phong's specular highlighting algorithm or volume shadow algorithm, are assigned to the GPU.

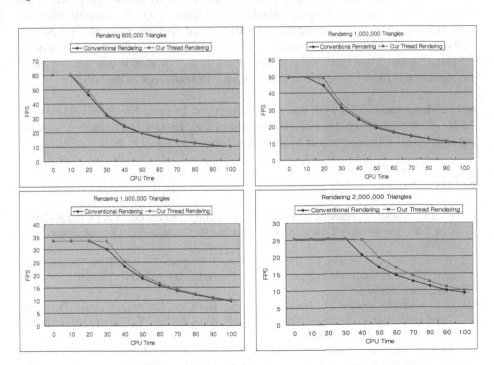

**Fig. 9.** Graphical representation of results

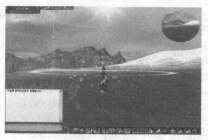

**Fig. 10.** Screen shots of an application example

# 5  Conclusion

The objective of our study is to optimize realtime graphics rendering by using parallel processing of the CPU and the GPU for a 3D game engine. In summary, we separated the CPU operations into two parts: pure CPU operations and operations exclusively dedicated for the communication between the CPU and the GPU concerning the flip operation. Then we assigned a dedicated thread to the second part. This can allow for maximizing the parallelism in processing the communication between the CPU and the GPU. Through some experiments, we concluded that the method proposed in this paper can allow faster rendering by reducing the bottleneck interval. In addition to our method using an exclusive thread for the GPU related operations, we also proposed a method for using the bottleneck which is implemented in our avatar based networked 3D game engine. The experimental results also lead us to conclude that our bottleneck use algorithm is more efficient in the case of a heavy bottleneck in the GPU.

**Acknowledgement.** This work was supported in part by grant No. RTI05-03-01 from the Regional Technology Innovation Program of the Ministry of Commerce, Industry and Energy(MOCIE) and in part by the Brain Korea 21 Project in 2006.

# References

[1] Akenine-Moller, T., Hainess, E.: Real-Time Rendering. 2nd edition, A K PETERS (2002)
[2] Gray, K.: The Microsoft DirectX 9 Programmable Graphics Pipeline. Microsoft Press (2003)
[3] Wimmer, M., and Wonka, P.: Rendering Time Estimation for Real-Time Rendering. In proceedings on Eurographics Symposium on Rendering 2003 (2003) 118-129
[4] http://www.gpgpu.org
[5] Cox, Michael, Sprague D., Danskin., Ehlers., Hook B., Lorensen B., and Tarolli G.: Developing High-Performance Graphics Applications for the PC Platform. In Course 29 notes at SIGGRAPH 98 (1998)
[6] Rohlf, J., Helman, J.: IRIS Performer: A High Performance Multiprocessing Toolkit for Real-Time 3D Graphics. In proceedings on SIGGRAPH 94 (1994) 81-394

# Distributed Data Visualization Tools for Multidisciplinary Design Optimization of Aero-crafts

Chunsheng Liu and Tianxu Zhang

Institute of Pattern Recognition and Artificial Intelligence, Huazhong University
of Science and Technology, Wuhan, 430074, P.R. China
liuchunsheng@buaa.edu.cn

**Abstract.** A user oriented grid platform for multidisciplinary design optimization (MDO) of aero-crafts based on web service highly requires to construct a tool for visualization of the computing data and visual steering of the whole process for MDO. In this paper, a distributed data visualization tool for MDO of Aero-crafts is described. And the visual steering scheme for MDO is described in detail, which is constructed under web service environment and is performed as a series of web pages. Visualization Toolkit (VTK) and Java are adopted in visualization service to process the results of MDO of Geometry and the distributed computational data.

## 1 Introduction

Multidisciplinary Design Optimization (MDO) is highly required in the development of novel high-performance aero-crafts, including flight performance, aerodynamic performance etc. Therefore, for many years MDO of aero-crafts has been a significant challenge for scientists and designers.

Generally, MDO of a complex system, especially an aero-craft system, usually involves various disciplines. Advances in disciplinary analysis in resent years have made those problems worse and those analysis model restricted to simple problems with very approximate approaches can not been used again. As those analysis codes for MDO of flight vehicles have grown larger and larger, it is indeed too incomprehensible and difficult for a designer-in-chief to maintain, since few know clearly what is included in the code and few can explain clearly the results from those codes. Therefore, the role of disciplinary scientist increases and it becomes more difficult for a designer-in-chief to manage the design process. To complete the design process smoothly, the designer-in-chief must joint all specialists from their own disciplines in a collaborative optimization process. Thus, a need exists, not simply to increase the speed of those complex analyses, but rather to simultaneously improve optimization performance and reduce complexity [1].

As the Grid technology developed, there appears a new way to solve the problem. Recently, significant progress has been made on the computational grid technology. The problem underlies of Grid concept is coordinated resource sharing and problem solving in dynamic, multi-institutional virtual organizations. In Grid computing environment, the computing resources are provided as Grid service. Then, we can construct

Y. Zhuang et al. (Eds.): PCM 2006, LNCS 4261, pp. 953–960, 2006.

a Computational Grid for MDO, to improve the performance of the MDO algorithms and gain many new characteristics that are impossible in traditional means for MDO of a large aero-craft system. This computational grid for MDO can make the design process be easily controlled and monitored and can be conducted interactively, and through this Grid system many specialists in various disciplines can be easily managed in one MDO group.

To construct a user oriented grid platform for multidisciplinary MDO of aero-crafts based on web service, visualization of the computing data and visual steering of the whole process for MDO is highly required. Presently there exists much software for distributed MVE (modular visualization environments), such as AVS/Express (Advanced Visual System), IBM's OpenDX (free source) and IRIS Explorer. As for the function, all those MVE toolkits can be adopted in this paper. However, the computational grid should have the characteristic for trans-platform. Then Java is the right developing toolkit for our grid system. To construct this Java system, it seems that Visualization Toolkit (VTK) is more attractive choice, which can be built as two layer architecture: one is kernel layer for pre-compiling and the other is packaging layer with interpreting computer language.

Therefore, in this paper, a distributed data visualization tool for MDO of Aero-crafts is described. And the visual steering scheme for MDO is described in detail, which is constructed under web service environment and is performed as a series of web pages. Visualization Toolkit (VTK) and Java are adopted in visualization service to process the results of MDO of Geometry and the CFD data.

This paper is organized as following: in Section 2, the framework of the computational grid for MDO will be described; In Section 3 the visual steering scheme for MDO will be discussed in details; In Section 4 the visualization service for computing data will be discussed; finally, Section 5 concludes what tools developed in the paper.

## 2   Grid Platform for MDO of Aero-crafts

### 2.1   Grid Framework for MDO of Aero-crafts

Procedure for Multidisciplinary Design Optimization (MDO) of aero-crafts by using genetic algorithms (GA) is shown in figure 1. When optimizing the aero-crafts, we will follow the steps listed by the figure. Firstly, set the range of a set of given designing parameters and use a random algorithm to select a specific value for each parameter from the given range. Secondly, use the analysis codes to compute each child task and get the result set. Thirdly, use a comparison algorithm to select the best result and use the best as the "seeds" to generate the next generation.

The Grid for MDO is composed of many Grid services. Each Grid service is built on the web and grid technology. Each service has some standard interfaces to support the registering of service, the querying of service, the communication and the interacting between the client and the service provider. A Grid service is a web service that conforms to a set of conventions (interfaces and behaviors) that define how a client interacts with a Grid service [2]. Some general features of the Grid service are: (1) Every Grid service is a web service, whose public interfaces and bindings are defined and described using XML[3]; (2) The Grid service has a set of predefined interfaces, such as Grid Service, Registry, Factory, Handle Map, Primary Key etc. [2]; (3) Each Grid service has the responsibility to maintain the local policy, which means the Grid service can decide what kind services it will provide and what kind of resources can be shared.

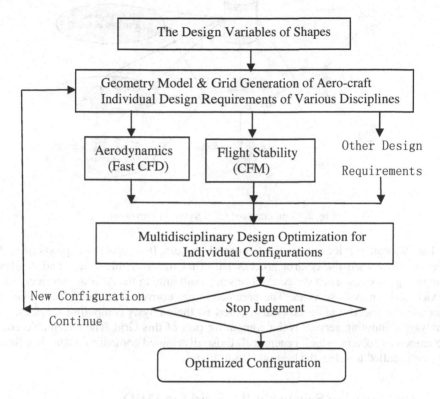

**Fig. 1.** Flowchart of the Optimization Procedure

## 2.2  Components of the Computational Grid for MDO

The Computational Grid System for MDO is composed of three modules as shown in figure 2. The first part is User service module. As shown in the figure 2, the executor and the co-designer are the specific users of this system. The user can submit the tasks, monitor the computing progress and get the middle and final results via the web pages. When received the requests from the users, the User service can query the UDDI (Universal Description, Discovery, Integration) center to find what kinds of services available now. The User service can supports the user accounts management, supports the task submitting and parameter adjusting. It can interact with other services to finish the computing work. The second part is the UDDI center module. The responsibility of this module is acting as an information exchange center. The third part is the Application services, including Allocate service, Select service and

Analysis service including CFD (Computational Fluid Mechanics) service, CFM (Computational Flight Mechanics)service and other Analysis services.

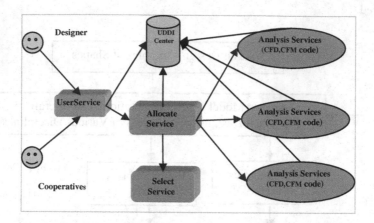

**Fig. 2.** Computational Grid System Framework

The Allocate service is a service to control process. It accepts the requests from the User service. Then the control process will find the available Select and Analysis computing services. Then the connections are built among the Allocate service, Select service and Analysis services. The parameters are conveyed to the Select service to generate the specific child tasks distributed to the analysis computing services. The Analysis computing service is the computing part of this Grid. The executable codes are named as solvers, which generate all those distributed computing Data. The Select service is called to select the best one from them.

## 3 Visual Steering Scheme in the Grid for MDO

The computational grid for MDO finally works well by connecting users and the Grid services. For users, if they want to start a new design, they only need submit their tasks through the web. To complete a MDO task, the designer-in-chief also can communicate with other designers from various disciplines through the web. There is a billboard on the web page. The task executor and the co-designers exchange information by it. When the co-designer finds some parameters are not suitable for the task, he leaves messages on the billboard. The task executer can adjust the parameters. Web services will help any designers complete their whole designing tasks mutually and interactively.

To provide users conduct their jobs from the special web server of the computational grid, a User Service with visual steering is constructed. The User service has following functions: (1) Support the user accounts management; (2) Support the Task submitting, parameter adjusting, process monitoring and the results obtaining; (3) It can interact with others services to finish the computing work; (4) Provide on-line instruction for users.

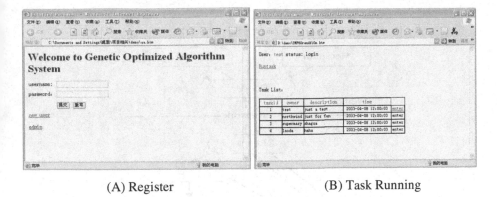

(A) Register                              (B) Task Running

**Fig. 3.** The prototype web pages of the Web services of the optimization Grid system

When a user login in the system via a Java Server Page (JSP), the daemon process of the web server redirect the request to a account manage process, and then the account manage process check the user's information form the database. After the user's identity has been identified, the User service will return some JSP to perform the task related works. As can be shown from Figure 3, where are some prototype web pages for the computational grid for MDO. (A) illustrates the web page entering the Grid system, which is a register service. (B) illustrates the web page of the Grid system, which gives the choice and service to run an optimization design task.

# 4  Visualization Service in the Computational Grid for MDO

Post-processing of MDO and Computational Fluid Dynamics (CFD) data is a very important aspect of scientific visualization. In this section, we describe how the Visualization Service be constructed in the computational grid for MDO of aero-crafts. It integrates the advantages of the distributed visualization and grid service technology.

As shown from figure 4., in this distributed visualization system of grid, computing data and metadata are saved in the server section and user, GUI interface and viewer are saved in the client section. visualization engine can be divided into two parts, one part locates in the server section, named as SVE (*server-side visualization engine*), and another part locates in the client section, named as CVE (*client-side visualization engine*). If SVE transports data to the server, visualization process will be completed by the client section; or SVE complete the visualization process of the data, and CVE transports data and 2-D image to be viewed through viewer.

According to the basic instruction of distributed visualization system and the characteristic of the Grid for MDO, Visualization Toolkit (VTK) and Java are adopted into the Visualization Service to process the optimized and CFD computation data. Figure 5 is the demonstration for Visualization Service System Architecture of the Computational Grid for MDO in this paper. The interface of the grid service is described by WSDL, and the internal implementation of the grid service is designed by using VTK as the visualization kernel.

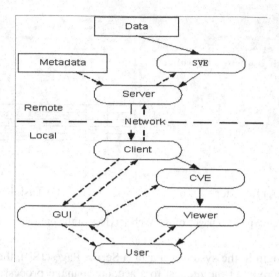

**Fig. 4.** Distributed Visualization System Architecture

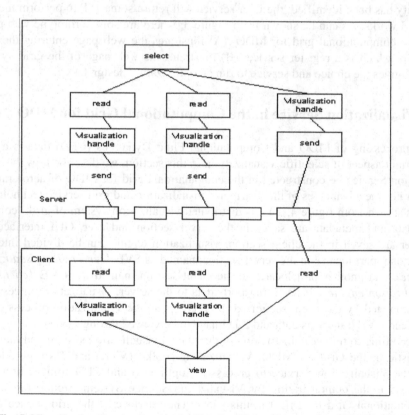

**Fig. 5.** Visualization Service System Architecture of the Computational Grid for MDO

In this Visualization Service System, there are those components as following. Firstly, Preliminary Data Module, including data selecting module (SelectFile), data preprocessing module (ReadFile) and data sending module (SendData). Secondly, Visualization Module, including Iso-surface processing module (Isosurface), mesh processing module (Mesh), streamline processing module (Streamline), contour processing module (Contour), vector data processing module (Vector), boundary processing module (Boundary), slice and clip processing module (Slice & Clip) and slice shrink processing module (Shrink).

As can be shown from figure 6, it is the streamline of flow field around an aero-craft with visualization system in this paper. As for the algorithms in the Visualization module, the Marching Cubes (MC) method is used to compute the iso-surface and the particle track method is used to compute the streamlines.

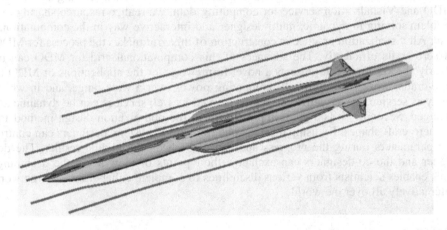

**Fig. 6.** Streamline of Flow Field Around an Aero-craft with Visualization Service System

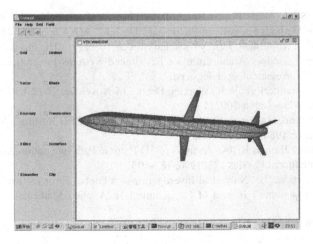

**Fig. 7.** The GUI in the Client Section of the Visualization System

Figure 7 is the GUI in the client section, user of the computational grid for MDO can download it from the result monitoring web page. The experimental result indicates that the Visualization Service can use remote powerful computing resources to provide strong visualization transactions for clients with weaker capabilities. And it is also shown that all visualization service by our VTK based software can view the optimized geometry and flow field of aero-crafts clearly and make the process for MDO of aero-crafts efficiently.

## 5  Conclusion

Visualization of the computing data and visual steering of the whole process for MDO is very important to construct a user oriented computational grid for MDO of aero-crafts based on web service. Through implementation the visual steering scheme for MDO and Visualization service for computing data, we realize resource sharing and problem solving in dynamic, multi-designer and interactive way in the computational grid. All visualization practice in construction of this grid makes the process for MDO of aero-crafts efficiently. The advances of this computational grid for MDO can be clearly shown. Firstly, it presents a novel framework for the applications of MDO of aero-crafts, which can utilize the computing power over a wide range, and in which analysis service and visualization service served as web services can be dynamically changed. Secondly, it is a great improvement in the optimization design method for the aero-craft shapes. By using this Computational Grid system, designers can control the parameters during the progress and can also check the middle results. The designer and the co-designers can exchange their points of view about the designing. This enables scientists from various disciplines to complete collaborative design work interactively all over the world.

## References

1. Kroo, Ilan., Steve Altus, Robert Braun, Peter Gage, and Ian Sobieski, "Multidisciplinary Optimization Methods For Aircraft Preliminary Design," AIAA paper 94-4325-CP, 1994.
2. Ian Foster, Carl Kesselman, Jeffrey Nick and Steven Tuecke. , "The Physiology of the Grid: An Open Grid Services Architecture for Distributed Systems Integration," 2002.2 http://www.globus.org/research/papers/ogsa.pdf.
3. Web Service Architecture, W3C Working Draft , 14 November 2002.,URL:http://www.w3.org/TR/2002/WD-ws-arch-20021114/.
4. Buning P, "Sources of Error in the Graphical Analysis of CFD Results", Journal of Scientific Computing, 1988 (3:2):149-164.
5. Darmfoal D and Haimes R, "An Analysis of 3D Particle Path Integration Algorithms", Journal of Computational Physics 123, 1996: 182-195.
6. Aid R and Levacher L, "Numerical Investigations on Global Error Estimation for Ordinary Differential Equations", Journal of Computation an Applied Mathematics, VOL82 (1-2), 1997:21-39.
7. Schroeder, W.J., Avila, L S and Hoffman, W., "Visualizing with VTK: a tutorial", IEEE Computer Graphics and Application. 2000, 20(5), 20.
8. William, J. S., Kenneth, M.M., Lisa, S.A.., "The VTK user's guide", New York: Kitware, 2000:1-355.

# An Efficient Clustering and Indexing Approach over Large Video Sequences

Yu Yang and Qing Li

Department of Computer Science, City University of Hong Kong, HKSAR, China
paul.yang@student.cityu.edu.hk,
itqli@cityu.edu.hk

**Abstract.** In a video database, the similarity between video sequences is usually measured by the percentages of similar frames shared by both video sequences, where each frame is represented as a high-dimensional feature vector. The direct computation of the similarity measure involves time-consuming sequential scans over the whole dataset. On the other hand, adopting existing indexing technique to high-dimensional datasets suffers from the "Dimensionality Curse". Thus, an efficient and effective indexing method is needed to reduce the computation cost for the similarity search. In this paper, we propose a Multi-level Hierarchical Divisive Dimensionality Reduction technique to discover correlated clusters, and develop a corresponding indexing structure to efficiently index the clusters in order to support efficient similarity search over video data. By using dimensionality reduction techniques as Principal Component Analysis, we can restore the critical information between the data points in the dataset using a reduced dimension space. Experiments show the efficiency and usefulness of this approach.

## 1 Introduction

As video data has been propagating rapidly over the Internet, it becomes an imperative task for the video research community to develop effective and efficient retrieval tools for video data. Due to the complexity of video data, retrieving similar video content according to user query is still a difficult task which requires: (a) compact representation model on video sequences, (b) efficient similarity search. Keyframe extraction and representation [1] is a widely researched topic to represent the whole video sequence by some representative frames; also, ViTri [2] clusters the video frames and use triplets of $< position, radius, density >$ to represent the video data. However, little work has been done on efficient similarity search over video data, which requires an efficient indexing scheme to reduce the computational cost in the similarity measurement. For multi-dimensional indexing, the performance of existing indexing structure degrades rapidly with the increase of dimensionalities [3,4]. Since video sequences are always represented by high-dimensional feature vectors, dimensionality reduction technique [5] can be used to transform the original high-dimensional space into reduced-dimensional one with the preservation of intra-distance between data points. However, this

Y. Zhuang et al. (Eds.): PCM 2006, LNCS 4261, pp. 961–970, 2006.

transformation is lossy and may cause false positives to occur; moreover, its performances varies under different distributions of the datasets. Hence, we need to understand the correlation between data points and make distinguishable clusters to let the corresponding indexing structure have better pruning power.

In this paper, we propose a Multi-level Hierarchical Divisive Dimensionality Reduction technique to index video data. The use of a multi-level structure is based on the observation that certain level of the lower dimensional subspaces may contain sufficient information to group the correlated clusters, and our target is to find more distinguishable clusters so that it can have a better pruning power (i.e., to decrease the number of unnecessary accesses on dissimilar data points) for video similarity search. The contributions of this paper are as follows: We provide an innovative multi-level clustering discovery algorithm designed for video dataset on reduced subspace by using Principal Component Analysis to find correlated clusters efficiently. Also, we provide a corresponding indexing structure to store clusters so that range query search only needs to be performed on specific clusters, thus yielding strong pruning power over video dataset. Being a general clustering approach, our method can be adopted into different video representation models.

The rest of the paper is organized as follows. In Section 2 we present some related work. Our clustering algorithm is described in Section 3, along with an indexing algorithm in Section 4. We conduct the experiment study in Section 5, and provide a conclusion with directions for future work in Section 6.

## 2   Related Work

For content-based video retrieval and identification, most existing approaches are based on the sequential correlation matching. Those sequential matching methods usually segment a video sequence into small fragments and use a similarity matching function in order to search desired video contents [6,7,8]; the search efficiency is ignored to some extent, as such video fragments are always represented by high-dimensional feature vectors, but the effect of "Dimensionality Curse" causes the existing indexing methods to be ineffective/or even worse than sequential scan. Although there exist some techniques to improve the speed of linear scanning, such as temporal pruning [9] or coarser granularity searching [10], their searching time-complexity still remains at least linear to the size of database due to the nature of exhaustive search over the whole database. An indexing structure is thus needed to index the fragments for similarity search.

Dimensionality reduction is a technique used to sooth the problem of efficiency degradation. The idea is to transform a dataset from a high-dimensional space to a lower dimensional space with the preservation of critical information. Principal Component Analysis (PCA) [11] is a typical dimensionality reduction technique to discover the proper axis for projections to perform the dimensionality reduction. It examines the variance structure in the datasets and determines the direction along which the data exhibits high variance. The first principal component (PC) accounts for the most variability of the data, and we can transform the data points from the original space to the 1-d space using the PC as the axis. Then the indexing and query processing can be done accordingly. This technique is referred to as Global Dimensionality Reduction (GDR), as the dimensionality reduction over the entire dataset is taken together. [2] is a typical GDR method for video dataset with an improved indexing structure to efficiently prune the (dis)similar frames. It works well when the dataset is globally correlated, i.e., most of the variation in the data can be captured by the first few PCs. However, when the dataset is locally correlated, GDR will generate a large set of false positives, and also, the loss in distance information then is non-trivial. In [12], a strategy called Local Dimensionality Reduction (LDR) is proposed to divide the whole dataset into separate clusters based on correlation of the data and then indexes each cluster separately. However, LDR fails to detect all the correlated clusters effectively, because it does not consider correlation nor dependency between the dimensions. [13] proposed a Multi-level Mahalanobis-based Dimensionality Reduction technique to discover correlated clusters; it shows the efficiency of using ellipsoid clusters by employing Mahalanobis distance measure. However, ellipsoid clusters suffers from high computational and indexing cost incurred from the transformation between the standard L-norm distance and the Mahalanobis distance.

Clustering has always been an interesting topic typically for researchers in the domain of data mining. Note that the aim of clustering in data mining is trying to find interesting clusters but not performing indexing and range queries, so different clustering algorithms focus on various perspectives to understand the construction of clusters. Projected clustering (ProClus [14]) finds subsets of features defining (or important for) each cluster: it first obtains clusters using B-medoid [15] by considering all the features and then finds the most important features for each cluster using Manhattan distance. OptGrid [16] finds clusters in a high-dimensional space by projecting the data onto each axis and partitioning the data by using cutting planes at low-density points. These approaches all suffer from the scenarios when clusters in the original space overlap in the projected axis.

# 3    Discovering Correlated Clusters

In this section, we first come with some terms and lemmas as the foundation and then present a multi-level clustering algorithm to discover correlated clusters.

## 3.1    Foundations

### Definition 1. Video Similarity Measure

For the purpose of our paper, we assume that a video sequence can be represented by a series of keyframes. Thus, for two video sequences $X$ and $Y$, they can then be represented as $X = \{x_1, x_2, ..., x_{f_x}\}$ and $Y = \{y_1, y_2, ..., y_{f_y}\}$, where $f_x$ and $f_y$ is the number of keyframes in the sequences respectively. We use $d(x, y)$ to denote the distance function to measure the (dis)similarity of two keyframes $x$ and $y$. A *keyframe similarity threshold* $\epsilon$ is predefined so that $x$ and $y$ are judged to be similar if $d(x, y) \leq \epsilon$. Then, the similarity between two sequences $X$ and $Y$ can be calculated by the following formulas, as in [7]:

$$sim(X,Y) = \frac{\sum_{x \in X} 1_{\{y \in Y : d(x,y) \leq \epsilon\}} + \sum_{y \in Y} 1_{\{x \in X : d(x,y) \leq \epsilon\}}}{f_x + f_y} \tag{1}$$

As discussed above, the computational cost of this similarity measure is extremely high for sequential scan over the whole dataset. Hence, we propose a clustering and indexing structure in the subsequent (sub-)sections to help reduce the accesses of dissimilar frames.

### Definition 2. Sum-Square-Error

Sum-square-error (SSE) is widely used as a criterion for clustering algorithm as K-means. If we denote our dataset to be $X = \{x_1, x_2, ..., x_n\}$, the overall SSE can be defined as follows:

$$SSE = \sum_{j=1}^{K} \sum_{x_i \in Cj} \| x_i - \mu_j \|^2 \tag{2}$$

where $\mu_j = \frac{1}{n_j} \sum_{x_i \in Cj} x_i$ denotes the mean of cluster $C_j$ and $n_j$ denotes the number of instances in $C_j$. Under the circumstances that two clustering algorithms generate the same number of clusters, the better clustering algorithm should result in a smaller overall SSE.

### Definition 3. Divisive clustering approach

K-means algorithm is one of the most popular and easy-to-implement clustering algorithms. However, one biggest problem of K-means is the selection of $K$ seed centroids to start with. Thus, we adopt a divisive approach by starting with one cluster and splitting it into two. We recursively perform the splitting algorithm until some predefined stop conditions are satisfied. When we perform the splitting, the change of SSE is calculated as follows:

$$\begin{aligned} \Delta SSE &= SSE_{old} - SSE_{new} \\ &= \sum_{x_i \in C_1} [\| x_i - \mu \|^2 - \| x_i - \mu_1 \|^2] + \sum_{x_i \in C_2} [\| x_i - \mu \|^2 - \| x_i - \mu_2 \|^2] \\ &= \Delta SSE_1 + \Delta SSE_2 \end{aligned}$$

where $C$ is the original cluster with centroid being $O$ and mean being $\mu$. The newly generated clusters are $C_1$ and $C_2$ with given centroids being $O_1$ and $O_2$ and given means being $\mu_1$ and $\mu_2$, respectively. Through observing this divisive approach, we get the following lemmas.

**Lemma 1.** *Points $O$, $O_1$ and $O_2$ (i.e., centroids of the above-mentioned clusters) are in a line and $O$ is the midpoint of $O_1$ and $O_2$.*

*Proof.* Assuming that these three points are not in a line, so we make a line across $O_1$ and $O_2$, and let $O_{mid}$ to be the midpoint of $O_1$ and $O_2$. Thus, $O_{mid}$ must be different from $O$. Then, there exists a dimension $d_p$, such that the value of $O_{mid}$ (denoted as $\mu_{mid}^{d_p}$ for dimension $d_p$) is not equal to that of $O$ (denoted as $\mu^{d_p}$). However, as $O_1$ and $O_2$ is the corresponding centroids of clusters $C_1$ and $C_2$, we have,

$$\mu_{mid}^{d_p} = \frac{\mu_1^{d_p} + \mu_2^{d_p}}{2} = \frac{\sum_{x_i \in C_1} x_i^{d_p} + \sum_{x_i \in C_2} x_i^{d_p}}{2}$$

$$= \frac{\sum_{x \in C} x_i^{d_p}}{2} = \mu^{d_p}$$

Thus, $O_{mid}$ and $O$ are in fact the same point, and points $O$, $O_1$ and $O_2$ are in a line.

**Lemma 2.** *When $O_1$ and $O_2$ falls in the first PC, the corresponding division of the cluster is a near-optimal one.*

*Proof.* Let each d-dimensional vector $x_i$ be represented by a weighted d independent orthonormal vector $\Phi = [\Phi_1, \Phi_2, ... \Phi_d]$ : $x_i = \sum_{s=1}^d \alpha_{is} \Phi_s$, with $\mu_j$ represented by $\mu_j = \sum_{s=1}^d o_{is} \Phi_s$. Assuming $n_1$ and $n_2$ denotes the number of points in cluster $C_1$ and $C_2$ respectively, we can get $\sum_{x_i \in C_1} \alpha_{is} = o_{1s} * n_1$. For $s^{th}$-dimensionality, we have:

$$\Delta SSE_1^s = \sum_{x_i \in C_1} [(\alpha_{is} \Phi_s - o_s \Phi_s)^2 - (\alpha_{is} \Phi_s - o_{1s} \Phi_s)^2]$$

$$= \Phi_s^2 (o_{1s} - o_s) \sum_{x_i \in C_1} (2 * \alpha_{is} - o_s - o_{1s})$$

$$= \Phi_s^2 (o_{1s} - o_s)^2 * n_1$$

As the first PC examines the dataset with the largest variance, both $\Phi^2$ and the distance between $O_1$ and $O$ will result in the largest possible value. Furthermore, as the sum of $n_1$ and $n_2$ equals to the number of points of the original clusters, we can conclude that this PCA-based partitioning approach is a near-optimal division method.

## 3.2    A Multi-level Clustering Algorithm

We are now ready to present our Multi-level Clustering Algorithm (MCA). As shown in Algorithm 1, the level $S$ of PC is initially set to 1. In GC1 and GC2, the algorithm tries to split the clusters with respect to the $S^{th}$-dimensionality. Within the same PC, it always chooses the cluster with largest SSE to split first. The splitting procedure stops when one of two conditions gets satisfied: (a) for the newly generated clusters whose sum of SSE denoted as $\Delta_{new}$ and the original cluster whose SSE denoted as $\Delta_{old}$, $\Delta' = \frac{\Delta_{new}}{\Delta_{old}}$ must be no smaller than a *Splitting threshold* $\epsilon_s$; (b) the distance between any two new clusters should

**Algorithm 1.** Multi-level Clustering Algorithm

| |
|---|
| **Clustering Algorithm:**<br>Input: Set of Points $A$, Original Dimensionality $D$, Level of PC $S$, Reduced Dimensionality Level $R$;<br>Output: Set of complete clusters, and some points not satisfying the stop conditions will be marked as outliers. |
| **GenerateCluster($A$, $D$, $S$)**<br><br>GC1:    Compute the eigenvector of the dataset $A$.<br><br>GC2:    Using Divisive clustering approach to generate Clusters from the $S$-th PC. Stop splitting when the stop conditions are satisfied.<br><br>GC3:    Reiteratively compute the generated clusters as follows:<br><br>GC3-1: Get the corresponding eigenvector of each clusters $C_i$.<br><br>GC3-2: Further generate clusters according to the corresponding largest PC. If no clusters can be generated, recursively perform cluster generating algorithm in the deeper PCs within the clusters. Stop only when the PC level is not smaller than $R$. |

be larger than $2 * \epsilon$, where $\epsilon$ is the *keyframe similarity threshold* as explained in Section 3.1. Note that Condition (b) helps in the indexing step to reduce the unnecessary accesses of clusters.

In GC3-1 and GC3-2 of Algorithm 1, we attempt to investigate possible PC in the deeper level by comprising a recomputation of PC in the sub-cluster (GC3-1), and an investigation of deeper PC of the sub-cluster (GC3-2). MCA reiterates until any of the stop conditions is satisfied.

## 4    Cluster Indexing

As the centroid of each clusters is still in the high-dimensional data space, the indexing of the data points and clusters remains a non-trivial task. In this section, we present an indexing scheme that can efficiently prune out dissimilar points within $\epsilon$-range.

### 4.1    Indexing Structure

Consider a dataset of $N$ data points, we first perform our MCA upon them as Figure 1 shows. In level 1 the whole space is partitioned into $n$ clusters $C_1$, $C_2$, ...,$C_n$ using the divisive clustering approach. In level 2, cluster $C_i$ is further partitioned into sub-clusters $C_{i1}$, $C_{i2}$, ..., $C_{im}$ using the recomputed PC of $C_i$. This process is repeated on each sub-cluster at each subsequent level $h$ where each subsequent clustering process operates on the its corresponding PC of $C_i$. At the leaf level $L$, the *indexed distance* is used as the indexed key on the corresponding PC of the internal cluster in level $L-1$. The leaf nodes correspond to the clusters of the actual data points.

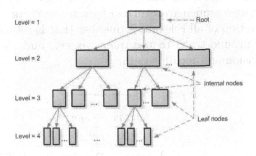

**Fig. 1.** Indexing structure

Here, each cluster (either an internal node or a leaf node) is represented by a triplet of $< O, R, D >$ in the proposed indexing structure, where $O$ is the centroid of the cluster, $R$ is the radius of the cluster, and $D$ is the *indexed distance* to be indexed in the indexing structure. For similarity measurement, given a keyframe $k$ in the cluster $j$, we first select out the *candidate clusters* which need to be accessed for further computation on similarity. For a leaf node cluster $j$ with its parent cluster $p$ (internal node), we first find out if a cluster with $O_j$ as centroid and $R_j + \epsilon$ as radius can be fully covered by cluster $p$. If so, this *candidate cluster* is just a sibling of cluster $j$ under cluster $p$. Otherwise, it may then have the possibility to have $\epsilon$-range data points outside of $p$. In the worst case, the *candidate clusters* may reside in different levels. This situation can be tracked down using a lookup table during the clustering step. With the increase of levels, the *projected distance* will be largely reduced and it will cause more clusters to have a radius much smaller than that of its parent; also, $\epsilon$ is a relatively small value. Therefore, most of the clusters are more likely to only have their sibling clusters as the *candidate clusters*, so that we only need to look up a few possible *candidate clusters* via the lookup table to get all the clusters needed for access.

## 5   Experiments

In this section we present our experimental study based on a real video data set. Our indexing structure can support different types of query such as range query and k-NN query, and experiments have shown the pruning power of our indexing structure.

### 5.1   Experiment Setup

The video database contains 140 video sequences obtained from the TRECVID 2005 news dataset with news video collected from different countries, with a total length of 170 hours. Each video sequence is then represented by a set of keyframes using 81-dimensional feature vectors via wavelet transformation, yielding a total number of 78034 keyframes.

For a typical query, precision and recall are defined as follows: precision is the percentage of video sequences returned by our search that are relevant, and recall is the the fraction of all relevant sequences that is returned by the search. Denote the set of ground-truth to the query as *rel*, and the result set of the search as *res*, precision and recall is defined as:

$$precision = \frac{rel \cap res}{res}$$

$$recall = \frac{rel \cap res}{rel}$$

The experiments are performed upon a Pentium-IV 3.2Ghz CPU PC with 1GB RAM. All our measurement are averaged over 100 queries. The default reduced dimensionality level is set to 10.

## 5.2   ε-Range Query

As described in Section 3.2, the user-defined value of the *keyframe similarity threshold* ε affects the performance of our algorithm. Experiments have been tested on different values of ε. As Figure 2 shows, when ε increases, if we perform a range query with radius ε, the number of false positives inside the ε range increase faster than the number of relevant keyframes, which results in the decrease in precision. On the other hand, we need to retrieve as much fraction of all relevant keyframes as possible. Therefore, even though a smaller ε can have a higher precision, it may result in lower recall. From Figure 2, ε is fixed to 0.4 to obtain a balance between precision and recall.

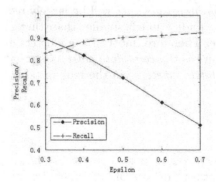

**Fig. 2.** Effect of ε on range query

## 5.3   Efficiency on Indexing

In the experiment, our input query is a video clip of a typical news topic selected from the video database. The similarity metrics is given by equation (1). By

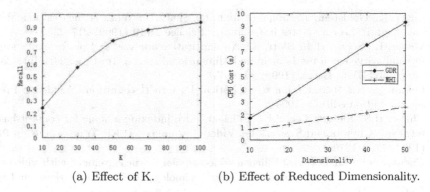

(a) Effect of K.                    (b) Effect of Reduced Dimensionality.

**Fig. 3.** Efficiency on Indexing

performing k-NN query with different K, different recall is as shown in Figure 3(a). When K is larger than 70, minor increase of recall is exhibited along with a rapid increase of false positives.

Meanwhile, considering reduced dimensionality level, for 50-NN query, a comparison study on CPU cost between General Dimensionality Reduction (GDR) method and our Multi-level Hierarchical Indexing algorithm (MHI) is tested. The GDR method only projects the features into reduced dimensionality level without clustering and are indexed using hybrid tree. Figure 3(b) shows the efficiency of our algorithm vis-a-vis the GDR method.

## 6   Conclusion and Future Work

In this paper we have presented an efficient clustering and modeling approach based on a Multi-level Hierarchical Divisive Dimensionality Reduction technique, which is able to discover clusters in subspaces while maintaining correlation information between the data points. We have also proposed a cluster-partitioning indexing scheme to index the clusters, which can efficiently prune out dissimilar frames and perform the $\epsilon$-range query for video similarity search. Experiments on large real video data also prove the effectiveness of our approach. For our future work, we plan to further incorporate some domain knowledge into the clusters to help understand the semantics feature of the frames. Meanwhile, our current work mainly considers the spatial relationship in the similarity measurement, and we will try to also take the temporal relationship into consideration in our subsequent work.

## References

1. Girgensohn, A., Boreczky, J.: Time-constrained keyframe selection technique. Multimedia Tools and Applications **11**(3) (2000) 347–358
2. Shen, H.T., Ooi, B.C., Zhou, X.: Towards effective indexing for very large video sequence database. In: SIGMOD '05: Proceedings of the 2005 ACM SIGMOD international conference on Management of data, New York, NY, USA, ACM Press (2005) 730–741

3. Beyer, K., Goldstein, J., Ramakrishnan, R., Shaft, U.: When is "nearest neighbor" meaningful? Lecture Notes in Computer Science **1540** (1999) 217–235

4. Weber, R., Schek, H.J., Blott, S.: A quantitative analysis and performance study for similarity-search methods in high-dimensional spaces. In: Proc. 24th Int. Conf. Very Large Data Bases. (1998) 194–205

5. Fukunaga, K.: Introduction to Statistical Pattern Recognition. Academic Press, second edition edition (1990)

6. Chang, H.S., Sull, S., Lee, S.U.: Efficient video indexing scheme for content-based retrieval. Circuits and Systems for Video Technology, IEEE Transactions on **9**(8) (1999) 1269–1279

7. Cheung, S.S., Zakhor, A.: Efficient video similarity measurement with video signature. Circuits and Systems for Video Technology, IEEE Transactions on **13**(1) (2003) 59–74

8. P. Indyk, G.I., Shivakumar, N.: Finding pirated video sequences on the internet. Tech. Rep., Stanford Infolab (1999)

9. Kashino, K., Kurozumi, T., Murase, H.: A quick search method for audio and video signals based on histogram pruning. Multimedia, IEEE Transactions on **5**(3) (2003) 348–357

10. Yuan, J., Tian, Q., Ranganath, S.: Fast and robust search method for short video clips from large video collection. In: Pattern Recognition, 2004. ICPR 2004. Proceedings of the 17th International Conference on. Volume 3. (2004) 866–869 Vol.3

11. Jolliffe, I.T.: Principle component analysis. In: Springer-Verlag. (1986)

12. Chakrabarti, K., Mehrotra, S.: Local dimensionality reduction: A new approach to indexing high dimensional spaces. In: VLDB '00: Proceedings of the 26th International Conference on Very Large Data Bases, San Francisco, CA, USA, Morgan Kaufmann Publishers Inc. (2000) 89–100

13. Jin, H., Ooi, B., Shen, H., Yu, C., Zhou, A.: An adaptive and efficient dimensionality reduction algorithm for high-dimensional indexing. In: Proc. of International Conference on Data Engineering (ICDE). (2003) 87–98

14. Aggarwal, C.C., Wolf, J.L., Yu, P.S., Procopiuc, C., Park, J.S.: Fast algorithms for projected clustering. In: SIGMOD '99: Proceedings of the 1999 ACM SIGMOD international conference on Management of data, New York, NY, USA, ACM Press (1999) 61–72

15. Kaufman, L., Rousseuw, P.: Finding Groups in Data - An Introduction to Cluster Analysis. Wiley Series in Probability and Mathematical Statistics (1990)

16. Hinneburg, A., Keim, D.A.: An optimal grid-clustering: Towards breaking the curse of dimensionality in high-dimensional clustering. In: The VLDB Journal. (1999) 506–517

# An Initial Study on Progressive Filtering Based on Dynamic Programming for Query-by-Singing/Humming

Jyh-Shing Roger Jang and Hong-Ru Lee

MIR Lab, CS Dept., Tsing Hua Univ., Taiwan, China
jang@cs.nthu.edu.tw, khair@wayne.cs.nthu.edu.tw

**Abstract.** This paper presents the concept of progressive filtering (PF) and its efficient design based on dynamic programming. The proposed PF is scalable for large music retrieval systems and is data-driven for performance optimization. Moreover, its concept and design are general in nature and can be applied to any multimedia retrieval systems. The application of the proposed PF to a 5-stage query-by-singing/humming (QBSH) system is reported, and the experimental results demonstrate the feasibility of the proposed approach.

**Keywords:** Progressive Filtering (PF), Dynamic Programming (DP), Query by Singing/Humming (QBSH), Melody Recognition, Music Retrieval, Dynamic Time Warping, Linear Scaling, Edit Distance.

## 1 Introduction

The idea of query by singing/humming was proposed [1] as an intuitive and natural method for music retrieval. Most people may think that the underlying technology is already mature and suitable for commercial application. However, most approaches proposed in the literature are not suited for real-world applications of music retrieval from a large music database. This is due to either excessive complexity in computation (which leads to a lengthened response time) or performance degradation (which leads to erroneous retrieval results). Finding an acceptable balance between computation and performance is a continuous goal for such retrieval systems. Therefore, this paper proposes the concept of progressive filtering (PF) with an efficient design method that can strike the right balance within a given response time constraint of the retrieval system. The proposed approach is applied to a query-by-singing/humming (QBSH) system with a database of 13,320 songs. The experimental results demonstrate that the proposed method can be used to construct an effective PF mechanism for music retrieval based on singing/humming input.

## 2 Progressive Filtering (PF) and Its Design Method

The basic idea of PF for a QBSH system is quite simple. We apply multiple stages of comparisons between a query and the songs in the database, using an increasingly more complicated comparison mechanism to the decreasing candidate pool such that the correct song remains in the final candidate pool with a maximum probability.

Y. Zhuang et al. (Eds.): PCM 2006, LNCS 4261, pp. 971–978, 2006.

Intuitively, the initial few stages are quick and dirty such that the most unlikely songs in the database are eliminated. On the other hand, the last few stages are much more discriminating (and time-consuming) such that the most likely songs are identified. Similar ideas of PF have also been proposed by Jang and Lee [4] and Adams et al. [5]. The initial application of two-stage PF to music retrieval for a commercial system is described in Jang et al. [6].

The multi-stage representation of PF is shown in Figure 1, where there are $m$ stages for data filtering, corresponding to $m$ different retrieval methods with varying complexity. For stage $i$, the input is the query and the candidate pool of $n_{i-1}$ songs from the previous stage; the only changeable parameter is the survival rate $s_i$, which is always between 0 and 1. The output is a reduced candidate pool of size $n_i = n_{i-1}s_i$ for the succeeding stage $i+1$. In other words, each stage performs a comparison and filtering process that reduces the size of the candidate pool by the factor of the survival rate $s_i$. We assume that the computation time $t_i$ of stage $i$ is proportional to the size of the input candidate pool, leading to the expression $t_i = n_{i-1}k_i$, where $k_i$ is a time constant that represents the one-to-one computation time (the time required to do the comparison between a query and a song in the candidate pool) of stage $i$. As a result, we have the following recurrent formula:

$$n_i = n_{i-1}s_i = n_0s_1s_2\cdots s_i,$$
$$t_i = n_{i-1}k_i = n_0s_1s_2\cdots s_{i-1}k_i,$$

where $n_0 = n$ is the original database size, and $n_m$ is the number of songs in the final output list.

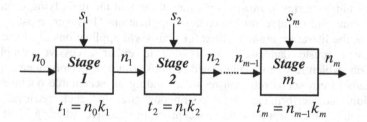

**Fig. 1.** Multi-stage representation of PF

In Figure 1, each stage is characterized by its capability to select the most likely candidates for the next stage. For a given stage, this capability can be represented by its recognition rate, which is defined as the probability that the target (ground-truth) song of a given query is retained in the output candidate pool of this stage. Intuitively, the recognition rate is a function of the survival rate, which can be represented by a function $r_i(s)$, satisfying the following two end-point conditions $r_i(0)=0$ and $r_i(1)=1$ for $i = 1\cdots m$. We shall refer to this curve as the RS (recognition rate vs. survival rate) curve for a given stage. Figure 2 demonstrates some typical RS curves for various comparison methods, which will be detailed in section 3.

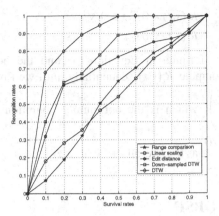

**Fig. 2.** Typical RS curves of various comparison methods

Once we have the effectiveness measure (the RS curve $r_i(s_i)$) and the efficiency measure ($k_i$, the time constant) for each stage, we can determine the optimum values of $s_i$ ($i = 1 \sim m$) such that the maximum recognition rate of the overall system can be achieved (on average) under a given limited computation time. More specifically, we have two constraints for the overall system. The first constraint states that the maximum allowable overall computation time should be less than or equal to a constant $T_{\max}$ (for instance, 5 seconds). The second constraint states that the number of the final output songs should be equal to a small integer, which is set to 10 throughout this paper. These two constraints can be expressed by the following equations:

$$\begin{cases} nk_1 + ns_1k_2 + ns_1s_2k_3 + \cdots + ns_1s_2 \cdots s_{m-1}k_m \le T_{\max} \\ \quad ns_1s_2s_3 \cdots s_m \le 10 \end{cases} \tag{1}$$

The objective function is the overall recognition rate:

$$R(s_1s_2 \cdots s_m) = r_1(s_1)r_2(s_2) \cdots r_m(s_m) \tag{2}$$

We can develop a dynamic-programming-based method to solve such an optimization problem. In particular, we define the optimum-value function $R_i(s,t)$ as the optimum recognition rate at stage $i$ with a cumulated survival rate $s$ and a cumulated computation time less than or equal to $t$. This function can be expressed in a recurrent formula as :

$$R_i(s,t) = \max_{s_i}\left\{ r_i(s_i)R_{i-1}\left(\frac{s}{s_i}, t - t_i\right) \right\} = \max_{s_i}\left\{ r_i(s_i)R_{i-1}\left(\frac{s}{s_i}, t - n\hat{s}_1\hat{s}_2 \cdots \hat{s}_{i-1}k_i\right) \right\} \tag{3}$$

where $\hat{s}_1, \hat{s}_2, \cdots \hat{s}_{i-1}$ are the optimum values of the survival rates at previous stages. The corresponding boundary conditions can be expressed as

$$R_i(s,t) = 0 \text{ if } s \leq 0, \forall i, \forall t$$
$$R_i(s,t) = 0 \text{ if } t \leq 0, \forall i, \forall s \tag{4}$$

By using the recurrent formula in Equation (3) and the boundary conditions in Equation (4), we can compute $R_i(s,t)$ sequentially until we find the overall objective function $R_m\left(\dfrac{10}{n}, T_{\max}\right)$, which is the optimum recognition rate with $T_{\max}$ as the computation time and $\dfrac{10}{n}$ as the overall survival rate.

# 3   Five Stages for QBSH

This section describes the comparison methods used for PF in a 5-stage QBSH system. It should be noted that each comparison method is itself a legitimate method for query by singing/humming, with varying degrees of computation time and discriminating power.

## 3.1   Range Comparison

Range comparison is an efficient method that can eliminate the unlikely songs in a quick and dirty manner. That is, a song is eliminated if the range of the query input (in terms of semitones) is different from that of the song by a given threshold $\theta$. Different values of the threshold $\theta$ lead to different recognition rates. Using the training data set, we can obtain the RS curve of this stage, as shown in Figure 2. It is evident that range comparison is not a method with good discriminating power. However, it is extremely fast since the range of the candidate songs can be computed in advance. The time constant $k_i$ is found to be 0.00008 second.

## 3.2   Linear Scaling

Linear scaling is the most straightforward method, in which the query pitch vector is linearly scaled several times and compared to the songs in the database. In practice, the query pitch vector is linearly scaled 9 times, ranging from 0.5 to 2 times the original length. The distance measure used in linear scaling is the Euclidean distance, with length normalization. To achieve key transposition, we can simply shift both pitch vectors to zero mean before invoking distance computation. The RS curve of this stage is shown in Figure 2. The time constant is 0.0001 second.

## 3.3   Edit Distance

Common operators used in edit distance for music retrieval [3] includes insertion, deletion, replacement, consolidation, and fragmentation. For two strings $A = a_1 a_2 ... a_m$ and $B = b_1 b_2 ... b_n$, the edit distance $d_{m,n}$ between them can be computed recursively via the following recurrent formula:

$$d_{i,j} = \min \begin{cases} d_{i-1,j} + w(a, \Phi) \text{ --------------} (deletion) \\ d_{i,j-1} + w(\Phi, b_j) \text{ ------------} (insertion) \\ d_{i-1,j-1} + w(a_i, b_j) \text{ ------------} (replacement) \\ \{d_{i-k,j-1} + w(a_{i-k+1},....,a_i, b_j), 2 \le k \le i\} \text{ ---} (consolidation) \\ \{d_{i-1,j-k} + w(a_i, b_{j-k+1},....,b_j), 2 \le k \le j\} \text{ ---} (fragmentation) \end{cases} , \tag{5}$$

where $w()$ is a function that represents the cost associated with various operators. In practice, we need to do note segmentation first and divide the music notes into pitch and duration vectors, which are processed separately using the edit distance. Zero-mean normalization is invoked for pitch vectors before using edit distance. Similarly, duration normalization [7] is also invoked before using edit distance. The final distance is an average of the pitch and duration distances. The RS curve of the edit distance is shown in Figure 2. It is obvious that edit distance has a much better discriminating power than range comparison and linear scaling. This is achieved at the cost of higher computation time, with a time constant of 0.0007 second.

### 3.4 DTW with Down-Sampled Inputs

Dynamic time warping (DTW) [2] is one of the most effective approaches to melody recognition. Before invoking DTW we need to consider key transposition. This is taken care of by a heuristic approach that involves 5-time pitch translation around the mean [4].

In this stage, in order to reduce the computation time, we down-sample the input vectors by a factor of 2 before invoking DTW. The RS curve of DTW with a down-sampled input is shown in Figure 2. The corresponding time constant is 0.0018 second.

Exact indexing of DTW has been proposed in the literature [10]. Employing the indexing method allows us to reduce the computation in this stage. (By doing so, the time constant becomes a function of the survival rate.) For the sake of simplicity we did not try any of the speedup mechanisms for DTW in this paper.

### 3.5 DTW

This stage invokes the same DTW formula of the previous stage, except that the input vectors are not down-sampled. The RS curve of DTW with a down-sampled input is shown in Figure 2. It is evident that DTW achieves the best recognition rate among all. However, it also has a higher time constant that equals to 0.0061 second.

## 4 Experimental Results

In this section, we start with the introduction of the singing corpus used in this study, and follow up with several experiments that serve to demonstrate the feasibility of the proposed approach.

### 4.1 Corpus for the Experiments

To evaluate the proposed approach, we use a singing corpus of 1230 clips from 40 subjects (25 males and 15 females), covering 623 songs out of a database of 13,320 songs. Each of the clips has 8-second duration, with 8KHz sampling rate and 8-bits resolution. Each sound clip is converted into a pitch curve via an auto-correlation-based pitch tracking method. The frame size is 500 without overlap. Rests or silences, represented by the value 0, are either removed or replaced by the previous nonzero elements, depending on the comparison method.

Half of the singing corpus (615 clips) is used as the training data for obtaining the RS curve $r_i(s)$ and the one-to-one computation time $k_i$ for stage $i$. The other half of the corpus is used as the test data for verifying the proposed approach. For the sake of simplicity, all the computation times referred to in this paper do not contain the computation of pitch tracking.

Each of the singing clips starts from the beginning of the target song. Therefore, our music retrieval task corresponds to the "anchored beginning, unanchored end" case, and we only keep the first 16 seconds of each song in the database.

## 4.2 Ordering of Each Stage

The DP-based design method for PF is very efficient so we can try all kinds of ordering exhaustively. Table 1 lists the results of the best ordering of the comparison methods under various values of $T_{max}$. Except for $T_{max} = 2$ where stages 4 and 5 are not used (due to insufficient allowable time), all the other larger values of $T_{max}$ correspond to the best ordering of range comparison as stage 1, linear scaling as stage 2, edit distance as stage 3, DTW with down-sampled input as stage 4, and DTW as stage 5. This is exactly as expected: quick but ineffective methods are used first; effective but slow methods are used last.

**Table 1.** Best ordering of comparison methods under various values of $T_{max}$

| $T_{max}$ | Best Ordering | | | | | Predicted RR | Test RR |
|---|---|---|---|---|---|---|---|
| | 1 | 2 | 3 | 4 | 5 | | |
| 2 | Range comparison | Linear scaling | Edit distance | (Not used) | (Not used) | 32.29% | 40.21% |
| 5 | Range comparison | Linear scaling | Edit distance | Down sampled | DTW | 58.50% | 57.58% |
| 10 | Range comparison | Linear scaling | Edit distance | Down sampled | DTW | 71.43% | 67.56% |
| 15 | Range comparison | Linear scaling | Edit distance | Down sampled | DTW | 81.02% | 77.43% |

## 4.3 Recognition Rates vs. Computation Time

One of the major advantages of PF is its scalability. That is, given an overall time constraint, the overall recognition rate can always achieve its highest possible value (statistically) via the adjustment of the survival rate at each stage. Therefore it will be interesting to see how the recognition rates degrade with decreasing allowable computation time. In this experiment, we assume the ordering of stages are: range comparison (stage 1), linear scaling (stage 2), edit distance (stage 3), DTW with down-sampled input (stage 4), and DTW (stage 5). Figure 3 demonstrates the curves (including predicted and actual) of the recognition rates vs. computation time. The predicted recognition rates are obtained from the training data set, while the test recognition rates are obtained from the test data set. Deviations between these two curves mostly come from the statistical differences between the training and test data sets.

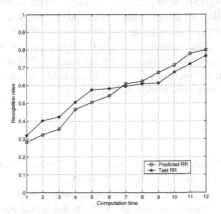

**Fig. 3.** Recognition rates vs. computation time

### 4.4 Survival Rates Versus Computation Time

Obviously, a shorter overall time constraint will ensure low survival rates at the first few stages of a PF system. On the other hand, a longer overall time constraint will allow a PF system to have high survival rates. Therefore we can plot the survival rates vs. computation time, as shown in Figure 4.

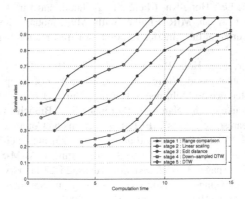

**Fig. 4.** Survival rates vs. computation time

From Figure 4 it can be seen that if the computation time is longer than or equal to 9 seconds, some stage will have a survival rate of 100%, indicating that the stage is not used at all.

## 5  Conclusions and Future Work

This paper introduced the concept of PF (Progressive Filtering) and proposed an efficient design method based on dynamic programming. The proposed method was applied to a 5-stage QBSH system, and several experiments were performed to demonstrate the feasibility of the proposed method. Related research on PF is still on-going, and there are several directions for immediate future work. First of all, this paper assumes that the time constant for each stage is a constant. In reality, we can apply some exact indexing techniques for linear scaling [8][9] or DTW [10]. This will make the time constant a function of the survival rate for each stage. Analysis based on this modification is currently under investigation.

## References

[1]  Ghias, A. J. and Logan, D. Chamberlain, B. C. Smith, "Query by humming-musical information retrieval in an audio database", ACM Multimedia '95, San Francisco, 1995.

[2]  Sakoe, H. and Chiba S., "Dynamic Programming Optimization for Spoken Word Recognition", IEEE Trans. on Acoustics, Speech and Signal Processing, Vol. 26, pp 623-625, 1980.

[3]  Hu, N. and Dannerberg, R. B., "A Comparison of Melodic Database Retrieval Techniques Using Sung Queries," in Proceedings of the second ACM/IEEE-CS joint conference on Digital libraries, pp. 301-307, New York: ACM Press 2002.

[4]  Jang, J.-S. Roger and Lee, Hong-Ru, "Hierarchical Filtering Method for Content-based Music Retrieval via Acoustic Input", The 9th ACM Multimedia Conference, PP. 401-410, Ottawa, Ontario, Canada, September 2001.

[5]  Adams, Norman, Marquez, Daniela and Wakefield, Gregory, "Iterative Deepening for Melody Alignment and Retrieval", in Proceedings of International Symposium on Music Information Retrieval (ISMIR), PP. 199-206, 2005.

[6]  Jang, J.-S. Roger, Lee, Hong-Ru, Chen, Jiang-Chuen, and Lin, Cheng-Yuan, "Research and Development of an MIR Engine with Multi-modal Interface for Real-world Applications", Journal of the American Society for Information Science and Technology, 2004.

[7]  Jang, J.-S. Roger, Lee, Hong-Ru, and Yeh, Chia-Hui, "Query by Tapping: A New Paradigm for Content-based Music Retrieval from Acoustic Input", The Second IEEE Pacific-Rim Conference on Multimedia, Beijing, China, October 2001.

[8]  Fukunaga, Keinosuke and M. Narendra, Patrenahalli "A Branch and Bound Algorithm for Computing K-Nearest Neighbors", IEEE Transactions on Computers, July 1975.

[9]  Yianilos, Peter N. "Data structures and algorithms for nearest neighbor search in general metric spaces," in Proceedings of the Fourth Annual ACM-SIAM Symposium on Discrete Algorithms, pages 311-321, Austin, Texas, 25-27 January 1993

[10]  Keogh, E., Exact indexing of dynamic time warping. in 28th International Conference on Very Large Data Bases. Hong Kong, pp 406-417, 2002.

# Measuring Multi-modality Similarities Via Subspace Learning for Cross-Media Retrieval

Hong Zhang and Jianguang Weng

The Institute of Artificial Intelligence, Zhejiang University,
HangZhou, 310027, P.R. China
zhanghong_zju@yahoo.com.cn, wengjg@cs.zju.edu.cn

**Abstract.** Cross-media retrieval is an interesting research problem, which seeks to breakthrough the limitation of modality so that users can query multimedia objects by examples of different modalities. In order to cross-media retrieve, the problem of similarity measure between media objects with heterogeneous low-level features needs to be solved. This paper proposes a novel approach to learn both intra- and inter-media correlations among multi-modality feature spaces, and construct MLE semantic subspace containing multimedia objects of different modalities. Meanwhile, relevance feedback strategies are developed to enhance the efficiency of cross-media retrieval from both short- and long-term perspectives. Experiments show that the result of our approach is encouraging and the performance is effective.

**Keywords:** Cross-media Retrieval, Heterogeneous, Multi-modality Correlation.

## 1 Introduction

Content-based multimedia retrieval is a challenging issue, which aims to provide an effective and efficient tool for searching media objects. Almost all of the existing multimedia retrieval techniques are focused on the retrieval research of single modality, such as image retrieval [1,2], audio retrieval [3], video retrieval [4], motion retrieval [5]. For example, in a traditional query-by-example system, users submit an image example and the system returns the retrieved images in database that are most similar to the submitted example. But few researches have done successfully on cross-media retrieval which breakthroughs the restriction of modality [6,7]. That is, can we retrieve audio objects of dog's bark by an image example of dog's portrait, or vice versa? In this paper, we use modality to represent different type of media sources such as image and audio, and define cross-media retrieval as a query mode in which the modality of query examples and that of query results are different.

The fundamental challenge of cross-media retrieval lies in the similarity mea sure between heterogeneous low-level feature spaces. For many media objects, there are different types of features to represent their content. Traditionally, images are represented with visual perceptual features, such as color, texture, and shape; audios are represented with auditory features. Thus, it's uneasy to judge the simil-arity between an image and an audio by estimating a measurement between a

Y. Zhuang et al. (Eds.): PCM 2006, LNCS 4261, pp. 979–988, 2006.

200-dimensional image feature vector and a 500-dimensional audio feature vector. In this paper, we propose a novel approach to build map from heterogeneous multi-modality feature spaces into a semantic subspace, where media objects of different modalities are represented in isomorphic structures and cross-media similarity can be accurately estimated.

The rest of this paper is organized as follows. Section 2 gives the representation of multi-modality data with multimedia bags. Section 3 models multi-modality content correlations and provides cross-media similarity estimation algorithm. We build the mapping to a semantic subspace and describe cross-media retrieval in section 4. Section 5 presents two relevance feedback strategies to extract semantic information from user interactions to improve cross-media retrieval. The experimental results are shown in section 6. Conclusions and future work are given in the final section.

## 2  Multi-modality Representation: Multimedia Bag

In our previous work [8], a supervised approach has been adopted to learn semantic correlations between labeled image database and labeled audio database. Although experimentally effective, this approach requires extensively training by labeling a large number of sample images and audios manually to achieve high accuracy. Moreover, it learns the correlation only between a pair of different modalities, and is not capable of understanding multi-modality correlations. Thus, we investigate an alternative approach to extend cross-media retrieval to a more generalized multi-modality environment with less manual effort in collecting labeled sample data.

Multiple Instance Learning (MIL) is a class of learning algorithms for handling problems with only partial label information expressed as the labels on bags of instances. Instead of receiving labeled instances as a conventional supervised method does, a MIL method receives a set of labeled bags, where each bag contains a number of unlabeled instances. Content-based image retrieval and classification has been a popular application of MIL [9,10]. Inspired by MIL, we represent multi-modality media objects with multimedia bags which are labeled with semantic concepts while their component multimedia instances are unlabeled. For example, a webpage of "car" consists of text information describing distinctive driving functions, images of overall car appearance and audios of engines and hoot. The multimedia bag labeled "car", including text instances, image instances and audio instances, is formed despite noisy data when collecting multimedia data from this webpage. With this strategy, the work of manual labeling is greatly reduced and initial category information is maintained. Multi-modality data is represented in an extendable and informative structure.

## 3  Learning Multiple Content Correlations

Since a multimedia bag contains multimedia instances of different modalities, cross-media retrieval can be feasible if the similarity between two arbitrary multimedia instances is accurately calculated. And the similarity between two multimedia bags can be estimated according to the similarity between component instances. In this section, by exploring multiple content correlations among multimedia instances, we learn the underlying semantics and accurately estimate cross-media similarity.

## 3.1 Multi-modality Correlation Matrix

Intrinsically, two kinds of content correlations need to be estimated: intra-media and inter-media correlations. Intra-media correlation is the similarity between multimedia instances of the same modality, while inter-media is that between multimedia instances of different modalities. By exploring each kind of pair-wise similarity, we work out a multi-modality correlation matrix to model both intra- and inter-media correlations.

Suppose there are $t$ different feature spaces $S_1, S_2, ..., S_t$. Let $R_m \subset S_m \times S_m$ denotes intra-media correlation, and $R_{mn} \subset S_m \times S_n (m \neq n)$ denotes inter-media correlation. $R_m$ can be represented as an adjacency matrix $L_{mm}$, with each cell $l_{xy}$ is the pair-wise distance from the $x_{th}$ to the $y_{th}$ multimedia instance in feature space $S_m$. Similarly, $R_{mn}$ can be measured with an adjacency matrix $L_{mn}(m \neq n)$, where the value of cell $l_{xy}$ is cross-media distance from the $x_{th}$ multimedia instance in $S_m$ to the $y_{th}$ multimedia instance in $S_n$. Specifically, given text, image and audio instances as training data, a multi-modality correlation matrix is constructed as follows:

$$L_{mmc} = \begin{vmatrix} L_{tt} & L_{ti} & L_{ta} \\ L_{it} & L_{ii} & L_{ia} \\ L_{at} & L_{ai} & L_{aa} \end{vmatrix} \tag{1}$$

where sub-matrices $L_{tt}, L_{ii}, L_{aa}$ are intra-media correlations: single modality similarity within text, image and audio instances respectively, and sub-matrices $L_{ti}, L_{ta}, L_{ia}$ represent text-to-image, text-to-audio and image-to-audio similarity respectively. Apparently, $L_{mmc}$ is a symmetrical matrix. If multimedia instances of the fourth modality are provided, such as video, matrix $L_{mmc}$ can be extended to include another four kinds of sub-matrices: video-to-video, video-to-text, video-to-image and video-to-audio.

## 3.2 Inter-media Correlation Estimation

Intra-media correlation can be calculated with single modality retrieval methods [1,2,3] which have been primary focus on research so far. In this subsection, we discuss inter-media correlation and solve the problem of heterogeneity.

We employ a distinct feature learning method of CCA [11] to analyze two heterogeneous feature spaces, and preserves inter-media correlation in an isomorphic subspace. Formally, consider image instances $I_x = (x_1, ..., x_n)$ and audio instances $I_y = (y_1, ..., y_n)$ where $x_i = (x_{i1}, ..., x_{ip})$, $y_i = (y_{i1}, ..., y_{iq})$, project $I_x$ onto a direction $W_x$, and $I_y$ onto a direction $W_y$:

$$I_x \xrightarrow{W_x} I_x' = <x_1', ..., x_n'>, \; x_i' = (x_{i1}', ..., x_{im}'); I_y \xrightarrow{W_y} I_y' = <y_1', ..., y_n'>, \; y_i' = (y_{i1}', ..., y_{im}') \tag{2}$$

Then the problem of correlation preserving boils down to finding optimal $W_x$ and $W_y$, which makes the correlation between $I_x'$ and $I_y'$ is maximally in accordance with that between $I_x$ and $I_y$. In other words the function to be maximized is:

$$\rho = \max_{W_x, W_y} corr(I_x W_x, I_y W_y) = \max_{W_x, W_y} \frac{(I_x W_x, I_y W_y)}{\|I_x W_x\|\|I_y W_y\|} = \max_{W_x, W_y} \frac{W_x' C_{xy} W_y}{\sqrt{W_x' C_{xx} W_x W_y' C_{yy} W_y}} \qquad (3)$$

where $C$ is covariance matrix. Since the solution of equation (3) is not affected by re-scaling $W_x$ or $W_y$ either together or independently, the optimization of $\rho$ is equivalent to maximizing the numerator subject to $W_x' C_{xx} W_x = 1$ and $W_y' C_{yy} W_y = 1$. Then with Lagrange multiplier method we can get $C_{xy} C_{yy}^{-1} C_{yx} W_x = \lambda^2 C_{xx} W_x$, which is a generalized Eigenproblem of the form $Ax = \lambda Bx$. And the sequence of $W_x$'s and $W_y$'s can be obtained by solving the generalized eigenvectors.

---

1. Select a semantic category, and extract low-level feature matrices for all training data.
2. Find optimal $W_x$ and $W_y$ for a pair of feature matrices, such as image feature matrix and audio feature matrix; map original features into m-dimensional subspace $S^m$ with formula (2).
3. Choose another pair of matrices, such as text and image feature matrices; repeat step 2 until all feature vectors are mapped into subspace $S^m$.
4. For every other semantic category, repeat step 2 to 3.
5. Calculate non-diagonal sub-matrices $L_{mn}(m \neq n)$ (see section 3.1) with the pair-wise distances between multi-modality data in $S^m$.

**Algorithm 1.** Inter-media correlation estimation

As multimedia bags are labeled with semantic concepts, we consider two multimedia instances belong to the same semantic category if their bag labels are the same, and then sort all multimedia instances into different semantic categories despite noisy data. Algorithm 1 shows how we calculate inter-media correlation.

# 4   Cross-Media Retrieval in Semantic Subspace

Multi-modality correlation matrix $L_{mmc}$ records pair-wise distances between multimedia instances from two arbitrary feature spaces. We need to find the mapping to a semantic subspace which is consistent with all kinds of multi-modality similarities. Research efforts show that manifold structure is more powerful than Euclidean structure for data representation [12]. In this section, we assume that multimedia instances of different modalities lie on a manifold, and learn this manifold structure to build a semantic subspace.

## 4.1 Constructing MLESS

Since multi-modality correlation matrix $L_{mmc}$ has been calculated in section 3.2, we use Laplacian Eignmaps [13] to find the mapping to MLESS (Multi-modality Laplacian Eignmaps Semantic Subspace). First a weight matrix $W$ with a locality preserving property is constructed as follows:

$$W_{ij} = \begin{cases} \exp(-L_{ij}/t), & \text{if } L_{ij} < \varepsilon \\ 0 & \text{otherwise} \end{cases} \qquad (4)$$

where $t$ and $\varepsilon$ are suitable constants, and $L_{ij}$ is the cell value from matrix $L_{mmc}$.

Suppose $y = \{y_1, y_2, ..., y_n\}$ is a one-dimensional map of multimedia instance $\{x_1, x_2, ..., x_n\}$ in the MLESS. A reasonable criterion for choosing a "good" map is to furthest ensure that if $x_i$ and $x_j$ are "close" then $y_i$ and $y_j$ are close as well. Then semantic subspace mapping can be formulated as an eigenvector problem:

$$Ly = \lambda Dy, (D_{ii} = \sum_j W_{ji}, L = D - W) \qquad (5)$$

where $D$ is a diagonal matrix, whose entry is column sum of matrix $W$. $L$ is called Laplacian matrix. By solving the first $k$ nonzero eigenvalues $\lambda_1 \le \lambda_2 \le ... \le \lambda_k$ and corresponding eigenvectors, we can find a k-dimensional map to MLESS. Therefore, we find a vector representation in semantic subspace for each multimedia instance.

## 4.2 Locating Multimedia Bags into MLESS

Once MLESS is constructed, all multimedia instances in training dataset are indexed by their coordinates in MLESS. A multimedia bag may consist of texts, images and audios, while another multimedia bag consists of only texts and images. Besides, component multimedia instances of a multimedia bag do not cluster together in MLESS. Thus it's not reasonable to locate multimedia bags into MLESS with weighted mean of their component instances. However, we can estimate the similarity between multimedia bags according to the similarity between their component multimedia instances. The distance between multimedia instances of the same modality but from different bags are as follows:

$$dis(Inst_1, Inst_2) = \|Cor_1 - Cor_2\|, if (Inst_1 \& Inst_2 \notin \Phi)$$
$$(Inst_1 \in Bag1, Inst_2 \in Bag2) \qquad (6)$$

Where $Inst_1, Inst_2$ are multimedia instances from two multimedia bags $Bag1 = \{text1, image1, audio1\}$ and $Bag2 = \{text2, image2\}$ respectively, $Cor_1, Cor_2$ are MLESS coordinates of $Inst_1, Inst_2$. Both $Bag1$ and $Bag2$ contain images, $dis(image_1, image_2)$ is then the distance between two images in MLESS. There is no audio instance in $Bag2$, so $dis(audio_1, audio_2)$ is not counted. $Mindis$ of two bags is defined as the minimal value of $dis(Inst_1, Inst_2)$, and $Maxdis$ is the maximum value.

Here are three heuristic rules for us to judge the similarity between two multimedia bags:

(1) If two multimedia bags have similar instances, the bags are usually similar too.

(2) If $Inst_1$ is more similar to $Inst_2$ than $Inst_3$ is, we often consider $Bag1$ is more similar to $Bag2$ than $Bag3$ is.

(3) $image_1$ is similar to $image_2$, but all other $Inst_1$ from $Bag1$ are quite dissimilar to $Inst_2$ from $Bag2$. Then $image_1$ or $image_2$ may be noisy data, also $Bag1$ and $Bag2$ are actually not as similar as $image_1$ and $image_2$ are.

Based on above heuristic rules, we define a balance parameter $F(i, j)$ between $Bag(i)$ and $Bag(j)$ as:

$$F(i, j) = \ln(\frac{\sum dis(Inst_i, Inst_j) - Mindis(i, j) - Maxdis(i, j)}{k - 2} - Mindis(i, j) + 1) \qquad (7)$$

Where $Inst_i \in Bag(i), Inst_j \in Bag(j)$ and $k$ is the number of $dis(Inst_i, Inst_j)$. The distance between $Bag(i)$ and $Bag(j)$ is given as:

$$Bagdis(i, j) = \alpha \times Mindis(i, j) + F(i, j) \qquad (8)$$

where $\alpha$ is the smoothing parameter.

### 4.3   Cross-Media Retrieval in MLESS

Users can query both multimedia bags and multimedia instances in MLESS with a query example. If the query example is in database, the question is very simple. The K-nearest text neighbors, K-nearest image neighbors and K-nearest audio neighbors in MLESS of the query example are returned as retrieval results. If the query example belongs to a multimedia bag in database, namely the host bag, we find K multimedia bags that are closest to this host bag with $Bagdis(i, j)$ and present them to user.

On the other hand, if the query example is outside database, we call it a new media object $NObj$. We must introduce $NObj$ into MLESS first. Since MLESS is a semantic subspace and there exists a well-known gap between low-level features and high-level semantics, it is not easy to accurately map $NObj$ into MLESS only based on content features. Suppose $NObj$ is a new image outside database, we develop the following strategies with the help of relevance feedback to find a good map.

Step 1: Find K-nearest images in database for this $NObj$ with Euclidean distance in low-level feature space, and return them to users.

Step 2: Let users mark positive images $\Omega = \{p_1, p_2, ..., p_s\}$, whose MLESS coordinates are represented as $p_s = (p_{s1}, ..., p_{sk})$. Then $NObj$ is located in MLESS at the coordinates $(n_1, ..., n_j, ..., n_k)$ where $n_j = (\sum_{i=1}^{s} p_{ij}) / s$.

In this way, *NObj* is mapped into MLESS according to the coordinates of positive examples $\Omega$, which describe similar semantics and cluster together in MLESS. Once *NObj* is accurately located in MLESS, cross-media retrieval with *NObj* is the same question we have thoroughly discussed above.

## 5   System Refinement with Relevance Feedback

Because of the noisy data, not all instances in a multimedia bag represent exactly the same semantic concept as the bag label does. Therefore, MLESS is not always consistent with human perception. Relevance feedback is a powerful method to learn better representation of multimedia content as well as the query concept. We present both short- and long-term learning strategies to enhance cross-media retrieval performance in a relevance feedback driven query-by-example system.

   **-Short-term learning:** *depend on query examples.* Initial query examples may not well represent the exact query concept. However, we can adjust query vector and refine query results. The following two situations need to be concerned differently:

- If the modality of query example $R$ is the same as that of positive examples $P$, the query vector of $R$ is moved towards the center of $P$; or else, if $P$ and $R$ are of different modalities, we employ query expansion method by generating single modality retrieval with query example of $P$.
- On the other hand, negative examples $N$ are treated differently. For each $n_i \in N$, find its k-nearest neighbors $C_i$ of the same modality, and move both $n_i$ and $C_i$ to the opposite direction of $R$.

   **-Long-term learning:** *independent with query examples.* Long-term learning strategy is provided to accumulate and incorporate the knowledge from past user interactions into multi-modality correlation matrix $L_{mmc}$, so that system's future retrieval performance can be enhanced. Specifically, we shorten the distances between positive examples and query examples by multiplying a suitable constant factor smaller than 1: $L_{xy} = \alpha L_{xy}, (x, y \in P \cup R, \alpha < 1)$, and lengthen the distance between positive examples and negative examples by multiplying a suitable constant factor greater than 1: $L_{xy} = \beta L_{xy}, (x \in P \cup R, y \in N, \beta > 1)$. When matrix $L_{mmc}$ is updated to a certain extent, MLESS is reconstructed with the input of updated $L_{mmc}$.

## 6   Experiment and Comparisons

We performed several experiments to evaluate the effectiveness of our proposed methods over a text-image-audio dataset, which consists of 6 semantic categories including dog, car, bird, war, tiger and plane. Multimedia datasets are collected from the Internet and Corel image galleries. In each semantic category there are 100 texts, 100 images and 100 audios. There are 423 multimedia bags in all. Among them 255 multimedia bags each consists of text, image and audio. Each of other 100 multimedia bags covers two of the three modalities. The remainder 68 bags are made up of image instances. Another unlabeled 60 images and 60 audios are used as new media objects outside database. Since audio is a kind of time series data, the dimensionalities of combined auditory feature vectors are inconsistent. We employ Fuzzy Clustering algorithm [14] on extracted auditory features to get cluster centroids as audio indexes.

## 6.1 Image-Audio Cross-Retrieval in MLESS

Cross-media retrieval between images and audios is performed to evaluate inter-media correlation learning results. To provide a systematic evaluation, we generate 5 random image queries and 5 random audio queries for each category, and conduct 3 rounds of relevance feedback for each query to perform short-term learning.

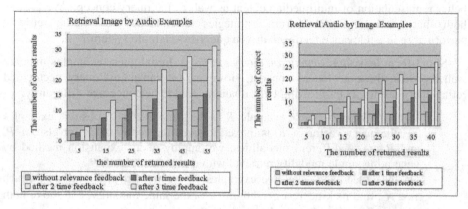

**Fig. 1.** Retrieval image by audio in MLESS    **Fig. 2.** Retrieval audio by image in MLESS

Figure 1 shows retrieval results of retrieving images by examples of audios in MLESS. Initial cross-media retrieval results without relevance feedback are not very satisfactory not only because of the existence of well-known semantic gap but also the noisy data in multimedia bags of about 9%. However, at the third round of relevance feedback the number of correct results is 22.4 while originally it is 9.2 when the number of returned results is 35. Figure 2 shows experiment results of retrieving audios by image examples. The number of correct results is 27.5 when the number of returned results is 40 at the third round of relevance feedback. This observation confirms that MLESS preserves inter-media correlations and becomes more and more consistent with human perceptions as user's relevance feedback is incorporated.

## 6.2 Multi-modality Retrieval in MLESS

The construction of MLESS is based on the analysis of multimedia content from heterogeneous feature spaces. Differently, traditional feature analysis methods only cope with low-level media content of single modality. We performed several experiments to compare multi-modality retrieval in MLESS with that in PCA subspace obtained by linear dimensionality reduction method of PCA. To construct PCA subspace, content-based feature vectors of texts, images and audios are respectively analyzed with PCA and mapped to the same dimensional PCA subspace.

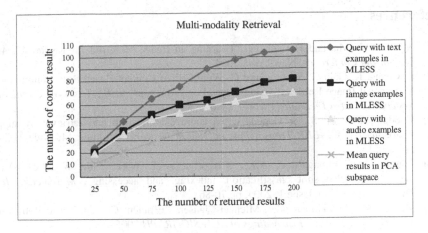

**Fig. 3.** Multi-modality Retrieval with different query examples

Figure 3 shows the comparison of multi-modality retrieval results. In our experiments, for each category we generate 5 random text queries, 5 random image queries and 5 random audio queries. For each query, the system returns 80 texts, 80 images and 80 audios that are most similar to the query example. In figure 3, "the number of correct results" means the total correct number among all returned 240 results in three modalities. The blue line in figure 3 indicates mean retrieval results in PCA subspace. It can be seen that our approach achieves a significant improvement over PCA-based methods. This confirms our approach from two aspects: (1) Multiple content correlation learning has discovered both intra- and inter-media correlations, so that our initial retrieval results are better than that of PCA-based methods. (2) Semantic subspace mapping successfully discover an embedded manifold structure to represent both intra- and inter-media correlations between multi-modality data.

# 7   Conclusions and Future Work

In this paper, we propose a discriminative and efficient approach to retrieve multi-modality dataset. The restriction of modality in content-based multimedia retrieval is eliminated by exploring semantic information of inter-media correlations. The experiments work well and clearly demonstrate the effectiveness of our approach from different aspects.

Our further work will focus on the following fields: (1) Seek for a more efficient cross-media distance estimation algorithm after canonical correlation analysis. (2) Explore active learning strategies to better utilize informative relevance feedbacks.

**Acknowledgments.** This work is supported by National Natural Science Foundation of China (No.60533090, No.60525108), 973 Program (No.2002CB312101), Science and Technology Project of Zhejiang Province (2005C13032, 2005C11001-05), and China-US Million Book Digital Library Project (www.cadal.zju.edu.cn )

# References

[1]   X. He, W.Y Ma, and H.J. Zhang, "Learning an Image Manifold for Retrieval", *ACM Multimedia Conference*, New York, 2004.

[2]   E. Chang, K. Goh, G. Sychay, and G. Wu, "CBSA: Content-Based Soft Annotation for Multimodal Image Retrieval Using Bayes Point Machine", *IEEE Trans on Circuits and Systems for Video Technology*, vol. 13, No.1, 2003.

[3]   Guodong Guo; Li, S.Z., "Content-based audio classification and retrieval by support vector machines", *IEEE Transactions on Neural Networks*, Volume 14, Issue 1, 2003, pp.209-215.

[4]   Jianping Fan, Elmagarmid, A.K., X.q. Zhu, Aref, W.G., Lide Wu, "ClassView: hierarchical video shot classification, indexing, and accessing", *Multimedia, IEEE Transactions*, Vol. 6, Issue 1, 2004, pp.70-86.

[5]   Meinard M¨uller, Tido R¨oder, Michael Clausen. "Efficient Content-Based Retrieval of Motion Capture Data". *Proceedings of ACM SIGGRAPH* 2005.

[6]   Fei Wu, Yi Yang, Yueting Zhuang, Yunhe Pan. "Understanding Multimedia Document Semantics for Cross-Media Retrieval", PCM 2005, pp.993-1004.

[7]   Yueting Zhuang, Fei Wu, Hong Zhang, Yi Yang. "Cross-Media Retrieval: Concepts, Advances and Challenges", 2006 International Symposium on Artificial Intelligence, Aug 1-3, 2006

[8]   Fei Wu, Hong Zhang, Yueting Zhuang. "Learning Semantic Correlations for Cross-media Retrieval". *The 13th International Conference on Image Processing (ICIP)* Atlanta, GA, USA 2006.

[9]   Chengcui Zhang, Xin Chen, Min Chen, Shu-Ching Chen, Mei-Ling Shyu. "A Multiple Instance Learning Approach for Content-based Image Retrieval Using One-class Support Vector Machine". *IEEE International Conference on Multimedia & Expo*, 2005. pp.1142-1145.

[10]  Maron O, Ratan AL. "Multiple-Instance Learning for Natural Scene Classification". In: Koller D, Fratkina R, eds. *Proceedings of the 15th International Conference on Machine Learning*. 1998. pp.341-349.

[11]  Hardoon, D. R., Szedmak, S. and Shawe-Taylor, J., "Canonical correlation analysis; An overview with application to learning methods", *Technical Report CSD-TR-03-02*, Computer Science Department, University of London, 2003.

[12]  H.S. Seung, D. Lee, "The manifold ways of perception", *Science*, vol 290, 2000.

[13]  M. Belkin and P. Niyogi, "Laplacian eigenmaps for dimensionality reduction and data representation", *Advances in Neural Information Processing Systesms*, 2001.

[14]  Xueyan Zhao Yueting Zhuang Fei Wu, "Audio Clip Retrieval with Fast Relevance Feedback based on Constrained Fuzzy Clustering and Stored Index Table", *The 3th IEEE Pacific-Rim Conference on Multimedia*, 2002, pp.237-244.

# SNR-Based Bit Allocation in Video Quality Smoothing

Xiangui Kang[1,2], Junqiang Lan[2], Li Liu[2], and Xinhua Zhuang[2]

[1] Dept. of ECE, Sun Yat-Sen Univ., Guangzhou 510275, China
[2] CS Department, Univ. of Missouri-Columbia, Columbia, MO, 65211
isskxg@mail.sysu.edu.cn

**Abstract.** Quality fluctuation has a major negative effect on perceptive video quality. Many recent video quality smoothing works target on constant distortion (i.e., constant PSNR) throughout the whole coded video sequence. In [1], a target distortion was set up for each frame based on a hypothesis that maintaining constant distortion over frames would boost video quality smoothing and extensive experiments showed the constant-distortion bit allocation (CDBA) scheme significantly outperforms the popular constant bit allocation (CBA) scheme and Xie et al's recent work [2, 3] in terms of delivered video quality. But during the scene changes, it has been observed that the picture energy often dramatically changes. Maintaining constant PSNR would result in dramatically different SNR performance and translate into dramatically different perceptive effects. Although computationally more complex, SNR represents a more objective measure than PSNR in assessing video quality. In this paper, a single-pass frame-level constant-SNR bit allocation scheme (CSNRBA) is developed for video quality smoothing throughout the video sequence. To achieve constant-SNR, a power series weighted actual SNR average of previous coded frames is adopted as the target SNR for the current frame. From the target SNR, the target distortion for the current frame is calculated. Then according to the analytic close-form $D$-$Q$ model and the linear rate control algorithm, the bit budget for the current frame can be estimated. Experimental results show that the proposed CSNRBA scheme provides much smoother video quality and achieve much better subjective video quality in terms of natural color, sharp objects and silhouette significantly on all testing video sequences than both CBA and CDBA schemes.

**Keywords:** Constant-SNR, Bit Allocation, Video Streaming, Quality Smoothing.

## 1 Introduction

Bit rate control, which is to achieve the best-perceived video quality under real-world constraints such as bandwidth, delay, and computation complexity, plays a key role in video coding. The actual bit rate control algorithm normally includes two parts: bit allocation and quantization control. In bit allocation, the target bit budget is allocated among different coding units such as GOPs (Group of Pictures), frames, slices, video objects or macroblocks. In quantization control, optimal quantization parameter $Q$ is determined to achieve the allocated bit budget.

Y. Zhuang et al. (Eds.): PCM 2006, LNCS 4261, pp. 989–998, 2006.

In many video communication applications, a lot of video coding applications pick the constant bit allocation (CBA or constant in shortly form) scheme [4-8]. The CBA scheme is implicitly based on the assumption that video content is stationary across frames. This assumption is not always valid, especially during fast motion or scene change video sequences. In video streaming applications, with a reasonable larger buffer size, it is possible to alleviate the quality fluctuation problem using content adaptive bit allocation scheme. In [9-16]. But almost all the existing schemes do not take account of that during the scene change the picture energy often dramatically change, maintaining constant distortion (i.e., constant PSNR) would result in dramatically different SNR performance and translate into dramatically different perceptive effects. The same PSNR means that two pictures have the same distortion. But one picture has larger energy than the other. The one with larger energy will tolerate distortion better than the other. Using both energy and distortion is the concept of using SNR. Although computationally more complex, SNR provides a more objective measure in video quality smoothing than PSNR.

In this paper, a novel single-pass frame-level SNR-based bit allocation scheme (CSNRBA) is proposed. To achieve constant SNR and have good content adaptive, we obtain the target SNR using a geometric power series weighted actual SNR average of previous coded frames. This target SNR together with the energy of the current frame determines the target distortion, then we adopt the linear rate model proposed in [17] to estimate the target bit budget for the current frame in our solution. We first use the analytic close-form $D$-$Q$ curve [1] to quickly localize the estimation in a very small $Q$ (or $\rho$) interval. Then the linear rate model is applied to the identified small region so that the parameter estimation will be more reliable/accurate. Close-form formulas for estimating the number of zero coefficients and the slope $\theta$ in the linear rate model, as well as the bit budget for the current frame are derived. Once the bit budget for the current frame is determined, any macroblock layer rate control algorithms, e.g. the one used in TMN8 can be used to determine the $Q$ for each MB. Experimental results show that the proposed CSNRBA scheme provides much smoother video quality on all testing video sequences than both the CBA and CDBA scheme [1].

The paper is organized as follows. In section 2, we will briefly review some related works, the standard H.263+ constant rate control algorithm TMN8 [7], the linear rate control algorithm [17] and the analytic close-form $D$-$Q$ model [1]. The proposed frame-level SNR-based bit allocation algorithm is discussed in details in Section 3. Performance evaluation is given in Section 4. In Section 5, we make our conclusion.

## 2    Related Works

TMN8 [7] is a model-based rate-distortion optimized bit rate control algorithm, in which the target frame bit rate is constant. In TMN8, both the rate $R$ and distortion $D$ are taken as the function of quantization stepsize $Q$.

$$D = \frac{1}{N} \sum_{i=1}^{N} \frac{Q_i^2}{12}; \quad B_i = A(\xi \frac{\sigma_i^2}{Q_i^2} + C) \tag{1}$$

where $D$ is the distortion; $Q_i$ is the quantization step size in the $i$-th macroblock; $N$ is the number of macroblocks (MBs) in a frame; $B_i$ is the bit budget allocated for the $i$-th macroblock, $A$ is the number of pixels in a macroblock; $\sigma_i^2$ is the standard deviation of the $i$-th macroblock; $C$ is the overhead (including header, syntax information and motion vectors) bit budget per pixel, assumed to be independent of macroblocks; $\xi$ is the model parameter. TMN8 selects quantization levels for all the macroblocks to minimize the overall distortion subject to the constant frame-level target bit rate constraint. The constrained minimization problem can be formulated as an unconstrained minimization problem by introducing a Lagrange multiplier, resulting in a closed-form solution:

$$Q_i^* = \sqrt{\frac{A\xi}{(\beta_i - ANC)}\frac{\sigma_i}{\alpha_i}\sum_{k=1}^{N}\alpha_i\sigma_i} \tag{2}$$

in which $\beta_i$ is the target bit rate for all the remaining uncoded macroblocks; $N$ is the number of remaining uncoded macroblocks; $\alpha_i$ is the distortion weight of the $i$-th macroblock. For details about the model and the rate control algorithm, please refer to [16].

Assume a video frame (either an I-frame or motion-compensated error frame) is encoded using DCT-based JPEG. Then, the bit rate $R$ and the distortion $D$ are observed to follow a linear relationship or an exponential relationship with the proportion $\rho$ of zero DCT coefficients, respectively [17].

$$R = \theta \times (N - \hat{N}); \quad D = \sigma^2 \times e^{-\beta(N-\hat{N})} \tag{3}$$

where $\sigma^2$ is the variance of a video frame; $\theta$ and $\beta$ are constants for a frame, $N$ is the total number of coefficients of a video frame, $\hat{N}$ is the number of zero coefficients. $\rho = \hat{N}/N$. This one-to-one relationship enables the $\rho$ domain algorithm to properly select $Q$ in video coding. The linear rate control or rate-distortion optimization has been successfully applied to the optimal bit allocation within a video frame, including bit allocation among video objects or different groups of macroblocks within a frame.

In [1], the distortion is approximated as:

$$D(Q) = \frac{1}{N}(\sum_{x=1}^{128}(x - r_Q(x))^2 H(x) + L\frac{Q^2}{12}) + \frac{1}{12} \tag{4}$$

in which $x$ is the original absolute DCT coefficient; $r_Q(x)$ is the quantized/reconstructed value of $x$; $H$ is the histogram; $N$ is the number of pixels, and $N = \sum_{x=0}^{M} H(x)$; $L$ represents the total number of the absolute DCT values that are larger than 128. In [1], it is shown that the $D$-$Q$ curve by Eq. (4) mimics the operational $D$-$Q$ curve very closely with a very low complexity.

## 3  Frame-Level Constant-SNR Bit Allocation (CSNRBA)

The same amount distortion distributed over a picture of larger energy affects the picture quality less than the one with smaller energy. It has been observed that during the scene changes the picture energy often dramatically changes. Thus we try to maintaining constant SNR. We do not use a simple arithmetic or geometric average of the actual SNR from previous frames for the target SNR; instead, we use a recursive formula to more efficiently calculate the target SNR as the weighted sum of the actual SNR and the target SNR of the previous frame:

$$sn\hat{r}_K = snr_{K-1} \times \lambda + sn\hat{r}_{K-1} \times (1-\lambda), \text{ if } K > 10, \tag{5}$$

where $snr_{K-1} = E_{K-1}/D_{K-1}$ is the actual SNR of the (K-1)-th frame, defined by the ratio of the energy $E_{K-1}$ of the original (K-1)-th frame over the distortion $D_{K-1}$ of the coded (K-1)-th frame. $\lambda$ should be chosen between 0 and 1. Bit allocation of the first 10 frames uses the constant bit allocation to have a stable average $SNR$. We use the constant bit allocation for each of the first 10 frames and an arithmetic average of their actual SNR for the target SNR of the 10-th frame, that is, $sn\hat{r}_{10} = \dfrac{1}{10} \sum_{i=0}^{9} snr_i$. Eq.

(5) can be expanded as:

$$sn\hat{r}_K = \sum_{i=10}^{K-1} snr_i \times a_i + (1-\lambda)^{K-10} snr_{10}, \text{ if } K > 10, \tag{6}$$

where $\sum_{i=10}^{K-1} a_i + (1-\lambda)^{K-10} = 1$. So $sn\hat{r}_K$ is a weighted sum of the actual SNR of all previous frames till and including the 10-th frame and the target SNR of the 10-th frame. The weight factor $a_i$ composes a geometric decreasing power series: $\lambda, \lambda \times (1-\lambda), \lambda \times (1-\lambda)^2, \dots, \lambda \times (1-\lambda)^{i-1}, \dots, \lambda \times (1-\lambda)^{K-11}$. The actual SNR of previous frames till and including the 10-th frame are weighed by this power series $a_i$ and the weight on the target SNR of the 10-th frame is diminishing as $K$ increases. If we adopt $\lambda = 0.1$, when $i > 23$, $a_i$ is less than $0.1\lambda$. If $i > M$, $a_i$ is less than $0.1\lambda$, we take $M$ as the virtual window size of the weight factors $\{ a_i \}$. A smaller $\lambda$ implies a lager (virtual) window size, which is in favor of global smoothness. On the other hand, a larger $\lambda$ implies a smaller (virtual) window size, producing more local smoothness. $\lambda$ is chosen as the inverse of the frame rate $\lambda = 1/F$ in our simulation based on the belief that the higher frame rate would require using more frames in video quality smoothing.

This target $SNR$ together with the energy $E_K$ of the current frame determines the target distortion $\hat{D}_K = (1/sn\hat{r}_K) \times E_K$. The target distortion $\hat{D}_K$ can then be used to determine the target bit rate for the current frame in four steps as follows: 1) Estimate number $\hat{N}$ of zero DCT coefficients corresponding to the target distortion; 2) Estimate the slope $\theta$ of the linear rate control algorithm; 3) Based on the estimated $\theta$

and $\hat{N}$, allocate a bit budget for the current frame; 4) Shape the allocated bit budget by the buffer constraints to guarantee no overflow neither underflow.

## A. Estimate of Number of Zeros

There are only two unknown parameters ($\sigma^2$ and $\beta$) in the $D$-$\hat{N}$ (distortion-number of zeros) model in Eq. (3), so any two known ($D$, $\hat{N}$) pairs would solve the equation and determine the $D$-$\hat{N}$ model. Then number of zeros, $\hat{N}$ corresponding to the average distortion $\hat{D}_K$ can be calculated immediately according to the determined model. But different $D$-$\hat{N}$ pairs will result in different parameter values. In order to avoid the model inaccuracy problem, we choose the two known ($D$, $\hat{N}$) pairs which are nearest to ($\hat{D}_K$, $\hat{N}$) as the model reference points. Since $D(Q)$ is a monotonically increasing function, without loss of generality we may assume that for some $Q^*$, $D(Q^*-1) < \hat{D}_K \leq D(Q^*)$. If the bit rate control algorithm works only on frame level, i.e. all the macroblocks in the frame share the same $Q$, then $D(Q^*)$ or $D(Q^*-1)$ would be the best approximation of $\hat{D}_K$. This best approximation, however, may still deviate from $\hat{D}_K$ significantly, especially when $Q^*$ is relatively small where the $D$-$Q$ slope is large. Accurate rate control algorithms such as TMN8 often work on macroblock layer so that each macroblock could have different $Q$s. In such cases, to minimize the quality fluctuation across frames, we need to find out the average fractional $Q$ or equivalently, the number of zeros corresponding to the target distortion of the frame. Denote the number of zeros for a specific $Q$ as $N(Q)$. From Eq. (3), we have:

$$D(Q^*) = \sigma^2 e^{-\beta(N-N(Q^*))}; \; D(Q^*-1) = \sigma^2 e^{-\beta(N-N(Q^*-1))}; \; \hat{D}_K = \sigma^2 e^{-\beta(N-\hat{N})} \qquad (7)$$

From the three equations in Eq. (7), the number of zeros $\hat{N}$, can be solved in close-form without explicitly knowing $\sigma^2$ and $\beta$ as:

$$\hat{N} = \frac{N(Q^*-1)\ln(\frac{D(Q^*)}{\hat{D}_K}) + N(Q^*)\ln(\frac{\hat{D}_K}{D(Q^*-1)})}{\ln(\frac{D(Q^*)}{D(Q^*-1)})} \qquad (8)$$

It can be seen that $\hat{N}$ is the linear combination of $N(Q^*)$ and $N(Q^*-1)$. The weights are determined by three log-ratio functions involving the target distortion $\hat{D}_K$ and two bounding reference values in the $D$-$Q$ function.

Because $D(Q)$ is a monotonically increasing function, we can adopt the binary search algorithm [18] to find out $Q^*$ from all the possible $Q$s, using our proposed simplified operational $D$-$Q$ determination. The number of search points to find out $Q^*$ in all the possible $Q$'s is $log(N_q)$, in which $N_q$ is the number of possible $Q$s. For example, in H.263, $N_q$ is 31, which means we only need maximal five $D(Q)$ values in order to locate $Q^*$.

## B. Estimate of $\theta$

According to our observation, the linear rate slope $\theta$ in Eq. (3) is relatively stable indeed. To estimate the slope $\theta$, we select the above mentioned $Q^*$ and count the number $N^*$ of zeros, then calculate the (run, level) pairs and their corresponding Huffman code lengths by look-up-table. At the end, we obtain the bit stream length $R^*$, and the slope $\theta$ is estimated as

$$\theta = R^*/(N - N^*) \tag{9}$$

## C. Bit Allocation

After both the slope $\theta$ and the number $\hat{N}$ of zeros are estimated, the bit budget $\hat{R}$ to meet the target distortion $\hat{D}_K$ can be determined as

$$\hat{R} = \theta(N - \hat{N}) \tag{10}$$

Since the estimated bit budget $\hat{R}$ only counts the bits for encoding DCT coefficients, headers and motion vectors will add more bits in the allocated bit budget as follows.

$$\hat{R} = \theta(N - \hat{N}) + R_{MV} + R_H \tag{11}$$

where $R_{MV}$ and $R_H$ are the bit budgets allocated for motion vectors and headers. To avoid buffer underflow and overflow, the allocated bit budget $\hat{R}$ by Eq. (11) needs to be further shaped using buffer constraints, and the final bit budget allocation scheme is given by:

$$R_t = \begin{cases} B_{max} - B; & if\ (\hat{R} + B - \dfrac{C}{F}) > (B_o = B_{max} - \dfrac{C}{F}) \\[2mm] 2 \times \dfrac{C}{F} - B; & if\ (\hat{R} + B - \dfrac{C}{F}) < (B_u = \dfrac{C}{F}) \\[2mm] \hat{R}; & otherwise \end{cases} \tag{12}$$

where $F$ is the target frame rate; $C$ is the target bit rate; $B_{max}$ is the buffer size; $B$ is the number of bits currently in the buffer; $B_o$ and $B_u$ are the overflow and underflow threshold respectively, which are set to $(B_{max} - C/F)$ and $C/F$ in the simulation. Eq. (11) and (12) together determine the final bit rate allocated for the current frame.

## 4  Performance Evaluation

Since our target application is video streaming and no frame skipping is preferred, CBA (Constant Bit Allocation) scheme is defined as

$$\hat{R} = \dfrac{C}{F} - \Delta; \quad \Delta = \begin{cases} B/F & if\ (B > 0) \\[2mm] (R_{K-1} - \hat{R}_{K-1})/(K-1) & Otherwise \end{cases} \tag{13}$$

where $\Delta$ is the discrepancy between the actual bits number $R_{K-1}$ for already encoded previous $(K-1)$-th frame and the allocated bits number $\hat{R}_{K-1}$. We compare CSNRBA with CDBA [1] and CBA. Three schemes have same buffer constraints as in Eq. (12). The buffer size for three algorithms is same, equals to one second's length, i.e. $B_{max} = C$. The thresholds for underflow $B_u$ and overflow $B_o$ are set to $C/F$ and $(B_{max} - C/F)$, respectively. In CDBA and CSNRBA algorithm, bit allocation of the first 10 frames uses the constant bit allocation to have a stable average SNR for CSNRBA or a stable average distortion for CDBA. TMN8 macroblock layer rate control algorithm is adopted to determine $Q$ for both allocation schemes.

Extensive simulations were performed on many standard sequences. Here we present a subset of representative results. The selected sequences are (all QCIF) News, Mother and Daughter, Foreman and a combined sequence of M&D, Akiyo and Car phone. The target bit rate and frame rate are all set to 48Kbps@10fps. The output bit rate may have control errors depending on how many bits are left in the buffer at the end of encoding. We re-adjust the target bit rate so that the actual output bit rates of all the algorithms remain the same.

From Table 1, it can be observed that at the same actual output bit rate, in terms of the output video quality measured by the average SNR value (dB), CSNRBA scheme has comparable SNR performance as the other two. To evaluate the SNR variation of video sequence, we use $V_{SNR} = \dfrac{1}{N_f - 1} \sum_{n=1}^{N_f-1} |SNR_n - SNR_{n-1}|$ (dB), where $N_f$ represents the total number of frames. A smaller $V_{SNR}$ means a smoother SNR behavior that translates into a smoother video quality. As seen from Table 1, CSNRBA delivers the smallest $V_{SNR}$ that generates the least perceptive quality fluctuation, as will be seen in the following.

**Table 1.** Performance comparison

| Sequence (QCIF) | Algorithm | Actual bit rate (Kbps) | SNR (dB) | $V_{SNR}$ (dB) |
|---|---|---|---|---|
| News | CBA | 48.48 | 26.3 | 0.34 |
| | CDBA | 48.48 | 26.3 | 0.19 |
| | CSNRBA | 48.48 | 26.3 | 0.13 |
| Combine | CBA | 52.03 | 30.4 | 0.75 |
| | CDBA | 52.03 | 30.6 | 0.37 |
| | CSNRBA | 52.03 | 30.7 | 0.23 |
| Foreman | CBA | 51.07 | 27.1 | 0.42 |
| | CDBA | 51.07 | 27.0 | 0.39 |
| | CSNRBA | 51.07 | 27.0 | 0.28 |
| M&D | CBA | 48.48 | 32.2 | 0.27 |
| | CDBA | 48.48 | 32.2 | 0.13 |
| | CSNRBA | 48.48 | 32.2 | 0.12 |

Fig. 1 further illustrates how SNR varies from frame to frame by each scheme. In both News and Combined video sequence, there are several scene changes, which cause a sharp SNR drop by the CBA scheme. It can be seen in Fig. 1 that CBA suffers the largest SNR fluctuation. As expected, the proposed CSNRBA algorithm holds SNR most stably around the scene changes. Maintaining a stable SNR is crucial for visual perception. Fig. 2 plots the encoding bits per frame for the "combined sequence". As expected, CSNRBA has the largest bit rate adaptation necessary for scene changes.

Subjective video quality is compared in Fig. 3 for the three algorithms. The frames compared are two scene change frames in the News and Combined sequence. CSNRBA achieves better perceptive video quality than the other two methods as expected. CSNRBA delivers clearer faces of man/woman in News (Fig. 3a-c), clearer eyes, clearer face in Combined (Fig. 3d-e) and more natural colors of faces comparing to CDBA and CBA

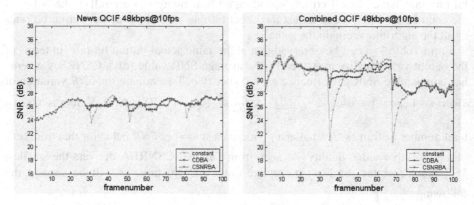

**Fig. 1.** Frame by Frame SNR comparison (48kbps@10fps)

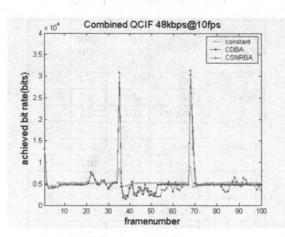

**Fig. 2.** Bit Rate vs. frame number

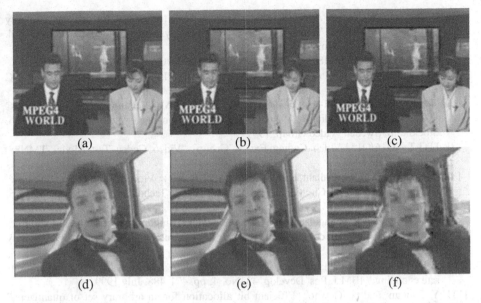

**Fig. 3.** The 50th coded frame of the News sequence: (a) CSNRBA; (b) CDBA; (c) CBA; The 67th coded frame of the combine sequence: (d) CSNRBA; (e) CDBA; (f) CBA

## 5  Conclusion

In this paper, we have proposed a single-pass frame-level constant-SNR bit allocation scheme for smooth video quality in video streaming applications. Experimental results on all testing video sequences show that the proposed CSNRBA scheme greatly alleviates the quality fluctuation problem observed in CBA scheme and provides smooth video quality in terms of natural color and sharp objects and silhouette significantly better than both the CBA and CDBA schemes. We also propose a practical way of estimating the rate slope in $\rho$ domain linear rate control algorithm. This slope estimation could be used in $\rho$ domain rate control as the initial slope value.

**Acknowledgement.** This work was supported by NSF of China (60403045, 60325208, 60572140) and NSF of Guangdong (04009742, 04205407, 04009739); also supported by NIH and NSF, under grant number NIH DHHS 1 R01 DC04340-01A2 and NSF EIA 9911095, respectively.

## References

[1] J. Lan, X. Zhuang and W. Zeng, "Single-Pass Frame-Level Constant Distortion Bit Allocation for Smooth Video Quality", IEEE international conference on multimedia and expo 2004 (ICME 2004), Taibei, Taiwan, July 2004.
[2] B. Xie and W. Zeng, "Sequence-based rate control for constant quality video," in Proc. 2002 International Conference on Image Processing, Rochester, New York, Sept. 2002.

[3] B. Xie and W. Zeng, "A sequence-based rate control framework for consistent quality real-time video," IEEE Transactions on Circuits and System for Video Technology. Vol. 16, No.1, pp. 56–71, Jan. 2006.

[4] "Test Model 5", Draft, ISO-IEC/JTC1/SC29/WG11/N0400, April 1993.

[5] Coding of Moving Pictures and Associated Audio, MPEG-4 Committee Draft, ISO/IEC 14496-2, Oct. 1998.

[6] "Text of ISO/IEC 14 496-2 MPEG4 video VM—Version 8.0," in ISO/IEC JTC1/SC29/WG11 Coding of Moving Pictures and Associated Audio MPEG 97/W1796. Stockholm, Sweden: Video Group, 1997.

[7] ITU-T SG16/Q15, Video Coding Expert Group, "Video Codec Test Model TMN8," Portland, June 1997.

[8] G. Cote, B. Erol, M. Gallant, and F. Kossentini, "H.263+: Video coding at low bit rates," IEEE Transactions on Circuits and System for Video Technology, vol. 8, pp.849–866, Nov. 1998.

[9] N. Mohawnian, R. Rajagopalan and C. A. Gonzales, "Single-pass constant- and variable-bit-rate MPEG-2 video compression," IBM J. Res. Develop. 43, No. 4, pp. 489-509, July 1999.

[10] P. H. Westerink, R. Rajagopalan, and C. A. Gonzales, "Two-pass MPEG-2 variable-bit-rate encoding," IBM J. Res. Develop. 43, No. 4, pp. 471-488, July 1999.

[11] Y. Shoham and A. Gersho, "Efficient bit allocation for an arbitrary set of quantizers," IEEE Trans. Acoust., Speech, Signal Processing, vol. 36, pp. 1445-1453, 1988.

[12] K. Ramchandran, A. Ortega and M. Vetterli, "Bit allocation for dependent quantization with applications to multiresolution and MPEG video coders," IEEE Transactions on Image Processing, vol. 3,no. 5, pp. 533-544, Sep. 1994.

[13] A. Ortega, K. Ramchandran and M. Vetterli, "Optimal trellis-based buffered compression and fast approximations," IEEE Transactions on Image Processing, vol. 3, no. 1, pp. 26-40, Jan. 1994.

[14] T. Chen and Z. He, "Signal-pass distortion-smoothing encoding for low bit-rate video streaming applications," International Conference on Multimedia and Expo, Baltimore, USA, Jul. 2003.

[15] Z. He, W. Zeng, C. W. When, "Lowpass Filtering of Rate-Distortion Functions for Quality Smoothing in Real-time Video Communication", IEEE Transactions on Circuits and System for Video Technology, vol. 15, no. 8, pp. 973-981, Aug. 2005.

[16] J. Ribas-Corbera and S. Lei, "Rate control in DCT video coding for low-delay video communications," IEEE Transactions on Circuits and System for Video Technology, vol. 9, pp. 172–185Feb. 1999.

[17] Z. He and S.K. Mitra, "A linear source model and a unified rate control algorithm for DCT video coding", IEEE Transactions on Circuits and System for Video Technology. vol. 12, pp. 970-982, Nov. 2002.

[18] T. H. Cormen, C. E. Leiserson, R. L. Rivest and C. Stein, "Introduction to Algorithms", MIT Press, 2nd Edition, 2001.

# Shadow Removal in Sole Outdoor Image

Zhenlong Du, Xueying Qin, Wei Hua, and Hujun Bao

State Key Lab of CAD&CG, Zhejiang University, P.R. China
{duzhl, xyqin, huawei, bao}@cad.zju.edu.cn

**Abstract.** A method of shadow removal from sole uncalibrated outdoor image is proposed. Existing approaches usually decompose the image into albedo and illumination images, in this paper, based on the mechanism of shadow generation, the occlusion factor is introduced, and the illumination image is further decomposed as the linear combination of solar irradiance and ambient irradiance images. The involved irradiance are achieved from the user-supplied hints. The shadow matte are evaluated by the anisotropic diffusion of posterior probability. Experiments show that our method could simultaneously extract the detailed shadow matte and recover the texture beneath the shadow.

## 1 Introduction

Shadow removal is significant in computer vision. In image segmentation, unwanted shadow boundaries may hinder the detection of true object boundaries. In motion estimation, the computation of optical flow is susceptible to illumination changes caused by shadows. In supervision, for the influence of shadow, erroneous target may be tracked. The problem of shadow identification becomes rather challenging if sole uncalibrated outdoor image is given. The luminance difference between illumination and shadow regions was exploited for shadow removal in single outdoor image [1]. In this paper, a novel method of shadow identification, extraction and removal is proposed, which only depends on an outdoor image. Shadow in natural scene has some particular properties that are different from the shadow in synthetic one.

1. Shadow always adheres to texture.

2. Umbrae does not appears totally black.

3. Umbrae and penumbrae are mutually interwoven.

4. The transition between umbrae and penumbrae is smooth.

Due to these characteristics, to identify the shadow from single outdoor image encounters three problems. How much radiance does the scene receive? how to evaluate the object reflectance? and how to determine the occlusion degree to light propagation? Unfortunately, these physical quantities are related to the scene, not directly to the image. But it does not mean it is impossible to evaluate them from image, in [2,7,13,14] a method of employing the radiance in image for

Y. Zhuang et al. (Eds.): PCM 2006, LNCS 4261, pp. 999–1007, 2006.
© Springer-Verlag Berlin Heidelberg 2006

estimating the incident irradiance of scene is proposed. Generally, the image is decomposed into albedo image $\mathcal{R}$ and illumination image $\mathcal{L}$, as illustrated by Eq. (1). At the pixelwise level, $\mathcal{R}$ essentially serves for the reflectance, and $\mathcal{L}$ for the received radiance. For approaching the true $\mathcal{R}$ and $\mathcal{L}$, Weiss [7] and Finlayson [12] exploited multiple images, while [1,2,8,13] only utilized single image. Because the third problems is not solved in [2,7,13,14], the penumbrae still influences the shadow identification.

$$I = \mathcal{R}\mathcal{L} \tag{1}$$

Based on the aforementioned observations, in this paper, $\mathcal{L}$ is further decomposed into the linear combination of solar irradiance $\mathcal{E}$ and ambient irradiance $\mathcal{A}$, as illustration in Eq. (2). Essentially speaking, $\mathcal{A}$ mainly refers to sky irradiance, and $\mathcal{E}$ to solar irradiance. For in natural scene object is illuminated by solar and sky lights, hence the proposed illumination decomposition is reasonable for outdoor image. $\alpha$ characterizes the occlusion, and the same time it depicts the shadow: $\alpha = 0$ corresponds to umbrae, $0 < \alpha < 1$ to penumbrae, and $\alpha = 1$ is the non-shadow region. Hence Eq. (3) is able to be derived.

$$I = \mathcal{R}(\mathcal{A} + \alpha\mathcal{E}) \tag{2}$$
$$I = \mathcal{M} + \alpha\mathcal{N} \tag{3}$$

Where $\mathcal{M} = \mathcal{R}\mathcal{A}$, $\mathcal{N} = \mathcal{R}\mathcal{E}$. $\mathcal{M}$ and $\mathcal{N}$ are the decomposed image. Corresponding to $\mathcal{A}$ and $\mathcal{E}$, $\mathcal{M}$ and $\mathcal{N}$ are the solar image and ambient image, respectively. Note that this kind of decomposition only fits for the illumination context with existence of point light.

In this paper, the user-assisted regions are employed for shadow identification, shadow extraction and shadow removal only in sole outdoor image, since user interference provides the information of irradiance and shading. Meanwhile, due to the feasible irradiance decomposition, shadow identification, extraction and removal could be accomplished in one outdoor image.

The rest of the paper is organized as follows. In next section the related works are reviewed. In section 3, three subproblems, shadow identification, shadow extraction and shadow removal, are discussed. In section 4, some results are shown, and the conclusion is put forward in the final section.

## 2    Related Work

In this section, we review the existed and possible solutions to shadow removal, which cover the approaches of the moving shadow elimination, static shadow removal, and shadow matting.

**Intrinsic Image** represents the illumination independent characteristic of image, it can be evaluated from one image or multiple images. Generally, multiple images record the reflected irradiance in different directions, and they can be used for converging $\mathcal{R}$ and $\mathcal{L}$. Reflectance image $\mathcal{R}$ sometimes is called the intrinsic image, Weiss [7] proposed a method for evaluating the intrinsic image from more than one image, but for capturing the illumination changes in natural scene, some images recording the different time of a day need to be taken, obviously, the acquisition manner is impractical to shadow removal from outdoor image. Meanwhile, registration between the images severely influences the result of shadow removal. Wu and Tang [2] suggested an approach of shadow removal based on the Bayesian optimization technique, and they composed the extracted shadow to another image, though the matte appears some color bleedings. Nadimi [10] discussed the method of eliminating the moving shadow, which is represented by Gaussian Mixture Model (GMM).

**Color Constancy** which characterizes the illumination independent descriptors, is evaluated by Finlayson [11], and estimated in the inverse chromaticity space by Tan [14]. On the basis of the color constancy, Finlayson et al [12] put forward an approach of shadow removal, since the removal is performed within the whole image, it easily influences the nonshadow regions. Additionally, Finlayson et al [13] employed the entropy minimization to derive an illumination invariant gray scale image for shadow removal, and achieved the convincing results.

**Relighting** technique could be exploited for shadow removal. When the sample images from natural scene are sufficient enough, applying the proposed method by Wong et al [4] is capable of eliminating the shadow. Sato et al [3] presented an approach which could estimate the irradiance within shadow region with known object shape. [1] suggested a shadow removal method by complementing the lost irradiance within shadow region.

**Passive Vision Technique** can be used for assisting the shadow removal. Chuang [9] moved an oriented stick to acquire the geometry of shadow caster, the proposed shadow matting method could effortlessly compose the pulled shadow matte into a novel scene. But the acquisition manner only fits for the small-scale scene. Cham [5] and Jaynes [6] presented the schema of shadow removal by employing the feedback information from the placed camera in scene, the suggested technique is appropriate for indoor cinema or exhibition hall.

**Matting** technique could be utilized for extracting the shadow matte. The direct matting within the gradient domain [17] can extract the underlying texture structure as well as shadow matte, and the shadow boundary is also preserved in the pulled matte. The gradient is much important for preserving the original structure in shadow-free image, so it is exploited in our approach.

Compared with the existed shadow removal approaches [2,13], our method has some advantages. The soft shadow is perfectly processed, and less color bleeding appears in shadow free image.

## 3    Shadow Removal

Shadow removal from single image is essential an ill-posed problem in computer vision, therefore some hints need to be provided for approximately solving this problem. That is to say, given one image and taken advantages of user-assisted cues, shadow could be removed. In our method, the initial $\mathcal{R}$, $\mathcal{A}$ and $\mathcal{E}$ is estimated by GMM, which is inspired by [2]. The rough shadow matte is extracted based on the initial estimate. A variational function is constructed and used for refining the shadow matte.

## 3.1    User-Supplied Regions

The user-supplied regions include three kinds of regions: "definitely shadow region" $\mathcal{S}$, "definitely non-shadow region" $\overline{\mathcal{S}}$ and "uncertain region" $\mathcal{U}$, as the illustration of Fig. 1. $\mathcal{S}$ indicates the umbrae (hard shadow) region, $\overline{\mathcal{S}}$ refers to the illumination region, and $\mathcal{U}$ describes the region to be processed. The user-provided configuration has slight difference from [2], it is that $\mathcal{S}$ should be the subset of $\mathcal{U}$. Additionally, the "excluded region" in [2] is accomplished by the user interference in this paper.

The goal of shadow removal is to obtain a shadow free image from $\mathcal{U}$ under the implicit information of $\mathcal{S}$ and $\overline{\mathcal{S}}$, which involves three inseparable procedures, shadow identification, shadow matting and shadow removal. Shadow identification is to determine the shadow region $\mathcal{F}$ from $\mathcal{U}$, it provides the approximate shadow region which all pixels' $\alpha$ is 1. The accurate $\alpha$ is decided by shadow matting. Shadow removal employs the extracted shadow matte to compensate the lost irradiance to solar light. In the paper, $\mathcal{S}$, $\overline{\mathcal{S}}$ and $\mathcal{U}$ are assume ed to bear the similar texture, which is the same to [1,2].

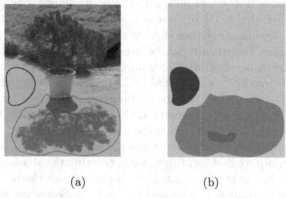

(a)                                    (b)

**Fig. 1.** (a) User-Supplied Regions, $\mathcal{S}$ = shadow(red), $\overline{\mathcal{S}}$ = nonshadow(blue) and $\mathcal{U}$= uncertain(pink) (b) Shows the filled regions $\mathcal{S}, \overline{\mathcal{S}}$ and $\mathcal{U}$, respectively

## 3.2    Shadow Identification

Since $\mathcal{S}$ and $\overline{\mathcal{S}}$ bear the similar texture, in statistical sense, their corresponding mean radiance should be nearly identical when the illumination is inexistent. The presence of shadow just shifts the mean intensity of $\mathcal{S}$ and $\overline{\mathcal{S}}$. It is easily found that the chrominance of $\mathcal{S}$ and $\overline{\mathcal{S}}$ remains nearly the same, but the luminance is far different. For avoiding the discrepant chrominance after shadow removal, the luminance and chrominance are still considered together. In the paper the procedure of shadow removal is performed in $La^*b^*$ color space, since luminance has little relevance with chrominance in $La^*b^*$. Consequently, the image is transformed to $La^*b^*$ color space, and the color vector of pixel $x$ is $\mathbf{I} = \{L_x, a_x^*, b_x^*\}$.

The existence of texture within shadow region modifies the pixel radiance, and generally it is subject to the probability distribution model, which is represented by GMM in the paper. $S$ and $\overline{S}$ are separately represented by GMM, denoted by $\{G_S(i; \mu_{S_i}, \Sigma_{S_i})\}$ and $\{G_{\overline{S}}(i; \mu_{\overline{S}_i}, \Sigma_{\overline{S}_i})\}$. Each gaussian involves the mean $\mu$ and variance $\Sigma$. $\pi$ is the mixing weight of Gaussian. The number of Gaussian is related to the size and shape of specified regions. Generally, more irregular the region is and more detailed texture the region bears, more number of gaussian is used. For instance, 6 gaussians are employed in Fig. 2.

The likelihood of pixel to GMM is evaluated and used for identifying the shadow region $\mathcal{F}$ of $\mathcal{U}$. Let $\mathcal{C} = \{S, \overline{S}\}$, the pixel likelihood to $\mathcal{C}$ is defined as that.

$$d_{\mathcal{C}}(\mathbf{I}) = \frac{1}{K} \sum_{i=1}^{K} [D_1(\mu_{\mathcal{C}}^i, \Sigma_{\mathcal{C}}^i) + D_2(\mathbf{I}, \mu_{\mathcal{C}}^i, \Sigma_{\mathcal{C}}^i)] \tag{4}$$

$K$ is the number of Gaussian, $D_1$ describes the probability of Gaussian, and $D_2$ characterizes the distance to Gaussian. $D_1$ and $D_2$ are evaluated as follows.

$$D_1(\mu_{\mathcal{C}}^i) = -\log \pi_{\mathcal{C}}^i + \frac{1}{2} \log \det \Sigma_{\mathcal{C}}^i$$

$$D_2(\mathbf{I}, \mu_{\mathcal{C}}^i, \Sigma_{\mathcal{C}}^i) = \frac{1}{2}(\mathbf{I} - \mu_{\mathcal{C}}^i)^T \Sigma_{\mathcal{C}}^i (\mathbf{I} - \mu_{\mathcal{C}}^i)$$

$d_S(\mathcal{M})$ and $d_{\overline{S}}(\mathcal{N})$ are regarded as the mean likelihood of $S$ and $\overline{S}$, respectively. The likelihood of pixel $x$ to $S$ and $\overline{S}$ are $d_S(\mathbf{I}_x)$ and $d_{\overline{S}}(\mathbf{I}_x)$. If $d_S(\mathbf{I}_x) < d_{\overline{S}}(\mathbf{I}_x)$ and $d_{\overline{S}}(\mathcal{M}) < d_{\overline{S}}(\mathbf{I}_x) < d_S(\mathcal{N})$ all hold, the pixel is deemed to belong to $\mathcal{F}$. Every pixel in $\mathcal{U}$ is evaluated under this decision rules, then the initial shadow matte which excludes the part illumination region is achieved.

### 3.3   Shadow Matting

After the shadow identification, $\mathcal{F}$ is achieved. The value of $\alpha$ within $\mathcal{F}$ need to be further determined. In this section, an approach of anisotropically diffusion to maximum a posterior probability (MAP) is employed for shadow matting. For each pixel $x$ in $\mathcal{F}$, its prior probability to user-assisted shadow region $S$ is evaluated by.

$$P(x|S) = \sum_{i=1}^{K} \pi_S^i G(\mathbf{I}_x - \mu_S, \Sigma_S) \tag{5}$$

The posterior probability of $x$ belonging to $S$ is able to derived by applying the Bayesian rule.

$$P(S|x) = P(x|S)P(x) \tag{6}$$

Where $P(x)$ is to set the normalization of $\alpha$, that is, $P(x) = \frac{\mathbf{I}_x - \mathcal{M}}{\mathcal{N}}$.

The influence of texture gives rise to the acute change of $\alpha$, which violates the propertoes of natural shadow. Meanwhile, radiance occurring in natural scene can not alter abruptly, so $\mathcal{F}$ is anisotropically diffused, as Eq. (7).

$$\frac{\partial P(\mathcal{S}|x)}{\partial t} = div\left[g\left(\nabla P(\mathcal{S}|x)\right)\nabla P(\mathcal{S}|x)\right] \tag{7}$$

Where $t$ is the iteration time, $div$ and $\nabla$ are separately divergence and gradient operator, $g(P(\mathcal{S}|x)) = \exp\left(\frac{\|\nabla P(\mathcal{S}|x)\|}{\eta}\right)$, and $\eta$ is the mean probability of $x$'s neighborhood. The smoothing procedure is stopped till the $\sum P(x|x \in \mathcal{S})$ remains unchanged. Additionally, because of the computational cost in smoothing procedure, the acceleration schema [18] is employed.

### 3.4  Shadow Removal

After the shadow matting, the rough shadow matte is obtained. However, when zooming in the shadow matte, $\alpha$ exhibits discontinuity, which corrupts the properties of natural shadow. Thus the shadow matte is required to refined. In the paper a schema of $\alpha$ refinement is devised, it requires that *alpha* matte should satisfy the energy minization, as that.

$$\alpha^* = \min_{\alpha} \int_{\mathcal{F}} \left(I_x - \lambda\left(\mathcal{M} - \alpha_x \mathcal{N}\right)\right)dx \tag{8}$$

where $\lambda$ is the adjusting factor to control the degree of matte smoothness.
Fig. 2(a) and (b) demonstrate the unrefined shadow matte and refined shadow matte, respectively. Fig. 2(b) shows the convincing soft shadow, and it perfectly satisfy the characteristics of natural shadow.
After $\mathcal{M}$, $\mathcal{N}$ and $\alpha^*$ are evaluated, the shadow-free image is achieved by complementing the quantity of irradiance $\overline{\alpha}\mathcal{N}$, where $\overline{\alpha}$ is $1 - \alpha^*$.

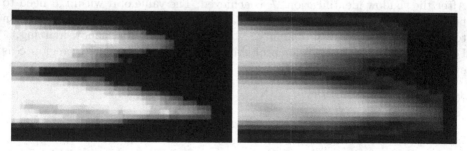

(a) Unrefined Shadow Matte        (b) Refined Shadow Matte

**Fig. 2.** Shadow Matte Refinement

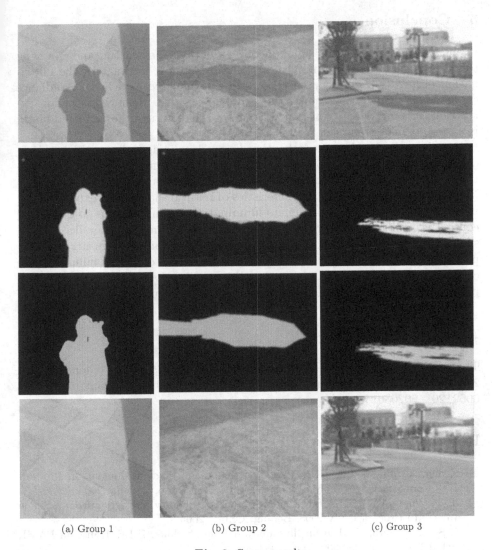

(a) Group 1            (b) Group 2            (c) Group 3

**Fig. 3.** Some results

## 4   Results

In this section, three groups of results are demonstrated for presenting the robustness and feasibility of our method. Each group is displayed by one column.
In Fig. 3, the first row is the outdoor image, the second one is the extracted
shadow matte, the third is the refined shadow matte, and the last one is the
shadow-free image in which the shadow is removed. The comparison of Fig. 3
and Fig. 4 shows that the refined shadow matte is very approaching the real
shadow. Moreover, it is the refined shadow matte that it is used for the recovering the texture, hence the shadow-free image is realistic too.

## 5  Conclusion

In one image, the problem of simultaneously identifying, extracting and removing the shadow is an ill-posed problem in computer vision, fortunately, the illumination occurring in outdoor image could be formulated as a linear irradiance combination model, which makes this problem solvable. Meanwhile, shadow extraction is a procedure of converging the actual shadow, and the extracted matte is an approximate reflect of true shadow.

Based on the irradiance constitution in outdoor image, the method of irradiance decomposition is proposed in this paper, it is different from the conventional approach which separates the image into albedo and illumination images. Moreover, depending on the characteristics of natural shadow and exploiting the user-supplied hints, the approximate illumination which conforms to the image context is constructed. In order to make the extracted matte as detailed as possible. The shadow matte is determined by the anisotropically diffusing maximal posterior probability, and it is refined in the procedure of energy minimization, consequently, the shadow free image is rather convincing. In future, how to compose the extracted shadow into the synthetic scene is our investigation.

## Acknowledgement

The work is supported by National Basic Research Program (China) Grant 2002CB312102, and Natural Science Foundation(China) Grant 60373035, 60021201, 60203014.

## References

1. Z. Du, X. Qin, H. Lin, H. Bao:Shadow removal in gradient domain, In Proc. of Intl' Conf. on Image Analysis and Recognition, Toronto, Canada, 2005.
2. T.-P. Wu, C.-K. Tang: A Bayesian Approach for Shadow Extraction from a Single Image, In Proc. of ICCV'2005, Beijing, China, 2005.
3. I. Sato, Y. Sato, K. Ikeuchi: Illumination from shadows, IEEE Trans. on PAMI, vol. 25, no. 3, pp. 290-300, Mar. 2003.
4. T.T. Wong, C.W. Fu, P.A. Heng, C.S. Leung: The plenoptic illumination function, IEEE Trans. on Multimedia, vol. 4, no. 3, pp. 361-371, Sep. 2002.
5. T.J. Cham, J. Rehg, R. Sukthankar, G. Sukthankar: Shadow elimination and occluder light supression for multi-projector displays, In Proc. of CVPR'2003, 2003.
6. C.Jaynes, S. Webb, R.M. Steele: Camera-based detection and removal of shadows from interactive multiprojector displays, IEEE TVCG, vol. 10, no. 3, pp. 290-301, May/June, 2004.
7. Y. Weiss: Deriving intrinsic images from image sequences, In Proc. of ICCV'2001, 2001.
8. A. Levin, Y. Weiss: User assisted separation of reflections from a single image using a sparsity prior, In Proc. of ECCV'2004, 2004.
9. Y.Y. Chuang, D.B. Goldman, B. Curless, D.H. Salesin, et al: Shadow matting and compositing, In Proc. of SIGGRAPH'2003, Aug. 2003.

10. S. Nadimi, B. Bhanu: Moving shadow detection using a physics-based approach, In Proc. of ICPR'2002, vol. 2, pp. 701–704, 2002.
11. G.D. Finlayson: Coefficient color constancy, Ph.D. Dissertation of Simon Fraser Univ. Apr. 1995.
12. G.D. Finlayson, S.D. Hordley, M.S. Drew: Removing shadows from images, In Proc. of ICCV'2001, 2001.
13. G.D. Finlayson, M.S. Drew, C. Lu: Intrinsic images by entropy minimization, In Proc. of ECCV'2004, 2004.
14. R.T. Tan:Illumination color and intrinsic surface properties - Physics-Based color analysis from a single image, Ph.D. Dissertation of Univ. of Tokyo, Dec. 2003.
15. P. Perez, M. Gangnet, A. Blake: Poisson image editing, In Proc. of SIG-GRAPH'2003, 2003.
16. M. Bertalmio, L. Vese, G. Sapiro, S. Osher: Simultaneous structure and texture image inpainting, IEEE Trans. on Image Processing, vol. 12, no. 8, pp. 882-889, Aug. 2003.
17. J. Sun, J. Jia, C.-K. Tang, H.-Y. Shum: Poisson matting, In Proc. of SIG-GRAPH'2004, 2004.
18. R. Deriche: Fast algorithms for low-level vision, IEEE Trans. on PAMI, vol. 1, no. 12, pp.78-88, Jan. 1990.

# 3D Head Model Classification Using KCDA

Bo Ma[1,2], Hui-yang Qu[2], Hau-san Wong[2], and Yao Lu[1]

[1] School of Computer Science and Technology, Beijing Institute of Technology
[2] Department of Computer Science, City University of Hong Kong
Bma000@126.com, quhy@cs.cityu.edu.hk, cshswong@cityu.edu.hk,
vis_yl@bit.edu.cn

**Abstract.** In this paper, the 3D head model classification problem is addressed by use of a newly developed subspace analysis method: kernel clustering-based discriminant analysis or KCDA as an abbreviation. This method works by first mapping the original data into another high-dimensional space, and then performing clustering-based discriminant analysis in the feature space. The main idea of clustering-based discriminant analysis is to overcome the Gaussian assumption limitation of the traditional linear discriminant analysis by using a new criterion that takes into account the multiple cluster structure possibly embedded within some classes. As a result, Kernel CDA tries to get through the limitations of both Gaussian assumption and linearity facing the traditional linear discriminant analysis simultaneously. A novel application of this method in 3D head model classification is presented in this paper. A group of tests of our method on 3D head model dataset have been carried out, reporting very promising experimental results.

**Keywords:** 3D head model classification, Kernel Linear Discriminant Analysis (KLDA), Clustering-based Discriminant Analysis (CDA), Kernel Fuzzy c-means, Kernel Clustering-based Discriminant Analysis (KCDA).

## 1 Introduction

3D model retrieval and classification have become one of the important research directions in pattern recognition and multimedia information processing with the proliferation of 3D scanners and digitizers [1], [2]. In particular, 3D head model classification is gaining prominence in view of its potential applications in computer animation and medical imaging [3]. In this paper, we focus on 3D head model classification based on subspace analysis method.

Subspace analysis methods constitute an important research branch of pattern recognition, and especially there have been a variety of works in the literature involving the related theoretical study and their applications in many fields like biometric feature recognition [4], [5], multimedia database retrieval and so on since the pioneering work of eigenface [6]. In principle, subspace analysis method is aimed at finding a set of directions onto which the projections of the original data samples should satisfy some predefined optimization criterion, which is, for example, maximum variance for the principal component analysis, or the maximum ratio between the between-class scatter and the within-class scatter for the linear discriminant analysis.

Y. Zhuang et al. (Eds.): PCM 2006, LNCS 4261, pp. 1008–1017, 2006.

Among these subspace analysis methods, LDA has been widely used for dimension reduction and enhancing the data separation ability. This method takes into account not only within-class scatter but also between-class scatter, leading to a highly effective solution to many pattern classification problems. It is well known that LDA can achieve the optimal Bayesian classification error when different classes have different means and the same covariance matrix. However, despite its popularity and advantages, LDA suffers from several limitations mainly including its linearity and Gaussian assumption.

In the traditional linear subspace analysis, the solution is a linear combination of the training data samples, therefore cannot solve the classification of the data samples having nonlinear separation hyperplane. Fortunately this limitation can be overcome by the introduction of the kernel trick to a certain amount. The main idea of kernel subspace analysis methods is to first map the original data into another high-dimensional space, and then to perform the traditional analysis methods like PCA or LDA [7], [8], [9]. Hopefully the mapped samples in the feature space can form linear separation hyperplane although in practice the performance of the kernel methods depends on the choice of both kernel function and the related kernel parameters.

To relax the Gaussian distribution assumption in the traditional LDA method, Xue-wen Chen and Thomas Huang made another effort by modeling each class structure as multiple clusters and then applying a LDA-like criterion that tries to find some directions such that the directional projections of every pair of clusters that lie in different classes are well-separated while the within-cluster scatter is minimized [10]. This method was named clustering-based discriminant analysis (CDA) and has been proved very effective in facial expression recognition.

In this paper, the 3D head model classification problem is addressed by a kernelized version of clustering-based discriminant analysis that we name KCDA. KCDA can integrate the merits of both Kernel LDA and CDA to improve the classical LDA method in the way that one hand multiple cluster structure is fully exploited and on the other hand kernel technique is imposed to get a nonlinear separation hyperplane. In addition, by expressing every cluster center as the sum of every sample weighted by its fuzzy member degree, we integrate CDA, KLDA and kernel fuzzy c-means algorithm [11] into a uniform framework. We illustrate a novel application of this method in 3D head model classification in this paper. A group of tests on 3D head model dataset have been performed to validate our developed method, reporting very promising experimental results.

## 2   CDA

In this section, we give a brief introduction to traditional LDA and CDA, and then show that LDA is factually a special case of CDA when the cluster number of each class degrades to 1.

To find discrimination features, LDA projects the original $a$-D vector $\mathbf{x}_k$ to a reduced feature space with the projected $b$-D feature $\mathbf{y}_k = \mathbf{A}^T \mathbf{x}_k$. The matrix $\mathbf{A} \in R^{a \times b}$ consists of $b$ eigenvectors corresponding to the $b$ largest eigenvalues of the eigensystem

$\mathbf{S}_B \mathbf{v} = \lambda \mathbf{S}_W \mathbf{v}$, where $\mathbf{S}_B$ is the between-class scatter matrix and $\mathbf{S}_W$ the within-class scatter matrix. The two scatter matrixes can be expressed as

$$\mathbf{S}_B = \sum_{i=1}^{l} (\boldsymbol{\mu}_i - \boldsymbol{\mu})(\boldsymbol{\mu}_i - \boldsymbol{\mu})^T \ , \ \mathbf{S}_W = \sum_{i=1}^{l} \sum_{k=1}^{N_i} (\mathbf{x}_k^i - \boldsymbol{\mu}_i)(\mathbf{x}_k^i - \boldsymbol{\mu}_i)^T \qquad (1)$$

where $\boldsymbol{\mu}_i$ denotes the mean vector of the $i$th class, $N_i$ the number of the samples of class $i$ ( $i=1,2,...l$ ), $\boldsymbol{\mu}$ the whole sample mean, and $\mathbf{x}_k^i$ the $k$th sample of the $i$th class. The main idea behind LDA is to maximize the ratio between the between-class scatter and the within-class scatter after projection. When all the classes have different mean vectors and the same covariance matrix under Gaussian distribution assumption, LDA can achieve the optimal Bayesian classification error. However, when the mean vectors of different classes are close to each other or the data distributions for some classes are multi-modal, the performance of LDA may be discounted.

Compared with LDA, CDA takes into account the case that there are multiple clusters embedded within certain classes [10]. Assume that there are $l$ classes, $d_i$ clusters ( $i=1,2,...,l$ ) for the $i$th class, and $N_{i,j}$ samples for the $j$th cluster of the $i$th class. $\mathbf{x}_k^{i,j}$ is used to denote the $k$th entity for the $j$th cluster of the $i$th class, and $\boldsymbol{\mu}^{i,j}$ the mean of the corresponding cluster. CDA computes the following eigensystem, $\mathbf{C}_B \mathbf{v} = \lambda \mathbf{C}_W \mathbf{v}$, where $\mathbf{C}_B$ and $\mathbf{C}_W$ are defined as

$$\mathbf{C}_B = \sum_{i=1}^{l-1} \sum_{e=i+1}^{l} \sum_{j=1}^{d_i} \sum_{h=1}^{d_e} (\boldsymbol{\mu}^{i,j} - \boldsymbol{\mu}^{e,h})(\boldsymbol{\mu}^{i,j} - \boldsymbol{\mu}^{e,h})^T \ , \ \mathbf{C}_W = \sum_{i=1}^{l} \sum_{j=1}^{d_i} \sum_{k=1}^{N_{ij}} (\mathbf{x}_k^{i,j} - \boldsymbol{\mu}^{i,j})(\mathbf{x}_k^{i,j} - \boldsymbol{\mu}^{i,j})^T \qquad (2)$$

According to the definitions, the derived eigensystem tries to maximize the distance of the projected features between clusters belonging to different classes while minimizing the within-cluster scatter.

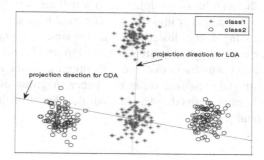

**Fig. 1.** Comparison between LDA and CDA

In addition, when each class only contains one cluster, we can see that CDA degrades to LDA from these equations in that $\mathbf{C}_B$ and $\mathbf{C}_W$ becomes exactly $\mathbf{S}_B$ and $\mathbf{S}_W$ of LDA respectively. Fig. 1 gives an illustrative comparison between the resulting projection direction of LDA and that of CDA in which we can see that along the direction computed by LDA, the projected features of one cluster of class 1 almost coincide with those of class 2, while along the direction of CDA, the projected features can be well-separated.

# 3  Kernel CDA

In this section, a kernelized version of clustering-based discriminant analysis is introduced. Our method works by first mapping the original data samples into another high dimensional space, and then applying CDA to the mapped data to extract features for subsequent classification tasks. Since multiple cluster structure for each class needs to be extracted after the original data samples are mapped into kernel space, we first give a brief introduction to kernel-based fuzzy c-means clustering algorithm in subsection 3.1 and then present our proposed method, i.e. kernel clustering-based discriminant analysis method in subsection 3.2.

## 3.1  Kernel-Based Fuzzy c-Means Clustering

The fuzzy c-means clustering algorithm minimizes an objective function $J_m$, which is the weighted sum of squared errors within groups and is defined as follows:

$$J_m = \sum_{k=1}^{n} \sum_{i=1}^{c} u_{ik}^m \|\mathbf{x}_k - \mathbf{\mu}_i\|^2, 1 < m < \infty \tag{3}$$

where $\mathbf{\mu}_i$ is a vector of unknown cluster prototype(centers). The value of $u_{ik}$ represents the grade of membership of data point $\mathbf{x}_k$ to the $i$th cluster. The inner product defined by the norm matrix defines a measure of similarity between a data point and the cluster prototypes. A non-degenerate fuzzy c-partition of the original space is conveniently represented by a matrix $\mathbf{U} = [u_{ik}]$ where $0 \le u_{ik} \le 1$.

Suppose that the original space $X$ is mapped into another high dimensional Hilbert space $F$ through a nonlinear mapping function $\phi: X \to F$ and $\mathbf{x} \to \phi(\mathbf{x})$. Similar to Eq. (3), in kernel fuzzy c-means clustering algorithm the objective function now becomes [11]

$$J_m = \sum_{i=1}^{c} \sum_{k=1}^{n} u_{ik}^m \|\phi(\mathbf{x}_k) - \overline{\varphi}_i\|^2 \tag{4}$$

where

$$D_{ik} = \|\phi(\mathbf{x}_k) - \overline{\varphi}_i\|^2 = k(\mathbf{x}_k, \mathbf{x}_k) + k(\overline{\varphi}_i, \overline{\varphi}_i) - 2k(\mathbf{x}_k, \overline{\varphi}_i) \tag{5}$$

and $k(\mathbf{x}, \mathbf{y}) = \phi(\mathbf{x})^T \phi(\mathbf{y})$, i.e. the so-called kernel function. In our current experiments, we adopt the Gaussian function as a kernel function, i.e.,

$$k(\mathbf{x}, \mathbf{y}) = \exp(-\|\mathbf{x} - \mathbf{y}\|^2 / \sigma^2) \tag{6}$$

In such a case, $k(\mathbf{x}, \mathbf{x}) = 1$ and the optimization criterion now becomes

$$J_m = 2 \sum_{i=1}^{c} \sum_{k=1}^{n} u_{ik}^m (1 - k(\mathbf{x}_k, \overline{\varphi}_i)) \tag{7}$$

The update equations for the clustering prototypes and membership degrees are

$$\overline{\varphi}_i = \frac{\sum_{k=1}^n (u_{ik})^m \phi(\mathbf{x}_k)}{\sum_{k=1}^n (u_{ik})^m} \quad for\ 1 \le i \le c \tag{8}$$

and

$$u_{ik} = \frac{1}{\sum_{j=1}^c \left( \frac{\|\phi(\mathbf{x}_k) - \overline{\varphi}_i\|_A^2}{\|\phi(\mathbf{x}_k) - \overline{\varphi}_j\|_A^2} \right)^{\frac{1}{m-1}}} \quad for\ 1 \le i \le c, 1 \le k \le n \tag{9}$$

## 3.2  Kernel Clustering-Based Discriminant Analysis

As defined in section 2, assume that there are $l$ classes, $d_i$ clusters ($i = 1,2,...,l$) for the $i$th class, and $N_{i,j}$ samples for the $j$th cluster of the $i$th class. $\mathbf{x}_k^{i,j}$ denotes the $k$th entity for the $j$th cluster of the $i$th class. Let $\overline{\varphi}^{i,j}$ be the center of the $j$th cluster of the $i$th class in the transformed space that is obtained by running the kernel fuzzy c-means algorithm for each class.

Similar to Eq. (2), the between-cluster scatter matrix $\mathbf{B}$ in the kernel space can be defined as

$$\mathbf{B} = \sum_{i=1}^{l-1} \sum_{e=i+1}^{l} \sum_{j=1}^{d_i} \sum_{h=1}^{d_e} (\overline{\varphi}^{i,j} - \overline{\varphi}^{e,h})(\overline{\varphi}^{i,j} - \overline{\varphi}^{e,h})^T \tag{10}$$

The within-cluster scatter matrix $\mathbf{V}$ in the kernel space can be defined as

$$\mathbf{V} = \sum_{i=1}^{l} \sum_{j=1}^{d_i} \sum_{k=1}^{N_{i,j}} (\phi(\mathbf{x}_k^{i,j}) - \overline{\varphi}^{i,j})(\phi(\mathbf{x}_k^{i,j}) - \overline{\varphi}^{i,j})^T \tag{11}$$

Given these two matrices, KCDA needs to resolve the following eigensystem:

$$\lambda \mathbf{V}\mathbf{v} = \mathbf{B}\mathbf{v} \tag{12}$$

whose largest eigenvalue gives the maximum of the following quotient of the inertia $\lambda = (\mathbf{v}^T \mathbf{B}\mathbf{v})/(\mathbf{v}^T \mathbf{V}\mathbf{v})$. Assume that the eigenvectors lie in the span of $N$ transformed samples $\phi(\mathbf{x}_t^{r,s})$, so there exists coefficients $\alpha_t^{r,s}$ ($r = 1,...,l; s = 1,...,d_r; t = 1,...,N_{r,s}$) such that:

$$\mathbf{v} = \sum_{r=1}^{l} \sum_{s=1}^{d_r} \sum_{t=}^{N_{r,s}} \alpha_t^{r,s} \phi(\mathbf{x}_t^{r,s}) \tag{13}$$

Next, we multiply Eq. (12) by $\phi(\mathbf{x}_p^{m,n})$ to obtain

$$\lambda \phi^T (\mathbf{x}_p^{m,n}) \mathbf{V}\mathbf{v} = \phi^T (\mathbf{x}_p^{m,n}) \mathbf{B}\mathbf{v} \tag{14}$$

The left term of this equation can be further organized as:

$$\lambda \phi^T (\mathbf{x}_p^{m,n}) \mathbf{V}\mathbf{v} = \lambda (\phi(\mathbf{x}_1^{1,1}), \phi(\mathbf{x}_2^{1,1}),..., \phi(\mathbf{x}_{N_{1,1}}^{1,1}), \phi(\mathbf{x}_1^{1,2}), \phi(\mathbf{x}_2^{1,2}),..., \phi(\mathbf{x}_{N_{1,2}}^{1,2}),..., \phi(\mathbf{x}_1^{l,d_l}),..., \phi(\mathbf{x}_{N_{l,d_l}}^{l,d_l}))^T \mathbf{V}\mathbf{v} = \lambda \mathbf{S}_V \boldsymbol{\alpha} \tag{15}$$

The right term of the Eq. (14) can be organized as

$$\phi^T (\mathbf{x}_p^{m,n}) \mathbf{B}\mathbf{v} = (\phi(\mathbf{x}_1^{1,1}), \phi(\mathbf{x}_2^{1,1}),..., \phi(\mathbf{x}_{N_{1,1}}^{1,1}), \phi(\mathbf{x}_1^{1,2}), \phi(\mathbf{x}_2^{1,2}),..., \phi(\mathbf{x}_{N_{1,2}}^{1,2}),..., \phi(\mathbf{x}_1^{l,d_l}),..., \phi(\mathbf{x}_{N_{l,d_l}}^{l,d_l}))^T \mathbf{B}\mathbf{v} = \mathbf{S}_B \boldsymbol{\alpha} \tag{16}$$

In the above two equations, $\alpha = (\alpha_1^{1,1}, \alpha_2^{1,1}, ..., \alpha_{N_{1,1}}^{1,1}, \alpha_1^{1,2}, \alpha_2^{1,2}, ..., \alpha_{N_{1,2}}^{1,2}, ..., \alpha_1^{l,d_l}, ..., \alpha_{N_{l,d_l}}^{l,d_l})^T$. The element of $\mathbf{S}_V$ with a row index corresponding to $\phi^T(\mathbf{x}_p^{m,n})$ and a column index corresponding to $\alpha_t^{r,s}$ is given by

$$\sum_{i=1}^{l} \sum_{j=1}^{d_i} \sum_{k=1}^{N_{i,j}} \phi^T(\mathbf{x}_p^{m,n})(\phi(\mathbf{x}_k^{i,j}) - \overline{\phi}^{i,j})(\phi(\mathbf{x}_k^{i,j}) - \overline{\phi}^{i,j})^T \phi(\mathbf{x}_t^{r,s}) \tag{17}$$

Similarly, the element of $\mathbf{S}_B$ with a row index corresponding to $\phi^T(\mathbf{x}_p^{m,n})$ and a column index corresponding to $\alpha_t^{r,s}$ is given by

$$\sum_{i=1}^{l-1} \sum_{e=i+1}^{l} \sum_{j=1}^{d_i} \sum_{h=1}^{d_e} \phi^T(\mathbf{x}_p^{m,n})(\overline{\phi}^{i,j} - \overline{\phi}^{e,h})(\overline{\phi}^{i,j} - \overline{\phi}^{e,h})^T \phi(\mathbf{x}_t^{r,s}) \tag{18}$$

Thus, we transform the original eigensystem (12) to an equivalent one as follows:

$$\lambda \mathbf{S}_V \alpha = \mathbf{S}_B \alpha \tag{19}$$

A simplest method to compute $\overline{\phi}^{i,j}$ is to adopt the following equation: $\overline{\phi}^{i,j} = \sum_{k=1}^{N_{i,j}} \phi(\mathbf{x}_k^{i,j})/N_{i,j}$. When kernel fuzzy c-means algorithm is used to extract the multiple cluster structure for each class, the cluster center can be expressed as

$$\overline{\phi}^{i,j} = \sum_{k=1}^{N} (u_k^{i,j})^m \phi(\mathbf{x}_k) / \sum_{k=1}^{N} (u_k^{i,j})^m \tag{20}$$

where both the class label and cluster label are omitted for the data sample since there is no ambiguity caused, $u_k^{i,j}$ denotes the fuzzy membership degree of the $k$th sample to cluster $j$ of class $i$, and $m$ the fuzziness parameter.

Finally note that when computing the eigensystem (19), the coefficients $\alpha$ need to be scaled by normalizing the corresponding vectors $\mathbf{v}$ in kernel space $F$: $\mathbf{v}^T\mathbf{v} = 1$.

## 4  Experiments

We have applied KCDA to 3D head model classification problem. In the 3D head model dataset, there are eight categories of heads, and each category contains 100 models. Here each category is composed of the 3D head models belonging to the same person, but with different expression such as laughing, surprise and depression. The class prototypes are selected from a subset of the Max Planck Institute (MPI) face database [12], which is based on real scanned data and has been adopted in previous facial modeling works [3], [13]. The original representation of the 3D head model is in the form of the concatenated 3D coordinates. For one head model there are totally 6292 vertices, so the dimension of the original representation is 18876. For the given dataset, by changing the size of the training set, we can report a group of experimental results. In addition, we present the comparisons between the proposed method and other three popular methods, namely, LDA, CDA, and Kernel LDA. There is only one parameter that needs to be adjusted for LDA, the suitable feature dimension, three for CDA, namely the feature dimension, fuzziness parameter and the cluster number combination, two for Kernel LDA, that is, feature dimension and kernel parameter, and four for Kernel CDA including all the parameters aforementioned. In current implementation, only the Gaussian kernel function is adopted.

For simplifying the parameter selection for each method, we first constraint the possible value of every parameter to a certain range, and then divide this range into several discrete values. The kernel parameter varies from 0.1 to 5 with a step length 0.1, and the fuzziness parameter from 1.1 to 3 with a step length 0.1. The cluster number varies from 1 to 7 for each class, and the feature number varies from 1 to the maximally allowed value, which is 1 for LDA, and is less than the number of the clusters for CDA, and the training set size for both Kernel LDA and Kernel CDA if no singularity problem arises. For every method and every possible combination of parameter values, we compute the classification rates and then choose the best parameters. Specifically, each time we take one sample out of the training database, and label it as the class that its nearest neighbor among all the rest samples belongs to. This process can be repeated until all the training samples have been counted.

In order to save the computation cost, before performing the LDA, CDA, KLDA and KCDA, we run PCA to reduce the data dimension to 20, which can keep over 90% variance of the data samples. We can also randomly choose several classes to form one single larger class so that the derived class has obvious multiple Gaussian structures. Fig. 2 gives several examples of our head model data.

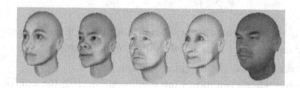

**Fig. 2.** Examples in the 3D head model database

Nearest mean classifier (NMC) and nearest prototype classifier (NPC) are used respectively to save computation cost of classification. In NMC, each class is represented by one mean vector, while, in NPC, each class is represented by several prototypes. In essence NPC is a compromise between NMC and NNC. In our experiments condensed nearest neighbor algorithm is used to get prototypes from the training set for each class. In the following we report the comparisons between LDA, CDA, KLDA and KCDA using NMC and NPC respectively.

From Table 1 to Table 3 we present the experimental results using nearest mean classifier for 2-class, 4-class and 8-class problem respectively. In 2-class problem, four classes of the original 3D head models forms one single class. In 4-class problem, two classes of the original 3D head models forms one single class. And in 8-class problem, one class of the original database stands for one class exactly. In each table, the top row corresponds to different training sizes. From these results, we can see KCDA almost always outperforms other three subspace analysis methods. In addition the difference between KCDA and other methods in 2-class problem and 4-class problem is bigger than that in 8-class problem, which explains that Kernel CDA can better make use of the multiple cluster structure in each class.

**Table 1.** Classification rates for 2-class problem using NMC

|      | 20     | 30     | 40     | 50     | 60     |
|------|--------|--------|--------|--------|--------|
| LDA  | 0.8806 | 0.8794 | 0.9031 | 0.9133 | 0.9107 |
| CDA  | 0.9056 | 0.9029 | 0.9375 | 0.9467 | 0.9536 |
| KLDA | 0.9111 | 0.9088 | 0.9344 | 0.9433 | 0.9464 |
| KCDA | 0.9472 | 0.9206 | 0.95   | 0.96   | 0.9679 |

**Table 2.** Classification rates for 4-class problem using NMC

|      | 80     | 100    | 120    | 140    | 160    |
|------|--------|--------|--------|--------|--------|
| LDA  | 0.5438 | 0.63   | 0.6393 | 0.6846 | 0.6292 |
| CDA  | 0.8844 | 0.8867 | 0.8831 | 0.8923 | 0.8958 |
| KLDA | 0.8813 | 0.8667 | 0.8786 | 0.9115 | 0.9125 |
| KCDA | 0.8969 | 0.8833 | 0.9034 | 0.9269 | 0.9208 |

**Table 3.** Classification rates for 8-class problem using NMC

|      | 240    | 280    | 320    | 360    | 400    |
|------|--------|--------|--------|--------|--------|
| LDA  | 0.4339 | 0.4212 | 0.4    | 0.4114 | 0.4114 |
| CDA  | 0.7964 | 0.7923 | 0.7896 | 0.7909 | 0.79   |
| KLDA | 0.85   | 0.8481 | 0.8542 | 0.8705 | 0.875  |
| KCDA | 0.8554 | 0.8558 | 0.875  | 0.875  | 0.8825 |

From Table 4 to Table 6 we present the experimental results using nearest prototype classifier for 2-class, 4-class and 8-class problem respectively. Again according to these tables we can easily find that KCDA almost always outperforms other three subspace analysis methods. Comparing Table 4~Table 6 with Table 1~Table 3, it also can be seen that the results using NPC is better than those using NMC due to more prototypes used in NPC.

**Table 4.** Classification rates for 2-class problem using NPC

|      | 20     | 30     | 40     | 50     | 60     |
|------|--------|--------|--------|--------|--------|
| LDA  | 0.8583 | 0.8794 | 0.9063 | 0.9233 | 0.9429 |
| CDA  | 0.9278 | 0.9353 | 0.9594 | 0.96   | 0.9643 |
| KLDA | 0.9278 | 0.9206 | 0.9469 | 0.9567 | 0.9607 |
| KCDA | 0.9444 | 0.9412 | 0.9625 | 0.97   | 0.975  |

**Table 5.** Classification rates for 4-class problem using NPC

|      | 80     | 100    | 120    | 140    | 160    |
|------|--------|--------|--------|--------|--------|
| LDA  | 0.7594 | 0.73   | 0.7679 | 0.7269 | 0.7458 |
| CDA  | 0.9563 | 0.9467 | 0.9571 | 0.9615 | 0.9625 |
| KLDA | 0.95   | 0.9367 | 0.9536 | 0.95   | 0.9625 |
| KCDA | 0.9625 | 0.9667 | 0.9714 | 0.9654 | 0.9792 |

**Table 6.** Classification rates for 8-class problem using NPC

|      | 240    | 280    | 320    | 360    | 400    |
|------|--------|--------|--------|--------|--------|
| LDA  | 0.3268 | 0.3432 | 0.3708 | 0.3636 | 0.3614 |
| CDA  | 0.8304 | 0.8346 | 0.85   | 0.8614 | 0.8636 |
| KLDA | 0.8482 | 0.8519 | 0.8583 | 0.8705 | 0.875  |
| KCDA | 0.8589 | 0.8615 | 0.8688 | 0.8841 | 0.8925 |

Note that an interesting thing is that in many cases CDA performs even better than Kernel LDA according to the numbers given in these tables. Our proposed method can integrate the merits of both CDA and Kernel LDA. In addition, it is needed to point out that when selecting the cluster number in clustering algorithm, validation method can often be used although this treatment may not guarantee to get the optimal cluster number for classification.

# 5 Conclusion

3D head model classification problem is addressed by use of a newly proposed subspace analysis method, i.e., kernel clustering based discriminant analysis method. Kernel fuzzy c-means clustering algorithm is first conducted for each class to extract the possibly embedded multiple cluster structure in the kernel space. Subsequently clustering-based discriminant analysis is performed in the kernel feature space to extract nonlinear features for classification tasks. The proposed method can integrate the merits of both CDA and Kernel subspace analysis method. We present a novel application of this method to 3D head model classification in this paper. According to the obtained experimental results, our method outperforms other currently popular subspace analysis methods.

**Acknowledgments.** The work described in this paper was partly supported by a grant from the Research Grants Council of Hong Kong Special Administrative Region, China [Project No. CityU 1197/03E].

# References

1. Funkhouser, T., Min, P., Kazhdan, M., Chen, J., Halderman, A., Dobkin, D.: A Search Engine for 3D Models. ACM Trans. Graphics. 22(1) (2003) 83-105
2. Motofumi, T., Suzuki, Y., Yaginuma, Y., Sugimoto, Y.: A 3D model retrieval system for cellular phones. In: Proc. IEEE Conf. Systems, Man and Cybernetics. Vol. 4. (2003) 3846-3851
3. Wong, H.S., Cheung, T.K., Ip, H.S.: 3D head model classification by evolutionary optimization of the extended Gaussian image representation. Pattern Recognition. 37(12) (2004) 2307-2344
4. Yang, M.H.: Kernel Eigenfaces vs. Kernel Fisherfaces: Face recognition using Kernel Methods. In: Proc. IEEE Conf. Automatic Face and Gesture Recognition. (2002) 215-220
5. Liu, Q., Huang, R., Lu, H., Ma, S.: Face Recognition using Kernel based Fisher Discriminant analysis. In: Proc. IEEE Conf. Automatic Face and Gesture Recognition. (2002) 205-211
6. Turk, M., Pentland, A.: Eigenfaces for recognition. J. Cognitive Neuroscience. 3(1) (1991) 71-86
7. Klaus-Robert Muller, Sebastian Mika, et.al: An introduction to kernel-based learning algorithms. IEEE Trans. Neural Networks. 12(2) (2001) 181-201
8. Baudat, G., Anouar, F.: Generalized discriminant analysis using a kernel approach. Neural Computation. 12(10) (2000) 2385-2404

9. Schölkopf, B., Smola, A.: Nonlinear component analysis as a kernel eigenvalue problem. Neural Computation. 10(5) (1998) 1299-1319
10. Xue-wen Chen, Huang Thomas: Facial expression recognition: a clustering-based approach. Pattern Recognition Letters. Vol. 24. (2003) 1295-1302
11. Kiyotaka Mizutani, Sadaaki Miyamoto: Possibilistic approach to kernel-based fuzzy c-means clustering with entropy regularization. Modeling Decisions for Artificial Intelligence. In: Proc. MDAI. (2005) 144-155
12. MPI Faces Database, Max Planck Institute for Biological Cybernetics, available online at http://faces.kyb.tuebingen.mpg.de/. (2004)
13. Ip, H.S., Wong, Y.F.: 3D Head Models Retrieval Based on Hierarchical Facial Region Similarity. In: Proc. Vision Interface. (2002) 314-319

# Framework for Pervasive Web Content Delivery*

Henry N. Palit[2], Chi-Hung Chi[1], and Lin Liu[1]

[1] School of Software, Tsinghua University, Beijing, China 100084
[2] School of Computing, National University of Singapore, Singapore
chichihung@mail.tsinghua.edu.cn

**Abstract.** It is generally agreed that traditional transcoding involves complex computations, which may introduce substantial additional delay to content delivery. Inspired by new multimedia data formats, like JPEG 2000, a new adaptation called modulation is devised. Unlike transcoding, modulation is fast since it basically generates an object's representation by selecting fragments of the object without decoding/encoding it. In this paper, a framework for pervasive Web content delivery is proposed to exploit the modulation's benefits.

## 1 Introduction

In pervasive Internet access with wide variation of client's hardware, network, and preference, a new direction for adoption of multi-presentation services is to generate various versions of the contents in advance (before service time) and let the client select the appropriate presentation himself/herself. This scheme seems easy, but in fact, it has some drawbacks. Firstly, the diversified contents may consume a large amount of disk space. Initially the content provider may be able to fulfill that need, but the consumption will get bigger and bigger as the services are expanded. Secondly, updating the contents is quite cumbersome. Any modification in a version of the contents may trigger modifications in the other versions. Thirdly, due to the earlier reasons, the number of versions is usually very limited. So, the overall system becomes rigid or inflexible. Lastly, the service would be better if the client need not select the suitable presentation. The client may get annoyed if he/she has to do the selection on every visit. Automatic selection of the presentation is preferable.

An alternative scheme is to adapt the contents on demand (during service time). This scheme is easier to maintain, more extensible, and less space-consuming than the former scheme. Yet, the client still needs to select the suitable presentation, unless the protocol is supplemented with a mechanism to get the client profile. In addition, the on-demand adaptation may introduce a latency delay to the client, especially if the content being adapted is a multimedia object. Compared to text-based objects, multimedia objects are commonly the target of adaptation due to their large data-size or unpresentability to the client. Multimedia objects will be the focus of our adaptation.

---

* This research is supported by the funding 2004CB719400 of China.

Y. Zhuang et al. (Eds.): PCM 2006, LNCS 4261, pp. 1018–1026, 2006.

The adaptation of multimedia objects is commonly known as transcoding (also called distillation [7]). As indicated by its name, transcoding involves conversions within and between media formats. It is lossy (inessential or unrenderable information is removed [12]), data-type specific, and generally irreversible. There are two main objectives of transcoding a multimedia object: 1) to make the object presentable to the client, and 2) to reduce the client's latency delay. Another benefit, reduced bandwidth consumption, may also be gained. Transcoding can be deployed either at the Web server (e.g., Quality Aware Transcoding [3] and InfoPyramid [13]) or the Web proxy (e.g., GloMop [7] and Mowser [1]). While server-based transcoding can well preserve the end-to-end object's semantics, proxy-based transcoding can help reduce the Web server's loads and offer scalability of service. Mogul et al. [10][12]proposed Server-Directed Transcoding (SDT) to reap benefits of the two approaches. Typical transcoding's workflow is as follows: a multimedia object is decoded into its plain format, parts of its data are then removed (e.g., by cropping, downscaling, color remapping, or quality reduction), and finally, the remaining data is encoded into a final object, which is indeed the former object's representation (note: we may interchangeably use the terms "version" and "representation" for the same meaning). Complex computations are usually involved in transcoding, and consequently, a latency delay is introduced. This is interesting. On the one hand, transcoding tries to reduce the client's latency delay; on the other hand, it introduces another latency delay. To achieve its second objective (i.e., reduction of the client's latency delay), transcoding should be employed only if the obtained reduction of latency delay can offset the introduced latency delay. Han et al [8]presented an analytical framework for determining whether and how much to transcode an image. Nevertheless, in other cases one may let this objective go in order to attain the first objective (i.e., the object's presentability to the client).

Recently we found that the emerging multimedia standards, like JPEG 2000 and MPEG-4, may open the way to efficient multimedia content delivery. Compared to their predecessors, both standards have many advanced features. Some features, in particular progressive transmission and compressed domain processing, are beneficial to multimedia data access. Through progressive transmission, a client can view a multimedia presentation immediately in increasing details: blurred to clear, small to big, or simple to complex. Hence, the client may comprehend the multimedia object's context earlier, even before the transmission is complete. Compressed domain processing allows operations such as rotation, flipping, cropping, and scaling without the need to decode the multimedia object. Inspired by these advanced features, we have devised a multimedia adaptation called modulation, which specifically adapts such a multimedia data-format. To illustrate its benefits, we have implemented modulation in the JPEG 2000 standard. Unlike transcoding, modulation involves no complex computation. As a result, it is very fast, taking less than 30 milliseconds to generate a 100 KB-sized representation of a 5 MB-sized JPEG 2000 image (tested on a 1.2 GHz Pentium III system, with 128 MB of RAM).

Picking up where we left off, this paper proposes a framework for pervasive Web content delivery. Here, "pervasive" means the Web contents can be distributed to any client using any wired or wireless device. In other words, it provides Web service to heterogeneous clients. The main objective of this framework is to deliver the Web contents within a minimal delay. To achieve that objective, this framework put considerable emphasis on high data reuse. Modulation, our previously proposed multimedia adaptation, fits well with the framework since it can offer high data reuse. In fact, the framework proposed here is to exploit the benefits of modulation. Data reuse in the Web content delivery cannot be separated from cache usage. Hence, the Web proxy equipped with a caching system is an important element in the framework.

The rest of this paper is arranged as follows. In our research, since we use the JPEG 2000 standard as an illustration to demonstrate how modulation works, a short overview of the JPEG 2000 standard is given in Section 2, followed by a brief description of modulation in Section 3. Section 4 details our proposed framework for pervasive Web content delivery. Section 5 presents related work that has not been covered in the paper's discussion. We conclude our discussion and highlight some future work in Section 6.

## 2   Overview of JPEG 2000

JPEG 2000 [2], developed by the Joint Photographic Experts Group (JPEG), is the latest multimedia standard for compression of still images. Superior low-bit rate performance, progressive transmission by pixel accuracy and resolution, and robustness to bit-errors are, among other JPEG 2000's features [4], beneficial to Internet data access. Owing to the progressive transmission, a client may view a JPEG 2000 image with increasing pixel accuracy, from blurred to completely clear. Alternatively, the image may be reconstructed with increasing resolution (*spatial scalability*), from small to original size.

In the JPEG 20000 standard, a source image is partitioned into packets through several processing stages. Packet is the smallest partition. It consists of 8-bit aligned data representing a particular tile, component, resolution, precinct, and layer of the JPEG 2000 image data. A sequence of packets constructs the JPEG 2000 codestream. In the codestream, packets can be interleaved in progression along four axes: layer, component, resolution, and precinct (position). When the codestream is transmitted to a client, this packet arrangement yields an image display with increasing quality and/or resolution.

There are several benefits of accessing the JPEG 2000 scalable image presentation over the Internet. Firstly, it provides resilience to transmission errors, as the most significant data may be sent over a channel with better error performance while the remainder may be sent over a channel with poor error performance. Secondly, it can shorten the client perceived latency time. Unlike images of the traditional data formats, a JPEG 2000 image can be displayed as soon as the first few packets are received. The displayed image may be blurred or small initially, but it improves in time. Since the client can see the image's context sooner than later, the perceived latency time is cut short. Lastly, the scalable image presentation can serve pervasive Internet access better. Any client device can choose the amount of quality and resolution that suits its constraints and drop the remaining data.

The image presentation – portrayed in the last sentence of the last paragraph – should be done better. Instead of wasting the Internet bandwidth by sending data that later are dropped by the client, those unused data should not be sent out in the first place. Since data in a JPEG 2000 image have been arranged in packets, it is unnecessary to decode the image. If one knows which data are not needed by the client and which packets correspond with those data, then the corresponding packets can just be dropped from the transmission. This is where modulation comes into play.

# 3  Modulation

## 3.1  Definition

The Oxford English Dictionary 1 defines modulation as the action of forming, regulating, or varying according to due measure and proportion. In this paper, we define modulation as the process to obtain an object's representation by means of adjusting (i.e., dropping and/or adding) the building blocks of the object. The building blocks of an object could be layers, packets, fragments, or whatever applicable (for simplicity, we use "fragments" for the rest of this section to represent the object's building blocks).

The modulating process is quite simple. One may liken it to playing a jigsaw puzzle. Each jigsaw's piece can be taken out or put into place as the player wishes, so long as it matches up well with the other pieces. Modulation has the following characteristics:

- Since modulation just drops and adds fragments from and to an object's representation, and no complex computation or whatsoever involved, the process is expected to be *minimal*, and consequently, fast. Thereby, it can be carried out by a Web server without noticeable decrease in performance.
- Modulation is an *exclusive* process. It is an object's transformation within a data format. Modulation cannot be used to transform a GIF image to a JPEG image, for example. If a client device does not support the modular data format, then transcoding is still required for conversion between data formats. This may be the only drawback of modulation.
- Unlike transcoding, which can only transform a high-fidelity representation to a low-fidelity one, modulation is *reversible*[2]. A representation can be generated out of an object by dropping some fragments. Conversely, the original object can be retrieved by putting back the missing fragments to the representation. This reversible property makes high data reuse possible in modulation.

## 3.2  Previous Experimentation with JPEG 2000

We have implemented modulation in the JPEG 2000 standard. The JPEG 2000 modulator can generate a variety of representations of a JPEG 2000 image. There are

---

[1] The Oxford English Dictionary, 2nd edition; prepared by J. A. Simpson and E. S. C. Weiner; Vol. IX, page 955; Oxford University Press, 1989.

[2] Another definition of modulation in The Oxford English Dictionary:
*Biol.* Reversible variation in the activity or form of a cell in response to a changing environment.

three parameters used to diversify the representations; they are: (color) component, resolution, and (quality) layer. Keeping only luminance component and dropping chrominance components, we get a grayscale representation of the JPEG 2000 image. Varying the resolutions yields representations with different dimensions (width x height). Reducing the layers of the JPEG 2000 image gives us a low quality representation. Of course, we can make a combination of the three parameters when generating a representation. For an instance, we can generate a grayscale, half-scaled-resolution, medium-quality representation of a JPEG 2000 image.

From the experiment, a low-fidelity representation can be generated successfully from a high-fidelity one. To construct a high-fidelity from a low-fidelity representation, a *supplement* is required. The supplement basically comprises the missing packets, which are required to construct the high-fidelity representation. Packets of the low-fidelity representation are combined with those of the supplement to form the high-fidelity representation.

We had measured the modulation's processing time. As a comparison, we also measured the transcoding's (of a JPEG image) processing time. While generating the JPEG representations by transcoding took between 1.9 and 2.3 seconds (depending on the resulting data-size), generating the JPEG 2000 counterparts by modulation just took between 25 and 60 milliseconds (also depending on the resulting data-size). Even constructing the original JPEG 2000 image from a representation – which requires two consecutive processes, i.e., generating a supplement and adding the supplement to the representation – was pretty fast, too (between 90 and 130 milliseconds). In conclusion, the modulation's processing time is quite minimal, taking only a small portion of the transcoding's processing time.

Minimal processing time (delay) is not the only advantage of modulation. Modulation offers high data reuse, as well. Thanks to its reversible property, any object's representation – either of high- or low-fidelity – can be used partially or fully to construct another representation. We should apply modulation to the Web content delivery and get benefited. It certainly helps reduce the bandwidth consumption. In the following section, we propose a framework for Web content delivery, which exploits modulation's benefits.

## 4   Framework for Pervasive Multimedia Content Delivery

As mentioned earlier, modulation is based on collaboration between servers and proxies. Based on modulation, our framework can be closely illustrated as in Figure 1. The server and proxy work together in adapting and delivering multimedia content to clients with heterogeneous devices. The role of proxy is particularly important in the framework since it has to match the client capabilities to the multimedia content presentation; hence, the proxy is the decision maker. To begin with, let us detail the framework's characteristics in the following subsection.

### 4.1   Characteristics

There are three key characteristics of the framework that we would like to highlight:

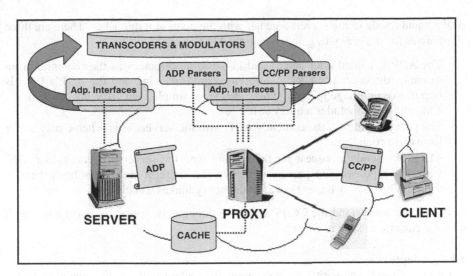

**Fig. 1.** Proxy-based pervasive multimedia content delivery

### 4.1.1  Meta-Data Documents

Two types of meta-data documents are depicted in Figure The first is CC/PP[3] (Composite Capability / Preference Profiles), an RDF-based document developed by W3C to describe device capabilities and user preferences. The second is ADP (Adaptation Profiles), also an RDF-based document that we devise to describe content's characteristics and to guide content's adaptation. Due to space limitation, we do not detail these meta-data documents. Instead, we would like to elaborate how they work in the framework.

CC/PP helps the proxy in identifying the client capabilities. The typical size of CC/PP (including its schema) ranges from 4 to 6 KB. Based on this document, the proxy can select the best presentation for the client. There are several ways for the client to deliver its CC/PP:

- The client can attach CC/PP within its requests, usually in the HTTP header. However, the XML-based document may need to be transformed into a compact form (like compact policy in P3P) to suit the HTTP header field's style. Alternatively, it may be included in the HTTP body, and instead of GET, POST is used as the request's method.
- The client only put a reference to CC/PP in its requests. The document can reside in any website (possibly in the device vendor's), and its URL is given in the request's header. The drawback is that there are extra roundtrips for the proxy to get client's CC/PP.

ADP is used by the proxy to identify content's characteristics (e.g., content-type, width, height, data-size, – and more importantly – list of representations) and to properly adapt the content. The size of ADP varies greatly and may be over 10 KB.

---

[3] http://www.w3.org/TR/2004/REC-CCPP-struct-vocab-20040115/

ADP should reside in the server, together with the content it describes. There are three alternatives for the proxy to gather content's ADP:

- The ADP is named after and placed in the same directory as the content. For an example, the content's URL is http://foo.com/image.jp2 and the ADP's URL is http://foo.com/image.jp2.adp. This scheme is simple, but may not work if the content's URL includes a query string.
- The proxy negotiates the content's ADP with the server. This scheme may suffer from extra roundtrips.
- The proxy sends a request for the content, and the server piggybacks the ADP with the response. The penalty is almost the same as the first scheme since a second request may be sent out after the proxy makes a decision.

In order to understand the CC/PP and ADP documents, the proxy is equipped with relevant parsers, as seen in Figure.

### 4.1.2  Adaptors
Since one of the framework's main purposes is to adapt multimedia content so that it can fit the client capabilities, a variety of adaptors are required. The adaptors include many kinds of transcoders and modulators. Both the proxy and server have access to the "database" of transcoders and modulators (see Figure). Most adaptors appear as stand-alone applications. Thus, an interface is needed for the proxy or server to access the adaptors. Commonly, one interface is for one adaptor.

### 4.1.3  Caching System
The proxy is also equipped with a cache. In addition to providing adaptation service, the framework can exploit the proxy's cache to store the contents locally for future use. Modulation, in particular, can offer high data reuse, thanks to its reversible nature. As a result, client latency delay can be reduced and bandwidth usage conserved.

The proxy's cache can also store the client's CC/PP, so that the proxy does not need to retrieve the document many times. Similarly, the content's ADP can be stored in the proxy's cache, and therefore, the proxy can quickly select the suitable multimedia presentation for the same client requests.

## 5  Additional Related Work

Caching a transcoded object was seldom discussed in most transcoding systems. This is understandable since transcoding may reduce the effectiveness of a caching system. Maheshwari et al. [11]proposed TranSquid, which is able to integrate transcoding and caching systems. TranSquid maintains separate, hierarchical caches for different categories of clients (high, medium, and limited capability). Moreover, TranSquid can transcode the high fidelity versions into the low fidelity ones at the proxy as opposed to re-fetching the object from the original server. Kangasharju et al. [9] proposed a Soft Caching Proxy, which allow a lower resolution version of an image object to be cached. In Soft Caching, recoding (i.e., transcoding) may be employed to an image being evicted from the cache. By recoding the image, the image's data-size becomes smaller, and therefore, it may be re-stored in the cache while freeing some cache's space for new objects. Similar to our model, both TranSquid and Soft Caching exploit data reuse to reduce client's latency and bandwidth consumption. Nevertheless, our model can offer higher data reuse by exploiting the reversible property of modulation.

The idea of exploiting the JPEG 2000 data stream is not new. Deshpande and Zeng [6] and Chi and Cao [5] used HTTP to stream JPEG 2000 images. They utilized the HTTP Range header to download an image's fragments, and then constructed the image presentation from the fragments. Deshpande and Zeng did not consider the use of a caching proxy to serve many clients, so there is no reduction in bandwidth consumption. Chi and Cao did not care much about the JPEG 2000 data format, and therefore, the resulting representations were solely based on quality. JPIP (JPEG 2000 Internet Protocol) [14] is an international standard for interactivity with JPEG 2000 files. It is developed under ISO/IEC Joint Technical Committee of Photographic Experts (JPEG), and presently becomes Part 9 of the ISO/IEC 15444 (JPEG 2000) standard. JPIP can run on top of HTTP, HTTP+TCP, or HTTP+UDP, either in a stateless or a stateful manner. Due to its interactive nature, JPIP only caches image data locally (on the client side); the HTTP responses are purposely made non-cacheable to avoid intermediary caching. Such scheme gives only little benefit.

## 6  Conclusion

With the emerging multimedia standards, such as JPEG 2000 and MPEG-4, we propose an alternative to deliver multi-presentation services. The scalable presentation is bestowed on the new multimedia standards. Utilizing this feature, a simple, fast adaptation can be devised. Using JPEG 2000 as an illustration, we devised a new adaptation, called *modulation*. Modulation is characterized as simple, exclusive, and reversible. Further, we have presented its specifications and comparison with transcoding. Inspired by modulation, we also built a framework for pervasive multimedia content delivery. The framework is proxy-centric, but emphasizes on collaboration between servers and proxies.

## References

1. H. Bharadvaj, A. Joshi, and S. Auephanwiriyakul. An Active Transcoding Proxy to Support Mobile Web Access. In *Proc. of 17th IEEE Symposium on Reliable Distributed Systems*, West Lafayette (IN), October 1998.
2. M. Boliek, C. Christopoulos, and E. Majani (eds.). *JPEG 2000 Part I Final Committee Draft Version 1.0*, March 2000. URL: http://www.jpeg.org/public/fcd15444-1.pdf.
3. S. Chandra, C. S. Ellis, and A. Vahdat. Differentiated Multimedia Web Services Using Quality Aware Transcoding. In *Proc. of INFOCOM 2000 – 19th Annual Joint Conference of the IEEE Computer and Communication Societies*, Tel Aviv (Israel), March 2000.
4. C. Christopoulos, A. Skodras, and T. Ebrahimi. The JPEG2000 Still Image Coding System: An Overview. *IEEE Transactions on Consumer Electronics, vol. 46, no. 4*, pp. 1103–1127, November 2000.
5. C. H. Chi and Y. Cao. Pervasive Web Content Delivery with Efficient Data Reuse. In *Proc. of 7th International Workshop on Web Content Caching and Distribution (WCW)*, Boulder (CO), August 2002.

6. S. Deshpande and W. Zeng. Scalable Streaming of JPEG2000 Images Using Hypertext Transfer Protocol. In *Proc. of 9th ACM Multimedia Conference*, Ottawa (Canada), October 2001.
7. A. Fox, S. D. Gribble, E. A. Brewer, and E. Amir. Adapting to Network and Client Variability via On-Demand Dynamic Distillation. In *Proc. of 7th International Conference on Architectural Support for Programming Languages and Operating Systems*, Cambridge (CA), October 1996.
8. R. Han, P. Bhagwat, R. LaMaire, T. Mummert, V. Perret, and J. Rubas. Dynamic Adaptation in an Image Transcoding Proxy for Mobile Web Browsing. *IEEE Personal Communications, vol. 5, no. 6*, pp. 8–17, December 1998.
9. J. Kangasharju, Y. G. Kwon, and A. Ortega. Design and Implementation of a Soft Caching Proxy. In *Proc. of 3rd International WWW Caching Workshop*, Manchester (England), June 1998.
10. B. Knutsson, H. H. Lu, J. Mogul, and B. Hopkins. Architecture and Performance of Server-Directed Transcoding. *ACM Transactions on Internet Technology (TOIT), vol. 3, no. 4*, pp. 392–424, November 2003.
11. A. Maheshwari, A. Sharma, K. Ramamritham, and P. Shenoy. TranSquid: Transcoding and Caching Proxy for Heterogeneous E-Commerce Environments. In *Proc. of 12th International Workshop on Research Issues in Data Engineering (RIDE): Engineering E-Commerce/E-Business Systems*, San Jose (CA), February 2002.
12. J. C. Mogul. Server-Directed Transcoding. *Computer Communication, vol. 24, no. 2*, pp. 155–162, February 2001.
13. R. Mohan, J. R. Smith, and C. S. Li. Adapting Multimedia Internet Content for Universal Access. *IEEE Transactions on Multimedia, vol. 1, no. 1*, pp. 104–114, March 1999.
14. D. Taubman and R. Prandolini. Architecture, Philosophy and Performance of JPIP: Internet Protocol Standard for JPEG2000. *Visual Communications and Image Processing 2003, eds. T. Ebrahimi and T. Sikora, Proc. of SPIE, vol. 5150*, pp. 791–805, June 2003.

# Region-Based Semantic Similarity Propagation for Image Retrieval

Weiming Lu[1], Hong Pan[2], and Jiangqin Wu[1]

[1] College of Computer Science, Zhejiang University 310027 Hangzhou, China
[2] Information Engineering College, Hangzhou Teacher's College 310012 Hangzhou, China
lwm_zju@hotmail.com, chin@hztc.edu.cn, wujq@cs.zju.edu.cn

**Abstract.** In order to reduce the gap between low-level image features and high-level image semantics, various long term learning strategies were integrated into content-based image retrieval system. The strategies always use the semantic relationships among images to improve the effectiveness of the retrieval system. This paper proposes a semantic similarity propagation method to mine the hidden semantic relationships among images. The semantic relationships are propagated between the similar images and regions. Experimental results verify the improvement on similarity propagation and image retrieval.

**Keywords:** similarity propagation, content-based image retrieval, long term learning, relevance feedback.

## 1 Introduction

Over the last decades, content based image retrieval (CBIR) has achieved a great advance, but it stands in nonplus recently and its performance is mainly limited by the semantic gap between low-level features and high-level semantics. To bridge this gap, three approaches have been widely used: image annotation [1][2][3][4], region object extraction [5][6][7] and relevance feedback [8][9][10].

Because manual image annotation is both time-consuming and costly process, it is impossible to precisely annotate all images in image database. Automatic image annotation technologies have been developed recently, but they are still impractical and ineffective. Furthermore, due to the multiplicity of contents in a single image and the complexity of image understanding, different users can make different annotation for the same image. We still can't annotate images correctly. In CBIR, user submit an image as query to express what he wants, which addresses the content expression problem by using the intrinsic features such as color, texture and shape to index and retrieve images. With the enlightenment of CBIR, an image can be indexed by other images with the same semantics in image database.

Relevance feedback technologies allow user to provide positive and negative judgments for images returned by CBIR system, then the system can dynamically learn the user's attention and quickly identify what user wants. Relevance feedback technologies can be classified as short term learning and long term learning. Short term learning is a memoryless process, it only works in a single query session, and the knowledge learnt from the previous session is forgotten when the session ends. In

Y. Zhuang et al. (Eds.): PCM 2006, LNCS 4261, pp. 1027–1036, 2006.

long term learning methods, knowledge obtained by relevance feedback is accumulated in system which can be used later. With this knowledge, semantic space can be created implicitly for images. Most long term learning methods generate the explicit semantic relationships between images using the knowledge. For example, the positive images in the same query session are considered as sharing some common semantics, and the positive and negative images in the same query session are irrelevant. Only when a user think two images are relevant in a single session directly, the two images will have the semantic relationships. It does not mine the hidden semantic relationships between images. For example, image A and image B have the same semantics, and image B and image C also have the same semantics. In intuition, image B and C may have similarity in their semantic content, but in previous methods, only the semantic relationships between A and B, B and C, excluding A and C, will be constructed in semantic space.

To address this limitation, we propose a region based image semantic similarity propagation method to mine the hidden semantics among images. In this method, we also mine the semantics between regions of images when user relevance feedback. Because of the multiplicity of contents in a single image, we segment the image into regions. Each region is thought as having a single semantic concept. There are semantics between two regions if two regions have the same concept. Intuitively, if two images are relevant, then there are semantic relationships between some regions of images; if two regions are relevant, then the images they belong to are relevant. The semantics can be propagated from images to regions and from regions to images. The rest of this paper is organized as follows: Session 2 describes the related researches on learning semantic space from user's relevance feedback and some efforts on mining hidden semantic relationships between images. Session 3 presents the proposed method for similarity propagation. The experiments and some compares are made in Session 4. Finally, Session 5 presents the conclusion of this paper.

## 2 Related Work

The traditional relevance feedback approaches have a common limitation. They do not have a mechanism to memorize or accumulate the semantic knowledge learnt from relevance feedbacks.

In the recent years, to overcome the aforementioned disadvantage, a number of researches [11][12][13][14][15][17] have been focused on exploiting long term learning to construct semantic space from user's feedback history. Furthermore, the inferred semantic space could be used later for continuously improving the retrieval performance.

[15] adopted LSI on inter-query information to extract the correlations of documents and terms in database. In this approach, user's inter-query relevance feedback information was stored in system. Each query result was regarded as a document and the images in image database were regarded as terms. The inter-query information with this form of a collection of documents can be subjected to latent semantic analysis. The semantic space can be used for future retrieval.

[13] and [17] proposed a statistical correlation model for image retrieval. This model captured the semantic relationships among images in the database from simple

statistics of user's feedback information. It can be trained from relevance feedback log and updated dynamically during image retrieval process. Then, the images were re-ranked based on the semantic correlations. The algorithm was effective and easy to implement. [17] described an image by semantically relevant peer images. The peer information was accumulated with the feedback information.

In [11], a long-term learning was proposed to infer a semantic space from user's relevance feedbacks for improving the retrieval performance over time. In addition, SVD was applied to compact the semantic space and reduce the subjectivity and noise from an individual user. In [14], He et al. tried to use other spectral method to construct the semantic space.

However, the methods mentioned above can only retrieve images which are marked as relevant directly during relevance feedback. In the semantic space, "direct semantic link" is only between their images. Due to the sparsity of the relevance feedback information, the problem is even more serious. Some researches [12][16] have focus on mining the "hidden semantic link" among images which are not regarded as relevant in feedback directly.

[16] proposed an approach named semantic propagation, which revealed the hidden semantic relationships among images given a set of relevance feedbacks. It was effective in propagating the semantic knowledge across all images in database, but the approach only considered indirect link of one intermediate image. [12] also used a simple statistical model to transform user's preferences during query sessions into semantic correlations among images. In addition, the model introduced a learning strategy to discover more relevant images that have not memorized. It can infer the hidden semantic correlation between two images according to the gathered semantic information. The hidden semantic similarity was estimated by a combination of image semantic clusters and image authoritative ranks.

## 3   Region-Based Semantic Similarity Propagation

Region based similarity propagation approach is stemmed from a simple and intuitive idea: semantic similarity can progressively propagate among images with the similar regions. Each image can be segmented into at least one region. Each region presents a semantic content for the image. If two images have the common semantics, then at least one region of each images share the common semantics. Similarly, if two regions have the common semantics, then the images they belong to also share the common semantics. Another intuition is that, the more important a region in an image, the more contribution it makes for the semantics of the image it belongs to. In this session, we firstly explain some notation and formulate the problem. A learning algorithm for the problem is then proposed.

### 3.1   Notation and Problem Formulation

The basic idea of semantic similarity propagation is that the semantic similarities among images and regions can influence mutually. The relationships between images and regions are shown in Fig. 1. It consist two layers, the image layer and the region layer. Each layer is an undirected graph. The dotted lines represent links between image and region. It means the image consists of such linked regions. The associated weight of the link means the importance of the region in the image. The real lines represent links between images or regions, with the means of having semantic relationships. The higher of the associated weight of the link, the more semantic similar of the two objects.

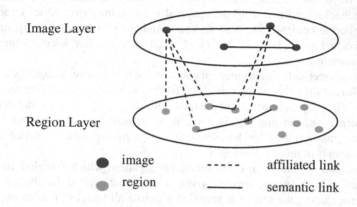

**Fig. 1.** The two-layered graph model

Let $I$ and $R$ denote the image and region similarity matrix. Let $I_{ij}$ present the semantic similarity between image $i$ and image $j$, so is the meanings of $R_{ij}$. Let $Z$ be the link matrix from image to region. Its transpose $Z'$ implies the links from regions to images. If $Z_{ij} > 0$, it means region $j$ belongs to image $i$, and the value of $Z_{ij}$ measures the importance of the region of image. So the region based semantic similarity propagation problem becomes how to update the semantic matrix $I$ and $R$ with the initial matrix $I^{(0)}$, $R^{(0)}$ and $Z$ iteratively.

### 3.2 The Algorithm

Motivated by the iterative similarity propagation approach in [18], we can describe the iterative process as follows:

$$
\begin{cases}
R^{(n+1)} = \alpha R^{(n)} + (1-\alpha)\lambda Z' I^{(n)} Z \\
I^{(n+1)} = \beta I^{(n)} + (1-\beta)\lambda Z R^{(n+1)} Z'
\end{cases}
\tag{1}
$$

where $\alpha$ and $\beta$ are parameters to linearly combine the original similarity and propagated similarity, and $\lambda$ is decay factor to make sure that the original similarity is more important than propagated similarity. $\alpha$, $\beta$ and $\lambda$ are all within $[0, 1]$. When $\beta = 1$, it degenerates to no similarity propagation between images. The convergence of this iterative process was proven in [18].

The matrix $R^{(0)}$ and $Z$ can be initialized before the first image retrieval process. Then the iterative approach will be applied in every relevance feedback process. It is presented as follows:

1. Construct image semantic matrix $I^{(0)}$ with the relevance feedback information.
2. Update the region importance matrix $Z$ optionally.
3. Apply the iterative process to update region and image semantic matrices.
4. Use the convergent matrix $I$ to update the semantic relationships.

The follows explain the approach in detail.

**Initialize matrix $R^{(0)}$ and $Z$ :** Without any semantic information of regions, $R^{(0)}$ is initialized with the information of region's low level features. Two regions can be considered as semantic similar if they have similar low level feature. The latter experiment shows that the noisy semantic links among regions infect the performance of similarity propagation. We first compute the $R^{(0)}$ as follows:

$$R^{(0)}_{ij} = \begin{cases} \exp(-\|r_i - r_j\|^2 / \sigma^2) & \text{if } \|r_i - r_j\|^2 < \varepsilon \text{ and } i \neq j \\ 0 & \text{otherwise} \end{cases} \qquad (2)$$

where $r_i$ and $r_j$ are two region features. Then, normalize the $R^{(0)}$ with $R^{(0)} = D^{-1/2} R^{(0)} D^{-1/2}$, where $D$ is a diagonal matrix with its $(i,i)$-element equal to the sum of the i-th row of $R^{(0)}$. The element of $Z$ measures the importance of a region in an image. It correlates with the area and the position of the region in an image. When the region is larger and closer to the image center, the region becomes more important. So the importance of region $j$ in image $i$ can be calculated as follows:

$$Z_{ij} = \frac{1}{Z_i} \left( \frac{area_{ij}}{dist_{ij}} \right) \qquad (3)$$

where $area_{ij}$ is the area of region $j$ in image $i$, $dist_{ij}$ is the distance of region $j$ to the center of image $i$, $Z_i$ is the normalize factor equal to $\sum_j \dfrac{area_{ij}}{dist_{ij}}$. The distance of region can be calculated as $dist_{ij} = \sum_j \| p_{ij} - c_i \|$, where $p_{ij}$ is a point in region and $c_i$ is the center point of image $i$.

**Construct image semantic matrix $I^{(0)}$ with the relevance feedback information:** When user judges the relevant and irrelevant images in the retrieval result, the set of relevant images $I_R$ and the set of irrelevant images $I_N$ can be collected. Then the semantic matrix $I^{(0)}$ can be initialized with the relevance information.

$$I^{(0)}{}_{ij} = \begin{cases} 1 & \text{if image } i \text{ and image } j \text{ are both in } I_R \\ -1 & \text{if image } i \text{ and image } j \text{ are in } I_R \text{ and } I_N \text{ respectively} \\ 0 & \text{otherwise} \end{cases} \tag{4}$$

**Update the semantic relationships:** After the n-th iteration, we get the incremental image semantic matrix $I^{(n)}$ propagated from the initial semantic matrix, which can be used to update the image semantic relationships. Let $K$ denote the image semantic similarity matrix with its element equal to the similarity among images. We can update the semantic relationships in system as follow:

$$K = \gamma K + (1 - \gamma) I^{(n)} \tag{5}$$

Then the updated $K$ can be used in semantic space construction or image retrieval.

**Learning region importance matrix $Z$ :** A region importance learning approach was proposed in [5]. The approach was inspired by the idea of TFIDF weighting, and assumed that important regions appears in more times in positive images and fewer times in all of the images. With the same assumption, if the similar regions appear in almost all positive images, they may be the regions having the most semantics in images, so the importance of such regions should increases. The details can be referred to [5].

# 4 Experiments

The image set used in out experiments is the Corel Image Gallery. We choose 5000 images with 50 semantic categories. Each category has about 100 images. In this paper, we focus on semantic similarity propagation by relevance feedback to improve retrieval performance.

Images are segmented into regions by meanshift algorithm [19]. The regions with area percentage less than 5% of the whole image are thrown. Three types of color features and three types of texture features are extracted for images: color histogram in HSV space with quantization 256, first and second color moments in Lab space, color coherence feature in Luv space with quantization 64, MSRSAR texture feature, Tamura Coarseness texture feature and Tamura directionality texture feature. Two types of color features are extracted for regions: color histogram in HSV space with quantization 150, first, second and third color moments in Luv space.

## 4.1 Performance Evaluation

We designed an automatic feedback schema to model the user's relevance feedback. The images sharing the same category with the query are considered as relevant examples. We random select images from each category as query images. At each relevance feedback, the system random select at most 6 relevant examples and at most 3 irrelevant examples from the top N search results (here we choose N=20). Then the similarity propagation will be performed based on the relevance information during the each query session of retrieval. To evaluate the performance of our algorithms, the retrieval accuracy is defined as

$$Accuracy = \frac{relevant\ images\ retrieved\ in\ top\ N\ returns}{N} \qquad (6)$$

We use Peerindex-based image retrieval [17] as baseline method. In our evaluation, we set $\alpha = \beta = \lambda = \gamma = 0.8$. Fig.2. shows the performance of image retrieval.

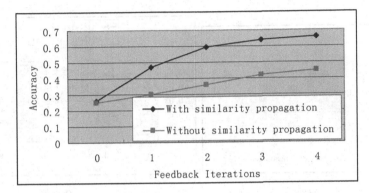

**Fig. 2.** Performance comparison on similarity propagation

As Fig.2. shows, with the similarity propagation, the Peerindex-based image retrieval system can retrieve more relevant images and improve the retrieval performance.

## 4.2 Propagation Analysis

After each iteration converges, we get the final image semantic matrix $I$. If $I_{ij} > \varepsilon$, we call the link between image $i$ and $j$ is valid, and moreover, if image $i$ and $j$ belong to the same category, the link is considered as correct. Because only valid links can bring more effect in image retrieval, we only take the valid links into account. In order to evaluate the function of similarity propagation, we define the semantic similarity propagation precision and recall as:

$$propagation\ precsion = \frac{Number\ of\ correct\ links\ propagated}{Number\ of\ all\ links\ propagated} \qquad (7)$$

$$propagation\ recall = \frac{Number\ of\ correct\ links\ propagated}{Number\ of\ all\ possible\ links} \qquad (8)$$

The propagation precision shows the accuracy of the propagation and the recall shows the rate to form the semantic relationships among images. Fig.3(a). shows the precision and recall increase along with the iteration until the value converges. Although the precision is not very high, we can eliminate the wrong links formed by propagation with user's relevance feedback. Fig.4. shows the increase of the number of correct links and valid links. The two lines have the same slope that means the links propagated in the succeeding iterations are all correct. The low precision is caused by the initial noisy semantic links among regions. Fig.3(b). shows that with the similarity propagation, the hidden semantic links can be found and it accelerates the construction of the semantic space.

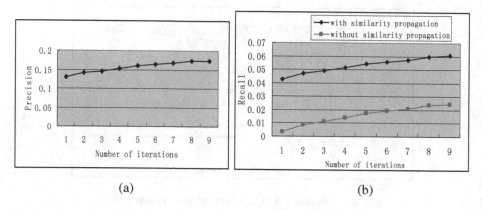

(a)                                                            (b)

**Fig. 3.** semantic link propagation precision (a) and recall (b)

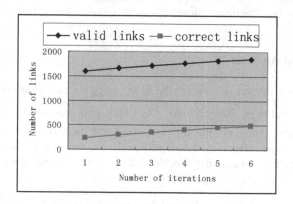

**Fig. 4.** The increase of semantic links

As we can see from the Fig2. and Fig.3, all lines are convergent. These empirical results prove the convergence of our approach.

## 4.3  Parameter Influence

Different parameters in system will affect the image retrieval. As analyzed before, the algorithm is degenerated to no similarity propagation when $\beta=1$. Fig.5 shows the variation of the retrieval accuracy after 6-th relevance feedback with the change of $\beta$. The best performance is achieved at $\beta=0.7$.

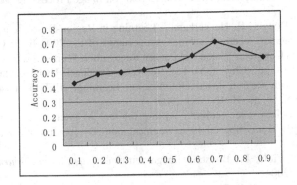

**Fig. 5.** Accuracy of image retrieval with the change of $\beta$

# 5  Conclusion

In this paper, we have proposed a semantic similarity propagation approach for image retrieval. Based on it, hidden semantic relations can be discovered which can accelerate the construction of semantic space for image database. Experimental results have verified the improvement on similarity propagation and image retrieval.

However, with the growth of the number of images, more storage is needed to store the semantic relations and more time is needed to propagate the similarity. Some noise semantic links will propagate in our approach. So in the future, we will develop an efficient approach that can eliminate the infection of noise semantic links.

**Acknowledgments.** This work is supported by National Natural Science Foundation of China (No.60533090, No.60525108, No.90412014), 973 Program (No.2002CB312101), Science and Technology Project of Zhejiang Province (2005C13032, 2005C11001-05), and China-US Million Book Digital Library Project (www.cadal.zju.edu.cn ).

# References

1. Blei, D. and M. Jordan.: Modeling Annotated Data. In Proceedings of 26th International Conference on Research and Development in Information Retrieval (SIGIR). 2003.
2. Rong Jin, Joyce Y.Cai, and Luo Si.: Effective Automatic Image Annotation Via A Coherent Language Model and Active Learning, ACM Conference on Multimedia(ACMM 2004), October 10–16, 2004, New York, New York, USA.

3. Jeon, J., V. Lavrenko, and R. Manmatha.: Automatic Image Annotation and Retrieval Using Cross-Media Relevance Models. in Proceedings of the 26th annual international ACM SIGIR conference on Research and development in information retrieval. 2003.
4. L. Wenyin, S. Dumais, Y. Sun, H. Zhang, M. Czerwinski, and B. Field.: Semi-automatic image annotation. In Proc. Interact2001 Conference on Human Computer Interaction, 2001.
5. F. Jing, M.J. Li, H.J. Zhang, and B. Zhang.: An Efficient and Effective Region-Based Image Retrieval Framework, IEEE Transactions on Image Processing, vol. 13, no. 5, May 2004
6. Iker Gondra, Douglas R. Heisterkamp.: Learning in Region-Based Image Retrieval with Generalized Support Vector Machines. Proceedings of the 2004 IEEE Computer Society Conference on Computer Vision and Pattern Recognition Workshops (CVPRW'04)
7. Chiou-Ting Hsu, and Chuech-Yu Li.: Relevance Feedback Using Generalized Bayesian Framework With Region-Based Optimization Learning, IEEE Transactions on Image Processing, vol. 14, no. 10, October 2005
8. Y. Rui, et al. Relevancefeedback: Apowerful tool in interactive content-based image retrieval, IEEE Trans. Special Issue Segmentation, Description and Retrieval of Video Content, 1998.
9. Tieu, K. and Viola, P.: Boosting image retrieval. *International Journal of Computer Vision*, 56(1), 2004.
10. P.Y. Yin, B. Bhanu, K.C. Chang, and A. Dong: Integrating relevance feedback techniques for image retrieval using reinforcement learning. IEEE Transactions on Pattern Analysis and Machine Intelligence. 27(10), 2005, 1536–1551.
11. X. He, O. King, W.Y. Ma, M. Li, and H.J. Zhang.: Learning a semantic space from user's relevance feedback for image retrieval, IEEE Trans. Circuit and Systems for Video Technology, vol. 13, no. 1, pp. 39-48, Jan. 2003.
12. J.W. Han, King N. Ngan, M.J. Li, and H.J. Zhang.: A Memory Learning Framework for Effective Image Retrieval. IEEE Transactions on Image Processing, vol.14, no. 4, April 2005
13. M. Li, Z. Chen, H.J. Zhang.: Statistical correlation analysis in image retrieval. Pattern Recognition 35 (2002) 2687–2693
14. X.F. He, W.Y. Ma, and H.J. Zhang.: Learning an Image Manifold for Retrieval. ACM Conference on Multimedia(ACMM 2004), New York, 2004.
15. Heisterkamp, D.R.: Building a latent semantic index of an image database from patterns of relevance feedback. In Proceedings of 16th International Conference on Pattern Recognition (ICPR 2002). Vol. 4., Quebec, Canada (2002) 134–137
16. Hoon Yul Bang, Cha Zhang and Tsuhan Chen.: Semantic Propagation from Relevance Feedbacks , 2004 IEEE International Conference on Multimedia and Expo (ICME 2004)
17. J. Yang, Q. Li, Y.T. Zhuang.: Towards Data-Adaptive and User-Adaptive Image Retrieval by Peer Indexing, International Journal of Computer Vision, 56 (1/3) p.47-63, 2004
18. X.J. Wang, W.Y. Ma, G.R. Xue, X. Li.: Multi-Model Similarity Propagation and its Application for Web Image Retrieval, ACM Multimedia'04, October 10-16, 2004, New York, NY USA.
19. D. Comaniciu and P. Meer.: Mean Shift: A Robust Approach Toward Feature Space Analysis. IEEE Trans. Pattern Analysis and Machine Intelligence, vol. 24, no. 5, pp. 603-619, May 2002.

# Author Index

# Lecture Notes in Computer Science

For information about Vols. 1–4194

please contact your bookseller or Springer

Printed in the United States
By Bookmasters